SPECIAL EDITION

# USING Mac® OS X Leopard

*Brad Miser*

Pearson Education

201 W. 103rd Street

Indianapolis, Indiana 46290

# CONTENTS AT A GLANCE

# Special Edition Using Mac® OS X Leopard



ISBN-13: 978-0-7897-3653-6
ISBN-10: 0-7897-3653-5

Library of Congress Cataloging-in-Publication Data

Miser, Brad.
Special edition using MACOSX Leopard / Brad Miser.
p. cm.
ISBN 0-7897-3653-5
1. Mac OS. 2. Operating systems (Computers) 3. Macintosh (Computer)—Programming. I. Title.
QA76.76.O63m57885 2007
005.4'4682—dc22

2007046235

Printed in the United States of America

First Printing: January 2008

11 10 09 4 3

**Trademarks**

All terms mentioned in this book that are known to be trademarks or service marks have been appropriately capitalized. Que Publishing cannot attest to the accuracy of this information. Use of a term in this book should not be regarded as affecting the validity of any trademark or service mark.

Mac OS X is a registered trademark of Apple Computer, Inc.

**Warning and Disclaimer**

Every effort has been made to make this book as complete and as accurate as possible, but no warranty or fitness is implied. The information provided is on an "as is" basis. The author and the publisher shall have neither liability nor responsibility to any person or entity with respect to any loss or damages arising from the information contained in this book.

**Bulk Sales**

Que Publishing offers excellent discounts on this book when ordered in quantity for bulk purchases or special sales. For more information, please contact

**U.S. Corporate and Government Sales**
**1-800-382-3419**
**corpsales@pearsontechgroup.com**

For sales outside the United States, please contact

**International Sales**
**international@pearsoned.com**

**This Book Is Safari Enabled**

The Safari® Enabled icon on the cover of your favorite technology book means the book is available through Safari Bookshelf. When you buy this book, you get free access to the online edition for 45 days.

Safari Bookshelf is an electronic reference library that lets you easily search thousands of technical books, find code samples, download chapters, and access technical information whenever and wherever you need it.

To gain 45-day Safari Enabled access to this book:

- Go to http://www.quepublishing.com/safarienabled
- Complete the brief registration form
- Enter the coupon code SUD2-5RYE-4ZBB-TKDM-7QC3

If you have difficulty registering on Safari Bookshelf or accessing the online edition, please email customer-service@safaribooksonline.com.

**Associate Publisher**
Greg Wiegand

**Acquisitions Editor**
Laura Norman

**Development Editor**
Laura Norman

**Managing Editor**
Gina Kanouse

**Project Editor**
Andy Beaster

**Indexer**
Lisa Stumpf

**Technical Editor**
Brian Hubbard

**Publishing Coordinator**
Cindy J. Teeters

**Designer**
Anne Jones

**Compositor**
Nonie Ratcliff

# Table of Contents

## IV Getting Things Done with Leopard's Applications

# About the Author

**Brad Miser** has written extensively about all things Macintosh, with his favorite topics being OS X and the amazing "i" applications that empower Mac OS X users to unleash their digital creativity. In addition to *Special Edition Using Mac OS X Leopard*, Brad has written many other books, including *My iPhone, Sleeping with the Enemy: Running Windows on a Mac (digital Short Cut); Special Edition Using Mac OS X, v10.4 Tiger*; *Absolute Beginner's Guide to iPod and iTunes*; *Absolute Beginner's Guide to Homeschooling*; *Mac OS X and iLife: Using iTunes, iPhoto, iMovie, and iDVD*; *iDVD 3 Fast & Easy*; *Special Edition Using Mac OS X v10.2*; and *Using Mac OS 8.5*. He has also been an author, development editor, or technical editor on more than 50 other titles. He has written numerous articles in *MacAddict* magazine and has been a featured speaker on various topics at Macworld Expo, at user group meetings, and in other venues.

Brad is or has been a sales support specialist, the director of product and customer services, and the manager of education and support services for several software development companies. Previously, he was the lead proposal specialist for an aircraft engine manufacturer, a development editor for a computer book publisher, and a civilian aviation test officer/engineer for the U.S. Army. Brad holds a Bachelor of Science degree in mechanical engineering from California Polytechnic State University at San Luis Obispo and has received advanced education in maintainability engineering, business, and other topics.

In addition to his passion for silicon-based technology, Brad likes to ride his steel-based technology, AKA a motorcycle, whenever and wherever possible.

A native of California, Brad now lives in Brownsburg, Indiana, with his wife Amy; their three daughters, Jill, Emily, and Grace; and a rabbit named Bun-Bun.

Brad would love to hear about your experiences with this book (the good, the bad, and the ugly). You can write to him at `bradmacosx@mac.com`.

## Dedication

*To those who have given the last full measure of devotion so that the rest of us can be free.*

## Acknowledgments

To the following people on the *Special Edition Using Mac OS X Leopard* project team, my sincere appreciation for your hard work on this book:

Laura Norman, my acquisitions and development editor, who helped me get the focus of the first edition of this book on track when I had gone astray and kept me in line the rest of the way. She also made sure that I kept the text flowing when we revised this tome for Mac OS X version 10.5. Laura, getting through such a big book with me as the author four times should earn you a medal of some kind!

Marta Justak of Justak Literary Services, my agent, for getting me signed up for this project. Marta was also a constant source of support for me during the process and was always ready to lend an ear to listen to whatever I needed to say. Marta, many times I needed to bounce an idea or complaint off someone—thanks for being there for me!

Brian Hubbard, my technical editor, who did a great job to ensure that the information in this book is both accurate and useful. Brian, I tried my best to sneak mistakes past you, but you caught me every time—thanks for a job well done! Brian also went way above and beyond the call of duty by revising the in-process manuscript to account for the many changes Apple made to Leopard during its long development process. Without Brian's hard work, this book would not have been possible.

Andy Beaster, my project editor, who skillfully managed the hundreds of files that it took to make this book. Andy, thanks for keeping everything current and making sure that things got where they needed to be when they needed to be there.

Ann Jones, for the interior design and cover of the book. You made this book a pleasure to look at! Also, a thanks for developing the book's cover. It is too bad that you can't judge a book by its cover because, if you could, everyone would believe that this book is top-notch—thanks!

Que's production and sales team for printing the book and getting it into your hands. Thanks, everybody!

And now for a few people who weren't on the project team, but who were essential to me personally:

Amy Miser, for supporting me while I took on this mammoth project for the fifth time and for being understanding about my need to do it yet one more time; living with an author isn't always lots of fun, especially with a big, complex book like this one. Amy, I promise, no more big books—until the next one! ;-)

Jill, Emily, and Grace Miser, for helping me remember that there is a lot more to life than pounding the keys—even though sometimes it seemed as if that was all I was doing. Girls, you brought lots of smiles to my face in stressful times. Thanks for reminding me of what is really important. And, a special thanks to Bun-Bun the rabbit for his early-morning visits to cheer me up while I was working!

Rick Ehrhardt for being such a good friend to me; I especially appreciate the occasional evening out—La Hacienda and Best Buy anyone?

# We Want to Hear from You!

As the reader of this book, *you* are our most important critic and commentator. We value your opinion and want to know what we're doing right, what we could do better, what areas you'd like to see us publish in, and any other words of wisdom you're willing to pass our way.

As an associate publisher for Que, I welcome your comments. You can email or write me directly to let me know what you did or didn't like about this book—as well as what we can do to make our books better.

*Please note that I cannot help you with technical problems related to the topic of this book. We do have a User Services group, however, where I will forward specific technical questions related to the book.*

When you write, please be sure to include this book's title and author as well as your name, email address, and phone number. I will carefully review your comments and share them with the author and editors who worked on the book.

Email: feedback@quepublishing.com

Mail: Greg Wiegand
Associate Publisher
Que Publishing
800 East 96th Street
Indianapolis, IN 46240 USA

For more information about this book or another Que title, visit our website at www.quepublishing.com. Type the ISBN (excluding hyphens) or the title of a book in the Search field to find the page you're looking for.

# INTRODUCTION

## In this introduction

# WELCOME TO MAC OS X

Now in its fifth major release (version 10.5), Mac OS X has been called many things, from revolutionary to evolutionary to being so innovative that it threatened the very existence of the Mac as we had come to know and love it. And all of those descriptions were appropriate.

The first release of Mac OS X was a giant leap forward for the Mac platform. Its innovations in basic architecture, the way it works, and even its user interface made Mac OS X the most significant event for Mac users since the first Mac was introduced back in the Jurassic period, circa 1984. Mac OS X was more stable, more powerful, and even more beautiful than any previous version. However, the first version of Mac OS X had some rough spots, not surprising at all because it was the first release of a brand-new OS (despite the version number implying it was the successor to Mac OS 9).

About a year later, version 10.2 was released. This release smoothed many of the rough edges left over from version 10.1 and added many new features. Due to some fundamental improvements in the core operating system, version 10.2 caused some ripples in the Mac universe because many applications had to be updated to run under that version.

Version 10.3 began to show the maturity of Mac OS X's more than two years of life. Version 10.3 continued the process of refining the OS along with adding some excellent new features, such as a totally redesigned Finder, Expose, improved applications, and so on. It also continued to improve the stability and performance of the OS. Much of the foundation work for the OS was accomplished by the previous two releases; version 10.3 was less disruptive than the previous releases while continuing to make major improvements in functionality, reliability, and performance.

Version 10.4 was less of a change than previous releases of Mac OS X were. This was good news because it meant that the core OS functionality has stabilized, and transitions to each subsequent version will have lots of benefits with less pain. While it was less disruptive than previous releases, new features abounded, such as the Dashboard and widgets, which provide instant access to accessory applications; the Spotlight, which enables you to quickly search your Mac for information of all kinds at the same time, and so on.

Now, version 10.5 continues to refine the OS while adding totally new features. For example, the new Time Machine application enables you to perform one of the most critical tasks (seldom done by most Mac users) that of backing up your data. Other areas have continued to improve such as new Finder functionality for the desktop and the cool web widget creation tool that enables you to capture parts of web pages as widgets on your Dashboard.

Of course, if you are new to the Mac or have never used Mac OS X before, all the previous versions don't matter. You get to enjoy the results of Mac OS X's evolution without having been through the growth process.

Mac OS X is a very powerful and feature-rich OS. Although many of the features of the OS are intuitive, some might not be obvious to you. And because of the amazing number of powerful applications that are part of the standard Mac OS X installation, such as Safari, iTunes, and many others, using Mac OS X effectively is much more than just manipulating the Finder and using the Dock. That is where this book comes in.

# INTRODUCTION TO *SPECIAL EDITION USING MAC OS X LEOPARD*

This book has two fundamental purposes:

- To help you make the jump to Mac OS X as efficiently as possible
- To provide a reference for you to use as you continue to grow in your Mac OS X use

To accomplish the first purpose, this book is written in a straightforward style; you won't find any fluff here. The book is designed to help you *use* Mac OS X as efficiently and effectively as possible. Everything about the book is an attempt to make specific information accessible and applicable to your daily Mac life. You will find only the background information you need to understand how to apply specific techniques and technologies; the focus is on the information you need to apply what you learn to your own Mac.

To accomplish the second purpose, this book covers an extremely broad range of topics. In addition to coverage of the core functionality of the desktop, you will find extensive coverage of topics to enable you to accomplish productive work with your Mac, such as surfing the Net, burning discs, and using Mac OS X's applications to accomplish specific tasks. This book also contains substantial amounts of information to help you add devices to expand your system so you can accomplish even more. Because Mac OS X has been designed to be networked, you will learn how to use its capabilities in this area to connect with other Macs, as well as to Windows networks. You'll learn how to both prevent and solve OS X problems along the way.

## HOW THIS BOOK IS ORGANIZED

This book consists of several parts, each of which contains at least two chapters. The following list provides an overview of this book's contents:

- **Part I, "Exploring the Core"**—This part gets you started on the right foot. You'll learn the core operations of the OS, from getting started with Mac OS X to working with the Finder, the Dock, the Dashboard, and more.
- **Part II, "Mastering the System"**—After Part I, you'll be ready to take your Mac use further. This part starts with information you need to be able to run Windows applications on your Mac. Then you'll explore Mac OS X in depth, such as customizing it. You'll also find out how to use Unix on your Mac. If you use a mobile Mac, you'll want to read the last chapter in this part, which shows you Mac OS X on one of these cool machines.

- **Part III, "Living in a Connected World"**—Mac OS X has been designed to facilitate your interaction with networks and with the Internet. This part of the book explains how to configure Mac OS X for the Internet and how to use the tools it provides after you are connected. You'll also learn how to create and manage wired and wireless networks.
- **Part IV, "Getting Things Done with Leopard's Applications"**—Mac OS X includes a number of useful applications, such as Mail, Safari, iTunes, Address Book, iCal, iChat, and others. In this part, you'll learn how to take advantage of these great applications.
- **Part V, " Expanding the System"**—No Mac is an island; this part of the book helps you understand the input and output technologies supported by Mac OS X to enable you to select and add the peripheral devices you need.
- **Part VI, " Protecting, Maintaining, and Repairing Your Mac"**—As great as Mac OS X is, you still need to know how to minimize problems with good preventive maintenance actions and be able to effectively solve any problems you do experience. You should also learn how to use Mac OS X's extensive security features to protect your Mac.

## Special Features

This book includes the following special features:

- **Chapter roadmaps**—At the beginning of each chapter, you will find a list of the top-level topics addressed in that chapter. This list will enable you to quickly see the type of information the chapter contains.
- **Troubleshooting**—Many chapters in the book have a section dedicated to troubleshooting specific problems related to the chapter's topic. Cross-references to the solutions to these problems are placed in the context of relevant text in the chapter as Troubleshooting Notes to make them easy to locate.
- **Mac OS X to the Max**—Some chapters end with a "Mac OS X to the Max" section. These sections contain extra information that will help you make the most of Mac OS X. For example, tables of keyboard shortcuts are included to help you work more efficiently. Other sections include summaries of information that is outside the scope of the book, but which you should be aware of.
- **Notes**—Notes provide additional commentary or explanation that doesn't fit neatly into the surrounding text. You will find detailed explanations of how something works, alternative ways of performing a task, and comparisons between Mac OS X and previous versions of the OS.
- **On the Web notes**—These notes provide you with URLs you can visit to get more information or other resources relating to the topic being discussed. They are distinguished by the special icon you see here.
- **Tips**—Tips help you work more efficiently by providing shortcuts or hints about alternative and faster ways of accomplishing a task.
- **Cautions**—These sidebars provide a warning to you about situations that involve possible danger to your Mac or its data.

- **Cross-references**—Many topics are connected to other topics in various ways. Cross-references help you link related information together, no matter where that information appears in the book. When another section is related to one you are reading, a cross-reference will direct you to a specific page in the book on which you will find the related information.

## Conventions

To make things as clear as possible, this book doesn't use many special conventions or formatting techniques to identify specific kinds of information. However, there are a few things you need to be aware of:

- Menu commands are referred to by starting with the menu name and moving down to the specific command while separating each layer with a comma. For example, rather than writing, "Open the Terminal menu, then select the Services command, then select the Mail command, and then select Mail Text," I use a shorthand technique. In this example, I would write, "Select Terminal, Services, Mail, Mail Text." This shorthand makes the command structure more clear and cuts back on the number of words you have to read.
- When you are working in the Terminal, the commands you enter and the output you see are in a `monospace font like this`.
- Variables that stand for text that is specific to you are usually in *italics*. For example, if I need to refer to your username in a specific location, I write, "Users/*username*, where *username* is your username," to indicate that you should look for your own information in place of the italicized phrase.

## Who Should Use This Book

In this book, I've made certain assumptions about your specific experience with the Mac OS and your general comfort level with technology. The biggest assumption is that you are quite comfortable with the fundamentals of using the Mac OS. For example, you won't find any explanations of how to use a mouse, how to copy and move files, the basics of drag and drop, and so on. When there are significant differences in these basic tasks under Mac OS X as compared to the previous versions of the OS, you will find those differences explained, but probably not in enough detail to teach you how to do them if you have never done them before.

If you are completely new to computers, you will still find this book very useful, but you will also need a companion book that explains the fundamentals of using a Mac in more detail than is provided in this book, such as *Easy Mac OS X Leopard* (0-7897-3771-X).

If you have used previous versions of the Mac OS, such as Mac OS 9 or earlier versions of Mac OS X, and are comfortable with basic tasks, this book will help you make the jump to Mac OS X version 10.5 in a short time. It also will serve as a comprehensive reference for you as you explore this amazing operating system.

PART I

# Exploring the Core

# CHAPTER 1

# Getting Started with Mac OS X

## In this chapter

1

# WELCOME TO MAC OS X

If you have not yet installed Mac OS X, before you go any further in this chapter, grab your Mac OS X 10.5 Installation disc and step through the installation process. Once you have Mac OS X installed on your Mac, come back here.

If you have already installed Mac OS X, you have created at least one user account because that is part of installing the OS. That's all you need to get started with Mac OS X, which is where this chapter comes in.

# STARTING UP MAC OS X

Mac OS X is truly a multi-user operating system. This offers many benefits to you, but it also means that when you use the OS, you have to log in as a particular user. When you do so, what you can see and do depends on the settings for the user account you use to log in to the system. Understanding and managing the user accounts on your Mac is critical to getting the most from your computer.

**NOTE**

> When you first start up Mac OS X after installing it, you didn't need to select a user account to log in. That's because by default Mac OS X uses the automatic login mode, which means that a designated user account is selected by your Mac automatically when it starts up. Because your Mac does it for you, you might not even realize that you have logged in. After your Mac starts up, the desktop appears just like when you log in to a user account manually. However, your Mac has gone through the login process–it just entered all the required information for you automatically.

In addition to the basic process of logging into your Mac, the user account under which you log in determines a lot of what you can do and the data you can see. The first user account you created during the installation process was an administrator user account, which provides you with pretty broad access to the system. But, you'll only have access to data associated with that user account.

In the rest of this section, you'll get an overview of the resources to which you have access with most types of user accounts.

⇨ To learn how to create, configure, and use user accounts, **see** Chapter 11, "Configuring and Working with User Accounts," **p. 231**.

---

**Directory Versus Folder**

Under Mac OS X, the terms *directory* and *folder* are basically synonymous. Typically, non-GUI operating systems use the term *directory*, whereas GUI operating systems, such as Mac OS X, use the term *folder*. Because Mac OS X has Unix as its foundation and the term *directory* is used under Unix, you will see folders referred to as *directories* in many places. The reason for this is that you can access the Unix command line; when you access your Mac's files using the command line, the concept of folders doesn't really apply (because there is no graphical element to the user interface). Practically speaking, however, the terms are equivalent and are interchangeable. You will see that I use both throughout this book.

---

## Understanding the Home Folder

Each user account on your Mac has a Home folder. This folder contains other folders that are used to store private files, public files, and system resources (such as preferences and keychains) for that user account. With two exceptions (the Public and Site folders), only someone logged in under a user account can access the folders in that user account's Home folder.

**CAUTION**

> The exception to the general rule about accessing the folders in another user's Home folder is the *root* account. The root user account can access everything on your Mac and is outside the normal security provided by user accounts. You should use the root account only in special situations, and you really need to understand it before you use it.

⇨ To learn about the root account, **see** "Enabling the Root User Account," **p. 261**.

By default, a user's Home folder contains the folders shown in Figure 1.1. However, the user can create additional folders within the Home folder. And, of course, users can create additional folders within the default folders contained in the Home folder as well. Any folders created with a Home folder take on the security settings of that folder. For example, if a user creates a folder within the Documents folder, that folder can only be accessed by that user.

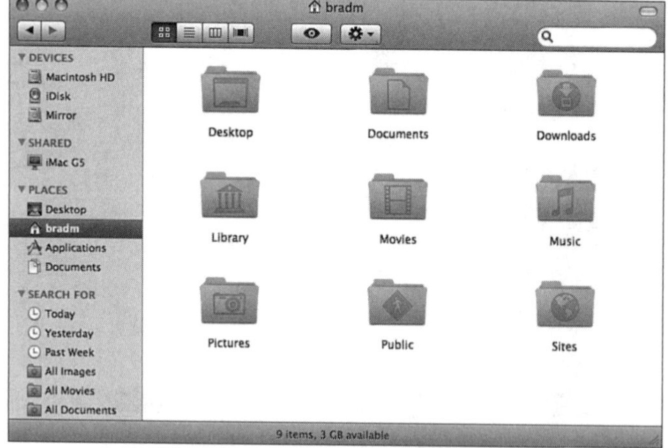


**Figure 1.1**
Every user account on your Mac has a Home folder; this folder contains folders that only that user can access (except for the Public and Sites folders).

Most of these folders are easy to understand because they are used to organize a user's files. For example, the Documents folder is the default location in which the user stores documents he creates. The Desktop folder contains items that are stored on that user's desktop (which, by the way, means that each user account has a unique desktop), and so on.

Some applications will automatically select a folder when storing files. For example, when you add music files to your iTunes Library, they are stored in the iTunes folder within the Music folder. Likewise, when you create movies with iMovie, they are stored in the Movies folder.

1

**TIP**

> You can quickly tell which user account is active by looking at the Home directory icon in the Finder window's Places sidebar, which is always located at the left side of Finder windows. It looks like a house for the current user's Home folder; the other Home directory icons are plain folders. The short name for a user account appears in the title bar of that user's Home folder (in Figure 1.1, the currently logged in account is called bradm).

Only someone logged in under a user account can access the contents of the folders in that user's Home folder—except for the Public and Sites folders that can be accessed by anyone using your Mac. Locked folders have an icon that includes a red circle with a minus sign (see Figure 1.2). If someone other than those who have permission attempts to open one of these protected folders, they only see a warning message and not any of the contents of the protected folder. Accessible folders in another user's directory have the plain folder icon, which means their contents are available to that user. Unlocked default folders in the current user's Home directory have the decorative Mac OS X icons (refer back to Figure 1.1). (Folders you create within your Home folder will have the generic folder icon but will be protected in the same way as its default folders.)

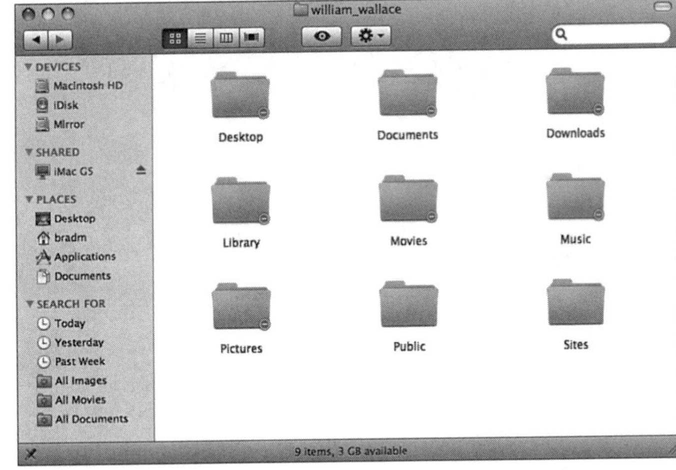


**Figure 1.2**
When you view another user's Home directory, the protected folders are marked with the minus icon to indicate that their contents are inaccessible to you.

**NOTE**

> Notice in Figure 1.2 that the title of the window shown is "william_wallace." This is the name of another user account; you can tell that it isn't the one currently logged in because it doesn't appear in the Places sidebar nor does its icon look like a house.

There are three folders in each Home folder that don't behave like the others; those are the Public, Sites, and Library folders.

## Understanding the Public Folder

A user's Public folder is accessible by users logged in under any account (see Figure 1.3). Its purpose is to enable users to share files that are stored within different user accounts on the same computer. To share your files with other users, simply store them in your Public folder. Other users can then open your Public folder to get to those files. Likewise, to access files other users have shared with you, you can open their Public folder.

**Figure 1.3**
In this example, I've opened another user's Public folder; I can work with any files it contains (as can other users) or I can place files in the Drop Box folder.

As you can see in Figure 1.3, the Public folder also contains a Drop Box folder. This folder can be seen by other users and they can place files in it, but it can't be opened by anyone except the owner of the user account under which that drop box is stored. This is useful when you want other users to be able to transfer files to you, but you want those files to be hidden from other users.

## Understanding the Sites Folder

The Sites folder contains files for each user's website. Part of each user account's resources is a website that can be accessed over a local network, from another user's account, or from the Internet (depending on how the Mac's Internet access is configured). You place the files for a user's website in the Sites folder to publish that site.

⇨ To learn how to create and serve a website from the Sites folder, **see** "Mac OS X to the Max: Using Mac OS X to Serve Web Pages," **p. 458**.

## Understanding the Library Folder

The Library folder is the only folder in the Home directory that is not intended for document storage. It contains items related to the configuration of the user account and all the system-related files for that account. For example, user and appplication preferences are stored here, as are font collections, addresses, keychains, and so on. Basically, any file that affects how the system works or looks that is specific to a user account is stored in the Library directory. You won't usually access this folder unless you are troubleshooting problems; you will learn more about the Library folder later in this book.

1

### UNDERSTANDING PARENTAL CONTROLS

In Mac OS X version 10.5, user accounts also include the parental controls feature. This feature enables you to tighten the security of a user account in specific situations, such as to limit email access, web browsing, and so on. For example, you can set the specific people with whom the user can exchange email.

While this feature is primarily intended to be used for younger people, it can be useful for any user account that you want to set some limits on. Parental Controls allow you to define what applications a user can run, and what changes they can make to their account.

⇨ To learn how to secure a user's access with Parental Controls, **see** Chapter 39, "Securing a Mac," **p. 941**.

## RESTARTING YOUR MAC

Although Mac OS X is very stable and you will generally leave it running for long periods of time, there are occasions when you need to restart your Mac to correct some problem that is occurring. Also, occasionally, you will need to restart your Mac after making system changes or installing new software.

Restarting Mac OS X is simple. You can restart Mac OS X in a couple of ways:

- Select Apple menu, Restart.
- Click Restart in a prompt dialog box or sheet, such as one that appears after you've installed software that requires your Mac be restarted (an OS X update, for example).
- Click Restart in the Login window.
- On a MacBook or MacBook Pro, press the Power button briefly and choose Restart in the resulting dialog box.

If Fast User Switching is enabled when you restart a Mac and other user accounts are logged in, you will see a warning dialog box. To be able to restart, you need to input an administrator user name and password and then click the Restart button.

⇨ To understand more about Fast User Switching, **see** "Enabling and Using Fast User Switching," **p. 255** (Chapter 11).

## SHUTTING DOWN YOUR MAC

There isn't really much reason to turn a Mac off. Using the Energy Saver settings, you can configure your Mac to sleep when you aren't actively using it; this saves wear on the Mac's moving parts and theoretically saves energy (but I doubt it will make any difference in your electric bill!). Most of the time, when you are done working with your computer and you want to secure it, you should simply log out. This stops all the processes that are running and puts your Mac in a safe condition. Logging in is much faster because you don't have to wait for your computer to start up. Even better, select Login Window on the Fast User Switching menu to keep your account logged in and protected.

Still, if you are leaving your Mac for a long time, you might want to shut it down. You can do so in the following ways:

- Select Apple menu, Shut Down.
- Press Shift-⌘-Q to log out, confirm the logout, and then click Shut Down in the Login window.

If you Mac doesn't respond to any commands, you might need to perform a hard shut down. Do so by pressing the Power key and holding it down until the Mac turns off. You won't have a chance to save any open files so you should use this method only when all other options have failed and your Mac is locked up. A hard shut down is definitely a last resort option, so use it only when you really need to.

# CHAPTER 2

# Viewing and Navigating Mac OS X Finder Windows

## In this chapter

## Working with Finder Windows

Mac OS X version 10.5 Finder windows provide the same function that Finder windows always have; that is, just like windows in your car, Finder windows enable you to see things. Of course, in the case of Mac OS X, you won't be looking for on-coming traffic, but rather you'll be looking for volumes, discs, folders, and files with which you want to work. In addition to their nice appearance, Finder windows offer lots of functionality, some of which are more obvious than others (see Figure 2.1). In this section, you'll learn everything you need to know to master using Finder windows.



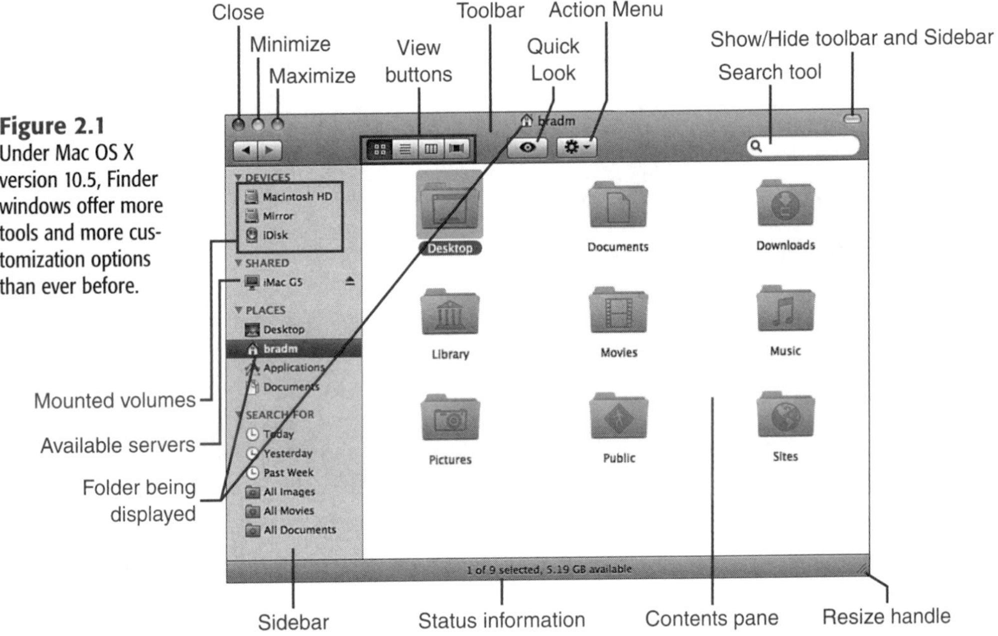


**Figure 2.1**
Under Mac OS X version 10.5, Finder windows offer more tools and more customization options than ever before.

### Opening Finder Windows

You can open Finder windows in several ways. If you click the Finder icon on the Dock (which is the Mac OS X icon), one of two things can happen. If no Finder windows are currently open, a new Finder window appears showing the contents of the default location you select. (Initially, this is your Home folder, but you can select any folder you'd like.) If at least one Finder window is already open, you will move to the Finder window in which you most recently worked.

You can also open a new Finder window by selecting File, New Finder Window (⌘-N). When you open a new Finder window, the result is always the same: The contents of your default location are displayed. (This is initially set to be your Home folder.)

The Mac OS X Finder uses a web-like model in that each new Finder window you open starts a "chain" of windows (thus, the Back and Forward buttons in the Finder window toolbar). The first window in every new chain you start by using the New Finder Window command is always the directory you define as the default. You can have many window chains open at the same time, which is another similarity to web windows. (You can quickly jump into specific folders using the toolbar, the Sidebar, the Go menu, and keyboard shortcuts.)

⇨ To learn how to navigate Finder windows, **see** "Navigating Finder Windows," **p. 31**.

By default, when you open an item (such as a folder), its contents replace the contents of the previous item that appeared in the Finder window you were viewing. (You can change this behavior globally with a preference setting.) You can also override this behavior so the new Finder window is separate from the first one by holding down the ⌘ key while you double-click an icon. This opens a new chain of Finder windows, with the contents of the item you opened displayed in the first window.



**TIP**

> This default behavior assumes that the toolbar and Sidebar are shown in a Finder window. If not, opening a folder always opens a new, separate chain of Finder windows.

After you have one Finder window open, you can open other Finder windows (either in the same chain of windows or by starting a new chain) to view the contents of a different folder, volume, disc, and so on. To view the contents of a folder, volume, or disc shown in the current Finder window, double-click the icon for the item you want to open, or select an item and select File, Open. The Open keyboard shortcut works, too—just select an item and press ⌘-O to open it. You can also open an item's contextual menu by right-clicking it and selecting Open. If those aren't enough options for you, here is one more: Select an item and choose Open on the Action menu. The contents of the item you opened replace the window's current contents and the name shown at the top of the window becomes the name of the item you opened.

As you probably know, you can choose different views for Finder windows. When you open a new Finder window, it always assumes the view you selected the last time you viewed that item in a Finder window. You'll learn more about Mac OS X Finder window views later in this chapter.

**NOTE**

> If you select an item while a Finder window is in the Column view, its contents are displayed in a new column.

To reiterate this sometimes confusing behavior of Mac OS X windows, the view in which a new window opens is determined by the view you used for that window the last time you viewed it. In other words, windows retain their view settings, even if the window from which you opened a separate Finder window is different. For example, if you viewed the Applications directory in List view, it appears in List view whenever you open it in a new Finder window until you change the view in which it appears.

Along the left edge of every Finder window is the Sidebar. This handy tool consists of several sections. In the Devices section are all the volumes mounted on your Mac, including hard disk volumes, disk image volumes, your iDisk, CDs, DVDs, and so on. The Shared section will display icons for the servers that are available on your local area network (LAN). In the Places section of the sidebar are some of the folders in your Home folder and the Applications folder. You can add any folders, applications, documents, or other files to or remove them from this area to completely customize it. Finally, the Search For section of the sidebar allows you to quickly find content base upon pre-determined searches, and you can also store smart folders and Spotlight searches here. The purpose of the Sidebar is to enable you to quickly open a Finder window that displays the contents of any item it contains.

When you select a volume or folder in the Sidebar, its contents appear in the Finder window. The currently selected item is highlighted so you can easily tell what is selected. (The name of the currently selected item appears at the top of the window as well.) If you select a document or application, that item opens just like when you double-click it.

**TIP**

If you hold down the ⌘ key while you click an item in the Sidebar, that item opens in a new Finder window chain. If you hold down the Option key when you click an item in the Sidebar, that item opens in a new Finder window and the previous window closes.

### CONFIGURING HOW NEW FINDER WINDOWS OPEN

To configure how Finder windows open, perform the following steps:

1. Press ⌘-, or select Finder, Preferences; when the Finder Preferences window opens, click the General tab if it isn't selected already (see Figure 2.2).

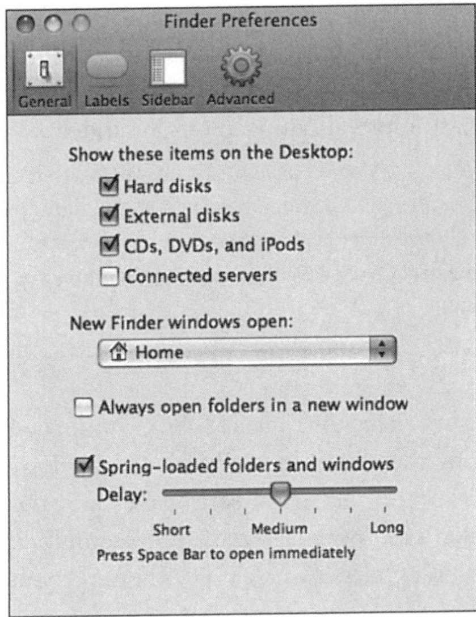


**Figure 2.2**
Use the General pane of the Finder Preferences window to configure how new Finder windows open.

2. On the "New Finder windows open" pop-up menu, select the location where you want new Finder window chains you open to start.

   On the pop-up menu, you see various volumes mounted on your Mac along with your Home and Documents folders. To choose one of these as the starting location for new Finder window chains, simply select it on the menu.

   To select a location not shown on the pop-up menu, choose Other. Then use the "Choose a Folder" dialog box to move to and choose the folder that you want to be your starting place. Navigating such dialog boxes is very much like navigating in a Finder window in the Column view.

⇨ To learn how to navigate in Finder windows using the Column view, **see** "Navigating Finder Windows," **p. 31**.

**NOTE**

> One of the nice features of Mac OS X is that most preference changes are made in real time—you don't have to close the Preferences window to see the results of your changes. For example, when you make the change in the previous steps, the window-opening behavior becomes active as soon as you make a selection on the pop-up menu. A good habit is to leave preference windows open as you make changes and close the windows only when you are happy with all the changes you have made.

3. If you prefer that when you open an item, the item's contents always appear in a new Finder window chain, check the "Always open folders in a new window" check box. However, because this option can lead to a proliferation of Finder windows, I recommend that you leave this option off. (Remember that you can always open a new Finder window chain by holding down the ⌘ key when you double-click an item.) A better way to view content is to use the Column view, which enables you to quickly move to any location, as you will see later in this chapter.

⇨ To learn more about Mac OS X directories, **see** "Understanding Mac OS X Directories," **p. 70**.

**NOTE**

> As you can see, you can choose a number of options for working with new Finder windows. Because my preferences are to have my Home folder open, and open new items in the current Finder window, that is what this chapter assumes. I point out differences along the way if you choose other preferences.

### Working with Spring-Loaded Folders

Mac OS X Finder windows can be *spring-loaded* (this feature is turned on by default), meaning that they pop open when you drag an item onto a closed folder. This enables you to quickly place an item within nested folders without having to open each folder individually. Simply drag an item onto a closed folder so the folder is highlighted and "springs" open. After the delay time (which you can set) has passed, the highlighted folder opens in a separate Finder window chain. (Unless you are viewing the window in Column view, in which case a new column appears for the item onto which you are dragging the item.) You can then drag the item onto the next folder and continue the process until you have placed it in its final destination. When you release the mouse button, what happens depends on the Finder preference you have selected. If new folders open in the same Finder window, you remain in the location where you placed the item. If new folders always open in a new Finder window, you return to the window where you started (however, the destination folder will remain open in its Finder window).

2

**TIP**

> You can cause a folder to spring open immediately by pressing the spacebar when you drag an item onto a closed folder.

You can configure your Mac's spring-loaded behavior by following these steps:

1. Click the General tab in the Finder Preferences dialog box.
2. Check the "Spring-loaded folders and windows" check box to turn this feature back on if you have turned it off (it is on by default).
3. Use the Delay slider to set the amount of delay time (the time between when you drag an item onto a folder and when that folder springs open).
4. Experiment to see whether the delay time is set correctly for you; if not, change it.

## SCROLLING FINDER WINDOWS

When the contents of a Finder window can't be shown in the amount of space the window currently has, you use the scrollbars to view contents that are out of sight. By default, the scrollbars are Mac OS X blue; you can change this to graphite with the Appearance pane of the System Preferences application. You can set the scroll arrows to both be located in the lower-right corner of Finder windows, or have an arrow located at each end of the scrollbars.

Mac OS X scrolling controls work as you expect them to. You have the following options:

- Drag the scrollbars.

**NOTE**

> As with previous versions of Mac OS X, the length of the scrollbar is proportional to the amount of the window you can see in the view. For example, if most of the scrollbar is filled in with color, you can view most of the window's contents. If the colored portion is relatively small, you can't view very much of the window's content.

- Click above or below or to the left or right of the bar to scroll one screen's worth at a time.
- Click the scroll arrows.

- Press the Page Up and Page Down keys to scroll vertically.
- Press the Home key to jump to the top of the window or the End key to jump to the bottom.
- Use the arrow keys or Tab (and Shift-Tab) to move among the items in the window (which also scrolls the window when you move outside the current view).

You can modify several aspects of scrolling behavior. You can change the location of the scroll arrows. And, rather than moving an entire page each time you click above, below, to the left, or to the right of a scrollbar, you can set the scrolling so that you move to the relative location you click instead. You can also turn on smooth scrolling, which smoothes the appearance of a window when you scroll in it. Follow these steps to modify these scrolling features:



1. Open the System Preferences application.
2. In the Personal section, click Appearance.
3. To change the locations of the scroll arrows, click the Together radio button to have the scroll arrows in the lower-right corner of windows or the "At top and bottom" radio button to place an arrow at each end of the scrollbars (see Figure 2.3).

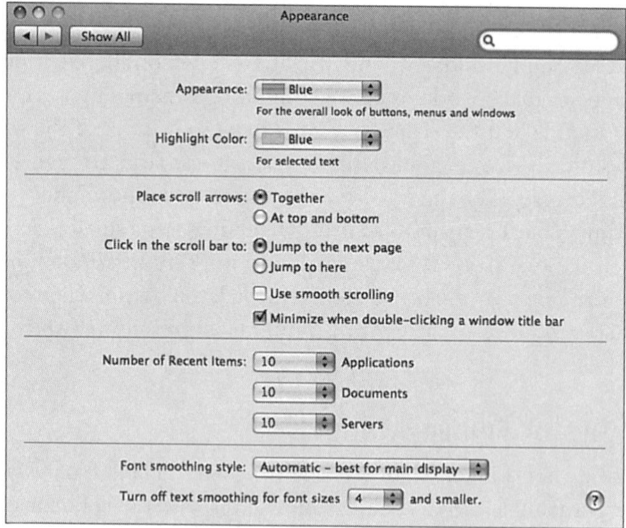


**Figure 2.3**
The Appearance pane of the System Preferences utility enables you to modify the behavior of window scrolling.

4. To change how scrolling works when you click in the scrollbar, click the "Jump to the next page" radio button to scroll a screen at a time or the "Jump to here" radio button to move to a position in the window that is relative to where you click in the scrollbar.
5. Check the "Use smooth scrolling" check box to turn on smooth scrolling.

**TIP**

> This is a good chance to practice Mac OS X preference setting techniques. Make your changes to the Appearance pane, but leave the System Preferences application open. Click in a Finder window; your changes immediately become active. If you are satisfied, jump back to the System Preferences application and quit it. If not, jump back into the Appearance pane and continue making changes until you are satisfied.



## RESIZING WINDOWS

Resizing windows also works as you might expect. To change the size of a window, drag its Resize handle until the window is the size you want it to be.

You can also use the Maximize button to make a window large enough to display all the items it contains or until it fills the screen, whichever comes first. Click the button and the window jumps to the size it needs to show all the items it contains or until it fills the available screen space. Click the button again to return it to its previous size.

You can also use this button to quickly swap between two sizes for a window. Make the window a size you like. When you click the Maximize button, it expands to its maximum size. Click the button again and it returns to the previous size. Each time you click the Maximize button, the window returns to the size it was previously (either the maximum size or the size you set).

If you are like me and have lots of Finder windows open on the Desktop, you can use this resizing behavior to make working between multiple windows more convenient. Select an open window and make it the size you want it to be so it is out of the way and you can store many windows of this size on your desktop; make it just large enough so you can see the window's title. You can click the Maximize button to open the window to work in it. Then, click the Maximize button again to return the window to its small size. Use the button to toggle between the two sizes. When you need to work in the window, make it large by clicking the Maximize button. When you are done, click the button again to make it small. You might find this even more convenient than minimizing windows (which you'll learn about shortly).

## RESIZING THE PANES OF FINDER WINDOWS

As you learned earlier, Finder windows have two panes. The left pane is the Sidebar, whereas the right pane is the Contents pane that displays the contents of the item you are viewing in the Finder window. You can change the relative size of the Sidebar by dragging the line that is located between the two panes. Drag this to the left, and the Sidebar takes up less room in the window. Drag it to the right, and the Sidebar takes up more window space.

The Sidebar retains your settings as long as you work within the same Finder window chain. When you open a new chain, the Sidebar becomes its default size.

## CLOSING, MINIMIZING, AND MAXIMIZING FINDER WINDOWS

Among the most distinctive features of Mac OS X are the three stoplight-type controls located in the upper-left corner of windows (refer to Figure 2.1). The red button (on the far left) closes the window. The gold button (in the middle) minimizes the window, which shrinks it and moves it to the right side of the Dock. The green button maximizes the window, which makes it as large as it needs to be to display all the items in the window until that window fills the screen (and returns it to the previous size, as you learned in the previous section).

⇨ To learn how to use the Dock, **see** Chapter 5, "Using and Customizing the Dock," **p. 107**.

By default, you can also minimize a window (thus moving it onto the Dock) by double-clicking its title bar.



**TIP**

If for some reason you don't want to minimize a window by double-clicking in its title bar, open the Appearance pane of the System Preferences application and uncheck the "Minimize when double clicking a window title bar" check box.

The Close, Minimize, and Maximize buttons work even if the window on which they appear is not active. For example, you can close a window that is in the background by clicking its Close button without making the window active first. (When you point to a button on an inactive window, the button becomes colored so that you know it is active, even though the window itself is not.)

**TIP**

You can close all open Finder windows by holding down the Option key while you click the Close button in one of the open windows.

## MOVING FINDER WINDOWS

You can move a Finder window around the desktop by dragging its title bar or its bottom border.

**NOTE**

If the Sidebar is collapsed, you can't move the window by dragging its bottom border. Only the title bar is visible to be able to move the window.

## USING THE ICON, LIST, COLUMN, OR COVER FLOW VIEWS FOR A FINDER WINDOW

You can view Finder windows in four different views: Icon, List, Column, and Cover Flow.

### VIEWING A FINDER WINDOW IN ICON VIEW

You can easily argue that icons made the Mac. Using friendly pictures to represent files and folders made the computer much friendlier and more approachable than any command line could ever hope to be. Mac OS X version 10.5 continues the use of icons to represent objects, and with their improved appearance under OS X, icons have never looked so good.

You can view Finder windows in the Icon view by opening a window and then selecting View, As Icons; by pressing ⌘-1; or by clicking the Icon view button in the toolbar (see Figure 2.4). The objects in the window become icons, and if you have never seen OS X icons before, prepare to be impressed.

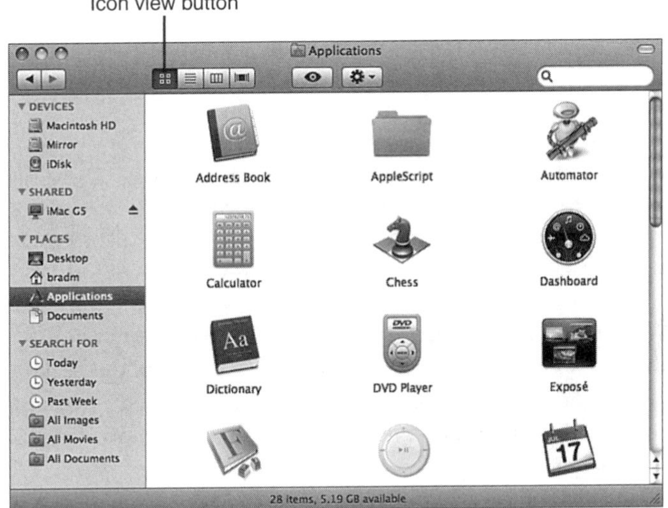


**Figure 2.4**
Other operating systems might have copied the Mac's icons, but none can compare to the snazzy look of Mac OS X.

⇨ You can customize the Icon view for Finder windows. **See** "Customizing Finder Windows," **p. 39**.

If you find that a window in the Icon view is messy, you can use the Clean Up command (View, Clean Up) to straighten up the window for you. This command neatly arranges icons so they line up in an orderly fashion.

**TIP**

> If you select one or more icons and open the View menu, you'll see that the command is now Clean Up Selection. This places the selected items back in an orderly location.

To arrange icons by a specific criterion, select View, Arrange By, and then select the criterion by which you want the window's icons ordered. Your options are the following: Name, Date Modified, Date Created, Size, Kind, or Label.

Although the Icon view is clearly the most pleasing view to look at, it is one of the least useful in terms of the information you see.

### Viewing a Finder Window in List View

The List view presents more information than does the Icon view (see Figure 2.5). To switch to the List view, click the List view button; select View, as List; or press ⌘-2.

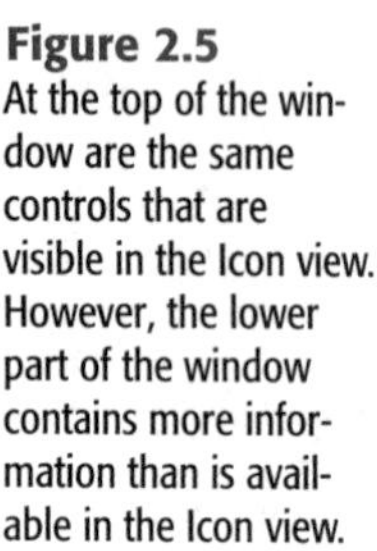

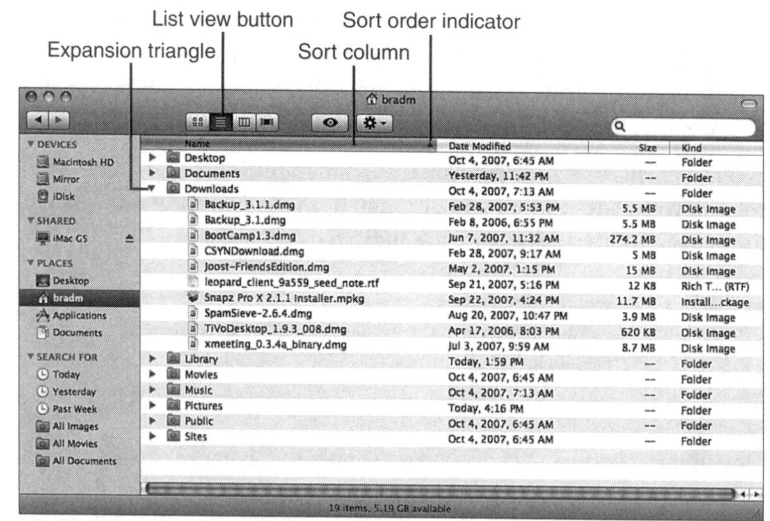


**Figure 2.5**
At the top of the window are the same controls that are visible in the Icon view. However, the lower part of the window contains more information than is available in the Icon view.



The information in the List view is organized into columns, with a header at the top of the column indicating the information in it. The information in the List view is always sorted—you can select the column that is used to sort the contents of the window. You can also determine the order in which the columns appear, change the width of columns, and expand or collapse the contents of folders. The information for each item you see in the default List view is the following:

- **Name**—This is the filename for files, the folder name for folders, the volume name for volumes, and so on.
- **Date Modified**—The most recent date and time when the object was changed. If the date is recent, it's indicated by a relative term, such as "Yesterday."
- **Size**—The size of the item, in kilobytes (KB), megabytes (MB), or gigabytes (GB). By default, the size of folders is not calculated. (You can set Mac OS X to calculate folder sizes if that information is important to you.)
- **Kind**—The type of object it is, such as folder, document, application, volume, and so on.

⇨ You can customize the List view for a single window or for all windows. **See** "Customizing Finder Windows," **p. 39**.

The column by which the window is sorted is highlighted with the highlight color (blue or graphite). To change the sort column, click the column heading of the column by which you want the list to be sorted. That heading is highlighted and the list is re-sorted by that criterion. At the right edge of the column heading for the column by which the window is sorted, you see the Sort order indicator. This shows you in which direction the list is sorted. For example, if the list is sorted by the Name column, an up arrow indicates that the list is sorted alphabetically and a down arrow indicates that the list is sorted in reverse alphabetical order. To change the direction of the sort, click the Column heading—the list is sorted in the opposite order (from ascending to descending or from descending to ascending).

You can resize a column by moving the pointer to the right edge of the column heading cell and clicking. When you do, the cursor changes from the pointer to a vertical line with outward-facing arrows on each side of it. When you see this cursor, drag the column border to resize the column.

You can change the order in which columns appear by dragging the column heading of the column you want to move and dropping it in the new location. The columns reshuffle and then appear in the order you have indicated.

**NOTE**

> You can't change the location of the Name column; it is always the first column in a window in List view.

One of the other benefits of the List view is that you can expand the contents of a folder so you can view them without having to open the folder's window first. To do this, click the right-facing expansion triangle next to the folder's name. The folder expands, and its contents are listed in the window. Click the triangle again to collapse the folder down to its icon.

**TIP**

> When you Option-click the expansion triangle for a collapsed folder, the folder and all the folders it contains are expanded. When you Option-click the expansion triangle for an expanded folder, the folder and all its contents are collapsed again.

## VIEWING A FINDER WINDOW IN COLUMN VIEW

The Column view was introduced for Mac OS X, and its benefit is that you can use it to quickly see and navigate levels of the hierarchy (see Figure 2.6). To switch to the Column view, click the Column view button on the toolbar; press ⌘-3; or select View, as Columns.

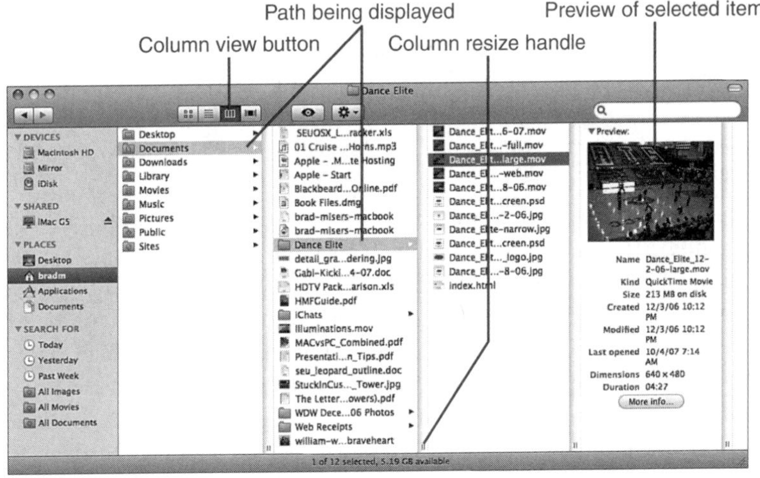


**Figure 2.6**
The Column view is a great way to see the hierarchical organization of directories and folders.

**NOTE**

> One reason the Column view is so important is that you use this view to navigate within Open, Save, and other dialog boxes. When you are using the Column view in dialog boxes, it works just as it does in Finder windows.

As you might suspect, in the Column view, the window is organized into columns, with each column representing a level of the file organization hierarchy. The leftmost column shows the highest level you can see; each column to its right shows the next level down the structure; and the column on the far right shows the lowest level you can see. When you select a file, the rightmost column shows a preview of the selected file. The "path" that you are looking at is indicated by the highlighted items in each column.



Folder icons have a right-facing arrow at the right edge of the column in which they appear, to indicate that when you select them, their contents appear in the column to the immediate right.

For example, put a Finder window in the Column view and click your Home folder on the Sidebar to see its contents. The Home folder's contents are shown in the first column in the window. If you click one of the folders in your Home folder, it becomes highlighted and its contents appear in one of the middle columns. As you select folders within folders, their contents appear in the column to their right. This continues all the way down into a folder until it contains no more folders.

You can move down into the hierarchy by clicking the item about which you want more detail. The column to the right of the item you click shows the contents of what you click. If you click something in the right column and the window is not large enough to display the contents of all the columns, the view shifts and the columns appear to move to the left. You can use this approach to quickly see the contents of any folder on your Mac, no matter how far down in the hierarchy it is stored.

**TIP**

> One of the best reasons to use the Column view is that you can move inside a window with the arrow keys on the keyboard. This is the fastest way to move among the folders and files on your Mac.

When there are more columns than can be displayed in the window, you can use the horizontal scrollbars to view all the columns. Scrolling to the left moves up the hierarchy, whereas scrolling to the right moves down the hierarchy. You can also make the window larger to view more columns at the same time.

You can resize the width of the columns in a window by dragging the resize handle located in the lower-right corner of each column. Each column in a window can have a different width.

When you click a file to select it, the far-right column shows a large icon or a preview of the file, and information about that file is displayed (refer to Figure 2.6).

If you click document files for which Mac OS X can create a preview, you see the preview in the column. If the file you select has dynamic content, you can play that content in the preview that you see in the Column view. For example, if you select a QuickTime movie, you can click the play or pause button (appears over the preview when you move your mouse above it) to watch the movie without opening the file. Certain types of text files are also displayed so you can read them (arrows appear on the preview to enable you to read the entire document). You can also see large thumbnail views of graphics stored in certain formats. For those items that Mac OS X cannot create previews of (an application is one example), you see a large icon instead of a preview.

2

**NOTE**

> If you switch from the Column view to one of the other views, the contents of the folder you most recently selected are shown in the window.

If you prefer not to see the preview, there are two ways to hide it. You can hide it in individual windows or you can hide it by using View Options.

To hide the preview in specific windows, click the Expansion triangle next to the word `Preview` that appears just above the preview of a selected file in the Preview pane. This hides all previews for the current window and shows detailed information about the item that is selected, along with the More info button (which opens the Info window that you will learn about later).

⇨ To learn about the Column view's View Options, **see** "Customizing the Column View," **p. 49**.

### Viewing a Finder Window in Cover Flow View

Mac OS X 10.5 introduces a new view for Finder windows. Originally a part of iTunes, Cover Flow provides a very interactive way to view previews of the files in a folder (see Figure 2.7). The Cover Flow view is especially useful if you are navigating a folder of photos or videos.

With a Finder window set to the Cover Flow view, you will see two panes. On the top is the actual Cover Flow preview of the files in the folder. The bottom pane is a list view of that same directory. Note that with the lower pane in list view, you can use the same steps to change the view as you do in a regular list view Finder window. For instance, you can sort by a different column or change the sort order.

The most noticeable feature of the Cover Flow view is the ability to scroll through the items in the folder. If you have a folder of photos, this view allows you to see a preview of each photo to find the one you are looking for. Resize the Finder window so that the Cover Flow preview area is big enough to see the preview. As you drag the Cover Flow scroll bar, the previews of the items in the folder flow in the direction you are scrolling. When you stop scrolling, the item that is selected displays at a slightly larger size than the other previews and is centered in the top pane. The name of the file, and the kind of file it is, are displayed under the preview.

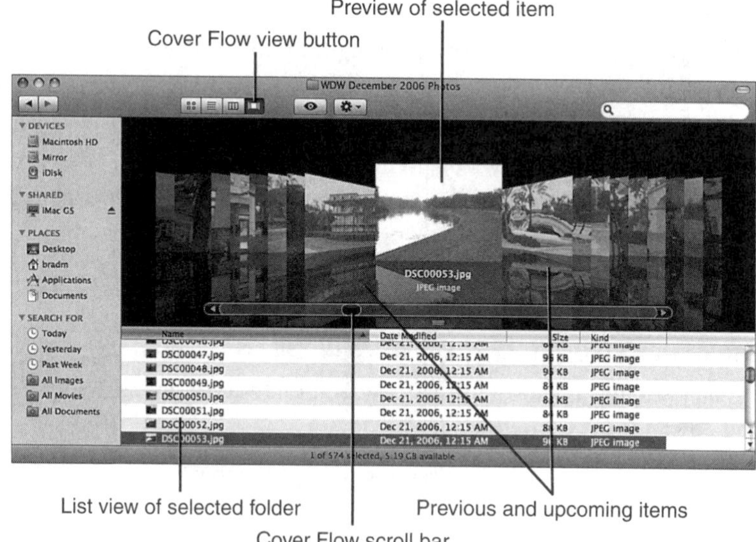


**Figure 2.7**
The Cover Flow view provides a very interactive way to preview photos and videos in a folder.

Browsing a folder that has QuickTime movies provides a preview of the movie. When you select a QuickTime movie and move the mouse over the preview, a play button appears on the preview. When you click the play button, the movie will start to play in the Cover Flow preview pane. Move your mouse over the preview again and a stop button appears. While a movie is playing, the other files no longer show previews of those documents; once you move the Cover Flow scroll bar the previews will appear again.

# Navigating Finder Windows

Mac OS X includes many features that enable you to navigate Finder windows. The two basic navigation tasks you do are moving around inside Finder windows (to select items, for example) and changing the contents of Finder windows to view other volumes or folders.

## Using the Keyboard to Select Items in a Finder Window

Although you can use the mouse to point to and click items to select them (or double-click to open them), moving to items and selecting them using the keyboard can be faster. There are two basic ways to navigate inside a window using the keyboard.

You can type an item's name to move to and select it. The OS matches item names as you type, so most of the time you don't need to type the item's whole name to move to it (for example, typing "mp3" moves you to the first item whose name begins with `mp3`). The more of the name you type, the more specific your movement becomes.

You can also move among items using the Tab and arrow keys. How this works depends on the view you are using for windows.

### Using the Keyboard to Select Items in the Icon View

When you are in the Icon view, pressing the Tab key selects the next item according to alphabetical order. Holding down the Shift key while you press Tab moves you among the items in reverse alphabetical order.

You can also use the arrow keys to move to and select items. The keys work just as you might expect. The up-arrow key moves you up the window, the right-arrow key moves you right, and so on.

The window scrolls automatically to keep the items you select in view.

### Using the Keyboard to Select Items in the List View

When a window is shown in List view, you can use the up- and down-arrow keys to move up and down the list of items in the window.

When you select an item, you can use the right-arrow key to expand it and the left-arrow key to collapse it.

**TIP**

> The Option key works with the arrow keys as well. If you hold down the Option key and press the right-arrow key, all the folders within the selected folder are expanded as well.

### Using the Keyboard to Select Items in the Column View

In the Column view, the right-arrow key moves you down the hierarchy, whereas the left-arrow key moves you up the hierarchy. The up- and down-arrow keys enable you to move up and down within a selected folder (which appears in a column).

Using these keys, you can move around your directories rapidly. As you move through the structure using these keys, the window scrolls so that you always see the currently selected item. It maintains your view at all times so you can quickly jump into different areas without scrolling manually.

When you get used to it, using the keyboard in combination with the Column view is one of the fastest ways to navigate Mac OS X Finder windows.

**TIP**

> After you have selected an item, press ⌘-down arrow to open it. For example, when you select an application and press these keys, the application launches.

### Using the Keyboard to Select Items in the Cover Flow View

Using your keyboard in Cover Flow view is very similar to List view. In fact, since the List view is present at the bottom of the Cover Flow Finder window, when you use the keyboard you will see the results in that pane as well. Using the right arrow, down arrow, or Tab key will move you to the next item. The left arrow, up arrow, and Shift-Tab will move you to the previous item. If you select a folder and hold the ⌘ key while pressing the down arrow, you will move into that folder.

### USING THE FINDER WINDOW'S SEARCH TOOL TO SELECT ITEMS

Under version 10.5, the Finder window toolbar's Search tool transforms a folder into a Smart folder. You can set the criterion used and the smart folder finds all folders and files that meet this criterion and displays them in the folder's Finder window. To search for files or folders, perform the following steps:

1. Open a Finder window.
2. Type the text or numbers that you want to search for in the Finder window Search box. As you type, the Finder starts finding folders and files that meet your search criterion and displays them for you (see Figure 2.8).

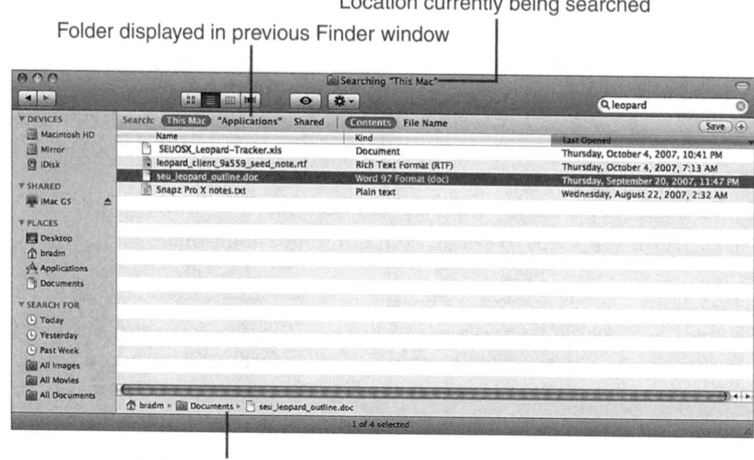


**Figure 2.8**
A smart folder gets its name for good reason; as you type something in the Search tool, files and folders that match what you type are displayed in the Finder window.

The locations of the items listed can be scoped by choosing the location in which you are interested. These are shown at the top of the window. From left to right they are This Mac, the location you were viewing when you started the search, or Shared.

**TIP**

> If you click the Other button, the "Search in specific locations" sheet appears. Check the boxes for the volumes you want to search, or use the Add and Remove buttons to add or remove locations. Click OK and the search is scoped based on the locations checked in the sheet.

3. Select the location in which you want to see items that match your search. For example, to find items anywhere on your computer, click This Mac. To narrow the search to your previous location, click its button. The window is refreshed, and you will see items that match your search criterion that are located in the location you selected.
4. When you find an item that you are interested in, click in the Contents pane and use the up- and down-arrow keys to select the item in the upper pane. Its location appears in the lower pane of the window (see Figure 2.9).

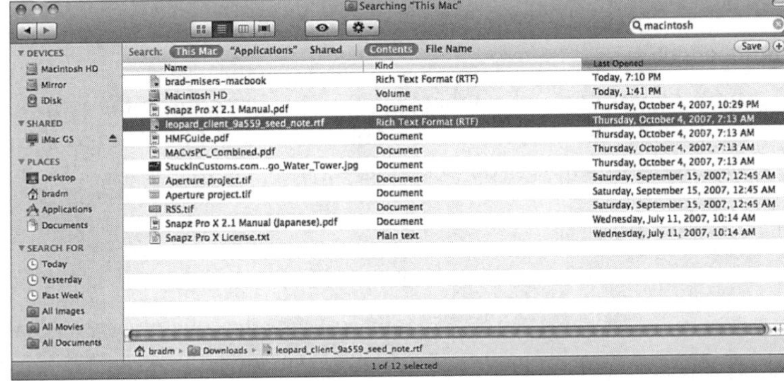

**Figure 2.9**
You can use the Finder window Search tool to search various areas of your Mac for files and folders that include specific text in their names.

5. To add more criteria to the search, click the Add button (+) next to the Save button. Use the resulting sheet to choose and configure additional search attributes.

**TIP**

> You can save a smart folder by clicking the Save button and using the Save sheet to name it, choose a save location, and indicate if you want it to be added to the Sidebar. After you've saved a search, you can run it again by opening it.

To clear the search and return to the previous Finder window, click the Clear Search button, which is the "x" located in the right end of the Search tool.

⇨ To learn more about Smart folders, **see** "Searching Your Mac with Smart Folders," **p. 101**.

## Navigating Up and Down the Directory Structure

There are several ways to move up and down the directory structure within Finder windows. You can use the keyboard as discussed in the previous section. You can also use the icons in the Sidebar as well as the Path pop-up menu. The Go menu enables you to jump to specific directories quickly.

### Changing Directories with the Sidebar

The Finder's Sidebar is a fast way to change the directory displayed in the current Finder window. The sidebar contains icons that take you to specific directories. As you read earlier, the Sidebar contains several sections. In the Devices section are all the volumes mounted on your Mac, including hard disk volumes, disk image volumes, your iDisk, CDs, DVDs, and so on. The Shared section will display icons for the servers that are available on your local area network (LAN.) In the Places section of the Sidebar are some of the folders in your Home folder and the Applications folder. You can add any folders, applications, documents, or other files to or remove them from this area to completely customize it. Finally, the Search For section of the sidebar allows you to quickly find content based upon pre-determined searchs, and you can also store smart folders and Spotlight searches here. The purpose of the Sidebar is to enable you to quickly open a Finder window that displays the contents of any item it contains.

⇨ To learn how to customize the sidebar, **see** "Customizing the Sidebar," **p. 39**.

2

To view the contents of an item shown in the sidebar, simply click its icon. The right pane of the Finder window shows the contents of the item you select. For example, if you click your Home folder (the icon with your user account short name as its name), you'll see the contents of your Home folder in the Contents pane of the Finder window.

### USING THE BACK AND FORWARD BUTTONS TO MOVE AMONG FINDER WINDOWS

Click the Back button on the toolbar to move back to the previous Finder window in the current Finder window chain. You can continue to click the Back button as many times as you want until you reach the first window you viewed using the current Finder window chain; at that point, the Back button is grayed out. Similarly, the Forward button moves you forward in a chain of Finder windows. You can also use the Go, Back and the Go, Forward commands to move back in the chain or forward in the chain, respectively.

**TIP**

> You can press ⌘-[ to move back and ⌘-] to move forward.

⇨ To learn how to customize the Finder toolbar, **see** "Customizing the Toolbar," **p. 41**.

If you open a new Finder window, the Back and Forward buttons are grayed out because there is no window to move back or forward to. Opening a new Finder window starts a new chain of windows, so both buttons are disabled. As soon as you open a second window within the same Finder window chain, the Back button becomes active. If you move back along that chain of windows, the Forward button becomes active.

### CHANGING DIRECTORIES WITH THE PATH POP-UP MENU

The Path pop-up menu enables you to quickly move up and down the directory structure of your Mac. To change directories, hold down the ⌘ key and click the window name in the title bar of a Finder window. When you do so, you see all the directories from the one currently displayed in the window up to the Computer directory (where Computer is the name of your Mac; this is the highest level on your Mac). Select a directory from the menu, and the Finder window displays the directory you chose.

You can add the Path button to your toolbar so you can select a directory without using the ⌘ key.

⇨ To learn how to add buttons to the Finder toolbar, **see** "Customizing the Toolbar," **p. 41**.

**TIP**

> You can also move up the directory structure one folder at a time by pressing ⌘-up arrow, which is the keyboard shortcut for the Enclosing Folder command that moves to the folder enclosing the item you are currently viewing.

2

### Changing Directories with the Go Menu

The Finder's Go menu enables you to move into many areas of your Mac. The menu is divided into several areas that contain various kinds of options (see Figure 2.10).

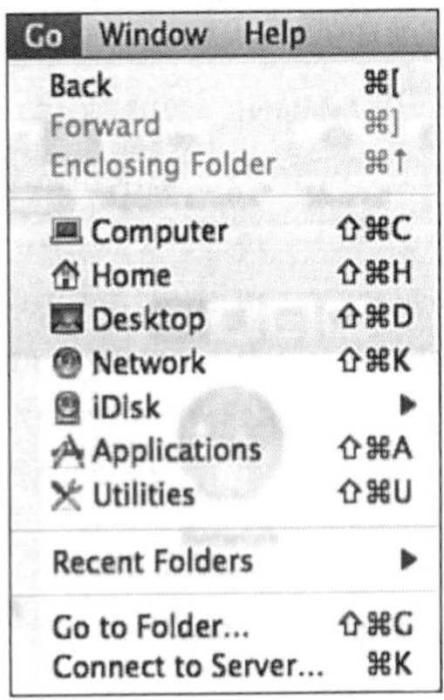


**Figure 2.10**
The Go menu provides quick access to various folders on your Mac.

At the top of the menu are the Back and Forward commands, which do the same thing as the Back and Forward buttons on the toolbar.

Just under these commands is the Enclosing Folder command. When you are displaying an item in a Finder window and press ⌘-up arrow or select Go, Enclosing Folder, the folder that contains the currently selected item is shown in the Finder window.

You can also use the Finder's Go menu to open specific directories. To do so, open the Go menu and select the directory you want to view. Its contents replace those shown in the active Finder window (if no Finder windows are active, the directory's contents appear in a new Finder window). For example, to display your Home folder, select Go, Home.

**TIP**

> Keyboard shortcuts are available for the specific directories on the Go menu. See the "Mac OS X to the Max" section at the end of this chapter for a list of these shortcuts.

If you select Go, Recent Folders, you can quickly move back to one of the folders you have recently viewed. (You can set the number of recent folders on this list using the Appearance pane of the System Preferences application.)

**TIP**

To clear the list of recent folders, choose Go, Recent Folder, Clear Menu.



You can also move to a folder using the Go to Folder command. Select Go, Go to Folder to see the Go to Folder dialog box (see Figure 2.11). You can type a pathname in this dialog box and click Go to open a Finder window for that directory. Following are some tips on how to type pathnames:

- Pathnames are case sensitive.
- A slash (`/`) separates each level in the path.
- Almost all paths should begin and end with the slash (`/`).
- The exception to the previous rule is when you want to move to a specific user's Home directory, in which case you can just type `~username/`, where `username` is the short name for the user's account.
- If the path begins with the directory on which Mac OS X is stored, you can skip that directory name and start the path beginning with the next level. If it is on another volume, you can include that volume's name at the beginning of the path.

**Figure 2.11**
This Go to Folder directory shows the path to the Movies folder within my Home folder.

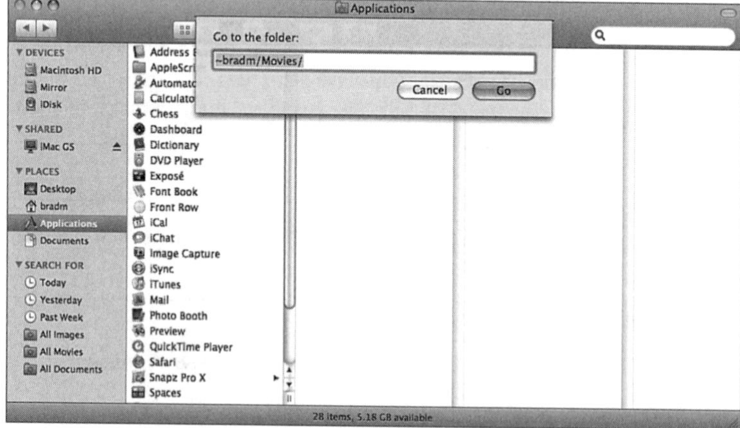


**NOTE**

Although you should be careful to use the proper case in pathnames, sometimes it doesn't make a difference. For example, the path to the Mac OS X System directory can be `/SYSTEM/`, `/system/`, or `/System/`. Sometimes, however, the case of the path you type must match exactly, so it is good practice to always match the case of the directory names you type.

Table 2.1 provides some examples of paths you would enter in the Go to Folder dialog box to move to specific directories.

**TABLE 2.1 PATHS TO SPECIFIC DIRECTORIES**

| Location | Path |
|---|---|
| Directory called Documents on a volume named Mirror | `/Mirror/Documents/` |
| Documents folder in the Home directory for the user account with the short name `bmiser` | `~bmiser/Documents/` |
| Mac OS X System Folder | `/System/` |
| Folder called `Ch_02_figs` located in the Documents directory in the user bmiser's Home folder | `~bmiser/Documents/Ch_02_figs` |

Following are some additional tips for the Go to Folder command:

- You can open the Go to Folder dialog box by pressing ⌘-Shift-G. Type the path, and press Return to move there.
- If you are patient when you type, Mac OS X will try to match the path you are typing and complete it for you. This usually takes more time than typing it yourself, but if the path is filled in for you, press Return to accept that path entered for you to move there.
- The most recent path you have typed remains in the Go to Folder dialog box; you can modify this path to move to a different directory.

**TIP**

> Although pathnames should end in `/`, you don't really have to type the last `/`. If it is needed, Mac OS X adds it for you. If not, the path works without it.

**NOTE**

> You can use the Connect to Server command to move to directories located on your network.

⇨ To learn how to connect to servers, **see** "Accessing Shared Files from a Mac OS X Computer," **p. 375**.

### CHANGING DIRECTORIES WITH THE KEYBOARD

One of the cool navigation features of Mac OS X is the capability to move up and down the directory structure using only the keyboard. Use the previous tips to select an item, and then press ⌘-down arrow to move into the item, such as a folder, an application, a document, and so on. For example, if you use the Tab key to select an application icon and then press ⌘-down arrow, that application opens. Similarly, if you press this key combination when you have a folder selected, the contents of that folder are shown in its previous view state.

**NOTE**

> This technique also works in the Column view to open applications or documents. When you are viewing folders and volumes, you don't need to hold down the ⌘ key because, in the Column view, the contents of a folder or volume are displayed when you select it.

To move up the directory structure, press ⌘-up arrow.



# CUSTOMIZING FINDER WINDOWS

Mac OS X enables you to customize many aspects of Finder windows, including the Sidebar, toolbar, status bar, and views you use.

## CUSTOMIZING THE SIDEBAR

The Sidebar provides a convenient way to access the mounted volumes on your Mac along with specific folders, documents, and applications (see Figure 2.12). As you read earlier, the Devices section of the sidebar shows all the mounted volumes on your Mac; the Shared section shows servers you are connected to; and the Search For section shows saved searches and smart folders. By default, the Places section of the Sidebar shows several of the folders within your Home folder and the Applications folder, but you can add or remove folders, documents, or applications to this area to customize it.

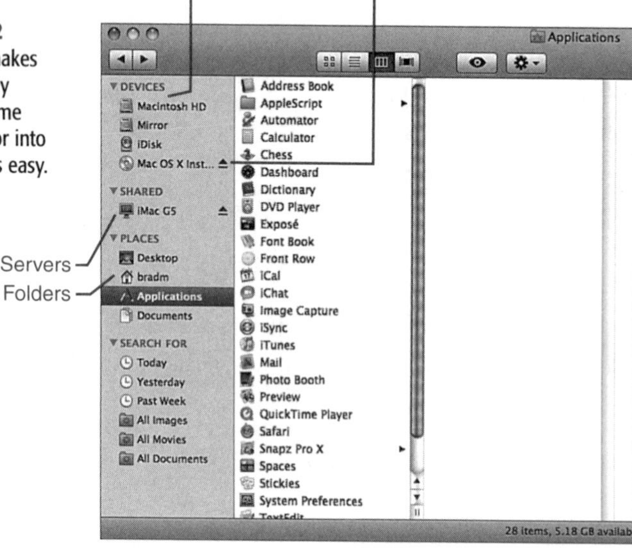


**Figure 2.12**
The Sidebar makes getting into any mounted volume on your Mac or into specific folders easy.

**TIP**

> You can also store files in the Places section of the Sidebar. Clicking a file icon on the Sidebar opens the file.

To view the contents of a volume or folder, click it; its contents appear in the Content pane of the Finder window. For volumes, a button enables you to perform an action. For example, when you have an ejectable volume, such as a disk image or DVD, you can click an Eject button. When you have inserted a blank CD or DVD, you can click the Burn button that appears next to a Burnable folder to burn the disc.

2

### Determining the Default Items in the Sidebar

Finder preferences determine which items appear in the Sidebar. To set them, follow these steps:

1. Select Finder, Preferences or press ⌘-,.
2. Click the Sidebar tab (see Figure 2.13).

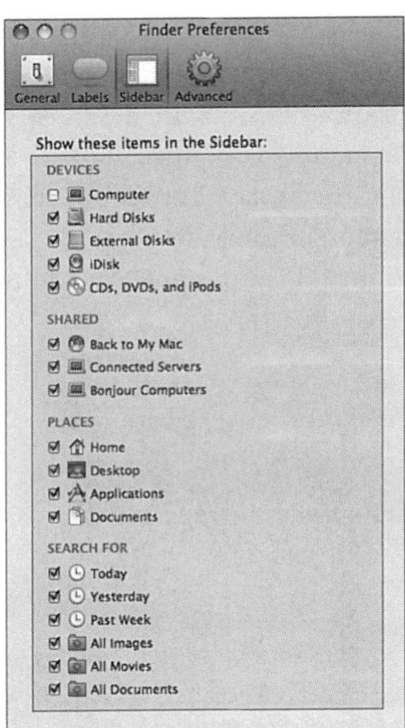


**Figure 2.13**
Use the Sidebar pane of the Finder Preferences window to configure the default items in the sidebar.

3. Check the check box next to each item you want to appear in the Sidebar.
4. Uncheck the box next to each item you don't want to appear in the Sidebar.

The next time you view a Finder window, its Sidebar contains the items you specified; these selections only impact default items; anything you've added or removed manually is not impacted.

### Organizing Your Sidebar

You can further organize the Sidebar by doing the following tasks:

- You can add any folder or file to the Places section of the Sidebar by dragging it into that section.

- You can also add a folder or file to the Sidebar by selecting it and selecting File, Add To Sidebar or pressing ⌘-T.
- You can remove folders from the Sidebar by dragging them out of the Sidebar. When you do, they disappear in a puff of smoke. Of course, the original item isn't affected.

**NOTE**

If you remove an item whose check box is checked on the Sidebar pane of the Finder Preferences window, that folder is removed and its check box becomes unchecked in the Preferences window.



- Resize the Sidebar to make it fill up more or less of the Finder window. (Your change lasts only as long as the current Finder window chain.)
- Show or hide the Sidebar by clicking the Show/Hide Toolbar button in the upper-right corner of Finder windows.
- Drag icons up and down within the Places section of the Sidebar to reorganize them.

## CUSTOMIZING THE TOOLBAR

Along the top of Finder windows, you see the toolbar. This toolbar contains the Back and Forward buttons, the View buttons, the Action menu (covered in a later section), Quick Look button and the Search tool. As with the sidebar, you can customize many aspects of this toolbar. You can show or hide it and customize the tools it contains.

**NOTE**

Many applications, especially those that come with Mac OS X, also provide a Mac OS X toolbar in their windows. You can use these same techniques to work with many of those toolbars.

### SHOWING OR HIDING THE TOOLBAR

You can hide or show the toolbar in a Finder window in any of the following ways:

- Click the Show/Hide Toolbar button in the upper-right corner of the Finder window.
- Select View, Hide Toolbar or View, Show Toolbar.
- Press Option-⌘-T.

The state of the toolbar controls how new Finder windows open when they are viewed in the Icon or List view. If the toolbar is displayed, new Finder windows open according to the preferences you set using the Finder Preferences dialog box. If the toolbar is hidden, new Finder windows always open in a separate window.

When you open a new Finder window from a window in which the toolbar is hidden (for example, by holding down the Option key when you open a new Finder window), the toolbar is hidden in the new window. When you open a Finder window from a window in which the toolbar is shown, the toolbar is shown in the new window as well.

The toolbar state in currently open Finder windows is independent. For example, you can show the toolbar in one Finder window while it is hidden in another. In fact, if you have two Finder windows for the same directory open at the same time, you can hide the toolbar in one window while it is shown in the other.

### CHANGING THE TOOLS ON THE TOOLBAR

The default toolbar contains various useful buttons, but you can customize its content by adding tools to it or removing tools from it:

2

1. Open a Finder window.
2. Select View, Customize Toolbar. The Toolbar customization sheet appears (see Figure 2.14).

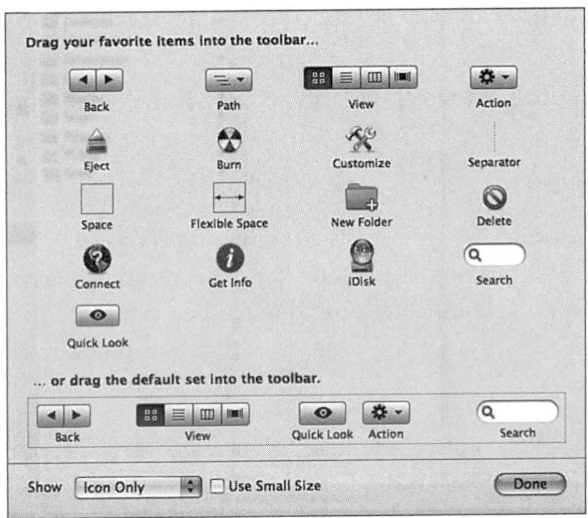


**Figure 2.14**
You can add buttons to or remove them from the toolbar using the Customize Toolbar sheet.

3. To add a button to the toolbar, drag it from the sheet to the toolbar, placing it in the location where you want it. (Table 2.2 lists the available buttons and what they do.)

   When you move a button between two current buttons on the toolbar, existing buttons slide apart to make room for the new button.

**NOTE**

> If you place more buttons on the toolbar than can be shown in the current window's width, a set of double arrows appears at the right edge of the toolbar. Click this to pop up a menu showing the additional buttons.

4. Remove a button from the toolbar by dragging it off the toolbar.
5. Change the location of the icons by dragging them. You can move buttons and menus that you add as well as those that are installed by default.

**TIP**

> You can return to the default toolbar by dragging the default toolbar set onto the toolbar from the Customize Toolbar sheet.

6. Use the Show pop-up menu to determine whether the buttons have text and an icon, text only, or an icon only.
7. To use the small icon size, check the "Use Small Size" check box.
8. Click Done.

2

The toolbar now reflects the changes you made (see Figure 2.15).

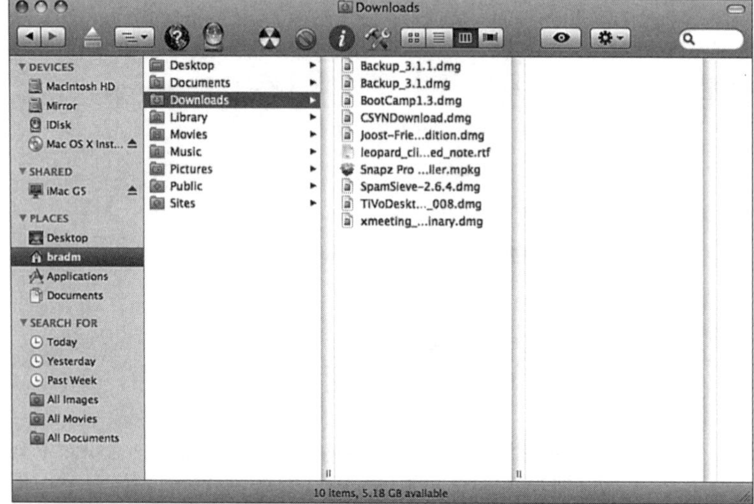


**Figure 2.15**
Now I am using a customized toolbar.

**TIP**

> You can rotate the toolbar among its views, such as Icon & Text, Icon Only, and so on by holding down ⌘ while you click the Show/Hide Toolbar button.

**Table 2.2 Useful Toolbar Buttons**

| Button Name | What It Does |
|---|---|
| Back/Forward | Moves you back or forward in a chain of Finder windows. |
| Path | Pops up a menu that shows the path to the current directory. You can select a directory on the pop-up menu to move there. |
| View | Changes the view for the current window. |
| Action | Provides a pop-up menu with access to various context-sensitive commands. |

*continues*

TABLE 2.2 CONTINUED

| Button Name | What It Does |
|---|---|
| Quick Look | Opens a floating window to preview or provide information about the selected item. If you have selected a folder you will be shown details about the contents of the folder. Selecting a document will provide a preview of that file. |
| Eject | Enables you to eject items, such as mounted volumes, discs, and so on, from the desktop. |
| Burn | Enables you to burn a CD or DVD from a burnable folder. |
| Customize | Enables you to open the Customize Toolbar sheet. |
| Separator | A graphic element you can use to organize your toolbar. |
| Space | Adds a block of space to the toolbar. |
| Flexible Space | Adds a block of flexible space to the toolbar. |
| New Folder | Creates a new folder. |
| Delete | Deletes the selected item. |
| Connect | Opens the Connect to Server dialog box. |
| Get Info | Opens the Get Info window for a selected item. |
| iDisk | Accesses your iDisk. |
| Search | Enables you to search Finder windows. |

**TIP**

If you add more buttons than can be displayed and then want to remove some of the buttons you can't see (you see the double arrows instead), you have to make the window wider so that you can see the button on the toolbar to remove it; you can't remove a button from the pop-up menu. You can also temporarily remove other buttons until you can see the one you want to remove.

## CUSTOMIZING THE STATUS BAR

The status bar provides status information for the current directory, volume, or whatever else is being displayed in the Finder window. Mostly, the status bar provides information about the number of items in the window and the amount of free space on the current volume.

Where the status bar is displayed depends on whether the toolbar is shown.

**NOTE**

In addition to the status bar, you can turn on the path bar to show the directory structure for the folder you are currently viewing. With the path bar displayed, you can also drag an item to a location in the path to move that item. To turn on the path bar go to the View menu and select Show Path Bar.

If the toolbar is shown, the status bar information is displayed at the bottom of the window. For example, if you are viewing a folder, the number of items it contains and the amount of space available on the drive where it is stored will be shown.

If the toolbar is hidden, the status bar appears immediately under the title bar (see Figure 2.16). As with the toolbar, you can hide or show the status bar using the View menu. Unlike the toolbar, however, you can't change the contents of the status bar.

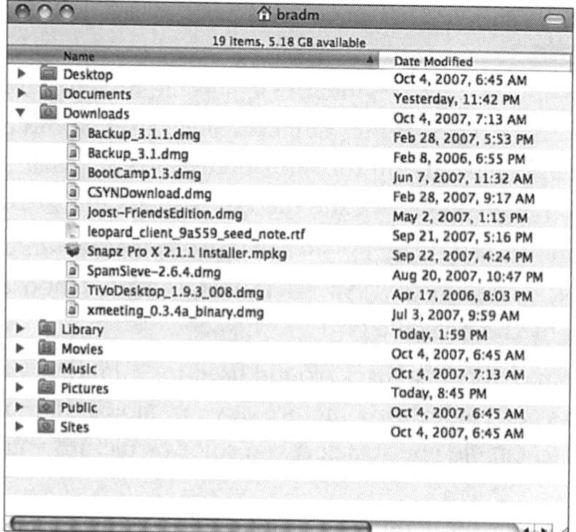


**Figure 2.16**
When the toolbar is hidden, the status bar appears immediately under the title bar. (Finder windows look a bit pitiful without the toolbar and Sidebar, don't they?)

## Customizing Finder Window Views

For each view type of Finder window view, you can set Default or global view preferences that affect all windows you open using that view type. You can then set options for individual windows to override the default settings for that view type for that specific window. For example, one of the customization options for the List view is the data you see in the window. You can choose to display the Comments column for a window in List view. If you set this as a default preference, each time you open a new window in List view, you see the Comments column. If there is a window in which you don't want to see the Comments column, you can change the preferences for that window so the Comments column is not displayed.

When you set a default preference, it affects all windows shown in that view. When you change a window's preference, it affects only the current window.

### Customizing the Icon View

The Icon view has the following view options:

- **Icon size**—You can set the relative size of the icons you see.
- **Grid spacing**—You can set the size of the grid Mac OS X uses to space icons in the window.

- **Text size**—You can set the size of text displayed next to the icons you see.
- **Label position**—You can set the location of the text next to icons. Your choices are on the bottom or to the right of the icon.
- **Show item info**—With this option enabled, you see information for the items in a window. The information you see depends on the items being displayed. For example, when the window shows volumes, you see the total space on the volume and the free space on each volume. When you view folders, you see the number of items in that folder. When you see files, information about the file is shown, such as the sizes of image files.
- **Show icon preview**—By default, graphic file icons contain a preview of the file's content within the icon. Some types of files don't include this icon information and their icon doesn't contain a preview. If you turn this preference on, Mac OS X creates a preview of the file in the file's icon even if the file type doesn't include one by default.
- **Arrange by**—You can choose to keep icons grouped by a criterion you select, including Name, Date Modified, Date Created, Size, Kind, and Label. Choose "Snap to Grid" to keep icons organized by the invisible grid.
- **Background**—You can choose the background used for a Finder window. Your choices are White, a color of your choice, or a picture of your choice. If you select Color or Picture, tools appear to enable you to select the color or picture you want to use.

Set your default preferences for the Icon view using the following steps:

1. Open a Finder window in the Icon view so you can preview the preferences you will set.
2. Select View, Show View Options or press ⌘-J. The View Options window appears (see Figure 2.17). You use this window to set both default and window settings. At the top of the window is the name of the folder you are currently viewing.
3. Use the "Icon size" slider to set the relative size of the icons you see. As you move the slider, the icons in the open window reflect the size you set. When you are happy with the size of the icons, release the slider.
4. Use the "Grid spacing" pop-up menu to set the size of the grid used to keep icons organized in the window.
5. Use the "Text size" pop-up menu to set the size of the icon labels.
6. Use the radio buttons in the "Label position" area to select the location of icon labels.
7. Use the two "Show" check boxes to enable or disable the options described in the previous bulleted list.
8. On the "Arrange by" pop-up menu, select the criterion by which you want icons grouped using the pop-up menu. (None is selected by default.) If you choose "Snap to Grid," icons are always arranged by the window's invisible grid.

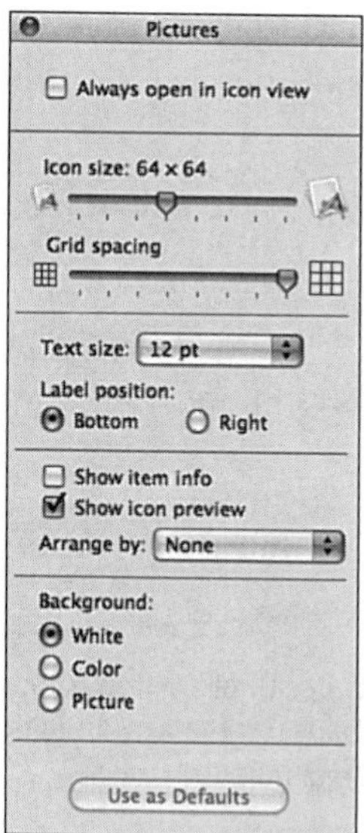


**Figure 2.17**
The View Options window enables you to customize Finder window views.

2

**NOTE**

> When you select Snap to Grid, a small grid icon will appear at the bottom left corner of the Finder window.

**TIP**

> You can also modify the view of the desktop, which is always in Icon view. Click anywhere on the desktop and open the View Options window. You can then set the icon size, text size, and other options just like a folder window (except for the folder background that is set using the Desktop pane of the System Preferences Utility).

9. Select the folder background option by selecting one of the radio buttons under Background.
10. If you chose Color, use the Color button to open the Color Picker to select the background color you want to use.
11. If you chose Picture, click the Select button, and then use the Select a Picture dialog box to select a background image.
12. Click the "Use as Defaults" button.

**NOTE**

> Supported image formats include PICT, TIFF, and JPEG. The background image you choose appears in folders you view using the default icon settings. This does not affect any image you are using as a background image on your desktop.

After you have made these settings, any window you view in Icon view is displayed using your default preferences, unless you override the global settings by setting a window's preference.

To change the preferences for an individual window, do the following:

1. Open the window you want to view and put it in the Icon view.
2. Open the View Options window by selecting View, Show View Options, or press ⌘-J.
3. Use the controls to set the Icon view preferences for the window you opened in step 1 (see the previous steps for help).

This window uses the preferences you set for it until you change them.



**TIP**

> You can leave the View Options window open while you select other windows. If you do so, the name shown at the top of the dialog box changes, as do the controls you see if the window you select is in a view different from the current one.

### CUSTOMIZING THE LIST VIEW

Customizing List view works pretty much the same way as Icon view, except that you have different options.

Set your default List view preferences using the following steps:

1. Open a Finder window in List view.
2. Open the View Options window by selecting View, Show View Options, or press ⌘-J.
3. Check the radio button for the icon size you want to use.
4. Select the text size on the "Text size" pop-up menu.
5. Check the boxes next to the data columns you want displayed in List view. The default data are Date Modified, Size, and Kind. The other data available are Date Created, Version, Comments, and Label. Data for which you check the boxes is displayed in columns in the List view.
6. Check the "Use relative dates" check box if you want to use relative dates. When you use the relative dates option, you see relative date information (such as yesterday) for some dates rather than the full date for all dates.
7. Check the "Calculate all sizes" check box if you want the size of folders to be displayed in the Size column. This option uses extra computing power, especially for those folders that contain many folders and files. You should usually leave this box unchecked unless folder size information is critical to you.
8. Check the "Show icon preview" check box to have the Finder display a preview icon of a selected item, rather than a generic icon.
9. Click the "Use as Defaults" button.

Every window you see in List view uses these options, unless you override the settings for a particular window.

Overriding the default options for a specific window is analogous to what you do for the Icon view. Open the window, open the View Options window, and use the controls to set the view options for the current window.

### CUSTOMIZING THE COLUMN VIEW

The Column view has fewer customization options than the other views. The Column view preferences you set apply to all windows in the Column view. Do the following:

1. Open a Finder window in Column view.
2. Open the View Options window by selecting View, Show View Options, or press ⌘-J.
3. Uncheck the "Show icons" check box to hide the icons in the window.
4. Uncheck the "Show preview column" check box if you prefer not to see the preview of a file you have selected in the window.



**NOTE**

> The Finder remembers the view you used the last time you opened a specific window and maintains that view each time you open that window–until you change that window's view. If you want a specific folder to always open in a particular view, click the check box at the top of the View Options dialog box to do so.
>
> Similarly, you can't tell the Finder to apply the default view preferences to all windows at the same time. If you have changed the view preferences for individual windows, you have to reapply the default view preferences to that window if you want to use them (by using the View Options window).

### CUSTOMIZING THE COVER FLOW VIEW

The view options for Cover Flow windows are identical to the options you have for a List view. Since the Cover Flow view includes a list view in the bottom pane, it is beneficial to be able to set these options.

Set your default Cover Flow view preferences using the following steps:

1. Open a Finder window in Cover Flow view.
2. Open the View Options window by selecting View, Show View Options, or press ⌘-J.
3. Check the radio button for the icon size you want to use.
4. Select the text size on the "Text size" pop-up menu.
5. Check the boxes next to the data columns you want to be displayed in the List porton of the Cover Flow view. The default data are Date Modified, Size, and Kind. The other data available are Date Created, Version, Comments, and Label. Data for which you check the boxes is displayed in columns in the List portion of the Cover Flow view.
6. Check the "Use relative dates" check box if you want to use relative dates. When you use the relative dates option, you see relative date information (such as yesterday) for some dates rather than the full date for all dates.

7. Check the "Calculate all sizes" check box if you want the size of folders to be displayed in the Size column. This option uses extra computing power, especially for those folders that contain many folders and files. You should usually leave this box unchecked unless folder size information is critical to you.
8. Check the "Show icon preview" check box to have the Finder display a preview icon of a selected item, rather than a generic icon.
9. Click the "Use as Defaults" button.



# WORKING WITH THE FINDER WINDOW'S ACTION POP-UP MENU

One of the default tools on the Finder window toolbar is the Action pop-up menu (see Figure 2.18). This menu provides access to context-sensitive commands, which means that commands on the menu depend on the item you have selected on the desktop. For example, when you select a file and open the menu, you see commands including New Folder, New Burn Folder, Open, Open With, Get Info, Compresss, Make Alias, Move to Trash, Duplicate, Quick Look, Copy, and Label.

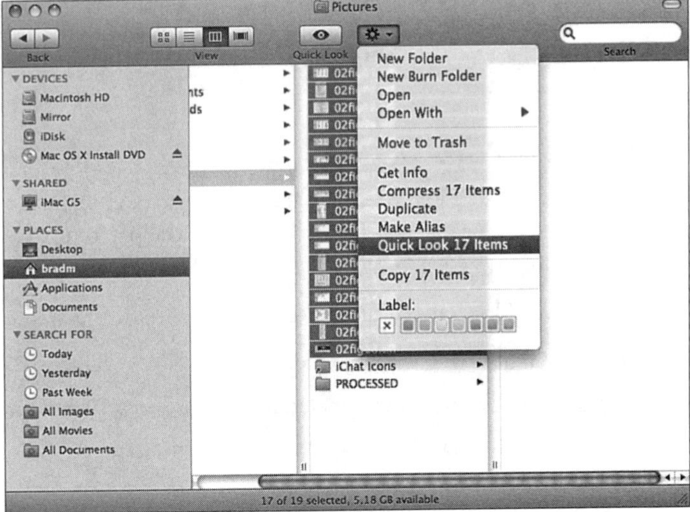


**Figure 2.18**
The commands on the Action pop-up menu change depending on the items you have selected.

**NOTE**

> As you probably suspect, the commands on the Action pop-up menu are similar to the commands on an item's contextual menu, which you can open by pointing to an item, holding down the Control key, and clicking the item (or right-clicking the item if you use a two-button mouse). If you do this, you'll see a couple more options on the contextual menu that you will learn about later in this book.

To use a command on the menu, select the item on which you want to use the command, open the menu, and select the command you want to use.

## WORKING WITH LABELS

Labels enable you to color code and text code files and folders as a means of identifying and organizing them. For example, you can assign all the folders for a specific project using the same label. In addition to making the relationship between these folders clearer, you can choose to group items within a window by label, which keeps them near one another as well. You can also use Smart Folders to automatically gather files and folders that have the same label.



### SETTING UP LABELS

You can assign text to the color labels by following these steps:

1. Open the Finder Preferences window.
2. Click the Labels button to open the Labels pane, which contains the seven label colors. Next to each color is its text label, which by default is the name of the color.
3. Edit the text labels for each color to match your label needs. For example, you can replace the color with the name of a project.

### APPLYING LABELS

You can apply labels to a folder or file by following these steps:

1. Select the items to which you want to apply a label.
2. Open the Action pop-up menu or the contextual menu.
3. Select the label you want to apply to the selected labels.

When an item has a label applied to it and you view the enclosing folder in Icon view, its name is highlighted in the label's color. When you view a window in the Cover Flow, Columns, or List view, a large dot filled with the label color appears next to the item you have labeled. If you view a window in the List view and select to show the Label column, the label text appears in the Label column for the item.

**TIP**

> If you view a window in Icon view, you can choose to keep items grouped by label. This keeps all the files you have associated with a specific location together in the window.

2

## MAC OS X TO THE MAX: FINDER WINDOW KEYBOARD SHORTCUTS

Table 2.3 lists keyboard shortcuts for working with Finder windows.

**TABLE 2.3 KEYBOARD SHORTCUTS FOR FINDER WINDOWS**

| Menu | Action | Keyboard Shortcut |
|---|---|---|
| None | Opens an item on the sidebar and closes the current window | Option-click |
| None | Opens an item on the sidebar in a new Finder window | ⌘-click |
| None | Closes all open Finder windows | Option-click the Close button |
| None | Opens an item in a new Finder window | ⌘-double-click a folder |
| Finder | Preferences | ⌘-, |
| File | New Finder Window | ⌘-N |
| File | New Folder | Shift-⌘-N |
| File | New Smart Folder | Option-⌘-N |
| File | Open | ⌘-O |
| File | Close Window | ⌘-W |
| File | Get Info | ⌘-I |
| File | Duplicate | ⌘-D |
| File | Make Alias | ⌘-L |
| File | Quick Look | ⌘-Y |
| File | Show Original | ⌘-R |
| File | Add to Sidebar | ⌘-T |
| View | as Icons | ⌘-1 |
| View | as List | ⌘-2 |
| View | as Columns | ⌘-3 |
| View | as Cover Flow | ⌘-4 |
| View | Show/Hide Toolbar | Option-⌘-T |
| View | Show/Hide View Options | ⌘-J |
| Go | Back | ⌘-[ |
| Go | Forward | ⌘-] |
| Go | Enclosing Folder | ⌘-up arrow |
| Go | Computer | Shift-⌘-C |

| Menu | Action | Keyboard Shortcut |
|---|---|---|
| Go | Home | Shift-⌘-H |
| Go | Desktop | Shift-⌘-D |
| Go | Network | Shift-⌘-K |
| Go | iDisk, My iDisk | Shift-⌘-I |
| Go | Applications | Shift-⌘-A |
| Go | Utilities | Shift-⌘-U |
| Go | Go to Folder | Shift-⌘-G |
| Go | Connect to Server | ⌘-K |
| Window | Minimize Window | ⌘-M |
| Window | Cycle Through Windows | ⌘-` |

# CHAPTER 3

# Working on the Mac OS X Desktop

## In this chapter

# The Mac OS X Desktop

The Mac's desktop has always been the place from which you work with files, folders, system configuration, and so on (see Figure 3.1). The desktop enables you to manipulate the files and folders on your Mac. You also can access commands that appear nowhere else and can control many aspects of how your system performs. And, of course, you can use the Finder to find folders and files stored on your machine.



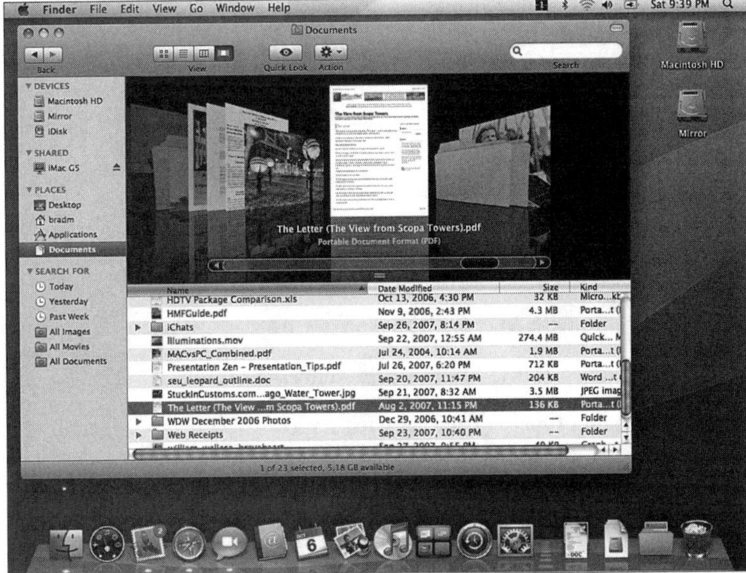


**Figure 3.1**
The most obvious aspects of the Mac OS X's desktop are the beautiful appearance of its icons, the controls provided in Finder windows, and the Dock.

⇨ For information on viewing and using Finder windows, **see** Chapter 2, "Viewing and Navigating Mac OS X Finder Windows," **p. 17**.

⇨ Because the Dock is such an important part of Mac OS X, it has a chapter dedicated to it; **see** Chapter 5, "Using and Customizing the Dock," **p. 107**.

# Working with Mac OS X Menus

One of the strengths of the Mac OS is that it has always featured certain menus that are very similar in all applications.

## The Mac OS X Apple Menu

The Apple menu has long been one of the staples of the Mac desktop. Its main purpose has always been to provide continuous access to specific commands whether you are working on the desktop or within an application. The Mac OS X Apple menu contains the commands listed in Table 3.1.

TABLE 3.1 COMMANDS ON THE MAC OS X APPLE MENU

| Command | What It Does |
|---|---|
| About This Mac | Opens a window showing the version of Mac OS X installed, the physical RAM installed, the number and type of processors, and the startup disk. You can also open Software Update to get the latest versions of Apple software and the System Profiler from this window to get more information about your Mac. |
| Software Update | Opens the Software Update tool, which you can use to get the latest versions of the Apple software installed on your Mac. |
| Mac OS X Software | Opens the default web browser and moves to the Mac OS X software downloads web page. |
| System Preferences | Opens the System Preferences application. |
| Dock | Provides control over the Dock's magnification, hiding, and position settings, and enables you to open the Dock Preferences pane of the System Preferences application. |
| Recent Items | Provides a menu of applications, documents, and servers that you have recently accessed; you can select an item to move back to it. The menu is organized into separate sections for each type of item. It also has the Clear Menu command, which clears the menu. |
| Force Quit | Opens the Force Quit Applications window that enables you to kill open applications (for example, when they are hung). |
| Sleep | Puts the Mac to sleep. |
| Restart | Restarts the Mac. |
| Shut Down | Shuts down the Mac. |
| Log Out *username* | Logs the current user (whose account name is `username`) off the Mac and opens the Login window. |

3

## MAC OS X APPLICATION MENUS

Under Mac OS X, every application has its own Application menu. The Application menu provides the commands you use to control the application in which you are working. A standard set of commands is consistent among all Mac OS X applications, however, specific applications can have additional commands on their Application menu (but they must support at least the standard commands on that menu). The name of the Application menu is the name of the application itself. For example, the desktop's Application menu is the Finder menu (because Finder is the name of the application that controls the desktop).

The following commands appear on all Application menus:

- **About *Application***—The About *Application* command, where *Application* is the name of the active application, displays version information about the application. Some About windows also provide links to support sites, the publisher's website, and so on. The About Finder command displays the version of the Finder you are using.

- **Preferences**—You use the Preferences command to set the preferences for an application. For example, you can use the Finder's Preferences command to control specific properties of the desktop.

⇨ To learn about Finder Preferences, see "Changing the Desktop's Appearance," **p. 87**.

**TIP**

> The keyboard shortcut for the Preferences command has been standardized (for all Apple applications and most of those from other sources) to be ⌘-,. This enables you to open the Preferences dialog box for any application with the same keys. This is a good thing.



- **Hide and Show commands**—The Hide and Show commands enable you to control which running applications are visible. There are three of these commands on the Application menu. The Hide *CurrentApplication* command (where *CurrentApplication* is the name of the running application) hides the current application. The Hide Others command hides all the running applications except the current one, and the Show All command shows all open applications.

**NOTE**

> Hiding an application causes all its windows and its menu bar to disappear. The application continues to run and any processes that are underway continue. You can also minimize application windows, which places open windows on the Dock; the application's menu bar continues to appear while the application is active, even if its windows are minimized.

All Application menus, except the Finder menu, also contain the following commands:

- **Quit**—The Quit command does what you would expect it to—it stops the running application.
- **Services**—The Services command provides commands to enable you to work with other applications from within the current application. For example, if you are using the TextEdit word processing application, you see the Grab command on its Services menu. Selecting this command activates the Grab application that enables you to capture something on the screen. After you capture the image, it is automatically pasted into the current TextEdit document. Many other commands appear on this menu; the commands available depend on the applications installed on your Mac and how those applications support the Services menu.

⇨ To learn more about using the Services command with Mac OS X applications, **see** "Working with Mac OS X Application Menus," **p. 150**.

**TIP**

> The keyboard shortcut for the Quit command is ⌘-Q. When you are working on the desktop, ⌘-Q doesn't do anything because you can't quit the Finder. However, you can relaunch the Finder using the Force Quit command.

The Finder's Application menu (the Finder menu) also has the Empty Trash and Secure Empty Trash commands, which are unique to its Application menu. The Empty Trash command deletes any files or folders located in the Trash. The Secure Empty Trash deletes files located in the Trash and overwrites the disk space where those files were stored so they can't be recovered. Because the Secure Empty Trash command overwrites the disk space where the files where written, it takes much longer to execute than does the Empty Trash command (of course, because it works in the background, that shouldn't slow down your work).

## MAC OS X FILE MENUS

Under Mac OS X, the File menu contains commands for working with files or folders.

The specific commands you see on an application's File menu depend on the application. Most applications' File menus have the New, Open, Save, Save As, Print, and Page Setup commands. Many other commands might appear on the File menu as well.

The Finder's File menu contains the commands listed in Table 3.2.



**TABLE 3.2 COMMANDS ON THE FINDER'S FILE MENU**

| Command | What It Does |
|---|---|
| New Finder Window | Opens a new Finder window |
| New Folder | Creates a new folder |
| New Smart Folder | Creates a new smart folder |
| New Burn Folder | Creates a new folder intended to be burned onto a disc |
| Open | Opens the selected item |
| Open With | Enables you to open a selected file with a specific application |
| Print | Enables you to print a selected file |
| Close Window | Closes the active window |
| Get Info | Opens the Info window |
| Compress | Compresses selected items and creates a .zip file to store the compressed versions |
| Duplicate | Creates a duplicate of the selected item |
| Make Alias | Creates an alias of the selected item |
| Quick Look | Opens the Quick Look view for selected items |
| Show Original | Exposes the original item for which an alias was created |
| Add to Sidebar | Adds an alias of the selected item to the Places Sidebar |
| Move to Trash | Moves the selected item to the Trash |
| Eject | Ejects the selected item (disc, disk image, server volume, and so on) |

*continues*

**Table 3.2 Continued**

| Command | What It Does |
|---|---|
| Burn | Burns the selected item to CD or DVD |
| Find | Opens the Finder's Find tool so you can locate files and folders |
| Label | Applies the label you choose to the selected items |

**NOTE**

> The Mac OS X Compress command is one of the most useful Finder commands. This command enables you to create compressed files from any folders and files on your Mac. Even better, Mac OS X supports the Zip compression format, which is the standard, native compression format on Windows computers. You no longer need a separate application to compress files. You can also expand any Zip file from the desktop by simply opening it.



## Mac OS X Edit Menus

Under Mac OS X, the Edit menu is pretty much as it has always been. The Edit menu contains commands for editing data. When you are working with most applications other than the Finder, the commands that appear on the Edit menu are Cut, Copy, and Paste. Applications can provide many more commands on this menu, such as Undo, Redo, Select All, and so on.

The Finder's Edit menu is somewhat different than this menu under most applications because you don't use the Finder to edit documents. Its commands apply to files and folders instead. For example, when you select a file and choose Edit, Copy, the file is copied. You can move to a different location and choose Edit, Paste to place a copy of the selected item in the new location. The Finder's Edit menu also has the Select All command, which selects everything in the active window; the Show Clipboard command, which shows what has been copied to the Clipboard; and the Special Characters command, which opens the Character palette.

## The Finder View Menu

The Finder's View menu contains the commands you use to view Finder windows.

⇨ To learn about using the Finder's View commands, **see** Chapter 2, "Viewing and Navigating Mac OS X Finder Windows," **p. 17**.

## The Finder Go Menu

The Finder's Go menu, as you might guess from its name, contains commands you use to go places. The Go menu enables you to move to the following locations:

- **Back or Forward**—You can move among the windows in a chain of open Finder windows by using the Back and Forward commands.
- **Enclosing Folder**—You can move into the folder that contains the currently selected item by choosing this command.

- **Frequently Used Folders**—You can move to any of the folders listed on the Go menu by selecting the folder into which you want to move.
- **Recent Folders**—This command lists the most recent folders you have used; select a folder to return to it. You can clear the Recent Folders menu by selecting Clear Menu.
- **Specific Folder**—Use the Go To Folder command to enter the path to a specific folder to open it.
- **Servers**—Use the Connect To Server command to open a server on your network.

⇨ To learn how to use the Go menu to navigate folders, **see** "Changing Directories with the Go Menu," **p. 36**.

⇨ To learn how to connect to servers, **see** "Accessing Shared Files from a Mac OS X Computer," **p. 375**.

## MAC OS X WINDOW MENUS



Another standard Mac OS X menu is the Window menu. This menu provides commands you use to work with windows that are currently open. Common choices on the Window menu include the following:

- **Minimize**—This does the same thing as clicking the Minimize button in a window—it moves a window onto the Dock.
- **Zoom**—This does the same thing as the Maximize button: It makes the active window as large as it needs to be to display all the window's contents or to fill the desktop, whichever comes first. Choosing it again toggles the window back to its previous size.
- **Cycle Through Open Windows**—This moves you among the open windows, one at a time.
- **Bring All to Front**—This command brings all open windows to the front. For example, if you have a lot of open Finder windows, then switch to an application, and then back to the Finder, you might not see all your open Finder windows. If you use this command, they all come to the foreground so you can see them.
- **List of Open Windows**—The Window menu always displays a list of the windows open for the application providing that menu. You can switch to an open window by selecting it on the menu.

On the Window menu, the active window in the application you are currently using is marked with some sort of icon. The active Finder window is marked with a check mark; other applications might use a different indicator (for example, a diamond). Be aware that a window can be both active and minimized, in which case the active icon on the Window menu can help you identify the active window even if you can't see that window (because it is on the Dock).

If you hold the Option key down while you open the Window menu, you'll see two additional commands that replace default commands. Minimize becomes Minimize All, which causes all open windows in the application, such as the Finder, to be minimized and moved to the Dock. The "Bring All to Front" command becomes the Arrange in Front command, which brings all open windows in the current application to the front and arranges them neatly on the desktop.

You might see more or fewer commands on the Window menu when you are working in specific applications.

## Mac OS X Help Menus

Most applications provide a Help menu that enables you to open their help system. And, most applications provide help through the standard Mac OS X Help application. You can also use Spotlight to search your Mac for specific information.

The Finder's Help menu contains two commands—Search and Mac Help.

You can use the Search box to use Spotlight to quickly search the Finder and the Mac's Help for information in which you might be interested. To use this tool, select Help and enter the term you want to search for in the Search box. As you type, the Help command is replaced by the results of the search (see Figure 3.2). The results are grouped by Finder items, such as menus, and Help Topics.



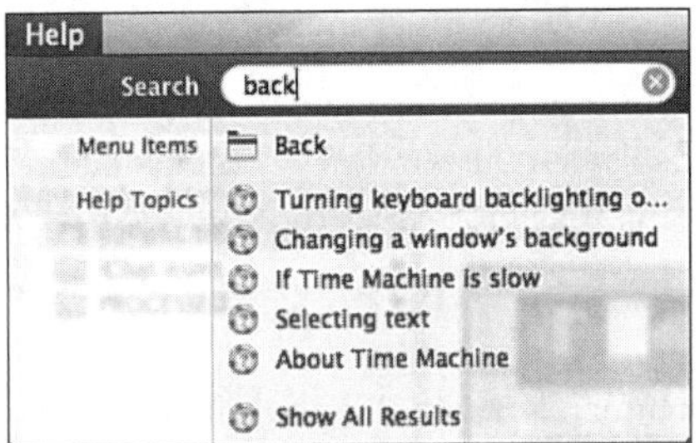


**Figure 3.2**
When you use the Search command on the Finder's Help menu, you search the Finder and Help.

If you choose a Finder item in the results, the item opens and a large, floating arrow points to it so you can't miss what you've searched for (see Figure 3.3).

If you choose a result in the Help Topic section, the Help system opens and takes you to that topic. This is a bit faster than opening the Help system and then doing the search, but you end up in the same place.

To clear a search so you see the original two commands, click the Clear button (X) in the Search tool.

The Mac Help command opens the Mac Help application, which provides extensive help for many areas of the OS (see Figure 3.4). Even better, many applications you install integrate their help systems into the OS help system. This enables you to access plenty of help using the same tool.

The Help application is based on HTML, so it works the same way web pages do. You can search for help and click links and buttons to access information and move around.

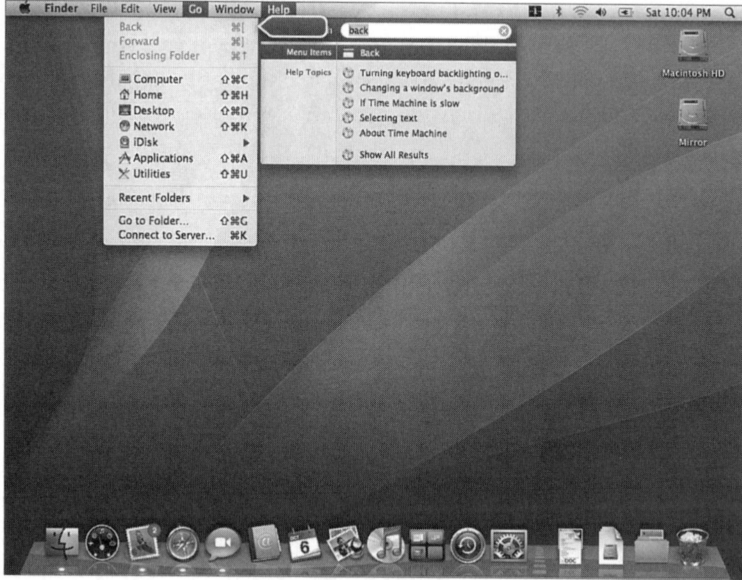


**Figure 3.3**
When you select a Finder item in the search results, the Finder isn't shy about showing it to you.

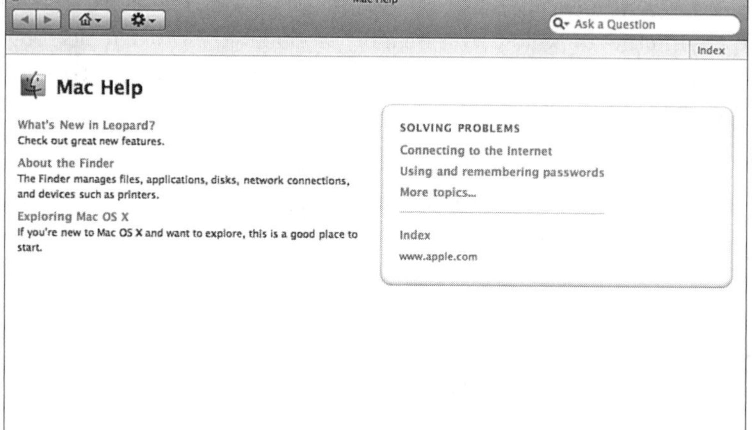


**Figure 3.4**
You can get a lot of Mac OS help by using the Help application.

The Home button in the Help Center's toolbar takes you back to the current help's home page. If you click and hold the Home button, you will see a list of all areas in which you can access help, such as AirPort Help, Mail Help, and so on. You can also view and choose these areas on the Help application's Library command.

**TIP**

> When you search for help, you frequently see the Tell Me More link. This link opens other pages that contain topics related to the one for which you searched.

When you have the Mac Help window open, there are a couple of tools you can use to help you find what you are looking for. The Index link will take you to, well, an index. Topics are listed alphabetically, and you can click on a letter of the alphabet to move to a certain term or phrase. The search field invites you to Ask a Question; enter a term and press Return to see the results.

The results window is organized into two areas: Help Topics and Support Articles.

The Help Topics section lists each help topic within the Help system that matches your search. By default, this area is sorted by the Relevance column, which is the Help system's judgment of how well a topic addresses your search criterion. You can open a topic by double-clicking it or selecting it and clicking Show. The topic appears in the window for viewing.



**TIP**

You can also browse most help systems from their home pages. This is often an even better way to find a specific topic because you don't have to be concerned about using specific words as you do when you search for help.

In the Support Articles section, you will see articles on the application's support web site that the Help application has found for you—of course, your Mac must be able to connect to the Internet to be able to search for information. Just like topics, you can access an article by double-clicking it or by selecting it and clicking Show. The article will be downloaded from the Web and will appear within the Help window.

**NOTE**

Articles on the Web are marked with the plus icon (+) while topics within the Help system are marked with the application's icon. For example, Mac OS X help topics are marked with the OS X icon (the "X").

Some help topics assist you in performing the action you are asking about by providing hyperlinks that open the related application or resource.

## The Spotlight Menu

The Spotlight menu, which is always located at the far right end of the menu bar, enables you to search for information on your Mac.

⇨ To learn how to use the Spotlight, **see** "Searching Your Mac with Spotlight," **p. 94**.

## Optional Finder Menus

As you work with various parts of the system, you can add menus to the Mac OS X menu bar to make those tools available at all times. For example, you can add the Displays menu, which has a display as its icon, to the menu bar so that you can jump immediately to the Displays pane of the System Preferences application. There are many possibilities as you will learn throughout this book.

## Mac OS X Contextual Menus

Mac OS X supports contextual menus. *Contextual menus* are pop-up menus that appear in various locations and contain commands specifically related to the context in which you are working. You can access contextual menus by pointing to an object that provides a contextual menu and clicking the right mouse button or holding down the Control key and clicking the left (or only, on a one-button mouse) mouse button. The contextual menu appears, and you can select a command on it.

**TIP**

Mac OS X supports a two-button mouse by default. You can open an item's contextual menu by right-clicking it. You can also program most multi-button input devices to perform a right-click. I strongly recommend that you use a mouse or trackball that has at least two buttons, if for no other reason than the convenience of opening contextual menus with one hand.



The desktop and Finder provide contextual menus, as do many applications, including those not provided by Apple. For example, the Microsoft Office application provides excellent support for contextual menus.

A summary of some of the more useful Finder contextual menu commands is provided in Table 3.3.

**Table 3.3 Useful Finder Contextual Menu Commands**

| Object | Command | What It Does |
|---|---|---|
| All | More, Automator | Opens the Automator so you can create a workflow. |
| Desktop | Change Desktop Background | Opens the Desktop & Screen Saver pane of the System Preferences application. |
| Desktop, Finder window | New Burn Folder | Creates a new burn folder on the desktop or within the current folder. (You'll learn more about these folders later in this chapter.) |
| Desktop, Finder window | New Folder | Creates a new folder. |
| Desktop, Finder window, folder, file | More, Folder Actions commands | Folder actions are AppleScripts you can attach to folders so those actions are performed automatically. You use the Enable Folder Actions command to select the actions associated with the selected item. You use the Configure Folder Actions command to configure how actions for an item work. You use the Disable Folder Actions command to disable an item's folder actions. |

*continues*

**Table 3.3 Continued**

| Object | Command | What It Does |
|---|---|---|
| Desktop, Finder window, folder, file, mounted volume | Automator | Enables you to create a workflow with the selected items or to create a new workflow. You can also choose workflows that you have already created to work with them. (You'll learn all about the Automator in Chapter 29.) |
| Desktop, Finder window, folder, file, volume | Get Info | Opens the Info window. (This is covered in more detail later in this chapter.) |
| Desktop, folder with no items selected | Show View Options | Opens the View options window for the desktop or the current folder. |
| File | Open With | Enables you to choose the application to use to open the selected file. |
| File | Print | Prints the selected files. |
| File | Quick Look | Opens the Quick Look tool. (This is covered in more detail later in this chapter.) |
| Folder | Paste item | Pastes the previously created copy of files or folders in the current location. |
| Folder, file | Color Label | Applies a label to the selected items. |
| Folder, file | Copy | Copies selected items. |
| Folder, file | Compress | Creates a Zip file containing the selected items. |
| Folder, file | Duplicate | Duplicates the selected items. |
| Folder, file | Make Alias | Creates an alias of the selected items. |
| Folder, file | Move to Trash | Moves the selected items to the Trash. |
| Folder, file | Open | Opens the selected item. |
| Mac OS X window toolbars | Customize Toolbar | Enables you to customize the current toolbar. |
| Mac OS X window toolbars | Toolbar Format commands | Use these to change the format of the toolbar, such as Text Only to hide the icons and display only text. |
| Mounted volume | Open Enclosing Folder | Opens the folder where the selected item is stored. |
| Mounted volume | Rename | Enables you to rename the selected volume. |
| Sidebar item | Remove From Sidebar | Removes the selected item from the Places sidebar. |
| Sidebar items | Rename | Enables you to rename the select Sidebar item. |

### THE FINDER ACTION POP-UP MENU

The Action pop-up menu, represented by a gear, is located on all Finder windows' toolbar by default. This pop-up menu provides contextual commands that work similarly to those on contextual menus. When you select an item or view a folder, commands appropriate to that object appear on the menu (see Figure 3.5).

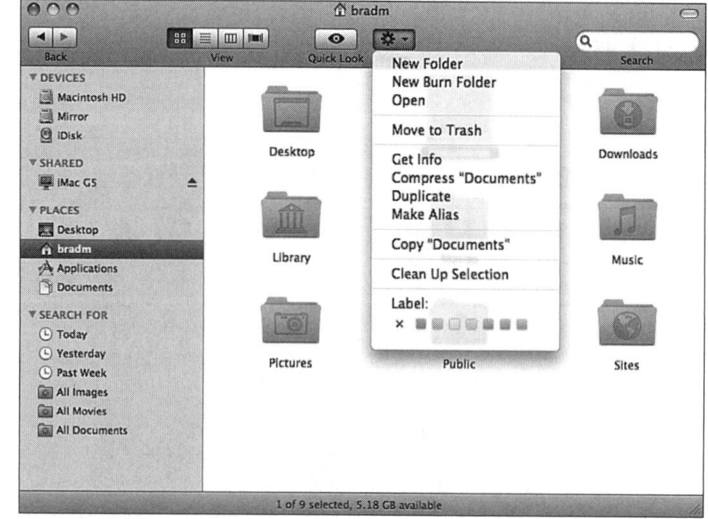


**Figure 3.5**
The Action pop-up menu provides contextual commands; in this case, the commands are for the selected folder.

The commands that appear on this menu are the same as those that appear on contextual menus (refer to Table 3.3).

**NOTE**

> Some applications, especially Apple applications, also provide an Action menu that is marked with the same gear icon.

## WORKING WITH THE SYSTEM PREFERENCES APPLICATION

The System Preferences application enables you to set preferences for many areas of Mac OS X and some third-party applications and peripheral devices. If you read through the previous chapters, you already have some experience with this application. However, because you will use the System Preferences application so frequently, it is worthy of a more detailed look.

You can open the System Preferences utility in various ways, including the following:

- Select Apple, System Preferences.
- Click the System Preferences icon on the Dock.
- Open the Applications folder and then open System Preferences using its icon.

3

**NOTE**

> Because the System Preferences application is used so frequently, Apple should have provided a keyboard shortcut to open it but didn't. If you use a macro utility, such as QuicKeys, you should set and use a keyboard shortcut to open this application.

The System Preferences application provides a window with a toolbar at the top and a series of icons or buttons in the bottom part (see Figure 3.6). To access the controls for a specific area, you click its icon. The System Preferences window will change to show a pane containing controls for that area (see Figure 3.7).



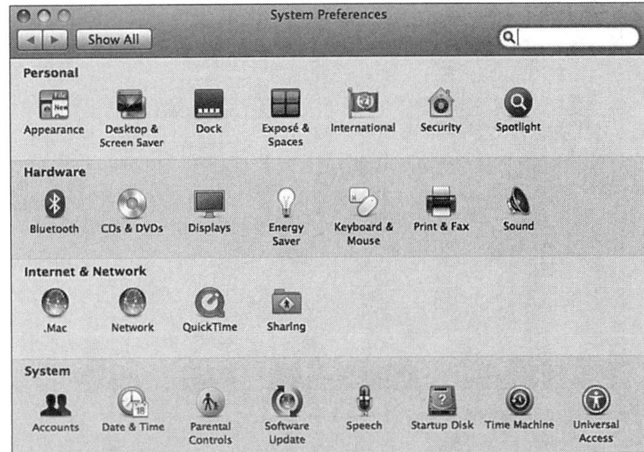


**Figure 3.6**
The System Preferences application enables you to configure and customize Mac OS X to suit your needs and personal preferences.

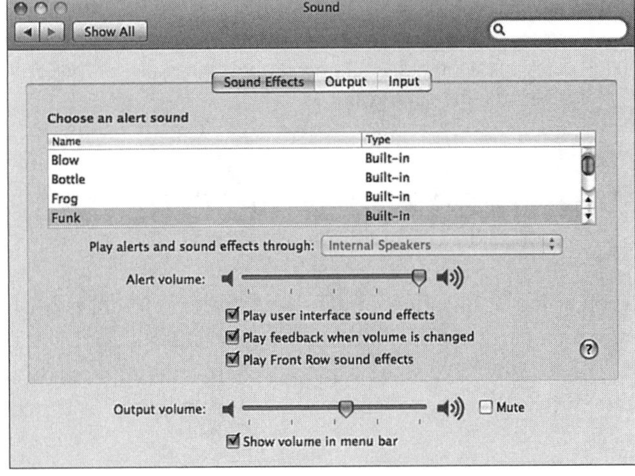


**Figure 3.7**
The Sound pane of the System Preferences application enables you to change your system's sound settings.

The default panes contained in the System Preferences utility (listed in alphabetical order) are the following:

- .Mac
- Accounts
- Appearance
- Bluetooth
- CDs & DVDs
- Date & Time
- Desktop & Screen Saver
- Displays
- Dock
- Energy Saver
- Exposé & Spaces
- International
- Keyboard & Mouse
- Network
- Parental Controls
- Print & Fax
- QuickTime
- Security
- Sharing
- Software Update
- Sound
- Speech
- Spotlight
- Startup Disk
- Time Machine
- Universal Access

3

By default, these buttons are organized into the following categories: Personal, Hardware, Internet & Network, and System. The Personal panes configure aspects of the user account that is currently logged in. The panes in the other three categories make system wide changes (and so require that you are logged in under or authenticate yourself as an administrator account).

You can choose to list the icons in alphabetical order if you prefer—just select View, Organize Alphabetically. The categories disappear and the icons are listed in alphabetical order (from left to right, top to bottom).

If you prefer to use a menu to open a pane, select the pane you want to open on the View menu.

After you have opened a pane, you can show all the panes of the window again by clicking the Show All button, by selecting View, Show All Preferences, or press ⌘-L.

**NOTE**

> Specific panes are covered in the parts of this book that explain the features they are related to. For example, the Accounts pane is explained in Chapter 11, "Configuring and Working with User Accounts."

Some panes appear only when your Mac has specific capabilities, such as the Bluetooth pane, which appears only if your Mac is Bluetooth capable. When you add hardware or software to your system, additional panes can appear to enable you to configure the device or software you added. One example of this is the Ink pane, which appears when you attach a handwriting recognition device (such as a tablet) to your Mac.

Panes added by Apple-produced tools, such as the Bluetooth pane, appear within the related categories, such as Hardware. Panes added by third-party tools, such as keyboard customization panes, are contained in the Other category.

## Managing Open Windows with Exposé

As you work on the desktop, you'll open lots of windows in the Finder. Plus, each time you work with an application, you'll open at least one window, and usually more than one. All those windows add up to a lot of desktop clutter. Mac OS X's Exposé helps you manage open windows by being able to move them out of the way quickly so that you can easily focus on specific windows in which you are interested.

⇨ To learn about Exposé, **see** "Managing Open Windows with Exposé," **p. 266**.



## Managing the Desktop with Spaces

Mac OS X's Spaces feature enables you to create sets of applications and related windows and switch among those sets easily and quickly. Spaces are a great way to manage your desktop because you can work with groups of windows at the same time and change the context in which you are working by simply changing your space.

⇨ To learn about Spaces, **see** "Creating, Using, and Managing Spaces," **p. 269**.

## Understanding Mac OS X Directories

Mac OS X includes many standard folders, often called *directories* in Mac OS X lingo. You have seen several of these as you learned about using the Go menu, working with Finder windows, and so on.

Some directories, such as the Mac OS X System folder, are critical to your Mac's operation, whereas others are merely organizational devices, such as the Documents folder within each user's Home folder.

There are two general groups of folders you will work with: those for the system and those for users.

### Mac OS X System Folders

Two main folders provide access to Mac OS X system-level files and folders.

#### The Computer Folder

The Computer folder is the highest-level folder on your Mac. It shows the volumes mounted on your machine, including hard drives, drive partitions, disk images, DVDs, CD-ROMs, and so on (see Figure 3.8). The name of the Computer folder is the name of your Mac.

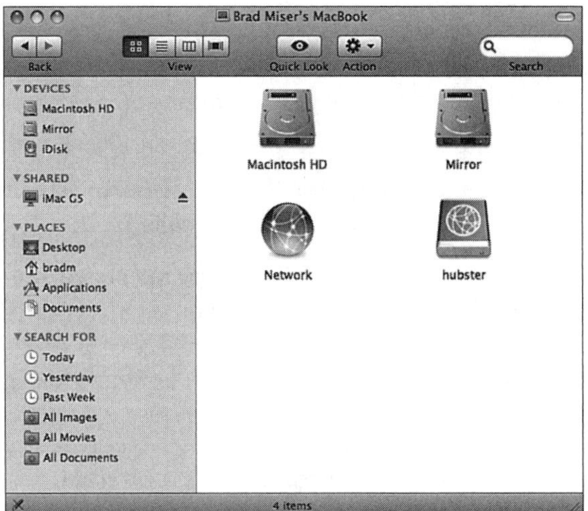


**Figure 3.8**
The Mac OS X Computer folder represents all the contents of your machine as well as the network resources you can access.

Most of the contents of the Computer folder should be familiar to you, such as volumes, CD-ROMs, and so on.

### The Mac OS X Startup Volume

One of the folders in the Computer folder is the one on which you installed Mac OS X. The name of this folder depends on what you named the volume.

By default, your startup volume folder contains the following four folders that are part of the Mac OS X installation:

- **Applications**—Under Mac OS X, all Carbon and Cocoa applications are stored in this folder.

⇨ To learn how to install applications, **see** Chapter 7, **p. 141**.

- **Library**—The Library folder contains many subfolders that provide resources to support applications, hardware devices, and other items you add to your Mac. This library folder contains the system folders that can be modified.
- **System**—This folder contains the Library folder that provides the core operating system software for Mac OS X. The items in this folder can't be modified except by installation applications, system updaters, or using the root account.
- **Users**—The Users folder contains the Home folder for each user for whom an account has been created. The Home folder of the user currently logged in has the Home icon; the Home folders for the rest of the users have plain folder icons. If you have deleted user accounts, it also contains a folder called "Deleted Users" that contains a disk image for each deleted user account (if you elected to keep the user's resources when you deleted his folder).

## Mac OS X User Folders

As you learned in Chapter 1, each user account includes a Home folder. By default, this folder contains nine folders where the logged-in user can store folders and files.

⇨ To learn about the specific folders in a user's Home folder, **see** "Understanding the Home Folder," **p. 11**.

Although the Home folder contains nine default folders, you can add folders within these folders as well as create new folders within the Home folder itself.

The benefit to using the standard folders is that they are integrated into the OS so you can access them quickly and in many ways. For example, you can select the Documents folder in Mac OS X Save and Open dialog boxes. This makes it easier to keep your documents organized than if you create your own folders outside your Home folder.



**TIP**

> You can add any folder to the sidebar, which is visible in all Open and Save dialog boxes along with Finder windows (when the sidebar is displayed). Adding a folder to the sidebar makes that folder accessible from many locations.

Another benefit of using the standard Mac OS X folders is that they take advantage of the default security settings that go with the user account. When you use folders outside a user account's Home folder, you should check and set the security of the folders you are using, if you want to limit the access to those resources by other people who use your Mac.

⇨ To learn how to configure an item's security, **see** "Understanding and Setting Permissions," **p. 385**.

Most of the user folders are self-explanatory, such as Documents, Movies, and Music. However, a few of them are worthy of more detailed attention.

### The Desktop Folder

The user's Desktop folder contains the items the user has placed on his desktop. Each user can have as much or as little on his desktop as he likes. When another user logs in, she sees only the contents of her desktop folder on the desktop.

### The Library Folder

In the Library folder are system files specifically related to the user account. The Library folder includes a number of subfolders (see Figure 3.9).

The particular folders you see depend on the applications you have used and what you have done. For instance, if you have installed iMovie, iPhoto, and iTunes, you'll find folders and files related to each of these applications. In the Fonts folder are fonts that only you can access. Your Internet plug-ins are stored in the Internet Plug-Ins folder, and the Preferences folder is where applications store your personal preferences.

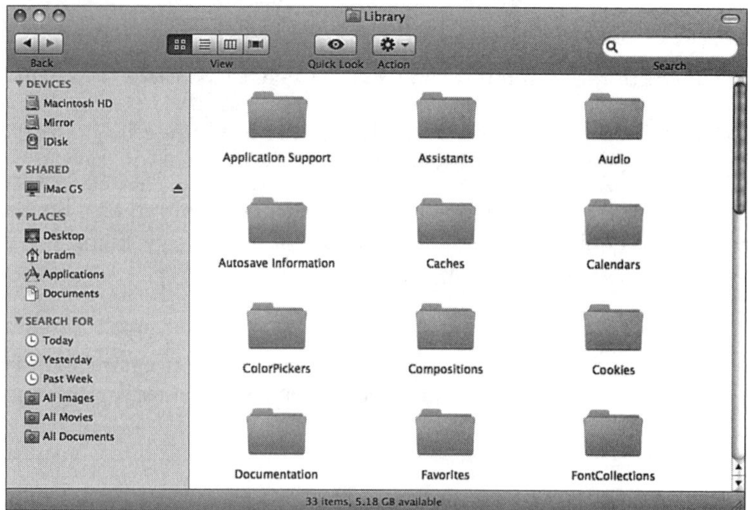


**Figure 3.9**
Each user has a Library folder where files that relate to that user's system resources, such as preferences, are stored.

3

### The Public Folder

A user's Public folder is available to all users who log in to a particular Mac. This folder lets users conveniently share or transfer files because placing files or folders within the Public folder makes them available to all the other users on a particular machine.

To access the files and folders in another user's Public folder, perform the following steps:

1. Open the Users folder. (Select your startup volume to see it.)
2. Open the Home folder for the user who has a file you want to share.
3. Open the Public folder and use the files contained within it.

**TIP**

> You can open a file or folder within another user's Public folder, or you can drag the file to your own folder to make a copy of it.

Within the Public folder, you will also see a Drop Box folder. Other users can place items into this folder, but no one else can open it. This is useful when you want others to transfer items to you but don't want all the other users to be able to see what has been shared.

### The Sites Folder

The Sites folder contains the files and folders that make up the website for each user account.

⇨ For more information on sharing a website under Mac OS X, **see** "Mac OS X to the Max: Using Mac OS X to Serve Web Pages," **p. 458**.

# Working with Files and Folders

Working with files and folders under Mac OS X version 10.5 is straightforward.

Under Mac OS X, you can move and copy files and folders as in previous versions of the OS. Just drag the folders or files to where you want them to reside.

To place a copy of an item in a different folder, hold down the Option key while you drag the item. To duplicate an item (make a copy of it in its current location), select it and select File, Duplicate (or press ⌘-D).

**NOTE**

> The Column view is one of the more useful views for moving files and folders around because it gives you a good view of the entire hierarchy of the volume you are working with.



You can also create copies of files and folders using the contextual menu commands and the commands on the Edit menu. You can place a copy of the items in a new location by selecting them, choosing the Copy command, and then pasting them in a new location.

When you move an object over a folder, it becomes highlighted so you can easily see in which folder the item you are moving will be placed. This is especially useful when you are viewing Finder windows in the Column view. Similarly, when you drag something over a folder on the Places section of the sidebar, the folder will be highlighted so it is clear which folder the object will be moved into when you release the mouse button.

## Creating and Naming Folders

The purpose of folders under Mac OS X is to enable you to organize files. You can create a new folder by using the New Folder command (such as File, New Folder, or press ⌘-Shift-N). The new folder will be created in your current location. Immediately after you create it, its name will be editable so you can simply type the name of the new folder.

Naming a folder is mostly a matter of personal preference; the maximum number of characters that you can use in a folder name is 256. Of course, you aren't likely to ever use a folder name that long because it would be very difficult to read, but at least you have lots of flexibility with folder names.

To name a folder or edit its current name, select the folder and press Return. The folder's name becomes highlighted and you can create a new name.

## Naming Files

Naming files is very similar to naming folders, with one exception. The underlying architecture of the Mac OS X uses *filename extensions*—for example, `.doc` at the end of a Word document filename.

File extensions are a code that helps identify a file's type and thus the application used to view or edit that file. Many Mac OS X applications also use filename extensions; the OS uses these extensions to launch the appropriate application for that document when you open the file.

⇨ To understand more about filename extensions under Mac OS X, **see** "Saving Documents in Mac OS X," **p. 161**.

When you name a document from within an application that uses filename extensions, the correct extension is appended automatically to the filename you enter. However, when you rename files on the desktop or in a Finder window, you need to be aware of a filename's extension if it has one (not all applications use an extension).

A complication in this is that you can choose to show or hide filename extensions on a file-by-file basis or at the system level. However, filename extensions are almost always in use, whether you can see them or not. Hiding them simply hides them from your view.

You can use the Info tool to associate applications with specific files so the lack of a proper filename extension is not a significant problem.

⇨ To learn how to associate files with specific applications, **see** "Opening Documents in Mac OS X," **p. 153**.



If you want to rename a file that has an extension, you should leave the extension as it is. If you change or remove the extension, the application you use to open the file might not be launched automatically when you try to open the file.

The filename extensions you see under Mac OS X include some of the three- or four-letter filename extensions with which you are no doubt familiar, such as `.doc`, `.xls`, `.html`, `.jpg`, `.tiff`, and so on. However, there are many, many more filename extensions you will encounter. Some are relatively short, whereas others (particularly those in the system) can be quite long. There isn't really any apparent rhyme or reason to these filename extensions so you just have to learn them as you go. Because you will mostly deal with filename extensions that are appended by an application when you save a document, this isn't a critical task. However, as you delve deeper into the system, you will become more familiar with many of the sometimes bizarre-looking filename extensions Mac OS X uses.

**NOTE**

> Depending on the file type, some files open properly even if you do remove or change the file's extension. But it is better to be safe than sorry, so you should usually leave the file extension as you find it.

You can choose to hide or show filename extensions globally or on an item-by-item basis. To configure filename extensions globally, use the following steps:

1. Select Finder, Preferences to open the Finder Preferences window.
2. Click the Advanced icon.
3. To globally show filename extensions, check the "Show all file extensions" check box.
4. To allow filename extensions to be shown or hidden for specific items, uncheck the "Show all file extensions" check box.

⇨ To learn how to show or hide filename extensions for specific items, **see** "Working with Name and Extension Information," **p. 81**.

## CREATING AND USING ALIASES

An alias is a pointer to a file, folder, or volume. Open an alias and the original item opens. The benefit of aliases is that you can place them anywhere on your Mac because they are very small in file size, so you can use them with little storage penalty.

There are several ways to create an alias, including

- Select an item and select File, Make Alias.
- Select an item and press ⌘-L.
- Hold down the Option and ⌘ keys while you drag an item.
- Open the Action menu for an item and select Make Alias.
- Open the contextual menu for an item and select Make Alias.



After you create an alias, you can work with it much like you can the original. For example, you can open it or move it to a new location.

Occasionally, you might need to find the original from which an alias was created. For example, if you create an alias to an application, you might want to be able to move to that application in the Finder. Do the following:

1. Select the alias.
2. Select File, Show Original (or press ⌘-R). A Finder window containing the original item opens.

Occasionally, an alias *breaks*, meaning your Mac loses track of the original to which the alias points. The most common situation is that you have deleted the original, but it can happen for other reasons as well. When you attempt to open a broken alias, you will see a warning dialog box that provides the following three options:

- **Delete Alias**—If you click this button, the alias is deleted.
- **Fix Alias**—If you click this one, you can use the Fix Alias dialog box to select another file to which you want the alias to point.
- **OK**—If you click OK, the dialog box disappears and no changes are made to the alias.

## TRASHING FILES AND FOLDERS

Since its inception, the Mac's Trash can has been the place where you move files and folders that you no longer want so that you can delete them from your computer. Under Mac OS X, the Trash is located at the right end or bottom of the Dock.

To move something to the Trash, use one of the following methods:

- Drag the item to the Trash on the Dock. When you are over the Trash icon, it is highlighted so you know you are in the right place.
- Select an item, open its contextual menu, and select Move to Trash.

- Select an item and choose File, Move to Trash.
- Select an item and press ⌘-Delete.

After you have placed an item in the Trash, you can access it again by clicking the Trash icon on the Dock. A Finder window displaying the Trash folder opens, and you can work with the items it contains.

When you want to delete the items in the Trash, do so in one of the following ways:

- Select Finder, Empty Trash. In the confirmation dialog box, click either OK (or press Return) to empty the Trash or Cancel to stop the process. You can skip the confirmation dialog box by holding down the Option key while you select Empty Trash.
- Open the Trash's Dock contextual menu and select Empty Trash on the resulting pop-up menu.
- Press Shift-⌘-Delete. In the confirmation dialog box, click either OK (or press Return) to empty the Trash or Cancel to stop the process. You can skip the confirmation dialog box by pressing Option-Shift-⌘-Delete instead.



To permanently disable the warning dialog box when you empty the Trash, perform the following steps:

1. Select Finder, Preferences to open the Finder Preferences window.
2. Click the Advanced icon.
3. Uncheck the "Show warning before emptying the Trash" check box. The warning will no longer appear, no matter how you empty the Trash.

You can also securely delete items from the Trash. When you do this, the data that makes up those items is overwritten so it can't be recovered. To perform a secure delete, place items in the Trash and select Finder, Secure Empty Trash.

## CREATING AND USING BURN FOLDERS

Burn folders are a special type of folder that are designed to help you move files and folders onto CD or DVD more easily. One of the differences between a regular folder and a burn folder is that everything you move into a burn folder becomes an alias. This means you can build a CD or DVD without disturbing the location of the items that you want to put on disc. Simply create a burn folder and place items into it. When you are ready to burn a disc, you can do so quite easily.

**TIP**

> You can use burn folders as back-up mechanism. For example, suppose you want to back up your iPhoto Library to DVD. Simply create a burn folder and place your Pictures folder in it. To create a fresh back up of your library, just burn the folder. (You don't need to move the files into it again because the aliases are updated automatically.)

To create a burn folder, use one of the following options:

- Choose File, New Burn Folder.
- Open the Action menu and choose New Burn Folder.
- Open the contextual menu and choose New Burn Folder.

When the new folder appears, you will see it has the radioactive icon and the name "Burn Folder." The name is highlighted so you can rename it immediately. Do so and press Return to save the new name.

After you have created a burn folder, move the files and folders that you want to place on a disc into it. As you move files and folders into it, aliases to the original items are created inside the burn folder. Continue placing items inside the folder until you have moved all files you want to place on disc into it (see Figure 3.10).

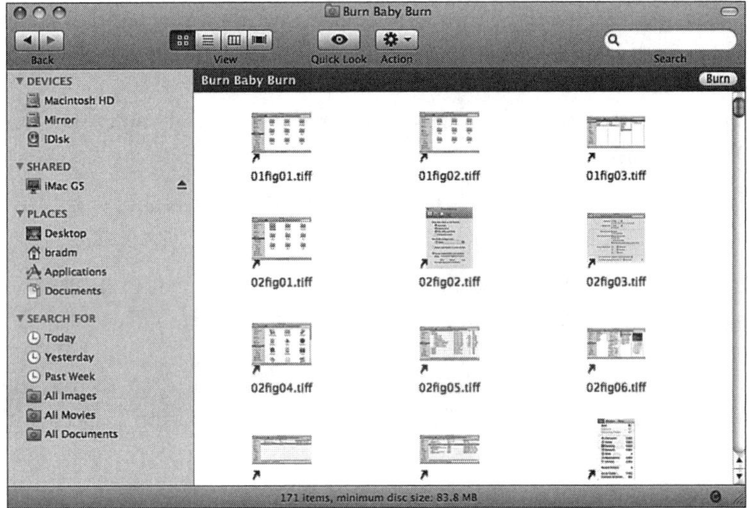


**Figure 3.10**
A burn folder contains aliases to items you place in it along with the black bar containing the folder name and Burn button shown at the top of its window.

**TIP**

For quick access, add a burn folder to the Places section of the sidebar so you can get into it easily to add more files to it.

You can organize files and folders within a burn folder just like other folders with which you work. For example, you can create new "regular" folders within the burn folder and place items within those folders.

**NOTE**

Unfortunately, using a burn folder supports burning to a disc in a single session. After you burn a folder to a disc, that disc is closed and can't be burned to again (unless it is an erasable disc, in which case you can erase its contents). Hopefully, someday the Finder will allow multi-session burns so you can add files to a disc you have burned.

When you are ready to burn a disc from the burn folder, view the folder and click its Burn button. You are prompted to insert a disc; in this prompt, you'll see the amount of space needed to burn the files on a disc. When your Mac mounts a disc that is ready to burn, you see the Burn prompt. Enter the name of the disc (it defaults to the name of the Burn folder), choose the burn speed on the Burn Speed pop-up menu, and click Burn. A progress bar appears, and the disc is burned.

You can quickly burn the contents of a burn folder at any time by repeating these steps, such as when you want to refresh your backups of important files.

**NOTE**

> You might wonder why it is better to create and use a burn folder than it is just to place files and folders directly on a disc. If you are only going to burn a disc once, there isn't a lot of benefit to creating a burn folder because it is just as easy to insert a blank disc into your burner and add files and folders to it. Burn folders become valuable when you want to re-create a disc, such as to refresh a back up or to make multiple copies of the same disc. Or, you might want to use them to organize files you are going to burn later in the order they will be on the disc.



## GETTING INFORMATION ON ITEMS

The Info window is a tool you use to learn about various items on your desktop and in Finder windows. For some items, you can also control specific aspects of how those items work and how they can be used.

You can access all the tools in the Info window from a single pane by using its expansion triangles. The window is organized into sections; you expose a section by clicking its expansion triangle. You can have multiple information windows open at the same time (which is helpful when you want to compare items).

The Info window has slightly different features and information for each of the following groups:

- Folders and volumes
- Applications
- Documents

The sections you see for each type of item are described in Table 3.3.

**TABLE 3.3 SECTIONS OF THE GET INFO WINDOW**

| Section | Applicable Items | Information/Tools It Provides |
|---|---|---|
| Spotlight Comments | Folders and volumes; applications; files | Enables you to enter comments that will be searched when you use Spotlight or as a criterion for a smart folder search. |

*continues*

TABLE 3.3 CONTINUED

| Section | Applicable Items | Information/Tools It Provides |
|---|---|---|
| General | Folders and volumes; applications; files | Provides identification information about the item, such as its name, type, and significant dates. |
| More Info | Folders and volumes; applications; files | Provides additional information about an item, such as the date on which it was last opened, resolution information (for images), and so on. |
| Name & Extension | Folders and volumes; applications; files | Gives the full item name, including its filename extension if applicable. |
| Preview | Folders and volumes; applications; files | Shows the icon of everything except files. For files, a preview of the file's content is provided. (This is the same preview the Column view provides.) |
| Languages | Applications | Displays and enables you to choose the languages that should be available in the application. |
| Open with | Files | Enables you to select an application to open a file. You can also set the application used for all files of the same type. |
| Sharing & Permissions | Folders and volumes; applications; files | Enables you to configure the access permissions for an item. |

Examples of how to use each of these parts of the Info Window are provided in the following sections.

## WORKING WITH THE SPOTLIGHT COMMENTS INFORMATION

The Spotlight Comments section enables you to add comments to a selected item:

1. Open the Info window for the item in which you are interested.
2. Expand the Spotlight Comments section.
3. Enter your comments in the field. The comments you enter remain with the item, and you can read them by either expanding the Comments section or by adding the Comments column to the List view and viewing a Finder window in that view.

**TIP**

> You can use the Comments field as a search criterion for a smart folder. This can be useful to create and easily gather a group of related items together in a smart folder.

## WORKING WITH GENERAL INFORMATION

The General section of the Info window is used mostly to provide detailed information about an item. However, for specific items, you can also use the controls it provides:

1. Select the item you are interested in and choose File, Get Info or press ⌘-I. The Info window appears.

> **TIP**
> You can also use the Actions pop-up menu or contextual menu to open the Info window.

2. Expand the General section if it isn't expanded by default.
3. View the information provided at the top of the window.
4. Use any tools that appear to configure the item.

Depending on the item you select, you have the following choices:

- You can select the Locked check box that appears when the selected item is a document, a folder, or an application to prevent the item from being changed.
- You can use the Stationery Pad check box to convert a selected document into a template.
- If the selected item is an alias, you can associate it with a different file by using the Select New Original button and then choosing the file you want it to point to.
- You can apply a color label by clicking the color you want to apply to the item. Click the "x" button to remove a label from the item.

## WORKING WITH MORE INFO INFORMATION

The More Info section provides a variety of data that depends on the kind of item you are viewing. For example, when you have selected an image file, this section displays resolution information. For most items, you see the date when the item was last opened. In some cases, Mac OS X can't generate any more information for an item in which case you'll see No Info in this section. To view more info for an item, do the following:

1. Select the item and press ⌘-I. The Info window will open.
2. Expand the More Info section.

## WORKING WITH NAME AND EXTENSION INFORMATION

The Name & Extension section enables you to view and change the name of the selected item:

1. Select the item you are interested in and press ⌘-I. The Info window appears.
2. Expand the Name & Extension section.

3. Edit the item name in the Name & Extension field that appears. Remember to add or edit filename extensions as appropriate. (Volumes and folders don't have filename extensions.)

**NOTE**

> Applications have the filename extension `.app`.

When you are displaying Name & Extension information for a document, the "Hide extension" check box is enabled. When this is checked, the filename extension for the file is hidden in Finder windows. This check box is overridden by the Finder's file extension preference. If the "Show all file extensions" check box in the Finder Preferences window is checked, filename extensions are shown regardless of the "Hide extension" check box for an individual file. The Finder preference must be unchecked for this box to hide or show a file's filename extension.

3

## WORKING WITH PREVIEW INFORMATION

The Preview section provides a preview of the selected item. For everything except documents, this preview is simply the item's icon. However, when you use this feature on a document, you get a preview of the item's content, just as you do when you view a Finder window in Column view. If the content is dynamic, such as a QuickTime movie, you can view or hear that content from the Preview section:

1. Select the item you are interested in, and press ⌘-I to open the Info window.
2. Expand the Preview section.
3. Use the Preview section to preview the item's content. For example, use the controls to view the item if it is a QuickTime movie. If you selected an image, you can view a preview of the image.

For documents for which Mac OS X can't generate a preview, you see the appropriate icon instead.

## WORKING WITH LANGUAGES INFORMATION

Mac OS X applications can support various languages. The Languages section of the Information window enables you to choose the languages you want to be available in an application. Do the following steps:

1. Select the application you are interested in, and press ⌘-I.
2. Expand the Languages section.
3. Uncheck the check box next to any language you want to disable for that application.
4. Check the check box next to any language you want to enable in the application.
5. To remove a language from the application, select the language and click Remove. After you confirm what you are doing, that language's support files are removed from the application's files and are no longer available.

6. To add language support to the application, click the Add button and select the language file you want to add.

**TIP**

> You can have more than one section of the Info window expanded at the same time. In fact, you can have as few as none expanded, or you can have all of them expanded.

## Working with "Open with" Information

You can use the "Open with" section to determine which application is used to open a file:

1. Select the document you are interested in, and press ⌘-I.
2. Expand the "Open with" section.
3. Select the application that you want the file to be opened with on the pop-up menu; the application currently associated with the document is shown in the pop-up menu. The "suggested" applications appear on the menu by default. If you want to select an application that is not shown on the pop-up menu, click Other and select the application you want to be used.
4. If you want all files of the same type to be opened with the application you selected, click the Change All button.

3

## Working with Sharing & Permissions Information

The Sharing & Permissions section is used to configure access to the item (see Figure 3.11). This area enables you to control who has access to an item, as well as defining the type of access provided.

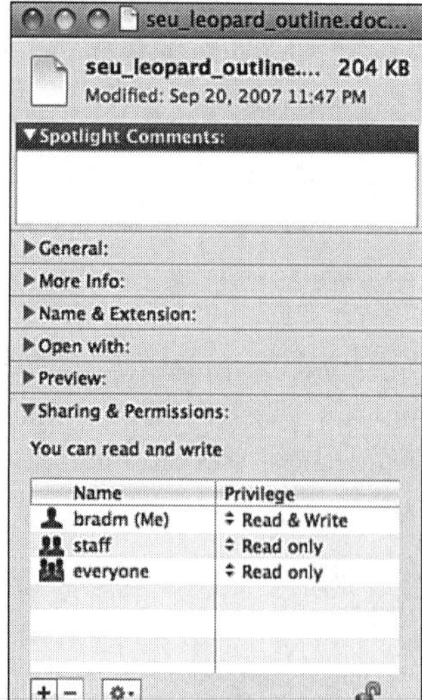


**Figure 3.11**
The Sharing & Permissions section of the Information window is an important security tool whether you share your Mac directly or across a network.

⇨ To learn how to configure access to an item, **see** "Understanding and Setting Permissions," **p. 385**.

### WORKING WITH THE INSPECTOR

When you work with the Info window, each item has its own window. This is nice because you can display the Info window for multiple items at the same time. However, it can get tedious when you don't want to do this because you have to select each item, open its Info window, and then close the Info window when you are done.

You can use the Inspector to see information about the *currently selected* item rather than the one that was selected when you opened the Info window. This is handy because you can leave the Inspector open, and as you select items, their information is displayed. You don't clutter up your desktop with lots of Info windows, and you don't have to keep opening the Info window for items.

To open the Inspector, hold the Option key down and choose File, Show Inspector, or press ⌘-I. The Inspector window appears. It looks just like the Info window except it has square corners instead of rounded ones. As you select items on the desktop, the information in the Inspector changes to reflect the currently selected item.

3

## GETTING A QUICK LOOK AT THINGS

The Finder's Quick Look command enables you to examine an item without opening an application. For example, if you see a number of image files, but don't know what they are, you can select them and use the Quick Look command to view them (without having to wait for an application to launch and then viewing the images in separate windows). To use the Quick Look command, perform the following steps:

1. Select the items you want to view.
2. Open the contextual menu, and choose Quick Look *x* Items, where *x* is the number of items you've selected, or Quick Look "*name*," where *name* is the name of a single item. The Quick Look window appears (see Figure 3.12).

**TIP** You can also choose File, Quick Look, or press ⌘-Y to open the Quick Look window.

3. Use the controls at the bottom of the Quick Look window to view the selected items. The controls you see depend on the items you selected. For example, if you select a group of images, you can play them in a slideshow, view an index sheet, and so on.
4. To view the Quick Look in full screen, click the Full screen button.
5. Select other objects and the Quick Look window refreshes to show information about the currently selected items (see Figure 3.13).

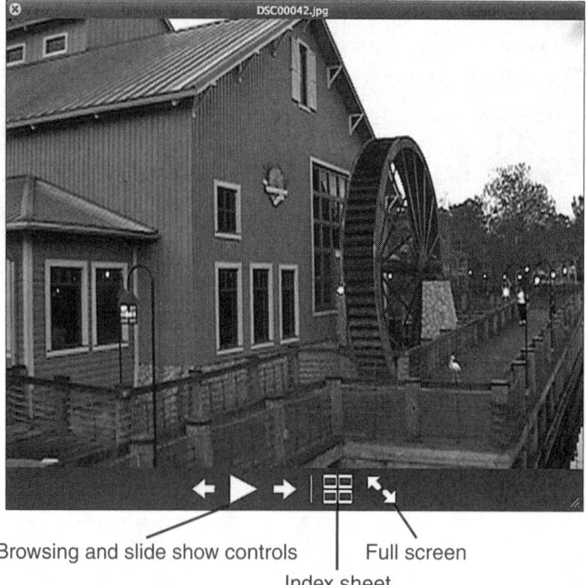


**Figure 3.12**
The Quick Look windows enables you to see what selected objects are without opening an application to view them. The tools you see at the bottom of the Quick Look window will change based on the items you are viewing.



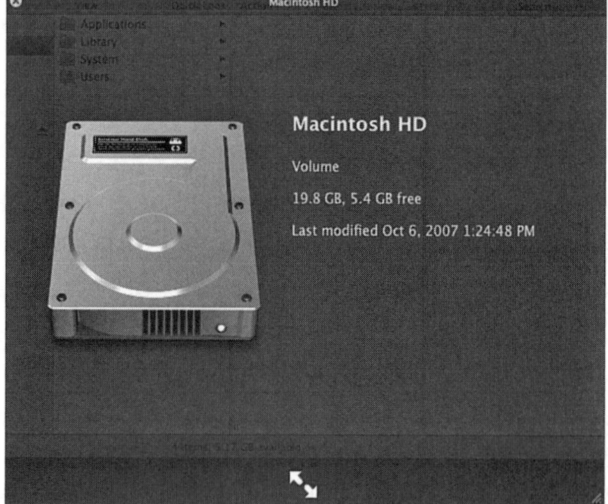


**Figure 3.13**
When you select different objects, the Quick Look window immediately updates.

6. Resize the window using its Resize handle.
7. Close the Quick Look by clicking its Close button located in the upper-left corner.

If you select a group of different kinds of objects at the same time, you can see each object's information in the window by clicking the right-facing arrow. The window updates for each object you've selected. The information shown in the Quick Look window depends on the kind of object in focus. For example, you see images in image files, the contents of text documents, and so on. For some objects, you only see an icon, such as volumes or files for which Mac OS X can't display a preview.

## CUSTOMIZING THE MAC OS X DESKTOP

Although the default Mac OS X desktop is very nice to look at, you will probably want to customize it to suit your preferences. You can customize the appearance of your desktop in many ways, including the following:

- Change the clock
- Change mounted disk behavior
- Change the desktop icon size
- Change the desktop icon arrangement
- Set desktop pictures



**NOTE**

> You can also change the Finder menu bar by adding menus to it, such as Displays, Volume, AirPort, and others. These menus are discussed in the related sections of this book. For example, you learn about the Displays menu in the section on configuring monitors using the Displays pane of the System Preferences application.

### CHANGING THE CLOCK DISPLAY

By default, Mac OS X provides a clock in the upper-right corner of the desktop. You can also configure the clock to be shown in a window that floats on the desktop if you prefer. You can control the appearance of the clock by using the System Preferences application:

1. Open the System Preferences application.
2. Click the Date & Time icon.
3. In the Date & Time pane, click the Clock tab (see Figure 3.14).
4. To hide the clock, uncheck the "Show the date and time in menu bar" check box. The clock is removed, and all the clock options are disabled.
5. If you want the clock to be displayed on the right end of the menu bar in the digital format, click the Digital radio button and complete steps 7-11.
6. If you prefer the time to be displayed in analog format, click the Analog radio button and skip to step 12.
7. Check the "Display the time with seconds" check box to include the seconds in the display.
8. If you want the AM/PM indicator to be shown, check the Show AM/PM check box.
9. Click the "Show the day of the week" check box to include the day in the clock display.

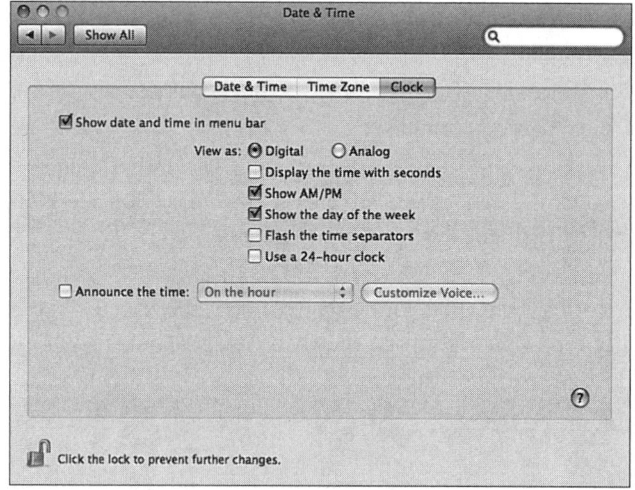


**Figure 3.14**
The Clock tab of the Date & Time pane of the System Preferences application enables you to customize the clock on the desktop.

3

10. If you want the colon between the hour and minutes to be displayed, check the "Flash the time separators" check box.
11. If you want to use a 24-hour clock, check the "Use a 24-hour clock" check box.
12. If you want the time to be announced, check the "Announce the time" check box. Then select the time interval on the pop-up menu. Finally, click the Customize Voice button to select the voice used to announce the time.

**TIP**

> You can click the menu bar clock to briefly display the full date. The menu on which the date appears also enables you to change the view option (analog or digital) and open the Date & Time pane of the System Preferences application.

## CHANGING THE DESKTOP'S APPEARANCE

You can customize other aspects of the appearance of the desktop using the following steps:

1. Select Finder, Preferences, or press ⌘- to open the Finder Preferences window.
2. Click the General tab.
3. Check the check boxes for the mounted items you want to appear on the desktop. Your choices are "Hard disks," "External disks," "CDs, DVDs, and iPods," and "Connected servers." If you uncheck the check boxes, you don't see the items on your desktop; you can access these items through the Computer folder or within any Finder window. If you check the check boxes, the items appear on the desktop.
4. Close the Finder Preferences window.
5. Click on the desktop.
6. Press ⌘-J to open the View Options window for the desktop.

7. Use the View Options controls to configure how icons on the desktop appear, such as size and grouping.

⇨ To learn about the details of these options, **see** "Customizing Finder Window Views," **p. 45**.

8. Close the View Options window.
9. Open the Desktop & Screen Saver pane of the System Preferences application. This pane has two tabs. The Desktop tab enables you to set your desktop picture, whereas the Screen Saver tab enables you to configure the screen saver.
10. Click the Desktop tab (see Figure 3.15). The Image well shows the desktop picture currently being used. In the left pane of the window, the Source pane shows the available image collections. The right pane shows the images contained in the selected source.

3

**Figure 3.15**
Aurora is the new default desktop in Mac OS X 10.5.

**TIP**

> If you just want to replace the current image with another one, drag the image you want to use onto the well. It replaces the image currently shown there and appears on the desktop immediately.

11. Select the source containing the image you want to apply to the desktop. You have the following options:
    - By default, Mac OS X includes several image collections (Apple Images, Nature, Plants, Black & White, Abstract, Solid Colors, and Pictures Folder); these appear in the Apple collection at the top of the Source pane.
    - You can select the Solid Colors source to apply a solid color to the desktop.
    - The Pictures Folder is the Pictures folder in your Home folder.

- The lower part of the pane contains iPhoto collections if you have iPhoto installed on your Mac. You can select your Photo Library to choose any image in your iPhoto Library or select any photo album to use its images.
- The Choose Folder option (+ sign at the bottom of the Source pane) enables you to select any other folder to use as a source of images. When you select the Choose Folder option, you can use the resulting sheet to move to and select a folder. When you do so, a Folders collection is added to the Source pane, and the images contained in that folder are shown in the preview pane.
- Except for the Choose Folder option, when you select an option, the images contained in the location appear in the preview pane in the right part of the window.
- When you select a folder, including the predefined ones, only the images at the root level of that folder are available on the preview pane. For example, if you select your Pictures folder, only the images that are loose in that folder are available. Any images contained within folders that are inside the Pictures folder are not available.



12. Apply the image to the desktop by clicking it on the preview pane. It appears in the Image well and on your desktop.
13. If you want to change desktop pictures automatically, check the "Change picture" check box. The image in the well becomes the "recycle" icon to show that you have selected to have the system change images periodically. The images contained in the source selected in the Source pane will be applied to the desktop based on the criteria you configure.
14. Use the pop-up menu to select the time at which you want the images to be changed. The options include "when logging in," "when waking from sleep," and a time interval from every five seconds to once per day.
15. To have the images selected at random, check the "Random order" check box. If you uncheck this, the images appear in the same order as they appear in the selected source (for example, alphabetically).

You can use just about any graphic file as a desktop image, such as .jpeg, .tiff, and .pict files.

If you want to install images in the Apple collection in the Source pane so they appear by default, just place them in the location `macosx/Library/Desktop Pictures/`, where *`macosx`* is the name of your Mac OS X startup volume.

This folder contains the collections of images that appear on the Collection pane. You can add your images to the default folders, and they will appear in those collections. Unfortunately, you can't add collections to the menu by creating folders within the Desktop Pictures folder.

**NOTE**

If you use more than one monitor, each monitor has its own desktop picture. A Desktop Picture pane appears on each desktop. You use that pane to configure the desktop images on each monitor.

**TIP**

If you want to change the image that is shown when the login window is displayed, name an image file "Aqua Blue.jpg" and copy it to the following location `Mac OS X/Library/Desktop Pictures/` where *`Mac OS X`* is the name of your startup volume. You will be prompted to replace the existing file. Do so. The next time the background image is displayed, such as when you log out, the new image will be shown. (If you will want to use the default image again, save a copy of the file before you replace it.)

3

# MAC OS X TO THE MAX: DESKTOP KEYBOARD SHORTCUTS

Table 3.5 lists keyboard shortcuts for working with the Finder.

**TABLE 3.5 KEYBOARD SHORTCUTS FOR THE FINDER**

| Action | Keyboard Shortcut |
|---|---|
| Add to Sidebar | ⌘-T |
| Close All | Option-⌘-W |
| Close Window | ⌘-W |
| Connect to Server | ⌘-K |
| Copy item | ⌘-C |
| Cut item | ⌘-X |
| Duplicate | ⌘-D |
| Eject | ⌘-E |
| Empty Trash | Shift-⌘-Delete |
| Find | ⌘-F |
| Force Quit | Option-⌘-Esc |
| Get Info | ⌘-I |
| Go Back | ⌘-[ |
| Go Forward | ⌘-] |
| Go to Applications Folder | Shift-⌘-A |
| Go to Computer Folder | Shift-⌘-C |
| Go to Enclosing Folder | ⌘-up arrow |

| Action | Keyboard Shortcut |
|---|---|
| Go to Folder | Shift-⌘-G |
| Go to Home Folder | Shift-⌘-H |
| Go to iDisk Folder | Shift-⌘-I |
| Go to Network Folder | Shift-⌘-K |
| Go to Utilities Folder | Shift-⌘-U |
| Hide Finder | ⌘-H |
| Hide Toolbar | Option-⌘-T |
| Log Out | Shift-⌘-Q |
| Mac Help | ⌘-? |
| Make Alias | ⌘-L |
| Minimize Window | ⌘-M |
| Minimize All | Option-⌘-M |
| Move to Trash | ⌘-Delete |
| New Finder Window | ⌘-N |
| New Folder | Shift-⌘-N |
| New Smart Folder | Option-⌘-N |
| Open | ⌘-O |
| Paste item | ⌘-V |
| Preferences | ⌘-, |
| Quick Look | ⌘-Y |
| Select All | ⌘-A |
| Show Original | ⌘-R |
| Show View Options | ⌘-J |
| View as Columns | ⌘-3 |
| View as Cover Flow | ⌘-4 |
| View as Icons | ⌘-1 |
| View as List | ⌘-2 |

CHAPTER 4

# FINDING THINGS ON YOUR MAC

## In this chapter

# LOOKING FOR THINGS IN ALL THE RIGHT PLACES

One of the problems that computer users have always faced is finding information, including documents, files, email messages, and other data, we need. It's easy to pile up lots of information on your Mac, and that information can come in many formats, such as contact information, documents, web pages, and so on. Over time, finding information you need can become a challenge. Fortunately, Mac OS X includes a couple of powerful tools you can use to find what you need on your Mac: Spotlight and Smart folders.

# SEARCHING YOUR MAC WITH SPOTLIGHT

Mac OS X includes an amazingly easy way to find things on your Mac, regardless of what it is. This tool is called Spotlight, and it enables you to search your entire Mac quickly and easily.

Spotlight works so amazingly well because it searches metadata. *Metadata* is information that is associated with every file on your computer. Metadata includes obvious information, such as the file name, creation date, modification date, and so on, but it also includes file type, content information, and much more. Because Spotlight searches metadata, it can search the entire contents of your computer without limiting you to searching for specific data (such as a folder or file name). A Spotlight search will return all files, folders, email, bookmarks, contact information, and so on that relate to your search. Spotlight will also search the web sites that you have visited recently. Both the names of sites and the content on those pages are indexed so that you can find information on the Internet that you have looked at before.



## CONFIGURING SPOTLIGHT

Before you start searching your Mac, configure Spotlight so it works as you intend. Do so with the following steps:

1. Open the Spotlight pane of the System Preferences application. By default, the Search Results tab is selected (see Figure 4.1).
2. Check the check boxes next to the items you want included in Spotlight searches, such as Applications, Folders, and so on. Uncheck the check boxes for items that you don't want to be searched.
3. Set the keyboard shortcut you use to launch Spotlight using the "Spotlight menu keyboard shortcut" check box and pop-up menu. The default is ⌘-spacebar, but you can change this to a function key if you prefer. If you don't want to be able to activate Spotlight with a key for some reason, uncheck the check box.
4. Use the "Spotlight window keyboard shortcut" check box and pop-up menu to configure the keys you use to move into the Spotlight search results window. The default is ⌘-Option-spacebar, but you can use the pop-up menu to choose a function key instead. If you don't want to use any keyboard shortcut, uncheck the check box.
5. Click the Privacy tab. You use this pane to select areas on your computer you don't want Spotlight to search. For example, if you keep sensitive documents in a folder within your Documents folder, you might want to block that folder from Spotlight searches.

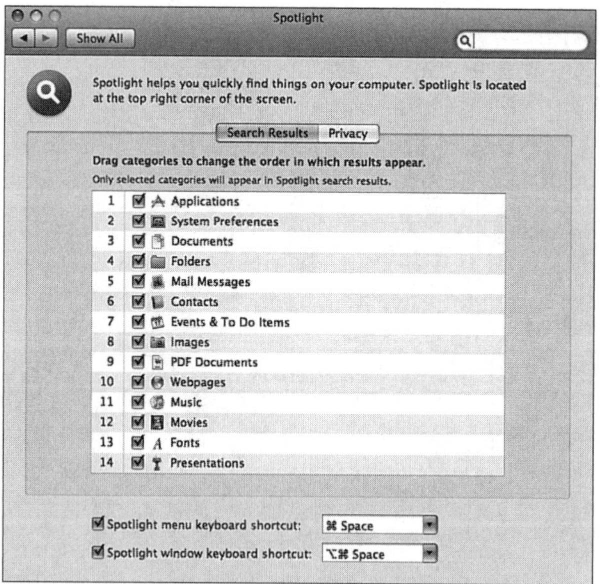


**Figure 4.1**
Use the Spotlight pane to configure the items for which Spotlight will search.

6. Click the Add button (+) at the bottom of the pane. The choose folder sheet appears.
7. Move to the folder you want to shield, select it, and click Choose. That folder is added to the list and won't be included in Spotlight searches.
8. Repeat steps 6 and 7 until you have protected all your sensitive folders.

4

## SEARCHING WITH SPOTLIGHT

To use Spotlight to search your Mac from the desktop, perform the following steps:

1. Click the Spotlight icon (the magnifying glass) in the upper right corner of your desktop, or press the Spotlight menu keyboard shortcut (⌘-spacebar by default). The Spotlight search bar appears (see Figure 4.2).
2. Type your search criterion in the search bar. As you type, Spotlight immediately begins searching your Mac and presents results in the Spotlight results window (see Figure 4.3). Within this window, you see that results are organized for you by type. At the top of the window is the Show All selection, which you'll learn about in the next step. Just under that is the Top Hit, which is the item that Spotlight believes best matches your search criterion. Under that, the remaining results are organized by type, including Applications, System Preferences, Documents, Folders, Mail Messages, and so on.

**TIP**

> You are probably used to typing a search term and then pressing the Return key. If you do this, you will be taken automatically to the Top Hit item. Try not to press the Return key so you can see all of the matching results.

**Figure 4.2**
You can enter any text or numbers in the Spotlight search bar to perform a search.

4

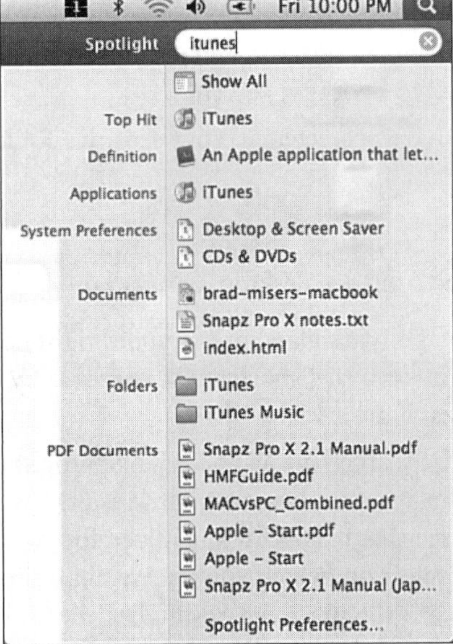


**Figure 4.3**
This search has found many items that are associated with the "itunes" criterion, including a Dictionary definition, applications, preferences, documents, and so on.

**NOTE**

If you used the Spotlight preference pane to prevent a type from being included in Spotlight searches, that category doesn't get searched and won't appear in the results window.

3. To open an item on the results list, select it. For example, if you select a document, it opens. If you select a folder, a Finder window opens so you can view its contents. If you select an application, it launches. As you move away from the results window, Spotlight is hidden so you can easily work with the result you selected.

4. To return to the search results, click the Spotlight icon again. Your previous search results appear because Spotlight remembers your search until you indicate that you are done with it.

   The results shown in the initial Spotlight window might be limited if there are a large number of them; as mentioned previously, the first item on the results list is the Show All option. This option presents every item that meets your search criterion.

5. To show all the results of a search, click Show All. The Spotlight window appears (see Figure 4.4). The Spotlight window behaves much like a Finder window, which is really what it is. For example, you can sort the window, change its view, and so on.

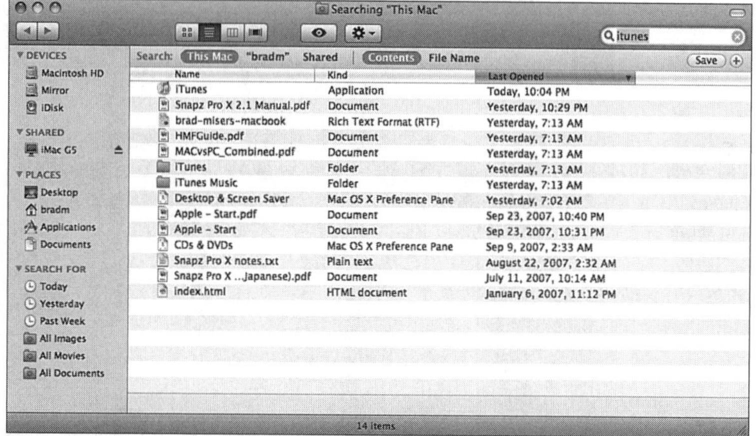


**Figure 4.4**
You can use the Spotlight window to display all of your search results and to change how they are listed.

The Spotlight window has many features, including the following:

- Click the quick view button (the "eye") to display a preview of an item (see Figure 4.5). You can use the quick view area to preview some items. For example, you can listen to audio files, watch movies, and so on. Click the arrow button at the bottom of the quick view to show the preview at full screen size.
- The Spotlight window has a list view, icon view, and Cover Flow view but not a columns view. The icon view allows you to resize the icons using the slider at the bottom right corner of the Spotlight window (see Figure 4.6).
- When you select a result, the path to it is shown at the bottom of the window.
- To open an item on the list, double-click it. The appropriate application or Finder window opens. You can return to the Spotlight window by moving back to the desktop.

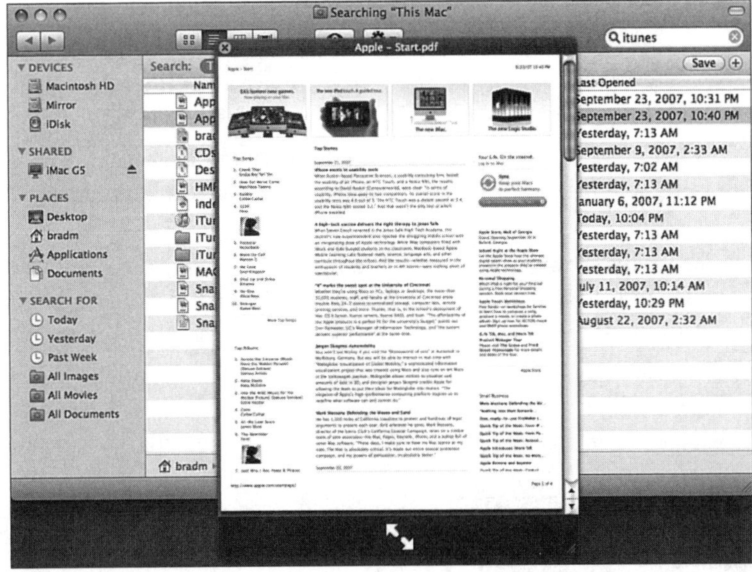


**Figure 4.5**
Here, the Quick View button has been clicked to a preview of a web page.

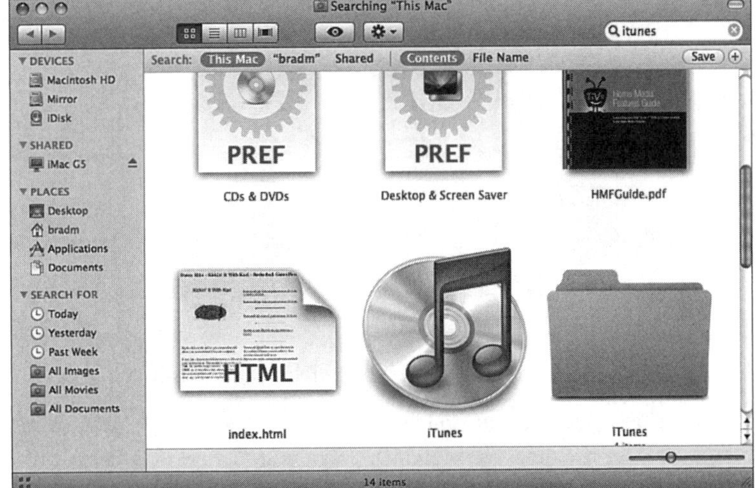


**Figure 4.6**
The icon view of the Spotlight window allows you to zoom in on the icon and see a preview of the document.

> **TIP**
>
> You can move back to the Spotlight window or open it any time using the keyboard shortcut, which is Option-⌘-spacebar by default.

- Minimize the Spotlight window to move it out of your way while you look at an item you found. You can jump back to the results by clicking the Spotlight menu button or by using the keyboard shortcuts for the menu or window.

TIP

> Take advantage of Exposé as you work with Spotlight results because that feature makes it easy to manage multiple open windows.

To clear a Spotlight search, click the "x" in the Spotlight search tool, or close the Spotlight window.

## SAVING SPOTLIGHT SEARCHES

You can save Spotlight searches and run them again at any time.

1. Use the information in the previous section to perform a Spotlight search and open the Spotlight window.
2. Configure the results as you want to see them.
3. Click on the Save button near the top right portion of the Spotlight window.
4. Name the search, and specify where to save it. The default is Saved Searches.
5. To add the saved search to the Sidebar, click the Add to Sidebar check box.
6. Press Return to save it.

To run a saved search, click on its icon in the Search For section of the Sidebar. The current results for that search are shown. When you save a Spotlight search, you save the search criterion, not the results. So, if new information that meets the search criterion has been added to your Mac, the next time you run the search, that information appears in the results.



TIP

> To edit a saved search, click on the search in the Search For section of the sidebar. Once the results of the search are shown, click on the Action menu, and select Show Search Criteria. The criteria for your search is shown, and you can modify how you are searching. Once you have completed your changes, click the Save button.

## USING SPOTLIGHT TO CREATE COMPLEX SEARCHES

When you use Spotlight, you'll probably get a lot of results. Because its searches are broad, the results are wide-ranging and might or might not be easy to work with. Perform the following steps to create and save complex searches:

1. Open the Spotlight window.
2. Open the Action pop-up menu, and choose Show Search Criteria. The search criteria bar is added to the Spotlight window (see Figure 4.7).
3. On the location bar, choose where the search should take place. For example, by default the search will take place across the entire computer. To limit the search to just your Home folder, click your username in the location bar. Select whether the Spotlight should just return file names that match your search or also search the content of those files.

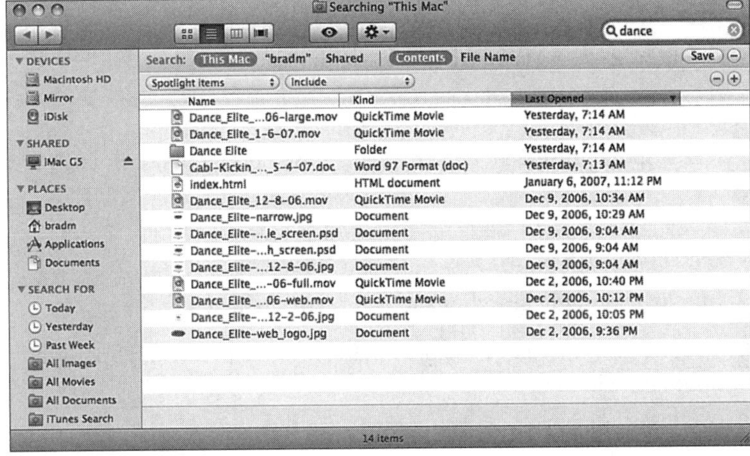


**Figure 4.7**
Use the search critera and the search location bars to create complex Spotlight searches.

4. Use the search criteria bar to fine tune your search. Click the first pop-up menu to select an attribute, such as Last Modified Date. The search criteria bar will then change to show specific things to search for related to that attribute.
5. Click the Add button (+). Another search criterion appears.
6. Repeat step 4 to configure the new criterion.
7. Repeat steps 5 and 6 until you've added all the criteria to the search that you want to include (see Figure 4.8).

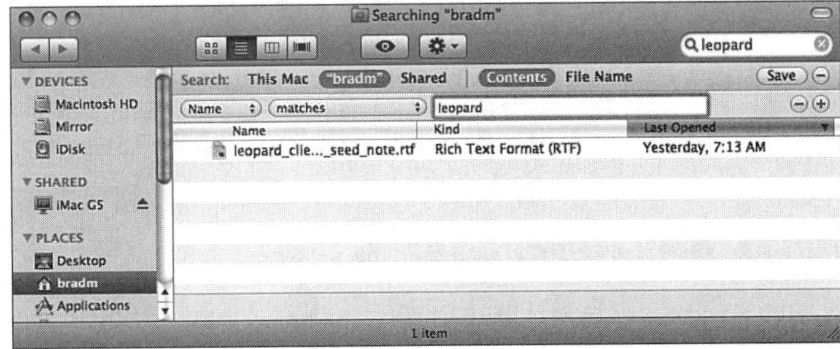


**Figure 4.8**
This search looks for documents in my Home folder that include text "leopard."

8. The search runs as you make the changes to the search criteria, and you see the results in the Spotlight window.
9. Click the Save button so that you can run this search again. You can re-run the search at any time by selecting it in Search For section of the Sidebar.

## ADDING SPOTLIGHT INFORMATION TO FOLDERS AND FILES

You can use the Finder's Info window to add metadata to files and folders so you can find them with Spotlight searches.

1. Select an item on the desktop and open the Info window.
2. Expand the Spotlight Comments section.
3. Add information to the Spotlight Comments box by typing it there. The information you add is searched when you perform Spotlight searches.

# Searching Your Mac with Smart Folders

The Finder enables you to create smart folders. A smart folder displays its contents based on search criteria that you define as opposed to a "regular" folder that displays items that have been manually placed within it. Even better, you can save smart folders so that you can repeat searches simply by refreshing the smart folders you create.

Just like Spotlight, smart folders search metadata so that there are many kinds of criteria you can use to search your Mac. Because of this, you can search by many different kinds of information, including the content of files and many attributes that aren't even displayed in the Finder.

Smart folders, the Finder's File, Find command (press ⌘-F), and the Spotlight window are all identical. You may get there in different ways, but the window, and the things you can do with it, are the same. As you further define your search criteria for a smart folder, you can save it to the Search For section of the Sidebar.



## Creating and Saving a Smart Folder

To search your Mac using a smart folder, perform the following steps:

1. Choose File, New Smart Folder, or press Option-⌘-N. A smart folder with the title "New Smart Folder" will appear (see Figure 4.9).

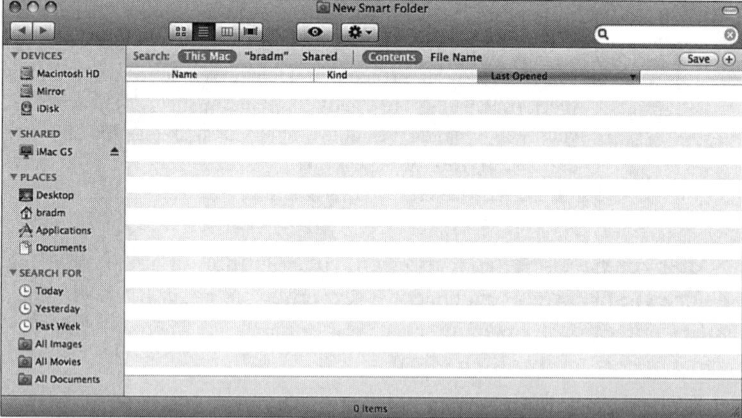


**Figure 4.9**
Don't let its simple-looking appearance fool you; a smart folder lives up to its name.

2. Choose the location in which you want to search by clicking the appropriate Search location button. To search your entire Mac, click the This Mac button. To limit the

search to your Home folder, click your short username. To search servers to which you are connected over a network, click Shared.

Next, you need to build the specific criteria that you want to use for the search.

3. Click the Add button to show the first Search Criteria bar, which shows Kind by default. When you do, you see a pop-up menu that lists a large number of options including Kind, Last Opened Date, Last Modified Date, Created Date, Name, Contents, and Other.

   Choose the first criterion by which you want to limit your search. For example, to limit the search by the date something was last changed, choose Last Modified Date.

   If you choose the Other option, you'll see a sheet that enables you to select from a very large number of options (see Figure 4.10). You can browse this list to see all of the criteria that are possible. A brief description for these options is provided in the sheet.

   To choose a criterion on this list, select it and click OK.

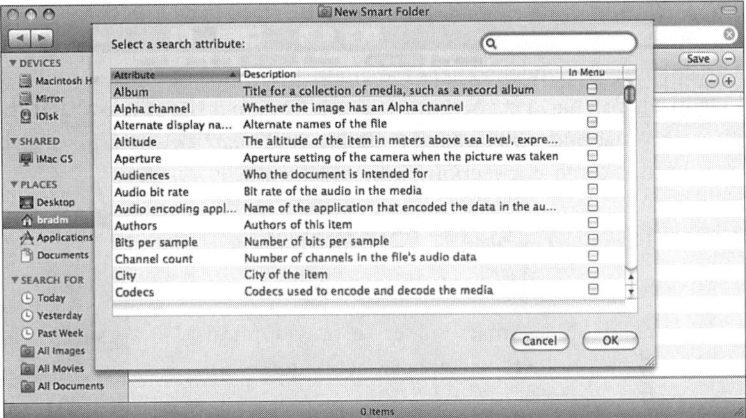


**Figure 4.10**
When you choose Other on a Search Criteria pop-up menu, you can choose from any of the possible search criteria.

**TIP**

> You can search for a criterion by typing text in the Search box at the top of the Other sheet. As you type, the criteria shown in the sheet will be limited to those that match your search. To add a criterion to the Search Criteria pop-up menu, select it and check the "Add to Favorites" check box.

After you have selected a criterion, controls appropriate for that criterion will appear. For example, when you choose a text criterion, a text box will appear. When you select a date criterion, a pop-up menu of options appears. If you choose Kind, a list of kinds of files appears as a pop-up menu.

4. Configure the criterion you selected by entering text, making a choice from the pop-up menu, and so on.

   In some cases, making a choice will result in additional tools you can use to configure the criterion. For example, if you choose Before for a date criterion, a date box will appear so that you can enter a date.

5. If an additional tool has appeared, such as a date box, complete the data for the criterion.

   As you define criteria, the location you selected will be searched, and items that meet the current search criteria will be shown in the Results section of the folder.

6. Click the Add button, which is the "+" at the end of each criterion's row, to add another criterion to the search.

7. Configure the next criterion with the same steps you did to configure the first one (steps 3 through 6).

8. To remove a criterion from the search, click the Remove button, which is the "-" at the end of each criterion's row. That criterion is removed from the smart folder and will no longer impact the search.

9. Continue adding, configuring, or removing criteria until you have fully-defined your search (see Figure 4.11).

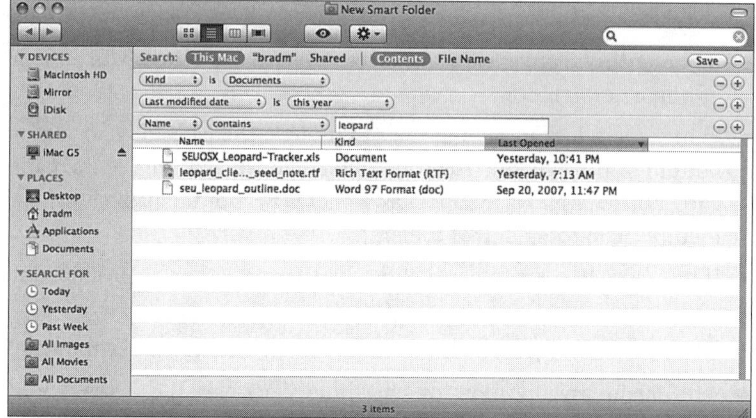


**Figure 4.11**
This search will find all documents solidified within the last week whose name includes "leopard."

10. When the search is configured, click the Save button. You see a Save sheet.

11. Name your search; choose a location in which to save it; determine if it will be added to the Search For section of the Sidebar by checking or unchecking the Add To Sidebar check box; and then click Save (see Figure 4.12).

    You return to the smart folder, which is named with the name you entered. If you opted to have the search added to the Search For section of the Sidebar, you see it there as well.

Following are some points to ponder when you are working with smart folders:

- If you don't want to limit your search, don't configure any search criteria and instead just type the text or numbers for which you want to search in the Search box at the top of the smart folder's window. This can be literally anything from text contained in documents, resolution of images, dates associated with documents, people's names, and so on. As you start to type, your Mac begins its search, and documents, folders, bookmarks, and anything else that meets your search text appear in the results section of the folder.

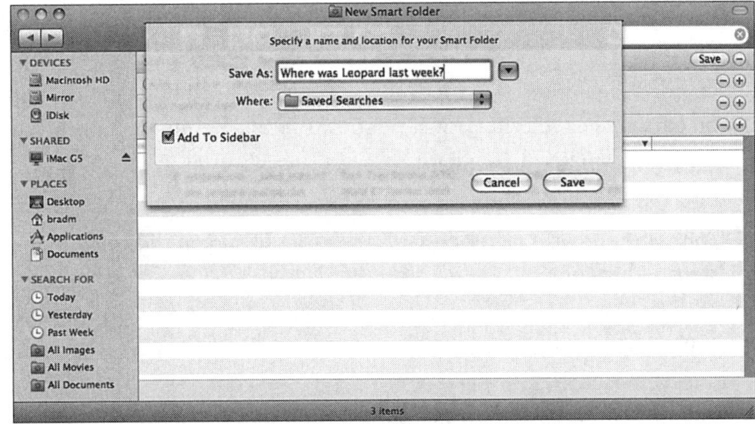


**Figure 4.12**
You can name and save the smart folders that you create so that you can repeat searches easily.

- You can open any item found by double-clicking on it. You can use any action or contextual commands on items as well, just as you can in a regular folder.
- If you click the quick view button (the "eye") associated with an item, you see a preview of it in a new window.
- When you select an item in the results area, the path to its location is shown at the bottom of the window. You can double-click on any part of the path shown to open that part. For example, if the Pictures folder is part of the path shown, double-click on the Pictures icon to open that folder.
- If you close a smart folder without first saving it, you're prompted to do so.
- After you have saved a smart folder and open it again, the search tools are not visible. Use the Action menu to select Show Search Criteria to see the search parameters again.
- The default save location for smart folder searches is the Saved Searches folder located at `/~username/Library/Saved Searches` where `/~username` is your username. If you want to remove searches, open this folder and delete any smart folder files you want to remove from your computer. If you also added the smart folder to your Sidebar, you'll need to remove its icon by dragging it off the sidebar.

**TIP**

> Want to find all the documents on your Mac that have changed recently so you can back them up? Create and save a smart folder with search criteria of Last Modified Since Yesterday and Kind Documents. The results will display all documents that have changed since yesterday.

## Using Smart Folders

After you have created a smart folder, you can perform the search again by opening the smart folder. If you choose to add it to the Search For section of your Sidebar, click its icon. You see the current results of the search.

The smart folder's window always shows the most current results of a search.

**NOTE**

> When you save a smart folder, you save the search criteria, not the results. This means that each time you use the smart folder, the search is repeated. If something has changed so that an item now meets the search criteria, it will appear in the smart folder.

There are several ways to search with a saved smart folder:

- Place it in the Search For section of the Sidebar, and click its icon.
- Drag the smart folder from its saved location onto the Dock. You can run the search by clicking the icon on the Dock.
- Select a smart folder's icon and choose File, Open, or press ⌘-O.
- Double-click the smart folder's icon.

**TIP**

> For immediate access to all your smart folders without cluttering up your Sidebar, store all the searches in one folder, and add that folder to the Dock. Right-click the folder, and you can immediately select any smart folder to open it.

### Changing Smart Folders

You can change an existing smart folder, by changing one or more of its search criteria.

1. Open the smart folder you want to change. The results are shown but the tools to edit your search do not appear.
2. Click the Action menu and select Show Search Criteria.
3. Reconfigure the search by changing existing criteria, adding new ones, or removing them. You can also change the search location.
4. Click Save. The smart folder now contains the revised search criteria.



## Mac OS X to the Max: Keeping Your Mac Organized

If I were the kind of writer who likes to use clichés, I would use one here. And the one I'd use would be, "An ounce of prevention is worth a pound of cure." You can make things easier to find on your Mac if you keep your files and information organized in logical ways and then are consistent about how you store data on your Mac. Often, this will eliminate the need to search because you'll already know where things are. Following are some pointers you might want to consider to reduce the time and effort you have to spend looking for information:

- **Folders in the Finder**—Your Home folder includes some defaults folders, such as Documents, Music, and so on, that you can use to organize files and other information. These should be just a start for you; create folders within these folders to further organize your files. There's really no limit to the number of folders you can create, and using the Column view, you can quickly get to any level of folder.
- **Folders within applications**—Many applications, including iTunes, Address Book, iPhoto, and so on, enable you to create folders to organize data in those applications. Making good use of these tools often reduces the searches you need to do because you know where information is stored.
- **Names**—Use meaningful names when you create files and folders. For example, when you are working on a project, apply the same prefix to all the folders and files associated with that project. When you view a Finder window in list or columns view, the files will naturally group themselves by the project prefix.
- **Trash**—Get rid of files and folders when you are done using them. The more junk you have on your Mac, the harder it is to find things in which you are interested.

# CHAPTER 5

# USING AND CUSTOMIZING THE DOCK

## In this chapter

# UNDERSTANDING THE DOCK

The Dock was one of the most revolutionary parts of the original Mac OS X desktop, and it remains one of the most immediately noticeable aspects of the OS under version 10.5. If you want to master Mac OS X, you should learn to take full advantage of the Dock's capabilities.

The Dock provides you with information about, control over, and customization of Mac OS X and the applications and documents with which you work (see Figure 5.1). By default, the Dock appears at the bottom of the desktop, but you can control many aspects of its appearance and location. You can also control how it works to a great degree.

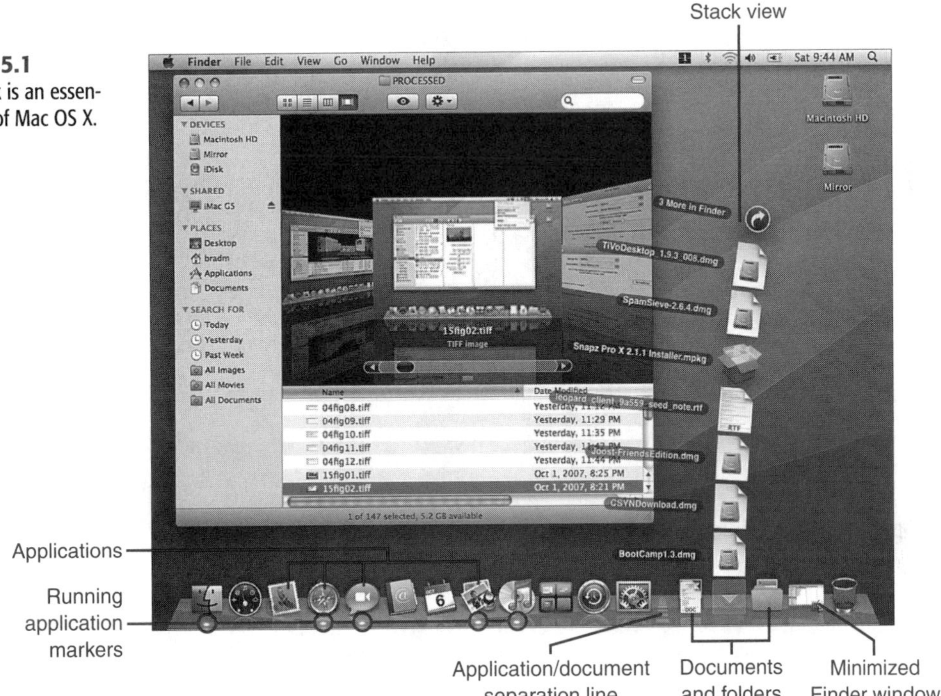


**Figure 5.1**
The Dock is an essential part of Mac OS X.



The Dock is organized into two general sections; the application/document separation line, as shown in Figure 5.1, divides them. On the left side of this line, you see application icons. On the right side of the line, you see icons for your Documents and Downloads folders, other folders that you place on the Dock, minimized Finder, document or application windows, and the Trash/Eject icon.

The Dock performs the following functions:

- **Shows running applications**—Whenever an application is running, you see its icon on the Dock. A small blue orb is located at the bottom of every running application's icon (refer to Figure 5.1). The Dock also provides information about what is happening in open applications. For example, when you receive email, the Mail application's icon changes to indicate the number of messages you have received since you last read messages.

- **Enables you to open applications, folders, minimized windows, and documents quickly**—You can open any item on the Dock by clicking its icon.
- **Enables you to quickly switch among open applications and windows**—You can click an application's or window's icon on the Dock to move into it. You can also use the ⌘-Tab key and ⌘-Shift-Tab keyboard shortcuts to move among open applications.
- **Enables you to control an application and switch to any window open in an application**—When you right-click (or Control-click with a one-button mouse) the icon of an open application, a pop-up menu appears. This menu lists commands as well as shows all the open windows related to that application; you can choose an item by selecting it from this menu.
- **Enables you to customize its appearance and function**— You can store the icon for any item (applications, folders, and documents) on the Dock. You can also control how the Dock looks, including its size, whether it is always visible, where it is located, and so on.

**TIP**

When you open an application whose icon is not installed on the Dock, its Dock menu includes the Keep in Dock command. If you choose this, the icon is added to the Dock.

**When the Trash Is Not the Trash**

Here is a question for you, "When is the Trash not the Trash?" If you have worked with Mac OS X before, you know the answer to this one! When you select an ejectable item, such as a CD or a mounted network volume, the Trash icon located on the right (or bottom if you use a vertical Dock) on the Dock becomes the Eject icon. When you drag an ejectable item onto this icon, it is ejected from your Mac.

5

# Using Items on the Dock

By default, the Dock is preconfigured with various icons you can begin using immediately. When you point to an item on the Dock, a Tool Tip appears above the icon that provides the name of the item. (You will probably recognize many of the items on the Dock by their icons.)

The default items on the Dock include the following:

- **Finder**—If no Finder windows are currently open, the Finder icon opens a new Finder window that shows your default new Finder window location (which can be to your Computer, Home folder, Documents folder, or just about any other location you choose. If at least one Finder window is open on the desktop, clicking the Finder icon while another application is frontmost takes you back to the Finder window that was most recently active. If you hold down the Control key while you click this icon (or right-click on it), you will see a list of all Finder windows that are open; choose a window from the list to move into it.

⇨ To learn how to set your default new Finder window location, **see** "Configuring How New Finder Windows Open," **p. 20**.

**TIP**

You can also open a Dock icon's menu by clicking the Dock icon and holding down the mouse button. After a second or two, the Dock item's menu appears.

- **Dashboard**—This icon takes you to the Mac's Dashboard so you can use its widgets. You can also use its menu to access tools to configure the Dashboard.
- **Mail**—Mail is Mac OS X's email application. When you receive email, an attention icon showing how many new messages you have received appears. If you open Mail's Dock icon menu, you can choose from several commands, such as Get New Mail and Compose New Message.
- **Safari**—This is Mac OS X's excellent web browser. Safari offers many great features as you will learn later in this book. When you open the Safari Dock icon's menu, you can quickly jump to any web page that is open, among other things.
- **iChat**—This is Apple's instant messaging application, which you can use to communicate with others on your local network or over the Internet via text chats or audio/video conferencing. It is compatible with AOL Instant Messenger and Google Talk.
- **Address Book**—Address Book is Mac OS X's contact manager application. You can store all sorts of information, such as email addresses and phone numbers, for everyone with whom you communicate.
- **iCal**—You can use iCal to manage your calendar; it offers other cool features such as the ability to publish your calendar to the Web so other people can access it.
- **Preview**—The Preview application enables you to view photos, image files, PDFs and other documents.
- **iTunes**—iTunes is the Mac's excellent digital music application. Its Dock menu offers selections you can use to control music playback.
- **Spaces**—New to Leopard, Spaces allows you to have separate virtual workspaces to help group the programs that you currently have running.

⇨ To learn how to work with Spaces, **see** "Creating, Using, and Managing Spaces," **p. 269**.

- **Time Machine**—Time Machine is Mac OS X 10.5's new automated backup tool. Once configured properly, the Time Machine icon in the Dock is how you view the Time Machine interface and find files and folders that you may have deleted.

⇨ To learn more about Time Machine, **see** "Backing Up Your Mac With Time Machine," **p. 907**.

- **System Preferences**—The System Preferences application enables you to configure and customize various aspects of Mac OS X. You will be using it frequently, which is why its icon is included on the Dock by default.

- **Documents**—Mac OS X 10.5 now includes an icon on the Dock to take you to your Documents. Combined with the Stacks view, this is a very convenient way to get to the files you need.

**The Stacks View**

In Mac OS X 10.5, Apple has introduced a new way to view items that are in a folder on the Dock. The Stacks view opens when you click on a folder in the Dock. Depending on the number of items in that folder, you will either see a vertical arc (or fan) of the icons in the folder, or you will see a grid of the icons. You can also change the view by right-clicking (or holding down the Control key when clicking) on the folder in the Dock, then selecting View As from the Dock menu. You can let Mac OS X select the view automatically, or select fan view or grid view. Clicking on an icon in the Stacks view will open that item.

- **Downloads**—Mac OS X 10.5 introduces a Downloads folder located in your Home directory. The Dock includes an icon for this folder so that you can access the items that you have recently downloaded from Safari and other applications.
- **Trash/Eject**—Some things never change; under Mac OS X, the Trash does what it always has. It is always located on the right end of the Dock (or the bottom if you use a vertical Dock). When you select an ejectable item, the Trash icon changes to the Eject symbol. When the Trash contains files or folders, its icon includes crumpled paper so that you know the Trash is "full."

**TIP**

To have an application whose icon is on the Dock open automatically when you log in, open its Dock menu and choose "Open at Login."

Using items on the Dock is easy: Simply click an icon to open whatever the item is. If the icon is for an application, that application opens (or moves to the front if it is already open). If the item is a document, the document opens, and if the item is a folder, the folder opens in a new Finder window.

**NOTE**

When you click a non-running application's icon, you might notice that it "bounces" as the application opens. This provides feedback to you that your selection was registered with the OS, and it is working on opening your application. You can turn off this feature, as you will learn later in this chapter.

Unless the application is permanently installed on the Dock (in which case the icon remains in the same position), the icon for each application you open appears on the right edge of the application area of the Dock. As you open more applications, the existing application icons shift to the left and each icon becomes slightly smaller.

**NOTE**

> The Dock is very insistent about getting your attention, even when it is hidden. If the Dock is hidden and an application needs to present information to you, such as an error dialog box, its icon appears to bounce up out of nowhere and continues to bounce up and down until you switch to that application to see what it has to say.

To move among the open applications you see on the Dock, you can press ⌘-Tab. As long as you hold down the ⌘ key, a menu appears across the center of the screen (see Figure 5.2). On this menu, you will see the icon for each open application (which, by no mere coincidence, are the icons that have the open application marker under them on the Dock). The icons are listed in the order in which you have most recently used the applications, with the current application being on the left side of the menu. Each time you press ⌘-Tab, the icon for the open application you are selecting becomes highlighted and you see the application's name below its icon. When you release the ⌘-Tab keys, the application you select becomes active (and visible, if it is hidden). You can move backward through the open applications on the menu by continuing to hold down the ⌘ key and pressing Shift-Tab.

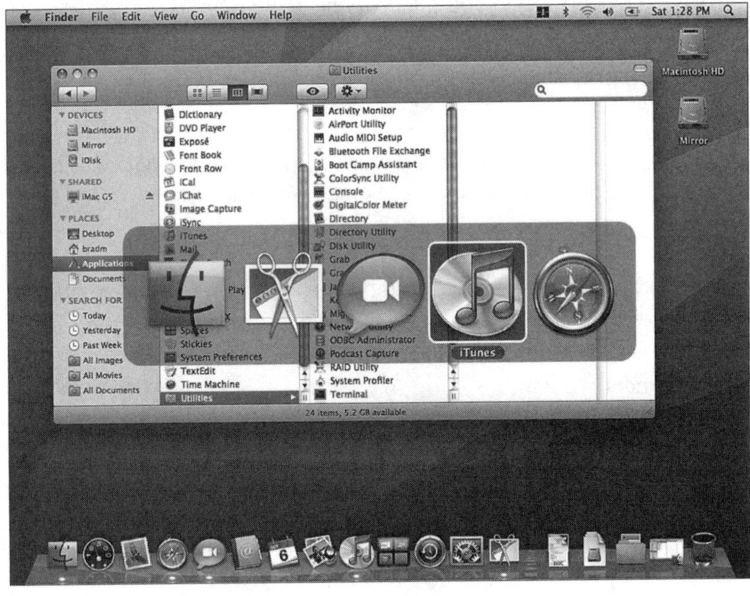


**Figure 5.2**
This list of open applications appears when you hold down the ⌘ key and press the Tab key.

If you don't hold down the ⌘ key and instead just press ⌘-Tab, the menu won't appear; instead you will move immediately into the next application on the list of open applications. Again, this list is organized according to the applications you have most recently used. For example, suppose you checked your email in Mail and then began working in Word. If you pressed ⌘-Tab once, you would jump back into Mail. If you pressed ⌘-Tab again, you would move back to Word because that was the application you were most recently using. Likewise, if you pressed ⌘-Tab twice in a row, you would move back to the application you were using before the most recent one. Although this might be a bit hard for me to describe, this technique enables you to easily switch among open applications by using only the keyboard.

**NOTE**

> If an application is open but the window you want to work in is minimized, when you select that application with the ⌘-Tab shortcut, you will move into the application. However, any windows that are minimized will not appear on the desktop because they are minimized. You have to click a minimized window's icon on the Dock for it to move back onto the desktop.

Unlike open applications, open documents don't automatically appear on the Dock. Document icons appear on the Dock only when you add them to the Dock manually or when you have minimized the document's window. Remember that, when you open an application's menu in the Dock, you will see a list of all the windows open in that application. You can then choose a listed window (such as a document window) to move into it.

**NOTE**

> Just like all icons on the Dock, the names of folders, minimized windows, and documents are shown above their icons when you point to them.

When you minimize a window, by default, the window moves into the Dock using the Genie Effect, during which it is pulled down into the Dock and becomes an icon that is a thumbnail view of the window. The icon for a minimized window behaves just like icons for other items do. To open (or maximize) a minimized window, click its icon on the Dock, and it is pulled back onto the desktop. You can change this so that the Scale Effect is used instead. This looks like the window is being quickly scaled down while it is placed on the Dock. Functionally, these effects do the same thing, but the Scale Effect is a bit faster, although not as impressive looking.



Minimized windows are marked with the related application's icon in the lower-right corner of the Dock icon so you can easily tell from which application the windows come. For example, minimized Finder windows have the Finder icon in the lower-right corner, minimized Safari icons have the Safari icon, and so on.

**TIP**

> You can quickly minimize an open window by pressing ⌘-M.

When you minimize an application window, it is moved onto the Dock, just like any other window. However, when you hide an application, its open windows do not appear on the Dock. The hidden application's icon continues to be marked with the arrow so you know that the application is running. You can open a hidden application's Dock menu to jump into one of its open windows.

As you add items to the Dock and as icons are added when you open applications, the icons on the Dock continue to get smaller. The Dock expands so it shows all open items as well as the icons that are permanently installed on the Dock (see Figure 5.3).

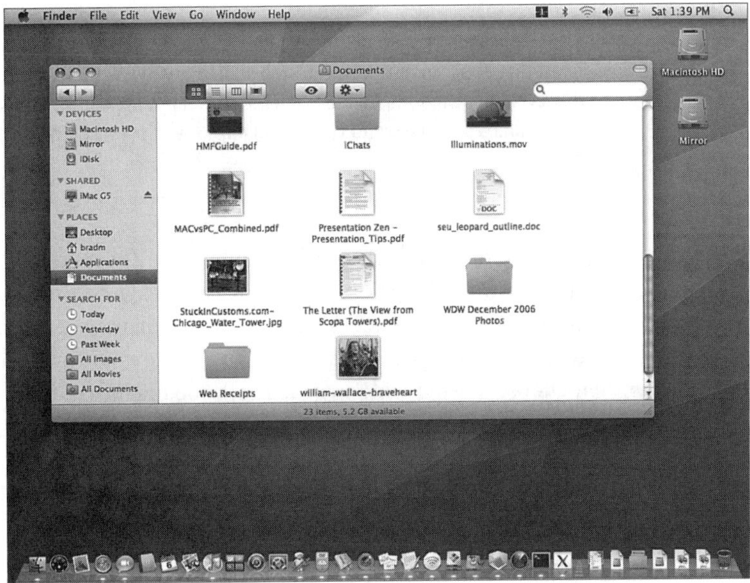


**Figure 5.3**
The items on the Dock shrink, and the Dock expands so you can have as many items on it as you'd like. (Compare this figure to Figure 5.1.)

Just as with an application's icon, if you point to a folder or a document icon on the Dock and right-click or Control-click it, a pop-up menu appears. What is on this menu depends on what you clicked.



**TIP**

> Remember that if you don't want to use the right button on your mouse or press the Control key while you click, just click an icon and hold down the mouse button. The menu will appear after a second or two.

When you use Dock icon menus, the following outcomes are possible:

- If you open the menu for the Finder Dock icon, the pop-up menu shows a list of all the open Finder windows, whether the windows are minimized or are on the desktop. Select a window on the menu to make it active. If you are working in another application, you can also select Hide to hide all open Finder windows.
- If you open the Dock menu for a closed application, folder, or document, you will see the Show In Finder command, which opens a Finder window containing the item on which you clicked; the item is selected when the Finder window containing it appears. This can be a quick way to find out where something is located. You can also choose the Open command to open the item; the Open at Login to have the item opened when you log in; and the Remove from Dock command that removes the icon from the Dock (only for icons that are actually stored on the Dock of course).

- If you open the Dock menu for a folder, you can specify how the Stacks view should display the items in the folder. You can select to view the stack as a fan or a grid, and you can determine how the items should be sorted. The Stack view is a great way to access items within specific folders fast and easy (see Figure 5.4).

**Figure 5.4**
Adding the Applications folder to the Dock enables you to choose any of your applications from the Dock.

- If you point to a URL reference or other item (such as a minimized document window) on the Dock, identification text appears above the icon to explain what the item is. If the icon is for a document, you can open the document by selecting Open on its Dock menu.
- If you open the Dock menu for an open application, you will see some basic commands, including Quit. You will also see a list of open windows; you can quickly jump to an open window by selecting it. Some applications also enable you to control what is happening from the Dock menu. For example, when iTunes is open, you can control music playback by using its Dock menu.



When you quit an open application, its icon disappears from the Dock—unless you have added that application to the Dock so that it always appears there. Minimized windows disappear from the Dock when you maximize them or when you close the application from which the document window comes.

**TIP**

> If you fill the Dock with many open applications, documents, and folders, it can be a nuisance to switch to each item and close it. Instead, log out (either select Apple menu, Log Out, or press Shift-⌘-Q). When you log out, all open applications are shut down, all documents are closed, and all minimized folder windows are removed from the Dock.

*continues*

*continued*

> When you log back in, the Dock is back to normal. All Finder windows that were on the Dock are gone from there, but they remain open on the desktop. Hold down the Option key, and click the Close box of one of the open windows to close them all.

# ORGANIZING THE DOCK

The default Dock is powerful, but it becomes even more useful when you include the items in it that you use often and organize the Dock to suit your preferences. You can move icons around the Dock, add more applications to it, remove applications that are currently on it, and add your own folders and documents to it so they are easily accessible.

## MOVING ICONS ON THE DOCK

You can change the location of any installed item on the Dock by dragging it. When you move one icon between two others, they slide apart to make room for the icon you are moving. However, you can't move most icons across the dividing line; for example, you can't move an application icon to the right side of the Dock.

If you move the icon of an open application that isn't installed on the Dock, that icon moves to the location to which you drag it and becomes installed on the Dock.

The Dock has two icons you can't move at all: Finder and Trash/Eject. The Finder icon always appears on the left end of the Dock (or top if you use a vertical Dock), and the Trash is always on the right end (or bottom if you use a vertical Dock). Other than these two end points, you can change all the other icons on the Dock as much as you like.

5

## ADDING ICONS TO THE DOCK

You can add applications, folders, and files to the Dock so it contains the items you want. Drag the item you want to add down to the Dock, and drop it where you want it to be installed. Application icons must be placed on the left side of the dividing line, and all others (folders and files) are placed on the right side. Just as when you move icons on the Dock, when you add items between other icons already installed on it, the other icons slide apart to make room for them. When you add an item to the Dock, an alias to that item is created, and you see its icon on the Dock.

**TIP**

> You can add multiple items to the Dock at the same time by holding down the ⌘ key while you select each item you want to add to the Dock and then drag them there.

## REMOVING ITEMS FROM THE DOCK

You can remove an icon from the Dock by dragging it onto the desktop. When you do this, the icon disappears in a puff of digital smoke and no longer appears on the Dock. Because the icons on the Dock are aliases, removing them doesn't affect the applications or files that those aliases represent.

If you drag a minimized window from the Dock, it snaps back to the Dock when you release the mouse button. You remove minimized windows from the Dock by maximizing or closing them.

### Adding Folders to the Dock

You can also add any folder to the Dock; when you click a folder's Dock icon, the contents of the folder are displayed in the Stacks view.

When you place a folder on the Dock, you can open its Dock menu that will list the contents of that folder (refer to Figure 5.4). All the subfolders also appear in hierarchical menus.

This feature is one of the most useful that the Dock offers. You can use it to create custom menus containing anything on your Mac (literally). The uses for this feature are almost unlimited. Some ideas include the following:

- Add your Home directory to the Dock so you can easily move to an item within it.
- Add your project folders to the Dock so you can easily get to the files you need for the project on which you are working.
- Create a folder that has aliases to your frequently used programs of documents. After you place that folder on the Dock you will be able to get to those items very quickly.
- Add the Applications folder to the Dock. This gives you quick access to all the applications on your Mac that are installed in the default Applications folder.

**NOTE**

> Although adding folders to the Dock is useful, it can be easier and just as useful to add folders to the sidebar in Finder windows. The benefit to adding folders to the Dock is that you can access them without bringing the Finder to the front.

5

You might find that adding folders to the Dock is even more useful than adding application or file icons to it. Remember that you can make more room on the Dock by removing items that you don't use from it. For example, you might choose to remove most or all of the application icons from the Dock and instead add the Applications folder to it.

## Customizing the Appearance and Behavior of the Dock

The Dock offers several behaviors you can change to suit your preferences. You can also change various aspects of its appearance, as follows:

- **Size**—You can change the default or current size of the Dock.
- **Magnification**—The magnification effect causes items on the Dock to magnify when you point to them. This can make identifying items easier, especially when many items

are on the Dock or when items are small (see Figure 5.5). You can set the amount of magnification that is used.

- **Hide/Show**—The Dock does consume some screen space. Because it is always topmost, it can get in the way when you are working near its location on the screen. You can set the Dock so that it is hidden except when you point to it. When this behavior is enabled and you point to the Dock's location, it pops onto the desktop so you can use it. When you move off the Dock, it is hidden again.

  If the Dock is hidden, you need to hover a moment in the area of the screen in which it is located before it will appear. This prevents the Dock from popping up when you are working in a document near the edge of the screen and unintentionally pass the mouse over the Dock's location.
- **Dock location**—The Dock can appear at its default location on the bottom of the screen, or you can move it to the left or right side of the desktop.
- **Minimize Effect**—You can choose either the Genie Effect or the Scale Effect.
- **Icon animation**—You already know about this one because it is on by default. When you click an application's icon to open that application, the icon bounces to show you that the application is opening.

**Figure 5.5**
The magnification effect makes identifying items easier (although the magnification level of this particular Dock would be a bit much for most Mac users).

**NOTE**

> The amount of magnification is not relative to the size of the Dock. For example, the magnified icons are the same size whether the Dock is large or small. Of course, because the Dock size is different, the magnified icons do make more contrast with a smaller Dock, but that is only because of the comparison your eye makes.

You can control these settings using the Dock pane of the System Preferences utility. Do the following:

1. Open the System Preferences application by clicking its icon on the Dock.
2. Click Dock to open the Dock pane of the utility (see Figure 5.6).

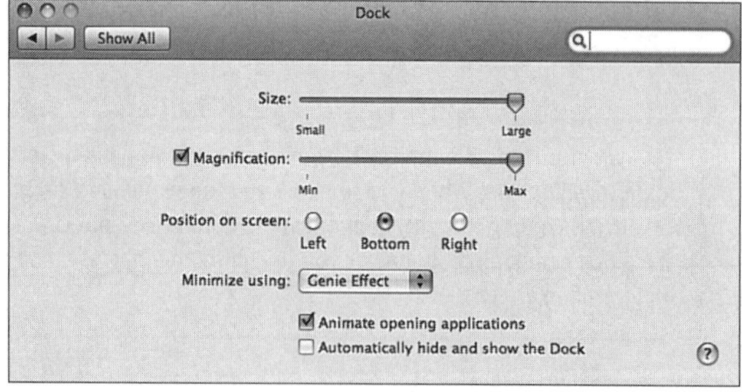


**Figure 5.6**
Use the Dock pane of the System Preferences utility to configure the appearance and behavior of the Dock.

**TIP**

You can also open the Dock preferences pane by selecting Apple menu, Dock, Dock Preferences. The Dock command on the Apple menu also enables you to quickly turn Dock magnification and hiding on or off; you can also change its location by selecting the location in which you want it to be.

3. Use the Size slider to set the default size of the Dock.

   Using the Size slider changes the size of the Dock as well as the items on it. The best practice is to configure the Dock with the items you will want it to contain. Then, use this slider to set its size when it contains those items. As you add items to it, it gets wider or taller until it fills the screen. After the Dock has expanded to the width of the screen, the items on it get smaller as you add more items to the Dock.

**TIP**

You can also change the size of the Dock by pointing to the line that divides the application side of the Dock from the document and folder side. When you do so, the cursor becomes a horizontal line with vertical arrows pointing from the top and bottom sides. Drag this cursor up to make the Dock larger or down to make it smaller.

4. Check the Magnification check box and use the slider to set the amount of magnification on the Dock.

**NOTE**

Changes you make in the Dock pane of the System Preferences application are live, and you see their effects on the Dock immediately. Of course, to see the magnification effect, you must point to an item on the Dock.

5. Click the Left, Bottom, or Right radio button to set the Dock's location on the desktop.
6. Use the "Minimize using" pop-up menu to choose the minimize/maximize effect; the options are Genie Effect or Scale Effect.
7. If you prefer that application icons not bounce when the application opens, uncheck the "Animate opening applications" check box.
8. Check the "Automatically hide and show the Dock" check box if you want the Dock to be visible only when you linger at its location on the screen.

**TIP**

> You can also configure the Dock by using its pop-up menu. Point to the application/folder dividing line. When you see the size-change pointer (the horizontal line with vertical arrows coming from it), hold down the Control key and click or right-click. You will see a pop-up menu that enables you to control the magnification, hiding, position, and minimization effects.

All Dock settings are specific to each user account, meaning that each user can have her own items installed on her Dock, configure the Dock to be hidden, and so on. One user's Dock settings do not affect any other user's Dock.

**NOTE**

> There are applications that are designed to be used only from the Dock; these are called Docklings. For example, you can add a calendar dockling to your Dock so that the current calendar is always displayed there. Docklings have never taken off even though the Dock has been part of OS X since its inception. In version 10.4, similar but better, functionality was added via the Dashboard and its widgets. You'll find that widgets are much more plentiful and easier to use than docklings.

⇨ To learn about widgets, **see** Chapter 6, "Working with Dashboard and Widgets," **p. 123**.

# MAC OS X TO THE MAX: USING DOCK KEYBOARD SHORTCUTS

Dock-related keyboard shortcuts are listed in Table 5.1.

TABLE 5.1 KEYBOARD SHORTCUTS FOR THE DOCK

| Action | Keyboard Shortcut |
|---|---|
| Turn hiding off or on | Option-⌘-D |
| Move to the next open application | ⌘-Tab |
| Move to the previous open application | Shift-⌘-Tab |
| Minimize a window | ⌘-M |
| Highlight/unhighlight the Dock | Control-F3 |
| Move among Dock items when it is highlighted | Left/Right arrow keys |

**NOTE**

If you are using a mobile Mac, you might need to press the Function key (fn) to cause its function keys to act like true function keys. For example, on some mobile Macs, the F3 key controls volume unless you press the fn key to make it function as the F3 key.

5

CHAPTER 6

# Working with the Dashboard and Widgets

## In this chapter

# USING THE DASHBOARD AND WIDGETS

Mac OS X's Dashboard is a way to quickly access and use mini-applications, called *widgets*. Some widgets are separate applications, while others enable you to access other, full-blown Mac OS X applications.

By default, the Dashboard application is always running so that its widgets are always available to you. Unless you remove it from the Dock, the Dashboard's icon is located to the immediate right of the Finder icon on the Dock (or below the Finder icon if you use a vertical Dock).

To use the Dashboard, you activate it. When you do so, the widgets that you have configured to appear will open on your desktop in the foreground and all other windows will move into the background. After you have used the widgets you want to use, you deactivate the Dashboard again and the widgets become hidden and open windows come to the foreground again in the same condition as when you activated the Dashboard.

## ACTIVATING AND DEACTIVATING THE DASHBOARD

By default, you can activate the Dashboard in the following ways:

- Press F12 on the keyboard for desktop Macs.

> **TIP**
>
> If you use a mobile Mac, such as a MacBook or MacBook Pro, open the Exposé & Spaces pane of the System Preferences application and look at the key listed on the Dashboard pop-up menu to determine what the default Dashboard activation key is on your Mac.

- Click the Dashboard icon on the Dock.
- Open the Dashboard Dock icon menu and choose Show Dashboard.
- Double-click the Dashboard's icon in the Applications folder.
- Double-click a widget's icon.



When you activate the Dashboard, the widgets that are configured to open when it is activated will appear (see Figure 6.1). You can then use those widgets or see the information they provide.

When you are done using widgets, you can deactivate the Dashboard again by pressing the default hot key, which is F12, or by clicking on the desktop outside of any open widget. All the widgets will disappear and you will return to your Mac's desktop.

**Figure 6.1**
When you activate the Dashboard, you'll be able access the widgets that are configured to open with it.

## Configuring the Widgets that Open When You Activate the Dashboard

You can configure the widgets that open when you activate the Dashboard by performing the following steps:

1. Press F12 to activate the Dashboard. The widgets currently configured to open will appear along with the Open Widget bar button (refer to Figure 6.1).
2. Click the Open Widget bar button. The Widget bar will open and you will see all of the widgets that are currently installed on your Mac (see Figure 6.2). Widgets are shown in alphabetical order from left to right.
3. Scroll through the installed widgets using the Browse arrows. At the bottom of each widget's icon, you'll see the widget's name.
4. To have a widget open when you activate the Dashboard, click its icon on the Widget bar or drag it from the Widget bar onto the screen at the location where you want it to appear. The widget will appear on the screen with a cool rippling effect (see Figure 6.3).



**TIP**

> You can open multiple instances of the same widget at the same time by continuing to click its icon or dragging it from the Widget bar onto the Dashboard. Each time you do so, a new version of that widget will appear. This is useful for some widgets such as the Weather widget if you are interested in information about the weather in more than one area.

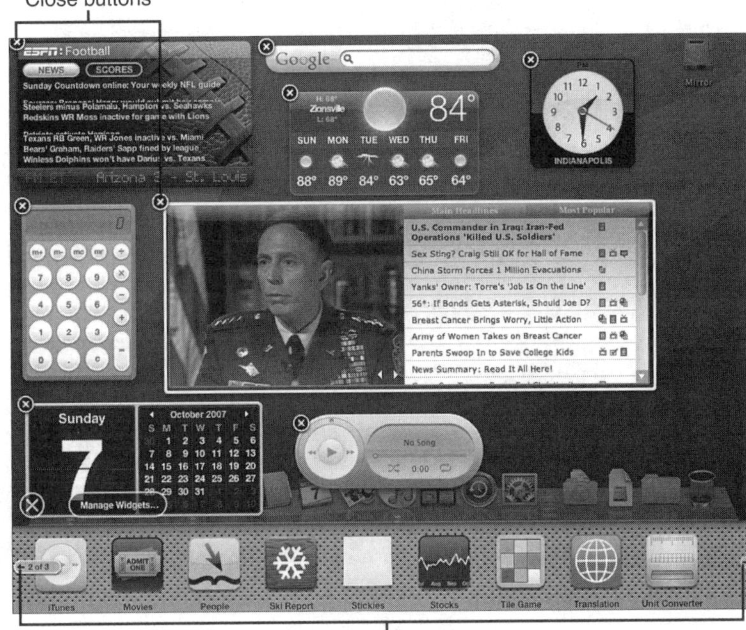


**Figure 6.2**
The Widget bar shows all of the widgets that are currently installed on your Mac.

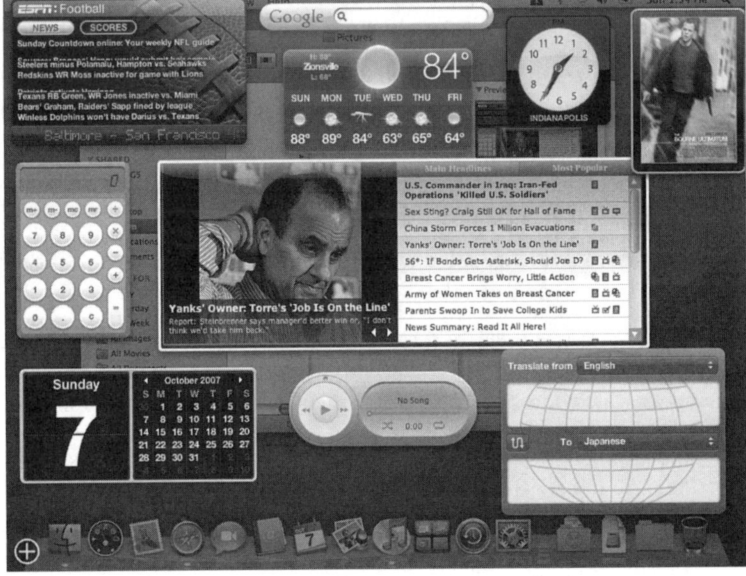


**Figure 6.3**
If you compare this figure to the previous one, you'll notice that the Translation and Movies widgets are now open.



5. Drag the open widget to the location on the screen where you want it to appear when you activate the Dashboard.

6. Close any widgets that you don't want to open when you activate the Dashboard by clicking the Close button, which is the "X" located in the upper-left corner of each widget's window.
7. Continue opening and placing widgets that you do want to use and closing those that you don't want to use until the Dashboard is configured to suit your preferences.
8. Close the Widget bar by clicking the Close button, which is the "X" located just above the Widget bar. The next time you activate the Dashboard, you will see and can use the widgets as you configured them.

**TIP**

> You don't need to close the Widget bar. When you deactivate the Dashboard, the Widget bar is closed automatically. The next time you activate the Dashboard, the Widget bar will remain closed.

## Using and Customizing Useful Widgets

Mac OS X includes a number of useful widgets along with some that aren't so useful. In this section, you'll find a mini-review of some of the default widgets I think are worth using.

⇨ To learn how to remove widgets that you don't use, **see** "Removing Widgets from the Dashboard," **p. 135**.

⇨ To learn how to install widgets in the Dashboard, **see** "Mac OS X to the Max: Finding and Installing More Widgets," **p. 136**.

### Using the Widgets Widget

The Widgets widget, which is the first one on the Widget bar even though it isn't the first one alphabetically, enables you to use a widget to manage the widgets on your Dashboard (see Figure 6.4).

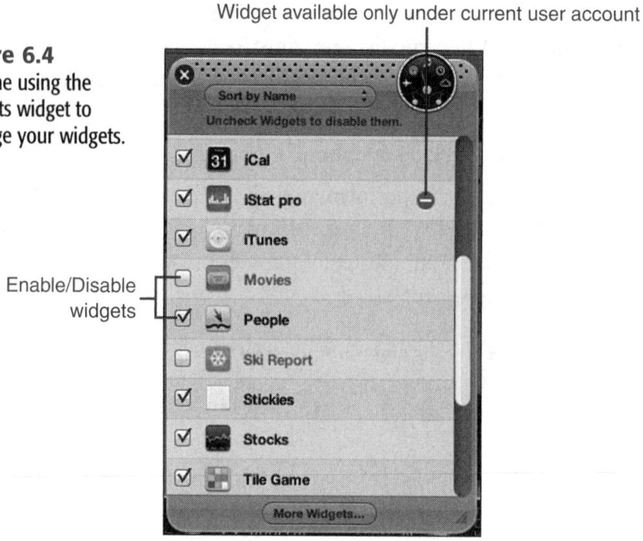

**Figure 6.4**
Imagine using the Widgets widget to manage your widgets.

Here's a quick list about this particular widget:

- You can open the Widgets widget by clicking the Manage Widgets button that appears when you open the Widget bar.
- The widget's list shows all of the widgets installed under the current user account. You can scroll the list or resize the widget to see more or fewer of the available widgets.
- Choose how you want the list sorted by choosing Sort by Name or Sort by Date on the drop-down list at the top of the widget.
- You can disable a widget by unchecking its check box. This causes the widget to be removed from the Dashboard (if it's been added there) and to be removed from the Widget bar. This doesn't actually remove the widget from your computer however. You can restore a widget by checking its check box again.
- Widgets marked with a red circle with a line in it are available only under the current user account.
- You can close the widget by clicking its Close button or you can look for more widgets on Apple's website by clicking the More Widgets button (more on this later).

### USING THE ADDRESS BOOK WIDGET

The Address Book widget enables you to access information in your Address Book more quickly than by using the Address Book application itself. The Address Book widget provides a number of useful tools as you can see in Figure 6.5 and in the following list:

- View a contact's information in the Address Book widget's window. If not all of a contact's information will fit in the window, use the scroll arrows that will appear to move up and down in the contact's information.
- Browse contact information by clicking the Previous or Next buttons.
- Search for a contact by typing the name of the contact in the Search tool. As you type, the contacts in the window will be reduced to include only those that meet your search text. You can only search by name. When the list contains the contact whose information you want to view, click it and the relevant information will fill the widget.
- To view information at a larger size, click it. It will be magnified on the screen. This works only for unlinked information, such as telephone numbers.
- Use the linked information for a contact to perform an action. Click an email address to send an email to the contact (when you do this, Mail will open and a message to the recipient will be created). If you click on an address, your web browser will open and the address will be shown on a Mapquest map.

⇨ To learn how to configure contact information in your Address Book, **see** "Configuring Your Address Book," **p. 644**.

6

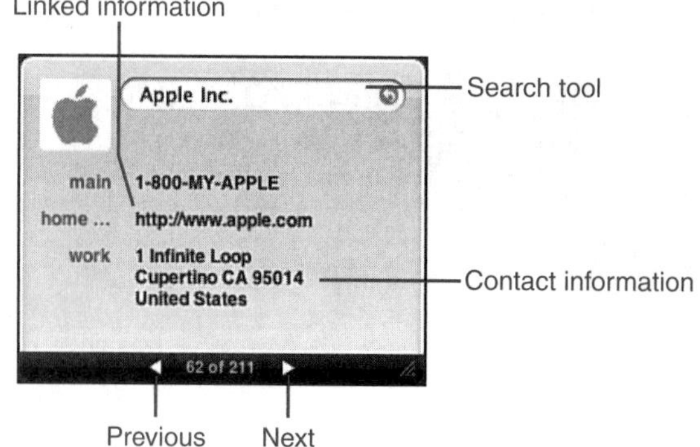


**Figure 6.5**
The Address Book widget is a quick way to get to your Address Book.

**TIP**

> You can remove a widget from the Dashboard anytime the Dashboard is active by holding the Option key down while you point to the widget. When you do so, the Close button will appear; click the button to close the widget.

### USING THE CALCULATOR WIDGET

The Calculator widget is simple, but useful. When it appears on the screen, you can use it to perform basic calculations (see Figure 6.6). You can "press" the Calculator's keys using the mouse or the keyboard.

**Figure 6.6**
It isn't much to look at, by the Calculator widget might be one of the more useful ones.

6

### USING THE ICAL WIDGET

The iCal widget presents an on-screen calendar that you can use to view dates, such as today's date or any date in the past or future (see Figure 6.7). You can see the iCal events you've scheduled for a day when you click the date on the left sie of the widget.

⇨ To learn how to configure iCal, **see** Chapter 26, Creating and Using Calendars with iCal," **p. 663**.

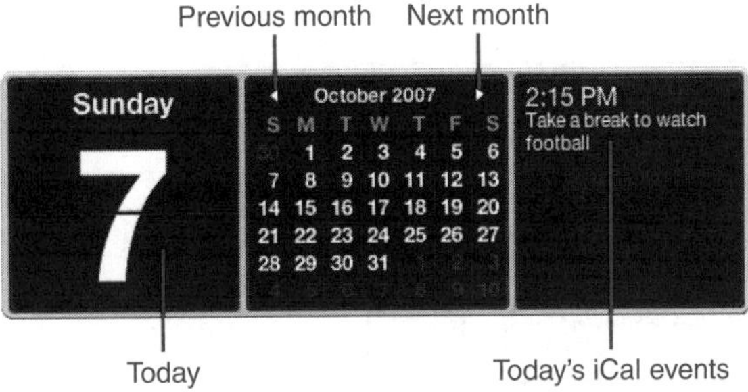


**Figure 6.7**
You can view your iCal events by clicking on a date in the iCal widget.

Following are some iCal widget pointers:

- Click on the date shown on the left side of the widget to expand it to show the month and click again to show the iCal events pane. Keep clicking to collapse the widget again.
- Move ahead or back by a month in the calendar using the Next or Previous buttons or the left and right arrow keys.
- When you expand the widget to see all three panes, the iCal events for the selected date will be shown in the far right pane. Unfortunately, only events on the current date are displayed; you'll have to go into the iCal application to look at events on future dates.

### USING THE DICTIONARY WIDGET

This is a very handy widget that you can use to access the Mac OS X Dictionary application. You can use the widget for both its dictionary and thesaurus functions. You can also search Apple resources with it. To use this widget, perform the following steps:

1. Activate the Dashboard and click Dictionary to use the dictionary mode or Thesaurus to use that mode (this assumes you have configured the Dictionary widget to be part of the Dashboard of course). There is also an Apple mode if you want to look for terms related to your favorite computing platform.
2. Start typing the word in which you are interested in the Search tool. As you type, the widget will find words that match your search text (see Figure 6.8).



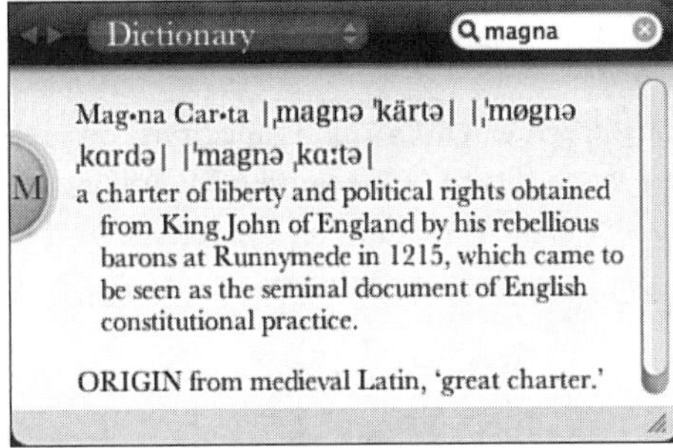


**Figure 6.8**
If you can spell as well as I, you'll find the Dictionary widget very helpful.

3. Continue typing until the word you are interested in appears in the widget's window.

**TIP**

> The Dictionary widget is one of the few whose window you can resize by dragging its Resize handle.

4. If a list of words appears, click the word you are interested in. Its definition will appear in the widget's window. It will also be moved into the Search tool.

**TIP**

> You can clear your current search by clicking the Clear button that appears in the Search tool.

5. To move back to the list of words, click the Back button. Your original search term will appear in the Search box again.
6. If the Scroll bar appears instead, use it to move up and down the window to view the entries that meet your search criteria.

**TIP**

> To see which dictionary is being used, click the Info button, which is the "i" that appears in the lower left corner of the widget.

## USING THE ITUNES WIDGET

You can use the iTunes widget to view and control music playback via iTunes. To use it, open iTunes. When iTunes is running, you can use the iTunes widget to select and play music (see Figure 6.9).

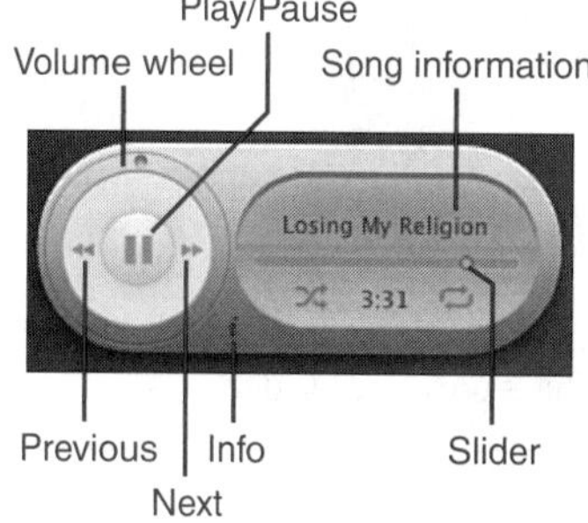


**Figure 6.9**
Use the iTunes widget to take control of your music.

6

To use the iTunes widget, take heed of the following notes:

- To choose a playlist, click the Info button. The Select Playlist pop-up menu will appear. Use this to choose the playlist you want to hear. Click Done to move to the widget's controls.

- Use the straightforward Play/Pause, Previous, and Next buttons to control the music.
- View the song currently playing in the Song information area.
- Adjust the volume by dragging the Volume wheel clockwise to increase it or counter-clockwise to decrease it.
- Drag the slider to fast forward or rewind in a song.

### USING THE UNIT CONVERTER WIDGET

If you ever need to convert from the English system to the Metric (or vice versa) or perform other such unit conversions, such as among different currencies, the Unit Converter widget can take all the work out of the process for you. To use this handy widget, perform the following steps:

1. Access the Unit Converter widget.
2. Choose the type of unit you want to convert on the Convert pop-up menu. There are many options from which you can choose, including Area, Currency, Energy, Time, and so on.
3. Use the lower left pop-up menu to choose the specific unit you want to convert. The options you see will depend on what you selected on the Convert pop-up menu. For example, if you choose Temperature, the options on this menu will be various units of temperature, including Fahrenheit, Celsius, and so on.
4. Use the lower right pop-up menu to choose the unit you want to convert the measurement into.
5. Type the data you want to convert in the lower left box. The converted measurement will be shown in the lower right box (see Figure 6.10).

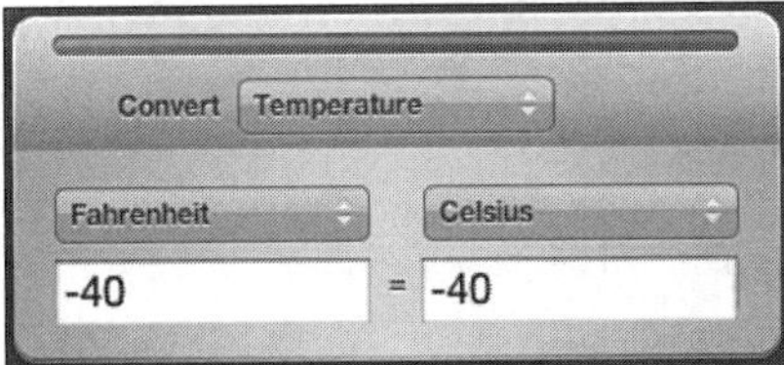


**Figure 6.10**
Ever wondered when the temperature in Fahrenheit is the same as it is in Celsius?

6

**TIP**

> If you choose a conversion for which data is provided by a third-party, such as Currency, click the Info button to see who is providing the data.

### USING THE WEATHER WIDGET

The Weather widget displays current weather conditions and temperature forecasts for an area that you select. To use it, perform the following steps:

**NOTE**

Many widgets, such as the Weather and World Clock widgets, require an Internet connection to work. Others, such as the Calculator, don't.

1. Open the Weather widget.
2. Move the pointer over the widget. When you do, the Info button will appear.
3. Click the Info button located in the lower-right corner of the widget's window. You'll see the configuration tools.
4. Enter the city or ZIP code for which you want to see weather information in the box. The simplest approach is to just enter the ZIP code, but you can enter the city and state if you don't know the ZIP code. When you enter a city's name, a list will pop up that shows you all the cities that might match your search. Click the city you want to use.
5. Choose the unit of temperature you want to be displayed on the Degrees pop-up menu. The options are Fahrenheit and Celsius.
6. If you want lows to be included in the 6-day forecast, check the "Include lows in 6-day forecast" check box.
7. Click Done. You'll return to the widget. You'll see the city you selected and an icon representing the current weather conditions in that area. Also displayed will be the current temperature and the current day's temperature forecast (see Figure 6.11).

**Figure 6.11**
Ah, another lovely day in Brownsburg, Indiana.

Following are a few tips to help you make the most of the Weather widget:

- To see a 6-day forecast, click the widget's window. It will expand and you'll see the latest predictions for the current day plus five days into the future. To collapse the widget again, click its window.
- You can track the weather in multiple areas at the same time by opening a Weather widget and configuring it for each area in which you are interested. When you activate the Dashboard, you'll see the weather in all your favorite spots (see Figure 6.12).
- Click the city shown in the Weather widget window. Your default web browser will open and you'll move to the AccuWeather.com web page for that city. Here, you can get into the details of the weather, present and future.

**NOTE**

The default city is Cupertino, California. I wonder what is important about that city?

**Figure 6.12**
Where would you like to be?

### USING THE WORLD CLOCK WIDGET

This simple widget displays the current time in a city of your choice.

1. Open the widget and click the Info button.
2. Choose the continent in which you are interested on the Continent pop-up menu.
3. Choose the city on the City pop-up menu.
4. Click Done. When you return to the widget, you'll see the hands on the clock zoom ahead or back until the current time in the city you selected is displayed (see Figure 6.13).

**Figure 6.13**
Use the World Clock widget to keep track of the time in your favorite cities.

## CONFIGURING WIDGETS



In a couple of the previous examples, you saw a step to click a widget's Info button. Some widgets have configurable options, such as setting a location or information source, configuring the information displayed in the widget's window, and so on. Not all widgets have the Info option, but many do. The button is located in various places on different widgets so there's really no way to know where to look for it on any given widget.

To see if a widget has options, move the pointer over the widget in which you are interested. If it has options, you'll see the Info button appear; this button is usually a lowercase "i" sometimes inside a circle, sometimes not (see Figure 6.14).

**Figure 6.14**
This Wikipedia widget has options.

When you click the Info button, the widget's configuration tools will appear (see Figure 6.15). You can use those tools to make the widget work or look the way you want it to. When you're finished making changes, click the Done button and the widget will be updated accordingly. You should always check out the Info options for any widgets that you use often because they usually provide options to make widgets even more useful to you.

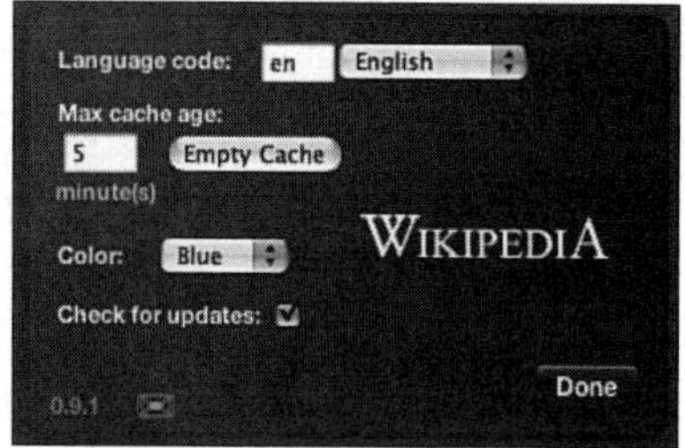


**Figure 6.15**
Check out the options for any widgets you use regularly.

# Configuring the Dashboard

There are a couple of things you can do to configure the Dashboard itself. You can change its hot key and active screen corner and you can remove any widgets you never use.

## Setting the Dashboard's Hot Key and Active Screen Corner

You can change the default hot key for the Dashboard by opening the Exposé and Spaces pane of the System Preferences application. Choose the new hot key on the Dashboard pop-up menu. Choose the mouse button to activate using the second Dashboard pop-up menu (if you have a multi-button mouse connected to your Mac of course).

You can also configure the Dashboard to open when you move the pointer to a corner of the screen by choosing Dashboard on the pop-up menu located at the corner you want to use. When you move the pointer to this corner, the Dashboard will activate just like it does when you press the hot key.

## Removing Widgets from the Dashboard

Some of the widgets that come with Mac OS X probably won't be useful to you (my least favorite is the Tile Game widget). You can remove any widgets you won't use by performing the following steps:

6

**NOTE**

> You have to authenticate yourself as an administrator to be able to remove widgets. And if you remove them, no one who uses your Mac will be able to use the widgets you remove. If you think you might use a widget someday, just remove it from the Dashboard instead of deleting it from your Mac.

1. Open the Widgets folder that is located in Library folder of your startup drive (see Figure 6.16).

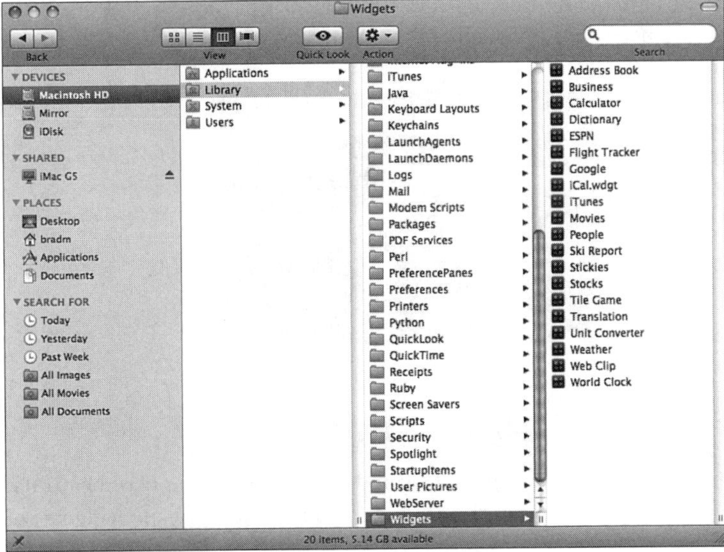


**Figure 6.16**
The Widgets in this folder will be on the Widget bar when you activate the Dashboard.

2. Drag the widget you don't want to use out of the Widgets folder. If you might want to install it again sometime, save the widget file. If not, you can delete it.
3. Restart your Mac. The undesirable widget will no longer be part of the Dashboard.

⇨ To learn how to install widgets in the Dashboard, **see** the following section, "Mac OS X to the Max: Finding and Installing More Widgets."

**TIP**

> Unlike other applications, the Dashboard's icon on the Dock doesn't serve much of a purpose. The Dashboard is always running, whether its icon appears on the Dock or not. To get rid of the Dashboard's Dock icon, open its menu and choose Remove from Dock. If you want it to be displayed there again, drag it from the Applications folder onto the Dock.

# MAC OS X TO THE MAX: FINDING AND INSTALLING MORE WIDGETS

Some of the default widgets are cool and some are lame. The good news is that your Dashboard isn't limited to just these widgets. There are three sources of widgets that you can add to your Mac. The first is by capturing sections of web pages as a widget. The second is to download widgets from the web and install them on your Mac. The third is to program your own widgets. In the remaining sections of this chapter, you'll learn about the first two options. The third one is beyond the scope of this chapter, but if you search the web, you'll find lots of information about how to create your own widgets.

## BUILDING YOUR OWN WIDGETS WITH WEB CAPTURE

For Leopard, a really nice feature was added to Safari and to the Dashboard. This is the ability to capture parts of web pages as a widget on your Dashboard. Here's how:

1. Open Safari and move to a web page containing information or tools you want to capture in a widget.
2. Click the "Open this page in Dashboard" button or choose File, Open in Dashboard. A selection box and capture toolbar appears.
3. Make the selection box enclose the part of the page that you want to be a widget and click Add (see Figure 6.17). The Dashboard will open and the part of the page you selected will become a widget (see Figure 6.18).

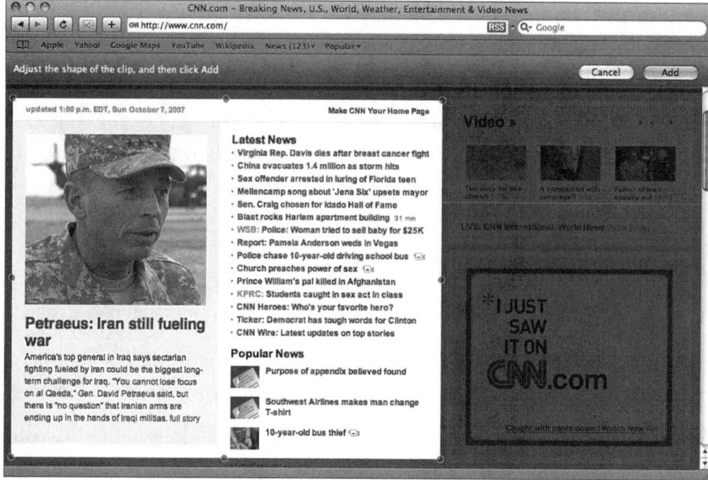


**Figure 6.17**
The selected part of this news web site will become a handy widget.

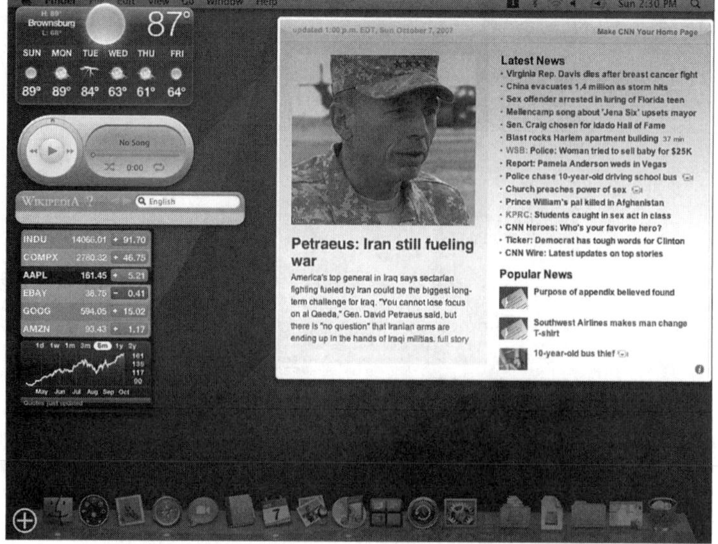


**Figure 6.18**
Here's my newly created CNN.com widget open in the Dashboard.

6

After you've created a widget via web capture, you can use that widget just like other widgets, well, mostly anyway. The links in the widget will take you to the related information on the source web page.

Some notes about this feature:

- The web capture selection captures a static portion of the web page based on what you select. If the information changes on the source web page, it might shift what's shown in the widget you create.
- To get rid of a web capture widget, open the Dashboard and the open the Widget bar. Click the Close button for the widget. Unlike other widgets, when you close a widget you've captured, it's gone forever.
- Capturing part of a web page is very complicated. It will work fine with some parts of some pages, but might not work with everything you try. It depends on how the page works, the part you select, and so on. Don't be too surprised if a widget you create doesn't work exactly as you expect. If not, just delete it and try again.
- Widgets that you create will have an Info button. Click this button to change the theme for the widget (which changes how the widget is framed) or to edit it by changing the part of the page that is selected.

## FINDING AND DOWNLOADING WIDGETS

The Dashboard can also be expanded with new widgets that you download from the Internet.

1. Activate the Dashboard and open the Widget bar.
2. Open the Widgets widget and click the More Widgets button. Your default web browser will open and take you to the widgets web page (see Figure 6.19).

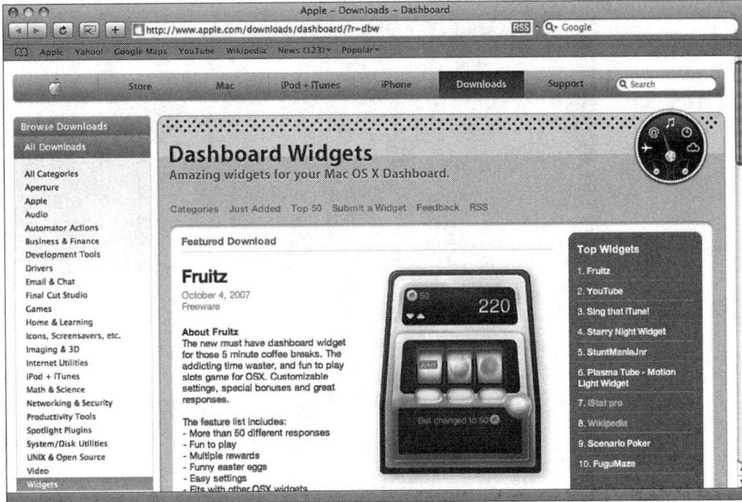


**Figure 6.19**
So many widgets, so little time.

3. Browse or search until you find a widget you want to try.
4. Download the widget. In most cases, you're prompted to install the widget after it has been downloaded.
5. Click Install at the prompt. You move to the Dashboard and see the new widget that you installed.
6. Click Keep to keep the widget or Delete to get rid of it. If you click Keep, the downloaded widget will be installed on your Dashboard.

## INSTALLING THIRD PARTY WIDGETS

If you download a widget from the Apple Dashboard website, you don't need to do any installation as it will be automatically recognized and installed as you learned in the previous section. However, you'll find widgets in other locations as well.

There are two ways widgets from other sources can be installed. One is to use an installer if one was provided with the widget. Otherwise, just place the widget file in the Widgets folder that is in the Library folder on your startup disk or in the Library folder in your Home folder; restart your Mac and then use the Widget bar to open and use the new widget. If it is installed in the startup disk's Library folder, the widget will be available to everyone who uses your Mac. If it is installed in the Library within a user's Home folder, it will only be available to that user.

**TIP**

> When you install a widget from the Apple website, it is installed only in the current user's Widgets folder. To make it available to all your users, move it from the Widgets folder in the user's Home folder to the Widgets folder in the startup disk's Library folder.

# CHAPTER 7

# Installing and Using Mac OS X Applications

## In this chapter

## Understanding Applications You Can Run Under Mac OS X

You can run the following types of applications under Mac OS X:

- **Unix applications**—Because Mac OS X is based on Unix, you can run many Unix applications on your Mac. Some of these applications have to be recompiled to run on the Mac, but most will work as they are. Of course, you will need to run them from the command line (unless you find and install a graphical user interface for the Unix subsystem). Because Unix is such a prevalent OS, thousands of Unix applications are available for you to use.

**NOTE**

> The X11 environment that is installed with Mac OS X provides a graphical interface for Unix applications. If you run Unix applications regularly, you can use this environment by launching the X11 application in the Appllication/Utilities folder.

- **Java applications**—You can run applications written in the Java and Java 2 programming languages. Because Java is a platform-independent programming language, the same applications work on Windows, Macintosh, and other platforms. You mostly encounter Java applications on the Web, but you will find some standalone Java applications as well.
- **Carbon applications**—These applications are written using the Carbon programming environment, which is designed to take advantage of the Mac OS X architecture. Many are existing applications that have been ported over to Mac OS X—in Mac OS X-lingo, they have been *carbonized*. Because carbonizing an application requires considerably fewer resources than creating a Cocoa application, most Mac OS X applications were carbonized Mac OS 9 applications. As Mac OS X has continued to mature, most applications have been written or rewritten specifically for Mac OS X.
- **Cocoa applications**—These applications are written using the Cocoa programming architecture, which means they take full advantage of the advanced features Mac OS X provides. Cocoa applications have to be written from the ground up in the new environment rather than being ported over like carbonized applications. Most new Mac OS X applications are based on Cocoa, and many applications written for previous versions of the Mac OS have been rewritten in Cocoa.
- **Windows applications**—With an Intel Mac, you can run Windows applications in a number of ways. Mac OS X 10.5 includes Boot Camp, a tool that allows you to install Windows XP or Vista and then boot your Mac from that operating systems. Programs from Parallels, VMware, and others provide the ability to have a Windows operating system running at the same time as Mac OS X.



⇨ To learn about running Windows applications, **see** Chapter 8, " Running Windows and Windows Applications on a Mac," **p. 171**.

# INSTALLING MAC OS X APPLICATIONS

Although carbonized and Cocoa applications behave somewhat differently, their similarities are as great as their differences. This is especially true when it comes to installing them.

Under Mac OS X, the two basic strategies by which applications are installed are the following:

- **Drag and drop**—Under this method, you simply drag the application files (usually just one file or folder) from one location to the location in which you want to install the application (usually the Applications folder).
- **Installer**—Some applications use an installation program to install the application and related files for you. Most applications use the standard Mac OS X Installation application as their installation mechanism. These applications are provided as package files, which have the file extension `.pkg`.

Because Mac OS X is designed as a multiuser OS, where you install Mac OS X applications is an important consideration. The two locations in which you should install Mac OS X applications are

- **The Applications folder**—If you want the application to be accessible to everyone who uses your Mac, you should install it in the Applications folder. To do this, you must be logged in as an administrator or authenticate as an administrator. Most applications that use an installer are installed in the Applications folder, and you usually don't have the option to install them elsewhere.

**TIP**

> Remember that you can also use the Parental Controls pane of the System Preferences application to limit access to specific applications.

- **The Home folder**—You can sometimes install applications in a user's Home directory (primarily applications that have drag-and-drop installation). You should install applications in a user's Home directory only if you don't want everyone who uses your Mac to be able to use that application. Because users can access only areas to which they have been granted permission through their security settings, you need to ensure that everyone who needs to use the application can access the location in which it is stored.

These installation locations are appropriate only for Mac OS X (carbonized or Cocoa) applications. You should install Unix or other types of applications in locations that are appropriate for those types of applications.

**CAUTION**

> If you have trouble installing an application, make sure you are logged in as an administrator. Many application installations can be done only while using an administrator account.

## INSTALLING MAC OS X APPLICATIONS WITH DRAG AND DROP

Under Mac OS X, applications can be provided as *bundles*. A bundle is a collection of the executable files and other resources required for an application. An application bundle can be presented as a single icon, which makes the drag-and-drop installation technique possible. Instead of having to deal with an installer application or a bunch of individual files, you can easily act on an entire application bundle by acting on its single icon.

Installing applications that use the drag-and-drop method is especially simple. Most of these applications are provided as self-mounting image (`.smi`) or disk image (`.dmg`) files. This means that the file behaves just as if it were a volume you mount on your desktop.

Many Mac OS X applications use this method, making installation of these applications almost trivially easy.

**NOTE**

> The only difference between the behavior of `.smi` and `.dmg` files is that `.smi` files automatically mount on your desktop when you launch them. Disk image files use Apple's Disk Utility software to mount. Because this application is installed on your Mac by default, these files behave quite similarly, and you probably won't notice any difference between them. However, you could use a `.smi` file even if Disk Utility wasn't installed on your machine, whereas you can't use a `.dmg` file without the Disk Utility application.

The general process to install an application provided in a `.smi` or `.dmg` file is the following:

1. Download and, if necessary, uncompress the `.smi` or `.dmg` file.
2. If the file isn't mounted on your Mac automatically, double-click the file (which is likely a `.dmg` file). Its volume is mounted on your desktop, just like any other volumes, such as a CD, DVD, or volume on a hard drive.
3. Open the resulting volume and drag the application's folder or file to the appropriate directory on your Mac. In most cases, you will place it in the Applications folder on your startup volume.
4. Unmount the mounted volume by selecting it and pressing ⌘-E (or select File, Eject).
5. Discard the `.smi` or `.dmg` files if you won't need to install the application again. However, in most cases, I recommend that you keep the original file in the event you need to reinstall the application. (For example, you can copy it to a CD or DVD.)

⇨ To learn how to download files from the Web and prepare them for use, **see** "Downloading and Preparing Files," **p. 536**.

7

**NOTE**

> Some applications don't even provide a `.smi` or `.dmg` file. After you download and uncompress the file, you will have the application's folder immediately. Drag this folder to where you want the application to be installed.

Many Mac OS X applications that you can download from the Web are provided in the `.dmg` format. As an example, download and install Netflix Freak, which is a great application if you use the Netflix DVD rental service like I do:

**NOTE**

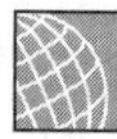

> You can get information about and download Netflix Freak at www.thelittleappfactory.com.

1. Log in as an administrator for your Mac.
2. Go to http://www.thelittleappfactory.com/, click the Our Software tab, and then click the Netflix Freak icon.

**TIP**

> Netflix Freak enables you to manage your Netflix account much more easily than using a web browser to access it. You can do all the functions you can from the Netflix website from within the Netflix Freak application, and these tasks are easier and faster.

3. Download Netflix Freak. After the file is downloaded, it is uncompressed and decoded automatically. You're warned that the file you are downloading is an application, which is not useful in this case since you know what you are doing, so just clear the prompt. When the download process is complete, you see the `netflixfreak.dmg` file. The disk image is the Netflix Freak volume on your desktop; its folder is opened for you automatically.
4. Open another Finder window and display the Applications folder.

**TIP**

> The fastest way to open the Applications folder is to press Shift-⌘-A.

5. Drag the Netflix Freak icon into the Applications directory to copy it there (see Figure 7.1).
6. Eject the Netflix Freak volume and store the original `.dmg` file in a safe location or delete it.
7. Launch Netflix Freak to start using it.

**TIP**

> If you want to save a little disk space, save the original `.sit` or `.zip` files that you download instead of the `.dmg` files. When you want to access the `.dmg` files again, you can uncompress the `.sit` or `.zip` files. You don't need to save both versions. The `.dmg` file is slightly more convenient than the `.sit` or `.zip` file, but it also requires slightly more disk space.

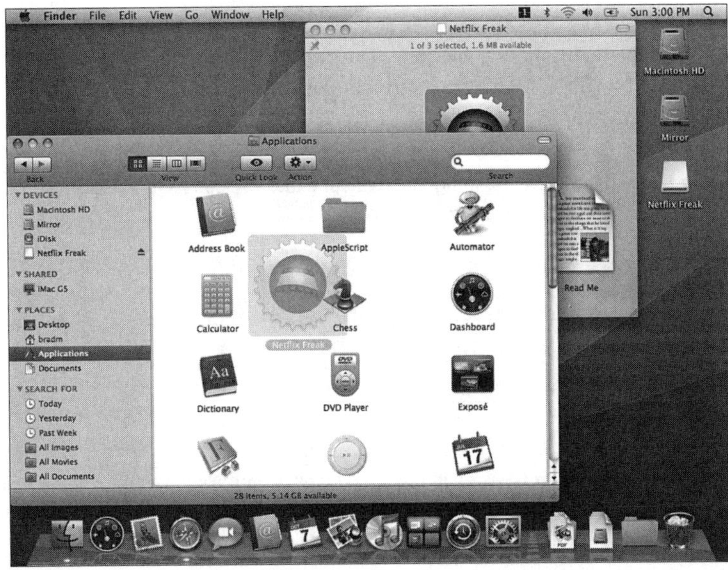


**Figure 7.1**
Installing the excellent Netflix Freak is a simple matter of drag and drop.

**CAUTION**

Some companies remove the installers for one version from their website when the next version is released. In such cases, you might not be able to download and install the application again without paying an upgrade fee to get the new version. Although this is not a very good practice in my opinion, some companies do have this policy. The only way to ensure that you will be able to reinstall the same version of an application you downloaded and licensed is to keep the original installer files. You should also keep any updates you download and install for that version.

*If you aren't able to place the application in the appropriate directory, see "I Can't Install an Application Because I Don't Have Sufficient Privileges" in the "Troubleshooting" section at the end of this chapter.*

## Installing Mac OS X Applications Using an Installer

All Mac OS X applications that use the standard Mac OS X installer application install in a similar fashion; however, minor variations can exist.

Under Mac OS X, applications that use the Installer application come in package files, which have the extension `.pkg`. For example, when you installed Mac OS X on your machine, you used this installer.



**NOTE**

When you download an application that comes in a `.pkg` file, it is often included in a `.dmg` or `.smi` file. This is usually done when there are files outside the application to be installed that the developer wants to include with the application but that should not be installed as part of it (readme files, for example).

The general process to install and use `.pkg` files is the following:

1. Download and prepare the file containing the application you want to install.
2. Mount the disk image and open it.
3. Double-click the `.pkg` file.
4. Work through the steps in the installer application.

An example of an application that uses this technique is the excellent Snapz Pro X screen capture utility:

1. Log in as an administrator for your Mac.
2. Go to www.ambrosiasw.com; move to the Utilities page; and click the Snapz Pro X icon.
3. Download Snapz Pro X. After you've clicked Continue in the warning prompt, the `.dmg` file is opened automatically; then the volume containing the software is mounted and appears on the desktop.
4. Look at the contents of the volume, and read any readme files you see.

**NOTE**

> Some installer packages also come with an uninstaller application. You should definitely keep the original files so you can run the uninstaller if you need to easily remove the application later. This is especially important for those applications that install resources in the system, such as software that supports peripheral devices.

5. If the installer doesn't launch automatically, open the package file, which has the `.pkg` file extension, such as `Snapz Pro X.pkg`. You will see the Installer window (see Figure 7.2). Just as when you installed Mac OS X, the left pane shows you the steps you will work through using the installer. The right pane provides information about each step. You use the Continue and Go Back buttons to move through the installation process.

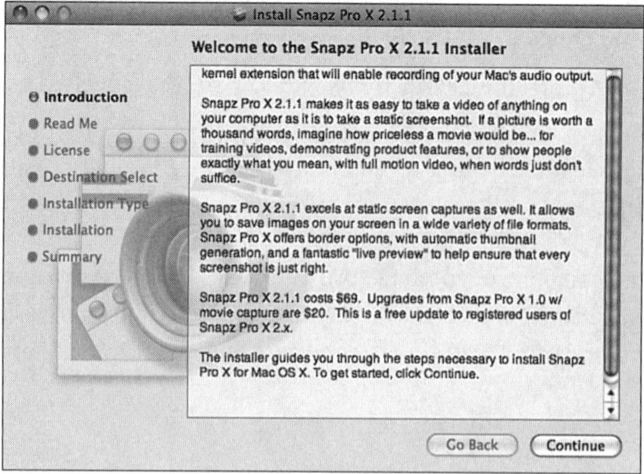


**Figure 7.2**
Running the installer for most applications is a simple of matter of following onscreen instructions.

6. If prompted, verify that you are an administrator by entering your administrator password (and username if you aren't logged in under an administrator account).

**NOTE**

> Some installations require that you authenticate yourself as an administrator before you can begin the installation—even if you are already logged in as the administrator.

7. Continue working through the steps in the installer until you get to the screen that tells you that the software was successfully installed.
8. Quit the Installer application.

**TIP**

> To unmount a disk image, click the Eject button next to it in the Sidebar; select it, and select File, Eject; or select it and press ⌘-E.

## LAUNCHING MAC OS X APPLICATIONS

There are many ways to launch Mac OS X applications, including the following:

- Select the application in a Finder window, and select the Finder's Open command (⌘-O).
- Double-click the application's icon.
- Single-click an application's icon on the Dock or Places sidebar.
- Open an alias to the application, such as one stored on your desktop.
- Open a document of the file type that the application is set to open.
- Drag and drop a document onto an application's icon or an alias's icon.
- Select an application's icon or an alias's icon, and press ⌘-down arrow.
- Launch the application from within another application. (For example, you can launch a web browser by clicking a URL in an email program.)
- Add the application to the Login Items window so it is launched automatically when you log in.
- Launch the application from a script created by the Automator, AppleScript, or another scripting utility.

If you have used a Mac before, you have probably used many of these methods to open applications. Most of them are very straightforward and require no discussion. A couple of them, though used less often, can be effective techniques for quickly opening an application.

**NOTE**

> The first time you launch an application under Mac OS X, you will see a dialog box that explains you are opening the application for the first time. In this dialog box, you'll see the name of the application that is trying to open, along with tools you can use to control it. The primary purpose of this is to warn you when an application first opens so you can confirm it is a legitimate application and not some Trojan horse or other application that is trying to launch without your knowledge. If you want to proceed with opening the application, click Open. If you aren't sure about the application, stop the process and check it out before opening it again.

One of the most powerful methods—although it's underused by many Mac users—is to launch an application by drag and drop. Macintosh drag and drop is a function of the OS whereby you move information from one location to another by simply selecting it, dragging it to where you want it to go, and then dropping it.

The drag-and-drop approach is especially efficient when you want to open a document with an application that wasn't used to create it initially. For example, if you receive a plain-text file and double-click it, it opens in TextEdit. If you want to open it in Word instead, you can simply drag and drop the document onto Word's icon and Word is used to open the file. Otherwise, you would have to first open Word, use the Open command, maneuver to the text file, and then open it. (You could also use the Open With command by opening the document's contextual menu.)

If the file type is compatible with the application on which you drag it, the application icon becomes highlighted to indicate that it is a compatible file.

**TIP**

> You can force an application to attempt to open a document with which it is not compatible by holding down the Option and ⌘ keys while you drag the document onto the application's icon. If the application is capable of opening files of that type, the file is opened. If not, either the application still launches but no document window appears or the document window appears and is filled with garbage.

You can also use drag and drop to open documents using applications installed on the Dock. Simply drag the file you want to open onto the application's icon on the Dock. If the application is capable of opening the document, its icon becomes highlighted. When you release the mouse button, the application launches, and the document is opened.

*If the drag-and-drop technique doesn't work, see "I Can't Drag a Document on an Icon to Open It" in the "Troubleshooting" section at the end of this chapter.*

*If a file opens, but its contents are scrambled, see "When I Open an Application, What I See Is Incomprehensible" in the "Troubleshooting" section at the end of this chapter.*

# Understanding and Using Standard Mac OS X Application Menus

Just like under all versions of the Mac OS, Mac OS X applications designed to work on the Mac follow certain conventions when it comes to the menus they provide. Although applications can provide more menus than the core set of standard menus, they are not supposed to provide fewer.

**CAUTION**

> The information in this section is based on standard Mac OS X menus for Cocoa applications. Carbonized applications might not follow the typical application menus. For example, all carbonized applications provide an Application menu, but not all provide Cocoa's Format menu.

## Working with Mac OS X Application Menus

All Mac OS X applications have an application menu, which provides the commands you use to control the application itself as well as to interact with the OS (see Figure 7.3).

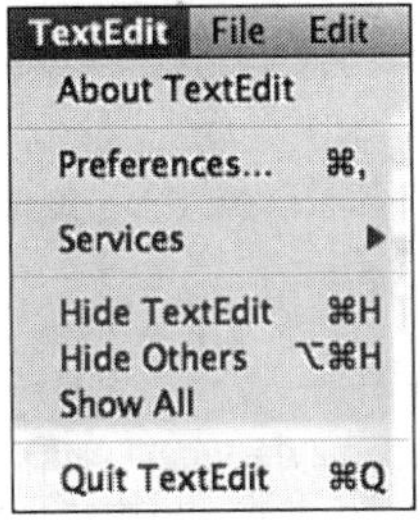


**Figure 7.3**
This TextEdit menu is typical of the application menu provided by Mac OS X applications.

Typical commands on an application's application menu are the following:

- About
- Preferences
- Services
- Hide/Show
- Quit

One of the more interesting commands on the application menu is the Mac OS X Services command. This command enables you to access functions provided by other applications to add information or perform functions while you are using the current application. Although it is not supported in all applications, when it is supported, it can be quite useful.

7

**NOTE**

> Game applications are the most likely to not provide standard menus, and that is okay. After all, who needs a Format menu when you are shooting bad guys?

There are various uses for the Services command, but as an example, suppose you are having trouble understanding an error message you are getting in a certain application, and you want to send an email to the technical support organization to get some help. That email might be a lot more meaningful if you can include an image of the actual error dialog box that you see with your explanation. Using the Services commands from within the Mail email application, you can do just that:

1. Move to the dialog box you want to capture; perhaps it is an error message that suddenly pops up on your screen.
2. Without doing anything in the dialog box (for example, don't click its OK button), launch the Mail application by clicking its icon on the Dock.
3. Create a new email message, and move into its body.
4. From the Mail menu, select Services, Grab, Timed Selection.
5. Bring the dialog box you want to capture to the front by clicking its window.
6. Wait for Grab's timer to go off.
7. Move back into the Mail application. The screen that Grab captured is pasted into the new email message.
8. Finish your message, and send it.

The specific services offered on the Services menu depend on the application you are using and the data with which you are working. You should explore Services options that you have with the applications you use most often. Most Apple applications do provide some services, but even with those, support for Services can be spotty. The only way to know is to explore the Services menu for the applications you use.

Even though Apple's basic Mac OS X text editing application, TextEdit, isn't all that great for word processing, it does provide a great example of how many Services commands can be supported. For a list of some of the Services commands available in TextEdit and what they do, see Table 7.1.

**TABLE 7.1 SAMPLE COMMANDS ON THE TEXTEDIT SERVICES MENU**

| Services Command | What It Does |
|---|---|
| Finder | Activates various Finder commands, such as Open, Reveal, and Show Info, on the selected item |
| Grab | Enables you to capture screen shots and paste them into the current document |
| Import Image | Enables you to import images from an imaging device, such as a digital camera, connected to your Mac |
| Mail | Emails selected text or the entire document via the Mail application |
| Make New Sticky Note | Creates a new sticky note from the selected text |

*continues*

**Table 7.1 Continued**

| Services Command | What It Does |
|---|---|
| Open URL | Opens a selected URL in the default web browser |
| Script Editor | Enables you to work with AppleScript, such as creating a new AppleScript or running an existing one |
| Search with Google | Searches for the selected text on www.google.com |
| Send File To Bluetooth Device | Sends a file to a Bluetooth device, such as a PDA |
| Speech | Enables you to have your Mac speak selected text |
| Summarize | Launches Mac OS X's Summary Service application that creates a summary of selected text |
| TextEdit | Opens a selected file in TextEdit, or creates a new TextEdit file from selected text |

**NOTE**

Some third-party applications can add their own commands to the Services menu. For example, QuicKeys, which enables you to create and run macros, adds a command to the Services menu that enables you to create a macro from within any application.

## Working with Mac OS X File Menus

The Mac OS X File menu provides the commands you use to work with files. Most of these are fairly obvious, such as New, Open, Save, Save As, and so on.

## Working with Mac OS X Edit Menus

Although all applications should provide an Edit menu, the commands on this menu can vary widely from application to application. At the least, the Cut, Copy, and Paste commands will appear on this menu. There might be others as well, such as Find, Spelling, Speech, and so on. As with the File menu, these commands should be familiar to you unless you are new to using a Mac.

## Working with Mac OS X Format Menus

As you might expect from its name, the Format menu provides commands that enable you to format the file with which you are working. The specific commands on the Format menu depend on the particular application you are using.

7

**NOTE**

The Mac OS X Format menu, including the Fonts panel, is available only in Cocoa applications that are designed to use it. Many Mac OS X applications provide format and font commands that are specific to those applications.

One of the most useful commands on most applications' Format menus is the Font command. This command enables you to work with the fonts you use in a document (see Figure 7.4). In addition to the commands you expect to see, such as Bold, Italic, and so on, you also will see the Show Fonts command, which opens the Font panel.

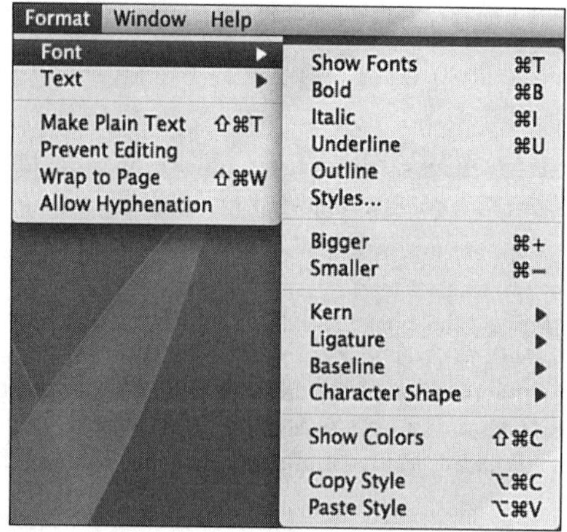


**Figure 7.4**
TextEdit's Font command is typical of this command on many applications' Format menus.

⇨ To learn how to install, manage, and use fonts, **see** Chapter 10, "Managing and Using Fonts," **p. 213**.

# Opening Documents in Mac OS X

Using most applications involves opening documents; Mac OS X offers several features that applications can use to make opening documents fast and easy.

There are several ways you can open documents:

- Select the document's icon in a Finder window, and select the Finder's Open command (press ⌘-O).
- Double-click a document's icon in the Finder.
- Single-click a document's icon on the Dock or Sidebar.
- Drag a document icon or alias onto an application's icon or alias (on the desktop, in a Finder window, or on the Dock).
- Select the document's icon or alias, and press ⌘-down arrow.
- Open the document using an Automator application, AppleScript, or other macro.
- Open a compatible application, and use its Open command to open a document.

**NOTE**

> If you see the document's icon on the Dock, an alias to that document has been placed there. If you see a thumbnail of the document's window on the Dock, that document is open, and its window has been minimized. In either case, single-clicking the icon causes the document to open so you can work on it.

7

Most of these techniques are simple. The Mac OS X Open dialog box is a good model of all the file selection dialog boxes you will encounter, so you should become very familiar with the way it works. Also, you need to understand how you can associate documents with specific applications so you can determine which application opens when you open a document.

## USING THE MAC OS X OPEN DIALOG BOX

Under Mac OS X version 10.5, Open dialog boxes are harmonized with Finder windows so behavior of these windows is similar.

As under previous versions of Mac OS X, different applications can add features to the Open dialog box for specific purposes, but most Open dialog boxes offer a similar set of features.

**NOTE**

> Many dialog boxes, although not called Open, are actually the Open dialog box with the name modified to suit the specific purpose at hand. These dialog boxes have names such as Choose a Picture, Choose a File, and so on. However, they all work in basically the same way and offer similar features as the Open dialog box.

A typical Open dialog box is shown in Figure 7.5.

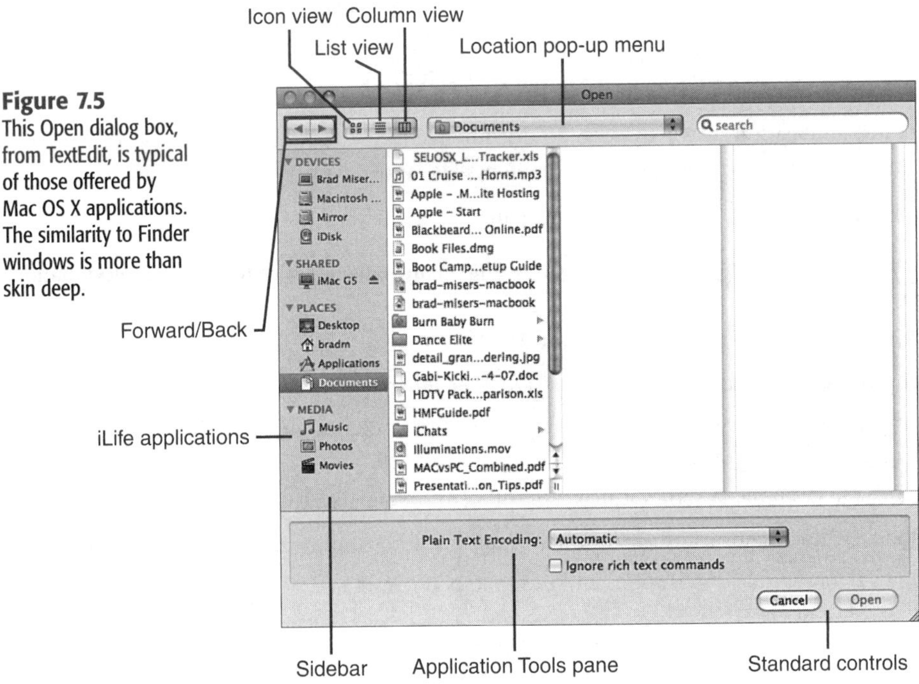


**Figure 7.5**
This Open dialog box, from TextEdit, is typical of those offered by Mac OS X applications. The similarity to Finder windows is more than skin deep.

If you read through earlier chapters in this book, you are quite knowledgeable of Finder windows, and Open dialog boxes work like Finder windows in many ways. For example, the Sidebar enables you to choose the location where you want to open a file. When you select a place, its contents appear in the center pane of the window. You can choose to view this pane in the Icon, List, or the Columns view; again, these views are the same as when you are viewing Finder windows. You can use the Icon, List, or Columns view buttons to change the view used in the dialog box. You can also use the Icon button's pop-up menu to configure how icons appear in the dialog box. You can use the Forward and Back buttons to move back to locations you viewed previously.

⇨ To learn how to work with Finder windows, **see** Chapter 2, "Viewing and Navigating Mac OS X Finder Windows," **p. 17**.

New in Mac OS X 10.5, the Media section of the Sidebar allows you to quickly access files that you have stored in your iLife applications. When you click on one of these familiar icons, you will be able to select a file from that application. This can be helpful, as the path to these files is often complex.

The location shown in the Location pop-up menu is the currently selected folder whose contents are displayed in the pane. For example, if Documents is shown in the Location pop-up menu, the Documents folder is selected and its contents are displayed. If you have selected the Columns view, the contents of the location selection on the Location pop-up menu appears in the leftmost column.

You can also use the Location pop-up menu to quickly access many areas of your Mac, from your current location up to the volume on which Mac OS X is installed (see Figure 7.6).

**Figure 7.6**
The Location pop-up menu in the Open dialog box enables you to move "up" from your current location along with places you've been recently.

If you use the Icon or List views to open a file or folder, simply move to it, select it, and click Open, or double-click the file or folder you want to open. If you use the Columns view and select a folder, that folder becomes selected and you see its contents in the pane to the right of the folder. You can then select a folder or document it contains. In either view, you can select a document, and double-click it or click Open.

You can change the Open dialog box in several ways, including the following:

- Change the view.
- Use the resize handle to make the dialog box larger or smaller.
- Click the Maximize button to make the dialog box its maximum size to fill up the screen.

> **NOTE**
>
> The Maximize button is not included in the Open dialog box under all applications—typically, only Cocoa applications include this feature.

- Drag the dialog box around the screen. Because the Open dialog box is an independent window, you can move it around to move it out of the way.

The Open dialog box might contain application-specific controls. For example, in Figure 7.6, you saw the Plain Text Encoding pop-up menu that lets you choose the type of encoding you want to use. In the Application Tools pane, you will also see different tools depending on the application in which you are working. As you locate and open files or documents, you should be aware of these additional options and apply them as needed.

## DETERMINING THE APPLICATION THAT OPENS WHEN YOU OPEN A DOCUMENT

When you open a document, the system determines which application should be used to open that file (other than when you open a document from within an application using its Open command, of course). Typically, the document's creator opens if it is installed on your Mac, such as Microsoft Word opening a `.doc` file

When opening a file from outside an application, several factors determine which application opens when you open a document, including the document's file type and creator information, as well as the file's filename extension. Mac OS X does a good job evaluating these properties to ensure that the correct application opens.

However, there might be situations in which you want to use a different application than the one the system selects, or you might not have the application that was used to create the document. In such cases, you can choose the application in which a document opens.

You can also change the association for all files of a specific type to determine which application opens when you open any file of that type.

There are two ways to associate document types with the applications used to open them. One is by using the Get Info window; the other is by using a document's contextual menu.

### USING THE GET INFO WINDOW TO ASSOCIATE DOCUMENTS WITH AN APPLICATION

You can use the Open with section of the Info window to determine which application is used to open a file.

1. Select the document you are interested in, and press ⌘-I. The Info window appears.
2. Expand the Open with section. The application that is currently associated with the document is shown on the pop-up menu. The associated application is called the default application—the text (default) appears after the application name when you open the pop-up menu.
3. Open the pop-up menu. You will see all the applications the system recognizes as being able to open the document, along with the Other selection (see Figure 7.7).

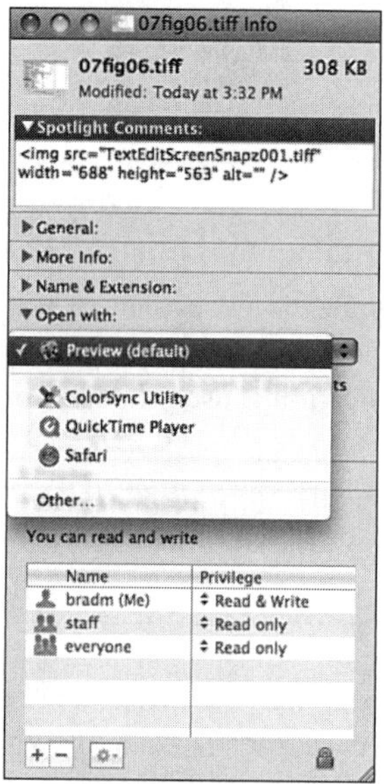


**Figure 7.7**
This menu lists all the applications Mac OS X thinks you can use on the document.

4. If one of the listed applications is the one you want to associate with the document, choose it on the menu. The document opens with that application the next time you open it.
5. If you want to select an application that is not shown on the pop-up menu, select Other. You will see the Choose Other Application sheet (see Figure 7.8).

   The Choose Other Application sheet moves to the Applications directory automatically, and by default, it shows you only the recommended applications, which are those that Mac OS X recognizes as being compatible with the document. This set of applications might or might not be the same as shown on the pop-up menu in the Info window. Mac OS X recognizes that some applications that can open files of that type might not really be intended to work with those files and so doesn't show them in the pop-up menu. However, they might be active in the Choose Other Application dialog box. Applications Mac OS X doesn't think can be used at all are grayed out.

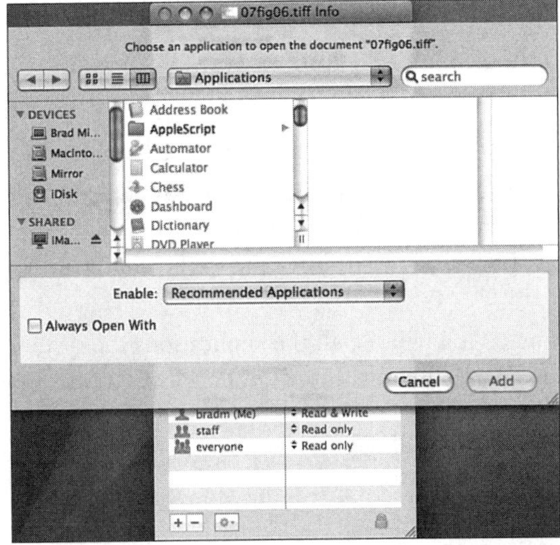


**Figure 7.8**
You can use the Choose Other Application sheet to select applications to open a document, even if Mac OS X doesn't recommend them.

6. To make all applications active, select All Applications from the Enable pop-up menu.
7. Use the sheet's controls to move to the application you want to select, select it, and click Add. After you click Add, you return to the Info window and the application you selected appears in the window. That application is used the next time you open the file.

**TIP**

> If you want to permanently change the application used to open the document, check the "Always Open With" box.

**CAUTION**

> Just because you told Mac OS X to use a specific application, even if it is the one that Mac OS X recommended, that doesn't mean you will actually be able to open the document with the application you select. If you try to open the document and generate error messages, you need to go back and select an application that can handle the type of file you are working with.

If you choose an application that Mac OS X isn't sure can open files of the selected type, you see a warning saying so in the sheet after you select the application. You can proceed even when you see the warning, but you might get unexpected results.

**TIP**

> Even though Mac OS X tries to recommend applications that are appropriate for the selected document, it doesn't always do a great job. In those situations, use the All Applications command on the Enable pop-up menu to add the application you want to use for the document.

You can also use the Info window to associate all files of a specific type with an application. Here's how:

1. Use the previous steps to associate a type of file with an application. After you have changed the application association, the Change All button becomes active.
2. Click the Change All button. You will see a warning dialog box that explains what you are about to do; for example, it lists the document types you are changing and the application with which you will associate documents of that type (see Figure 7.9).

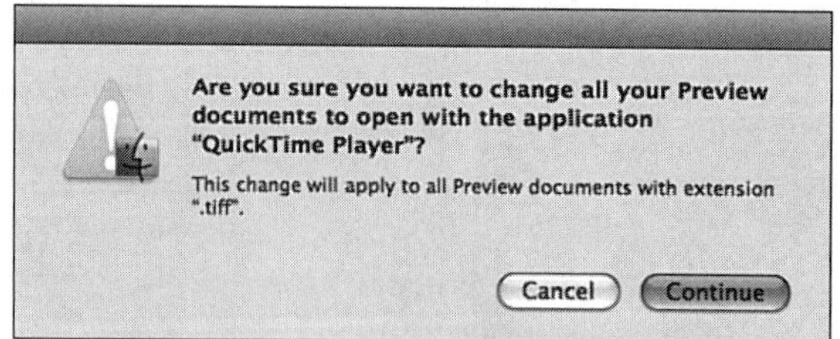
Are you sure you want to change all your Preview documents to open with the application "QuickTime Player"?
This change will apply to all Preview documents with extension ".tiff".
Cancel
Continue

**Figure 7.9**
This warning dialog box provides the information you need to ensure that the file association you are creating is the correct one.

3. If you are sure that you want to make the change, click Continue. All files of the selected type become associated with the application you selected. The application you selected becomes the default application for all documents of that type.

### Using a Contextual Menu to Open a Document with a Specific Application

You can also use a file's contextual menu to determine which application is used to open it by doing the following:

1. Select a document that you want to open with a specific application.
2. Hold down the Control key, and click the file to open its contextual menu.
3. Select Open With. Another menu appears that lists all the applications the system recognizes as being compatible with the document you are trying to open. The application currently associated with the document is marked as the default (see Figure 7.10).
4. Select the application with which you want to open the document from the list. If you want to use an application that is not on the list, select Other, and use the Choose Other Application sheet to move to and select the application you want to use. (See the preceding section for detailed information on how this sheet works.) The document opens in the application you selected.

When you use this technique, the document is associated with the application only if you save the document from within that application. If you simply open it and view it, the previous application continues to be associated with the document.

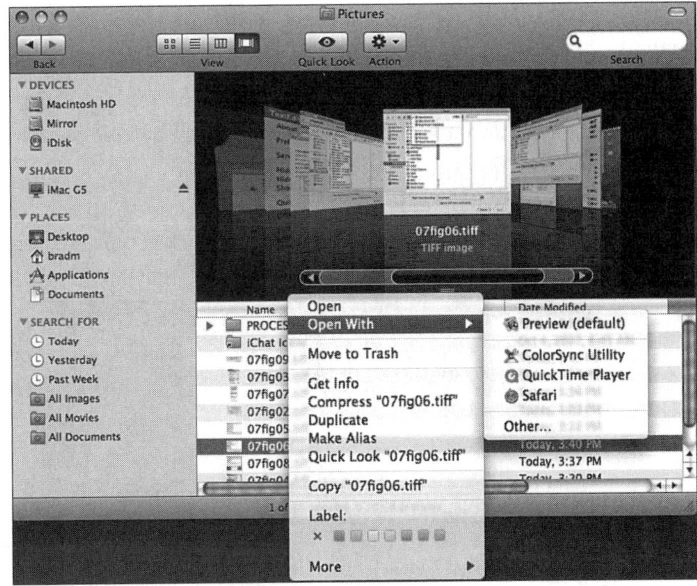


**Figure 7.10**
This menu provides the same controls as the Open with section of a document's Info window.

If you want the file to always open with a different application, even if you don't make any changes to it, open the contextual menu, and then press the Option key. The Open With command becomes the Always Open With command. After you choose an application, the file is associated with that application and always opens in it.

**NOTE**

> Note that setting an application for all files with a specific type and creator combination does not override any documents for which you have set a specific application. For example, suppose you set the application to use for a specific document. Then, using another document, you change the application used for documents of that type and creator to be a different application. The first document would still open with the specific application you selected previously.

**TIP**

> You can also access the same Open, Open With, and Always Open With commands on the Action pop-up menu in the Finder window's toolbar.



### USING FILENAME EXTENSIONS TO ASSOCIATE DOCUMENTS WITH APPLICATIONS

You can also try to change the application associated with a specific document by changing the document's filename extension. For example, to associate QuickTime Player with a document, you would change its extension to `.mov`. When you do so, the file's icon might change to reflect that extension, and the document opens with the application that extension is associated with. But this doesn't always happen. Do the following:

1. Edit the filename extension of the file you want to associate with an application so the extension is unique to that application. For example, you can change `.rtf` to `.doc` to associate a file with Microsoft Word.

   The filename extension you use must be specific to an application for this to work. For example, some filename extensions, such as `.tiff`, can be associated with many applications. You must use the Info window or contextual menu to change the association for such files.

   A warning dialog box appears (see Figure 7.11). In this dialog box, you see two buttons: One keeps the file's current filename extension, and other causes the new one to be used.

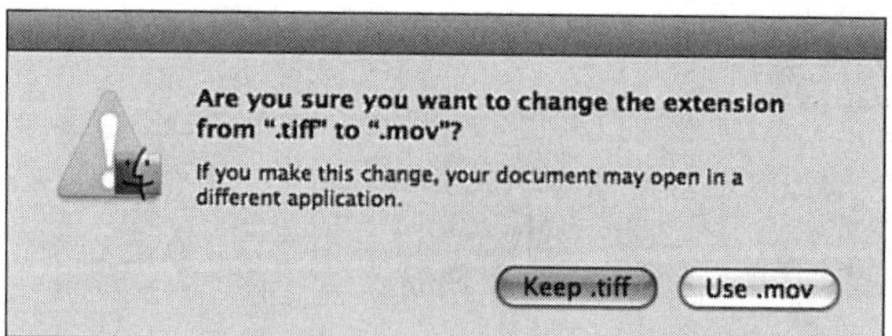


**Figure 7.11**
When you change a filename extension, you have to confirm the change by clicking the Use button in a dialog box like this one.

2. Click the Use button; the filename extension is changed. The file is associated with the application currently associated with files that have the filename extension you chose to use. (If you click the Keep button, nothing is changed.)

Changing the filename extension does not override a selection you have made with the Info window. If you associate an application with a document by using the Info window tools and then subsequently change the filename extension, the choice you made with the Info window overrides the filename extension and determines the application used to open that document.

# Saving Documents in Mac OS X

When you use applications, you will also be saving documents frequently. Fortunately, Save sheets under Mac OS X are also similar to Finder windows, just like Open dialog boxes.

The specific Save sheet or dialog box you see depends on the application you are using. Cocoa and some carbonized applications use the Save sheet that is described in this section. Some carbonized applications use the older Save dialog boxes.

A typical Mac OS X Save sheet is shown in Figure 7.12.

**NOTE**

> You can resize the Save sheet using its Resize handle. It's size is independent of the document window from which it comes, but it always remains attached to the top of that window.

7

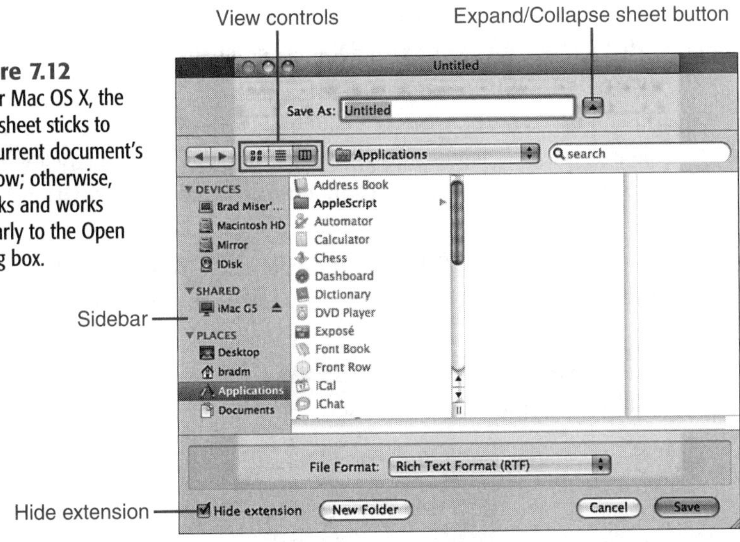


**Figure 7.12**
Under Mac OS X, the Save sheet sticks to the current document's window; otherwise, it looks and works similarly to the Open dialog box.

The sheet contains the Save As text box in which you enter the filename. If you click the Expand/Collapse button, the sheet expands so you see a window that is very similar to the Open dialog box you learned about in the previous section. If you click this button again, you see the collapsed version of the sheet.

**NOTE**

> One of the benefits of a sheet is that an open sheet will not prevent you from working with other documents, even within the same application. The sheet stays with the document to which it is attached. You can open, work with, and save other documents without closing the sheet.

Save sheets and Open dialog boxes look and work very similarly, but a couple of items on Save sheets aren't on Open dialog boxes so you need to pay attention to them.

One is the Format pop-up menu, which is sometimes called File Format depending on the application in which you are working. You use this pop-up menu to choose the format of the file you are saving.

The other is the Hide extension check box. If you check this box, the filename extension is hidden. If you uncheck this box, which I recommend that you do, the filename extension is shown in the Save As box. Because filename extensions are important clues about how a document will open, you should generally choose to display them.

Some applications work in an opposite way: Instead of the Hide extension check box, their Save sheets include the "Append file extension" check box. When this box is checked, the filename extension is added to the file's name.

**TIP**

> Creating a new folder (using the New Folder button) in the Save As sheet can be a bit confusing. The new folder is created in the currently selected directory, which is shown in the Location pop-up menu. Because viewing multiple levels of the hierarchy using the Columns view controls is easy, you might be creating a new folder in a location you didn't realize you had selected. Before using that command, double-check the Location pop-up menu to ensure that you have selected the correct location to create the new folder.

In some applications' Save As sheet, you will see additional controls, such as an Options button that enables you to configure options for the file format you select.

## UNDERSTANDING FILENAMES AND FILENAME EXTENSIONS

An important aspect of saving documents under Mac OS X is that it uses filename extensions. Filename extensions consist of a period and three or more characters that are added to the end of the filename. When you save a document, most Cocoa and carbonized applications automatically append the correct filename extension for the type of file you are saving. Mac OS X uses the filename extension to associate the file with a particular application.

The addition of filename extensions to Mac filenames can be confusing because one of Mac's strengths has traditionally been the lack of such extensions. However, because most applications tack the appropriate filename extension onto the filename you enter automatically, you generally don't have to worry about them.

**NOTE**

> In fact, if an extension is left off a filename, the Mac still uses the file creator and type information to open the file in a compatible application. However, you should include filename extensions for all documents you save.

Most Mac OS X files have a filename extension, including documents, system resources, and so on. In fact, a bewildering number of filename extensions exist under Mac OS X, and because it is based on the Unix operating system, Mac filename extensions are not limited to a certain number of characters. However, most document filename extensions consist of three or four characters. Some examples are shown in Table 7.2.

**TABLE 7.2 EXAMPLES OF MAC DOCUMENT FILENAME EXTENSIONS**

| Filename Extension | What It Stands For | Default Application Associated with It |
|---|---|---|
| `.mov` | Movie | QuickTime Player |
| `.tiff` | Tagged Interchange File Format | Preview |
| `.rtfd` | Rich Text Formatted Document | TextEdit |
| `.rtf` | Rich Text Format | TextEdit |

*continues*

**TABLE 7.2 CONTINUED**

| Filename Extension | What It Stands For | Default Application Associated with It |
|---|---|---|
| `.jpg` or `.jpeg` | Joint Photographic Experts Group | Preview |
| `.pdf` | Portable Document Format | Preview |
| `.html` | Hypertext Markup Language | Default web browser (such as Safari) |
| `.doc` | Microsoft Word Document | Word |
| `.xls` | Microsoft Excel Spreadsheet | Excel |
| `.mp3` | Motion Picture Experts Group, Audio Layer 3 | iTunes |

**System Filename Extensions**

Although dealing with document filename extensions is fairly straightforward, dealing with system filename extensions can get really ugly. Some are straightforward, such as `.app` for applications and `.dock` for docklings, but many seem to be gibberish. Usually, you can just take system filename extensions as they are (because you can't change them), and sometimes you can even figure out what they stand for. For example, the `.kext` filename extension stands for kernel extension, which is an extension to the operating system software.

One system filename extension that is useful to know is `.plist`. It indicates a preference file, as in `iTunes.plist`, which is the preferences for the iTunes application.

At the top of the Save sheet, you enter the filename you want to use. Under Mac OS X, you can use long filenames—up to 255 characters, including the filename extension and the period between the filename extension and the filename itself (so be sure to allow room for the filename extension when you enter a filename). When you save a document in many applications, the appropriate filename extension is added to the filename automatically. (You won't see it if the Hide extension check box is checked.) As mentioned previously, in some applications, you have to check a box to add the filename extension to the filename.

If you intend to share your files with people who use older operating systems (such as Mac OS 9 or Windows 95), you need to keep the name under 31 characters, including the filename extension the application will add to the name you enter.

If you want to share your files with Windows computer users, you need to ensure that the filename extension used is comprehensible to Windows PCs.



**NOTE**

> Some applications provide a File Format pop-up menu in the Save As sheet that you can use to choose the file format in which you want to save the document. Sometimes, the options on it are disabled. In such cases, look for the Save To command. This command enables you to save one file type to another type. The Save To dialog box looks and works exactly as the Save As sheet does, except that the options on the File Format pop-up menu are enabled.

## VIEWING OR HIDING FILENAME EXTENSIONS

Under Mac OS X, you have the option to view or hide filename extensions. However, filename extensions are usually used whether you can see them or not. Generally, I recommend that you always view them because they provide valuable information.

You can choose to hide filename extensions for specific files, or you can set the Finder to always display filename extensions for all files (regardless of the filename extension setting for a specific file).

You can show or hide the filename extensions for specific files by using the following steps:

1. In a Finder window, select the file for which you want to hide the filename extension.
2. Open the Info window.
3. Expand the Name & Extension section.
4. Check the "Hide extension" check box. (To show the extension for a file, uncheck this box.)
5. Close the Info window.

**TIP**

> You can edit a file's name and filename extension in the box in the Name & Extension pane of the Info window.

To override the filename extension display setting for every file, use the following steps:

1. Open the Finder Preferences window.
2. Click the Advanced button to make the Advanced pane appear.
3. Check the "Show all file extensions" check box.
4. Close the Finder Preferences window.

Filename extensions will always be shown, regardless of the "Hide extension" check box in the Info window.

Under most applications, the filename extension status (hidden or not) for specific files is saved, even when you use the Finder preferences to always display filename extensions. If you turn off "Show all file extensions" again, the filename extensions for any files you have hidden become hidden again.

Some applications, especially carbonized applications, don't automatically add filename extensions unless the appropriate check box is checked in the Save sheet.



## SAVING DOCUMENTS AS PDFS

One of the many benefits of Mac OS X is that the Portable Document Format (PDF) is a native format. This means you can create a PDF from *any* application without using Adobe's Acrobat or Distiller (although those tools offer some special features that are not available to Mac OS X natively).

PDF documents are useful for two primary reasons. First, they retain their appearance regardless of the fonts and applications installed on the viewing computer. Second, PDF documents can be viewed natively in Mac OS X (using the Preview application) or by Adobe's free Reader application (which is available for all platforms). These reasons make PDF the ideal format for distributing and viewing documents electronically.

PDFs also retain their formatting when they are printed. This makes PDF a good way to distribute documents that you know the recipient will want in hard copy. You can email a PDF, and the receiver can print it. Unlike faxing, in which the document format degrades significantly, when the recipient prints the PDF, it will look as good as it does when you send it.

An additional benefit to PDFs is that they can't be easily modified. When you send a PDF to someone, he will have a difficult time changing it. (It can't be changed at all without special tools.) So, PDFs are also a good way to secure documents you provide to others.

To create a PDF version of a document, you use the Print command to "print" the document to a PDF file:

1. Create your document using the appropriate application.
2. Save the document.
3. Select File, Print to open the Print sheet.

**NOTE**

> You probably noticed that the Print dialog box is also a sheet. This means you can leave it open and work with other documents in the same or different applications.

4. Open the PDF drop-down menu, and select "Save as PDF."
5. Use the Save dialog box (its not a sheet when you save to PDF) to name the file and choose a location. You can also add identification information and configure security options.
6. Click Save.

A PDF file is created in the location you specify. This document can be viewed using the Preview application or with Adobe Reader.

⇨ To learn about using Preview to view PDFs, **see** "Using Preview to Read PDFs," **p. 702**.

⇨ To learn more about creating PDFs, **see** "Creating PDF Files," **p. 828**.



**NOTE**

> You can also choose to print documents in the PostScript file format. To do this, select "Save as PostScript" on the PDF drop-down menu on the Print sheet. Then use the Save to File sheet to choose a location and save the document.

# TROUBLESHOOTING

## I CAN'T INSTALL AN APPLICATION BECAUSE I DON'T HAVE SUFFICIENT PRIVILEGES

*When I try to install an application, I see an error message stating that I do not have sufficient privileges.*

To install an application in the Applications folder, you must be logged in as an administrator. If you can't log in as an administrator, try installing the application in your Home folder instead.

If this doesn't work, you might have to log in as root to install the application.

⇨ To get additional help, **see** "Enabling the Root User Account," **p. 231**.

## I CAN'T DRAG A DOCUMENT ON AN ICON TO OPEN IT

*When I try to open a document by dragging its icon on top of an application's icon, the icon doesn't highlight so that it will open.*

This happens when you try to open a document for which the application is not recommended. You can force it to open by holding down the Option-⌘ keys while you drag the document's icon onto the application's icon.

You can also associate an application with a document using the document's Info window.

## WHEN I OPEN AN APPLICATION, WHAT I SEE IS INCOMPREHENSIBLE

*I opened a document, but what appears onscreen is a bunch of gobbledy-gook.*

This happens when you open a file that contains data the application can't interpret. Use the Info window for the document to associate a different application with the document; using an application that Mac OS X lists as a recommended application makes it more likely to open successfully. You can also try opening the document from within an application rather than from the Finder.

PART II

# MASTERING THE SYSTEM

# CHAPTER 8

# Running Windows and Windows Applications

## In this chapter

## CHOOSING HOW TO RUN WINDOWS ON A MAC

Over the years, I've tried to get a lot of people to switch from Windows computers to the Mac. There was one argument that I could never overcome and when we hit it, the conversation was over and the person I was speaking with was left with Windows. The "winning" argument was, "I'd like to use a Mac, but I have to run XYZ and it's only available for Windows." In most cases, the person was right and she had a legitimate need for the application. Using a Windows PC was the only choice. As badly as I felt, I had to turn away and let the Windows havoc be wrought.

With the rise of Intel Macs, this vexing argument is finally slain. Windows and Windows applications can be run just as well (and even better in many cases) on a Mac than they can on hardware designed for Windows. You can enjoy Mac bliss most of the time, but when you do need to run Windows, you can fire it up on your Mac and use the Windows applications.

There are two basic options to get Windows running on a Mac.

### BOOT CAMP

The option that is native to Mac OS X is running Windows via Boot Camp. When you use this option, you can choose to boot your Mac up in the Mac OS or in Windows. When you boot up in Windows, you have a fully-functional Windows PC on your hands (it will probably outperform many dedicated Windows machines too). This option is great because it provides you with the ability to run Windows and its applications on your Mac. And you don't have to pay anything else for the Boot Camp software because it's built into Mac OS X. However, this method has one significant, and in my opinion, fatal flaw. That is that you have to restart your computer each time you want to switch from Mac to Windows and then back again. If you run Windows applications only very rarely, this might not be so bad, but if you're like me and regularly run a couple of Windows applications, you waste a lot of time restarting the computer.

### VIRTUALIZATION SOFTWARE

The second option is to use virtualization software. This approach provides a virtual environment (also called a virtual machine) in which you install and run Windows. Because the virtualization software is just another application running on the Mac, you can switch to it as easily as moving to any open Mac application. So, you can leave Windows running all the time and jump into it when you need it. This makes using Windows much more convenient than the Boot Camp option. Surprisingly (to me anyway), the performance of Windows in the virtual environment isn't noticeably slower than running it under Boot Camp or even on some Windows hardware. The only downside is the cost of the virtualization software itself. If you use Windows more than rarely, the time you save switching back and forth more than makes up the cost of the software. Plus, with a virtual approach, you can easily share data and files between the Mac OS and Windows.

In the remainder of this chapter, you'll get information about each of these methods so you can choose the one that works the best for you.

**NOTE**

> To run Windows on a Mac, you do have to purchase a *full* copy of Windows to install whether you use Boot Camp or a virtualization application. The cost for this varies depending on the flavor of Windows you purchase and how you purchase it. If you are getting Windows only to run specific applications, see whether the applications you need are supported on Windows XP. If so, you might be able to save a few dollars using this older version of Windows. At press time, a full version of Windows Vista Home Basic Edition was about $180. If you're only going to be using Windows to run Windows applications, the Basic Edition should be sufficient. Make sure you get a full version; an upgrade version won't work.

# Using Boot Camp to Run Windows on a Mac

The general steps to get Windows running under Boot Camp are the following:

1. Run the Boot Camp Assistant to prepare your Mac for Windows and install it.
2. Run Windows.

**NOTE**

> To get support for Boot Camp, visit www.apple.com/support/bootcamp/.

## Running the Boot Camp Assistant and Installing Windows

The Boot Camp Assistant prepares your Mac for a Windows installation. One of the things it does is to partition a hard drive to create a volume on which Windows will be installed and from which you'll boot up when you want to run Windows. To use the Boot Camp Assistant, do the following:

**CAUTION**

> Part of the Boot Camp preparation is to partition your Mac's internal hard drive. Before you do this, make sure you have all your data backed up in case something goes wrong.

1. Launch Boot Camp Assistant (Applications/Utilities). You see the first screen of the assistant (see Figure 8.1).
2. Click Continue. You see the Create a Partition for Windows screen (see Figure 8.2). On the left, you see the partition for Mac OS X, whereas on the right you see the partition for Windows, which is a minimum of 5GB.
3. Set the size of the Windows partition by dragging the Resize handle between the two partitions to the left, clicking the Divide Equally button to divide the disk in two partitions, or clicking the Use 32 GB button to set the Windows partition at 32GB. The 32GB option is a reasonable size for many Windows environments, but remember that you'll be limited to the partition's size when you run Windows so make sure you allow plenty of space if you are going to install lots of Windows applications.

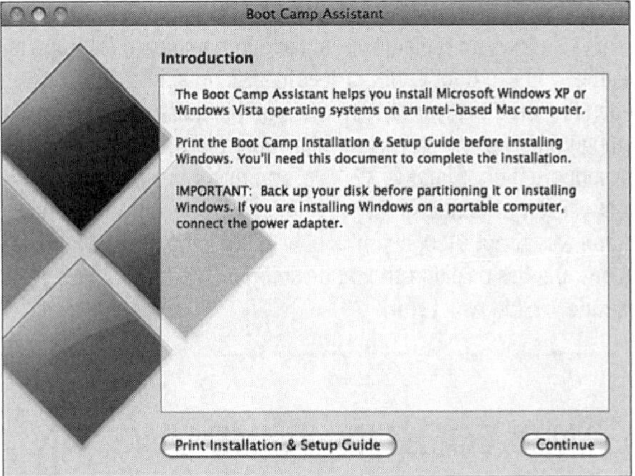


**Figure 8.1**
The Boot Camp Assistant walks you through the process of preparing for Boot Camp.

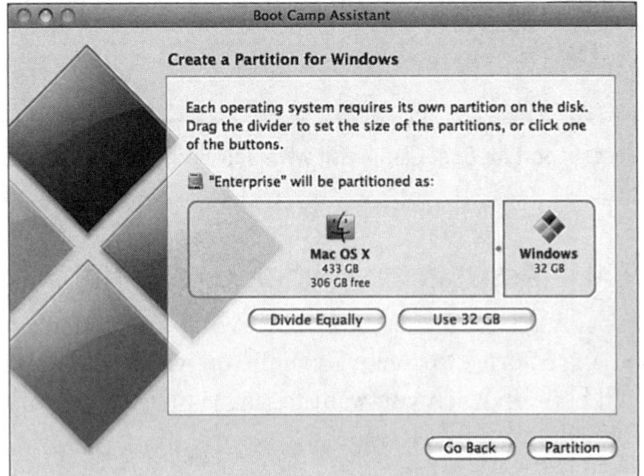


**Figure 8.2**
In order to run Windows under Boot Camp, you must create a Windows partition on your Mac's internal hard drive.

4. Click Partition. The partition process starts and you see its status in the window. When the process is complete, you're prompted to insert your Windows installation disc (see Figure 8.3).
5. Insert the Windows installation disc, wait until it is mounted on the Mac, and click Start Installation.

   The Mac restarts and boots from the Windows installation disc. The installation application starts installing files; you see the progress at the bottom of the blue Windows Setup screen.

**NOTE**

> These steps are based on Windows XP. If you install a different version of Windows, some of the details might be a bit different.

**Figure 8.3**
When you see this screen, insert your Windows installation disc to start the installation process on the partition you just created.

6. When the Welcome To Setup screen appears, press the Return key (which is the equivalent to the Enter key on Windows).
7. Press F8 to agree to the Windows license information.
8. Select the BOOTCAMP partition and press the Return key.
9. Select either the FAT (Quick) or NTFS (Quick) format option. Choose NTFS if you want Windows to be more secure and reliable. Choose FAT if you want to be able to save files to the Windows partition while using Mac OS X.

**CAUTION**

> Make sure you select the correct partition to install Windows on. If you don't, you might overwrite a partition with Mac OS X or your data on it, in which case those data are lost. You should install Windows only on the BOOTCAMP partition.

10. Double-check to make sure you have the BOOTCAMP partition selected and press the F key. The partition is formatted according to the format selection you made.

    When the format process is complete, the Mac restarts with Windows instead of the Mac OS. The Windows Setup Wizard runs.
11. Work through the various screens of the Setup Wizard to configure Windows. Read the information on each screen and make the appropriate selections based on your preferences. For example, you'll need to enter the Windows product key, set time and date, name the computer, configure how you'll connect to the Internet, and so on. You can expect this process to take about 30 or 40 minutes.

**NOTE**

> Another benefit of using a virtualization approach is that the virtualization software does almost all the Windows configuration for you automatically, making installing Windows much easier and faster to install.

When the process is complete, the Mac restarts again. This time it starts up in Windows and you see the Windows Setup application.

12. Follow the onscreen prompts to do some basic configuration, including selecting security settings and creating one or more user accounts.
13. When you complete the Setup application, click Finish. The Windows desktop appears.
14. Eject the Windows installation disc.
15. Insert the Mac OS X installation disc.
16. Follow the onscreen instructions to complete the installation of the various drivers Windows needs to work with the Mac hardware.
17. At the prompt, restart the computer. Windows starts up.

    If you're prompted by the New Hardware Wizard, follow the onscreen prompts to work through them. Most of the time, the default selections work.
18. To return to the Mac, choose Start menu, Shut Down, Turn Off (Windows XP Home edition).
19. Restart the Mac and hold the Option key down.

**NOTE**

> Some wireless keyboards or mice won't be recognized during the startup process. If yours isn't, connect a wired keyboard to control the startup process.

20. Choose the Mac OS X startup volume and press the Return key. The Mac starts up under Mac OS X again.

## RUNNING WINDOWS

After you've installed Windows under Boot Camp, you can transform your Mac into a Windows PC by performing the following steps:

**CAUTION**

> Windows is constantly under attack from viruses. Running Windows on a Mac doesn't protect you from these threats when you are using the Windows environment; it's as susceptible to attacks as Windows on Windows hardware is. You should install and use security software under Windows as soon as you get your Windows environment running. See "Mac OS X to the Max: Protecting Windows on a Mac from Attack" at the end of this chapter for some suggestions.

**TIP**

> You can choose the startup volume during the startup process by holding the Option key down while the Mac restarts. You see all the available startup volumes, such as your Mac OS X and Windows volumes. Click the volume you want to use and press Return. The Mac starts up under the selected volume.

1. Open the System Preferences application.
2. Select the Startup Disk icon.
3. Choose the Windows startup disk (see Figure 8.4).

**Figure 8.4**
When you see this screen, insert your Windows installation disc to start the installation process on the partition you just created.

4. Click Restart and then click Restart again at the prompt. The Mac restarts and the Windows desktop appears.

**CAUTION**

You must activate a copy of Windows to keep it running for more than 30 days. When you do this, the copy of Windows you run is registered to the specific computer on which you activate it as a means to limit illegal copies of Windows. Unfortunately, you can activate Windows under only one environment (Boot Camp or a virtual machine) on the same computer. Don't activate your copy of Windows until you're sure which method you are going to run it under (Boot Camp or a virtual machine) because you'll have to pay for a new copy of Windows to activate it under a different scheme (or try to explain the situation to Microsoft to get the previous activation "undone" so you can activate it under a different environment).

5. Launch existing Windows applications or install new applications from the Web or from installation discs.
6. When you're done with Windows, choose Start menu, Shut Down, Turn Off (Windows XP Home edition). Windows shuts down as does the Mac.
7. Power up the Mac and hold the Option key down.
8. Select the Mac OS X startup volume and press Return. The Mac starts up in Mac OS X again.

8

**TIP**

> If you decide that you don't want to use Boot Camp to run Windows, launch the Boot Camp Assistant, click Continue, choose Create or remove a Windows partition, click Continue, and the click Restore. The Windows partition will be deleted and the space returned to the Mac OS. Any files you've stored on the Windows partition will be lost so make sure they are backed up before doing this.

# USING PARALLELS DESKTOP FOR MAC TO RUN WINDOWS VIRTUALLY ON A MAC

Following are the general steps to get Windows running under a virtual environment:

1. Purchase, download, and install the virtualization software.
2. Configure a virtual environment and install Windows.
3. Run Windows in the virtual environment.

There are several virtualization applications available, but the one that works best for me is Parallels Desktop for Mac. This application is simple to install and configure and it performs very well. It has lots of great features, including the ability to easily share data and files between the Mac OS and Windows. You can download and try it before you purchase the application; at press time, it cost about $80 to continue using the application beyond the 15-day trial period. The remainder of this section focuses on using Parallels Desktop for Mac.

**NOTE**

> For more detailed information about Parallels and to download a trial version, visit www.parallels.com/en/products/desktop/.

## INSTALLING PARALLELS DESKTOP

To install Parallels Desktop, perform the following steps:

1. Move to www.parallels.com/en/products/desktop/.
2. Click the Download Trial link. You move to the download page (see Figure 8.5).
3. Download the Parallels Desktop for Mac installer.
4. While you're waiting for the download to complete, click the "free 15-day trial activation" link.
5. Create a new account to request the activation link be sent to your email address. The activation code will be emailed to the address you entered.
6. When the download process is complete, move back to the desktop and run the Install Parallels Desktop application (see Figure 8.6).

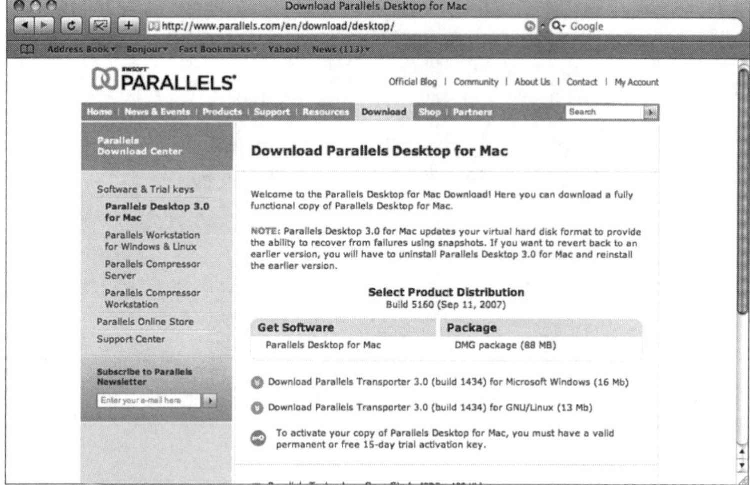


**Figure 8.5**
From the Parallels Desktop for Mac download page, you can download the application and request an activation code for the free trial period.

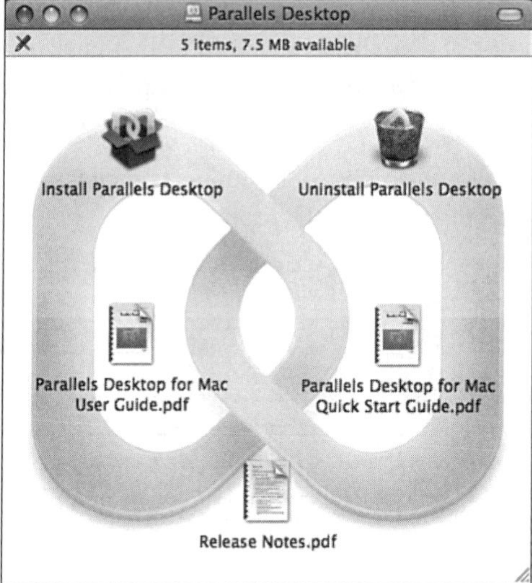


**Figure 8.6**
After Parallels Desktop has downloaded, run its installer.

7. Follow the onscreen instructions to complete the installation. When the process is done, you see the completion screen (see Figure 8.7).
8. Click Close to quit the installer. You're ready to launch Parallels and configure a virtual environment.

**Figure 8.7**
Installing Parallels Desktop takes only a few minutes.

## Configuring a Virtual Environment and Installing Windows

Each OS you run under Parallels has its own virtual environment for which you can set various settings, such as the amount of disk space dedicated to that environment, which the environment is stored, and so on. Before you can install Windows, you create and configure a virtual environment for it.

1. Launch Parallels Desktop (Applications folder unless you chose a different installation location). You're prompted to enter an activation code.
2. Click Enter Activation Key. The Enter Activation Key sheet appears (see Figure 8.8).

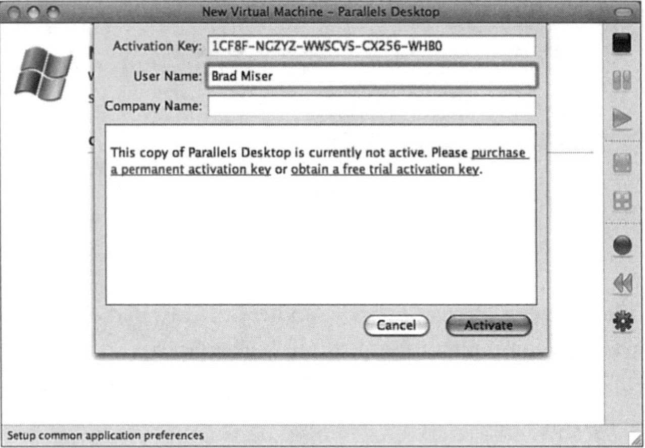


**Figure 8.8**
To create a virtual environment, you need to enter an activation key, such as one for the free trial period.

3. Enter the activation key, your name, and click Activate. You see the OS Installation Assistant window. This assistant will lead you through the creation of the virtual environment.

4. If you will install Windows XP or Vista, choose the Windows Express mode and click Next.
5. Select Windows XP or Windows Vista and click Next.
6. Enter the Windows product key from your Windows installation disc, enter your name, and click Next (see Figure 8.9).

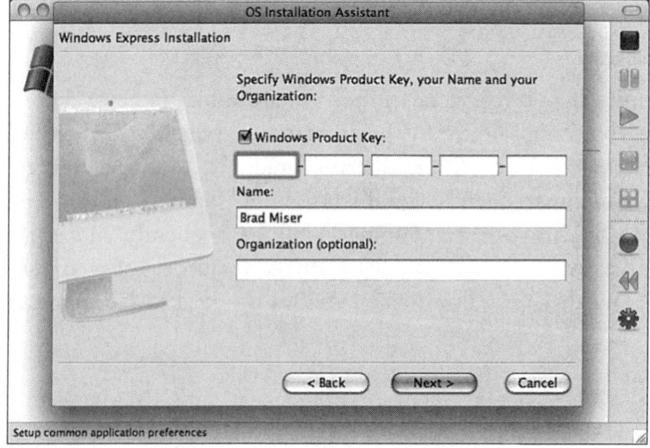


**Figure 8.9**
To create a virtual environment, you need to enter the product key from your Windows installation disc.

7. Name the virtual environment; the default name is the name of the version of Windows you chose to install, but you can call it something else if you'd like (see Figure 8.10).

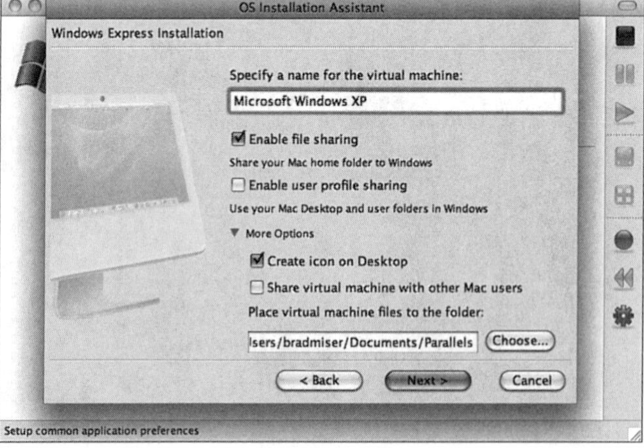


**Figure 8.10**
These settings configure several important aspects of your Windows environment, such as whether you can share files with the Mac OS and whether other users will be able to access the environment you create.

8. Check the Enable File Sharing check box if you want to be able to share your Mac Home folder with the Windows environment.
9. Check the "Enable user profile sharing" check box if you want to be able to access your Mac's desktop and user folders from within Windows.

10. Expand the More Options section.
11. If you want a Parallels icon on your desktop, check the "Create icon on Desktop" check box.
12. To enable other users on your Mac to access Windows, check the "Share virtual machine with other Mac users" check box.
13. If you didn't check the check box in step 12 and want to specify a different location for the environment's files, click Choose and select the installation location.
14. Click Next.
15. To optimize the performance of the Windows environment, choose the Virtual machine radio button. To maximize the performance of Mac OS X when Windows is also running, choose the Mac OS X applications radio button. The choice you make here depends on how frequently you'll be running Windows and the kind of applications you'll be using. If you'll be running Windows frequently, choose the Virtual machine option to experience the best performance. Because it's easy to start and stop Windows, you can quickly shut it down when you want to make Mac applications run as quickly as possible.
16. Click Next.
17. Insert your Windows installation disc, wait until the disc mounts, and click Finish. The virtual machine starts and launches the lovely Windows installer. You see the Parallels window with various Windows installer messages as the installation progresses (see Figure 8.11). You can expect the installation process to take 45 or more minutes to complete, and it is resource intensive so it's better if you don't use your Mac for anything else while it runs.

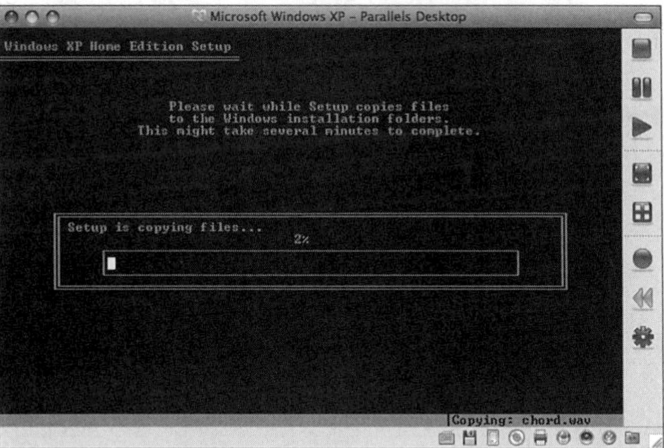


**Figure 8.11**
Parts of the Windows Installer aren't pretty, but it works (mostly, anyway).

Windows will start and stop a time or two, and you see a variety of messages from Windows itself and from Parallels Desktop. Read and respond to the messages as seems best; in most cases, you just click OK at various prompts.

After the basic installation process and initial Parallels Desktop configuration are complete, you see the Windows OS Logon screen in the virtual machine window (see Figure 8.12). You're ready to start running Windows.

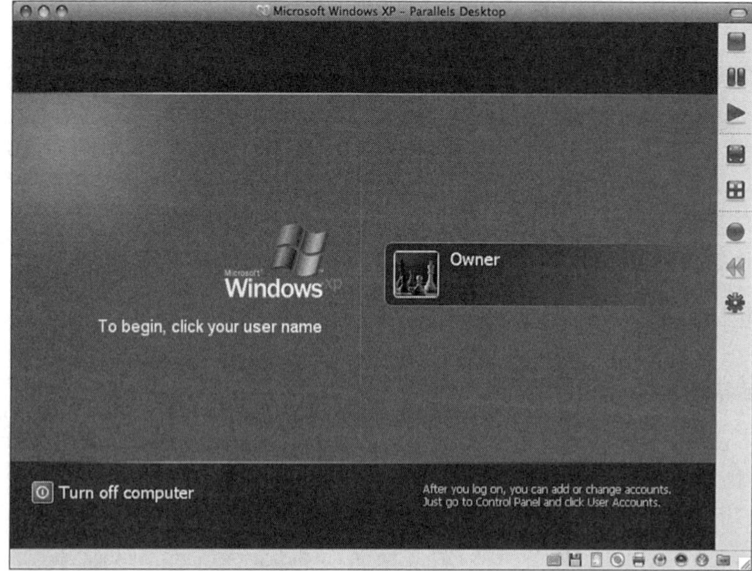


**Figure 8.12**
When you see the Windows Logon screen, the installation process is complete and you are ready to start running Windows.

18. Click the Owner user account to log on to Windows. The Windows desktop appears and you start using it (see Figure 8.13).

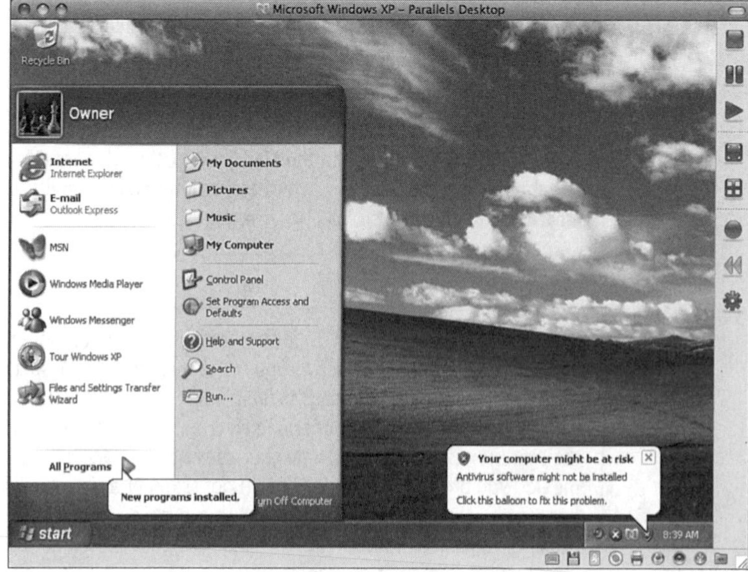


**Figure 8.13**
If you used Windows on a Windows PC, this screen should look quite familiar to you even though Windows is actually running on a Mac.

19. Choose Start menu, Turn Off Computer, Turn Off. The Windows environment closes.
20. Quit Parallels Desktop.
21. Eject the Windows installation disc.

**NOTE**

> One of the great things about Parallels Desktop is that the Windows environment gets its network settings from the Mac. So if the Mac on which you install Parallels is connected to a network and the Internet, the Windows environment is too without any additional configuration by you. Also, because the Windows environment gets its connection from the Mac, any protection from hacking through the network (such as NAT protection from an AirPort Extreme Base Station) is also applied to the Windows environment.

## Running Windows

**CAUTION**

> Windows is constantly under attack from viruses. Running Windows in a virtual environment on a Mac doesn't protect you from these threats when you are using the Windows environment; it's as susceptible to attacks as Windows on Windows hardware is. You should install and use security software under Windows as soon as you get your Windows environment running. See "Mac OS X to the Max: Protecting Windows on a Mac from Attack" at the end of this chapter for some suggestions.

Running Windows under Parallels Desktop is simple.

1. Launch Parallels Desktop by double-clicking its icon on the desktop or its icon in the Applications folder. The application launches and you see information about the virtual machine in the window and Windows launches (see Figure 18.14).

**NOTE**

> Only one environment can be using a CD or DVD at the same time. If you've inserted a CD or DVD, but don't see it on the Mac desktop, the odds are that Windows is running and the disc is mounted there, which makes it unavailable to the Mac. Stop the Windows environment and the disc will appear on the Mac desktop.

**CAUTION**

> You must activate a copy of Windows to keep it running for more than 30 days. When you do this, the copy of Windows you run is registered to the specific computer on which you activate it as a means to limit illegal copies of Windows. Unfortunately, you can activate only Windows under one environment (Boot Camp or a virtual machine) on the same computer. Don't activate your copy of Windows until you're sure which method you are going to run it under (Boot Camp or a virtual machine) because you'll have to pay for a new copy of Windows to activate it under a different scheme (or try to explain the situation to Microsoft to get the previous activation "undone" so you can activate it under a different environment).

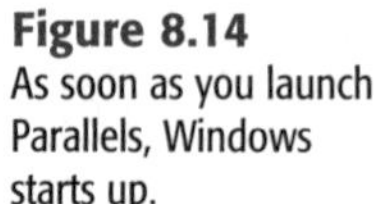

**Figure 8.14**
As soon as you launch Parallels, Windows starts up.

2. Launch existing Windows applications or install new applications from the Web or from installation discs.

There isn't much difference in running Windows in a virtual machine than there is running it on a Windows PC. However, you can jump back to the Mac by switching to the specific application you want to run, such as by pressing ⌘+Tab. You can leave Windows running as long as you need to; if you won't be using it for a while, it's a good idea to shut it down to maximize the resources available to the Mac OS.

Parallels Desktop has lots of great features that you can use to make Windows work the best for you. For example, you can use the Coherence mode so that the Parallels window disappears and all you see on the Mac desktop is the Windows Start menu and any Windows applications you are running. You can also run Parallels in full screen mode, which is especially useful if you have two displays connected to your Mac because you can run the Mac OS on one display and have the Windows environment fill the other. For additional information, see the documentation included in the Parallels installation disk image.

## Mac OS X to the Max: Protecting Windows on a Mac from Attack

Running Windows, whether via Boot Camp or a virtual machine, is hazardous. There are thousands and thousands of viruses, trojan horses, worms, and other threats to the Windows OS and to the files you store under it. One of the first things you should do when you get a Windows environment running is to install security software on it. At the least, you need a package that protects Windows from viruses, but that is really only the basic protection you need. The application you get should also protect Windows from other threats as well, such as worms and macro viruses. Because there are so many Windows computers and so many threats to those computers, there are many Windows security applications from which to choose. Symantec makes a number of security applications, such as Norton AntiVirus and Norton 360.

The following steps provide a general guide to installing security software under Windows:

1. Launch your Windows environment.
2. Open Internet Explorer and move to www.symantec.com.
3. Find the product you want to use, purchase it, and download it (see Figure 8.15).

**CAUTION**

> It's not clear whether the threats to Windows on a Mac also expose the Mac OS and its files to attack. There's no doubt some clever hacker is working on a way to attack the Mac OS through Windows running under Boot Camp or a virtualization application to show it can be done if for no other reason. Protecting the Windows environment from attack should also lower the already small chance that the Mac environment can be attacked via Windows.

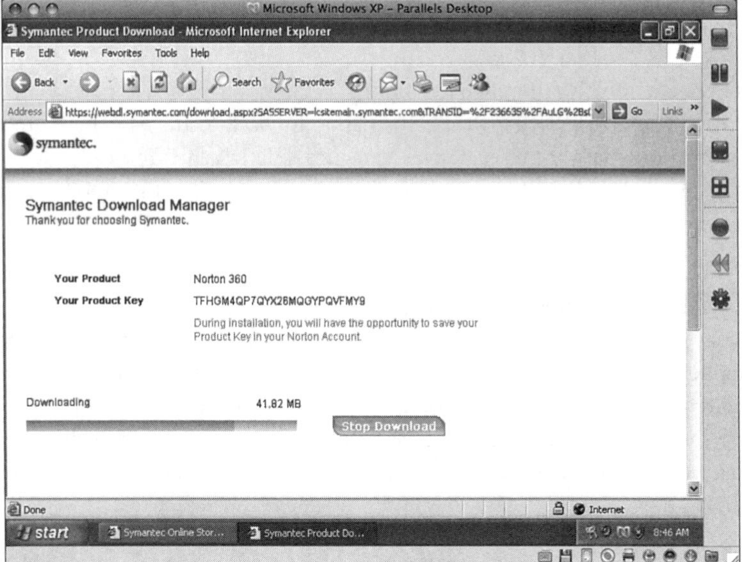


**Figure 8.15**
Downloading a security application works under Windows quite similarly to download applications using Safari on the Mac.

4. Install and configure the security software (see Figure 8.16).

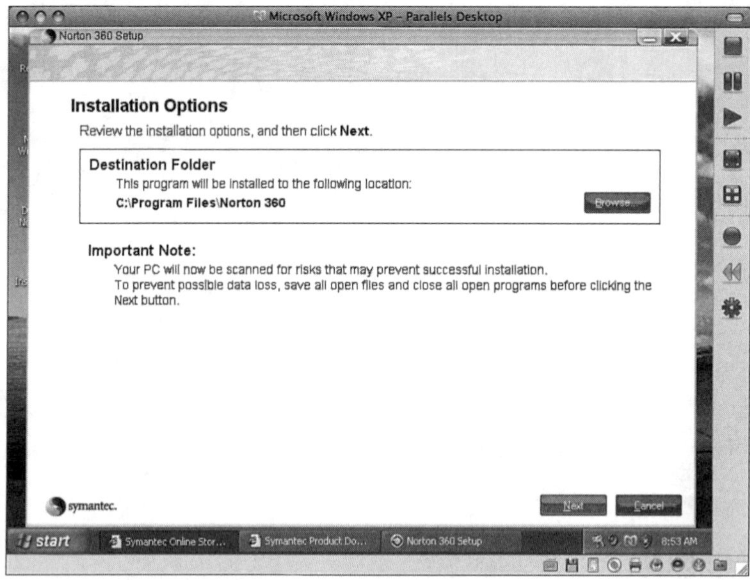


**Figure 8.16**
Install the security application under the Windows environment and then configure the protection it provides.

Make sure, in whichever software you use, that you configure it to automatically update its virus definitions frequently because new Windows viruses emerge constantly so you need to ensure your security software is as current as possible.

CHAPTER 9

# Setting System Preferences

## In this chapter

9

# Setting Your Preferences

The System Preferences application is an important tool you use to control how your Mac OS X system works and looks. If you have read through other chapters this book, you have already used some of the panes it contains to work with various parts of the system. Table 9.1 provides a summary of each pane and tells you where in this book you can learn more about it.

**Table 9.1 System Preferences Application Panes**

| Category | Pane | What It Does | Where You Can Learn More about It |
|---|---|---|---|
| Personal | Appearance | Controls several aspects of how your desktop looks, how scrolling happens, number of recent items, and font smoothing | "Setting Appearance Preferences," p. 193 |
| Personal | Desktop & Screen Saver | Sets the desktop picture and configures the screen saver | "Setting Desktop Pictures and Choosing a Screen Saver," p. 196 |
| Personal | Dock | Controls how the Dock looks and works | "Customizing the Appearance and Behavior of the Dock," p. 117 |
| Personal | Expose & Spaces | Enables you to set hot keys for Expose and to configure spaces on your Mac | "Managing Your Desktop with Exposé, Spaces, and Other Tools," p. 265 |
| Personal | International | Configures the languages and formats your system uses | "Setting International Preferences," p. 205 |
| Personal | Security | Enables you to protect your Mac with FileVault, a firewall, and system security controls | "Securing a Mac," p. 921 |
| Personal | Spotlight | Configures how Spotlight works | "Configuring Spotlight," p. 94 |
| Hardware | Bluetooth (only appears if your Mac is Bluetooth capable) | Configures Bluetooth communication between your Mac and other devices | "Finding, Installing, and Using Bluetooth Devices," p. 775 |

| Category | Pane | What It Does | Where You Can Learn More about It |
|---|---|---|---|
| Hardware | CDs & DVDs | Sets default behaviors when you work with CDs or DVDs | "Setting Default Disc Behaviors," p. 206 |
| Hardware | Displays | Configures the settings of displays connected to your Mac | "Configuring a Mac's Display," p. 786 |
| Hardware | Energy Saver | Manages your Mac's power use | "Managing Your Mobile Mac's Power," p. 318 |
| Hardware | Ink (only appears if you have a tablet device connected to your Mac) | Controls the Ink handwriting recognition system when you connect a tablet device to your Mac | Use this pane to configure how your Mac recognizes your handwriting as input if you use a tablet input device |
| Hardware | Keyboard & Mouse | Configures mice and keyboards you use | "Working with Mice, Keyboards, and Other Input Devices" p. 763 |
| Hardware | Print & Fax | Configures printers your Mac can access and provides fax settings | "Installing, Configuring, and Using Printers," p. 813 |
| Hardware | Sound | Provides the settings you use to manage your Mac's sound | "Working with Your Mac's Sound," p. 801 |
| Internet & Network | .Mac | Sets up and manages your .Mac account | "Using .Mac to Integrate a Mac onto the Internet," p. 435 |
| Internet & Network | Network | Enables you to configure a Mac for network access | "Building and Using a Wired Network," p. 359<br>"Creating and Managing AirPort Wireless Networks," p. 393 |
| Internet & Network | QuickTime | Configures your Mac's QuickTime settings | "Configuring QuickTime," p. 604 |
| Internet & Network | Sharing | Enables you to share your Mac's services and Internet connection over a network | "Configuring the Services on a Network," p. 369<br>"Sharing an Internet Connection," p. 421 |

*continues*

9

**TABLE 9.1 CONTINUED**

| Category | Pane | What It Does | Where You Can Learn More about It |
|---|---|---|---|
| System | Accounts | Enables you to create and manage user accounts | "Configuring and Working with User Accounts," p. 231 |
| System | Date & Time | Sets your Mac's date and time | "Configuring Your Mac's Date and Time," p. 207 |
| System | Parental Controls | Enables you to customize the access specific user accounts have to your Mac's resources and allows you to limit someone's time on a Mac | "Securing a Mac," p. 921 |
| System | Software Update | Keeps your version of Mac OS X and Apple applications current | "Using Software Update to Maintain Your Software," p. 876 |
| System | Speech | Configures speech recognition and text to speech settings | "Making Your Mac Accessible to Everyone," p. 277 |
| System | Startup Disk | Configures your Mac's statup volume | "Choosing a Startup Volume with System Preferences," p. 209 |
| System | Time Machine | Configures a back-up system for your Mac's data | "Backing Up a Mac," p. 895 |
| System | Universal Access | Enables you to make your Mac more accessible to those who have disabilities | "Making Your Mac Accessible to Everyone," p. 277 |
| Other | As Installed | The Other section appears when you've added hardware or software to your system that has a preference component. After you install the hardware or software, it's preference pane will be shown in the Other section. | Documentation or help system provided with hardware or software |

**NOTE**

You might see more or fewer panes in the System Preferences application than are listed in Table 9.1 depending on the hardware and software you have installed. For example, if your Mac doesn't support Bluetooth hardware, you won't see the Bluetooth pane.

Following are some tips to work with the System Preferences application:

- You can open a pane by selecting it on the application's View menu.
- Right-click on the System Preferences application's icon on the Dock, and choose a pane on the pop-up menu to work with it.
- To see all the panes again, select View, Show All Preferences; press ⌘-L; or click the Show All button on the System Preferences application's toolbar.
- You can search for a pane by typing text in the System Preferences application's Search tool. (You can move into the tool by clicking in it; selecting View, Search; or pressing ⌘-F.) As you type, the panes that meet your search will become "spotlighted" and the rest of the panes will be darkened.
- If you prefer that the panes be listed alphabetically rather than by category, select View, Organize Alphabetically. The System Preferences application will be reorganized and the panes will appear alphabetically from the upper left to the bottom right.
- Use the toolbar's Back and Forward buttons to move among panes you have opened.



# Setting Appearance Preferences

How your Mac's desktop looks is likely an important thing; since you are going to be looking at it so much, it should look as pleasing to you as possible. Likewise, it should work in the way that makes the most sense to you. You can use the Appearance pane of the System Preferences application to configure certain aspects of how Mac OS X looks and works. And if the default colors provided in the pane aren't up to snuff, you can use the Color Picker to add colors you'd like to see.

## Configuring the Appearance Pane

Use the Appearance pane of the System Preferences application to control several basic settings for your system. This pane is organized into four sections. From top to bottom, they control basic appearance settings, scroll behavior, the number of recent items tracked, and font smoothing (see Figure 9.1).

The Appearance pop-up menu includes these options:

- Select Blue if you want color in the buttons, menus, and windows.
- Select Graphite if you want to mute the color so the color elements are gray instead.
- Use the Highlight Color pop-up menu to select the highlight color. You can choose one of the default colors on the pop-up menu or choose Other to open the Color Picker, which is described in the next section.

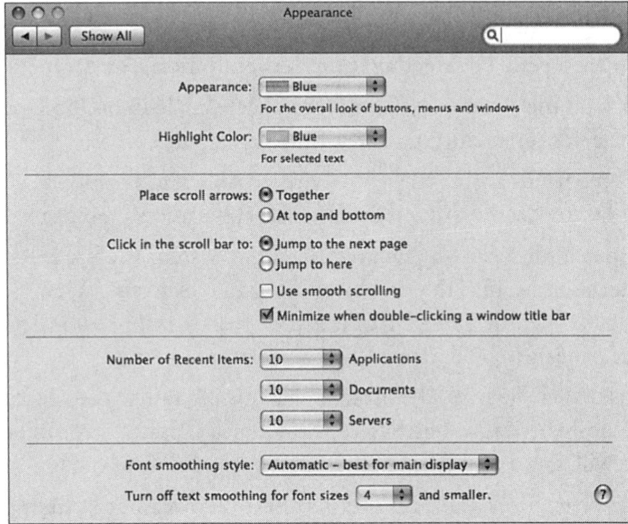


**Figure 9.1**
The Appearance pane can be used to configure several different aspects of how Mac OS X looks and works.

Use the "Place scroll arrows" radio buttons to set the following scrolling behaviors:

- Choose the Together radio button to place the scroll arrows together.
- Choose the "At top and bottom" radio button to have a scroll arrow placed at each end of the scrollbar.
- Select "Jump to here" to cause a window to jump to the relative position in the scrollbar on which you click, or "Jump to the next page" to scroll a page at a time when you click above or below the scroll box.
- If you want scrolling to be smooth (instead of jumping when you scroll, your Mac kind of strolls to the new location), check the "Use smooth scrolling" check box.
- Uncheck the "Minimize when double-clicking a window title bar" check box if you don't want to be able to minimize a window by double-clicking its title bar for some reason.

Set the number of recent items tracked on the Apple menu for applications, documents, and servers using the Number of Recent Items pop-up menus. You can track as few as none or as many as 50 recent items with a number of choices in between.

The bottom section of the pane provides the controls you use to configure how font smoothing is enabled on your Mac. *Font smoothing* (known as antialiasing for graphics) reduces the jaggies that occur when you view certain fonts onscreen; this is most noticeable when you use larger sizes or thick fonts or when you apply bold or other formatting. Font smoothing is always turned on, but you can configure it specifically for your system:

1. Open the Appearance pane of the System Preferences application.
2. Using the "Font smoothing style" pop-up menu, select the smoothing style you want your Mac to use. Your options are:
   - Automatic—best for main display
   - Standard—best for CRT
   - Light
   - Medium—best for Flat Panel
   - Strong

   You will probably be satisfied with the option appropriate for the display type you use, but you can experiment with the other options to see whether one of them matches your needs better.
3. Select the font size at or below which text smoothing is disabled on the "Turn off text smoothing for font sizes" pop-up menu. Because the effect of smoothing is less noticeable at small font sizes, your system can save some wasted processing power by not smoothing fonts displayed at small sizes. The default value is 4 points, but you might not even notice if you increase this value slightly.



## USING THE COLOR PICKER TO CHOOSE COLORS

There are many areas in which you choose to use colors for certain things, such as when you apply colors to text or apply a color to the background of a Finder window. To apply colors, you use the Color Picker, which you can open by choosing Other on the Highlight Color pop-up menu on the Appearance pane (see Figure 9.2). Within applications, you use the Colors panel to apply colors to text and images, and it works in the same way as the Color Picker.

**TIP**

> How you open the Colors panel depends on the application you are using. However, in some applications, such as TextEdit, you can open it by pressing Shift-⌘-C.

The five modes in the Color Picker are represented by the five buttons along the top of the window. From left to right they are the Color Wheel, Color Sliders (including Cyan Magenta Yellow Black [CMYK], Hue Saturation Balance [HSB], Gray Scale, and Red Green Blue [RGB]), Color Palettes, Image Palettes, and Crayons. Each of these modes work similarly. Select the mode you want to use, and the controls in the Color Picker window change to reflect the mode you are in. Use the mode's controls to select or configure a color to apply. When you want to apply the color to the selected object, click it.

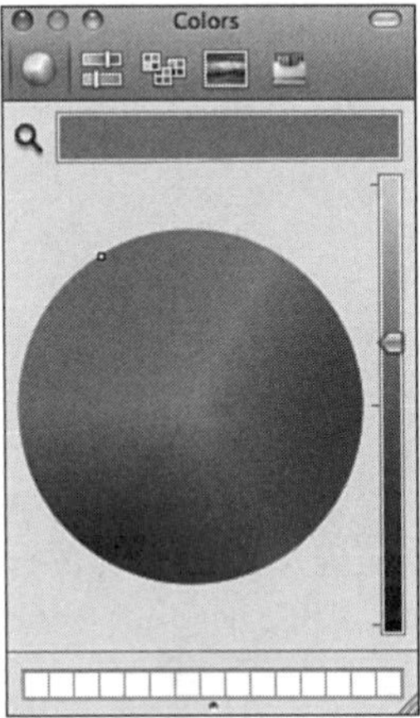


**Figure 9.2**
The Color Picker enables you to create and apply custom colors to selected elements, such as to the background of a Finder window or the color your Mac uses to highlight interface elements.

**TIP**

> You can add the configured color to the list of favorite colors at the bottom of the window by dragging the color from the top of the dialog box to the boxes at the bottom so you can easily apply the color again in the future.
>
> If you click the Magnifying Glass icon, the pointer turns into a magnifying glass. If you move this over an area and click, the color in that area appears in the current color box of the Color Picker.

**NOTE**

> The Colors panel you see within particular applications might have the same or slightly different modes.

# SETTING DESKTOP PICTURES AND CHOOSING A SCREEN SAVER

Setting a desktop picture is a great way to personalize your Mac and make it more pleasing to look at; using a screen saver is a good way to protect your screen from damage that can be caused by a static image being displayed on it for a long period of time. You can use the Desktop & Screen Saver pane of the System Preferences application to configure both these aspects of your system.

## CHOOSING DESKTOP PICTURES

You use the Desktop tab of the Desktop & Screen Saver pane of the System Preferences application to configure a desktop picture (see Figure 9.3). You can choose to use one of Mac OS X's default images, any image or folder of images in your Pictures folder, any images or folder of images located elsewhere, or any photos you have in your iPhoto Library. You can use images in just about any image format as desktop pictures, such as .tiff, .jpg, and so on.

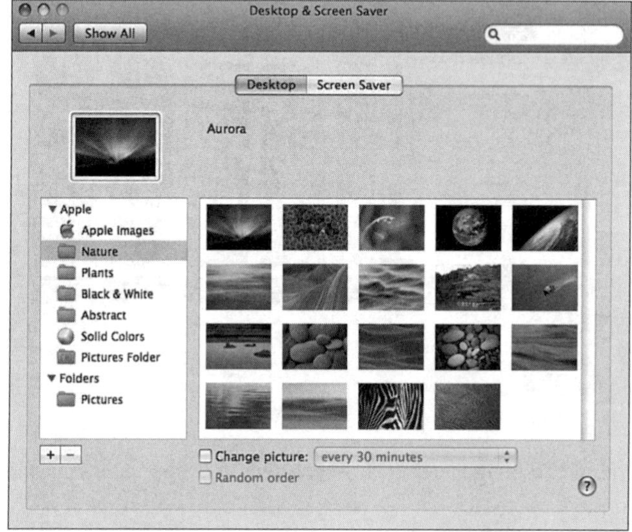


**Figure 9.3**
Although you probably won't see your desktop picture all that much assuming you have lots of windows open, it's nice to have something pleasant to look at from time to time.



**TIP**

> If your Mac is connected to multiple displays, the desktop on each display can have its own desktop picture. When you open the Desktop tab, a pane will appear on each display. Use each screen's pane to configure its desktop picture; the desktop picture on each display is independent so you can have the picture on one display be dynamic while the picture on the other is static.

Configuring desktop pictures is easy:

1. Open the Desktop tab of the Desktop & Screen Saver pane of the System Preferences application. At the top of the tab, you see the current desktop picture in the Image well and the name of the image next to the Image well. Beneath that on the left side of pane is the list of available sources of pictures. On the right side of the pane are the pictures in the source that is selected on the left side of the pane.
2. Choose the image source that you want to use on the desktop by selecting it on the Source list. There are a number of default sources including Apple Images, Nature, Plants, and so on. Choose Pictures Folder to use the Pictures folder in your Home folder as the source. If iPhoto is installed on your Mac, expand the iPhoto Albums source to see your photo albums; select an album to use it as the source. You can add any other folder as a source by clicking the Add Source (+) button at the bottom of the pane. After you select a source, its images appear in the right part of the pane (see Figure 9.4).

**Figure 9.4**
Here I've selected a folder with photos from a recent vacation.



3. To use one of the images being shown, select it. The image you select will be placed on the desktop.

**TIP**

> You can also place a single image on the desktop by dragging it from the desktop onto the Image well.

4. To have your Mac rotate the desktop picture among those in the selected source, check the "Change picture" check box and choose the amount of time each picture should be displayed on the pop-up menu; there are many options including each time you log in, when waking up from sleep, and various times from every 5 seconds to every day. If you want the images to be selected at random, check the "Random order" check box; if you leave this unchecked, the images will be used in the same order as they are in the source. When you do this, the Image well will be filled with an icon that indicates that images will be rotated. The first image is selected and placed on the desktop and is changed according to the timing you selected.

**TIP**

> To remove an image source from the list, select it and click the Remove Source button (-).

## Configuring a Screen Saver

Mac OS X was the first version of the Mac OS that included a built-in screen saver. Many Mac users enjoy having a screen saver. Mac OS X's version provides the features you would expect, and the quality and style with which the screen saver displays images are quite nice. It can be especially nice when you use your own images.

You use the Screen Saver tab of the Desktop & Screen Saver pane of the System Preferences application to configure a screen saver for your computer (see Figure 9.5).

**Figure 9.5**
You can use one of Mac OS X's built-in screen saver modules, create your own screen saver, or add a screen saver that someone else created (such as by using one that has been posted to a user's .Mac account).

**Display Sleep Time**

If you really want to protect your screen, use the Energy Saver pane to set a display sleep time. Display sleep actually turns off the display mechanism, which saves the screen. Of course, a blank screen isn't nearly as interesting as the screen saver.

To be safe rather than sorry when it comes to the health of your Mac's display, you should keep the display sleep setting at a relatively short amount of time so it sleeps when you aren't actively using your Mac. This will prevent possible damage to your display more effectively than the screen saver does.

Along the left side of the pane, you see two general categories of screen saver modules you can use. The Apple group includes modules provided by Apple, such as Flurry or iTunes Artwork. The Pictures section includes sources of photos that can be used as a screen saver module, including a .Mac module and photos from your iPhoto Library. The Preview pane shows a preview of the selected module and you see various controls you can use to configure and test the module you select; these work similarly for all the modules.

### Using a Built-in Screen Saver Module

The general steps for using one of Mac OS X's built-in modules are the following:

1. Open the Screen Saver tab of the Desktop & Screen Saver pane.
2. If you want your Mac to randomly select and use a screen saver, check the "Use random screen saver" check box and skip to step 9. Each time the screen saver activates, your Mac will select a different module to use.

3. Select the screen saver module you want to use from the Screen Savers list; you see a preview in the Preview window.
4. Use the Options button to set various parameters for the screen saver you select. The options that are available depend on the specific module you select. Some modules don't have options and the Options button will be disabled.
5. If you select a module that uses photos, use the Display Style buttons to choose how the photos are displayed. You can choose a Mosiac style, Collage style, or you can have each image be presented using transition effects to create a slideshow.

9

**NOTE**

Most of the default Mac OS X screen saver modules use standard images Apple has provided. One of them—the iTunes Artwork module—is more interesting, however. It creates a screen saver using the artwork associated with albums in your iTunes Music Library. When you select this module, the artwork is gathered from iTunes automatically and the album covers appear in a large square consisting of subsquares, each of which rotates through various album covers.

6. If you want the clock to be displayed along with the screen saver, check the "Show with clock" check box. The time will appear on screen along with the screen saver images.
7. If your Mac is connected to multiple displays, but you want the screen saver to be shown only on the main display, check the "Main screen only" check box. The images will be displayed on the display with the Mac title bar; other displays will be blank.

**NOTE**

If you use multiple displays, a different image from the selected screen saver module is shown on each display.

8. Test the screen saver by clicking the Test button. The images that are part of the screen saver are rendered and displayed with the configuration options you selected.
9. Use the "Start screen saver" slider to set the idle time that must pass before the screen saver is activated.

**NOTE**

If the display sleep time set on the Energy Saver pane is less than the time you set in step 9, you will never see the screen saver because the display will sleep before the screen saver is activated. If this is the case, a warning appears on the Screen Saver tab pane and a button enables you to jump to the Energy Saver pane. You can either decrease the time for the screen saver to activate or increase the time for Display sleep.

10. Click the Hot Corners button.
11. On the resulting sheet, select the corners where you can move the mouse to manually start or disable the screen saver. Select the action you want to occur on the pop-up

menu located at the corner you want to configure and click OK. For example, if you select Start Screen Saver on the pop-up menu located in the upper-left corner of the sheet, you can start the screen saver by moving the cursor to the upper-left corner of the display. The default is to have no action occur at any corner.

### Creating a Custom Screen Saver Module

Some of the built-in modules are pretty cool (I especially like iTunes Artwork), but you can have even more fun by creating or using a custom module. There are several ways to do this:



- Gather the images you want to use for a screen saver in a folder, and use the Choose Folder module to select that folder.
- Create a screen saver from a collection of your own images by creating a photo album for that purpose in iPhoto. You can access any image in your iPhoto Photo Library as well as any of its photo albums on the Screen Savers list.
- Use a screen saver that someone has made available through .Mac or as an RSS feed.
- Use a screen saver you download from the Internet.

To create a screen saver from your own images, use the following steps:

1. Create a folder containing the images you want to use. The images can be in the standard image formats, such as .jpg or .tiff.
2. Open the Screen Saver tab, and select the Choose Folder module.
3. Use the Choose Folder sheet to move to and select the folder containing the images you want to use; then click Choose.
4. Use the other controls on the tab to configure the screen saver. You have the same display options as for the built-in screen saver modules.

You can choose to use the images within your Pictures folder by selecting it on the list of Screen Savers. Only the images located in the root folder (not within folders that are inside the Pictures folder) are used. You configure the screen saver using the same steps you use for other options.

If you have installed and use iPhoto, you can choose any images in your iPhoto Photo Library as a screen saver by selecting Library, which is located under the Choose Folder module. You can also select any photo album you have created in iPhoto as a screen saver by selecting it on the list that appears under the Photo Library on the screen saver list.

### Using .Mac Screen Saver Modules

Using the .Mac service, people can make their screen savers available to you, and you can make your screen savers available to other people.

You can also choose an RSS feed as a screen saver.

⇨ To learn how to use .Mac services, **see** Chapter 20, "Using .Mac to Integrate a Mac onto the Internet," **p. 435**.

To use a module available via .Mac, perform the following steps:

1. Open the Screen Saver tab, and select the .Mac and RSS module.
2. Click Options to see the Configuration sheet (see Figure 9.6). The top of the sheet contains a list of .Mac screen savers and RSS feeds to which you are subscribed. If the check box is checked, the images in the screen saver are used. If not, they aren't used.



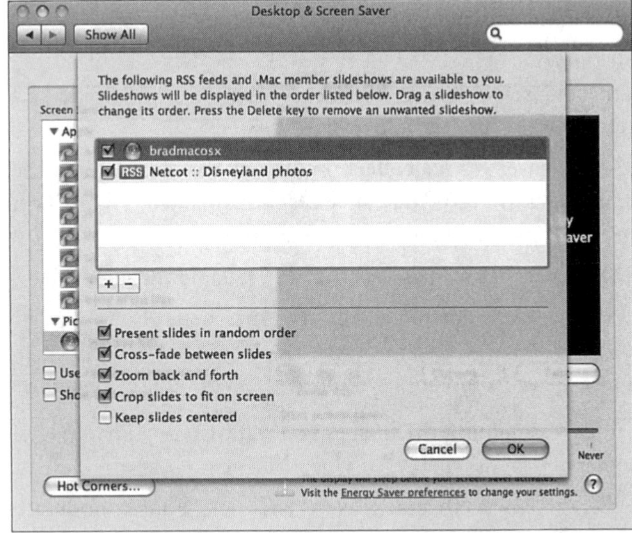


**Figure 9.6**
Choosing a screen saver published via .Mac or an RSS feed can make your screen more interesting when you aren't actively using your Mac.

3. Click the Add button (+) and choose "Add .Mac subscription" or "Add RSS feed."
4. If you choose to create a .Mac entry, enter the .Mac member name of someone whose slideshow you would like to use as your screen saver in the .Mac Membership name field. The person whose .Mac name you enter will appear on the list of slideshows to which you are subscribed. If you select RSS feed, enter the address to that feed. Press Return; your Mac will check the information you entered. If it isn't valid, you'll need to fix it.
5. Use the Display Options check boxes to configure the slideshow. (The same display options apply to all the .Mac screensaver modules you use.)
6. Check the check box for each .Mac or RSS feed you want to use in your screen saver. If an item's check box is unchecked, the slideshow is still available to you but isn't displayed.
7. Click OK.

**TIP**

> To unsubscribe from a public slideshow, select the slideshow, and press Delete or click the Remove button (-). Of course, you can always just uncheck the box to prevent the images in that screen saver from being included.

8. Configure and test the screen saver just like one of Mac OS X's built-in screen savers.

**TIP**

> If you have people who are interested in you (such as relatives), you can create a .Mac public slideshow and inform those people who are interested that it is available. As you update your slideshow, people who subscribe to and use it see the images you add to the collection.



### Using Screen Savers Acquired from the Internet and Other Sources

You can also download screen savers from the Internet or obtain them from other sources. Screen saver modules have the `.saver` filename extension. To do this, follow these steps:

1. Download the screen saver you want to use and prepare it for use.
2. Place the `.saver` file in the directory *`Mac OS X`*`/Library/Screen Savers`, where *`Mac OS X`* is the name of the startup volume.
3. Use the Screen Saver tab to choose and configure the screen saver you added.

## Setting International Preferences

Mac OS X includes support for a large number of languages, language behaviors, and date, time, and number formats. You control these properties through the International pane of the System Preferences application (see Figure 9.7).

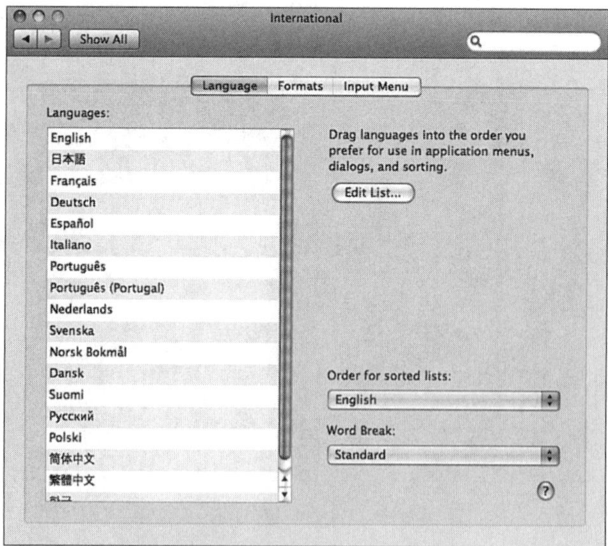


**Figure 9.7**
You can use the International pane of the System Preferences application to control various language and format properties based on a language and the conventions of particular nations.

## Setting the Language Tab Options

Use the Language tab to configure the languages you want to use. The Languages list shows the languages that are currently active. You can drag these languages up and down in the list to set the preferred order you want to use them on menus and in dialog boxes. If you click the Edit List button, a sheet will appear on which you can choose the languages that you want to appear in the Languages list. (The languages on this list are those that were installed when you installed Mac OS X.) After you click OK, the languages whose check boxes you unchecked will no longer appear on the language list. Use the "Order for sorted lists" pop-up menu to choose the language by which lists will be sorted. Use the Word Break pop-up menu to choose how you want word breaks to occur.

**NOTE**

> Changes you make to languages will become active in the Finder the next time you log in.

## Setting the Formats Tab Options

Use the Formats tab to configure the format of the dates, times, and numbers used on your Mac. When you open this tab, you see a section for each of these areas along with the Region pop-up menu (see Figure 9.8).

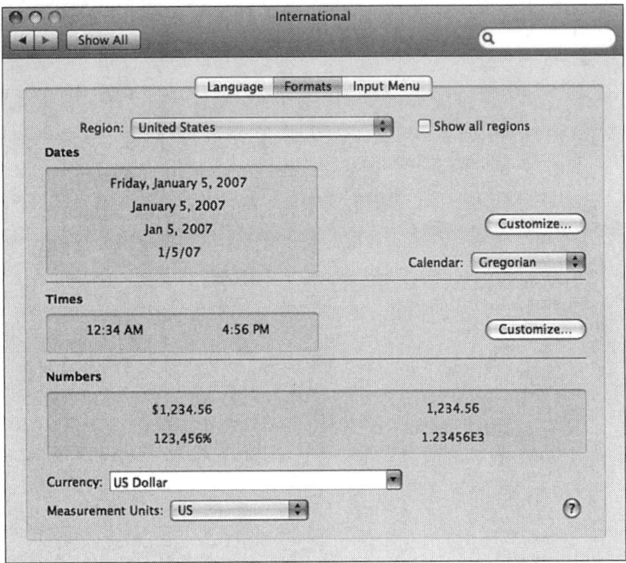


**Figure 9.8**
Use the Formats tab of the International pane to set the format of dates, times, and numbers for your system.

### Choosing a Region

Select the region setting for your Mac on the Region pop-up menu. By default, you see region choices that relate to the languages you have installed. If you want to see all possible region options, check the Show all regions check box. When you make a selection, default formats for the region you selected are applied to each setting area (dates, times, and numbers).

After you have set general format preferences via the Region pop-up menu, you can customize the format in each area.

**NOTE**

> The options described in the following paragraphs are for the United States region. If you choose a different region, different options might be available to you, but they can be set using similar steps.



### CUSTOMIZING DATE OPTIONS

In the Dates section, click the Customize button. The Customize Dates sheet will appear. Use the controls on this sheet to set the date formats displayed in Finder windows and other locations. There are four general date formats: Short, Medium, Long, and Full. Use the pop-up menus, check boxes, and text fields to set the format for each type of date. Choose the date format you want to configure on the Show pop-up menu. The default format will be shown in the box below the pop-up menu. Click each element, such as the month, to customize it. For example, you can customize the month format by selecting the abbreviated form. Drag the elements around to change the order in which they appear. If you want to add more elements to the default format you selected, drag them from the Date Elements section of the sheet to the location in which you want the elements to appear. Repeat these steps to configure each of the date format options (such as for the Short format). Click OK to save your settings and close the sheet. On the Calendar pop-up menu, choose the calendar you want to use, such as Gregorian or Japanese.

**TIP**

> To remove an element from the date or time customization, select it and press the Delete key.

### CUSTOMIZING TIME OPTIONS

In the Times section, click the Customize button. The Customize Times sheet will appear. Choose the time format you want to configure on the Show pop-up menu. The default format will be shown in the box below the pop-up menu. Click each element, such as the minute, to customize it. For example, you can customize the minute display by choosing to show the leading 0 or not. Drag the elements around to change the order in which they appear. If you want to add more elements to the default format you selected, drag them from the Time Elements section of the sheet to the location where you want the elements to appear. Repeat these steps to configure each of the time format options (such as for the Short format). To determine the modifier that is displayed when the time is before or after noon, enter the modifier in the Before Noon and After Noon boxes. Click OK to save your settings and close the sheet.

**NOTE**

> The settings you make in the Dates and Times sheets affect the format of these values in the Finder and other locations. They do not affect the clock display; you control the format of the clock using the Time & Date pane.
>
> Is time really important to you? With Mac OS X, you can choose to display milliseconds by adding the Milliseconds element to one of the standard time formats.

#### Customizing Number Formats

You can see the format of numbers using the region you have selected in the Numbers section. You can't change the number format except with the following two controls.

- Use the Currency pop-up menu to choose the currency format you want to use, such as U.S. Dollar or Euro.
- Use the Measurement Units pop-up menu to select the default measurement units used (U.S. [aka English] or Metric).

**NOTE**

> When you make changes to a standard format, the selection on the Region pop-up menu becomes Custom to indicate that you have customized your settings.

### Setting the Input Menu Tab Options

Use the Input Menu tab to control and configure the Input menu that can appear on the menu bar.

⇨ To learn how to configure the Character Palette, **see** "Working with the Character Palette," **p. 226**.

⇨ To learn how to configure a keyboard for different languages, **see** "Configuring a Keyboard," **p. 765**.

## Setting Default Disc Behaviors

Use the CDs & DVDs pane of the System Preferences application to determine your Mac's default behaviors when you insert a disc (see Figure 9.9).

**Figure 9.9**
The CDs & DVDs pane of the System Preferences application enables you to determine what your Mac does when you insert a disc into it.

You set a behavior for your Mac when you insert a music CD, picture CD, or video DVD. On the pop-up menu for each of these, you'll see a similar set of commands. At the top of the menu is a list of all applications that Mac OS X thinks might be suitable for the type of disc you insert. Choose the application that you want to use by default; for example, you can choose DVD Player or Front Row for video DVDs. To select an application not on the list, choose "Open other application" and then choose the application you want to use. To have an AppleScript run, choose "Run script" and then select the script you want to use. To have your Mac do nothing, choose Ignore.

The next time you insert a disc, your Mac will take the default action that you set.



# CONFIGURING YOUR MAC'S DATE AND TIME

The Date & Time pane of the System Preferences application enables you to set and maintain your system's time and date (see Figure 9.10). You can set the time and date manually, or you can use a network timeserver to set and maintain your system's time and date for you.

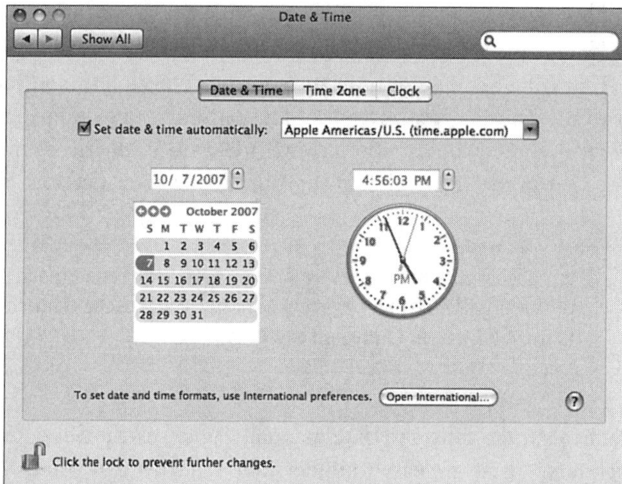


**Figure 9.10**
The Date & Time pane enables you to determine how your Mac keeps track of time.

To set your system's date and time, do the following:

1. Open the Date & Time pane of the System Preferences application.
2. Click the Time Zone tab, and use the map to set your time zone (see Figure 9.11). Drag the highlight bar over your location to select the correct time zone. Then, use the Closest City pop-up menu to select the specific time zone for the area where you are located.

**NOTE**

> If you specified a .Mac account when you installed Mac OS X, the time zone information has been configured for you.

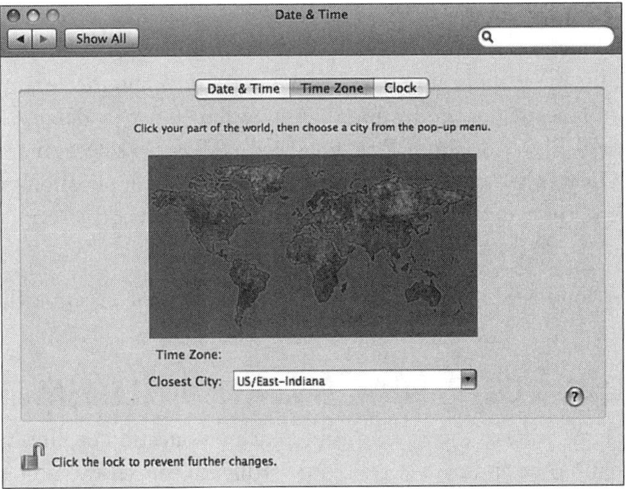


**Figure 9.11**
Use the Time Zone tools to set the time zone where you and your Mac are currently located.



3. Click the Date & Time tab.
4. If you are going to use a network timeserver to maintain the time and date for your machine, check the Set date & time automatically check box, and select the timeserver you want to use on the drop-down list. The options you see depend on where you are. Apple provides three primary timeservers: one for the Americas, one for Asia, and one for Europe. Select the server that is appropriate for your location.

**NOTE**

It probably goes without saying that you have to be connected to the Internet to use one of Mac OS X's built-in timeservers. Similarly, you must be connected to a local network to use a timeserver located on that network.

5. If you want to set the time and date manually, uncheck the Set date & time automatically check box. There are easy to understand controls that you use to set the date and time. You can use the Calendar tool to choose a date, type a date in the date box, or use the arrows next to it to select a date. You can then use similar controls to set the time.

⇨ To learn how to use the Clock tab to configure the desktop clock, **see** "Changing the Clock Display," **p. 86**.

**NOTE**

You can find the official time for any time zone in the United States at www.time.gov. Of course, this is useful only if you live in the United States and can not handle the time being off by as much as 0.1 seconds.

# Controlling System Startup

Under Mac OS X, there are several ways to configure and control the startup process. The most straightforward way is to use the Startup Disk pane of the System Preferences application to select a startup volume. There are other ways you can control system startup as well, such as selecting a startup volume during the startup process, starting up in the single-user mode, and starting up in the verbose mode.



## Choosing a Startup Volume with System Preferences

The Startup Disk pane of the System Preferences application enables you to select a startup volume (see Figure 9.12). Open the pane to see a list of the valid startup volumes on your machine. Select the volume from which you want to start up, and click Restart. You are prompted to confirm this action by clicking the Restart button. Your selection is saved and your Mac restarts from the volume you selected.

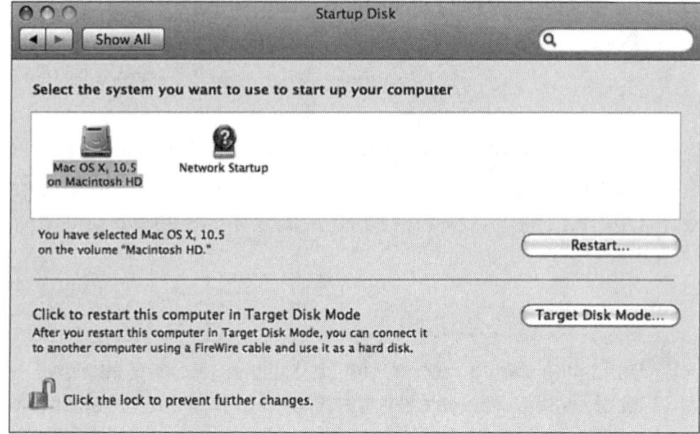


**Figure 9.12**
The Startup Disk pane allows you to select a startup volume for your Mac.

**TIP**

For troubleshooting purposes, it's a good idea to install Mac OS X on more than one volume. Use one of these as your working startup volume. Don't use the other one except for troubleshooting purposes. This can be a great help when you are having trouble with your Mac.

If you want your Mac to start up in Target Disk mode so it acts as if it is only a hard disk, click Target Disk Mode and then click Restart at the prompt sheet.

⇨ To learn more about Target Disk Mode, **see** "Starting Up in Target Disk Mode," **p. 211**.

## Choosing a Startup Volume During Startup

During the startup process, you can select the startup volume by holding down the Option key while the machine is starting up. As the Mac starts up, you see icons for each of the valid startup volumes on your machine. The currently selected startup volume is highlighted. You can select a startup volume by clicking the arrow below the volume's icon. The Mac will then startup from the volume you selected.

## STARTING UP IN SINGLE-USER MODE

The single-user mode starts up your Mac in a Unix-like environment. In this environment, you can run Unix commands outside of Mac OS X. This can be useful in a couple of situations, mostly related to troubleshooting problems.

9

**NOTE**

Single-user mode is also called *Console mode*.

**CAUTION**

When you start up in single-user mode, you will be using the root account. Under this account, you can do anything to the files on your Mac. Some actions you perform under the root account can't be undone, so be careful that you don't do something you didn't mean to do.

To start up in single-user mode, hold down ⌘-S while the machine is starting up. Many system messages appear and report on how the startup process is proceeding. When the startup is complete, you will see the `root#` Unix prompt. This means you can start entering Unix commands.

**NOTE**

During the startup process, you are likely to see some information that doesn't make a lot of sense to you unless you are fluent in Unix and the arcane system messages you see. You might also see some odd error messages, but typically I wouldn't worry about them too much. However, if you have particular problems you are trying to solve, some of these messages might provide valuable clues for you.

One of the more useful things you can do is to run the Unix disk-repair function, which is `fsck`. At the prompt, type

```
/sbin/fsck -y
```

and press Return. The utility checks the disk on which Mac OS X is installed. Any problems it finds is reported and repaired (if possible).

**NOTE**

If the startup disk is Journaled, type **`/sbin/fsck -yf`** to force the utility to run.

You can use many other Unix commands at this prompt, just as if you were using the Terminal application from inside Mac OS X.

⇨ To learn more about using Unix commands, **see** Chapter 14, "Unix: Working with the Command Line," **p. 297**.

To resume the startup process in Mac OS X, type the command `reboot` and press Return. Additionally, even more arcane Unix messages will appear and then the normal Mac OS X startup process continues. When that process is complete, you end up at the Login window or directly in the Mac OS X desktop, depending on how your Login preferences are configured.



**TIP**

> If you want to eject a disc when you restart your Mac, hold down the mouse button while you restart.

## Starting Up in Verbose Mode

If you hold down ⌘-V while your Mac is starting up, you start up in the verbose mode. In this mode, you see all sorts of system messages while the machine starts up. The difference between verbose mode and single-user mode is that the verbose mode is not interactive. All you can do is view the system messages; you can't control what happens. Many of the messages you see will probably be incomprehensible, but some are not (particularly messages about specific system processes starting up). This mode is likely to be useful to you only in troubleshooting. And even then, the single-user mode is probably more useful because it gives you some control over what is happening.

## Starting Up in Safe Mode

If you are having trouble starting up your Mac, try starting in Safe mode. When you do this, you'll start up in a basic system where many features and peripherals are disabled. However, this can be useful when you are troubleshooting problems. To start up in Safe mode, start or restart your Mac. When the startup sound plays, hold down the Shift key. When you see the spinning progress indicator underneath the Apple logo, release the Shift key. You will then start up in Safe mode.

## Starting Up in Target Disk Mode

If you'd like to connect two computers together so you can easily move files between them, you can use FireWire to have one computer act like a mounted volume on another. The computer you want to use as a disk must start up in Target Disk mode.

**NOTE**

> Target Disk Mode is different than networking computers because the computer that is operating in Target Disk mode works like a hard drive instead of like a computer. You can't use it to do anything beyond what an external drive can do.

First, configure the Mac you want to use as a disk to start in Target Disk mode. Open the Startup Disk pane of the System Preferences application, and click the Target Disk Mode button located at the bottom of the pane. Click Restart at the prompt. When the Mac restarts, you'll see a FireWire symbol on its screen. This indicates that it is in Target Disk mode.

Connect the Mac to another one using a FireWire cable. The Target Disk Mac will appear as a mounted disk on the second Mac. You can then use its hard drive just like one installed on the second machine. For example, you can move files to it, install software on it, and so on.



To return the Mac to normal condition, press and hold the Power button until the Mac shuts down. Disconnect the FireWire cable and then press the Power button again to restart it normally.

**TIP**

Using Target Disk mode can be an easy way to back up all the files on a mobile Mac. Restart the mobile Mac in Target Disk mode and connect it to a desktop machine with some free hard drive space. Drag all the files from the mobile Mac onto the disk on which you want to store the backed-up files.

## USING OTHER STARTUP OPTIONS

Table 9.2 lists various startup options and their keyboard shortcuts.

**TABLE 9.2 MAC OS X STARTUP OPTIONS**

| Startup Option | How to Select It |
|---|---|
| Prevent automatic login | Hold the left Shift key and mouse button down when you see the progress bar during the startup process. |
| Start up from a computer connected via FireWire in Target Disk Mode | Hold T down during startup. |
| Eject a CD during the startup process | Hold down the mouse button during startup. |

CHAPTER 10

# Managing and Using Fonts

## In this chapter

# INSTALLING AND MANAGING MAC OS X FONTS

Mac OS X offers a lot of great features related to fonts. For example, the Quartz Extreme graphics layer renders Mac OS X fonts clearly at any size and makes using special font features such as kerning controls, ligatures, and so on, easy. You can configure and select fonts within applications using the Font panel. The Font panel offers several useful features such as the ability to create and use sets of your favorite fonts.

⇨ To learn how to work with fonts using the Fonts panel, **see** "Using the Font Panel," **p. 219**.

Mac OS X includes a large number of high-quality fonts in the default installation. You can install additional fonts you want to use.

You use the Font Book application to manage the fonts on your Mac. With the Font Book it is easy to group fonts together that you use often; quickly see a preview of a specific font; and manage the fonts that are available on your Mac.



## UNDERSTANDING MAC OS X FONTS

Fonts with the file extension `.dfont` are Datafork TrueType fonts that are single-fork files, meaning all the data for that font is stored in the single fork of its file. This is the native Mac OS X font format. However, under Mac OS X, you can also install and use any of the following types of fonts:

- Windows TrueType fonts (`.ttf`)
- TrueType collections (`.ttc`)
- OpenType fonts (`.otf`)
- Bitmapped fonts (`.sfont`)
- Fonts and font suitcases used by Mac OS 9 and earlier versions of the Mac OS (these might or might not have a filename extension)

**NOTE**

One advantage of Mac OS X font files being able to provide all their information in a single fork is that these fonts can be shared with operating systems that do not recognize files with resource forks (Windows, Unix, and so on).

There are two locations in which fonts are installed under Mac OS X. To make a font available to everyone who uses your Mac, it is installed in the directory `[`*`Mac OS X`*`]/Library/Fonts`, where *`Mac OS X`* is the name of your Mac OS X startup volume. Within this directory are at least three types of font files. Those with the filename extension `.dfont` are the single-fork font files; you'll also see TrueType fonts, which have the `.ttf` extension. You might also see fonts whose names have other extensions or that do not have a filename extension (font suitcases).

**NOTE**

> Under Mac OS X, you can install or remove fonts while applications are open; fonts you install instantly become available to the system and any active applications.

To make a font available to only specific users, it is installed in the following directory: `/users/[`*`shortusername`*`]/Library/Fonts`. A user's `Library` directory also contains the `FontCollections` folder. The `FontCollections` directory contains the set of font collections available to the user in the Font Book application and the Font pane.

**NOTE**

> Any user can install fonts into the `Fonts` folder in the `Library` folder in her Home directory.



## CONFIGURING FONTS WITH THE FONT BOOK

The Font Book enables you to manage all the fonts installed on your Mac. There are two levels of font groups you can use: libraries and collections. A *library* is a means of storing fonts on your computer or on a server; you can then access the fonts stored in those libraries. You can organize fonts into *collections* and then enable and disable individual fonts or font collections. Collections are a means to gather fonts into groups to make them easier to select and apply. For example, when you work with the Mac OS X Font panel, its fonts are organized by collection. You can use these collections to group fonts into smaller, focused groups to make font selection easier and faster.

When you open the Font Book application (`Applications` folder), you see three panes by default (see Figure 10.1). The Collection pane contains two sections. The upper section shows the libraries currently being managed by Font Book, whereas the lower section shows you the font collections on your Mac.

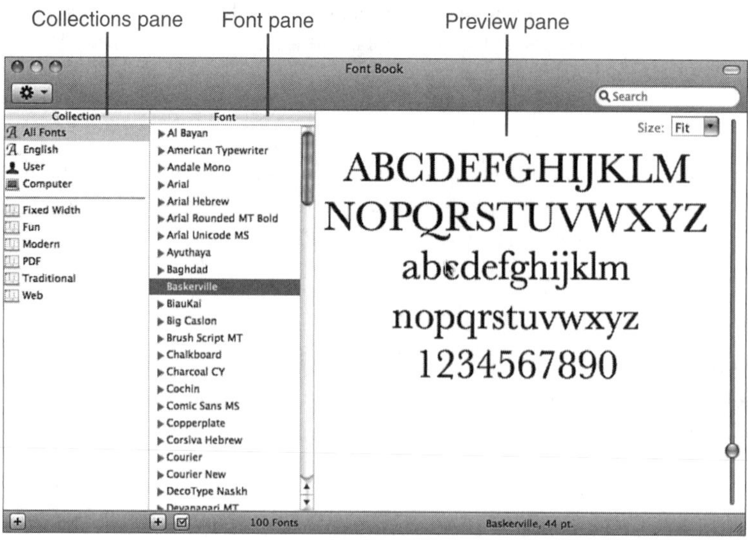


**Figure 10.1**
The Font Book application enables you to manage the fonts on your Mac.

Four libraries are available to you by default.

- All Fonts contains all the fonts on your computer.
- The language collection contains just the fonts for the main language you set for your computer and is named for the chosen language.
- User contains fonts stored so that only the current user can access them.
- Computer contains all the fonts on your Mac (in the default condition, these are the same as those in the All Fonts library).
- Some applications create collections that are installed by default, and you can create your own collections.

## WORKING WITH FONT LIBRARIES



To view the contents of a library, select it on the library list at the top of the Collection column. The fonts it contains will be displayed in the Font pane. You can also perform the following library actions:

- Create a new library by choosing File, New Library. An empty library will appear on the list; edit the name of the new library.
- Disable a library by opening its contextual menu and selecting the Disable command. The word "Off" will be shown for that library and it won't be able to be used. You can enable a library by opening its contextual menu and selecting the Enable command.
- Add fonts to a library by clicking the library in the Collections pane and selecting Add Fonts from the contextual or Action menu. Use the resulting Open dialog box to move to and select the fonts you want to add to the selected library.

**NOTE**

> The most likely use for a new library is to work with files that aren't stored on your computer. For example, if fonts are stored on a server on your network, create a library for those fonts and add them to it. To use the fonts stored on a server, you must be connected to that server via the network, even after you have stored the fonts in your Library.

- Delete a library by selecting it and selecting the Delete command on the contextual or Action menu, or by pressing the Delete key. Confirm the deletion at the prompt and the library will be removed from the Font Book window.

## WORKING WITH FONT COLLECTIONS

Font collections are groups of fonts created for any number of reasons, such as to make selecting the fonts you use most frequently easier. You can use the default font collections included with Font Book and create your own collections.

To view the fonts that are currently part of a collection, select that collection on the Collection list. The fonts it contains are listed on the Fonts pane. You can view the typefaces provided with font families shown on the Fonts pane by clicking the expansion triangle next to that font (see Figure 10.2).

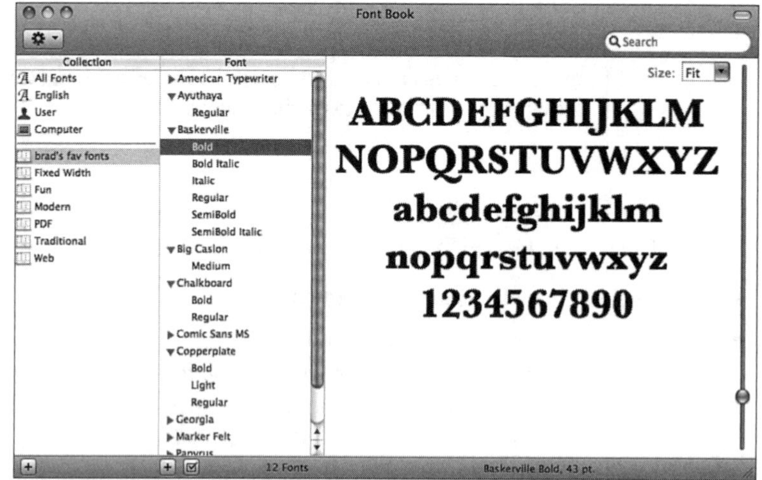


**Figure 10.2**
Here, you can see that I have created a collection called brad's fav fonts and placed the fonts I use most frequently in it.



**TIP**

> If a bullet appears next to a font's name, multiple versions of that font are installed. To remove the multiple versions, select the font and select Edit, Resolve Duplicates. This causes Font Book to turn off the duplicate fonts so that they won't clutter things up when you select a font.

### Creating a Font Collection

To create a font collection, do the following steps:

1. Click the New Collection button (the plus sign) below the bottom of the Collection list, select File, New Collection, or press ⌘-N. A new collection appears on the list; its name is selected and ready for you to edit.
2. Select the default name of the new collection and click the mouse button; when the field becomes editable, type the name of the collection and press Return. The collection will be renamed.
3. View libraries or other collections, such as the All Fonts collection, to look for fonts to add to the collection you just created.

**TIP**

> To locate a specific font, select the All Fonts collection and type the font name in the Search tool on the Font Book toolbar.

4. Drag a font you want to install in the new collection from the Fonts pane and drop it on the collection in which you want to place it. You can drag an entire font family to add it to the collection or expand it and drag only the typefaces that you want to be available in the collection onto it.
5. Repeat steps 3 and 4 to add more fonts to the collection.

**TIP**

You can move multiple fonts at the same time by holding down the ⌘ when you select each font you want to add to another collection.

### Editing Font Collections



After you have created a font collection, you can change it in the following ways:

- Double-click the collection name and edit it.
- Select the collection; select a font you want to remove from the collection; and select File, Remove [*font*], where *font* is the name of the font family or a specific typeface that you selected. Click Remove in the Confirmation dialog box; the font is removed from the collection (the font remains installed on your Mac).
- Select a font within a collection and choose Edit, Disable [*font*], where *font* is the name of the font family or a specific typeface that you selected. Click Disable in the Warning dialog box. The font is no longer able to be selected from within applications. The word `Off` appears next to the font to indicate it has been disabled.
- Select a font that has been disabled and select Edit, Enable [*font*], where *font* is the name of the font family or a specific typeface that you selected. The font is again available within that collection from within applications.
- Select a collection, open its contextual menu, and choose Disable [*font*], where *font* is the name of the font family or a specific typeface that you selected. Click the Disable button in the warning dialog box. The collection is no longer selectable within applications. The word `Off` appears next to the collection to indicate it has been disabled.
- Select a collection that has been disabled, open its contextual menu, and choose Enable [*font*], where *font* is the name of the font family or a specific typeface that you selected. The collection is again available within applications.

**TIP**

If you use specific sets of fonts in specific applications, consider creating a font collection for each application and placing the fonts you use within it. Then, you can easily choose fonts from this group by selecting the application's font collection.

## Configuring the Font Book Window

You can also configure the Font Book window itself in the following ways:

- Select Preview, Show Font Info. When you do, information about the selected font appears in the Preview pane.

- Change the size of the font preview in the Preview pane by either selecting a point size on the Size pop-up menu or by dragging the vertical slider along the right side of the pane. If you select Fit on the pop-up menu, the preview size is adjusted so you can see all the preview within the pane.
- Change the relative size of the panes by dragging their resize handles.

**TIP**

> The panes are limited to certain relative sizes. If you try to make a pane larger but are unable to do so, increase the size of the Font Book window itself and then make the other panes larger. You should then be able to resize the first pane.

- Change the size of the Font Book window by dragging its Resize handle.
- Change the configuration of the preview shown in the Preview pane by selecting one of the options on the Preview menu. The Sample option shows each letter and number in the selected font, whereas the Repertoire option shows all the characters included in the selected font. The Custom option enables you to type characters in the Preview pane to preview them.



**TIP**

> If you have trouble with a font, try validating it by selecting it and selecting File, Validate Font. Use the resulting Font Validation tool to check the font. When you do, the tool will report on the condition of the font.

### INSTALLING FONTS WITH THE FONT BOOK

You can use the Font Book to install fonts by performing the following steps:

1. Select or create the library into which you want to place the fonts and select File, Add Fonts (⌘-O). The Open dialog box will appear.
2. Move to and select the font you want to install.
3. Click Open. The font will be added to the selected library. You can add it to collections and work with that font within Font Book and from within applications.

**TIP**

> To see where a font is installed, select it and select File, Reveal in Finder (⌘-R). A Finder window opens that shows the location in which the file has been installed.

## USING THE FONT PANEL

The Font panel gives you control over the particular fonts used in your documents and also enables you to manage any font installed on your Mac, no matter which application you are using. The Font panel provides control over the particular fonts used in your documents and also enables you to manage all the fonts installed on your Mac.

In most applications, you can open the Font panel by choosing Format, Fonts, Show Fonts or by pressing ⌘-T (see Figure 10.3).

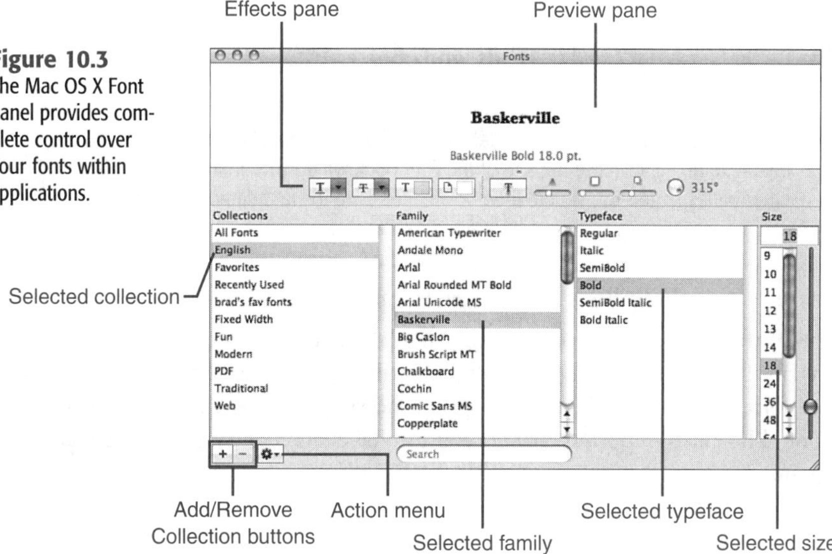


**Figure 10.3**
The Mac OS X Font panel provides complete control over your fonts within applications.



**CAUTION**

> Not all applications support Mac OS X's Font system. If an application doesn't use this system, it provides its own set of formatting tools that you use to format a document. For example, Microsoft Word does not support Mac OS X's font system so you can't access the Font panel from within the application. If an application doesn't support the Mac OS X Font panel, you have to use its own font tools instead.

The Font panel has a number of panes. You can choose to hide or display certain panes, whereas others are always visible. The various panes of the Font panel are the following:

- **Collections (always displayed)**—As you learned earlier, you can use collections to group fonts together. Font collections make selecting fonts easier because you can group fonts into collections, so you can select a set of fonts by choosing the collection in which those fonts are contained. The collections you see in the Collections pane of the Font panel include all those fonts and collections that are installed and enabled via the Font Book application. Applications can also provide distinct collections. For example, in TextEdit, you see the Favorites collection, which contains a set of fonts, typefaces, and sizes you have added via the Add to Favorites action, and the Recently Used collection, which contains the fonts, typefaces, and sizes of text formatting you have recently applied in the current document.
- **Family (always displayed)**—The Family pane lists all the font families that are part of the selected collection. You select the family you want to work with on the list of available families in the selected collection.

- **Typeface (displayed except when working with the Favorites and Recently Used collections)**—In the Typeface pane, you choose the typeface for the selected font family, such as Regular, Bold, and so on.
- **Size (always displayed)**—You choose the size of the font you are applying in the Size pane.
- **Preview (displayed when you select Show Preview on the Action menu)**—This pane, which appears at the top of the Font panel, provides a preview of the font you have selected.
- **Effects (always displayed)**—This pane provides buttons you use to configure underline, strikethrough, text color, background color, and text shadow effects.

The Action menu at the bottom-left corner of the panel provides access to the following commands:

- **Add to Favorites**—This command adds the current font, typeface, and size to the Favorites collection.
- **Show/Hide Preview**—This choice opens or hides the Preview pane.
- **Show/Hide Effects**—This command opens or hides the Effects pane.
- **Color**—Choosing this causes the Color Picker to open.
- **Characters**—This command opens the Characters palette.
- **Typography**—This command opens the Typography panel that you can use to choose ligatures, adjust the space before and after characters, and shift the text baseline.
- **Edit Sizes**—Using this command, you can customize the sizes that appear in the Size pane.
- **Manage Fonts**—This command opens the Font Book that enables you to manage the fonts installed on your Mac.



### Previewing Fonts

If you select Show Preview on the Action menu, the Preview pane appears at the top of the panel. This pane provides a preview of the currently selected family, typeface, and size. You can use this preview to help you make better selections more quickly. To hide the Preview pane, select Hide Preview on the Action menu.

### Using Font Favorites

When you select a font family, typeface, and size and then use the Add to Favorites command on the Action menu, that font is added to your Favorites collection. When you select the Favorites collection in the Font panel, you can quickly choose one of your favorite fonts to use; this saves you a couple of steps (see Figure 10.4).

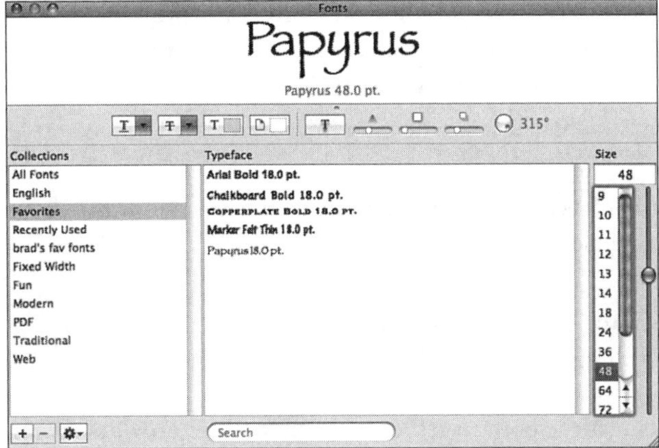


**Figure 10.4**
When you add a font, typeface, and size to your Favorites collection, you can easily apply that formatting to selected text in a document.



**NOTE**

> The capability to save specific combinations of family, typeface, and size as a favorite makes using specific fonts easy. This is much like the styles feature offered in Word and other text applications. By designating a combination as a favorite, you can reapply it quickly and easily. Unfortunately, you can't make changes to the favorite and have those changes be made wherever that favorite is used as you can with styles.

## CREATING OR REMOVING FONT COLLECTIONS

You can add or remove font collections from the Font panel. When you do so, the font collection is also added or removed to the collections available in the Font Book application (which contains all the fonts installed on your Mac).

From the Font panel, you can make the following changes to the collections shown in the Collections list:

- Add new font collections.
- Remove font collections.
- Add fonts to collections.

Although you can manage font collections from within the Font panel, you should generally use the Font Book application. This is because font collections are really a system-level resource, so it is better practice to manage them using a system tool—that being the Font Book.

**TIP**

> Using the Font Book, you can disable both font collections and individual fonts from within collections. This is the best technique because you can prevent collections and fonts from being available within an application but maintain those collections and fonts on your Mac.

### APPLYING EFFECTS TO FONTS

Using the Effects tools, you can apply the following effects to selected text:

- Apply underline effects
- Apply strikethrough effects
- Apply color to text

> **NOTE** You can also apply color effects by selecting Color on the Action menu.

- Apply color to a document's background
- Apply text shadow effects



To apply effects to text, do the following steps:

1. Select the text to which you want to apply the effects.
2. Open the Font panel.
3. Open the Action menu and select Show Effects (if the Effects pane isn't visible). The Effects pane provides a number of tools you can use to apply effects to your text (see Figure 10.5).

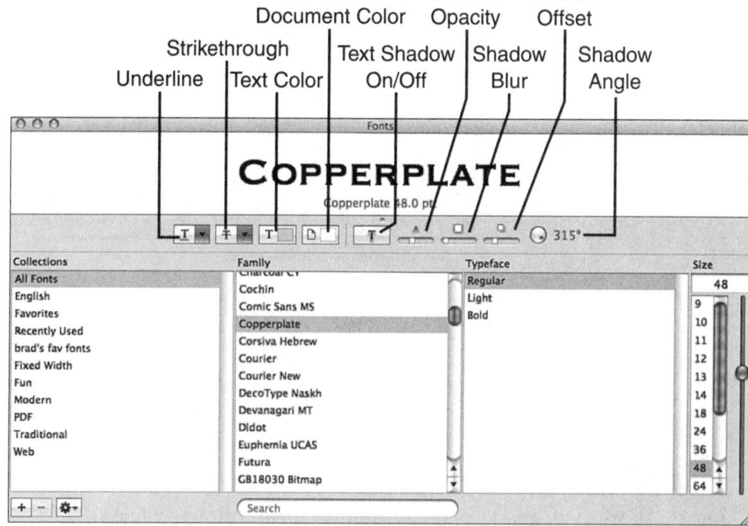


**Figure 10.5**
You can use the Effects pane to apply various effects to selected text.

4. Select from the underline effects on the Underline pop-up menu. The options are None, Single, Double, or Color. If you select Color, use the Color Picker to choose the color of the underline.

5. Select the strikethrough effects on the Strikethrough pop-up menu. The options are None, Single, Double, or Color. If you select Color, use the Color Picker to choose the color of the strikethrough.
6. Click the Text Color button and use the Color Picker to choose the text color.
7. Click the Document Color button and use the Color Picker to select the background color of the document on which you are working.
8. To apply a shadow to the text, click the Text Shadow button; when a shadow is applied, the button is blue.
9. Use the Shadow Opacity, Shadow Blur, and Shadow Offset sliders to configure those properties of the shadow.
10. Use the Shadow Angle wheel to set the angle of the shadow.



**NOTE**

Unfortunately, you won't see the text effects you apply in the Preview pane of the Font panel. You need to be able to see the document on which you are working to see the results of the effects you apply.

### EDITING THE SIZES THAT APPEAR ON THE SIZE PANE

If you select Edit Sizes on the Action menu on the Fonts panel, you will see the Font Size sheet, which you can use to change the sizes that appear in the Size pane of the Font panel (see Figure 10.6).

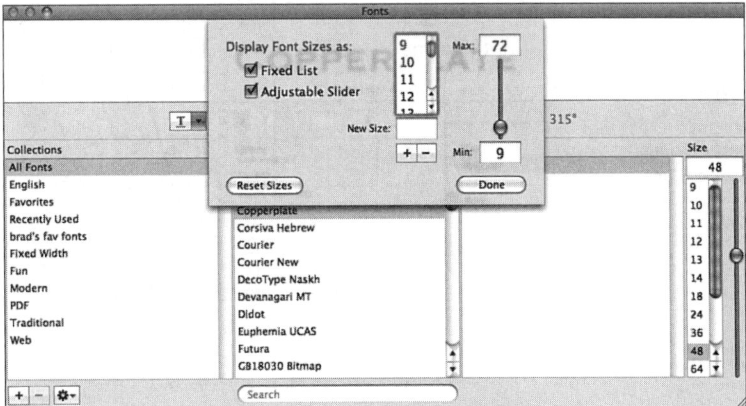


**Figure 10.6**
You can control the specific sizes of font that appear in the Fonts panel using the Font Size sheet.

Using the Font Size sheet, you can perform the following tasks:

- To add a size to the Size pane, enter the size you want to add in the New Size box and click + (the plus sign).
- To remove a size from the Size pane, select it on the size list and click – (the minus sign).

- To remove the list of fixed sizes from the Size pane, uncheck the Fixed List check box. Check that box again to display the list of fixed sizes again.
- To show the Size slider in the Size pane, check the Adjustable Slider check box. Then, enter the minimum font size and maximum size to be included on the slider in the Min Size and Max Size text boxes.
- To reset the sizes to the default values, click the Reset Sizes button.

Save your changes by clicking the Done button. The sheet disappears and the changes you made are reflected in the Size pane.

### APPLYING TYPOGRAPHY EFFECTS TO FONTS

The Font panel enables you to apply some basic typography effects to text. To do so, use the following steps:



1. Open the Action menu and select Typography. The Typography tools appear (see Figure 10.7).

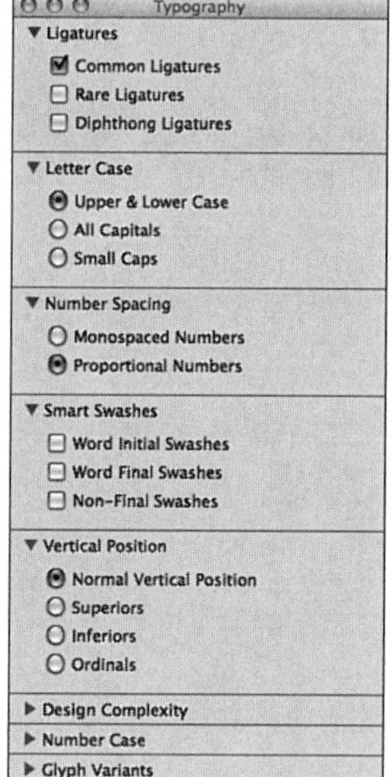


**Figure 10.7**
You can use the Typography tools to apply typography effects to text.

2. Use the resulting tools to apply a variety of typographical effects to the selected text.

**NOTE**

> The specific typography effects you see in the Typography window depend on the font family currently selected. Try selecting various families with the Typography window open to see the options that become available.

# WORKING WITH THE CHARACTER PALETTE

Special characters can be a pain to use because remembering which font family the character you need is part of is often difficult. The Character Palette is designed to help you find special characters in various languages and quickly apply those characters to your documents. You can also add favorite characters you use frequently for even easier access.

You can open the Character Palette from within applications that use the Mac OS X Font panel, or you can install the Character Palette menu on the Mac OS X menu bar.

## OPENING THE CHARACTER PALETTE FROM THE FONT PANEL

To open the Character Palette from the Mac OS X Font panel, select Characters on the Action menu. The Character Palette will open (see Figure 10.8).

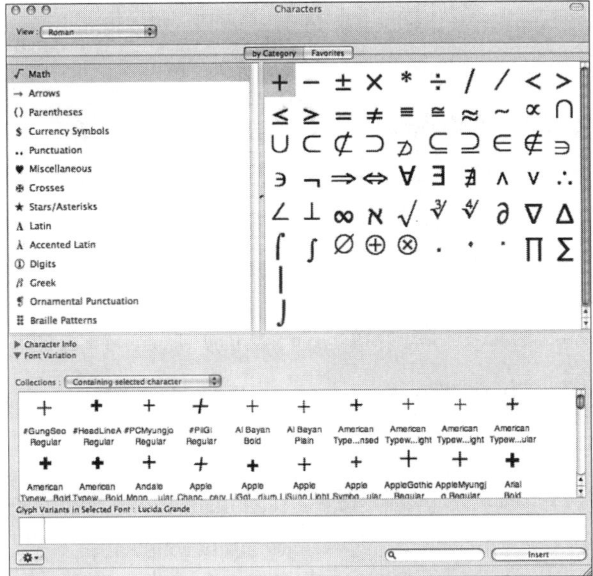


**Figure 10.8**
The Mac OS X Character Palette enables you to efficiently work with special characters.

You can now work with the palette as described in the "Using the Character Palette" section later in this chapter.

## INSTALLING THE CHARACTER PALETTE ON THE FINDER MENU BAR

You can also install the Character Palette on the Input menu on the Mac OS X menu bar so it is available in all applications, whether they use the Mac OS X Font panel or not. To install the palette, perform the following steps:

1. Open the System Preferences application.
2. Click the International icon. The International pane opens.

3. Click the Input Menu tab and check the On check box next to Character Palette. The "Show input menu in menu bar" check box is checked automatically and the Input menu appears on the Finder's menu bar. This enables the Input menu that appears on the right end of any application's menu bar, including the Finder (see Figure 10.9).
4. Check the boxes next to any languages you want to install on the Input menu.

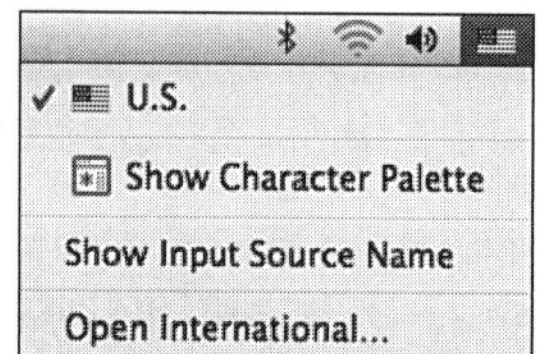


**Figure 10.9**
The Input menu enables you to access the Character Palette from any application.

After you have installed the Character Palette on the Input menu, you can open it by selecting Input menu, Show Character Palette.

10

## Using the Character Palette

The Character Palette has two tabs. The "by Category" tab enables you to select and insert characters you need. When you find a character you use regularly, you can add it to the other tab, which is the Favorites tab, so you can grab it easily and quickly.

To find and use a character, carry out the following steps:

1. Open the Character Palette (either through the Action menu in the Font panel or from the Mac OS X Input menu).
2. On the Character Palette, select the language sets you want to view on the View pop-up menu. For example, to see Roman characters, select Roman.
3. Click the "by Category" tab and choose the category of character you want to view in the left pane. For example, select Math to view mathematical symbols.
4. Select the character with which you want to work by clicking it.
5. Expand the Character Info section. You will see a large version of the selected character along with its name. You'll also see characters to which the selected one is related. You can choose to work with one of the related characters by clicking it. The one you click will become selected, even if it is not in the currently selected category.
6. To apply different fonts to the character, click the expansion triangle next to the Font Variation tab. Select the font collection you want to use on the Collections pop-up menu. Then, click the font you want to apply to the character you selected. When you expand the Font Variation section, a preview pane appears; this shows a preview of the character you have selected along with its name. You can see a version of the character in each font family in the collection selected on the Collections pop-up menu.

**TIP**

> To limit the fonts shown in the Font Variation pane to only those that contain the character you are working with, select "Containing selected character" on the Collections pop-up menu. The character is shown with the fonts that contain it.

7. Continue adjusting the character until it is the way you want it.
8. Click Insert with Font. The character is pasted into the active document at the insertion point.

**NOTE**

> If you don't apply a font to the character, the Insert with Font button is just the Insert button.

*If the symbol you selected doesn't appear correctly in the document you inserted it in, see "The Special Character I Inserted Doesn't Look Correct" in the "Troubleshooting" section at the end of this chapter.*

**TIP**

> You can search for special characters by description or code using the Search tool that appears at the bottom of the Character Palette window.

# Troubleshooting

## The Special Character I Inserted Doesn't Look Correct

*I inserted a special character from the Character Palette into a document, but the character that appeared wasn't the one I selected.*

This can happen if the application you are working with does not support the Mac OS X font and formatting tools. The most likely case is that the format information you associated with the character, such as the font, was not translated into the application properly.

To solve the problem, use the application's formatting tools to apply the same font to the character as is selected in the Character Palette. The symbol should then appear just as it does in the Character Palette.

# Mac OS X to the Max: Setting Up Character Favorites

You can create a set of favorite characters on the Character Palette to let you quickly choose a special character to insert into a document. This is especially useful when you have applied specific fonts to a character.

To create favorite characters, take the following steps:

1. Open the Character Palette.
2. Create the character just as you would to insert it into a document.
3. Open the Action menu and select Add to Favorites. This copies the character onto the Favorites tab (see Figure 10.10).

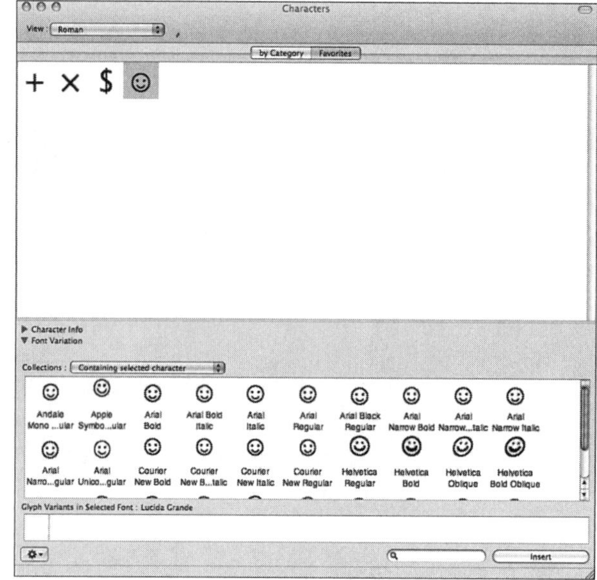


**Figure 10.10** The characters shown on the Favorites tab can be inserted into a document quickly and easily.

To insert a favorite character from the Favorites tab into a document, perform the following steps:

1. Open the Character Palette.
2. Click the Favorites tab.
3. Select the character you want to insert.
4. Click Insert.

You can remove a character from the Favorites tab by selecting it and selecting "Remove from Favorites" on the Action menu.

CHAPTER 11

# Configuring and Working with User Accounts

## In this chapter

# USING MAC OS X USER ACCOUNTS

When you started using Mac OS X Leopard, whether that was when you purchased a new Mac or upgraded from an earlier Mac OS X version, you might not have taken advanatage of one of the system's most important, and frequently underused, features, which is the ability to create and use multiple user accounts.

Unfortunately, the Mac OS X installer and configuration application that runs the first time you use Mac OS X doesn't really encourage multiuser set up. To get you started as fast and as easily as possible, the initial configuration creates a single user account and configures your Mac to log in to that account automatically. That's all well and good to get started, but certainly no place to stop. It's important that you understand how to use multiple user accounts on your Mac, especially if you share your Mac with other people. However, even if you are the only person who ever touches your Mac's keyboard and mouse, you should still have at least two user accounts.

**NOTE**

> To be at least somewhat fair to Windows, this is one place where the Windows XP installer is actually better than Mac OS X's. When you install Windows XP, you are prompted to create multiple user accounts. I wish the Mac OS installer had a similar feature so Mac users would be more likely to create multiple user accounts.



## UNDERSTANDING WHY YOU SHOULD USE MULTIPLE USER ACCOUNTS

If you share your Mac with other people, it's pretty easy to see why having more than one user account is a good thing.

One reason is that each user account on your Mac has its own set of preferences and resources that are specific to that user account. This means that how the OS looks and works is unique to each user. A simple example is the desktop picture, which is stored as a preference within each user account. Under each account, the user's desktop environment can look different. Most other customizable aspects of Mac OS X, such as the Dock, are also specific to each user account. Applications also store preferences specific to each user account so that those applications can be tailored to each person who uses your Mac. Because of this, Mac OS X and the applications it supports can be customized for every one who uses your Mac (as long as each person has his own user account, of course).

Another important reason to make your Mac a multiuser machine is that an account defines a user's ability to perform specific actions that are either allowed or denied by the account's security privileges. Actions controlled by a user's account security privileges include whether the user can view or change specific files, change certain system preferences, and so on. For example, a user account must have administrator privileges to modify a Mac's network settings or to install applications. Even though you share your Mac with others, you probably want to retain control of how the machine is configured. You can allow others to access and use your Mac without giving them carte blanche to make changes to it.

If everyone who uses your Mac also uses the Internet for email or web browsing (which is highly likely), user accounts also keep each person's Internet configuration, such as email account, separate too.

Lastly, user accounts also come with a set of resources to which only the user has access. Most of these are contained in the user's Home folder. This helps keep your Mac organized. When other people create documents and other files, those files are visible only to that user and won't clutter up your desktop.

If you don't share your Mac with others, you still need to configure at least two user accounts on it. You'll of course need the account you primarly use while working on your Mac. You'll also need a "clean" account that you can use to troubleshoot problems.

**NOTE**

> User accounts are not a natual concept for some Mac users. Although you can use the automatic login mode so that you don't have to log in to your Mac, the fact remains that Mac OS X is a multiuser system. To get the most out of it, you need to get comfortable with user accounts because whether you have to log in or not, you will always be utilizing user accounts under Mac OS X at some level. At the least, you need to be comfortable with user accounts for troubleshooting purposes.

11

## UNDERSTANDING USER ACCOUNT TYPES

There are several types of Mac OS X user accounts I'll address in this chapter:

- **Administrator** accounts have broad access to the system; the initial account set up by the Mac OS X installation application is of this type.
- **Clean** accounts are administrator accounts that you use solely for troubleshooting (this isn't a formal type, but rather a functional one).
- **Standard** user accounts don't have administrator permissions and can have other limitations as well.
- **Shared** user accounts are intended to be used by multiple people.
- **Guest** user accounts are temporary accounts that don't have permanent resources on your Mac.
- The **root** user account is the extremely powerful and equally dangerous account you use mostly for troubleshooting.

You can also create groups of user accounts to enable you to configure security properties to provide specific kinds of access to system resources, folders, and files.

### UNDERSTANDING ADMINISTRATOR ACCOUNTS

The account created when you installed Mac OS X is an administrator account. Administrator accounts are special because they provide wide access to the system and are one of only two accounts that can control virtually every aspect of Mac OS X (the other being the root account). A user who logs in as an administrator for your Mac can do the following:

- **Create other user accounts**—An administrator for your Mac can create additional user accounts. By default, these user accounts have more limited access to the Mac than does an administrator account, but you can allow other accounts to administer your Mac as well (so you can create multiple administrator accounts).
- **Change global system preferences**—The administrator can change global system settings for your Mac; other user accounts can't. For example, to change the network settings on your Mac, you must be logged in as the administrator (or you must authenticate yourself as an administrator).
- **Configure access to files and folders**—An administrator can configure the security settings of files and folders to determine who can access those items and which type of access is permitted.
- **Install applications**—Applications you install under Mac OS X require that you be logged in as an administrator or that you authenticate yourself as one.



When you are logged in under an administrator account, you can perform most of these actions without inputting more information because your account configuration gives you permissions to do so. However, when you are logged in under a non-administrator user account (and sometimes in specific situations while logged in under an administrator account), you'll need to authenticate yourself as an administrator to be able to complete the action.

You should control who has access to the administrator accounts for your machine. If someone who doesn't understand Mac OS X—or who wants to cause you trouble—logs in with your administrator account, you might be in for all kinds of problems.

*If you forget the username and password for your administrator account, see "I Forgot My Administrator User Account Username or Password" in the "Troubleshooting" section at the end of this chapter.*

### UNDERSTANDING THE CLEAN ACCOUNT

There's one user account you should create, but seldom use. I call this the clean account not because the others are dirty, but because no customization or personalization should be done under this account. It should remain in its just-created state so that all the preferences and other files stored under it are as close to being in their default states as possible.

You use the clean account to troubleshoot problems. By logging in under the clean account, you can often isolate problems that are related to a user account preference or a change made by an application that only affects the user account under which that change was made.

When a problem occurs, you log in to the clean account and attempt to replicate the problem. If it doesn't recur, you know that the issue is specific to the user account you were logged in under when it happened. If it recurs, you know that it is a system problem. This information can be critical to being able to solve a problem efficiently and effectively.

You should always create a clean user account on your Mac, whether you create any of the other types or not.

### UNDERSTANDING NON-ADMINISTRATOR (STANDARD) USER ACCOUNTS

When you share your Mac with others, you'll most likely want to provide them with non-administrator user accounts, which are called *standard* user accounts. Because these accounts don't have administrator permissions, the types of activities they can do are limited. For example, people using these accounts can't install applications or make certain changes that affect the system. This is a good thing because it prevents other people from making changes to your system without your knowledge or permission.

You can further limit the access of standard accounts too, such as using the Simple Finder or Parental Controls features to more extensively control the resources to which people using these accounts can access. When you limit an account like this, it becomes a managed account.

### UNDERSTANDING THE GUEST ACCOUNT

The guest account is a good way to let people use your Mac on a temporary basis. You don't need a password to log in as a guest; all the user has to do is select the guest account. Once logged in, the user can access the Mac as if he were using a standard or managed account.The primary difference between the guest account and other accounts is that as soon as the user logs off, all the information associated with that account is deleted so no permanent changes are made to your Mac.



You also use the guest account to allow others to connect to your Mac over the local network. When someone logs in as a guest they can access shared folders, as well as upload files to those public directories.

### UNDERSTANDING SHARING-ONLY ACCOUNTS

Sharing-only accounts are designed to allow a user to have access to your Mac over a network without being able to physically log in to to your computer. Similar to a guest account, a sharing-only account can access shared folders, as well as upload files to those public directories. However, the benefit of using a sharing-only account is an added layer of security by requiring the person to know a username and password to access these resources. Depending on the environment your Mac is in, a sharing-only account may be a more secure choice for providing others access to your files.

### UNDERSTANDING USER GROUPS

Mac OS X uses the group concept to assign permissions to access files and folders. You can create user groups and assign user accounts to those groups. This makes providing permissions simpler because you only have to choose one group to give the members of that group the appropriate permissions.

### UNDERSTANDING THE ROOT ACCOUNT

Because Mac OS X in based on Unix, it includes the root account. In a nutshell, the root account is not limited by *any* security permissions. If an action can be done on your Mac, the root account can do it. This is both good and bad. It's good because you can often solve problems using the root account that you can't solve any other way. It's bad because you can also cause problems that it might not be possible to recover from, at least not easily. For example, when you are using an administrator account, you have limited access to certain system files so there is no way you can delete them. However, under the root account, anything goes so it's possible you can do things that cause your system to be unusable.

Like the clean account, you'll likely only use the root account for troubleshooting. But, when you need it, you'll really need it.

# CREATING AND CONFIGURING USER ACCOUNTS

Hopefully, you are convinced that you need at least two user accounts on your Mac. Because one administrator account was created when you installed Mac OS X, you'll need to at least create one more administrator account to use as your clean account.



If you share your Mac with others, you can choose to create a user account for each person. Or, you can create a user account that several people share. This can be useful if there are people who use your Mac but don't necessarily need private folders or individual customization. For example, if you share your Mac with children, you might want to create a single user account for them to use.

The good news is that three of the four types I described earlier are created and configured using the steps you'll find in this section. (The root account is an animal of an entirely different type; you'll learn how to work with the root account later in the chapter.)

## CREATING USER ACCOUNTS

To create user accounts, use the System Preferences application and follow these steps:

1. Open the System Preferences application.
2. Click the Accounts icon in the System area to open the Accounts pane of the System Preferences application (see Figure 11.1).

   Along the left side of this pane is the list of user accounts currently configured on the Mac. At the top of this list in the My Account section, the user account under which you are logged in is shown. If you've not created additional user accounts, this will be the account you created when you installed Mac OS X. Under the Other Accounts heading are the other user accounts that exist on the machine; click the expansion triangle next to the heading to see the other accounts on your Mac. Under each username, you will see the type of account it is, such as Admin, Managed, and so on. At the bottom of the user list is the Login Options button, and just below that are the Add User (+) and Delete User buttons (-). The right part of the pane shows the tools you use to configure the selected user account.

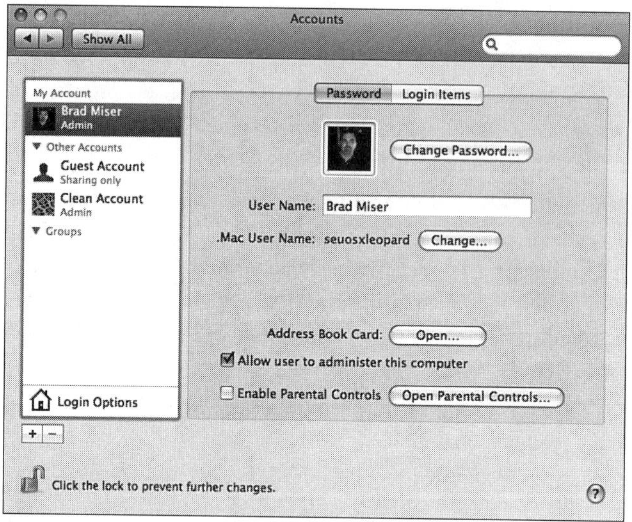


**Figure 11.1**
You create and manage user accounts with the Accounts pane of the System Preferences application.

Only an administrator can create or change user accounts. If you aren't logged in as an administrator for your Mac, you have to authenticate yourself as being an administrator before you can create an account. To do so, click the Lock icon located in the lower-left corner of the System Preferences window, enter the username and password for an administrator account, and click OK. This identifies you as an administrator so that you can make changes, such as adding and changing user accounts.

3. Click the New User button, which is the plus sign located under the list of users. A sheet appears in which you enter basic information for the user account you are creating.
4. Choose the type of user to create on the New Account pop-up menu. If you want the new account to be an administrator account, select Administrator on the menu. Of course, you should allow this only on accounts you control or for people you trust not to cause you problems.
5. Enter the name for the user account in the Name box. The name is the "full" name for the user account; it doesn't have to be a real full name—the name can be pretty much whatever you want it to be.
6. Press Tab to move to the Short Name box. When you do, Mac OS X creates a short name for the user account. The short name is used for specific areas under that user account (such as the name of the user's Home folder) and for access to services provided under that account (such as the account's website). The short name can be used instead of the name to cut down on the number of characters you have to type in specific situations, such as when you log in to the account (in which case the short name and name are interchangeable). However, the Home directory is always identified by the short name only.

Mac OS X automatically creates a short name for the account; it just places all the letters in the name together with no spaces. You can choose to use this one, or you can change it to something else.

7. Edit the short name as needed, such as by replacing it if you don't like the one Mac OS X created for you automatically.

   The short name can be as few as one character and can't contain any spaces, dashes, or other special characters (Mac OS X won't let you enter any characters that are unacceptable). Underscores are acceptable. You should adopt a general rule about the short name for an account, such as using the first initial of the first name and the complete last name. Keeping the short name consistent will help you deal with other user accounts more easily.

   After it's created, you can't change the short name for a user account, so be deliberate when you create it.

**TIP**

> You can use a user account for any purpose you want. For example, because each user account has its own website, you might want to create a user account simply to create another website on your machine. For example, you might want to create a user called "Group Site" (with a short name of "group_site") to serve a web page to a workgroup of which you are a member.



8. Create the password that the user will enter to log in under the user account. For better security, use a password that is eight characters long and contains both letters and numbers (this makes the password harder to crack). Passwords are case sensitive; for example, mypassword is not the same as MyPassword. If you want help creating a password, move to step 9 without typing a password. If you want to type it in without help, enter it in the Password and Verify fields and skip to step 16.

   If you leave the Password field empty, a password will not be required to log in to the account. When you choose to do this, you will see a warning dialog box when you attempt to save the account. If you ignore this warning, the account is created without a password. When the user logs in to the account, he can select it on the list of user accounts and log in without entering a password. Obviously, this is not a secure thing to do, but it can be useful nonetheless. For example, you might choose to create an account for children whom you don't want to have to use a password. When you create such "unprotected" accounts, you should use the Parental Controls tools to limit access to your Mac, such as by using the Simple Finder option.

**TIP**

> You can remove a password from an existing account even though the system tells you this can't be done. Just remove the password, save the account changes, click Ignore in the warning dialog box, and then click OK in the dialog box that tells you this change won't be accepted. It is actually accepted and the account no longer requires a password.

9. Click the Key button to the right of the Password field. The Password Assistant will open (see Figure 11.2).

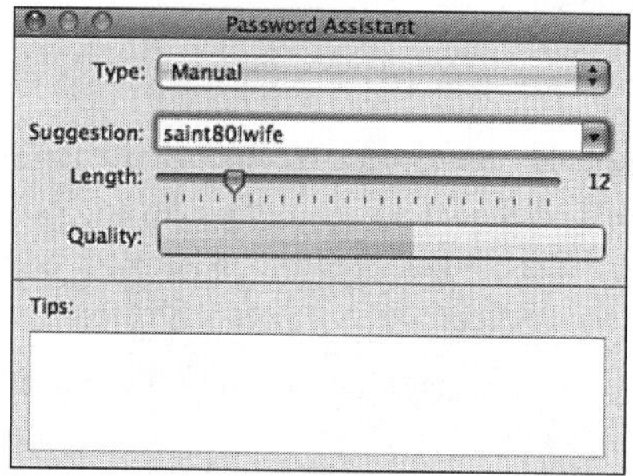


**Figure 11.2**
The Password Assistant can help you create passwords.

10. Select the type of password you want to create on the Type pop-up menu. There are several options:
    - **Manual**—Enables you to type a password manually. When you choose this option, you can use the Password Assistant to help you gauge the quality of the password you create.
    - **Memorable**—Creates a password that your Mac thinks that users will be able to remember.
    - **Letters & Numbers**—Creates a password consisting of letters and numbers.
    - **Numbers Only**—Creates a password consisting of only numbers.
    - **Random**—Creates a random password.
    - **FIPS-181 compliant**—Creates a password that is compliant with the federal requirements for automatic password generation.
11. To create a password yourself, choose Manual and type the password in the Suggestion box. As you type, the Assistant will provide tips for you in the Tips box (see Figure 11.3). It will also display the quality of the password on the Quality gauge. The more of the bar that is filled in with green, the more secure the password is. If the bar has red or yellow, the password you've created is not very secure. When you're satisfied with the password you've created, enter the password you've created in the Verify field and skip to step 16.

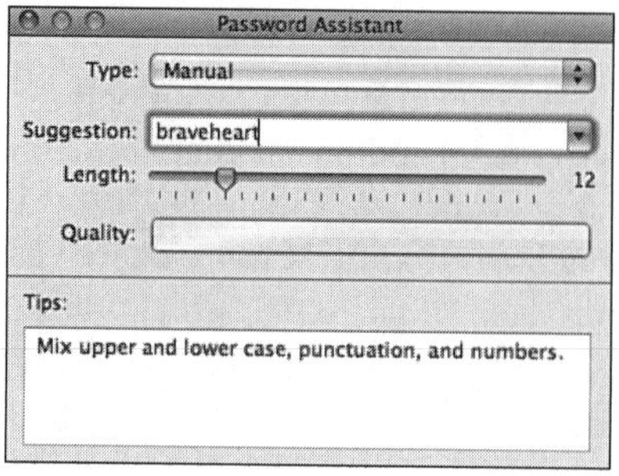

**Figure 11.3**
The Assistant is suggesting I mix case and add punctuation and numbers to make this password more secure.

**NOTE**

> If you close the Password Assistant before you create the user account, the password you entered manually will be deleted from both fields. Leave the Assistant open while you finish configuring the sheet.

12. To have the Assistant suggest a password, choose a type other than Manual. The Assistant will generate a password of that type in the Suggestion box.
13. Select the length of the password you want to create using the Length slider. The minimum number of characters is 8. The maximum is 31, but I suspect your users won't be happy with a password that long! More characters mean a more secure password, but also one that is harder to remember and type.

    After you choose the length, your Mac will generate a new password of the type you selected and it will appear in the Suggestion box.
14. If you don't like the suggested password shown, use the Suggestion pop-up menu to select another option. You can generate more suggestions by choosing More Suggestions.

    As you select passwords, the Quality gauge shows you a relative measure of the quality of the password you are choosing. The more of the bar that is filled with green, the more secure the password will be. Of course, this is from the security perspective, which isn't necessarily the same as the user's preferences!
15. When the Suggestion box contains the password you want to use, click in the Verify box and retype the password.
16. Move into the Password Hint field (press Tab) and enter a hint to remind the user what the password is. This reminder is optional; if a user fails to log in successfully after three attempts, this hint can appear to help him remember his password.



**NOTE**

> If you have not turned off the Automatic Login mode and you create a new user account, you will see a dialog box asking whether you want that mode to be turned off. The account that is logged in automatically is also shown in this dialog box. (If you have disabled the Automatic Login mode already, you won't see this dialog box.)

17. If you want the new account's Home folder to be protected with FileVault, check the "Turn on FileVault protection" check box.

⇨ To learn more about FileVault, **see** "Securing Your Mac With FileVault," **p. 922**.

18. Review the information you have entered and update it as needed; when you are ready to create the account, click Create Account (see Figure 11.4). If you didn't enter a password, you'll be warned in a dialog box, click OK if you are sure you want to create a user account without a password.

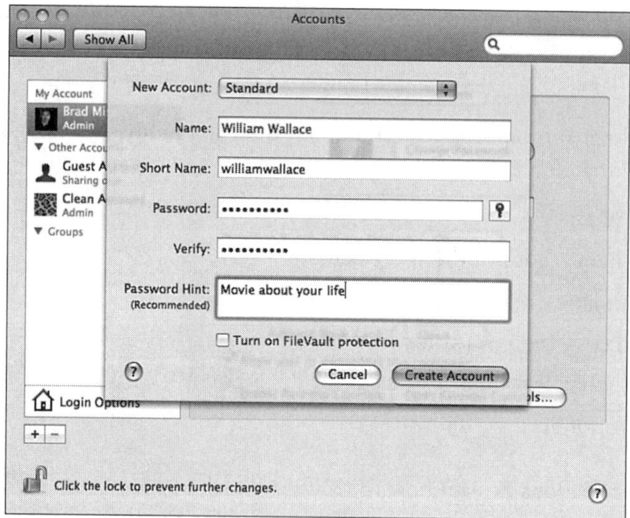


**Figure 11.4** When you complete the information on this sheet, you are ready to create a new user account.

You'll return to the Accounts pane and the user account you created will be shown at the bottom of the Other Accounts list (see Figure 11.5). Under the account, you'll see the type of account it is. *Standard* means that the account can't administer the Mac and it doesn't include parental controls. *Admin* means that the account can administer the Mac. *Managed* means that parental controls have been used to limit the account's access to the Mac in some way.

11

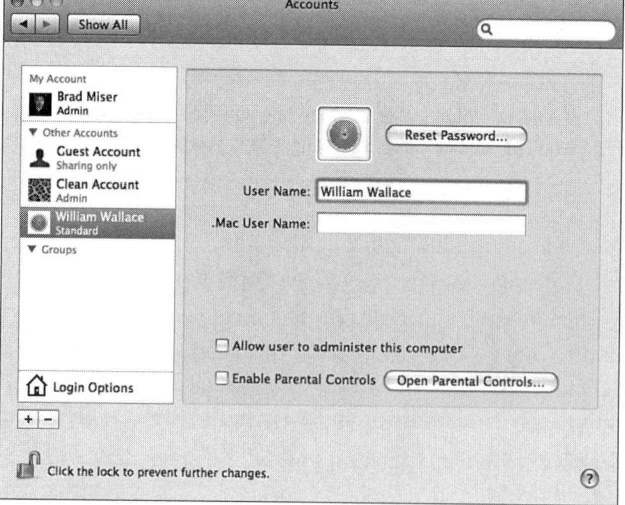


**Figure 11.5** The account called William Wallace has been created and is ready to configure.

## Configuring User Accounts

After you have created a user account, you can configure it to determine the kind of access that account has to your Mac and to customize certain aspects of it.

When you select the account under which you are currently logged in (the one shown in the My Account area), the Password and Login Items tabs appear. You use these tabs to configure these elements of the current account.

If you aren't logged in under the account you want to modify, you can configure the following aspects of that account:

- Account picture
- Account name (but not the short name)
- .Mac username
- Password (you can reset it for the user)
- Parental controls to limit the access of the account
- Administrator access

The following sections explain how to configure each of these areas for the current account as well as others you have created. You'll see notations about the differences in the steps.

*If you are unable to select a user account to modify it, see "I Can't Change a User Account" in the "Troubleshooting" section at the end of this chapter.*



### Configuring a User Account's Full Name or Password

You can change the password for the current account or reset another account's password by peforming the following steps:

1. Open the Accounts pane of the System Preferences application and select the user whose account you want to update.

**NOTE**

> If a user account (other than the one you are currently using) is logged in to the Mac, you won't be able to make any changes to it. Log out of that account first and then change it.

2. To change the account's full name, enter a new full name in the Name box. (Remember that you can't change a user account's short name.)
3. If you are changing the password for the current account, click the Password tab and then click the Change Password button. If you are chaning the password of another account, click the Reset Password button. The sheet that appears will look slightly different, but you use either version in a very similar way.
4. If you changing the current account's password, enter the current password in the Old Password field.
5. Configure the new password using the same steps that you use when you create a password for a new user account.

⇨ For detailed information about creating passwords, **see** "Creating User Accounts," **p. 236**.

6. If you are changing the current account's password, click Change Password or if you are changing another account's password, click Reset Password. The sheet will close and the new password will take effect.
7. To enable a user to administer your Mac, select the user and click the "Allow user to administer this computer" check box. To prevent a user from administering your Mac, uncheck this check box. (You'll have to log out and back in for this change to take effect.)

## CONFIGURING A USER ACCOUNT'S PICTURE

You can associate a picture with a user account. This picture shows up in a number of places, such as next to the user's account in the Login window, in the user's Address Book card, in iChats, and so on. There are two sources of images that you can use. One is the default images that are part of Mac OS X. The other is any other image that you create or that you download from the Internet. To configure a user's image, perform the following steps:

1. Open the Accounts pane of the System Preferences application and select the user whose picture you want to set. You can do this for admin, standard, and shared accounts.
2. Click the image well, which is above the Name field (it will contain an image assigned by Mac OS X or selected when you created the first user account). The Picture sheet will appear (see Figure 11.6). At the top of this sheet, you'll see the Edit Picture command that you can use to customize the image. In the lower part of the sheet, you'll see all the default images from which you can choose.



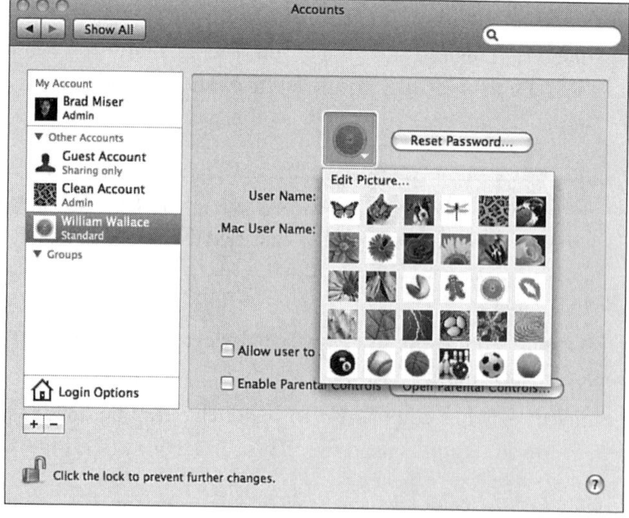


**Figure 11.6**
On this sheet, you can select an image for a user account or click the Edit Picture link to open an image editor.

3. To select a different default image, click the one you want to use. The current image will be replaced with the one you select.

4. To capture an image to use or to choose one from an image file, click the Edit Picture command. The Image sheet apopears (see Figure 11.7).

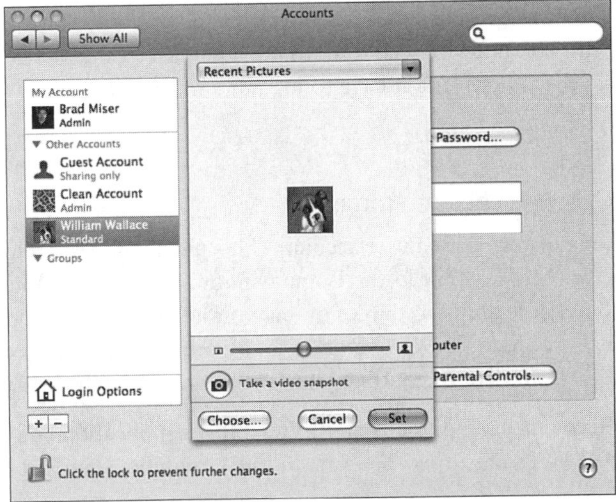


**Figure 11.7**
Use the Image sheet to create a more customized image for an account.



5. To place an image in the sheet, drag an image onto the image well in the center of the sheet, click Choose and move to and select an image (such as one you've downbloaded from the Internet), or click Take Video Snapshot to capture an image from a video camera connected to your Mac (such as the iSight cameras that are built-in on most Macs).

   The image formats you can use as the login picture include JPEG and TIFF. However, you can't use a GIF as a login picture.

6. When the image is shown in the image well, use the slider to crop the image to the part you want to use. Drag the slider to the right to zoom in on part of the image you want to use.

> **TIP**
>
> If you have worked with other images recently, click the Recent Pictures pop-up menu at the top of the Images dialog box and select the image you want to use.

7. Drag the image around in the image well to select the portion of it to be used as the account's picture (see Figure 11.8).

8. When the picture is what you want it to be, click Set. The image is shown in the image well on the Picture tab and is used for that user account (see Figure 11.9).

> **TIP**
>
> The default login pictures (those shown on the scrolling list) are stored in the directory `Mac OS X/Library/User Pictures`, where *`Mac OS X`* is the name of your Mac OS X startup volume. You can install additional images in this directory to make them available as part of the Apple Pictures collection.

**Figure 11.8**
I've downloaded an image of William Wallace from the Internet and associated it with this user account.

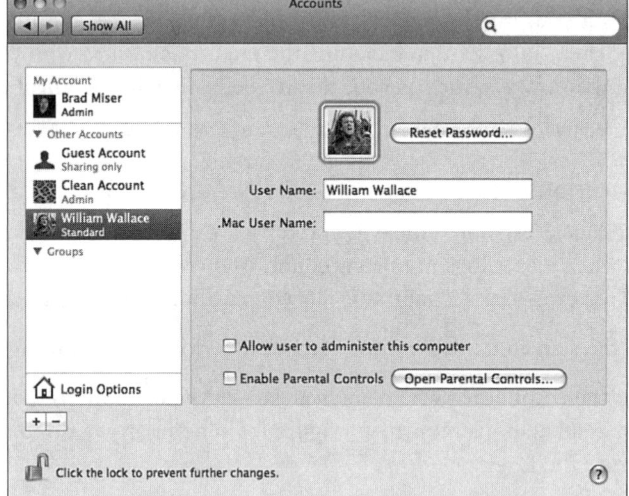


**Figure 11.9**
This image seems a much better fit for William's user account as I am sure you will agree.

11

### Limiting Access of a User Account Using Parental Controls

You might want to limit the access a user has to your Mac. For example, if the user is a child, you might not want that child to be able to use certain applications or to burn CDs or DVDs. You can use the Parental Controls to set these kind of limits on a user account. Follow these steps:

1. Open the Accounts pane of the System Preferences application and select the user whose access you want to limit.
2. Check "Enable Parental Controls."

3. Click Open Parental Controls. The Parental Controls pane will appear. In this pane, you will see the various areas on which you can set limits.
4. Use the various panes and tools to set limits on the account. Because these controls are tightly connected to your Mac's overall security, they are convered in Chapter 39, "Securing a Mac." After you've configured these controls for a user account, that account will only be able to perform tasks and access data according to the limits you set. In addition, the user will now be a managed account, as noted in the list of users.

⇨ To learn about parental controls in more detail, **see** "Using Parental Controls to Safeguard a Mac," **p. 941**.

⇨ To learn how to use Parental Controls to limit Internet access to and from a user account, **see** "Defending Your Mac from Internet Attacks," **p. 937**.

### Configuring Your Address Book Card

In the Address Book application, each person has a card that provides her contact information. When viewing the user account pane for the currently logged in account (the one listed in the My Account section), the Address Book Card Open button will appear. If you click this button, the Address Book application will open and you will move to your Address Book card. You can then edit your card as needed. After you've done this, your Address Book card will contain your current information, including the picture associated with your account. This is useful in a number of ways, such as your picture being included in email sent with Mail.

⇨ To learn how to edit your address card information, **see** "Editing Your Own Address Card," **p. 649**.

11

### Setting Applications and Documents to Open Automatically at Login

To make your Mac even more efficient, you can have applications automatically start or documents open when a user logs in to an account. And you can have a different set of applications start up for each user account; this lets you customize each user's startup experience.

To configure the startup items for a user account, perform the following steps:

1. Log in to the account for which you want to set the login items (you don't have to be logged in as an administrator to configure login items as you do to create user accounts or configure the Login window).
2. Open the System Preferences application.
3. Click the Accounts button, select the current user account, and then click the Login Items tab. The Login Items pane appears (see Figure 11.10). You place any items you want to open on the list to have them open when the user logs in. The order in which they are listed in the window determines the order in which they open (the topmost item opens first).
4. Click the Add button, which is the plus sign (+) at the bottom of the pane.
5. Use the Add sheet to move to the item you want to be opened at login, select it, and click Add. When the sheet first appears, the Applications folder is selected automatically and you can select the applications that are installed there. If you want to add documents

or applications stored elsewhere to the list, use the Add sheet to move to the files you want to be opened, select them, and click Add.

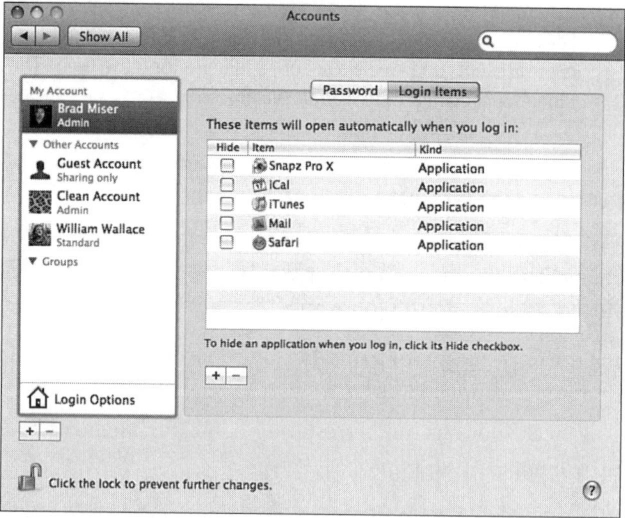


**Figure 11.10**
When you add applications or documents to the Login Items list, they automatically open when you log in.

**TIP**

> You can also drag application or document icons directly onto the Login Items list instead of using the Add button.

When you place an item in the window (by using the Add button or dragging it there), an alias to that item is created.

6. If you want the item to be automatically hidden when it is opened, check the Hide check box. This is useful for applications that you don't need to see right away but still want to open. For example, you might want to open your email application but leave it hidden until you receive new email.
7. When you have all the items in the window, drag them up to make them open earlier in the process or down to have them open later in the sequence.

**NOTE**

> Some applications might rely on others to function. In that case, you want the dependent application to open after the application on which it depends, so it should be lower on the list.

8. To remove an application or document from the list (so that it doesn't open on login), select it and click the Remove button, which is the minus sign (–) at the bottom of the pane. This doesn't affect the item at all—it only removes it from the Login Items list.
9. Continue adding, removing, and rearranging items until all the startup items are listed in the window in the order in which you want them to open.

11

The next time the user logs in, the login items will open automatically, in the order you specified.

**TIP**

> Login items are a great way to customize your Mac for other users. Simply log in to the other accounts and create a set of login items for those users. The applications and documents will open for them automatically.

### CONFIGURING AN ACCOUNT'S ADVANCED OPTIONS

There is a set of advanced options you can configure for user accounts. It is rare that you will need to change these options, but they can be useful in some situations. To configure an account's advanced options, do the following:

1. Right-click (or Ctrl-click with a one-button mouse) the user in the Accounts pane of the System Preferences application.
2. Choose Advanced Options on the resulting contextual menu. The Advanced Options dialog box will appear (see Figure 11.11).

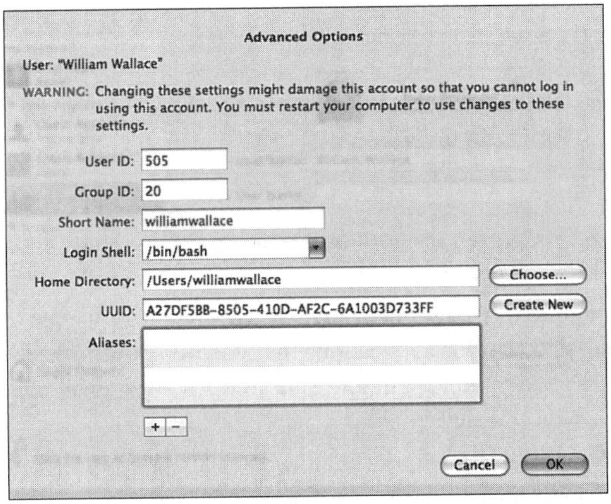

**Figure 11.11**
The Advanced Options dialog box enables you to configure a user account in more detail.

**CAUTION**

> Changing the advanced options can result in you not being able to use the account. You should make a note of all the options settings before you change them. If you change the options such that the account become unusable, you might be able to reset them to the working state (which is where your record of the original values comes in).

3. Use the fields in the dialog box to change any of the following properties:
    - **User ID**—This is an identification number assigned by the system when you created the user account. You can change it if desired.

- **Group ID**—This identifies the group of which the user is a member. Security to access folders and files on the Mac can be configured by this group along with some other administrative actions.
- **Short Name**—This is the account's short username. Changing the short username here enables you to log in using the new short name, but doesn't change the short name as it appears on the user account's home folder or website.
- **Login Shell**—This associates a Unix shell with the user account. You can choose from the available shells using the drop-down list.
- **Home Directory**—Use the field to change the user's Home directory. You can type a path to the new folder in the field or use the Choose button to choose one.
- **UUID**—This is the Univerally Unique Identifier. This number is used to identify the user without accessing a central database. You can generate a new UUID for the user account by clicking the Create New button.
- **Aliases**—You can create aliases for the user account by clicking the "+" button and entering the alias. You can remove aliases by selecting them and clicking the "-" button. If you create an alias then go to either the login window or an authentication dialog, you can enter that alias name instead of the full name or the short name. For instance, my short name is bradm, but if I create an alias for seuosxbrad I can then authenticate as seuosxbrad and then the password. This is especially useful for web sharing. You could create multiple aliases that would point to the same Sites folder for my user account. Basically, you can use the alias any place you would use the full or short name to login.

⇨ To learn more about setting permissions, **see** "Securing Your Mac with Privileges," **p. 922**.

⇨ To learn more about Unix shells, **see** "Shells," **p. 298**.

⇨ To learn more about .Mac, **see** "Understanding Mac OS X Directories," **p. 70**.

4. Click OK. The changes you made to the user account will take effect.

## ENABLING THE GUEST ACCOUNT

A guest account enables someone to temporarily log in to your Mac without a password. Guest accounts have limited access to your Mac's resources and any files or folders the guest user creates are deleted when the user logs out. The guest account is a good way to let someone use your Mac without making any changes to it. To enable the guest account, do the following:

1. Open the Accounts pane of the System Preferences application.
2. Select Guest Account on the account list (you might have to expand the Other Accounts section to see it).
3. Check the "Allow guests to log into this computer" check box. The Guest account will be ready to use.

If you want to allow a guest to be able to access shared folders on your Mac from across your network, check the "Allow guests to connect to shared folders" option.

## CREATING A SHARING-ONLY ACCOUNT

A sharing-only account is designed to be a more secure method for allowing others to connect to the shared folders on your Mac. Unlike a guest account, which anyone could attempt to use to connect to your shared folders, the sharing-only account requires the person to know the username and password to gain access to the resources you are sharing.

You create a sharing account just like a standard user account, with a couple of differences. On the Account sheet, choose Sharing Only on the New Account drop-down list. Unlike other accounts, you can't provide administrator permissions to a sharing account nor can you turn on FileVault protection or Parental Controls for them.

## CREATING GROUPS OF USERS

You can create a group and assign users to that group to configure permissions for folders and files. Groups make it easier to set the same level of access to specific objects for multiple people.

⇨ To learn more about setting permissions, **see** "Securing Your Mac with Privileges," **p. 922**.

To create a user group, do the following steps:

11

1. Open the Accounts pane of the System Preferences application.
2. Click the Add Account button (the "+" sign).
3. On the Account sheet, choose Group on the New Account drop-down list.
4. Enter the name of the group in the Name field.
5. Click Create Group. You'll return to the Accounts pane and will see the user accounts, sharing accounts, and groups that can be placed into the group you created (see Figure 11.12).

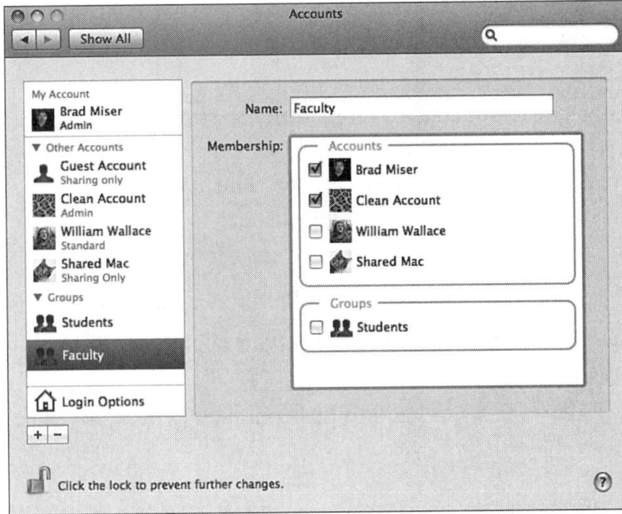


**Figure 11.12**
When you check the box next to a user account, sharing account, or group, it will be placed in the group selected on the account list.

6. Check the box next to each user account, sharing account, or group that you want to place in the group. When the group you created is assigned permissions, all the members of the group will get those permissions.

# Logging In, Logging Out, and Configuring Login Options

Basic tasks like logging in, logging out, restarting, and shutting down Mac OS X are performed frequently as you and others use your Mac. The sections that follow briefly outline these processes.

## Logging In to a User Account

As you learned previously, you must log in to be able to use a Mac OS X–powered Mac. To log in, you simply select or enter the name of the user account, enter the password (for accounts that have passwords), and press Return. You then move to the desktop for that user account.

## Logging In to a Guest Account

As you learned earlier, a Guest account can be used to provide temporary access to your Mac. It's temporary because as soon as the guest logs out, the Mac "forgets" everything that user did, such as the files and folders created, websites visited, and so on. Logging in to a guest account is even simpler than other accounts; simply choose the guest account and login.



## Logging Out of a User Account

Under Mac OS X, rather than shutting the computer down, most of the time you will log out instead. When you log out, all the processes currently running are stopped and the user account is "closed." To log out of the current user account, select the Apple menu, and then select Log Out (or press Shift-⌘-Q). In the resulting confirmation dialog box, press Return or click Log Out (if you don't do this within 2 minutes, the system logs you out automatically). The processes that are currently running are stopped (you are first prompted to save any open documents that have unsaved changes), and you return to the Login dialog box.

If you have enabled Fast User Switching, you can also select the Login window command on the User Switching menu to protect access to your account while keeping it logged in.

**TIP**

> Logging out and then logging back in is a lot faster than stopping and starting your machine. In fact, there aren't many reasons to shut down your machine, and if you use it to serve web pages, you shouldn't shut it down at all. To secure your Mac when you aren't using it, just log out.

## Configuring Automatic Login

When you started Mac OS X for the first time, you were in the Automatic Login mode. In this mode, you don't have to enter login information; Mac OS X does it for you. This means that you don't have to enter a username and password each time you start or restart your machine; by default, the first user account (created during the Mac OS X installation process) is used for the automatic login.

**CAUTION**

You should enable Automatic Login mode only if you are the only person who uses your Mac. If you enable Automatic Login mode with the administrator's account, you provide access to many of your system's resources, which is an unsecure way to operate. However, if you have a Mac in a secure location and are the only person who uses it, the Automatic Login mode eliminates the need to log in every time you start or restart the machine.

**TIP**

If you are going to enable Automatic Login mode, create a non-administrator account to use. That way, even if someone does get access to your Mac, he won't be able to use the administrator account. Of course, you might have to log out and then log back in as the administrator to perform certain tasks, but this strategy provides a good compromise between security and convenience.



To configure Automatic Login mode, use the following steps:

1. Open the Accounts pane of the System Preferences application.
2. Click the Login Options button. You'll see the Login Options pane (see Figure 11.13).

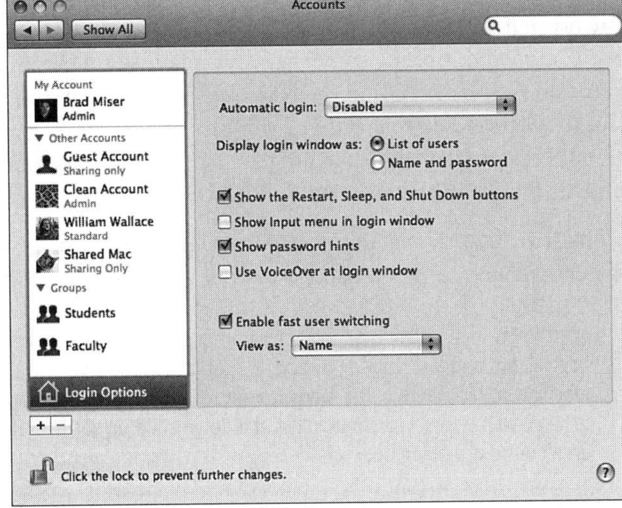


**Figure 11.13**
Use the Login Options pane to configure how you log in to your Mac.

3. To enable automatic login mode, open the "Automatic log in" drop-down list and select the user account that should automatically be logged. The password prompt sheet will appear, and the user account you selected on the pop-up menu is selected in the sheet.
4. Enter the password for the account that you selected in step 3.
5. Click OK.

The next time you start or restart your Mac, the account you specified is automatically logged in and you move directly to the desktop for that account.

This setting affects only the start or restart sequence. When you log out instead of shutting down or restarting, you still see the Login window again and have to log in to resume using the Mac.

To disable automatic login, choose Disabled on the "Automatic log in" drop-down list.

## Controlling How User Accounts Appear in the Login Window

You can configure several aspects of how user accounts appear in the Login window:

1. Log in under an administrator account and open the Accounts pane of the System Preferences application.
2. Click the Login Options button.
3. To display empty Name and Password fields in the Login window instead of a list of the user accounts you have configured, click the "Name and password" radio button. When this button is selected, you have to type the name or the short name and password for an account to log in to it. To display the list of user accounts, click the "List of users" radio button instead. With this option, each account (and its picture) appears onscreen. To log in, the user clicks her account, enters her password, and clicks the Login button.



## Hiding the Sleep, Restart, and Shut Down Buttons

If you enable Automatic Login mode, you might run into trouble if you leave the Restart and Shut Down buttons in the Login window enabled. Here's how that could happen. Say you are using your Mac and decide that you want to take a break for a while, but there are people in your area whom you don't want to be able to use the machine while you step away. You log out, and your machine is protected, right? Not necessarily. If the Restart and Shut Down buttons are enabled, someone can restart the Mac from the Login window and then it would start up in the automatic account, giving the person access to the machine. Disabling these buttons prevents someone from using them to access an account that is automatically logged in to.

The previous scenario might make you pause to ask a question before you enable Automatic Login mode. If you do disable the Restart and Shut Down buttons and then log out, can someone simply press the hardware Restart or Reset button on the CPU to start up the Mac to automatically log in to the automatic login account? This would bypass the protection offered by disabling the buttons, right? Nope; when the Mac is not shut down properly (by using the Shut Down command), the automatic login feature is disabled when the machine is started or restarted the next time. So, if you have to use one of those buttons, you must log in the next time you start or restart the machine.

To disable the Sleep, Restart, and Shut Down buttons, do the following:

1. Open the System Preferences application and then the Accounts pane, and then click the Login Options button.
2. Uncheck the "Show the Restart, Sleep, and Shut Down buttons" check box.

When the Login window appears, these buttons are hidden and the only way to use the Mac is to log in using a valid account. If you want these buttons to appear in the Login window again, simply check the check box. When these buttons do appear in the Login window, the related actions can be performed without being logged in to a user account.

## Showing the Input Menu in the Login Window

You can use a variety of languages with Mac OS X. The specific language you use at any point in time determines the keyboard layout you should be using. This is controlled on the Input menu from which you can select the keyboard configuration you want to use. To show this menu on the Login window, check the "Show Input menu in login window" check box on the Login Options pane of the Accounts pane of the System Preferences application. When the Login window appears, the keyboard layout can be selected on the Input menu. When it isn't shown, the layout associated with the currently selected language is used.

⇨ To learn about working with languages, **see** "Configuring Your Keyboard's Language Settings and the Input Menu," **p. 768**.

## Using VoiceOver in the Login Window

Mac OS X's VoiceOver feature causes the computer to read text on the screen. You can enable this feature for the Login window by checking the "Use VoiceOver at login window" check box located on the Login Options pane of of the Accounts pane of the System Preferences application. When the Login window appears, the Mac will read its content aloud. This can be used to help people who are visually impaired to access the computer.

⇨ To learn about VoiceOver, **see** "Understanding and Using VoiceOver," **p. 279**.

## Showing Password Hints

You learned earlier that you can configure password hints that are displayed to help a user remember her password. If you check the "Show password hints" check box, the Forgot Password button is displayed on the Login window. When a user clicks this button, the password hint appears.

If the user tries to log in, but is unsuccessful in three attempts, the password hint appears even if he doesn't click the Forgot Password button.

**NOTE**

> If the user clicks the Forgot Password button, it becomes the Password Reset button. If this button is clicked, the steps to reset a password by using the installation disc are shown. This is usually a last resort. It is better to reset a user's password via the Account tools.

## ENABLING AND USING FAST USER SWITCHING

When a user logs out of his account, all documents are closed and all applications and processes are quit. When a user logs in again, any of these must be restarted to get back to where the user was when he logged out. However, you can take advantage of *fast user switching*. What this means is that you can log in to another user account without logging out of the accounts that are currently logged in. This is very nice because you can leave applications and documents open in an account and display the Login window to prevent someone from using those items. And, another user can log in and work with his account. When he is done, you can log back in to your account and everything will be as it was when you left it. This saves a lot of time and hassle reopening items, and processes you are running can continue to run while another user is logged in to the machine.

**NOTE**

> If your Mac has limited RAM, you might not want to enable Fast User Switching because applications running under other user accounts will consume resources even if your user account is the active one. This means performance might be slower for you because the applications under other user accounts are using RAM and so it isn't available to your applications.

11

To enable this feature, do the following steps:

1. Open the Accounts pane of the System Preferences application and click the Login Options button.
2. Check the "Enable fast user switching" check box. A new menu appears in the upper-right corner of the desktop that enables other users to log in.
3. Use the "View as" pop-up menu to determine how the Fast User Switching menu appears on the Finder toolbar. Your options are
   - **Icon**—A silhouette appears at the top of the menu.
   - **Short name**—The short name of the user account currently logged in appears at the top of the menu.
   - **Name**—The full name of the user account currently logged into appears at the top of the menu.

Then, logging in and out of accounts can be done fast and easily with the Fast User Switching menu (see Figure 11.14).

**Figure 11.14**
The Fast User Switching menu enables you to log in to other accounts without logging out of the current one.



To log in under another account, select it on the menu. You will see the Login window with the account you selected (see Figure 11.15). Enter the password for the account and click the Log In button or press Return. After a cool, 3D spinning effect, that user is logged in and his desktop appears.

**Figure 11.15**
You can see that the Restart and Shut Down buttons don't appear in this Login window.

**TIP**

> If you create a user account without a password and enable the Fast User Switching feature, you can log in to the account without a password immediately by selecting it on the Fast User Switching menu. You will bypass the Login window altogether.

To temporarily block access to the current user account without logging out, open the Fast User Switching menu and select Login Window. The Login window will appear. You can leave the machine without worries that someone will be able to access your account. When you are ready to log in—or when anyone else is, for that matter—select the user account, enter a password, and click Login (you get to see the cool 3D spin again, too).

**NOTE**

> On the Fast User Switching menu and in the Login window, users who are currently logged in have the circle with a check mark icon next to them.

If another user account is logged in and you attempt to restart or shut down the machine, a warning dialog box appears that explains that other users are logged in and the action you are taking could cause them to lose data. If you enter an administrator username and password and click Shut Down or Restart, the other users are logged out and the action you want is performed. Be careful about doing this though because the other users can lose unsaved data.

**TIP**

> You can jump quickly to the Accounts pane of the System Preferences application by selecting Account Preferences on the Fast User Switching menu.



# TESTING AND CHANGING USER ACCOUNTS

After you have created user accounts, you should log in under those accounts to test and configure them (some configuration can be done only while logged in under an account).

## TESTING USER ACCOUNTS

After you create a new user account, you should test it by logging in under that account to make sure it works:

1. Select Apple menu, Log Out (or press Shift-⌘-Q).

**TIP**

> If you have enabled fast user switching, you can use the Fast User Switching menu instead. It really is faster and easier.

2. When the logout confirmation dialog box appears, press Return (or click the Log Out button). You will return to the Mac OS X Login window. At the top of the Login window, you see the computer name. If you have configured the window to show a list of users, in the center part of the window, you see the login picture and name of each user account on the machine. If several user accounts appear, this will be a scrolling pane. At the bottom of the window are the Sleep, Restart, and Shut Down buttons (unless they are hidden).

**NOTE**

> The system automatically logs you out 2 minutes after you select the Log Out command, even if you don't click the Log Out button.

3. If the Login window shows the user accounts on the machine, click the user account under which you want to log in. The dialog box will contract and you see the selected user account and an empty Password box. If the User Name and Password fields appear instead, enter the username (name or short name) for the account you want to log in to.

**NOTE**

> If the user account does not have a password, you are logged in as soon as you select that account's icon.

   You can return to the full login window by clicking the Back button.

4. Enter the password for the user account and click Log In (or press Return or Enter).

   If the user account information is not valid, the login dialog box "shudders" to indicate that the information you entered is invalid (remember that this information is case sensitive). After three unsuccessful attempts, the password hint appears if one has been entered for the user account and that feature is enabled.

   When you enter correct information for the user account, the login process is completed and you see the desktop for that user account, which might look quite different from the administrator's desktop.

5. After you have logged in to the new account, you can make any changes to the configuration of the user account that you want; for example, create a startup configuration by adding items to the Login Items pane or customize the Dock.

⇨ To learn about login items, **see** "Logging In, Logging Out, and Configuring Login Options," **p. 251**.

⇨ To learn about customizing the Dock, **see** Chapter 5, "Using and Customizing the Dock," **p. 107**.

6. Make sure that the security of the account is correct. For example, if you used Parental Controls to block access to some applications, check to ensure that you can't access those applications.
7. From the desktop, press Shift-⌘-Q and then press Return to log out of the account.

*If you are unable to log in to a user account you have created, see "I Can't Log In on a User Account" in the "Troubleshooting" section at the end of this chapter.*

## EDITING USER ACCOUNTS

You can make changes to an existing user account. To do so, use the following steps:

**NOTE**

> If a user account is logged in, you won't be able to change it. Log out of that account before trying to edit it.

11

1. Open the Accounts pane of the System Preferences application.
2. Select the user account you want to edit. That user's information appears in the right part of the window.
3. Make changes to the user's information (such as changing the Picture or Parental Controls) as needed. If you aren't logged in as an administrator, you can change only a few items, such as the picture and login items.

**TIP**

> Remember that, even if you aren't logged in under an administrator account, you can authenticate yourself as an administrator so that all the account-editing tools become available to you. To do this, click the closed lock icon in the lower-left corner of the System Preferences application window, enter an administrator username and password, and click OK. The lock icon opens and you can do all the actions that are allowed while logged in as an administrator.

**NOTE**

> Because it is used as the Home directory name for the account as well as for other items (such as in the website address for the user account), you can't make any changes to the short name. Once created, the short name can never be changed.

4. Use the controls on each tab to make changes to the account. These work just like they do when you create a user account.

⇨ To learn how to create a user account, **see** "Creating User Accounts," **p. 236**.

**NOTE**

> Even if you are logged in as an administrator and are changing your own name, password, or password hint, you have to confirm your password by entering it at the prompt before you can make those changes.
>
> If the current user account has permission to change the password, it can be changed by selecting the current password and trying to change it. When this is done, a sheet prompts the user for the current password. If the user enters the current password successfully, the Name, Password, Verify, and Password Hint fields become editable and the user can change the data in these fields as needed (the short name still can't be changed).

5. Test the account to make sure it works with the changes you have made.

*If you are unable to use the buttons in the Accounts pane of the System Preferences utility, see "The Buttons in the Accounts Pane Are Inactive" in the "Troubleshooting" section at the end of this chapter.*

11

**NOTE**

> After you have entered a password, you won't be able to see it, even when you edit the user account. The only way to recover from someone forgetting his password is to reset it to a new one by editing the user account.

After you have tested and verified users' accounts, provide the names and passwords for the user accounts you created to the people who need them. You should explain the limitations of the accounts to the users as well.

## DELETING USER ACCOUNTS

You can also delete user accounts that you no longer need by doing the following:

1. Open the Accounts pane of the System Preferences application.
2. Select the account you want to delete.
3. Click the Delete User button, which is the minus sign at the bottom of the user list. You will see the delete user confirmation sheet.

   When you delete a user, you have three options for the contents of that user's Home folder: You can choose to save the user's Home folder as a disk image in the Deleted Users folder so the files it contains can be accessed, you can leave the folder in its current location, or you can choose to delete the folder immediately.

   This doesn't apply when you delete a group because a group doesn't have resources to delete.
4. If you choose to save the user's Home folder as a disk image, click "Save the home folder in a disk image." The deleted user account's Home directory will be moved to the Deleted Users folder. Within this folder, you will see a disk image for the deleted user's Home folder. Administrator accounts can open this disk image to work with its contents.
5. To leave the user's Home folder as it is, click "Do not change the home folder." The Home folder will remain in the Users folder.
6. To delete the user's Home folder, click "Delete the home folder."
7. Click OK. The user account will be deleted and its Home folder will be acted upon according to the option you selected.

**TIP**

> The one account you can't delete is the guest account. However, you can disable it if you don't want people to be able to use it.

After you delete it, the user account you deleted is no longer available in the Login window and can no longer be used.

If you elected to preserve the user's Home folder as a disk image, the Home directory for that account is converted into a disk image file that is stored in the location `Mac OS X/Users/Deleted Users`, where *`Mac OS X`* is the name of your Mac OS X volume.

The name of the disk image is `shortusername.dmg`, where `shortusername` is the short username of the account that was deleted. To access the files that were in the account's Home directory, open its disk image file. The Home directory for that account will then be a mounted volume on your machine, which you can use just like another volume you mount.

The Deleted Users folder is accessible only to those accounts that have administrative privileges on your Mac. If you want other users to be able to access files that were in the deleted account's Home directory, you must change the permissions associated with the disk image.

⇨ To learn how to configure permissions, **see** "Securing Your Mac with Privileges," **p. 922**.

# ENABLING THE ROOT USER ACCOUNT

Because Mac OS X is based on Unix, a user account called root exists on every Mac OS X machine. The root account has permission to do everything that is possible; the root account permissions go way beyond even administrator account permissions. Because of this, logging in under this root account is very powerful, and it is also dangerous because it isn't that hard to mess up your system, delete folders (whether you intend to or not), and so on. However, because you sometimes need to log in under the root account to accomplish specific tasks, you should understand and become comfortable with it.

You should be logged in under the root account only for the minimum time necessary to accomplish specific tasks. Log in, do what you need to, and then log out of root again. This minimizes the chance of doing something you didn't intend to do because you forgot you were logged in under root.

11

**CAUTION**

> Be careful when you are working in your Mac under the root account. You can cause serious damage to the system as well as to data you have stored on your machine.

The root account is a very special user account, but it is still a user account. The full name of the root account is System Administrator, and its short name is root. One difference between the root account and other accounts is that the root account exists without having to create it. However, you have to assign a password to it before you can begin using it.

You can create a password for the root account by following these steps:

1. Open the Terminal application found in the Applications/Utilities folder (see Figure 11.16).

⇨ To learn more about the Terminal application, **see** "Terminal," **p. 298**.

2. At the prompt, type **`sudo passwd root`** and press Return. You'll see a prompt explaining that you are changing the password for the root account.
3. At the password prompt, enter an administrator password for your Mac and press Return. You'll be prompted to enter a new password for the root account.
4. Type the new password for the root account and press Return.

**Figure 11.16**
The Terminal doesn't look like much of a destination, but it is very powerful if you know the right Unix commands.

5. Type the new password a second time at the "Retype new password" prompt and press Return. The new password is now set.

After you have created the root password, you can log in under the root account by performing the following steps:

1. Log out of the current account.
2. Log in under the root account. If the login window is configured to show user accounts, select Other on the list and then enter **root**, type the root password, and click Login. If the Login window just shows the User Name and Password fields, enter **root** and the password and click Login.
3. Confirm that you are logged in as root by opening the Home directory; root appears as the username and as the label of the Home folder in the Places sidebar (see Figure 11.17).

> **NOTE** If you enable Fast User Switching, the root account isn't listed on the Fast User Switching menu. To log in to the root account, you must bring up the Login window by choosing Login Window on the Fast User Switching menu.

Because the root account has unlimited permissions, you can add or remove files to any directory on your Mac while you are logged in under the root account, including those for other user accounts. You can also make changes to any system file, which is where the root account's power and danger come from.

Use the root account only when you really need to. Make sure that other people who use your Mac do not know the root password; otherwise, you might find yourself with all sorts of problems.

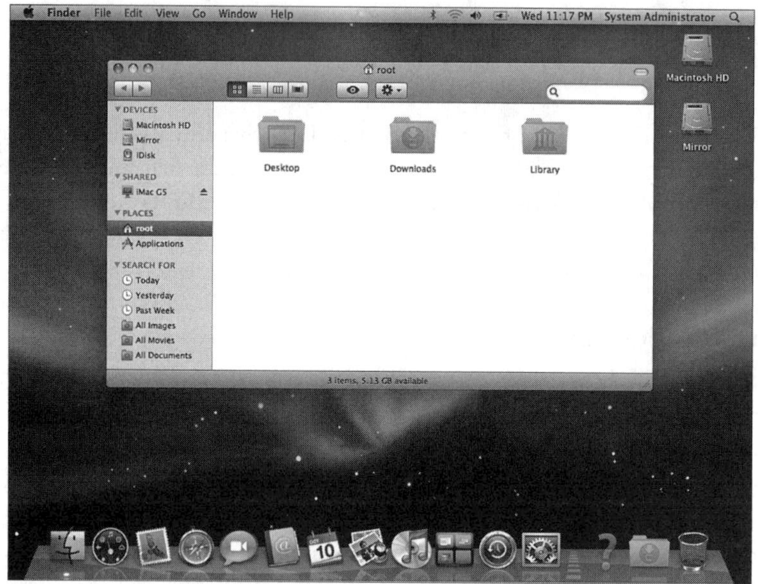


**Figure 11.17**
When you can see the Home directory for the root user, you are logged in as root.

**TIP**

> You can also log in to the root account directly in the Terminal window to enter Unix commands using the command line. This can be a faster way to enter a few commands if you are comfortable with the command-line interface.

# TROUBLESHOOTING

## I FORGOT MY ADMINISTRATOR USER ACCOUNT USER NAME OR PASSWORD

*When I try to authenticate myself as an administrator, I can't because I don't remember my account information.*

If you forget the password for your administrator account, you have two options. If you can remember the password for your clean account, log in under that account and reset your admin password. If you can't remember that password either or don't have a clean account (shame on you!), the process is slightly more complicated.

1. Restart your Mac from the Mac OS X installation disc. (You can insert the disc and use the Startup Disk pane to select it or restart your Mac while holding the C key down.)
2. After the installer application starts, choose Utilities, Reset Password.
3. Enter and verify the new password and click OK.
4. Quit the installer and restart your Mac.
5. As it restarts, hold the left mouse button down so the installation disc will be ejected. The Mac will restart from the previous startup disc and you should be able to log in using the new password.

### I CAN'T CHANGE A USER ACCOUNT

*When I try to select a user account in the Other Accounts list, it is grayed out and I am unable to work with it.*

The most likely cause of this error is Fast User Switching is turned on and the user account is currently logged in. You can't modify a user account that is currently active. To see if this is the problem, look closely at the user account's icon in the account list. If there is a checkmark in a circle next to it, the user account is logged in. Switch to that user account and log out. Then you will be able to modify its settings.

### I CAN'T LOG IN ON A USER ACCOUNT

*When I try to log in under a particular user account, the login window shudders and I can't log in.*

The most likely cause of this error is that you are entering the user account information incorrectly. If you are selecting a user account from the list, you must be entering the password incorrectly. If you are entering both the account name and password, you have to ensure that you use the correct combination. Try entering the information again. Remember that both name and password are case sensitive.

If you are logging in using the short name, try using the full name instead. Also, if you created an alias using the Advanced Options for the account, you could try to log in using that name and the appropriate password.

If you are still not able to log in under that account, log in as the administrator and open the Users pane of the System Preferences utility to check the account or edit it. You can also delete the account and start over.

### THE BUTTONS IN THE ACCOUNTS PANE ARE INACTIVE

*When I open the Accounts pane of the System Preferences utility, the buttons are all inactive.*

The Lock icon in the lower-left corner of the window enables you to lock or unlock the ability to make global system changes. If this icon is in the locked mode, you need to authenticate yourself as the administrator (even if you are logged in under that account). Click the Lock icon, enter the administrator username and password in the Authentication dialog box, and press Return. If you enter valid information, the buttons become active and you are able to make changes to the account configurations.

CHAPTER 12

# Managing Your Desktop with Exposé, Spaces, and Other Tools

## In this chapter

# TAKING CONTROL OF YOUR DESKTOP

Mac OS X and modern Macs are powerful. This power enables you to have many applications and documents open at the same time, which is great for your productivity. At some point though, you'll have so many open windows on your desktop that finding the specific document or application that you want to work on can start to become laborious. Fortunately, Mac OS X includes a couple of features designed to help you manage all the desktop clutter. Exposé helps you manage windows that are open on your desktop. Spaces enables you to create collections of applications and open windows so that you can switch among them easily.

As you run all these applications at the same time, you'll also need to know how to manage the applications that are running.

# MANAGING OPEN WINDOWS WITH EXPOSÉ

Because it is so useful to have multiple applications and multiple documents within each application open at the same time, you might have dozens of windows open simultaneously with those windows layered one on another. Getting to the specific window in which you are interested can be difficult. That is where Exposé comes in. It is designed to help you quickly manage all the open windows on your desktop.

**TIP**

> You can customize the controls used to activate Exposé functions, as you will learn in the next section.



## USING EXPOSÉ

Exposé offers a number of useful functions, which are noted in the following list:

- **See all open windows at the same time**—If you press the F9 key (default), all open windows will be reduced in size and tiled such that they can all be displayed on the desktop at the same time (see Figure 12.1). When you point to a window, its title will appear so you can definitely identify it if you can't do so just by its appearance. (In Figure 12.1, I am pointing to the Mail application so you can see information about the Inbox.) You can click a window to move into that window, and the other windows return to their previous sizes and locations. You can also move into a window in which the cursor is located by pressing F9 again; if you don't point to a different window, pressing F9 will return you to your previous location.

**NOTE**

> If you use multiple monitors and activate Exposé, the windows on all monitors shrink and remain on the monitor they were originally on when you activated Exposé.

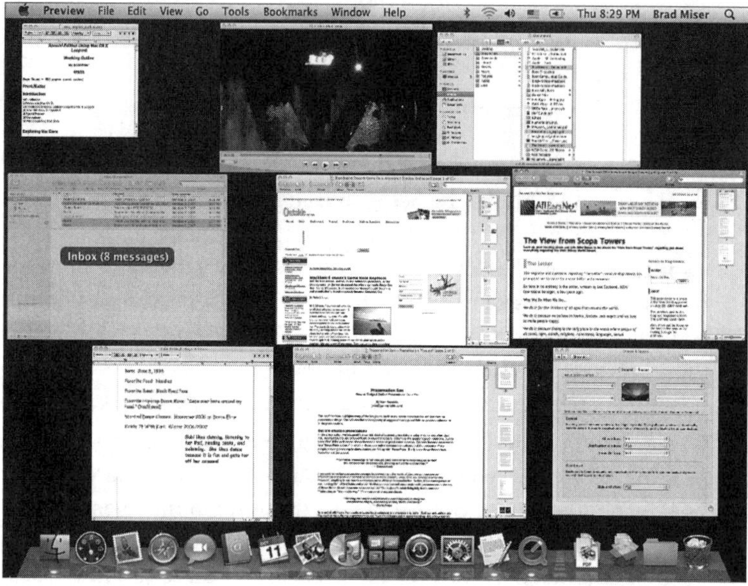


**Figure 12.1**
Using Exposé, you can show all open windows on your desktop at the same time.

- **See all the windows in the current application at the same time**—If you press the F10 key (default), all the windows in the current application will be shown (see Figure 12.2). Just like the previous command, you can point to a window to see its title, click it to move into it, and so on.

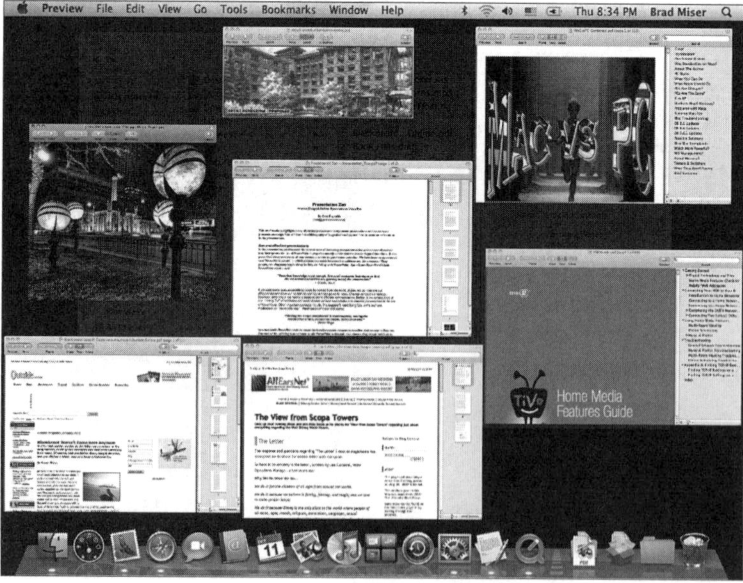


**Figure 12.2**
Here, I've pressed F10 so that all the windows open in Preview are shown.

**TIP**

> If you hold down the Shift key while you activate Exposé, you see its effects in slow motion. Why is this useful? I have no idea.

- **Hide all open windows and show the desktop**—If you press F11 (default), all open windows will be hidden by being moved off the sides of the desktop and you will see your desktop in all its beauty. This is useful if you have a bad case of desktop clutter and want to work on the desktop without closing or moving the current windows. You can return all windows to their previous locations by pressing F11 again. You can also open an item on the desktop by double-clicking it; when you do, the other windows return to their previous locations. Another option is to click one of the window borders that will be visible along the edges of your screen to return windows to their previous states.
- **Cycle through the Open windows in each application**—If you activate Exposé by pressing F9 or F10, you can cycle through the set of open windows in each application by pressing the Tab or Shift-Tab keys (to move in the opposite direction). Each time you do, the next application becomes active and you see all its open windows. Windows open in other applications remain at their current sizes and are unselectable. When the window you want to work in is exposed, click in it to deactivate Exposé and start using the application with which the window is associated.

## Configuring Exposé

You can customize the following aspects of Exposé using the Exposé tab of the Exposé & Spaces pane of the System Preferences application (see Figure 12.3):

12

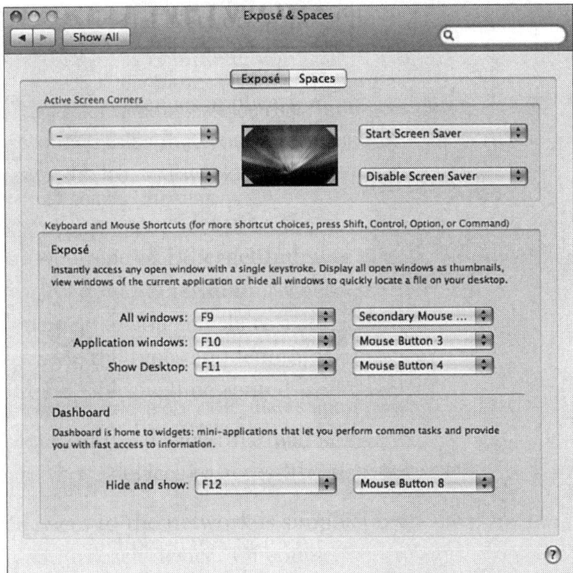


**Figure 12.3**
The Exposé & Spaces pane of the System Preferences application enables you to customize various aspects of Exposé.

- **Active Screen Corners**—Use the pop-up menu located at each corner of the preview monitor to set an action that happens when you move the cursor to that corner. The actions you can set are All Windows (the default F9 key), Application Windows (the default F10 key), Desktop (the default F11 key), Dashboard, Spaces, Start Screen Saver, Disable Screen Saver, and No Action (-). To set an action for a corner, select the action on the related pop-up menu. When you point to that corner of the screen, that action will occur.
- **Keyboard**—Use the Keyboard pop-up menus to set the keys to activate each Exposé action. In addition to the keys on the menus, you can see other combinations by scrolling down the pop-up menu. If you hold down a modifier key (such as the ⌘ key), you can add that modifier to the shortcut.
- **Mouse**—If you use an input device with more than one button, such as a two-button mouse, the Mouse pop-up menus appear. Use the Mouse pop-up menus to set Exposé actions for specific buttons on the device you use, such as the right button on a two-button mouse.

- **Dashboard**—Use the pop-up menus to select which keyboard and mouse (if you have a mouse with multiple buttons) controls will activate the Dashboard.

⇨ To learn more about the Dashboard, **see** Chapter 6, "Working with the Dashboard and Widgets," **p. 123**.

# CREATING, USING, AND MANAGING SPACES

Being able to use Exposé to manage open windows and applications is nice, but if you use a large amount of applications and windows at the same time, getting to the windows you want to work with can still be tedious. Spaces enables you to create environments that contain specific applications so that you can easily switch between them to perform specific actions. For example, you can create an Internet space that has all your Internet applications open and a Project space that contains applications and documents related to a project you are working on. When you want to move from the project to the Internet, simply move into the Internet space and all your applications are immediately available. Getting back to your project space is just as easy.



## ENABLING AND BUILDING SPACES

To get started with Spaces, you need to enable the feature and build your spaces. After you create spaces, you assign applications to those spaces. Only applications that are bound to a space are available to you when you access that space. To enable Spaces and create spaces, perform the following steps:

1. Open the Spaces tab of the Exposé & Spaces pane of the System Preferences application (see Figure 12.4).
2. Check the Enable Spaces check box. If you want to have the Spaces menu appear in the menu bar, check that check box, as well.

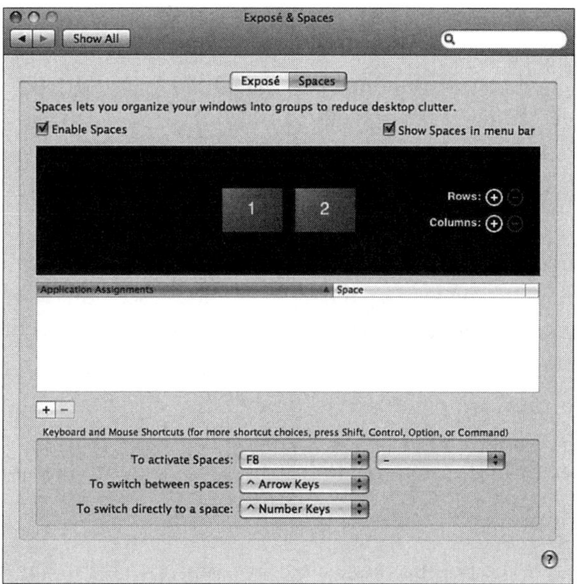


**Figure 12.4**
Use the Spaces tab to create and configure spaces on your Mac.

3. At the top of the pane, you see the preview window that shows a thumbnail of each space you have configured; initially there are two spaces in the same row. As you create spaces, you'll add them by row or by column. Below the preview window is the Application Assignments section; here, you see the applications are part of the selected space. At the bottom of the pane are the controls you use to set keyboard shortcuts for specific actions.
4. Use the keyboard pop-up menu to set the keyboard shortcut to activate Spaces.
5. If you have a multi-button mouse, use the mouse pop-up menu to set the mouse control to activate Spaces.
6. Add applications that you want to be part of the spaces you are creating. There are several ways to do this:
    - Drag an application's icon from the desktop and drop it on the space where you want it contained; when the icon is over a space, the space's thumbnail is highlighted to show you that you can drop it on the space.
    - Drag an application's icon from the desktop and drop it on the application list. Then, choose the space where you want the application to be used on the pop-up menu in the Space column (more on that in a bit).
    - Click Add Application and use the resulting sheet to move to and select the application you want to add. Then use the pop-up menu in the Space column to choose the space where you want that application to appear.
7. Add spaces by clicking the Add button in the Row section to add a new row of spaces or the Add button in the Column section to add a new column of spaces.
8. Add spaces until you've added all that you want to have available.

9. To remove spaces, you must remove an entire row or column by clicking the Remove button in the Row or Column section.
10. Use the pop-up menu in the Space column to assign an application to a space (see Figure 12.5). The choices on the menu are each space you've created and Every Space which makes the application available in all spaces. When you select an application, the spaces to which it is assigned are highlighted in the preview window.

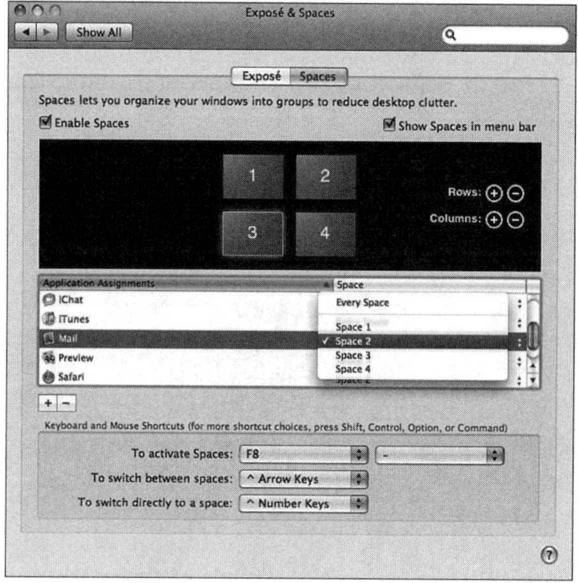


**Figure 12.5**
Assign applications to spaces to make them available when you choose a space.

11. To remove an application from the list, select it and click Remove.
12. Use the "To switch between spaces" pop-up menu to choose the keyboard shortcut to move among the spaces you have created.

**TIP**

Hold a modifier key down to see more shortcut choices on these menus.

13. Use the "To switch directly to a space" pop menu to choose the keyboard shortcut you can use to jump directly into a space.

12

## Using and Managing Spaces

After you've created spaces, you can use them to more efficiently manage your desktop. Here are some space pointers:

- Press the keyboard shortcut you set for switching between spaces (the default is Ctrl-Arrow key). The Spaces manager appears on the screen (see Figure 12.6). The manager has a box representing each of the spaces you've created. To jump to a space, keep pressing the shortcut keys until the space you want to use is highlighted. When you release the keys, you jump into that space and return to the last application you were using in that space.

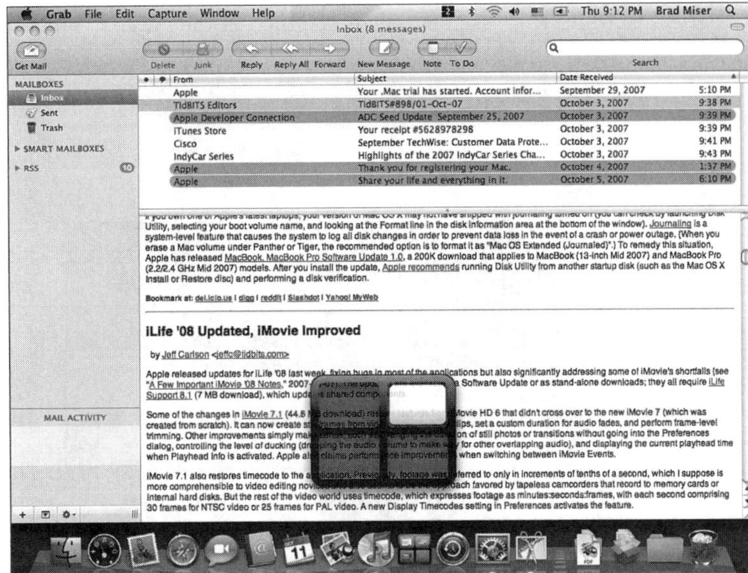


**Figure 12.6**
When you activate Spaces, you see the Spaces manager that indicates how many spaces are available to you.



- Press the keyboard shortcut for jumping directly to a space (the default is Ctrl-number key) to move directly into a space. When you do, the Space manager will appear briefly, you move into the space you selected, and applications in that space are available to you.
- When you are in a space, you can open applications that aren't part of that space, just as you can when you aren't using Spaces. That application will be available in the current space, but not in any others. If you open an application that is already assigned to a different space, you jump to the space that it has been assigned to.
- The Finder is available in all spaces.
- If an application isn't running when you move into the space that it has been assigned to, you need to launch it to be able to use it.
- Spaces retain window configurations. If you use multiple monitors and have windows on each display in a space, they will resume their former positions as soon as you move back into that space.
- You can use the Dock to move into open or closed applications. If you open an application in a space, you move into that space. If the application is not part of a space, it opens as usual, but is available only when you are using the space you were using when you opened it. In other words, it is temporarily bound to the space you were using when you launched it.

- If you assign an application to all spaces, its windows will always appear in the same positions in all spaces.
- If you press the Spaces keyboard shortcut (the default is F8), you see large thumbnails of all your spaces (see Figure 12.7). In each space, you see smaller thumbnails of all the applications running in that space. If you use multiple displays, you see a thumbnail for each display. Click a space to move into it.

**Figure 12.7**
Pressing the Spaces keyboard shortcut shows you all your spaces.

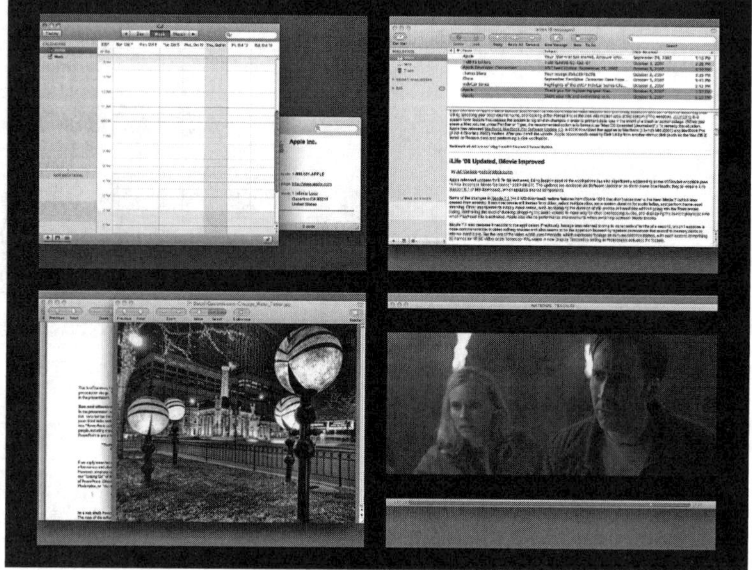

- To turn Spaces off, open the Spaces tab of the Exposé & Spaces pane of the System Preferences application and uncheck the Enable Spaces check box. All open applications will return to the desktop. You can start using your spaces again by checking the Enable Spaces check box.



# MAC OS X TO THE MAX: CONTROLLING RUNNING APPLICATIONS

Exposé and Spaces enable you to control which applications and windows you view on the desktop and use. Mac OS X also provides many ways to control open applications, including these:

- You can switch among open applications by clicking the icon of the open application that you want to switch on the Dock. If you're using Spaces and the application is bound to a space, you move into that space.
- You can move among open applications using the ⌘-Tab or Shift-⌘-Tab keys. When you press these keys, the Application Switcher menu, which is a list of the currently

open applications, appears (see Figure 12.8). The active application is always located on the far left edge of the menu. You can move into a different application by pressing the ⌘-Tab or Shift-⌘-Tab keys until the application you want is selected, or you can click an application on the Application Switcher menu to move into it. If you select an application that is bound to a space, you'll move into that space as well.

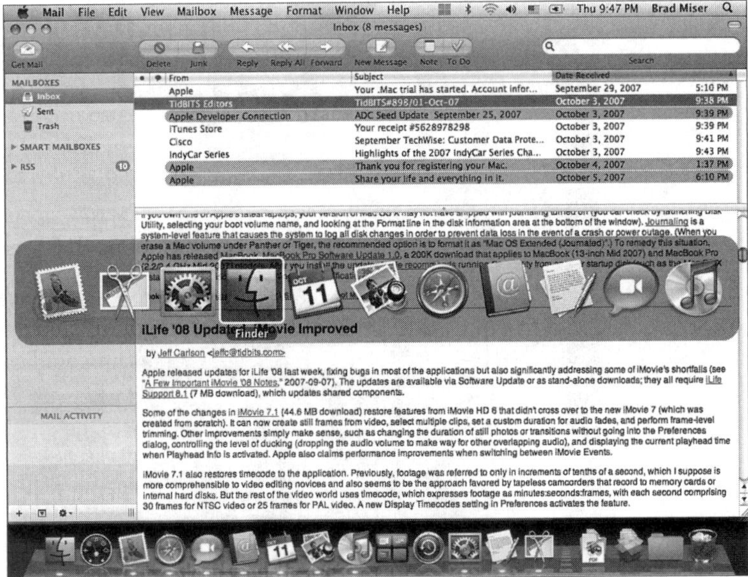


**Figure 12.8**
The Application Switcher menu appears when you press the ⌘-Tab or Shift-⌘-Tab keys.



- Use Exposé (press F9) to show all open windows and click a window in the application you want to switch to.
- Move into a space where an application has been assigned; if the application is open, you'll be able to use it immediately. If not, you'll have to launch it.
- Hide applications quickly by either pressing ⌘-H or choosing *Application*, Hide where *Application* is the name of the active application.
- Quit an open application by opening the application's Dock icon and selecting Quit on the pop-up menu.
- There are several ways to force a hung application to quit. Press Option-Command-Esc to open the Force Quit Applications window, select the application you want to quit, and click Force Quit (see Figure 12.9). (If an application is hung, its name appears in red in the Force Quit Applications window and "Not Responding" is shown next to the application's name.) Open the Activity Monitor application (Applications/Utilities); select the application (process) you want to quit; and select View, Quit Process (or press Option-⌘-Q). You can also use the Unix `kill` command in the Terminal application along with the process number of the application you want to force to quit. Yet another way is to choose the Apple menu and then Force Quit; this also opens the Force Quit Applications window.

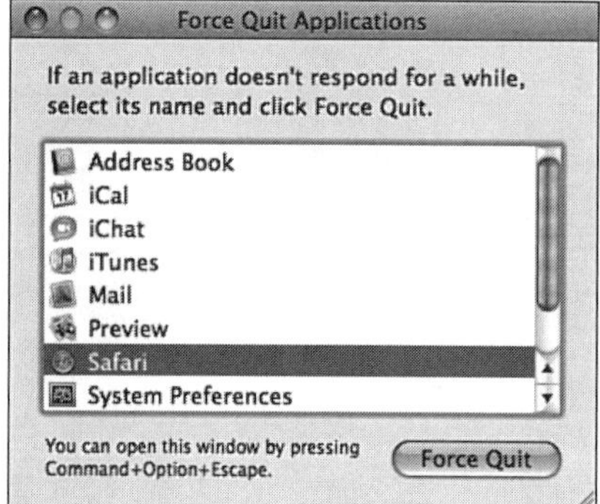


**Figure 12.9**
You can force an application to quit by opening the Force Quit Applications window, selecting the application you want to quit, and clicking Force Quit.

> **TIP**
>
> When you select the Finder in the Force Quit Applications window, the Force Quit button becomes Relaunch–the Finder must always be running when you are using Mac OS X. If the Finder hangs, force it to relaunch.

⇨ To learn more about using Unix commands, **see** Chapter 14, "Unix: Working with the Command Line," **p. 297**.

⇨ To learn more about the Activity Monitor, **see** "Using the Activity Monitor to Understand and Manage Processes," **p. 961**.

> **TIP**
>
> You can also use the Force Quit Applications window to quickly move into open applications. Just open the window by pressing Option-⌘-Esc and then double-click an application shown on the list. That application moves to the front. You can leave the window open all the time if you want to; because it is always on top, it makes a convenient application palette. Of course, if you don't have a lot of screen real estate, this window can get in the way.

CHAPTER 13

# Making Your Mac Accessible to Everyone

## In this chapter

## Understanding Universal Access

The Universal Access pane of the System Preferences application is where you can make your Mac more accessible to users who have various physical or mental challenges. However, even if you don't have such challenges or don't provide technical support to other users who do, you can use the Universal Access tools to make your Mac better suited to the way in which you like to work. For example, using the Zoom feature, you can zoom using the same keyboard shortcut in any application.

Setting up Universal Access involves configuring any of or all the following areas:

- **Seeing**—Using the Seeing controls, you can configure visual aspects of your system. You can use VoiceOver to have your Mac speak interface elements and you can use zoom to increase the size of items on the screen. You can change the display to be white on a black background or grayscale. You can also configure the display's contrast.
- **Hearing**—The Hearing controls enable you to set the screen to flash when the alert sound plays.
- **Keyboard**—Using the Keyboard controls, you can configure Sticky Keys that enable users to choose key combinations by typing only one key at a time. You can also provide assistance to users who have difficulty with initial or repeated keystrokes with the Slow Keys feature. Slow Keys enables you to set a delay for the time between when a key is pressed and when the input is accepted by the system.
- **Mouse**—The Mouse controls enable you to control the mouse by using the numeric pad on the keyboard and to control the size of the cursor that appears on screen.

**NOTE**

> On mobile Macs, the Mouse controls are the Mouse & Trackpad controls.

Although not technically part of the Universal Access configuration tools, you can also use your Mac's Speech Recognition and Text to Speech capabilities to add audio elements to the interface.



## Configuring and Using Seeing Assistance

The Seeing assistance functions are designed to make the Mac's display more visible to users who have difficulty seeing the screen. There are three basic areas of configuration: VoiceOver, Zoom, and Display. You start configuring all of these areas by moving to the Universal Access pane of the System Preferences application and clicking the Seeing tab (see Figure 13.1).

**NOTE**

> If you have an assistive device, such as a Braille display, you can click the check box on the Universal Access pane of the System Preferences application to enable that device. You can also display the Universal Access status in the menu bar by selecting the appropriate check box.

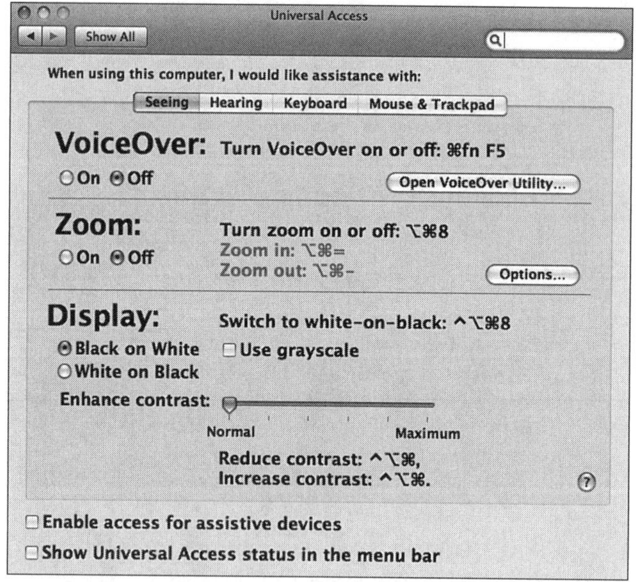


**Figure 13.1**
The Seeing tab of the Universal Access pane enables you to configure how your Mac displays information and to have the OS use VoiceOver to speak interface elements.

## UNDERSTANDING AND USING VOICEOVER

VoiceOver causes your Mac to speak the current position of the VoiceOver cursor in the interface so that you can tell where you are on the screen even if you can't see it clearly. For example, if you have VoiceOver active when you open the Universal Access pane, your Mac would speak the following text to you, "System Preferences, Universal Access, Tool bar" because that is the first interface element that gets selected with the VoiceOver cursor when you open that particular pane. VoiceOver also speaks commands you issue when you activate them. When VoiceOver is active, your Mac will also speak the contents of dialog boxes and other interface elements.

You can customize VoiceOver to work in very specific ways by using the VoiceOver Utility.

### USING DEFAULT VOICEOVER SETTINGS TO HAVE YOUR MAC SPEAK TO YOU

Activating and using VoiceOver with default settings is a simple task. To turn VoiceOver on, use the following steps:

1. Open the System Preferences application and click the Universal Access icon to open the Universal Access pane.
2. Click the Seeing tab.
3. Click the On radio button in the VoiceOver section. On the screen, you will see the VoiceOver cursor (which is a box around the specific interface element currently selected) and the Mac will speak its current location to you (see Figure 13.2).

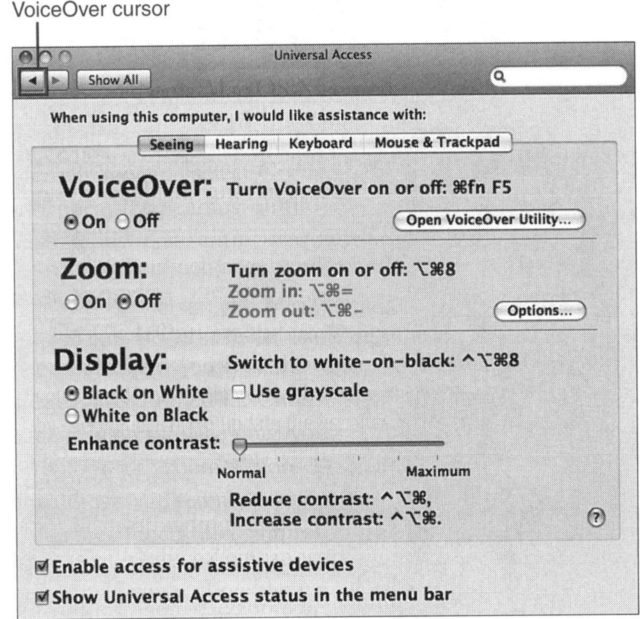


**Figure 13.2**
When VoiceOver is active, the VoiceOver cursor is used to speak a specific part of the interface (in this case, the Back button).

After you have activated VoiceOver, your Mac will begin to speak to you. Each time something changes, the Mac will always speak the current location of the VoiceOver cursor to you. You move the VoiceOver cursor by pressing the Control-Option-Arrow keys to move the VoiceOver cursor around the screen. Each time it moves onto a new element, that element will be spoken to you as it becomes highlighted by the cursor (that is, when the VoiceOver cursor's box is placed around the element).

**NOTE**

> When something appears on the screen that needs your input, such as a sheet, your Mac will speak the words "Interactive dialog" to let you know that such an element has appeared on screen.



When you change applications, VoiceOver will speak the application name and the current location of the VoiceOver cursor within that application.

If you move into an editable text field, your Mac will speak each letter of the text as you move onto it.

**NOTE**

> If you move around quickly, your Mac might not be able to speak each element as you move to it. It will continue speaking each element you have moved the cursor over until it catches up with you.

By default, the position of the mouse cursor is not tied to the VoiceOver cursor. In order to activate a command or control, you must still use the mouse cursor to point to it. The idea is that you use the VoiceOver cursor to point to interface elements so that you know what they are because the Mac will speak them to you. When you want to activate an element, you still select it with the mouse cursor. For example, suppose that you are looking at a screen with tabs on it. You can use the Control-Option-Arrow keys to move the VoiceOver cursor to each tab. When you find the tab you want to move into, you would move the mouse cursor to the tab and then click the mouse button to open the tab.

### Using the VoiceOver Utility to Configure VoiceOver

Using VoiceOver "out of the box" can be useful, but you can also customize it in many ways by using the VoiceOver utility. To access this utility, click the Open VoiceOver Utility button. The button is located on the Seeing tab of the Universal Access pane in the System Preferences application. The VoiceOver Utility has nine sections, each of which enables you to configure a specific aspect of how VoiceOver works (see Figure 13.3).

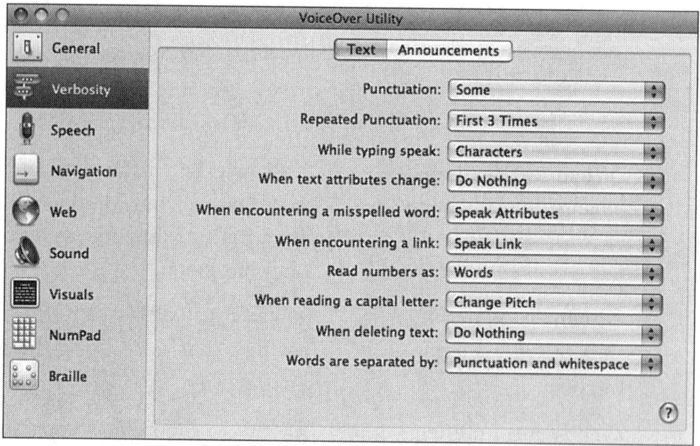


**Figure 13.3**
The VoiceOver Utility enables you to customize nine aspects of how it works.

Unfortunately, going into the details of each control in the VoiceOver Utility is beyond the scope of this book. However, Table 9.1 provides a description of some of the configuration tools available to you.

13

**TABLE 9.1 USEFUL VOICEOVER UTILITY CONFIGURATION CONTROLS**

| Section | Control | What It Does |
|---|---|---|
| General | Login Greeting box | This field contains the text that is spoken when you turn on VoiceOver and log in; you can change the text to change the greeting. |
| General | Portable preferences pop-up menu | Allows you to select what this Mac should do if it detects portable preferences. VoiceOver allows you to save your preferences to removable media so you can take those preferences and apply them on other Macs you might use. |
| Verbosity | Punctuation pop-up menu | Use this to determine how punctuation is spoken to you; for example, choose None to prevent any punctuation from being spoken or All to have all punctuation spoken. |
| Verbosity | Repeated Punctuation pop-up menu | Choose how you want your Mac to speak repeated punctuation, such as Spoken with Count which causes your Mac to speak the punctuation followed by the number of times it appears (for example, “Comma, three). |
| Verbosity | While typing speak pop-up menu | Choosing Every Word causes your Mac to speak every word as you type it; choosing Every Character causes your Mac to speak each character you type; choosing choosing Characters & Words causes your Mac to speak both; choosing Nothing turns off this feature. |
| Verbosity | When text attributes change pop-up menu | When a text attribute changes, such as something being bolded, your Mac can speak the attributes, play a tone, or do nothing; make your selection using this menu. |
| Verbosity | When encountering a misspelled word pop-up menu | Your Mac can alert you to spelling errors by either playing a tone or speaking the attributes of the spelling error. |
| Verbosity | When encountering a link pop-up menu | Use this to choose how your Mac acts when a link is encountered; choices include Do Nothing, Speak Link, Change Pitch, and Play Tone. |
| Verbosity | Read numbers as pop-up menu | You can specify whether the Mac should read numbers as words or as digits. |
| Verbosity | When reading a capital letter pop-up menu | Use this to choose how your Mac speaks when it reaches an uppercase letter; choices include Do Nothing, Speak Cap, Change Pitch, and Play Tone. |

| Section | Control | What It Does |
|---|---|---|
| Verbosity | When deleting text pop-up menu | If you would like your Mac to warn you when you are deleting text, you can select from changing the tone when the text is read, playing a tone, speaking the change. |
| Verbosity | Words are separated by pop-up menu | Select from punctuation and whitespace, or just whitespace to help your Mac know how to treat words as it reads them. |
| Verbosity | Announcement Settings tab | This tab opens the Announcement Settings pane. |
| Announcement Settings pane | Announce when mouse cursor enters a window check box | When this is checked, your Mac will tell you when the mouse cursor moves into a different window by speaking the window name (and application name if applicable). |
| Announcement Settings pane | Announce when a modifier key is pressed check box | This causes your Mac to speak when you press a modifier key, such as the ⌘ key. |
| Announcement Settings pane | Announce when the caps lock key is pressed check box | This causes your Mac to speak when you press the Caps Lock key. |
| Announcement Settings pane | Speak header when navigating across a table row check box | This causes your Mac to speak the headers in the table as you move across a row. |
| Announcement Settings pane | Automatically speak text in dialog boxes | Your Mac will read dialog boxes to you when this is checked. |
| Announcement Settings pane | Speak when status text changes | If you have a status window open and there is a change to the status, that change will be spoken. |
| Announcement Settings pane | Speak text under mouse after delay check box and slider | Check the check box and your Mac will speak the element at which the mouse cursor is currently pointing; use the slider to set the amount of time between when you point to something and when your Mac speaks it. |
| Speech | Mute speech | Select this check box to temporarily stop the speech on your Mac without turning off VoiceOver. |
| Speech | Default Voice | Select the voice that your Mac should use to speak the VoiceOver elements. Use the additional controls to change the rate, pitch and volume of the voice. |
| Speech | Pronunciation | This pane provides you with a number of special characters, abbreviations, and terms. You can then modify how each should be pronounced when spoken by your Mac. Use the Add button at the bottom of the pane to add specific items that you want to have pronounced correctly. |

*continues*

13

**TABLE 9.1 CONTINUED**

| Section | Control | What It Does |
|---|---|---|
| Navigation | Initial position of VoiceOver cursor pop-up menu | Select whether VoiceOver should initially be positioned on the first item in the window or on the keyboard focus. |
| Navigation | Keyboard focus follows VoiceOver cursor check box | This keeps the keyboard focus in sync with the VoiceOver cursor; when you move the VoiceOver cursor, the keyboard focus moves too. |
| Navigation | Mouse cursor follows VoiceOver cursor check box | This makes the mouse cursor always be in the same location as the VoiceOver cursor. |
| Navigation | Mouse cursor follows VoiceOver cursor | Selecting this check box will make your mouse cursor move automatically to where you have the VoiceOver cursor. |
| Navigation | VoiceOver cursor follows mouse cursor | If you want the VoiceOver cursor to follow your mouse, select this check box. |
| Navigation | Insertion point follows VoiceOver cursor check box | This control causes the insertion point to be in the same location as the VoiceOver cursor. |
| Navigation | VoiceOver cursor follows insertion point | You can have the VoiceOver cursor move to where the insertion ppoint is for entering text by clicking this check box. |
| Web | Web Navigation radio buttons | Choose DOM navigation to move through a web page via its DOM (Document Object Model) elements or Group navigation to move via the groups on a page. |
| Web | Navigate Images check box | Check this box to navigate to images. |
| Web | Only navigate images with a desciption | If you check the Navigate Images check box, this check box includes only images with a description that can be read to the viewer. |
| Web | VoiceOver cursor moves to newly loaded web page | Check this box to cause VoiceOver to automatically move to a new web page when it loads. |
| Sound | Mute sounds check box | Allows you to temporarily mute the VoiceOver sounds without changing your VoiceOver preferences. |
| Sound | Enable positional audio check box | If you are listening through headphones or very good speakers, this selection will let you hear a relative position in stereo where an element is on your Mac's screen. |

| Section | Control | What It Does |
|---|---|---|
| Visuals | Show VoiceOver cursor check box and slider | With the box checked, the VoiceOver cursor appears as a box on the screen; use the slider to change its size. |
| Visuals | VoiceOver Menus Magnification slider | This slider changes the font size used on the VoiceOver menu. |
| Visuals | Caption Panel tab | Opens the Caption Panel pane. |
| Caption Panel pane | Show Caption Panel check box and slider | With the box checked, VoiceOver will display a panel at the bottom of the screen that shows what it most recently spoke; use the slider to set the size of the panel. |
| Caption panel pane | Rows in Caption Panel slider | Use this to set the number of rows allowed in the Caption Panel. |
| Caption Panel pane | Caption Panel Transparency slider | Use this to determine how transparent the Caption Panel is. |
| Visuals | Braille tab | Opens the Braille Panel. |
| Braille Panel | Braille Panel tab and slider | Opens the Braille Panel pane. |
| Braille Panel pane | Show Braille panel check box | When you select this check box, a black panel will appear near the bottom of the screen with the Braille characters for the words your Mac speaks in VoiceOver. Use the slider to control how large the panel is on your screen. |
| Braille Panel pane | Braille Panel transparency slider | Allows you to select how transparent the Braille Panel should appear on screen. |
| NumPad | Numeric Keypad Settings button | This button opens the Numeric Keypad pane. |
| Numeric Keypad pane | Numeric Keypad controls | Use this pane to activate the numeric keypad to navigate on the desktop; once activated, you can use each key's pop-up menu to determine how that key navigates. |
| Braille | Braille translation pop-up menu | Displays American English as the language supported by the Braille display connected to the Mac. |
| Braille | Show contracted Braille | Select this check box to specify whether VoiceOver should contract words not shown by the VoiceOver cursor, as well as display words in the cursor in uncontracted Braille. |
| Braille | Status cells check boxes | Use the check boxes to specify how status windows should be shown and in what style for the connected Braille display. |

*continues*

13

**Table 9.1 Continued**

| Section | Control | What It Does |
|---|---|---|
| Braille | Show status on radio buttons | Select which side the status messages should appear on the Braille display connected to your Mac. |
| Braille | Input tab | The Input tab opens a pane that allows you to change which Braille display keys map to specific VoiceOver functions. You can use this sheet to add or remove mappings, as well as modify existing input key mappings. |

## Understanding and Using Zoom

The Zoom function enables you to zoom in on the screen to make things easier to see.

### Using Zoom

First, activate zoom by using the following steps:

1. Open the Seeing tab in the Universal Access pane of the System Preferences application.
2. Click the On radio button in the Zoom section.

**TIP**

> You can also turn Zoom on or off by pressing ⌘-Option-8.

After Zoom is turned on press ⌘-Option-= to zoom in or ⌘-Option-- to zoom out (see Figure 13.4). When you are zoomed in, you can move around in the display by moving your mouse.

13

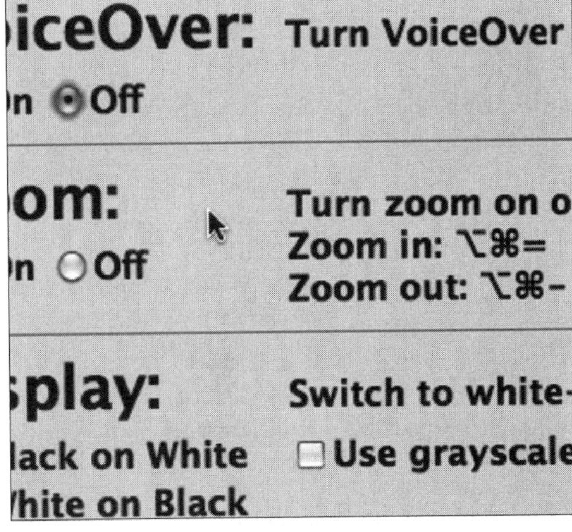


**Figure 13.4** Here, I have zoomed in on the Zoom controls.

### CONFIGURING ZOOM

There are several options you can configure for Zoom as listed in Table 9.2. You can access these controls by clicking the Options button in the Zoom section. When you do, the Options sheet will appear. Choose the options you want and click Done to save them.

**TABLE 9.2 ZOOM CONTROLS**

| Control | What It Does |
| --- | --- |
| Maximum Zoom slider | Sets the amount of magnification that can be achieved by pressing the zoom in keys once. |
| Minimum Zoom slider | Sets the amount of magnification that can be achieved by pressing the zoom out keys once. |
| Show preview rectangle when zoomed out check box | When this is checked, a black box will appear around the mouse cursor; this box shows the area that will be zoomed in on when the zoom in keys are pressed when no zoom is currently applied; the box disappears when you zoom in. |
| Smooth images check box (Press Option-⌘-\ to turn smoothing on or off) | When checked, your Mac will smooth zoomed images; you can turn this on or off using the keys listed. |
| Zoom follows the keyboard focus check box | When checked and you zoom, the zoom focus occurs for the area of the screen that you are focused on using the keyboard. |
| When zoomed in, the screen image moves radio buttons | Choose "Continuously with pointer" to have the zoomed image move with mouse movements; choose "Only when the pointer reaches an edge" to have the image moved only when the mouse cursor reaches the edge of the image or screen; choose "So the pointer is at or near the center of the image" to always keep the cursor near the center of the image. |
| Use scroll wheel with modifier keys to zoom check box and field | Check this box to use the scroll wheel on a mouse to zoom and enter the modifier key you'll use to activate zoom. |

## UNDERSTANDING AND USING DISPLAY OPTIONS



The Display options section of the Seeing tab enables you to configure the following settings:

- **Black on White**—Check this check box to use the default black text on a white background in Mac OS X screens.
- **White on Black**—This check box causes your Mac to display white text on a black background.

- **Use grayscale**—This check box removes the color from the display and instead uses shades of gray.
- **Enhance contrast**—Use this slider to change the contrast of the display. Contrast is the visual difference between the light and dark elements presented on screen.

> **TIP**
> Use the keyboard shortcuts listed next to the Display options on the Seeing tab to be able to turn them on or off quickly.

# CONFIGURING AND USING HEARING ASSISTANCE

The Hearing tab of the Universal Access pane enables you to have your Mac display an on-screen visual alert when it needs to get your attention (see Figure 13.5). To set this, open the tab and check the "Flash the screen when an alert sound occurs" check box. When your Mac plays the alert sound, it will also flash the screen. Click the Flash Screen button on the Hearing tab to see what the flash alert looks like.

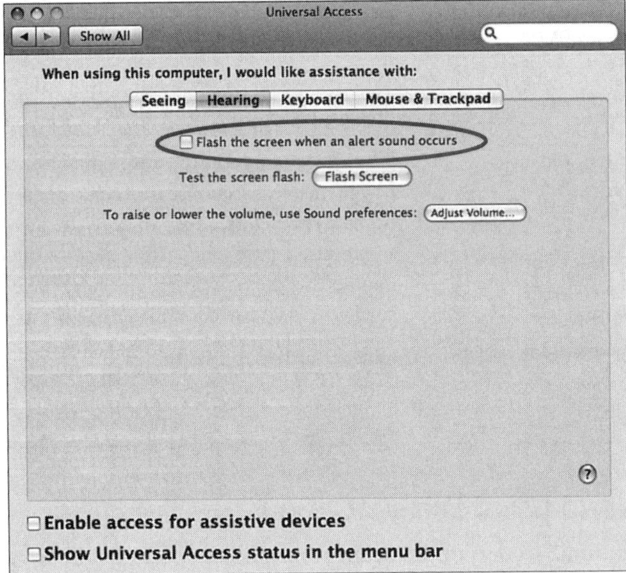


**Figure 13.5**
If you prefer your Mac to flash the screen when it needs your attention, use this check box to make it so.

13

# CONFIGURING KEYBOARD ASSISTANCE

The Keyboard tools make your Mac easier to control for those who have difficulty manipulating the keys on the keyboard. There are two general features: Sticky Keys and Slow Keys. Sticky Keys helps users press more than one modifier key at a time because each key pressed "sticks" on. You can also configure Slow Keys to tailor how keys can be pressed to register them with the system. To configure the Keyboard settings, perform the following steps:

1. Open the Keyboard tab on the Universal Access pane of the System Preferences application.
2. Click the Sticky Keys On radio button to activate that feature.
3. If you want users to be able to enable or disable Sticky Keys by pressing the Shift key five times, check the "Press the Shift key five times to turn Sticky Keys on or off" check box.
4. If you want audio feedback when the modifier key is set, check the "Beep when a modifier key is set" check box.
5. If you want each keypress to be shown on the screen, check the "Display pressed keys on screen" check box.
6. Turn Slow Keys on by clicking the Slow Keys On radio button.
7. To play a key sound each time a key is pressed, check the "Use click key sounds" check box.
8. Use the Acceptance Delay slider to set the amount of time a key must be pressed before it is registered. Move the slider to the left to increase the delay between the time the key is pressed and when it is registered as a keypress by the system.

## CONFIGURING AND USING MOUSE ASSISTANCE

Mouse Keys enables users to control the location of the pointer by using the numeric keys on the keypad; this can be useful if a person has difficulty manipulating a mouse or trackpad. To configure Mouse Keys, perform the following steps:

1. Open the Mouse (or Mouse & Trackpad on a mobile Mac) tab of the Universal Access pane of the System Preferences application.
2. Click the On radio button to turn Mouse Keys on.
3. You can enable Mouse Keys to be turned on or off from the keyboard by checking or unchecking the "Press the Option key five times to turn Sticky Keys on or off" check box.
4. Use the Initial Delay slider to set the amount of time a key must be pressed before the pointer starts moving. Move the slider to the left to make the pointer start moving sooner when a key is pressed or to the right to increase the delay.
5. Use the Maximum Speed slider to determine how fast and far the pointer moves when a key is pressed. Drag the slider to the right to increase the speed of movement or to the left to decrease it.
6. To change the size of the pointer on the screen, use the Cursor Size slider. Drag the slider to the right to increase the size of the cursor (see Figure 13.6).
7. If you are using a mobile Mac you can check the "Ignore trackpad when Mouse Keys is on" so that moving your hand across the trackpad does not interfere with using the keyboard to navigate.

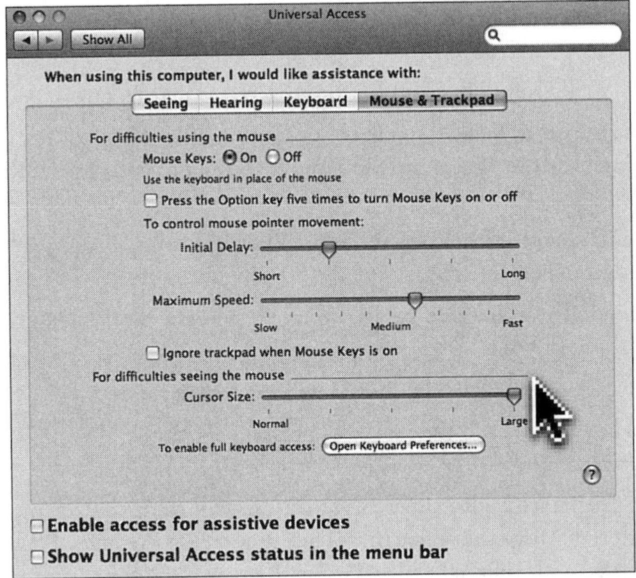


**Figure 13.6**
You can increase the size of the cursor if someone who uses your Mac has difficulty seeing the standard pointer.

# Mac OS X to the Max: Configuring and Using Speech Recognition

Mac OS X has built-in support for speech recognition. This works both ways—you can speak to your Mac to issue commands and your Mac can read onscreen text to you. Whether controlling your Mac with speech works for you or not depends on a lot of variables, such as your speaking voice, the position of your mouth relative to your Mac's microphone, the microphone itself, and so on. Also, don't expect your Mac to start working like the computer on the *Starship Enterprise*; it will take some time for you to get voice recognition working effectively.



**TIP**

> I've tried several voice recognition systems, including the Mac's built-in one. Frankly, beyond the initial gee-whiz factor of being able to speak a command and have the computer respond by doing something, I have found that using the keyboard and mouse is a much more effective way to work. But, you might want to experiment to see whether it works better for you, particularly if you have special needs when it comes to interacting with your Mac. This section will get you started, but is certainly not intended to explain all the details.

## Configuring Your Mac for Voice Control

To configure speech recognition on your Mac, perform the following steps:

1. Open the Speech pane of the System Preferences application.

2. Click the Speech Recognition tab and use the controls to configure how speech recognition works. This pane has two tabs: Settings and Commands (see Figure 13.7). Use the Settings tab to configure basic settings of speech recognition.

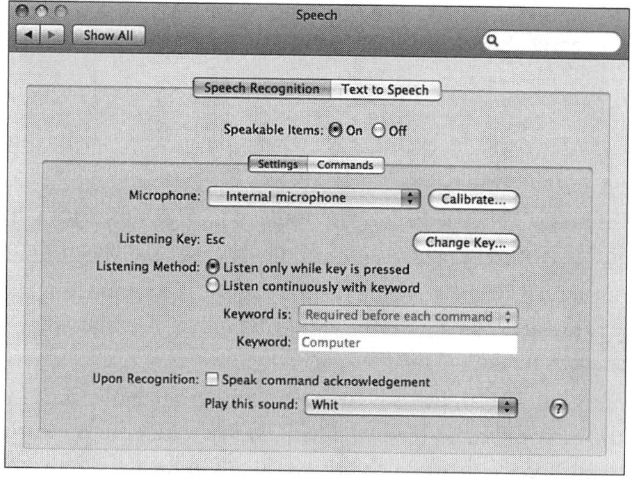


**Figure 13.7**
Use the Settings tab of the Speech Recognition pane to configure how your Mac listens to you.

3. Use the Microphone pop-up menu to choose the microphone you want to use. The options you have will depend on the configuration of your system.
4. Click the Calibrate button. The Microphone Calibration window will appear (see Figure 13.8).

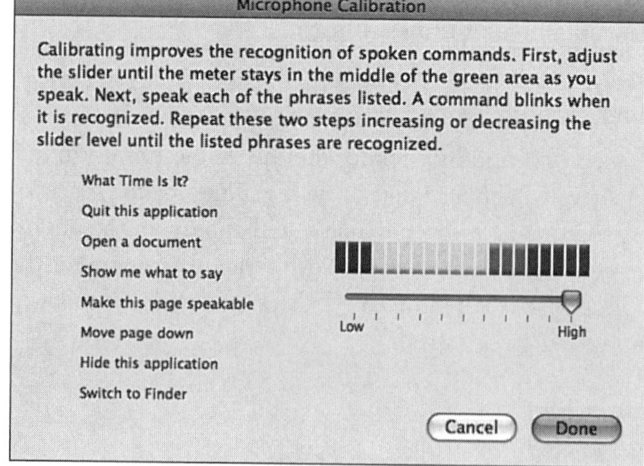


**Figure 13.8**
Using the Microphone Calibration window, you adjust your microphone's input to easily pick up spoken commands.

5. Speak some words and drag the slider to the left or right until what you speak is mostly registered near the center of the green band above the slider.
6. Speak each phrase listed along the left edge of the window. If the phrase is recognized by your Mac, it will flash. If it isn't recognized, adjust the slider and repeat the phrase until it is.

13

7. Continue this process until you can speak all the phrases and have them recognized without changing the slider.

> **TIP**
> When you speak to your Mac, you'll probably have to slow down and make sure you enunciate each word more clearly than you probably do in normal conversation.

8. When your Mac registers each phrase when you speak it, click Done. The Microphone Calibration window will close.
9. By default the listen key is Esc; if you want to change this, click Change Key and choose the key you want to use. The listen key makes your Mac listen for spoken commands.
10. If you want to press the listen key before you speak a command, click the "Listen only while key is pressed" radio button. With this active, you must press the listen key before you speak a command.
11. If you want your Mac to listen continuously for commands, click the "Listen continuously with keyword" radio button. Then, choose when the keyword is required on the "Keyword is" pop-up menu. The options are "Optional before commands," "Required before each command," "Required 15 seconds after last command," and "Required 30 seconds after last command." Then, enter your keyword in the Keyword field. The default is "Computer," which means you need say the word "Computer" to get your Mac to listen to your commands, but you can change this to something else if you prefer to use a different term.
12. If you want your Mac to acknowledge your command by speaking it, check the "Speak command acknowledgment" check box. When your Mac acknowledges your command, it will speak the command it thinks it heard.
13. Choose the sound you want your Mac to play when it recognizes a command on the "Play this sound" pop-up menu.
14. Activate speech recognition by clicking the Speakable Items On radio button at the top of the pane. A sheet will appear that provides some tips for success; read these tips and click Continue. A round feedback window will appear on the desktop. In the center of this, you'll see either the current listen key or the phrase you need to speak (see Figure 13.9). When your Mac is listening to you, the lower part of this window will show you how the sound is being registered.

**Figure 13.9**
The feedback window indicates that the word "Computer" needs to be spoken before voice commands.

15. Click the Commands tab. You use this pane to determine the command sets you can speak (see Figure 13.10).

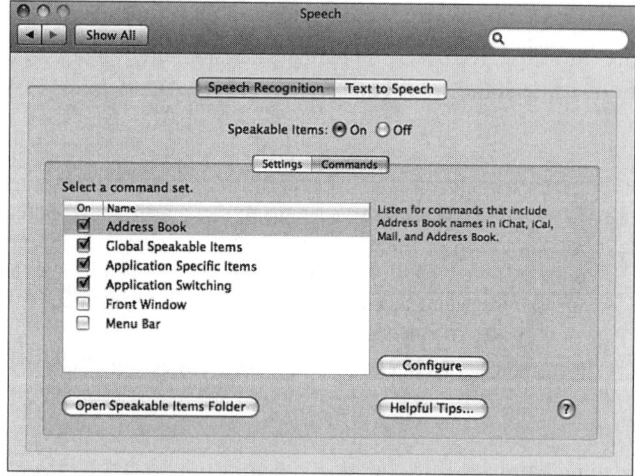


**Figure 13.10**
Use the Commands tab to choose command sets that you want to be able to speak.

16. Select a command set, such as the Front Window set. A description of the commands will appear to the right of the list.
17. To activate a command set, check its check box. You will then be able to speak the commands in that set. You will be ready to start talking to your Mac.

**TIP**

If a command set has additional configuration options, the Configure button will become active when you select that command set. Use this button and resulting sheet to set options for the command set.

**NOTE**

There are a number of commands available in the Speakable Items folder. When you activate the Global Speakable Items command set, these commands will be available to you. To see these commands, click the Open Speakable Items Folder button. A Finder window will appear and you will see Speakable items available to you. (For kicks, check out the "Tell me a joke" command.)

13

## USING SPEECH RECOGNITION

After you have configured speech recognition, it will either be easy to use or extremely frustrating depending on how well your Mac recognizes the commands you speak. The only way to find out is to try it.

If you configured speech recognition to require the listening key, press it and speak a command. If your Mac recognizes the command, it will act on it and provide you with the feedback you configured it to, such as repeating the command or playing the sound you selected.

If you have your Mac listen continuously, speak the keyword you set and then speak the command. If your Mac recognizes the command, it will act on it and provide you with the feedback you configured it to, such as repeating the command or playing the sound you selected.

If your Mac does nothing, it doesn't recognize the command. This can be because it didn't "hear" you, didn't understand what you said, or the command you spoke isn't a speakable command.

> **TIP**
>
> To see which commands you can speak, click the arrow at the bottom of the feedback window and select Open Speech Commands window. In the Speech Commands window is the list of commands you can speak. When you open an application that supports speech recognition, that application appears in the Speech Commands window and the list of spoken commands it supports is shown.
>
> If you double-click the feedback window, it moves to the Dock.

If you find speaking commands useful, you can continue to talk to your Mac to control it. However, if you are like me, you will quickly grow tired of trying to get it to work reliably and even if you do get it to work well, it is still faster to use your hands to control your Mac. But, this can be kind of fun to play around with.

## Using Text to Speech

As you saw earlier in this chapter, using VoiceOver, your Mac can speak to you. The Text to Speech feature takes this concept much further and can be used across many applications and OS to have your Mac speak to you.

To configure Text to Speech, perform the following steps:

1. Open the Text to Speech tab of the Speech pane of the System Preferences application.
2. Select the voice you want your Mac to use on the System Voice pop-up menu and then set the rate at which the voice speaks using the slider. Click the Play button to hear a sample.
3. If you want your Mac to speak alerts to you, check the "Announce when alerts are displayed" check box and use the Set Alert Options button to open a sheet that enables you to configure the voice used, the alert phrase, and the delay time. Click OK to set the options you selected.
4. If you want applications to speak when they need your attention, check the "Announce when an application requires your attention" check box.
5. If you want to be able to quickly have your Mac read selected text to you, check the "Speak selected text when the key is pressed" check box. In the resulting sheet, type the key combination you want to use to cause your Mac to read text you select and click OK.

TIP

> You can change this key combination later by clicking the Set Key button.

TIP

> Your Mac can speak the time to you, as well. Use the Date & Time Preferences pane to configure this option.

Your Mac will start speaking to you when the conditions you selected occur, such when an alert is played.

If you enabled the "speak selected text" feature, you can select any text and press the keyboard shortcut to cause your Mac to read it.

In applications that support Text to Speech, you can have your Mac read to you by choosing Edit, Speech, Start Speaking. You can shut your Mac up by choosing Edit, Speech Stop Speaking.

CHAPTER 14

# Unix: Working with the Command Line

## In this chapter

# A COMMAND LINE WITH THE MAC OS?

As you learned earlier in the book, Mac OS X is running on top of a version of the Unix operating system. This means that Mac OS X can use many Unix applications. It also means you can enter Unix commands directly in the command-line interface to manipulate your system. In fact, in some situations, using a Unix command might be the best way you can accomplish a task (such as deleting a rogue file that you can't delete by dragging it to the Trash).

Unix is a very powerful language/operating system; however, it is also enigmatic, and many of its commands require you to use complicated syntax to get them to work properly. Unix commands are incomprehensible to most people by just looking at them, so don't expect to be able to figure out how a particular command works without some help. Mostly, you will learn about commands you want to use from various Unix resources (such as this chapter, other books, websites, and Unix manual pages). You might find using the command line to be so counter to the Mac OS X interface experience that you don't want to use it; if so, that is fine because few situations exist in which it is required in everyday Mac use. However, if you want to master Mac OS X, you should become familiar with the command line and learn some basic Unix commands. You might find that Unix provides ways of doing things that are both powerful and efficient.

There is so much you can do with Unix that there is no way you can learn how to work proficiently with it in the few pages of this chapter. To become even remotely fluent in Unix, you will need to do some additional learning outside of this book. What you can learn here is generally how the command-line interface works, and you can also learn how to use some basic Unix commands as examples. In the "Mac OS X to the Max" section at the end of the chapter, I provide references for you so you can learn more about using Unix if you choose to.

## TERMINAL

You use the Terminal application (Applications/Utilities) to enter Unix commands in the command-line interface (see Figure 14.1). When you first open it, the Terminal window is simple; all you see are your last login date and time, the hostname, the user account under which you are logged in, and the command prompt.

**NOTE**

Hostname is the name of the machine that is hosting your Unix session. When you are running a Unix session from your local machine, this will be your computer's name for most default configurations. If you are providing services over the network, the computer's network name is used.



## SHELLS

In Unix, the *shell* is the user interface you use to interact with Unix. You can use different shells for the same set of Unix tools; each shell will have slightly different features, but they all work somewhat similarly (although the specific commands you use can differ). You can change the specific shell you use if you find one that offers features in which you are interested.

The default shell for working with Unix under Mac OS X is called `bash`. Other shells are available, but `bash` is a good place to start.

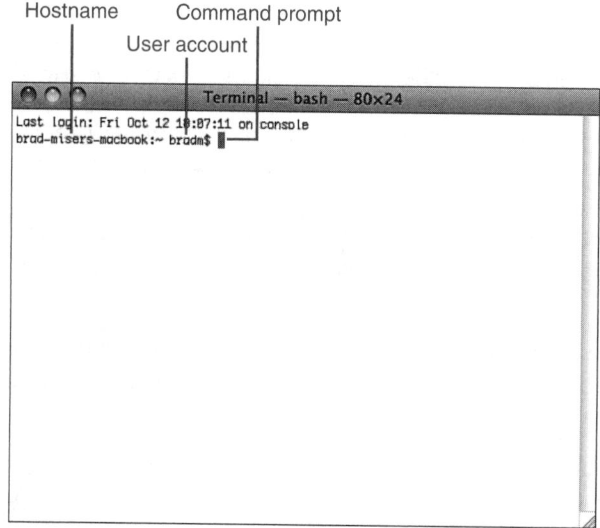


**Figure 14.1**
The command-line interface in Terminal isn't much to look at, but it is very powerful.

**NOTE**

> There are different shells installed in Mac OS X by default, and you can also download additional shells. After you download and install the shell, you use the Terminal's Preferences to set the shell you want to use. The details of using different shells are beyond the scope of this chapter. See some of the references listed at the end of this chapter for help.

## UNIX COMMAND STRUCTURE

To enter commands, you type them at the command prompt. All Unix commands use a specific syntax and consist of the following three parts:

- Command
- Options
- Argument

The *command* is the specific action you want to take, such as listing the contents of a directory using the `ls` command.

You can enter *options* for a command to make the command work in a specific way. To add an option to a command, you type a hyphen followed by a letter. The options you can use are specific to each command. For example, when used with the `ls` (`list`) command, the `-l` option tells Unix to list the contents of the directory in the long format.

14

The *argument* is the "thing" on which the command will be executed, such as a file or directory. For example, to list the contents of a directory called `mydirectory`, the argument would be that directory name and the path to that directory.

When you enter specific commands, you might not use options or arguments; in some cases, you won't use either and will simply enter the command by itself.

**NOTE**

> Unix is case sensitive, so you must always follow the case conventions for specific commands. Most of the time, you will type everything in lowercase letters for commands and options, but paths can include both uppercase and lowercase letters.

You can run several commands in sequential order by separating the commands with a semicolon, as in `command1; command2`. Each command will be activated in the order in which you list it.

You can send the output of one command to be the input of another command by separating them with the pipe symbol (`¦`), as in `command1 ¦ command2`. This is called *piping*.

When entering commands, you will frequently need to use the path to a directory or file you want to manipulate. The path is the means by which you locate a file in the hierarchy; levels of the hierarchy are indicated by the slash (`/`). Also, Unix uses relative pathnames. When you refer to something within or below the current directory, you need to enter only the portion of the path from the current directory to the subdirectories and files rather than the full path from the top level of the hierarchy. For example, to refer to a directory called `projects` within your `Documents` folder when you are currently in the `Documents` directory, you would enter the path `projects`. When you want to move above or outside the current directory, you must type the full path. In Unix, full paths always start with `/`.

**NOTE**

> The full path to your Home directory is `/`*`startupvolume`*`/Users/`*`shortusername`*`/`, where *`startupvolume`* is the name of your Mac OS X startup volume and *`shortusername`* is the short username for your account. However, because you can use relative paths, you can leave out the first `/` and the name of your Mac OS X startup volume to get to this directory. You only need to add the volume name when you are working outside the current volume.



Unlike graphical interfaces, such as Mac OS X, Unix does not like spaces in filenames, volume names, or paths. To enter a space in one of these, use the backslash (`\`) followed by the space. For example, to refer to the volume called Mac OS X, you would enter `/Mac\ OS\ X`.

To get to the root of the startup volume, the path is simply `/`. However, unless you are logged on under the root account, you won't be able to do anything with the files and directories you see using a command line because of the system security.

One of the best ways to become familiar with entering pathnames is to drag items from a Finder window onto the Terminal window. When you do so, the pathname to that item is entered in Terminal. You can use this trick to make entering paths easier because you can drag the item onto the prompt after you have entered a command and option to quickly add the argument to complete the command. And, after you drag several onto the window, you will get a good idea of how to type pathnames at the prompt manually. Follow these steps:

1. In a Finder window, open the Home directory for your user account.
2. Open a new Terminal window from within the Terminal application by selecting File, New Shell. A new Terminal window will appear.

**TIP**

> When using Terminal, you can have multiple windows open at the same time. Each window is independent, so you can have multiple sessions running independently. You can save each session separately too, which you will learn about later in this chapter.

3. Drag the `Documents` directory from the Finder window onto the new Terminal window. The path to the directory is shown at the prompt (see Figure 14.2). Note that you can't drag the folder from the Places sidebar; you must drag it from a Finder window.

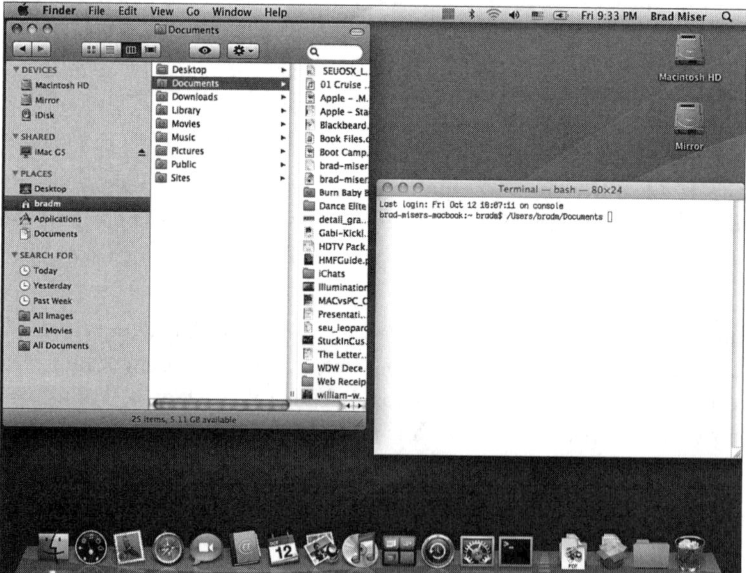

**Figure 14.2**
You can quickly enter a path at the prompt by dragging an item from a Finder window onto Terminal; in this case, I dragged the `Documents` folder from my Home directory onto the Terminal window.

**NOTE**

If you deal with Unix systems outside of Mac OS X, you will notice that paths almost never include spaces. Unix can have trouble properly interpreting spaces, so you can run into problems if the path you want to use includes spaces. Generally, if you plan to use Unix frequently, you should include underscores when you name your files and directories instead of spaces. Or, you can simply drag the object into the Terminal window and let the Mac enter the path for you. Spaces will be replaced by a backslash and a space (\ ).

⇨ To see examples of specific Unix commands, **see** "Learning Unix by Example," **p. 302**.

### UNIX APPLICATIONS

Because Unix has been around so long, thousands and thousands of Unix applications are available. You can run many of these under Mac OS X, and the OS includes several of these applications as part of the standard installation. For example, the Apache web server application enables you to host your own web pages. Mac OS X comes with a couple of Unix text editors, which are vi (Visual Editor) and emacs (an abbreviation of editing macros).

⇨ To get some examples of running these Unix applications, **see** "Working with Basic Unix Applications," **p. 311**.

### SHELL SCRIPTS

You can invoke a series of commands using a shell script; you can save the script and run it at any time to save yourself from having to retype the commands over and over. You create a script using the same syntax as in regular Unix commands. The difference is that you save those commands to a text file. When you want to run the commands, you execute the file instead. You can also run scripts that others have written just as easily.

The details of writing and running scripts are beyond the scope of this book. See the references listed at the end of this chapter for information about creating and using shell scripts.

### UNIX FLAVORS

Finally, you should be aware that various versions of Unix are available. And, different releases of different versions exist as well. Mac OS X is built upon a version of the Berkeley Software Distribution (BSD) version of Unix called Darwin. As this version is updated, the version that is part of Mac OS X is updated as well.



## LEARNING UNIX BY EXAMPLE

Many Unix commands are available, and there is no way you can do more than scratch the surface in a single chapter. However, you can learn how Unix commands work in general by trying some specific examples of useful Unix commands.

⇨ For references in which you can learn more Unix commands, **see** "Learning Unix," **p. 314**.

Each of the following sections provides information about specific commands. For each command, you will see four areas of information about that command. First, you will read a general description of what the command does. Second, you will see the command's syntax and some of the useful options for that command. Third, you will see a more specific description of the command's effect. Fourth, you will see the steps you can take to use the command.

**NOTE**

> For the commands in this section, you won't see all or even many of the options that are possible for each command. You will need to access a more detailed reference for that type of information, such as the command's manual pages.

## LEARNING ABOUT THE ENVIRONMENT

When you are troubleshooting, it can be helpful to understand the environment in which you are running Unix. You can use the `uname` command to get information about the computer on which you execute the command. Or, you might need to check this information to make sure some software or hardware is compatible with your system:

Command: `uname`

Options: `-a` provides all the information about your machine; `-s` shows the operating system name; `-n` lists the machine name

What it does: Provides information about various aspects of the machine on which you are running Unix

1. Launch the Terminal application and at the command prompt, type **`uname -a`**; then press Return. You will see various items of information about your machine, such as the core operating system (`Darwin`), the version of the kernel you are running, and so on (see Figure 14.3).

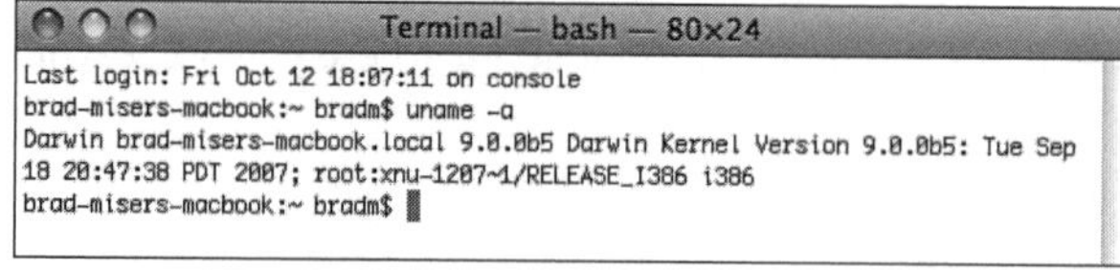

Terminal — bash — 80×24
Last login: Fri Oct 12 18:07:11 on console
brad-misers-macbook:~ bradm$ uname -a
Darwin brad-misers-macbook.local 9.0.0b5 Darwin Kernel Version 9.0.0b5: Tue Sep
18 20:47:38 PDT 2007; root:xnu-1207~1/RELEASE_I386 i386
brad-misers-macbook:~ bradm$


**Figure 14.3**
The `uname` command provides information about the machine on which you are running Unix.

2. Type **`uname -s`** and press Return. You will see only the core operating system (`Darwin`).
3. Type **`uname -n`** and press Return. You will see the name of the machine hosting the Unix session.

Command: `env`

What it does: Provides extensive information about your Unix session (your Unix environment)

14

Type **env** and press Return. You will see information including your Home directory, the shell you are running, the username you are using, the language being used, the application you are using to enter Unix commands, and so on.

**TIP**

> The Terminal application has been updated to include a number of new features that you might want to take advantage of. You can now have multiple tabs, similar to tabs in Safari, that allow you to have several command-line sessions at the same time in the same application window. You can also specify the theme of your window, which will change the color scheme that you see. Both the Terminal Preferences and the Shell menu provide access to these new features.

**NOTE**

> You have the ability to save all of the configuration of how you use Terminal into a window group. This allows you to have all of your window settings and shell preferences setup the way you want each time you open Terminal. Use the Window menu and select Save Windows as Group. You will be prompted to name the new window group and you can check the check box to use your new window group each time Terminal is launched. If you save multiple window groups, you can use the Window Groups pane of the Terminal preferences to select the window group to be used when Terminal launches.

## VIEWING THE CONTENTS OF DIRECTORIES

You will frequently need to move up and down the directory structure to work with specific files or other directories. Unix has many commands that enable you to do so, including

Command: `pwd`

What it does: Shows you the full path to your current location

Use the `pwd` command when you aren't sure about the directory in which you are currently located. When you use the command, you will see the full path in which you are working. This can be helpful if you become confused about where you are as you move around the directories.

Command: `cd` *`pathname`*

What it does: Changes your directory location to the one in the path *`pathname`*

**NOTE**

> When a specific command is listed in a step, you should ignore the period at the end of the command. For example, in the following steps, don't type the period after the command `cd Music` in step 1.

14

1. Type **`cd Music`**. The prompt will change to `[computername:Music]` to indicate you are in the Music directory in your Home directory.

**TIP**

> The ~ in a pathname represents your Home directory, so `~/Music` means you are in the `Music` directory that is within your Home directory. This can help you take some shortcuts when entering paths, as you will see in the next step.
>
> Also remember that the forward slash (/) in a path indicates a change in level in the hierarchy. If you are in your Home directory and type `cd /Music`, you will get a message telling you that no such directory exists. When you enter the forward slash, Unix looks back to the highest level in the structure and there is not a directory called `Music` in that directory. Leaving the / out indicates that Unix should look in the current directory, which is where the directory is actually located.

2. Type **`cd /Users/`*`shortusername`***, where *`shortusername`* is the short username for your account. This moves you back into your Home directory. You include `/Users/` because you are moving above the `Music` directory and so need to include the full pathname.

**NOTE**

> In a pathname, the tilde character (~) indicates that you are in your Home directory. In step 2, you could have just entered `cd ~` to move back into your Home directory. In addition, if you are in a directory and just want to move up a level, type `cd ..` and press Return.

Command: `ls`

Options: `-F` differentiates between files and directories; `-l` shows full information for all the files in the directory

What it does: Lists the contents of a directory in various formats and with various information

**NOTE**

> Although most commands and options are in lowercase, they aren't always. For example, the `-F` option is different from the `-f` option (both are valid for the `ls` command).

1. Use the `cd` command to move into the directory of which you want to see the contents.
2. Type **`ls`**. You will see a multiple-column view of the directory; files and directories are listed by name.
3. Type **`ls -F`**. You will see the same list as before except that now directories are indicated by a / after their names.
4. Type **`ls -l`**. You will see the contents of the directory listed along with lots of information about each file and directory within the current directory (see Figure 14.4). If there are many items, the information will scroll so quickly that you might not be able to see all of it. This is a good opportunity to see an example of piping two commands together.

14

5. Type **`ls -l | more`**. This time, the same list will appear, but the display will stop when the screen is full and you will see the `byte` prompt at the bottom of the window. Press the spacebar to see the next screenful of information. Once you see the `end` prompt, you can scroll the window using the scrollbars to see all the items in the window. Press the spacebar one more time to return to the command prompt.

**TIP**

> If you type the command `ls -la`, you will also see the invisible files in a directory.

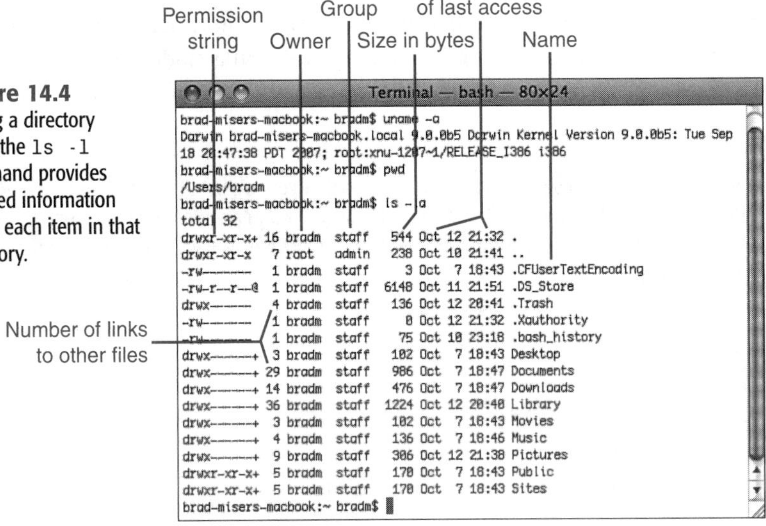


**Figure 14.4**
Listing a directory using the `ls -l` command provides detailed information about each item in that directory.

The permissions string you see at the start of each item in the full listing indicates how the item can be accessed. The first character indicates whether the item is a file (`-`) or a directory (`d`). The next three characters indicate what the owner of the file can do; `r` is for read, `w` is for write, and `x` is for execute. If any of these characters is the hyphen (`-`), that action can't be taken. The next three characters indicate the permission that the group has to the file. For example, if these characters are `r-x`, other members of the group can read, not write, and execute the file. The last three characters indicate what everyone else can do.

The execute permission applies to a directory. To access a directory, you must have both read and execute permission. If you also have `w` permission, you can change the contents of the directory as well.

Command: `file` *`filename`*

What it does: Indicates what type of file *`filename`* is

Type **`file`**, followed by the filename you would like information about (it's often easiest to drag the file from the Finder and drop it next to the command rather than typing the pathname to that file), and press Return. Information about the file is displayed.

## CHANGING THE CONTENTS OF DIRECTORIES

You can use Unix commands to change the contents of directories as well. For example, you can delete files using the `rm` command. This can sometimes be faster than using the Trash. Once in a while, you might not be able to use the Trash to get rid of a file; you can often use the Unix commands to accomplish the task when other means fail.

Command: `rm`

Options: `-i` prompts you before deleting each file; `-r` removes the entire directory

What it does: Deletes everything that you indicate should be deleted

1. Use the `cd` and `ls` commands to find a file you want to delete.
2. Type **`rm`** ***`filename`***, where *`filename`* is the name of the file you want to delete, and press Return. The file is deleted.
3. Type **`rm -i`** ***`filename`*** and press Return. You are prompted about removing the file; type **`Y`** to remove the file or **`N`** to cancel.
4. Type **`rm -r`** ***`directoryname`***, where *`directoryname`* is the name of a directory you want to delete, and press Return. The directory and all its contents are deleted.

**NOTE**

> You can't remove the current directory unless you enter the full path to it.

**TIP**

> The asterisk (*) is a wildcard character. For example, to delete all the files in a directory that have the file extension `.tiff`, you can type `rm *.tiff`.

Command: `cp`

What it does: Copies a file

1. Type **`cp`** ***`filename filenamecopy`***, where *`filename`* is the name of the file you want to copy and *`filenamecopy`* is the name of the file to which it will be copied; then press Return. The first file is copied into a new file that has the second name you typed.
2. Type **`cp`** ***`filename path`***, where *`filename`* is the name of the file you want to copy and *`path`* is the location in which you want the copy to be created; then press Return. A copy of the file is placed into the location you specified.

Command: `mv`

What it does: Moves a file or directory

Type **`mv`** ***`filename path`*** and press Return. The file or directory *`filename`* is moved to the location *`path`*.

Command: `mkdir`

What it does: Creates a directory (folder)

1. Use the `cd` command to move into the directory in which you want to create a new directory.
2. Type **`mkdir`** ***`directoryname`*** and press Return. A new directory with the name *`directoryname`* is created in the current directory.

## Using the Manual

All Unix commands have a manual associated with them. This manual lists the syntax for the command and defines its options; manuals can be a good reference when you are using a specific command but can't remember an option or the command's exact syntax. Many manual pages also provide some explanation about how the command works.

Command: `man`

What it does: Brings up the manual pages for the command you enter

1. Type **`man ls`** and press Return. The manual pages for the `ls` command appear (see Figure 14.5).

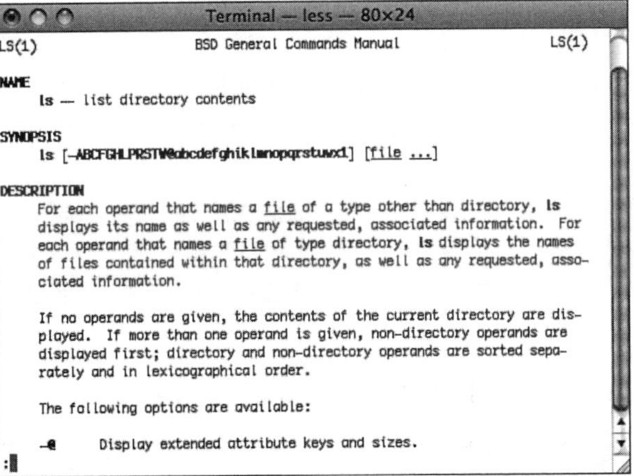


**Figure 14.5**
You can get extensive information about any command by using the `man` command.

2. Press the spacebar to move to the next page.
3. Continue reading the manual pages until you have the information you need.
4. Press Q to return to the command prompt.

It is a good idea to take a look at the manual pages for any Unix commands you use. Pay special attention to the list of options that are available for the command.

14

**NOTE**

Some Unix applications provide manual pages using the help argument. For example, `perl --help` brings up information about the Perl application.

**TIP**

> Pressing the spacebar moves you down the manual page one screen's worth at a time; you can move down a manual page one line at a time by pressing the Return key instead.

## USING SUPERUSER COMMANDS

As you learned earlier in the book, the root account is the fundamental user account that can do *anything* under Mac OS X. The root account has more access to the system than even an administrator account does. Using this account can be hazardous to your system because, when you are under root, the OS assumes that you know what you are doing and doesn't provide any checks on your activities. You can easily delete things you don't mean to or mess up the system itself.

**CAUTION**

> Be very careful about the commands you enter while logged into the root account. You can potentially do damage to your system—even an inatverdant mistype of a keystoke could result in unexpected and undesired results. You should use this only when you really have to, and even then, you need to be very careful about the commands you enter while you are working on the root prompt.

However, when you need to use a specific command at a specific time that you can't do under another user account, it can be helpful to enter commands as root.

Command: `sudo`

Option: `-s`, which runs the command in the default shell

What it does: Gets you into the root account so you can enter a command that you can't enter under another account

**NOTE**

> Not all account types can access the root account. You must be logged in as an administrator account to be able to properly run the `sudo` command.

⇨ For help activating the root account and creating a password for it, **see** "Enabling the Root User Account," **p. 261**.

1. Open a new Terminal window or a new tab in an existing window. The prompt shows the short name of the user account you are logged in under.
2. Type **`sudo -s`** and press Return. If you are using the `sudo` command for the first time in a session, you may see a warning regarding what you are about to do and will be prompted to enter your password; enter your password and press Return. If you have logged in as root previously, you won't have to enter the password again. When the `sudo` command is successful, the prompt shows the shell you are using (see Figure 14.6).

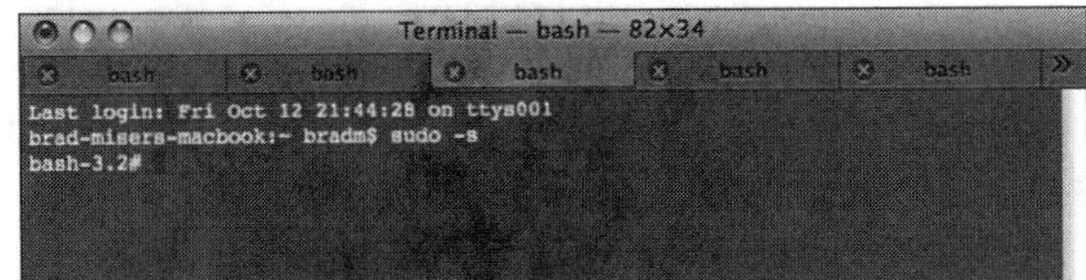


**Figure 14.6**
The `bash-3.2#` prompt indicates that you are logged in under the root account; be careful when you see this prompt.

To return to the previous account, type **`exit`** and press Return. You'll return to the prompt showing your previous user account. You should do this as soon as you finishing entering commands under the root account to lessen the chance that you'll do something you don't intend.

## KILLING A PROCESS

When a process goes wrong, it can cause problems, such as hanging, or it might start consuming tremendous amounts of processing power, thus bringing your system's performance to a crawl. You can tell that a process has gone out of control by monitoring its percentage of CPU usage. If this number gets high and stays there, the process is likely hung.

The `top` command allows you to view information about the different applications and processes that are running on your Mac. Because the information generated by the `top` command is dynamic, you should open it in a Terminal window and then open another window or tab to enter commands. Under Mac OS X, there are several ways to stop an out-of-control process. For applications, you can use the Force Quit command. At the process level, you can use the Process Viewer to force a process to quit. You can also use the powerful Unix command `kill` to stop a running process.

Command: `kill` *`ProcessID`*

Options: `-9` kills the process no matter what; `-3` quits the process

What it does: Stops the process with the ID number *`ProcessID`*

1. Launch the Terminal.
2. Type **`top`.** You will see a listing of all the processes currently running on your Mac (see Figure 14.7). Use the information in the table to identify the problematic process, such as one that is consuming an unreasonable amount of processing power. In this example, assume that Safari has gone out of control (although, as you can see in the figure, it is using only 29.6% of the CPU so it really doesn't have a problem at this point). In the figure, Safari's process ID number is 644.
3. Open a new tab by selecting File, New Tab (⌘-T).
4. Type **`kill -9 644`**. (Of course, you would actually type the process number for the process you want to kill.) The `-9` option specifies that the compuer cannot ignore the `kill` command.
5. Switch back to the Terminal tab showing `top`. You will no longer see the process that you killed listed in the process list. You can use the same steps to kill any process by using the process ID of that process.

   You can stop the `top` process by pressing Ctrl+C.

14

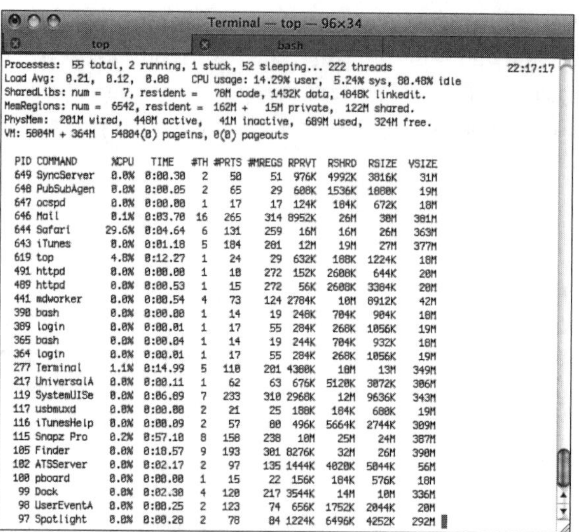


**Figure 14.7**
This top window shows all the processes running on your Mac; you can use the process ID with the `kill` command to stop any running process.

**NOTE**

> If the process you are trying to kill is an Administrator process, you will have to use the `sudo -s` command to get into the root account before you use the `kill` command.

# Working with Basic Unix Applications

You learned earlier that several Unix applications are included with Mac OS X. Although you aren't likely to use these instead of your Mac OS X applications for your everyday work, sometimes these applications can be quite useful. For example, you might want to use the vi text editor to create shell scripts. A couple of simple examples will show you how such applications work.

## Editing Text with vi

The Unix application vi is a basic text editor. You can use it to create and edit text files, but it is most useful for creating shell scripts. You are unlikely to use it to create text documents, but you can use it to create plain-text documents if you would like.

The vi program has two modes: Edit and Command. In Edit mode, you can enter and edit text. In Command mode, you issue commands to the program. Do the following:

1. Type **`man vi`**. Read the manual pages to get an idea of how vi works.

**TIP**

> To save long manual pages for a command, use the `man` command on that command and press the spacebar to reveal the entire text of the manual pages. Select the manual text you want to save in a file and select File, Save Selected Text As. Name the text file and save it. You can then refer to that file when you need help with that command.

2. Open a new Terminal window (⌘-N) or a new Terminal tab (⌘-T) and type **vi** and the name of the text file you want to create, such as `vi newtestfile.txt`. The program opens, the file is created in the current directory, and you see a screen containing tilde symbols in the editing area. At the bottom of the screen, you will see the vi command line.
3. Type **i** to enter Insert mode.
4. Type your text.
5. Press Esc to move into Command mode. While you are in Command mode, you will hear an alert sound if you try to type anything that isn't a recognized vi command; you will also see a prompt at the bottom of the vi window telling you that the text you typed isn't a recognized command.

**NOTE**

> Determining which mode you are in can be confusing. When you enter Command mode, the cursor appears to jump back a couple of spaces and the bottom line of the window is empty. You can then type a command. If you see text on the screen when you type, you are in Edit mode. You will also see `-INSERT-` at the bottom of the screen.

6. Type **:w** and press Return to write the text to the file you created. At the bottom of the vi window, you will see confirmation that the text has been written to the file (see Figure 14.8).

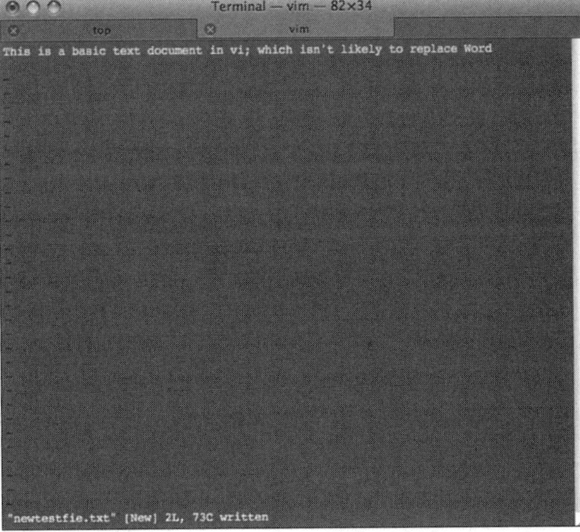


**Figure 14.8**
The message at the bottom of this vi window indicates that one line of text has been written to the file `newtestfile.txt`.



7. To continue adding text to the file, type **a**. The command line disappears and the cursor becomes active after the last text you entered.

8. Continue adding text and writing it to the file.
9. When you are done, press Esc to enter Command mode; then type **`:wq`** and press Return to quit vi. You will return to the command line.

Because GUI text editors are available, you might not want to use Unix text editors such as vi, but for short, plain-text documents, such as a shell script, these editors can be useful.

To edit an existing file with vi, type **`vi`** ***`filename`***, where *`filename`* is the name of the file you want to edit, and press Return. The file opens and you can begin editing it.

If you intend to use vi, make sure that you read its manual pages in detail; vi has many commands available, but they are hard to figure out without help.

## Compressing, Uncompressing, and Extracting Files

Unix has some built-in programs to enable you to work with compressed files, including the following:

- To compress a file, type **`compress`** ***`filename`***. The file named *`filename`* is compressed and a `.Z` is appended to its name.
- To uncompress a file, type **`uncompress`** ***`filename`***, where *`filename`* is the name of the compressed file. The file is uncompressed.
- You can also use the gzip compression application by typing **`gzip`** ***`filename`***. Uncompress the file using the `gunzip` command. gzip offers various options; check its manual pages to see them.

Many Unix files are archived in the tar (tape archive) format before they are compressed. After you compress such files, you will see a file that has the `.tar` extension. You can extract a tar file using the command `tar xvf` *`filename`*, where *`filename`* is the name of the tar file.

**NOTE**

> The `tar` command also has various options; check its manual pages for help.

# Mac OS X to the Max: Unix Resources

Using Unix proficiently requires some additional learning—Unix is a very complex and sophisticated tool that you should become familiar with to master Mac OS X. In this part of this chapter, you will learn the keyboard shortcuts that will help you use the Terminal application more efficiently. You also will find references to websites and books that can help you learn Unix in more depth.

## USING TERMINAL KEYBOARD SHORTCUTS

Table 14.1 lists keyboard shortcuts for the Terminal application.

**TABLE 14.1 TERMINAL KEYBOARD SHORTCUTS**

| Action | Shortcut |
|---|---|
| Use Selection for Find | ⌘-E |
| Find Next | ⌘-G |
| Find | ⌘-F |
| Find Previous | Shift+⌘-G |
| Jump to Selection | ⌘-J |
| Line Down | ⌘-Down arrow |
| Line Up | ⌘-Up arrow |
| New Command | Shift+⌘-N |
| New Shell | ⌘-N |
| Next Page | Spacebar |
| Cycle Through Windows | ⌘-' |
| New Window | ⌘-N |
| New Tab | ⌘-T |
| Save Selected Text As | Option+Shift+⌘-S |
| Save Text As | Option+⌘-S |
| Send Reset | ⌘-R |
| Set Title | Shift+⌘-T |
| Show Inspector | ⌘-I |

## LEARNING UNIX

The following list describes websites for learning more about Unix:

- www.uwsg.indiana.edu/usail/—Site name: Unix System Administration Independent Learning. This is an online course about administering Unix.
- www.eco.utexas.edu/Help/Unixhelp/TOP.html—Site name: Unixhelp for Users. This is a nicely organized and fairly extensive reference site.
- www.comet.ucar.edu/strc/unix/index.htm—Site name: SOO/STRC Unix Resources. This is a page containing links to other Unix learning sites.

The following list describes some recommended books for learning more about Unix:

- *Sams Teach Yourself Unix in 10 Minutes*—Author: Robert Shimonski. This is a good "fast and easy" entry into the world of Unix.
- *Sams Teach Yourself Unix in 24 Hours, Second Edition*—Authors: Dave Taylor and James C. Armstrong, Jr. This contains 24 one-hour lessons to get you into Unix.
- *The Complete Idiot's Guide to Unix*—Author: Bill Wagner. This book's friendly approach to Unix is good if you prefer a less-structured approach than the *Sams Teach Yourself* books.
- *Special Edition Using Unix, Third Edition*—Author: Peter Kuo. This is a comprehensive Unix reference. This is a good resource to have when you become comfortable with Unix and want to explore it in great detail.

# CHAPTER 15

# Computing on the Move with MacBook Pros and MacBooks

## In this chapter

# Using Mac OS X on a Mobile Computer

Using Mac OS X on a laptop Mac, such as a MacBook or a MacBook Pro, isn't that much different than using it on a desk-bound machine. The three primary tasks unique to mobile Macs are the following:

- Managing your Mac's power
- Controlling your Mac with function keys
- Configuring and using the trackpad

Although managing locations isn't unique to mobile Macs, you are more likely to need to switch among network configurations when using a MacBook Pro or a MacBook, so you need to understand how to use the Location Manager to make reconfiguring your Mac's network connections fast and easy.

Many users who have a mobile Mac also have a desktop Mac. When you use more than one machine, it is annoying to have to try to re-create certain information, such as your Safari bookmarks, on each machine you use. Fortunately, with Mac OS X you don't need to do that if you also have a .Mac account. Using .Mac and Sync preferences, you can synchronize key items that you use frequently on all your Macs so they are available to you at any time. When you make a change on one machine, such as updating an address in your Address Book, that change is made on each computer you have synchronized via .Mac. This is especially useful for keeping a mobile Mac in sync with your desktop Mac, and vice versa.

⇨ To learn how to use .Mac to synchronize computers, **see** "Using .Mac to Synchronize Important Information on Your Macs," **p. 454**.

Another challenge to using more than one Mac, such as a mobile and desktop Mac, is accessing the same versions of the files you use. For example, you might work on a Word document on your mobile Mac and then want to use that same file on your desktop Mac. Fortunately, there are many ways to access the same files from different computers.

⇨ To learn how to use the same files on different computers, **see** "Mac OS X to the Max: Keeping Your Files in Sync," **p. 331**.

# Managing Your Mobile Mac's Power

The factor that makes a mobile Mac mobile is the capability to run using battery power. This is obviously an advantage, but it also adds another task for you, which is managing that power so you maximize your battery life and thus your working time while on the move.

## Using the Power Management Menu

When you run Mac OS X on a mobile Mac, by default you see the power management icon (see Figure 15.1). If you click this icon, the power management menu appears. At the top of this menu is an icon that keeps you informed about the power state of your Mac. When the battery is fully charged and you are running on the AC adapter, you see the plug icon. When the battery is charging, you see the battery with lightning bolt icon. If you open the menu, you see information about the state of the battery, such as whether it is charging, is fully charged, or how much running time it has; the Show command that you can use to change what's displayed; the current source of power for your mobile Mac (Power Adapter or Battery); power setting options from which you can choose; and the Open Energy Saver command to open the Energy Saver pane of the System Preferences application.

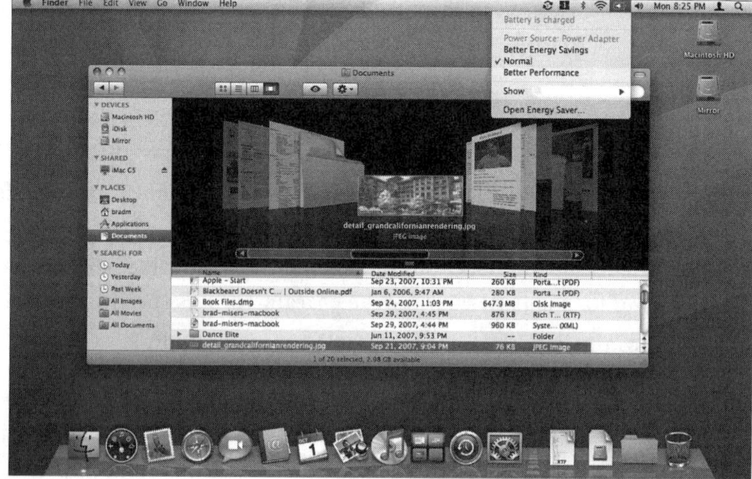


**Figure 15.1**
The power management icon and menu on the menu bar keep you informed of the power state of your mobile Mac.

When you are running on battery power, the icon is always the battery. The battery icon is filled proportionally to represent the amount of power you have left (see Figure 15.2). At the top of the power management menu, you see the time or percentage remaining until you are out of power (you can also choose to show neither).

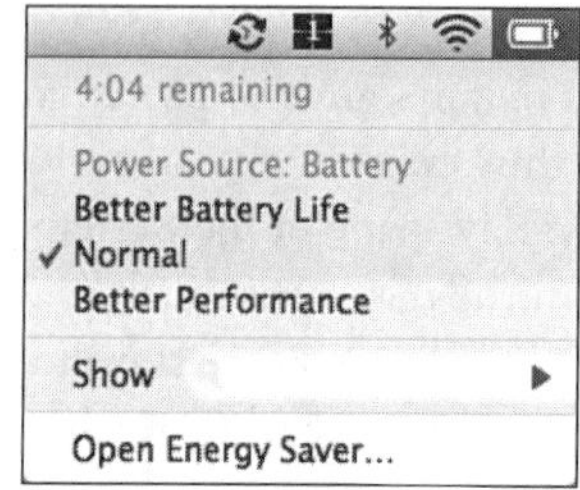


**Figure 15.2**
This Mac is running on battery power and has 4 hours and 4 minutes of running time left at current power usage levels (because it isn't doing anything at the moment, power usage is low).

**NOTE**

> When you are running on battery power and choose to show time or percentage, the first item on the power management menu is always the opposite of what you have selected to display. For example, when you choose to display time on the icon, the percentage is shown on the menu, and vice versa. If you don't show time or percentage, you see only the battery icon.

When you plug the power adapter back in to the Mac, the icon changes to a battery with a lightning bolt to indicate that the battery is charging.

**NOTE**

> The battery icon takes a few seconds to update. For example, if you unplug the AC adapter and then immediately point to the icon, you still see the charging status information. While your Mac is calculating how much time you have left, you see the word `Calculating` next to the icon; just wait a few moments and the information shown is updated.

You can configure the power management icon on the menu bar in the following ways:

- Open the menu and select Show, Time to show the time remaining for the battery or for the charging process next to the icon.
- Open the menu and select Show, Percentage to show the percent of power/time remaining for the battery or for the charging process next to the icon.
- Return to the icon alone by selecting Show, Icon Only.

**TIP**

> To remove the power management icon and menu from the menu bar, open the Energy Saver pane of the System Preferences application, click the "Show Details" button, then click the Options tab, and uncheck the "Show battery status in the menu bar" check box.

## MAXIMIZING BATTERY LIFE

The ultimate and constant challenge of using a mobile Mac when running on the battery is to make your power last as long as possible. You should consider the following steps to maximize your battery life

- **Dim your screen**—Your Mac's screen is a major source of power consumption. If you dim the screen, it requires less power and thus extends your battery life. To dim your screen, use the Brightness slider on the Displays pane of the System Preferences application or the appropriate function key. Dim the display as much as you can while still being able to see it comfortably. For example, when you are traveling on a darkened airplane, you can set your display brightness to a lower level than when you are using it in a well-lit room.

**TIP**

> MacBook Pros and MacBooks have dedicated function keys to control screen brightness, typically F1 to lower brightness and F2 to increase it. When you press one of these, an onscreen level indicator pops up to show you the relative brightness level and how you are changing it.

- **Configure the Energy Saver pane for the work you are doing while you are on the move**—Use the Energy Saver pane to configure your mobile Mac's power usage to maximize battery life. You'll learn how a bit later in this chapter.
- **Avoid applications that constantly read from a CD or DVD**—The CD or DVD drive is another major source of power use. If you can copy files you need onto your hard drive and use them from there, you will use power at a lower rate than if your Mac is constantly accessing its removable media drive. In some cases, such as when you are watching a DVD movie, this isn't possible. At other times, however, you can store the files you need on the hard drive. For example, when you want to listen to music, you can add the songs to your iTunes Music Library so you don't need to use the CD or DVD drive.
- **Put your Mac to sleep whenever you aren't actively using it**—You can put your Mac to sleep by selecting Apple menu, Sleep or by closing your mobile Mac's lid. When you open your Mac or press a key, the Mac instantly wakes up so putting it to sleep frequently doesn't cause a lot of wasted time for you.

**NOTE**

> When your Mac sleeps, all active processes are stopped, the screen goes dark, and the disk or disc drives stop. This reduces your Mac's power use to the bare minimum. A Mac in Sleep mode can survive a long time, but of course, it can't do anything while it is asleep. You need to strike a balance between the length of pauses in your work and the sleep time.

## CONFIGURING POWER USE

One of the most important power management tasks is to actively use the Mac's Energy Saver pane of the System Preferences application. This enables you to customize your Mac's energy settings to maximize battery life for the type of work you are doing.

You can do this in two ways. One is to use the pane's standard energy setting configurations. The other is to configure the details yourself.

### USING A STANDARD POWER SETTING

To use the standard configurations, perform the following steps

1. Open the System Preferences application and click Energy Saver, or click the power management icon to open the power management menu and select Open Energy Saver. You see the Energy Saver pane. At the top of the pane is the "Settings for" pop-up menu. This enables you to choose the energy settings for running on the battery or on the power adapter. Just below this is the Optimization pop-up menu. This enables you to configure your Mac to use power settings appropriate for specific tasks.
2. On the "Settings for" pop-up menu, select Battery. This enables you to configure your mobile Mac's energy usage while it is running on battery power.

3. Open the Optimization pop-up menu and select the setting you want to use. Better Battery Life reduces the performance and power usage of the processor, Normal is balance of performance and battery life, and Better Performance sacrifices battery life for performance. Custom opens the detailed configuration settings, which are explained in the next section. When you choose an option, a summary of its settings appears below the menu (see Figure 15.3).

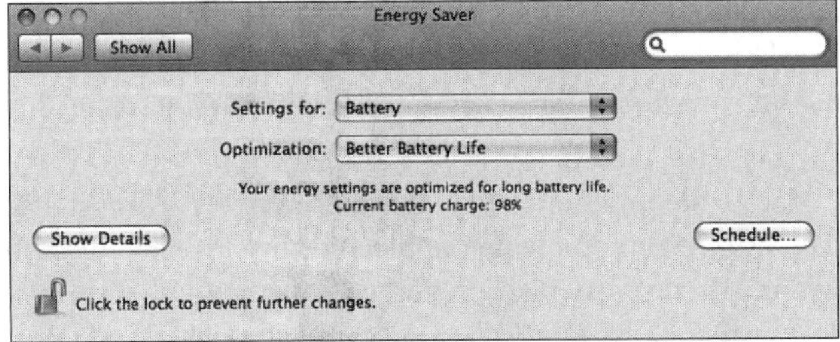


**Figure 15.3**
Here, I've selected Better Battery Life on the Optimization pop-up menu; the current settings for my expected running time are shown under the menu.

**CAUTION**

When your battery power starts getting low (about 10% remaining), you will start to see low-power warning dialog boxes. If you continue to use your Mac to lower power levels, eventually the screen dims. When your Mac is on its last electron, it goes to sleep. The only way to revive it is to connect it to the power adapter or change to a fresh battery. This (hopefully) prevents you from losing data because the Mac shuts off unexpectedly when the battery is completely drained. Even in sleep mode, your Mac uses some power, so if it enters the sleep mode because of low battery power and you don't do anything about it, eventually, your Mac turns off. And poof, there goes any data you have left unsaved.

### CUSTOMIZING YOUR MAC'S POWER SETTINGS

If you prefer a more hands-on approach, you can use the Detail mode to customize the energy-saving settings yourself. Do the following:

1. Open the System Preferences application and click Energy Saver, or open the power management menu and select Open Energy Saver.
2. Click the Show Details button. The pane expands and you see controls you can use to configure the energy-saving settings in detail (see Figure 15.4). By default, the Sleep tab is selected; you use the controls on this tab to configure the sleep settings for your system.
3. Select Custom on the Optimization pop-up menu (or just start making changes and it is selected automatically).

**TIP**

If you choose one of the standard settings on the Optimize Energy Settings pop-up menu with the Details shown, you can see the details of that configuration. For example, select Better Battery Life and you see that the sleep timer is set for 5 minutes, display sleep is set to 1 min, and hard disk sleep is on.

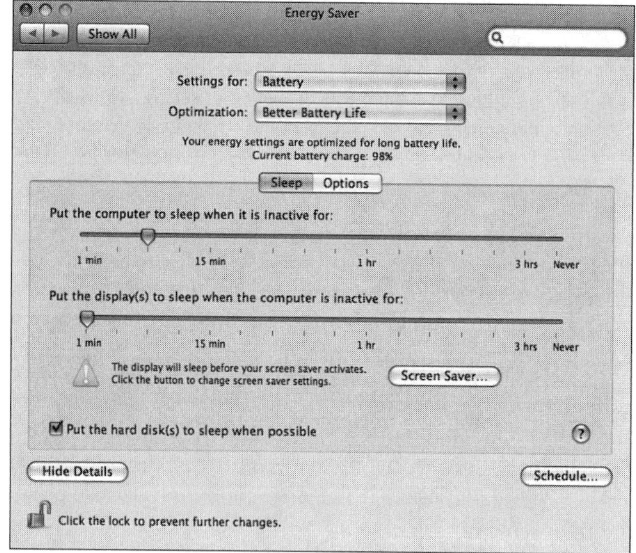


**Figure 15.4**
When you show details, you can adjust several aspects of the energy-saving settings independently.

4. Choose the power source for which you want to configure energy savings on the Settings for pop-up menu; your choices are Power Adapter or Battery. You can have a separate configuration for each power mode. (The mode in which you are operating is selected by default.)
5. Use the top slider to control the amount of inactive time before the entire system goes to sleep. Setting a shorter sleep time causes your Mac to sleep frequently, thus conserving battery power. But, this can also interrupt your work. Set the Sleep slider to a value that is just longer than normal pauses in your work.
6. Use the "Put the display(s) to sleep when the computer is inactive for" slider to set the amount of inactive time before the screen goes dark.

**TIP**

As you move the sliders, the current time at which the slider is pointing will appear above the slider at its right edge. This is helpful in selecting a precise time on the slider.

Because the screen is such a major consumer of power, you should have the display sleep after only a few minutes of inactivity when you configure your mobile Mac for operating in battery power. This also protects the flat-panel display in your mobile Mac from damage and early failure.

There is also a dim function, which is different from sleep. Dimming causes the screen to go to a lower brightness setting before the display sleeps (when it goes totally dark). You configure this option on the Options tab.

15

**NOTE**

> If you set the display sleep time to be less than the time at which your screen saver activates, you will see a warning saying so and the Screen Saver button appears. You can click this button to change your screen saver settings. Normally, when you are running on battery power at least, you want the screen to sleep rather than using the screen saver because the screen saver consumes battery power for processing and screen display.

7. Unless you have a very good reason not to, leave the "Put the hard disk(s) to sleep when possible" check box checked. The hard disk is another major consumer of power, and putting it to sleep saves significant amounts of energy. This setting causes your Mac to put the hard drives to sleep when they aren't actively being used, which is a good thing when your goal is to minimize power consumption.
8. Review the settings summary that appears just below the pop-up menus to ensure that the settings are what you desire. If you are running on battery power, you see an estimate of the time remaining.
9. Click the Schedule button. You use the resulting sheet to set an automatic startup/wake or shutdown/sleep time for the computer.
10. To set an automatic startup or wake time, check the "Start up or wake" check box and choose the day (using the pop-up menu) and time (by typing a time or using the Up and Down arrow buttons) at which the machine should start if it is powered off or wake up if it is in sleep mode. For example, you can set your Mac to start at a specific time everyday, on weekdays or weekends, or on a specific day only.

**NOTE**

> If your mobile Mac's lid is closed, the automatic start up/wake settings have no effect.

11. To set an automatic restart, shutdown or sleep time, check the lower check box on the sheet and select Restart, Shut Down or Sleep on the pop-up menu. Then select the day and time you want this action to happen on the Day pop-up menu and using the time box and arrow buttons. Click OK to activate these settings and close the sheet.
12. Click the Options tab. Use the check boxes on this tab to further configure Energy Saver. Like the Sleep settings, you set the Options for Battery and Power Adapter, which have slightly different options.
13. Choose Battery on the "Settings for" pop-up menu.
14. Check the "Slightly dim the display when using this power source" check box if you want your Mac's display to have a lower brightness when operating on the power source shown on the "Settings for" pop-up menu. When this box is checked, the brightness of the display will be reduced slightly when you are using the selected source. In my experimentation, it appears that this function reduces screen brightness by about two ticks on

the brightness indicator. This isn't a huge reduction in brightness, but it can save some power. And when you are running on battery power, every minute of power saved is a minute you can keep using your Mac.

**TIP**

A better way to save battery power by dimming the screen is to just develop a habit of manually setting the screen to a low, but comfortable, level for the various environments in which you work.

15. The "Automatically reduce the brightness of the display before display sleep" check box determines if your display's brightness will be reduced automatically before it goes to sleep. This causes the screen to dim before it goes completely to sleep. If you move the cursor or press a key, the screen will return to its previous brightness setting. I find this feature annoying, but if it doesn't bother you, it can be a way to save more power.
16. Use the "Show battery status in the menu bar" to determine whether the power management icon and menu appear on the menu bar. You should leave this checked so you can easily see the current status of your battery.
17. Choose Power Adapter on the "Settings for" pop-up menu. You see additional options on the pane along with some of the same options for the battery.
18. Check the "Wake for Ethernet network administrator access" check box if you want the Mac to wake up when an administrator tries to access it via an Ethernet network.
19. Uncheck the "Automatically reduce the brightness of the display before display sleep" check box. There's even less reason to use this setting when you're connected to the power adapter because you don't need to worry about maximizing your power to keep working.
20. If you want your Mac to restart automatically after power has been removed at the source, check the "Restart automatically after a power failure" check box. Because a mobile Mac has a battery, it keeps going even if the power adapter loses power so this setting really doesn't apply for mobile Macs.

**NOTE**

The battery status menu setting is the same for both modes so you only need to set it once.

You should configure all these settings for each power mode (battery and power adapter). To configure the other source's settings, select the other power mode on the "Settings for" pop-up menu, and configure the Sleep and Options tabs for that mode.

**NOTE**

Energy Saver settings are global, meaning they are the same for all user accounts on your Mac.

15

### CHOOSING YOUR MAC'S POWER USE

You can determine which power settings your Mac uses in the following two ways:

- Open the power management menu on the menu bar and select the setting you want to use.
- Open the Energy Saver pane of the System Preferences application and select the settings you want to use on the Optimization pop-up menu.

In addition to the default settings, you'll see that Custom is a choice in both locations. This makes the settings be the last that you set them at manually. In other words, Custom remembers the last group of settings you adjusted yourself.

**TIP**

> If you operate your mobile Mac on battery power frequently, consider getting a second battery. This effectively doubles your working time because you can swap out batteries without shutting down your Mac. Just put it to sleep and change the battery. As long as you are fairly quick about it, you can change the battery and go back to where you were. This is especially nice for long plane flights.

## CONTROLLING YOUR MOBILE MAC WITH FUNCTION KEYS

The function keys on mobile Macs enable you to control the following:

**NOTE**

> Different models and generations of mobile Macs can use different keys for the functions listed here. Just look at your mobile Mac's keys to determine which keys control which functions. The keys are marked with icons, such as the speaker icon for keys that control volume, the sun icon for brightness, and so on.

- Use the F1 and F2 keys to change the display's brightness.
- Use F3 to mute the volume.
- Use F4 and F5 to set the volume level.
- Use F6 to turn Numbers Lock on or off. When this is on, you get the alternate characters shown in the lower right corners of several keys, such as "J" and "K." These keys let you replicate the numeric keypad that is standard on desktop keyboards.
- When your mobile Mac is connected to an external display, press F7 to switch between mirrored displays (both displays show the same image) and extended desktop (the desktop is displayed across both displays).
- The key on the farthest right is the Eject key, which causes your mobile Mac to eject a CD or DVD.

To activate these functions, just press the appropriate key. When you change display brightness or system volume, an indicator appears on the screen to graphically show you the changes you make.

**TIP**

> If you prefer to have the function keys work as function keys without having to hold the FN key down while you press them, open the Keyboard tab of the Keyboard & Mouse pane of the System Preferences application. Check the "Use all F1, F2, etc. keys as standard function keys" check box. If you do this, you have to hold down the FN while pressing the appropriate hardware control key (such as F1 to lower the screen's brightness).

# Using and Configuring the Trackpad

Configuring and using the trackpad is straightforward. You use the Keyboard & Mouse pane of the System Preferences application to control how your trackpad works. When you are using a mobile Mac, the Trackpad tab becomes available. Follow these steps:

1. Open the Keyboard & Mouse pane of the System Preferences application and click the Trackpad tab (see Figure 15.5).

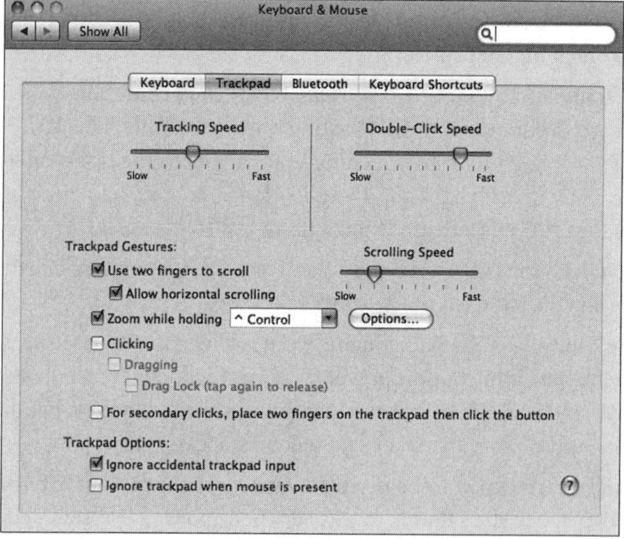


**Figure 15.5**
When you are running Mac OS X on a mobile Mac, you can set the trackpad options using the Trackpad tab.

2. Use the Tracking Speed slider to set the speed at which the pointer moves relative to your finger's speed on the pad.
3. Use the Double-Click Speed slider to control how rapidly you have to click the trackpad button or the trackpad itself to register a double-click.

4. To be able to scroll by dragging two fingers along the trackpad, check the "Use two fingers to scroll" check box and then set the scrolling speed using the Scrolling Speed slider.
5. To also be able to scroll horizontally with two fingers, check the "Allow horizontal scrolling" check box.

   With these options enabled, you can scroll in a window by simply dragging two fingers around the trackpad.
6. To be able to zoom in on web pages and other documents using the trackpad, check the "Zoom while holding" check box and choose a zoom key on the pop-up menu; the Ctrl key is the default. Click Options and use the resulting sheet to configure zooming behavior. Choose "Continuously with pointer" to have the screen image move with your pointer while you are zoomed in. Choose "Only when the pointer reaches an edge" to have the image remain in place until you get to the edge of the window at which point it will move to allow the zoom. Choose "So the pointer is at or near the center of the image" to have the image remain centered around the pointer while you zoom. Check the "Smooth images" check box to turn on smoothing while zoomed in. Click Done to save your changes and close the sheet.

   To zoom in a window, hold the zoom key down and drag two fingers around the trackpad.
7. If you want to be able to "click" the mouse/trackpad button by tapping on the trackpad, check the Clicking check box.
8. Use the Dragging and Drag Lock check boxes to control how you can drag items with the trackpad. If you turn on the Clicking option and then check the Dragging check box, you can drag an item by touching your finger to the trackpad and dragging your finger across it. If you check the Drag Lock check box, the item continues to be locked to the cursor until you release it by tapping the trackpad again.
9. To "right-click" using the trackpad, check the "For secondary clicks, place two fingers on the trackpad then click the button" check box.
10. To disable the trackpad while you are typing, check the "Ignore accidental trackpad input" check box. This option prevents unwanted interference from the unintentional taps on the trackpad while you are typing or just moving your hand across the pad. When you stop typing, the trackpad becomes active again.
11. If you want the trackpad to be disabled when you connect an external mouse to your mobile Mac, check the "Ignore trackpad when mouse is present" check box.

## CONFIGURING AND USING LOCATIONS

As you move your mobile Mac around, you will probably want to connect to different networks from different locations. For example, you might use an AirPort network to connect to the Internet at home, an Ethernet network to connect when you are at work, and a temporary connection when you are on the road.

The Mac OS X Location Manager feature enables you to configure multiple network configurations on your Mac. You can then switch among these configurations easily (rather than having to manually reconfigure your Mac each time you change locations).



**NOTE**

> You can have more than one active port on the same machine, meaning you can have different means of connecting to a network active at the same time (such as AirPort and Ethernet). You don't need to have a location for each active port. You should use locations when you want to have different *sets* of active ports that you want to be able to switch among easily. For example, suppose you connect to the Internet using Ethernet at your office and at home. But, at the office you have a fixed IP address while at home you use a DHCP server. You can create a location for each situation and easily switch between them by using the appropriate location.

## Creating a New Location

To configure a new network location, use the following steps:

1. Open the Network pane of the System Preferences application (see Figure 15.6).

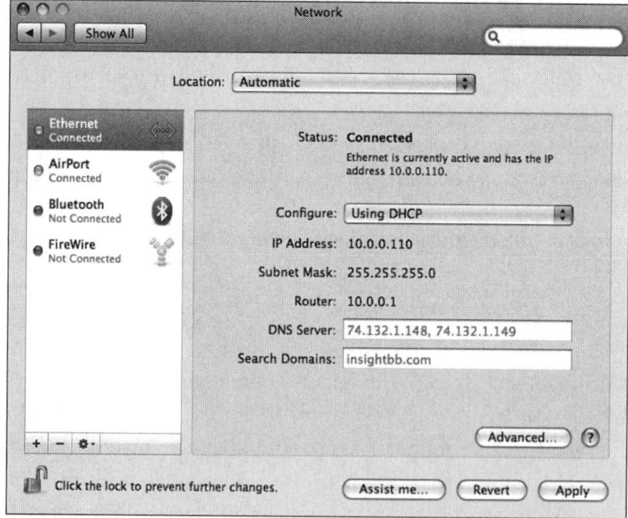


**Figure 15.6**
If you regularly change networks, configure a location for each network you use so you can easily switch between them.

2. On the Location pop-up menu, select Edit Locations. The Locations sheet appears. In the pane, you see the locations on your Mac.
3. Click the Add Location button (plus sign) at the bottom of the Locations. A new location is created and its name is highlighted to show you it can be edited.
4. Name the new location (see Figure 15.7).

15

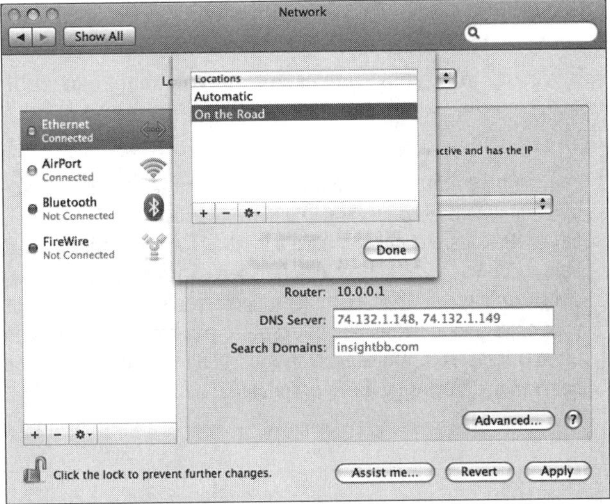


**Figure 15.7**
Use the Location sheet to create and configure a new location.

5. Click Done. The sheet closes and you return to the Network pane.
6. Choose the location you created on the Location pop-up menu. The services your Mac supports and their status are shown in the Services pane.
7. Select and configure each service for the location. For example, select Built-in Ethernet and then use the tools in the right pane of the window to configure the Ethernet connection for the new location.

⇨ For help configuring an Internet connection, **see** Chapter 16, "Connecting a Mac to the Internet," **p. 335**.

⇨ For help configuring an Ethernet network connection, **see** Chapter 17, "Building and Using a Wired Network," **p. 359**.

⇨ For help configuring an AirPort connection, **see** Chapter 18, "Creating and Managing AirPort Wireless Networks," **p. 393**.

8. Open the Action menu at the bottom of the Services pane and choose Set Service Order.
9. In the resulting sheet, arrange the order of the connection methods in the list to be the order in which you want your Mac to try to connect to the network. Drag the first method you want to be tried at the top of the list, the second one in the second spot, and so on. For example, if you want to use Built-in Ethernet first and then AirPort, drag Built-in Ethernet to the top of the list and place AirPort underneath it. When your Mac connects to the network, it will try these connections in the order in which they are listed. Click Set. When you return to the Network pane, you see the services in the order you configured them.
10. Quit the System Preferences application. The network location you configured will be used.

## Changing Your Mac's Location

To change the location your Mac is using, open the Network pane of the System Preferences application and choose the location you want to use on the Location pop-up menu. If the Apply button becomes active, click it to Apply the location; some configuration changes require this while others don't.

### EDITING OR DELETING LOCATIONS

You can edit or remove locations by following these steps:

1. Open the Network pane of the System Preferences application.
2. Select Edit Locations from the Location pop-up menu. The Locations sheet appears.
3. Select the location you want to change.
4. Rename the location by selecting it, pressing the Return key, entering the new name, and pressing Return again.
5. Delete a location you no longer use by selecting it and choosing Delete Location (minus sign).
6. To duplicate a location, select it, open the Action menu at the bottom of the Locations pane, and choose Duplicate Location; you can then rename it to something that describes that location.
7. Click Done. You return to the Network pane.
8. Make any other changes to the location selected in the Location pop-up menu and click Apply.
9. Close the System Preferences application.

**TIP**

> To protect your mobile Mac's data in the event someone swipes it, use Mac OS X's FileVault feature to encrypt your data so any rat who takes your mobile Mac won't be able to use its data.

⇨ To learn how to use FileVault, **see** "Securing Your Mac with FileVault," **p. 922**.

## MAC OS X TO THE MAX: KEEPING YOUR FILES IN SYNC

As you move around with your mobile Mac, I'm sure you'll find all kinds of great things to do with it (one of my favorites is to watch DVDs while I travel). Some of these might even involve work! If you work on files on your mobile Mac, it is highly likely that you will want to move those files to or from another Mac, such as your desktop Mac. There are lots of ways to accomplish this:

- Store the files you are going to share between your mobile Mac and other machines on your .Mac iDisk. Then set your iDisk to synchronize automatically on all machines. The same versions of those files will be accessible on all your Macs automatically (and they will be backed up on your iDisk, too).

⇨ To learn how to use an iDisk, **see** "Using Your iDisk," **p. 441**.

- Before and after a session on your mobile Mac, connect the mobile Mac to the network that your desktop Mac is on and use file sharing to move the files back and forth between the machines. (Make sure you move the correct version so you don't accidentally replace a newer version with an older one.)
- Email files to yourself. This is easier to do if you have more than one email account. For example, use a .Mac email account for your regular email and another account just on one machine. You can send files to yourself via that address. The big problem with this method is that most email gateways allow only relatively small files to be sent (usually less than 5MB).
- Use a folder cloning or synchronizing application to keep specific folders synchronized. You select one or more folders on each machine that you want to keep in sync and the application will ensure the latest version is in the folder on each computer. My favorite is ChronoSync.

⇨ To learn more about ChronoSync, **see** "Using ChronoSync," **p. 906**.

- Put files on CD, DVD, or an external hard drive (an iPod is excellent for this), and then copy them onto a different machine.

One of the harder aspects of keeping files synchronized between a mobile Mac and other machines is knowing exactly which files changed during your most recent use of the mobile Mac. With Mac OS X's smart folders, you can make even this easy to do:

1. Create a new smart folder.
2. Configure it to find files whose Kind is Documents and that were Last Modified Within Last 2 Days (or some other timeframe).
3. Save the smart folder.

Each time you open this smart folder, you will see the document files that have changed within the timeframe you specify. This makes it simple to know which files you need to move to your desktop Mac or other location.

⇨ To learn how to configure and use smart folders, **see** "Searching Your Mac with Smart Folders," **p. 101**.

PART III

# Living in a Connected World

# CHAPTER 16

# Connecting a Mac to the Internet

## In this chapter

## CONNECTING TO THE INTERNET

The Internet is one of the most significant social and economic movements—it is a movement as much as it is technology—in human history. In just a few years, the Internet transformed from an obscure scientific and government computer network to become a dominant means of global and local communication, commerce, entertainment, and information. Fortunately, Mac OS X has equipped you to make the most of the Internet.

Finding, installing, and configuring an Internet account can be complex. You can use many technologies to connect to the Internet, and you can obtain an Internet account from many different Internet service providers (ISPs).

The general steps to connect your Mac to the Internet are the following:

1. Determine the technology you will use to connect to the Internet.
2. Find an ISP and obtain an account.
3. Install and configure the modem or other hardware you need.
4. Configure your Mac to connect to the account you have established.
5. Test your configuration and troubleshoot any problems you find.

Depending on how you are going to connect to the Internet, you might have to do most of these steps yourself or your ISP might handle them for you—at least for the initial installation and configuration. Even if your ISP handles the initial configuration for you, you will need to understand how to reconfigure your Mac when the inevitable happens and you have to reinstall the system, move your account to another Mac, and so on.

While many ISPs provide always-on Internet access, in most cases you won't end up leaving a Mac connected directly to the Internet because you'll use a network (wired, wireless, or both) to connect to the Internet and then connect Macs to that network to gain Internet access. This has many benefits including sharing a single Internet account among many computers and, more importantly, having a much safer way to connect. Networks are covered in Chapter 17, "Building and Using a Wired Network," and Chapter 18, "Creating and Managing AirPort Wireless Networks." Chapter 19, "Sharing an Internet Connection," discusses sharing Internet connections and Chapter 39, "Securing a Mac," looks at securing your Mac.

## CHOOSING YOUR INTERNET CONNECTION TECHNOLOGY

There are six general technologies you can use to connect your Mac to the Internet. These technologies are summarized in Table 16.1 and explained in more detail in the following subsections.

**TABLE 16.1 MOST COMMON INTERNET CONNECTION TECHNOLOGIES**

| Technology | Connection Method | Advantages | Disadvantages |
|---|---|---|---|
| DSL | DSL modem via standard phone line | Broadband connection speeds (both directions)<br>Always-on, reliable connection<br>Consistent connection speed | Availability depends on location relative to specific aspects of phone infra-structure |
| Cable | Cable modem via fiber-optic cable | Broadband connection speeds (both directions)<br>Always-on, reliable connection | Availability depends on cable infrastructure<br>Connection speed can fluctuate based on traffic over local cable hub |
| Dial-up | Dial-up modem via standard phone line | Available anywhere<br>Inexpensive<br>Accessible from any location | Very slow<br>Connection must be established each time services are needed<br>Not as reliable as other connection methods<br>Can be difficult to achieve maximum performance<br>Ties up phone line for voice calls when connected<br>Will need to buy an external dial-up modem<br>Configuration can be complicated |
| Satellite | Satellite dish and modem | Fast download speed<br>Always-on connection | Expensive<br>Upload speed is some-times much slower than download speed<br>Most difficult installation and configuration<br>Limited availability |

*continues*

16

TABLE 16.1 CONTINUED

| Technology | Connection Method | Advantages | Disadvantages |
|---|---|---|---|
| T-1/ Fractional T-1 | Direct cabling | Fastest connection<br>Always-on connection<br>Most reliable connection | Very expensive<br>Requires complex and expensive installation and configuration |

**TIP**

Some broadband ISPs, such as cable providers, offer dial-up accounts as part of their services. (Some include the cost in the basic account, whereas others charge an additional fee for the dial-up access.) Typically, these dial-up services are intended for those times when you are traveling and need to access your account from locations other than where the service was initially installed. If you are able to use a broadband connection and will need to access it from multiple locations, check with your ISP to see whether it offers dial-up access to your account. Of course, most hotels and other locations offer high-speed Internet access so you rarely need one of these dial-up accounts.

There are other connection technologies that can be used. One is connecting to the Internet via a Bluetooth cell phone or PDA. The cell phone makes the connection and shares it with your Mac. Another is a broadband connection delivered by a cell phone provided through an access card; these are intended for mobile access. Some providers might offer Integrated Services Digital Network (ISDN) connections; at one point, ISDN was poised to become the connection technology of choice, but has been replaced by better technologies (DSL and cable). Exploring the details of these additional types are beyond the scope of this chapter because they are fairly specialized.

Generally, you want to choose the fastest connection method that is available in your area and that you can afford. A broadband Internet connection makes the Internet even more useful when compared to a slower connection (such as a 56K dial-up connection). For example, with a broadband connection, you can download files as large as 10MB or more in just a few moments. A broadband connection makes downloading even very large files, as much as 100MB or more, practical. Just to give you a reference point about how large the files you download can be; using a cable modem, I have routinely downloaded 400MB and larger files in less than 20 minutes. Try that with a dial-up account!

In addition to making downloading files faster, a broadband connection enables you to experience online video and audio in a fashion quite similar to watching cable TV or listening to a radio. Finally, a broadband connection enables you to avoid the delays and hassles of waiting for a dial-up account to connect to the Internet each time you want to use it because it is always on. With a broadband connection, the Internet actually becomes an extension of your desktop.

For most people, choosing a connection technology isn't very difficult. If cable or DSL is available in your location, choose one of them because you'll get great service for a relatively low cost. If one of those is not available to you, you're next best option is a satellite connection, but those aren't available everywhere and can be expensive. If no other type is available to you, dial-up will be your last resort; and because of its very slow connection speed, dial-up should be used only if you can't afford another connection type or another type isn't available to you.

## DSL



Digital subscriber line (DSL) accounts communicate over standard phone lines through a DSL modem. DSL accounts offer broadband communication speeds and always-on access.

The primary downside to DSL is that the technology requires that you be within a maximum distance from a central office or hub for the telephone company that provides service to your location. This maximum distance is fairly short (usually about 3 miles), and this single factor makes DSL unavailable for many locations. As telephone infrastructures improve, DSL service should become more widely available.

Because it is an always-on connection and you have the same IP address for long periods of time, security is a very important consideration when you use a DSL modem to access the Internet. You must install some type of protection to keep your machine from being hacked or used in an Internet attack on other sites. Fortunately, Mac OS X includes a firewall that does this for you, and most Internet sharing hubs protect your machines as well.

If DSL is available in your location, you should consider obtaining a DSL account.

**NOTE**

You might notice that I am not being specific when I mention connection speeds. This is because most of the connection speeds quoted in advertisements or even in technical information are theoretical maximums. The actual speed you experience will depend on your specific situation and how your account is configured (for example, DSL accounts can offer various speeds). Generally, you need to consider whether you are dealing with a broadband connection (such as cable or DSL) or not (dial-up).

## CABLE

Cable modem access is provided through a cable modem using the same cable over which cable TV service is provided. Cable Internet accounts offer broadband speeds (in fact, the speed of cable accounts is faster than most other technologies) and always-on access.

As with DSL, cable modem service is not available in every location. However, if your area is covered by cable TV service, there is a good chance that cable modem service is currently offered in your area or soon will be. Because the cable infrastructure is already in place, companies can offer Internet access without making major infrastructure changes.

One downside to cable Internet access is that you share the data pipeline with other users of the service and the cable TV viewers who are on the same cable trunk you are on (such as in a neighborhood). This means that the speed you experience is dependent on the load on the system at any point in time (whereas DSL uses a dedicated line to provide service to you so that you always experience the same speed—bear in mind that even at peak times, cable access is still usually somewhat faster than DSL). Another downside to cable is that it tends to be relatively expensive (typically about $50 per month). And you have to deal with the local cable company; these companies are not noted for having the best service practices.



Because it is an always-on connection and you have the same IP address for long periods of time, security is a very important consideration when you use a cable modem to access the Internet. You must also install some type of protection to keep your machine from being hacked or used in an Internet attack on other sites. Fortunately, Mac OS X includes a firewall that does this for you, and most Internet sharing hubs protect your machines as well.

Even with these downsides (which are relatively minor compared to the benefits), a cable modem account can offer excellent performance and is worth exploring if available to you.

## SATELLITE

Satellite Internet access works much like satellite TV. The data is downloaded through a small satellite dish and fed to your Mac. The speed of communication is quite fast.

However, satellite Internet access has several disadvantages. The biggest is that some satellite accounts support only downloads, so you still have to maintain a separate account for uploading information. Second, you have to install the satellite dish. Third, and perhaps most importantly, not all satellite providers support Macs.

You should consider a satellite Internet account only in those cases in which DSL or cable is not available to you. Because of its limited applicability, additional information on satellite access is beyond the scope of this chapter.

## DIAL-UP

Even with the rapid rise of broadband connections, the dial-up Internet account is still widely used. Because you can access a dial-up connection over standard phone lines, dial-up accounts are available just about everywhere. Dial-up accounts are also relatively inexpensive.

The primary problem with dial-up connections is that they are slow—really, really slow. Even in the ideal case, with a true 56K connection, a dial-up connection is just not fast enough to enable some of the more interesting applications on the Internet, such as video, audio, and moving large files (such as those 3MB or larger). And most of the time, you won't be connecting at your account's maximum speed—phone-line noise and other factors often limit the speed you can achieve. Another problem is that you have to establish a connection each time you want to use an Internet service. The connection process can take anywhere from ten seconds to a minute or more depending on the particular situation. When you frequently need to access Internet services throughout the day, the time you have to wait for a connection to be established can be quite annoying, not to mention a waste of your time.

Another problem with dial-up accounts is that they can be unreliable. You can experience busy signals, and your connection is dependent on the quality of the phone lines between you and your provider. Internet sessions are occasionally disconnected in the middle of doing something, such as downloading a file. This can be a huge waste of time, as well as frustrating.

If you use the Internet as much as most Mac users do, you should use a dial-up account only if one of the broadband connection technologies is not available to you or you can't afford one of the faster connection technologies.

Because dial-up accounts really don't deliver the Internet experience that most Mac users need, the details of obtaining and configuring a dial-up account are beyond the scope of this chapter.



### T-1

A T-1 line is a dedicated broadband connection delivered over a line consisting of 24 channels, with each channel delivering up to 64Kb per second. T-1 connections are very fast but are also expensive and are usually limited to businesses to provide access for many people through a single account. Some providers also offer fractional T-1 service, in which only a portion of the 24 channels is dedicated to the subscriber.

Finding a T-1 provider is much like finding other providers; you should typically start with local ISPs who offer this service. After you have purchased a T-1 account, the ISP handles the installation and initial configuration of the line for you. Because T-1 and fractional T-1 connections are fairly complex and their costs limit them to business use, additional information about T-1 lines is beyond the scope of this chapter.

## PICKING THE TECHNOLOGY

After you have an understanding of all the possibilities, you need to determine which technology is appropriate for you. Most Mac users will be better off with a broadband connection of some type; dial-up accounts just don't cut it for the most interesting Internet resources. However, if no broadband services are available in your area or you can't afford a broadband connection, dial-up certainly beats having no Internet connection.

To determine which technologies are available to you, you need to obtain information from various ISPs that offer services in your area. Following are some tips to help you find an ISP:

- **One of the best sources of information about local ISPs is the people you know**—Many people in your immediate circle probably have Internet access through a local provider. You should ask these folks if they are happy with their providers. You can also find out which services are available, whether the provider has good technical support, how much the services cost, and so on. Using your personal network is an excellent way to find ISPs to contact.

- **If you have cable TV service, check with your cable company to see whether it offers Internet access**—Most cable companies advertise their Internet service to death, but some don't—especially when they first introduce it and want to test it on a limited number of users.
- **If you have access to the Internet, use the Web to locate a provider**—Go to http://www.thelist.com/, which enables you to find local access providers for just about every location in the world (see Figure 16.1).



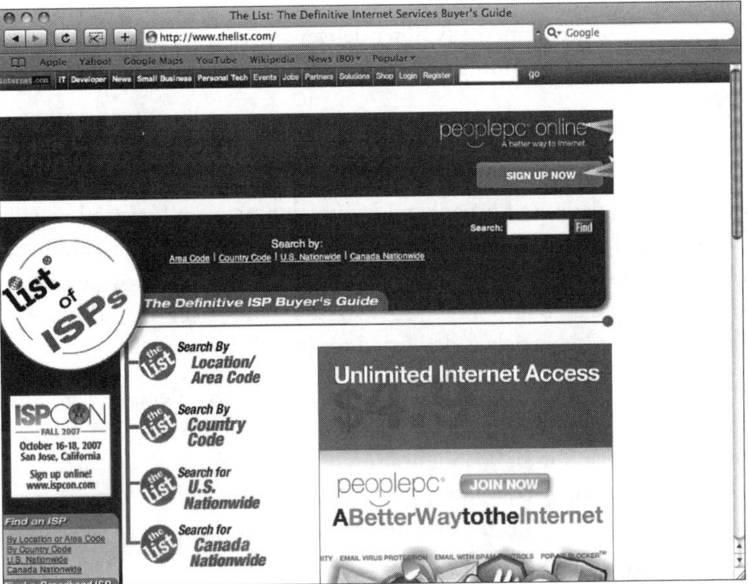


**Figure 16.1**
The List website lives up to its claims; it truly is the definitive ISP buyer's guide.

- **Check out the local news broadcasts in your area**—Almost all local TV stations have websites that are maintained by a local ISP. At the end of the broadcast, you will see a credits screen saying that Internet services are provided by XYZ Company. XYZ Company might be a good choice for you to check out.
- **Check with your company's ISP**—If the company you work for has a website that is administered by an outside ISP or if an outside ISP provides Internet access for your company, check with that ISP to see which services it offers and whether it offers a discount for employees of your company. Often, an ISP will provide inexpensive Internet access to the employees of a company to which it provides business services.
- **Watch and listen for advertisements**—Most service providers advertise, more than you'd probably like, in local newspapers and on the radio and TV.

You should also check with national Internet access providers, such as EarthLink (www.earthlink.net), to see which services are offered in your location.

**TIP**

> Many ISPs provide more than one connection technology for their accounts. When you contact an ISP, make sure that you ask about all the possible ways you might connect. Sometimes, especially when introducing a new access method, an ISP might not promote all its options.

The process of determining which connection technology is available to you should be fairly simple. If you have access to cable TV service, check with the cable provider to see whether it also offers Internet access. If so, obtain cost information. Most cable TV companies have a monopoly on the areas to which they provide service, so you usually have only one source to check for cable Internet access.

Next, try to determine whether DSL service is available in your location. The best way to do this is to search the Web for DSL providers in your state (see Figure 16.2). You can use a general search site to search for information about DSL providers in your state. Also, check the national DSL providers to see whether a company in their network provides local DSL access. Typically, you can go to the provider's site and check availability of DSL service at your location by entering your phone number. If the service is available, obtain information about the cost and whether Mac is supported. You can also check with your telephone service provider because they typically offer DSL if your location supports it. If DSL service from one provider is not available at your location, it is likely that it is not available from any provider because they all use the same telephone infrastructure.

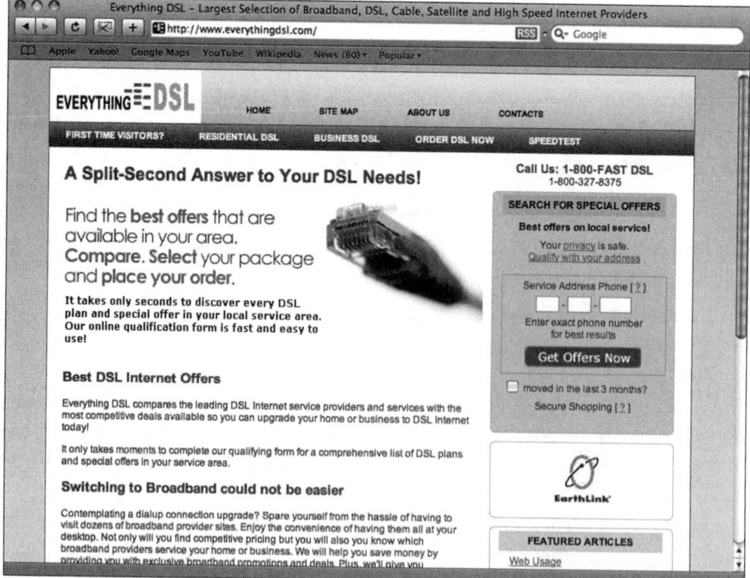


**Figure 16.2**
The EverythingDSL website is a good example of a web resource you can use to determine whether DSL is available in a specific area.

Beware that DSL service is one of the most over-advertised and over-hyped services around. Just because you hear or see advertisements for local DSL service does not mean that it is actually available. Some of this advertisement is for "future" service, even though your location might not be close enough to a central phone node to be capable of accessing DSL from any provider. Even worse, sometimes the checks these organizations do on your phone line to see whether you can access this service are not reliable. I have heard more than one case in which the initial contact, even up to the point of signing a contract, indicated DSL service was available, but when the installation was attempted, it failed because the service was not really available.

Be careful about eliminating companies that claim not to provide Mac support. Most of the time, this just means they won't be able to provide tech support if you use a Mac. The service probably will work just fine because an Internet connection is not really tied to the type of operating system you are using. If you are comfortable that you will be able to solve any problems you encounter, not having tech support available might not be a problem for you. I prefer not to do business with companies that don't support Mac, but you might have to choose otherwise to get the Internet access you want.

If DSL or cable service isn't available to you, search the web for satellite providers that service your area.

**TIP**

> If DSL providers aren't available to you, you might want to explore Internet service provided by cell phone companies. This could be a viable option for you, especially if you use a mobile Mac.

If all other types aren't available to you or are too expensive, locate ISPs in your area that provide dial-up Internet access. This should be the most commonly available option, even if it isn't the most productive.

After you have obtained all the available connection information, you should be able to decide which technology is appropriate for you. If possible, try to locate a cable or DSL provider because you will get the most out of a broadband account. If all else fails, locate a good provider of dial-up access.

**NOTE**

> In some cases, such as a DSL or dial-up account, you will have several ISP options. One of the most fundamental considerations is whether you use a national provider or a local one. National providers offer several advantages. In many cases, a national provider offers more extensive resources for you, such as better access to technical support, a self-install kit, and so on. National providers can enable you to access your account in different ways (such as DSL or dial-up) from many locations; if you travel often, this should be an important consideration for you. Local providers, on the other hand, often offer more personalized service and local resources.

# Obtaining and Configuring an Account

After you have decided on the technology you will use, contact the provider to obtain an account. You usually have to call to set up your account, but some ISPs enable you to request service over the Internet; others provide self-install kits that enable you to obtain and configure an account without any human intervention (one example is EarthLink).

If you use a broadband account of some sort, the provider sometimes installs any needed hardware for you, such as a cable modem, and configures your machine to use it (although self-install kits are becoming more common). If you use a dial-up account, you usually receive instructions about how to configure that account; some providers, such as EarthLink, provide software that does the installation and configuration for you.



**CAUTION**

> Be wary about any dedicated "front-end" software a provider might want to install on your machine. Most of the time, this software consists of an application that gives you a specialized interface for using the service. This software is almost never necessary and can cause problems for you. It is better to just use the configuration information the provider gives you and then use Mac OS X software to access the Internet.

Even if the provider handles the initial installation and configuration for your account, you still need to understand how to configure your account yourself. You should try to understand the configuration information related to your account. You at least should ensure that you have all the information you need to configure your account for the inevitable situation in which you must reconfigure it on your machine.

**TIP**

> If your provider offers more than one way to connect, such as via a cable modem and a backup dial-up account, be sure you get the information you need for all connection methods available to you.

The following data is required to configure your Mac for Internet access:

- **Type of configuration**—This information tells your computer which protocol to use to connect to the Internet. If you are using a broadband connection, several possibilities exist, which include a static IP address, Dynamic Host Configuration Protocol (DHCP), PPP over Ethernet (PPPoE), DHCP with a fixed IP address, or the Bootstrap Protocol (BootP). A static IP address means that your Mac always has the same IP address. When you use DHCP, your provider assigns your Mac an IP address along with most of the other information you need to connect; this is the most common type and is also the easiest to configure. PPPoE is most often used for DSL accounts. DHCP with a fixed IP address means that your IP address is fixed, but the DHCP server provides the other information for you. BootP access is used for "diskless" machines that use a server to provide the operating system.

- **IP address, subnet mask, and router**—These addresses locate your machine on the Internet and provide it with its address. Most broadband accounts use dynamic IP addressing, which simply means that your Mac has an IP address assigned each time it connects rather than having a static address. If you have a manual or static IP address, it never changes and is permanently assigned to your machine. When you have a static IP address, you also need the subnet mask and router; with dynamic addressing, this information is provided by the server.
- **DHCP client ID**—If you use DHCP access, you sometimes have a client ID name for your computer. In most situations this is optional; however, if your provider includes a DHCP Client ID with your account, you need to use it. If you are configuring an account using a local DHCP server, you probably don't have to use a client ID.
- **Domain name server**—A domain name server (DNS) translates the addresses the computers use into English that we humans can usually understand. The DNS enables you to use an address, such as www.companyname.com, rather than having to deal with a series of numbers such as 192.169.x.x. The DNS number you need from your provider will be something such as 192.169.x.x. Ideally, your provider will include several DNS addresses so you have a backup in case the primary DNS fails. (If your DNS fails, you won't be able to access websites unless you know their numeric IP addresses.)
- **Search domain**—This information is related to the particular part of the provider's network where you are located. It is usually optional. You might be provided with more than one search domain.
- **Usernames and passwords**—These are the two pieces of information that uniquely identify you and enable you to access your account. You probably chose your own username when you established your account. Your password might or might not have been assigned by the ISP.

  You might have more than one username or password. Sometimes, your ISP gives you one username and password that enable you to connect to the Internet and another set (or maybe just a different password or username) to let you use your email account. Make sure that you know which is which, and use the right ones in the right setting fields. If you use a PPPoE account, your username is your account name.

**NOTE**

> In some cases, you might not need a username and password to access the Internet. For example, if you have a static IP address, you don't need a username and password to connect to the Internet. However, you will need a username and password to access your email accounts. You usually don't have a username and password for cable access either because the physical location of the modem determines whether the access is valid or not.

- **Phone number**—If you use a dial-up account, you need to have the phone number that you need to dial to reach your ISP. Some ISPs offer different numbers for different modem speeds, so be sure you get the phone number for your modem's speed.

- **Email account information**—You will be given your email address (probably something such as username@isp.net). You will also need an address for the server that receives your mail (this often has a "pop" in it, such as pop.isp.net). The third piece of information you need is the address of the server that sends your mail (this often has "smtp" in it, such as smtp.isp.net). Some broadband accounts have simpler server configuration for both sides, such as mail.isp.net.
- **Web customer support address**—If your account offers additional services, such as multiple email accounts, obtain the information you need to access that site so you can manage your account.



**TIP**

Make sure that you collect and organize the information you need to access your account. You will need to reconfigure your Mac at some point and, if you don't have the information handy, this will be harder than it needs to be. One way to do this is to configure your account and after you are sure it works properly, you can take screenshots (Shift-⌘-3) of the various configuration screens. This enables you to quickly re-create your specific configuration. Of course, you should also keep copies of any information your provider gives you.

Most broadband providers include the modem hardware (such as a cable modem) you use to connect with your account. In some cases, they also install the hardware for you. However, you can usually supply your own hardware if you prefer. (This is usually less expensive over the long haul.) And, many providers offer "self-install" kits at local retailers. These kits include the hardware, software, and instructions you need to install the service yourself. (One benefit to these kits is that you don't have to wait all day for the cable guy to show up!)

If you need to install the modem you will be using, do so. In the case of an Ethernet-based connection, this requires you to connect the modem to your Mac's Ethernet port or the WAN port on your network hub and then connect the modem to the source (the cable that comes into your house).

**NOTE**

My bias has probably already shown through, but in my experience cable Internet access is the way to go if it is available to you. The access speed is fast and the connections tend to be reliable. (It is delivered over the same infrastructure as cable TV service, and we know that people can't live without TV!) Because cable TV reaches a significant proportion of homes (in the United States at least), cable Internet access is more likely to be available to you than even DSL. Typically, cable service is provided via DHCP, which makes configuration simple.

## CONFIGURING YOUR MAC FOR INTERNET ACCESS

Providing the details of configuring every type of Internet account is beyond the scope of this chapter, but some examples of configuring cable and DSL connections should enable you to configure your particular account.

If you have a network, you'll usually only configure a Mac to access the Internet to make sure the configuration information is correct or if you need to troubleshoot problems. The rest of the time, your Mac will get its connection from the network. Information about configuring Internet access through a network is provided in the next three chapters.

When you connect to the Internet through a network, you'll configure the network's hub just like you configure a Mac, using the same settings. More on this in the following chapters.



**NOTE**

> When you install Mac OS X, the Internet Setup Assistant leads you through the configuration of your Internet account. You can launch the Internet Setup Assistant at other times to walk you through the configuration process by clicking the "Assist me" button on the Network pane of the System Preferences application.
>
> If you use a provider that includes configuration software with your account, such as EarthLink, you can configure your account by using that software. In this section, you learn how to configure your account manually.

**CAUTION**

> Here's another caution about any specific access software a provider might give you to access the Internet. This software tends to be more problematic than it is worth, especially if it is web-based. When you get an account and such software is provided, ask the provider whether it is required. Many times, this software is mostly a way for the provider to generate revenue by using it to advertise. I recommend you avoid this kind of software if you can.

You can configure multiple sets of Internet configurations for your machine so that you can switch between them easily. And, you can have multiple accounts configured and active on a machine at the same time (they will be used according to the priority you determine). This is useful when you use your Mac in different locations—for example, with a MacBook that you use at a work location and at home or while traveling. Another case in which this is useful is if you have several ways of connecting from the same location, such as via a cable modem or dial-up account. You use the Location Manager to manage the Internet configurations on your machine. If you envision needing to do this, you should set up a location before configuring it. If you will need only one set of configurations, you don't need to use the Location Manager. Also, a single location can include multiple configurations, such as Ethernet and wireless connections to a network connected to a cable modem.

⇨ To learn how to configure and use locations, **see** "Configuring and Using Locations," **p. 328**.

The Internet accounts you configure on your Mac will be available to all users who have accounts on your machine.

## Connecting Through DSL or Cable Using an Ethernet Connection

**CAUTION**

> As soon as you connect your Mac to the Internet with an always-on connection, especially one with a fixed IP address, your Mac will be subjected to attacks from hackers. You shouldn't directly connect a Mac to the Internet unless you have some type of firewall protection in place; fortunately, Mac OS X includes a built-in firewall.
>
> However, best practice is to install a hub between your Mac and the modem. Most hubs offer protection and also enable you to share an Internet account.

⇨ To learn how to install and use a wired hub to share an Internet account, **see** Chapter 17, "Building and Using a Wired Network," **p. 359**.

⇨ To learn how to install and use an AirPort base station as a hub, **see** Chapter 18, "Creating and Managing AirPort Wireless Networks," **p. 393**.

⇨ To learn how to protect your Mac from Internet attacks, **see** "Defending Your Mac from Internet Attacks," **p. 937**.

Configuring an Internet account for Ethernet connection is usually simple. The three main options you use for an Ethernet-based Internet account are Manual IP Settings, DHCP Server, and PPPoE. DHCP Server is the most likely option you will use. However, your ISP will tell you which option is appropriate for your connection.

Connect your Mac's Ethernet port to the cable modem or to the hub to which the cable or DSL modem is connected. Then, configure the OS to use that connection

**NOTE**

> Some broadband modems connect to a USB port rather than an Ethernet port, but configuring the account on your Mac works in the same way.

## Configuring TCP/IP Using a DHCP Server

If your provider provides access through a DHCP server, configuring your account is straightforward.

**NOTE**

> Many local area networks provide Internet access by installing a DHCP server on the network and connecting that server to the Internet (often with a T-1 line). In such cases, you can configure your Mac to use that DHCP server to connect to the Internet just as you can when you deal directly with an ISP for an account.

To configure your account, do the following:

1. Open the Network pane of the System Preferences application.
2. From the Services list on the left side of the pane, select Ethernet (see Figure 16.3).

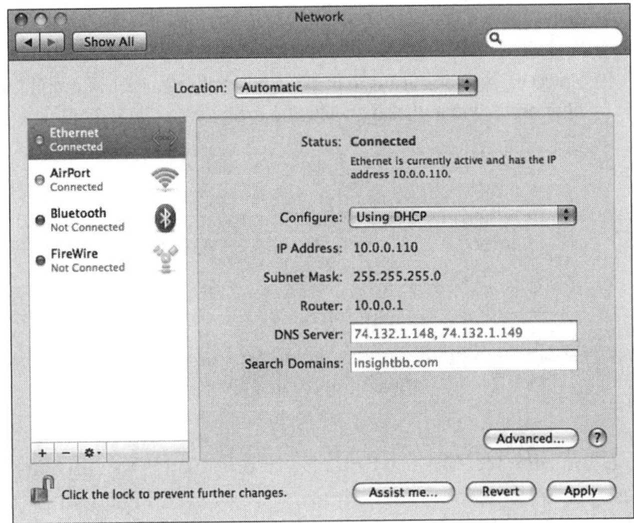


**Figure 16.3**
Use the Ethernet option on the Services list to configure an Ethernet Internet connection.

3. Select Using DHCP from the Configure menu.
4. If you have a DHCP Client ID (your ISP will tell you if this is the case), click on the Advanced button and select the TCP/IP tab. You can then enter it in the DHCP Client ID field. (If you are using a DHCP server on a local network, you can probably leave this field empty. In most cases, you can leave this field empty even when you are using an ISP to gain Internet access.) Click OK to return to the Services list and the configuration of the Ethernet service.
5. If you have DNS and search domain information, enter it in the appropriate fields. (These are optional when you use a DHCP server and in most cases, you will leave these fields empty.) You might see information in these fields already; Mac OS X will try to obtain the information from your ISP automatically.
6. If you are on a network that uses a proxy server, click the Advanced button and select the Proxies tab, and configure the proxies for your network.

⇨ For more information about proxy servers, **see** "Understanding and Configuring Proxy Servers," **p. 351**.

7. Click Apply to save your changes.
8. Open an Internet application, such as a web browser. If you can access Internet resources, your configuration is complete.

*If you are unable to access Internet resources after configuring your account with a DHCP server, see "My Ethernet Connection Can't Connect" in the "Troubleshooting" section at the end of this chapter.*

## CONFIGURING STATIC TCP/IP SETTINGS

If your provider supplies a static or manual address for you, use the following steps to configure it:

1. Open the Network pane of the System Preferences application.
2. From the Services list, select Ethernet.
3. Select Manually from the Configure pop-up menu.

**NOTE**

> You can also use a static IP address with the router being assigned dynamically. If this is the case for you, select "Using DHCP with manual address" instead of Manually. The rest of the steps are the same, except you don't configure the router because that is done for you by the DHCP router.

4. Enter the IP Address, Subnet Mask, Router, DNS, and Search Domains information your ISP provided in the appropriate fields.
5. Click Apply to save your changes.
6. Open an Internet application, such as a web browser. If you can access Internet resources, your configuration is complete.

*If you are unable to access Internet resources after configuring your account manually, see "My Ethernet Connection Can't Connect" in the "Troubleshooting" section at the end of this chapter.*

**NOTE**

> IPv4 is the current Internet protocol standard in almost all situations. However, IPv6 is a newer standard that is being used in some research institutions. If you need to configure a connection based on IPv6, you can do so by clicking the Advanced button and using the Configure IPv6 section of the resulting sheet to configure the service. In most cases, the automatic settings should work fine, but you can also enter manual settings if you need to.

## UNDERSTANDING AND CONFIGURING PROXY SERVERS

A *proxy server* is a server that sits between end-user computers on a network and the Internet. All Internet traffic of a specific type (such as HTTP for web pages) passes through a specific proxy server. There can be separate proxy servers for each type of service (such as HTTP, FTP, and so on), or a network can use a single proxy server for all Internet services.

When a machine on the network requests a resource (such as a web page), the proxy server downloads the resource and serves it to the machine as if the resources originated from the proxy server itself (although the user doesn't notice that the page is being served by the proxy server instead of the server hosting the requested page).

Proxy servers serve two main purposes:

- **They can improve speed in some cases**—Because the Internet resources are downloaded to the proxy server and then served to users on the local network, after the first access, subsequent accesses to that resource are much faster. This is true because the resource must be downloaded from the Internet to the proxy server only once; from there, it can be served to users on the local network rather than downloading it from the Internet each time.
- **They can be used to filter requests**—Because all information from the Internet flows through a proxy server, that server can be set to block access to specific Internet resources.

**NOTE**

For more information on proxy servers, see http://webopedia.internet.com/TERM/p/proxy_server.html.

If you are on a network that uses proxy servers, you use the Proxies tab of the Advanced section for the Network pane of the System Preferences application to configure them (see Figure 16.4). You configure a proxy for a specific service by checking the check box for that service and entering the proxy address and port in the appropriate fields. Typically, you obtain the proxy server information you need from your network administrator.

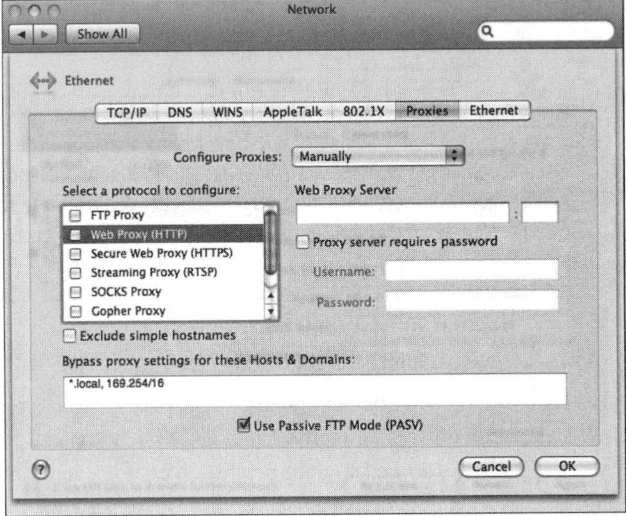


**Figure 16.4**
If you need to configure Internet access through a proxy server, you use the Proxies tab to do so.

## Configuring a PPPoE Account

Configuring a PPPoE account is more complicated than the other Ethernet options, but it doesn't take more than a few minutes:

1. Open the Network pane of the System Preferences application.
2. From the Services list, select Ethernet.
3. Use the Configure pop-up menu to select Create PPoE Service. You are prompted to provide a name for the service. Enter a name and click Done.
4. The new service you just created and named is now shown on the Services list and you can use the right side of the Network pane to configure the service (see Figure 16.5).



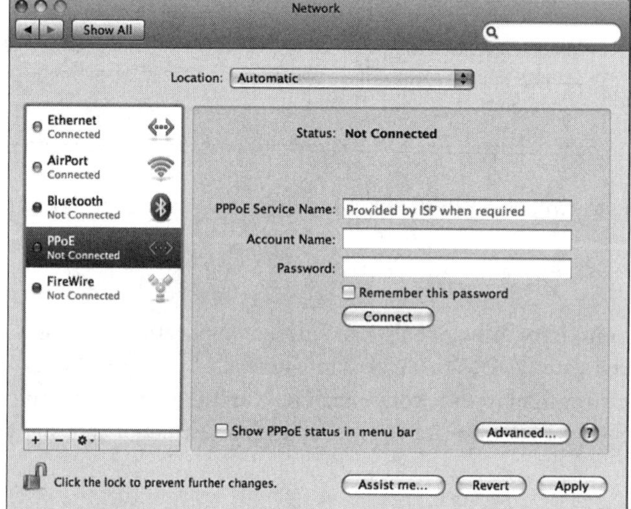


**Figure 16.5**
Create a new service to configure a PPP over Ethernet connection.

5. Enter the service name in the PPPoE Service Name field. (This is also optional.)
6. Enter your access account name in the Account Name field.
7. Enter your access password in the Password field; again this might be different from your email account password. If you leave this field empty, you must enter your password each time you connect. (If you enter a password, click the "Save password" check; if you uncheck the check box, your password is deleted from the field.)
8. Check the "Save password" check box to enable other user accounts to access the account without entering the connection password.
9. Check the "Show PPPoE status in menu bar" check box. This puts a menu on the menu bar that you can use to control your PPPoE connection.
10. Click the Advanced button and select the PPP tab to view the Session Options. Use the controls on this sheet to configure your Internet access.
11. In most cases, you should check the "Connect automatically when needed" check box. This enables your Mac to automatically connect to the Internet when it needs to.
12. Use the next four check boxes to control how your Mac monitors your connection. If you want to be prompted when your Mac is connected but is not actively using the connection, check the "Prompt every XX minutes to maintain connection" check box and

enter the time after which you want to be prompted to maintain the connection. If you want your Mac to automatically disconnect after a specific period of time, check the "Disconnect if idle for" check box and enter the idle time. Most users should check the "Disconnect when user logs out" check box so that the connection is broken when the current user logs out of the machine. Check the "Disconnect when switching user accounts" check box if you want the connection to be shut down when a different user account becomes active.

16

**NOTE**

> In only rare cases will you need to use the controls in the Configuration area of the Settings pop-up menu. Those options can be useful when troubleshooting a PPPoE connection.

13. Click OK to close the PPPoE Options sheet, and then click Apply to save your changes.

### Testing a PPPoE Connection

You can test your account by opening an Internet application, such as a web browser (assuming you enabled your Mac to connect automatically). If you are able to access Internet resources, your configuration is complete. Or, you can use the application that you use to manually connect and disconnect from your account, which is Internet Connect. Do the following:

1. Open the Network pane of the System Preferences application.
2. Select the PPoE service you created from the Services list. You will see the PPPoE account information you configured earlier.
3. Click the Connect button. You will see the status of the connection in the window. If your connection is successful, you will see the connected message and status information in the lower part of the Internet Connect window.
4. Click Disconnect to shut down the connection.
5. Quit System Preferences.

If you are able to connect successfully, you can use Internet applications, such as your email and web browser. You can monitor and control your connection from the PPPoE status menu on the menu bar.

*If you aren't able to connect to the Internet, see "My Ethernet Connection Can't Connect" in the "Troubleshooting" section at the end of this chapter.*

## Managing Multiple Internet Accounts

If the Internet is vital to you, such as for business purposes, you might have more than one Internet account you access in different ways. For example, you might use a cable modem as your primary access and maintain a dial-up account as a backup. You can maintain multiple Internet accounts on a single Mac.

You can manage the network ports and associated Internet accounts on your machine through the Services list on the Network pane of the System Preferences application.

Four network ports are shown by default. Active ports are indicated by a green circle next to the service name and will say Connected, while inactive ports have a red circle and will say Not Connected. The order in which the ports are listed determines which port is tried first when a connection is needed. Each of these ports could be configured with a different Internet connection so that if the connection on one port is not available, the connections on the other ports will be used.



To configure multiple accounts, do the following:

1. Open the Network pane of the System Preferences application.
2. Select the port you want to be your primary connection method on the Services list.
3. Configure that port for the related account (see the previous sections in this chapter for details). For example, configure your machine to use an Ethernet network to connect to the Internet.
4. Apply your changes to save the configuration of the port.
5. Make sure the connection you configured is turned on (its got a green circle) and that it is at the top of the Services list. If it is not the first connection listed, use the Action menu at the bottom of the Services list and select Set Service Order. A sheet will appear with the list of connection types (see Figure 16.6). Drag the connection you just configured to the top of the list, and change the order of the other services as well. Click OK to save your changes and return to the Network pane of the System Preferences application.

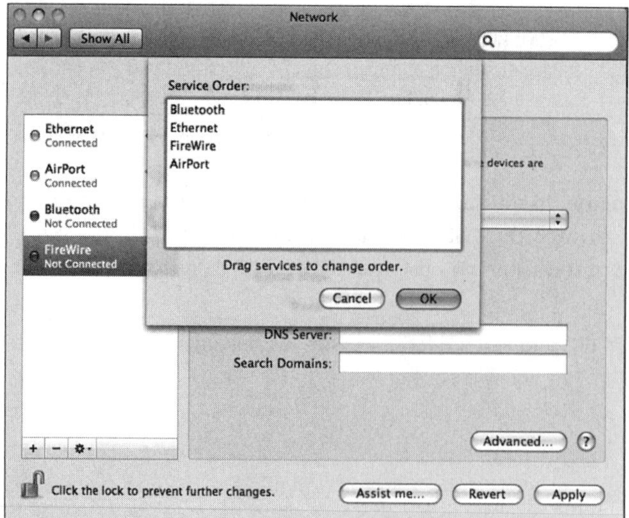


**Figure 16.6**
Use the Set Service Order list to specify the order in which network connections should be established.

6. From the Services list, select the port you want to be the second connection option, such as AirPort.
7. Configure the Internet connection for that port.
8. Make sure that the port is turned on; it should appear second in the Services.
9. Continue configuring the Internet connections on each port that you want to be active. Use the Set Services Order option of the Action menu to arrange the ports on the list in the order in which you want them to be used.
10. Click Apply and then quit the System Preferences application.



When your machine needs to connect to the Internet, it tries the ports and associated Internet accounts you specified in the order in which they are listed from top to bottom. Following are some other points about managing multiple connections:

- **You can have more than one configuration of the same port**—To create a new instance of a port, click the New button at the bottom of the Services list. Name the port and then select the type of port it is (Ethernet, AirPort, and so on). Click OK and the new port appears on the list. You can configure it in the same way as the default ports.
- **You can duplicate a port configuration**—This can be useful when you are configuring more than one port of the same type. Select the connection you want to duplicate in the Service list and click on the Action menu to select Duplicate Service. Provide a new name, and click Duplicate. Your new connection will be listed in the Service list and ready for you to configure.
- **You can edit a port's name by selecting Rename Service on that connections Action menu.**

**TIP**

> Inactive ports will appear on the Services list. You can permanently delete a port by using the Delete button at the bottom of the Services list. If you find you need that port again, just use the Add button at the bottom of the Services list to create it again.

You can also maintain multiple sets of network and Internet configurations that you create and maintain through the Location Manager. For example, if you use a MacBook, you might have a configuration when you use the machine from home, another when you use it from work, and so on.

⇨ To learn how to configure and use locations, **see** "Configuring and Using Locations," **p. 328**.

# TROUBLESHOOTING

## MY ETHERNET CONNECTION CAN'T CONNECT

*I've followed the steps for configuring my Ethernet connection, but I still can't get a successful connection. How do I figure out where I'm going wrong?*

The most common cause of problems connecting with an Ethernet account is an incorrect configuration. Still, there can be other problems as well. The following guidelines should help you troubleshoot problems you experience when trying to connect with an Ethernet-based connection:

- If you are using a modem (such as a cable modem), make sure that the modem you are using is powered up and properly connected to your Mac, either directly or through a network. Most modems have power, PC link, and activity lights. If any of these don't indicate the proper status, check your modem installation.
- If your Mac gets its access through a network, power down the modem and hub (such as an AirPort Base Station) and wait for about 20 seconds. Then turn each device back on. Many times, resetting a modem and hub in this way will restore the Internet connection.
- Make sure that the ISP services are currently available. Most broadband connections are very reliable, but they can go down from time to time. Usually, ISPs provide a status hotline you can call to see whether problems with service have been reported in your area. If there are problems, you will have to wait for the provider to correct them before you will be able to connect. (In these situations, it is nice to have a backup account, such as a dial-up account.)
- If your Mac gets its access through a network, remove the Mac from the network, connect it directly to the modem, and reconfigure the Mac as needed to access the account directly. (It's a good idea to save a location with this configuration for troubleshooting purposes.) Don't do this unless the Mac is protected with the Mac OS X firewall as it will get hacked if the connection works. If the connection works, you know the problem is with the network, in which case, you'll need to troubleshoot the network. If the connection doesn't work, you know the issue is with the modem, the configuration, or the connection itself.
- Work through the configuration steps for your account again, being especially careful to check all the configuration information you enter.
- If you are using a DHCP server, see whether you can obtain static settings for your account. Sometimes, you will be able to connect to an account with static settings when the automatic (DHCP) settings fail. If you use DHCP, check the IP address listed in the Sharing pane of the System Preferences application. If you see one that starts with 169, that means your Mac is not obtaining an IP address from the provider and will not be able to connect to the Internet. You must either figure out why it isn't able to obtain an IP address from your ISP or use a manual IP address.

- If you use a DHCP service and something changes, your Mac's IP address can become invalid. When this happens, you lose your Internet connection. You can force the system to get a new address by clicking the Advanced button for the service, opening the TCP/IP tab and clicking the Renew DHCP Lease button. This attempts to obtain a new IP address and might solve the problem.
- If you are still unable to connect, contact the service provider or network administrator from whom you obtain your service. Confirm that you are using the correct installation information for your account. If you are, ask for assistance in troubleshooting the connection from the provider's end.

---

**Getting Help**

Be aware that you might get flak from your ISP's technical support when you tell them you are using a Mac. Because the Mac has a smaller number of users, the tech support person to whom you talk will probably have less experience with Macs than with Windows machines. Also, many technical support people, such as those with cable companies, are overloaded and will try to get you off the line as soon as possible. If your problem doesn't fit into a checklist, they might want to stop before your problem is solved. Try to stay positive; you might have to be assertive (not aggressive) to get the support you need. Sometimes, it is better to explore the support area of a provider's website (which, of course, assumes that you can connect in some fashion, perhaps from another computer) before calling for help.

---

CHAPTER 17

# Building and Using a Wired Network

## In this chapter

# Local Area Networking with Mac OS X

Wherever there is more than one computer (whether those machines are running the Mac OS, Windows, Linux, or another operating system) in the same general physical area, there is an opportunity to network those computers into a local area network (LAN). A LAN offers many benefits, including the following:

- Sharing an Internet connection
- Sharing devices, such as printers
- Sharing files
- Providing a local web
- Providing FTP, email, and other services



A LAN can be as simple as two Macs (or a Mac and a network device such as a printer) connected together using an Ethernet crossover cable. A LAN can be as complex as hundreds of computers, dozens of printers, and many other devices communicating with each other among many buildings on a college or business campus. Local networks can also be anything in between, from a small home office with a couple of Macs and a Windows machine to a workgroup that has 10 or more workstations in it.

Creating and managing a large Ethernet network (such as one with hundreds of devices on it) is a major task, coverage of which is beyond the scope of this book. This chapter assumes a more modest network that includes several Macs; a Windows PC or two; and a couple of network devices, such as printers. Not coincidentally, this is the environment in which Macs are most likely to be used. The principles of managing larger networks are the same, but the details are much more complicated.

Similarly, this chapter focuses on one of the two networking technologies for which support is built in to the Mac OS: Ethernet. The other, AirPort, is covered in the next chapter. Ethernet is a *wired* scheme, meaning that a physical cable connects all the devices on the network. AirPort is a wireless scheme that broadcasts the network data over the air.

There are other means of networking machines together, but they are specialized and beyond the scope of this book. For most networks that you will manage with Mac OS X, Ethernet and AirPort are the best tools to create a LAN.

There are two general steps to preparing a wired Ethernet network. The first is to connect the devices on that network using Enthernet cables. The second is to configure the services you'll be providing on the network.

## Networking Services Supported by Mac OS X

Mac OS X supports a variety, in both range and depth, of network services as you can see in Table 17.1.

TABLE 17.1 NETWORKING SERVICES PROVIDED BY MAC OS X

| Service/Protocol | Abbreviation | Function |
|---|---|---|
| Apple File Protocol | AFP | Enables file sharing on machines running older versions of the Mac OS, such as Mac OS 8 and Mac OS 9. |
| AppleTalk | AppleTalk | Set of services used to communicate on Macs running older versions of the Mac OS or AppleTalk devices such as printers. |
| Bluetooth | Bluetooth | Enables Macs to communicate with various wireless devices, such as cell phones and PDAs. |
| Bonjour | Bonjour | Enables Bonjour-compatible devices on a network, such as computers and printers, to automatically discover and configure other Bonjour-compatible devices. |
| Common Internet File System | CIFS | Provides remote file access on many platforms, such as Windows. |
| Dynamic Host Configuration Protocol | DHCP | Provides automatic assignment of IP addresses to devices on a network. |
| Bootstrap Protocol | BOOTP | Enables computers to use the operating system installed on a different computer on the network to start up and operate. |
| File Transfer Protocol | FTP | Enables the fast transfer of files over TCP/IP networks. |
| Hypertext Transport Protocol | HTTP | Provides the transmission and translation of data between a web server and web client. |
| Internet Protocol | IP | Enables communication across a wide variety of devices and services. |
| Lightweight Directory Access Protocol | LDAP | Enables users to log on to a network and to locate resources, such as files and hardware devices, on a network. |
| Network File Service | NFS | Enables file sharing on Unix-compatible devices, such as Mac OS X computers. |
| Network Time Protocol | NTP | Synchronizes time across devices on a network. |
| Open Transport | OT | Another set of networking protocols that was introduced under earlier versions of the Mac OS. |
| Point-to-Point Protocol | PPP; PPPoE | Provides TCP/IP services over dial-up connections (PPP) and over Ethernet (PPPoE). |
| Printer Access Protocol | PAP | Provides services necessary to print to network printers. |

*continues*

17

**Table 17.1 Continued**

| Service/Protocol | Abbreviation | Function |
|---|---|---|
| Service Location Protocol | SLP | Enables devices on a network to be discovered automatically. |
| Short Message Block | SMB | Enables Macs to connect to Windows and Unix file servers. |
| Transmission Control Protocol/Internet Protocol; User Datagram Protocol/ Internet Protocol | TCP/IP; UDP/IP | Enables the transmission of data across extended networks, such as the Internet. These protocols do not provide services in themselves but are the means by which data is transmitted across networks. |
| Web-Based Distributed Authoring and Versioning | WebDAV | Extends HTTP to provide collaboration and file management on remote web servers. iDisk services are provided via WebDAV. |

17

**Note**

Support for SMB and CIFS enables you to integrate Macs onto Windows and Unix networks with no additional software installations. You can also integrate Windows computers into networks that mostly consist of Macs.

All the services listed in Table 17.1 can be useful, but in this chapter, you will learn how to implement the two services you are most likely to use: file sharing and FTP. After you have learned to configure these, you can apply similar principles to configure additional services on your network.

⇨ To learn how to configure Mac OS X's built-in web server to implement HTTP services, **see** "Mac OS X to the Max: Using Mac OS X to Serve Web Pages," **p. 458**.

**Note**

The WebDAV standard provides a much better environment for file sharing and other services across HTTP networks, primarily the Web. For example, when you use an iDisk under Mac OS X, you are using the WebDAV standard. This enables you to remain connected to the iDisk for long periods of time without being disconnected during idle periods.

## Implementing a Network

To implement a network, you should do the following:

1. Design your network.
2. Build your network.
3. Configure the services that will be available on the network.
4. Monitor and administer your network.

# DESIGNING A NETWORK

Before you implement a network, you need to design the network you want to create. As a starting point, answer the following questions:

- **What types of services do you want to provide over the network?**—Will you provide file serving? Do you want to share an Internet connection? How about FTP or web services? The answers to these questions will drive the rest of your network design. For example, if you plan to share an Internet connection, you will most likely want to include a hub that can act as a DHCP server in your network design.
- **How many devices do you want to be on the network?**—The devices for which you plan must include all the workstations on the network as well as shared devices, such as printers, modems, and so on. The answer to this question determines how many access points into the wired network you will need to provide.
- **How will you connect the devices together?**—For example, will you use Ethernet for all devices or will you include an AirPort hub (hardware or software base station) in the network? The answers to these questions determine the connecting devices you will need to use, such as Ethernet hubs, AirPort base stations, and so on.
- **Who will need access to the services you are providing?**—How will they connect to the network? The answers to these questions help you identify the users on your network.
- **What are the security implications of the services you are providing on the network?**—This question should drive you to ensure that you protect machines that will have access to the network. For example, you need to be very careful about providing FTP access to machines on which sensitive or critical data is stored. There are security concerns with any network service you provide; you should understand these when you design your network so you know how to provide proper security for it.

As you answer the previous questions, you should be ready to start designing your network. You should document your network design with at least a simple sketch of the network, the list of the devices you need to include on the network, and so on. Also, include the services you will be providing from specific machines on the network. An example of a design for a small office network is shown in Figure 17.1.

**TIP**

> Having your network design documented enables you to expand it more easily when you outgrow it. It is much simpler to determine what needs to be done to expand a network when you see it on paper than it is by looking at it in the real world. (Besides, unless all the machines are in the same room, you probably won't be able to see them all at the same time, anyway.)

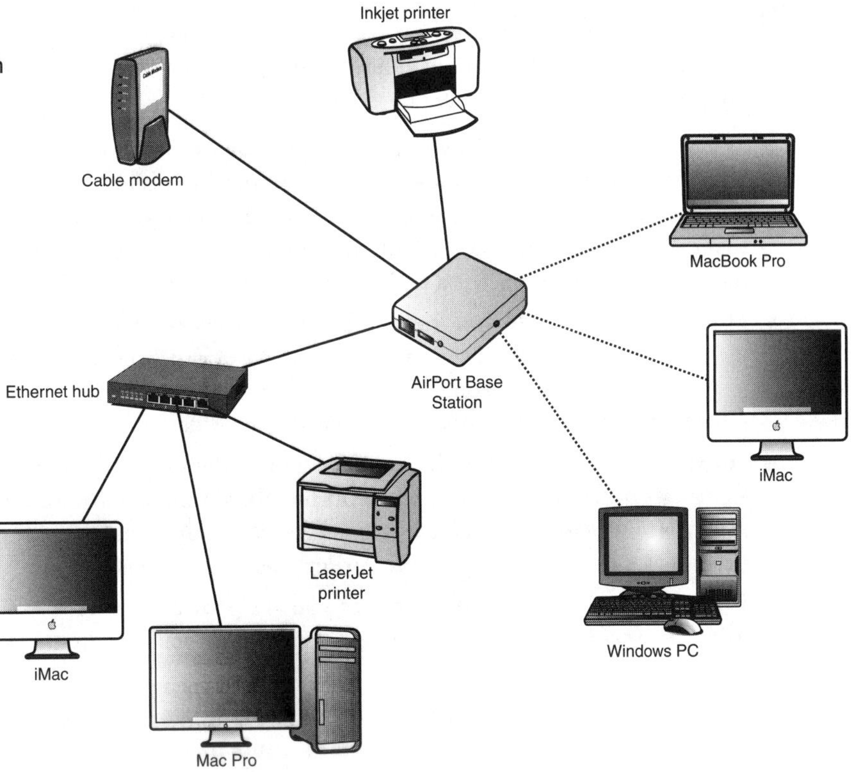

**Figure 17.1**
A simple network design document, such as this one for a small office network, can aid network design, implementation, and maintenance.

# BUILDING A WIRED NETWORK

After your network design is complete, you can start building the wired part of your network.

Obtain the devices and cables that you determined you need for the network you want to build, and then assemble the network.

Your network design document identifies the devices you need on the network. For example, you can determine the type of Ethernet hub you need by counting the number of devices you are connecting to it and determining whether it must provide services to the network, such as a DHCP server, so you can share a single Internet account among the devices. You also need to determine the types and length of cable you will need to attach the devices to the network, how the cables will be routed, and so on.

After you have obtained the devices that will be installed on the network, you need to connect and configure those devices to access the network.

Connecting the devices to the network is simply a matter of attaching an Ethernet cable to an Ethernet hub and to each device. Of course, depending on the physical locations of the devices on the network, this can be quite a challenge, especially if you have to traverse long distances or connect machines located on different floors. For complicated cable runs, it's often much easier to connect a device to the network wirelessly.

Configuring the devices attached to the network includes configuring the Internet access and firewall (if needed) for each machine, configuring computers to connect to networked printers, and so on.

⇨ To learn how to configure Mac OS X machines for Internet access, **see** Chapter 16, "Connecting a Mac to the Internet," **p. 335**.

⇨ To learn how to create and configure an AirPort network, **see** Chapter 18, "Creating and Managing AirPort Wireless Networks," **p. 393**.

⇨ To learn how to share an Internet connection among the devices on the network, **see** Chapter 19, "Sharing an Internet Connection," **p. 421**.

⇨ To learn how to protect machines on your network from Internet attacks, **see** "Defending Your Mac Against Internet Hackers," **p. 940**.

**NOTE**

> When you create a LAN, you are actually creating an intranet. You can provide most services on an intranet that are available on the Internet. The only difference is that you can control what happens on the intranet much more closely than you can control anything on the Internet.



As you install a device, be sure to test its basic access to the network by accessing various resources on the network, such as networked printers and Internet access if that is provided through the network. This step confirms that the physical aspects of the network are working properly and that the basic network configuration for Internet access is done properly.

After you have confirmed that the devices are correctly attached to and configured for the network, you need to configure the particular services each machine will use and the access that others on the network will have to those services; examples of such configuration are provided in the next section.

**NOTE**

> Tutorials on creating and managing Ethernet networks are located at www.lantronix.com/learning/index.html.

# Finding and Installing an Ethernet Hub

Ethernet is a hub-based network architecture, meaning that all the data that flows through an Ethernet network must flow through a hub of one type or another. To implement a wired network, you'll need to install a hub.

**NOTE**

> There are two exceptions to this rule. One is using an Ethernet crossover cable to connect two devices directly. This special cable acts as a very basic hub, so you don't need to use a specific hub device. The other is that many modern Macs support direct computer-to-computer Ethernet connections using a standard Ethernet cable.

## UNDERSTANDING ETHERNET HUBS

The basic function of an Ethernet hub is to enable data to flow through an Ethernet network. The various types of Ethernet hubs are as follows:

- **Passive or *dumb* hubs**—These hubs don't do anything but allow data to be passed back and forth between the devices to which they are connected. All the traffic through a passive hub goes to every device on the network, thus compromising the performance of the network because much of the data being communicated is wasted.
- **Intelligent or manageable hubs**—In addition to the basic function, which is used to connect various Ethernet devices, these hubs offer features that can be used to monitor and manage the data flowing through the network.
- **Switching hubs**—This type of hub is the most active; it actually directs the flow of each packet of information based on the destination of that packet. Because data is sent only where it is actually needed, the data flow on the network is efficient. Switching hubs offer the best performance of any hub type. Fortunately, most hubs that you can buy are of this type.

  These hubs can also accomplish *load balancing*, which means they analyze the flow of information and direct information such that the load on various devices on the network is balanced. This prevents particular devices from being overloaded while others sit idle. Load balancing is particularly important for situations in which active web servers, or other types of servers, are on a network. A web server can easily generate large amounts of traffic; load balancing can smooth the data flow around such servers so that no one server gets overwhelmed, thus slowing network traffic to a crawl.

17

**TIP**

For most small networks, a good configuration is one AirPort Base Station to provide all services to the network, such as Internet sharing and protection from attacks, with additional dumb Ethernet hubs to connect all the wired devices on the network. This is the design that was shown in Figure 17.1.

In addition to the core features of enabling the communication of data to multiple devices on a network, many hubs also offer additional features, which include the following:

- **Support for multiple speeds**—Hubs can support the various speeds of Ethernet; many hubs support multiple speeds and can intelligently switch between speeds so that you can have both lower- and higher-speed devices attached to the same network. The hub manages the differences in speeds to prevent bottlenecks and other performance problems.
- **Number of ports**—Every Ethernet hub offers a specific number of ports, such as 5 or 10. The more ports a hub has, the more devices it can support. Hubs can also be attached to other hubs to enable even more devices to be attached to a network.
- **Firewall**—Some hubs can act as firewalls to protect the networks to which they are connected from outside attack.

- **Internet account sharing**—Hubs offering this feature enable everyone on a network to share a single Internet account. Such hubs usually include a DHCP server and often offer firewall protection, too.
- **Wireless communication**—Hubs can enable devices to communicate with the network wirelessly.
- **Network analysis and management software**—Some hubs include software you can use to analyze the traffic flow on the network to which they are attached so you can identify problems, such as a *bottleneck* (which is a spot on the network at which point the data flow is slowed, usually because of a device being overloaded).

## CHOOSING AND INSTALLING AN ETHERNET HUB

Choosing the right Ethernet hub for your network is a matter of identifying the features you need and then locating a hub that offers those features. Some features to consider are the following:

17

- **Speed**—All modern Macs can communicate at speeds of at least 1000Mbps (1Gbps), so you should make sure that the hub you get can handle this speed. Most hubs are capable of switching speeds and are rated with the speeds they support, such as 10/100/1000 for a hub that can support 10Mbps, 100Mbps, and 1000Mbps.
- **Number of ports**—Hubs support multiple devices through the ports they offer. You need a port for each device on the network, such as each Mac, Windows PC, printer, cable modem, and so on. Generally, you should get a hub with more ports than you think you will need to allow room for your network to grow.
- **Internet account sharing**—If you plan on sharing an Internet account, you should get a hub that supports this.

**NOTE**

> Internet account sharing is built in to the Mac OS X. However, using a hub to share an account is often a better choice because a Mac that provides account sharing always has to be on, and it takes a performance hit to share an account. Sharing hubs are dedicated devices and are always on by design. Because such hubs are inexpensive and easy to use, they are usually the best choice.

- **Firewall**—If you connect your network to the Internet, you should use a hub that offers a firewall—such hubs often support sharing an Internet account as well.

**NOTE**

> Configuring Mac OS X's built-in firewall to protect individual machines is simple. However, if you have other machines that don't offer a firewall, you should ensure that the hub you use provides one.

- **Mac OS X compatibility**—Because Ethernet is not platform specific, most hubs support Macs, Windows, and other machines. If you have a managed hub, you most likely will use a web browser to configure that device. However, some hubs offer particular features that are platform specific. In addition, some hubs can only be updated using Windows-based computers.
- **Other features**—If there are specific features you need, such as network management software, look for hubs that offer those features.

**NOTE**

> An Aiport Base Station is a good example of a multifunction hub. In addition to providing a wireless network, shieliding your network from Internet attack, and enabling you to share an Internet connection, current models also have three Ethernet ports that act as an Ethernet hub. You'll learn more about AirPort in the next chapter.



Hubs generally fall into two camps: those designed for small networks with few or no features and those designed to support a larger number of devices or that offer other features.

Typically, if you evaluate the list of factors provided previously, the type of hub you need becomes clear fairly quickly. Then it is a matter of choosing among the brands that offer the type of hub you need.

In theory, installing an Ethernet hub is easy; you simply connect power to the hub and then connect each device (computers, printers, and so on) to it using the appropriate Ethernet cables with RJ-45 connectors at each end. In practice, routing the cables can be a major challenge, especially if you are covering large distances in a building that is not designed to allow easy installation of such cables.

---

**Ethernet Cards**

To attach a specific device to an Ethernet network, that device must have an Ethernet card installed in it. Although all Macs have Ethernet cards built in, other devices might not. For example, Ethernet cards are not installed in every printer, even those that are capable of being networked.

The type of Ethernet card you need to install in a device depends on the specific device you are installing on the network. For example, the interface card for a printer needs to match the specifications for a particular brand and model. On the other hand, devices that can use PCI cards can accept a standard Ethernet PCI card to enable that device to be attached to a network.

---

After an Ethernet hub is physically installed on the network, you might have to install some software or configure that hub (for example, if you will be sharing an Internet connection over it, you have to configure the hub's DHCP server).

**NOTE**

> Most hubs include an *uplink* port to which you can attach other hubs. This enables you to expand a network by adding more devices to it than a single hub has ports. After you have filled the ports on one hub, you can attach another hub to the first hub's uplink port and begin using the ports on the second hub to add more devices to the network.

### Using an Ethernet Hub

For most applications, after a hub is installed and configured, you don't need to think about it anymore. It simply does its work. If you use network-monitoring software, you run that from a device connected to the hub.

Most hubs offer a basic set of diagnostic lights you can use to monitor the traffic across each port on the hub. These lights can be useful if your network has problems you need to diagnose. One type of diagnostic light included for each port on most hubs is an activity light that illuminates when the hub senses activity from the device connected to that port. Most hubs also include a speed indicator light for each port to give you information about the speed of communication with a specific device; this light can help you ensure that each device is communicating with the network at the maximum possible speed.



## Configuring the Services on a Network

As noted in Table 17.1, Mac OS X supports a large number of network services. To access these services, you must configure each machine that will be using them. This involves configuring the particular machine that will be providing those services (the *server*) and then enabling access to those services on various machines on the network that will be accessing those services (the *clients*).

Explaining how to configure each of the possible services is beyond the scope of this book. However, learning about some examples of services you are likely to use will enable you to configure the others.

Some services you'll want to take advantage of on most networks are the following:

- File sharing
- FTP server
- Windows file sharing
- Printer sharing
- Web server

⇨ To learn how to share files with Windows computers, **see** "Mac OS X to the Max: Networking Mac OS X with Windows Computers," **p. 389**.

⇨ To learn how to share the printers attached to a Mac OS X machine, **see** "Working with Shared Printers," **p. 822**.

⇨ To learn how to host websites from a Mac OS X machine, **see** "Mac OS X to the Max: Using Mac OS X to Serve Web Pages," **p. 458**.

### Configuring and Using File Sharing

The Mac OS has long provided peer-to-peer file-sharing capabilities to enable Macintosh computers on a network to share files. Mac OS X provides much more robust file sharing services along with more tools you can use to control and configure a network.

**NOTE**

> Peer-to-peer file sharing implies that the files being shared are stored on workstations that people use to accomplish work. The other type of file sharing is based on a sever/client arrangement in which the primary purpose of the server machine is to provide network resources, such as files to share. The technology involved is similar. If you are managing a relatively small network, you are probably not likely to have a dedicated server on it, but that's okay because peer-to-peer file sharing works just as well for these kinds of networks.

Under Mac OS X, you can share files with Macs running Mac OS X, Macs running OS 9 and earlier, Windows file servers, and Unix file servers. For other Macs running Mac OS X, you can use AppleTalk for file sharing or use TCP/IP. For Macs running earlier versions of the Mac OS (such as Mac OS 9), you can use AppleTalk to share files. For Windows and Unix, you can use SMB and CIFS services.



When connecting to other Macs for file sharing, the machines communicate through either TCP/IP or AppleTalk. To log in to a Mac OS X file-sharing machine serving files via TCP/IP, that machine must have an IP address. Typically, this IP address is assigned as part of connecting that machine to the Internet, such as by a DHCP server provided by an Ethernet hub or an AirPort Base Station.

Mac OS X includes support for Bonjour, which enables devices to seek out other Bonjour-compatible devices on a network and automatically configure access to those devices. All Macs that have Mac OS X version 10.2 or later are Bonjour aware and can therefore take advantage of this technology to easily and quickly connect to other Macs. However, other devices, such as printers, can also support Bonjour, so those devices can be configured automatically as well.

**NOTE**

> Interestingly enough (to me anyway), Bonjour is also being used in some "non-computer" devices. For example, TiVos use Bonjour.

AppleTalk is the Mac's original network protocol and continues to be supported in Mac OS X. When you are connecting to Macs running OS version 8.6 or earlier, you have to use AppleTalk as support for file sharing over TCP/IP, which was added in Mac OS 9.0.

In Chapter 19, you will learn how to share an Internet account using a DHCP server. Such a server assigns IP addresses to the machines connected to it. The *D* stands for dynamic, meaning these addresses can change. This can make locating a specific machine by its IP address tough because each machine's address can be changed by the DHCP server. Fortunately, with most DHCP servers, you can choose to manually assign IP addresses to the devices attached to it. When you do this, machines have the same IP address even though they are using a DHCP server to obtain that address.

With Bonjour, you don't need to worry about the IP addresses of individual machines because your Mac seeks out the devices that are communicating on a network and automatically configures access to those devices.

**NOTE**

> If other devices on your network, such as printers, have dynamic IP addresses assigned to them and you use the IP address to configure that device, you can lose the connection to those devices when the DHCP server assigns a new address to them. (This typically happens if the hub loses power for some reason or the device is removed from the network for a while.) In such cases, you need to reconfigure any computers that access the device with the new address assigned by the DHCP server. For such devices, consider assigning a static address that remains constant for that device.

To identify the current IP address of a Mac OS X machine, open the Network pane of the System Preferences application. Select a connection type from the Services list and the machine's current IP address will be shown in the Status section (see Figure 17.2).

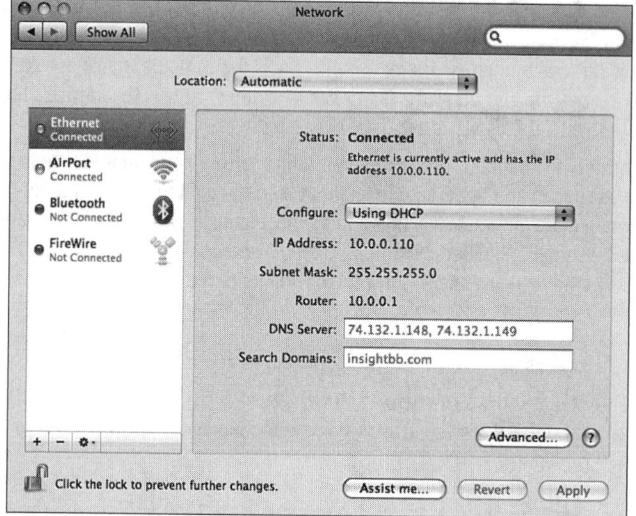


**Figure 17.2**
On the Network pane, you see the current IP address of a Mac OS X computer; the address is shown next to the active network port (in this case, the address is 10.0.0.110).

On the Sharing pane of the System Preferences application, you can also use the machine's name to identify it from other machines that support Bonjour. The machine name is shown in the Computer Name field at the top of the Sharing pane. Unless you've changed it, this will usually be something creative such as *Your Name*'s Computer, where *Your Name* is, amazingly enough, your name.

**TIP**

> To identify the current IP address of a Mac OS 9 machine, open the File Sharing control panel.

## CONFIGURING FILE SHARING ON A MAC RUNNING MAC OS X

To share the files stored a Mac OS X machine, you must enable the Personal File Sharing service on that computer. This includes turning on the File Sharing service, turning on AppleTalk (if you will be sharing files with Mac OS 9 machines), naming the machine, and so on.

**TIP**

> If your purpose in file sharing is one-way—for example, enabling others to download files from a specific machine but not to upload files to it—consider using FTP services rather than file sharing. You will learn how to provide FTP services in a later section of this chapter. You can also use web sharing to enable people to download files from a Mac OS X machine.

17

**What's in a Name?**

Your Mac actually has two names associated with it. One is the computer name, which by default is a combination of the first user's name and the word *Computer*. The other name is that device's hostname, which is actually the name used when the device is accessed over a network.

By default, the hostname and the computer name are the same, except your Mac automatically removes any characters, such as spaces, and uppercase letters that aren't permitted in a hostname. Any changes you make to the computer name are automatically made in the hostname. However, you can manually set the hostname for a machine to be something different from its computer name. To do this, click the Edit button at the top of the Sharing pane. In the resulting sheet, enter the hostname of the Mac. The hostname always ends in `.local`.

The following steps assume that a Mac has access to the network (via Ethernet or AirPort) and that the default security privileges are in place on the file-sharing machine. You can change the default privileges for items you share to make them more or less available, as you will learn in a later section of this chapter.

To provide file sharing services from a Mac running Mac OS X, do the following steps:

1. Open the System Preferences application.
2. Click the Sharing icon to open the Sharing pane (see Figure 17.3). At the top of the pane are the computer's name and just below that, its hostname.

   When you click the name of a service in the Services list, the details for configuring that service will appear to the right. You use the check box next to the name of a service to turn it on or off.

⇨ To learn how to share an Internet connection among the devices on the network, **see** Chapter 19, "Sharing an Internet Connection," **p. 421**.

3. Provide the computer's name by entering a name in the Computer Name text box; use a name that will help others on the network easily identify the machine. The default computer name is the first user's name entered when the machine was registered, with an apostrophe, an *s*, and the word *Computer* (where *Computer* is the type of Mac you have) tacked onto it. You can use the default computer name or change it to one you prefer.

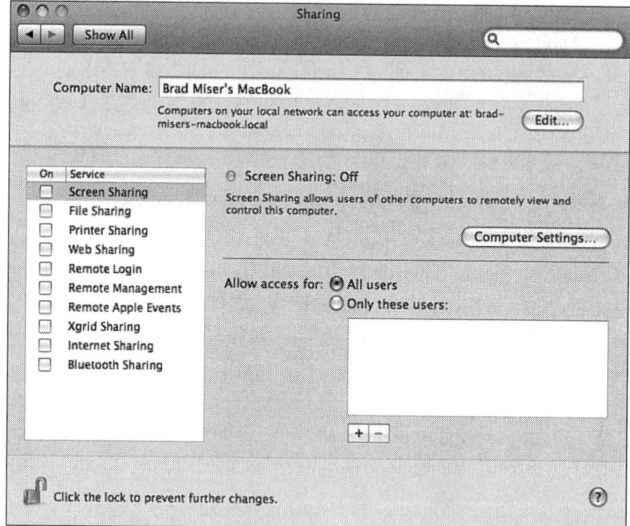


**Figure 17.3**
You enable the network services a Mac provides by using the controls on the Services list of the Sharing pane.



After you provide a name, the machine's hostname is automatically created. Some characters, such as spaces, aren't allowed in a hostname, which is the name by which the machine is identified on the network. If you enter such characters in the computer name, the machine name that people see on the network won't be exactly what you entered. For example, if you include a space in the computer name, it is replaced by a hyphen for the machine's network name. The Mac automatically removes and replaces any disallowed characters.

4. If you want to manually enter a hostname, click the Edit button; then, in the resulting sheet, enter the hostname for the machine and click OK. The extension `.local` is added to the hostname you type to indicate that the host is on the local network.
5. Identify the service you want to activate on the machine, such as File Sharing.
6. Click the On check box to turn on the selected service. For example, if you click the On check box for File Sharing, that service is activated; after a moment or two, you see the AFP address of the machine and the browsing name (which is the name by which others on the network will be able to identify the computer when they browse the network) at the bottom of the pane. When you select and enable other services, information related to those services is shown in the pane instead. When a service's check box is checked, that service is on and can be accessed by others on the network.

   If you will be sharing files with Macs running a version of the Mac OS older than Mac OS X and those machines don't support file sharing over TCP/IP, you need to make AppleTalk active on the Mac OS X machine. If the machines to which you will be providing file-sharing services do allow file sharing over TCP/IP, you don't need AppleTalk and can skip to step 12.

**CAUTION**

> If you don't need to use AppleTalk to use file sharing, leave it off. AppleTalk can sometimes interfere with other network services, such as TCP/IP services to the Internet. AppleTalk can also make your machine visible to a local or wide area AppleTalk network.

7. Open the Network pane of the System Preferences application.
8. Select the network port over which AppleTalk access will be provided on the Show menu. For example, select Ethernet to enable machines to use the AppleTalk protocol over Ethernet. Select AirPort to provide AppleTalk over an AirPort network. Once you have selected the port, click on the Advanced button.

**NOTE**

> You can provide AppleTalk over only a single network port at a time. For example, you can provide AppleTalk over Ethernet or over AirPort, but not both at the same time.



9. Click the AppleTalk tab and check the "Make AppleTalk Active" check box.
10. If you have AppleTalk zones on your network, select the zone from the AppleTalk Zone pop-up menu (if there aren't any zones, this pop-up menu will be inactive). You can configure AppleTalk zones using the Configure pop-up menu (select Manually if you want to manually configure the network or Automatically to have your Mac configure it automatically).
11. Click OK. AppleTalk services will become active on the computer.
12. Review the services you have configured on the Sharing pane (see Figure 17.4).

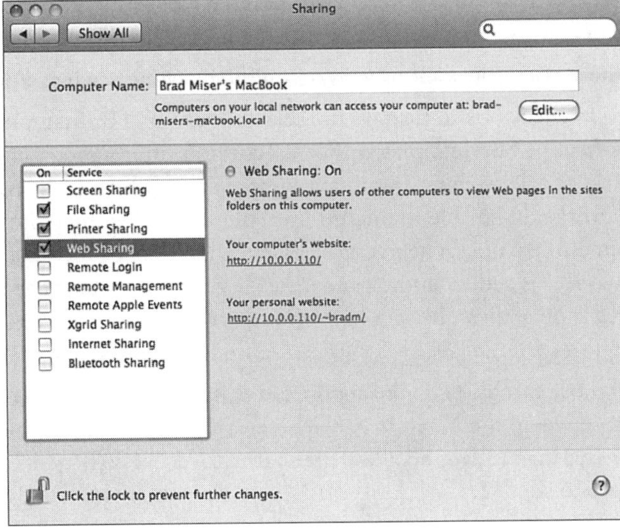


**Figure 17.4**
This Mac is providing file-sharing services to other Macs and Windows computers, is providing a website, and is sharing the printers connected to it.

### USING FIREWALLS AND NETWORK SERVICES

If you have a firewall installed on the machine you are configuring as a server, you must configure that firewall to allow the type of access needed for others to access it from the network. For example, to enable the machine to provide file-sharing services, you must configure the firewall to allow machines from the network to connect to the file server. With some firewalls, you can allow access to specific services, such as AFP, only from specific IP addresses. All other requests for services will be denied.

If you use the Mac OS X built-in firewall, the services you enable on the Services pane are allowed automatically. You can use the Firewall tab of the Security pane to manually configure the services that are allowed if you need to.

If you use another type of firewall or configure the built-in firewall using another method (such as the Unix commands), you must enable access to the services you are providing through that firewall.

Similarly, if some machines on your network are connected through an AirPort Base Station, you won't be able to access those machines from machines connected outside the network. Because an AirPort Base Station provides protection for the machines it connects, machines outside the network can't see any of the machines on the network.



Always be aware of the security settings of the networks you are configuring and using. Sometimes, you can waste a lot of time troubleshooting a network problem that is actually a case of things working just as planned (such as when you try to figure out why no one can connect to a machine protected by a firewall that isn't configured to allow those services to be accessed on the machine).

### ACCESSING SHARED FILES FROM A MAC OS X COMPUTER

There are two basic ways you can access shared files. One is to browse the network for available machines sharing files. The other is to move to the services on a machine directly using the URL for the specific service you want to access.

In either case, when you connect to a server, you must log in to that server to access its resources. You can log in under a user account that is valid for that server, or you can log in as a guest. When you log in under a valid user account, you have access to all the items on that machine just as if you were logged in to the machine directly (rather than over a network). If you are logged in as a guest, you can access only the items on the machine that allow public access, such as each user's Public folder.

**NOTE**

> To access a network resource by browsing, it must support Bonjour, SMB, or AppleTalk. If not, you have to access it by entering its URL via the Connect to Server command.

New with Mac OS X 10.5, the Shared section of the sidebar always shows the network resources that are visible to your Mac. You may need to click the triangle to the left of

Shared to see the list of available servers. When you click a server, you will be able to connect to and then browse what is being shared.

To access shared files stored on a Mac OS X computer that is sharing its files from a Mac OS X machine by browsing the network, do the following steps:

1. Open a Finder window and select Go, Network or press Shift-⌘-K. The Network directory will appear. Depending on the network to which you are connected, you will see a number of icons representing various network resources available to you.

**NOTE**

> It can take a few minutes for your Mac to successfully browse the network to which it is connected. After you start the browse process, if you don't see the resources you think you should, refresh the Network window by moving away from it and then back again or by clicking its icon to update the list of available network resources.



2. To access other Macs providing services, open the Network icon if you see it; if not, the individual servers with which you can work will appear directly under the Network folder. In either case, you will see the names of the computers on your network that are providing services to you (see Figure 17.5).

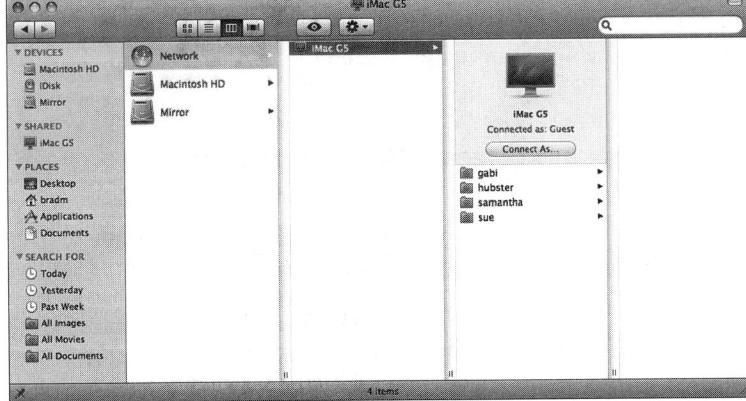


**Figure 17.5**
The Network folder provides access to other Macs providing services on your network; in this case, I can access an iMac on my network. Note you also see this iMac in the Shared section of the sidebar.

3. Double-click the icon for the server and services you want to access. The Connect to Server dialog box appears (see Figure 17.6).

**TIP**

> View the Network folder in Column view and select the server you want to access. In the Preview column, you'll see the server's icon and the Connect As button. Click the Connect As button to connect to the machine providing services to you.

**Figure 17.6**
You use this dialog box to log in to a server.

4. To log in as a registered user, which provides the same access to resources you would have when you log in directly to that machine, click the Registered User radio button and enter the username and password for the account under which you want to log in. If you don't have login information for a specific user account on the machine to which you are connected, click the Guest radio button instead. Click Connect to connect to the server. A window will appear that lists each volume or user's Home folder (which will be the Home folder of the user account under which you logged in) you can access.

**TIP**

> Check the "Remember this password in my keychain" check box in the Connect to Server dialog box to add a network resource's login information to your keychain. The next time you access that resource, the login information will be input automatically so you can just click Connect to connect to it.

5. Select the resource that was mounted to work with it (see Figure 17.7). It is easiest to select from the Shared section of the Sidebar. The resources that appear depend on the user account under which you are logged in. If you logged in as a guest, you can access only public resources.

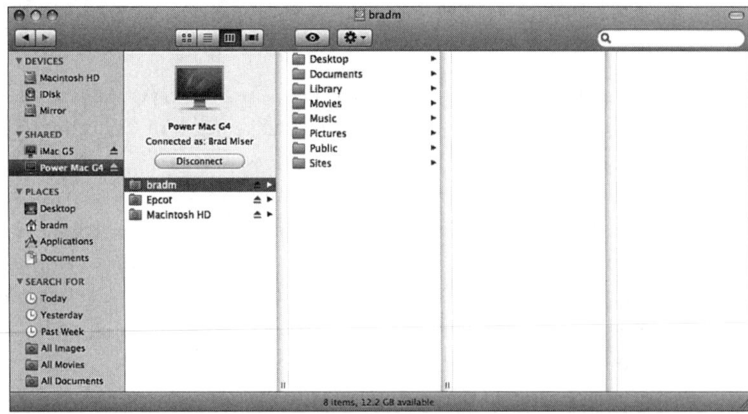


**Figure 17.7**
I can access my Home folder on an older Macintosh that is available on my network.

**NOTE**

Network volumes are represented by icons with a globe on them, as you can see in Figure 17.7.

6. Open the folders available via the shared resource to work with them. For example, you can open files, drag them to your Mac to copy them, and so on.

*If you can't see a server when you browse, see "I Can't Access a Server" in the "Troubleshooting" section at the end of this chapter.*

For more precise access to services on a Bonjour machine (such as to choose to access FTP services when file sharing and FTP are being provided) or to access services on a machine that doesn't support Bonjour, you can use a computer's address to access it manually. To do so, perform the following steps:

1. From the Finder, select Go, Connect to Server (⌘-K) or open the Finder's Dock menu and choose Connect to Server. The Connect to Server dialog box will appear (see Figure 17.8).

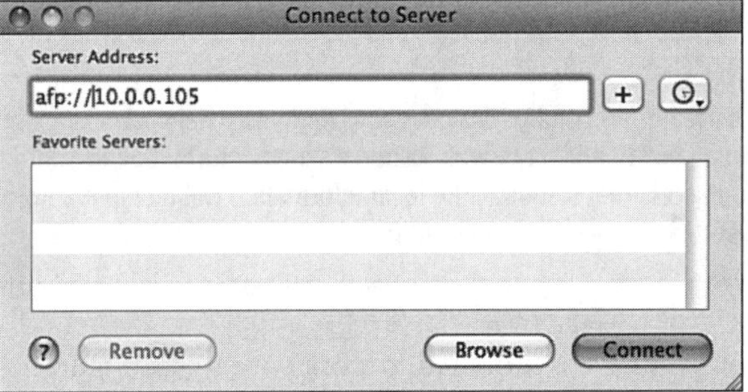


**Figure 17.8**
Use the Connect to Server dialog box to move to a server by entering its URL.

**TIP**

If you click the Browse button, you move to a Finder window showing the Network directory; this does the same thing as selecting Network on the Places sidebar.

2. Type the server address you want to access in the Server Address box. The address you use depends on how you want to access the server. For example, to open all of a computer's resources, type its hostname, which is `hostname.local`, where *`hostname`* is the hostname of the machine you are accessing. To access file-sharing services, use the URL for File Sharing services, which will be something such as `afp://10.0.1.4/`. You can obtain the address for the specific service you want to access on the Sharing pane of the System Preferences application on the computer you are accessing over the network. Select the specific service you want to access and the related address will appear at the bottom of the pane.

3. Click Connect. Your Mac will attempt to locate the resource via the address you entered. You can monitor the progress of this via the Connecting To Server progress window. If the connection is made successfully, you will see the Connect to Server dialog box (see Figure 17.9).

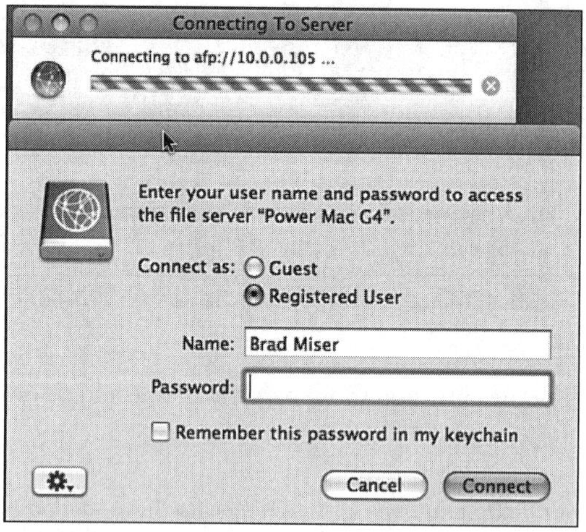

**Figure 17.9**
Notice the progress window that indicates the Mac is trying to connect to the specified URL. Use this dialog box to log in to a network server.



4. Enter the username and password for the account under which you want to log in and click Connect or click the Guest radio button and click Connect instead. The server's volumes that you can access appears in the Select Volume dialog box (see Figure 17.10). The resources that appear depend on the user account under which you are logged in. If you logged in as a guest, you can access only public resources.

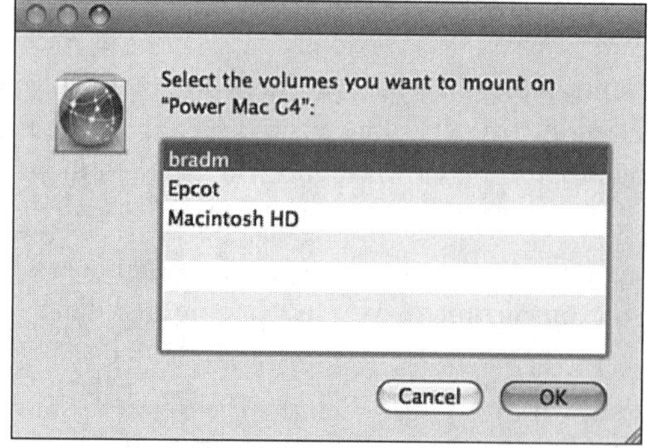


**Figure 17.10**
The machine called Power Mac G4 has a number of volumes that can be mounted on the computer being used to access that server.

5. Select the volume you want to mount—hold down the Shift or ⌘ key to select multiple volumes—and click OK. A Finder window opens and the server you chose to access is shown in the Shared section of the Places sidebar (see Figure 17.11). If you have set mounted servers to appear on the desktop using the Finder preference, they appear on your desktop as well.

**Figure 17.11**
My MacBook is currently connected to my iMac and Power Mac G4. Both those servers appear in the Shared section of the sidebar, and I am accessing my Home directory on the G4.



6. Access the network volumes just like those directly connected to or installed in your Mac.

*If the connection is never made and quits or the Connect to Server dialog box never appears, see "I Can't Access a Server" in the "Troubleshooting" section at the end of this chapter.*

Following are some additional tips about using a Mac OS X machine to access file-sharing services via the Connect to Server command:

- When you sign on to a Mac OS X file-sharing machine as a registered user, meaning you have a username and password, the Action pop-up menu in the Connect to Server dialog box is enabled. If you open this menu, you can change the password for the account under which you are logging in (if the account allows this) by choosing the "Change password" command.
- When you are logged in to a file-sharing machine, you can quickly choose other volumes to mount by clicking the server in the Shared section of the Places sidebar. All the volumes that have access to are shown here, and you can then move to the resources you need.
- The address to which you most recently connected is remembered in the Connect to Server dialog box so you can reconnect to it by opening that dialog box and clicking Connect.
- To remove access to a network resource, click the Eject button shown next to it in the Shared section of the Places sidebar or select the mounted folder or volume and choose File, Eject or press ⌘-E.
- To log back in to the same file-sharing machine under a different user account, such as an administrator account, you must log off that machine and repeat the initial login process. You do this by ejecting all the mounted volumes provided by that server.

- At the upper-right corner of the Connect to Server dialog box is the Recent Servers pop-up menu (the Clock icon) that shows a list of the most recent servers you have accessed. You can select a server from this list to return to it, or you can clear the list by selecting Clear Recent Servers.
- Just below the Server Address box on the Connect to Server dialog box is the Favorite Servers list. You can add a server to your favorites list by entering its URL and clicking the Add to Favorites button (+). You can return to any favorite server by selecting it on the list and clicking Connect. Remove a favorite by selecting it and clicking the Remove button.
- You can place an alias to a networked volume on your Mac, such as by adding it to the Dock. When you open such an alias, you are prompted to log in to the server and, upon doing so, you can access that volume. If you add the password to your keychain, you will skip the login process.

*If you are unable to access the file server, see "I Can't Access a Server" in the "Troubleshooting" section at the end of this chapter.*



**TIP**

> You can add a volume from a network server to the Login Items tab of the Accounts pane of the System Preferences application to mount that server each time you log in.

## CONFIGURING AND USING FTP SERVICES

Among its other network services, Mac OS X also includes a built-in FTP server. Using an FTP server can be an even more convenient way to enable others to access files stored on a particular machine. Other people can use a standard web browser or FTP application to download files stored on your Mac via the FTP services you enable on a machine.

**CAUTION**

> Granting FTP access to a machine has security implications that are beyond what I have room to cover in this chapter. If you intend to use the FTP services on a machine that has sensitive data on it, you should investigate the implications of running FTP services on a Mac under Mac OS X that has data on it you need to protect.
>
> You can sometimes move outside the particular Home directory for the account under which you log in to the FTP site, so be very careful about granting FTP access to a machine unless you are very sure about the person who will be using it.

Configuring FTP services under Mac OS X is similar to providing file-sharing services:

1. Open the Sharing pane of the System Preferences application.
2. Click the File Sharing service in the Services list. Click the Options button.

3. On the resulting sheet, you can select which file-sharing protocols should be enabled. Click the check box next to "Share files and folders using FTP" and take note of the IP address that you should give to others so they can connect to your Mac.
4. Click Done to return to the Sharing pane.
5. Click the On check box next to File Sharing. The File Sharing services will start up. You can use the Shared Folders and Users areas on the Sharing pane to determne which users have access to which resources.

To access the FTP server, browse for the network resource or move to the FTP address via the Connect to Server dialog box. You can also use a web browser or an FTP client and use the URL `ftp://ip_address/`, where *`ip_address`* is the IP address of the machine providing FTP services (remember that the FTP URL for the machine is shown on the Options sheet when you select the File Sharing service). You will see the FTP File System Authentication dialog box (see Figure 17.12). In this dialog box, you are prompted to enter the username and password for the services you are accessing; enter the short name and the password for the user account whose Home directory you want to access and click OK.



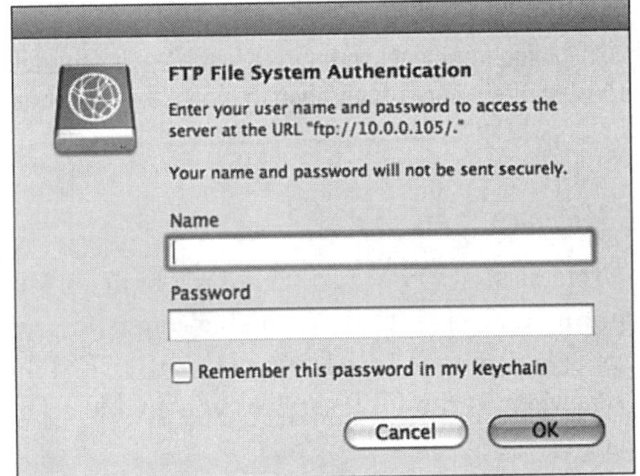


**Figure 17.12**
When you access an FTP server, you will use this dialog box to log in to that service.

If you use the Finder or a web browser to access the FTP services, a Finder window opens, the FTP server (named with its IP address) appears in the Shared section of the Places sidebar, and the folders you can access appear. You can open any accessible folders to see the files they contain. To copy a file onto your Mac, drag it from the FTP resource onto your computer.

**NOTE**

> When you use the Finder or a web browser, FTP is a one-way service. You can only copy files from the FTP server to your Mac; you can't move files from your Mac to the FTP server as you can with file sharing. For this reason, use FTP when you don't want people changing files on your Mac but only want to provide copies of files stored on your machine. If you use a dedicated FTP application, you can move files in both directions via FTP.

If you use a non-administrator account to log in to the FTP server, you have access to the entire Home directory for that user account. If you log in under an administrator account, you have wider access to files on the machine.

*If you can't access the FTP site on a machine, see "I Can't See the FTP Site" in the "Troubleshooting" section at the end of this chapter.*

*If you are initially able to enter the FTP site, but then it stops working, see "FTP Access Was Working but Now It Isn't" in the "Troubleshooting" section at the end of this chapter.*

# Using the Network Utility to Assess Your Network

The Network Utility application provides a set of tools you can use to assess the condition of communication across machines on your network as well as a set of tools that enable you to get information about various sites on your network and the Internet.

When you launch the Network Utility (Applications/Utilities), you will see a window with nine tabs, one for each service the application provides (see Figure 17.13).

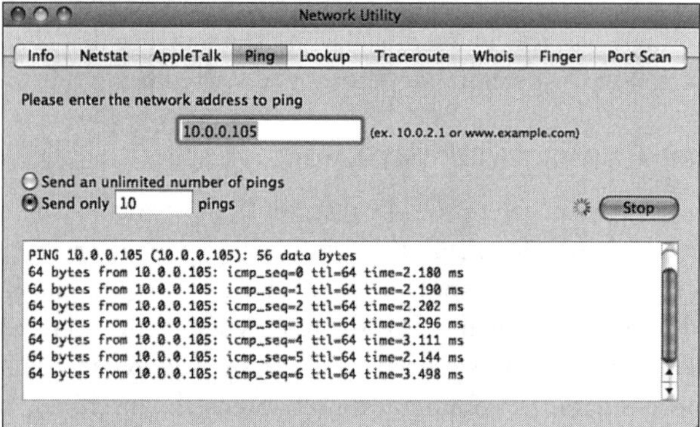


**Figure 17.13**
Ping is a useful way to test your connection to another machine (in this case, I pinged `10.0.0.105`, which is another Mac on my network).

Table 17.2 summarizes the tabs in the Network Utility application.

**Table 17.2 Tabs in the Network Utility Application**

| Tab | Function |
|---|---|
| Info | Provides information about the interface selected on the pop-up menu. For example, you can get the IP address, connection speed, connection status, and hardware information. You also see the statistics about the transfers over the selected interface. |
| Netstat | Presents various statistics about the performance of the various network protocols. To access this data, select the Netstat tab, choose one of the options by selecting a radio button, and click Netstat. The data appears in the Netstat pane. |
| AppleTalk | Provides information about active AppleTalk services on the machine. |

*continues*

Table 17.2 Continued

| Tab | Function |
|---|---|
| Ping | Contacts a specific server to assess network performance between the current Mac and a network resource. When you can't connect to a resource, ping its address to see whether your Mac can communicate with it. If the ping isn't successful, you will know that the machines are unable to communicate. If it successful, you know that the machines can communicate and the problem is related to the specific service you are trying to use. |
| Lookup | Provides various information about a specific Internet address. For example, you can enter a URL and get the IP address for that site. |
| Traceroute | Traces a specific route between machines and provides statistics about that route, such as the maximum number of hops needed. |
| Whois | Enables you to look up information about a domain or an IP address, such as to whom it is registered. |
| Finger | Reports information about a specific individual based on the person's email address. |
| Port Scan | Enables you to scan for open access ports on a specific domain or IP address. |



Covering each of these services in detail is beyond the scope of this chapter, but the next couple of examples should be helpful in getting you started using this tool.

## Checking Network Connections with Ping

Troubleshooting network problems can be difficult because identifying where the source of the problem is can be hard—for example, with the machine you are using, with the machine you are accessing, with an application, and so on. Ping is a way to check on the fundamental communication between two machines. If the ping is successful, you know that a valid communication path exists between two machines. If it isn't successful, you know that a fundamental problem exists with the communication between the machines, and this helps you know where to troubleshoot.

To ping a machine, perform the following steps:

1. Open the Network Utility application and click the Ping tab.
2. Enter the IP address or URL for the machine you want to ping.
3. Click "Send an unlimited number of pings" to send a continuous number of pings, or click "Send only ___ pings" and enter the number of pings if you want to send a specific number.
4. Click Ping.

Watch the results in the lower part of the window. You will see your machine attempt to communicate with the machine whose address you entered. If they are able to successfully communicate, you see statistics about how fast the pings are (refer to Figure 17.13). If the pings are successful, you know the communication path between the machines is valid. If not, you know you have a fundamental connection problem between the two machines.

### Tracing a Route with Traceroute

Sometimes looking at the specific route between two machines can help identify the source of problems you might be having:

1. Open the Network Utility application and click the Traceroute tab.
2. Enter the domain name or IP address to which you want to trace a route, and click Trace. The lower pane of the window will be filled with information that shows each step of the path from your machine to the one whose information you entered (see Figure 17.14).

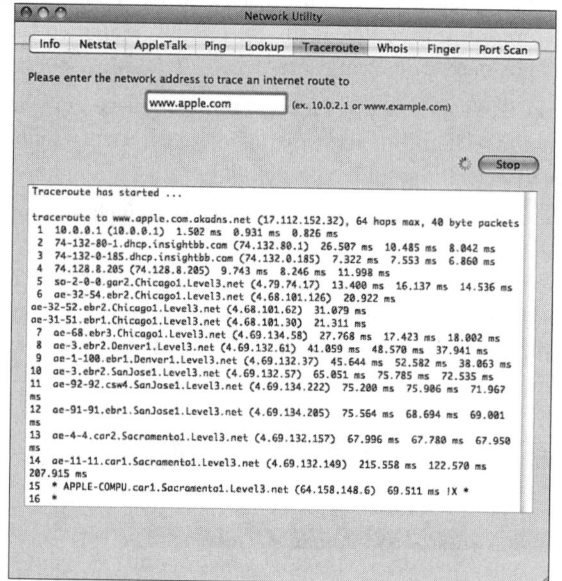


**Figure 17.14**
This Traceroute window shows the path from my machine to www.apple.com.

17

## Understanding and Setting Permissions

Access to items on your Mac OS X machine, whether from the machine directly or over a network, is determined by the access privileges set for those items. Three levels of access privilege can be set for any item; these are the following:

- Owner
- Group
- Others

The owner is the owner of the item. When you are the owner of an item, this will be your short username followed by "(Me)."

17

The group is a set of users. By default, Mac OS X includes several groups for which various permissions are assigned to different volumes and directories. Many of these default groups look odd, and some are even nonexistent (for example, in certain places, you will see Members of group “”). You can also create your own groups and place users in those groups to provide access to a collection of people.

⇨ To learn about creating user groups, **see** “Creating Groups of Users,” **p. 250**.

Others include those users who are neither the owners nor members of a group.

For any object, there are four levels of access that can be assigned to people or groups:

- **Read & Write**—This is the broadest level of access and lets the user to whom it is assigned read and write to the item to which it is assigned.
- **Read only**—This privilege lets a user see items in a directory but not change them. For example, if a user has read-only access to a folder, he can copy its files, but he can’t change the files stored in that folder. If this permission is applied to a file, the user can open the file, but not make any changes to it.
- **Write only (Drop Box)**—With this access, a user can place items in a directory but can’t see the contents of that directory. By default, each user has a Drop Box folder in the Public folder in her Home folder.
- **No Access**—The user can’t do anything with the item, including seeing it.

If you open the Info window for an item and expand the Ownership & Permissions area, the current access permissions for the item will be shown. For example, Figure 17.15 shows the Permissions information for a document, whereas Figure 17.16 shows similar information for the current startup volume.

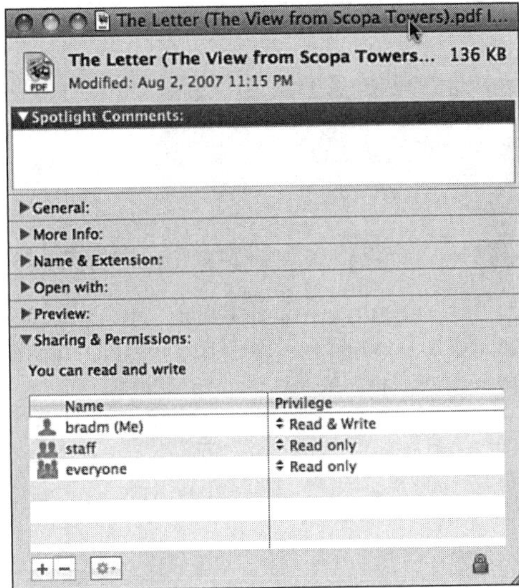


**Figure 17.15**
This Info window for a document shows that the user account bradm has Read & Write access to it, but so do others.

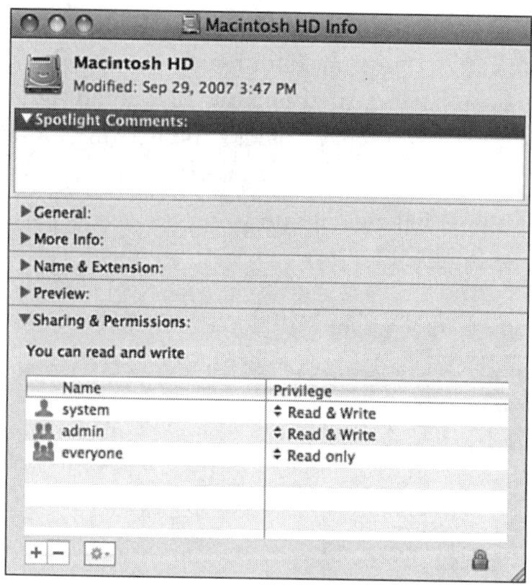


**Figure 17.16**
This Info window for the current startup volume shows that only the root account (system) and administrator account (admin) have Read & Write access while others only have Read-only access.



There are several things you need to know about the Ownership & Permissions information shown in the Info window.

First, unless you are logged in under the root or administrator account, you can't use the pop-up menus to change the permissions assigned to items on the Mac OS X startup volume above the current user's Home directory. However, when you open the Ownership & Permissions area of the Info window for an item on another volume or within a user's Home directory, the pop-up menus become active and you can use them to change the privileges for the items that folder contains. You can select the user or group on the pop-up menu in the Name column and set the privilege for that user or group using the pop-up menu in the Privilege column.

You can add more users or groups to the list, or remove users or groups from the list, using the Add (plus) or Remove (minus) buttons at the bottom of the Info window.

Second, the groups you see in the Info window are default groups created when you install Mac OS X. The user accounts that are members of these groups can access the item with the group's privileges. You can use the Accounts pane of the System Preferences application to create and manage user groups.

To configure access privileges for most items, you need to either be logged in as an administrator or authenticate yourself in the Info window.

To set the access privileges for any item, perform the following steps:

1. Log in under an administrator account or the root account.
2. Select the item for which you want to set permissions and press ⌘-I.
3. Expand the Ownership & Permissions section in the Info window.
4. If you are the owner of the item, use Privilege pop-up menu to set your access to the item.

5. If you click the Add button at the bottom of the Name column, you see the People tool. This tool presents all the contact information in your Address Book along with all the user accounts and groups you have created on your Mac. Find the user with which you want to share the item, select it, and click Select. The person you selected will be shown on the user list and you can configure the user's permission.
6. Use the pop-up menu in the Privilege column to set the access permission for the user or group you selected (see Figure 17.17).

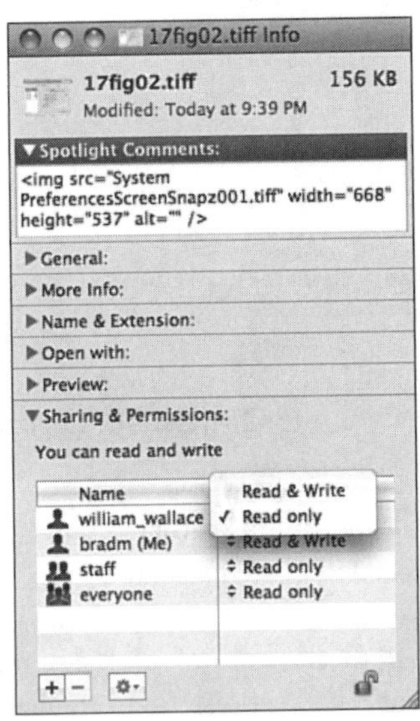


**Figure 17.17**
Use the pop-up menus in the Ownership and Permissions section of the Info window to set access permission for people and user groups.

7. To add additional users or groups, click the Add button (the plus sign). Then choose the user or group and select the access permission.
8. To remove a user or group from the list, select it and click the Remove button (the minus sign).
9. Continue adding, configuring, and removing users and permissions until you have configured all the permissions for the item.

Under Mac OS X, you can open multiple Info windows at the same time. This is a handy way to compare and contrast the permissions provided for different items.

## TROUBLESHOOTING

### I CAN'T ACCESS A SERVER

*When I try to browse for a server, I can't see the resource I am trying to access. Or, when I access a specific address via the Connect to Server command, the connection is never made because the process quits or the Connect to Server dialog box never appears.*

First, make sure that the network resource you are trying to access is available. Go to that machine; ensure it is running; and check its Sharing pane to make sure the services, such as file sharing, are turned on. Check the machine's network connections to ensure it is communicating successfully with the network. For example, check its Internet connection or access a network printer.

Second, if you are trying to browse for the machine and it is properly configured and communicating with the network, ensure it supports Bonjour—it must be running Mac OS X version 10.2 or later to do so. If not, you need to access it via its address. If you are trying to access the machine via the address for a specific service, check the address you need to access to ensure you are using the correct one.

Third, go back to the machine on which you are attempting to access the network resources and make sure its network connections are active, such as by accessing the Internet.

Fourth, if you can't find a Bonjour-enabled computer by browsing, access it via its address. If you are accessing the network resource via its address, be sure you are using the correct address for the service you are trying to access. For example, make sure you are using the File Sharing address if that is the service you are attempting to use.

#### I Can't See the FTP Site

*When I try to move to the FTP site, I get a connection refused or site not found error.*

First, check whether any TCP/IP services are working. Turn on web sharing for the machine you are attempting to use for FTP. If you can successfully connect to its website, a problem exists with the FTP services themselves. If you can't successfully connect, you have a network problem.

If the problem is related to the FTP service, make sure you don't have a firewall installed that blocks FTP services. Also, try shutting down the FTP machine and then starting it up again.

#### FTP Access Was Working, but Now It Isn't

*I have successfully accessed FTP services on a machine before, but now it isn't working.*

If you are using a web browser to access the FTP site, quit the browser, restart it, and try again.

If several unsuccessful logins to an FTP service have been attempted, subsequent logins will be denied. When this happens, restart the machine providing the FTP services.

## Mac OS X to the Max: Networking Mac OS X with Windows Computers

Because support for Windows and Unix file-sharing protocols is built in to Mac OS X, using a Mac on a Windows or Unix network is easy. It is simple to add a Windows computer to a Mac-based network.

## SHARING FILES WITH WINDOWS COMPUTERS

You can use Mac OS X to access files provided on a Windows computer on your network via the SMB protocol without doing any additional configuration. To use files provided on a Windows or Unix network that uses SMB, perform the following steps:

1. Connect your Mac OS X machine to the network.
2. Open the Connect to Server dialog box and click Browse. Depending on the SMB servers on your network and how the network is configured, the SMB servers might or might not appear in the list of available servers when you browse the network, so you might have to enter the server address manually.
3. If you don't see the SMB server to which you want to connect, enter the address of the server to which you want to connect; the form of the address is `smb://`*`ServerName`*`/`*`ShareName`*`/`. *`ServerName`* is the IP address for the Windows machine you are attempting to access, and *`ShareName`* is the name of the item being shared with you, such as a volume or folder.

17

**TIP**

> To determine the IP address (*`ServerName`*) for a Windows machine, open the Command Prompt window, type **`ipconfig`**, and press Enter. The IP address of the Windows machine will be shown.

4. Click Connect. You are prompted to enter your workgroup/domain, username, and password for that server.
5. Enter the required information and click OK. You are logged in to the shared resource and can use the files it contains just like a Mac that is acting as a file server.

**NOTE**

> Connecting to Windows computers can be problematic depending on the specific network you are using. If the preceding steps don't enable you to connect to a Windows computer, try using the Apple support document located at the following address: http://docs.info.apple.com/article.html?artnum=106660.

To enable Windows users to access files stored on your Mac, carry out the following steps:

1. Open the Sharing pane of the System Preferences application.
2. Click the File Sharing service in the Services list. Click the Options button.
3. On the resulting sheet, you can select which file sharing protocols should be enabled. Click the check box next to "Share files and folders using SMB."
4. You must enable a user account for Windows sharing to be accessed from a Windows computer. Check the On check box for a user account that you want to be accessible from a Windows computer. A password sheet appears.
5. Enter the password for the account and click OK.

6. Repeat steps 4 and 5 for each account you want to enable.
7. When you have finished enabling accounts, click Done to return to the Sharing pane of the System Preferences application. Take note of the IP address to provide to users so they can access your Mac from their Windows computer.
8. Provide the user account, password, and address to the Windows users you want to be able to log in.

A Windows user can use the URL, username, and password you provided to log in to your Mac to share files just like Macs on your network (see Figure 17.18).

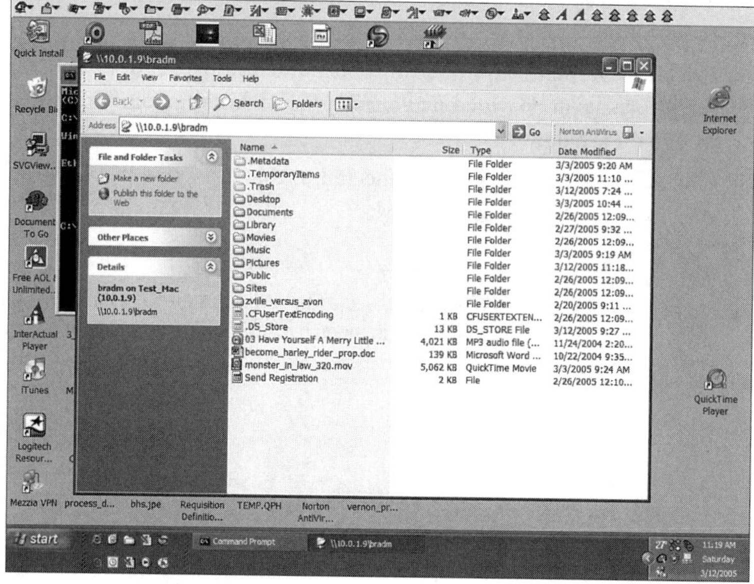


**Figure 17.18**
This Mac OS X folder is being accessed from a Windows XP computer.



## ACCESSING VIRTUAL PRIVATE NETWORKS

Virtual Private Network (VPN) service enables networked computers to access file servers, email servers, and other network resources over a WAN connection just like machines connected via a LAN can. Using Mac OS X, you can connect a Mac to a VPN. To access a VPN, perform the following steps:

**NOTE**

> Before you will be able to access a VPN, you'll need to talk to that network's administrator to get all the information you will need such as connection method, address, username, password, and so on.

1. Open the Network pane of the System Preferences application.
2. Click the plus sign to add a service at the bottom of the Services list.

3. On the resulting sheet, select VPN from the Interface pop-up menu. When you do, you will be presented with two additional pop-up menus to work with.
4. Use the VPN Type pop-up menu to specify which VPN protocol to use. Your network administrator should specify which to use. L2TP over IPSec is more secure.
5. Enter a name for the service. This name will appear in the Services list on the Network pane.
6. Click the Create button. You will return to the Services list and the new VPN service will be selected.
7. Enter a server address. This can be in the form or a URL or an IP address.
8. You may need to enter an account name. Some VPN servers that you might connect to require this.
9. Click the Authentication Settings button to configure how you login to the VPN. Use the information provided by your network admin to configure this sheet. Click OK when you are done.
10. Click Connect. You will be connected to the VPN and should be able to access the resources on the remote network.



**TIP**

> If you use VPN regularly, add the VPN status menu to the Finder menu bar by checking the "Show VPN status in menu bar" check box in the Internet Connect window.

CHAPTER 18

# Creating and Managing AirPort Wireless Networks

## In this chapter

# AirPort Wireless Networking

AirPort is an amazing technology that makes wireless networking affordable and simple to install and configure. Wireless networking offers many benefits over a wired network, the most important of which is that you don't need to physically connect devices to be able to include them on a network. It's also easy to connect a wireless network to a wired one so you can have the best of both.

**NOTE**

> AirPort is Apple's name for its implementation of IEEE 802.11a/b/g/n wireless standards, which are also the standards for Windows computers and other devices. That's good news because it means that AirPort devices are compatible with any networks or devices that implement these standards. So, you can use non-Apple devices on AirPort networks and use AirPort-equipped Macs on non-AirPort networks as long as those networks comply with the 802.11 standards, which almost all do.

With AirPort, you can quickly and easily set up and manage a wireless network to do the following tasks:

18

- **Connect to the Net**—You can use AirPort to connect to the Internet wirelessly, and you can easily share a single Internet connection among multiple Macs and Windows PCs on the network. An AirPort base station also protects your network from attack via Network Address Translation (NAT) technology.
- **Create or connect to a wired network**—Through a base station, you can connect an AirPort-equipped Mac to an Ethernet (wired) network. With an AirPort Extreme Base Station, you can connect Ethernet devices to it directly to create a wired network along with the wireless one.
- **Share a USB printer**—You can connect a USB printer directly to an AirPort base station to share that printer with AirPort devices.
- **Share a hard drive**—With an AirPort Extreme Base Station, you can share a USB hard drive across a wireless and wired network, easily creating a shared file space among all the devices on the network. This is especially useful for backing up multiple computers on the same hard drive.
- **Connect directly to other AirPort-equipped computers**—You can directly network to one or more AirPort-equipped computers. As long as all the computers are set up to use the same AirPort connection, they can communicate with each other making instant, temporary networks fast and easy.

**NOTE**

> For more detailed information about wireless networks, see my book *Mac User's Guide to Living Wirelessly*.

AirPort functionality is provided through the following components:

- **AirPort-ready Macs**—If your Mac is AirPort ready, it has built-in antennas that are used to transmit and receive signals to and from the wireless network. It also has a slot in which you can install an AirPort card. The good news is that all modern Macs are AirPort compatible and most include an AirPort card as standard equipment.
- **AirPort card**—To use AirPort, your Mac must have an AirPort card installed in it. If your Mac doesn't have a card, you can add one inexpensively because AirPort Extreme cards cost only about $49. AirPort cards are simple to install yourself, or you can order one as an option when you purchase a new Mac. AirPort cards are standard on most current Macs.
- **AirPort software**—The AirPort software is necessary for Macs to communicate through the AirPort hardware. The software to configure and use an AirPort network is part of the standard Mac OS X installation.
- **AirPort base station**—An AirPort base station transmits the signals for the AirPort network. There are three basic types of base stations. The AirPort Extreme Base Station is a dedicated hardware device that contains ports for a cable or DSL modem, USB printer or hard drive, and up to three Ethernet devices. Another option is an AirPort Express Base Station, which performs a similar function to the full-size base station but doesn't offer as many features (for example, it has only one Ethernet port to which you connect a cable or DSL modem or a single Ethernet device). You can also configure any AirPort-equipped Mac to act as a base station by using Mac OS X's built-in Internet sharing capabilities.



**NOTE**

Functionally, an AirPort Extreme or AirPort Express Base Station and an AirPort-equipped Mac OS X machine sharing its Internet connection are identical from the perspective of providing an Internet connection (although using a dedicated base station offers many benefits). In this chapter, when I use the term *base station*, it can refer to any of these means of providing an AirPort network. When referring to a specific base station, I'll use the full name, such as AirPort Express Base Station.

The general steps to create and manage an AirPort network are the following:

1. Design your network.

⇨ For help with designing a network, **see** "Designing a Network," **p. 363**.

2. Obtain, install, and configure the base station you'll use for the wireless part of the network.
3. Configure AirPort-equipped Macs and other wireless devices to use the AirPort network.
4. Configure the services provided on the network, such as file sharing.

An AirPort network provides access to a similar set of services that a wired network does, and the two networks can work together seamlessly. For example, computers connected to a wired network via AirPort can print to printers connected to the base station, use file sharing with Macs connected to the network wirelessly, and so on. If you connect a USB printer to an AirPort Extreme or Express Base Station, you can share that printer with any AirPort-equipped Mac. If you connect a USB hard drive to the USB port on an AirPort Extreme Base Station, you can share that drive with all the computers on the network, whether they connect via a wire or wirelessly.

⇨ To learn how to configure network services over a network, **see** "Configuring the Services on a Network," **p. 369**.

Before getting into the meat of this chapter, there are a few AirPort tidbits you need to understand.

Like Ethernet, there are several flavors of AirPort. There are a number of technical differences between these types, but the most import one is communication speed.

AirPort was the original incarnation and offered many wireless benefits. AirPort communicates at 11Mbps and is compatible with wireless devices based on the 802.11b standard. AirPort is no longer supported by modern Macs, which support AirPort Extreme instead (that's a good thing). However, modern AirPort technologies are backward compatible, so you can connect an AirPort Mac to a network using one of the newer standards and still enjoy its benefits (at a lower speed than the other types, but it works well enough).

AirPort Extreme is the newer standard and offers even more benefits. First, is speed. AirPort Extreme communicates at 54Mbps, which is almost five times the speed at which the original AirPort communicates. AirPort Extreme is compatible with devices using the 802.11g Wi-Fi standard. Second, AirPort Extreme can support more computers at the same time than does AirPort. Third, AirPort Extreme enables you to share a USB printer or hard drive from an AirPort Extreme Base Station. Fourth, with AirPort Extreme, you can wirelessly link base stations together to expand the range of an AirPort network to cover large areas.

The newest standard is also called AirPort Extreme, but supports the 802.11n specification, which is up to five times faster than 802.11g networks. The newest AirPort Extreme Base Station also has a much larger range than previous models, which is also good news.

Mac OS X supports all flavors of AirPort, but specific Mac models support either AirPort or one of the AirPort Extreme versions; in other words, older Macs can support an AirPort card, whereas all modern Macs support AirPort Extreme cards. The two cards are not interchangeable. To find out which flavor your Mac supports, check its documentation. All shipping Macs support AirPort Extreme.

Fortunately, even though the hardware for the two standards is different, it is compatible. AirPort machines can connect to AirPort Extreme networks, and vice versa. The primary difference is that AirPort networks are much slower than AirPort Extreme networks are. And, AirPort Extreme Base Stations offer more features than AirPort Base Stations do.

Because it is the newer standard, this chapter focuses mostly on AirPort Extreme. I do my best to use the term *AirPort Extreme* when discussing something that is specific to AirPort Extreme technology or *AirPort Standard* when referring to the older technology. When I use the term *AirPort*, I mean to refer to something that is applicable to both technologies.

**NOTE**

> Because it is based on the 802.11 standards, AirPort is compatible with 802.11 networks and devices. For example, you can connect an AirPort-equipped Mac to any wireless network that supports 802.11b, 802.11g, or 802.11n devices, such as those designed for Windows computers. Similarly, Windows machines equipped with 802.11b, 802.11g, or 802.11n devices can also access an AirPort network.

# SETTING UP AN AIRPORT BASE STATION

Setting up an AirPort base station is slightly different depending on the type of base station you use: an AirPort Extreme or Express Base Station or an AirPort-equipped Mac OS X machine that provides Internet sharing.

There are many benefits to using an AirPort Extreme or Express Base Station to provide a wireless network. One is that they don't place any processing load on an individual Mac and are intended to run at all times, so the AirPort network is always available. They also provide the ability to share an Internet connection with devices to which they are networked using an Ethernet connection. One of the most important benefits of a base station is that it can shield your network from attack using Network Address Translation. The disadvantage of this device is its cost (currently $159 for an AirPort Extreme Base Station and $99 for an Express Base Station).

18

⇨ To learn about when and how to use an AirPort Express Base Station, **see** "Working with an AirPort Express Base Station," **p. 418**.

The benefit of using an AirPort-equipped Mac OS X machine as a base station is that you don't need to purchase any additional hardware (except for the AirPort card in the Mac that will act as the base station if it doesn't already have one). You get most of the functionality from an AirPort base station but don't have to support another dedicated device. Using this method does have several disadvantages, though. One is that it places additional processing load on the machine that acts as the base station. Another is that the network can be affected by the state of that machine. For example, if the machine is shut down or crashes, the network is taken down as well. Another is that a Mac acting as a base station doesn't support all the base station's features, such as the option to wirelessly link base stations together to increase the range of a network. Using an AirPort-equipped Mac isn't as secure as using a dedicated AirPort base station either.

**NOTE**

> You can have multiple base stations operating in the same area at the same time to grow your AirPort network to be quite large.

## SETTING UP AN AIRPORT EXTREME BASE STATION

Apple's AirPort Extreme Base Station is a relatively simple device. It contains a transmitter that broadcasts the signal over which the network is provided. It has four Ethernet ports. One, the WAN port, is used to connect to a broadband Internet connection, such as a cable modem. The other three are used to connect to a wired Ethernet network or to Ethernet-equipped devices so the base station can also share its Internet and network connection with the devices connected to it via a network or directly to one of its Ethernet ports. Along with the power adapter port, it offers a USB port to which you can connect a USB printer or USB hard drive to share one of those devices with the network.

Setting up an AirPort Extreme Base Station consists of the following two tasks:

1. Install the base station.
2. Configure the AirPort network, including the Internet connection the base station will use to connect to the Internet.

### INSTALLING THE BASE STATION

First, locate the device in a central area so it provides the maximum amount of coverage where you install it. In most houses, the AirPort Extreme Base Station provides adequate signal strength even if you locate it at one end of the house and place machines you want to network at the other end. However, the closer the machines are to the base station, the stronger the signal is.



Of course, a major consideration for the location of the base station is where your Internet connection will come from. If you use a cable modem, you need to locate the device so that you can connect the cable modem to it. If you use a DSL modem, you need to locate the base station relatively close to the phone line port to which the DSL modem is attached.

After you have placed the base station in its location, attach its power adapter to the station and plug it in to a wall outlet. Use an Ethernet cable to connect the cable or DSL modem to the WAN (Wide Area Network) Ethernet port.

You can connect an Ethernet device to each of the three LAN Ethernet ports on the base station. For example, you can connect a network printer, a computer, or to add more than three devices, connect one of the ports to an Ethernet hub.

If you want to share a USB printer with all Macs that can access the network, connect the printer's USB cable to the USB port on the base station. Likewise, you can connect a USB hard drive to the base station's USB port to share that drive on the network.

### CONFIGURING THE BASE STATION

After you have installed the base station, you need to configure it. You can configure it manually through the AirPort Utility, or you can use the guided approach. With either method, you configure the base station from a machine with which it can communicate either via AirPort or through an Ethernet network.

**NOTE**

> The machine you use to configure a base station must be AirPort-capable to be able to configure the base station wirelessly. It does not need to have an AirPort card if it is connected to the base station via Ethernet.

### CONFIGURING THE BASE STATION USING THE GUIDED APPROACH

Use the following steps to configure the base station using the guided approach:

**NOTE**

> The specific steps you use to configure a base station with the AirPort Utility depend on what you are doing. For example, you see different options when configuring a base station for the first time than you do when you are reconfiguring a base station. These steps provide an example of reconfiguring an existing base station, but the steps to configure a new one are similar, just in a slightly different order and differences in minor details.

1. Open the AirPort Admin application (Applications/Utilities) to see the first window, which shows all the base stations with which the Mac can communicate (see Figure 18.1).



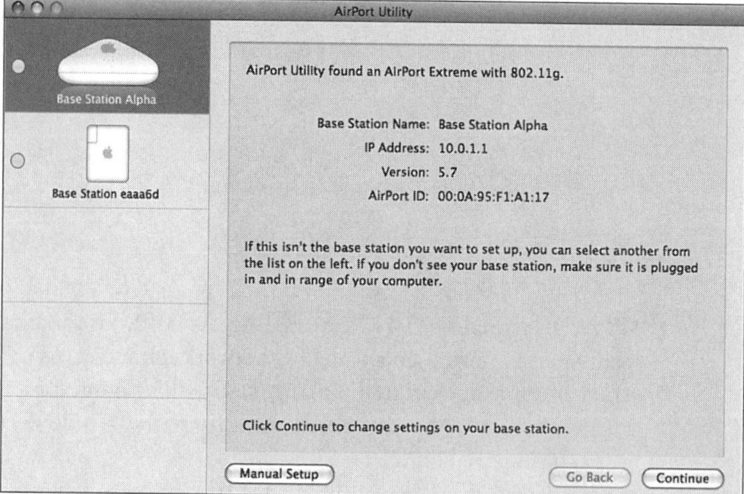


**Figure 18.1**
Use the AirPort Utility application to configure AirPort base stations.

**CAUTION**

> If you are configuring a base station that has already been configured and is protected by a password, you have to enter that password before you can proceed.
>
> If the base station you are configuring has outdated software installed on it, the AirPort Utility application attempts to update it. To do so, you must be able to connect to the Internet, which is sort of a Catch-22 in that it assumes that it is already configured and you are reconfiguring it. You can download the update to the Mac you are going to use to configure the base station and then the base station can update its software from there.

2. Select the base station that you want to configure.
3. Click Continue.
4. Click the “Create a new wireless network” radio button and click Continue.
5. Enter the name for the wireless network you are creating. This is the name that you’ll select to join a machine to the network.
6. Enter the name of the base station. This simply identifies the base station for configuration purposes.
7. Click Continue.
8. Choose the level of security for the wireless network. You have the following options (see Figure 18.2):

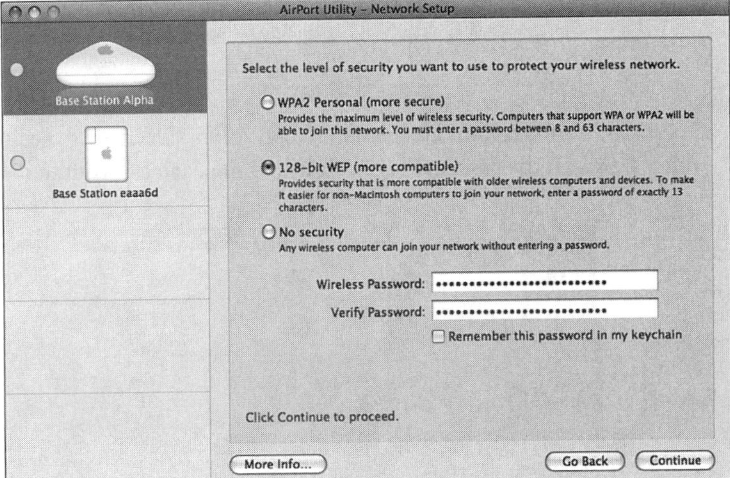


**Figure 18.2**
You should use WPA2 or WEP security on an AirPort network.



- **WPA2 Personal**—Wi-Fi Protected Access (WPA) is the most secure encryption technique supported on an AirPort network. However, using WPA2 can limit the access of some devices to the network. Use this option for a network that includes only Macintosh computers unless you’re sure the Windows computers you connect can support WPA2.
- **WEP**—Wired Equivalent Privacy (WEP) is an encryption strategy that attempts to provide wireless networks with the same level of protection that wired networks have. This option provides a good level of security, while being more compatible with Windows and other devices. For networks that include older Macs or Windows computers, choose this option.
- **No security**—If you select this option, your network won’t be secured and anyone within range can join it without a password. You should never use this option unless you are very sure no one whom you don’t know about will be able to access your network. This option leaves your network, and all the devices connected to it, vulnerable to attack.

After you select an option, the controls in the sheet change to reflect the option you select. For example, if you choose WEP, you see two password fields and the strength pop-up menu.

9. Enter the network password in the Wireless Password and Verify Password fields, unless you selected No security, in which case you don't enter a password.

**TIP**

> Various types and versions of other operating systems support specific kinds of security and can require passwords to be of specific lengths. When you create a password for a network that includes computers running different operating systems, you need to make sure the password you create is compatible. For example, if you connect a computer running Windows XP SP2 to an AirPort network using 128 bit WEP security, create a password that is exactly 13 characters. Fortunately, on Macs and Windows machines, the password can be remembered so you don't need to enter it each time you connect to the network.

10. Check the "Remember this password in my keychain" check box.
11. Click Continue.
12. Configure the base station for Internet access. The information you enter should be exactly the same as you use to connect a Mac to the Internet. In most cases you'll choose the "I connect to the Internet with a DSL or cable modem using DHCP" radio button. If you use another technology, click "I do not use DHCP" and follow the onscreen instructions.

⇨ To learn how to configure a Mac for the Internet, **see** Chapter 16, "Connecting a Mac to the Internet," **p. 335**.

13. Click Continue.
14. Enter the password that will be required to change the base station's settings in the Base Station Password and Verify Password fields. This should be different from the network password you created in step 10.
15. Check the "Remember this password in my keychain" check box (see Figure 18.3).
16. Click Continue. You see the Summary screen that shows the information that will be used to configure the base station (see Figure 18.4).
17. Review the information shown. If it's not correct, click Go Back and use the previous screens to correct it.
18. When you're ready to configure the base station, click Update. The base station is configured according to the settings you entered. When the process is complete, the base station restarts and the network is available for use.

*If you see an error message stating that the required AirPort hardware was not found when you started the AirPort Setup Assistant, see "No AirPort Hardware Is Found" in the "Troubleshooting" section at the end of this chapter.*

*If you can't access the base station because you don't know the password, see "I Don't Know the Base Station Password" in the "Troubleshooting" section at the end of this chapter.*

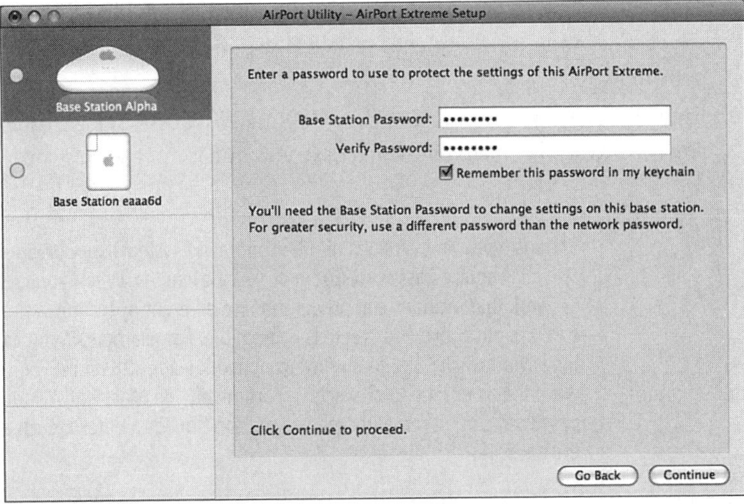


**Figure 18.3**
Enter a password that will be required to change the base station's settings.

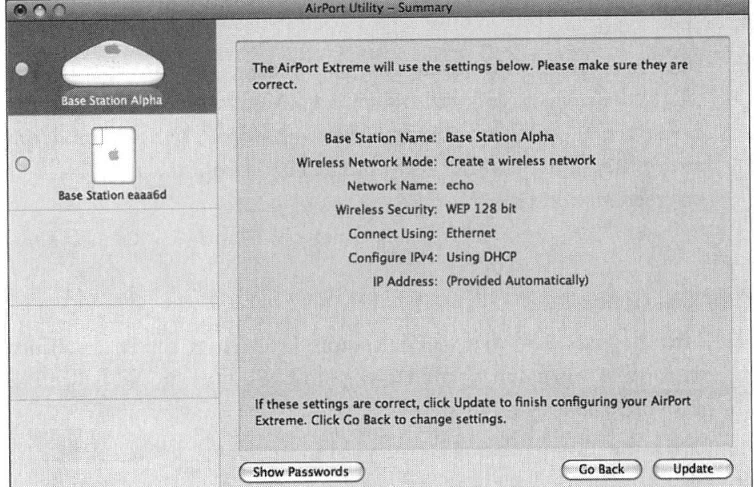


**Figure 18.4**
The Summary screen shows how the base station will be configured when you click Update.



## CONFIGURING A BASE STATION MANUALLY

You should also know how to manually configure the base station. Manual configuration can be a better and more complete way to configure a base station, and there are some options you can configure only using the manual technique. If you want to change only one aspect of a base station's configuration, using the manual method is also the way to go. And, it can also be a faster way to configure a base station. For example, you need to manually configure a base station when you want to share an Internet account with other machines on an Ethernet network or to use the AirPort base station as a bridge between the wireless network and a wired one (for example, to allow AirPort-equipped machines to use a printer connected to a wired network). You also use the AirPort Utility application to configure a base station manually by performing the following steps:

1. Open the AirPort Utility (Applications/Utilities). You see all the base stations currently in range of the Mac you are using, whether they can communicate wirelessly or over an Ethernet connection.
2. Select the base station you want to configure and click Manual Setup (if there is only one base station in range, it is selected automatically).

*If you get an error message when trying to configure your base station manually, see "I Can't Configure My Base Station Manually" in the "Troubleshooting" section at the end of this chapter.*

3. If the base station has been reset, you see a dialog box informing you that the base station has been reset and is not currently configured. (If the base station has not been reset, you won't have to do this step.) Click Automatic and then authenticate yourself using an administrator name and password. The software reconfigures the base station and restarts it. When it is complete, you return to the Select Base Station window. Click Manual Setup again.

**NOTE**

When you have problems with a base station, sometimes you must reset it so that it returns to its default settings (in effect, you start over).

If new AirPort firmware is available, the application will prompt you to do download and install it. Do so and your base station's firmware will be updated and it will be restarted. You return to the Select Base Station window. Select the base station again and click Manual Setup.

You next see a window that has the base station name as its title that includes several tabs; some tabs also have subtabs (see Figure 18.5).

18

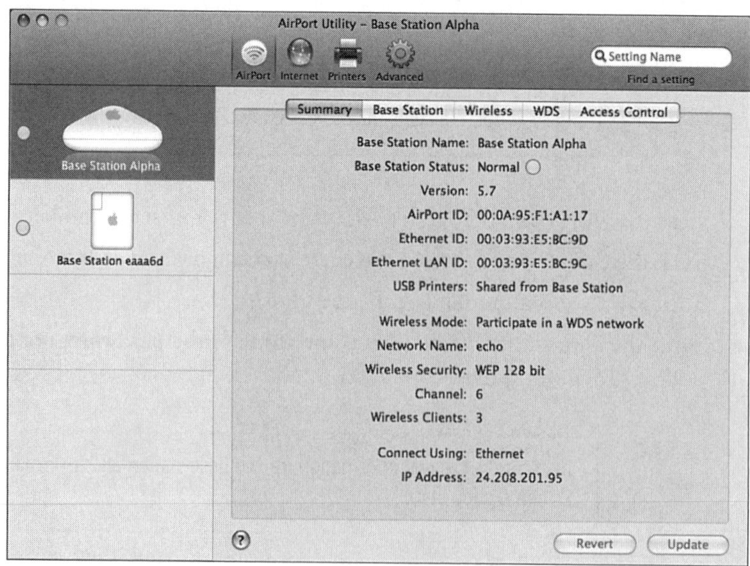


**Figure 18.5**
This Manual Setup mode enables you to configure all aspects of a base station.

In the manual mode, the AirPort Utility has the following tabs:

**NOTE**

> The tabs you see depend on the type of base station you are configuring. For example, an Extreme Base Station has different options than does an Express Base Station. For example, an Express Base station has the Music tab that you can use to configure music broadcast from iTunes. The rest of this information reflects an AirPort Extreme Base Station.

- **AirPort**—Use this tab to configure various aspects of the AirPort network, such as the base station name, network name, and expanding the range of a network with WDS.
- **Internet**—With this tab, you determine how the base station connects to the Internet and how it distributes addresses to the other devices on the network.
- **Music**—On this tab (AirPort Express Base Station only), you configure AirTunes services to broadcast iTunes music to speakers connected to the base station.
- **Printers**—On this tab, you configure a printer attached to the base station.
- **Disks**—On this tab, you configure a hard disk attached to the base station.
- **Advanced**—Although you are unlikely to need to use this tab, you should know in general what is does, which is to enable you to create logs to store messages that can be helpful in diagnosing network problems. You can also configure specific ports on the base station to provide access to devices outside the network. On the third subtab, you can configure PPP dial-in accounts.



Covering all these options is beyond the scope of this chapter, but the following steps demonstrate how to configure some of the most common settings.

**NOTE**

> These steps assume that the base station you are configuring has been configured previously. If not, the steps might be slightly different.

1. Select the AirPort tab if it isn't selected already. You see a number of subtabs.
2. Click the Summary tab to see the current configuration of the AirPort network.
3. Click the Base Station tab (see Figure 18.6).
4. Enter the base station name (this is the name of the hardware, not the name of the network it provides) in the Name field.

**TIP**

> To enter the contact information for the base station and its location, click the Base Station Options tab.

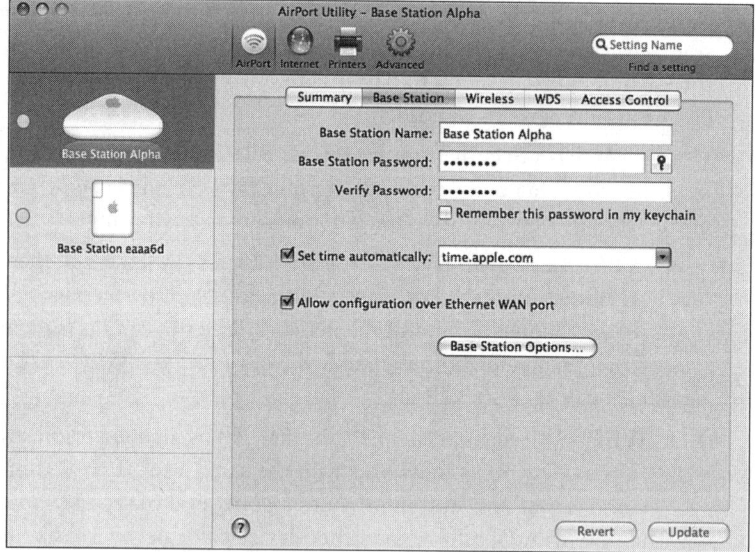


**Figure 18.6**
Use the Base Station tab to configure the base station name, password, time server, and whether it can be configured via Ethernet.

5. To change the base station's password (not the network's password), use the Base Station Password and Verify Password fields and check the "Remember this password in my keychain" check box.
6. To have the base station's time set automatically, check the "Set time automatically" check box and choose the timer server on the pop-up menu.
7. To allow the base station to be configured over its Ethernet WAN connection, check the "Allow configuration over Ethernet WAN port" check box.
8. Click the Wireless tab. On this tab, you configure the wireless network being provided by the base station.
9. Use the Wireless Mode pop-up menu to determine whether the base station is part of a WDS network.
10. Enter the network name in the Network Name field.

**NOTE**

> If the base station is already providing a network and you change the name or password of the network, people who use the network need to change the network they use. The new network name appears as an available network on the client machines, but you must provide the new password to those whom you want to use the network.

11. Use the Radio Mode pop-up menu to determine the specific standards supported on the network, such as 802.11b/g compatible.
12. Use the Channel pop-up menu to select the channel over which the base station communicates. Generally, the default channel works fine, but if you are having trouble

communicating with devices, you can try different channels to improve signal transmission and reception. If you have multiple AirPort networks in the same area, you can use the Channel pop-up menu to have each network use a different channel so that they don't interfere with one another.

13. Use the Wireless Security pop-up menu, Wireless Password field, the Verify Password field, and the "Remember this password in my keychain" check box to set the security of the wireless network. The basic options are the following:
    - **WPA2 Personal**—Wi-Fi Protected Access (WPA) is the most secure encryption technique supported on an AirPort network. However, using WPA2 can limit the access of some devices to the network. Use this option for a network that includes only Macintosh computers unless you're sure the Windows computers you connect can support WPA2.
    - **WEP**—Wired Equivalent Privacy (WEP) is an encryption strategy that attempts to provide wireless networks with the same level of protection that wired networks have. This option provides a good level of security, while being more compatible with Windows and other devices. For networks that include older Macs or Windows computers, choose this option.
    - **No security**—If you select this option, your network won't be secured and anyone within range can join it without a password. You should never use this option unless you are very sure no one whom you don't know about will be able to access your network. This option leaves your network, and all the devices connected to it, vulnerable to attack.

18

**NOTE**

> For WEP and WPA, you have two additional options when configuring security manually. You can choose a lower level (40 bit) of WEP security and also have the WPA/WPA2 Personal option.

14. Click the Wireless Options button. The Wireless Options sheet appears (see Figure 18.7).
15. Use the Multicast Rate pop-up menu to set the multicast rate. Choosing a higher value improves performance but also reduces range.
16. Use the Transmit Power pop-up menu to change the strength of the base station's signal. If many base stations exist in the same physical area, reduce the signal strength to limit the interference of these stations with one another. You can also reduce the strength to limit the size of the AirPort network's coverage, such as if the base station is in a small space and you don't want to extend the network past that space.
17. If you want to create a closed network, check the "Create a closed network" check box. A closed network does not appear on other users' AirPort menus. To join closed networks, users have to know the name and password for that network (because they can't see the network on a menu). Using a closed network is a good way to keep your network more secure.

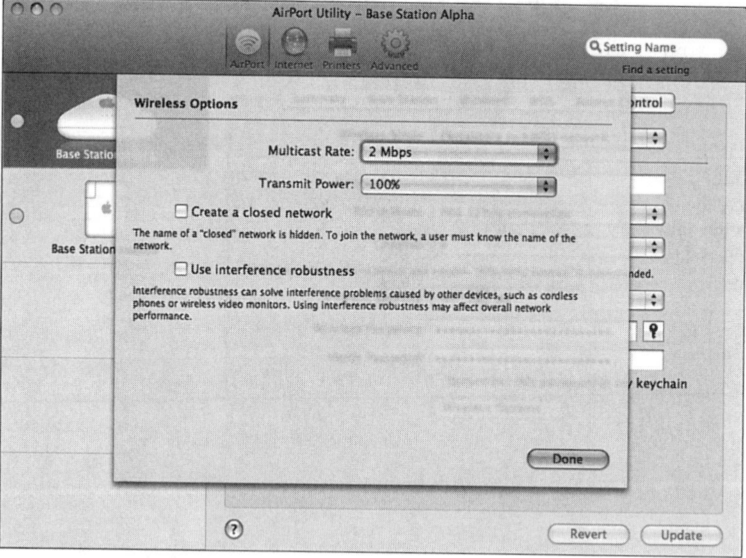


**Figure 18.7** Wireless Options include transmission power and a closed network.

18. Use the "Use interference robustness" check box to make the AirPort signal less sensitive to interference.
19. Click OK to save your changes and return to the Wireless tab.

⇨ To learn how to configure WDS, **see** "Making AirPort Go Farther," **p. 417**.

20. Click the Internet tab and then the Internet Connection subtab.
21. Configure the base station for Internet access. This works similarly to configuring a Mac for Internet access. Choose the connection method from the Connect Using pop-up menu and then enter the settings you want to use in the lower part of the window. For example, if the Internet connection is provided via a cable or DSL modem using DHCP, choose Ethernet on the Connect Using pop-up menu and Using DHCP on the Configure pop-up menu. Enter the domain name in the Domain name field and a client ID if required.

⇨ To learn how to configure a Mac for the Internet, **see** Chapter 16, "Connecting a Mac to the Internet," **p. 335**.

**NOTE**

> One additional control available for a base station's Internet access that is not present for a Mac is the WAN Ethernet Port pop-up menu. Use this menu to set the speed at which the base station communicates with a wired network over its WAN port. In most cases, the Automatic (Default) value is the best choice, but you can choose a specific speed.

22. Click the DHCP subtab to control how the base station provides IP addresses to the network (see Figure 18.8). Use the DHCP Range pop-up menu and field to select the base configuration of IP addresses. If you want to use a specific set of IP addresses,

enter the starting and ending IP numbers you want to assign. As machines connect to your network, these IP addresses are assigned to each machine that connects (you have to have enough addresses in the range so one is available for each machine).

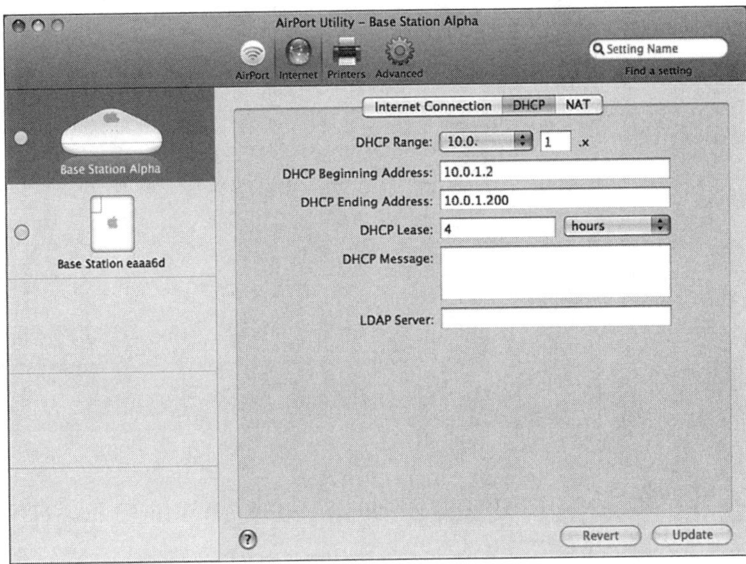


**Figure 18.8**
Use the DHCP subtab to configure the IP addresses the base station provides to the network.



23. Use the DHCP Lease box and pop-up menu to set the number of hours for the DHCP lease on each machine. When this time passes, a new address is assigned to each machine. You can enter a DHCP lease message in the DHCP Message box.
24. Click the NAT subtab (see Figure 18.9).

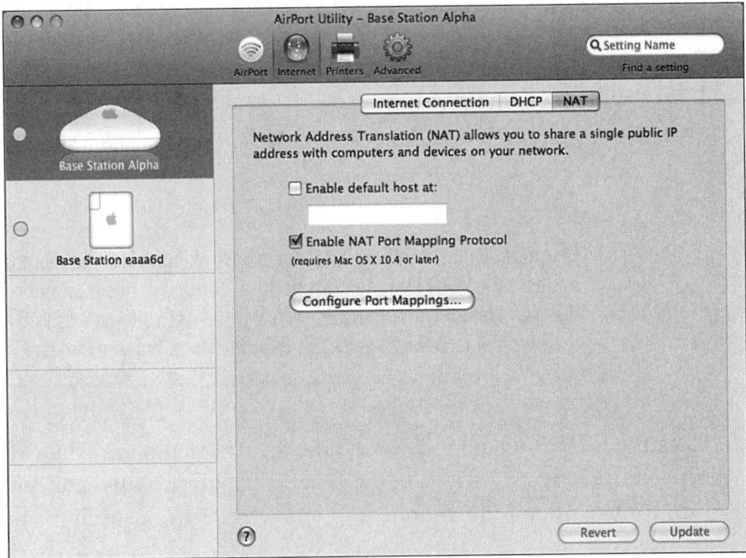


**Figure 18.9**
Use a base station's NAT protection for your network to shield the addresses of the devices connected to it from the outside.

25. Make sure the Enable NAT Port Mapping Protocol box is checked.
26. Click the Printers tab (see Figure 18.10).

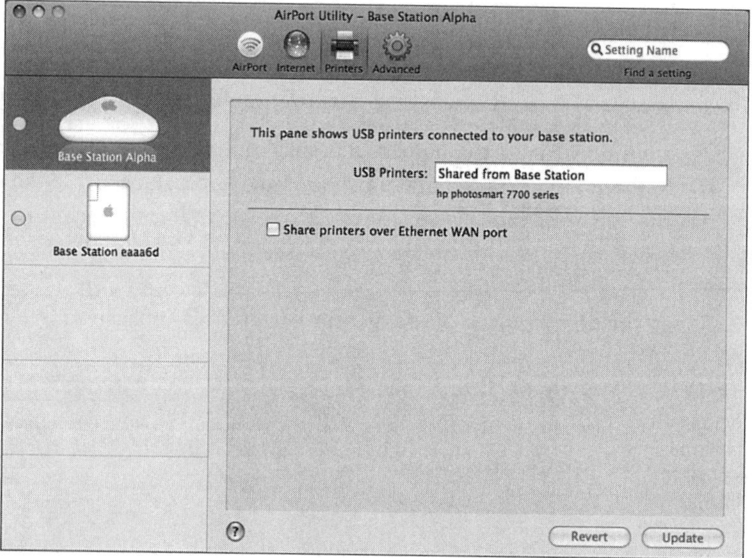


**Figure 18.10**
Configuring access to a printer connected to a base station is simple.

27. Enter the name of the printer connected to the base station.

**NOTE**

To be able to print to a printer attached to a base station, each computer must have the printer driver installed on it.

28. When you're ready to configure the base station, click Update. The base station is configured according to the settings you entered. When the process is complete, the base station restarts and the network is available for use.
29. Quit the AirPort Utility.

**NOTE**

For more detailed information on AirPort, visit Apple's Knowledge Base at www.apple.com/support/airport.

You can now access the Net and other network services from an AirPort-equipped Mac using the AirPort network. The base station also provides services to a wired network if it is connected to one.

## CONFIGURING AN AIRPORT-EQUIPPED MAC TO ACT AS A BASE STATION

As you learned earlier, you can use any AirPort-equipped Mac running Mac OS X to act as a base station. When you do this, the Mac OS X machine provides services similar to those that a dedicated base stations provides, but you don't have as much control over the AirPort network.

To configure a Mac as a base station, perform the following steps:

1. Configure an AirPort-equipped Mac so it can connect to the Internet, such as through DHCP services provided on an Ethernet network, and activate the AirPort connection via the Network pane.

⇨ To learn how to configure a Mac for the Internet, **see** Chapter 16, "Connecting a Mac to the Internet," **p. 335**.

2. Open the Sharing pane of the System Preferences application (see Figure 18.11).



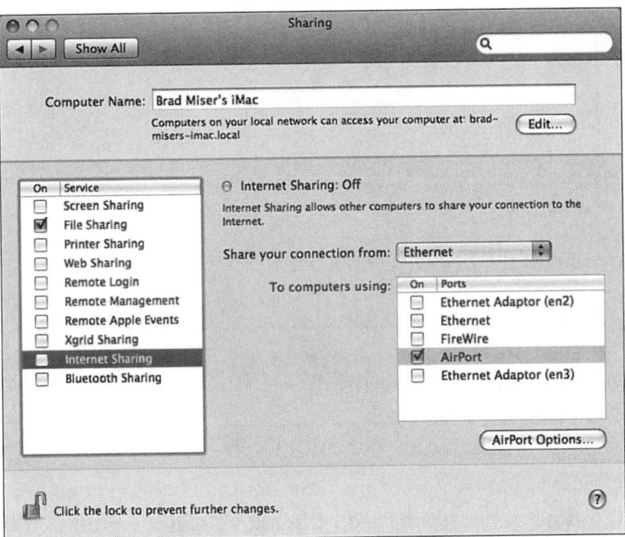


**Figure 18.11**
You use the controls on the Sharing pane to enable a Mac to share its Internet connection with other computers.

3. Select the Internet connection you want to share with other machines on the "Share your connection from" pop-up menu. For example, if your computer gets its Internet connection from a wired network, select Ethernet.

**NOTE**

> You can choose to share a connection from a wired network to AirPort-equipped machines or from an AirPort-equipped machine to a wired network.

4. Select the type of connections with which you are going to share the machine's Internet connection by checking the appropriate "To computers using" check boxes. For example, if you want to share the connection with computers via AirPort, check AirPort, and

if you want to share the connection via FireWire, check the FireWire check box. You can choose more than one connection type with which to share the connection.

5. If you share the connection over AirPort, select AirPort and click the AirPort Options button. The AirPort network configuration sheet appears.
6. Edit the default network name as needed. The default name is the name of your computer, but you can make it something more interesting if you want to.
7. Unless you have multiple AirPort networks active in the same area or you experience interference that prevents your network from operating properly, leave the Channel pop-up menu set to Automatic. If you want to choose a channel manually, select it on the pop-up menu.
8. For a more secure network, check the "Enable encryption (using WEP)" check box.

**NOTE**

WEP is an encryption strategy that attempts to provide wireless networks with the same level of protection that wired networks have. WEP does provide improved security compared to nonencrypted transmissions, but be aware that it does have some flaws as do almost all security measures. If the information transmitted over your network is very sensitive, you should use WEP to provide at least some protection.

9. Enter the network password in the Password and Confirm Password fields. This is the password users will enter to connect to the network.
10. Select an encryption key length on the WEP Key Length pop-up menu. The options are 40-bit and 128-bit. If only newer Macs running Mac OS X will be connecting to the network, select 128-bit. If you aren't sure which level of encryption other machines can support, select 40-bit. If you don't want to use the encryption at all, uncheck the "Enable encryption (using WEP)" check box.

**TIP**

If you'll be sharing the network with computers not running Mac OS X, make sure the password you create is 13 characters if you use 128-bit encryption or 5 characters if you use 40-bit.

11. Click OK. The Options sheet closes.
12. Check the Internet Sharing check box. The Internet connection is shared with other computers via AirPort or built-in Ethernet.
13. Use the other services check boxes to configure other services you will provide over the network, such as File and Printer Sharing. Your Mac then begins providing services over AirPort and its network becomes available to AirPort-equipped Macs.

⇨ To learn how to configure sharing services, **see** "Configuring the Services on a Network," **p. 369**.

18

**TIP**

> If Printer Sharing is enabled, USB printers connected to the Mac acting as a base station are also available to the AirPort network. This is a great way to share USB printers with other Macs. Also, the AirPort menu on the menu bar on a Mac acting as a base station is different from the menu on a client machine. This menu also has different options than a client menu.

---

**Using a Mac As a Base Station**

One of the disadvantages of using a Mac as a base station is that the Mac must be on for the network to be available. If that Mac is turned off or crashes, the AirPort network is lost.

If the Mac that is acting as the base station goes into Sleep mode, its services are also lost. Use the Energy Saver pane of the System Preferences utility to ensure that the software base station machine never sleeps while you want the AirPort network to be available. Also, if Sleep interrupts AirPort network services, client machines might have to quit and then restart Internet applications, such as Safari, to resume using the network.

---

⇨ To learn how to control sleep, **see** "Managing Your Mobile Mac's Power," **p. 318**.

# Connecting to an AirPort Network with Mac OS X

18

After an AirPort network has been established, you can access it from any AirPort-equipped Mac.

To access an AirPort network, you must configure a Mac OS X machine to connect to it.

You can do this in several ways. For example, you can configure a Mac's Airport configuring using the AirPort tools on the Network pane of the System Preferences application be completing the following steps:.

1. Open the System Preferences application and click the Network icon to open the Network pane.
2. Click the AirPort option in the left part of the pane (see Figure 18.12). The AirPort tools appear in the right part of the pane.
3. If AirPort is currently off, turn it on by clicking the Turn AirPort On button. AirPort services start. If your Mac has connected to a network, you see information about that network at the top of the pane.
4. To join a network, select the network's name on the Network Name pop-up menu and enter the password if the network requires one. The Mac joins the network and starts receiving services over the network.
5. If you want to be prompted to join new networks, check the "Ask to join new networks" check box.
6. Check the "Show AirPort status in menu bar" check box to put the AirPort menu on your menu bar. You can use this menu to quickly select and control your AirPort connection.

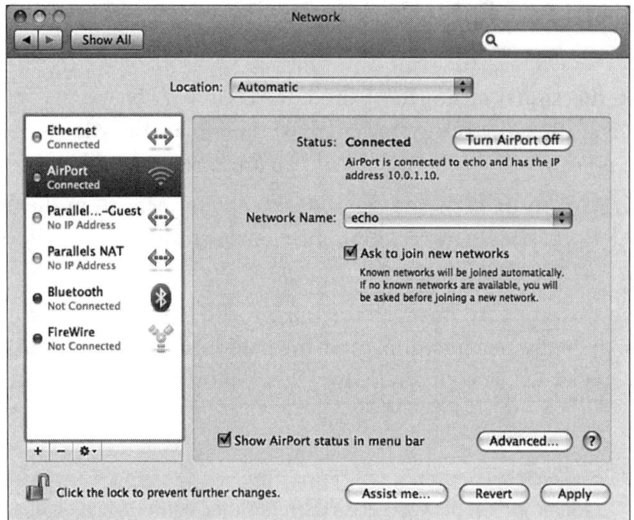


**Figure 18.12**
Use the AirPort tools to configure how your Mac connects to AirPort networks.

7. Click the Advanced button. You will see the Advanced options sheet, which you can use to configure additional aspects of your AirPort connection. It's unlikely you'll ever need to use most of these options, but they enable you to configure specific aspects of your connection, such as your preferred networks and the TCP/IP settings.
8. Click OK to close the Advanced sheet.
9. Click Apply and quit the System Preferences application.

18

**NOTE**

As your Mac connects to the network, the name of the network to which you are connecting briefly appears next to the AirPort icon in the menu bar.

If you want to use an AirPort network other than your preferred one, open the AirPort menu on the menu bar and select the AirPort network to which you want to connect. If its password is not already stored on your keychain, you will be prompted to enter it. Do so and you will be logged on to that AirPort network.

**TIP**

When prompted to enter your password, check the "Add to Keychain" check box to have Mac OS X remember the password so you don't have to enter it again.

*If you can access an AirPort network but can't access the Internet, see "I Can't Access the Internet Through AirPort Even Though I Can Connect to the AirPort Network" in the "Troubleshooting" section at the end of this chapter.*

You can use the AirPort menu on the menu bar to control AirPort in several ways, including the following:

- **Measure the signal strength of the connection**—The "waves" emanating from the AirPort icon show the relative strength of the signal your Mac is receiving. As long as you see two or more waves, the signal you are receiving is plenty strong.
- **Turn AirPort on or off**—You can disconnect your Mac from the AirPort network and disable AirPort services by selecting Turn AirPort Off. Turn AirPort on again by choosing Turn AirPort On.
- **Choose a different AirPort network from the list of available networks**—When you do so, you are prompted to enter the password for that network—unless you have saved the password to your keychain. Do so and you will move onto to the network you select.

NOTE

Some AirPort networks are hidden (a closed network) and do not broadcast their identities. To join such a network, you must know the name and password of the network you want to join. To join a hidden network, select Other on the AirPort menu on the menu bar, enter the name and password for the network, and click OK.



- **Create a computer-to-computer network**—When you select Create Network, you can create a network between two or more AirPort-equipped Macs. In the Computer to Computer dialog box, enter the name and password of the network you are creating, select the channel you want to use, and then click OK. Other users can select the network on their AirPort menus (of course, you need to provide the password for your network to those users if you require one). When your Mac is hosting a computer-to-computer network, the AirPort icon changes to a Mac "inside" a quarter circle to show that you are in the computer-to-computer mode.

  The channel you choose for a network controls the frequency of the signal used to create an AirPort network. If you have trouble connecting to other machines over the network you create, try a different channel.

  When you create and use a computer-to-computer network, other AirPort connections, such as the one you use to connect to the Internet, are deselected and therefore can't be used.

  To require and configure a password for the network, click Show Options in the Computer to Computer dialog box.

  Check the Use Interference Robustness check box to make the network less susceptible to interference (it will have a smaller range).

TIP

Computer-to-computer networks are a great way to play network games. You can create an AirPort network and host a game. Other users can connect to the network and join the game by selecting your network using their AirPort controls.

*If you are getting no signal or a weak signal from the AirPort network you want to join, see "Weak Signal" in the "Troubleshooting" section at the end of this chapter.*

Using AirPort is a great way to quickly create and use wireless networks. After you have connected to the Net without wires (especially when roaming with a mobile Mac), you won't want to settle for anything else.

Although this chapter has focused on using AirPort to access the Internet, an AirPort connection works just like any other network connection (such as an Ethernet connection). For example, you can access the files on another machine over an AirPort network just as you can with an Ethernet network.

⇨ For more information about configuring other network services; **see** Chapter 17, "Building and Using a Wired Network," **p. 359**.

# TROUBLESHOOTING

## NO AIRPORT HARDWARE IS FOUND

*When I launch the AirPort Setup Assistant, I see an error message stating that the required AirPort hardware can't be found.*

The AirPort software requires that you have an AirPort card installed on the machine you use to configure a base station. If an AirPort card is not found, the software won't run.

If you don't have an AirPort card installed in your Mac, you need to install one before running the AirPort Setup Assistant.

If you do have an AirPort card installed, it is not properly installed. Repeat the installation steps to ensure that the card is properly installed.

## I DON'T KNOW THE BASE STATION PASSWORD

*I can't access the base station because I don't know its password.*

When you have trouble with an AirPort base station, you can reset it to its factory defaults by inserting a paper clip into the reset button hole on the bottom or back of the unit. Hold down the button for 5 seconds and the base station is reset—all settings are returned to the default and the password becomes `public`.

## I CAN'T CONFIGURE MY BASE STATION MANUALLY

*When I try to configure a base station manually, I get an error stating that the base station can't be configured.*

This problem can occur for various reasons. First, try resetting the base station (see the previous section). If that doesn't work, try opening the AirPort Setup Assistant and configuring the base station using the assistant. Then, go back into the AirPort Admin Utility and try to configure the base station again. This sometimes clears the error.

### I CAN'T ACCESS THE INTERNET THROUGH AIRPORT EVEN THOUGH I CAN CONNECT TO THE AIRPORT NETWORK

*My Mac is connected to an AirPort network, but I can't access the Internet.*

If you are connecting to the Internet through a base station, the most likely cause is that the base station has lost its Internet connection. Use some means to confirm that Internet services are available to the base station, such as by using a machine connected independently or calling your service provider. If services are available, use the AirPort Admin Utility to check its configuration to ensure that it is correct. If all else fails, reset the access point.

If none of these steps works and you have a broadband modem connected to the base station that provides DHCP services, use the following steps to attempt to reset the connection:

1. Unplug the modem for at least 20 seconds, and then plug it back in again. This forces the modem to get a new address.
2. Reset the base station by pressing its reset button for 5 seconds.
3. Open the AirPort Setup Assistant and select the Join an Existing Network option.
4. Follow the onscreen instructions to update the base station.

### WEAK SIGNAL

*My AirPort signal strength is low. Or, I can't find the network to which I want to connect.*

Two primary factors affect the strength of the AirPort signal your Mac receives from a base station (hardware or software) or from Macs providing a computer-to-computer network. One is the distance from the base station to your Mac; the other is the amount of interference in the area.

If your Mac is within range of the base station you want to use, there should be no trouble getting a strong enough signal. If you are at the edge of or beyond that range, move your Mac closer to the base station or move the base station closer to you. You can also try repositioning the base station because it can sometimes be affected by materials or other fields between it and your Mac.

If you are close to the base station but can't get a strong signal, try changing the frequency of the network in the event that it is being interfered with by another signal of some type.

⇨ To learn how to change an AirPort network's frequency, **see** "Configuring a Base Station Manually," **p. 402**.

## MAC OS X TO THE MAX: MAKING THE MOST OF AIRPORT

AirPort is an amazingly powerful yet easy-to-use technology. In the section, you learn a couple of tricks to make the most of it.

## Making AirPort Go Farther

AirPort provides large range in most circumstances, and a single base station can usually provide coverage for an entire house easily.

However, you can extend the range of an AirPort network to make it cover an even larger area.

You can also link AirPort Extreme and Express base stations together wirelessly so that the signal is rebroadcast from one base station to the next. You can continue this chain of base stations to extend a network over a very large area. This is called a *wireless distribution system (WDS)*. Following are the general steps to create a WDS:

1. Configure one base station to connect to the Internet.
2. Open the AirPort Utility, select that base station, and click Manual Setup.
3. Click the AirPort tab and the WDS subtab (see Figure 18.13).

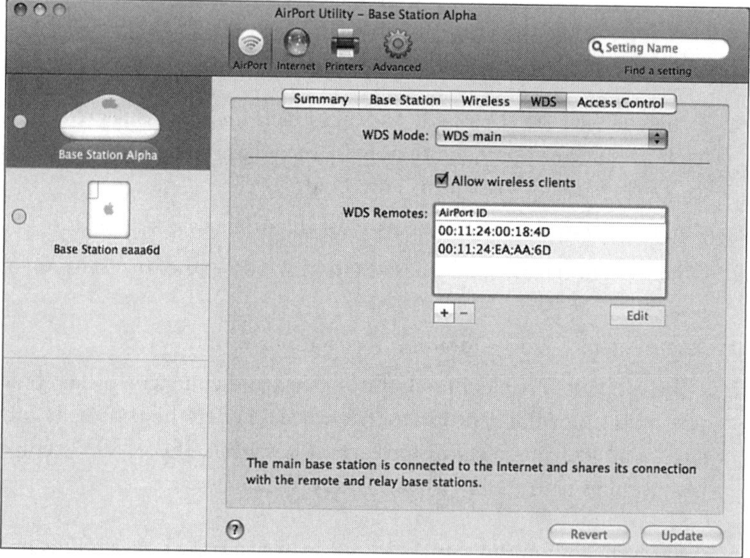


**Figure 18.13**
Using WDS, you can dramatically extend the range of an AirPort network.

4. Choose WDS main on the WDS Mode pop-up menu. For other base stations, choose the appropriate type for the base station that you are configuring. A *remote* base station shares the Internet connection of the main base station. A *relay* base station shares the main base station's Internet connection and can also share its connection with additional base stations.
5. Check the "Allow wireless clients" check box.
6. Click the Add Base Station button, which is the plus sign next to the list of base stations. The Base Station Selection sheet appears (see Figure 18.14).

18

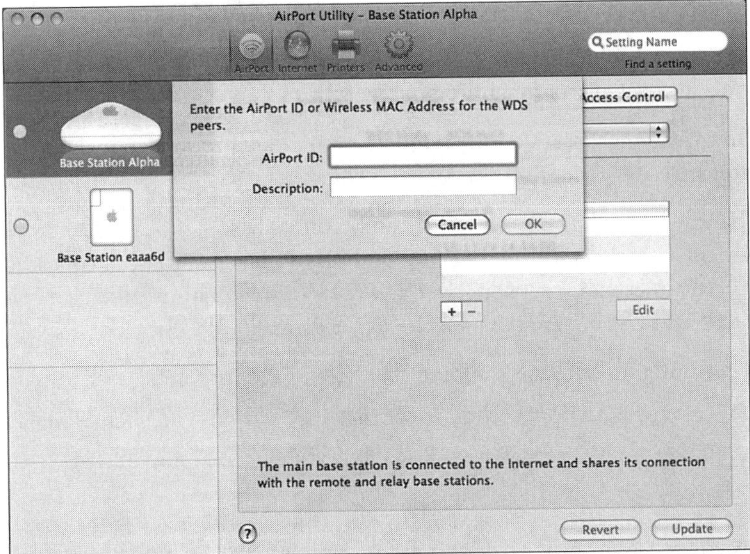


**Figure 18.14**
Use this sheet to configure a base station to add to the WDS you are creating.



7. Enter the AirPort ID for the base station. This address is provided on the base station itself or you can select the remote or relay base station in the AirPort Utility and copy its AirPort ID and past it into the field.
8. Enter a description of the location of the other base station.
9. Click OK to return to the Base Station window; the base station you added is shown on the list.
10. Repeat steps 6–9 to add other base stations to the WDS.
11. Click Update. The AirPort Utility selects and connects to each base station. As it does, you must enter the appropriate passwords. When the process is complete, you see a sheet that provides a status for each base station. If the WDS setup was successful, you can use that base station as part of the WDS.

After you have configured the WDS, you can place the base stations on it in various locations throughout an area to increase the coverage. The WDS network will appear to each machine as a single AirPort network even though it's being provided by multiple base stations.

## Working with an AirPort Express Base Station

An AirPort Express Base Station is a small AirPort base station that is designed to be mobile and also offers some other features not found in the larger base stations.

In addition to being able to provide an AirPort network, you can connect speakers to the Express audio port to broadcast music from iTunes using the AirTunes feature. You can also store up to five profiles for an Express Base Station and switch between them easily. Because it's so small, you can take an Express with you and quickly set up a wireless network anywhere you go, such as a hotel room. Plus, at $99, the Express is quite inexpensive for the features it provides.

**TIP**

> An Express is a great addition to an AirPort network to extend its range using the WDS feature. It's less expensive than the AirPort Extreme Base Station and is a perfect choice for a remote or relay base station.

The Express does have one limitation: It has only one Ethernet port so you can't connect both a broadband modem and an Ethernet network. If you use an Express as the only base station on a network, you won't be able to connect any wired devices to it via Ethernet. If you have all wireless devices, this won't be a limitation for you, but in most cases, you'll want to have an AirPort Extreme Base Station on the network so you can combine the wireless network with a wired one.

Other than this limitation, you can configure and use an Express just like the larger base station.

# CHAPTER 19

# Sharing an Internet Connection

## In this chapter

# ENABLING MULTIPLE MACS TO USE A SINGLE INTERNET ACCOUNT

One of the primary advantages of networking computers together is that they can share a single Internet account. You can also share a single Internet account on mixed networks that include both Macintosh and Windows computers.

Most means of sharing an Internet account rely on the Dynamic Host Configuration Protocol (DHCP). This protocol enables IP addresses to be dynamically assigned to each device on a network. A DHCP server assigns and manages these addresses. This protocol means that each device doesn't have to have be assigned a unique IP address through manual configuration; the DHCP server has a unique address and assigns IP addresses to the machines under it, as they are needed.

**NOTE**

> Each device for which a DHCP server provides an address must have a unique IP address; the DHCP server provides these addresses and ensures that they are unique. Most DHCP servers also provide network address translation (NAT) protection for the devices to which they provide services. When NAT protection is active, all the machines under the server appear to be from one IP address, which is that of the DHCP server. Using a DHCP server with NAT isolates the machines it serves from direct contact with other machines on the Internet and protects those machines from Internet attacks to a great degree.



In this chapter, you will learn how to share an Internet account using the following techniques:

- AirPort
- Mac OS X's built-in Internet sharing feature
- Multiple IP addresses for a single account
- A hardware DHCP server/hub

# USING AIRPORT TO SHARE AN INTERNET ACCOUNT

One of the easiest and best ways to share an Internet account is to use AirPort. In fact, using AirPort automatically enables you to share an Internet account among computers using an AirPort-compatible, wireless connection. You can also use an AirPort base station or an AirPort-equipped Mac to share an Internet connection with machines on a wired Ethernet network.

When you install and configure an AirPort base station, you can share the Internet account with which it is configured among other AirPort-equipped Macs and other wireless computers that can access that network. You can also share an Internet account among computers that are connected to an AirPort Extreme Base Station via Ethernet. This is because the base station is capable of acting as a DHCP server for the network and can provide unique IP addresses to computers connected via AirPort and via Ethernet at the same time.

**NOTE**

> Just because Windows computers don't call their wireless connections AirPort, that doesn't mean they can't share an Internet connection through an AirPort base station. They can, in fact, join an AirPort network as long as their wireless device supports the same protocol the AirPort network does. Because AirPort uses standard wireless protocols, in most cases PCs running Windows with wireless networking capabilities can also join AirPort networks.

When used with a broadband connection, an AirPort base station also provides your network with basic firewall protection when you use NAT, which is explained later in this chapter. Because the only thing directly connected to the Internet is the base station itself, hackers can't see the computers that are connecting to the Internet through the base station. They can see the base station, but because it isn't a computer, there isn't much they can do to it.

Because AirPort is easy to install, configure, and maintain, and because you also provide wireless access for AirPort-equipped devices, using AirPort is one of the best ways to share an Internet account.

➪ To learn how to install, configure, and use an AirPort network to share an Internet connection, **see** Chapter 18, "Creating and Managing AirPort Wireless Networks," **p. 393**.

## USING A MAC RUNNING MAC OS X TO SHARE AN INTERNET ACCOUNT

19

Mac OS X includes a built-in DHCP server you can use to share a single Internet connection with other devices on your local network. And if the Macintosh on which you configure the DHCP server includes an AirPort card, you can also provide a wireless AirPort network without the use of an AirPort base station.

**NOTE**

> The function of the DHCP server is to provide and manage IP addresses to devices on the network. The DHCP server doesn't actually provide the Internet access itself; that comes from the connection method you use (such as a cable modem). The DHCP server manages the traffic between the Internet connection and the other devices on the network.

One advantage of this approach is that you don't need to add dedicated Internet sharing hardware (such as a sharing hub or an AirPort base station) to your network. A standard Ethernet hub enables you to share your Internet account over an Ethernet network, and an AirPort card enables you to share that account over a wireless AirPort network. Another advantage is that it doesn't cost anything to share an account (assuming that you already have the connection hardware, such as for an Ethernet network).

**NOTE**

> You can use Mac OS X's built-in firewall to protect the DHCP machine from attacks from the Internet (and because it sits between the Internet and the other devices on your network, it protects those devices as well).

⇨ To learn how to configure the Mac OS X firewall, **see** "Defending Your Mac from Internet Attacks," **p. 937**.

This approach does have one significant disadvantage and one minor drawback, however. The significant disadvantage is that the Mac providing DHCP services must always be running for the machines that share its account to be capable of accessing the Internet. If the DHCP machine develops a problem, no device on the network can access the Internet. Similarly, if the machine from which the account is shared goes to sleep or is shut down, the Internet connection is lost by all the computers on the network. The less significant issue is that the DHCP services do require some processing power. These services will most likely not result in any noticeable performance decrease, but if your machine already runs at its limits, asking it to provide these services might slightly slow down other tasks.

**NOTE**

> DHCP servers are not platform specific. For example, if you have a DHCP server running on a Macintosh, you can connect a Windows computer to the network and use the same DHCP server to share the Internet account with it. Or, you can install a DHCP server on a Windows machine and use it to share the account with Macs on the network.



Configuring a Mac to provide DHCP services to a network requires the following general steps:

1. Connect the Mac to the Internet.
2. Install the network you will use to connect the Mac with other machines.
3. Configure the Mac to share its Internet account.

## CONNECTING THE DHCP MAC TO THE INTERNET

It goes without saying (but I will say it anyway) that to use a Mac to share an Internet account, that Mac must be connected to the Internet. The method you use to connect to the Internet doesn't matter. You'll get the best results if you use a broadband connection, such as a cable or DSL modem, but you can also share a dial-up connection if you want (don't expect speedy operation, though).

⇨ To learn how to connect a Mac to the Internet, **see** Chapter 16, "Connecting a Mac to the Internet," **p. 335**.

## INSTALLING THE DHCP MAC ON A NETWORK

The next step is to install the DHCP Mac on the network with which you are going to share the Internet connection. You can build a wired network using Ethernet, or you can use AirPort to connect the Mac to other AirPort-equipped Macs (you can share an account with other machines using both networking methods at the same time).

⇨ To learn how to build and manage a wired network, **see** Chapter 17, "Building and Using a Wired Network," **p. 359**.

⇨ To learn how to install, configure, and use an AirPort network, **see** Chapter 18, "Creating and Managing AirPort Wireless Networks," **p. 393**.

## CONFIGURING THE DHCP MAC TO SHARE AN ACCOUNT

After you have configured the Mac for Internet access and connected it to other computers (with or without wires), you need to configure the Internet sharing services on it.

The three possibilities when you configure Internet sharing on your Mac are as follows:

- Your Mac is connected to the Internet via an Ethernet connection, and it has an AirPort card installed in it.
- Your Mac is connected to the Internet via Ethernet but does not have an AirPort card installed in it.
- Your Mac is connected to the Internet via an AirPort base station, in which case you can share the Internet account by connecting that Mac to other computers via Ethernet to share its account via an Ethernet network (you wouldn't need to share the Internet connection with the AirPort-equipped Macs because the base station already does that).

**NOTE**

AirPort Extreme Base Stations include Ethernet ports you can use to connect the base station to an Ethernet network. When you do this, the base station can also share a connection with machines connected to the Ethernet network. In that case, you don't need to use a Mac to share a connection.

19

When you configure Internet sharing on your Mac, it automatically determines which case is true for your machine and presents the appropriate options for you. To configure Internet sharing, use the following steps:

1. Open the System Preferences application and click the Sharing icon to open the Sharing pane.
2. Click Internet Sharing in the Services list on the left side of the pane. What you see depends on how the Mac is connected to the Internet. For example, in Figure 19.1, you see the Internet Sharing configuration for a machine connected to the Internet via AirPort; you can tell this is so because AirPort is selected on the "Share your connection from" pop-up menu. In Figure 19.2, you see an example of a machine connected to the Internet via Ethernet. Because that machine also has an AirPort card installed in it, it can share its connection with other machines using both built-in Ethernet and AirPort.

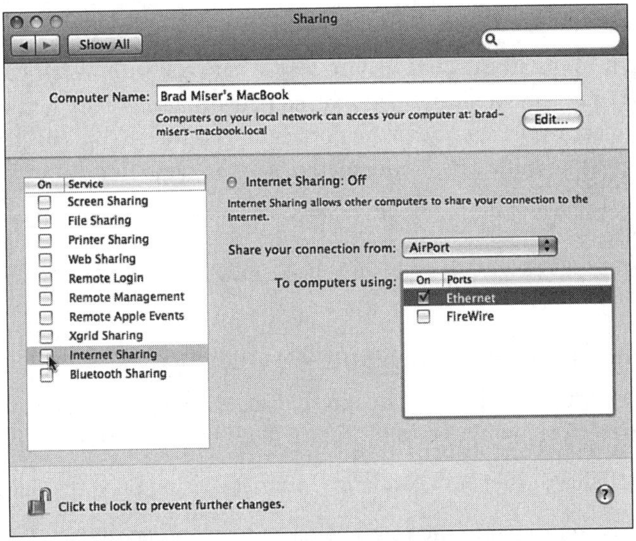

**Figure 19.1**
This Mac is connected to the Internet via AirPort.

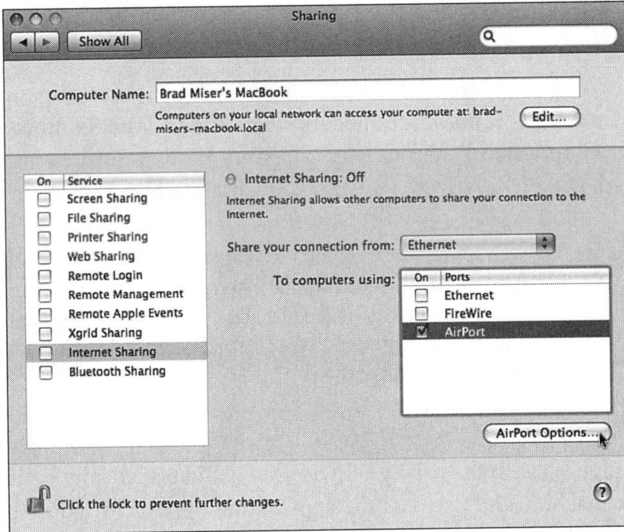


**Figure 19.2**
The Sharing pane shows a machine that is currently connected to the Internet via Ethernet, but that also has an AirPort card installed in it.



**NOTE**

> The ports you see listed in the "To computers using" list will be those that are active under your current network settings (determined by the location setting currently active). For example, if in your current location, the Built-in FireWire port is active, that port will also be available for you to share an Internet connection with other computers.

⇨ To learn how to configure your network settings, **see** "Managing Multiple Internet Accounts," **p. 354**.

⇨ To learn how to use locations, **see** "Configuring and Using Locations," **p. 328**.

3. On the "Share your connection from" pop-up menu, select the Internet connection you want to share. In most cases, you will be connected by only one means, such as AirPort or built-in Ethernet, so the choice should be obvious. However, if the Mac can connect in multiple ways, choose the option you want to share. For example, if you are connected to an Ethernet network that has Internet access and you also have access to the Internet through an AirPort base station, you can share either connection with other computers.

   In the "To computers using" box are the means by which you can share the connection that you selected with other computers. For example, in Figure 19.2, you can see that the Mac can share its connection with other machines over Ethernet and AirPort.

4. Mark the On check box for the ports over which you want to share the connection. For example, to share the Mac's connection with computers via AirPort, mark the On check box next to AirPort on the list of ports.

   If you use an Ethernet port to share a connection, you might see a sheet warning you that activating sharing might cause problems for other ISP customers or violate your service agreement (some providers prohibit sharing an individual account on multiple machines, but most allow a reasonable amount of sharing such as with five or fewer computers). Read the dialog box and click OK to close it.

5. If you made an AirPort port active in step 4, select the AirPort port and click the AirPort Options button. Then configure the AirPort network you are creating using the resulting sheet. For example, you will name the network (if you don't want to use the default name), choose a channel and password, and so on. When you are done configuring the AirPort network, click OK.

⇨ To learn how to configure an AirPort network, **see** Chapter 18, "Creating and Managing AirPort Wireless Networks," **p. 393**.

**CAUTION**

> Be careful about sharing an account over the same port by which you are receiving it. For example, if your Mac is already getting an Internet connection through an Ethernet network, don't also share its Internet connection with that same network. For one thing, you don't need to because the device providing the connection to your Mac is already sharing its connection with other devices on the network. For another, you can cause confusion for yourself and potentially IP address conflicts by sharing the same connection on the same network. Generally, unless you have multiple networks of the same type operating in the same location (such as more than one AirPort network), a port that is selected on the "Share your connection from" pop-up menu shouldn't also be turned on in the "To computers using" list.

6. Click the check box next to Internet Sharing in the Services list (you can't click the check box until you turn on at least one port on the "To computers using" list). Your Mac will start providing DHCP services.

You might see a warning sheet that explains that activating sharing might disrupt services on the network. If you are administering the network, click Start in the sheet. If someone else administers the network on which you are sharing your connection, make sure you coordinate with that person before starting Internet Sharing.

Your connection will be shared with all the devices with which your Mac can communicate via the ports that you have turned on. For example, if your Mac is connected to a local network via Ethernet and you made that port active, other devices on the network can use the account via the DHCP services your Mac provides.

7. Quit the System Preferences application.
8. Configure the other devices on the network to obtain their IP addresses from a DHCP server. Those devices should now see your Mac and be able to access the Internet through the shared connection.

**TIP**

If you share an Internet account over AirPort, an upward pointing arrow is added to the center of the AirPort icon in the menu bar. This indicates that the connection is shared and that you can access the sharing controls from the menu.

**CAUTION**

If the machine sharing the connection goes to sleep or is shut down, the Internet connection is lost on the network and no other machine using the network can access the Internet. You should disable sleep using the Energy Saver pane of the System Preferences application when you use Internet Sharing.

*If other machines with which you are sharing a connection are unable to connect to the Internet, see "The Machines with Which I Am Sharing a Connection from My Mac Can't Connect at All" in the "Troubleshooting" section at the end of this chapter.*

*If other machines with which you are sharing a connection lose the connection to the Internet, see "The Machines with Which I Am Sharing a Connection from My Mac Have Lost Internet Access" in the "Troubleshooting" section at the end of this chapter.*

In this section, I've focused on using built-in Ethernet and AirPort to share a connection. That's because they are by far the most likely way you will do so. However, there are other ports by which you can share a connection, including built-in FireWire and Bluetooth. Basically, you can share a connection via any means by which your Mac can communicate with other devices. Using these less common ports is really no different from using the ones described in this chapter. Just choose the appropriate port by which the sharing machine is accessing the Internet on the "Share your connection from" pop-up menu and turn on the ports through which you want to provide an Internet connection in the "To computers using" list.

## Using Multiple IP Addresses to Share an Internet Account

With some broadband accounts, such as cable, you can purchase additional IP addresses (or DHCP names) so you can configure multiple machines to access the same account. The requirements to do this are an address for each device that will be using the account and an Ethernet or other network, which typically consists of a hub with the cable or digital subscriber line (DSL) modem connected to the wide area network (WAN) port and each device connected to a local area network (LAN) port.

**NOTE**

> Some Internet service providers use DHCP to provide IP addresses to you. In these cases, you assign a DHCP name to your computer. The ISP's DHCP server assigns IP addresses to you as you need them. To share an Internet account among several devices, you need a unique DHCP name for each device; you use this DHCP name to configure the network on each device.

To share an account using multiple IP addresses, do the following:

1. Contact your ISP to determine whether this option is available.
2. If it is, obtain additional addresses (or DHCP names); you will need one address for each machine or device (such as an AirPort base station) you want to share the account. You will probably need to pay an additional fee for each IP address you obtain.
3. Connect the cable or DSL modem to the WAN port on the hub for your network.
4. Connect each device to a LAN port on the hub.
5. Configure each machine with one of the available addresses (or DHCP names).

19

*If you can't use a device on your network because of an error message about the same IP address being used on more than one device, see "I Get an Error Message Telling Me That Multiple Devices Have the Same IP Address" in the "Troubleshooting" section at the end of this chapter.*

One advantage to this method is that you can use a standard Ethernet hub to facilitate sharing the account; these hubs are quite inexpensive and are simple to install and use. Setting up each device to use its address is straightforward as well. You simply configure each machine as if it were the only one using the account.

One possible disadvantage is that you might have to pay an additional fee for each address you use. The typical cost of additional addresses is $5–$7 per month per address on top of the address included with your base account. This can get expensive if you have several devices on your network; however, you can balance that cost against not needing a hub (Ethernet or AirPort) that has Internet account sharing built in.

Another disadvantage is that you don't get any special features, such as a built-in firewall. The IP addresses that you configure on each machine are usually publicly accessible on the Internet, which means hackers can see them. You have to add protection for each device on your network in some other way.

Typically, using a hub with built-in Internet sharing (such as an AirPort base station) or using a Mac to share its account is a more secure and easier to manage option. But, some providers require you to have a unique address for each machine that will be using the account, and this might be your only legal option.

## USING A HARDWARE DHCP SERVER TO SHARE AN INTERNET ACCOUNT

One of the best ways to share an Internet account is to use a hub device that provides DHCP services to the network. These devices have the DHCP software built in and handle the administration of IP addresses for the network automatically.

In addition to basic DHCP services, some of these devices also include special features, such as built-in firewall protection for your network.

The general steps for installing and using such a device are the following:

1. Choose and obtain the device.
2. Install the device on your network.
3. Configure the device to connect to the Internet.
4. Attach the computers and other devices to the network and configure each device to use the DHCP server you configured in step 3.



---

**ISPs and Sharing a Connection**

Not all ISPs support sharing a single Internet connection. Check the agreement you have with your provider to ensure that sharing an account is within your rights under that account. Some configurations can actually block access to your account by a hub or other sharing device, thus preventing you from sharing the account using a hardware device. Before you purchase a hub, make sure that it is acceptable under the terms of your Internet account; otherwise, you might end up wasting your money. Fortunately, most providers allow you to share the account on a reasonable number of machines.

Some providers use sort of a "don't ask, don't tell" policy. They provide support for one machine per account and make it clear that they don't support networks, in which case you are on your own if you have problems connecting through your own network. However, because using a sharing hub is so straightforward, this isn't really much of a drawback.

---

AirPort Extreme and AirPort Express Base Stations are examples of hardware DHCP devices that also happen to provide wireless communication. One unique thing about these devices is that they are produced by Apple and the wireless technology is called AirPort. The other, and more important, unique thing about them is that AirPort software is built-in to Mac OS X. Because of these factors, AirPort Base Stations are the easiest to use.

However, there are many other kinds of DHCP hubs, also often called Internet sharing hubs, that you can buy and use. Some of these will work with a Mac just fine, whereas others require Windows-only software. Although the AirPort base stations are a bit more expensive than some other devices, I believe the convenience and reliability for Mac users make the additional cost well worth it. However, if the cost of an AirPort base station is prohibitive, you can easily find and use a similar device made by another manufacturer. Before you purchase one, make sure that it is compatible with Mac OS X. The main area of compatibility is the software you use to configure the hub. In many cases, you use a web browser to access and configure it, but some hubs have specialized software that might be Windows only.

# TROUBLESHOOTING

## THE MACHINES WITH WHICH I AM SHARING A CONNECTION FROM MY MAC CAN'T CONNECT AT ALL

*I have started Internet Sharing on a Mac, but other devices on the network can't access the Internet.*

Attempt to connect to the Internet from the Mac that is sharing the account. If that machine can't connect, something has happened to its Internet connection. If that machine can connect, check that Internet Sharing is configured properly.

Then, check the Internet connection settings for each machine to make sure they are set to connect via a DHCP server.

⇨ To learn how to troubleshoot a Mac connected to the Internet, **see** Chapter 16, "Connecting a Mac to the Internet," **p. 335**.

⇨ To learn how to configure Internet Sharing, **see** "Configuring the DHCP Mac to Share an Account," **p. 425**.

## THE MACHINES WITH WHICH I AM SHARING A CONNECTION FROM MY MAC HAVE LOST INTERNET ACCESS

*The machines with which I am sharing an Internet connection were able to connect, but now they can't.*

First, check whether all the machines with which the connection is being shared have this problem or only some do. If all the machines are unable to connect, the problem stems from the Mac sharing the account (see the next paragraph). If some of the machines with which the connection is being shared can access the Net, the problem lies with those machines. Check the configuration of those machines to ensure that they are configured to use a DHCP server. Also, check their network connections to make sure they are communicating with the network properly.

⇨ To learn how to troubleshoot a Mac connected to the Internet, **see** Chapter 16, "Connecting a Mac to the Internet," **p. 335**.

⇨ To learn how to build and manage a network, **see** Chapter 17, "Building and Using a Wired Network," **p. 359**.

⇨ To learn how to install, configure, and use an AirPort network, **see** Chapter 18, "Creating and Managing AirPort Wireless Networks," **p. 393**.

If none of the machines can access the Internet, something has happened to the Mac that is sharing the connection.

Make sure that the Mac is still running and that sleep is disabled. If both of these conditions are true, move to the next paragraph. If the Mac is shut down, restart it to restart Internet Sharing. If the Mac has gone to sleep, you need to wake it up to restart Internet Sharing.

Attempt to connect to the Internet from the Mac that is sharing the account, such as by opening a web browser. If that machine can't connect, something has happened to its Internet connection. If that machine can connect, reconfigure Internet Sharing.

⇨ To learn how to troubleshoot a Mac connected to the Internet, **see** Chapter 16, "Connecting a Mac to the Internet," **p. 335**.

⇨ To learn how to configure Internet Sharing, **see** "Configuring the DHCP Mac to Share an Account," **p. 425**.

### I Get an Error Message Telling Me That Multiple Devices Have the Same IP Address

*When I attempt to start up one of the devices on my network, I see an alert stating that a device has already been assigned the IP address and that IP services are being shut down. How do I correct this problem?*

Two devices on the same network cannot have the same IP address. If you start up one device and see this error message, you have two or more devices trying to use the same address. Check the configuration of each device to see which devices are using that address (for Mac OS X machines, select the network service that is being used from the Services list on the Network pane of the System Preferences application to see how the computer is configured). Check that each device has a unique address, including an AirPort base station or other device that is sharing the account.

Occasionally, your hub will "remember" the devices that are using specific IP addresses and you will see this error even though you made sure that each device had a unique address. If this happens, power down your entire network, including the hub and all other devices attached to it. Wait a few seconds and power up everything again, starting with your broadband modem and hub, and then your computers. The error should be cleared as each device registers its unique address on the network.

## Mac OS X to the Max: Troubleshooting a Network Connection

Troubleshooting a network connection to the Internet can be quite challenging. Your approach should be to eliminate potential sources of the problem one by one until you find the specific problem you are having.

If you are unable to connect to the Internet after you have installed and configured an Internet Sharing hub, try the following steps:

1. Power down all the devices and the network, including the modem and hubs, and wait a few seconds. Turn on the power to the modem and hub first, and then turn on your computers. This will often reset the network and restore access.

2. Check the modem to see whether its status lights indicate it is connected to the Internet. If it isn't connected, check with the ISP to make sure service is currently available. If service is down, you'll need to wait until its restored before you'll be able to connect. If service is available, the issue is with the modem. Your ISP may be able to remotely reconfigure the modem for Internet access. If that fails, the modem itself might have failed, in which case you need to repair or replace it.

   If the modem appears to be connected, the problem lies with a device on the network.
3. Check two or more devices on the network. If at least one computer can connect to the Internet, you know that account is available, therefore the problem lies with specific computers or with some other hardware connected to the network such as the hub. If possible, try to connect with one device wirelessly and one connecting through the wired part of the network. This can identify which part of the network is having problems.
4. If you determine the problem is with a specific computer, reconconfigure that computer to connect to the appropriate network.
5. If you determine the problem lies with part of the network, such as devices connected via an Ethernet hub, check the hubs to make sure they are still working. Most hubs have status lights you can use for this. If the hub seems to have a problem, remove its power and the restart it. This will often clear the problem.
6. If it appears that Internet service is available, but no device on the network can connect to it, connect the modem directly to a Mac and configure that Mac to access the Internet (make sure the Mac's firewall is turned on before you do this). Once the Mac can connect successfully, you know that the service is available and that the problem lies at the hub or other part of the network.
7. Install the hub that was connected to the modem again and configure it to connect to the Internet. Connect and configure the Mac you used in step 6 to the hub to see if it can still connect. If it can't, the hub is not working or is not configured correctly. You'll need to correct that problem to continue.
8. Once the Mac can connect to the Internet through the hub, start connecting other devices to the network one by one. Check each device for Internet connection.
9. Repeat step 8 for each device. If you discover a problem with a device, check its configuration and its connection to the Internet.
10. In some cases, you might need to configure your hub to use media access control (MAC) address cloning. A MAC address uniquely identifies each node on a network. In some cases, you will need to clone, or copy, the MAC address of one of the computers on your network onto the router. See the instructions that came with the hub to learn how to configure MAC cloning on your router.



**NOTE**

> You might be able to share an account using a software DHCP server even if you can't use a hardware device to do so. For example, try using the Mac's built-in Internet Sharing to share your account on a network. Connect the Mac directly to your cable or DSL modem and then use Internet Sharing to share the connection with the network. Remember to enable the Mac's firewall to protect it and your network from attacks from the Internet.

CHAPTER 20

# Using .Mac to Integrate a Mac onto the Internet

## In this chapter

## Understanding and Using .Mac

Apple's .Mac is a suite of services you can access that literally integrate your Mac into the Internet. These services include the following:

- **Email**—Using .Mac provides you with an email account you can use to send and receive email. Your .Mac email address ends in `@mac.com`, so using it is a good way to identify yourself as a Mac user. Using the Webmail service, you can also access your .Mac email account from a web browser. You can add more email accounts to your .Mac account for a nominal fee.
- **iDisk**—An iDisk is a virtual disk space you can use to store files just like a disk attached to your Mac. A number of folders exist on an iDisk by default. For example, you can place items in your Public folder, and any Mac users who know your .Mac member name can access the files in that folder (which is an excellent way to share files with other Mac users around the world). And, you can create a website to share the files in your Public folder with anyone. You also store the data that forms your .Mac web page on your iDisk. You can configure your Mac to create a local copy of your iDisk and keep it automatically synchronized with the online version. An iDisk might be the best benefit of having a .Mac account.
- **HomePage**—The HomePage service enables you to create and serve a website. You can use HomePage templates to create a site, or you can use a web page application, such as iWeb, to create your site and use .Mac to serve it.
- **Synchronization**—If you use more than one Mac, you can use .Mac to synchronize information across those Macs, such as your Safari bookmarks, your Address Book, and so on. You can also access your calendar and contact information via the Web.
- **iLife publishing**—.Mac makes it incredibly easy to share your iLife content over the Web. For example, you can easily create and publish a website using iWeb. Likewise, you can quickly share photos from iPhoto.
- **Software**—The .Mac service enables you to download and use software free, such as utilities and games. You can also access a lot of other software, such as demos, updates, and more.
- **Online chat**—Your .Mac email account enables you to take advantage of iChat to chat online via text, audio, and video.
- **iCards**—These are electronic greeting cards you can send to others via email. There are numerous card combinations you can send—these are great for the artistically challenged because you can create a customized greeting card by selecting from the available images and styles.

The only requirement to use .Mac is that you can connect to the Internet, can have a .Mac account, and are using Mac OS 9 or later.

**NOTE**

> You can use .Mac with any kind of Internet connection. Like all Internet services, .Mac will work much better with a broadband connection, especially for iDisk and HomePage. If you do use a broadband connection, you'll soon find that .Mac does become an extension of your Mac.

# GETTING STARTED WITH .MAC

Your first steps to start using .Mac are to obtain a .Mac account and then configure your Mac to access that account. The following sections give you a quick overview of these steps; however, if you already have a .Mac account, you can skip to the section titled "Working with Your .Mac Email Account."

## OBTAINING A .MAC ACCOUNT

Before you can access .Mac services, you need to obtain a .Mac account. At press time, the cost of a .Mac account started at $99.95 per year for a single membership with 10GB of total storage space. However, you can obtain and use a trial .Mac account that provides access to most of the .Mac services free for 60 days.

There are various types of accounts you can purchase starting with the single user account with 10GB of disk space. Other types include email only (you have to have a full membership to purchase these), an upgrade to 20GB of storage space, a family pack that includes multiple accounts, and an upgrade to the family pack.

Because you can upgrade your account at any time, I recommend that you start with the base account and see how that works for you. If you need more disk space or to add other people, you can easily upgrade your membership later.

You will need to create your .Mac member name. You should put some thought into this step. The member name you choose will be part of your .Mac email address (which will be `membername@mac.com`), and it will also be part of the URL to your .Mac website. Typically, you should choose some variation of your name so people can remember your email address and URL and can easily associate both with you. Your member name has to be at least 3 characters long and can't be longer than 20 characters. Again, you should keep your member name fairly short to make it easier for other people to work with. When you installed Mac OS X, you were prompted to enter your existing .Mac account information or to create a .Mac account. If you entered your .Mac account information or created a .Mac account at that time, you are all set and can skip to the next section.

20

To obtain a .Mac account manually, do the following:

1. Open the System Preferences application and click the .Mac icon to open the .Mac pane.
2. Open the Account tab and click the Learn More button. Your default web browser will open and you will move to the .Mac home page (see Figure 20.1).

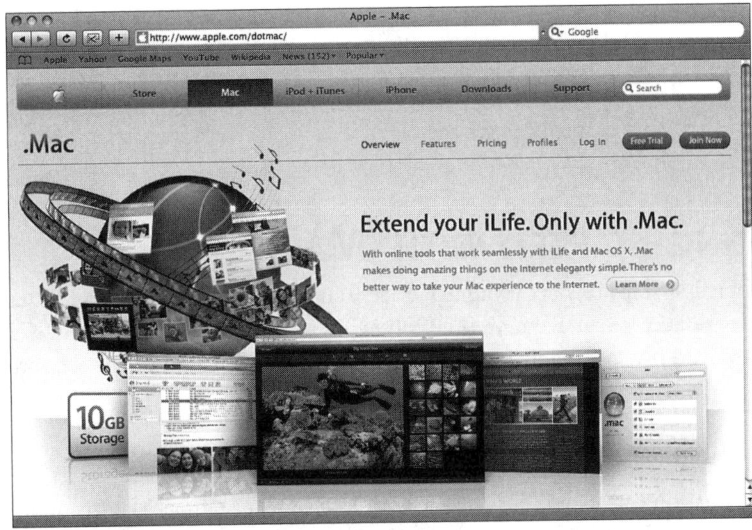


**Figure 20.1**
The .Mac website enables you to obtain a .Mac account and to use .Mac services.

**TIP**

> You can also get to the .Mac website by going to www.apple.com/dotmac.

3. Click the Join Now button.
4. Follow the onscreen instructions to create your .Mac account. You will have to provide personal information and accept a license agreement. As part of the process, you create a member name and password for your account. You can choose to create a free trial account, or you can pay for a full account. If you create a full account, you must provide payment information, such as a credit card.

When you have successfully created an account, you will see a page that displays your member name, password, email address, and email server information. You should print this page so you will have the information if you need to retrieve it at a later time.



## Configuring Your .Mac Account

After you have obtained a .Mac account, you configure Mac OS X to access its services:

1. Open the Account tab of the .Mac pane of the System Preferences application.
2. Enter your .Mac member name and password in the pane.

By completing these simple steps, your Mac will be able to access your .Mac account automatically.

**NOTE**

> Each user account on your Mac can have its own .Mac account. The settings in the .Mac pane of the System Preferences application of one account do not affect the other accounts. The steps to work with other .Mac accounts are exactly the same as those to work with the first one you create.

# Working with Your .Mac Email Account

One of the cool things about using a .Mac account is that you get an email account with the distinctive "@mac.com" domain. You can use .Mac email accounts with Mac OS X's Mail application very easily. You can also access your .Mac email via the Web. And, you can add more email addresses to your .Mac account.

## Using Your .Mac Email Account with Mail

To use your .Mac email account with Mail, you need to configure that account in the Mail application. This is simple because support for .Mac email accounts is built in to Mail and adding a .Mac email account requires only that you enter your .Mac member name and password.

⇨ To learn how to configure email accounts in Mail, **see** "Configuring Email Accounts," **p. 467**.

**NOTE**

> If you created or configured an existing .Mac account when you installed Mac OS X, your .Mac email account was configured in the Mail application for you automatically.

After you have set up your .Mac email account in Mail, you use it just like other email accounts you have.

⇨ To learn how to use Mail, **see** Chapter 21, "Managing Your Email with Mail," **p. 465** .

**NOTE**

> With a .Mac account, you share your allocated disk space between your iDisk and email. You can choose the proportion of the space dedicated to each, as you'll learn later in this chapter.



## Accessing Your .Mac Email Account from the Web

You can access your .Mac email from any computer that has web access, which makes it convenient to use your .Mac email account even if you aren't at your own Mac. To access your .Mac email via the Web, perform the following steps:

1. Use a web browser to move to www.apple.com/dotmac.
2. Click the Login link at the top of the page.

3. On the .Mac login page, enter your member name and password and click Login.
4. On your .Mac home page, click the link for Mail in the .Mac toolbar. You will move into your .Mac email account (see Figure 20.2).

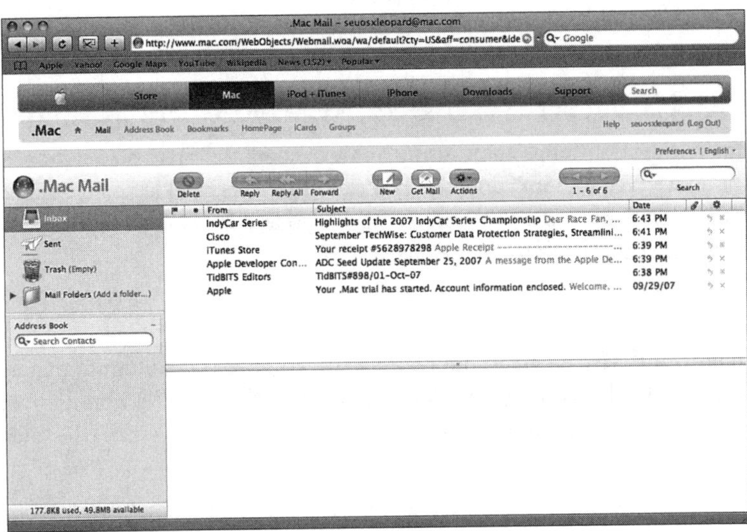


**Figure 20.2**
Using the .Mac website is a great way to access your .Mac email from any computer that can connect to the Web.

5. Use the tools to work with and manage your email.

Using the .Mac website to access your email is similar to using the Mail application from the Mac OS X desktop. You can read your email, send email, organize it, and so on.

## ADDING EMAIL ACCOUNTS TO YOUR .MAC ACCOUNT

One .Mac email account might not be enough for you. For example, you might want to provide a .Mac email account for each user of your Mac. The good news is that you can add email accounts to a .Mac account for a nominal fee (at press time, additional email-only accounts were only $10/year). To do so, perform the following steps:



1. Open the Account tab of the .Mac pane of the System Preferences application.
2. Click the Account Details button. You'll move to the .Mac website.
3. Log in using your member name and password. You'll move to the Account Settings page.
4. Click the Manage Accounts button. You'll move to the email account status page, which will display your current email accounts.
5. Click the Buy More button. You'll move to the Buy More page.
6. Choose the number of email accounts you want to purchase on the "Email-Only Account(s)" pop-up menu and click Continue.
7. Follow the onscreen instructions to create the additional accounts.

After you have purchased the additional email accounts, you can configure those accounts in email applications or use the .Mac website to access them.

## USING YOUR IDISK

iDisk is among the most useful things about having a .Mac account. The uses for an iDisk are almost limitless; the bottom line is that your iDisk is additional disk space that you access via the Internet. You can use this space to store any files you choose. It is also vital to certain .Mac services, such as HomePage, because you store all the files you use on your web page in the appropriate folders on your iDisk.

**TIP**

> Although your iDisk isn't likely to be large enough to perform system backups, you can use it to back up important documents. This keeps them separate from your computer and enables you to access them from any Mac. With your .Mac account, you can download and use the Apple Backup application to back up your files on your iDisk.

You can configure a Mac to create a local copy of your iDisk and keep it synchronized with your online iDisk. This is especially useful when you work with the same set of files from multiple locations, such as a work Mac and your home Mac.

When you purchase a .Mac account, the combination of iDisk and email storage space is 10GB. You can configure this to shift more space to the iDisk or to your email, and you can upgrade the disk space available to your account.

### SETTING THE SIZE OF YOUR IDISK

In most cases, you should increase the size of your iDisk relative to the space used by your email account.

**TIP**

> Only email that you store on the .Mac server counts against the email portion of your .Mac disk space. Make it a practice to download your .Mac email to your Mac and to regularly delete your email to keep your disk use for email to a minimum so you can have more iDisk space.



1. Open the Account tab of the .Mac pane of the System Preferences application.
2. Click the Account Details button. You'll move to the .Mac website.
3. Log in using your member name and password. You'll move to the Account Settings page.
4. Click the Storage Settings button. You'll move to the Storage Settings page (see Figure 20.3).

**Figure 20.3**
Using this page, you can set the balance of storage space between your iDisk and .Mac email.

5. Choose the split between disk space for your iDisk and email account using the pop-up menu. In the "In use" column, you see the current space being used for the iDisk and that being used for mail. In the Allocated column, you see the amount currently allocated for each type of storage. To change the split, choose the amount you want to be available for email using the pop-up menu. The choices you see on this menu depend on the storage space associated with your account.
6. Click Save. Your .Mac disk space will be allocated according to your selection.

**TIP**

> As you have probably figured out, you use the Account Settings web page to configure various aspects of your .Mac account, such as changing your password, billing information, and so on.

20

## CONFIGURING YOUR IDISK

You can configure your iDisk for your Mac OS X user account by opening the iDisk tab of the .Mac pane of the System Preferences application (see Figure 20.4).

**TIP**

> If the iDisk tab doesn't reflect your most recent account changes, quit the System Preferences application and restart it.

The most important configuration you will do is determining whether you will create a local copy of your iDisk on your computer. If you do this, you can work with the local copy just like other volumes on your computer. Then, you can either synchronize the local version with the online version manually or have your Mac do it automatically.

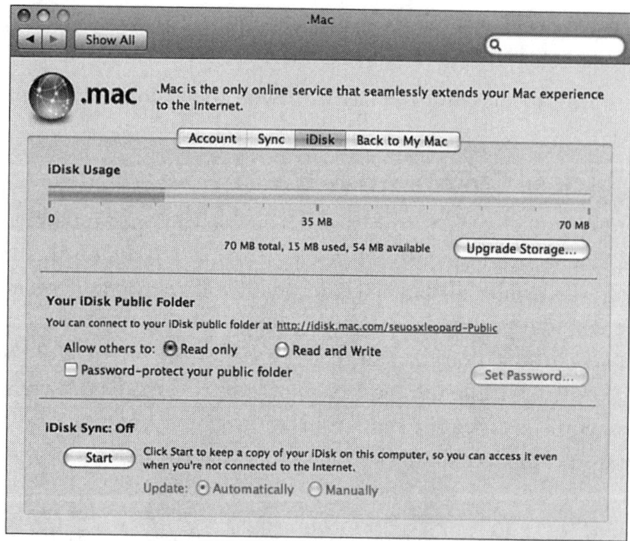


**Figure 20.4**
Using the iDisk tab of the .Mac pane, you can configure your iDisk; here, you can see that I have 70MB of space available in this trial .Mac account but am currently using only 15MB.

If you have a broadband connection, this is less important because there won't be as much difference accessing your online iDisk compared to the local copy. However, if you are going to work on files while they are on your iDisk (as opposed to just storing them there), using the local version will improve performance.

To configure your iDisk, perform the following steps:

1. Open the System Preferences utility and click the .Mac button to open the .Mac pane.
2. Click the iDisk tab.
3. Use the Disk Space bar to assess the status of your disk space. The total length of the bar represents the current size of your iDisk, and the colored portion represents how much of that space is currently being used.
4. To create a copy of your iDisk on your Mac, click the Start button. This causes your Mac to download a copy of your iDisk so you can access it directly from your desktop. If you want your Mac to keep the local copy and the online iDisk synchronized at all times, click the Automatically button (this option should be selected only if you have a broadband connection to the Internet). If you prefer to manually synchronize your local and online iDisks, click the Manually button (this option should be selected if you have a relatively slow Internet connection).
5. To control whether others can input information to the Public folder on your iDisk, use the radio buttons in the "Your iDisk Public Folder" section. Click the "Read only" button if you want users to only be able to read files in the Public folder on your iDisk but not be able to change any information there. Click the "Read and Write" button if you want them to also be able to change files there. If you chose the latter option, you should protect your iDisk with a password.

6. To protect your iDisk with a password, check the "Password-protect your public folder" check box and click the Set Password button.
7. In the resulting sheet, enter the password you want to use, confirm it, and click OK.

## Working with a Local Copy of Your iDisk

If you chose to create a local copy of your iDisk, you can open it from the Finder by clicking its icon in the sidebar. You can also select Go, iDisk, My iDisk or press Shift-⌘-I (see Figure 20.5). In the resulting Finder window, you will see the folders on your iDisk. At the bottom of the window, you can see the current space being used along with information about the last synchronization that was performed (or the progress of the current one if it is still being performed). While the local copy of your iDisk is being syncrhonized with the online version, you'll also see the synchronization symbol rotating next to the iDisk icon in the sidebar and information about the sync process at the bottom of the Finder window.

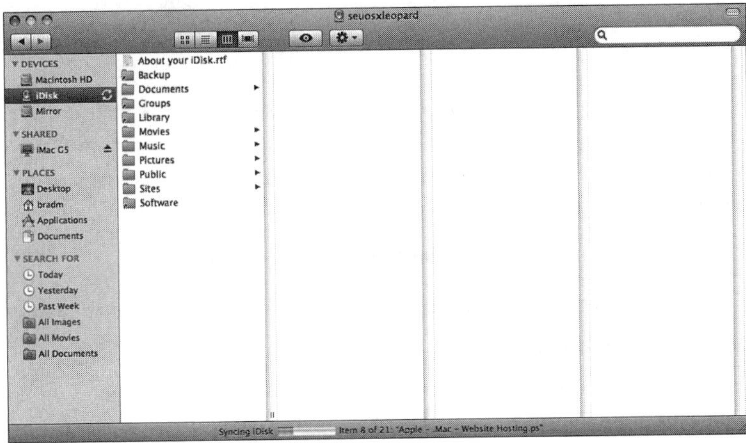


**Figure 20.5**
You can access your local copy of your iDisk by clicking its icon in the sidebar of a Finder window.

> **NOTE**
> The local iDisk is actually a disk image file called `Previous local iDisk for` *`username`*`.dmg`, where *`username`* is your member name.

If you set the local copy of your iDisk for manual synchronization, you can perform the synchronization by clicking the "Synchronize now" button located to the right of the iDisk icon in the sidebar. The two versions of the iDisk will be synchronized; a progress bar at the bottom of the Finder window will inform you about the status of the process.

> **TIP**
> If you click the Action button for a Finder window showing your iDisk, you can select the Sync Now command to perform synchronization or the Automatic Syncing command to set your iDisk to be synchronized automatically.

20

## WORKING WITH YOUR ONLINE IDISK

If you choose not to create a local copy of your iDisk, you can still work with your iDisk from the Finder. However, when you move files to and from the iDisk, you will actually be moving those files across the Internet rather than just between locations on your hard drive. In most cases, you should use a local copy instead. However, you can directly access your online iDisk to work with it.

To do so, click the iDisk icon on the sidebar and the contents of your iDisk will be shown in a Finder window.

If you have set your desktop preferences so that mounted disks appear on your desktop, you will see a disk with an icon of a hard disk in front of a globe—this is your iDisk. Your iDisk will also appear in the Devices section of the sidebar.

⇨ To learn how to set the preference for disks being shown on the desktop, **see** "Customizing the Mac OS X Desktop," **p. 86**.

**TIP**

> Look for the Synchronize symbol to the right of the iDisk volume in the sidebar of the Finder window to tell the difference between the online iDisk and a local copy of your iDisk. If you don't see any symbol, you are working with the online iDisk. If you do see the Synchronization symbol, you are working with a local copy.

**TIP**

> If you use more than one .Mac account, you can download and use the iDisk Utility application to make working with multiple .Mac accounts more convenient. You can download this application from the .Mac website.

## WORKING WITH AN IDISK

After your iDisk is mounted on your Mac (whether it is a local copy or the online version), you can work with it just like the other volumes and disks on your machine. Open your iDisk and you will see a number of folders, including the following:

- **Backup**—The Backup folder is where your data is stored if you use the Apple Backup application to backup your Mac via your iDisk.
- **Documents, Movies, Music, and Pictures**—These folders contain elements for web pages you might want to add to your .Mac website using HomePage. For example, if you want to include a Pictures page on your site, you can store the images you want to include on the page in the Pictures folder.
- **Library**—The Library folder contains files that support the use of iDisk, such as application support files.
- **Public**—The Public folder is where you can store files you want other .Mac users to be able to access via .Mac or those you want to publish via a files web page so anyone can download them.

- **Sites**—The Sites folder is where you store your own HTML pages to be served from the .Mac website (rather than using the HomePage service).
- **Software**—The Software folder contains software you can download to your Mac. Apple stores system and application software updates here so you can easily access and download them. To see what software is available, simply open the Software folder. To download any of the files you see to your Mac, drag the file from the Software flder to a folder on your machine. For example, a folder called Mac OS X Software contains applications you can download to your Mac by simply dragging them from the folder to your hard drive. The contents of the Software folder do not count against your iDisk storage space.

## ACCESSING IDISKS FROM THE GO MENU

The iDisk commands on the Finder's Go menu are the following:

- **My iDisk**—This command opens your own iDisk.
- **Other User's iDisk**—When you select this command, you see the Connect To iDisk dialog box. Enter the member name and password of the user's iDisk that you want to access and click Connect. That iDisk is mounted on your Mac and you can work with it just like the iDisk that is configured as part of your .Mac account. For example, if you have two .Mac accounts, you can configure one iDisk as part of your Mac OS X user account and use this command to access the iDisk that is part of another .Mac account.
- **Other User's Public Folder**—When you select this command, the Connect To iDisk Public Folder dialog box appears. Enter the member name of the user whose Public folder you want to access and click Connect. If the user has not selected the option to protect the Public folder with a password, that user's Public folder on her iDisk is shown in a Finder window. If the folder is protected with a password, enter the password and click Connect when prompted to do so.

20

**TIP**

> When you need to enter a password to access someone else's Public folder, your username is Public, which is entered for you. If you add the password to your keychain, you don't have to enter it again. The Public folder will be unlocked for you automatically when you access it.

## SHARING INFORMATION ON YOUR IDISK WITH OTHERS

One of the most useful things about an iDisk is that you can place files in the Public folder and then share them with other users. You can do this in a couple of ways.

If the people with whom you want to share files are Mac users, they can access your files via the commands on their Mac's Go, iDisk menu. All you need to do is place the files you want to share in your iDisk's Public folder and then provide your .Mac member name to the people with whom you want to share files. If you protect your Public folder with a password, you need to provide the password to them as well.

**NOTE**

> If you use a local iDisk and chose the Manual synchronization option, remember to synchronize your iDisk after you place new files in your Public folder for others to access.

You can also publish the contents of your Public folder so others can access it using a web interface. This means you can share files with anyone, whether they use a Mac or not.

⇨ To learn how to create a .Mac website, **see** "Using .Mac to Publish a Website," **p. 448**.

## Upgrading Your iDisk

You might need to have more space available than the 10GB that is provided as part of a standard .Mac account. In fact, if you want to create a website with lots of movies, music, and photos on it, up to 10GB might not be enough for you even if you've allocated most of your space to your iDisk. If you will be using the .Mac Backup application to back up your data, you are also likely to want more .Mac disk space.

At press time, you could increase the total storage space for your .Mac account to 20GB for an additional $49.95/year.

To add more space to your .Mac account, go to the iDisk tab of the .Mac pane and click the Upgrade Storage button. You'll move to the .Mac website. Log in and you'll move to the Upgrade Storage page. Follow the onscreen instructions to add more space to your .Mac account.

After you have added more disk space to your .Mac account, allocate the portion you want to make available to your iDisk.

⇨ To learn how to allocate disk space between your .Mac email and iDisk, **see** "Setting the Size of Your iDisk," **p. 441**.

## Using Your iDisk to Work with the Same Files on Multiple Macs

If you regularly work on more than one Mac (such as one at work or school and one at home), you can use .Mac to make sure you can access the same files on each Mac you use. To do this, perform the following steps:

1. Configure each Mac to use your .Mac account.
2. On each Mac, configure your iDisk so you use a local copy and choose the synchronization option.

   You don't need to choose the same synchronization option on each Mac. For example, if one Mac connects via a broadband connection, you could choose the Automatic option. If another uses a slow connection, you could choose the Manual option for that Mac.
3. Store the files on which you are working in a folder on your iDisk. (Don't use the Public folder unless you want other people to be able to access these files.) As you save files, they will be saved on your iDisk.
4. When you are done working on a Mac for which the Manual synchronization option is active, synchronize the iDisk. The files on which you are working will be moved to the online iDisk.

5. When you get to a different Mac, synchronize the iDisk (if you have configured that Mac for automatic synchronization, you don't need to do this step). The files on which you work will be available in the Mac's iDisk folder.

**TIP**

> After you have finished working on files and no longer need to access them, move them out of your iDisk so they no longer affect your available space.

# USING .MAC TO PUBLISH A WEBSITE

Using a .Mac account, you can publish your own website. There are two basic ways you can use .Mac to do so. The first is to use .Mac's HomePage tools to build your web pages. You add content to these pages by placing files in the related folders on your iDisk. The second, and more flexible, way is to add your own website files to the Sites folder on your iDisk to publish that site. For example, you can create your website using your favorite web page application and then post the site's files in the Sites folder on your iDisk. The iWeb application that is part of the iLife suite is perfect for this because it makes creating and publishing a web site very easy. Whichever way you publish, Apple's .Mac server takes care of serving the site for you.

## CREATING A .MAC WEBSITE USING HOMEPAGE

When you build a website using .Mac HomePage tools, you create each page on the site using HomePage templates. You can also create a set of sites and place different pages on each site. People can access each site directly, or you can provide a site menu to help them navigate among your sites.

You can use HomePage templates to add any of the following pages to your site:

- **Photo Album**—I bet you can guess what you store on these pages. Use these pages to share your photos via the Web.

**TIP**

> If you use iPhoto 6 or later, it's easier just to publish photos directly from iPhoto, such as by using the Photocast tool.

20

- **File Sharing**—Pages using this template present the files in your Public folder for easy downloading.
- **Site Menu**—These pages help you create a menu so visitors can explore your site by clicking links.
- **iMovie**—You can serve iMovies you create so others can watch them over the Web.
- **Writing**—These pages are formatted as personal newsletters.
- **Résumé**—You can publish an online résumé to land that next big job.
- **Baby**—Use these pages to make a grandparent's day.

- **Education**—These pages are designed for those involved in education. The template pages include pages for school events, a school album, teacher information, and so on.
- **Invite**—You can use these pages to create custom web invitations.
- **Advanced**—You can use this option to publish pages stored in your iDisk's Sites folder.

Before you get started adding pages to your website, decide what kinds of pages you want to have on your site or what types of sites you want to include. Add the files for each page to the appropriate folder on your iDisk. For example, if you are going to have an iMovie page, add your movie files to the Movies folder. Add photos you want to post by placing the files in the Pictures folder, and so on, until you have added the content you want to have on your site to the appropriate folder on your iDisk.

The process to add each type of page is similar. You can create pages based on any of the available templates by following these steps:

1. Move to the .Mac web page and log in to your .Mac account if you aren't already logged in.
2. Click the HomePage icon or tab. You will see the HomePage screen (see Figure 20.6). This screen contains the tools you need to build and edit your pages and the sites on which you store those pages. In the upper part of the window you will see all the sites and pages that are currently part of your site. You will also see the URL to your site. In the lower part of the screen, you will see the tools you use to create pages.

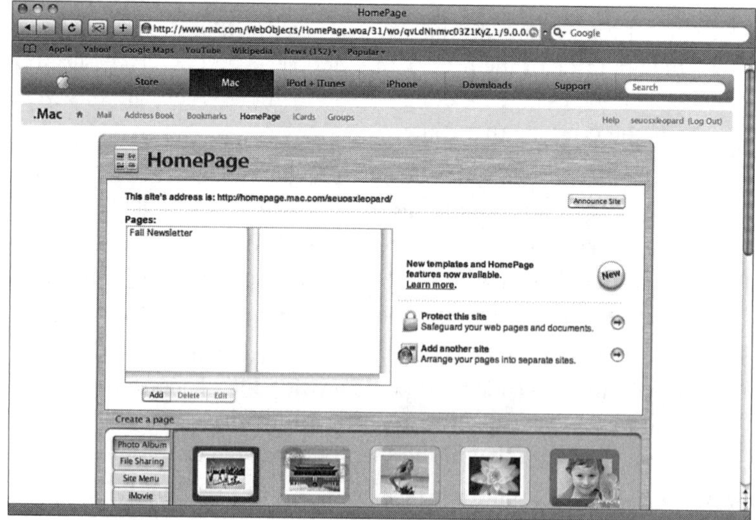


**Figure 20.6**
The HomePage web page enables you to build your own website quickly and easily.



**TIP**

> The page shown in bold is the Start Page—your home page—which is the first page people see when they access your website.

3. In the Create a page area, click the tab for the type of page you want to create (for example, click iMovies to create a movie page). You will see buttons for each of the various themes (templates) available for the type of page you selected.

> **TIP**
>
> If you have more than one site, select the site on which you want to place the file-sharing page before doing step 4.

4. Click the button for the template you want to use. If the page serves files of some kind that must be stored in a specific location, such as pictures for a slideshow, you'll be prompted to select the folder on your iDisk that contains the files you want to publish on the page you are creating. If the page doesn't require files in a specific location, you'll move directly to the Edit page for the page you are creating (skip to step 6).
5. Use the tools on the "Choose a folder" page to move to and select the folder containing the files required by the page; then click Choose. You will move to the edit page that is based on the template you selected.

> **NOTE**
>
> If you work with a local copy of your iDisk, it must be synchronized before the files will be available on the Web. If you use the Manual synchronization option, click the Synchronize button after you put the files in the appropriate folder.

6. On the Edit screen, edit the text associated with the page. For most pages, this will include the title of the page, a title of objects on it, and a description of the page's contents. For pages that are designed to provide text content, this will include boxes in which you can type that content.
7. If the page serves files of some kind, such as a QuickTime movie, click the Choose button. The "Choose a file" page will appear. The folders on your iDisk possibly containing appropriate files will be shown in the far left pane.
8. Move to the file you want to place on the page, select it, and click Choose. You'll return to the edit page window and the file will be placed on the web page you are creating.
9. Scroll to the bottom of the window. Check the Show check boxes for any special features you want to add. Most pages provide for a counter that shows the number of people who have visited the page (the Show check box next to the 0) and a "Send me a message" feature that enables visitors to send email to you.
10. Click the Preview button to see how your page will look. The page will be presented as it will be when you publish it.
11. If you need to make changes, click the Edit button and use the instructions in the previous steps to make your changes.
12. When you are done with the page, click Publish. The web page you created will be added to your site and you will see its URL.
13. Click the URL to visit your new page (see Figure 20.7).

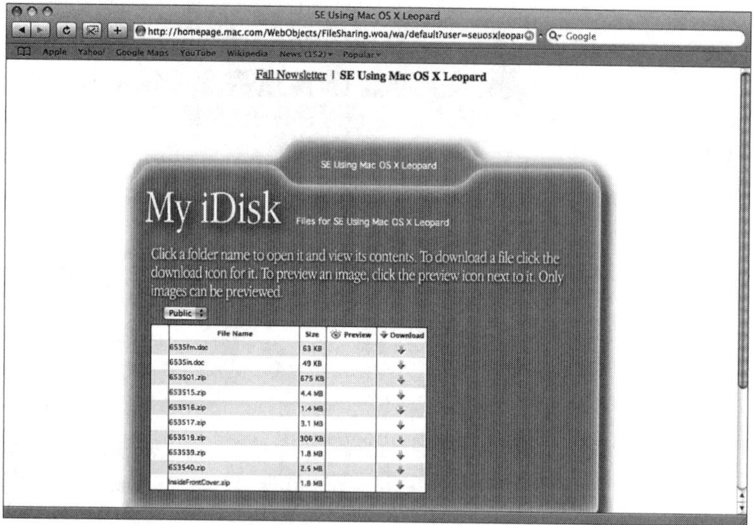


**Figure 20.7**
Hopefully, you will use HomePage to publish more interesting pages than this one, but you get the idea.

**NOTE**

When HomePage creates a page for you, the URL ends in the name of the template you selected to create the page followed by a sequential number (such as FileSharing27.html). These URLs aren't likely to be easy for others to type. However, you can create site menu navigation pages on your site that link to each page. People can access your site menu at http://homepage.mac.com/*membername*/, where *membername* is your member name. This makes locating your site and moving to its pages much easier.

Continue adding pages to your site until it contains all you want it to. When you are done, you will see all the pages on your site in the upper-left corner of the HomePage window.

You can also create additional sites and then add pages to those sites using the same process. Each site is independent so you can create completely different web experiences for different purposes.

To create another site, carry out the following steps:

1. On the HomePage page, click the arrow button next to "Add another site." You will move to the "Create a site" page.
2. Enter the name of the site you are creating in the Site Name field.
3. If you want a password to be required for someone to be able to view your site, check the On check box and enter the password in the Password field.
4. Click Create Site. You will return to the HomePage page and see the new site you have created. The HomePage page now contains boxes for your sites and the pages on those sites.
5. To see the pages included in a site, select the site on the Sites pane; its pages appear in the Pages pane. Select a page and a preview appears in the third column on the screen (see Figure 20.8).

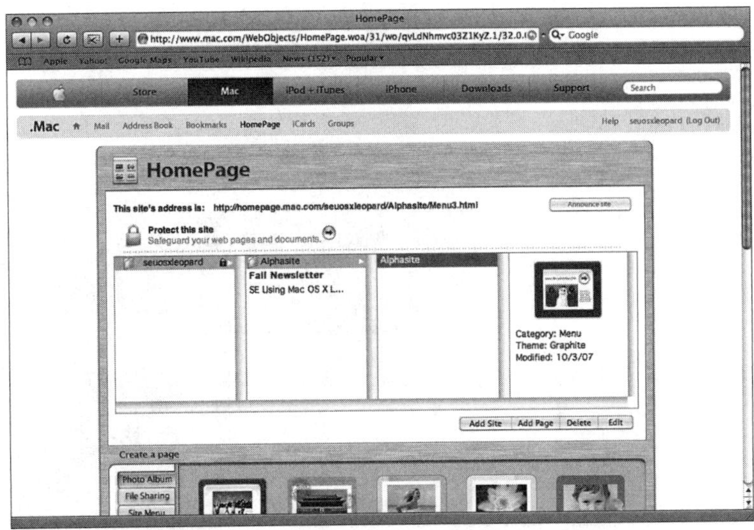


**Figure 20.8**
My website now includes sites: One is called alphasite, and the other is the default site that is called seuosxleopard.

The URL for the website you create is http://homepage.mac.com/*yourmembername*/. (Don't include the period shown in this URL—that is only to please my editors!)

When someone visits this URL, she sees the page you designated as the start page. She can use the links on this page to move to the other pages on your website.

You can move directly to a specific page using the URL for that page. For example, if you create an iMovie page, the URL for that page will be http://homepage.mac.com/*yourmembername*/iMovieTheater.html, where *yourmembername* is your member name. As you add more pages of each type, the names are differentiated by sequential numbers, as in iMovieTheater1, iMovieTheater2, and so on.

Creating websites using HomePage is easy and powerful. Following are some additional tips for your consideration:



- Set the home page for each site (called the *start page* in .Mac lingo) for your website by dragging the page you want to use to the top of the Pages list for that site.
- You can see the URL for any site by selecting it. Its URL appears at the top of the HomePage screen.
- n The Home site is always the one with your member name as its URL. Any other sites you create have URLs based on this one. For example, if you create a site called Book_Information, its URL is http://homepage.mac.com/*yourmembername*/Book_Information, where *yourmembername* is your member name.
- To add more pages to a site, select that site on the Sites list and click the Add Page button.
- To add more sites, click the Add Site button.

- You can delete sites or pages by selecting what you want to delete and clicking Delete. Then click Yes on the resulting confirmation screen.
- Password-protect any sites that contain information to which you want to limit access.
- Use site menu pages to organize your site and enable visitors to move around using links. You can also place images on site menu pages as a preview of the pages that are linked to the site menu page.
- To add a custom page to your site, create it using any tool that outputs HTML files. Place the resulting file in the Sites folder on your iDisk and then use the Advanced page template to publish it.
- To place a counter on a page, use the Show check box next to the counter icon (a box with a zero in it) that becomes available when you edit the page. This counter counts the number of visitors to that page.
- Use the Show check box next to the "Send me a message" text to place an email link on a page. Visitors can click this link to send email to your .Mac email address.

## CREATING YOUR WEBSITE BY ADDING YOUR OWN PAGES TO THE SITES FOLDER

Although you can quickly and easily create a basic website using the HomePage templates and tools, you are somewhat limited in what you can do. The available templates might or might not be suitable for the site you want to create. Even if you want to do more than you can with the .Mac web page templates, .Mac is still valuable because you can use .Mac to host *any* website you create using any other website editing tools, such as Adobe's GoLive or Macromedia's Dreamweaver. In this scenario, .Mac acts just like any other web-hosting service you might use.

**TIP**

> Apple's iWeb application, part of the iLife suite, is about the easiest way to create and publish websites. It's even easier than HomePage. iWeb is integrated with .Mac so to publish a site is literally a single click. The only downside to iWeb is that it is a template-based approach so you have to work with the templates provided in the application. That isn't much of a limitation unless you like to design your sites from the ground up.



The general process to get your customized website on the .Mac site is the following:

1. Create your website using the tools you prefer.

**NOTE**

> Name the home page of your site `index.html`. This ensures that a viewer is taken to the right start page for your site when he moves to its URL.

2. Test the site by accessing it while it is stored on your Mac. You can test a website by opening it from within a web browser. For example, open your site using Safari by selecting File, Open File. Then, maneuver to the home page for your site and open it.

The site will work just as it will after you post it on your .Mac website (except that it will be faster, of course). You should test your site in various browsers and operating systems to ensure that it can be viewed properly.

3. Fix any problems you find.
4. When your site is ready to post, copy all its files and folders into the Sites folder on your iDisk.
5. Test your site again by accessing it over the Internet.

To access the website in your Sites folder, use the following URL: http://homepage.mac.com/*yourmembername*/. (For this to work, you must have named the home page for the site `index.html`.)

When you move to your .Mac website URL, you see the page you named `index.html`.

The website you store in the Sites folder is not integrated into a .Mac website you create using the .Mac template. In fact, any pages you create using the .Mac templates are not accessible after you copy your own site into the Sites folder because your custom site replaces any HomePage sites you have created.

## USING .MAC TO SYNCHRONIZE IMPORTANT INFORMATION ON MULTIPLE MACS

You can also use .Mac to keep important information synchronized on all the Macs you use. For example, you can make sure you have access to the same set of Safari bookmarks on each Mac you use. Similarly, you can keep the same set of information in the Address Book on each of your Macs. To synchronize your Macs, perform the following steps:

1. Click the Sync tab found on the .Mac pane of the System Preferences application (see Figure 20.9).
2. Check the "Synchronize with .Mac" check box.
3. Choose the frequency at which you want information to be synchronized on the pop-up menu. To have information synchronized constantly, choose Automatically. Other options include Every Hour, Every Day, Every Week, and Manually.
4. Check the check box next to each type of information that you want to be synchronized. For example, to synchronize your Safari bookmarks, check the Bookmarks check box. To synchronize your contact information, check the Contacts check box.
5. Click Sync Now. The synchronization process will start and you'll be prompted to choose how you want information to be synchronized.
6. When prompted, choose the synchronization option you want to use from the pop-up menu. The "Merge data on this computer and .Mac" option adds new data on your Mac to that stored in your .Mac account and adds data stored in your .Mac account onto the Mac. The "Replace data on .Mac" replaces all the related data in your .Mac account with information on the Mac. The "Replace data on this computer" option causes data on .Mac to replace the data currently on your Mac.

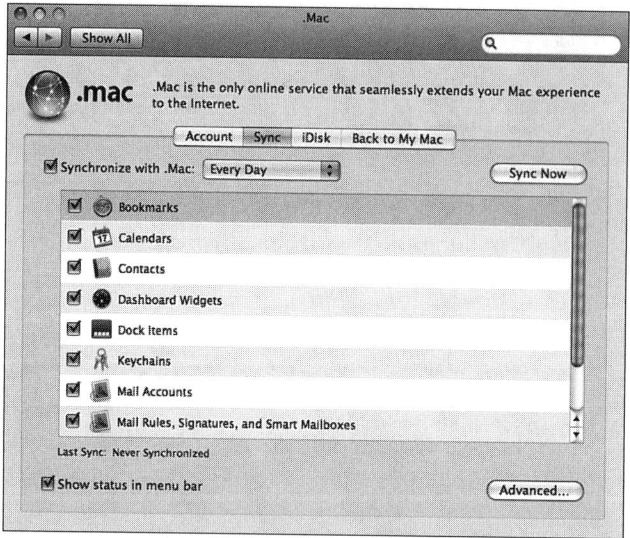


**Figure 20.9**
Use the options on the Sync tab to keep information on multiple Macs synchronized.

7. Click Sync. The data you selected to be synchronized will be moved to and from the Mac and .Mac until it is synchronized according to the option you selected. From this point forward, it will be synchronized according to the option you selected on the pop-up menu.
8. Repeat steps 1–7 for each Mac you want to keep in sync.

The time and date of the last synchronization will be shown under the .Mac icon.

If you configured the sync with something other than Manual, you don't need to bother with it anymore; your Mac will keep its information in sync with what is on your .Mac account. If you chose Manual, you'll need to click the Sync Now button to synchronize your Mac's information.

If you check the "Show status in menu bar" check box, the Sync menu will appear in the Finder menu bar. On this menu, you can see the time and date of the last synchronization, choose the Sync Now command, or open the Sync tab.

You can manage the Macs being synchronized using the Advanced button of the Sync tab (see Figure 20.10). On the list, you'll see each computer that is being synchronized via the .Mac account. The computer you are currently using will be indicated by the `(This Computer)` text. In addition to the computer name, you'll see the time and date of that computer's last synchronization.

You can remove a computer from the synchronization list by selecting it and clicking the Unregister button. In the resulting prompt, click Unregister. The computer will be removed from the list and will no longer be available for synchronization.

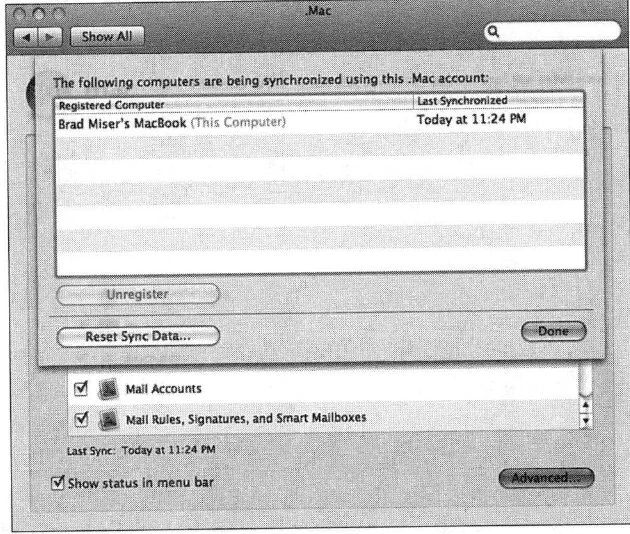


**Figure 20.10**
The Advanced tab of the .Mac pane provides information about all the computers you are synching via .Mac.

If you want to reset how data is being synchronized on a computer, select it and click the Reset Sync Data button. In the resulting sheet, you can configure the reset (see Figure 20.11). On the Replace pop-up menu, choose the kind of information you want to reset; choose All Sync Info to reset all the information you have chosen to sync. Click the left or right arrow to determine the direction in which you want to do the reset. To replace the data on the Mac with data on .Mac, click the left arrow. To replace the data on .Mac with data on the computer, click the right arrow. Then click Replace. The data will be reset in the direction you indicated.

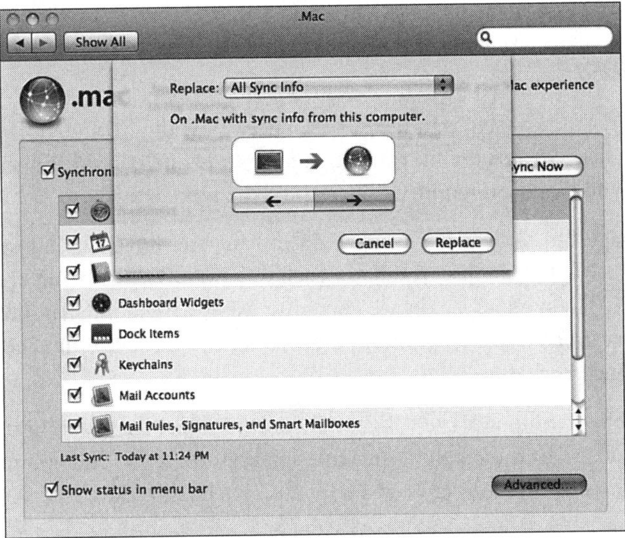


**Figure 20.11**
Use this prompt to reset the synchronization options for a computer.

20

## GETTING FREE SOFTWARE VIA .MAC

Purchasing a .Mac account includes lots of benefits, including free versions of commercial applications and discounts on the purchase prices of others. To download the free applications, move to the .Mac website and click the Member Central link. You'll move to the Members Central page from which you can download applications and see special offers. For example, you can download the Backup application to perform backups.

## REMOTELY ACCESS YOUR MAC WITH BACK TO MY MAC

Mac OS X 10.5 introduces a new way for Mac users to access the data on their computer. Back to My Mac allows you to access files on the Mac OS X computers that use your .Mac account. In addition, enabling the Screen Sharing service allows you to remotely control your Mac over the Internet. Back to My Mac requires a paid .Mac account, and the Mac you want to access or control must be turned on and connected to the Internet. To enable Back to My Mac, perform the following steps:

1. Click the Back to My Mac tab found on the .Mac pane of the System Preferences application (see Figure 20.12).

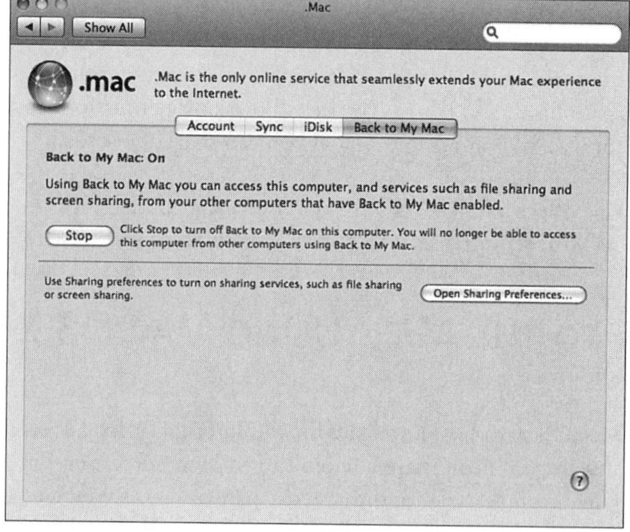


**Figure 20.12**
Back to My Mac enables you to share files with or remotely control any Mac configured with your .Mac account.

2. If the Back to My Mac service is not enabled, click the Start button to enable it. You can see the status of the service at the top of the pane.
3. Click on the Open Sharing Preferences button to move to the Sharing pane of the System Preferences application. Here you can configure the Screen Sharing and File

20

Sharing services and turn them on so that you will be able to remotely access this computer. Be sure to specify the accounts that can access this Mac remotely for Screen Sharing.

⇨ To learn how to enable network services on your Mac, **see** "Configuring the Services on a Network," **p. 369**.

4. When you use another computer that is configured with your .Mac account, the computer that has Back to My Mac turned on will appear in the Sharing section of the sidebar.

**TIP**

> If you do not see the remote Mac in the Sharing section of the sidebar, open the Finder preferences and click the Sidebar tab. Make sure that Back to My Mac is checked so that it will appear in the sidebar.

5. Select the computer you want to remotely access. Click Connect As to access shared files on the remote Mac. You will be prompted to log in so that you can access the correct user account on the remote Mac. After you authenticate as a user on that computer, you will see the files you have access to, and you can copy files to and from the remote Mac.
6. To control the remote Mac, click Share Screen. Click "As a registered user" and enter your username and password. You will then take control of the Mac. Note that this will take over control of the computer; if someone else is using that remote computer this may be a bit of a shock. You could click "By asking permission" instead, which will ask the current user of that remote Mac if you can share the screen.

Back to My Mac offers a new level of resource sharing. Because it is integrated with .Mac, communicating with remote Mac OS X 10.5 computers is very easy to do.

## MAC OS X TO THE MAX: USING MAC OS X TO SERVE WEB PAGES



You can use Mac OS X to host a website for the Internet or for a local intranet because the web server software you need is already built in to Mac OS X. Serving a website to the Internet is a fairly complex task, and there are many nuances you need to consider. However, serving a website to a local network is fairly straightforward. In either case, you can use Mac OS X to get your site online.

Mac OS X includes very powerful and sophisticated web server software: Apache. This software is widely used across the Internet to serve web pages, and Mac OS X users can take full advantage of it out of the box. Although Apache is a Unix application, you can perform the basic tasks of serving a website without messing around with text commands. Of course, to really customize and master Apache, you do need to get your hands into the command line. However, you can get a site up and running without ever interacting directly with Apache.

Establishing and maintaining a web server is a complex and challenging task, and explaining all the details associated with hosting a website is beyond the scope of this book.

The general process for using your Mac to host a website is the following:

1. Create your website using any tools you prefer.
2. Test it to make sure that it works.
3. Register your domain.
4. Move the files for your website to the appropriate location on your Mac.
5. Start the web server.
6. Monitor your site to ensure that it has adequate performance and is available 24/7.

Each user account on your Mac can serve its own website; this means you can serve many websites from your Mac at the same time. To provide a website for a user's account, you place the files for that site in the Sites folder that is contained in that user's Home directory.

There is also an overall website for the Mac itself. You should ensure that you add a website for the Mac so that when people move to the home page for your machine, they will see a meaningful site.

To start serving a website from your Mac, perform the following steps:

1. Place the files for the site you want to post in the Sites folder of the user account you want to use. Each user's Sites folder contains an `index.html` file that provides a default home page for that user's website. You replace this file with your own `index.html` file to serve your specific site (you can also modify the default index page if you want). The default `index.html` page contains information about how web sharing works and is worth reading if you are new to the topic.

> **TIP**
>
> You can test any user's website without actually adding web pages to the Sites folder. Because the `index.html` page is part of each Sites folder, that page is served up for every account. So, if you move to the URL for a user account on your machine, you should see the Mac OS X Web Sharing page. If you do, that means web sharing is working. All you need to do is replace the default content with your content.

2. Open the System Preferences application and open the Sharing pane.
3. In the Services lick, check the "Web Sharing" On check box. This starts the web server on your Mac. On the right side of the Sharing pane, you will see the URL of the Mac along with the URL for the user's website. You build the URL for your site based on either of these. For example, if your IP address is 12.34.567.89, the basic URL for your site is http://12.34.567.89/. Similarly, if the registered domain name for your Mac is agreatmac.com, the URL to your machine is also http://www.agreatmac.com/. If you use the IP address to access the site, it is resolved to the hostname and that is what appears in the address bar of the browser.

The URL to a specific user's website on your Mac is the URL for the Mac itself with a ~ (tilde character) followed by the short version of the username appended to it. For example, if the short name for my user account is bmiser, the URL to my website would be http://12.34.567.89/~bmiser/ or http://www.agreatmac.com/~bmiser/ (if I had registered a domain name appropriately, of course).

**TIP**

> The tilde (~) character in the URL indicates that the address points to that user's Home directory, in which the Sites folder is stored. If you leave this out of the URL, the user's site won't be found.
>
> Although it is technically more accurate to include the end slash (/) in the URL, you do not have to insert it: The Apache server will insert if when it returns the page.

4. Close System Preferences.
5. Use another machine to access the URL for your website.

If you see the site, everything is in great shape and your pages are "available."

**TIP**

> The concept that each user who has an account on your Mac can have a unique website opens many possibilities for you. You can create user accounts for the sole purpose of providing specific websites. For example, if I wanted to host a website for this book, I could create a user account called SEUsing MacOSX with the short name usingosx. I could then place the website in the Sites folder for this account and the site would be published.

**TIP**

> Mac OS X 10.5 allows a user account to have alias names, as well. This can become very handy for web sites, as you could provide different alias names that all point to the same web site. For example, `usingosx` could be an alias for my `bradm` account. This would allow `http://12.34.567.89/~bradm` and `http://12.34.567.89/~usingosx` to both point to the same web site.

20

⇨ To learn how create account aliases, **see** "Configuring an Account's Advanced Options," **p. 248**.

If you are going to be hosting any web pages on your Mac, you should also configure the root-level website for your Mac. This site will appear if someone accesses the website on your Mac without including a specific user's account in the URL. For example, if someone enters only **`http://12.34.567.89/`**, he would see the root-level web page.

**TIP**

> Consider creating a web page that provides URL links to all the websites that are hosted on your Mac and posting that at the root level. This would make it easy for a visitor to get to any of the sites on your machine.

If you open the directory located at Mac OS X/Library/WebServer/Documents/, where Mac OS X is the name of your Mac OS X startup volume, you will see many index pages. Each of these has an abbreviation for the language for which that page is applicable at the end of its filename (for example, the file `index.html.en` is the English version of the page). The version that Apache serves depends on how your machine is configured.

To post a root-level web page, do the following:

1. Create the website you want to be at the root level of your machine.
2. Name the home page for this site; again, the name of the home page for the site should be `index.html`.
3. Place the files and folders for the site in the following location: *Mac OS X*/Library/WebServer/Documents/, where *Mac OS X* is the name of your Mac OS X startup volume. Make sure the index file is in this directory.

**NOTE**

> The web server continues to run as long as your Mac is turned on and the website for each user account is served continuously, even if no one is logged in to the system. You can stop the server by shutting down the Mac or by turning off web sharing using the Sharing pane of the System Preferences application.

The information in this section has barely scratched the surface of Apache specifically and web serving in general. However, a great deal of information on both topics is available within Mac OS X as well as on the Internet.

To access the Apache documentation included with Mac OS X, open the manual alias in the Documents folder in the WebServer folder. The Apache folder will open. Open the `index.html` file and the Apache User Guide will open.

To find information on the Web about Apache, visit www.apache.org. There is plenty of information on this site, including some nice tutorials.

PART IV

# Getting Things Done with Leopard's Applications

# CHAPTER 21

# Managing Your Email with Mail

## In this chapter

# WORKING WITH MAIL

Email is an important tool for most Mac users. Fortunately, Mac OS X includes the Mail email application. In addition to being easy to use, Mail packs a lot of powerful features to enable you to take control over your email.

# CONFIGURING MAIL

Before you can start using Mail to work with your email, you need to configure the accounts it uses. If you entered account information in the Setup Assistant when you installed Mac OS X, those accounts are configured for you already. For example, if you set up or entered the information for your .Mac account in the Setup Assistant, your .Mac email account is configured in Mail automatically.

If you are like most Mac users, you probably have more than one email account; you can use Mail to access any or all of them.

There are also several other areas that you don't necessarily have to configure to use Mail, but I have included them in the section so that all the configuration information is together for your reference.

## CONFIGURING GENERAL MAIL PREFERENCES

Using the General pane of the Mail preferences dialog box, you can configure the following preferences:

- **Default email application**—Use the "Default Email Reader" pop-up menu to select the email application you will use by default. If you want to use Mail, you don't need to make a selection on this menu. If you want to use another application, choose Select on the menu and use the resulting sheet to select the application you want to use instead of Mail.
- **Frequency of mail checking**—Use the "Check for new mail" pop-up menu to determine how often Mail checks for new mail. Select Manually to disable automatic checking or the frequency at which you want Mail to check for new email automatically, such as "Every 5 minutes" to have Mail check every 5 minutes.
- **Mail sounds**—Mail can play sounds for the following events: new mail received, mail error, and mail sent. You can choose the sound that is played when new mail is received by choosing the sound for that event on the "New mail sound" pop-up menu. To turn this sound off, choose None. To disable the sound for other events, uncheck the "Play sounds for other mail actions" check box.



**TIP**

> You can use custom mail sounds by selecting Add/Remove on the pop-up menu and selecting the custom sound you want to use. Mail will place the sound file you select in the `Library/Sounds` folder in your Home folder. You can then choose it on the pop-up menu in Mail and other applications, such as iChat.

- **Dock indicator**—Mail's icon on the Dock can indicate when you have new mail and how many new messages you've received. Use the "Dock unread count" pop-up to configure the Mail Dock icon. Choose Inbox Only to have only unread messages in your inbox displayed on the icon. You can also choose All Mailboxes or one of Mail's default smart folders, such as Last 7 Days. To disable the Dock indicator, choose None.
- **iCal invitations**—Use the "Add invitations to iCal" pop-up menu to determine how Mail handles iCal invitations you receive. Select Automatically to have them added to your iCal calendar when you receive them, or select Never if you don't want them added to your calendar.
- **Downloads**—Use the Downloads Folder pop-up menu to determine where Mail stores file attachments from the email messages you receive. Leave the default Main Downloads folder selected, or choose Other and specify a different folder.
- **Remove unedited downloads**—Use the "Remove unedited downloads" pop-up menu to determine when Mail deletes file attachments that you haven't changed. The options are Never, When Mail Quits, and After Message is Deleted.
- **Unavailable email server**—Use the "If outgoing server is unavailable" pop-up menu to select what to do when the server you use to send email is not accessible. You can have Mail display a list of alternative servers, or have Mail automatically try to deliver the email again later.
- **Search folders**—Use the "When searching all mailboxes, include results from" check boxes to determine whether the Trash, Junk, or Encrypted Messages folders are included in searches. If a folder's box is checked, it will be included. If not, it won't be.
- **Synchronize**—If you use .Mac and have more than one Mac, you can keep your Mail information synchronized on each machine you use. Check the check boxes for the synchronization options you want to use ("Rules, Signatures, and Smart Mailboxes" and "Accounts") and then click the .Mac button. Use the resulting .Mac pane to configure the synchronization you want to use.

⇨ To learn how to use .Mac to synchronize information, **see** "Using .Mac to Synchronize Important Information on Multiple Macs," **p. 454**.

## Configuring Email Accounts

The most basic configuration for Mail is the email accounts you are going to access with it. Before you get started, gather the following information for each mail account you want to configure in Mail:

- **Account type**—There are four types of email accounts with which Mail can work. A .Mac account is one provided by Apple's .Mac servers. A Post Office Protocol (POP) account is provided by most ISPs. An Internet Message Access Protocol (IMAP) account is similar to a POP account but offers additional features, and an Exchange account is provided by an Exchange server, which is used on many business networks.

**NOTE**

> When you use a .Mac email account with Mail, it is configured as an IMAP account. In Mail, it is treated as its own category because it is part of your .Mac account.

- **Your email address**—This should be self-explanatory.
- **Incoming mail server**— This is the address of the server that handles retrieving your email. For POP accounts, it often looks something like pop.isp.net.
- **Your email username**—This is your username for your email account, which might or might not be the same as your username for your Internet account. Typically, this is everything before the @ in your email address.
- **Your email password**—This is the password for your email account, which might or might not be the same as that of your Internet access account.
- **Outgoing email server or Simple Mail Transfer Protocol (SMTP) host**—This is the address of the server that handles sending your email.
- **Authentication**—You need to know whether your SMTP server uses authentication.
- **SMTP username**—This is the username for your SMTP server; it is usually the same as your email username, but it isn't always.
- **SMTP password**—Again, this is usually the same as your email password.

After you have gathered this information, you are ready to configure the email accounts. You can use the Accounts pane of the Preferences dialog box or the Add Account command.

### Adding Accounts Using Preferences

To add email accounts to Mail using the Preferences option, do the following:

1. Launch Mail.
2. Select Mail, Preferences (or press ⌘-,).
3. Click the Accounts button to see the Accounts pane of the Preferences window (see Figure 21.1). This pane has three tabs: Account Information, Mailbox Behaviors, and Advanced. In the left part of the pane is the list of email accounts that are currently configured.
4. Click the Add Account button (the plus sign at the bottom of the list of accounts). The General Information sheet appears.
5. Select the account type from the Account Type pop-up menu.
6. Enter a description of the account in the Description field.
7. Enter the rest of the information for the account including the full name and email address or full name, username, and password for a .Mac account.

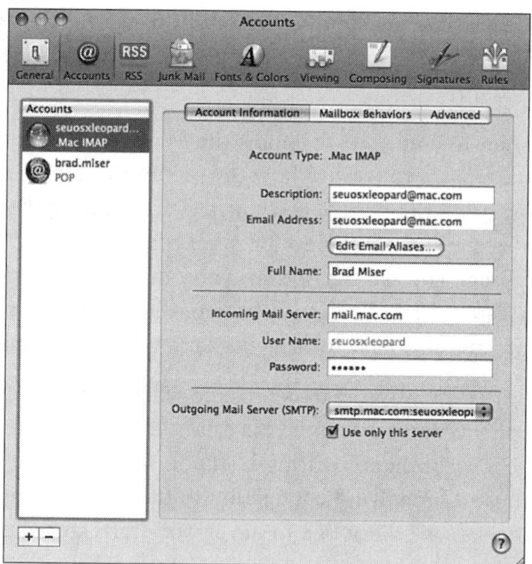


**Figure 21.1**
If you configured a .Mac account when you installed Mac OS X, your .Mac email account is configured in Mail automatically.

**NOTE**

> What you enter in the Full Name field is what appears next to your return email address shown in the Email Address data field. If a recipient uses Mail, he sees your full name instead of your email address.

8. Click Continue. For all account types except .Mac, the incoming Mail Server sheet appears. For .Mac accounts, Mail will check the information you entered and if it is correct, the account is configured and you move directly to the Conclusion sheet; skip to step 12.
9. Enter the Incoming Mail Server, enter your username (typically everything before the @ in your email address) and password, and then click Continue. Mail will check the connection using the information you entered. If the information works, you see the Outgoing Mail Server sheet. If not, you'll need to correct it before you can move ahead.
10. Enter the SMTP server address for the account in the Outgoing Mail Server box. If an SMTP server is already configured, you can choose to use it by selecting it on the drop-down list.
11. If the SMTP server for the account uses authentication, check the Use Authentication check box and configure the User Name and Password fields in the sheet; the username and password might or might not be the same as those for the incoming mail server. Click Continue when you are finished configuring the outgoing mail server. Mail will check the connection to make sure it can communicate with the server. If it can, you see the Account Summary sheet, which means the account has been configured successfully. If not, you'll need to correct the configuration until it can communicate with the server.
12. Click Continue. You see the Conclusion sheet. Click Done if you are finished creating accounts, or click Create Another Account to start the process again.

After you have created one or more accounts, you return to the Accounts pane and the accounts you have configured are shown in the left part of the pane. Next, configure mailbox behavior for each account.

Select the account you want to configure and click the Mailbox Behaviors tab. This tab provides several controls you can use to control how the account you are configuring behaves. The options you see depend on the type of account you are creating. For example, you see fewer options for a POP account than you do for other types. Because .Mac accounts are popular with many Mac users, you see the options you can configure for .Mac accounts in the following list and in Figure 21.2. You can configure the options on this tab for other account types in a similar way, although the specific options you have might be different:

- Use the check box in the Drafts area to determine whether messages are stored on the .Mac server when you are writing them. This causes email that you are writing to be saved on the .Mac server as you are writing it. If you write email offline, you don't want to select this. If you use a broadband connection to the Net, you can check the "Store draft messages on the server" check box to have your drafts stored online as you write them.
- You can use Mail to create and manage notes, which are text documents you can create and store within Mail. If you want your notes to be stored in your Inbox, check the "Store notes in Inbox" check box. If you leave this unchecked, you can access notes via the Notes folder.
- Use the controls in the Sent area to determine whether sent messages are stored on the server and when sent messages are deleted. Usually, you don't want to save sent messages on the server because those messages count against your total storage allowance for your account. If you do want sent messages to be stored on the server, check the "Store sent messages on the server" check box. Then use the "Delete sent messages when" pop-up menu to select how often the sent messages will be deleted. The options are Never, One day old, One week old, One month old, or Quitting Mail.
- Use the Junk controls to configure how Mail handles messages that are classified as junk. Similar to the first two options, you can select to have junk mail stored on the server; if you select to allow this, use the pop-up menu to determine when junk mail is deleted from the server.
- Use the Trash controls to configure how trash is handled. If you want deleted messages to be moved to the Trash mailbox, check the "Move deleted messages to the Trash mailbox" check box. If you want deleted messages to be stored on the server, check the "Store deleted messages on the server" check box, and to determine when deleted messages are actually erased, use the "Permanently erase deleted message when" pop-up menu. The options are Never, One day old, One week old, One month old, or Quitting Mail.

Configure these behaviors for each account using similar options.

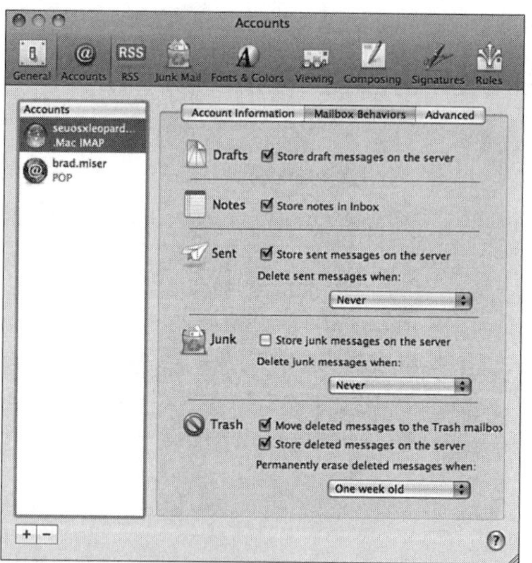


**Figure 21.2**
You can configure these special mailbox actions when using a .Mac mail account.

**TIP**

> You can also add a new account by selecting File, Add Account. The New Account Assistant will open and lead you through creating the account. The steps you use are the same as those you use when creating an account via the Preferences dialog box.

Finally, configure the Advanced options for each account using the following steps (again, these assume a .Mac account; other account types might have different options):

1. Select the account you want to configure and click the Advanced tab. Just like the Mailbox Behaviors tab, the specific controls you see depend on the type of account you are configuring (see Figure 21.3).
2. Use the "Enable this account" check box to enable or disable the account. If you disable an account, it won't be used.
3. Check the "Include when automatically checking for new mail" check box if you want this account always included when Mail automatically checks for mail. If you uncheck this check box, you must manually check for mail for this account.
4. If enabled, check the "Comapct mailboxes automatically" check box to have Mail automatically compress your mailboxes to minimize the storage space they require.
5. Use the "Keep copies of messages for offline viewing" pop-up menu to determine what Mail does with the messages it receives when you are not connected to the Internet. For example, if you select "All messages and their attachments," all your messages and any attachments they contain are downloaded to your Mac so you can view them even if you aren't connected to the Net. If you select "Only messages I've read," only the messages you have read are downloaded to your Mac. Choose "All messages, but not attachments" to download messages but not their attachments or "Don't keep copies of any messages" if you don't want any information to be downloaded to your Mac (you'll have to be connected to the Internet to be able to read messages).

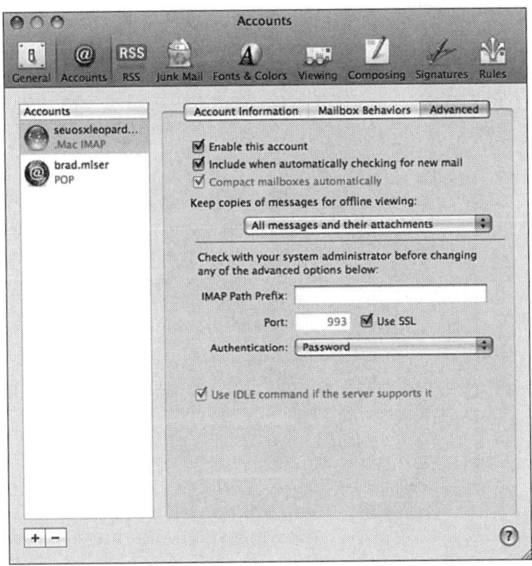


**Figure 21.3**
These are the Advanced controls for a .Mac email account.

**NOTE**

Other options are available at the bottom of the Advanced pane, but you aren't likely to use them unless you are specifically directed to do so by the administrator of the email system you are using.

6. Select another account or close the Preferences dialog box. You will be prompted to save your changes.

---

**IMAP Accounts**

One area in which an IMAP account (such as a .Mac account) is significantly different from a POP account is in how email is stored. Under an IMAP account (such as a .Mac email account), mail is always left on the server until you delete it. The benefit of this is that you can access that mail from different machines without forwarding it to each machine or having duplicate copies (on the server and in the inbox in your email applications). As you will learn later, when you work with an IMAP account that has a limited amount of storage for email messages, you have to be aware of how full your email storage is and make sure that you keep it under its limit.

When you use a POP account, the mail you read is actually downloaded to your Mac. So, a copy exists in both places. With POP accounts, you should check the "Remove copy from server after retrieving a message" check box and select a timeframe for messages to be deleted on the pop-up menu. Otherwise, the email you read remains on the server, and you might download it again the next time you check your email.

---

Using steps similar to these, you can add the rest of your email accounts to Mail to work with them all from the Mail application. As you read previously, the steps for a specific account depend on the type of email account you are adding. Just use the specific configuration information provided for each account and repeat the previous steps.

**NOTE**

> Mail can't access an AOL email account. However, you should be able to add just about any other email account to it. In fact, Mail is pretty smart about some other email services. For instance, if you add a Google GMail account, Mail will automatically connect and add all the settings for you.

## SETTING OTHER MAIL PREFERENCES

There are various other Mail preferences you might want to set. The general steps you use to set these preferences are shown here:

1. Select Mail, Preferences to open the Mail Preferences window.
2. Click the button for the area of preferences you want to set.
3. Set the preferences.
4. Set more preferences or close the Preferences window.

In the following sections, you will get an overview of each preference area and a description of some of the more useful preferences you can set.

### SETTING RSS PREFERENCES

You can use Mail and other applications to receive and read RSS feeds. The RSS preferences can be used to determine how RSS feeds are handled on your Mac.

⇨ To learn how to work with RSS feeds, **see** "Working with RSS Feeds," **p. 503**.

### SETTING JUNK MAIL PREFERENCES

You use the Junk Mail pane to configure Mail's Junk Mail feature.

⇨ To learn how to configure and use Mail's junk mail feature, **see** "Handling Junk Mail," **p. 496**.

### SETTING FONTS & COLORS PREFERENCES

Use the Fonts & Colors pane of the Mail Preferences window to control how text appears in Mail windows:

- Use the font and size pop-up menus to select the font and size for the mailbox font, message list font (the pane in which all the messages in a mailbox are listed), the message font (which is the font used for messages you read), the note font, and the fixed-width font.
- If you prefer a fixed-width font for plain-text messages, check the "Use fixed-width font for plain text messages" check box.
- If you want different levels of quoted text to use different colors, check the "Color quoted text" check box and select the colors for each level using the pop-up menus.

**Email Formats**

Mail enables you to send and read email in two formats: plain text and Rich Text Format (RTF). (You can also read email in the HTML format, but you can't compose your own mail in this format.) Plain-text messages contain no formatting, but RTF messages can be formatted. Whether the formatting you apply in an RTF message will be seen depends on the email application the recipient of your email uses. Most can interpret RTF messages correctly, but others cannot.

Email purists prefer plain-text format because any email application can handle them and plain-text messages are quicker to compose and read (which is part of the point of email in the first place). Also, proper quoting is much easier with a plain-text message. I prefer plain text myself for these very reasons.

Many mailing lists enable you to select the format in which you receive messages. You often can select between the plain-text or HTML format. Selecting the plain-text format results in much faster performance, although you won't see all the bells and whistles that can be contained in an HTML email message. However, plain-text messages usually contain links to that content on the Web so you can easily view the specific content you want to see.

## SETTING VIEWING PREFERENCES

Using the Viewing pane of the Mail Preferences window, you can control the following viewing options:

- Use the "Show header detail" pop-up menu to determine how much information is shown in the header of email messages you receive. Your choices are Default, None, All, or Custom. If you select Custom, you can select the specific data you want to see in the header of your messages.

**NOTE**

Note that the "Show header detail" pop-up menu affects mail you have already downloaded. For example, you can select an email message to read and then select a level of header detail from the "Show header detail" pop-up menu to change the header information for the mail you are reading.

**TIP**

You can show all header information in messages by selecting View, Message, Long Headers or by pressing Shift-⌘-H.

- Check the "Show online buddy status" check box if you want the status of people whom you have designated as being online buddies to be displayed. This helps you know when these people are online so you can chat with them.
- Check the "Display unread message with bold font" check box if you want messages that you haven't read yet to appear in bold in the Mail List pane.
- Uncheck the "Display remote images in HTML messages" check box if you want only the text portion of HTML messages that you receive to be displayed. If you receive a lot of spam, it's a good idea to uncheck this box so you can choose which images are displayed; otherwise, you might be unpleasantly surprised by images in spam messages.

**NOTE**

> Mail uses the Safari HTML rendering engine to display HTML messages. This improves the formatting you see when you view HTML messages and makes HTML messages fully interactive.

- Uncheck the Use Smart Addresses check box if you don't want Mail to substitute a person's name (from the Address Book) for her email address when you receive mail from her.
- Check the "Highlight related messages using color" check box, and select a color by using the color button. *Threads* (a series of messages connected by replies to an original message) in your mailbox are highlighted with the color you select so you can spot related messages more easily.

### Setting Composing Preferences

The Composing pane of the Preferences window controls various composing options, which include the following:

- Use the Message Format pop-up menu to set the default format for new messages you can create. Your options are Plain Text and Rich Text. You can override your default choice for specific messages.

**TIP**

> For example, if you select Plain Text as your default format, you can create a message in the Rich Text format by creating the message and selecting Format, Make Rich Text (Shift-⌘-T). If you select Rich Text, you can select Format, Make Plain Text (Shift-⌘-T) to create a plain-text message.

- Select "as I type" on the "Check spelling" pop-up menu to have Mail check your spelling as you type messages. Choose "when I click Send" to have Mail check spelling when you send a message or "never" to disable spell check.
- Check the Automatically check box and then select Cc: on the pop-up menu to include yourself in the Cc block of every message you send. If you prefer to include yourself on the address list for a message but hide your address from the other recipients, select Bcc: on the pop-up menu.
- Check the "Automatically complete addresses" check box to have Mail look up addresses in your Address Book or on specific LDAP servers. Then click the Configure LDAP button and use the resulting sheet to configure the servers on which you want Mail to look up addresses.
- Check the "When sending to a group, show all member addresses" check box to list members of a group by their names in an email that you send to a group (rather than listing just the group name).

- If you want to highlight email addresses when you are sending them outside of "safe" domains, check the "Mark addresses not in this domain" check box and enter the domain you want Mail to consider safe in the box. For example, you might want to be careful about sending messages outside your work domain. In that case, you would check the box and enter your company's domain (such as `company.com`) in the box. Whenever you address messages to someplace other than that domain, the address is highlighted in red.
- Use the "Send new mail from" pop-up menu to choose the account from which new email will be sent (your default account). You can choose "Account of last viewed mailbox" to choose the account in which you most recently read email, or you can choose a specific account. This affects only the default email account from which new email will be sent. You can always override this choice when you compose a new message.
- Use the "Create Notes & To Do's in" pop-up menu to choose the default account for notes and To Do items you create in Mail. The options are the same as for the default send account.
- Use the controls in the Responding area to configure how Mail handles reply messages. To use the same mail format as the original message (such as plain text), check the "Use the same message format as the original message" check box. If you don't check this, your reply uses your default format. To include the original message's text in your reply (which is a good idea so you can use quoting), check the "Quote the text of the original message" check box. Check the "Increase quote level" box to have Mail indent each message's text by one level; this makes an email conversation clearer because you can more easily see the flow of the mail threads. If you choose to use quoting (which you should), use the radio buttons to determine whether the entire message is quoted or only the selected part. The second option is preferable because, if you don't select any text in the original message when you reply to it, the entire text is quoted, which is the same thing the "Include all" option does anyway. However, if you want to reply to only a specific part of a message, you can select it and only that part is included in the message. This provides better context for your reply.

### SETTING SIGNATURE PREFERENCES

You can configure signatures to be attached to your email messages. You can have as many signatures as you would like, and you can select a default signature or select one each time you compose a new message:

1. Click the Signatures icon to open the Signatures pane of the Mail Preferences window. The accounts you have configured will be shown in the far left pane. The list of signatures you have configured will be shown in the middle pane, whereas the far right pane will show the detail for a selected signature (see Figure 21.4).
2. Select the account for which you want to configure a signature, or select All Signatures to make the signature available to all accounts.

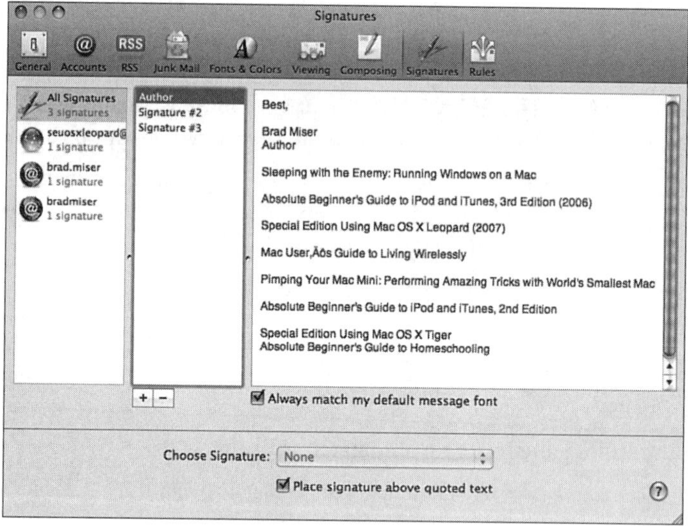


**Figure 21.4**
Adding a signature to your emails is easy to do and can be shared across your email accounts.

3. Click Add Signature (+). A new signature will appear in the center pane and its name will be highlighted to indicate that it is ready to edit. Default text for that signature will be shown in the far right pane.
4. Name the signature by typing a name in the highlighted area.
5. Edit or replace the signature text in the far right pane. You can use just about anything you'd like for your signature.
6. If you want your signature to always appear in your default font, check the "Always match my default message font" check box. Underneath this check box, you'll see what your default font currently is.
7. If you created signatures under the All Signatures category, drag them onto each account under which you want to be able to use them.
8. Select one of the email accounts in the far left pane.
9. If you want a signature to be added to messages from that account, select an option on the Choose Signature pop-up menu. You can choose a signature by name, At Random to have Mail select one of the signatures each time you create a new message, or In Sequential Order to have Mail choose each signature in the order in which they are listed. If you choose None, no signature will be added automatically. In any case, you can always choose from the available signatures on the Signature menu in the New Message window.
10. Check the "Place signature above quoted text" check box, and your signature will be placed above any text that is quoted when you reply to a message. Signatures appear at the bottom of a message by default. When you use quoting, this can be odd because your signature appears after the quoted text instead of after the part you wrote. Use this check box to ensure that your signature appears after what you write and above the quoted text.

Here are a few more signature tips:

- **Change signatures**—To change a signature, select it and edit it in the far right pane.
- **Select a default signature**—When you have more than one signature created for an account, drag the one you want to be the default to the top of the Signature list.
- **Copy a signature**—You can make a copy of a signature by selecting its text and selecting Edit, Copy. Then paste the text into a new signature. This is useful if you want to base a new signature on one you have previously created.
- **Delete a signature**—You can delete a signature by selecting it and clicking Remove (-). After you confirm the deletion in the prompt, the signature is no longer available.

#### Setting Rules

You use the Rules pane to set up automated mail rules.

⇨ To learn how to create rules for your email, **see** "Configuring and Using Rules for Email," **p. 494**.

### Configuring the Mail Toolbar

As with other Mac OS X toolbars, you can configure Mail's toolbar to be more compatible with the way you work:

- Use the Hide Toolbar or the Show Toolbar command on the View menu to hide or show Mail's toolbar. You can use the Show/Hide toolbar button in the Mail title bar as well.
- Select View, Customize Toolbar to add buttons to, remove buttons from, and reorganize the toolbar. Just like other toolbars, you can drag icons onto the toolbar to add them to it or drag them off it to remove them. You can also select how the buttons are displayed and their size.

**TIP**

> Hold down the ⌘ key and click the Hide/Show Toolbar button to cycle through various views, such as large icons, text only, and so on.

## Sending, Receiving, and Replying to Email

If you have used an email application before, such as Entourage or Eudora, using Mail to send, receive, and reply to email will be familiar to you after you learn about the Mail interface.

The main Mail window has four panes. The top pane contains the Mail toolbar. The second pane from the top is the Message List, in which you see the list of items in the selected mailbox. The lower pane of the Mail window is the Reading pane in which you read the mail item that is selected in Message List. All your mailboxes are in the Mailbox pane, which appears along the left side of the Mail window (see Figure 21.5).

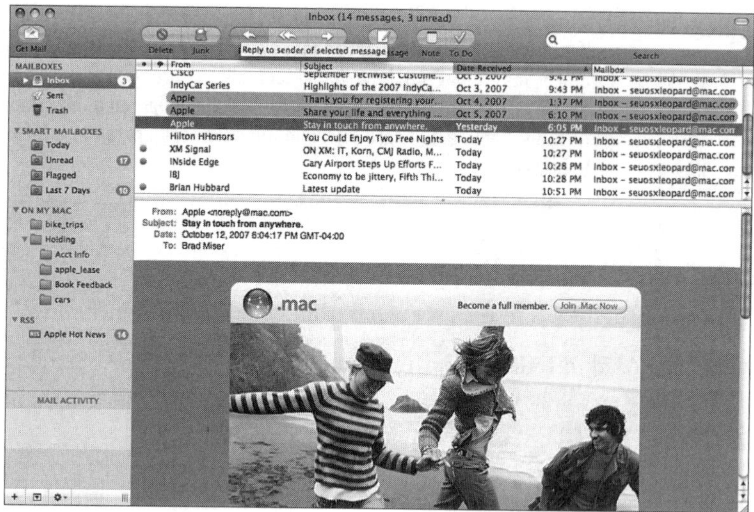


**Figure 21.5**
The Mail application uses four panes to enable you to browse, view, and organize your email.

The Message pane of the Mail window behaves much like a Finder in List view. For example, you can change the width of the columns, sort the list of messages, and so on. The columns in the default Mail window are the following (from left to right in Figure 21.5):

- Message Status
- Buddy Availability
- From
- Subject
- Date Received
- Mailbox

The Mailbox pane shows all your mailboxes. You can show the Mailbox pane by selecting View, Show Mailboxes (Shift-⌘-M). You can close the pane by selecting View, Hide Mailboxes (Shift-⌘-M). You can control the width of the pane by dragging the handle located at the bottom of the edge it shares with the other panes so it is the width you want it to be. At the bottom of the Mailbox pane you will see Mail Activity, which displays the progress of Mail when it is sending or received email messages.

The Mailbox pane contains several mailboxes and folders by default. The Inbox is used to store all your received mail; within the main Inbox is a mailbox for each of your email accounts. You can expand or collapse the contents of a mailbox by using its expansion triangle. You also see Drafts, Sent, and Trash mailboxes; the purpose of each of these should be self-evident. You might also see Drafts and Sent Messages folders for specific types of email accounts.

**NOTE**

> If you use a .Mac, IMAP, or Exchange email account, the Drafts, Junk, and Sent Messages mailboxes appear and have folder icons. These are folders stored on your Mac, whereas the other mailboxes are stored online. If you configured a .Mac email account to store messages online, they are stored in the online folders rather than those stored on your Mac.

## RETRIEVING AND READING EMAIL

There are several ways to retrieve email from your accounts, including

- Setting Mail to retrieve your mail automatically using the General pane of the Mail Preferences window
- Clicking the Get Mail button on the Mail toolbar
- Pressing Shift-⌘-N to get new mail in all your accounts
- Selecting Mailbox, Get New Mail in *accountname*, where *accountname* is the account from which you want to retrieve your mail

**NOTE**

> The first three methods listed retrieve mail for all the email accounts you have configured in Mail (for those accounts that are enabled and that you set to be included in the "retrieve all" action using that account's settings).

**TIP**

> You can temporarily hide the Reading pane by double-clicking the border between the Message List and the Reading pane. The Reading pane disappears and the Message List consumes the entire Mail window. Double-click the bottom of the Mail window to reopen the Reading pane. You can change the relative height of the two panes by dragging the resize handle located in the center of the bar between the two panes.

When you get mail, it is placed in the Inbox mailbox for the account to which it was sent. All email is accessible via the top Inbox account, which includes the contents of each account's inbox.

When you receive email, Mail's Dock icon indicates that you have new email and shows you the total number of new messages you have received. If you chose to have Mail play a sound when new mail is received, you hear that sound when mail is received. When you open the Mail icon on the Dock, a list pops up that shows you all the windows open in Mail, as well as some useful commands (see Figure 21.6).

When you select Inbox on the Dock menu, you move into Mail to read your email; each unread message has a blue dot in the Status column to indicate that it is a new message. The number of new messages is also indicated next to the Inbox mailbox.

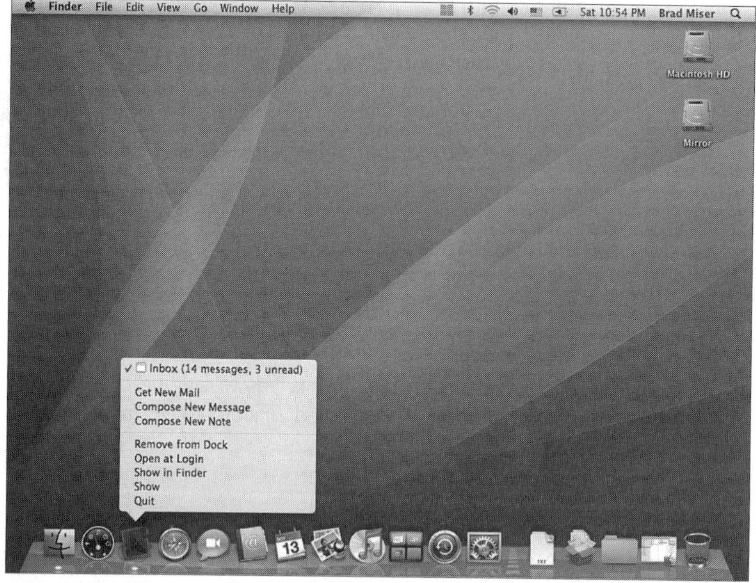


**Figure 21.6**
When you receive new mail, Mail lets you know how many messages you have received (three in this case); you can quickly access the mailboxes containing the new messages by opening the Mail icon on the Dock and selecting Inbox.

**TIP**

> You can also create a new message or check for new email from the Mail Dock menu.

If you have more than one email account, each account has its own Inbox. To see all your Inboxes, click the expansion arrow next to the Inbox icon (see Figure 21.7). The Inbox for each of your accounts appears. Select an Inbox to see the messages for that account only, or select the Inbox icon to see all your messages at the same time.

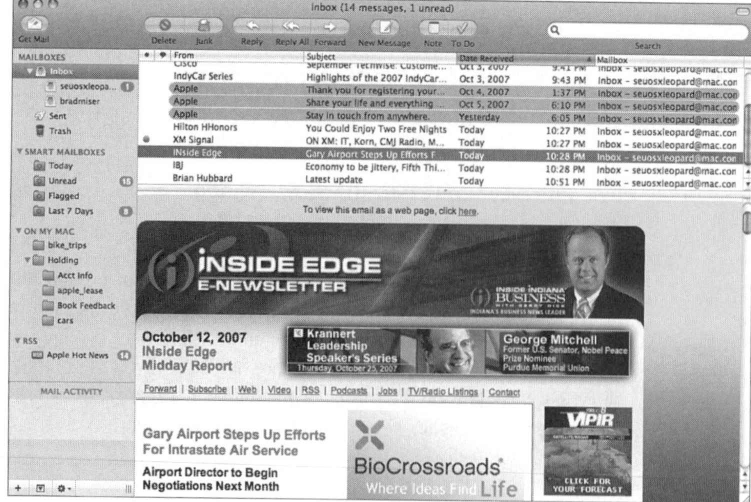


**Figure 21.7**
Each of my email accounts has its own Inbox, as you can see listed under the Inbox icon.

**TIP**

In Mail, you can display the contents of more than one mailbox at a time. To do so, select File, New Viewer Window (Option-⌘-N). In the new Viewer window, select the mailbox whose contents you want to view. You can have as many Viewer windows open as you want. For example, you might select to have a Viewer window open for each of your mail accounts.

*If you are unable to retrieve your mail, see "My Mail Can't Be Retrieved" in the "Troubleshooting" section at the end of this chapter.*

**NOTE**

You can see the activity of Mail as it downloads messages in a separate Activity window. To see the Activity window, select Window, Activity (or press ⌘-0).

### Reading Individual Messages

To view the contents of a mailbox or folder, select it in the Mailbox pane. The Message List shows the messages contained in that mailbox or folder. To read a message, select it in the Message List and read it in the Reading pane.

**TIP**

If the sender of a message is included in your Address Book, the name on that person's card is shown in the From box instead of the person's email address (assuming you leave the Smart Addressing preference enabled). If you click the From name or email address, a pop-up menu appears. This menu shows the email address that the message is from and enables you to reply to the message, create a new message, or add the contact to your Address Book.

To read your mail, use the following shortcuts:

- Scroll down in a message by pressing the spacebar.
- Move up and down the messages in the Message List using the up- and down-arrow keys.
- Double-click a message to read it in its own window.

**TIP**

If the mailbox you are viewing has several messages in it, select those that are interesting to you; hold down the Shift key to select contiguous messages or hold down the ⌘ key to select messages that are not contiguous. Select View, Display Selected Messages Only. The other messages in the mailbox are hidden and you can quickly read the messages you selected (using the shortcuts mentioned in the previous list). To see all the messages in the mailbox again, select View, Display All Messages.

### WORKING WITH EMAIL THREADS

As you read and reply to messages, each message and its replies become a thread, as in a thread of conversation about a topic (or at least started from a topic). If the "Highlight related messages using color" preference is set, Mail highlights all the messages in a thread with the color you select (it is light blue by default). You can also select to organize a mailbox by threads so that all the mails that form a conversation are grouped together.

To organize messages in the Message List pane by threads, select View, Organize by Thread. A thread column is added to the left side of the Message List pane. Messages that are part of a thread are highlighted in the selected color and are grouped together. Select View, Organize by Thread again to return the Message pane to its previous organization. The messages in a thread are sorted just like other messages in the Message List pane.

**NOTE**

If you don't organize by threads, messages in threads are still highlighted with the color indicated in Mail's preferences settings.

Following are some thread tips (these apply when you use the Organize by Thread command):

- The first message in the thread is a summary of the other messages. Select that message to see each sender, title, and date of each message in the thread. At the top of the summary message is the name of the first message in the thread, who started it, and when the first message was sent.
- You can collapse a thread by clicking the expansion triangle next to the summary message. The thread collapses so you see only the summary message. You can also collapse a thread by clicking the up and down arrow icon in the Status column for a message in the thread.
- Select View, Expand All Threads to expand all the threads in a selected mailbox, or select View, Collapse All Threads to collapse all the threads in a selected mailbox.

**TIP**

Mail defines the messages that make up a thread by a special header element. This means you can change the subject of a reply in a thread and Mail will still recognize that the message is part of the thread. However, not all applications can do this and sometimes header information is removed from a message; therefore, it is usually better to leave the subject as it was when the thread was started.

If the person who sent you a message is in your Address Book and has an image on the related address card, that image appears in the upper-right corner of the email message.

## Writing and Sending Email

Writing email in Mail is also quite similar to other email applications. You can create a new mail message in several ways, including the following:

- Click the New button on the toolbar.
- Select File, New Message.
- Press ⌘-N.
- Point to a name in the To, From, or Cc block for a message you are reading in the Reading pane; click it; and select New Message on the resulting pop-up menu. A message is created and is addressed to the person whose name you clicked.
- Open the Mail's menu on the Dock and select Compose New Message.

**TIP**

> If you point to the From block on an email message and click, a pop-up menu appears. On this menu, you can see the email address of the person, chat with the recipient, create a new message, open the related address card (if the recipient has a card, that is), or create an address card. You can also create a smart mailbox for all the mail from that person (you'll learn about smart mailboxes later in this chapter).

When you create a new message, you see the New Message window (see Figure 21.8). Creating the message is straightforward. If the message is not already addressed, type the email address(es) in the To and Cc fields. Mail attempts to match what you type to the addresses in your Address Book or on the list of previous recipients that Mail maintains automatically. The addresses that match what you type appear on a drop-down list. You can move up and down this list with the up- and down-arrow keys. To select an address on the list, highlight it and it is entered in the message's address box. (If there is only one address for the name you type, it is selected by default.) You can enter multiple addresses in an address field by typing a comma and then repeating the previous steps to add more addresses. When you have added all the addresses in the To field, press Tab to move to the next field.

**TIP**

> Mail automatically tracks a list of people to whom you have sent email. This list is called the Previous Recipients list. When you enter an email address in the To field, Mail attempts to match what you are entering to the recipients on this list. If it finds a match, it fills in the rest of the address for you. You can view the list by selecting Window, Previous Recipients. On this list, you can view addresses of people who have sent you email or delete addresses from the list, or add addresses to your Address Book.



**TIP**

> When an address is selected on the drop-down list that appears when Mail attempts to match the address you are typing, you can add it to the message and be ready to enter the next address by pressing comma.

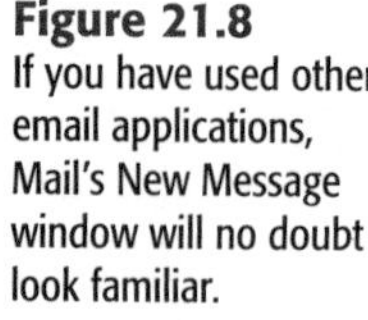

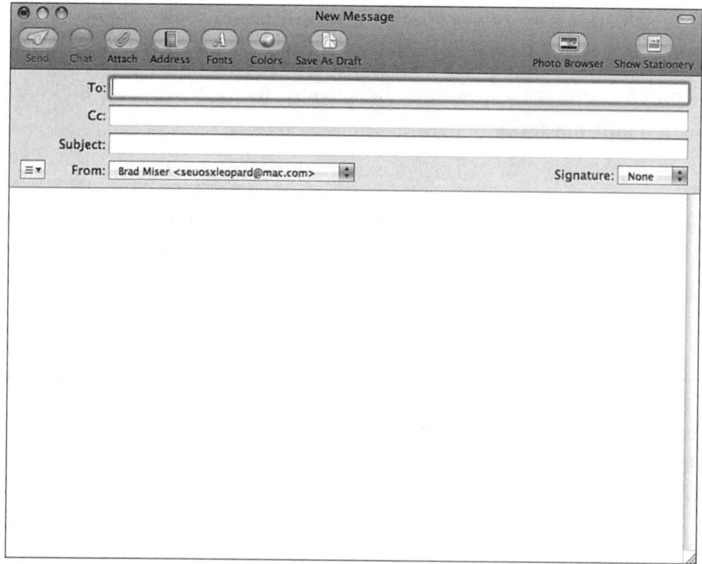


**Figure 21.8**
If you have used other email applications, Mail's New Message window will no doubt look familiar.

To use your Address Book to address a message, open the Address Book by clicking the Address icon on the New Message window's toolbar or by pressing Option-⌘-A. An Addresses window appears that contains the contacts in your Address Book. Browse or search the window to find the people or groups to which you want to send the message. Select the person or group to whom you want to send mail, and click To or Cc to send those addresses to the respective fields in the New Message window.

**TIP**

> You can add a Bcc (blind carbon copy) address line by selecting View, Bcc Address Field or by pressing Option-⌘-B. You can add a Reply To address line by selecting View, Reply-To Address Field (or by pressing Option-⌘-R). You can use the Reply-To Address field to enter an address to which people should reply if it is different from the return address associated with the account selected on the Account pop-up menu. You can also add either of these fields by opening the pop-up menu just to the left of the Account pop-up menu.

Enter the subject of the message in the Subject field.

Select the account from which you want to send the mail using the Account pop-up menu (your default account is listed automatically). If you have configured only one account, this menu isn't displayed.

Mail uses the following three rules to determine the account that is used to send a new message:

- If you have selected a mailbox associated with an account (such as the Inbox for an account), that account is the default for a new message.

- If you selected a default account for new mail on the Composing pane of the Preferences dialog box, that account is used for new mail.
- When you reply to a message, the account to which the original message was sent is selected automatically.

**TIP**

The New Message window has its own toolbar; you can customize its toolbar just as you can other Mail and Mac OS X toolbars (View, Customize Toolbar).

Select the signature you want to use from the Signature pop-up menu. The default signature for the selected account will be inserted, but you can use the menu to choose a different one.

There are two ways to create the body of the message. One is to just type the text and use Mail's formatting tools to format if you use the RTF format. The other is to use one of Mail's email templates.

To create your own message, move into the body and type your message. As you type, Mail checks your spelling according to your preferences. If you use the "check as I type" option, when Mail identifies a misspelled word, it underlines the word in red. You can Control-click or right-click a misspelled word to pop up a menu that enables you to change the word to the correct spelling, ignore the spelling, or learn the word that Mail thinks is misspelled.

You can right-click or Control-click any word, misspelled or not, to perform a number of actions on it, such as searching for the word on your Mac using Spotlight, searching the Web via Google, looking up the word in the Dictionary application, and so on.

**TIP**

You can also control Mail's spell checker using the Spelling commands on the Edit menu. You can open the Spelling window by selecting Edit, Spelling, and then Spelling again. You can configure the spell checking by selecting Edit, Spelling and Grammar, Check Spelling and then choosing the option you want, such as While Typing.

**NOTE**

Because I encourage the use of plain-text email rather than formatted email, I won't be addressing formatting email in this chapter. However, if you elect to create RTF messages, use the commands on the Format menu to format them. You can change the format of a new message (plain text or rich text) by selecting Format, Make Plain Text or Format, Make Rich Text.



To use a template, do the following:

1. Click the Show Stationery button in the toolbar. The available templates appear below the header information.
2. Select a category to see the templates in that category.

3. Select a template, and it appears in the lower pane.
4. Change its content to be what you want to be; some templates include images that you can't change (see Figure 21.9). You can change the template for a message without deleting any text you've input.

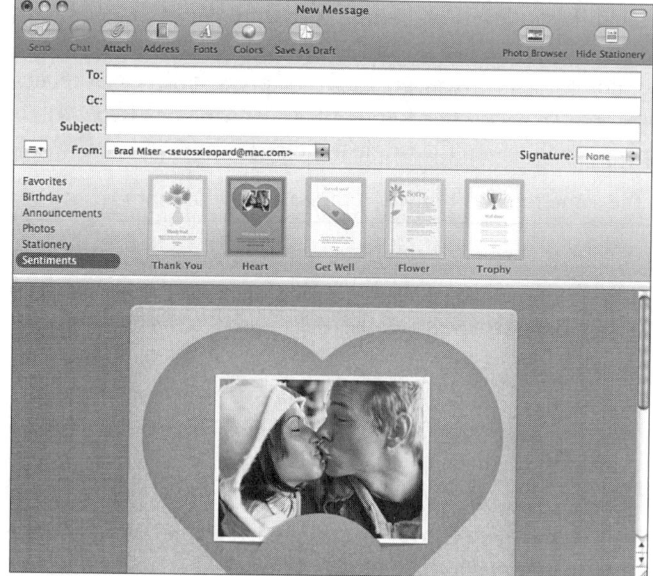


**Figure 21.9**
Mail's stationery enables you to create fancy emails with just a click.

As you work with a new message that you create, open its contextual menu to gain quick access to various commands, such as formatting commands for an RTF message, Spell Checker controls, and quoting commands.

To send a message, do one of the following:

- Click the Send button on the toolbar.
- Select Message, Send.
- Press Shift-⌘-D.

**TIP**

> While you're composing a message, you can save it in the Draft mailbox by either selecting File, Save (⌘-S) or clicking the Save As Draft button on the New Message toolbar. You can leave a message you are working on in your Draft folder as long as you'd like. If you close it, you can open it to work on it again by selecting the Draft folder and double-clicking the message. As you work, Mail saves your messages as drafts periodically, but you can use the command to save them manually.

*If your mail can't be sent, see "My Mail Can't Be Sent" in the "Troubleshooting" section at the end of this chapter.*

## REPLYING TO EMAIL

Replying to messages you receive in Mail is also similar to other applications. By default, Mail marks the different levels of quoting with different colors along with a change bar. As with other applications, you can select the message to which you want to reply and click Reply on the toolbar; select Message, Reply; or press ⌘-R, which replies to only the sender of the message. You can also click Reply All; select Message, Reply All; or press Shift-⌘-R to reply to everyone to whom the original message was sent.

You can use the same tools to reply to a message as you use to write a new message.

**NOTE**

> You should always quote carefully in your replies. Quoting makes email much more effective because it gives the reader a good context for the information you are providing. Quoting is one reason I prefer plain-text messages. Quoting in a plain-text message is much easier; formatting often gets in the way of clear quoting.

You can also perform the following actions on mail you have received:

- **Reply with iChat**—Select Message, Reply with iChat or press Shift-⌘-I if the sender of the message is available via iChat.
- **Forward**—Select Message, Forward or press Shift-⌘-F to forward a message to other recipients.
- **Redirect**—Select Message, Redirect or press Shift-⌘-E to redirect the message to someone else. The difference between redirecting and forwarding a message is that when you redirect a message, the message's original sender's email address still appears in the From field so the person to whom you redirect the message can reply to the message to send email to the person who sent the message. If you forward a message and the recipient replies to it, the reply comes to you because your address becomes the From address on a forwarded message.
- **Bounce**—Select Message, Bounce or press Shift-⌘-B to bounce a message back to the sender. When you do so, the bounce message that is sent makes it appear as if your email address is not valid.

**TIP**

> You can open a message's contextual menu to access many useful commands, such as Reply, Reply All, Forward, and so on.

**NOTE**

> You might be tempted to bounce spam email that you receive. However, this usually doesn't do any good because most spam includes a bogus return address so your bounced message has no legitimate place to go. You can use the Bounce command to respond to email from legitimate organizations that have sent unwanted email to you. Hopefully, the bounce results in your address being removed from the related mailing list. Use Mail's Junk Mail feature to deal with spam.

## DELETING EMAIL

You can delete messages by selecting the messages you want to delete and doing one of the following:

- Click the Delete button on the toolbar.
- Select Edit, Delete.
- Press the Delete key.

Deleted messages are stored in the Trash folder in the Mailbox pane. You can open this folder just like other folders you have. Messages aren't actually removed until the Trash folder is emptied.

When you use an IMAP account, such as a .Mac email account, you have to empty the Trash folder to actually remove the messages from the server. If you don't, those messages continue to count against the total storage space you have on the server. Typically, you are limited to a certain storage space for *all* your messages (under an IMAP or a .Mac account, all your messages remain on the server). Because messages in the Trash folder count against this limit, you should empty this folder more frequently under an IMAP account than you do with POP accounts.

Because they are actually IMAP accounts, .Mac email accounts are limited to a certain amount of storage. If the messages stored in your .Mac email account approach or exceed this limit, you receive email messages warning you that you are exceeding your allotted storage space. To move messages off the server, you need to move them from the Inbox for that account to one of your personal mailboxes stored on your Mac or to the Trash and then empty it.

You can determine whether deleted messages are stored on the server by using the Mailbox Behaviors tab of the Accounts pane of the Mail Preferences window. Open this tab and uncheck the "Store deleted messages on the server" check box. This causes the messages you delete to be downloaded to your Mac, so they won't count against your storage limit.

You can also use the "Permanently erase deleted message when" pop-up menu to select a time period for your deleted messages to be permanently erased.

**NOTE**

> Just like the Inbox, each email account has its own Trash.

To empty Mail's Trash, do one of the following:

- Select Mailbox, Erase Deleted Messages, In All Accounts or press ⌘-K.
- Select Mailbox, Erase Deleted Messages, *accountname*, where *accountname* is the name of the account whose Trash you want to empty.
- Select Mailbox, Erase Junk Mail or press Option-⌘-J to erase the messages stored in the Junk folder (more on that later).
- Use Mail's preferences to set an automatic deletion point, such as a time period or when you quit Mail.

# Customizing Your Email

Mail provides many tools you can use to customize various aspects of your mail. These include customizing the Mail window, organizing your email, sorting your email, and automating your mail with rules.

## Customizing the Viewer Window

You can customize the Viewer window by using the commands shown in Table 21.1.

**Table 21.1 Ways to Customize the Viewer Window**

| Command | What It Does |
|---|---|
| View, Columns | Enables you to select the columns displayed in the Viewer window. In addition to the columns shown by default, you can select from many columns, including Attachments, Date Sent, and so on. |
| View, Sort By | Sorts the Message List pane by the column you select. |
| View, Hide/Show Mailboxes | Hides/shows the Mailbox pane. |
| View, Hide/Show Toolbar | Hides/shows the Mail toolbar. |

**NOTE**

> Remember that you can also customize the Message List window by moving the columns to change the order in which they appear, resizing them, changing the column by which the pane is sorted, and so on, just as you can in Finder windows in the List view.

## Organizing Your Email

There are a number of ways to organize your email, including using mailboxes, smart mailboxes, and smart mailbox groups.

### Using Mailboxes to Organize Your Email

You can create your own mailboxes to organize your messages. The mailboxes you create are also shown in the Mailbox pane. You can also create nested mailboxes to create a hierarchy of mailboxes in which you store your messages.

1. Select Mailbox, New Mailbox or click the Add Mailbox button (+) at the bottom of the Mailbox pane to see the New Mailbox sheet (see Figure 21.10).

**Figure 21.10**
You use the New Mailbox sheet to create a new mailbox either on your Mac or on a server.

2. On the Location pop-up menu, select the location of the mailbox you are creating. If you select On My Mac, the folder is created on your computer. If you use an IMAP or .Mac account, you can select that account to create a folder on that account's server.

   Remember that if you store the folder on a server, the contents of that folder count against your storage quota.
3. In the New Mailbox sheet, enter the name of the mailbox you want to create. To create a nested mailbox, enter the name of each mailbox separated by a slash (/). For example, to create a mailbox called Receipts within a mailbox called Mail to Keep, you would enter **`Mail to Keep/Receipts`**.
4. Click OK.



The mailbox will be created and will appear on the Mailbox pane. If you have created a mailbox that contains other mailboxes, you can use its expansion triangle to expand or collapse it. In Figure 21.11, you can see that I have created a folder called Apple that is nested within a folder called Mail To Keep. Messages you place in folders stored on a server count against your storage limit on that server, so it is generally a better idea to create folders on your Mac instead of storing them on the server.

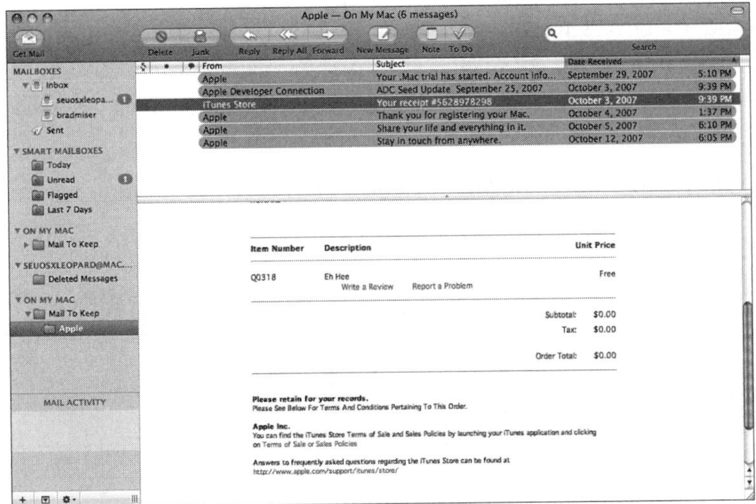


**Figure 21.11**
You can created nested folders to organize your email.

> **TIP**
>
> You can place a folder within another folder by dragging its icon onto the folder in which you want to place it.

You can move messages from one mailbox to another in the following ways:

- Drag and drop a message from the Message List pane to a mailbox.
- Drag messages from the Message List pane in one Viewer to the Message List pane in another Viewer; this copies the messages in the mailbox shown in the second Viewer window.
- Select messages and select Message, Move To; then select the mailbox to which you want to transfer the messages.
- Select messages and select Message, Copy To; then select the mailbox to which you want to create a copy of the selected messages.
- Select messages and select Message, Move Again to move the selected messages into the same mailbox into which you most recently transferred mail (Option-⌘-T).
- Open a message's contextual menu and select the Move To, Copy To, Move Again, or Apply Rules command.
- Select messages and select Message, Apply Rules (Option-⌘-L); then select a rule that transfers the messages.

### Using Smart Mailboxes to Organize Your Email

You can use smart mailboxes to organize your email automatically based on criteria you define. For example, you might want to store all the email you receive from a group of people with whom you are working on a project in a specific folder. Rather than having to place these messages in the folder by dragging them out of your Inbox individually, you can create a smart mailbox so that mail you receive from these people is automatically placed in the folder. You can create smart mailboxes for many needs like the one mentioned here; if you can define a set of conditions for which you want something done, you can create a smart mailbox to have the action you want to happen done for you automatically.

Smart mailboxes have the gear icon and are purple. By default, Mail includes a smart mailbox called Today so you can easily see your most recent emails.

To create a smart mailbox, complete the following steps:

1. Select Mailbox, New Smart Mailbox or open the Action pop-up menu and select New Smart Mailbox. The Smart Mailbox sheet appear.
2. Name the smart mailbox by typing its name in the "Smart Mailbox Name" box.
3. Select the first condition for the mailbox on the first pop-up menu in the conditions box; by default, this menu shows From, which will base the condition on the name or email address in the From field. There are many other choices, including Entire Message, Subject, Date Received, and so on. If you want to place all the mail you receive from a specific person in a smart mailbox, select From.
4. Select the operand for the condition on the second pop-up menu. What you see on this menu depends on the condition you selected. Common choices include "Contains," "Does not contain," "Is equal to," and so on. In the example of creating a smart mailbox for mail from a specific person, select Contains.
5. Enter the condition text or date in the box. For example, enter a person's name if you are creating a smart mailbox to collect mail from a specific person.
6. To add another condition, click the + button.
7. Repeat steps 3–5 to configure the second condition.
8. If you have configured more than one condition, select "all" on the pop-up menu above the condition list if all the conditions must be true for mail to be stored in the smart mailbox, or select "any" if only one of the conditions must be true.

**TIP**

> To remove a condition, click the Remove (-) button next to the condition you want to remove.



9. If you want messages that are in the Trash or the Sent folders to be included in the smart mailbox, check the related "Include" check boxes.
10. Review the conditions for the smart mailbox and click OK if you are ready to create it (see Figure 21.12). The mailbox is created and any mail that meets its conditions is placed in it.

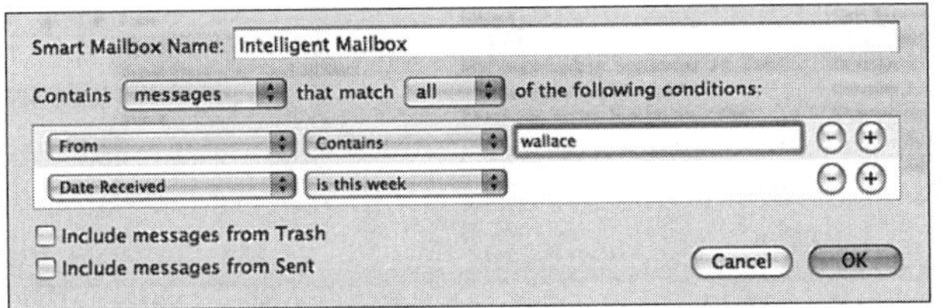


**Figure 21.12** This smart mailbox will contain mail I have received from anyone whose name includes "Wallace" and has been received this week.

**TIP**

> To change the conditions for an existing smart mailbox, open its contextual menu and select Edit Smart Mailbox. Use the resulting Smart Mailbox sheet to make changes to the smart mailbox.

### USING SMART MAILBOX FOLDERS TO ORGANIZE YOUR SMART MAILBOXES

If you want to organize your smart mailboxes, you can create a smart mailbox folder and then place your smart mailboxes within it (you can't put smart mailboxes within regular mailboxes/folders):

1. Select Mailbox, New Smart Mailbox Folder.
2. In the sheet that appears, name the new smart mailbox folder and click OK. The smart mailbox folder will be created.
3. Drag smart mailboxes into the smart mailbox folder to place them there. When you do, an expansion triangle appears so that you can expand the folder to see its contents.

## CONFIGURING AND USING RULES FOR EMAIL

You can automate the handling of your email by configuring and using rules. For example, you might want to create a mailbox for the mail from a certain person and have that mail automatically transferred into that mailbox (you could use a smart mailbox to do this, too). Or, you might have the messages from a mailing list to which you are subscribed placed in a specific mailbox for later reading.

To create and implement rules, you use the Rules pane of the Mail Preferences window:

1. Open the Mail Preferences window and click the Rules icon to open the Rules pane. Some rules are installed by default.
2. Click Add Rule to open a Rule sheet to define the rule you are creating.
3. Name the rule by entering a description.
4. Use the If pop-up menu to determine whether at least one criterion (select "any") or all the criteria (select "all") in the rule must be met for the actions in the rule to be taken.
5. Use the first condition pop-up menu to select the first criterion on which the rule will act. You can select any of the fields in a mail message. You can also select from various criteria, such as whether the sender is in your Address Book.

6. Use the Contains pop-up menu to select how the criteria will relate to the value you enter (such as "Contains," "Is equal to," and so on).
7. Enter the value for which the rule will be implemented, if applicable, or use a pop-up menu to select a value. (Some conditions, such as "Sender is in my Address Book," don't require any values.)
8. To add more criteria, click the Add button (+) and repeat steps 5–7 to create additional conditions for the rule.
9. Use the Action area to select the actions that will be performed by the rule by making a choice from the first pop-up menu and making other choices from the other pop-up menus or fields related to that choice.

   The actions you can select are Move Message, Copy Message, Set Color of Message, Play Sound, Bounce Icon in Dock, Reply to Message, Forward Message, Redirect Message, Delete Message, Mark as Read, Mark as Flagged, Run AppleScript, or Stop Evaluating Rules. You can include multiple actions in the same rule.
10. Click the Add button next to the action and repeat step 9 to create and configure additional actions. When you are done, review the rule you have created. For example, the rule shown in Figure 21.13 checks to see whether a message is from me, the subject contains Special Edition Using Mac OS X, or is from my email address; if any of these conditions is true, the message is moved to the Trash and the Frog sound plays.

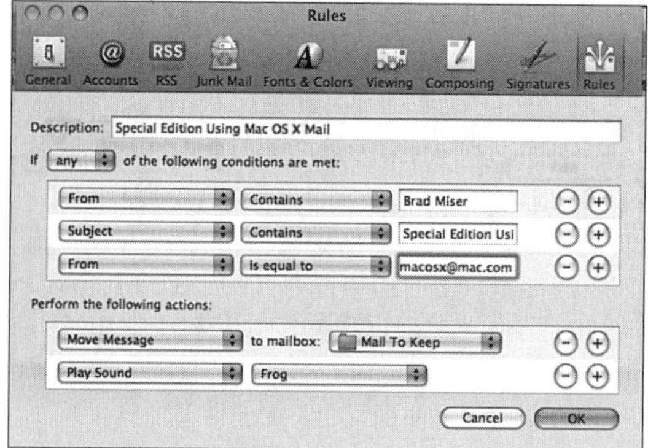


**Figure 21.13**
Hopefully, you won't want to create a rule like this one!

**TIP**

> You can remove conditions or actions by clicking the Remove button (–).

11. Click OK. The rule is created and you are prompted to apply the rule to the messages currently in selected mailboxes.
12. Click Apply or Don't Apply and the appropriate action is taken. You return to the Rules pane and see the rule you created on the list of rules.

**NOTE**

> If you apply a color in a rule, that rule appears in that color in the Rules pane. Messages already in a mailbox that meet the rule's criteria are also shown in the color applied by the rule.

You can use the Edit and Duplicate buttons to edit or duplicate rules and the Remove button to delete rules.

Any future messages you receive that meet the criteria for a rule are acted upon by that rule. You can also manually apply rules to messages by selecting messages and selecting Message, Apply Rules (Option-⌘-L).

**TIP**

> Manually applying rules is a good way to test your rules to ensure that they do what you intended.

## Handling Junk Mail

Unfortunately, no matter how careful you are with your email address, it might eventually get on a junk mail list. And after it gets on one such list, it will probably get on many, and your inbox will overflow with junk mail. Fortunately, Mail includes some built-in tools for dealing with junk mail.

**TIP**

> Although Mail's Junk mail feature is a good way to deal with spam, it doesn't eliminate it. See the sidebar at the end of this section for recommendations about how to deal with spam more effectively.

You can configure Mail's Junk feature via the Junk Mail pane of the Mail Preferences dialog box (see Figure 21.14).

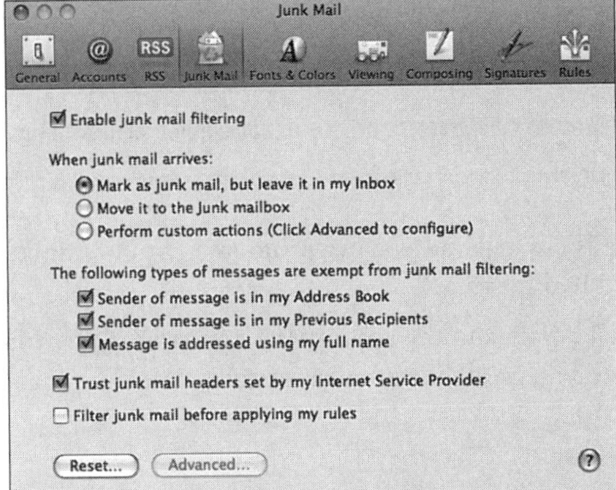


**Figure 21.14** Use the Junk Mail pane to configure Mail's junk feature.

21

The Junk feature has four modes.

In the Disabled mode, the Junk feature is inactive and doesn't do anything. You can disable the Junk feature by unchecking the "Enable Junk Mail filtering" check box on the Junk Mail pane of the preferences dialog box.

In the Training mode (which is the default mode), Mail applies its Junk rules to your messages. This causes Mail to color the message brown or gold (depending on your color perception), indicating that Mail thinks the message is junk. You use this mode to fine-tune the Junk Mail feature so it correctly filters your messages to identify the junk. When you view a message that has been correctly identified as junk, don't do anything. When a message has been identified as junk but it isn't, click the Not Junk button. If you find a message that is junk, but Mail has not identified it as such, click the Junk button on the toolbar. You can place the Junk Mail feature in the Training mode by clicking the "Leave it in my inbox, but indicate it is junk mail" radio button.

After some time has passed and you are confident that Mail's Junk filter is working properly, you can move into Junk Mail's Automatic mode. When you do so, Mail creates a Junk folder in the Mailbox pane and prompts you to ask whether it should move all the identified junk mail to this folder. Click Yes. You move into the Automatic mode by clicking the "Move it to the Junk mailbox" radio button.

When the Junk feature is in the Automatic mode, it moves all the messages it identifies as junk into the Junk folder. You should review the contents of this folder periodically to ensure that no messages you want to keep are in this folder by mistake. If there are messages you want, move them to a different folder. Then delete all the messages in the Junk folder.

You can also use the Custom mode to configure the rules used by the Junk filter. To use this mode, click the "Perform custom actions (Click Advanced to configure)" radio button. Then click the Advanced button to open the Advanced configuration sheet.

If you click the Advanced button, you move to a Rules sheet and the default Junk rule is ready to edit. (Mail's Junk Mail feature is actually just a special mail rule.) You can change this mail rule just like any rule you create on the Rules pane to change how Mail handles junk mail. If you open the Junk rule, you see that this is simply a rule that acts on any messages that are from people who are not in your Address Book, are not on your Previous Recipient list, are not addressed to your full name, or are marked as Junk. In the Training mode, this rule changes only the color of the messages. In the Automatic mode, it moves the messages to the Junk folder.

By checking the related check box on the Junk Mail pane of the preferences dialog box, you can exempt email messages from the Junk Mail filter in the following situations:

- The sender of a message is in your Address Book.
- The sender of a message is on the list of previous recipients.
- The message is addressed to your full name (most spam uses an email address).

If your Internet service provider (ISP) provides junk mail headers that attempt to identify junk mail by its own rules and you want Mail to recognize and use those headers, check the "Trust Junk Mail headers set by my Internet Service Provider" check box.

You can also specify whether the Junk Mail filter should run before your other rules are applied. This makes sense because spam should be removed or tagged as such before Mail does anything else with it.

If you click the Reset button, the Junk Mail feature is returned to its default state. This also removes any learning the filter has done so you have to repeat the training process.

## THE END OF SPAM

With all due respect to Mail's Junk feature, there are certain circumstances in which providing your email address is likely to result in your address being obtained by a spammer. And after it gets into one spammer's hands, it will get into lots of spammers' hands and you will start receiving dozens or even hundreds of spam messages every day. The only real way to stop spam is to stop using the email address that has been spammed. Junk mail filters, such as Mail's Junk feature, are really only a way to make dealing with spam easier; they don't eliminate the spam from your life.

Several situations should be considered to have high risk of your address being spammed. One is public discussion forums, such as on websites, in newsgroups, in chat rooms, and so on; in fact, getting spammed from these locations is guaranteed. Another is when you are shopping online; many online retailers have valid privacy policies that allow you to opt out of your address being provided to others, but some don't have such policies. Another is any time you are asked for an email address, such as when you are taking a survey, registering for a "free" prize, and so on. Providing an email address in any of the situations will likely get you spammed.

If that happens and you use an email address for work or to keep in touch with people, you aren't likely to want to change the address you use.

There is a solution to this dilemma: You can create "disposable" email accounts for use in the situations that are more likely to result in an addressed getting spammed. If that happens, you can simply stop using the spammed email account and create another disposable account to use in the high spam risk situations.

Meanwhile, you can keep your permanent email address close the vest by providing it only to people you know or to companies that you are sure are legit and won't sell your address to spammers.

There are many sources of good disposable email accounts, including the following:

- Yahoo Mail (mail.yahoo.com) or Google GMail (mail.google.com).
- Other similar sites that enable you to create and use email accounts at no or low cost. For example, you can add additional email accounts to your .Mac account for relatively little cost.

- Your own Internet access account. Many ISP accounts provide multiple email accounts under your primary access account. Even better, most of the time you can create and delete your own subaccounts, which is the ideal situation. Keep your base email account private; never use it under any circumstance. Then create an email account as your permanent address and provide that to the people with whom you really want to communicate. Finally, create your disposable address and use that in high spam risk situations. If that address gets spammed, just delete it and create another one.

**NOTE**

> You might have noticed that in this book I provide my email address which is `bradmacosx@mac.com`. I like to receive email from readers, and spammers aren't likely to read a book to get a single address. So, even exposing an email address in a public place like a book isn't all that risky. However, I use the practice described in the last bullet in the previous list to manage my own email. For example, I have an email address for personal email and another disposable address I use when shopping online (mostly Mac stuff and DVDs). If that address ever gets spammed, I can just delete it and create a replacement.

# SENDING AND RECEIVING FILES WITH EMAIL

One of the most valuable uses of email is to send and receive attachments. Again, Mail handles file attachments similarly to other email applications you might be accustomed to.

## ATTACHING FILES TO YOUR EMAIL

Attaching files to messages you send can be done in the following ways:

- In the message to which you want to attach files, select File, Attach File (Shift-⌘-A). Then, use the Choose File sheet to select the files you want to attach.
- Click the Attach button on the New Message window's toolbar. The Choose File sheet appears; use it to select the files you want to attach to a message.

**TIP**

> In the Choose File sheet, check the Send Windows-Friendly Attachments check box if you are sending files to Windows users. This makes these users more likely to be able to use the files you send. You can turn on this feature so it applies to all attachments by selecting Edit, Attachments, Send Windows Friendly Attachments.

- Drag the files onto the New Message window.

When you place a file in a new message window, you see a thumbnail preview of the file with its icon, the filename, and its size in parentheses. If the file type is one that can be displayed in the message, such as a TIFF image or a PDF file, you actually see the contents of the file in the body of the message.

By default, Mail displays the contents of files you attach if it can. If the contents of the file are being displayed and you would rather see just an icon, open the file's contextual menu and select View as icon. The file is displayed as an icon instead. To view the file's content again, open the menu and select View in Place.

File attachments must be *encoded* before they can be sent. When a file is encoded, it is translated into a string of text. The application that receives the message must then decode that message so the files become usable. Encoding and decoding is handled automatically, and you can't select the encoding method used.

*If recipients of your file attachments have trouble with them, see "Recipients of My Attachments Are Seeing Odd Things" in the "Troubleshooting" section at the end of this chapter.*

You should also compress files you attach to email messages. Under Mac OS X, you can compress any file in the Zip format using the Finder's Compress command. Simply select the files you want to attach to an email message, open the contextual menu, and select Compress. The files you selected are placed in a Zip file. You can then rename the file (don't change the `.zip` file extension) and attach the Zip file to the message you are sending.

Sending file attachments is simple except for one thing—the Windows versus Mac situation, which raises its ugly head in the area of file attachments, too. Basically, Mac and Windows operating systems use different file format structures. Mac files have two "forks," whereas Windows files have only one. This is sometimes a problem when you send files to Windows users because they end up with two files. One is the usable file and one is unusable to them (the names of the files are *`filename`* and *`_filename`*). Recipients can use the first one and safely ignore the second one. However, it is still confusing for them.

Mail includes a solution for this problem, which is called sending Windows-Friendly Attachments. This causes Mail to strip the second file away, so the Windows recipient receives only one file for each attachment. That is a good thing.

However, Mac users who receive Windows-friendly attachments might lose some features, such as thumbnail preview or information about the file. In the worst case, the file might be unusable.

You can choose to attach files as Windows-friendly by checking the box in the Attach File dialog box. If you always want to send files in the Windows-friendly format, select Edit, Attachments, Send Windows Friendly Attachments.

Unless you always send files to other Mac users or only to Windows users, you have to decide whether to use the Windows-friendly option each time you attach files. You should either use this option when you send files to Windows users (if you don't know which type of computer the recipient uses) or not use it if you are certain the recipient uses a Mac.



## Using Mail's Photo Browser

Because you're likely to use Mail to email photos that you manage in iPhoto, you can access the Photo Browser by clicking the Photo Browser button in the New Message toolbar. You can use the Photo Browser to easily find photos in your iPhoto Library and drag them onto a new message window to add them to an email you create (see Figure 21.15). Use the Browser's tools to find the images you want to send and then drag them onto a new message window.

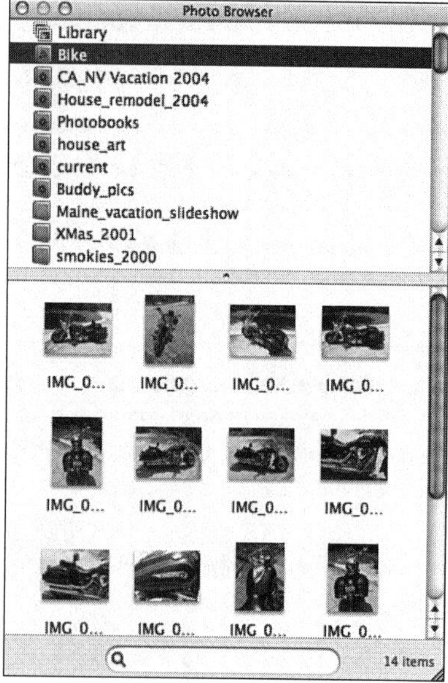


**Figure 21.15** The Photo Browser makes it easy to attach iPhoto photos to email messages.

## USING FILES ATTACHED TO EMAIL YOU RECEIVE

When you receive a message that has files attached to it, you see the files in the body of the message. As when you send files in a message, you see the file's icon, name, and size. If the file can be displayed in the body, such as a TIFF or PDF, the contents of the file are displayed in the message. You can use the file attachments in the following ways:

- Select File, Save Attachments. Use the resulting sheet to move to a location and save the attachments.
- Select File, Quick Look Attachments. A Quick Look window will appear and show a preview of the document. Depending on the document type, you might be able to scroll and navigate the Quick Look to see more of the document.
- Click the Save button next to the attachment information at the top of the message. Use the resulting sheet to move to a location and save the attachments.
- Click the Quick Look button next to the attachment information at the top of the message. Depending on the document type, you might be able to scroll and navigate the Quick Look to see more of the document.
- If multiple files are attached, click the expansion triangle next to the attachment line in the message's header and work with each file individually.
- Double-click a file's icon to open it.

- Drag a file's icon from the message onto a folder on your Mac's desktop to save it there.
- You can open the attachment's contextual menu and select one of the listed actions, such as Open Attachment, which opens it in its native application; Open With, which enables you to select the application in which you want the file to open; Save Attachment; or Save to Downloads folder, which saves the attachment in your designated Downloads folder.

**TIP**

> If the contents of the file are being displayed and you would rather see just an icon, open the file's contextual menu and select View as icon. The file is displayed as an icon instead. To view the file's content again, open the menu and select View in Place.

**TIP**

> If you have trouble viewing a message and the folder into which you want to store the file attachments, double-click the message to open it in its own window. Then you can resize the window so you can more easily see the folder into which you want to drag it.

If the files you receive are compressed, you must uncompress them before you can open them.

⇨ To learn more about uncompressing files, **see** "Downloading and Preparing Files," **p. 536**.

# SEARCHING EMAIL

As you collect email, you will probably need to search it. You can quickly search for messages, or you can search for specific text in a message.

In the Mail Search tool in the upper-right corner of the Mail window, type the text you want to search for. As you type, the messages shown in the Message List pane are reduced to those that meet your criteria. You also see a toolbar above the Message List pane that helps you quickly scope the search, such as by specific fields or in the selected mailbox or all mailboxes (see Figure 21.16). The Rank column appears in the Message List pane to show you how well the found messages meet the criteria you configure. You can read a message found by the search by selecting it and reading it in the Reading pane. Click the Show in Mailbox link to move to the message as it is stored in a mailbox.

To clear a search, click the Close button (the "x") in the Search tool.

You can also search for text within a specific message using the Find Panel.



1. Select Edit, Find, Find (⌘-F). The Find Panel appears.
2. Enter the text for which you want to search.
3. Click Next to search for the text.

You can use the Replace with box in the Find panel to replace the text you find with different text.

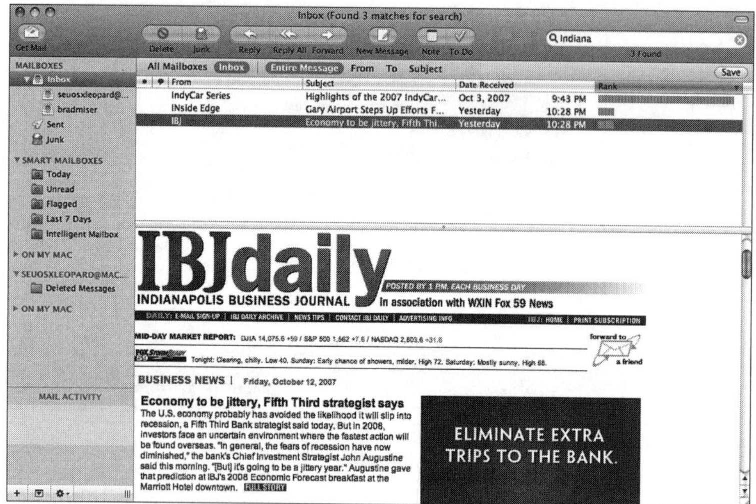


**Figure 21.16**
Mail's search tool enables you to quickly search for email.

**TIP**

> You can also search by creating a smart folder based on your search criteria. This enables you to search by multiple attributes at the same time. Consider creating a smart mailbox for this purpose. Edit it each time you want to search for mail by more than a single attribute.

**NOTE**

> You can also search your email by using the Finder's Spotlight search tool because it includes your email in its search domain.

# Working with RSS Feeds

RSS feeds are streams of information that change as times passes. Many websites, especially news sites, offer RSS feeds to which you can subscribe. You can use Mail to read RSS feeds, which is convenient because they are delivered to your Inbox automatically.

## Adding RSS Feeds and Configuring Mail to Manage Them

To add an RSS feed to Mail, choose File, Add RSS Feeds. The RSS Feeds sheet appears (see Figure 21.17). In the Collections pane, you see your bookmarks from Safari. At the top of this pane, the All RSS Feeds option is selected and you see all the RSS feeds available to you in the right pane. To add one of these feeds, select it and click Add.

To enter the URL to a feed, click "Specify a custom feed URL" in the RSS Feeds sheet; then enter the URL in the resulting Feed URL sheet and click Add.

All feeds appear in the RSS Feeds mailbox by default, but you can place them in your Inbox if you prefer. If you want feeds from either source to appear in your Inbox, check the "Show in inbox" check box.

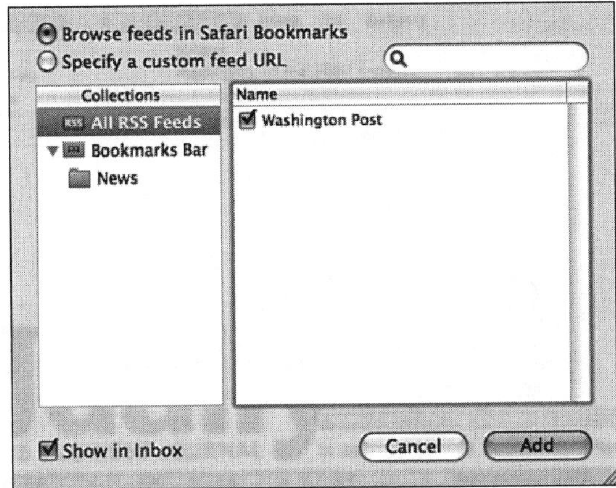


**Figure 21.17** Adding RSS feeds to Mail makes keeping up with dynamic information easier.

You can also move feeds from the RSS Feeds mailbox to your Inbox by clicking the up arrow button that appears when you select a feed. Likewise, you can move a feed from your Inbox to the RSS Feeds mailbox by pointing to a feed in the Inbox and clicking the down arrow button.

Lastly, configure your RSS feed preferences by opening the RSS pane of the Mail Preferences dialog box. Use the following pop-up menus to configure how RSS feeds are managed:

- Use the Default RSS Reader menu to choose the application that you want to use by default to read feeds. The three options are Mail, Safari, or Other (which you can use to choose a different application).
- Use the Check for Updates menu to determine how frequently Mail checks for updates to your feeds. The choices are Manually, Every 30 minutes, Every hour, or Every day.
- Use the Remove Articles menu to determine when Mail removes articles in your feeds. The options are Manually or after specific periods of time, such as a day, one month, two months, and so on.

### Reading RSS Feeds

After you added feeds to Mail, you can read them by selecting a feed in the Inbox if that is where it is stored or by selecting the RSS Feeds maibox. The articles in the selected feed appear in the Message List. Choose one to read it in the Reading pane.



## Working with Notes

Mail notes are a way you can capture text and images and save them in Mail. To create a note, choose File, New Note or click the Note button in the Mail toolbar. The Note window appears (see Figure 21.18). You can enter text in the note and format it using the Fonts and Colors buttons. You can create lists by adding the Lists button to the Notes toolbar, or by using the Format menu and selecting Lists to insert a bulleted or numbered list. To add images to a note, drag them from the desktop onto the note window. You can also attach files to a note by clicking the Attach button. To save a note, click the Done button. To send a note via email, click Mail Note.

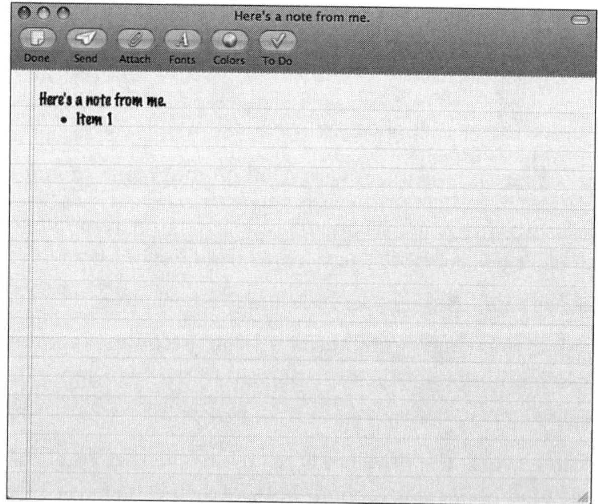


**Figure 21.18**
Use Mail Notes to save information so you can access it easily.

When you save notes, they are stored in the Notes mailbox. They can also be viewed in the Inbox if you checked that option in the Account preferences for your email account. Select the Notes mailbox and the notes you've saved appear in the Message List pane. Select a note to read it in the Reading pane or double-click it to open it in a separate window.

# WORKING WITH TO DO ITEMS

You can track tasks you need to accomplish by creating To Do items. If you use iCal, To Do items in Mail and To Do items in iCal are synchronized for you automatically. So, when you create a To Do item in Mail, it appears in iCal and vice versa.

To create a To Do item in Mail, click the To Do button on the toolbar. You move to the To Do mailbox and an empty To Do item box appears. Enter the name for the To Do item and use the other tools to configure it; these work just like configuring To Do items in iCal.

⇨ To learn how to configure To Do items in iCal, **see** "Working with Your To Do List," **p. 673**.

After you've configured To Do items, you'll receive alarms that you set. When you complete an item, select the To Do mailbox and check the check box for the item you've completed. It will be marked as completed and you won't be bothered with alarms.

You can delete To Do items by selecting them and clicking Delete.

# TROUBLESHOOTING

## MY MAIL CAN'T BE RETRIEVED

*When I check my mail, I get a "Fetch Error," saying that Mail couldn't connect to my mail server.*

This can happen for various reasons, such as a problem with your Internet connection, a misconfigured email account, and so on. Use the following information to correct the problem.

Open and use another Internet application, such as a web browser.

If it works properly, there is a problem with Mail or your mail account configuration.

If it doesn't work properly, you are having trouble with your Internet access, which is why your mail account can't be accessed. You need to troubleshoot your Net connection.

⇨ For help troubleshooting your Net connection, **see** "Troubleshooting," **p. 357**.

If you have more than one email account, try all your accounts. If you have problems with all your accounts, something might have happened to the Mail application.

⇨ For help with troubleshooting applications, **see** Chapter 40, "Solving Mac Problems," **p. 949**.

If your other accounts work, the problem is related to the specific account. If you have successfully retrieved email under this account before, the problem is likely a temporary one with the server from which you retrieve email or a temporary interruption in your communication with that server. In this case, wait awhile and try again later. If you continue to have problems or you have never been able to retrieve email from this account, try the following:

1. In Mail, select Mail, Preferences.
2. Click the Accounts button.
3. Select the account with which you are having trouble.
4. Check the account information for that account—especially the Server Name, User Name, and Password fields—and correct any errors you find. If no errors exist in these fields, the account is configured properly.
5. Allow some time to pass and try the account again. If you are still unable to retrieve your mail, the problem might reside with the provider of the mail account.
6. Contact the technical support for the organization providing your mail service for further help.

You can also use Mail's Connection Doctor to help you troubleshoot your accounts. Select Window, Connection Doctor. The Mail Connection Doctor window will open and check each of your accounts (incoming and outgoing) to see whether there is a problem. If there is a problem, select the account with the problem and click the "Assist me" button.

### MY MAIL CAN'T BE SENT

*When I try to send mail, I get an error message stating that my mail can't be sent.*

Troubleshooting this problem is similar to troubleshooting a problem retrieving mail. The only difference is in step 4. You should carefully check the SMTP server address, SMTP User, and SMTP password boxes. If authentication is used for your SMTP account, make sure the Authentication check box is checked.

When you run Connection Doctor, it also checks outgoing mail accounts.

*For help troubleshooting a problem with sending mail, refer to "My Mail Can't Be Retrieved," earlier in this section.*

### RECIPIENTS OF MY ATTACHMENTS ARE SEEING ODD THINGS

*People to whom I send attachments see duplicate files, missing file attachment messages, and other odd things.*

This happens when the recipient's email application does not fully support the encoding scheme Mail uses to encode files you attach to your messages. Most email applications decode files well enough for the files to be used, although some strange things can happen on the recipient's end. A few email applications can't decode the Mail file attachments at all. Problems can be experienced with very old Mac email applications, some Windows email applications, and some Unix email applications.

In some cases, Windows recipients receive two files for each file you attach. Mail sends two files: one contains the file data and the other contains the resource information. Most of the time, the recipient can safely ignore the resource file, and work with the data file. Tell the recipients who are having problems to try opening the files to determine which one is the correct file. The recipients can discard the unused resource files.

The missing file attachment message can usually be ignored, or you can try to resend the attachments using the Windows-friendly setting.

If the recipient's email application is incapable of decoding the files at all, you must find another means to transmit the files to her, such as an email application that enables you to select a different encoding scheme. Or, you can create a .Mac website to share the files.

⇨ To learn how to use .Mac to share files, **see** "Using .Mac to Publish a Website," **p. 448**.

## Max OS X to the Max: Using Mail Keyboard Shortcuts

Table 21.2 shows keyboard shortcuts for the Mail application.

**Table 21.2 Keyboard Shortcuts for Mail**

| Action | Keyboard Shortcut |
|---|---|
| Activity | ⌘-O |
| Add Reply-To Header | Option-⌘-R |
| Add Sender to Address Book | Shift-⌘-Y |
| Address Panel | Option-⌘-A |
| Append Selected Messages | Option-⌘-I |
| Apply Bcc Header | Option-⌘-B |
| Apply Rules | Option-⌘-L |
| Attach File | Shift-⌘-A |
| Bigger | ⌘-+ |
| Bounce | Shift-⌘-B |
| Check Spelling | ⌘-; |
| Copy Style | Option-⌘-C |
| Decrease Quote Level | Option-⌘-' |
| Delete | Delete |
| Erase Deleted Messages in All Accounts | ⌘-K |
| Erase Junk Mail | Option-⌘-J |
| Find | ⌘-F |
| Find Next | ⌘-G |
| Find Previous | Shift-⌘-G |
| Forward | Shift-⌘-F |
| Get All New Mail | Shift-⌘-N |
| Go to In | ⌘-1 |
| Go to Out | ⌘-2 |
| Go to Drafts | ⌘-3 |
| Go to Sent | ⌘-4 |
| Go to Trash | ⌘-5 |
| Go to Junk | ⌘-6 |
| Go to Notes | ⌘-7 |

| Action | Keyboard Shortcut |
|---|---|
| Go to To Do | ⌘-8 |
| Go to RSS | ⌘-9 |
| Hide Deleted Messages | ⌘-L |
| Hide/Show Mailboxes | Shift-⌘-M |
| Increase Quote Level | ⌘-' |
| Jump to Selection | ⌘-J |
| Mailbox Search | Option-⌘-F |
| Message Long Headers | Shift-⌘-H |
| Make Plain Text | Shift-⌘-T |
| Mark as Flagged | Shift-⌘-L |
| Mark as Junk Mail | Shift-⌘-J |
| Mark as Unread/Mark as Read | Shift-⌘-U |
| Move Again | Option-⌘-T |
| New To Do | Option-⌘-Y |
| New Message | ⌘-N |
| New Note | Control-⌘-N |
| New Viewer Window | Option-⌘-N |
| Next Alternative | Option-⌘-] |
| Open Message | ⌘-O |
| Paste as Quotation | Shift-⌘-V |
| Paste and Match Style | Option-Shift-⌘-V |
| Plain Text Alternative | Option-⌘-P |
| Preferences | ⌘-, |
| Previous Alternative | Option-⌘-[ |
| Raw Source | Option-⌘-U |
| Redirect | Shift-⌘-E |
| Reply All | Shift-⌘-R |
| Reply | ⌘-R |
| Reply with iChat | Shift-⌘-I |
| Save As | Shift-⌘-S |
| Save | ⌘-S |
| Select All Messages in This Thread | Shift-⌘-K |

*continues*

**TABLE 21.2 CONTINUED**

| Action | Keyboard Shortcut |
|---|---|
| Send Again | Shift-⌘-D |
| Show Colors | Shift-⌘-C |
| Show Deleted Messages | ⌘-L |
| Show Fonts | ⌘-T |
| Show Spelling and Grammar | ⌘-: |
| Smaller | ⌘- - |
| Use Selection for Find | ⌘-E |

CHAPTER 22

# Surfing the Web with Safari

## In this chapter

# BROWSING THE WEB WITH SAFARI

Apple's Safari is Mac OS X's default web browser. Safari offers many great features and excellent performance (see Figure 22.1).

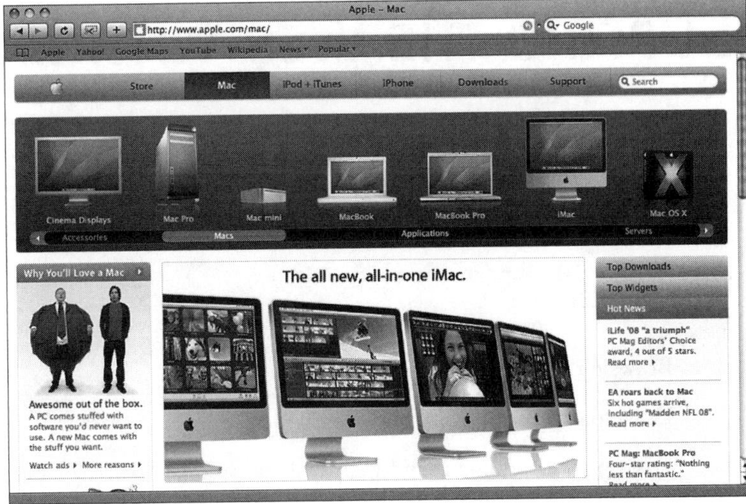


**Figure 22.1**
Safari works as good as it looks.

Because you are reading this book (indicating that you know your way around a Mac), I assume that you are quite comfortable with the basics of using Safari, such as using its buttons, navigating the Web by clicking links and entering URLs in the Address bar, and so on. In this section, you will learn about some of Safari's great features that might not be quite so obvious.

## BROWSING AND CONFIGURING RSS PAGES

Safari supports Rich Site Summary (RSS) web pages. RSS feeds provide a summary of articles and other information on a website so you can more efficiently browse information and then drill down into the information in which you are interested (see Figure 22.2). On an RSS feed page, you'll see a headline for each element on the page. You can scroll up and down the page to browse the headlines. When you find something in which you are interested, click the headline or the "Read more" link. You'll move to the article on a "regular" web page and can read its information. When you are done, click the SnapBack or RSS button to return to the RSS feed.

**NOTE**

> The articles you move to from some RSS feeds will cause the SnapBack button, RSS button, or both to appear in the Address bar. It doesn't matter which button you use—both will return you to the RSS feed.

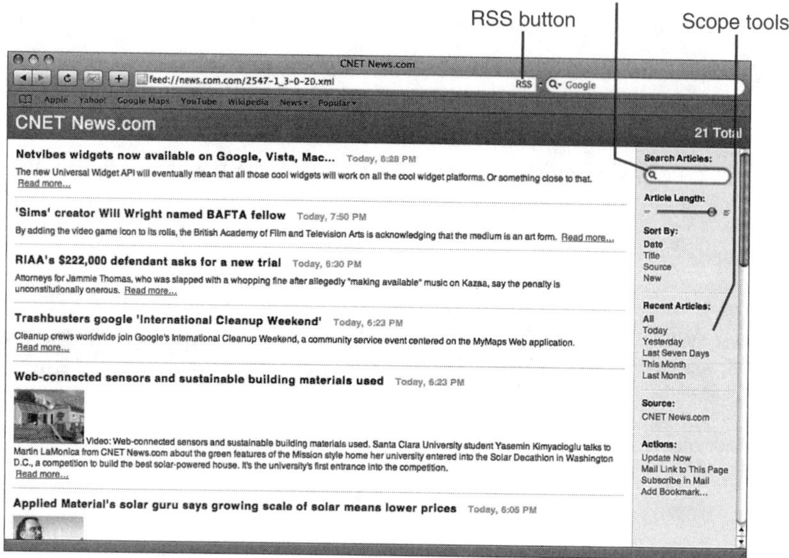


**Figure 22.2**
This CNET News.com RSS feed isn't as pretty to look at as a regular web page, but it is much more efficient to use.

## BROWSING RSS FEEDS

In addition to these handy features, there are several other things you need to know about RSS feeds:

- The URL for an RSS feed will start with `feed://` rather than `http://`. When an RSS feed is loaded into your browser, you'll also see the RSS button at the right end of the Address bar.
- When you view a "regular" website and the RSS button appears in the Address bar, an RSS feed is available for that website. Click the RSS button to view the RSS feed.
- Use the Search Articles tool to search the contents of the feed. If you enter a search term and then create a bookmark, your search will be saved as a bookmark so you can repeat it easily.
- Use the Article Length slider to set the length of the summaries you see on a feed page. With the slider all the way to the right, you see the headline and first sentence or two. If you move the slider all the way to the left, you'll only see the headline and date for each story.
- Use the scope tools to configure the contents of the RSS page. For example, you can sort the articles using the Sort By options. You can choose the timeline for the articles you see with the Recent Articles options, such as by choosing Today to see only articles that are published on the current day.
- The source of information for an RSS feed will be shown in the Source area.
- Any actions available for the feed, such as a link to enable you to email it, will be shown in the Actions area.

- Safari includes a number of bookmarked RSS feeds by default. To view these, choose Bookmarks, Show All Bookmarks. Then click the All RSS Feeds collection.
- Safari can automatically check for updates to RSS feeds and add them to the feed page. When new articles appear for a feed, the number of new articles is shown next to the feed's bookmark in the Bookmarks bar.
- You can view all the RSS feeds referenced in a bookmark folder that contains them by opening the Bookmarks menu and choosing "View All RSS Articles." In the resulting page, you'll see all the RSS feeds from all bookmarks in that folder (see Figure 22.3).

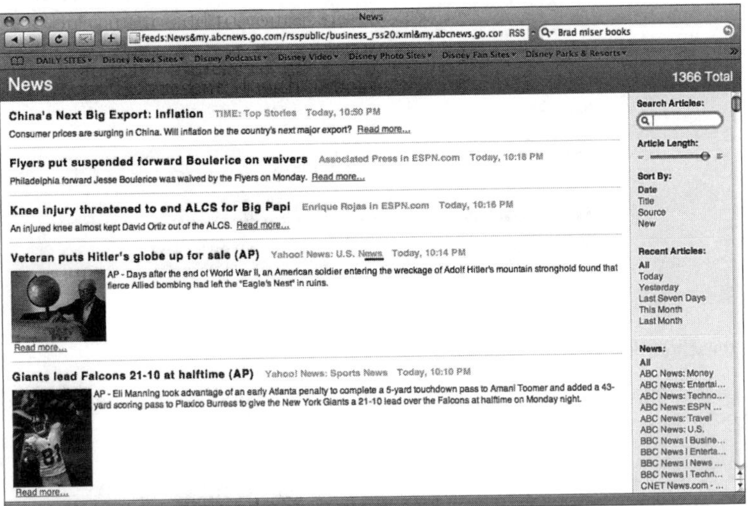


**Figure 22.3**
If you choose View All RSS Articles, you see a page containing articles from all the RSS feeds in that folder of bookmarks.

⇨ To learn how to read RSS feeds in Mail, **see** "Working with RSS Feeds," **p. 503**.

## CONFIGURING SAFARI'S RSS PREFERENCES

There are many aspects of working with RSS feeds that you can configure using the RSS pane of the Safari Preferences dialog box (see Figure 22.4):

- Set the default RSS reader on the Default RSS Reader pop-up menu. If you want to use something other than Safari or Mail, choose Select and then navigate to and choose the application you want to use to read RSS feeds.
- Use the Bookmarks Bar and Bookmarks Menu check boxes to tell Safari whether you want the RSS feeds in these areas to be updated automatically. If you check at least one of these, use the "Check for updates" pop-up menu to set how frequently Safari updates the checked items. The options are "Every 30 minutes," "Every day," "Every hour," and "Never" (select "Never" if you don't want articles to ever be automatically downloaded to your Mac).
- If you want new articles highlighted with a color, check the "Color new articles" check box and choose the color you want used on the pop-up menu.

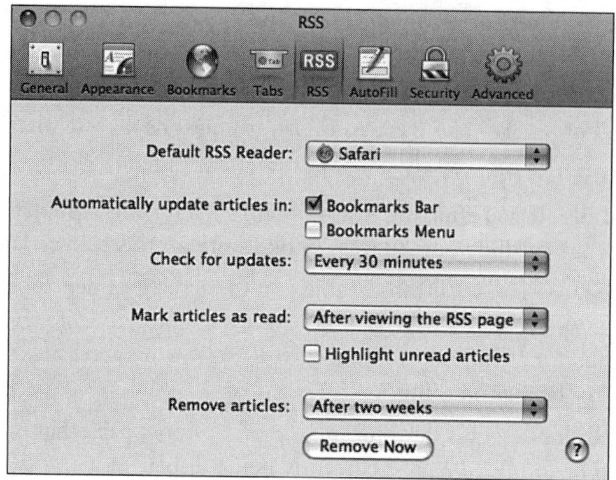


**Figure 22.4**
Use the RSS pane of the Safari Preferences dialog box to customize the way RSS feeds work.

- If you want RSS articles automatically removed after a specific amount of time, choose the time on the "Remove articles" pop-up menu. The times available range from after one day to never.
- To remove all articles, click the Remove Now button. If you click Remove Now in the resulting prompt, all RSS articles that have been downloaded to your Mac will be deleted.

## Configuring Safari

There are a number of ways in which you can configure Safari to match your browsing preferences. The most commonly used options are outlined in the sections that follow.

### Configuring Safari's Window

By default, Safari's window is pretty standard looking (refer to Figure 22.1). However, using the options on the View menu, you can customize the Safari browser experience to suit your preferences. On that menu, you have the following options:

- **Show/Hide Bookmarks Bar**—The Bookmarks bar provides easy access to your favorite bookmarks. It appears under the Address bar if it is being displayed.
- **Show/Hide Status Bar**—The Status bar provides useful information about what Safari is doing at any point in time or information about a link to which you are pointing, such as its URL.
- **Show/Hide Tab Bar**—You can open web pages in tabs within the Safari window. This command shows or hides the Tab bar regardless of tabs being open or not. The Tab bar opens automatically when you open at least two tabs.
- **Hide/Show Toolbar**—This command shows or hides the Safari toolbar. At its most basic, the toolbar includes the Address bar that displays the URL of the page currently being shown along with default buttons for a number of actions, such as Refresh.

- **Customize Toolbar**—When you choose this command, you can select the tools that appear on the toolbar via a standard Customize toolbar sheet. The tools available on this sheet are described in the following bullets:
  - **Back/Forward**—The Back and Forward buttons do just what you expect.
  - **Home**—This button takes you back to your home page.
  - **AutoFill**—If you click the AutoFill button, a form is completed with information from your card in your Address Book (more on this feature later).
  - **Text Size**—These buttons enable you to increase or decrease the size of text being displayed on a page (if you have ever squinted while trying to read a page designed for Windows computers, you know why increasing the size of text on a page can be a good thing!).
  - **Stop/Reload**—This button can be used to stop a page that is currently being loaded or to reload a page currently being displayed.
  - **Open in Dashboard**—This button enables you to capture all or part of a web page as a widget on the Dashboard. More on this tool later in this chapter.
  - **Add Bookmark**—Use this to show or hide the Add Bookmark button.
  - **Print**—Use this to print the page being displayed.
  - **Report Bug**—When you click this button, you can send a bug report about Safari to Apple.
  - **Address**—This tool can be used to enter or show a URL.
  - **Google Search**—The Google Search tool is a great way to search for information, as you will learn in a later section.

> **TIP**
>
> Some of the optional tools are also available as commands on the View menu, such as Reload Page, Make Text Bigger, and so on.

## CONFIGURING SAFARI'S GENERAL PREFERENCES

Press ⌘-, to open the Safari Preferences dialog box, and click the General button to open its General pane (see Figure 22.5). The general preferences are explained in the following list:

- **Default Web Browser**—Use the "Default Web Browser" pop-up menu to choose your default web browser, which is the browser Mac OS X will use to view web pages and to open web links. Initially, Safari is the option selected on the pop-up menu. However, you can choose Select and then pick another browser. This sets your browser preference for all areas of the OS.
- **New Window Behavior**—Use the "New windows open with" pop-up menu to choose what happens when you open a new Safari window. The options are Home Page, Empty Page, Same Page, or Bookmarks. In most cases, Empty Page is the best choice because it doesn't cause Safari to download a page that you probably don't want to view anyway. However, if you frequently use bookmarks to move to a new page, that can be a useful option as well.

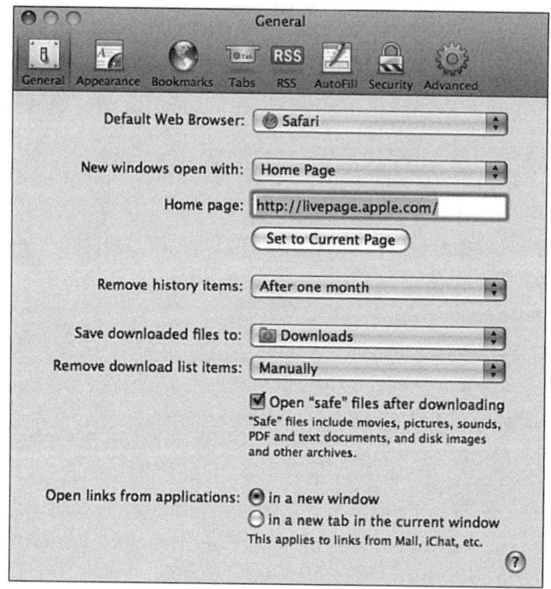


**Figure 22.5**
Although simple in appearance, the General pane enables you to configure important Safari behaviors.

- **Home Page**—Type a URL in the Home page field to set it as your home page. Alternatively, you can move to the page you want to be your home page, open the General pane, and click "Set to Current Page." The home page is displayed when you use the Home button or if you have it set to be displayed when you open a new Safari window. If you leave the field empty, moving to the home page opens a new empty page.
- **History**—As you move among pages, Safari keeps a log of the pages you've visited. On the "Remove history items" menu, you can choose the timeframe on which the history items are removed. The options range from one day to one year or Manually (in which case you need to manually delete history items).
- **Download Behavior**—You will frequently use Safari to download files. Use the "Save downloaded files to" pop-up menu to select the location in which you want those files to be placed by default. With Mac OS X Leopard a new Downloads folder comes standard, and is where you ought to have your downloads stored. That way, you will always know where files you download are located.

**NOTE**

> Setting a file download location, similar to choosing a default web browser, affects the OS—not just Safari. For example, if you use a download tool that uses your download location preference, such as Mail, that application uses the preference you set within Safari.

Use the "Remove download list items" pop-up menu to choose when items are removed from the Downloads window (you'll learn about that later).

If you want "safe" files to be opened as soon as you download them, check the "Open 'safe' files after downloading" check box (it is checked by default). When Safari downloads image, movie, text, sound, and other content files, they are opened automatically. For those files that might cause damage to your system, such as applications, macros, and other suspicious files, you must open them manually after you download them.

- **Link behavior**—When documents, such as email messages, contain URL links, two radio buttons determine how those links open when you click them. If you click the "in a new window" radio button, a new Safari window opens and displays the page at which the link points. If you click "in a new tab in the current window," the content at which the link points opens within a new tab in the current window.

### Configuring Safari's Appearance Preferences

Click the Appearance tab in the Safari Preferences dialog box to move to the Appearance pane. Here you can set the standard font, fixed-width font, and default encoding that are used when pages are displayed. (If a page uses a built-in style sheet, your options might be overridden by the style sheet, but most of the time, your preferences will be used.) To select a font, click the related Select button and use the Font panel to configure the font. To choose an encoding method, use the pop-up menu.

If you want images to be displayed when a page is opened, check the "Display images when the page opens" check box (it is checked by default). If you use a slow connection, you might want to uncheck this check box so you don't waste time downloading images you aren't interested in.

### Configuring Safari's Security Preferences

Safari has a number of good security features, some of which you can configure on the Security pane of the Safari Preferences dialog box (see Figure 22.6).

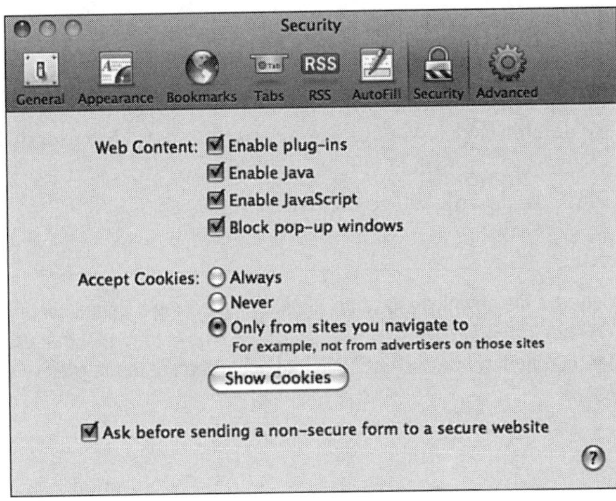


**Figure 22.6**
Use the Security pane to set how Safari manages the security of your Mac; the best part is the ability to block pop-up windows.

The Web Content controls determine whether certain types of content are enabled. These controls include

- **Enable plug-ins**—Determines whether any Safari plug-ins, such as those for QuickTime, Flash, and so on, are enabled. If you disable the plug-ins, content that requires them is not displayed. I recommend you leave this check box checked because most content that requires such plug-ins is safe. And, except for the plug-ins installed by default, you will choose the plug-ins you want to install.
- **Enable Java and Enable JavaScript**—Java and JavaScript are two programming languages that can be used to execute complex operations within the Safari browser. For example, if you use a bank service, it likely uses JavaScript to deliver its functionality. Again, you should typically allow these types of content.
- **Block pop-up windows**—If you have ever been annoyed by the numerous and obnoxious pop-up windows that appear when you visit some websites, you might think that this is the single best feature of Safari. If this option is checked, Safari does not allow a web page to open additional windows. This means that all pop-up windows that point to different URLs are blocked and you never have to see them.

  Although blocking pop-up windows is mostly a good thing, some pop-up windows actually provide useful information and are necessary to get the most out of a website. If you block them, a site might not work well, or at all.

**TIP**

If you block pop-up windows and a site that needs them doesn't work properly, you can enable them again by selecting Safari, Block Pop-Up Windows or by pressing Shift-⌘-K. This toggles the pop-up window setting, so you can also use it to quickly allow pop-ups if you generally prevent them.

You use the Cookies radio buttons to determine how Safari deals with cookies it encounters. Typically, "Only from sites you navigate to" is the best setting because cookies often provide a useful service for the sites you intentionally visit, such as shopping sites. If you want to block all cookies, click Never. I don't recommend that you use the Always option.

To see the cookies that have been accepted, click the Show Cookies button. A sheet appears that shows you all the cookies that have been downloaded to your Mac (prepare to be astounded at their number!). In addition to the information you see about the cookies, you can select cookies and either click Remove to delete them or click Remove All to delete all the cookies on your Mac. It's not a bad idea to review this list from time to time and delete any cookies you can't recognize (or at least recognize where they came from). If a site needs a cookie to function, it will create it again, although you might lose some of your customized information on that site.

**Cookies**

On the Web, *cookies* are small text files websites use to track information about you. When you visit a site that uses cookies, the site can check the cookies it previously installed on your machine to serve you or capture more information about you. For example, a cookie can contain areas of interest so you are automatically taken to spots on the site that are more likely to generate a purchase from you.

Most cookies are relatively harmless and some even serve a good purpose, but you do need to be aware that a lot of information about you and what you do on the Web is captured whether you know it or not. If this thought bothers you, select the Never radio button so cookies are never accepted. If you do this, be aware that some sites might not work for you or you might have to spend more time re-entering information, such as a username, each time you visit a site.

If you want Safari to warn you when you send nonsecure information to a secure site, check the "Ask before sending a non-secure form to a secure website" check box.

**The Greatest Browser Feature Ever**

That might be a bit of an overstatement, but if you frequently access secured services over the Web using usernames and passwords, such as banking or shopping sites, you might find the following feature to be the best thing about Safari. Safari is fully integrated with Mac OS X's Keychains. Basically, this means you can store usernames and passwords within Safari and Safari will automatically enter that information for you when you return to the related sites. All you then have to do is move to the URL for the service, and the username and password are entered for you automatically. Click Login, Enter, or a similar button or link and you are in.

To enable this, Safari creates the Safari Forms AutoFill keychain item and stores usernames and passwords there.

⇨ To learn how to configure and use AutoFill for usernames and passwords, **see** "Using Safari AutoFill," **p. 530**.

⇨ To learn more about Keychains, **see** "Securing Your Mac with Keychains," **p. 928**.

## CONFIGURING SAFARI'S ADVANCED PREFERENCES

To see Safari's Advanced preferences, click the Advanced tab on the Safari Preferences dialog box. The Advanced preferences consist of universal access, style sheet options, and proxy settings.

Use the Universal Access controls to set a minimum font size or control Tab key behavior.

If you have a style sheet you want Safari to use, you can add it by selecting Other on the Style Sheet pop-up menu and then selecting the sheet you want to install. If you add more than one sheet, you can select the sheet you want to use on the Style Sheet pop-up menu.

**NOTE**

> Cascading style sheets can be used to determine the formatting for web pages. Many pages use these sheets. If not, a page is presented based on Safari's own interpretation of the HTML and the other code of which the page is composed.

You can use the Proxies button to access the Proxies tab of the Network pane of the System Preferences application.

## SEARCHING WITH SAFARI

Of course, you can use Safari to access the many web search engines available, such as Yahoo!, Lycos, and so on. You do this by visiting that search engine's site.

However, you can access one of the best search engines, Google, directly from the Safari Address bar. This enables some great features, most notably the SnapBack button.

**NOTE**

> **If you don't see the Google search tool, make sure the Address bar is displayed and that the Google search tool has been added to the Address Bar (it is by default).**

To search the Web using the built-in Google search tool, do the following:

1. Type the text for which you want to search in the Search tool and press Return. You jump to Google and the results of your search are displayed (see Figure 22.7).

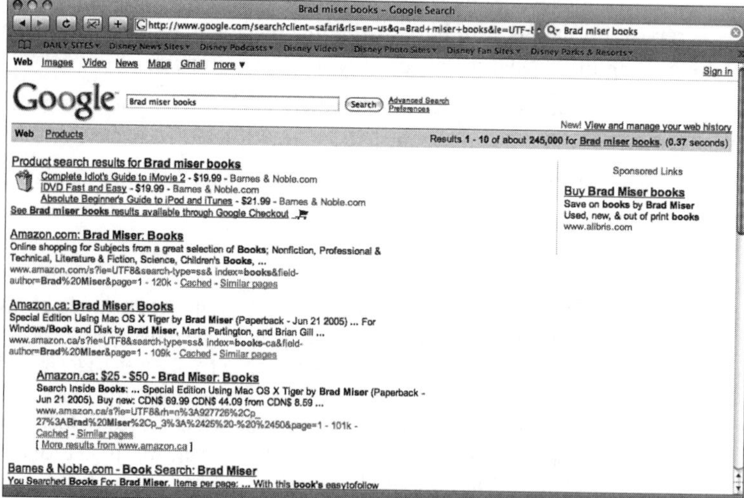


**Figure 22.7**
Safari's built-in search tool enables you to quickly search on Google.

2. Use a link on the results page to move to a page that looks promising (see Figure 22.8).
3. To return to the results page so you can try other links, click the SnapBack button; select History, Search Results SnapBack; or press Option-⌘-S.

Snap Back

**Figure 22.8**
The SnapBack button enables you to return to the Google search results page.

Performing a Google search from within Safari is fast and easy. Here are few tips:

- To repeat a previous search, click the magnifying glass icon in the search tool; then on the pop-up menu, select the search you want to repeat.
- To clear the searches you have performed, click the magnifying glass icon in the search tool; then on the pop-up menu, select Clear Recent Searches.
- To clear the current search (when the Google page is being displayed), click the x button inside the search field.

**TIP**

> Sometimes when you search for something on the web it can be hard to find the exact word or phrase you were searching for on the result page. If you type ⌘-f in Safari you will see a search bar just above the content of the web page. At the far right is a search tool where you can type the word or phrase; as you type, Safari will start to look for matches to what you are entering. To the left of the search tool is a counter of all of the instances of what you have searched for. On the web page each instance of that word or phrase will be highlighted (in some cases a box may be drawn around the match because of the background color of the page) so that you can see matches. Left and right arrow buttons let you easily move to the previous or next instance of a match.

## USING SAFARI SNAPBACK

Using the SnapBack button when you search with the Google search tool is great, but you can also use this feature when you are browsing. Safari marks the first page you visit on any site as the SnapBack page. As you move to other pages on the site, you can return to the SnapBack page by clicking the SnapBack button shown at the end of the URL of the page you are currently viewing. You then move back to the SnapBack page for that site.

Here are a couple more SnapBack tips:

- You can mark a page to be the SnapBack page for a site by either selecting History, Mark Page for SnapBack or pressing Option-⌘-K. Whenever you click the SnapBack button, you return to this page. (If you don't set a SnapBack page, you return to the first page on the site.)
- You can also return to the SnapBack page by selecting History, Page SnapBack or pressing Option-⌘-P.

## Using Safari Bookmarks

Like all other browsers, Safari enables you to bookmark web pages so you can easily return to them. And, also similar to other browsers, Safari provides tools you can use to organize your bookmarks. However, Safari's bookmark tools are more refined and powerful than most of the browsers I've used.

### Configuring Safari Bookmarks Preferences

Open the Bookmarks pane of the Safari Preferences dialog box to configure your bookmark preferences. On this pane, you have the following options:

- **Bookmarks Bar**—The two Include check boxes determine whether Address Book and Bonjour sites are accessible from the Bookmarks bar.

  If you make your Address Book available from the Bookmarks bar, you can access any websites associated with cards in your Address Book by selecting the site you want to visit on the Address Book menu. This is a very cool way to quickly access the website for anyone or any company in your Address Book.

  Similarly, you can make all the Bonjour computers that provide services Safari can access available via the Bonjour menu. This enables you to quickly move to web, FTP, or other resources on your local network.
- **Bookmarks Menu**—This area enables you to add your Address Book and Bonjour sites to the Bookmarks menu. Additionally, you can include all the Bookmarks bar's bookmarks on the Bookmarks menu by checking the Include Bookmarks Bar box.
- **Collections**—Safari uses the term *collections* for groups of bookmarks. You can use collections to organize bookmarks; a number of collections are included by default. You use the Bookmarks window to work with these (this is covered later in this section).
- **Synchronize**—If you use machines in different locations, you might find yourself adding bookmarks on one machine and not being able to use those bookmarks when you are working on another machine. If you have a .Mac account, you can synchronize your bookmarks across many machines so they all have the same set. To do this, check the "Synchronize bookmarks with other computers using .Mac" and click the .Mac button. The .Mac pane of the System Preferences application opens and you can use the Sync tab to configure synchronization.

⇨ To learn how to configure .Mac synchronization, **see** "Using .Mac to Synchronize Important Information on Multiple Macs," **p. 454**.

### Accessing Safari Bookmarks

You can use bookmarks in the following ways:

- Click a bookmark on the Bookmarks bar.
- Select a bookmark on the Bookmarks menu.
- Press ⌘-1 to move to the first bookmark on the Bookmarks bar (not counting menu items on the bar), ⌘-2 to move to the second one, and so on up to ⌘-9 to move to the ninth one listed on the Bookmarks bar. This only works for bookmarks not for folders. If an item is a folder, you must select it using the mouse.
- Open the Bookmarks window and double-click a bookmark.
- Open the Address Book or Bonjour menu on the Bookmarks bar and select a site to visit.
- Open a bookmark's contextual menu and select either Open, Open in New Window or Open in New Tab.

### Setting Safari Bookmarks

You can bookmark web pages with the following steps:

1. Move to the page you want to bookmark.
2. Select Bookmarks, Add Bookmark or press ⌘-D. The Add Bookmark sheet opens.
3. Edit the name of the bookmark. You can use the default name, change it, or replace it with one of your choosing.
4. On the pop-up menu, select the location in which you want the bookmark to be stored. You can select Bookmarks Bar to add the bookmark to the Bookmarks bar, any folder to place the bookmark in that folder, or Bookmarks Menu to place the bookmark on the Bookmarks menu.
5. Click Add or press Return. The bookmark will be added in the location you selected.

**TIP**

> You can add a bookmark to the Bookmarks bar by dragging across the URL in the Address bar and dropping it on the Bookmarks bar. In the resulting name sheet, edit the name of the bookmark and click OK. The bookmark will be added to the Bookmarks bar so you can access it from there.

### Organizing Safari Bookmarks

Use Safari's Bookmark tools to organize your bookmarks. You can determine the location of bookmarks, place them in folders to create hierarchical bookmark menus, rename them, and so on. To do these tasks, open the Bookmarks window by clicking the Bookmarks button at the left end of the Bookmarks bar; by selecting Bookmarks, Show All Bookmarks; or by pressing Option-⌘-B. The Bookmarks window opens (see Figure 22.9).

In the left pane of the window is the list of *collections* (groups or folders of bookmarks). At the top of the list are the Bookmarks Bar and Bookmarks Menu collections that contain the bookmarks in those areas. Under those are the Address Book and Bonjour collections, and under those is the History collection that contains a list of sites you have visited. Below that is the All RSS Feeds collection that contains all your RSS feeds. Under that are the rest of the bookmark folders; Safari includes several folders with many bookmarks by default. You can add your own folders and bookmarks, as well as adding your bookmarks to existing collections.

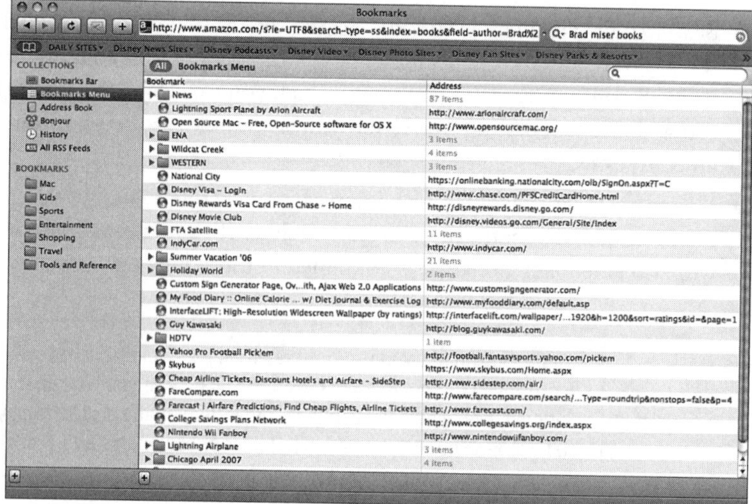


**Figure 22.9**
The Bookmarks window enables you to organize your bookmarks.

To view the contents of a collection, select it. The bookmarks it contains are shown in the right pane. For each bookmark, its name and address will be shown. If an item in the collection is a folder, you will see the folder along with its expansion triangle; click this to expand the folder's contents.

Organizing bookmarks is straightforward:

- Move bookmarks from one collection to another by dragging them onto the collection in which you want to place them. For example, to move a bookmark from the Bookmarks bar to the Bookmarks menu, drag it from the Bookmarks Bar collection to the Bookmarks Menu collection.
- Create new collections by clicking the New Collection button (the +) at the bottom of the Collections pane.
- Create a new folder in a collection by clicking the New Folder button (the +) at the bottom of the Bookmarks pane.
- Rename a collection, folder, or bookmark by selecting it, opening the contextual menu, and selecting Edit Name.
- Change the URL for a bookmark by selecting it, opening the contextual menu, and selecting Edit Address.
- Move to a URL by double-clicking it or opening its contextual menu and choosing Open or "Open in New Window."

- Add a folder to the Bookmarks Bar or Bookmarks Menu collections by selecting Add Bookmark Folder from the Bookmarks menu. Then place bookmarks in the folder you created. When you select the folder in either location, a pop-up menu appears to enable you to quickly select any bookmarks in that folder.
- If you check the Auto-Click check box for a folder, all the bookmarks in that folder will open, with each bookmark appearing in a separate tab, when you click the folder's button on the Bookmarks bar or choose it on a menu.
- Search your bookmarks using the Search tool at the top of the Bookmarks pane. Using the Magnifying Glass pop-up menu, you can choose to search in the selected collection or in all collections. After you've searched, you can scope the results by clicking the button with the name of the collection you are searching or All to show the bookmarks in all collections.
- Delete a collection, folder, or bookmark by selecting it and pressing Delete or by opening its contextual menu and choosing Delete. If you delete a folder or collection, you will also delete any bookmarks contained in those items.

**TIP**

> Put the bookmarks you use most often on the Bookmarks bar or Bookmarks menu because you can get to them most quickly there (if you have so many that these become cluttered, use folders to keep them organized). In the next section, you learn a technique that enables you to open an entire folder of bookmarks with a single click.

## USING SAFARI TABS

If you have spent any time on the Web, you have no doubt seen the benefits of having many web browser windows open at the same time. Of course, you can do this with Safari by selecting File, New Window or pressing ⌘-N. If you have done this, you also know that after opening more than a couple of windows, moving back to specific windows can be cumbersome. That is where Safari's Tabs feature comes in. You can open many pages within the same window; each web page appears as a tab. You then select the tab to view that page.

### CONFIGURING TABS

First, configure the Tab feature by opening the Tabs pane of the Safari preferences dialog box (see Figure 22.10).

To configure tabbed browsing, follow these steps:

1. To open a new tab when you ⌘-click a link, check the "⌘-click opens a link in a new tab" check box. As you come across links on pages, you can open the link in a new tab by pressing the ⌘ key when you click the link.
2. If you want new tabs to be selected, so the page on the tab is displayed, as soon as they are created, check the "Select tabs and windows as they are created" check box.

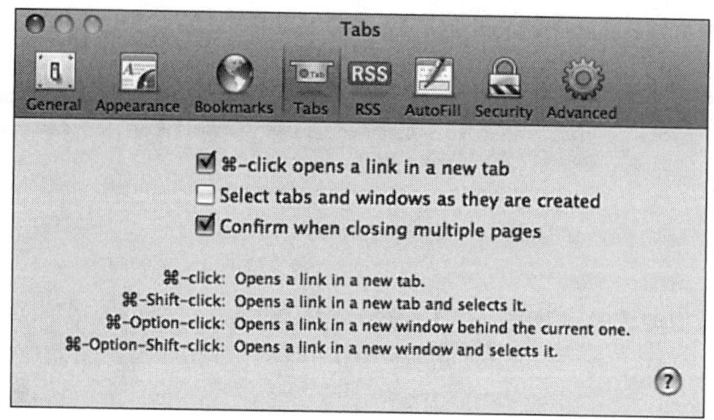


**Figure 22.10**
Configure tabs to open many windows on the Web in a single Safari window.

**TIP**

The previously mentioned preference affects what the tab keyboard shortcuts do. If you don't enable this preference, you have to physically select a tab after you create it to view it. I have assumed that this preference is enabled for the rest of this section.

3. If you want to confirm when you close multiple pages at the same time, check the "Confirm when closing multiple pages" check box. If this isn't checked, you can close multiple pages without being prompted to confirm that action.

**TIP**

Notice the keyboard shortcuts at the bottom of the Tabs pane. These are important tips that help you effectively work with tabs. If you can't remember them, they are listed in the next section and in Table 22.4 at the end of this chapter. The keyboard shortcuts you see depend on the check boxes that are checked. For example, if you uncheck the first check box, you see a different set of actions for the keyboard shortcuts than you do with it checked.

### Using Cool Safari Tab Tricks

After you have enabled tabs, the Safari window contains a tab for each web page you have opened. To open a new tab and display it, hold down the ⌘ key while you click a link or bookmark. The page will open and be on a new tab. You can open as many tabs as you like (see Figure 22.11).

Following is a list of tab tricks:

- Click a tab to view its web page. The tab currently being displayed is highlighted.
- To close a page, click the x button in its tab. The tab and page close.
- To open a page in a new tab and move to it, ⌘-click a link or bookmark.
- To open a new tab without viewing it, ⌘-Shift-click a link or bookmark.
- To open a link or a bookmark in a new window and view it, ⌘-Option-click it.
- To open a link or a bookmark in a new window but move the new window to the background, ⌘-Option-Shift-click it.

22

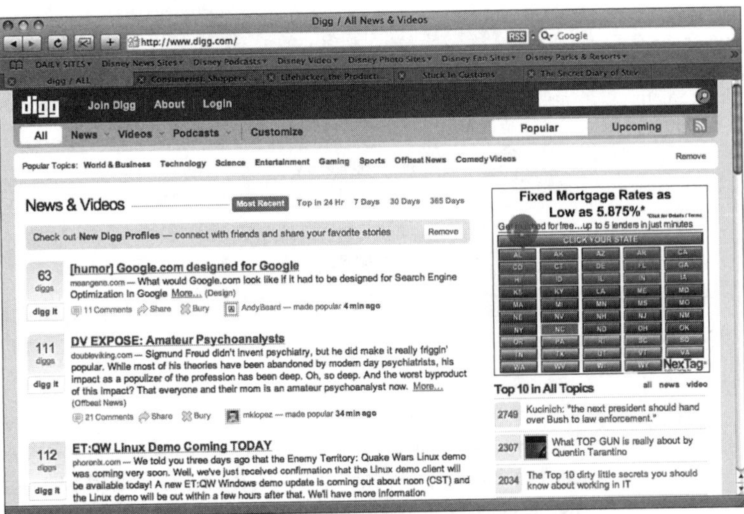

**Figure 22.11**
Each tab is a separate and independent web page; very cool!

**NOTE**

> The previous four actions are reversed if you uncheck the "Select tabs and windows as they are created" preference. For example, you would ⌘-Shift-click a link or bookmark to open it in a tab and view it.

- To move into the next tab, choose Window, Select Next Tab or press Shift-⌘-].
- To move into the previous tab, choose Window, Select Next Tab or press Shift-⌘-[.
- Rearrange your tabs by clicking and dragging a tab to a different location on the tab bar.
- If you want a tab to become a new window, just click and drag the tab down into the content pane; you will see a small preview of the web page. Release the mouse button a new window will be created for the page you are viewing.
- Create one bookmark for an entire set of tabs. If you have a set of web site you visit often, open them all into tabs in a Safari window then go to the Bookmarks menu and select Add Bookmark For These *Number* tabs, where *Number* is the number of tabs in the window.

Okay, I have saved the coolest thing about Safari for this moment: Safari enables you to open as many pages as you want by clicking a single bookmark for a collection. Each page included in the group opens in a new tab. If you frequently open the same set of pages, you can click a single bookmark to open them all at the same.

**TIP**

> If you don't enable Auto-Click for a folder of bookmarks, you can open all the bookmarks it contains in tabs by opening its menu on the Bookmarks bar and choosing the Open in Tabs command. Also, you can open individual bookmarks within an Auto-Click collection by opening the collections menu on the Bookmarks bar and choosing the page you want to open.

First, create the group of bookmarks you want to open:

1. Open the Bookmarks window and create a folder in the Bookmarks Bar collection.
2. Check the Auto-Click check box for the folder you created.
3. Place bookmarks for all the sites you want to open simultaneously in the folder you created in step 1 (see Figure 22.12).

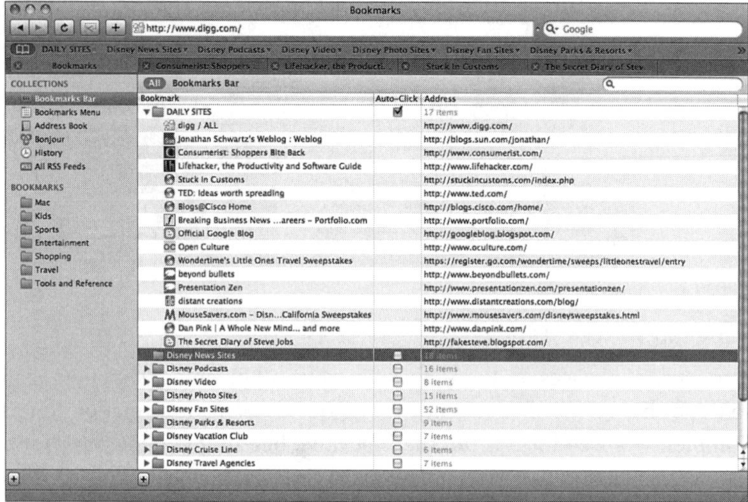

**Figure 22.12**
Because the Auto-Click check box is checked, I can open all the pages inside the folder called DAILY SITES with a single click.

**TIP**

> To make moving bookmarks into folders within collections easier, open a second Safari window and view the Bookmarks window. You can drag bookmarks from the first window onto the second to move them among collections.

Close the Bookmarks window and click the button on the Bookmarks bar for the folder you created in the previous steps. Every page opens in its own tab (see Figure 22.13). Working with a set of web pages has never been so easy.

**TIP**

> You can use Automator to create an application that will open websites for you. You can add this application to your Login Items so they automatically open for you each time you log in.

⇨ To learn how to use the Automator, **see** Chapter 29, "Making Your Mac Do the Work for You with the Automator," **p. 721**.

**Figure 22.13**
I opened all the pages in this window just by clicking the Favorite Podcasts button in the Bookmarks bar!

## USING SAFARI AUTOFILL

If you access services on the Web, such as travel planning, shopping, banking, and so on, you no doubt have a lot of experience filling out the same information time and time again. Completing a web form is fun the first time, but after completing your address, phone number, username, and password a few dozen times, it gets old. This is where Safari's AutoFill feature comes in. It enables you to complete various kinds of information automatically or at the click of the AutoFill button.

Using AutoFill, Safari can enter the following types of information for you:

- **Your Address Book information**—Safari can access the information stored on your card in your Address Book. This can include your address, phone number, website, and so on.

⇨ To learn how to configure the information on your card in your Address Book, **see** "Editing Your Own Address Card," **p. 649**.

- **Usernames and passwords**—Safari can capture your username and password at many websites. When you return to those sites, your username and password are entered for you automatically.
- **Information entered on various websites**—As you provide information in other types of websites, Safari can gather this data and remember it so that the next time you visit a site, you can complete any information by clicking the AutoFill button.

### CONFIGURING AUTOFILL

First, you need to tell Safari which AutoFill features you want to use by configuring your AutoFill preferences:

1. Press ⌘-, to open the Preferences dialog box.
2. Click the AutoFill tab to open the AutoFill pane (see Figure 22.14).

**Figure 22.14**
Using Safari's AutoFill feature saves you a lot of typing.

3. If you want Safari to be able to enter the information from your Address Book card, check the "Using info from my Address Book card" check box.

> **TIP**
>
> If you click any of the Edit buttons, you can edit the AutoFill information for that area. For example, if you click the Edit button for the Address Book, the Address Book application will open and you will see your Address Book card in edit mode so you can make changes to it. If you click Edit for "User names and password," a sheet appears on which you see the websites for which Safari has remembered this information. You can remove individual sites by selecting them and clicking Remove.

4. If you want Safari to capture usernames and passwords at various websites you use, check the "User names and passwords" check box.
5. If you want Safari to capture other types of information you enter on the Web, check the "Other forms" check box.
6. Close the Preferences dialog box.

### USING AUTOFILL

Using AutoFill is straightforward.

To enter your personal information from your Address Book card, use the following steps:

1. Move to a web page that requires your personal information, such as name, address, and so on.
2. Click the AutoFill button on the Address bar; select Edit, AutoFill Form; or press Shift-⌘-A. Safari will transfer the information from your card in your Address Book and place it in the appropriate fields on the web form.

3. Review the information that was entered to ensure that it is correct. AutoFill isn't perfect and sometimes web forms use slightly different terms for data.

**TIP**

> If you find AutoFill consistently not entering specific information, add that information to your card in your Address Book.

To use the username and password feature, complete the following steps:

1. Move to a website that requires a username and password.
2. Enter your username and password on the page.
3. Click Login. You will be prompted about whether you want Safari to capture the username and password for this site.
4. In the prompt, make one of the following choices:
    - Click Yes if you want the information to be added to AutoFill.
    - Click Not Now if you don't want the information to be captured at this time but want to be prompted the next time you access the site.
    - Click "Never for this Website" if you don't want the information captured and never want to be prompted again.

If you click Yes, the next time you visit the website, your username and password will be filled in automatically. All you have to do to log in to the site is click the Login button or link.

**CAUTION**

> The username and password feature is convenient, but you shouldn't use it unless you are the only one who uses your Mac OS X user account or the people who share your Mac OS X user account are very trustworthy. Because the usernames and passwords for your accounts are entered automatically, anyone who uses your Mac OS X user account and moves to the related websites can log in to your account on that website.

If you decide you don't want to provide automatic access to a specific website, you can remove that site's username and password:

1. Open the AutoFill pane of the Safari Preferences dialog box.
2. Click the Edit button next to the text "User names and passwords." A sheet appears that lists each website and username you have captured in Safari.
3. Select the website you want to remove.

**TIP**

> Click Remove All to delete all the websites for which you have captured usernames and passwords.

4. Click Remove. Continue removing websites until you have removed all the sites you no longer need.
5. Click Done and close the Preferences dialog box.

**NOTE**

> If you don't turn off the username and password feature by unchecking the "User names and passwords" check box, you will be prompted by AutoFill the next time you visit any websites you deleted from the list.

Using the AutoFill feature for other kinds of forms is similar to the first two. When you enable the "Other forms" feature and enter information in websites, that information is captured. When you return to those sites in the future, you can enter the information again by clicking the AutoFill button; selecting Edit, AutoFill Form; or pressing Shift-⌘-A. You can edit the list of websites for which information is remembered by clicking the Edit button next to the text "Other forms" on the AutoFill pane of the Safari Preferences dialog box.

## CREATING WEB WIDGETS

Mac OS X's Dashboard feature is a great way to quickly get to specific information and tools. You can use Safari to add websites or parts of websites as widgets on your Dashboard so you can work with your custom web widgets just like other widgets on your Dashboard.

To create a web widget, do the following steps:

1. Move to the web page you want to capture.
2. Click the "Open this page in Dashboard" button (it is the button on the toolbar that looks like a pair of scissors) or choose File, Open in Dashboard. The Dashboard capture bar appears along with the selection box that jumps to the element of the page that can be captured as a unit. The rest of the page is darkened to show it is not part of the capture (see Figure 22.15).

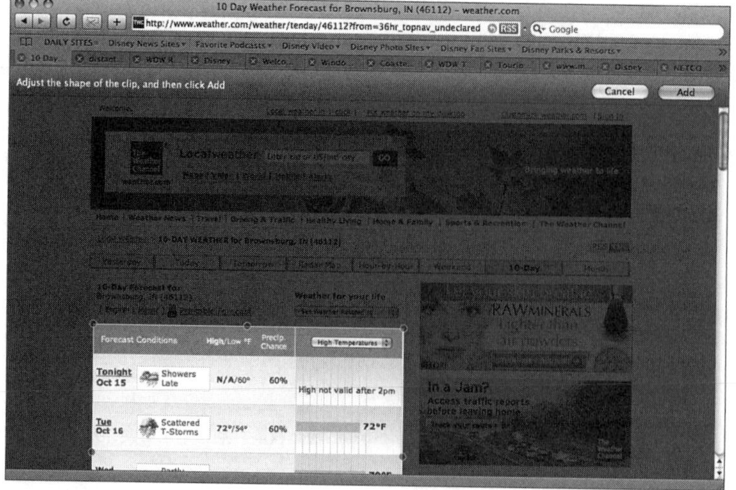


**Figure 22.15**
You can capture part of a web page and place it on your Dashboard with just a couple of mouse clicks.

3. If the selected portion of the page is not the part you want, move the mouse pointer around the page. As you do, other "boxes" on the page are highlighted.

   The capture tool is designed to capture specific document object model (DOM) elements of a page. As you move the pointer, the next closest DOM element is highlighted. These elements are rectangular boxes of various sizes; some will have content, others may not.

4. After the element you want to capture is selected, click it. Resize handles appear around the selection box (see Figure 22.16).

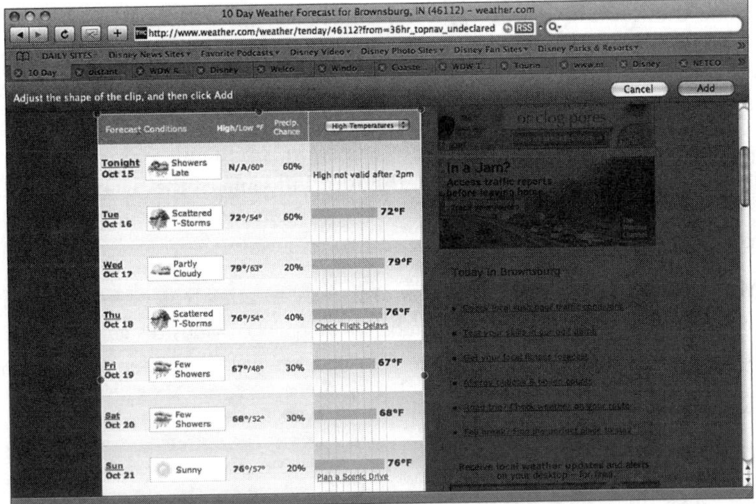


**Figure 22.16**
You can change the size of the selection box by dragging its Resize handles.

5. Change the size of the selection box to include only the portion of the page you want to capture.
6. When the selection box reflects the widget you want to create, click the Add button. The widget is created, the Dashboard opens, and you see the widget you created (see Figure 22.17).
7. Click the info button (the lowercase "i") on the widget you created. The configuration controls appear.
8. Choose a theme for the widget by clicking it; themes change the borders of the widget.
9. If the widget includes audio, check the "Only play audio in Dashboard" check box so that its audio only plays while the Dashboard is active. Otherwise, the widget's audio might play all the time, which is probably not what you want.
10. To change the size of the widget, click Edit and then resize it. Click Done.
11. When you're happy with the changes you made, click Done to save your changes and return to the widget.

⇨ To learn about the Dashboard, **see** Chapter 6, "Working with the Dashboard and Widgets," **p. 123**.

**Figure 22.17**
This section of the weather.com website is now a widget on my Dashboard.

Here are some tidbits about creating web widgets:

- Each time you open a web widget by opening your Dashboard, its content is refreshed.
- If the website on which you captured content changes layout or other aspect, your widget may no longer work.
- To remove a web widget from your Dashboard, click the Manage Widgets button and click the x button on the widget. After you remove a web widget, it is deleted and you have to re-create it to add it to your Dashboard again.
- Web widgets work best for viewing information that doesn't require authentication or for which a cookie stores any personalization information. Most sites that require secure logins can't be accessed via web widget you create. To see whether a site can be captured in a widget, try capturing its login box as a widget and then try to log in. If it works, you can log in to the site quickly by opening the widget and logging in. In most cases, you'll move to an error page or the actual login page in which case you should just delete the widget.
- Most links in a web widget should take you to the appropriate place on the related web page. Some links might not work, it depends on how the page is built and how the widget was captured.
- Getting a web widget just right can be tricky. The only way to tell is to try capturing the widget you want. If it doesn't work the way you expect, try capturing more of the web page (remember you can use the widget's Edit button to change the size of the widget). For information pages, you'll usually get what you want on the first try. For pages with which you interact, a bit more experimentation may be required. In some cases, you won't be able to capture the part of a page that you want to be able to use, but at least it won't take very much work to find out.

### USING SAFARI'S ACTIVITY VIEWER

As you move around the Web, Safari tracks the sites you have visited. You can view this information on the Activity window. To do so, select Window, Activity or press Option-⌘-A. The Activity window appears. In this window, you will see a list of the sites you have visited during the current browsing session. You can expand each site to see the individual pages you have visited and double-click any of these to return to that page.

### BROWSING PRIVATELY

As you travel around the Web, Safari helpfully tracks where you have been, usernames and passwords, cookies, AutoFill information, and other items to make using the Web more convenient. However, sometimes you might not want all this information recorded and would instead prefer to browse without any sort of recordkeeping on Safari's part. For example, you might be using a public Mac or be logged in under someone else's user account. In Safari terminology, this is called *private browsing*. When you browse privately, web pages you visit are not tracked in the History folder, items you download are removed from the Downloads window, any cookies stored on the Mac are deleted, information isn't retained for AutoFill, and your searches aren't saved.

To browse privately, choose Safari, Private Browsing. Click OK in the resulting prompt and private browsing will be in effect. When you are ready to resume normal browsing, choose Safari, Private Browsing again. Safari will clear any cookies and downloads stored during the private browsing session and return to normal browsing mode.

### EMAILING WEB PAGES

When you surf, you'll likely encounter web pages you'd like other people to view. Using Safari's built-in web page emailing ability, you can easily send information about web pages to other people via email:

1. View the web page you want to send to someone else.
2. Choose File, Mail Contents of This Page or press ⌘-I if you want to send the actual contents of the web page to someone; choose File, Mail Link to This Page or press Shift-⌘-I if you want to send a link to the page. Your default email application opens, a new message is created, and the web page contents or a link to the page is inserted into the new message.
3. Address the email message, add any information you want, and send it.

## DOWNLOADING AND PREPARING FILES

One of the best things about the Web is that you can download files from it. These files can be applications, graphics, audio files, text files, updaters, or any other file you can think of. Downloading files is simple; the only two areas that might give you some trouble are finding the files you download and preparing them for use.

The general process for downloading and preparing files is the following:

1. Locate the file you want to download.
2. Download the file to your Mac.
3. Prepare the file for use by decoding and uncompressing it.

There are two basic ways to download files. You can use a web browser to download files, or you can use an FTP client (or the Finder) to download files from FTP and other sites. Using a web browser to download files is simpler, but it is also slower. A dedicated FTP client can dramatically speed up file downloading.

⇨ For information on using the Finder to download files from an FTP site, **see** "Downloading Files via FTP in the Finder," **p. 545**.

**TIP**

> To make accessing downloaded files as easy as possible, a default Downloads stack is included on the Dock. Click the stack's icon to see the files you've downloaded. The icon of the stack is the icon of the file you've downloaded most recently.

## Configuring a Downloads Folder

By default, your web browser stores files you download in the Downloads folder in your Home directory. If this isn't where you want downloaded files to be stored, you should create a folder into which your web browser will always download files. That way, you will always know where to find the files you download and they won't clutter your desktop.

**NOTE**

> Because a directory is modified when you store files in it, you must use a directory that you have permissions to write to. On your Mac OS X startup volume, you are limited to downloading files to a directory within your Home directory. However, you can choose a location outside your Mac OS X startup volume if you want.
>
> If you want other users of your machine to be able to access the files you download, you can use your Public folder as your downloads folder.

After you have created your downloads folder, open the General pane of the Safari Preferences dialog box and use the "Save downloaded files to" pop-up menu to choose that folder.

## Downloading Files Using Safari

Downloading files is as simple as anything gets. Safari uses its Downloads window to show you information about the files you are downloading. To start the download process, just click the download link for the file you want to download.

**TIP**

> You can download multiple files at the same time. Start one; then, move back to a web window, move to the next, and start it downloading.
>
> You can also continue to browse the Web while your files are downloading. The speed decreases a bit, but at least you can do something while the file is downloading. If you use a fast connection, you probably won't notice the slowdown.

Some sites simply provide the file's name as its link, whereas others provide a Download button. Whichever way it is done, finding the link to click to begin the download process is usually simple.

After you click the link to begin the download, the Downloads window opens showing the progress of the file you are downloading (see Figure 22.18). As a file is downloaded, you see its name, the download progress, and the file size. During the download process, you see the Stop button for the files you are downloading; you can stop the process by clicking this button.

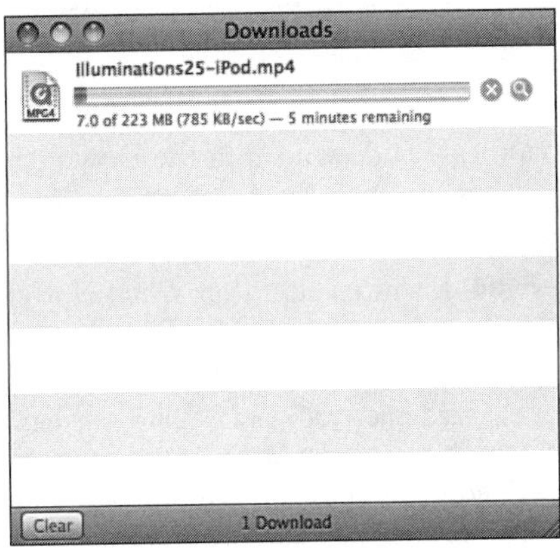


**Figure 22.18**
The Downloads window provides the information and tools you need to manage your downloads.

When the download is complete, you will see the file's icon in the Downloads window. Also, the Stop button becomes the Find in Finder button, which contains a magnifying glass. Click this button to move to the file you downloaded in the Finder.

**TIP**

> If the download process is interrupted for some reason (such as a connection problem or if you clicked the Stop button), the Stop button becomes the Retry button, which contains a circular arrow. Click this button to try to download the file again.

As you download files, Safari continues to add them to the list in the Downloads window. You can clear them manually by clicking the Clear button. You can have Safari remove them automatically by selecting either When Safari Quits or Upon Successful Download on the "Remove download list items" pop-up menu on the General pane of the Safari Preferences dialog box.

After the download is complete, Safari tries to prepare the file that downloaded so you can use it. Most of the time, this works automatically, but in some situations, you must perform this task manually. This process can be somewhat complicated depending on the file you download. If the file you are downloading contains an application you may be warned about this and prompted to verify that you want to complete the download.

## PREPARING FILES FOR USE

Most files you download are encoded and compressed. *Encoding* is the process of translating an application or other file into a plain-text file so it can be transferred across the Internet. *Compressing* a file is a process that makes the file's size smaller so it can be transferred across the Internet more quickly.

Before you can use a file you have downloaded, it must be decoded and it might also need to be uncompressed. Depending on the type of file it is, these two actions might be done at the same time or might have to be handled separately. An application is required for both tasks; a single application can usually handle them, but occasionally the file might need to be uncompressed with one application and decoded with another.

### UNDERSTANDING FILE EXTENSIONS FOR COMPRESSED FILES

Knowing what will happen in any situation requires that you understand the types of files you are likely to download. You can determine this by the filename extension. The most common extensions with which you will have to deal are listed in Table 22.1.

**TABLE 22.1 COMMON FILE EXTENSIONS FOR COMPRESSED OR ENCODED MAC FILES**

| File Extension | What It Means | Comments |
|---|---|---|
| `.bin` | Binary file format | A common encoding format for the Mac. |
| `.gz` | Unix compression format | The dominant compression format for Unix files. |
| `.hqx` | Binhex encoding | Another very common encoding format for the Mac. |
| `.dmg` | Disk Image file format | A file that is a disk image and must be mounted with the Disk Utility application before it can be used. |
| `.pkg` | Package format | Package files are installed with the application installer. |
| `.sea` | StuffIt compression format that can be uncompressed by double-clicking the file | Useful because the recipient of the file doesn't have to have a decompression tool. He simply double-clicks the file to decompress it. |
| `.sit` | StuffIt compression | One standard compression format for Mac files. |
| `.tar` | Tape Archive format | An archiving format for Unix computers that is used for some files you might want for Mac OS X. |
| `.zip` | Zip compression format | The dominant compression format for Windows PCs and Mac OS X's standard compression format. |

If the file you download is in the `.bin`, `.hqx`, `.img`, or `.pkg` format, you don't need to do anything to prepare the file for use. Safari will handle that for you. Some of the other formats, however, will require some manual intervention to prepare the file for use.

#### MANUALLY PREPARING A FILE FOR USE

Although you can usually rely on Safari's preconfigured helper applications to handle most of the files you download, it is useful to know how to manually decode and uncompress files you download so you can handle them yourself and better understand how to configure a helper application to do it for you.

By default, Safari attempts to launch the appropriate helper application to handle files you download. If a file you download can be handled successfully by the helper application, it is prepared and a usable version of it is placed in the same folder into which it was downloaded.

If you download a `.zip` file, double-click it to uncompress it. A file or a folder containing usable files (if the `.zip` includes more than one file) will be created.

If you download a `.sit` or other file type, you'll need to also download and install a copy of the freeware StuffIt Expander to be able to expand and then use the file.

**NOTE**

> You can get information about and download StuffIt Expander at www.stuffit.com.

## WORKING WITH PLUG-INS AND HELPER APPLICATIONS

Many file types are available on the Internet. In addition to HTML, JSP, GIF, JPEG, and other files that are used to present a web page, there are graphics, movies, sounds, PDFs, and many other file types you can open and view. Safari can't work with all these file types directly, and fortunately, it doesn't have to. Safari and other web browsers use plug-ins and helper applications to expand their capabilities so they can work with files they don't natively support.

### WORKING WITH PLUG-INS

*Plug-ins* are software that can be incorporated into a web browser when it opens (thus, the term *plug-in*). Internet plug-ins enable applications to display files that are of the specific types handled by those plug-ins. For example, the QuickTime plug-in enables web browsers to display QuickTime movies.

#### INSTALLING INTERNET PLUG-INS

As you travel around the Web, you might encounter file types for which you do not have the required plug-in. In that case, you must find and install the plug-in you need. Usually, sites have links to places from which you can download the plug-ins needed for the file types on the site. There are a couple of places in the system where plug-ins can be stored.

Plug-ins that are available to all user accounts are stored in the folder *`Mac OS X`*`/Library/Internet Plug-Ins/`, where *`Mac OS X`* is the name of your startup volume.

You must be logged in under an Administrator account to store a plug-in in this directory.

Internet plug-ins can also be stored in a specific user account, in which case they are available only to that user. A user's specific plug-ins are in the location *`shortusername`*`/Library/Internet Plug-Ins/`, where *`shortusername`* is the short name for the user account.

To install a plug-in, simply place it in the directory that is appropriate for that plug-in (to be available either to all users or to only a specific user). Quit the web browser and then launch it again to make the plug-in active.

**NOTE**

> Some plug-ins are installed using an installer application, in which case you don't need to install the plug-in manually.

If you open the Internet Plug-Ins directories, you will see the plug-ins currently installed. Any plug-in installed in these folders can be used by a supported web browser.

Many plug-ins are available for web browsers. The QuickTime plug-in is installed by default so you can view QuickTime movies in web browsers. Additionally, the Shockwave Flash plug-in is installed by default, as is the Java Applet plug-in. There are many other plug-ins you might want to download and install.

You can see the plug-ins installed for Safari by selecting Help, Installed Plug-ins. A new window opens displaying all the installed plug-ins (see Figure 22.19).

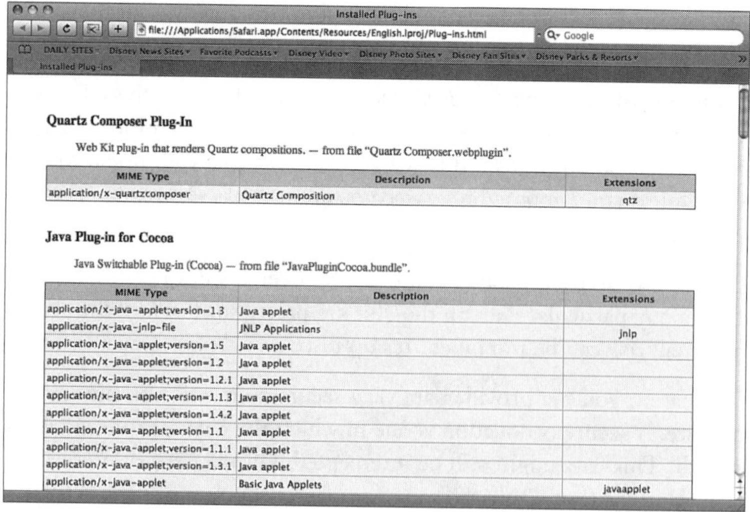


**Figure 22.19**
Safari's Installed Plug-ins window shows you all the plug-ins to which Safari has access.

When you attempt to view a file for which you do not have the appropriate plug-in, you see a warning dialog box that tells you what to do. Usually, you see instructions to help you find, download, and install the plug-in as well.

#### Using Internet Plug-Ins

After a plug-in is installed in the appropriate folder, it works with a web browser to provide its capabilities. When you click a file that requires the plug-in to be used, the appropriate plug-in activates and enables you to do whatever it is designed to do. For example, when you open a QuickTime movie, you see the controls that enable you to watch that movie within the web browser.

### Working with Helper Applications

Although plug-ins provide additional capability by "plugging in" to a web browser, *helper applications* are standalone applications web browsers can use to work with files of specific types. Any application on your Mac can be used as a helper application.

Safari determines the helper applications it uses to open files based on the file type and file-name extensions with which specific applications are associated via the Finder. For example, if PDFs are set to open in Preview, Safari launches Preview when you download a PDF file (assuming that the "Open 'safe' files after downloading" preference is enabled).

⇨ To learn how to associate files with applications, **see** "Determining the Application That Opens When You Open a Document," **p. 156**.

## The Basics of Web Security

Security on the Internet is a very important, complicated topic. Because this is not an Internet book, you won't find much detail in this section. But there are really only three things you need to know.

If you are visiting a site and don't see the lock or `https` in the URL, don't provide any data you don't want someone else to see—such as credit card information, your Social Security number, and so on. In fact, this is a general principle you should follow while you are on the Net. Unless you are *sure* the service you are using is secure, don't provide any information you don't want transmitted to the world.

This sounds pretty dramatic, and it is a bit overstated. I believe the chances of anyone intercepting any particular data on the Net are pretty small, but if the potential loss is great, even that small risk can be too much. It's up to you to choose how much risk you want to assume.

Fortunately, you can provide data via a secure connection to sites running the proper server software. A secure connection is one in which the data transmitted is scrambled, encrypted, or both. This data might still be intercepted, but the person intercepting it won't be able to do anything with it. Only the server receiving the data will be able to decode and unscramble it. Although this system isn't perfect, it's about as close to perfect as you'll get. After all, the only way to be perfectly safe is to never do anything at all.

How do you tell you are using a secure connection? Look for the lock icon in the upper-right corner of the Safari window. If it is there, you are using a secure connection. You can also tell by looking at the URL. If it begins with `https` instead of just `http`, you are visiting a secure location.

You can usually find secure sites in places where you have the opportunity to buy things and need to transmit your credit card information to do so. Of course, how you want to deal with sensitive data is up to you. Some people can accept more risk than others. However, here is the guiding principle that I use:

*Do not transmit—via an unsecured means—any data for which you can't accept the risk of a third-party intercepting that data.*

Like me, you might find shopping via the Web extremely convenient, easy, and inexpensive, but I suggest that you transmit credit card data only via secure sites. And always remember: Do not judge what you do on the Net against a perfect world (where there is no chance of your data being misused). Consider the risks you are willing to accept in the non-Net world. For example, you probably think nothing of using your credit card in one of those gas pumps with an integrated card reader. That is certainly no more secure, and might be much less secure (especially if your card number is printed on the paper receipt), than using your credit card on a secure website.

Web browsers have many security features. The details of these are beyond the scope of this book, but you can explore on your own to see whether you need to make changes—the default security capabilities of most browsers work for most people.

Third, some sites provide digital certificates to verify data from that site. When you view a site that uses such a certificate, you see a window that gives you some options. One option is to install the certificate on your machine. When you do so, the certificate is installed in the appropriate directory and your browser can access that certificate as needed. You can also choose to always trust data from the site so you don't see any security warnings during future visits.

# Mac OS X to the Max: Going Further on the Web

There is a lot you can do to take your browsing on the Web to the max, including using keyboard shortcuts and exploring useful Mac and other websites.

## Using Safari Keyboard Shortcuts

Table 22.3 lists keyboard shortcuts for Safari.

**NOTE**

> Table 22.3 assumes that you have enabled Safari's Tab feature.

**TABLE 22.3 KEYBOARD SHORTCUTS IN SAFARI**

| Menu | Command | Keyboard Shortcut |
|---|---|---|
| Safari | Preferences | ⌘-, |
| Safari | Block Pop-Up Windows | Shift-⌘-K |
| Safari | Empty Cache | Option-⌘-E |
| File | New Window | ⌘-N |
| File | New Tab | ⌘-T |
| File | Open File | ⌘-O |
| File | Open Location | ⌘-L |
| File | Close Window | ⌘-W |
| File | Save As | ⌘-S |
| File | Mail Contents of This Page | ⌘-I |
| File | Mail Link to This Page | Shift-⌘-I |
| Edit | AutoFill Form | Shift-⌘-A |
| View | Show/Hide Bookmarks Bar | Shift-⌘-B |
| View | Show/Hide Status Bar | ⌘-/ |
| View | Show/Hide Tab Bar | Shift-⌘-T |
| View | Show/Hide Toolbar | Shift-—-\ |
| View | Stop | ⌘-. |
| View | Reload Page | ⌘-R |
| View | Make Text Bigger | ⌘-+ |
| View | Make Text Normal Size | ⌘-0 |
| View | Make Text Smaller | ⌘-- |
| View | View Source | Option-⌘-U |
| History | Back | ⌘-[ |
| History | Forward | ⌘-] |
| History | Home | Shift-⌘-H |
| History | Mark Page for SnapBack | Option-⌘-K |
| History | Page SnapBack | Option-⌘-P |
| History | Search Results SnapBack | Option-⌘-S |
| Bookmarks | Show All Bookmarks | Option-⌘-B |
| Bookmarks | Add Bookmark | ⌘-D |
| Bookmarks | Add Bookmark Folder | Shift-⌘-N |
| Bookmarks | Go to first bookmark | ⌘-1 |

| Menu | Command | Keyboard Shortcut |
|---|---|---|
| Bookmarks | Go to second bookmark | ⌘-2 |
| Bookmarks | Go to third bookmark | ⌘-3 |
| Bookmarks | Go to fourth bookmark | ⌘-4 |
| Bookmarks | Go to fifth bookmark | ⌘-5 |
| Bookmarks | Go to sixth bookmark | ⌘-6 |
| Bookmarks | Go to seventh bookmark | ⌘-7 |
| Bookmarks | Go to eighth bookmark | ⌘-8 |
| Bookmarks | Go to ninth bookmark | ⌘-9 |
| Window | Select Next Tab | Shift-⌘-] |
| Window | Select Previous Tab | Shift-⌘-[ |
| Window | Downloads | Option-⌘-L |
| Window | Activity | Option-⌘-A |
| Help | Safari Help | ⌘-? |

## DOWNLOADING FILES VIA FTP IN THE FINDER

Using the Finder, you can download files directly from an FTP site to your Mac:

1. Use Safari to open the FTP site from which you want to download files. The FTP site will be mounted on your desktop.
2. Drag the files you want to download from the FTP site volume onto your Mac. The files will be downloaded, and the Copy progress window will show you the progress of the download process.
3. Prepare the files for use.

# CHAPTER 23

# MANAGING AUDIO WITH ITUNES

## In this chapter

## Using iTunes

iTunes is one of the best reasons to use a Mac. Since this isn't an iTunes book, there's no way I can cover even a part of what iTunes can do for you, but here's a short list to get things started:

- Listen to audio CDs.
- Listen to Internet radio and podcasts.
- Store all the music you like in a single place so you never need to fuss with individual CDs again.
- Search and organize all this music so listening to exactly the music you want is fast and easy.
- Create custom playlists containing the specific songs you want to hear.
- Create smart playlists that are based on a set of criteria, such as all the jazz music you have rated at four or five stars.
- Burn your own music CDs to play in those oh-so-limited CD players in your car, a boombox, or in your home.
- Share your music collection with other people over a wired or wireless network; you can listen to music other people share with you as well.
- Transfer photos from your computer onto an iPod so you can view them there.
- Build a video library that includes music videos, TV shows, movies, and other content; watch that video in iTunes or move it onto an iPod for viewing on the move.
- Shop the iTunes Store so you can add to your music, video, and podcast collections.
- Do the Party Shuffle, iMix your music, and much more.

iTunes works as well with video, podcasts, and other content as it does with music, but for space reasons, I've limited this chapter to core music-related functionality.

**NOTE**

> For more information about iTunes, including everything you need to know about video, iPods, and so on, see my book *Absolute Beginner's Guide to iPod and iTunes*.

## Listening to Audio CDs and Other Sources

Listening to audio CDs and other sources with iTunes is simple:

1. Choose the source to which you want to listen on the Source list along the left side of the iTunes window. For example, insert an audio CD. In a moment, the CD is mounted and is selected on the Source list in iTunes. Or, choose the Music source to view all the contents stored there.

By default, iTunes automatically connects to the Internet and attempts to identify a CD you have inserted. If it finds it, it displays the CD's information, including the CD name, track names, times, artist, and genre, in the Content pane. iTunes does most of the labeling work for you; this comes in handy when you want to search or browse for music to create playlists or just to listen to specific tracks.

If iTunes finds information for a CD, it remembers that information and displays it each time you insert the CD.

If you choose a source within iTunes, it skips this step because it already knows all the information about the source.

At the bottom of the iTunes window is the Source Information display. This shows you the total number of songs in the source, how long it plays, and the total disc space used.



2. To play the source, do any of the following: click the Play button in the upper-left corner of the window (when playing, this becomes the Pause button); select Controls, Play; or press the spacebar.

   The source plays. As a song plays, a speaker icon appears next to it in the Content pane to indicate it is the current song, and information about that song appears in the Information window (see Figure 23.1).

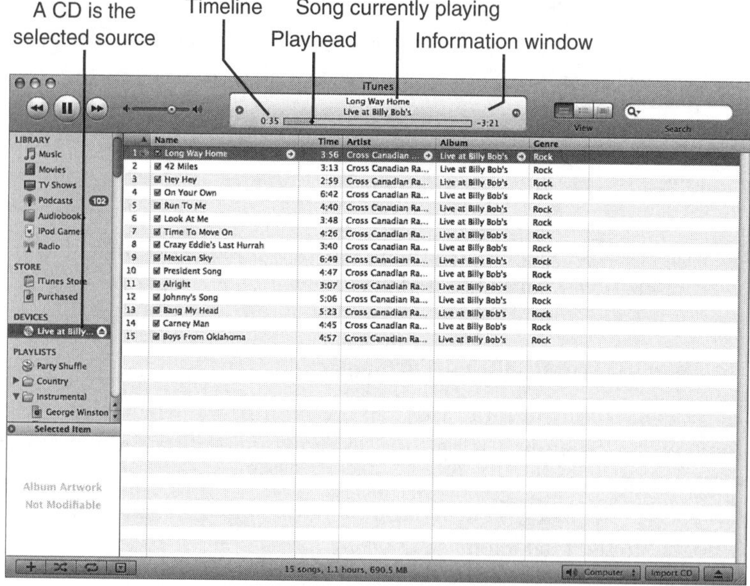


**Figure 23.1**
You can tell this CD is playing because the Play button has become the Pause button and the speaker icon appears next to the song currently being played.

3. Control the volume of the sound by dragging the Volume slider to the left to turn it down or to the right to turn it up. You can also control the volume by selecting Controls, Volume Up or Controls, Volume Down. For yet another option, press ⌘-Up arrow and ⌘-Down arrow keys.

To mute the sound, select Controls, Mute. You can press Option+⌘+Down arrow to do the same thing.

4. To pause a song, click the Pause button; select Controls, Pause; or press the spacebar.

**NOTE**

> Using the Volume slider within iTunes changes the volume of iTunes relative to your system's volume. If you can't make the music loud or quiet enough, set your system volume level and then change the iTunes volume with the slider.



There are lots more ways to control tunes, some of which are in the following list:

- Double-click any song to play it.
- When a song is playing and you click and hold the Rewind or Fast Forward button, the song rewinds or fast-forwards until you release the button.
- When a song is playing, drag the Playhead on the Timeline to the right to move ahead in the song or to the left to move back in a song. When you release the Playhead, the song resumes playing at that point.
- When a song is playing, click the Timeline at the point you want the song to play. The Playhead jumps to the point where you clicked, and the song plays from that position.
- If a song is not playing or a song is playing but you single-click (but don't hold down) the Rewind or Fast Forward button, the previous or next song, respectively, is selected. (If the previous song was playing, the next one starts to play when you jump to it.) You can also select Controls, Next or Controls, Previous to move to the next or the previous song.
- To remove a CD, select it in the Source list and select Controls, Eject Disc; press ⌘-E (Macintosh); click the Eject button that appears next to the CD on the Source list; or click the Eject button located in the lower-right corner of the iTunes window.

## VIEWING INFORMATION WHILE LISTENING TO TUNES

You can view different information in the Information window, such as the name, artist, and album of the currently playing song. When you first view this window, it contains a timeline bar that represents the total length of the song being played. A black diamond (the Playhead) indicates the relative position of the music you are hearing at any point in time compared to the total length of the song.

At the top of the Information window is a line of text that shows the song currently playing (even if it is paused). What appears on the second line of text changes over time; it rotates between the artist name and the album name. You can freeze this display on a specific attribute, such as album name, by clicking the text. Each time you click, the information changes from album to artist to album again. Whichever one you last clicked remains showing in the window.

**NOTE**

> When you "freeze" information in the Information window, it remains frozen until the next track is played, at which point it starts rotating again.

Underneath the album, artist, and song name line is the Timeline. The value shown on the left end of the Timeline is always the time position of the Playhead. As a song plays, the Playhead moves to the right; the portion of the Timeline representing the amount of song that has been played is shaded (everything to the left of the Playhead). The value shown on the right end of the Timeline can be either the total time of the track or the track's remaining time (indicated by a negative value). You can choose the value that is displayed by clicking the time; if total time is shown, it becomes remaining time and vice versa.



**NOTE**

> When you play a CD containing music from various artists, the artist will be shown on the top line of text next to the song name for each song. The artist displayed on the lower line of text will be Various Artists.

If you click the Show Current Song button, which is the curved arrow located at the right side of the Information window, the song currently playing is selected in the Content pane; this is indicated by blue highlighting. This can be handy when you are working with other music sources while listening to a song because you can click this button to quickly return to the song that is playing.

Finally, if you click the Change Display button, the display becomes a graphical representation of the volume levels at various frequency groups (see Figure 23.2). You can return to the song information by clicking the button again.

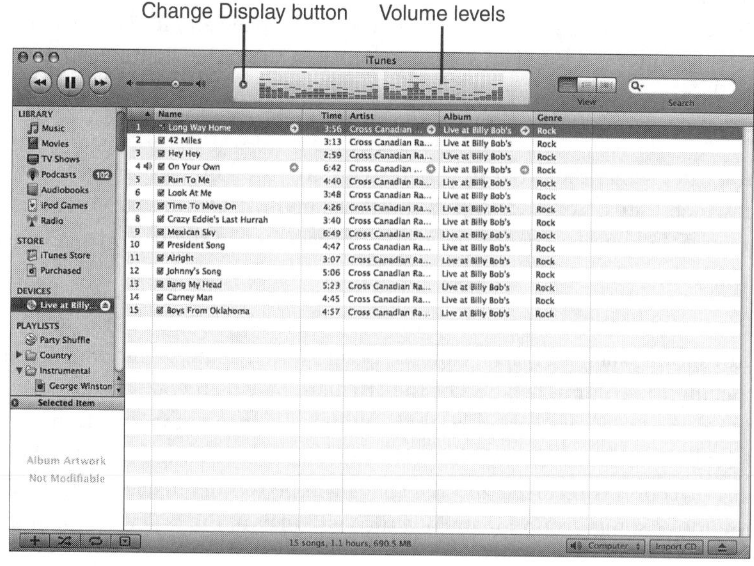


**Figure 23.2**
Why would you want to use the volume level display in the Information window? No real reason I know of, but it does look kind of cool.

**NOTE**

> The neat thing about the Information window is that it changes based on the context of what you are doing. You have seen how it works when you listen to music. When you add music to your Library, the information and tools in the window become those you use for the import process. Likewise, when you burn a CD, the information shown is relevant to that process.



## Controlling the Order of Tunes

Playing a source from start to finish and controlling the volume are useful and required tasks, but with iTunes you can take control of your music so that you hear only what you want to hear, in the order in which you want to hear it. The following sections show you how iTunes lets you take control of your tunes. For example, in the next section you'll learn how to choose the songs you want to hear.

Let's face it, you probably don't like every song on a CD no matter how much you like the CD on the whole. With iTunes, you can choose the songs that play when you play a source. You can cause a song to be skipped by unchecking its check box. When the source plays, every song whose check box is unchecked is skipped.

To have iTunes include and thus play the song again the next time you play the source, simply check its check box again.

**TIP**

> Along with a CD's information, iTunes remembers the settings you make for a CD and reuses them each time you insert and play the CD. This includes skipping songs, changing the order in which they play, and so on.

iTunes determines the order in which songs play by the order in which they are shown in the Content pane, starting from the top of the pane and moving toward the bottom. By default, songs are listed and therefore play in the order they appear on a CD, from track 1 to the last track on the disc. However, you can make songs in a source play in any order you choose. There are a couple of ways to do this.

You can change the order in which songs are listed in the Content pane (and thus the order in which they play) by dragging the songs up or down (you can't do this when Music is the source). When you change the order of the songs in the pane, you change the order in which they play.

You can also change the order of tracks by sorting the Content pane by the various attributes shown, such as Track Number, Song Name, Time, Artist, and so on. You can do this by clicking the column heading of the attribute by which you want to sort the list. When you do so, the tracks are sorted by that column. To change the direction of the sort (from ascending to descending or from descending to ascending), click the Sort Order triangle; the sort direction is reversed and the songs will be reordered accordingly. Just as they do when you move songs around manually, they will play in the order in which they are listed in the pane. (This isn't so useful when you listen to a CD because many of the attributes, such as artist, genre, and album are the same. However, when you use playlists or display more attributes, this can be very handy.)

The column by which the pane is sorted is indicated by the column heading being highlighted in blue—this defaults to the first column, which is the Track Number (which, by the way, is the only unnamed column because it applies only to audio CDs and to no other sources). (When a CD is the source, the Track Number column is always the first or leftmost column in the Content pane.) When you select a different column, its heading becomes blue to show that it is the current sort column.



You can also tell which column is the current sort column by the Sort Order triangle. It appears only in the sort column. When the triangle points down, the sort is descending. When the triangle points up, the sort is ascending.

**NOTE**

If you have manually reordered a CD by dragging songs up and down in the Content pane, that order is remembered and used when you sort the CD by the first column (Track Number). To put songs back in their original order, drag them so that track 1 is at the top, track 2 is next, and so on.

## PLAYING MUSIC RANDOMLY

For a little variety, you can have iTunes play songs in a source randomly using its Shuffle feature. To use this feature, click the Shuffle button located at the bottom of the window (second one from the left) or select Controls, Shuffle. The songs are reordered in the Content pane and play in the order in which they are listed (which should be in a random fashion). The Shuffle button is highlighted in blue to indicate that it is active.

To return the source to the order you have set for it (or its original order if you haven't changed it), click the Shuffle button again or select Controls, Shuffle.

You can control how the Shuffle command works by using the Shuffle preferences. Here's how:

1. Open the iTunes Preferences dialog box and select the Playback pane.
2. Choose how likely it is that you'll hear songs from the same artist or from the same album by using the Smart Shuffle slider. Move the slider toward "more likely" to increase the chances of hearing songs by the same artist or from the same album in a row. Move the slider toward "less likely" to decrease the odds of hearing songs from the same artist or from the same album in a row.
3. Choose how you want songs to be shuffled by clicking one of the Shuffle radio buttons. Choose Songs if you want songs to shuffled randomly. Choose Albums if you want iTunes to randomly select an album, play all its songs, and then choose the next album to play. Likewise, choose Groupings if you want iTunes to randomly choose groupings of songs to play (such as compilations).

4. Click OK. The next time you use the Shuffle function, it works according to the preferences you set.

## REPEATING TRACKS

Sometimes, you just can't get enough of the music to which you are listening. In that case, you can set iTunes to repeat an entire source or to repeat only a single song. To repeat your tunes, check out these pointers:



- To have iTunes repeat an entire source, select Controls, Repeat All or click the Repeat button located at the bottom of the window (third one from the left). The Repeat button becomes highlighted to show you that it is active, and the source repeats when you play it.
- To repeat only the selected song, select Controls, Repeat One or click the Repeat button a second time. A 1 appears on the Repeat button to indicate that only the current song will be repeated.
- To turn off the repeat function, select Controls, Repeat Off or click the Repeat button until it is no longer highlighted in blue.

**TIP**

Using Repeat, you might hear a song you don't like all that much more than once. Remember to uncheck the Select check box for any songs you don't want to hear. They are skipped no matter how you play the source.

## CONTROLLING ITUNES FROM THE DOCK

The iTunes icon on the Mac OS X Dock enables you to control iTunes at any time, even when the iTunes window is in the background, when its window is minimized, or when the application is hidden. When you Ctrl-click the iTunes Dock icon (or right-click if you have a two-button mouse), the iTunes menu appears (see Figure 23.3). At the top of this menu is the iTunes command, which moves you into the iTunes window. Just under that is the Now Playing section that provides information about the song currently playing (if no music is selected or playing, you won't see this section). You can control iTunes by selecting a command on the iTunes Dock menu. For example, you can pause the music by selecting Pause. After you select a command, the menu disappears and you can get back to what you were doing.

**TIP**

If you use iTunes as much as I do, you'll want the application running all the time. Open the iTunes Dock menu and select the Open at Login command. This adds iTunes to your list of Login items so it opens each time you log in to your Mac.

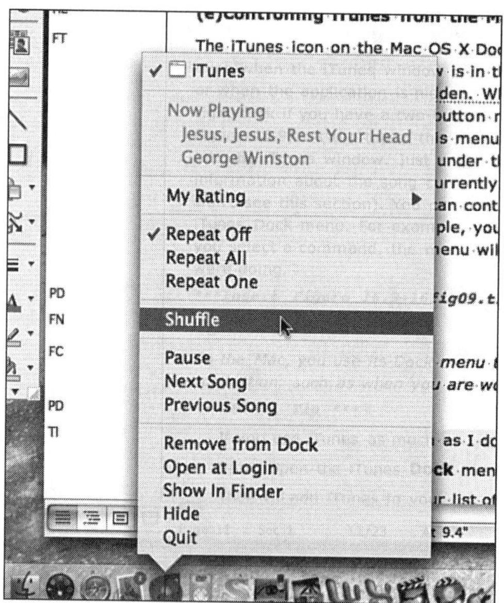


**Figure 23.3**
Use the its Dock menu to control iTunes even when you can't see the application.



## CONTROLLING ITUNES WITH THE ITUNES WIDGET

First, configure the iTunes widget to appear when you use the Dashboard by performing the following steps:

⇨ To learn more about the Dashboard, **see** "Using the Dashboard and Widgets," **p. 124**.

1. Open the Dashboard.
2. Click the + located in the lower-left corner of the desktop. The Dashboard bar appears.
3. Drag the iTunes widget from the bar onto the location on your desktop where you want it to be when you open the Dashboard.
4. Close the Dashboard.

When you want to use the iTunes widget, open the Dashboard. Your widgets appear, including the iTunes widget (see Figure 23.4). Some of the controls look slightly different than they do within iTunes, but they work in the same way. Use the controls, such as rotating the Volume wheel to change volume, and then hide the Dashboard again by pressing its key or clicking someplace else.

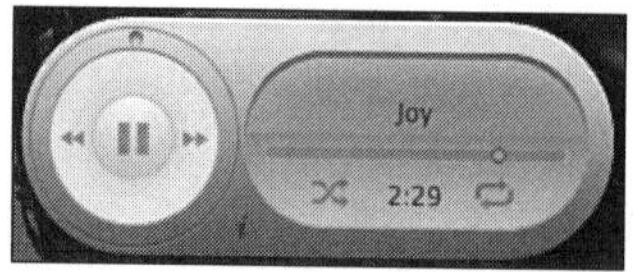


**Figure 23.4**
The iTunes widget is another way to control iTunes when you aren't working with the application directly.

One control that isn't so obvious is the one that enables you to select a music source from within the iTunes widget. Open the widget and wait for a moment or two. An *i* appears at the bottom of the widget near its center. Click this button and you see the "Select a Playlist" pop-up menu. Choose a playlist on this menu and click Done. You can play the source you selected by clicking the widget's Play button and control the music with the widget's other controls.



# Customizing iTunes

You can configure iTunes in various ways to suit your preferences. You can also change the size of the iTunes window in different ways.

## Setting General iTunes Preferences

On the General pane of the iTunes Preferences dialog box are several settings you might want to use:

- **Source Text**—Use this drop-down list to change the font size of the sources shown in the Source list. The options are Small (default) and Large.
- **Song Text**—This setting changes the size of the text used in the Content pane. Again, your options are Small and Large.
- **Show sources check boxes**—Use the Show check boxes to determine whether specific sources appear on the Source List. For example, to hide the iPod Games source, uncheck its check box. By default, all sources are shown.
- **Show genre when browsing**—This check box controls whether the Genre column appears in the Browser (the check box is checked) or not (the check box is not checked).
- **Group compilations when browsing**—Compilations are what iTunes calls CDs that contain music from various artists (you know, like that *Greatest TV Theme Songs from the 1970s* CD you like so much). If you check this check box, these compilations are grouped as collections of music even though the artists might be different on one or more tracks. If you don't want your compilations grouped and prefer to have each track be grouped by artist, uncheck the check box.
- **Show links to iTunes Store**—When this is checked, arrow buttons appear next to songs, artists, and albums in the Content pane and in other locations. When you click one of these buttons, you move to related music in the iTunes Store. If you don't want these links displayed, uncheck the check box.
- **Show content ratings in Library**—Content in the iTunes Store is rated. Check this check box to show the ratings in your Library or uncheck it if you don't want ratings to be shown.
- **Automatically download missing album artwork**—You can display album artwork in iTunes. With this check box checked, iTunes automatically downloads artwork for music that currently doesn't have artwork associated with it. If you have not configured or created an iTunes Store account, you will see a warning that this needs to be configured before iTunes can downoad the artwork.

- **Remember view setting for each source**—There are many ways to change the view you use for the Content pane, such as changing the columns of information shown. When you check this check box, iTunes remembers the settings you used for each source so that they are used each time you work with that source.
- **Shared Name**—When you share music across a network, use this field to name your Library so other users know what it is.
- **Check for iTunes updates automatically**—This check box controls whether iTunes checks for updates and lets you know when they are available. Because it is a good idea to use the current version, you should leave this check box checked. Mac OS X's Software Update feature also checks for iTunes updates.



## CHANGING THE SIZE OF THE ITUNES WINDOW

Like the windows of other applications, you can change the size of the iTunes window. For example, you might want to make the window smaller so that it doesn't consume so much desktop space (remember that you can minimize or hide the window and use its Dock controls to control it). You can change the window's size in the following ways:

- **Hide the application**—Press ⌘-H to hide iTunes. Its window is hidden from the desktop. You can control iTunes by using its Dock menu or widget. Click the iTunes Dock icon to show the window again.
- **Toggle the size of the window**—If you click the Zoom button (the green "light") on the window's title bar, the iTunes window collapses so that only the playback controls and the Information window are shown. Click the button again to return the window to its full size.

**TIP**

> Within the iTunes window, you can change the relative width of the Source list pane versus the Content pane/Browser or between the Browser and the Content pane by dragging their borders to the left or right or up or down. Move your cursor over the border; when you are in the right place to be able to drag it, the cursor changes to a vertical line with arrows coming out its side (Source pane) or a hand (Browser). When this cursor appears, drag the border to change the pane's width or height.

- **Change the size of the window**—In either the full or collapsed state, you can change the size of the window by dragging its resize handle located in the bottom-right corner of the window.

**TIP**

> If you toggle the window to its reduced size and then make it even smaller with the Resize handle, the window contains only the playback controls.

## Setting iTunes Playback Preferences

You can use iTunes Playback preferences to control how your music plays. For example, you can get rid of the gap of silence between songs or make songs play back at a consistent volume level. You can take advantage of these features by using the Playback pane of the iTunes Preferences dialog box. On this pane, you can configure the following preferences for your music (see Figure 23.5):



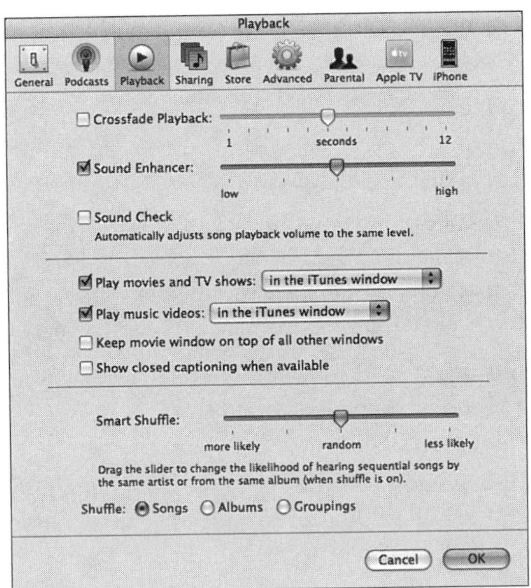


**Figure 23.5**
Control how your music sounds with the Playback preferences.

- **Crossfade Playback**—This effect causes one song to fade out and the next one to fade in smoothly, eliminating the gaps of silence between songs. To activate it, check the Crossfade Playback check box and use the slider to see the amount of fade time. If you move the slider to the left, songs fade out more quickly. If you set it to 0, there is no fading and as soon as one song ends, the next one starts. If you move the slider to the right, songs overlap; as one song starts to fade out, the next start to fade in so you hear them both at the same time. Click OK and the effect takes effect.

**NOTE**

> This Crossfade setting does not affect audio CDs. Because there is a physical gap between tracks on the CD, iTunes can't do anything about it. This setting applies to other sources, such as your Music source and playlists.

- **Sound Enhancer**—This effect is iTunes' attempt to "add depth and enliven" the quality of your music. The actual result of this effect is a bit difficult to describe, so the best thing to do is try it for yourself. Check the Sound Enhancer check box and use the slider to set the relative amount of enhancement. Click OK and then listen to some music. It if sounds better to you, increase the amount of the effect. If not, decrease it or turn it off.

- **Sound Check**—This effect sets the relative volume level of all songs to be the same. It is useful if you have changed the relative volume level of songs and want to have all your music play at the same volume level. To implement this effect, check its check box and click OK.



# ADDING MUSIC FROM AUDIO CDS TO YOUR ITUNES MUSIC LIBRARY

If you have audio CDs, you'll want to import them to your iTunes Library so the music they contain is always available to you.

## CONFIGURING ITUNES TO IMPORT MUSIC

When you import CDs into your Library, you choose the encoding format you use. The options are:

- **MP3**—MP3 is the acronym for the audio compression scheme called *Moving Picture Experts Group (MPEG) audio layer 3*. The revolutionary aspect of the MP3 encoding scheme is that music data can be stored in files that are only about 1/12 the size of unencoded digital music without a noticeable degradation in the quality of the music. A typical music CD consumes about 650MB of storage space, but the same music encoded in the MP3 format shrinks down to about 55MB. Put another way, a single 3.5-minute song shrinks from 35MB on audio CD down to a paltry 3MB or so in MP3 format. The small size of MP3 files opened up a world of possibilities.

  Although the MP3 format is still widely used, when you work with iTunes, you're better off using one of the newer formats it supports, such as AAC.

- **AAC**—The primary successor to MP3 is called *Advanced Audio Coding (AAC)*. This format is part of the larger MPEG-4 specification. Its basic purpose is the same as that of the MP3 format: to deliver excellent sound quality while keeping file sizes small. However, the AAC format is a newer and better format in that it can be used to produce files that have better quality than MP3 at even smaller file sizes.

  The AAC format also enables content producers to add copy protection schemes to their music. Typically, these schemes won't have any impact on you (unless of course, you are trying to do something you shouldn't).

  One of the most important aspects of the AAC format is that all the music in the iTunes Store is stored in it; when you purchase music from the store, it is added to your computer in this format.

- **WAV**—The *Windows Waveform (WAV)* audio format is a standard on Windows computers. It has been widely used for various kinds of audio, but because it does not offer the "quality versus file size" benefits of the MP3 or AAC formats, it is mostly used for sound effects or clips people have recorded from various sources. Millions of WAV files are available on the Internet that you can play and download.

You can load WAV files into iTunes, and you can even use iTunes to convert files into the WAV format. However, because MP3 and AAC are much newer and better file formats, you aren't likely to want to do this very often.

- **AIFF**—The *Audio Interchange File Format (AIFF)* provides relatively high-quality sound, but its file sizes are larger than MP3 or AAC. As you can probably guess from its name, this format was originally used to exchange audio among various platforms and applications.

  As with the WAV format, MP3 and AAC formats provide a better sound quality versus file size trade-off, so you aren't likely to use the AIFF format very often. The most typical situation in which you might want to use it is when you want to move some music or sound from your iTunes collection into a different application that does not support MP3 or AAC.

- **Apple Lossless**—The goal of this format is maximum sound quality. As a result, files in this format are larger than they are in AAC or MP3. However, Apple Lossless files are slightly smaller than AIFF or WAV files. If you have a sophisticated ear, high-quality sound systems, and discriminating taste in music (whatever that means), you might find this format to be the best for you. However, because storing music in this format requires a lot more space on your computer and on an iPod, you will probably use the AAC or MP3 format more often.

Before you start importing music to your Library, choose the import options (mainly format and quality levels) you want to use. Here are the steps to follow:

1. Open the Importing subtab of the Advanced pane of the iTunes Preferences dialog box (see Figure 23.6).
2. Select the format in which you want to add music to your Library on the Import Using menu. For example, to use the AAC format, select AAC Encoder. To use the MP3 format, select MP3 Encoder. Or, select Apple Lossless Encoder to maximize the quality of your music.
3. Select the quality level of the encoder you want to use on the Setting menu. The options you see in this list depend on the format you selected in step 2. If you chose AAC Encoder, you have four quality options: High Quality, Higher Quality, Spoken Podcast, and Custom. If you chose MP3 Encoder, you have four options: Good Quality, High Quality, Higher Quality, and Custom. If you selected the Apple Lossless Encoder, you have only the Automatic option.

**NOTE**

> The Custom option enables you to configure specific settings the encoder uses. If you want to check it out, select Custom on the Setting menu and explore the options you see.

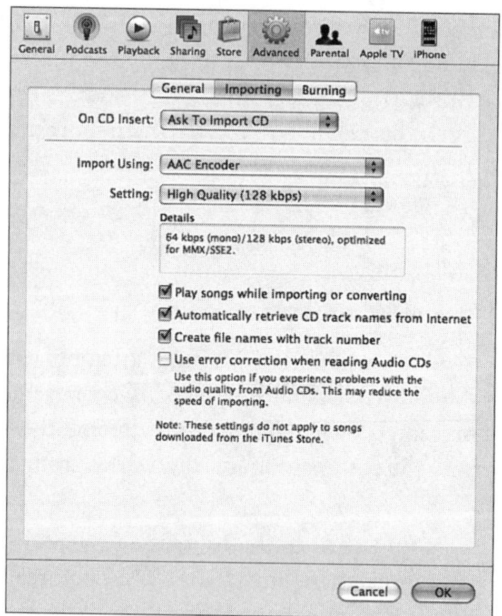


**Figure 23.6**
Here, you can see that the AAC format (the AAC Encoder) is selected.



In the Details box, you see a summary of the settings you have selected. For example, you see the data rate of the encoder, such as 128Kbps, and the processor for which the encoder has been optimized. (Do you need to worry about these details? Not really.) If you use the AAC encoder, the High Quality setting likely be all you ever need.

**TIP**

> In most cases, choosing an encoder isn't a difficult decision. If hard drive space is a factor for you, you use an iPod, or you don't have the ears of a music expert, the AAC encoder is the way to go. If you demand perfection, use the Apple Lossless Encoder. Because I don't have musically trained ears, I use the AAC encoder. (Although my music collection does contain a number of MP3 files that I created before the AAC format became available.)

4. If you want music you add to your Library to play while it is being added, check the "Play songs while importing or converting" check box. This is a personal preference, and it doesn't affect the encoding process significantly.
5. If you want the files that iTunes creates when you import music to include the track number in their filenames, check the "Create file names with track number" check box. Because this helps you more easily find files for specific songs, I recommend that you keep this preference active.
6. Check the "Automatically retrieve CD track names from Internet" to have iTunes download information about a CD so that information is added to the Library when you import the CD.

7. Check the "Use error correction when reading Audio CDs" check box to cause iTunes to more closely control the encoding process. You should use this option only if you notice problems with the music you add to your Library, such as cracking or popping sounds. If that happens, check this check box and try the import process again.
8. Click OK to close the dialog box.



## ADDING AUDIO CDS TO YOUR LIBRARY

Use these steps to add a CD to your Library:

1. Insert the CD you want to add to your Library. iTunes attempts to identify it. When it does, the CD appears in the Source list and is selected. Depending on your importing preferences, you may be presented with a dialog box to import the CD. You can click Yes to have iTunes import all the songs automatically, or No so that you can determine what you want to import.
2. If there are songs you don't want to add to the Library, uncheck their check boxes; only songs with their check boxes checked are imported. Unless you really hate a song or disk space is at a premium, it is generally better to import all the songs on a CD. If you don't like to hear specific songs, you can use the check box in another source, such as in your Library, to cause those songs to be skipped when you play that source.
3. Click the Import CD button. The import process starts (see Figure 23.7).

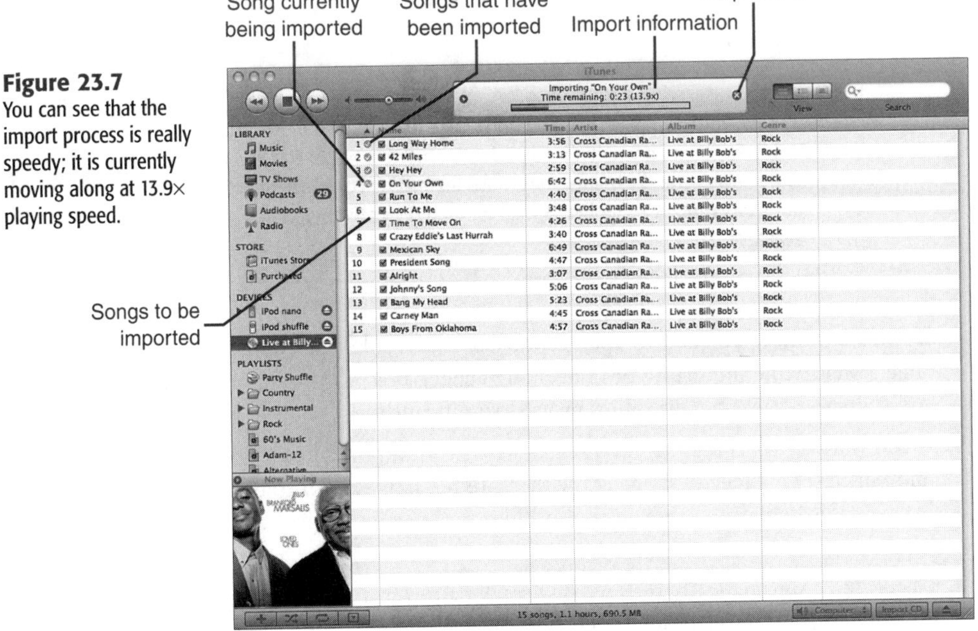


**Figure 23.7**
You can see that the import process is really speedy; it is currently moving along at 13.9× playing speed.

If you left the "Play songs while importing or converting" preference active, the music plays as it is imported.

The Information window shows information related to the import process, such as the name of the song currently being imported and the rate at which the import process is happening.

The rate of the import process depends on the hardware you are using, the import settings, and other tasks your computer might be performing. In most cases, the import process occurs at a much greater rate than the playing process. For example, with moderate hardware, you can usually achieve import rates exceeding 7x, meaning 7 minutes of music be imported in 1 minute of time.



An orange circle with a "squiggly" line inside it marks the song currently being imported. When a song has been imported, it is marked with a green circle containing a check mark.

If you want to stop the import process for some reason, click the Stop button (the small *x* within a circle) in the Information window.

When the process is complete, you hear a tone, and all the songs are marked with the "import complete" icon.

If you have the "Play songs while importing or converting" preference active, the music keeps playing long after the import process is complete (because importing is much faster than playing is). Listen for the Complete tone or keep an eye on the screen to determine when all the music on the CD has been imported.

During the import process, you don't have to listen to what you are importing. You can select a different source, such as a playlist, and play it while the CD is being imported. This slows the import speed slightly, but probably not enough to bother you.

4. Eject the CD when the import process is complete. You can put the CD away somewhere because you probably won't need to use it again.

## ADDING AUDIO CDS TO THE ITUNES LIBRARY QUICKLY

The import process moves along pretty quickly, but you can make it even faster by following these steps:

1. Gather a pile of your CDs in a location close to your Mac.
2. Set the import preferences (encoder and quality) for the import session.
3. Open the Importing subtab of the Advanced pane of the iTunes Preferences dialog box.
4. Select "Import Songs and Eject" on the On CD Insert menu. This causes iTunes to begin the import process immediately when you insert a CD. When the import process is complete, the CD is ejected automatically, too.
5. Click OK to close the dialog box.
6. Insert the first CD you want to import. iTunes starts importing it automatically. When the process is complete, the CD is ejected automatically.

7. Insert the next CD you want to import. Again, iTunes imports the music and ejects the disc when it is done.
8. Repeat step 7 until all the CDs you want to be able to use in iTunes have been imported.

**TIP**

> When you are finished batch importing your CDs, you might want to reset the On CD Insert menu to Show Songs to prevent unintentionally importing a CD more than once.

23

# ADDING MUSIC FROM OTHER SOURCES TO YOUR ITUNES MUSIC LIBRARY

Although audio CDs are likely to be a major source of the music you add to your Library, they certainly don't need to be the only one. You can purchase music from the iTunes Store easily and quickly. And, you can add any audio file to your Library, such as files your download from the Internet.

## PURCHASING MUSIC FROM THE ITUNES STORE

When you select the iTunes Store source, you move to Apple's online iTunes Store (see Figure 23.8). You can use the various links, buttons, and search tool to find music in which you are interested. You can then preview that music; adding the music to your Library is as simple as clicking the Buy Now button for albums or individual songs. Once downloaded, the music is added to your Library and you can listen to it and use it mostly like music you import from CD. (There are some limitations imposed by the copyright protection, but you aren't likely to encounter those.) All the music you purchase is also stored in the Purchased playlist.

**Figure 23.8**
The iTunes Store offers lots of great music, not to mention videos and podcasts.

### Importing Audio Files into Your Library

Another potential source of music for your Library is the Internet. There are millions of audio files there, and you can download these files and add them to your Library.

1. Locate the files you want to add to your Library. For example, find the MP3 files on your hard drive or go to a website that has audio files, such as MP3 files, and download them to your computer.
2. Select File, Add to Library. You see the Add To Library dialog box.
3. Use the dialog box to move to and select the folder containing the files you want to add or to select the files you want to add to the Library.
4. Click Open. The files you selected are imported into your Library.



## Browsing and Searching Your Music Library

It won't be long until you have a large Library with many kinds of music in it. In fact, you are likely to have so much music in the Library that you won't be able to find songs you are interested in just by scrolling up and down the screen. In this section, you learn how to find music in your Library, first by browsing and then by searching. When you browse, you can choose to use three views: List, Grouped, and Cover Flow.

### Browsing in the Library with the List View

The Browser enables you to find music by, well, browsing:

1. Click the List View button, which is the View button closest to the Information window.
2. Select Music on the Source list. This focuses iTunes' attention on the music content in your collection.
3. If the Browser isn't showing, click the Browser button, which is located in the lower-right corner of the iTunes window (it looks like an eye). The Browser appears between the Information window and the Content pane (see Figure 23.9). The Browser has three columns: Genre, Artist, and Album. The columns start on the left with the most general category, Genre, and end on the right with the most specific category, which is Album.

   If you don't see the Genre column in the Browser, open the General pane of the iTunes Preferences dialog box and check the "Show genre when browsing" check box.

   The contents of the "path" selected in the Browser are shown in the Content pane that now occupies the area below the Browser. At the top of each Browser column is the All option, which shows all the contents of that category. For example, when All is selected in the Genre column, you see the contents of all the genres for which you have music in the Library.
4. To start browsing your Library, select the genre in which you are interested by clicking it. When you do so, the categories in the other two columns are scoped down to include only the artists and albums that are part of that genre.

**Figure 23.9**
The Browser offers a good way to find songs in your Library.

**NOTE**

> The Source information at the bottom of the window always reflects the selections you've made in the Browser.

5. To further limit the browse, click an artist in which you are interested in the Artist column. The Album column will be scoped down to show only those albums for the artist selected in the Artist column (see Figure 23.10). Also, the Content pane shows the songs on the albums listed in the Album column.

**Figure 23.10**
Now I am browsing all my music in the Blues/R&B genre that is performed by B.B. King.

6. To get down to the most narrow browse possible, select the album in which you are interested in the Album column. The Content pane shows the tracks on the selected album.
7. When you have selected the genre, artist, and album categories in which you are interested, you can scroll in the Content pane to see all the tracks included in the music you are browsing.

To make the browse results less narrow again, select All in one of the Browser's columns. For example, to browse all your music again, click All in the Genre column.



I hope you can see that you can use the Browser to quickly scan your Library to locate music you want to hear or work with. As you use the Browser more, you come to rely on it to get you to a group of songs quickly and easily.

## BROWSING IN THE LIBRARY USING THE GROUPED VIEW

The List view is useful, but it doesn't really provide you with a good sense of the collections of music you browse because the tracks appear in a list with no respect to how the tracks are collected. Use the Grouped view to browse the Music source while seeing the groups of music you are browsing:

1. Click the Grouped View button, which is the middle View button. The music in the Content pane is grouped by album or collection and you'll see the artwork associated with each group.
2. Use the Browser to narrow the music you are browsing to find what you are looking for (see Figure 23.11). It works just as it does in List view.

**Figure 23.11**
Using the Grouped view, you get to see how the music you are browsing is grouped, along with its artwork.

## BROWSING IN THE LIBRARY WITH THE COVER FLOW VIEW

I admit that browsing music only in a digital format does lose something when compared to looking through a collection of CDs. There's something appealing about flipping through a set of CDs, especially when you stumble upon one you haven't listened to in a while. If you like to do this, the Cover Flow view will appeal to you. To use it to browse your music, perform the following steps:

1. Click the Cover Flow View button, which is the rightmost View button. The Browser is replaced by the Cover Flow browser (see Figure 23.12). Here, you see the "album" art associated with the music you're browsing; this looks similar to a collection of CDs. The album facing the screen directly is associated with the music at the top of the Content pane (this is the music currently in focus). You see the album name and artist just below the album in focus. The covers to the right of this one represent music lower in the Content pane, whereas the covers to the left represent music higher in the Content pane.

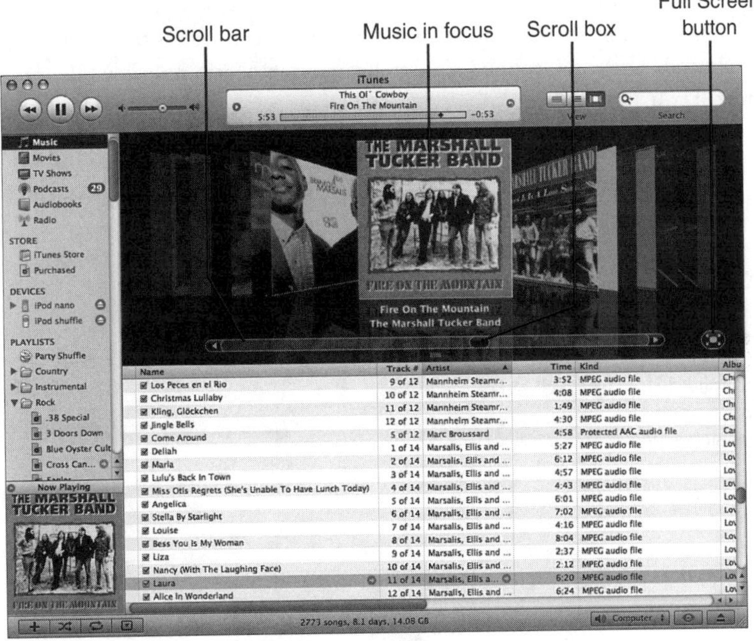


**Figure 23.12**
The Cover Flow view enables you to "flip" through your music collection to browse it.

2. To browse "ahead" in your music, click an album cover to the right of the one in focus; to browse "back" in your music, click a cover to the left of the one in focus. The farther to the left or right you click, the more covers you jump ahead or back, depending on which direction you click. For example, if you click an album immediately next to the one in focus, you move ahead or back one album. If you click all the way to edge of the screen, you jump ahead or back by multiple albums.

   As albums come into focus, you see their content at the top of the Content pane.

**TIP**

> You can also use the scrollbar and scroll box to browse your music. Click the right arrow button at the right end of the scrollbar or drag the scroll box to the right to move ahead, or use the left arrow button or drag the scroll box to the left to move back. The scroll tools enable you to browse even a large collection of music quickly. But it isn't quite as fun as using the flip technique.

3. When music comes into focus that you want to hear, double-click it to start playing it.



As you flip through albums, music you happen to be playing continues to play as you bring other music into focus. If you don't play the music you are browsing, after a couple of seconds of inactivity the covers flip back to the music currently playing so that it comes back into focus.

To see a full screen browser with playback controls, click the Full Screen button, which is just to the right of the scrollbar. The desktop is replaced by a full screen browser; use the controls at the bottom to control playback or browse the source (see Figure 23.13).

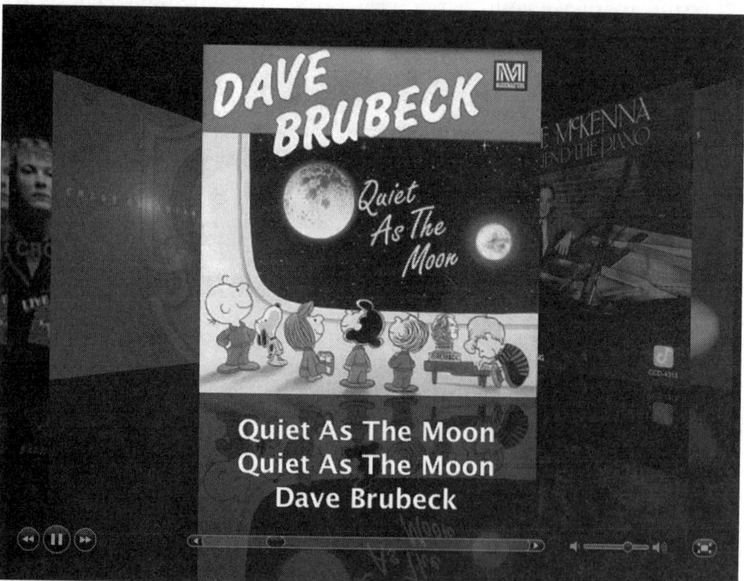


**Figure 23.13** The Full Screen browser is nice to look at, but you can't use anything else on your Mac while it appears.

## Searching Your Music Library

You can use iTunes Search tool to search for specific content. You can search for content (music, audiobooks, video, and so on) by any of the following criteria:

- Artist
- Album
- Composer
- Song (track name)

To search for music in your Library, perform the following steps:

1. Select the source you want to search. (For example, click the Music source to search your entire music collection.) As you might surmise, you can search any source in the Source list—such as a CD, playlist, and so on—by selecting it and then performing a search.
2. To choose a specific attribute by which to search, such as Album, click the Magnifying Glass icon and choose the search attribute on the drop-down list that appears. If you don't choose a specific attribute, All is used, which searches all the available attributes.
3. Type the data for which you want to search in the Search tool. As you type, iTunes searches the selected source and presents the songs that meet your criterion in the Content pane. It does this on the fly, so the search narrows with each keystroke. As you type more text or numbers, the search becomes more specific.
4. Keep typing until the search becomes as narrow as you need it to be to find the content in which you are interested.
5. To refine your search by attribute, open the Magnifying Glass icon and choose the attribute to which you want to limit the search. For example, if you want to see only results that have your search term as the Artist attribute, choose Artist. The search results are limited to only those tracks that match the current criteria (what you typed and the attribute you selected).

**TIP**

The current search attribute is marked with a check mark on the Magnifying Glass drop-down list.

By the way, searching works the same way regardless of the current view.

After you have found content with a search, you can play it, add it to playlists, and so on.

To clear your search, click the Clear Search button that appears in the Search tool after you have typed in it. The songs shown in the Content pane are again determined by your selections in the current view.

## Removing Tunes from the Music Library

Not all that glitters is gold, nor are all tunes that are digital good. Sometimes, a song is so bad that it just isn't worth the hard disk space it consumes. To remove songs from your Library, ditch them with the following steps:

1. Find the songs you want to delete by browsing or searching.
2. Select the songs you want to trash. They become highlighted to show you they are selected
3. Press the Delete key. You are prompted to confirm that you really want to delete the songs you have selected.

**TIP**

> Remember that you can stop a song from playing by unchecking its check box in the Content pane. If you aren't sure you want to dump a song permanently, use that method instead so you can always listen to the song again should you change your mind about it.

4. If you see the warning prompt, click Remove to confirm the deletion. You see another prompt asking whether you want the selected files to be moved to the Trash or you want to keep the files on your computer. (If you have disabled the warning prompt, you move directly to the second dialog box.)
5. Click "Move to Trash" to move the files so you can get rid of them entirely. The selected songs are deleted from your Library, and their song files are be moved to the Trash. The next time you empty that receptacle, those songs are gone forever.

   If you just want to remove the references to files from the iTunes Library but not delete the song files, click "Keep Files." The songs are removed from the Library, but the song files remain in their current locations (and so you could always add the songs to your Library again later).



You should never delete music you purchased from the iTunes Store unless you are absolutely sure you never never never want it again or you have that music backed up elsewhere. You can download music you purchased from the store only one time. After that, you have to pay for it to download it again.

Of course, songs you delete probably might not really be gone forever. You can always add them back to the Library again by repeating the same steps you used to place them in there the first time. This assumes that you have a copy somewhere, such as on a CD or stored in some other location. If you imported the music from your hard disk and had iTunes move the songs files to your iTunes Music folder, your only copy resides in your iTunes Library, so make sure you have such music backed up before you delete it if you might ever want it again.

## UNDERSTANDING AND USING TAGS

Browsing and searching music is fast and easy, even if you have thousands of songs in your Library. This functionality is enabled because each track in your Library has data items—also called *tags*—that categorize and identify that track for you. Genre, artist, and album are just three of the possible tags for each track in iTunes. There are many more items of information that iTunes manages.

Tags fall into two groups: tags that iTunes assigns for you and that you can't change, and tags that you or iTunes assigns and that you can change.

Tags that iTunes assigns and that you can view but can't change include the following:

- **Kind**—This identifies the type of file the track is, such as Protected AAC audio file, AAC audio file, MP3, and so on.

- **Size**—The amount of disk space required to store the track.
- **Bit Rate**—The quality level at which the track was encoded. Larger numbers, such as 128Kbps, mean the track was encoded at a higher quality level (and also has a relatively larger file size).
- **Sample Rate**—The rate at which the music was sampled when it was captured.
- **Date Modified**—The date on which the track file was last changed.
- **Play Count**—The number of times the track has been played.
- **Last Played**—The last time the track was played.
- **Profile**—A categorization of the track's complexity.
- **Format**—The format in which the track was encoded, such as MPEG-1, Layer 3.
- **Channels**—Whether the track is stereo or mono.
- **Encoded With**—The tools used to encode the track, such as the version of iTunes used, the version of QuickTime, and so on. This applies only when you use iTunes to encode the track.

**NOTE**

> Not all tracks have all the data fields listed. You will see only data that is applicable to a specific track. For example, only music purchased from the iTunes Store has information about the purchase.

- **ID3 Tag**—ID3 tags are data formatted according to a set of specifications. If a track's data has been formatted with this specification, the ID3 version number will be shown.
- **Purchased by, Account Name, and FairPlay Version**—If a track was purchased from the iTunes Store, this information identifies who purchased the music and which account was used. The FairPlay version information relates to the means by which the track is protected.
- **Owner, Narrator, Published**—This information is provided for audiobooks that you add to your Library, such as those from Audible.com. The owner is whoever purchased the book. The narrator is who reads the book. Published identifies when the book was published.
- **Where**—This shows a path to the track's file on your computer along with its filename.

Tags collected for songs that you can change include the following:

- **Name**—This is the name of the track.
- **Artist**—The person or group who performs the track.
- **Album Artist**—Often used to indicate Various Artists for soundtracks and other compilation albums.
- **Album**—The name of the album or compilation from which the song comes.
- **Grouping**—This is a label you can assign to group tracks together. You can then organize tracks by their group, collect them in playlists, and so on.

- **Composer**—The person who is credited with composing the track.
- **Comments**—This is a free-form text field in which you can make comments about a track.
- **Genre**—This associates a track with its genre, such as Jazz or Classical.
- **Year**—The year the track was created.
- **Track Number**—The track's position on the CD from which it came, such as "2 of 12."
- **Disc Number**—The number of the CD or DVD. This is meaningful for multiple-disc sets.
- **BPM**—The track's beats per minute.
- **Part of a Compilation**—When checked, this check box indicates that the track is part of a compilation, meaning a CD or other grouping that contains tracks from a variety of artists.



When you add a song to your Library, no matter how you add it, iTunes adds as much of this data as it can find for each song.

When you insert a CD, iTunes attempts to get that CD's information from an online CD database, which is why it connects to the Internet. If iTunes finds the CD in this database, the information for that CD is applied to the CD and carried into the Library if you import the tracks from that CD into iTunes. If you purchase music from the iTunes Store, it also contains many of these tags. If content you add to your Library doesn't have tags, you'll have to add them yourself (which isn't hard to do, as you'll soon see).

Even if content you add does have tags, you can add or change the data in the previous list.

So, why should you care about all these tags? There are a couple of reasons.

The first is that, as you already know because you learned how to browse and search your Library in the previous chapter, tags can be used to find music in which you are interested. That reason alone should be enough to convince you that these types of data are important to you. But wait, there's more.

The second reason is that when it comes time to create playlists, you can use tags to determine which tracks are included in your playlists. For example, you can configure a playlist to include the last 25 songs you have played from the Jazz genre. This is just a basic example—you can get much more sophisticated than this. In fact, you can include several combinations of tags as criteria in playlists to create interesting sets of music to listen to.

When you view music in the Browser and in the Content pane, all the information you see results from the tags associated with that music, such as artist, title, album, time, kind, and so on. You can also view tags in other contexts.

## VIEWING TAGS IN THE INFO WINDOW

To view the Info window, select a track in your Library and select File, Get Info or press ⌘-I. The Info window appears; at the top of the window, you see the name of the track whose information you are viewing (see Figure 23.14). This window has six panes that apply to music and a seventh that can be used with video content.

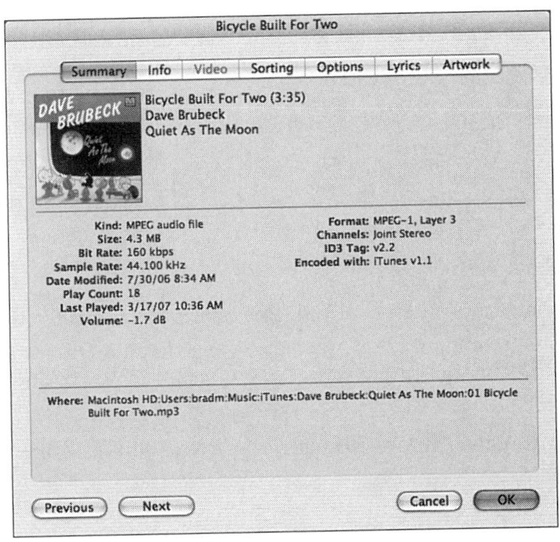


**Figure 23.14**
The Info window enables you to view the tags associated with tracks, and you can change many of them.

23

The Summary pane provides a summary view of the track's tags that you can't change on the tab, starting at the top with any album art associated with the track and including its name, length, artist, and album. In the center part of the pane, you see the data that iTunes manages. (You can view this data, but you can't change it.) At the bottom of the pane, you can see the path to the track's file on your computer.

When you click the Info tab, you see the tags you can change.

The other three panes of the window that relate to music content—Sorting, Options, Lyrics, and Artwork—are used to configure specific aspects of a track.

You can view information for other tracks in the selected source without closing the window. Click Next to move to the next track in the source you are viewing (such as your Music) or Previous to move to the previous track. When you do so, the next or previous track's information is displayed in the Info window.

## Labeling a Track in the Info Window

Typically, if you have imported a CD or purchased music from the iTunes Store, you shouldn't change the data that came from the source, such as name, artist, album, track number, and so on. Occasionally, a CD's information will include an error when it is added (such as a misspelling in the artist's name); you'll probably want to fix such mistakes. You can certainly add data to empty fields.

You can use the Info window to change a track's tags, as you can see in the following steps:

1. Open the Info window for the track that has tags you want to add or change.
2. Click the Info tab, and the Info pane appears.
3. Enter or change the information shown in the various fields. For example, you can change the track's name or artist. Or, you might want to add comments about the track in the Comments box.
4. To change a track's genre, select the new genre from the Genre menu.

**TIP**

> If a genre by which you want to classify music isn't listed on the menu, you can add it to the menu by selecting Custom on the menu and then typing the genre you want to add. That genre will be added to the menu and associated with the current track. You can use the genres you create in this way just as you do the default genres.

5. When you are done entering or changing tags, click OK. The Info window closes, and any changes you made are saved.



## TAGGING MULTIPLE TRACKS AT THE SAME TIME

You can change some tags, such as Genre, for a group of tracks at the same time. This can be a faster way to enter tags because you can change multiple tracks in one window. Here are the steps to follow:

1. Select the tracks whose tags you want to change.
2. Open the Info window. You're prompted to confirm that you want to change the information for a group of tracks.
3. Click Yes to clear the prompt. The Multiple Item Information window appears (see Figure 23.15). The information and tools in this window work in the same way as they do for individual tracks. The difference is that the information and settings apply to all the tracks you have selected.

**TIP**

> Many iTunes dialog boxes have a check box you can check to prevent the dialog from being displayed again. For example, if you don't want to be warned when you use the Multiple Item Information tool, check the "Do not ask me again" check box.

4. Enter data in the fields, make changes to existing data, or use the other tools to configure the tracks you have selected. As you change information, the check box next to the tag becomes checked to show that you are changing that tag for all the selected tracks.
5. When you are finished making changes, click OK. The window closes, and the changes you made will be saved.

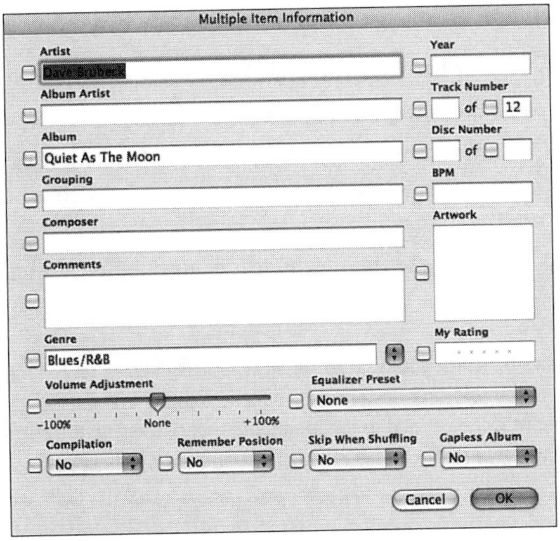

**Figure 23.15**
You can use this window to change the data for multiple tracks at the same time.

Most of the fields in the Multiple Item Information dialog box are pretty straightforward, such as Artist, Album, and so on. You'll learn about others when you read about changing a track's options in a bit. The same options apply as for an individual track; you can just change multiple tracks at the same time by using the Multiple Item Information dialog box.

## Setting Tags in the Content Pane

You can also edit tags within the Content pane:

1. Click a track once to select it.
2. Click once on the tag you want to edit. The tag is highlighted to show that it is ready to be edited.
3. Type the new information, choose a value on the tag's drop-down list (such as to set equalization for a track), or click to set a value (for example, to rate a track).
4. Press Return. The changes you made are saved.

## Changing Sorting Tags

By default, iTunes uses a track's default tags for sorting purposes, such as its title, artist, and so on. However, you can add sorting tags in case the default tags aren't sufficient. To do this, perform the following steps:

1. Select a track, open the Info window, and click the Sorting tab.
2. Enter the information by which you want iTunes to sort the track in the related "Sort" fields. For example, enter information in the Sort Artist field. You can change the name of the artist for sorting purposes without changing the name of the artist that is associated with the track on audio CD or from the iTunes Store.
3. Click OK. When you sort music, any information you entered in the "Sort" fields is used instead of the default tags.

# Configuring a Track's Options

You can configure a number of options for the tracks in your Library, including the following:

- **Volume Adjustment**—You can change a track's relative volume so it is either louder or quieter than "normal." This is useful if you like to listen to tracks recorded at a variety of volume levels because the volume remains somewhat similar as you move from track to track.
- **Equalizer Preset**—You can use the iTunes Equalizer to configure the relative volume of sound frequencies. When you set an Equalizer preset for a track, the settings in that preset will be used each time the track plays.
- **My Rating**—You can give tracks a rating from one to five stars. You can use ratings in various ways, such as to create criteria for playlists (for example, include only my five-star songs) or to sort the Content pane.
- **Start and Stop Time**—You can configure tracks to start or stop playing at specific times in the track. This can be useful if you don't want to hear all of a track, such as when a track has an introduction you don't want to hear each time it plays.
- **Remember playback position**—When this option is enabled, iTunes (and an iPod) starts playing a track from the point at which you last played it. This is an incredibly useful option for tracks that are audiobooks, podcasts, or videos because you can stop playing that content and do something else, such as listen to or watch other content. When you come back to a track with this option enabled, iTunes and an iPod will pick up where you left off. This prevents you from hearing or seeing the same content again or from searching for the point at which you stopped listening or watching.
- **Skip when shuffling**—If this option is enabled for a track, the track is skipped when you play iTunes in the Shuffle mode. This is useful for tracks you don't want to hear when you shuffle (such as those that make sense only in the content of the album from which they come) or for content that doesn't make sense when you shuffle (such as episodes of a podcast or an audiobook).
- **Part of a gapless album**—Some tracks are designed to be heard with no gap between them, such as those from a live album. When a track is part of such an album, checking this option removes any gap between songs. iTunes recognizes most gapless albums automatically, but you can manually configure this setting if you need to.

**NOTE**

> iTunes is pretty smart and makes your listening and viewing life as easy as possible. For example, when you add podcasts, video, or audio books from the iTunes Store to your Library, the Playback Position, Skip, and Gapless options are set appropriately. If you add this kind of content from other sources, you should make sure these options are set the way you want them to be.

## Configuring Track Options in the Info Window

You can configure a track's options in the Info window by performing the following steps:

1. Select the track whose options you want to set.
2. Open the Info window.
3. Click the Options tab (see Figure 23.16).



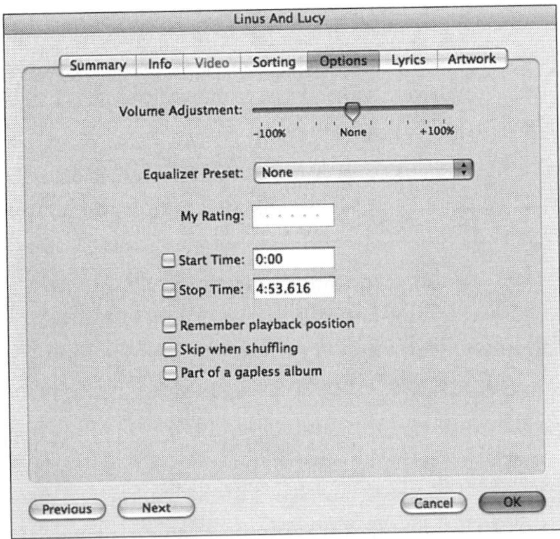


**Figure 23.16**
Using the Options tab, you configure a track's optional settings.

4. To set the track's relative volume, drag the Volume Adjustment slider to the left to make the track quieter or to the right to make it louder.
5. To apply an equalizer preset to the track, choose the preset you want to be used when the track plays on the Equalizer Preset menu. On this menu, you see a large number of presets that are available to you. When you choose one, the track's playback is adjusted accordingly. For example, if you choose Bass Booster, the relative volume of the bass frequencies is increased.
6. To rate the track, click the dot representing the number of stars you want to give it in the My Rating field. For example, to give the track three stars, click the center (third) dot. Stars appear up to the point at which you click. In other words, before you click, you see a dot. After you click a dot, it becomes a star, as do the rest of the stars to its left.

**TIP**

> If you want to configure options for a group of tracks, select those tracks and open the Info window. Use the resulting Multiple Item Information window to make changes to all the tracks at the same time.

7. To set a track's start time, check the Start Time check box and enter a time in the format *minutes:seconds*. When you play the track, it starts playing at the time you enter. The default value is 0:00, which makes sense because that is the starting point for a track.

**NOTE**

> When you set a start or stop time, you don't change the track file in any way. You can play the whole track again by unchecking the Start Time or Stop Time check box.

8. To set a stop time, check the Stop Time check box and enter a time in the format *minutes:seconds*. When you play the track, it stops playing at the time you enter. The default stop time is the total track length, which also makes sense. Notice that the default stop time is very precise, even going to two decimal places beyond a second.

**TIP**

> To determine the start or stop times you want to use, play the track and use the times displayed when the Playhead is at the position where you want the track to start or stop playing.

9. If you want iTunes to remember the point at which you stopped playing a track and to start playing the track at that point the next time you play it, check the "Remember playback position" check box. If you always want the track to start playing at the current Start Time, leave the box unchecked.
10. If you want the track to be skipped when you shuffle (when the track is an audio book, for example), check the "Skip when shuffling" check box.
11. If the track is part of a gapless album, check the "Part of a gapless album" check box.
12. Click OK.

### Rating Tracks in the Content Pane

You can also rate tracks in the Content pane. To do so, follow these steps:

1. Scroll in the Content pane until you see the My Rating column.
2. Select the track you want to rate. Dots appear in the My Rating column for that track.
3. Click the dot representing the number of stars you want to give the track. The dots up to and including the one on which you clicked become stars.

## Working with Lyrics

In the Info window, you've seen that there is a Lyrics tab. As you probably can guess, you can store lyrics, or any other text for that matter, for a track on this tab. You can then view the text you store there by using the Info window, or you can display the lyrics on an iPod.

23

## Adding Lyrics to a Track

The first step is to find or create the lyrics you want to associate with a track. Although it might be lots of fun figuring out the lyrics for tracks by listening to them and writing them down yourself, I'm going to assume that you have better things to do with your time. In that case, it's easy to look up lyrics for most artists on the Web.

Most of the lyrics available on the Web come from a person who listened to the music (as opposed to the published source). This means that there can be errors in the lyrics you find. You can correct them yourself or look for a more reliable source.

You can then copy and paste the lyrics you find onto the Lyrics tab. Here's how:

1. Open your web browser and move to www.google.com.
2. Search for *artistname* and lyrics, where *artistname* is the name of the artist with which the track is associated. The result is likely to be several sites that provide lyrics for that artist.
3. Click a link to move to one of the sites. These sites typically organize lyrics by album.
4. Find the track for which you want lyrics, and click it. The lyrics appear.
5. Select the lyrics and copy them to your Mac's Clipboard.

Now that you have the lyrics, you can apply them to a track by performing the following steps:

1. In iTunes, open the Info window for the track whose lyrics you just copied.
2. Click the Lyrics tab.
3. Paste the lyrics you copied into the Lyrics pane (see Figure 23.17).
4. Click OK. The lyrics are saved with the track.

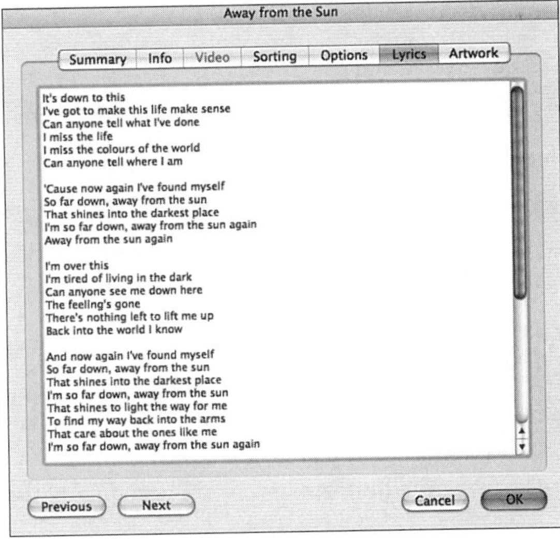


**Figure 23.17**
I've pasted the lyrics for the song "Away from the Sun" into the Lyrics tab.

### Viewing Lyrics for a Track

After you have added lyrics for a track, you can view those lyrics in iTunes by selecting the track and opening the Lyrics pane of the Info window.

**TIP**

> You can also view lyrics on newer iPod models by clicking the Select button until the lyrics are displayed on its screen.



## Adding and Viewing Album Artwork

Many CD and album covers are works of art (although many aren't!), and it would be a shame never to see them just because your music has gone digital. With iTunes, you don't need to miss out, because you can associate artwork with tracks and display that artwork in the iTunes window.

To enjoy artwork with your tunes, you need to first associate artwork with your music. There are a number of ways to do this. All the music you purchase from the iTunes Store includes artwork, so any music you buy has artwork automatically. And, if you have an iTunes Store account, iTunes can be configured to automatically download artwork for music you add to your Library in other ways, such as when you import an audio CD. If the artwork for music isn't in the iTunes Store because the music itself isn't there, you can add artwork to music manually or semi-automatically.

After artwork has been added to your music, you can easily view it in iTunes.

If you burn discs for your music, having artwork associated with your music is good because you can use iTunes to print jewel case covers that include this art.

### Configuring iTunes to Download Album Artwork Automatically

One of the cool features of iTunes is that it automatically downloads artwork from the iTunes Store. As you read earlier, when you purchase music from the store, its art comes with it. What you might not expect is that as long as you have an iTunes Store account, iTunes also downloads art associated with music you add to the Library from other sources, such as audio CDs you import.

After you have an iTunes Store account, open the iTunes Preferences dialog box, click the General tab, check the "Automatically download missing album artwork" check box, and click OK. iTunes automatically retrieves artwork for all the albums in your Library that it can. As you add other music to your Library by importing it, iTunes retrieves any artwork it can automatically.

The limitation to this feature is that for iTunes to automatically download an album's artwork, that album must be available in the iTunes Store. This isn't a big limitation because a huge amount of music is available there, so the odds are good that any music you add to your Library will be there, which means most of your music will get artwork automatically.

## ADDING ARTWORK FOR SONGS MANUALLY

If music isn't available in the iTunes Store, you can add it manually. Or, you might want to associate artwork that isn't the default album cover with a track. For example, you might want to add the artist's picture or some other meaningful graphic to tracks.

You can add one or more pieces of art to tracks by using the following steps:

1. Prepare the artwork you are going to associate with a track. You can use graphics in the usual formats, such as JPG, TIFF, GIF, and so on.

> **TIP**
> You can often find album artwork on Amazon.com by searching for the artist, album or song title. Click the album art and save the image to your Mac so you can use it in iTunes using the following process.

2. Select the track with which you want to associate the artwork.
3. Open the Info window and then click the Artwork tab (see Figure 23.18). If the selected track has artwork with it, you see it in the Artwork pane.

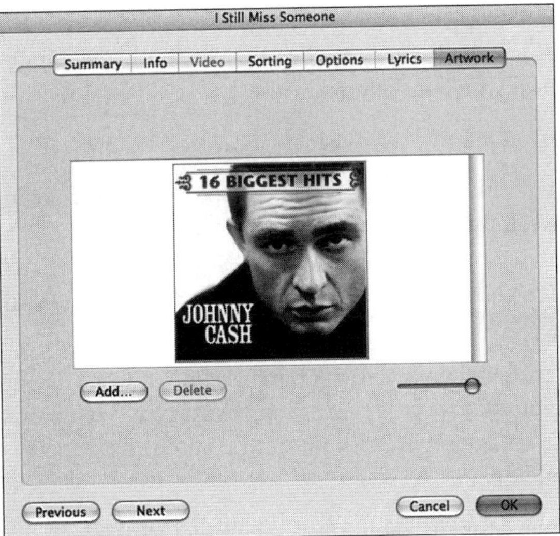


**Figure 23.18**
You use the Artwork pane to add artwork to a song.

4. Click Add. A dialog box that enables you to choose an image appears.
5. Move to and select the image you want to associate with the track.
6. Click Choose. The image is added to the Artwork pane of the Info window.

   You can use the slider under the image box to change the size of the previews you see on the Artwork pane. Drag the slider to the right to make the image larger or to the left to make it smaller. This doesn't change the image; instead, it only affects the size of the image as you currently see it in the Info window. This is especially useful when you associate lots of images with a track because you can see them all at the same time.

7. Repeat steps 4–6 to continue adding images to the Artwork pane until you have added all the images for a track.
8. To change the order of the images, drag them around in the image box. If a track has more than one graphic, place the image that you want to be the default on the left side of the image box.
9. Click OK. The window closes and the images are saved with the song.



**TIP** You can also add artwork to a track by dragging the image file from your desktop onto the Artwork pane of the Info window or onto the Artwork pane of the iTunes window.

## Adding Artwork to Songs Semi-Automatically

The odds are that if you have an iTunes Store account and you allow iTunes to download artwork automatically, most of your music has artwork associated with it. If not, in the previous section you learned how to manually add artwork to tracks. The results are good, but the process is kind of laborious. There's a path between fully automatic and manual, which is what I've cleverly called semi-automatic. What this means is that you can add software to your computer that will assist you in downloading artwork for your music. These tools use different sources of album artwork than the iTunes Store, such as Amazon.com, so you might be able to obtain artwork that isn't available in the iTunes store.

Because I'm on a tight page count, I don't have room to review all the available tools or show you how they work. What I can do is tell you how to find them and show you how my personal favorite works as an example. Then you can find and use the one that you like best.

Use Google to search for "automatic artwork for iTunes." Read about the options and choose the one you want to try; most are freeware or shareware, so you can try lots of them for free. Some of these tools are standalone applications, some plug into iTunes, and others are widgets.

My current favorite is Amazon Album Art Widget by The Widget Foundry (www.widget-foundry.com) for Mac OS X. After you add this widget to the Mac OS X Dashboard, you can easily add art to any tracks in your Library based on the tracks you have selected, the track currently playing, or the album currently playing. When you open the widget, it looks up the related artwork on Amazon.com and copies it into the widget. You then click the Set as album art in iTunes link to save the art in iTunes for the selected or playing music. With this tool, it takes only about 10 seconds and three mouse clicks to add art to tracks.

## Viewing Album Artwork

To view a track's artwork, do one of the following:

- Click the Show/Hide Song Artwork button, which is the fourth button from the left under the Source list. The Artwork pane appears and displays the artwork associated

23

with either the currently playing song or the currently selected song (see Figure 23.19). At the top of the artwork, you see Selected Item, which indicates you are viewing the artwork associated with the selected track, or Now Playing, which indicates you are viewing artwork associated with the track currently playing.

**Figure 23.19** You can view the artwork associated with a track in the Artwork pane.

- Move the pointer over the artwork and click when the pointer becomes the hand icon to see a larger version in a separate window. The title of the window is the name of the track with which the artwork is associated.
- To choose between viewing artwork associated with the selected track or the track currently playing, click the arrow button or text at the top of the Artwork pane. The artwork changes to the other option (for example, if you click Now Playing, it becomes Selected Song), and you see the appropriate artwork for that track.
- If you select the Now Playing option, the artwork changes in the Artwork pane and in the separate art window as the next track plays (unless, of course, the tracks use the same artwork, and even then the track title in the separate artwork window will change). When nothing is playing or selected, you see a message saying so in the Artwork pane.
- If the track has more than one piece of artwork associated with it, click the arrows that appear at the top of the pane to see each piece of art. You can click each image to open it in a separate window too.

# CUSTOMIZING THE CONTENT PANE

There are a number of ways to customize the columns (tags) that appear in the Content pane. What's more, you can customize the Content pane for each source. The customization you have done for a source (such as a CD or playlist) is saved and used each time you view that source.

To be able to save the view settings for each source, open the iTunes Preferences dialog box, click the General tab, check the "Remember view setting for each source" check box, and click OK. If you don't check this box, all sources use the same view setting.

23

You can select the tags (columns) that are shown for a source by using the following steps:

1. Select the source whose Content pane you want to customize. Its contents appear in the Content pane.
2. Select View, View Options or press ⌘-J. You see the View Options dialog box (see Figure 23.20). At the top of the dialog box, you see the name of the source for which you are configuring the Content pane. You also see all the available columns that can be displayed. If a column's check box is checked, that column is displayed; if not, it won't be shown.

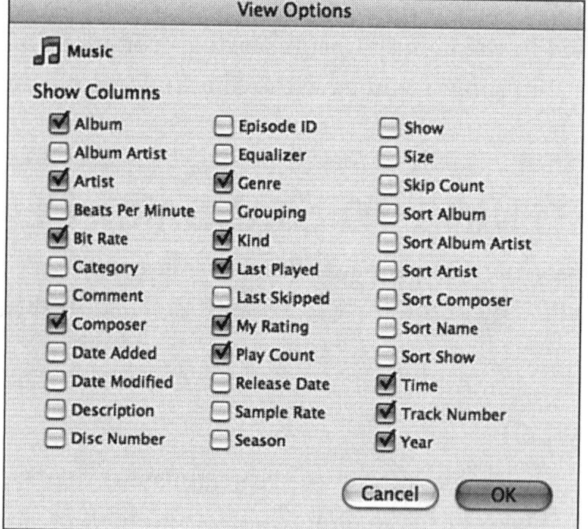


**Figure 23.20**
You can set the columns shown in the Content pane with the View Options dialog box.

3. Check the check boxes next to the columns you want to see.
4. Uncheck the check boxes next to the columns you don't want to see.
5. Click OK. When you return to the Content pane, only the columns you selected are shown for the source.

If you can't see all the columns being displayed, use the horizontal scrollbar to scroll in the Content pane. You can also use the vertical scrollbar to move up and down in the Content pane.

Not all columns apply to all types of content. For example, the Season column is intended for TV shows to display what season a particular track (episode) appeared in. iTunes doesn't limit the columns available in the View Options dialog box based on the source you've selected. If you include a column for a source that doesn't really apply, just open the View Options dialog box again and uncheck its check box.

Following are some other ways to customize the Content pane:

- You can change the width of columns in the Content pane by pointing to the line that marks the right boundary of the column in the column heading section. When you do, the cursor becomes a vertical line with arrows pointing to the left and right. Drag this to the left to make a column narrower or to the right to make it wider. The rest of the columns move to accommodate the change.
- You can change the order in which columns appear by dragging a column heading to the left or to the right. When you release the mouse button, the column assumes its new position and the other columns move to accommodate it.
- You can sort the Content pane by any of the columns shown, by clicking the column heading by which you want the pane to be sorted. The tracks are sorted according to that criterion, and the column heading is highlighted to show it is the current sort column. To change the direction of the sort, click the Sort Order triangle, which appears only in the Sort column. When you play a source, the tracks play according to the order in which they are sorted in the Content pane, starting from the top of the pane and playing toward the bottom (unless you have the Shuffle feature turned on, of course).

# Building and Listening to Standard Playlists

Although they aren't as smart as their younger siblings (smart playlists), standard playlists are definitely useful because you can choose the exact songs included in them and the order in which those songs play.

## Creating a Standard Playlist

You have two ways to create a playlist. One is to create a playlist that is empty (meaning it doesn't include any songs). The other is to choose songs and then create a playlist that includes those songs.

The place you start depends on what you have in mind. If you want to create a collection of songs but aren't sure which specific songs you want to start with, create an empty playlist. If you know of at least some of the songs you are going to include, select them first and then create the playlist. Either way, creating a playlist is simple and you'll end up in the same place.

### CREATING AN EMPTY STANDARD PLAYLIST

You can create an empty playlist from within iTunes by using any of the following techniques:

- Selecting File, New Playlist.
- Pressing or ⌘-N.
- Clicking the Create Playlist button, which is the "+" at the bottom of the Source list.

Whichever method you use will result in an empty playlist whose name is highlighted to show you that it is ready for you to edit. Type a name for the playlist and press Return. The playlist is renamed and selected. The Content pane is empty because you haven't added any songs to the playlist yet. You will learn how to do that later in this section.



**TIP**

> iTunes keeps playlists in the Source pane in alphabetical order within each group (standard and smart playlists). So, when you rename a playlist, it jumps to the location in the standard playlist section on the Source list to be where it belongs.

### CREATING A STANDARD PLAYLIST WITH SONGS IN IT

If you know some songs you want to place in a playlist, you can create the playlist so it includes those songs as soon as you create it. Here are the steps to follow:

1. Browse or search the Library to find the songs you want to be included in the playlist. For example, you can browse for all the songs in a specific genre or search for music by a specific artist.
2. In the Content pane, select the songs you want to place in the playlist.

**TIP**

> You can select songs that are next to one another by holding down the Shift key while you click them. You can select multiple songs that aren't next to one another by holding down ⌘ key while you click them.

3. Choose File, New Playlist from Selection. A new playlist appears on the Source list and is selected. Its name is highlighted to indicate that you can edit it, and you see the songs you selected in the Content pane.

**TIP**

> When you add a new album to your Library, use this technique to quickly create a playlist to make it easy to listen to. Select all the songs in the album and then use the New Playlist from Selection command. You can use the resulting playlist to easily select the new album for your listening pleasure.

iTunes attempts to name the playlist by looking for a common denominator in the group of songs you selected. For example, if all the songs are from the same artist, that artist's name is the playlist's name. Similarly, if the songs are all from the same album, the playlist's name is the artist's and album's names. Sometimes iTunes picks an appropriate name, and sometimes it doesn't.

4. While the playlist name is highlighted, edit the name as needed and then press Return. The playlist is ready to listen to and for you to add more songs.



**TIP**

> For still another way to create a playlist, try this: Select a group of songs and drag them onto the Source list. When you do so, iTunes does the same thing it does when you create a playlist using the steps in this section.

## ADDING SONGS TO A PLAYLIST

The whole point of creating a playlist is to add songs to it. Whether you created an empty playlist or one that already has some songs in it, the steps to add songs are the same:

1. Select the Music source.

**TIP**

> You can also move songs from one playlist to another one. Just select a playlist containing tracks you want to add to the playlist instead of the Library in step 1.

2. Browse or search the Music source (or other source) so that songs you want to add to the playlist are shown in the Content pane.
3. Select the tracks you want to add to the playlist by clicking them (remember the techniques to select multiple tracks at the same time).

**TIP**

> You can add the same song to a playlist as many times as you'd like to hear it.

4. Drag the selected songs from the Content pane onto the playlist to which you want to add them. As you drag, you see the songs you have selected in a "ghost" image attached to the pointer. When the playlist becomes highlighted and the cursor includes a plus sign (+), release the mouse button (see Figure 23.21). The songs are added to the playlist.
5. Repeat steps 2–4 until you have added all the songs you want to include in the playlist.

**TIP**

> If you double-click a playlist, it opens in a separate window. You can drag songs onto this window to add them to the playlist. This is helpful when you have a lot of playlists and other items on your Source list because you can arrange the iTunes window and the playlist window so you can see both easily at the same time.

**Figure 23.21**
You can add songs to a playlist by dragging them from the Content pane onto the playlist in the Source pane.

6. Select the playlist on the Source list. Its songs appear in the Content pane (see Figure 23.22). Information about the playlist, such as its playing time, appears in the Source Information area at the bottom of the iTunes window.

**NOTE**

> The Source Information area becomes very important when you are creating a CD because you can use this to make sure a playlist will fit onto a CD.

**Figure 23.22**
This playlist, called "Songs to Write By," are tunes that are a good to listen to while writing a book.

**TIP**

> You can add a song to a standard playlist by opening its contextual menu, choosing Add to Playlist, and then choosing the playlist to which you want to add that song.

### Removing Songs from a Playlist

If you decide you don't want one or more songs included in a playlist, select the songs you want to remove in the playlist's Content pane and press the Delete key. A warning prompt appears. Click Yes and the songs are deleted from the playlist. (If this dialog box annoys you as it does me, check the "Do not ask me again" check box and you won't ever have to see it again.)

**NOTE**

> When you delete a song from a playlist, it *isn't* deleted from the Library. It remains there so you can add it to a different playlist or listen to it from the Library. Of course, if it is included in other playlists, it isn't removed from those either.

### Setting the Order in Which a Playlist's Songs Play

Just like other sources, the order in which a playlist's songs play is determined by the order in which they appear in the Content pane (the first song is the one at the top of the window, the second is the next one down, and so on). You can drag songs up on the list to make them play earlier or down in the list to make them play later.

You can also change the order in which songs will play by sorting the playlist by its columns. You do this by clicking the column title in the column by which you want the Content pane sorted. You can set the columns that appear for a playlist by selecting View, View Options, as you learned to do earlier.

**NOTE**

> You can't sort a playlist by dragging songs up or down unless the playlist is sorted by the Track Number column (always the first column in the Content pane unless you are viewing the Library, in which case it is always the first column with information in it). If songs "bounce back" when you try to reorder them, click the Track Number column to make it the sort column. Then you'll be able to drag songs around to change their order.

### Listening to a Standard Playlist

After you have created a playlist, you can listen to it by selecting it on the Source list and using the same controls you use to listen to other sources. You can even search in and browse playlists just as you can the Library or CDs. (That's the real beauty of iTunes; it works the same way no matter what the selected source is!)

### Deleting a Standard Playlist

If you decide you no longer want a playlist, you can delete it by selecting the playlist on the Source list and pressing the Delete key. A prompt appears; click Yes and the playlist is removed from the Source list. (Be sure to check the "Do not ask me again" check box if you don't want to be prompted in the future.) Even though you've deleted the playlist, the songs in the playlist remain in the Library or in other playlists for your listening pleasure.

**NOTE**

The only time tracks or other content are actually removed from your Library is when you delete them while the Music source is selected. You should do this only when you are absolutely sure you won't want those tracks again. If you are working with playlists, deleting tracks removes them from only the current playlist so you can always add them again later if you change your mind.



# Building and Using Smart Playlists

The basic purpose of a smart playlist is the same as a standard playlist—that is, to contain a collection of tracks to which you can listen, put on a CD, and so on. However, the path smart playlists take to this end is completely different from that of standard playlists. Rather than choose specific songs as you do in a standard playlist, you tell iTunes the kind of tracks you want in your smart playlist and it picks out the tracks for you and places them in the playlist. For example, suppose you want to create a playlist that contains all your classical music. Rather than picking out all the songs in your Library that have the Classical genre (as you would do to create a standard playlist), you can use a smart playlist to tell iTunes to select all the classical music for you. The application then gathers all the music with the Classical genre and places that music in a smart playlist.

## Understanding Why Smart Playlists Are Called Smart

You create a smart playlist by defining a set of criteria based on any number of tags. After you have created these criteria, iTunes chooses songs that match those tags and places them in the playlist. Another example should help clarify this. Suppose you are a big-time Elvis fan and regularly add Elvis music to your Library. You could create a playlist and manually drag your new Elvis tunes to that playlist. But by using a smart playlist instead, you could define the playlist to include all your Elvis music. Anytime you add more Elvis music to your Library, that music is added to the playlist automatically so it always contains all the Elvis music in your Library.

You can also base a smart playlist on more than one attribute at the same time. Going back to the Elvis example, you could add the condition that you want only those songs you have rated four stars or higher so the smart playlist contains only your favorite Elvis songs.

As the previous example shows, smart playlists can be dynamic; iTunes calls this *live updating*. When a smart playlist is set to be live, iTunes changes its contents over time to match changes to the music in your Library. If this feature isn't set for a smart playlist, that playlist contains only those songs that met the criteria at the time the playlist was created.

Finally, you can also link a smart playlist's conditions by the logical expression All or Any. If you use an All logical expression, all the conditions must be true for a song to be included in the smart playlist. If you use the Any option, only one of the conditions has to be met for a song to be included in the smart playlist.

## CREATING A SMART PLAYLIST

You can create a smart playlist by performing the following steps:

1. Select File, New Smart Playlist or hold down the Option key and click the New Playlist button, which becomes the New Smart Playlist button when the Option key is pressed down. You see the Smart Playlist dialog box (see Figure 23.23).

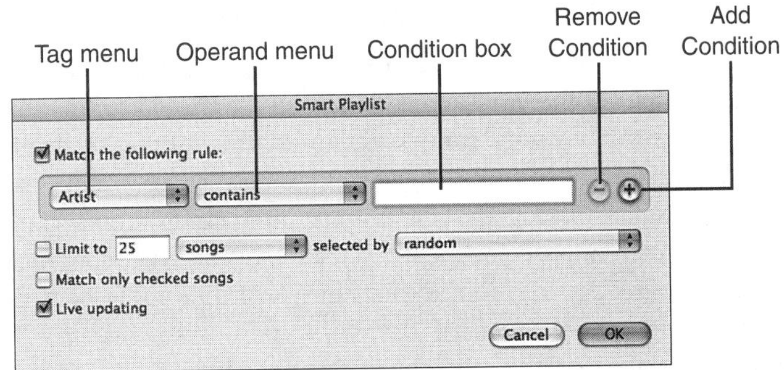


**Figure 23.23**
The Smart Playlist dialog box enables you to create playlists based on a single tag or on many of them.

**TIP**

> You can also create a new smart playlist by pressing Option-⌘-N.

2. Select the first tag on which you want the smart playlist to be based from the Tag menu. For example, you can select Artist, Genre, My Rating, or Year, among many others. The Operand menu is updated so that it is applicable to the attribute you select. For example, if you select Artist, the Operand menu includes contains, does not contain, is, is not, starts with, and ends with.
3. Select the operand you want to use on the Operand menu. For example, if you want to match data exactly, select is. If you want the condition to be more loose, select contains.
4. Type the condition you want to match in the Condition box. The more you type, the more specific the condition is. As an example, if you select "Artist" in step 1, select "contains" in step 2, and type "Elvis" in this step, the playlist finds all songs that include Elvis, Elvis Presley, Elvis Costello, Elvisiocity, and so on. If you type Elvis Presley in the Condition box and leave the contains operand, iTunes includes only songs whose artist includes Elvis Presley, such as Elvis Presley, Elvis Presley and His Back-up Band, and so on.

**NOTE**

> As you make selections on the Attribute menu and type conditions in the Condition box, iTunes will attempt to automatically match what you type to tags in your Library. For example, if your Library includes Elvis music and you use Artist as an attribute, iTunes will enter Elvis Presley in the Condition box for you when you start typing "Elvis."

5. To add another condition to the smart playlist, click the Add Condition button. A new, empty condition appears. At the top of the dialog box, the all or any menu also appears.
6. Select the second tag on which you want the smart playlist to be based in the second condition's Tag menu. For example, if you want to include songs from a specific genre, select Genre on the menu.
7. Select the operand you want to use in the Operand menu, such as contains, is, and so on.
8. Type the condition you want to match in the Condition box. If you selected Genre in step 6, type the genre from which the music in the playlist should come. As you type, iTunes tries to match the genre you type with those in your Library.
9. Repeat steps 5–8 to add more conditions to the playlist until you have all the conditions you want to include (see Figure 23.24).

**Figure 23.24**
This smart playlist is approaching the genius level; it now includes three conditions.

**TIP**

> If you want to remove a condition from a smart playlist, click the Remove button (the minus sign) for the condition you want to remove.

10. Select "all" on the menu at the top of the dialog box if all the conditions must be met for a track to be included in the smart playlist, or select "any" if only one of them must be met. For example, you could create a smart playlist based on multiple Artist conditions and the playlist would feature music by those artists. In this case, you would choose "any" so that if a song is associated with *any* of the artists for which you created a condition, it would be included in the playlist. As a contrasting example, if you want the playlist to include songs you have rated as three stars or better by a specific artist, you would include both of these conditions and then select "all" in the menu so that both conditions would have to be met for a song to be included (a song is both by the artist and is rated with three or more stars).

**NOTE**

> If you include more than one condition based on the same tag, you usually don't want to use the "all" option because the conditions will likely be mutually exclusive, and using the "all" option will result in no songs being included in the playlist because no song will be able to meet all the conditions at the same time.

You can limit the length of a smart playlist to a maximum number of songs, the time it plays, or the size of the files it includes. You set these limits using the "Limit to" check box and menus.

11. If you want to limit the playlist, check the "Limit to" check box. If you don't want to set a limit on the playlist, leave the check box unchecked and skip to step 15.
12. Select the parameter by which you want to limit the playlist in the first menu; by default, this menu has songs selected. Your choices include the number of songs (just songs on the menu), the time the playlist will play (in minutes or hours), and the size of the files the playlist contains (in MB or GB).

**TIP**

> Limiting a playlist by disk space is useful when you want to do something else with that playlist, such as burning a CD. You could set the playlist to be limited to 700MB to ensure all its songs will fit on one disc. (The exact limit depends on the specific drive and disc media you use.)

13. Type the data appropriate for the limit you selected in the "Limit to" box. For example, if you selected minutes in the menu, type the maximum length of the playlist in minutes in the box. If you selected songs, enter the maximum number of songs that can be included in the playlist.
14. Select how you want iTunes to choose the songs it includes based on the limit you selected by using the "selected by" menu. This menu has many options, including to choose songs randomly, based on your rating, how often the songs are played, and so on.
15. If you want the playlist to include only songs whose check box in the Content pane is checked, check the "Match only checked items" check box. If you leave this check box unchecked, iTunes includes all songs that meet the playlist's conditions, even if you have unchecked their check boxes in the Content pane.
16. If you want the playlist to be dynamic, meaning that iTunes updates its contents over time, check the "Live updating" check box. If you uncheck this check box, the playlist includes only those songs that meet the playlist's conditions when you create it.
17. Click OK to create the playlist. You move to the Source list, the smart playlist is added and selected, and its name is ready for you to edit. Also, the songs in your Library that match the criteria in the playlist are added to it and the current contents of the playlist are shown in the Content pane.
18. Type the playlist's name and press Return. The smart playlist is complete.

## Listening to a Smart Playlist

Listening to a smart playlist is just like listening to other sources: You select it on the Source list and use the playback controls to listen to it. The one difference is that, if a smart playlist is set to be live, its contents can change over time.

**NOTE**

> Just like other sources, when you select a smart playlist, its information is shown in the Source Information section at the bottom of the window. This can be useful if you want to create a CD or just to see how big the playlist is (by number of songs, time, or file size). Remember, though, that because a smart playlist's contents can change over time, its source information can also change over time. So, just because a smart playlist fits on a CD today doesn't mean it still will tomorrow (or even later today).



### Changing a Smart Playlist

To change the contents of a smart playlist, you change the smart playlist's criteria (remember that iTunes automatically places tracks in a smart playlist based on your criteria). Use the following steps to do this:

1. Select the smart playlist you want to change.
2. Select File, Edit Smart Playlist. The Smart Playlist dialog box appears, and the playlist's current criteria are shown.

**TIP**

> You can also edit a smart playlist by selecting it and opening the Info window (which also opens the Smart Playlist dialog box). Plus, you can open the playlist's contextual menu by right-clicking (two-button mouse) or Ctrl-clicking it (one-button mouse) and selecting Edit Smart Playlist.

3. Use the techniques you learned when you created a playlist to change its criteria. For example, you can remove conditions by clicking their Remove buttons. You can also add more conditions or change the other settings for the playlist.
4. Click OK. Your changes are saved and the contents of the playlist are updated to match the current criteria.

**TIP**

> To delete a smart playlist, select it on the Source list and press Delete. Confirm the deletion at the prompt (if you see it), and the playlist is removed from the Source list.

You can also change a smart playlist by using the same techniques you use on other sources such as sorting it, selecting the columns you see when you view it, and so on.

## Organizing Playlists

As you use iTunes, you are likely to create lots of playlists. Over time, your list of playlists can get huge, making your Source list long and unwieldy. Fortunately, you can create folders to organize your playlists and then drag your playlists into the folders you create. By doing this, you can keep your Source list neat and tidy and also make your playlists easier to use.

Just like folders on your desktop, you can create folders for any kind of playlist on your Source list. You might want a folder for all your playlists from specific genres or maybe another folder for all your playlists that contain albums.

To create a folder, choose File, New Folder. A new folder appears on the Source list; its name is highlighted to indicate it's ready for you to give it a name. Type the folder name and press Enter to save it.

**TIP**

> You can also create a new folder by pressing Option-Shift-⌘-N.

To place a playlist within a folder, drag its icon onto the folder until that folder's icon becomes highlighted, and then release the mouse button. The playlist is moved into the folder; as soon as you add at least one playlist to a folder, an expansion triangle is added to the folder's icon. You can click this to expand or to collapse the folder so that you see or don't see the playlists it contains.

A folder can contain both kinds of playlists and they can even contain playlists containing different types of content. For example, you can create playlists of rock music videos and include them in a folder you've created for your playlists that also include rock music.

Just because you can create folders for your playlists, that doesn't mean you have to do so. You can place some playlists in folders and leave others at the top level of the Source list. The point is that you can use folders to organize your Source list however you see fit (see Figure 23.25).

**Figure 23.25**
On this Source list, you can see three folders; the Soundtracks folder is expanded so you can see the playlists it contains.

On the Source list, your folders appear between the "special playlists" (you'll learn about these in the next section) and the playlists that aren't in folders. Folders are listed in alphabetical or numerical order based on their names.

Within folders or not, playlists are listed in alphabetical order based on their names (just like folders). You can make your playlists and folders be listed in another order by appending numbers before their names, such as adding "1." before the name of the playlist you want to appear at the top of the list. You could add "2." to the one you want to be listed next, and so on. (Remember that you can change the name of a folder or playlist by selecting it, clicking the name so it becomes highlighted, changing the name, and then pressing the Return key.)

# Mac OS X to the Max: Using iTunes Sources



In this chapter, you've focused on CDs, the Music source, and playlists that you create. However, there are many more sources with which you'll work when you use iTunes.

## Understanding Sources

In the area between the Library Music source and your playlists and folders, you see a number of sources (some really are playlists, whereas others are tools, but they work similarly). These sources include the following:

- **Movies**—This Library sources contains all the movie content you've added to iTunes.
- **TV Shows**—When you purchase TV shows from the iTunes Store, they are sorted in this source.
- **Podcasts**—This source is used to manage your podcasts. As you subscribe to podcasts, you can access them by selecting Podcasts on the Source list.
- **Audiobooks**—When you add audiobooks to iTunes, they are stored here.
- **iPod Games**—A number of iPod games are available in the iTunes Store. If you buy any of these, they are stored in the iPod Games source.
- **Radio**—This playlist contains Internet "radio" stations to which you can listen.
- **Ringtones**—If you use an iPhone, you can create ringtones using music you've purchased from the iTunes Store. When you do, your ringtones are listed in this source.
- **iTunes Store**—This is the source you select to work with the iTunes Store.
- **Purchased**—This playlist contains music and videos you purchase from the iTunes Store.
- **iPods**—When you connect an iPod to a Mac, it appears as a source. When you select an iPod, the Content pane is replaced by the tools you use to configure and work with the iPod.
- **Party Shuffle**—You'll learn how to use the Party Shuffle playlist next.

**TIP**

> Remember that you can show or hide these sources by using the check boxes on the General tab of the iTunes Preferences dialog box.

## USING THE PARTY SHUFFLE

The Party Shuffle playlist enables you to play a source you select in shuffle mode; you can also set several options to liven things up even more. If you like to keep things interesting, the Party Shuffle is a good way to do so because you can hear the songs in any source in a random order without having to change the source itself. After you try this special playlist, you'll probably use it as often as I do, which is to say, quite a lot. To do the Party Shuffle, follow these steps:



1. Select Party Shuffle on the Source pane. You see a dialog box explaining what the Party Shuffle is; read it, check the "Do not show this message" again check box, and click OK. You see songs fill the Content pane and some controls appear at the bottom of the pane (see Figure 23.26).

**Figure 23.26**
The Party Shuffle source might seem odd to you at first, but once you get to know it, you'll love it.

2. Select the source of music you want to shuffle on the Source pop-up menu. You can choose your Library, any playlist (standard or smart), or any folder (that contains standard or smart playlists). The playlists and folders appear in alphabetical order and the different kinds of playlists look the same on the menu.
3. If you want songs you have rated higher to be played more frequently, check the "Play higher rated songs more often" check box. This causes iTunes to choose songs with higher star ratings more frequently than those with lower or no star ratings.
4. Use the two Display pop-up menus to choose how many songs are shown that have been played recently and that are upcoming. Your choices range from 0 to 100 on both menus. When you make selections, the songs in the Content pane reflect your choices.

   The current song is always highlighted in the Content pane with a blue bar. Songs that have played are grayed out and are listed above the current song. Songs that will be played are in regular text and appear below the current song.

5. If you want to change the order in which upcoming songs will play, drag them up or down in the Content pane.
6. When you are ready to hear the tunes, use the same playback controls that you use with any other source.

The Party Shuffle source plays forever. After it plays a song, it moves one of the recently played songs off the list, moves the song it just played into the recently played section, highlights and plays the next song, and adds another one to the upcoming songs section. This process continues until you stop the music.



**NOTE**

The Party Shuffle is one item for which the Source Information data doesn't make a lot of sense. Because the list is always changing, the source information doesn't really mean a lot. It simply shows information based on the songs currently shown in the Content pane, which changes after each song is played.

As the Party Shuffle plays, you can keep moving upcoming songs around to change the order in which they will play. You can also press the right-arrow key to skip to the next song.

In addition, you can add songs manually to the Party Shuffle. View a source to find the song you want to add. Open the song's contextual menu by right-clicking it. Select "Play Next in Party Shuffle" to have the song play next, or select "Add to Party Shuffle" to add the song to the end of the upcoming songs list.

**TIP**

One interesting command on a track's contextual menu is the Show in Playlists command. Choose this to see a list of all the playlists in which a song is contained.

# CHAPTER 24

# Using Leopard's Other Digital Media Applications

## In this chapter

# Going Beyond iTunes

iTunes is the Mac's premiere digital media application, and it's so good it even dominates on the Windows platform for listening to audio and watching video (of course, the iPod has something to do iTunes' popularity on both platforms). Although iTunes gets the most press, it isn't the only digital media application that comes with Mac OS X. In this chapter, you'll learn about some of the other valuable members of the Mac's digital entertainment team: QuickTime, DVD Player, Front Row, and Photo Booth.

# Being Quick with QuickTime



Apple's QuickTime is the technology your Mac uses to handle dynamic data. *Dynamic data* simply means data that changes over time. This includes video, audio, and other such media. In fact, QuickTime technology and the QuickTime framework enable all the iLife applications, including iTunes. Without QuickTime, using Mac OS X wouldn't be nearly as interesting as it is.

Under Mac OS X, except for viewing QuickTime movies on your computer and on the Web, you likely won't deal with QuickTime directly very often. But, in addition to knowing how to handle those tasks, you should have a good understanding of the QuickTime technology.

Since its introduction, Apple's QuickTime has been one of the most successful multimedia standards on any platform. In fact, it has been so successful that it is also widely used on Windows computers; QuickTime movies on Windows play the same way they do on the Mac. QuickTime has also been widely adopted on the Web, with many websites serving video and animation files as QuickTime movies. And, as on the Mac, QuickTime technology drives iTunes on Windows computers.

Although you are most likely to encounter QuickTime movies on the Web, you will encounter them in many other places, including interactive games, reference titles, entertainment titles, learning tools, and of course web pages.

## Understanding QuickTime Versus QuickTime Pro

QuickTime comes in two flavors: QuickTime and QuickTime Pro. With QuickTime, you get a basic set of capabilities that enable you to watch all sorts of QuickTime content. But that is about all you can do with it. QuickTime Pro, on the other hand, enables you to create and edit QuickTime movies, along with various other useful things—the most useful of which is downloading QuickTime movies you encounter on the Internet and saving them on your Mac.

### QuickTime

With the version of QuickTime included as part of Mac OS X, you'll get substantive QuickTime capabilities. These features include the following:

- Viewing all flavors of QuickTime movies on and off the Internet
- Working with more than 30 audio and video file formats
- Changing the size at which movies are played
- Printing frames of movies

### QuickTime Pro

When you pay for the QuickTime Pro upgrade, you'll get many more features. One of the most important features is the ability to create and edit your own QuickTime movies. QuickTime Pro provides you with all the capabilities of QuickTime plus much more, including the following:

- Playing full-screen video
- Viewing files in a wider variety of formats
- Creating your own QuickTime movies
- Editing and saving movies in various formats, one of the most important being the video format for iPods
- Copying and pasting material from various formats into QuickTime movies
- Preparing QuickTime movies for streaming delivery via the Web
- Using sharpening, color tinting, and embossing filters on movies and images
- Creating slideshows from a series of still images



The additional features in QuickTime Pro become part of the QuickTime framework. Therefore, any applications that use that framework—such as iTunes, iMovie, iPhoto, iDVD, Final Cut Express, and so on—also benefit from the additional QuickTime Pro features, such as the capability to apply custom compression schemes. In fact, a QuickTime Pro license is included with Apple's professional media applications, such as Final Cut Pro.

**NOTE**

Apple maintains an extensive website dedicated to QuickTime. This site includes software and updates you can download, information on how QuickTime works, links to QuickTime showcases, and so on. The site is at www.apple.com/quicktime and has some great samples of QuickTime movies you can view.

Before the iLife applications came into being, upgrading to QuickTime Pro was essential for anyone who wanted to create or edit digital media. That's because it was about the only way to do these tasks without spending thousands of dollars on specialized software. Since the rise of iLife and other consumer applications (such as Final Cut Express), you probably won't have much need for QuickTime Pro. You would likely need to use QuickTime Pro only if you prepare media files for web delivery, need to access some of its more specialized features, or don't want to use the iLife applications for some reason.

**NOTE**

> One of the most interesting capabilities of QuickTime Pro is that you can download many movies from websites, such as movie trailers, to your computer. Once there, you can use these movies like other content on your Mac, such as importing them into your iLife projects.

## CONFIGURING QUICKTIME

You'll need to do some basic configuration of QuickTime to customize it for your system. This configuration is done with the QuickTime pane of the System Preferences application. Open the System Preferences application and click the QuickTime icon to open the QuickTime pane. Across the top of the pane, you will see the following tabs: Register, Browser, Update, Streaming, and Advanced.

24

### REGISTERING QUICKTIME

You need to use the Register pane of the QuickTime pane only when you upgrade to QuickTime Pro.

⇨ To learn how to register QuickTime Pro, **see** "Upgrading to QuickTime Pro," **p. 607**.

### CONFIGURING QUICKTIME FOR WEB BROWSING

One of the most useful things about QuickTime is that you can view QuickTime movies on the Web. Because QuickTime is a framework, web browsers such as Safari can use its tools to present content to you. To configure how QuickTime is used when you view web movies, perform the following steps:

1. Open the Browser tab of the QuickTime preferences pane (see Figure 24.1).

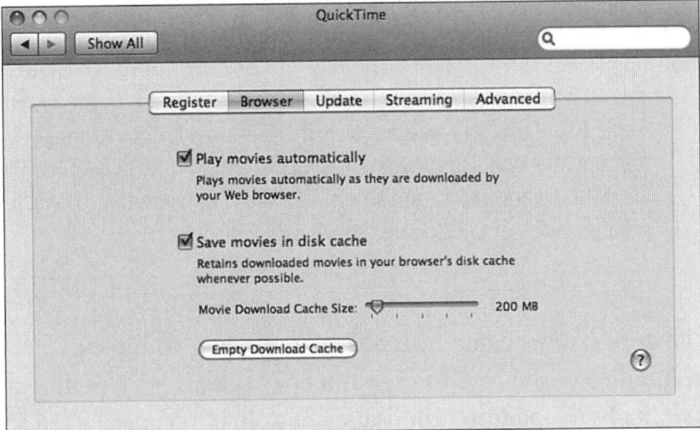


**Figure 24.1**
Use the Browser tab to configure how your web browser handles QuickTime movies.

2. If you don't want QuickTime movies to automatically play in your web browser for some reason, uncheck the "Play movies automatically" check box. In most cases, you will want them to play automatically. However, if you use a very slow Internet connection, you might want to disable this feature.

3. Uncheck the "Save movies in disk cache" check box if you don't want movies you view on the Web to be saved in your browser's disk cache. In most cases, this is a useful option, especially if you like to view a movie more than once during a single browsing session; subsequent viewings are much faster because the movie is read from your disk rather than being downloaded from the Web again. Most users should check this box.
4. Use the slider to set the amount of cache you want to be used for storing downloaded content.

**TIP**

> To empty your download cache, click the Empty Download Cache button.

### Installing and Updating Third-Party QuickTime Software

The Update pane enables you to install third-party QuickTime software on your Mac and control how updates to that software are handled. Open the pane and click the Install button. You move to a website from which you can download and install QuickTime software from a number of companies. After you've done this, you can use the Update controls on the Update pane to install updates for the software you have installed (updates to QuickTime itself are handled via the Mac's Software Update tool).



### Configuring QuickTime Streaming

The Streaming pane enables you to configure how your Mac works with streaming content. *Streaming content* is that which plays on your Mac as it is being downloaded from the Internet or from other networks to which you are connected. Configure streaming for your system with the following steps:

1. Open the Streaming tab of the QuickTime preferences pane.
2. Use the Streaming Speed pop-up menu to set the speed at which your Mac is connected to the Internet. The Automatic option enables your Mac to determine the connection speed automatically. Or, you can use the menu to set a specific speed, such as Intranet/LAN if your Mac is connected to a local network that provides your Internet access.
3. Check the Enable Instant-On check box if you want streaming content to start "instantly." This feature enables streamed content to play as soon as it starts to download to your Mac.
4. If you turn on the Enable Instant-On feature, you can set the amount of delay that occurs before a movie starts playing by using the Play slider. With a shorter delay, movies start playing faster but less buffered data is stored on your Mac. Thus, should some network congestion occur and the download process be slowed, interruptions in movie playback will be more likely. If this happens, move the slider to the right to increase the amount of time content is downloaded before it starts to play.

### Setting Advanced QuickTime Options

The Advanced tab enables you to configure some specialized aspects of how QuickTime works (see Figure 24.2).

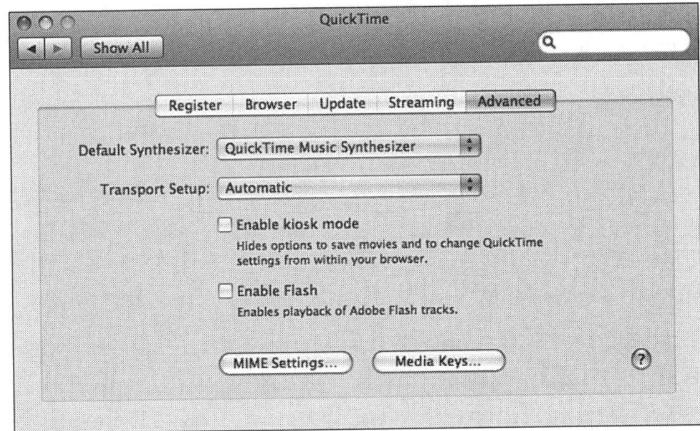


**Figure 24.2**
You probably won't need to use QuickTime's Advanced settings, but you should know where they are just in case.

Following is a brief description of the Advanced settings:

- **Default Synthesizer**—QuickTime can play music using different synthesizers (a *synthesizer* transforms digital or other signals into specific musical notes, tones, and so on). This pop-up menu is useful if you work with a Musical Instrument Digital Interface (MIDI) device. By default, the standard QuickTime Music Synthesizer is used. However, you can install various synthesizers and use them to produce the music that is part of QuickTime movie files. If you are involved in creating MIDI files or using a MIDI instrument, you can use this pop-up menu to select the default synthesizer that should be used.
- **Transport Setup**—The Transport Setup pop-up menu enables you to change the protocol and port QuickTime uses to download QuickTime streams from the Internet. In almost all cases, the Automatic option will be the setting you need. However, if you choose Custom on the pop-up menu, you can choose to use User Datagram Protocol (UDP) or Hypertext Transfer Protocol (HTTP) and configure the port used for the protocol you select. You won't likely ever need to change this unless you are connected to a network that requires specific settings.
- **Kiosk mode**—If you check the "Enable kiosk mode" check box, the QuickTime interface is hidden when you play QuickTime content from within your web browser.
- **Enable Flash**—Check this check box to enable Flash content to be played with QuickTime tools.
- **MIME settings**—The MIME Settings button enables you to choose the types of files handled by QuickTime when you encounter them on the Internet. Click the MIME Settings button, and you will see the MIME Settings sheet. In that sheet, you will see a listing of various groups of file formats, such as Streaming, Video, and so on. Click the expansion triangle next to each group to see the file formats it contains. Check the box

next to each file format you want to be handled in QuickTime; to have QuickTime handle all the formats in a group, check the group's check box. Click OK to save the settings you select.

**NOTE**

> *MIME* is the acronym for Multipurpose Internet Mail Extensions. As you might guess, MIME was originally developed as a means of exchanging files via email. Now, the term refers to the general encoding schemes used to encode files transferred over the Internet.

- **Media keys**—Media keys enable you to manage your access to protected data files. If you need to get to QuickTime files that are sensitive, you need to use a password (called a *key*) to access the files. Individual tracks can also be secured with a key. If you use such secured QuickTime files, you can enter the keys needed to play them by clicking the Media Keys button.



## Upgrading to QuickTime Pro

Upgrading to QuickTime Pro does not require any additional software installation. All you need is a registration code, which unlocks the additional features of QuickTime Pro. There are several ways to obtain your QuickTime Pro registration code, but the easiest ways are to use the Web:

- Go to www.apple.com/quicktime/upgrade and click the Upgrade Now link.
- Open the System Preferences application, open the QuickTime pane, click the Register tab, and then click Buy QuickTime Pro. You will move to the registration website.

Using the website to upgrade is quite simple—just follow the onscreen instructions. You will receive your registration code via the order confirmation web page or via the phone, depending on how you order the upgrade. Save this code because you will need it each time you have to configure QuickTime Pro.

The QuickTime Pro upgrade costs $29.99. Whether it is worth it depends on how much you need the specialized features it provides. If you have the iLife applications, you probably don't need to upgrade. However, being able to download QuickTime content from the Web might just be worth the upgrade cost because you can incorporate that content into your projects. And if you have content you want to save in the iPod format, it can also be worthwhile.

After you have obtained your QuickTime Pro registration code, you use the Register pane of the QuickTime pane of the System Preferences application to upgrade. Enter your name and QuickTime Pro registration code to upgrade to the Pro version.

*If you weren't able to upgrade successfully, see "My Attempt to Upgrade to QuickTime Pro Failed" in the "Troubleshooting" section at the end of this chapter.*

## Opening QuickTime Player and Setting QuickTime Player Preferences

QuickTime Player is the basic application you use to view QuickTime content stored on your computer or in the QuickTime format on CD or DVD, such as those you create using iMovie. Although the appearance of the QuickTime Player controls varies a bit among these contexts, the controls you use to watch movies work similarly.

To launch QuickTime Player, open it from within the Applications folder. When QuickTime Player opens, by default, it will download and display the Content Guide that leads you to content on the Web each time you open the application (see Figure 24.3).

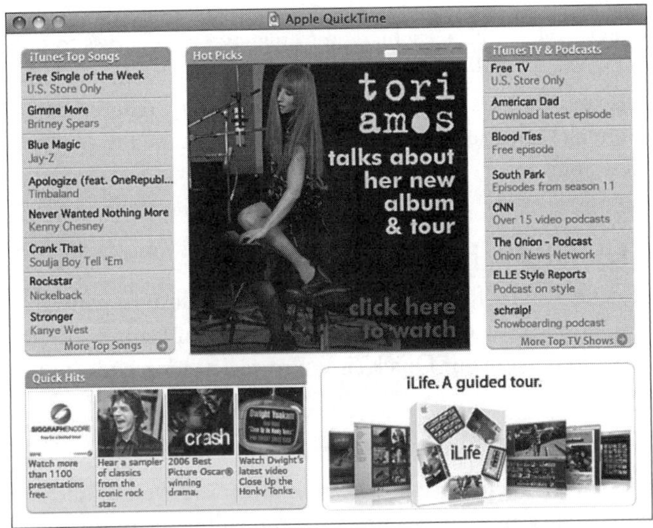


**Figure 24.3**
The Content Guide leads you to QuickTime content on the Web.

> **TIP**
> If you want to view the content the Content Guide shows you, click the links provided in the QuickTime Player window.

There are some general preferences you might want to set by selecting QuickTime Player, Preferences. The options in the resulting Player Preferences dialog box are as described here:

- **Open Movie**—If you check the "Open movies in new players" check box, each movie you open appears in a new QuickTime Player window rather than replacing the current movie.
- **Auto-Play**—If you check the "Automatically play movies when opened" check box, movies begin to play as soon as you open them. If this is not checked, you have to click the Play button to start movies you open.
- **Playback Quality**—If you check the "Use high quality video setting when available" check box, the QuickTime Player application will choose the best possible video settings for the types of content you play.

- **Closed Captioning**—If you check the "Show closed captioning when available" check box, the QuickTime Player application will display any close captioning that is included in the video you are watching.
- **Timecode**—QuickTime can display timecode information for the content being displayed. Use the two check boxes in this section of the QuickTime Player preferences to specify how the timecode information is displayed.
- **Only Front Movie Plays Sound**— If the "Play sound in frontmost player only" check box is checked and you have more than one movie playing, only the movie in the frontmost QuickTime Player window produces sound.
- **Play Sound in Background**—When the "Play sound when application is in background" check box is checked, a movie's sound continues to play when you move it into the background.
- **Show Equalizer**— When the "Show equalizer" check box is checked, you will see the QuickTime Player equalizer.
- **Content Guide**—Checking the "Show Content Guide automatically" check box means that, when you launch QuickTime Player, it presents content available to you and displays links to that content in the QuickTime Player window (you can choose to watch it or not). This is checked by default. If you don't want to see the Content Guide each time you launch the application, you should uncheck the box.
- **Fast User Switching**—If the Fast User Switching feature is enabled, users can log in to your Mac without other users having to completely log out first (which means running applications can continue to run). If you check the "Pause movies before switching users" check box, movies that are playing when another user logs in are paused until the previous user logs back in.
- **Selection indicators**—You can use QuickTime Player's selection indicators (crop markers) to select parts of a QuickTime movie. If you check the "Hide selection indicators for empty selection," the markers are hidden when nothing is selected.
- **Recent Items**—Use the "Number of Recent Items" pop-up menu to choose how many movies QuickTime Player retains on its File, Open Recent list.

**NOTE**

> If you haven't upgraded to QuickTime Pro, you might not have access to all the preferences described here.

If you click the Full Screen button in the Preferences dialog box, you'll be able to set the following preferences:

- **Full Screen playback**—Use the Movie Size pop-up menu to choose how content is presented, which means the QuickTime Player interface is hidden. The options include Fit to Screen, Double Size, and so on. If you have multiple displays, click the thumbnail of the display on which you want the content presented; the thumbnail with the QuickTime logo will be used.

- **Background color**—Use the Background color button to open the Color Picker to choose the background color for QuickTime Player.
- **Movie or Presentation**—Click Movie if you want content to play using the movie controls. Click Slideshow if you want to control the movie using the arrow keys.
- **Background color on all screens**—Check "Display background color on all screens" if you want the background color to be used on all screens shown in QuickTime Player.
- **Stay in Full Screen**—Check "Remain in full screen when player is inactive" if you want QuickTime Player to remain in full screen mode when content is done. If not check, the QuickTime Player interface will reappear when a movie finishes.
- **Full Screen controls**—Check "Display full screen controls" if you want QuickTime Player controls to appear on the screen; use the Hide after pop-up menu to determine how long the controls remain on the screen.



If you have a camera connected to your Mac, such as an integral iSight camera, you can use the Recording preferences to determine how content is recorded in QuickTime Player:

- **Video Source**—Use this pop-up menu to determine the device you'll use to record video.
- **Microphone**—Use this to select the audio input when you record in QuickTime Player.
- **Quality**—Choose the format in which you'll record on this pop-up menu.
- **Save to**—Use the "Save files to" pop-up menu to choose the location in which recorded content will be saved.

## Watching QuickTime Movies Stored Locally

If you use a VCR, CD player, or DVD player, you won't have any trouble using the QuickTime Player controls to view QuickTime content. Find a QuickTime movie on your hard drive or on a disc and open it. QuickTime Player launches and you see the QuickTime Player window (see Figure 24.4). If the auto-play preference is turned on, the movie will start to play automatically.

**TIP**

> To see which features are enabled by the QuickTime Pro upgrade (if you haven't upgraded), open each QuickTime Player menu. Commands available only to Pro users are grayed out and the word PRO is listed next to them. As you can see, there isn't a whole lot you can do without the upgrade. But, QuickTime Player works fine for viewing content, so that's okay. You most likely use other applications, such as iMovie, for many of the QuickTime Pro functions.

**TIP**

> QuickTime movie files use the extension `.mov`. If you don't know where a QuickTime movie is, use Spotlight to search for files with this extension.

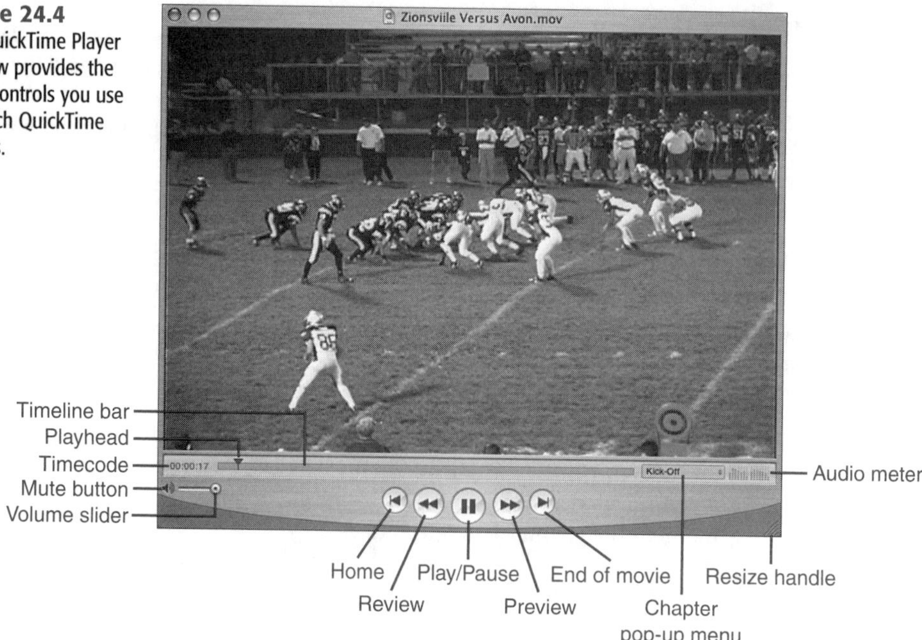


**Figure 24.4**
The QuickTime Player window provides the basic controls you use to watch QuickTime movies.



Most of the controls in the QuickTime Player window are easy to understand. For example, the Review button plays the movie in reverse, the Preview button plays the movie in fast forward mode, and so on.

However, you need to become familiar with the less obvious parts of the QuickTime Player window, especially if you have never worked with digital video before. The current frame is shown in the viewing window (if you haven't played the movie, it is the first frame in the movie). Just below the viewing window is the movie's Timeline bar (also known as the *Scrubber bar*). This represents the total length of the movie. The location of the Playhead shows where in the movie the current frame is located. As you play a movie, the Playhead moves to the right in the Timeline bar so that it always shows the location of the frame displayed in the viewing window.

At the left edge of the Timeline bar is the timecode. The timecode represents the location of the Playhead in the following format: minutes:seconds:frame number. For example, if you see 2:34:10, the Playhead is located on the 10th frame of the 34th second of the 2nd minute of the movie.

Control the size of the movie using the commands on the View menu. You can view it at half size, actual size, double size, or fit to screen. Increasing the size of a movie beyond the size at which it was created sometimes decreases its image quality and frame rate. With some movies, this is hardly noticeable; with others, increasing the size can make them unwatchable. You can experiment to see which size is the best compromise for a particular movie on your specific system.

**TIP**

> You can also change the size of the QuickTime Player window using the Resize handle. The window remains in proportion to the size in which the movie was created. If you hold down the Shift key, you can resize the window any way you want (with sometimes amusing effects on the movie itself). You can quickly return a movie to its default size by selecting View, Actual Size or by pressing ⌘-1.

Click the Play button (or press the spacebar) to view the movie and use the Volume slider to adjust its sound level.

⇨ QuickTime Player offers many keyboard shortcuts; to learn which shortcuts are available, **see** "Using QuickTime Player Keyboard Shortcuts," **p. 636**.

If the movie contains chapter markers, such as those you can add to your iMovie projects, jump to a specific chapter in the movie by opening the Chapter pop-up menu and selecting the chapter you want to view. If you are playing the movie when you use this menu, you will jump to the chapter you selected and the movie will continue to play. If it isn't playing, you'll see the first frame in the chapter you selected.



You can move to any point in the movie by dragging the Playhead to the frame you want to view.

You can get more control over the sound using the A/V controls; display them by selecting Window, Show A/V Controls. The A/V Controls window appears (see Figure 24.5). You can use the controls in the Audio pane of the window to further adjust the audio portion of the movie by setting volume, balance, bass, treble, and pitch shift. Use the controls in the Video section to set brightness, color, contrast, and tint. You can use the Jog Shuttle slider to move the movie forward or in reverse at various speeds (move the slider further to play the movie faster in that direction). You can set the movie's playback speed with the Playback Speed slider.

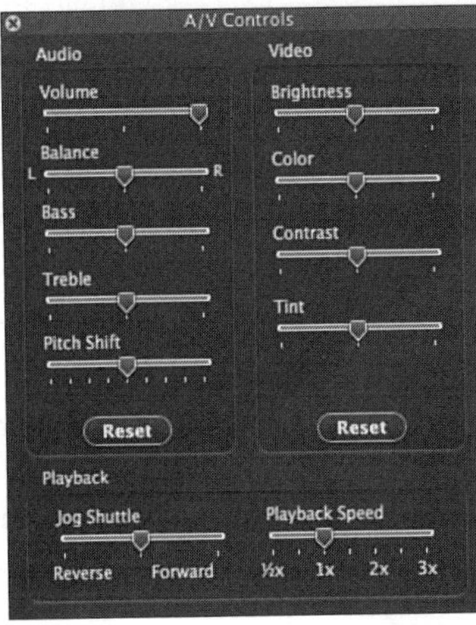


**Figure 24.5**
Use the A/V Controls window to control your movie in more detail.

**TIP**

> To mute a movie, click the speaker icon at the left edge of the Volume slider.

You can get more information about a movie by selecting Window, Show Movie Inspector. In the resulting window, you will see technical information about the movie, such as its format, resolution, and size.

**NOTE**

> When you minimize a movie you are watching, it moves onto the Dock and continues to play.

You can cause a movie to loop so that it plays over and over again by selecting View, Loop or by pressing ⌘-L.



**NOTE**

> QuickTime movies can also be inserted into many types of documents, such as Word files, presentations, and so on. When you view such a file, you will see a "mini" QuickTime controller that enables you to watch the movie embedded in a particular document. Applications can add or remove controls to customize the interface you see in that application, but when you understand how to view movies with QuickTime Player, you won't have any trouble with these other controllers.

## Watching QuickTime Movies Stored on the Web

QuickTime is a major format for movies on the Web. Using the QuickTime plug-in, you can watch QuickTime movies from within a web browser, such as Safari. When you do so, you use controls that are similar to those in the QuickTime Player application.

One of the best places to view QuickTime movies is at Apple's Movie Trailer site. Here, you can view trailers for the latest creations from Hollywood.

**CAUTION**

> If you use a slow Internet connection, watching movies, such as the movie trailers on the Apple website, can be an exercise in patience. High-quality movie files are *big*. Watching them on the Web, even with the streaming feature and the MPEG-4 format, can take more time than it is worth. If you use a slow connection, try watching some movies to see whether you can tolerate the length of time it takes to download enough of the movie so you can begin watching it. If you can, great. If not, you might have to find smaller movies to watch or, even better, move up to a faster connection. You can also use the Instant-On preference to configure the delay before a movie begins to play.

To view some cool trailers online, do the following steps:

1. Go to www.apple.com/trailers.
2. Click a trailer to view it. What happens next depends on how the particular trailer has been created. Related to the previous caution, many of the trailers on the Apple site are offered in different versions, which are sized to be appropriate for various connection speeds. Usually, there are four choices: iPod (for downloading and placing on your iPod), small (for dial-up connections), medium (for DSL, slower cable, or ISDN connections), and large (for broadband connections). You might also be presented with an HD option to view a high-definition version of the trailer.
3. If a size option is presented, click the size your connection supports; if not, just click the "Click here to play movie" link. The movie will start to download. As soon as enough has been downloaded that the movie can play without interruption the rest of the way, it will begin. The movie will appear in a window that contains QuickTime controls you can use to watch the trailer (see Figure 24.6). Note that if you open an HD version, the QuickTime Player application will launch for you to watch the trailer.

24

**Figure 24.6**
This trailer, for *National Treasure: Book of Secrets*, is an example of how movie trailers can be viewed from the Web.

4. The movie begins to play as soon as enough has been downloaded to your Mac so the trailer plays continuously. If you use a fast connection and use the Instant-On feature, this happens quickly. If you use a slow connection or have configured a delay using the Instant-On slider, it can take longer. You can see how much of a movie has been downloaded by looking at the dark shaded part of the Timeline bar.

**TIP**

> You can start a movie at any time by pressing the spacebar. If you don't wait for the automatic start, the movie might stop before it finishes if it runs out of downloaded movie before it gets to the end.

5. Use the QuickTime controls listed in Table 24.1 to control playback.

*If you can only download a QuickTime movie from the Web rather than being able to view it, see "I Can't View QuickTime Movies on the Web" in the "Troubleshooting" section at the end of this chapter.*

**Table 24.1 QuickTime Controls for Web Movies**

| Control | Function |
|---|---|
| Volume | Click the volume button and a slider will pop up. Use the slider to set the volume level. |
| Play/Pause | Use this to play or pause the movie. The spacebar does the same thing. |
| Slider | Drag this to move to any point in the movie. |
| Step Backward/Step Forward | Moves back or ahead in the movie by one frame. |
| QuickTime controls | Pops up a menu of additional commands. |

Depending on how the movie is presented, you might not see the window shown in Figure 24.6. For example, some QuickTime content will play in the iTunes window. Others, especially those that offer full-screen versions, will provide a customized playback window or will play in QuickTime Player.

## Watching DVD Movies with DVD Player

DVDs are a great way to watch movies, TV shows, and other content. Because they are digital, the image and sound quality of DVD movies is superb (well, except for poorly produced ones that is). And the digital format enables special features that can't be duplicated with other means, such as videotape. For example, with DVD movies, you can get true 5-, 6-, or even 7-track soundtracks to provide unbelievable surround sound and sound fidelity. Plus, DVDs usually have a lot of features—missing scenes, trailers, and so on.

Mac OS X supports the playback of DVD movies with its DVD Player application. When you insert a DVD, your Mac automatically starts the DVD Player application. In most cases, DVD Player will enter into Full Screen mode and start playing your DVD. Moving your mouse to the top of the screen reveals the Image bar, along with the menu bar. Moving your mouse to the bottom of the screen reveals the Controller. Your movie plays in the Viewer, which is the main part of your screen.

24

**Figure 24.7**
With DVD Player, you can enjoy all the amazing content available on DVD.



**NOTE**

If you try to capture screenshots of a DVD using the Mac's built-in tools, such as the Grab application, you won't be allowed to or all you will get is a black screen. To capture DVD content in a screenshot, you need to use the excellent Snapz X Pro.

In Full Screen mode, the Mac OS interface disappears and you can see only the DVD content and the DVD windows you choose to display by moving the mouse to reveal them. If you need to resize the window so that you can have your movie running while you work on other things, move your mouse to the top of the screen to reveal the menu bar and use the View menu to change the window size. Your options include Half Size, Actual Size, Double Size, and Fit to Screen.

**NOTE**

When you view a movie at a size other than full screen, DVD Player will have a separate Viewer window, a Controller that you can move around to different locations on the screen, and the ability to open a window to see the chapters/bookmarks/video clips.

**NOTE**

To really enjoy DVD content, you should connect your Mac to a digital sound system.

⇨ To learn how to add digital sound to your Mac, **see** Chapter 33, "Working with Your Mac's Sound," **p. 801**.

The Controller contains the controls you use to watch movies (see Figure 24.8).

**Figure 24.8**
The Controller does just what you think: It enables you to control DVD playback.

The Player settings and Streams/Closed Captioning buttons provide additional control over what you hear and see from your DVD (see Figure 24.9). Clicking the Streams/Closed Captioning button presents you with a menu to select different languages, subtitles, closed captioning, and viewing angles.

If you have used a standard DVD player or VCR, the DVD Player controls will be easy to understand. To play and control a movie, use the following steps:

1. Insert the DVD into your Mac's DVD drive. After a moment, the DVD is mounted on the machine. By default, DVD Player opens and begins to play the DVD. Depending on the DVD, the disc's main menu might appear or you might be prompted to select a soundtrack or other features.

*If you see a message about the DVD's region code, see "When I Play a Movie, I See a Message About the Region Code Needing to Be Set" in the "Troubleshooting" section at the end of this chapter.*

**TIP**

> To configure what action your Mac takes when you insert a DVD, use the CDs & DVDs pane of the System Preferences application.

**Figure 24.9**
You can modify your DVD viewing experience with these tools on the Controller.

2. Select the menu option you want, such as Play Movie, by clicking it. You can also use the arrow keys to move among the menu options and then press Return to select an option. The movie begins to play in the Viewer. When you activate a control, the upper-left corner of the Viewer briefly displays an icon or text describing the control you used most recently (such as Play).

**TIP**

> Click in the Disc information section on the Controller to cycle through the available data, such as chapter, remaining time, and so on. Click the title or chapter text to change the display to the related information.

3. Use the commands on the View menu to control the size of the Viewer.
4. To bring the Controller back, move the pointer, press a key, or press Option-⌘-C.

**NOTE**

> If you're running a fairly powerful Mac and you minimize the Viewer, it moves into the Dock and the movie continues to play. Be sure to take a look at the DVD Player preferences and uncheck the Pause Playback option when the viewer is minimized.

5. If you move the pointer to the bottom of the screen, the Controller will appear and display the Timeline bar. At the left end, you see the current position of the Playhead, whereas at the right end you see the time remaining. You can drag the Playhead to move to a different position in the movie.

*If you see the* `NOT PERMITTED` *message when you use a control, see "An Action I Try Isn't Permitted" in the "Troubleshooting" section at the end of this chapter.*

*If you see a green screen when you attempt to view a disc, see "When I View a DVD, I See a Green Screen" in the "Troubleshooting" section at the end of this chapter.*

6. Use any of the controls on the Player settings button on the Controller to modify how the DVD Player application displays your movie. You can modify the video zoom and color, as well as display an audio equalizer using the small triangle at the top right corner of the Player Settings window.

**TIP**

You can also control a movie by selecting onscreen controls with the mouse.

Following are some other DVD playback notes:

- **DVD menus**—All DVD movies include a menu that provides access to the content of the disc and its special features. You can highlight and select commands on these menus by using the keyboard's arrow buttons, using the mouse to point to them, or using the mouse to point to them on the Controller. You can move back to the most recent menu you viewed by clicking the menu button on the Controller; selecting Go, DVD Menu; or pressing ⌘-D. Depending on how the DVD is structured, clicking the title button might take you to the same place or it might move you to the DVD's main menu.

**TIP**

When you move to a menu and then back to the DVD, you will move back to same spot at which you were viewing the DVD when you selected the menu command.

- **Use the Controller to quickly change the movie's settings**—For example, you can control subtitles, closed captioning, and select different angles (when available) from the Streams/Closed Captioning button.
- **Scan forward or backward**—When you scan forward or backward, you can control the rate of the scan by selecting Controls, Scan Rate, and then the rate at which you want to scan (such as 8x speed). DVD Player supports scan rates up to 32x, which is really flying. The scan rate you select controls both forward and backward scanning.
- **Go menu**—Many commands are available on this menu that you can use to quickly access various areas on the DVD, including the DVD menu, the beginning of the disc, the content you were viewing the last time you played the disc, bookmarks, titles, chapters, and so on.
- **Bookmarks**—You can use this feature to mark specific areas of a DVD so you can quickly return to them. When viewing content to which you want to add a bookmark, select Controls, New Bookmark. In the New Bookmark sheet, name the bookmark and click Add. You can return to that bookmark by selecting Go, Bookmarks, *Bookmarkname*, where *Bookmarkname* is the name of a bookmark you have created.

You can also jump to a bookmark by selecting it on the Bookmark menu on the Image bar or by using the Bookmarks window. (You learn more about bookmarks later in this chapter.)

- **Chapters**—Most DVD content is organized by chapter. Moving your mouse to the top of the screen will reveal the Image bar; click the icon of a book to see the chapters on your DVD. Choose Go, Chapter Number to jump to a chapter. You can also choose Window, Chapters (⌘-B) to move into the Chapters window on which you can click a chapter's thumbnail to jump to it.

**TIP**

> If thumbnails don't appear for the chapters, open the Action pop-up menu and choose Generate Missing Thumbnails.

- **Keyboard commands work best**—As you watch movies, you will find that the best way to control them is using the keyboard. Most of the major functions in the Player have keyboard shortcuts. For the best DVD experience, learn to use these shortcuts.

⇨ To learn about bookmarks, **see** "Working with Bookmarks," **p. 625**.

⇨ To learn the many keyboard shortcuts for playback and configuration DVD Player offers, **see** "DVD Player Keyboard Shortcuts," **p. 637**.

## Configuring DVD Player

DVD Player is a relatively simple application, but you can do some configuration to make it work the way you want it to. The DVD Player preferences window has six panes: Player, Disc Setup, Full Screen, Windows, Previously Viewed, and High Definition. These preference settings are summarized in Table 24.1.

**NOTE**

> You can't control a movie while the Preferences dialog box is open.

**Table 24.1 DVD Player Preferences**

| Pane | Preference | Effect |
|---|---|---|
| Player | When DVD Player opens: Enter Full Screen mode | These preferences determine which action DVD Player takes when it opens. Because it is typically in the Full Screen mode when you watch a movie, this preference selects the Full Screen mode automatically when a DVD is mounted on your desktop and DVD Player starts (which it does by default when a DVD containing movie content is mounted on your Mac). |
| Player | When DVD Player opens: Start playing disc | If you want discs to start playing when DVD Player opens, make sure the "Start playing disc" check box is checked. |

| Pane | Preference | Effect |
|---|---|---|
| Player | When DVD Player is inactive: Pause Playback | When enabled, this preference pauses DVD playback when you move out of DVD Player. |
| Player | When a disc is inserted: Start playing disc | With this enabled, a DVD starts to play when you insert it into your Mac. |
| Player | When muted: Show Closed Captioning | When enabled and you mute DVD Player, closed captioning will automatically be turned on. |
| Player | During iChat with audio: Mute audio or Pause playback | Use these radio buttons to determine which action DVD Player takes when you enter a chat session. You can have DVD Player either mute its audio or pause the playback of the DVD. |
| Player | When viewer is minimized: Pause playback | If you select this preference, when you minimize the viewer (and it moves onto the Dock), the pause function is selected automatically. This is handy when you need to move DVD Player out of the way to do something else (such as when your editor calls and you need to act like you are working). When you return to the DVD Player window, you can start viewing at the same point you left off. |
| Disc Setup | Language: Audio | Use this pop-up menu to choose the default audio track for discs you play. If you choose "Use Disc Default," DVD Player will start with the default audio track for the disc. If you choose a language, it will try to start with that instead. |
| Disc Setup | Language: Subtitle | Use this pop-up menu to set the default Subtitle options. |
| Disc Setup | Language: DVD menu | This option sets the default menu language for discs you view. |
| Disc Setup | Internet: Enable DVD@ccess web links | Many DVDs offer content on the Web. Use this preference to enable or disable links on DVDs you view. |
| Disc Setup | Audio output: | Use this pop-up menu to choose the output sound source for DVD playback. If you have only one sound option, your only choice is System Sound Output. If you have more than one option, you can choose the sound output you want to use on this menu. |
| Disc Setup | Disable Dolby dynamic range compression | If your Mac supports digital audio out, use the pop-up menu to select Digital Out to take advantage of that output, such as 5.1 digital surround sound. Use the check box to determine whether dynamic range compression is used (this evens out the volume level of a disc). |

*continues*

**Table 24.1 Continued**

| Pane | Preference | Effect |
|---|---|---|
| Full Screen | Hide controller if inactive for x seconds | Use this to control the automatic hiding of the separate Controller window when you aren't using it. By default, the Controller window is hidden after 10 seconds. You can change this time or turn off the feature if you want to manually hide and show the Controller window. |
| Full Screen | Dim other displays while playing | If you have more than one monitor connected to your Mac, this preference causes all of them except the one on which the DVD is being shown to go black while you are playing a DVD. |
| Full Screen | Remain in full screen when DVD Player is inactive | If you want DVD Player to remain in Full Screen mode whenever it is inactive, check this box. By default, DVD Player switches to Maximum Size mode when you move to the Finder or another application. With this preference active, it remains in Full Screen mode instead. |
| Full Screen | Use Current video size in full screen | With this checked, the size of the video content is not maximized when you move to full screen, but remains at its current size. Use this when you are viewing low resolution content whose quality looks poor at large sizes. |
| Full Screen | Kiosk Mode (disable menu bar) | Check this check box if you want to disable the DVD Player menu bar. |
| Full Screen | Allow Screensaver on DVD menu in kiosk mode | When you enable this preference, you are operating in kiosk mode, and the disc is playing on a menu screen, your Mac's screen saver will activate. This prevents a static image on the DVD menu from appearing on your display for a long time (possibly damaging the display). |
| Windows | Display status information | The status information appears at the top of the and provides information about what is happening, such as when you click a control. Uncheck the "Display status information" check box to hide this information. |
| Windows | Fade controller when hiding | To have the Controller window fade slowly out of existence when it hides, check this box. With it unchecked, the Controller blinks out of existence. (Your Mac must support Quartz Extreme for this to happen.) |

| Pane | Preference | Effect |
|---|---|---|
| Windows | Closed Captioned, Text | Use this button to set the color of text used when closed captioning is displayed. |
| Windows | Closed Captioned, Background | Use this button to set the color of the background over which closed captioning text is displayed. |
| Windows | Closed Captioned, Transparency slider | Use this slider to set the transparency of the closed captioned text box. |
| Windows | Closed Captioned, Font | Use the Font pop-up menu to choose the font for closed caption text. |
| Windows | Closed Captioned, Font size for separate window | Use this box to enter the font size when closed captioned text appears in a separate window. |
| Previously Viewed | Start playing discs from: Beginning, Last position played, Default bookmark, or Always ask | Choose the radio button to select the location from which you want discs to start playing. For example, if you choose "Last position played," a disc will start playing at the same point you stopped playing the last time you viewed it. |
| Previously Viewed | Always use disc settings for: Audio EQ, Video Color, or Video Zoom | DVD Player includes tools you can use to adjust the audio, video color, and zoom settings for a disc. If you want DVD Player to use disc settings for these, check the appropriate box for the setting you want to always use from the disc. If you uncheck a box, you can configure the related setting manually (you learn how later in this chapter). |
| High Definition | For Standard Definition: Actual video size or Disc default | Use these radio buttons to determine how DVD Player handles discs in the standard definition format. Choose Disc Default to have DVD use the disc's default size or Actual video size to use the current size of the Viewer. |
| Higher Defintion | For High Definition: Actual video size, 720 height, 1080 height | When you view an HD disc, this setting determines how the Viewer window is sized. Choose the size you want to be the default, such as 720 height if you always want HD content to be displayed in a Viewer with 720 pixels in height. |

24

**TIP**

If you watch a TV series on DVD and choose the "play from last position played" preference, it can be somewhat confusing for you because when you insert a new disc, DVD Player will sometimes resume playing from a point that you haven't viewed previously. This happens because the markers on the discs for different episodes during the same season might be the same. Thus, DVD Player can't tell the difference between discs within the same season or series and moves to the same spot on the new disc that you left off on the previous one. If this happens, just select Go, DVD Menu to move to the disc's menu. Then you can choose which part you want to view.

24

**CAUTION**

> Many DVDs that claim to offer DVD-ROM or web content are not compatible with the Mac. However, you can often open these DVDs via the Finder to access some of this additional content.

## Working with Disc Info

You can use the Disc Info window to rename a disc and set an image to display in the Viewer window when the disc isn't playing, such as an image from the DVD. Here's how:

1. Insert the DVD you want to work with.
2. Move to the frame in the DVD that you want to display when the DVD is stopped—this image will be shown instead of a black Viewer window.
3. Select File, Get Disc Info. The Disc Info window will appear. This window has four panes. The Info pane provides detailed information about the disc including its audio and video formats, media type, and so on.
4. To rename a disc, type the name of the disc in the Title box. This doesn't actually change the disc, but Mac OS X will substitute the name you enter for the disc's name when it appears at the top of the separate Viewer window. Because discs are often named according to filename limitations, it's often better to have DVD Player use a more meaningful name.
5. Click Jacket Picture. The image that appears in the image well is the image that will be shown on the screen when you stop playback. In most cases, this is the image from the DVD's case. However, you can set this to be the frame at which you are currently located by clicking Current Frame. You can also choose a different graphic by clicking Choose and selecting the graphic you want to use instead (see Figure 24.10). You can return the image to the disc jacket's image by clicking Disc Jacket Picture.

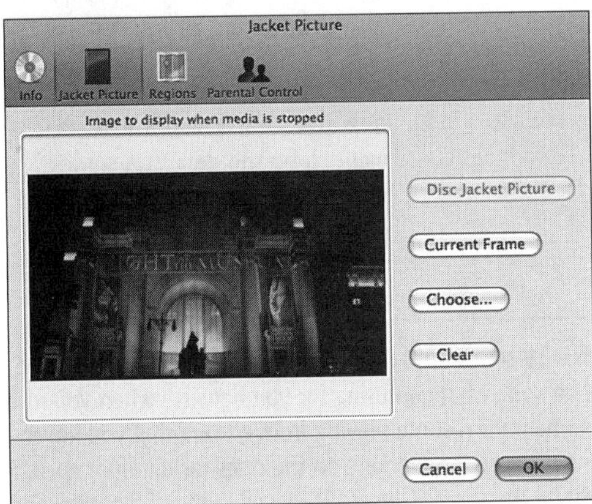


**Figure 24.10**
When this disc is stopped, the image shown in the image well will be displayed in the Viewer.

6. Click the Regions icon to open the Regions pane. All DVDs are encoded with specific geographic regions. Likewise, all DVD players are encoded with a region. In order for a disc to be played, the player and disc's region must be the same. On the Regions tab, you see the disc's region and the drive's region. When you insert a disc from a different region, you'll be prompted to change the region setting for the drive to match so that you can play the disc. However, this can be done only 4 times so you should be sure you want to change the drive's region setting because once you've hit the limit, you won't be able to change it again and you'll only be able to play discs from that region from that point on. At the bottom of the Regions pane, you see how many region changes you have left.
7. Click the Parental Control icon to open that pane. When you've enabled Parental Controls for a user account, you can use the controls on this pane to determine what happens when the disc is inserted. For example, you can require authorization before the disc will be able to be played.
8. Click OK. The Disc Info window closes and any changes you made are saved. All your settings are remembered for the specific disc. For example, the name you gave the disc will be the title of the Viewer window. When you stop the disc, the image you selected will be shown in the Viewer.



## USING CLOSED CAPTIONING

Closed captioning presents text on the screen for the speaking parts and some sound effect portions of a disc's soundtrack. You can control closed captioning for a disc using the following pointers:

- Turn on closed captioning by selecting Features, Closed Captioning, Turn On. You can also press Option-⌘-T or you can select Streams/Closed Captioning from the Controller when viewing your DVD in Full Screen mode.
- To have the closed captioning appear in a window separate from the Viewer, select Features, Closed Captioning, Separate Window. (Remember that you can configure this window using preferences you learned about earlier in this chapter.) When you play this disc, the closed captioning will appear in a window called Closed Caption.
- Turn off closed captioning by selecting Features, Closed Captioning, Turn Off. You can also press Option-⌘-T.

**NOTE**

> If you have closed captioning displayed in a separate window, when you close the Closed Caption window, the closed captioning will move back into the Viewer window.

## WORKING WITH BOOKMARKS

Bookmarks enable you to set locations within a disc and move back to them easily. Bookmarks work just like chapters on a disc, except that you set them rather than the disc's producer.

### Setting Bookmarks

To set a bookmark, perform the following steps:

1. Move to the point at which you want to set a bookmark.
2. Select Controls, New Bookmark or press ⌘-=. The disc will be paused and the New Bookmark sheet will appear.
3. Name the bookmark. You can name the bookmark almost anything you want.
4. If you want the bookmark to be the default for the disc, check the "Make Default Bookmark" check box.
5. Click Add. The bookmark will be added for the disc.

### Using Bookmarks

There are a number of ways to work with the bookmarks you create, including the following:

- To jump to a bookmark, select Go, Bookmarks, *bookmarkname*, where *bookmarkname* is the name of a bookmark you have created. You'll move to the bookmarked frame and the disc will play from there (if it was playing when you selected the bookmark).
- When viewing a DVD in Full Screen mode, move your mouse to the top of the screen to reveal the Image bar. Click the icon at the left end of the Image bar that looks like a bookmark; the Image bar will display the bookmarks you have created for the movie.
- Select Window, Bookmarks. The Bookmarks window will open (see Figure 24.11). Here, you'll see a list of all the bookmarks you have set for a disc.

**Figure 24.11**
You can use the Bookmarks window to work with a disc's bookmarks.

- Double-click a bookmark in the window to jump to it.
- Click the Add button (+) to add a new bookmark.
- Select a bookmark and click the Delete button (-) to delete it.
- Open the Action menu and select Show Thumbnails. A thumbnail will be shown for each bookmark.
- Select a bookmark and open the Action menu. Select Rename and then rename the bookmark, or select Delete to delete it.
- If you make a bookmark the default, you can use the Default bookmark preference to have the disc always start playing from the bookmark each time you view it.

## Working with Video Clips

You can mark video clips from DVDs you view and watch them. For example, there might be scenes you love to watch over and over. You can mark these segments as video clips and then easily view them anytime you want.

24

**NOTE**

The term *video clip* is a bit misleading. You aren't actually creating a clip. Instead, you are marking a portion of the DVD as a clip so that you can watch that clip easily. It isn't really a clip, which implies that you are saving the clip as a QuickTime movie or some other object that you could use in another application.

### Capturing a Video Clip

To create a video clip, perform the following steps:

1. Move to the point at which you want the video clip to start.
2. Select Controls, New Video Clip or press ⌘--. The New Video Clip sheet appears, and the start time is set to the current location (see Figure 24.12).

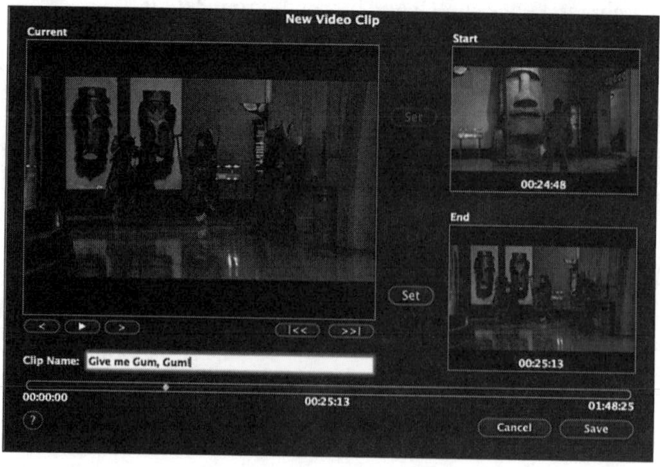


**Figure 24.12**
Using the New Video Clip sheet, you can create custom video clips for a disc.

3. Use the playback controls or Playhead to move the point at which you want the video clip to end.

**TIP** You can use the same steps to set the starting point of the clip as well. The default start is set to be the current frame.

4. Click the Set button next to the End preview window. The endpoint of the clip is set.
5. Name the clip.
6. Click Save. The sheet closes and the clip is saved.

24

### Working with Video Clips

There are a number of ways to work with video clips you create, including the following:

- To jump to a video clip, select Go, Video Clips, *videoclipname*, where *videoclipname* is the name of a video clip you have created. The clip will play; when it starts, you will see its name in the upper-left corner of the window. When the clip is done, it will stop playing and you'll see the complete message.
- To exit Clip mode, select Go, Video Clips, Exit Clip Mode.
- To repeat a clip, select Go, Video Clips, Repeat Clip.
- When viewing a DVD in Full Screen mode, move your mouse to the top of the screen to reveal the Image bar. Click the icon at the left end of the Image bar that looks like a film strip; the Image bar will display the video clips you have created for the movie.
- Select Window, Video Clips. The Video Clips window opens. In this window, you'll see the video clips you have created for a disc.
- Double-click a video clip in the window to play it.
- Click the Add button (+) to add a new clip.
- Select a clip and click the Delete button (-) to delete it.
- Open the Action menu and select Show Thumbnails. A thumbnail will be shown for each clip.
- Select a clip and open the Action menu. Select Rename and then rename the bookmark, or select Delete to delete it. Select Exit Clip Mode to move back to regular playing mode or Repeat Clip to repeat the video clip.

## Using the DVD Player Timer

The Timer feature will cause a specific action to be performed when an event happens. For example, if you tend to fall asleep watching DVDs, you can configure the Timer to put your Mac to sleep at a specific time.

To configure the Timer, do the following:

1. Start playing a DVD.
2. Select Controls, Timer, Set Timer or press ⌘-T. The Timer sheet appears.
3. Choose the action you want to be performed on the Action pop-up menu. The options are Quit DVD Player, Sleep, Shut Down, and Log Out.
4. Use the radio buttons to set when the action you selected will happen. The options are in a specific amount of time or when the DVD ends.
5. Click OK. You return to the Viewer and the Timer On message is displayed briefly. When the time you specified occurs, the action you selected will be done.

Following are a few other Timer tricks:

- Select Controls, Timer, Display Timer to cause the current time remaining and action to be performed to appear on the screen. They disappear again after a few seconds.
- Select Controls, Timer, Pause to pause the timer.
- Select Controls, Timer, Cancel Timer or press Option-⌘-. to stop the timer.



## Setting Custom Playback Size

You can customize the size of the video shown in the Viewer window by using the Video Zoom controls.

**NOTE**

> Some discs prevent you from resizing video. If this is the case, you will get the `NOT PERMITTED` message when you try to use the Video Zoom function.

1. Select Window, Video Zoom. The Video Zoom window appears (see Figure 24.13).

**NOTE**

> Using the Video Zoom tool changes the size of the video being displayed in the Viewer window, not the size of the Viewer window itself. To change the size of the Viewer, use the commands on the Video menu.

2. Check the On check box to turn on the Video Zoom.
3. Use the sliders to set the width and height of the video.
4. If you want to maintain the video's aspect ration, check the "Lock Aspect Ratio" check box. When you move one slider, the other will also move to keep the same proportion between the two dimensions.

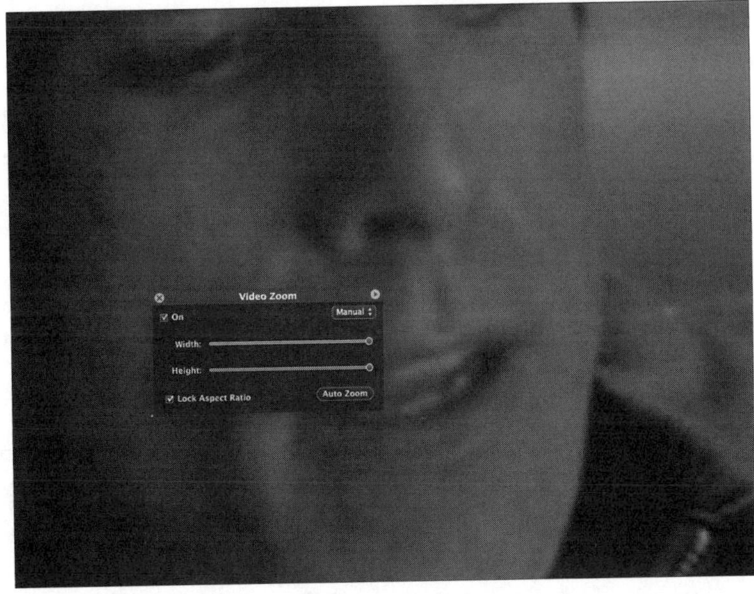


**Figure 24.13**
You can use the Video Zoom controls to set the size of the video being displayed relative to the size of the Viewer.



**TIP**

> Open the pop-up menu located in the upper-right corner of the window for additional options, such as presets including Standard Display – Widescreen Movie. You can also create your own presets.

## CONTROLLING A DISC'S COLOR

Similar to the Video Zoom tool, you can use the Video Color tool to customize the color settings of a disc. Do the following:

1. Select Window, Video Color. The Video Color window appears.
2. Check the On check box to turn on the tool.

**NOTE**

> Some DVDs prevent any sort of adjustment, in which case you'll see the `NOT PERMITTED` message when you attempt to do something that isn't allowed.

3. Use the sliders to adjust the images you see.

**TIP**

> Explore the pop-up menu located in the upper-right corner of the Video Color window to work with presets or return a disc's settings to the default values (called the Normal setting).

### Configuring DVD Player Audio

DVD Player also includes a built-in graphic equalizer so you can customize audio playback for your DVDs and sound system. Here's how:

1. Select Window, Audio Equalizer. The Audio Equalizer window appears.
2. Turn it on by clicking the On check box.
3. Use the sliders to set the relative volume levels of various frequencies.

TIP

> Just like the Video Zoom and Video Color tools, you can use the Audio Equalizer's pop-up menu to work with presets. Also, you can open any of these tools from the same window by selecting the tool with which you want to work from the pop-up menu in the window's title bar.



## Sitting on the Front Row

Front Row is Mac OS X's "remote control" application. The idea is that you might want to control music, DVDs, and other content from a distance, such as when your Mac is on the other side of the room. All Macs except the Mac Pro ship with the Apple Remote that you use with Front Row to control specific content on your Mac from afar. The default content you can play with Front Row is

- **DVDs**—Using this option, you can view DVD content and control it using the remote. You don't have as many options as you do with DVD Player, but for long distance viewing, it's easier to use than is DVD Player.
- **Movies**—This option enables you to access movie trailers from the Apple Trailers website.
- **TV Shows**—If you have purchased any episodes or full seasons of TV shows from the iTunes Store, those shows are available with this option.
- **Music**—This option gets you to audio content in your iTunes Library.
- **Podcasts**—Selecting this option provides easy access to podcasts that you have subscribed to within iTunes.
- **Photos**—Use this to view photos and slideshows in your iPhoto Library.
- **Settings**—The Settings option allows you to configure the use of sound effects, as well as specify whether a screen saver should turn on if your Mac has been inactive while in Front Row.
- **Sources**—If your Mac is on a network with other Macs that are sharing their iTunes and iPhoto Libraries, you can select one of those other Macs as the source for the content you see in Front Row.

Using Front Row is straightforward. The basic steps follow:

1. Press the Menu button on the remote. The Front Row menu takes over the Mac's screen (see Figure 24.14).

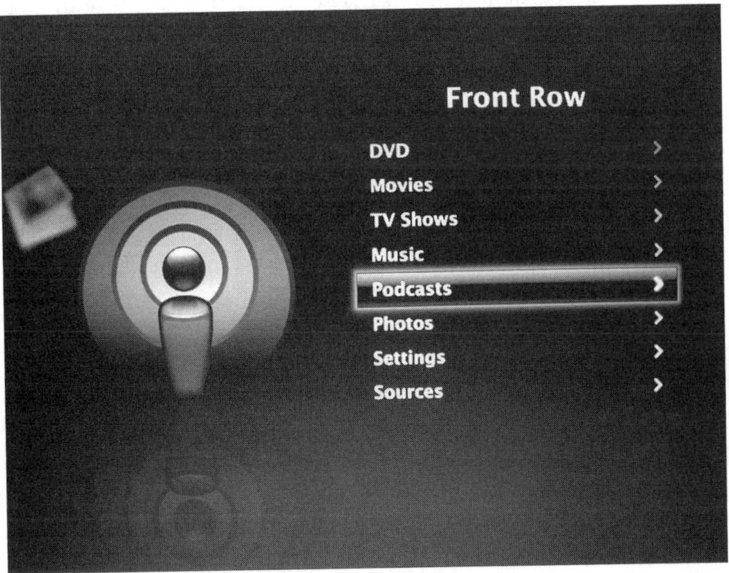


**Figure 24.14**
Front Row enables you to enjoy digital entertainment on your Mac from a distance.



2. Use the remote's control wheel to select the type of content you want. Each time you press the Rewind or Fast Forward button, the options rotate around the screen. When the one you want is front and center, press the Play button. A menu for that type of content will appear (see Figure 24.15).

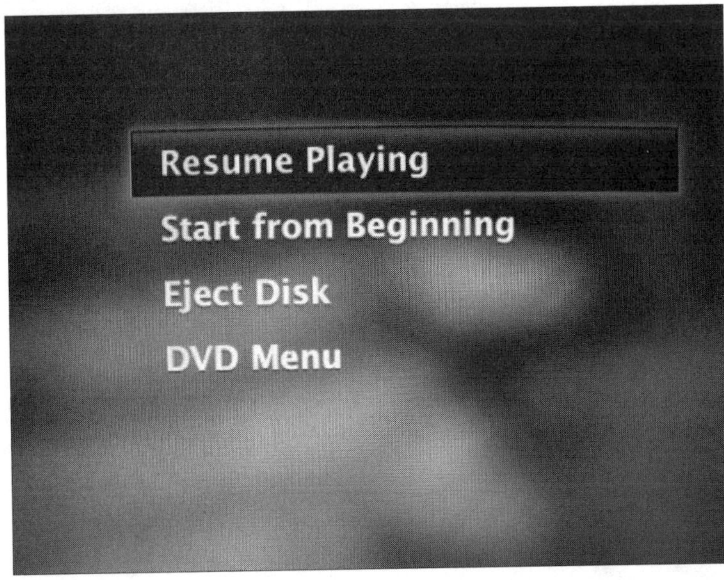


**Figure 24.15**
Viewing DVDs with Front Row is even simpler than with DVD Player.

**TIP**

> You can also control Front Row using your keyboard. Because Front Row is an application, you can also put it on your Dock to easily launch.

3. Use the remote's buttons to move up and down the menu; when the command you want is highlighted, press the Play button.
4. Continue moving into the menu until you select the content you want to play.
5. Play the content; what you see depends, of course, on the type of content you are playing.

**NOTE**

> Front Row displays content only on your Mac's primary display.

6. Use the remote to control the content. For example, to move back to the previous menu, press the Menu button.
7. When you're done with Front Row, press the Menu button until Front Row yields control of your Mac back to you.



## Taking Photos in the Photo Booth

Photo Booth is a simple application whose purpose is to enable you to capture photos and GIF animiations using an iSight camera, such as those built-in to iMacs and mobile Macs. It's sort of a one-trick pony, but it can be useful occasionally and just might be fun if you like to play around with its effects. If you have an iSight camera connected to your Mac, you can use Photo Booth as the following steps reveal:

1. Launch Photo Booth. The top pane of the window shows the image currently being captured. In the bottom pane, you see images and GIF animimations that have already been captured.
2. To spice up the image with effects, click the Effects button. The top pane will be replaced with the many effects that Photo Booth offers. You see previews of the current image with the effects applied. Page through the available effects until you find the one you want; select it and you return to the Photo Booth window, which shows the modified image (see Figure 24.16).
3. Click the Capture button (the red circle with a camera icon). A countdown will appear below the image preview. This gives you time to make the image what you want it to be. When the countdown ends, the image is captured and added to the captured image collection at the bottom of the Photo Booth window.

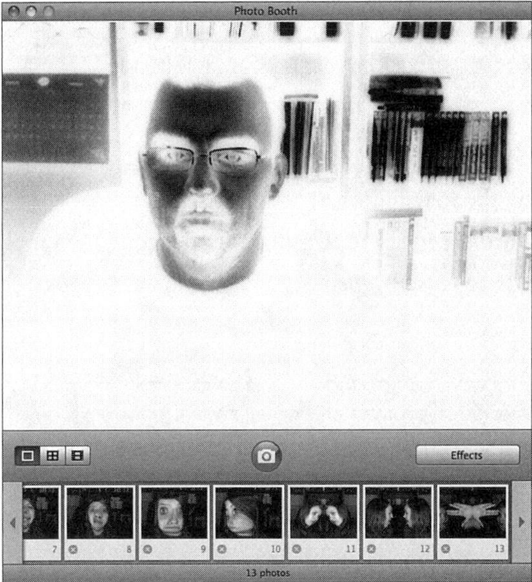


**Figure 24.16**
I kind of like the X-Ray effect myself.



Here are some other things you can do with Photo Booth:

- To capture a series of images and create a 4-up image of the shot, click the "Take four quick pictures" button to the left of the Capture button. Click the Capture button for Photo Booth to enter Burst mode. You will have a countdown, then the photo is taken, and then you go into another countdown. A total of four photos are taken, and then put into a single image with all four images displayed.
- To create a short movie clip, click the "Take movie clip" button. The Capture button now looks more like a video camera; when you click it you will get a countdown, and then a timer appears to the left. In place of the Capture button you will now see a Stop button. Click the Stop button when you are done recording your movie clip.
- After you have captured your images and video, they appear in the bottom pane of the window. To view an image, select it and it fills the preview window.
- Scroll through the captured images using the scroll arrows.
- To delete an image, click its Delete button (the "x").
- Flip a photo around a verical axis by selecting it and choosing Edit, Flip Photo.
- After you've selected an image, you can email it by clicking the Email button, save it to your iPhoto Library by clicking iPhoto, make it the account picture for the current account by clicking Account Picture, or make it your chat picture by clicking Buddy Picture.
- Print a proof sheet of the photo or photos that you have selected. Expand the print dialog box so that you can see the Photo Booth settings and select the style of proof sheet that you want to print.

# Troubleshooting

### My Attempt to Upgrade to QuickTime Pro Failed

*When I entered my QuickTime Pro registration information, I saw an error dialog box stating that the registration information is not correct. Or, it appeared to work, but when I returned to the Registration sheet, the* PRO *commands were still disabled and no registration information appeared in the sheet.*

The QuickTime Pro registration code is tied to the name you used when you obtained it. You must enter this name exactly as you used it; otherwise, the registration code will not be accepted. Also, double-check the registration code you entered. These codes are long and complex, so it is easy to make a mistake. The code and name are case sensitive, so be sure you enter them exactly as shown in the information you receive from Apple.

### I Can't View QuickTime Movies on the Web

*When I attempt to view a QuickTime movie on the Web, I'm unable to do so and am forced to download the file to my Mac instead.*

This happens if the QuickTime plug-in has been moved or damaged. To reinstall the plug-in, you need to update QuickTime. When the updater runs, it will reinstall the plug-in in the appropriate location and you will be able to use it with your web browser. To update QuickTime, choose Apple menu, Software Update. The appropriate files will be downloaded and installed on your Mac. Restart your Mac and you should be able to view QuickTime movies on the Web.

### When I Play a Movie, I See a Message About the Region Code Needing to Be Set

*When I try to play a DVD movie, I get a message about region codes.*

All DVD movies contain a code so they play in only one of six regions in the world. This ensures that the format is supported by the display systems in that part of the world and also helps with piracy issues.

If you try to play a movie that has a code other than the one with which your player is set, you will see a dialog box enabling you to change the code for your player (in this case, the DVD drive in your Mac). If you choose to change the code, your DVD drive's code is changed. However, you can make this change only four times. At that point, the drive's code becomes permanent. I don't recommend that you change your drive's region code unless you are sure that most of the DVDs you will play in the future will have that code. If a code different from most of your movies becomes permanently set for your drive, you will be able to play only movies with that region code.

### An Action I Try Isn't Permitted

*When I try to use a control, a* `NOT PERMITTED` *message appears onscreen.*

The controls for a DVD movie can be activated only at specific times. For example, sometimes you can't scan forward through the warnings at the beginning of every DVD. The only solution is to wait until you are able to use the control.

### WHEN I VIEW A DVD, I SEE A GREEN SCREEN

*When I try to view a DVD, all I see is a green screen.*

This can happen for two reasons. One is that you are viewing a disc in the wrong region; the other is that DVD Player sometimes suffers from an occasional glitch. Try resizing the Viewer window with one of the commands on the Video menu. Most of the time, this clears any temporary problems DVD Player is having. If this doesn't work, the region code is the likely culprit. Or, the DVD drive in your Mac might be failing. Try another disc to see whether that is the case.

## MAC OS X TO THE MAX: GOING FURTHER WITH DIGITAL ENTERTAINMENT TOOLS

Learn to use keyboard shortcuts in QuickTime Player and DVD Player to use these applications efficiently and easily.

### USING QUICKTIME PLAYER KEYBOARD SHORTCUTS

Some useful QuickTime Player keyboard shortcuts are shown in Table 24.2.

**TABLE 24.2 KEYBOARD SHORTCUTS FOR QUICKTIME PLAYER**

| Menu | Action | Keyboard Shortcut |
|---|---|---|
| File | Close Player window | ⌘-W |
| File | Open URL | ⌘-U |
| File | New Player | ⌘-N |
| None | Move Playhead backward one frame | Left arrow |
| None | Move Playhead forward one frame | Right arrow |
| None | Pause movie (movie playing) | Spacebar or Return |
| None | Play movie (movie paused) | Spacebar or Return |
| None | Turn down volume | Down arrow |
| None | Turn up volume | Up arrow |
| None | Turn volume to maximum | Shift-Option-up arrow |
| None | Turn volume to minimum | Shift-Option-down arrow |
| View | Loop | ⌘-L |
| View | Play movie at half size | ⌘-0 |
| View | Play movie at actual size | ⌘-1 |
| View | Play movie at double size | ⌘-2 |
| View | Play movie and fit to screen | ⌘-3 |
| View | Play movie at full screen | ⌘-F |

| Menu | Action | Keyboard Shortcut |
|---|---|---|
| Window | Add movie as favorite | ⌘-D |
| Window | Show A/V controls | ⌘-K |
| Window | Show Movie Inspector | ⌘-I |

## DVD PLAYER KEYBOARD SHORTCUTS

Table 24.3 contains keyboard shortcuts for DVD Player.

**TABLE 24.3 KEYBOARD SHORTCUTS FOR DVD PLAYER**

| Menu | Action | Keyboard Shortcut |
|---|---|---|
| | Highlight DVD menu options | Up, down, left, right arrows<br>Tab; Shift-Tab |
| | Select DVD menu options | Return |
| Controls | Scan Backward | Shift-⌘-left arrow |
| Controls | Scan Forward | Shift-⌘-right arrow |
| Controls | Close/Open Control Drawer | ⌘-] |
| Controls | Closed Captioning, Turn On/Off | Option-⌘-T |
| Controls | Eject DVD | ⌘-E |
| Controls | Mute | Option-⌘-down arrow |
| Controls | New Bookmark | ⌘-= |
| Controls | New Video Clip | ⌘-- |
| Controls | Play/Pause | Spacebar |
| Controls | Stop | ⌘-. |
| Controls | Timer, Cancel Timer | Option-⌘-. |
| Controls | Timer, Set Timer | ⌘-T |
| Controls | Volume Down | ⌘-down arrow |
| Controls | Volume Up | ⌘-up arrow |
| DVD Player | Preferences | ⌘-, |
| File | Get Disc Info | ⌘-I |
| Go | DVD Menu | ⌘-D |
| Go | Next Chapter | Right arrow |
| Go | Beginning of Disc | Shift-⌘-D |
| Go | Previous Chapter | Left arrow |

*continues*

TABLE 24.3 CONTINUED

| Menu | Action | Keyboard Shortcut |
|---|---|---|
| Go | Switch to Finder | Option-⌘-F |
| Video | Enter/Exit Full Screen | ⌘-F |
| Video | Half Size | ⌘-0 |
| Video | Actual Size | ⌘-1 |
| Video | Double Size | ⌘-2 |
| Video | Fit to Screen | ⌘-3 |
| Window | Show/Hide Controller | Option-⌘-C |

24

TIP

When scanning, each time you press the related key combination, the scan rate increases by one increment. If you use the Controller's scan buttons, the scan is performed at the speed selected on the Scan Rate command on the Controls menu.

# CHAPTER 25

# Tracking Your Contacts with Address Book

## In this chapter

# Using Address Book

Mac OS X includes the Address Book application, in which you can store all the information about your contacts. The most obvious use for this information is within Mail for addressing email you send, but other applications can access the Address Book as well. This is useful because it enables you to use a single contact database for other applications that use information about your contacts, such as iChat. You can store as much information as you want, and you can customize each entry in the Address Book as much as you like. You can also print Address Book information in a number of ways.

**TIP**

> If you enter a website address for a contact, you can access that website from within Safari's Address Book bookmarks. You'll learn more about this in Chapter 22, "Surfing the Web with Safari."

Address Book is based on *virtual cards*, or *vCards*. A vCard is an electronic information card that you can drag and drop between applications to transfer the information contained on that card. You can also share vCards with other users to exchange information. For example, you can drag someone else's vCard onto your Address Book to quickly add that person's information to your contacts.

25

**TIP**

> Address Book is not the only application that can work with vCards. Many other applications can use vCards. For example, Microsoft Entourage can read vCards, so you can provide your vCard to someone who uses that application and that person can easily add your contact information to her contact database. Microsoft Outlook, the dominant email, calendar, and contact information application on Windows computers, also uses vCards.

## Exploring Address Book

When you open Address Book, you will see that its window consists of three columns. The first two columns are Group and Name. The Group column shows the groups you have created, and the Name column lists each card in your Address Book. The third column is the Card column, which shows the card that is selected in the Name column (see Figure 25.1). Before you add any contact information, your Address Book includes a card for you and one for Apple. You can build your Address Book over time so that it includes all your contacts.

**NOTE**

> The contact information entered for you is whatever you provided when you registered your copy of Mac OS X. If you entered a username and password for an Apple ID account when you installed Mac OS X, your contact information is retrieved from your Apple account as well.

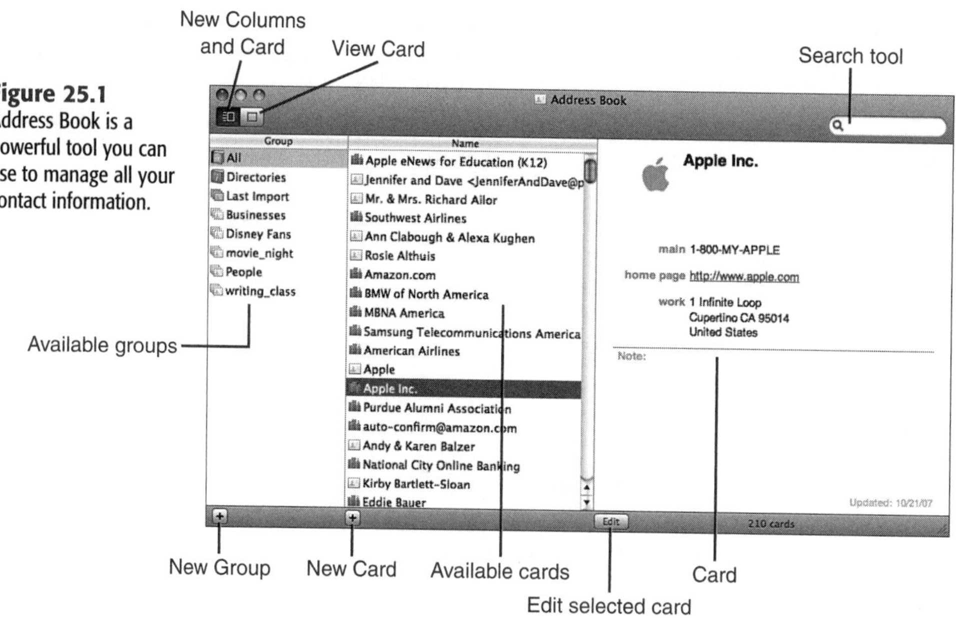


**Figure 25.1**
Address Book is a powerful tool you can use to manage all your contact information.

Just above the Group column are buttons you can use to control the look and features of Address Book. Click the View Columns and Card button to present Address Book's default three-column view. Click View Card to have Address Book show only the Card column.

If you use a Bluetooth-equipped Mac, a third button is shown to the right of the View Card button. This button enables you to pair your Address Book with a Bluetooth-capable cell phone, PDA, or other device that you can use for contact information. For example, you can keep contact information on your phone synchronized with information stored in your Address Book and vice versa.

In the upper-left corner of each card is an image well that you can use to place an image for your contact, such as a photo of the person for whom you created the card or the logo for a company (such as the apple for Apple). You can add a photo to a card by dragging a photo onto this well. The photo you use can be a JPEG, GIF, TIFF, or PDF file and should be 64×64 pixels.

The card marked with a silhouette is your card. This is important because your card can be used to add your contact information in various locations automatically.

**NOTE**

> When you send email to or receive email using Mail from a contact who has an image in the related Address Book card, that image appears in the email.

Although Address Book provides the standard functions you expect, such as email addresses and phone numbers, the information in Address Book is dynamic. For example, when a contact's card includes an email address, you can click the address to send the contact email. When you include a URL for a contact, you can click it to visit that web page, and when the contact has a .Mac account, you can open the contact's iDisk. You can also use the contact's card to chat with the person using iChat and visit the contact's website from within Safari. Address Book information is also accessible in many other places, such as when you are faxing documents using Mac OS X's built-in fax capability.

## Finding Information in Address Book

To locate information within Address Book itself, you can browse your contacts or search for specific contacts.

To browse your contacts, perform the following steps:

1. Open Address Book by clicking the Address Book icon on the Dock or by opening the Applications folder and double-clicking the Address Book icon.
2. Scroll in the Name column to find the contact you are interested in.
3. Select the contact whose information you want to view. The contact's card is displayed, and you can see the person's contact information.

The information in Address Book is extremely flexible. The fields displayed for each contact can be configured individually. When you display a card, only the fields that contain information are displayed. For example, compare Figure 25.1 and Figure 25.2 to see how Address Book has reconfigured the card display for cards with different amounts of information.

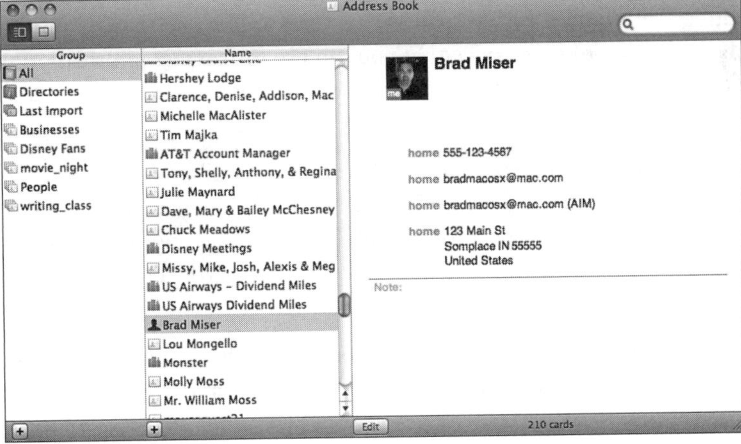


**Figure 25.2**
Come now, you didn't really expect me to include my real phone number and address in this book did you? (The email address is real.)

You can also search to locate a contact's information:

1. Open Address Book by clicking the Address Book icon on the Dock or by opening the Applications folder and double-clicking the Address Book icon.
2. Enter text in the Search tool. You can enter text found in any of the contact's information, including name, address, home page, and so on. As you type, the list of names

shown in the Name column is narrowed so it includes only those contacts whose data contains the text you enter.

3. Select the contact whose information you want to view. The contact's card is displayed, and you can see the contact's information.

To view all your contacts again, click the X button that appears in the Search tool when you perform a search.

## Using Information in Address Book

When working with Address Book, you can easily do the following tasks:

> **NOTE**
>
> When you click a data label, such as an email or physical address, the pop-up menu that results has different commands for different items. For example, when you open an email address's pop-up menu, one of the options is Send Email. However, if you click a physical address, you see different options including Map Of, which enables you to retrieve a map for the address.

- **Send an email**—To send an email to one of your contacts, view the contact to which you want to send an email. Then click the label next to the email address to which you want to send an email. A pop-up menu appears. Select Send Email (see Figure 25.3). Your default email application will open and a new message addressed to the contact will be created.



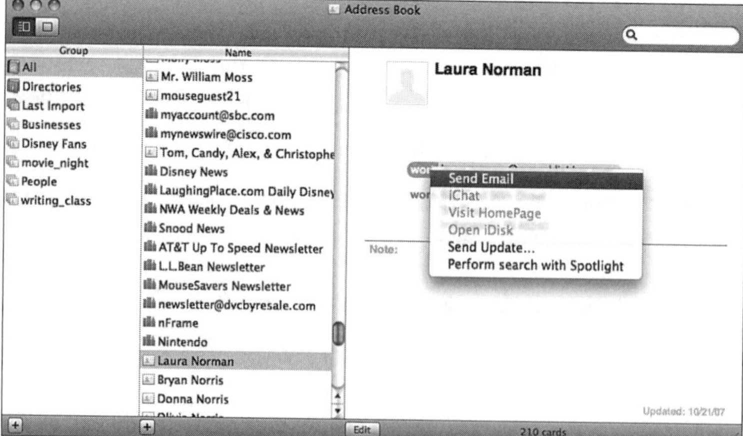


**Figure 25.3**
Sending an email from Address Book can be done with the Send Email command.

- **Visit the contact's website or home page**—Click the label next to a website you want to visit. From the resulting pop-up menu, select Go to Location. Or, click a URL shown on the card. Your default web browser will open and you'll move to the website.

- **View a map to an address**—Click the label next to an address and select Map Of from the resulting pop-up menu. Your default web browser will open and move to the Google Maps website. A map to the selected address is then displayed.
- **Copy a mailing label**—Click Copy mailing label to copy a physical address so you can paste it into an application you use to create envelopes or print mailing labels.
- **Chat**—Select iChat to use the iChat application to text, audio, or video chat with the contact.
- **Open an iDisk**—If the contact has a .Mac account and you have configured his .Mac email address, you can open the person's iDisk by clicking the label next to the .Mac email address and selecting Open iDisk. The contact's iDisk will open in a new Finder window.
- **Visit a HomePage website**—If the contact has a .Mac account and has a HomePage website, select the Visit HomePage command to go there.
- **Scroll through your contacts**—Select Card, Next Card (or press ⌘-]) or select Card, Previous Card (or press ⌘-[) to browse through your contacts.
- **Edit your contacts**—Click the Edit button to move into Edit mode (more on this later).



**TIP**

> Explore the contextual menus for various card elements along with the options in the menus to discover even more Address Book commands.

# Configuring Your Address Book

You can change the view of Address Book to show only cards by clicking the View Card Only button; selecting View, Card Only; or pressing ⌘-2. The window collapses down to the card only. You can add cards, edit cards, or browse cards from the collapsed window.

Show the other columns again by selecting View, Card and Columns or by pressing ⌘-1.

You can configure several aspects of the Address Book by using its Preferences dialog box (see Figure 25.4). To open this dialog box, select Address Book, Preferences or press ⌘-,.

## Configuring Address Book General Preferences

Using the General tab of the Preferences dialog box, you can configure the following preferences:

- **Display order**—Click the "First name Last name" radio button to have Address Book display contact information in the first name, last name format. Click the "Last name First name" radio button to display contacts in the last name, first name format.
- **Sort criterion**—Select First Name or Last Name on the Sort By pop-up menu to have Address Book sort the Cards column by that criterion.

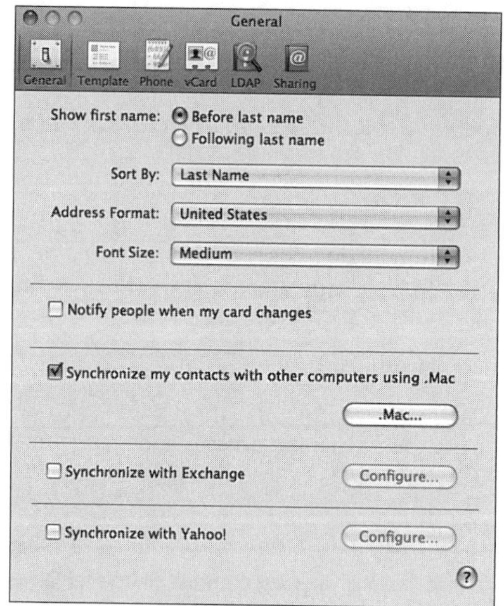


**Figure 25.4**
Maximize the benefits of your Address Book by customizing it using the Preferences dialog box.

- **Address format**—Use the Address Format pop-up menu to select the address format you want to use by country.
- **Font size**—Use the Font Size pop-up menu to select the Small, Medium, or Large font size for the information shown in the Address Book window.
- **Notifications about changes to your card**—If you want contacts to be notified when your contact information changes and want to send them your revised information, create at least one group containing the contacts whom you want to be notified (you'll learn how to do this later in this chapter) and check the "Notify people when my card changes" check box. Whenever you change something on your own vCard, you can notify people in the group by selecting File, Send Updates. In the resulting Send Updates dialog box, select the groups to which you want to send the update by checking their check boxes; then enter a subject and text for the message and click Send. The message you send includes your updated vCard that the recipients can use to replace the outdated version of your card in their own contact lists.
- **Synchronization via .Mac**—If you use more than one Mac and have a .Mac account, you can keep your Address Book synchronized on all your computers. Check the "Synchronize my contacts with other computers using .Mac" and click the .Mac button. You'll move to the .Mac pane of the System Preferences application, where you can configure your options.

⇨ To learn how to use .Mac to synchronize information, **see** "Using .Mac to Synchronize Important Information on Multiple Macs," **p. 454**.

- **Synchronization with Exchange**—Many organizations use an Exchange server to provide email and contact information services to the network.

- **Synchronization with Yahoo!**—If you have a Yahoo! account, you can now synchronize the contacts in that account with your Address Book.

You can synchronize your Address Book with the information stored on an Exchange server by doing the following:

1. Check the "Synchronize with Exchange" check box.
2. Click Configure. In the resulting dialog box, enter your username, password, and the Outlook Web Access server address with which you want to synchronize your Address Book.
3. If you want to synchronize this information every hour, check the "Synchronize every hour" check box.
4. Click OK; information from the Exchange server is added to your Address Book and your Address Book information is added to the Exchange server.

**CAUTION**

For synchronization to work, you must enter the address for Outlook Web Access server rather than the Exchange server address itself. Address Book uses the Web Access address to retrieve your information. If you don't know what this address is, contact the administrator for the Exchange server you are trying to access. To confirm that you are using the right server address, access the address through Safari. If you can access your email this way, you should be able to synchronize Address Book with your Exchange information.



## CUSTOMIZING YOUR ADDRESS BOOK CARD TEMPLATE

You can customize the information and layout of the cards in your Address Book.

Open the Address Book Preferences window and click the Template button to open the Template preferences pane (see Figure 25.5).

**TIP**

You can also edit the card template by selecting Card, Add Field, Edit Template.

To change the layout of and the information contained on the cards in your Address Book, you can do any of the following:

- **Add fields**—Use the Add Field pop-up menu at the top of the dialog box to add fields to the cards in your Address Book. To add a field, select it on the menu. The field will be added and it will be grayed out on the pop-up menu to indiciate that it is part of the current template.
- **Remove fields**—Click the minus sign next to a field to remove it from the card.
- **Add more fields of the same kind**—Click the plus sign next to a field to add another field of the same type to the card.

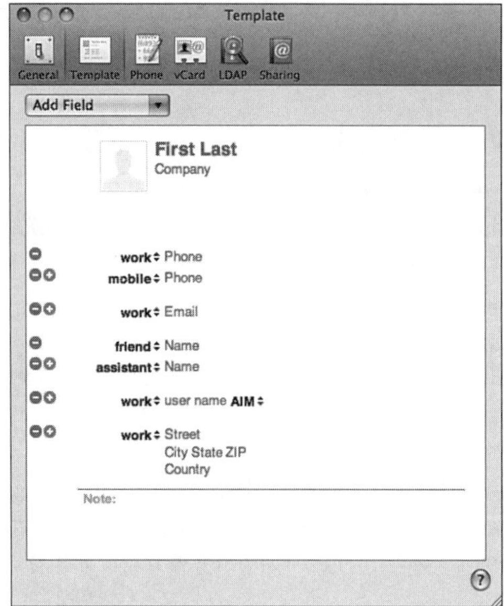


**Figure 25.5**
You can use Address Book's Template preferences to design the cards in your Address Book.

- **Change a field's label**—Use the pop-up menu next to a field's label to change that label. You can select one of the labels on the menu or select Custom and create a custom label.

25

Using these tools, you can customize the contents of cards and the specific fields they contain as much as you like. Because Address Book displays only those fields that contain data (when you view a card), you don't need to be concerned about having too many fields on your cards because on each card, you'll only see those fields that contain data.

## Configuring Address Book's Phone Number Format

You can change the phone number format used in Address Book by using the following steps:

1. Open the Phone pane of the Address Book Preferences dialog box.
2. To have Address Book format phone numbers automatically, check the "Automatically format phone numbers" check box. With this active, Addresss Book will automatically add hyphens, periods, or other formatting elements to phone numbers when you enter them on a card.
3. If you do check the check box mentioned in the previous step, use the Formats pop-up menu to select the format that should be used.

**TIP**

> You can create custom phone number formats by clicking the down arrow next to the Formats pop-up menu, which opens a pane showing the configured formats. Select one and click Edit to change it. To add a new format, click the plus sign. To remove a format, select it and click the minus sign.

### CHOOSING VCARD PREFERENCES

On the vCard pane of the Address Book Preferences dialog box, you can set the following preferences:

- **vCard Format**—Click the 3.0 radio button to use the newer vCard format. Click the 2.1 radio button to use an older version of the vCard standard.
- **Encoding**—Use the Encoding pop-up menu to choose the encoding you want to use, such as Western (Mac OS Roman). This is only used with the older 2.1 vCard format.
- **Enable private me card**—You can use this option to hide information on your vCard so that information won't be exported when you provide your vCard to someone else. To do so, check the "Enable private me card" check box. Edit your card and uncheck the check boxes for the data that you don't want to include on your vCard when you share it.
- **Export notes in vCards**—If you check the "Export notes in vCards" check box, when you export vCards, any notes you have entered for a card are exported with the card. Be careful with this one because any information you put in notes will be exported with the vCards!
- **Export photos in vCards**—If you check the "Export photos in vCards" check box, when you export vCards, any vCards you export that contain photos will have those photos included when you export them.



**NOTE**

> Address Book can also work with Lightweight Directory Access Protocol (LDAP) directories that can provide address information over a network. Such directories appear when you click the Directories icon in the Group column. You can add directories to your Address Book by using the LDAP tab of the Address Book Preferences dialog box. Explaining how to use such directories is beyond the scope of this chapter. If you need help, see the administrator of the network that is providing one or more LDAP directories to you.

## SHARING YOUR ADDRESS BOOK WITH .MAC USERS

You can share your Address Book information with other people who use .Mac. To do so, perform the following steps:

1. Open the Sharing pane of the Address Book Preferences dialog box.
2. Check the "Share your Address Book" check box.
3. Click the Add button (+). The information in your Address Book will appear in the resulting sheet.
4. Select the people who use .Mac with whom you'd like to share your Address Book and click OK. You'll move back to the Sharing pane and the people whom you selected will be shown in the list.

5. Check the "Allow Editing" check box for those people whom you want to be able to change information in your Address Book.
6. Select the people you have added and click the Send Invite button. An email will be created and addressed to those people. This email will contain the link they need to be able to access your Address Book information.

**TIP**

> To remove someone from the list of people who can access your Address Book, select his name on the list and click the Remove button (-).

# ADDING ADDRESSES TO YOUR ADDRESS BOOK

Obviously, before an address book is of much value, it has to have some information in it. There are several ways to get information into your Address Book:

- Edit your own address card.
- Add cards manually.
- Add a card from an email message you have received.
- Import a contact's vCard.
- Import address information from an email application.
- Import address information by syncing with a Bluetooth cell phone or PDA.
- Synchronize your Exchange contact or Yahoo! account contacts wth your Address Book.



## EDITING YOUR OWN ADDRESS CARD

The first time you open Address Book, a card is created for you automatically based on the information you entered when you installed Mac OS X. If you entered one or more email addresses when you installed Mac OS X, those addresses are included in your address card automatically. You should edit this card, mostly so that you can easily send your contact information to other people simply by sending them your vCard.

**NOTE**

> Another place your card's information is used is for Safari's AutoFill feature. When you complete a form on the Web, your card's information is used if you choose to enable Safari's AutoFill feature.

You can jump to your card by selecting Card, Go to My Card. Your card will be selected. Your card's icon has a silhouette next to your name. When you select your name in the Name column, your card appears; its image well is marked with the text *me*.

**TIP**

> You can export a vCard by viewing it and selecting File, Export vCard.
>
> You can export your own card, or any other card for that matter, as a vCard by selecting the card, opening its contextual menu, and selecting Export vCard. Select a location, name the vCard, and click Save.

If you want to create a different card for yourself for some reason, you can create a new card and enter your contact information in it. After you have created your new card, select it and select Card, Make This My Card (this is disabled if you have already selected your card).

You can edit your own card using the same steps you use to edit any other cards (editing cards is explained shortly).

## Adding Addresses Manually

As you might expect, you can add people to your Address Book by inputting their information manually.

To manually add an address, do the following:

25

1. Click the Plus button in the Name column; select File, New Card; or press ⌘-N to see a new, empty address card. The fist name is highlighted by default so you can edit it immediately (see Figure 25.6). The fields on the card are those that are defined in your current template.

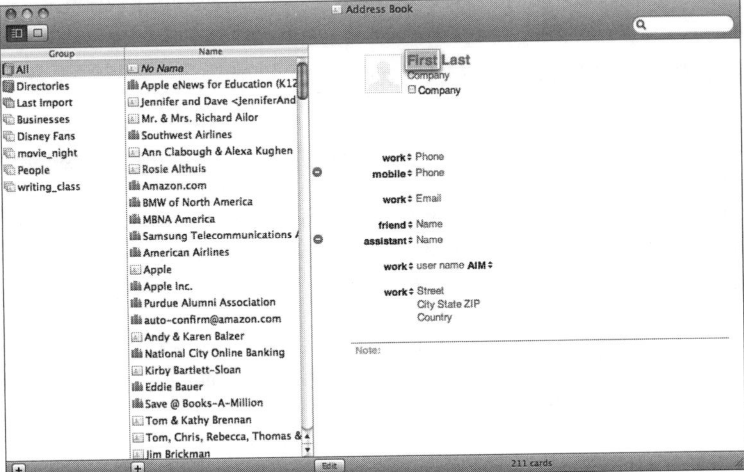


**Figure 25.6**
This is a new card, ready for the contact's information.

2. Input the first name.
3. Press Tab to move to and select the Last field, and then enter the contact's last name.
4. Press Tab to move to and select the Company field, and then enter the person's company information if applicable.

5. If you want the company to be listed above the name, check the Company check box.
6. Press Tab to move to and select the first contact information, which is “work phone” by default.
7. Click the menu icon to reveal the label pop-up menu (see Figure 25.7).

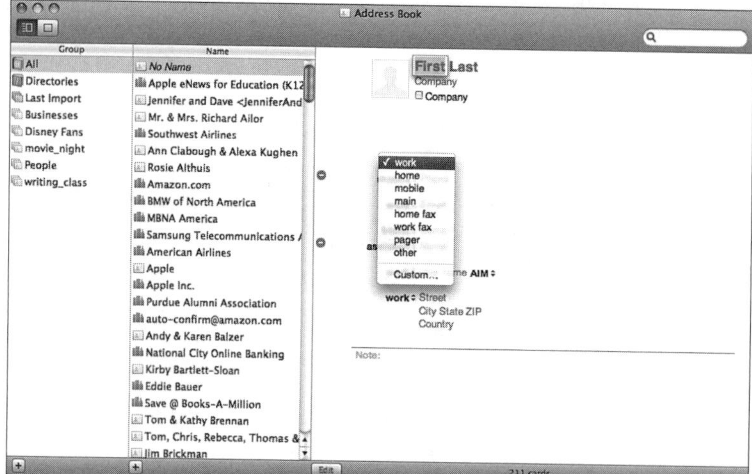


**Figure 25.7**
You use this pop-up menu to label contact information.

8. Select the label for the contact information, such as “home.”

**NOTE**

> Two entries on the label pop-up menu require some explanation. The selection called other inserts the label “other.” If you select Custom, you can create a custom label for a field.

9. Enter the contact information, such as a work phone number if you chose the label “work.”
10. Continue tabbing to each field on the card, selecting the label for that field and editing the information to fill in the rest of the card.
11. If the contact has a home page, select the home page field and enter the URL of the home page with which you want to associate the contact.
12. If you want to remove fields from the card, click the Remove Field button (the minus sign) next to the field you want to remove. The field is removed from the current card only.
13. If you want to add more fields of the same type to the card, click the Add Field button (+) next to one of the existing fields. After you have added a field, you can edit it in the same way as the default fields. Similar to removing a field from a card, when you add a field to the card, it is added on the current card only.

⇨ To learn how to add a field to all cards in the Address Book, **see** "Customizing Your Address Book Card Template," **p. 646**.

14. If you have an image you want to associate with the contact, drag the image onto the contact's image well. (You can add images in the usual graphics formats, such as JPEG or TIFF.) When you are over the image well, the cursor changes to a green circle with a plus sign in it. Release the mouse button and you see the image in a new window (see Figure 25.8).

**Figure 25.8**
Okay, I don't really know Gandalf, so sue me.



15. Use the slider at the bottom of the window to crop the image.
16. When the image appears as you want it, click the Set button.

**TIP**

> When you are editing a card, you can double-click an image or the image well to open the image editing window. You can also select Card, Choose Custom Image to open the same window. In that window, click the Choose button to move to and select an image to display in the window. If you have a camera, such as an iSight camera, connected to your Mac, click the camera button to capture the image being taken by the camera. With either an imported or captured photo you can apply Photo Booth effects by clicking the effects gallery button.

17. Add notes for the card by clicking next to the Note label and typing the note.
18. Click the Edit button to move out of Edit mode. Your new card is now ready to use (see Figure 25.9).

**NOTE**

> When you edit your own card and have the "Notify people when my card changes" preference selected, you are prompted to send a message notifying others that your information has changed.

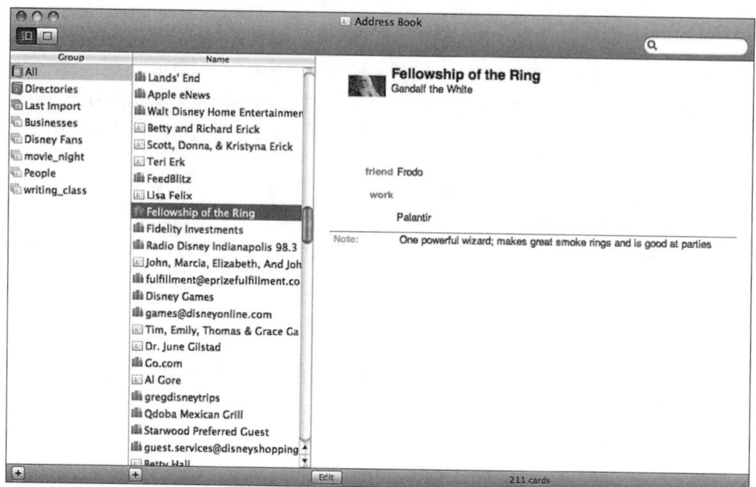

**Figure 25.9** You can create an address card for anyone you know (or even for those you don't know!).

## Adding an Address from an Email Message

You can create a contact in your Address Book by adding the sender's information from an email message to it. To add a contact from an email that you receive in the Mail application, do the following:

1. Use Mail to open an email message from the person whom you want to add to your Address Book.
2. Select Message, Add Sender to Address Book (or press Shift-⌘-Y). The person's name and email address are entered on a new address card.



## Using vCards to Add Information to Your Address Book

The benefit to using a vCard is that you can add a lot of information about a contact with very little work on your part. When you receive a vCard from someone, use the following steps to add that person's address card to your Address Book:

1. Drag the vCard onto the Name column in Address Book.
2. Click OK when prompted. The vCard will be added to your Address Book.
3. Select the card and click the Edit button.
4. Edit the information as needed (you learn how to edit cards later in this chapter).

**NOTE**

> When you import vCards to your Address Book, the group called Last Import always contains the cards you most recently added.

**NOTE**

> vCard files have the filename extension `.vcf` (virtual card file).

## Importing Addresses from Another Application

If you have used another email application in the past, you probably have an Address Book or Contact database in that application. If that application supports vCards, you can easily export vCards from the application and then add them to Address Book.

As an example of how this works, the following steps show you how to export contacts from Microsoft's Entourage email application and then add those contacts to Address Book. Because Entourage supports vCards, you can create vCards for your Entourage contacts and then import those contacts into Address Book:

1. Create a folder to temporarily store the vCards you export from Entourage. You will probably want this folder visible on the Desktop or in the Dock so you can access it easily.
2. Open Entourage.
3. Click the Address Book button to move into Address Book mode.
4. Drag the contacts for whom you want to create vCards from the Entourage window onto the folder you created in step 1, and drop them in that folder. A vCard is created for each of your Entourage contacts.

25

**NOTE**

> If you drag an Entourage group to create a vCard, a text clipping file is created instead. You need to re-create your groups within Address Book.

5. Open Address Book.
6. Drag the vCards from the folder in which you stored them onto the Name column. The contacts you added are now available for you to use and edit.

It is unlikely that all the information in your current address book or contact list will make it into the Address Book application. For example, if you have added Category information for your Entourage contact list, that information is not imported into Address Book. After you have imported contacts into Address Book, you should check them over so you know exactly what information made it in, and what didn't. If you lost any important information, you might have to spend some time re-creating it within Address Book.

**NOTE**

> When you import addresses into your Address Book and it finds duplicates, you have the opportunity to review the addresses you are adding so you can remove the duplicated entries. You can also merge the multiple entries together.

## Syncing Contact Information with a Cell Phone or PDA and Address Book

If you store contact information on a cell phone or PDA, you might be able to sync that device with Address Book. First, you establish a connection between your Mac and the device, such as using Bluetooth or connecting it via a dock or cradle. Second, you use iSync to synchronize information between your Mac and the device.

This doesn't work for all types of mobile devices, but you should definitely check it out for the device you use because this enables you to manage your contact information from your Mac and update your mobile device's information easily and vice versa.

⇨ To learn how to synchronize a mobile device with a Mac, **see** Chapter 36, "Synchronizing Information on Macs and Other Devices," **p. 859**.

# Editing Addresses in Your Address Book

To edit an address in your Address Book, use the following steps:

1. In Address Book, view the card containing the information you want to edit.
2. Click the Edit button. Address Book moves into Edit mode. The first name is selected and is ready to edit.
3. Use the same steps to change the information on the card that you do to create a card (see the earlier section on creating cards for the details).

**TIP**

> You can use the Add Field button on the Template pane of the Address Book Preferences dialog box to add fields to the card. You can also add fields by using the Card, Add Field command. On the Add Field menu, you can select the type of field you want to add.



Many of the data fields have pop-up menus containing the data field's label. You can open these menus and select a new label for that field. The changes you make by doing this affect only the current address card; this means you can configure the information for a specific card independent of other cards. For example, if you know someone who has three mobile phones, you can select "mobile" as the label for three of the fields on that person's address card. You can also select "Custom" to create custom field labels for existing or new fields.

You can quickly swap the last name with the first name for the card by viewing the card and selecting Card, Swap First/Last Name.

To remove an image from a card, view the card and select Card, Clear Custom Image.

If you don't want a field's data to appear on a card, select the data and click the Delete data button (the minus sign). The data is replaced with the type of data it is, such as Email for an email address. The data does not appear on the card when it is viewed.

**NOTE**

> After you add a field, you can't remove it. You can only delete its data so that it doesn't appear on the card any more.

To delete a card from Address Book, select it and press Delete. Click Yes in the resulting prompt and the card is removed from Address Book.

**TIP**

> You can view a card in an independent window by viewing it and selecting Card, Open in Separate Window (or by pressing ⌘-I). You can also edit a card when it is displayed in a separate window.

# Working with Address Groups

Address groups (just called *groups* in Address Book) enable you to email multiple people using a single object. Working with an address group is similar to working with other address cards in your Address Book.

There are two types of groups. A *group* is a collection of cards that you add to the group manually. A *smart group* defines a set of criteria; cards that meet these criteria are added to the group automatically.

## Creating and Configuring a Basic Address Group

Creating an address group is simple, as you can see in the following steps:

1. Click the New Group button, which is the plus sign in the Group column; select File, New Group; or press Shift-⌘-N. You will see a new group in the Group column, and the name of the group will be selected and ready to edit.
2. Change the group's name to something meaningful and press Return.
3. Click All in the Group column to view all the cards in the Address Book.
4. Search or browse for the cards you want to add to your Address Book.
5. Drag the cards you want to be included in the group onto the group's icon in the Group column. Those cards become part of the group.



**TIP**

> You can create a new group and add selected address cards to it by first selecting the cards you want to place in the new group and selecting File, New Group From Selection. A new group is created and includes the cards you selected.

You can view a group by selecting it on the Group column. The Name column shows only those cards that are included in the group. You work with the cards in a group just as you do individual cards. For example, you can edit a card, use it to send email to that individual, and so on.

To remove a card from a group, view the group, select the card you want to remove, and press Delete. After you confirm the action, the card is removed from the group. However, the card still exists in Address Book.

You can also export a group as a vCard. Select the group, Control + click it or right-click with a two-button mouse, and select Export Group vCard. Select a location, name the card, and click Save. You can use the group's vCard in the same way you use vCards for individuals.

If any of the cards you add to a group includes more than one email address, you can edit the mailing list for the group to set the specific addresses that are used:

1. Select the group for which you want to configure the mailing list.
2. Select Edit, Edit Distribution List. The Edit Distribution List dialog box will appear.
3. Select the email address you want to use for an individual by clicking it. The address that will be used appears in bold; other addresses are grayed out to show that they won't be used.

> **TIP**
>
> You can change all the email addresses used for the group to be of the same kind by selecting a type on the Change All Labels pop-up menu. For example, to use only home email addresses, select "home."

4. Click OK. When you send a message to the group, the addresses you selected are used.

## CREATING A SMART ADDRESS GROUP

You can use the Smart Groups feature to have Address Book populate a group based on criteria you define rather than manually placing contacts in the group. Smart groups work just like other smart objects, such as smart playlists in iTunes or smart photo albums in iPhoto. To create a smart address group, perform the following steps:

1. Choose File, New Smart Group or press Option-⌘-N. The Smart Address Book sheet appears (see Figure 25.10).



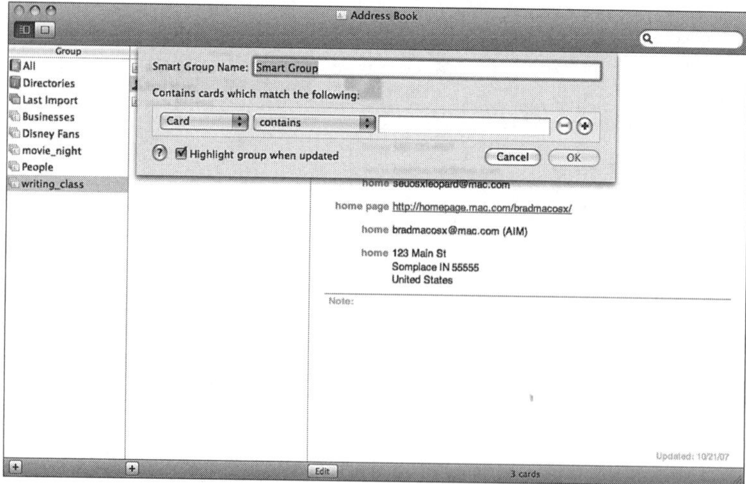


**Figure 25.10**
To create a smart address group, define the criteria for contacts that you want included in the group and Address Book will put them there automatically.

2. Enter the name for the group in the Smart Group Name field.
3. On the first pop-up menu, choose the field on which you want to base the first criterion. For example, to base it on last name, choose Other and then choose Last. Choose Card to base on the criterion on any data on a card.
4. On the second pop-up menu, choose the operator for the condition, such as “contains,” “is,” and so on.
5. In the box, type the data for the condition, such as the last name.
6. To add another condition, click the Add Condition button (the plus sign). An empty condition is created.
7. Configure the new condition by repeating steps 3-5.
8. Continue adding conditions until you have all that you want to use.
9. Choose the pop-up menu at the top of the sheet to choose “all” if all the conditions you configured have to be met to have a card included in the group or “any” if you want a card included as long as it meets at least one condition.
10. Check the “Highlight group when updated” check box if you want Address Book to highlight the group when any changes are made to it. Because Address Book automatically includes or excludes cards in the group based on its conditions, it’s not obvious when the group changes. Use this setting if you want to know whenever a smart group changes.
11. Click OK. The smart group is created and any cards that meet its criteria are added to it automatically (see Figure 25.11).



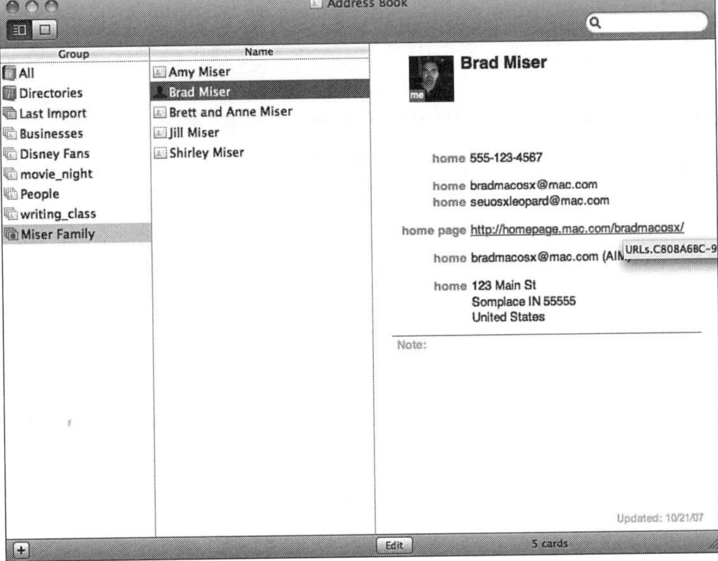


**Figure 25.11**
A smart group is a good way to collect all the cards for a family.

Following are a few tidbits about smart groups:

- To change the contents of a smart group, open its contextual menu and choose Edit Smart Group. The Smart Group criteria sheet will appear. Use that sheet to change the group's conditions. When you click OK, the group's content will reflect its current conditions.
- To remove a condition from a smart group, edit it and click the Remove Condition button (the minus sign) next to the condition you want to delete. That condition no longer affects the cards included in the group.
- You can perform similar tasks with a smart group that you can with basic groups, such as sending email to the group.

## ADDRESSING EMAIL

There are several ways in which you can address email to people in your Address Book:

- View the contact to whom you want to send a message and click the label for the email address you want to use. Select Send Email on the pop-up menu.
- Drag the contact's vCard to the To, Cc, or Bcc box of a Mail email message.
- Open a group's contextual menu and select "Send email to *groupname*," where *groupname* is the name of the group you clicked.
- Drag a group's vCard to the To, Cc, or Bcc box of a Mail email message.



**NOTE**

> When you send email from Address Book, the email application used is your default email application.

## PRINTING YOUR ADDRESS BOOK

As you work with your Address Book, you might want to print it to take it with you, to print address labels, and so on. When you print from Address Book, you have the following four layout options:

- **Envelopes**—This option prints envelopes for your contacts.
- **Lists**—This option prints the cards you select in a list. You can select the attributes that are included on the list for each card.
- **Pocket Address Book**—This option prints a small version of your Address Book that is designed to be carried.
- **Mailing Labels**—This prints the cards as mailing labels.

To print Address Book as a list, use the following steps:

1. Select the cards you want to print. To print the entire Address Book, select All in the Groups column.
2. Select File, Print or press ⌘-P. The Print dialog box opens. The first time you go to print in Address Book the dialog box is collapsed; click the downward-facing arrow at the right to expand the dialog box and see all the options.
3. On the Style pop-up menu, select Lists.
4. Configure the printer, presets, paper size, and orientation just as you do with any print job.
5. Select the attributes you want included for each card by checking their check boxes. You will see a preview of the list in the left side of the dialog box.
6. Select the font size on the Font Size pop-up menu.
7. Print the list.

To print mailing labels, use the following steps:

1. Select the cards you want to print. To print the entire Address Book, select All in the Groups column.
2. Select File, Print or press ⌘-P. The Print dialog box opens.
3. On the Style pop-up menu, select Mailing Labels.
4. Click the Layout tab.
5. If you are printing on standard Avery or DYMO labels, select the label type on the Page pop-up menu. If you are creating a custom label, select Define Custom instead; in the Layout Name sheet that appears, enter the name of the label you are creating and click OK. As you make choices, a preview of the labels will appear in the left pane of the dialog box.
6. If you selected a standard label, select the specific label number you are printing on the label number drop-down list that appears next to the Page pop-up menu. If you selected Define Custom in the previous step, use the controls under the Layout tab to design the label, such as by defining the margins, number of rows and columns, and the gutters.
7. Click the Label tab.
8. Select the address type for which you want to print labels on the Addresses pop-up menu. If you want to print labels for all addresses, select All.
9. On the "Print in" pop-up menu, select how you want the labels to be sorted. The options are Alphabetical Order and Postal Code Order.
10. If you want to include the contact's company name on the label, check the Company check box. If you want country to be included on the labels, check the "Country" check box. If you don't want your own country to be included, check the "Except my country" check box.
11. Click the Color box and use the Color Picker to select the color of the text on the labels.

12. Click the Image Set button to place an image on the labels.
13. Click the Font Set button to open the Font panel and select the font you want to use on the labels.
14. Check the labels in the preview pane.
15. Print the labels.

**NOTE**

> The other two types of printing can be done in a similar way. Choose the type of print job you want to do on the Style pop-up menu and use the controls in the dialog box to configure the print job.

# Using the Address Book Widget

You can also access your Address Book through the Address Book widget.

⇨ To learn how to use the Address Book widget, **see** "Using the Address Book Widget," **p. 128**.

# Subscribing to an Address Book

If other .Mac users have shared their Address Book with you, you can subscribe to it to view or edit its information by using the following steps:

1. Select File, Subscribe to Address Book.
2. In the resulting sheet, enter the .Mac user's username and click OK. You'll be able to view the other user's Address Book information, and you can edit it if you have permission to do so.



# Mac OS X to the Max: Using Address Book Keyboard Shortcuts

Table 25.2 shows keyboard shortcuts for the Address Book application.

**Table 25.2 Keyboard Shortcuts for the Address Book**

| Action | Keyboard Shortcut |
|---|---|
| Address Book Help | ⌘-? |
| Edit Card | ⌘-L |
| Hide Address Book | ⌘-H |
| Import vCards | ⌘-O |
| Merge Selected Cards | ⌘-I |

*continues*

**Table 25.2 Continued**

| Action | Keyboard Shortcut |
|---|---|
| Minimize Address Book Window | ⌘-M |
| Move Between Fields on an Address | Tab and Shift-Tab |
| New Card | ⌘-N |
| New Group | Shift-⌘-N |
| New Smart Group | Option-⌘-N |
| Next Card | ⌘-] |
| Open in Separate Window | ⌘-I |
| Preferences | ⌘-, |
| Previous Card | ⌘-[ |
| This is a Company | ⌘-\ |
| View Card and Columns | ⌘-1 |
| View Card Only | ⌘-2 |
| View Directories | ⌘-3 |

# CHAPTER 26

# CREATING AND USING CALENDARS WITH ICAL

## In this chapter

# MANAGING YOUR CALENDAR WITH ICAL

We all have busy lives and, if you are like me, you have trouble remembering where you are supposed to be and when you are supposed to be there. Fortunately, Mac OS X's iCal calendar application can help you keep your schedule under control. With this tool, you can maintain multiple calendars at the same time, such as a work calendar, family calendar, and so on. Even better, you can share your calendar with others so coordinating activities is much easier. You can also access other people's calendars to see how your schedule meshes with theirs.

# CONFIGURING ICAL

You don't need to configure many preferences in iCal, but if you open the General tab of the iCal Preferences dialog box, you will see the following options (see Figure 26.1):

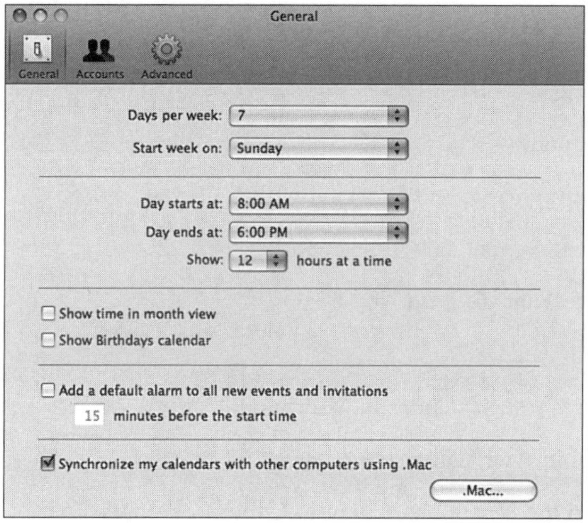

**Figure 26.1**
Configuring iCal isn't hard to do.

- **Week**—Use the "Days per week" and "Start week on" pop-up menus to configure how iCal manages and displays weeks. You can select 7- or 5-day weeks and set the start day of the week.
- **Day**—Use the pop-up menus in this area to set the start and end times for your days and to choose how many hours are displayed at a time.
- **Month**—The "Show time in month view" check box determines whether the time is displayed next to events when you are viewing your calendar in the Month view.
- **Birthdays**—If you have stored birthdays for your contacts in Address Book, check the "Show Birthdays calendar" check box to display the Birthday calendar that shows those birthdays.
- **Alarms**—For many people a gentle remnder about an upcoming event is very helpful. You can specify if you want all of your new events and invitations to have an alarm and how many minutes before the event the alarm should go off.

- **Synchronization**—As with other applications, such as Address Book, you can use .Mac to synchronize calendar information on different Macs. Use the "Synchronize my calendars with other computers using .Mac" check box and the .Mac button to configure this.

⇨ To learn how to use .Mac, **see** Chapter 20, "Using .Mac to Integrate a Mac onto the Internet," **p. 435**.

If you open the Advanced pane of the iCal Preferences dialog box, you'll see the following options:

- **Time Zone**—iCal's Time Zone Support feature enables the application to add time zone information to your calendar. You can then associate events with specific time zones and change the time zone for which you are viewing events. This feature is most useful when you are using iCal while traveling. As you change time zones, you can set iCal to use the time zone you are currently in. Then, it adjusts the time for each event so it is appropriate to the time zone you are in. To activate this feature, check the "Turn on time zone support" check box. If you leave this check box unchecked, time zone is ignored.
- **Events and To Do items**—Use the "To Do" and "events" tools to configure how events and To Do items are managed. The "Hide To Do items with due dates outside the calendar view" check box enables you to hide any To Do items that don't need to be done during the period you are currently viewing or that have been completed prior to the current time being displayed. The "Hide To Do items" check box and text box enable you to have iCal hide To Do items after they are completed and to set the number of days that must pass until completed items are hidden. Use the "Delete events" and "Delete To Do items" check boxes and text boxes to determine whether iCal deletes these items and, if so, the number of days after they occur that must pass before these items are deleted from your calendar. If you want to use iCal as a means to document tasks you have done and events in which you have participated, leave these last two check boxes unchecked to ensure that these data are maintained in iCal.
- **Alarms**—If you check the "Turn off alarms when iCal is not open" check box and iCal is not running, you won't be notified of events or To Do items via iCal alarms. You can also turn off all alarms so that you are never reminded about an event or invitation.
- **Invitations**—Check the "Automatically retrieve invitations from Mail" if you use Mail and want iCal invitations you receive to be retrieved automatically. This feature makes it easy to schedule events with other people who use iCal or a compatible application because you can send invitations to them and they can accept (or not) and you'll be notified of their decision.



Use the Accounts pane of the iCal Preferences dialog box to configure access to calendars available to you via CalDAV services on a network. This pane enables you to configure the information you need to access these calendars so they will be displayed within iCal. You need to have access to the server addresses, usernames, and passwords to access this information and then use the Accounts preferences to configure iCal to access that information. You aren't likely to use this unless your Mac is connected to an organization's network, in which case you will need to contact your network administrator to be able to configure iCal to access this information.

## Using iCal

Like other *i* applications, iCal is pretty simple to use. If you have used other calendar applications, you probably will have an easy time moving to iCal. By default, the iCal window has three panes (see Figure 26.2).

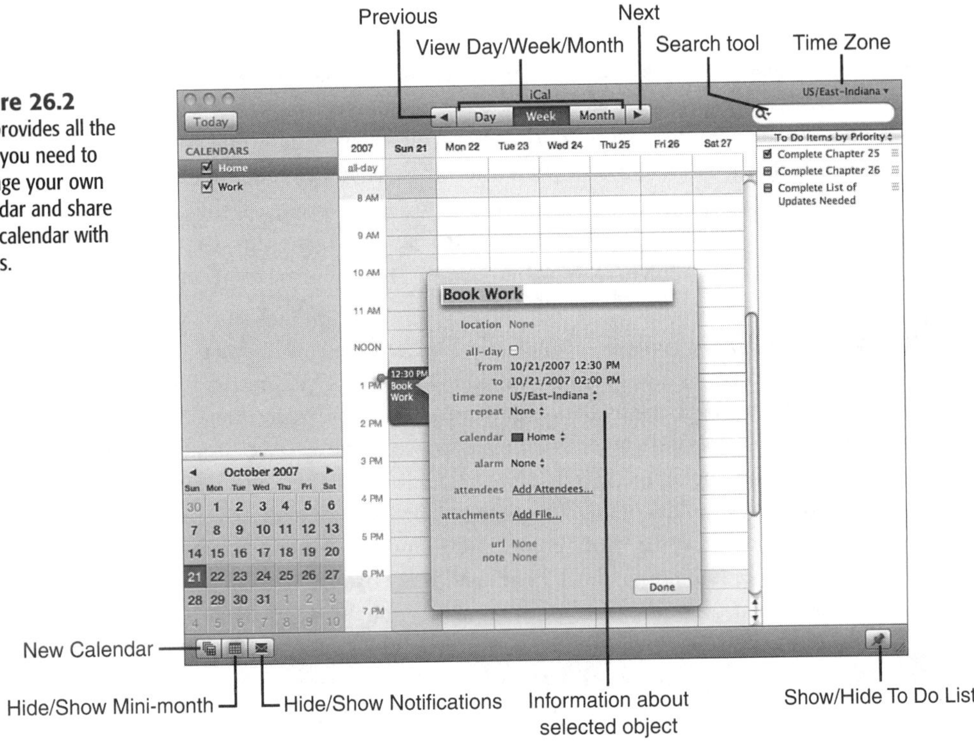


**Figure 26.2**
iCal provides all the tools you need to manage your own calendar and share your calendar with others.

26

Along the upper-left side of the window is the Calendar pane. In this pane, you see each calendar you have created along with those to which you have subscribed. If a calendar's check box is checked, its events are being displayed. If not, they are hidden.

The lower part of the Calendar pane contains the Mini-month pane, which shows you a month at a glance, or the Notifications pane, which shows you information about notifications. You choose the pane you want to view by clicking the related button.

You can also access your calendar information via the Dashboard iCal widget.

⇨ To learn about the Calendar widget, **see** "Using the iCal Widget," **p. 129**.

In the center pane is the calendar itself. There are three views for this: Day, Week, and Month.

Along the top of the window are the following tools:

- **Previous**—Use this to go back by a day, week, or month (whichever is currently displayed).

- **Day/Week/Month**—Use these three buttons to change the view of the calendar window.
- **Next**—Use this to go forward by a day, week, or month (whichever is currently displayed).
- **Time Zone**—If iCal is configured to use time zones, the current time zone is displayed. You can use the Time Zone pop-up menu to change the time zone being used, such as when you are traveling.
- **Search tool**—Use this to search for events and To Do items. This tool works similarly to the Search tool in other areas, such as iTunes or the Finder. To search, click the Magnifying Glass pop-up menu to open it and choose the kind of search you want to do (if you don't select anything, all calendar items are searched). Enter your search text; as you do, items that match your search will be found. When you enter search text, iCal's Search Results pane opens automatically (see Figure 26.3). This pane lists all the events and To Do items that meet your search criterion. When you are done with a search, click the Clear button (the "x"). The search is cleared and the Search Results pane closes.

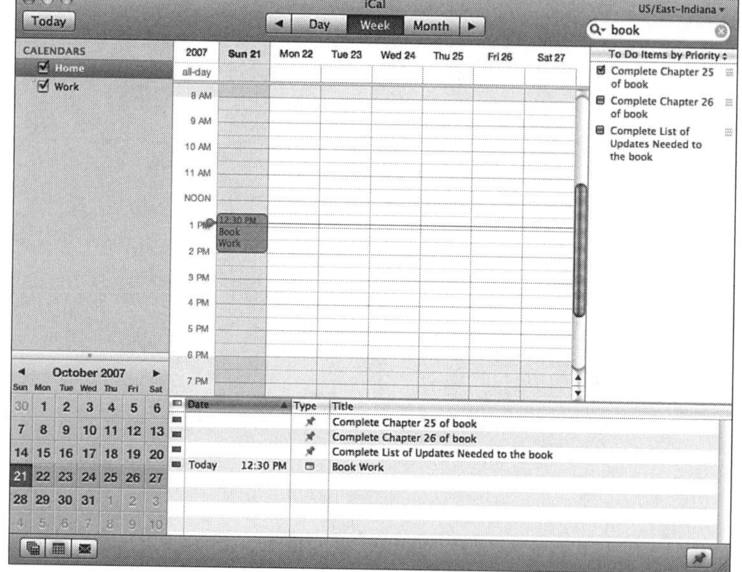

**Figure 26.3**
Here, I have searched for items related to the term *book*. The resulting events and To Do items are shown in the Search Results pane that appears under the calendar.

- **New Calendar**—Click this to create a new calendar.
- **Hide/Show Mini-month**—This shows or hides the mini-month tool. When you are viewing the mini-month, you can move back in time by clicking the Previous button (the left arrowhead next to the current mini-month), or forward by clicking the Next button (the right arrowhead). The current date is highlighted on the mini-month calendar.

> **TIP**
>
> You can drag the Mini-month pane's top border up to display more months or down to show fewer.

- **Hide/Show Notifications**—You can send and receive notifications for events scheduled with iCal. Click this button to show the Notifications pane on which you can see and work with your notifications.
- **Show/Hide To Do List**—This button opens the To Do Items pane, which shows the To Do items on your plate. This pane appears to the right of the calendar.
- **Show/Hide Info**—To see the detail of a calendar event, double-click it on the calendar. The Info sheet will be displayed; if you need to edit the details, click the Edit button to make changes to the event (see Figure 26.4).

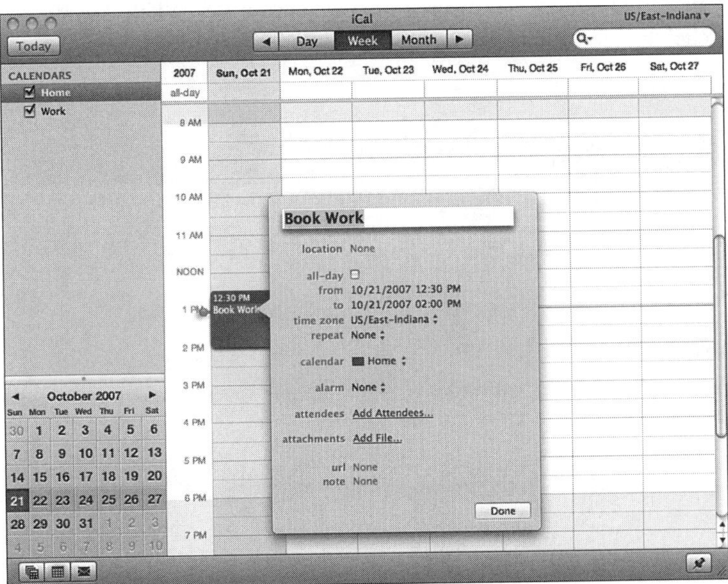


**Figure 26.4**
In this example, I have selected a very important event on my calendar and opened the Info sheet so I can see and configure the details for that event.



> **TIP**
>
> You can always return to the current day on your calrendar by pressing ⌘-T.

# CREATING, CONFIGURING, AND WORKING WITH CALENDARS

As you read earlier, you can manage multiple calendars within the iCal application. For example, you might want to create separate calendars for home and work activities, for special projects, and so on. Each calendar can include its own events and To Do items. To create a new calendar, do the following steps:

1. Click the New Calendar button. A new, untitled calendar will appear in the Calendar pane.
2. Enter the name of the new calendar and press Return.
3. Select the new calendar and right-click or Control-click to display the contextual menu. The calendar Info sheet opens. At the top of the sheet, the name of the calendar is shown so that you know which calendar you are getting information about.
4. Enter a description of the calendar.
5. Use the Color pop-up menu to associate a color with the calendar. When you add events to the calendar, they appear in the color you select. Having different colors for different calendars is useful because you can easily see which events came from which calendars when you are viewing multiple calendars at the same time.
6. If you do not want alarms to be displayed for the items on just this calendar, click the "Ignore alarms" check box.
7. Click the Publish button to share your iCal calendar with others using either .Mac or a private server.

⇨ To learn how to publish your calendar, **see** "Publishing Your iCal Calendar," **p. 676**.

To include a calendar's events and To Do items in the calendar being displayed, check its check box. If you uncheck a calendar's box, its events and To Do items are hidden (you can check its box to see its events and To Do items again).

To remove a calendar, select it and press Delete. The calendar, along with all its events and To Do items, will be removed from iCal. Most of the time, you're better off hiding a calendar because it won't appear in iCal any more, but you can still access its information at any time. When you delete a calendar, all its information is deleted with it.



# WORKING WITH EVENTS

You can use iCal to track life events of all kinds. You can associate events with specific calendars, set reminders, and so on. To create an event, do the following steps:

1. Select the calendar and then the day on which you want the event to appear.
2. Select File, New Event (⌘-N), or open the contextual menu on the day on which you want the event to appear and select New Event. A new event will appear on the selected date.

**NOTE**

> You can also create an event by dragging over the time on the day which the event occurs.

3. Type the name of the event and press Return.
4. Double-click the event to see the Info sheet. The basic information is displayed first; click the Edit button to see all the details.

5. Enter information about the location of the event by clicking the word None next to `Location` that appears under the event's title.
6. Check the "all-day" check box if the event is an all-day event.
7. If it isn't an all-day event, use the "from" and "to" fields to set a start and end time for the event.

> **TIP**
> You can also change or set the date of the event using the "from" and "to" fields.

8. If the time zone is enabled, choose the time zone for the event on the "time zone" pop-up menu.
9. If you want the event to repeat, use the "repeat" pop-up menu. You can choose a standard frequency for the event or select Custom to set a custom frequency. When you choose a frequency, the "end" pop-up menu appears. Use this to choose an end date for the repeating event.
10. If you want to change the calendar on which the event appears, use the "calendar" pop-up menu to choose the calendar on which you want the event to appear.
11. If you want to set an alarm for the event, use the "alarm" pop-up menu. Your options for the alarm are the following: "None," which has no alarm; "Message," which displays a text message; "Message with sound," which displays a text message and plays a sound; "Email," which causes an email to be sent to an address you select; "Open file," which opens a file of your choice; or "Run Script," which causes a script you select to run. If you select an alarm with sound, the sound pop-up menu appears. If you choose any type of alarm, a pop-up menu that enables you to set the alarm time appears. If you select Email, a pop-up menu that enables you to select the email address to which the alarm should be sent appears.

    You can set multiple alarms for an event by configuring the first alarm and then clicking the second "alarm" pop-up menu that gets created automatically. Use the alarm configuration tools to configure the second alarm. You can repeat this as many times as you need to set as many alarms as you want.

> **TIP**
> The email addresses that appear on the "alert" pop-up menus for events or To Do items are those that are on your card in the Address Book application. To add more addresses, add them to your card in Address Book.

12. Select the sound for the alarm if applicable and the amount of time before the event that you want the alarm to be activated.
13. Set the time for the alarm using the lowest pop-up menu in the "alarm" section. The times you can choose are all relative to the event start time, such as 1 hour before.

14. Enter attendees for the event in the "attendees" field. You can type in names or drag them from your Address Book. To show people in your Address Book, select Window, Address Panel (Option-⌘-A). You can drag people from the Addresses window onto the "attendees" list. You can enter multiple attendees by dragging each onto the attendees field.

**NOTE**

> If your calendar is on a CalDAV server, you can view attendee availability by clicking the Show Availability button that appears on the Info sheet. You can also reserve rooms and meeting equipment for your event.

15. You can add attachments to a calendar item so that you can access items you need for that event. Click Add File and use the resulting Open dialog box to navigate to and select the file. Click Open and the file will be attached to the event.
16. If a URL is associated with the event, enter it in the "url" field.
17. Enter any notes about the event in the Notes field.
18. Review the event and make any necessary changes; you can then click Done to save the event (see Figure 26.5).

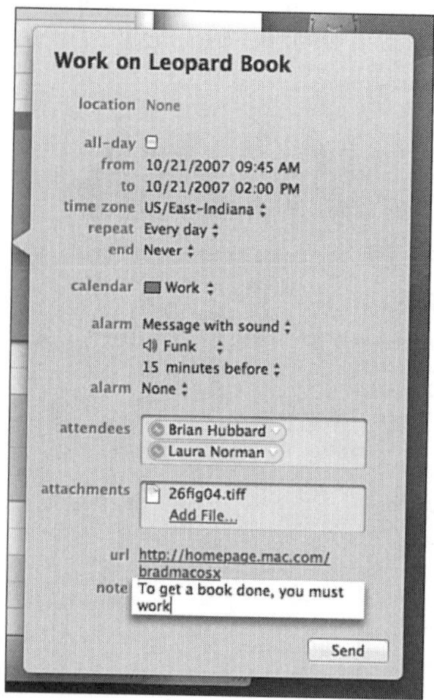


**Figure 26.5**
An author's work is never done.

19. If you want to send email invitations for the event to the people on the attendees list, open the detail of the event again and click in the area where the attendees are listed. The Done button changes to Send; click the Send button. This is active only if you added attendees with email addresses to the event. After you've clicked Send, an email will be created in your default email application and the event will be attached to it.

Depending on the email application you use, the email may send automatically. The people who receive these invitations can easily add the event to their own calendars by accepting them.

To view or change the details of an event, double-click the event in the calendar and then click the Edit button. Make changes to the event as needed and the changes are saved automatically.

Here are some additional tips for working with events:

- You can change the date on which an event occurs by dragging it from one date in the calendar to another.
- You can change the calendar on which an event occurs by opening its contextual menu (Control-click the event) and selecting the event's new calendar.
- You can duplicate an event by opening its contextual menu and selecting Duplicate; selecting Edit, Duplicate; or pressing ⌘-D. You can drag the copy onto a different date.
- You can email an event to others by opening its contextual menu and selecting "Mail event." (This is the same action that happens when you click the Send button for an event. The difference is that you can address the email that is created to anyone. When you click Send, the email is sent to only those people listed as attendees for the event.) Your default email application will open and the event will be included as an attachment (see Figure 26.6). The recipient can then click the attachment, which has the extension `.ics`, onto iCal to add it to her calendar.



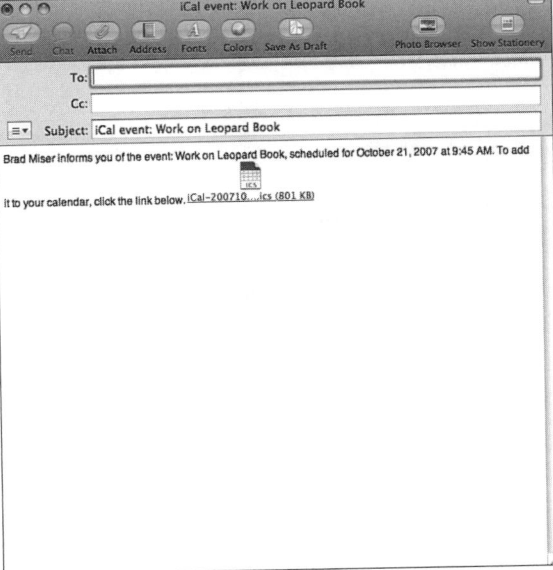


**Figure 26.6**
You can email events to others so they can easily add them to their own calendars.

- If you use the Send command, as people add the event to their calendars, you'll see a green check next to their names. This indicates that the attendee has accepted the event by adding it to his calendar. This tracking doesn't occur when you use the Mail event command.
- When you change an aspect of a repeated event, such as the alarm, you'll be prompted to make the change to all the events or only to the current one. If you choose only the current one, the current event is detached from the series and will no longer be connected to the other instances of the same event. This will be indicated by "(detached event)" being appended to the frequency shown in the "repeat" section for the event.
- Several of the data elements for events have contextual menus to enable you to perform actions. For example, if you click the alarm element, you can add more alarms or remove an existing alarm. If you add a URL, you can use its contextual menu to visit that website.
- As you configure an event, icons will appear at the top of the event on the calendar to indicate when an alarm has been set, whether the event is a repeating event, and so on.
- If you have turned on the time zone feature, the "time zone" pop-up menu appears in the Info sheet when you view the event. You can use this to set the time zone for the event. This is especially useful if you will be inviting people who are not in your current time zone. If they've enabled time zones in iCal, the event will be adjusted on their calendar automatically for their time zone.

## WORKING WITH YOUR TO DO LIST

To create a To Do item, use the following steps:

1. Either open the To Do pane or select File, New To Do (⌘-K). A new To Do item appears on the To Do list and the name is selected.
2. Type the name of the To Do item and press Return.
3. Double-click the To Do to open the Info sheet. Information about the event will appear.
4. Use the "priority" pop-up menu to set the To Do item's priority. As you set priorities, To Do items will be sorted on the To Do list accordingly.
5. If the event has a due date, check the "due date" check box and use the date fields that appear to set the due date.
6. If you want to set an alarm for the event, open the "alarm" pop-up menu and select the alarm you want to set (this is enabled only when the To Do item has a due date). The options are the same as those for an event.
7. Select the calendar with which the To Do item should be associated on the "calendar" pop-up menu.
8. If a URL is associated with the To Do item, enter it in the "url" field.
9. Enter any notes for the To Do item in the Notes field.

Following are some tips for working with To Do items:

- You can change a To Do item by double-clicking it to open the Info sheet. Then use the tools to change the item's information; these work just like when you create a To Do item.
- When you have completed a To Do item, mark it as complete by checking the box next to its name on the To Do list or by checking the "completed" box on the Info sheet. (Remember that you can show or hide the To Do list.)
- The priority of To Do items is indicated by the number of bars that appear to the right of their names on the To Do items list (see Figure 26.7).

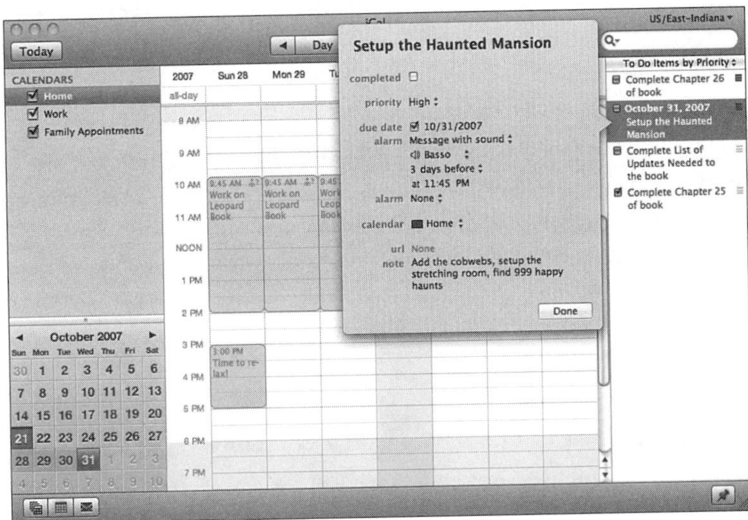


**Figure 26.7**
The priority of items on your To Do list is indicated by the number of bars shown next to its name.



- Sort the order in which To Do items appear on the list by using the pop-up menu at the top of the To Do pane. You can sort the list by due date, priority, title, calendar, or manually.
- On the To Do pop-up menu, choose Hide Items Outside of Calendar view if you want to see only To Do items related to the days you are currently viewing. When this option is not selected, you'll see all your upcoming To Do items.
- If you want to see all the items you've completed, open the To Do pop-up menu and choose Show All Completed Items.
- Open a To Do item's contextual menu to duplicate it, change the calendar with which it is associated, mark its priority, email it, or change the sort order for the To Do items pane.
- When the due date for an item is the current date or the due date has passed, its "complete" check box becomes a warning icon to indicate that the item is overdue. You can check the warning icon to mark the item as complete.

**TIP**

> When you email an event or a To Do item to someone, the recipient can add the item to his calendar by clicking its link or by dragging it onto the iCal window. If the recipient uses Mail and his preferences are set to add invitations to iCal automatically, the iCal information will be added to his calendar when he receives your email.

## Printing from iCal

From iCal, you can print calendars that show events, To Do items with due dates, mini-months, and your calendar keys (showing the calendars with which events and To Do items are associated). Open the Print dialog box to view and set the straightforward options for printing calendar information (see Figure 26.8). For example, you can choose the date range you want to print, which calendars are included, and the specific items you want to be included.

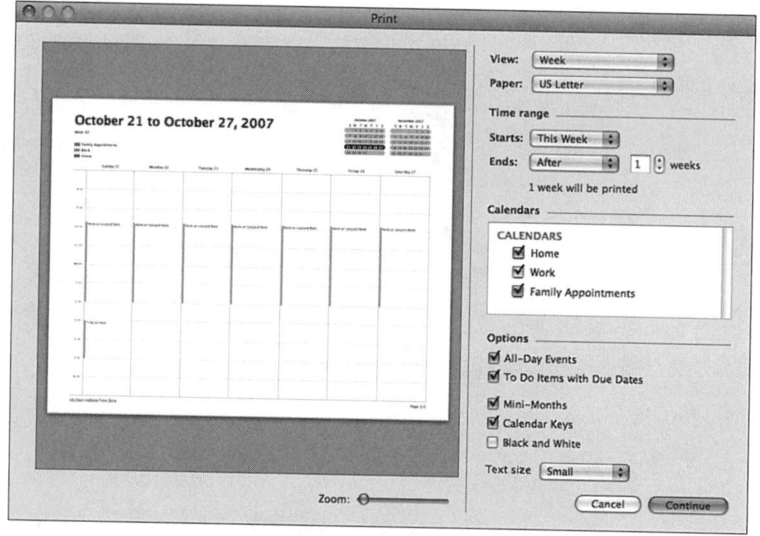


**Figure 26.8**
iCal offers flexible printing options.

26

## Synchronizing Your Calendar in Multiple Locations

If you use more than one Mac, you will probably want to keep your iCal calendar on each machine synchronized. To do this, you use .Mac and iSync.

⇨ To learn how to synchronize information on multiple machines, **see** "Using .Mac to Synchronize Important Information on Multiple Macs," **p. 454**.

# PUBLISHING YOUR ICAL CALENDAR

One of the cool things about iCal is that you can publish your calendars online so other people can view them. You can choose to share an iCal calendar via your .Mac account or use any other server.

**TIP**

> Because you can access a shared calendar over the Web, sharing your calendar provides a way for you to view your calendar even if your Mac isn't available. As long as you can access the Web, you can get to and view your calendar.

To publish your calendar, use the following steps:

1. Select the calendar you want to share.
2. Select Calendar, Publish. The Publish sheet appears (see Figure 26.9).

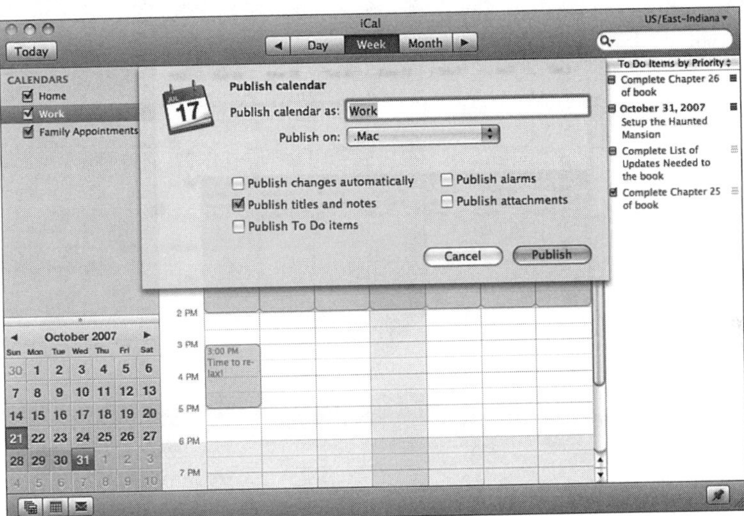


**Figure 26.9**
You can easily publish your calendars via .Mac.



3. Type the name of the calendar as you want it to appear online; by default the calendar's name is entered, but you can change this if you want to.
4. Choose how you want to publish the calendar on the "Publish on" pop-up menu. Select ".Mac" to use your .Mac account or "a Private server" to choose a different server. If you chose the latter option, you need to enter the server's URL along with your username and password for that server.

**NOTE**

> If you haven't configured your .Mac account when you start to publish your calendar using .Mac, you will be prompted to do so.

5. If you want changes you make to your calendar to be published automatically, check the "Publish changes automatically" check box. In most cases, you should check this so your calendar is always up-to-date.
6. If you want both the title and notes associated with an item to be published, check the "Publish titles and notes" check box.
7. If you want the alarms and To Do items to be published, check the "Publish alarms" and "Publish To Do items" check boxes. You can also publish attachments that are associated with events on your calendar.
8. Click Publish. When the calendar has been published, you will see the confirmation dialog box. This dialog box provides the URL for the calendar and enables you to visit the calendar online or send an email announcing the calendar (see Figure 26.10).

**Figure 26.10**
This published calendar can be viewed on the Web at any time.

9. Click the button for the action you want to take, such as OK to close the dialog box and return to iCal or Visit Page to see the calendar online (see Figure 26.11).

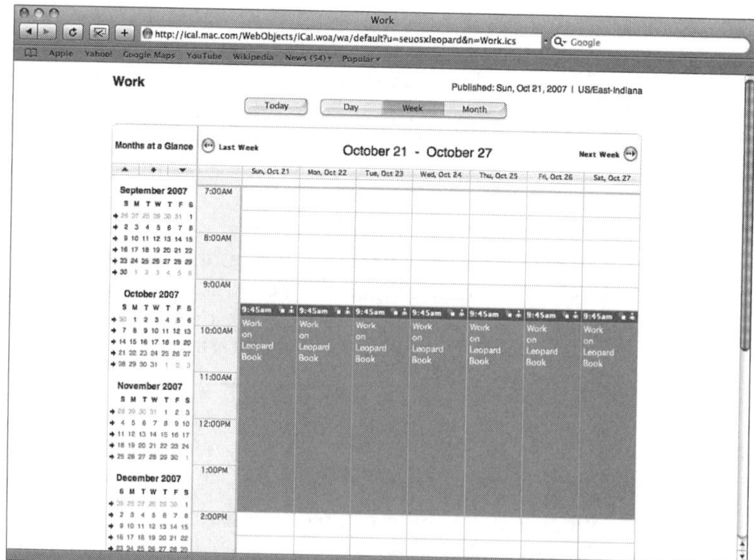


**Figure 26.11**
Here's the published calendar.

Following are some more pointers on publishing your calendars online:

- When a calendar is published, the published icon (which looks like a dot radiating waves) appears next to the calendar's name.
- If you open a published calendar's contextual menu, you see several interesting commands. These include Unpublish, which removes the calendar from the Web; Send Publish Email, which enables you to send an email announcing the published calendar and its URL; Copy URL to Clipboard, which copies the calendar's URL to the Clipboard so you can easily paste it into documents; Refresh, which publishes any changes you have made to the calendar; and Change Location, which enables you to move the calendar to a different site.
- People can subscribe to your shared calendars so they appear in their iCal windows. More on this in the next section.
- You can view your own shared calendar at any time from any computer by moving to its URL. This is a great way to maintain access to your own calendar when you aren't at your Mac.
- You can change a shared calendar by selecting and opening the Info drawer. Use the controls in the drawer to make changes to the calendar's publishing settings.

# MAC OS X TO THE MAX: SUBSCRIBING TO OTHER CALENDARS

You can subscribe to other people's personal calendars or public calendars to add them to your iCal window.



## SUBSCRIBING TO PERSONAL CALENDARS

You can add other personal calendars to your iCal window by doing the following steps:

1. Select Calendar, Subscribe (Option-⌘-S). The Subscribe sheet appears.

> **TIP**
>
> If you are part of a family of iCal users, each person can publish her own calendar and subscribe to each family member's calendar. This provides a great way for everyone in the family to know what's happening in each other's schedule because all they have to do is look in iCal to see all the calendars at the same time.

2. Enter the URL for the calendar to which you want to subscribe and click Subscribe. The Subscribing configuration sheet appears (see Figure 26.12).
3. Enter the title that you want to be used for the calendar in iCal. You can also add a description for the calendar and select which color the items for the calendar should be. If you need to change the URL for the calendar you can edit it here, as well.

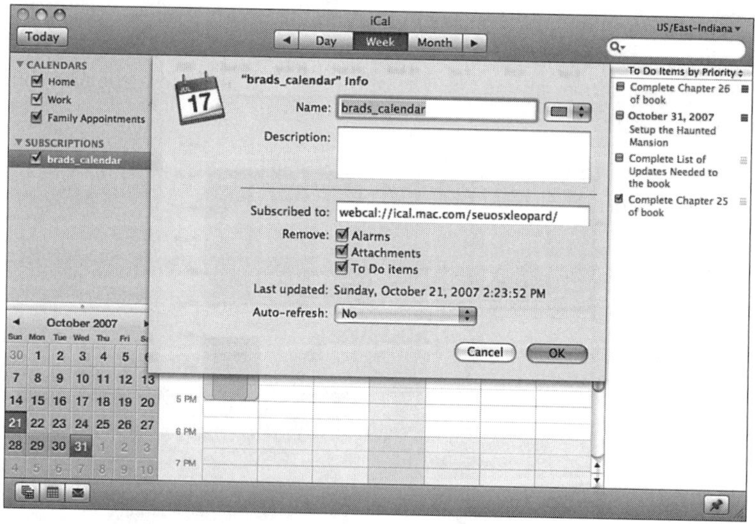


**Figure 26.12**
When you subscribe to a calendar, you can name it and set several other options.

4. If you want the calendar's information to be refreshed automatically, select the frequency at which you want the refresh to occur on the pop-up menu.
5. If you don't want the calendar's alarms to appear in your iCal window, check the "Remove alarms" check box.
6. If you don't want the calendar's To Do items to show up in your iCal window, check the "Remove To Do items" check box. You usually don't want to display the To Do items on a calendar to which you are subscribing unless you have To Do items on it.
7. If you don't want the calendar's attachments showing up in your iCal window, check the Remove Attachments check box.
8 Click OK. The calendar is added to your iCal window, and you can view it just like your own calendars. iCal creates a Subscriptions section in the Calendars pane and displays the new calendar here. If you set the calendar to be refreshed automatically (refer to step 3), it is kept current for you too.



**TIP**

> If you don't set a calendar to be refreshed automatically, you can refresh it manually by opening its contextual menu and selecting Refresh.

**NOTE**

> You can't make any changes to a calendar to which you are subscribed. You can only view it.

## SUBSCRIBING TO PUBLIC CALENDARS

Many public calendars are available to which you can subscribe. For example, most professional sports teams have calendars that show games and other events. You can also find

DVD release calendars, TV schedules, and many other types of calendars to subscribe to. Just like personal calendars, when you subscribe to public calendars, the events on those calendars are shown in your iCal window. To find and subscribe to public calendars, do the following steps:

1. Use Safari to go to one of several iCal sharing sites, such as iCalShare.com (see Figure 26.13).

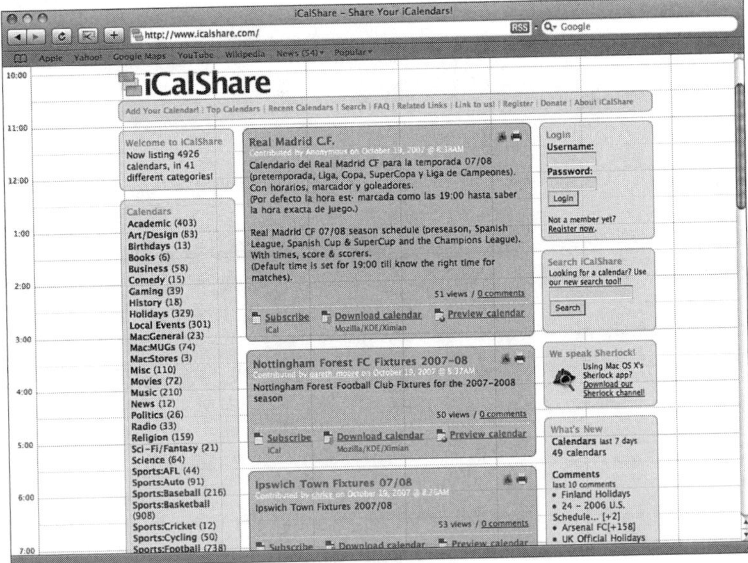


**Figure 26.13**
The iCalShare.com site provides all sorts of interesting calendars to which you can subscribe.



2. Use the search tool or browse through the available calendars that are published on the site. When you find a calendar you want to subscribe to, select it and view the information page. At the bottom are several links; click on Subscribe. You move into iCal and the Subscribe To sheet appears. The URL information is filled in automatically.
3. Click Subscribe. The Subscribe To configuration sheet appears.
4. Review the subscription options and change them as needed.
5. Click OK. The calendar will be added to your iCal window, and you can view its events.

# CHAPTER 27

# Conferencing in Text, Audio, and Video with iChat

## In this chapter

## Communicating with iChat

When you need to communicate with someone else in real-time, there's no easier or more powerful way to do it than with iChat. Of course, you can also use it to do instant text messages. Although useful, that isn't anything to write home about. However, with iChat, a broadband Internet connection, and a FireWire camera (such as the iSight camera built into iMacs, MacBooks, and MacBook Pros), you can use iChat to conduct videoconferencing and audio conferencing. And that is something to write home about, or actually, that is something to have a videoconference with home about.

To text chat, each person must have an a .Mac, AOL Instant Messenger (AIM), or Google Talk account. To chat with audio or video, both parties must be using a .Mac account and must have a broadband Internet connection along with the hardware needed, such as a camera to have a video chat.

## Configuring a Mac for iChat

If you are going to use iChat to have audio- and videoconferences, you must have a FireWire or USB camera attached to your Mac. If you have a modern iMac, MacBook, or MacBook Pro, an iSight camera is built in. If you don't have one of these, you can use an external webcam or some FireWire camcorders for this purpose. You also need a broadband connection to the Internet. Finally, you will need a Mac that is capable of handling the workload of a video chat. All modern Macs are videoconference capable. The best way to find out whether your Mac can handle a videoconference is to try it.

**NOTE**

> To use a camcorder for chatting, the camera must support *play through*, meaning the input coming through the camera's lens must play through the FireWire out port at the same time. If your camera doesn't offer this, you won't be able to use it to chat. Fortunately, many camcorders work with iChat.

Connect the camera you are going to use to your Mac. If it is a camcorder, power it up and place it in Camera mode.

If you don't have a FireWire camera or a broadband connection to the Internet, you can still use iChat for text chatting.

**NOTE**

> Many camcorders are set to go to sleep after a certain period of inactivity passes. When you are using a camcorder during a video conference, it thinks it is inactive because you aren't recording. When it goes to sleep, your conference suddenly ends. Use your camcorder's controls to set its sleep to a large value or to turn off its Sleep mode.

To get started, launch iChat and use the following steps to configure it:

1. Review the information in the welcome screen and click Continue. The "Set up a new iChat Account" window appears. If you have a .Mac account configured for the current user account, the account information is configured automatically. If not, enter the .Mac, AIM, or Google Talk account information in the window and click Continue.

**TIP**

> If you want to apply for an iChat account, click the Get an iChat Account button and follow the onscreen instructions to register for a trial .Mac account. The accompanying iChat account remains valid even if you let the .Mac account expire.

2. Click Done. The basic configuration of iChat is complete and you move into the chatting windows.

iChat offers a number of preferences you can use to configure the way it works. The general preferences you can configure and a description of some specific preferences that might interest you include the following:

- **General**—Use the General tab of the iChat Preferences dialog box to configure some general iChat behaviors (see Figure 27.1). The Settings check boxes enable you to configure various settings. For example, you can add the iChat status to the menu bar. Use the "When fast user switching, set my status to" pop-up menu to determine your iChat status when you switch to a different user account on your Mac. Use the radio buttons to determine what happens when you log in to your user account and your iChat status is Away; for example, you might want your status to be updated to Available automatically. Use the "Save received files to" pop-up menu to select a location in which you save files you receive via iChat.

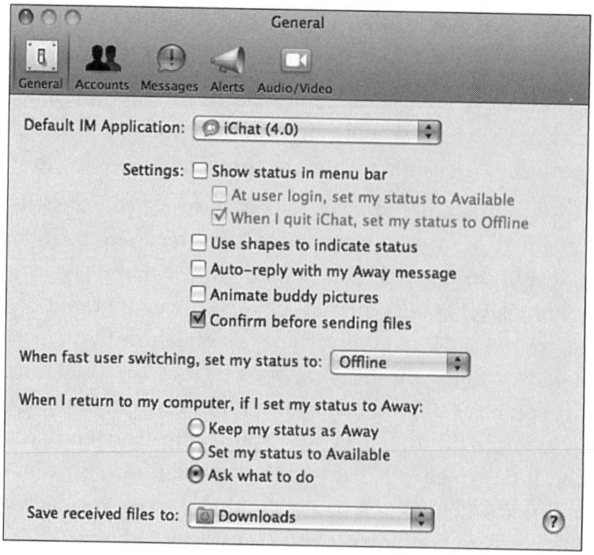

**Figure 27.1**
Use the General pane to configure various iChat settings.

- **Accounts**—Use the Accounts pane to configure the accounts over which you want to chat. Click the Add button (+) at the bottom of the Accounts list to add new accounts. Select an account and use the tools that appear in the right pane of the window to configure it.

**NOTE**

New in Mac OS X 10.5 is the ability to have multiple accounts in iChat and to have them logged in at the same time. In addition to .Mac, AIM, and Google Talk accounts, if there is a Jabber server on your network, you can connect to it to chat with others. You can also enable Bonjour chatting so that you can communicate directly with others on your network that your Mac can discover.

**TIP**

If you have a mobile phone that will support text messaging, you can sign-up for AOL Mobile to receive instant messages on your phone. This can make you truly available anywhere to chat with the people you know. Note that you may be charged by your wireless provider for the messages that you send and receive through your phone.

- **Messages**—The Messages pane enables you to set various formatting options for your messages (see Figure 27.2). Use the Set Font button to configure the font in which you want to view text messages. Use the balloon and font color pop-up menus to choose the color of those items. Check the "Reformat incoming messages" check box and use the corresponding Set Font button and pop-up menus to have iChat reformat text you receive according to your preferences. In the lower part of the pane, you see various options for how iChat works. For example, if you want to save the transcript for chat messages, check the "Automatically save chat transcripts" check box and use the Open Folder button to choose the location in which you want the transcripts to be stored. If you are a fan of tabbed web browsing, you will appreciate the "Collect chats into a single window" feature. All of your chat sessions will be displayed as tabs in a window for the specific account you are using.
- **Alerts**—Use the Alerts pane to set the alerts and notifications iChat uses to get your attention. Select the event for which you want to configure an alert on the Event pop-up menu and then select the specific alert on the check boxes and pop-up menus to configure it. Repeat these steps for each event for which you want to set an alert.
- **Audio/Video**—Use these preferences to configure AV conferencing (see Figure 27.3). In this pane, you will see the current image being received from the camera connected to your Mac. Just under the image is an audio meter that provides a graphic representation of the volume level being received. Choose the audio input on the Microphone pop-up menu; for example, to receive audio via the built-in mic, choose Internal microphone. If you have a Bluetooth headset, click the Set Up Bluetooth Headset button to configure it. If you want to set a bandwidth limit for conferencing, use the Bandwidth Limit pop-up menu to do so. Check the "Automatically open iChat when camera is turned on" check box to have iChat launch when you turn on your camera. Check "Play repeated ring sound when invited to a conference" to be notified via a ringing sound when someone wants to conference with you.

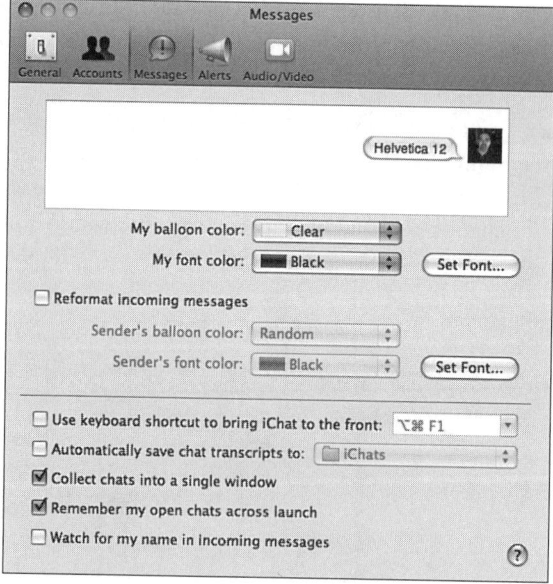


**Figure 27.2**
Using the Messages preferences, you can control the formatting used for chatting.

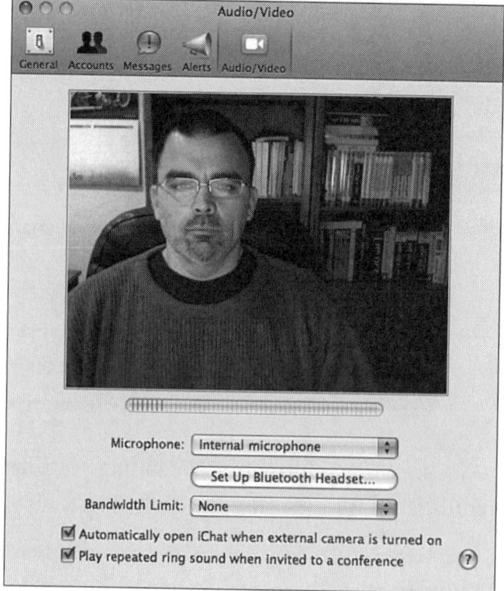


**Figure 27.3**
Use the Audio/Video pane to configure AV conferencing.

27

# Setting Up Chatting Buddies

There are three sources of people with whom you can chat; in iChat lingo these are called *buddies*. One source is the people whom your Mac can see via Bonjour. The second source is people who are configured in your Address Book and have either a .Mac email address, Jabber account, or an AIM screen name. The third source is the buddies you have defined with your .Mac, AIM, or Google Talk accounts because the info about these buddies is retained by these services so that you can log in from any computer and be able to access your buddies.

When you open iChat, you might see two windows: One is titled Bonjour, and the other is labeled Buddy List (see Figure 27.4). The people shown on the Bonjour list are found automatically when your Mac searches your local network for Bonjour users. You add people with whom you want to chat on the Buddy List. You can chat with people on either of these lists in the same way.

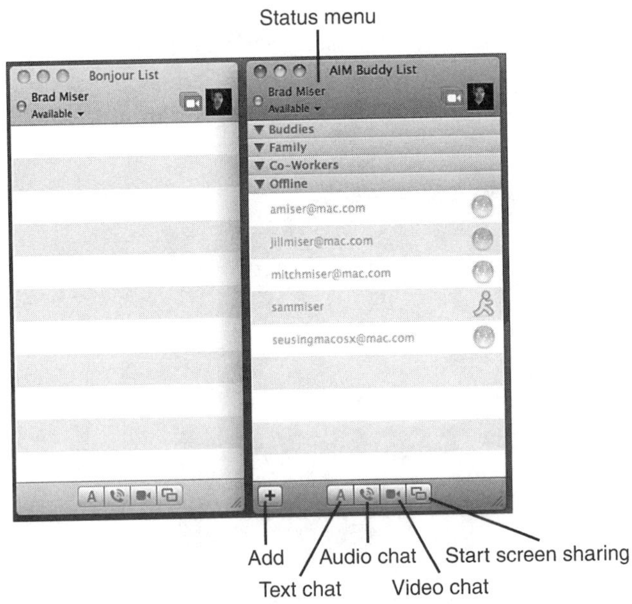


**Figure 27.4**
The Bonjour window shows users who are available to chat on your local network, whereas the Buddy List shows users who have been added to your permanent Buddy List.

**NOTE**

> If you haven't enabled Bonjour messaging, you don't see the Bonjour List window.



At the top of each window, you see your information, including your name, status, video icon (if you have a camera configured for use), and the photo associated with your name.

In the Buddy List window, buddies are placed into one of several categories. AIM Bots are those buddies who use AIM bots to chat. Buddies are your buddies who are currently online. There is a category for Family and a category for Co-Workers to easily get to these groups of contacts. If you chat with someone not on your buddy list, a new category called Recent Buddies will appear. The Offline category contains all your buddies who are currently offline. Use the expansion triangles to expand or collapse the categories.

To add people to your Buddy list, do the following steps:

1. If you want to have the person's contact information available in your Address Book, add the person you want to place on your Buddy List to your Address Book; include either a .Mac address or an AIM username.
2. In iChat, click the Add button (+) located in the lower-left corner of the Buddy List window and choose. The resulting sheet enables you to manually enter information or to choose a person from your Address Book.
3. To manually add a buddy, enter the account name, choose the type on the top pop-up menu, choose the group in which you want the buddy placed (Buddies, Family or Co-Workers), and enter the first and last name. Skip to step 5.
4. To select the person you want to add to your Buddy List, click the expand button next to the Last Name field. The lower pane of the sheets expands and you see a mini–Address Book viewer. Search or browse for the person you want to add and select the name.
5. Click Add.
6. Repeat steps 2 and 5 to add more people to your Buddy List.

After you add buddies, you return to the Buddy List window and the new buddies appear in the appropriate sections when they are online or in the Offline section when they aren't.

# CHATTING WITH TEXT

Instant messaging is a preferred way of communicating for many people. Text chats are easy to do, fast, and convenient. Using iChat, you start your own text chats or answer someone's request to text chat with you.

## STARTING A TEXT CHAT

You can text chat with others by using the following steps:

1. Select the person in the Bonjour window or on the Buddy List with whom you want to chat. If the person is on the Offline list, she isn't available for chatting so you'll need to communicate some other way. Even if the person is online, make sure the status indicator shows they she is available for chatting before you initiate a chat session.
2. Click the Text Chat button, which is the A located at the bottom of the respective window. An empty Instant Message window appears. The name of the window is "Chat with *buddy*" where *buddy* is the name of the person with whom you are chatting.
3. Type your message in the bar at the bottom of the window. You can use the pop-up menu at the end of the window to add smileys to what you type.
4. When you are ready to send what you typed, press Return. You see the message you typed near your name at the top of the window. It is sent to the person with whom you are chatting.

Your message appears in a text bubble on that user's desktop. When the user clicks the bubble, she is able to accept your request, type a reply, and send it you.

When you receive a reply to your message, you see the person's picture along with the text she sent (see Figure 27.5).

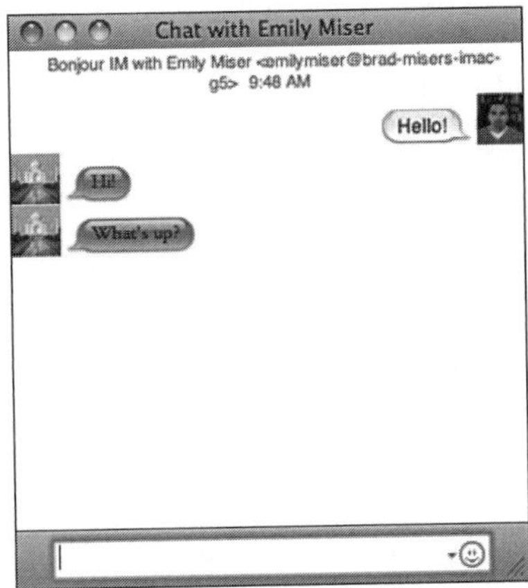


**Figure 27.5**
Once a buddy accepts your chat request, you see what she types along with the picture associated with her username.

> **TIP**
> You can change the picture others see of you when chatting by going to the iChat menu and selecting Change My Picture. Use the resulting dialog box to either capture an image of yourself with the built-in iSight camera, or select an image on your Mac. iChat supports animated GIFs as buddy icons for iChat, as well as a number of other image formats.

5. Type your response in the message box at the bottom of the window and press Return.

> **TIP**
> Click the emoticon icon at the end of the text box to include a smiley with your text.

6. Continue chatting to your heart's content (see Figure 27.6).
7. When you are done chatting, let the person you are chatting with know and close the chat window. If you keep iChat open, you could chat with that person again. If you quit iChat, or go offline, the person with whom you were chatting will see that your status has changed.

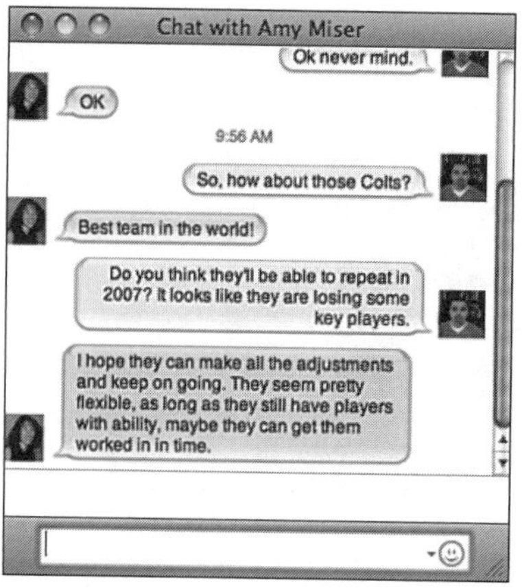


**Figure 27.6**
Text chats are a great way to communicate about the topics you care about.

### Answering a Text Chat Request

When a person wants to chat with you, a box will appear on your screen. Click it and it expands to a chat window (see Figure 27.7). To accept the chat, click the Accept button, type your reply, and press Return to send it (you don't need to click the Accept button, you can just type to accept). If you don't want to talk, click Decline. If you want to block the person trying to chat with you, click Block.

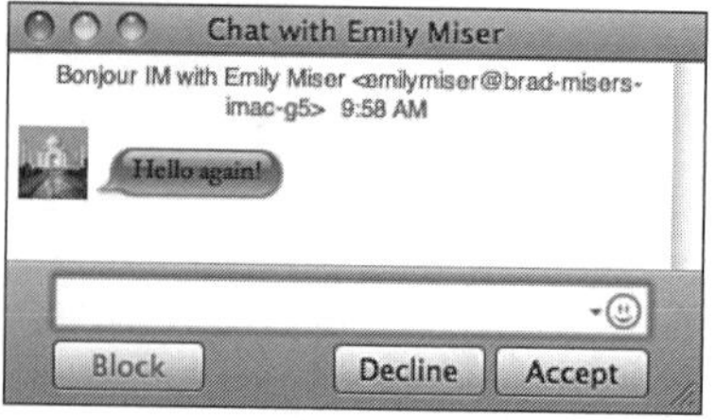


**Figure 27.7**
When someone requests a text chat with you, you can accept it or not.

If you accept the chat request, use the chat window just like when you start a session.

To end a session, close the chat window.

When someone leaves the chat, you'll see a status message saying so at the bottom of the window.



## Chatting with Sound

Text chats are great, but audio chats are sometimes even better. Using an audio chat is pretty much like talking on the telephone.

To start an audio chat, select one or more people with whom you want to chat and click the Audio chat button. You see the Audio Chat window and invitations are sent to each buddy you selected. When a person accepts the invitation, you see that person's name above an audio level indicator and their image (see Figure 27.8). When you see that, start talking. Audio chats work just like talking on the telephone.

**Figure 27.8**
Audio chats allow you to talk with someone, or groups or people, just as if you were using a telephone.

**NOTE**

> If you are listening to iTunes when you start an audio or video chat, it automatically stops playing.

To mute your microphone, click the Mute button, which looks like a microphone. When muted, the audio bar is filled and both the bar and button are orange.

Control the volume with the Volume slider.

To remove a person from an audio chat, point to their name and click the x button that appears.

When someone wants to audio chat with you, you'll receive an invitation. Accept it and you'll join the chat.

## Conferencing with Video and Sound

If a person you want to talk to and see meets the requirements for AV chatting, click the camera icon next to the person with whom you want to conference or select one or more video-ready buddies and click the Video Chat button. A request for conference is sent to the buddies you selected. You also see a Video Chat window showing the image being transmitted by your camera.

The people with whom you are trying to communicate see a Video Chat invitation window. If they click your name in that window, it expands to show a Video Chat window on each person's machine. They can then select to accept or deny your request.

If a person accepts, you will see a message that video conferencing is starting. As other people accept, you see a video window for each (see Figure 27.9). You appear in a window as well; your window is highlighted.

**Figure 27.9**
When you have more than one person in a chat, each person appears in her own window.

Speak normally, and you should keep your movements a bit slower than usual so the motion is smoother on the other end. Depending on how many servers the data has to flow through and how fast each person's connection is, considerable delay might occur. You need to adjust your speech and movement to fit the specific conference in which you are participating. In most cases, this delay won't be a problem for you. To see the conference in full screen, click the Make Full Screen button.

To remove someone from the conference, point to their window and click the x button that appears.

To add more people to the conference, click the Add Buddy button and choose the person you want to invite to join you.

When you are done with the chat, close the window.

When someone wants to video chat with you, you receive an invitation similar to other invitations. You can accept it to start the conference or decline.

## SHARING YOUR SCREEN IN A CHAT

27

If you've ever tried to explain to someone how to do something on their computer or if you've ever tried to have someone explain to you what he is doing, you'll see why the ability to share screens in iChat is so useful.

To share your screen with someone you need to first initiate a video chat with them. In addition, they must be using Mac OS X 10.5. After you have established your video chat, go to the Buddies menu and select Share My Screen if you want that person to be able to remotely control your computer. If you want to control their computer, select Ask to Share Remote Screen from the Buddies menu.

After a screen-sharing session has started, iChat will will enable an audio chat between you and your buddy. You can then talk about what is being accomplished. A screen-sharing session allows you to control your buddy's computer by giving you control of her keyboard and mouse; she will be able to see you doing whatever it is you are doing on her computer. You can copy files from her computer to yours, or from yours to hers. Anything she could do on her computer, you can do on her computer. The same is true if you had shared your screen with her.

Screen sharing has many practical applications, especially if you are trying to troubleshoot an issue on a remote computer. But there are security issues to be aware of. If you share your screen with someone they have full access to everything you have access to. Be certain to only share with people that you know and trust.

## Presenting in the iChat Theater

The ability to chat with someone via text, audio, or video can be very effective. But sometimes you need to be able to show someone a file or a presentation. iChat Theater provides you with the opportunity to share a file, photos, a presentation, or other type of document while you have a video chat with a buddy.

To see whether the file you want to present will work in the iChat Theater, return to the Finder, click on the file, and then click the Quick View button in the Toolbar. If Quick View shows a preview of the file, it will work in the iChat Theater. If the file does not show a preview, but shows the icon for the file, it will not work.

To use the iChat Theater, you need to establish a video conference with your buddy. They do not need to have a video camera; you can create a one-way video chat with them. After you have established the video chat, go to the File menu and select Share a file with iChat Theater. You are presented with a standard Open dialog box; navigate to the file and click the Share button. Your buddy will then see file that you have shared while he continues to hear you speaking in the chat. You will see a Quick View window of the file being shared. Depending on the file, you may be able to control what your buddy sees. For example, if you are sharing a Keynote slideshow you will be able to advance to the next slide. When you are done presenting the file, just close the Quick View window to return to your video conference.

When you are done sharing the document, close the Quick View window and your video conference will resume. If you have another file to present, you can follow the same steps to present another document to your buddy.

**Figure 27.10**
Using the iChat Theater, I am sharing a QuickTime video with a buddy. You can see the controller for the video that allows me to pause and play the video.

# MAC OS X TO THE MAX: CHAT AWAY

Following are some additional iChat tidbits:

- You can have multiple chats of various types going on with different people at the same time. Each chat appears in its own, independent chat window unless you check the "Collect chats into a single window" check box on the Messages pane of the iChat Preferences dialog box.
- Manage your status by clicking the pop-up menu next to your name at the top of the Buddy List. When the green dot appears, your status is online and people will be able to see you; when the red dot appears, your are unavailable for chatting. There are a number of status options that can appear for you as you see on the menu. For example, if you choose Current iTunes Song, the artist and song currently playing in iTunes will be shown when your status appears in other people's Buddy List. Choose Edit Status Menu to see a sheet on which you can customize your status menu.
- Use your status settings to prevent unwanted interruptions. For example, if you are online, but busy with something, open your status menu and choose Away or one of the other unavailable statuses.
- You can be logged in and initiate chats without others knowing you are online by setting your status to Invisible.
- Right-click a buddy on the Buddy List and choose Show Profile. You see the Info window that has three panes. The Profile pane shows you the person's profile including chat name account, capabilities, photo, and notes. On the Alerts pane, you can configure actions specific to that buddy, such as sounds that play when that person logs in. Use the Address Card pane to associate a card in Address Book or to enter additional information for the buddy.

- To block someone with whom you don't want to chat, select the buddy and choose Buddies *blockbuddy* where *blockbuddy* is the name of the person whom you want to block.
- Use the Video menu to configure and control various video and audio settings. For example, choose Video, Full Screen to put a video conference in Full Screen mode. Choose Video, Record Chat to record a chat session. Use the Enabled commands at the bottom of the menu to enable or disable the microphone, camera, and screen sharing feature.
- To add effects to your image in a video chat, Video, Show Video Effects. In the resulting Video Effects window, click the effect you want to apply.
- You can add backgrounds to your video chat sessions. Select Video, Video Effects and a new window opens. You will see different special effects on the first page; use the arrows at the bottom corners to move to the next or previous pages. Page 3 of the video effects includes video clips you can use as backgrounds. For instance, a video of the Eiffel Tower or Yosemite can be used. Page 4 is where you can add your own still or video backdrops.

**Figure 27.11**
Backdrops can make a video chat with friends or co-workers a lot more interesting and fun.

Just drag a photo or video file from iPhoto, iMovie, or the Finder onto one of the User Backdrop areas. Open the Video, Video Preview to see a preview of the backdrop; you will be asked to move out of the camera's view so that it will be able to replace the real background items behind you with the backdrop you have selected. After the backdrop has been applied you can move back in front of the camera and initiate your video chat. You can change to another backdrop at any point after that, as iChat now knows enough about what is really behind you that it can replace those items with the backdrop you select.

CHAPTER 28

# WORKING WITH LEOPARD'S TEXT AND GRAPHIC APPLICATIONS

## In this chapter

# WORKING WITH TEXT AND GRAPHICS

Although not as well known as iLife, iWork, Word, Acrobat, and other more mainstream applications, Mac OS X does include several very useful text and graphics applications. These include TextEdit, which is a basic word processor; Preview, which enables you to preview lots of different kinds of content; Image Capture, which captures images from a camera; and Grab, with which you can capture images on your Mac's screen. Even though none of these are likely to replace their more full-feature counterparts, they can be very handy.

# WORKING WITH TEXTEDIT

Mac OS X's TextEdit application is a fairly powerful word processor hidden behind a simple and humble-looking interface (see Figure 28.1). It doesn't look like much, but TextEdit can probably handle most of what you use a word processor for. I'm assuming you've used a similar application before and so don't need to know the very basics of creating a text document.

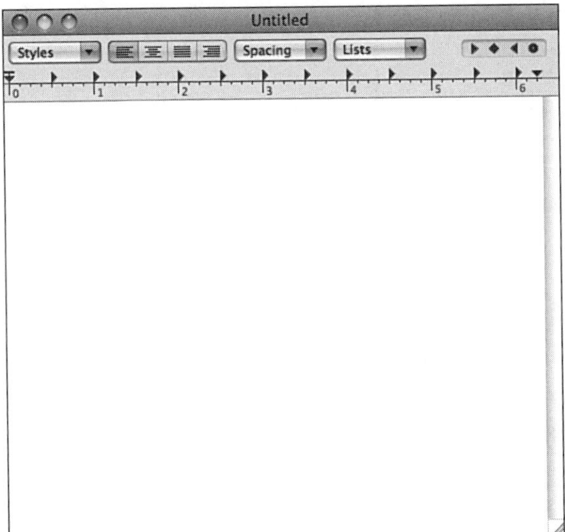


**Figure 28.1**
No, it isn't much to look at, but don't let its simple appearance fool you—TextEdit packs some powerful features in a plain-looking package.

However, check out the following list features that you might not spot at first glance:

- **File formats**—TextEdit is compatible with a number of file formats in the context of opening and saving documents. Its basic file format is the Rich Text Format (RTF), but it supports many others including: HTML, web archive, and most importantly, various flavors of Word (see Figure 28.2). You can save or open documents in any of these formats.
- **Formatting**—TextEdit's Format menu includes the Font command that enables you to apply a large variety of formatting to text, including using the Mac OS X Font panel.

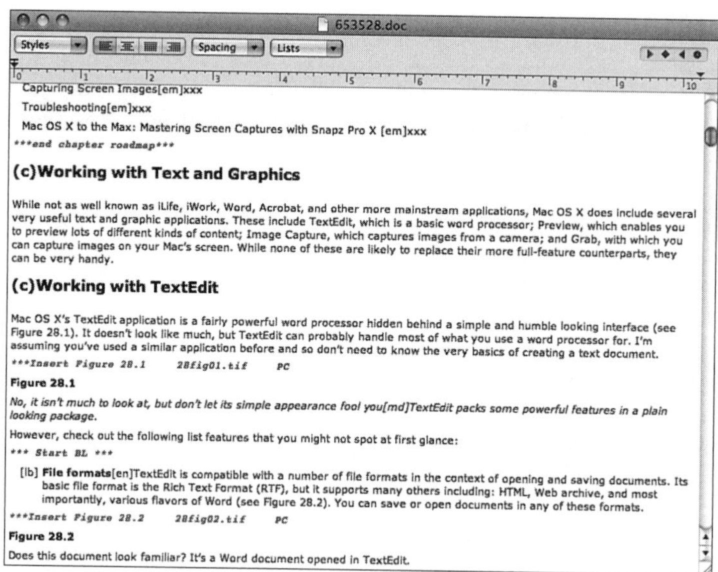


**Figure 28.2**
Does this document look familiar? It's a Word document opened in TextEdit.

- **Styles**—Styles are collections of formatting elements that you can save and reapply to text by choosing the appropriate style name. To create a style, enter text and format it as you want the style to be saved and select it. Then, open the Styles pop-up menu located in the upper-left corner of the TextEdit window and choose Other. The Styles sheet appears; click Add To Favorites; in the resulting sheet, enter a name for the style, and configure whether you want the font and ruler to be included as part of the file. After you click Add, the style you created will be added to the Styles pop-up menu and you can reapply it to text easily by selecting the text and choosing the style on the pop-up menu.

  After you've defined a style, you can easily select text in the document with that style by selecting an instance of the style, choosing Other on the Styles menu, and clicking Select. You can then choose to select text within the document or within an existing selection. Once the text is selected, you can make changes to it consistently throughout a document.

  To remove a style, open the Styles menu and choose Other. Use the preview buttons to display the style in the preview pane (see Figure 28.3).

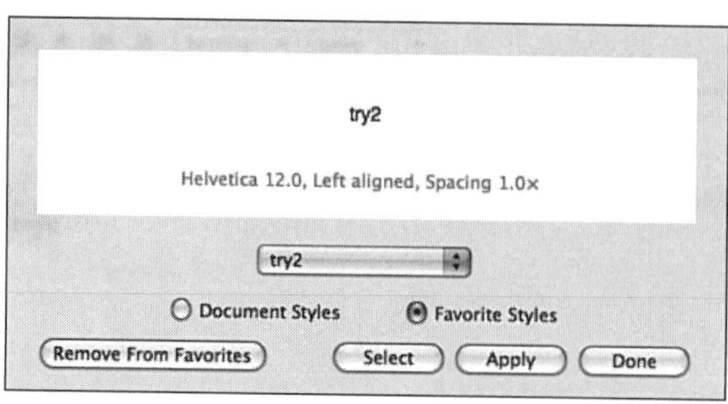


**Figure 28.3**
The Styles sheet enables you to preview and select text in the styles defined.

28

- **Tables**—Like other word processors, TextEdit supports the creation of tables. To insert a table into a document, choose Format, Text, Table. The Table tool appears (see Figure 28.4). Use the tool to define the number of rows and columns, the alignment (vertical and horizontal), cell border and color, and cell background and color. You can also create nested tables.

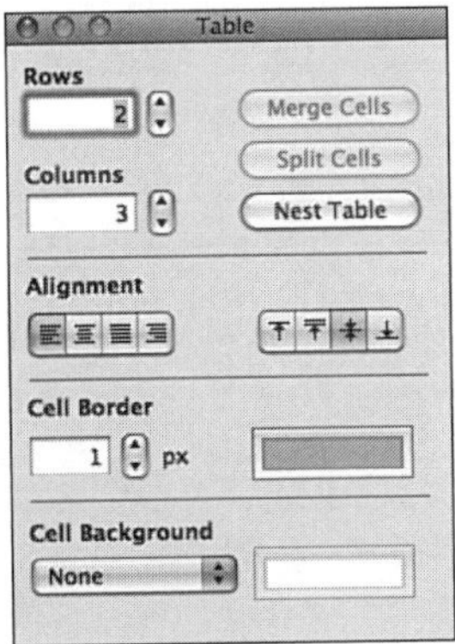


**Figure 28.4**
The Table tool enables you to create tables in your TextEdit documents.

  After you've created your table, you can drag the borders of cells to resize them. You can also use styles and apply the other formatting tools to a table's content.

- **Lists**—Using the List tool, you can create a variety of lists. To start a list, open the Lists menu and choose the style of bullet you want to use in the list. You can choose from symbols, such as bullets, or organized lists, such as numbers for a numbered list. Each time you press Return, a new list item will be created using the bullet style you selected. To end the list, choose None on the Lists menu or press Return twice.

  If you choose Other on the Lists menu, a sheet appears in which you can define customer lists by adding a prefix, choosing a bullet, and adding a suffix.

- **HTML creation**—You can use TextEdit to create or edit HTML documents for web pages. You can save any document in HTML; if you use TextEdit's tables and lists, those elements will be maintained and formatted properly in the resulting web page.
- **Spelling and grammar checking**—TextEdit has a full-featured spell checker that can check as you type or on a entire document. It's available on the Edit menu. If you open the Spelling and Grammar tool, you can choose to have grammar checked when you check spelling.
- **Hyperlinks**—Use the Format, Text, Link command to add hyperlinks to your TextEdit documents.



If you find TextEdit useful, check out its preferences. You can use these to set default formats, formatting, options (including spell checking and page numbering), and open/save settings.

# Working with Preview

As its name implies, Preview's primary function is to let you preview (perhaps the application would be more accurately called View) documents. In the context of Preview, *documents* include many kinds of files, such as image files, PDFs, and many more. Preview is useful for viewing a wide variety of documents and allows you to make some minor editing changes to some of those documents.

**NOTE**

> Preview is Mac OS X's default PDF viewing application.

## Working with Images in Preview

Many of the image file types you commonly use under Mac OS X are configured to open in Preview by default.

**NOTE**

> Preview might not be the default application for viewing image, PDF, or other files. If not, you can open any image file by first opening Preview and then using the Open command, or by setting Preview to be the application associated with a specific image file.

⇨ To learn how to associate files with an application, **see** "Determining the Application That Opens When You Open a Document," **p. 156**.

To open and view images in Preview, use the following steps:

1. Open one or more image files. Preview will open and you will see the selected image in the Preview window (see Figure 28.5). You'll see the other open images in the sidebar. If the image doesn't fill the Preview window, you'll see gray borders around it.

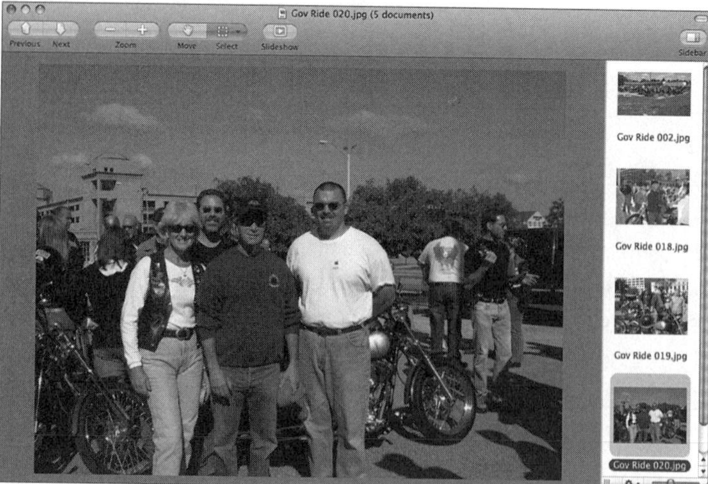


**Figure 28.5**
Preview enables you to view images and perform some basic image editing tasks.

**TIP**

> If an application other than Preview opens when you open an image file, open the file's contextual menu and select Open With, Preview.

2. Use the tools in the toolbar to control how the images appear, such as the Zoom In button to make the image larger.

**TIP**

> To zoom in on part of an image, select the part on which you want to zoom and select View, Zoom to Selection (or press ⌘-*). To remove the selection box, click the image outside of the box.

Many of Preview's commands are straightforward, such as the Zoom to Fit command that sizes the current image so it fills the Preview window. If you have used any graphics application, you won't have any trouble with these basic viewing commands.

Preview also features the sidebar, which is useful when you are working with more than one image at a time. Each image appears as a thumbnail in the sidebar. Select an image's thumbnail to view it in the Preview window.

**NOTE**

> If you open images one at a time, a Preview window will open for each image file.

You can open and close the sidebar by clicking the Sidebar button on the toolbar; by selecting View, sidebar; or by pressing Shift-⌘-D. You can change the size of the thumbnails in the sidebar using the slider located at the bottom of the sidebar; use the Action pop-up menu to change how the images in the sidebar are organized.

**TIP**

> You can customize Preview's toolbar just like you can in many other Mac OS X applications, including the Finder.

To get information about an image, choose, Tools, Inspector. In the Inspector window, you see various information about the image, such as its resolution, type, file size, and so on (see Figure 28.6). Click the Metadata tab, which has the exclamation point icon, to get even more detailed information. You can use the third tab, which has the magnifying glass icon, to associate keywords with an image; you can use these keywords to find images using Spotlight.

To perform basic image correction on an image, choose Tools, Adjust Color. Use the resulting Adjust Color tool to change exposure, white- and black-point, saturation, contrast, and other aspects of an image (see Figure 28.7). You can use the Sepia slider to apply the sepia effect to an image.

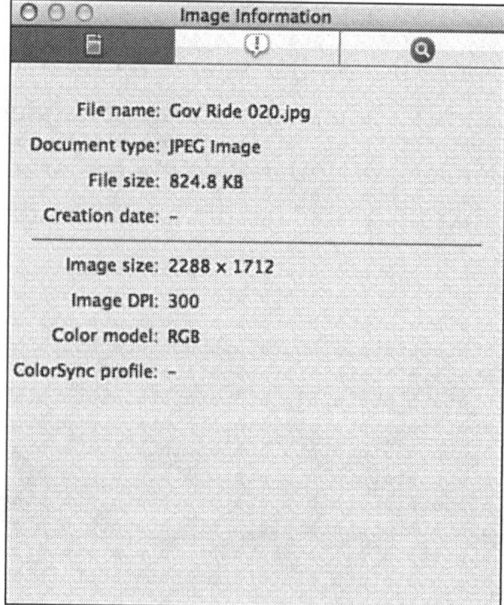


**Figure 28.6**
Preview's Inspector provides detailed information about an image.

**NOTE**

Some digital cameras have the ability to include Global Positioning System (GPS) coordinates about where an image was captured. If you are working on an image that has this data, the Inspector will include a GPS section with the data from the camera. You can see on a map where the image was taken, as well as use the coordinate information for a tool like Google Earth.

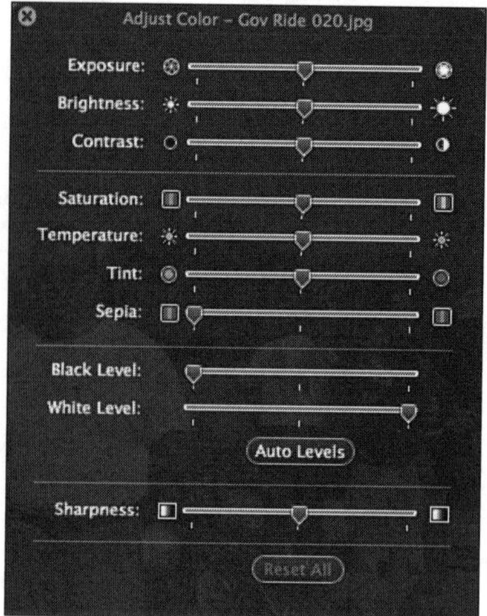


**Figure 28.7**
Use the Adjust Color tool to improve your image.

You can resize an image by choosing Tools, Adjust Size. In the resulting sheet, you can change the image's dimensions based on pixels or inches.

Cropping is one of the most basic and useful image editing options. Fortunately, you can use Preview to easily crop images, as you can see in the following steps:

1. Open the image you want to crop.
2. Choose the selection tool you want to use on the Select pop-up menu and drag in the image to select the portion of the image you want to keep (see Figure 28.8).
3. To adjust the selected part of the image, drag the selection box around or resize it by either dragging a corner or dragging the resize handle located in the center of each side of the selection box.

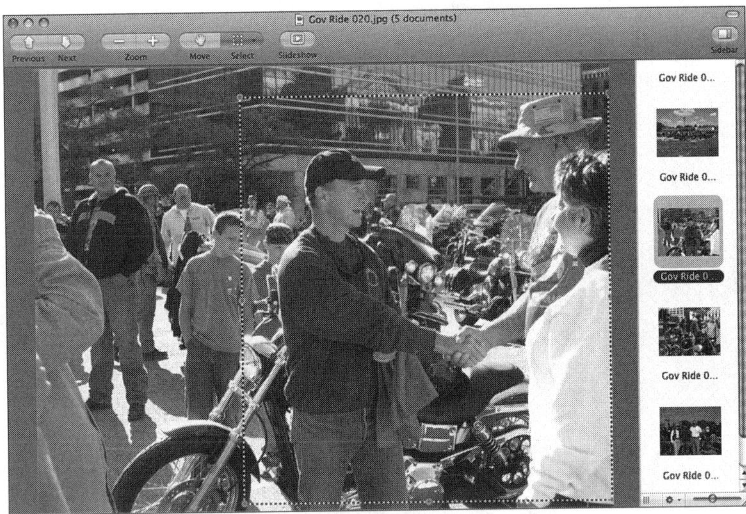


**Figure 28.8**
Select the portion of the image you want to keep before you use the Crop command.

**TIP**

> To keep the selection box proportional to the original image, hold down the Shift key while you drag.

4. When you have selected the part of the image you want to keep, select Tools, Crop or press ⌘-K. All the image outside of the selection box will be removed.

**TIP**

> You can move to back to the most recently saved version of an image by selecting File, Revert.

28

## Using Preview to Read PDFs

Portable Document Format (PDF) files are a common way to distribute electronic documents. You are likely to encounter many PDFs on the Web, as file attachments to emails, and so on. Preview is Mac OS X's default PDF viewer.

⇨ You can create your own PDF documents. To learn how, **see** "Saving Documents As PDFs," **p. 165**.

To view PDFs with Preview, do the following:

1. Open a PDF document in Preview.
2. Open Preview's sidebar. The sidebar has three views: Thumbnails, Table of Contents, and Annotations. To see the document's table of contents, click the pop-up menu on the tool bar at the bottom of the sidebar and select Table of Contents. You see the document's table of contents; you can expand or collapse sections by clicking their expansion triangles (see Figure 28.9).

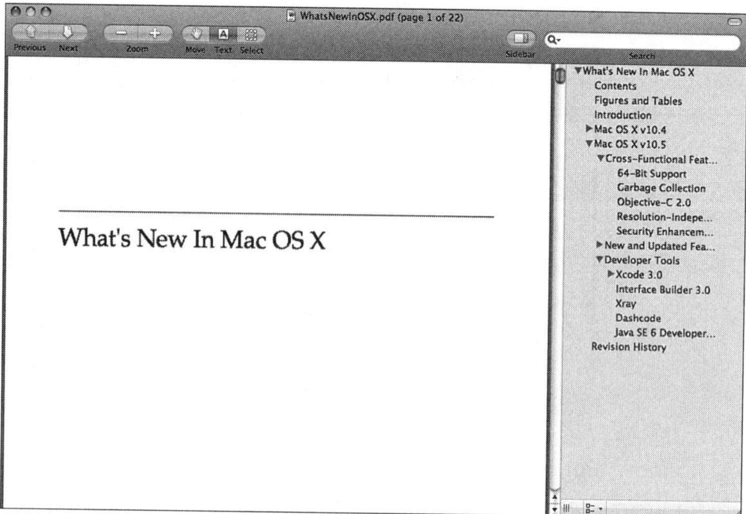


**Figure 28.9**
You can click a section in the table of contents to jump to it.

3. To view the document via thumbnails, select Thumbnails from the pop-up menu, which is located on the left side of the sidebar toolbar; click a thumbnail to move to a specific page.
4. Move to pages one at a time by clicking the Next or Previous button in the toolbar or by pressing the Down or Up arrow keys.
5. Adjust the display of a PDF document by using the commands shown when you select View, PDF Display. The options include Single Page, which shows the document page-by-age; Two Pages, which shows two pages at a time; and so on.
6. You can add notes to your PDF by selecting text and using the Mark Up and Annotate pop-up menus. Choose the Text selection tool on the Preview toolbar and select the text you want to annotate. On the Tools, Mark Up menu, choose the type of marking you want to apply, such as highlighting or strikethrough. Or, choose an annotation, such as a box, on the Tools, Annotate menu. You can use both types of tools on the same page, and you can include multiple annotations on the same page. If you select Annotation from the pop-up menu in the sidebar, you'll see the list of all annotations you've made (see Figure 28.10).

**TIP**

> You can add Mark Up and Annotation tools to the toolbar by going to View, Customize Toolbar. On the resulting sheet, select the tools you want to add and move them to the toolbar. This can be much faster than using the menus to select these tools.

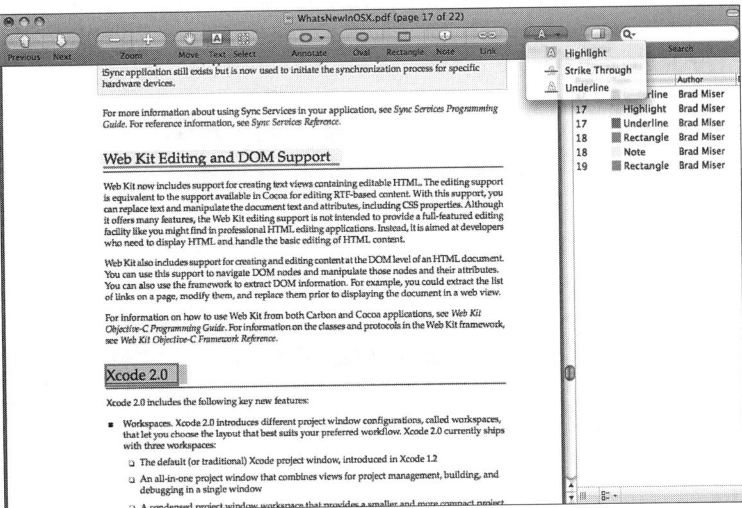


**Figure 28.10**
You can annotate PDF documents using Preview's Annotation tools.

7. To move around inside a document, select Tools, Move Tool, click the Move tool on the toolbar, or press ⌘-1. The cursor will become the hand and you can drag around a page to move it within the Preview window (unless the entire page fills the window, in which case you can't do this).
8. To select text so you can copy and paste it into other documents, select Tools, Text Tool or press ⌘-2. Select the text you want to copy and select Edit, Copy. The text will be moved to the Clipboard, from which you can paste it into other documents, such as TextEdit. (A PDF's security settings determine whether you can do this.)
9. To select parts of a page using a selection box, select Tools, Select Tool or press ⌘-3. Drag on the page to select part of it. You can then copy that part and paste it into other documents. To remove the selection box, choose a different tool.
10. To add a bookmark to a PDF, move to the location at which you want to set a bookmark and select Bookmarks, Add Bookmark or press ⌘-D. In the resulting sheet, name the bookmark and click Add. You can return to this point in the document at any time by selecting it on the Bookmarks menu.
11. To search a PDF document, type the text for which you want to search in the Search box that appears at the right end of the toolbar. As you type, Preview will search the document for your search text. When it finds the first instance, the page on which it appears will be shown and the occurrence of the search term is highlighted. In the sidebar, each occurrence of the search term appears on the list of results (at the top of the

list, you will see how many occurrences there are in the document). When you click an occurrence, the page on which it appears is shown in the Preview window and the search term is highlighted on the page.

12. If you made annotations to the document, save it before you close it.
13. Preview gives you the ability to change the order of the pages in a PDF. Click on one of the pages in the Sidebar and drag it to the position you want that page to be in now. You can also click on a page and then press Delete to remove the page from the document. Save your changes (you might want to Save As so that you keep the original version if you need it again.) Finally, you can also merge PDF documents by opening one PDF then selecting another PDF in the Finder and dragging and dropping the second PDF into Preview's Sidebar.

**TIP**

Check out the Inspector when you are working with PDF documents. It has five tabs that provide lots of information about and control over the PDF document.

## VIEWING A SLIDESHOW IN PREVIEW

iPhoto, iDVD, and iMovie can be used to create slideshows. Although not nearly as sophisticated as those applications, you can create a basic slideshow in Preview by performing the following steps:

1. Use Preview to open the image files you want to view in a slideshow.
2. Select View, Slideshow; press Shift-⌘-F; or click the Slideshow button that appears on the toolbar. The Preview interface will disappear and the images will be displayed as a slideshow.
3. Move the mouse and a set of controls appears at the bottom of the screen (see Figure 28.11). From left to right, the buttons are
   - **Back**—Moves the slideshow back one image
   - **Pause/Play**—Pauses or plays the slideshow
   - **Next**—Moves to the next image
   - **Index Sheet**—Displays thumbnails of each image so you can click one to move to that image
   - **Fit to Screen/Actual Size**—Adjusts the size of the image to fill the screen or be the actual size
   - **Close**—Stops the slideshow
4. Use the appropriate buttons to control the slideshow.
5. When you are done, click the Close button or press Esc. You move back to the standard Preview window.

**Figure 28.11**
Preview's slideshows aren't fancy, but they are a quick way to view a batch of images.

## Using Preview to Convert Files to Different Formats

One of the nice things Preview does for you is enable you to convert an image from one format to another. Here's how:

1. Open the image you want to save in a different format.
2. Select File, Save As. The Save As sheet appears.
3. Select the file format in which you want to save the file in the Format pop-up menu (see Figure 28.12).
4. If the format you selected has options, use the slider, check boxes, or other controls to configure its settings.
5. Rename the file, choose a save location, and then click Save. A new file in the format you selected will be created.

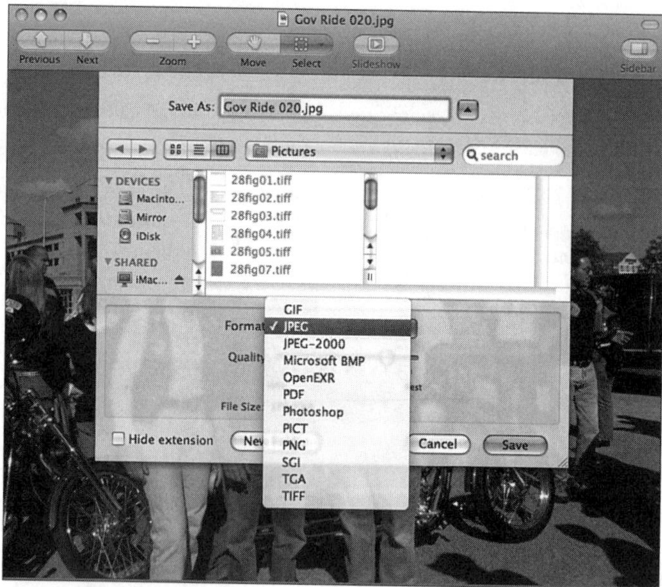


**Figure 28.12**
One of Preview's most useful functions is its capability to convert image files to different formats.

## Setting Preview Preferences

You can configure several Preview preferences to tweak Preview to suit your needs. These options are summarized in Table 28.1.

**Table 28.1 Preview Preferences**

| Tab | Preference | What It Does |
|---|---|---|
| General | User name | Used to track who made annotations to PDF files. |
| General | Window background color | Sets the color of the area outside an image in the Preview window (the default is gray). |
| Images | When opening images: Open all images in one window | No matter how you open images (one at a time or many at once), they all appear in the same window and you can use the Drawer to work with them. |
| Images | When opening images: Open groups of images in the same window | When you open multiple images at the same time, they all appear in the same window and you can use the Drawer to work with them. |
| Images | When opening images: Open each image in its own window | No matter how many images you open at once, they each appear in a separate Preview window. |
| Images | Default image size: Actual size | Opens images at their default sizes. |

*continues*

**Table 28.1 Continued**

| Tab | Preference | What It Does |
|---|---|---|
| Images | Default image size: Scale large images to fit window | Automatically zooms out in large images so the entire image is displayed in the Preview window. |
| Images | Respect image DPI for Actual Size | This causes the Actual Size command to take the image's resolution into account when resizing it. |
| PDF | Default document scale | Choose "Auto-scale" to use the default size settings stored in the PDF file; choose "Use scale of" and enter a value to cause Preview to use the scale value you enter when you open a PDF. |
| PDF | Remember last page viewed | Causes Preview to display the page you last viewed when you open a document. |
| PDF | Use logical page numbers | Causes Preview to show the correct overall page number of a document including the frontmatter pages (which might be numbered with Roman numerals or another number scheme). |
| PDF | Greeking threshold | Sets the size at which greeking is used to display text; this is done when text becomes too small to be displayed legibly and instead is replaced by symbols that look like Greek. |
| PDF | Anti-alias text and line art | When checked, Preview will smooth out text and art through antialiasing. |
| PDF | Open sidebar only for Table of Contents | Causes Preview to open the sidebar only when a PDF has a table of contents element included in it. |
| Bookmarks | Remove | This pane shows all the bookmarks that have been created using Preview; for each, the label, file, and page are shown. Select a bookmark and click Remove to delete it from the document in which it was created. |



## Working with Image Capture

Mac OS X was designed to work with digital images; it includes the basic Image Capture application that provides a consistent interface for various models of digital cameras. Its single purpose is to download images from digital devices (cameras, scanners, and so on) to your Mac. When you are working with a digital camera, you are better off using iPhoto to download images because it has more powerful tools and enables you to build and organize your image library. Still, Image Capture has a few tricks up its sleeves and might be the best way to scan images.

Image Capture works with devices that support the Picture Transfer Protocol (PTP). If you aren't sure whether your device supports this protocol, check the manufacturer's website and product specifications to see whether your particular model supports PTP. Fortunately, almost all modern digital imaging devices do.

**NOTE**

> The more technical name for PTP is ISO 28740.

Image Capture can be configured so it automatically downloads images when you plug your camera or scanner into your Mac. Mac OS X also has built-in support for many digital cameras that can transmit the captured photos via 802.11 networking or Bluetooth. By default, Mac OS X is configured to open iPhoto when it detects a camera. You can change this behavior with the Image Capture Preferences command.

**NOTE**

> Image Capture works pretty much the same way whether you are downloading images from a scanner or a camera. However, your best bet is to use iPhoto to download images from your camera so you have all its photo-related tools at your fingertips.

## USING IMAGE CAPTURE TO DOWNLOAD IMAGES FROM A CAMERA TO YOUR MAC

If you don't have iPhoto installed on your Mac (perhaps you don't want to purchase the iLife software), you can use Image Capture to download images from a camera to your Mac so you can work with them, such as viewing them or creating a simple slideshow in Preview. Use the following steps to get images from a camera to your Mac:

1. Connect your camera to your Mac using its USB cable.

**NOTE**

> If iPhoto is installed on your Mac, by default your Mac opens iPhoto when you connect a camera to it. You can allow that to happen and then open Image Capture. Both applications can be running at the same time. You can also change the Image Capture preferences to specify that Image Capture should open when you connect your camera to your Mac.



2. Power up your camera (if it has a mode selector to communicate with a computer, choose that mode—most cameras switch to this mode automatically). If you haven't configured Image Capture to open automatically, open it (Applications folder). If you have configured Image Capture to open automatically, it will do so when your Mac

detects the camera. You will see the Image Capture window (see Figure 28.13). The application communicates with the camera to determine how many images need to be downloaded. When the camera is ready to begin downloading images, the Download Some and Download All buttons become active (see Figure 28.13).

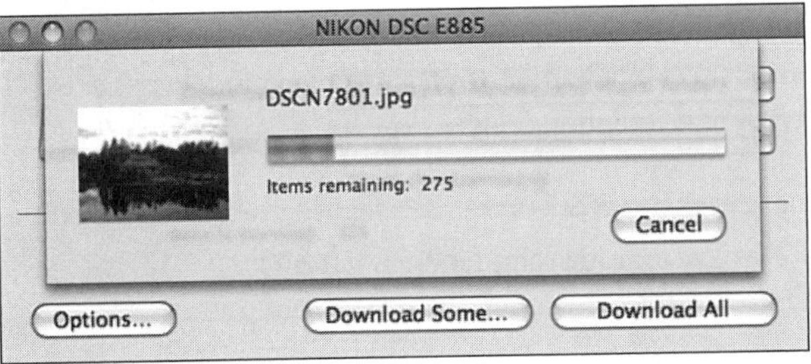


**Figure 28.13**
When you connect a supported camera to your Mac, Image Capture displays the number of images that are ready to be downloaded.

> **NOTE**
> If your camera is not recognized by Image Capture, it probably does not support PTP. In that case, you have to use the camera's software to download images from it.

3. Select the folder into which you want the images to be downloaded on the Download To pop-up menu. By default, Image Capture selects the Pictures, Movies, and Music folders option. You can select Other on the menu to choose a different folder to which to save images instead.
4. To download all the images on the camera, click Download All. The images you download are saved into the appropriate directories in your Home folder or in the folder you selected on the Download To pop-up menu. For example, photos are downloaded to the Pictures directory. As the images are downloaded, you see a progress dialog box that shows you a preview of the images being downloaded (see Figure 28.14). When the application is done downloading images, it moves to the background and the directories into which it downloaded images are opened.

   After the images have been downloaded, a Finder window containing the images you downloaded opens so you can work with them.

**Figure 28.14**
As Image Capture downloads your photos, you see a preview of each image it is downloading.

**NOTE**

Notice that the default download folders are Pictures, Movies, and Music. Some cameras can capture movies and sound. If your camera has QuickTime movies on it, those are placed in the Movies directory in your Home directory. Likewise, sounds are placed in the Music directory.

*If Image Capture does not recognize your camera, see "The Digital Camera Is Not Recognized by Image Capture" in the "Troubleshooting" section at the end of this chapter.*

**TIP**

When you connect a camera, the Options button in the Image Capture window becomes active. You can use this feature to configure various aspects of how your camera interacts with your Mac. For example, you can set the camera's time and date, cause images to be automatically deleted from the camera after they are downloaded, and so on.

To download only selected images, use the following steps:

1. Connect your camera and open Image Capture.
2. After the application is ready to begin downloading images, click Download Some. You will see a window that shows a preview of each image stored in the camera (see Figure 28.15). By default, the window appears in the Icon view.

**Figure 28.15**
You can use the preview window to select images to download; you can also rotate images or delete them.

3. Click the List View button or select View, as List to see the images in the List view. In this view, you see the images in a Finder-like window. You see a lot of information for each image, including its name, file size, date and time of capture, width and height in pixels, and so on.

**NOTE**

> You can change the width of the columns in the List view; you can also change which column the List view should sort by and in which direction.

4. Return the window to the Icon view by clicking the Icon view button or by selecting View, as Icons.
5. If you need to rotate images, select the images you want to rotate and click the Rotate Left or Rotate Right button.
6. Select the folders into which you want to download the images on the Download folder pop-up menu. The default is the same as when you download all images, but you can change it to be any folder you'd like to use.
7. Select the images you want to download (use the Shift key or ⌘ key to select multiple images) and click Download. The images are downloaded into the selected folder.

**TIP**

> You can connect multiple cameras to your Mac at the same time. To choose the one with which you want to work, use the Camera pop-up menu.

## Choosing Image Capture Options

Image Capture has other options that are useful:

- **Automatic Task**—You can attach AppleScripts to Image Capture so it performs an action you select from the Automatic Task pop-up menu when you download images. A number of actions are on the menu by default, including Build Web Page, Build Slide Show, Crop to 3×5, and so on. You can use any of these tasks or add your own. To add a task to the menu, place it in the `*Mac OS X*/System/Library/Image Capture/Automatic Tasks` directory, where `*Mac OS X*` is the name of your Mac OS X startup volume.
- **Options dialog box**—If you click the Options button in the Image Capture window, you will see a sheet that contains two tabs. The Options tab enables you to configure how downloads are handled, such as whether all images are downloaded automatically or whether images are deleted from the camera after they are downloaded. The Information tab displays information about the device you are using, such as the type of camera and the application your Mac is using to interface with it. If you use Image Capture regularly, you should explore these options.

**NOTE**

> Image Capture downloads only those images that aren't already in the selected folder. So, you won't get duplicate files if you have previously downloaded images on the camera and then perform another download with new images.

### Setting Image Capture Preferences

If you use Image Capture to download images from a camera or a scanner, you should configure it to suit your preferences.

**NOTE**

> Although the Image Capture Preferences is accessed via the Image Capture application, what you choose here affects other applications. For example, you must use this preference to set the application that opens automatically when you connect a camera to your Mac. This is because Image Capture provides the basic framework your Mac uses to interact with cameras and scanners regardless of the specific application you use.

To set your image-handling preferences, perform the following steps:

1. Select Image Capture, Preferences. The Image Capture Preferences dialog box opens.
2. On the "When a camera is connected, open" pop-up menu, select Image Capture (if iPhoto is installed on your Mac, it is selected by default) to have your Mac open Image Capture when it detects that a camera is connected to it.

**TIP**

> If you want an application other than Image Capture or iPhoto to open when you connect a digital camera, select Other and select the application you want to open automatically.

3. If you want to the scanner window to open automatically when you launch Image Capture, check the "When Image Capture is launched, open scanner window" check box.
4. Close the Preferences window.

## Sharing Imaging Devices on a Network or via the Web

With Mac OS X, you can share imaging devices on a network or over the Web. This enables others to access devices connected to your Mac and you to access devices others are sharing.

⇨ To configure a local network, **see** Chapter 17, "Building and Using a Wired Network," **p. 359**.

⇨ To learn how to configure web sharing, **see** "Mac OS X to the Max: Using Mac OS X to Serve Web Pages," **p. 458**.

### Sharing a Camera over a Network or the Web

To share a device connected to your Mac with a network, use the following steps:

1. Open Image Capture; then choose Devices, Browse Devices. The Image Capture Device Browser appears and you see all the imaging devices with which Image Capture can communicate.

2. Select the device you want to share and click the Sharing button. The Sharing sheet appears (see Figure 28.16).

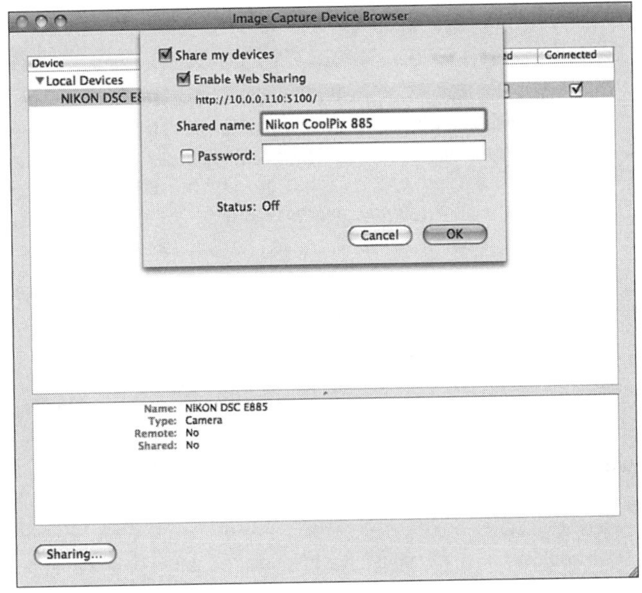


**Figure 28.16**
You can share a digital camera or other device with those on your network or via the Web.

3. Check the "Share my devices" check box.
4. If you want to enable devices to be shared over the Web, check the "Enable Web Sharing" check box.
5. Provide a name for the devices in the Shared name box. This is the name people who access the device will see.
6. If you want to require a password to be entered to access the device, check the Password check box and enter a password in the Password field.
7. Click OK. The device will be shared.

**CAUTION**

> For a device to be shared over a network, the computer to which it is connected must be on the same subnet as the computer trying to access it. For small networks, this is not an issue. However, if you are using a large network, make sure the machines are on the same subnet because sharing will not work if they aren't. Of course, you can use web sharing to share a device regardless of the subnet.



## Accessing a Shared Camera

There are two basic ways to access devices that have been shared: via a local network or over the Web. The method you use depends on how the device has been shared with you.

To access a device that has been shared with you over a network, use the following steps:

1. Open Image Capture.
2. Select Devices, Browse Devices. You'll see the Image Capture Devices window.
3. Expand the Remote Devices section. You'll see a list of all shared imaging devices over the network.
4. Select the specific imaging device you want to access (see Figure 28.17).

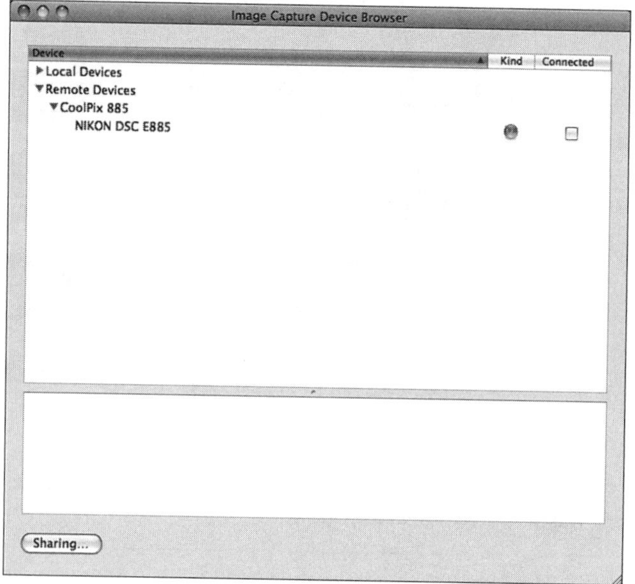


**Figure 28.17** The Nikon DSC E885 is physically connected to another computer on a network.

5. Click the Connected check box. The same Image Capture window will appear as does when a device is physically connected to your computer.
6. Use the Image Capture tools to download images from the device. These work in exactly the same way as they do when a device is connected to your Mac.

You can also access a device that has been shared with you over the Web by doing the following:

1. Launch Safari.

**NOTE**

> For Bonjour devices to be available in Safari, you must turn on that preference in the Bookmarks pane of the Safari Preferences dialog box.

⇨ To learn how to configure Safari to access Bonjour services, **see** "Browsing the Web with Safari," **p. 512**.

2. Select Bookmarks, Bonjour, *devicename*, where *devicename* is the name of the device you want to access. Your Mac connects to the device and you see its contents in a web page called "Digital Cameras on *machinename*," where *machinename* is the name of the Mac sharing the camera, assuming that the device is a camera of course (see Figure 28.18).

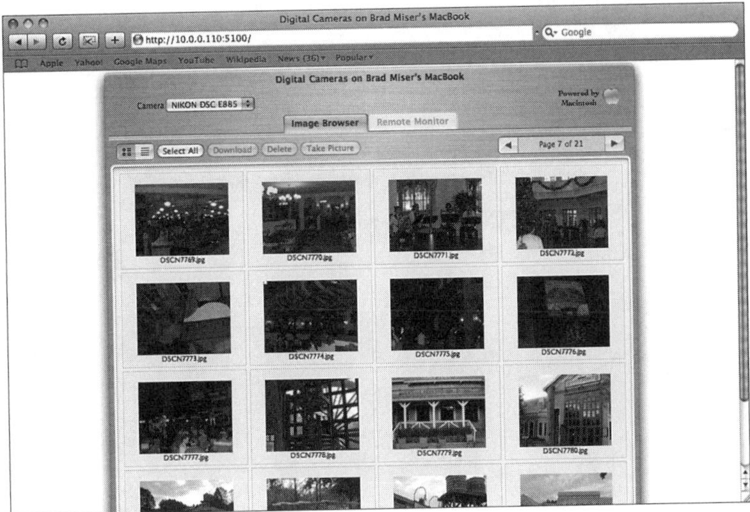


**Figure 28.18**
This web page shows the contents of a camera being shared over a local area network.

**TIP**

> If more than one device is being shared with you, select the device you want to work with on the Camera pop-up menu.

3. Use the Browse arrows to view each page of content being provided by the device.
4. To download images to your Mac, select them and click Download.

Accessing a camera over the Web offers many cool features, including the following:

- Click the List View button to view the page as a list instead of with icons.
- To select all the images on the device, click Select All.
- You can delete images from the shared device by selecting them and clicking Delete.
- To take a picture with the shared device, click Take Picture. The camera takes a picture. To see the new picture, refresh the web page by selecting View, Reload Page (or by pressing ⌘-R).

**NOTE**

> For this to work, the imaging device must support Image Capture while it is in computer mode. Some devices can't capture images and communicate with other devices at the same time. To find out whether yours can, set it in Image Capture mode and open Image Capture. If no imaging devices are found, you won't be able to use this feature.

- You can view a larger version of an image by double-clicking it. To return to the thumbnail views, click the Return button (it is an upward-pointing, curved arrow). You can browse through all the images at the large size by using the Browse arrows.

### Using Device Sharing to Monitor an Area

If you want to feel like Big Brother, you can use a shared device to monitor an area remotely. You can set the remote device to capture an image periodically and display that image on a website. Here's how:

1. Set up the camera so it captures the image you want to be able to monitor, such as a doorway into a room or some other part of a room.

**NOTE**

> For this to work, the imaging device must support Image Capture while it is in computer mode. Some devices can't capture images and communicate with other devices at the same time. To find out whether yours can, set it in Image Capture mode and open Image Capture. If no imaging devices are found, you won't be able to use this feature.

2. Share the camera over the Web.
3. Access the shared camera (see the previous section for details).
4. Click the Remote Monitor tab. The camera takes a picture and transfers it to the web page; to see the results immediately, reload the page. Just below the tab is the time at which the image was last updated and the time at which it will be updated again.

**NOTE**

> Images capture via Remote Monitoring are not stored on the camera; they are only displayed. You can capture an image and store it on a camera by clicking the Take Picture button.

The camera keeps taking pictures at the set interval and displaying them on the web page. This enables you to see what is happening in an area over time.

**TIP**

> By default, a new image is captured every 60 seconds. To change this, click the Preferences button located just under the Remote Monitor tab. Enter the interval at which you want images to be captured and click Set. Setting a shorter interval provides more active monitoring.



## Capturing Screen Images

In many instances, capturing an image of what is happening on your Mac's screen is useful. One example is if you are writing instructions about how to do a particular task, such as when you are writing your own book about Mac OS X. Another is when you want to capture an error message or some other anomaly you want to be able to explain to someone (for example, you might want to capture the image of an error dialog box so you can email it when you try to get technical support).

With Mac OS X, you have two built-in ways to capture screen images. One is to use keyboard commands. The other is to use the Grab application.

## Capturing Screen Images with Keyboard Shortcuts

Mac OS X includes keyboard commands you can use to capture desktop images. After you capture an image, it is stored on your desktop as a Portable Network Graphics (PNG) file and is called `Picture X.png`, where `X` is a sequential number. You have the following three options:

- Shift-⌘-3 captures the entire desktop.
- Shift-⌘-4 changes the pointer to a plus sign. Drag this pointer to select the part of the screen you want to capture. When you release the mouse button, an image of the selected area is captured.
- Shift-⌘-4-spacebar enables you to capture a window, menu bar, Dock, or other area of the screen. First, open the area you want to capture, such as a window or menu. When you press the key combination, a large camera pointer icon appears. Move this icon over the area that you want to capture, which becomes highlighted. Click the mouse button to capture the image.

**TIP**

> To choose not to capture an image after you have pressed these key combinations, press Escape. If you want to save an image to the Clipboard so you can easily paste it into a document, hold down Control while you press the keys for the kind of screenshot you want to take.

## Capturing Screen Images with Grab

Mac OS X includes the Grab application. As its name implies, using Grab, you can "grab" an image of your Mac's desktop. There are several options you can use to capture a specific image. To capture a desktop image, follow these steps:

1. Open Grab (Applications/Utilities).
2. Select the Capture mode you want for your screenshot using the Capture menu. Your options are as follows:
    - Selection captures an area of the screen you select.
    - Window captures the active window.
    - Screen captures the entire screen.

- Timed Screen provides a timer so you can set up a screen before it is captured (so you have time to switch to a window and open a menu before the image is captured, for example).

3. Follow the instructions you see. For example, if you select Timed Screen, the Timed Screen Grab dialog box appears. Then open the area you want to capture, such as a document window with a menu open. When you are ready to take the shot, click Start Timer in the Timed Screen Grab dialog box and get the window as you want it to be captured. After 10 seconds have passed, Grab captures the image.

   When the capture is complete, you see a new window containing the image you captured.

4. To see the size of the image you captured and its color depth, select Inspector from the Edit menu or press ⌘-1. The Inspector window appears and you see information about the image.

5. Save the image. Grab's default file format is TIFF.

The images you capture with Grab are just like images you create in other ways. You can open them in image-editing applications, preview them in Preview, print them, and so on.

**TIP**

> Grab's capturing capabilities are provided to the OS so that other applications can use them. For example, if you are working in a Carbon or Cocoa application, you can easily grab an image of its screen by selecting the Services command from that application's menu. Then, select Grab and select the type of grab from the menu. When you release the mouse button, the image you captured is displayed. How it is displayed depends on the application from which you captured it. For example, if you grab an image while you are using TextEdit, a Rich Text Format file is created.

# TROUBLESHOOTING

## THE DIGITAL CAMERA IS NOT RECOGNIZED BY IMAGE CAPTURE

*When I connect a digital camera to my Mac, Image Capture doesn't recognize the camera, so I can't download images.*

The most likely cause of this is that Mac OS X does not support the camera you are using, probably because your camera does not use PTP. In this case, you can try to obtain Mac OS X–compatible software for your camera and use that to download images. You will probably have to use software that came with the camera to download its images to your Mac.

In rare cases, a cable or hardware problem might exist. Use the Apple System Profiler to ensure that your Mac is capable of communicating with the camera.

⇨ To learn about the System Profiler, **see** "Using System Profiler to Create a System Profile," **p. 954**.

# Mac OS X to the Max: Screen Captures with Snapz Pro X

Mac OS X's built-in screen capture capabilities work fairly well, but if you are serious about capturing screen images, you simply must use Ambrosia Software's Snapz Pro X. This utility enables you to capture screen images in any way and in any file format. You can also use its QuickTime option to record QuickTime movies of actions you perform, such as if you want to create a QuickTime movie of the steps you use to perform a specific task.

**NOTE**

> You can get information about and download a trial version of Snapz Pro X at www.ambrosiasw.com.

After you download and install Snapz Pro X, using it to capture images is, well, a snap:

1. Activate the application by pressing the default keyboard shortcut, which is Shift-⌘-3.

**NOTE**

> By default, Snapz Pro X replaces the default Mac OS X screen capture keyboard shortcut. That's okay because after you use Snapz Pro X, it is likely that you won't ever use the built-in utility again.

2. In the resulting window, select the option for the type of image you want to capture, such as Screen to capture the entire screen (see Figure 28.19).

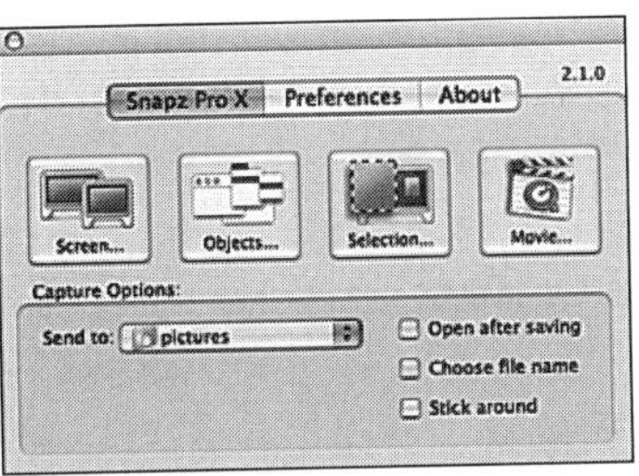


**Figure 28.19** Don't let this simple window fool you; Snapz Pro X is a very powerful application.

3. Use the Object Settings dialog box to configure the capture, such as by choosing whether you want the cursor to be captured as part of the image.
4. Click the image to capture it.

Snapz Pro X has many preferences and options you can use to configure it to work exactly how you want it to, such as choosing filenames, the file format to use, and so on. Take my word for it—if you capture screen images, try Snapz Pro X. Fortunately, you can download and try it for free so it won't cost you more than a few minutes of time to give it a spin. You won't be sorry if you do.

CHAPTER 29

# Making Your Mac Do the Work for You with the Automator

## In this chapter

# UNDERSTANDING THE AUTOMATOR

The Automator enables you to automate actions that you repetitively perform on your Mac. You can create a series of steps that Automator will perform for you and then repeat those steps by running the script you create. Automator is extremely powerful because you can use it to automate actions involving many applications at the same time. Although Automator enables complex actions to be performed, its graphical interface makes building complex scripts as easy as drag-and-drop.

## UNDERSTANDING THE AUTOMATOR APPLICATION

The Automator window has several panes (see Figure 29.1). Across the top of the window is the toolbar that provides access to the Library pane, a button to access your iLife media quickly, and controls for recording and running your scripts. The left side of the window contains a pane for the library of applications that Automator can work with. You can click the Actions button to see what functions a specific application can support, or click the Variables button to see what information you can pass from one application to another. When you click an action or variable, the details about that item are displayed in the Information pane at the bottom-left corner of the Library pane. Use the Search tool to find a specific action or variable that you need for your workflow. By far the largest pane on the Automator window is the workflow window where you can drag actions onto and build your workflow.

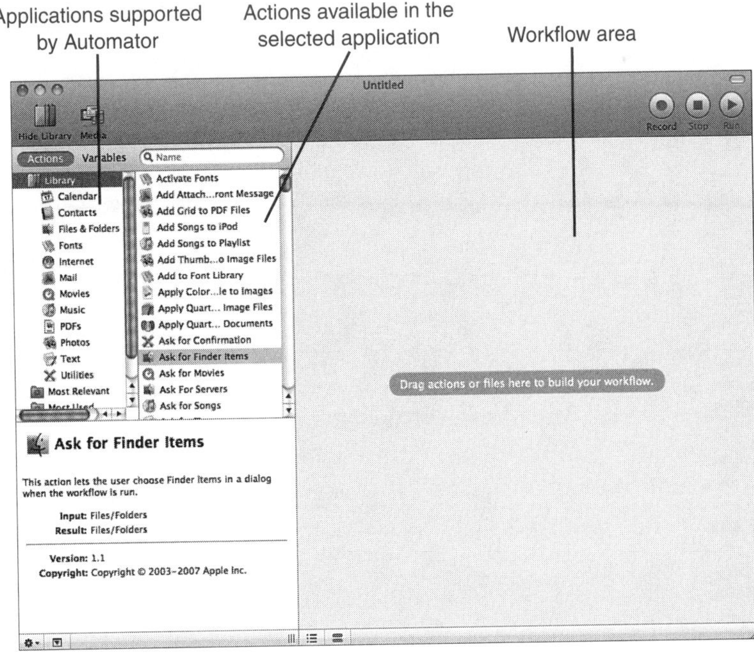


**Figure 29.1**
Automator makes creating complex programs easy because you can drag steps onto the Workflow area of the Automator window.

Understanding how the Automator works requires that you understand the following concepts:

- **Actions**—These are the basic building blocks of any automated workflow. An *action* is a single step that is performed when your automated tasks run. Actions can be relatively simple, such as asking the user to input text, or complex, such as applying photo editing tools to a series of files. Each application supported by the Automator supports a number of individual actions.
- **Input**—Some steps require input, which is something that is needed for the action to be performed. For example, if an action applies to a file, that file is the input of the action. Different actions require different kinds of input. Automator helps you understand what kind of input an action requires.
- **Output**—Most actions end up providing output, which is the result of that action. For example, if an action makes a change to a file, that changed file becomes the output of the action. When actions are linked together, the output of one action becomes the input to the next one.
- **Workflow**—A *workflow* is a series of actions you save to automate work; that is, a script of actions that you want to be able to run easily. A workflow consists of one or more steps that are linked together and result in something you would normally do by manually performing each step. You can save workflows so you can run them from within the Automator, edit them, and so on.
- **Variables**—Variables represent attributes that are part of a workflow. You use a variable when the attribute changes. For example, if you want to perform an action based on today's date, you can include the Today's Date variable when configuring a workflow.
- **Application**—You can also save a workflow as an application. You can run the applications you create with the Automator just like other applications on your Mac. When you run an application you have created, the actions you programmed will be performed.

## Knowing When to Automate Tasks

Using the Automator is relatively easy given how powerful it is. Still, it does require some learning, especially if you have never programmed or written macros or scripts using other applications. You'll need to balance the time and effort required to learn to use the Automator to create workflows against the time you save by automating your Mac. In the beginning, while you are learning how to use Automator, it might take more time to create a workflow than it would to perform tasks manually. As you get more proficient with the Automator, though, you'll be able to create workflows more quickly, which in turn will improve your overall efficiency in getting things done on your Mac.

29

**NOTE**

In Mac OS X 10.5, Automator now has the capability to record what you are doing on your Mac and create a workflow from those steps. You must first access the Universal Access pane of the System Preferences application and select "Enable access for assistive devices" so that Automator can record what you do with the mouse and keyboard. Once the steps are recorded you will see a new action called Watch Me Do that you can incorporate into a workflow.

Good candidates for automation with the Automator are any series of steps you find yourself repeating again and again. The steps you perform manually can be exactly the same, or you might perform the same series of steps but use different files or folders each time. In such cases, the time you invest in creating an Automator workflow can pay off because you can have your Mac repeat those steps for you.

Perhaps the most important consideration when deciding to automate is that the applications you use during the steps you are automating must be supported by the Automator and, more specifically, the individual actions you perform must be available in the Automator for that application.

## Determining Which Applications Are Supported by the Automator

To automate tasks, the applications you use to perform those tasks must be supported by the Automator. Most Apple applications do support the Automator, including those that are part of Mac OS X and those that are included in the iLife suite.

To determine which applications are supported by the Automator, launch the Automator application, located in the Applications folder. Automator presents you with several options for starting points that are designed around specific types of projects. Click the button for a Custom workflow; you will then see the Automator window with the Library pane open. Click the Actions button, and look at the applications shown under the Library folder (see Figure 29.2). If an application appears on this list, it supports the Automator. If not, you'll have to use a different automation tool to automate tasks involving that application.

⇨ To learn about some other automation tools, **see** "Mac OS X to the Max: Automator Alternatives," **p. 738**.

## Understanding Actions That Are Supported by the Automator

Each application supported by the Automator has one or more actions that you can use in your workflows. Some applications, such as the Finder, support many actions, whereas others support only a few. If all the steps you need to perform to complete a task are available as actions, you can automate a task. You can also create actions by recording them. If neither of those approaches works, you'll need to use a different automation tool.

To see which actions are supported, select an application on the Library list. The actions supported for that application will be shown in the Action pane (see Figure 29.3).

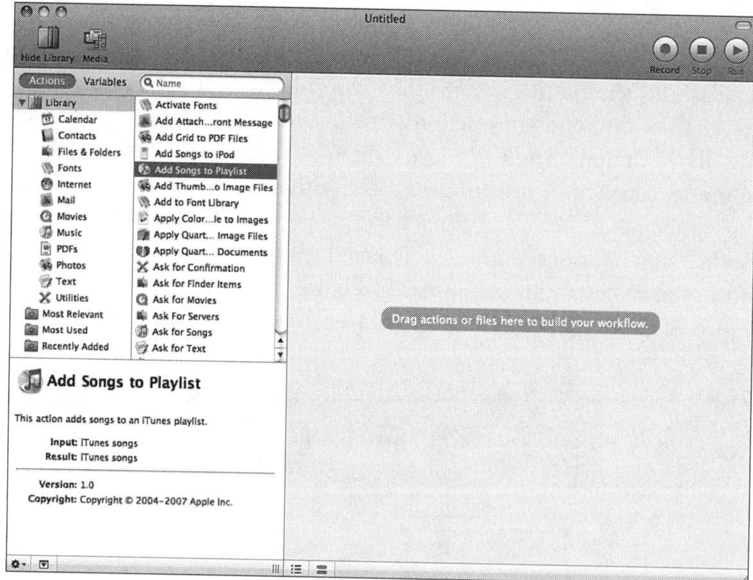


**Figure 29.2**
With Actions selected in the Library pane, you see all the applications on your Mac that support the Automator.

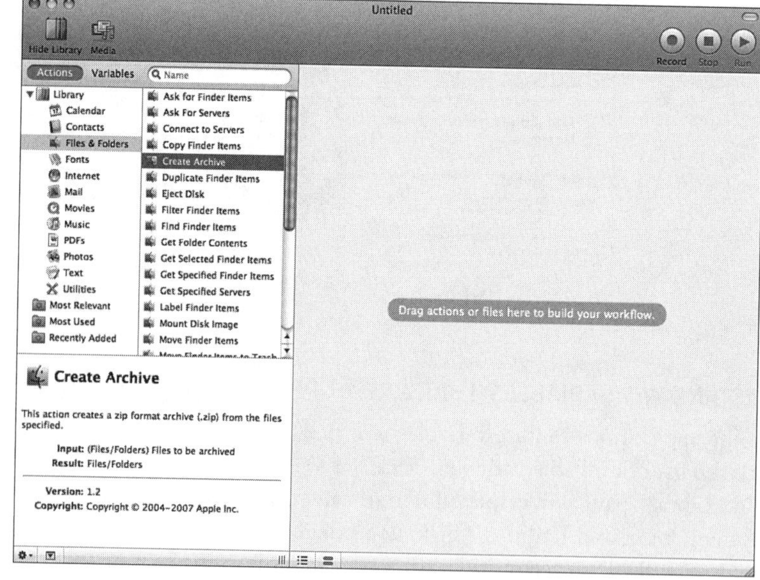


**Figure 29.3**
Here you can see that the Finder application supports many actions, including the Create Archive action, which creates a `.zip` archive of selected files.

When you select an action on the Action pane, information about the action is shown in the Information pane located at the bottom of the Action pane of the Library window. This information includes a summary of what the action does along with its input and output. For example, when you select the Finder's Create Archive action, you'll see that this action creates a zip format archive (`.zip`) from the files specified. Its input is the files to be archived. The output, called `result`, is the archived file.

To understand an action in more detail, drag it from the Action pane and drop it onto the Workflow area (see Figure 29.4). The action is added to the workflow, and you see its details. The action's title bar has the expansion triangle at the far left to show or collapse the detail of the action, the action's title in the center, and the delete button on the right side. In the action's window, you see the tools you use to configure the action; these depend on the specific action you are using. These tools can include text boxes, check boxes, and pop-up menus. When you connect actions together in a workflow and one action's output is another action's input, they are connected with a downward-facing arrow to indicated output and a semi-circle to indicate input. In Figure 29.4, you can see the "Ask for Finder Items" output becomes the input for the "Add attachments to Front Message" action.

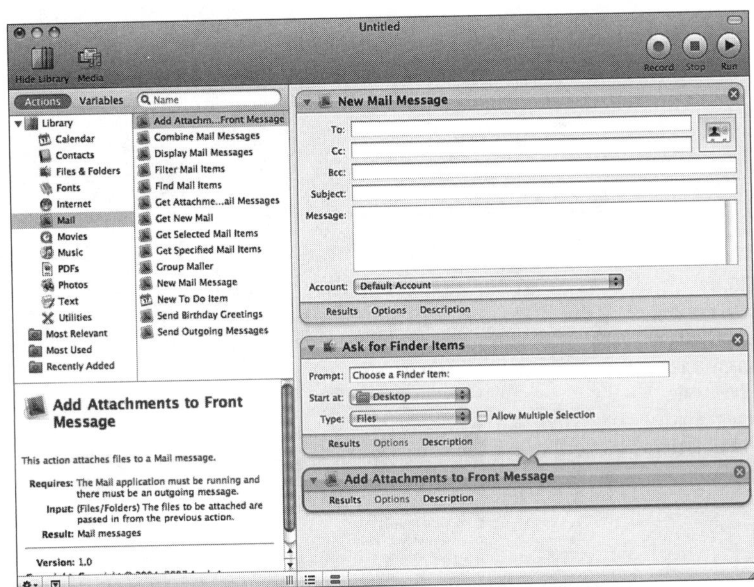


**Figure 29.4**
To build a workflow, you drag actions onto it.

### UNDERSTANDING VARIABLES THAT ARE SUPPORTED BY THE AUTOMATOR

Some applications can use variables to represent attributes that are used in a workflow. To see the list of available variables, click the Variables button at the top of the Library pane. The Library pane will display different categories of variables, such as Date & Time, System, User, and Utilities. Clicking a category will display the variables that are available. Select a variable to see more information about it in the bottom of the Library window. Variables allow you to use their values in your workflow.

## CREATING YOUR OWN WORKFLOWS

Any type of programming, which is what you are doing when you use the Automator, requires that you follow a logical path (well, logical to your Mac anyway) that ends up in the result you want. This isn't always easy to do. For best results, you should tackle any automation project by performing a series of steps, as you will learn about in the following sections.

## DESIGNING A WORKFLOW

The first step when creating any workflow is to determine the tasks you want to automate. You need to identify the applications those tasks involve and the specific steps that are required. For best results, you should manually perform each step that is required to complete these tasks and document what you do during each one. Create a list of specific applications the tasks involve and the specific steps performed in that application. This might seem tedious, but creating a workflow that actually does what you expect will be much easier if you take the time to design it before you jump into the Automator and start dragging steps into a workflow.

**NOTE**

> After you have listed the steps in your workflow, you need to make sure that Automator supports both the applications and actions you need to perform to accomplish those tasks. If it doesn't, you'll need to use a different automation tool.

⇨ To learn about some other automation tools, **see** "Mac OS X to the Max: Automator Alternatives," **p. 738**.

A less systematic approach is to just use trial and error. You can sometimes develop workflows effectively by just adding an action at a time running the workflow after each to make sure it does what you expect.

A third approach is to try recording a workflow. Even if this doesn't result in the end product, it will often add most of the actions you need so that you can just refine them to complete the workflow.

## CREATING AND SAVING A WORKFLOW

After you have designed a workflow, you are ready to jump into the Automator to create and save it. At this stage, you should save the workflow in the Workflow format so you can continue to work with it.

When you save a workflow, you will give it a name. Usually, you'll want its name to describe what it does so you can remember it later.

## BUILDING A WORKFLOW MANUALLY

To build your workflow, perform the following general steps:

1. Use your design document to identify the first step that needs to be done.
2. In the Library pane, select the application you use to perform that step. Then select the specific action that should occur during the step.
3. Drag the action into the Workflow area.
4. Configure the action for the workflow.
5. Refer to the next step in your workflow design document.
6. Repeat step 2.

7. Drag the action into the Workflow area. The output of the previous step will be become the input of the step you just placed in the workflow.
8. Check the output/input connection to ensure they match. For example, if the previous step outputs a file or folder, the input of the next step should be a file or folder.
9. Repeat steps 5–8 to systematically create the workflow to match your design.
10. Save the workflow.

## RECORDING A WORKFLOW

You can also build a workflow by recording actions you perform. When viewing a workflow, click the Record button and then perform the steps you want to record. As you perform them, they are added to the workflow. Once there, you can configure them and refine the workflow by recording more tasks or adding and configuring actions manually.

## TESTING AND EDITING A WORKFLOW

After you have created the workflow, you should go through a testing process to ensure that the workflow works as you expect it to. It is typical that it won't work quite right at first, so plan on needing to edit it a few times before you get it working properly. The general steps to test and edit a workflow are the following:

1. Click the Run button. The workflow executes and performs the steps you have designed.
2. Check the results of the workflow. If they are what you intended, you are done (this isn't likely the first time through unless you are working with a very simple workflow). If not, edit the workflow by proceeding to step 3.

> **NOTE**
>
> Some workflows won't complete because one or more steps fail. In that case, you'll usually see an error message that should help you figure out what went wrong.

3. Identify the specific step (action) that is not working properly. Sometimes, this will be the last step executed, but at other times, it might be a step earlier in the workflow. This process can take some detective work; your clues will be the results of the workflow, error messages, and so on.

   To help in the troubleshooting process, click an action in the workflow and select Show Results from the Action menu, or click the Results button on the action. The action's tools are replaced by the results of the action. This can be extremely useful when troubleshooting a workflow.
4. Edit the workflow by reconfiguring an action that is not working properly, adding new actions, reordering the actions in the workflow, and so on.
5. Run the workflow again. If it works properly, you are done.
6. If the workflow doesn't result in what you expect, repeat steps 3–5 until it does.

You should expect to spend some time testing and editing a workflow until it does just want you want it to. You can increase the odds of your workflow working right the first time by designing it in a good amount of detail before you start creating it. Generally, the more prep work you do designing and documenting your workflow, the less time you will have to spend testing and editing it.

### SAVING A WORKFLOW AS AN APPLICATION

After your workflow does what you want it to, you can save it as an application. You can then run the workflow by launching the application, which you do just like other applications on your Mac, such as by double-clicking it, putting it on the Dock and clicking its icon, adding it to your login items so it runs when you log in, and so on.

## LEARNING HOW TO AUTOMATE YOUR MAC BY EXAMPLE

Once you understand the general way the Automator works and how you should go about building workflows, the only way to really learn how to create your own workflows is to start creating them. The first few you create might take a while, but as you gain more experience with Automator, you'll become more proficient creating new workflows. To get you started, in this section you'll find two sample workflows you can re-create on your Mac. Doing this will give you some experience using the Automator; then you'll be ready to start designing and creating your own workflows.

### OPENING WEBSITES

If you visit the same websites regularly, you can create a workflow and application that opens Safari for you and takes you to as many websites as you'd like. To create this workflow, perform the following steps:

⇨ To learn how to use Safari to browse the Web, **see** "Browsing the Web with Safari," **p. 512**.

1. Launch the Automator and select Custom as the starting point.
2. On the Library pane, select Internet. You see the actions available for Safari.
3. Select the "Get Specified URLs" action. In the Information area, you see an explanation of the action ("This action passes the specific URLs into the next action.") along with its results (URLs).
4. Drag "Get Specified URLs" from the Action pane onto the Workflow area (see Figure 29.5). In the center of this action is a table that contains each URL you want to open. By default, Apple's home page is on the list of URLs that will be opened.

**TIP**

> To remove a URL, such as the Apple home page, from the list of URLs, select it and click the Remove button.

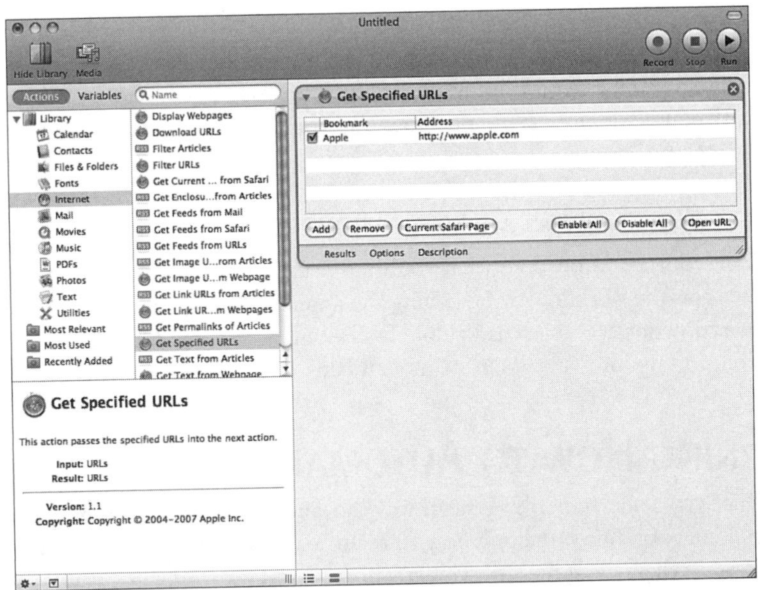


**Figure 29.5**
The "Get Specified URLs" action is now part of this workflow.

5. Click the Add button. A new address appears on the list.
6. Double-click the Bookmark portion of the URL line so it becomes highlighted, and then enter a name for the website.
7. Press Tab so the Address part of the URL line becomes highlighted, and then type the URL.

**TIP**

> You can add a website more easily by opening it in Safari and clicking the Current Safari page button. The URL of the current web page is added to the URL list.

8. Continue adding URLs until you have all that you want to be opened in the list.

**TIP**

> To test a URL on the list, select it and click Open URL. Safari launches and moves to the URL.

9. Choose File, Save; name the workflow; and save it.
10. Select the "Display Webpages" action. In the Information area, you see that this action displays web pages in Safari when provided with URL addresses. Its input is URL addresses and its output is Safari documents.
11. Drag the "Display Webpages" action onto the Workflow area and drop it after the "Get Specified URLs" action (see Figure 29.6).

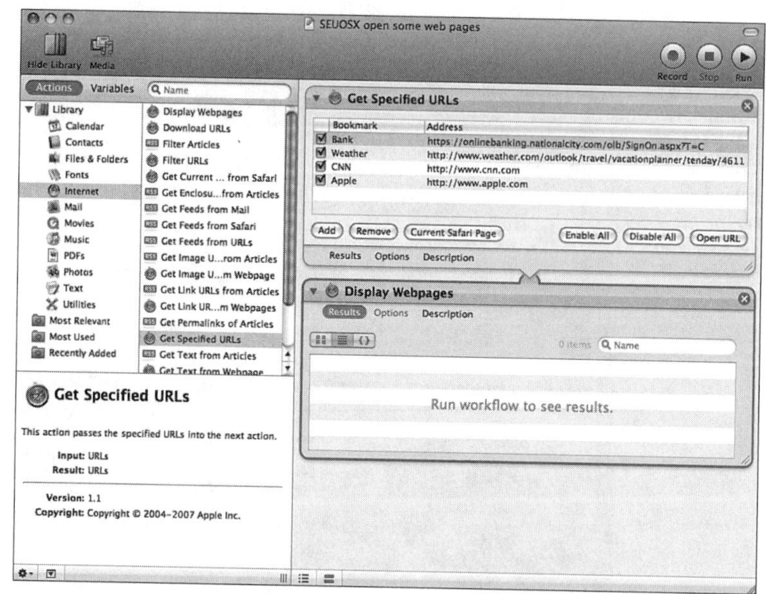

**Figure 29.6**
This workflow now has two actions.

**TIP**

You can also add an action to a workflow by double-clicking it on the Actions pane.

12. Check that the output of the first action, which is URLs, matches the input of the section action, which is also URLs. Notice how the output arrow of the first action fits into the input receptor of the second to graphically show you that the output and input of these actions match.
13. Click the Run button. Automator runs the workflow. As each action runs, you see a progress wheel next to the action's Delete button. When it completes, you see a green check mark next to the action's Delete button to show you the action was completed successfully. The next action runs in the same way. When the entire workflow is done, you'll hear a whistle tone.
14. Switch to Safari and you see that a Safari window has opened for each URL that is part of your workflow (see Figure 29.7).

    Each web page opens in a new window, which can clutter your desktop. It would better if each opened in a new tab within a single Safari window. However, if you look for actions for Safari, you won't see the Merge All Windows command that combines all open windows into a single tabbed window.

    In these kind of situations, you can often use the recoding tool to add actions to a workflow, even if they are provided for an application. Add this to the workflow.
15. Close all open Safari windows.
16. Move back to the workflow and run it again. The same set of windows will open.

29

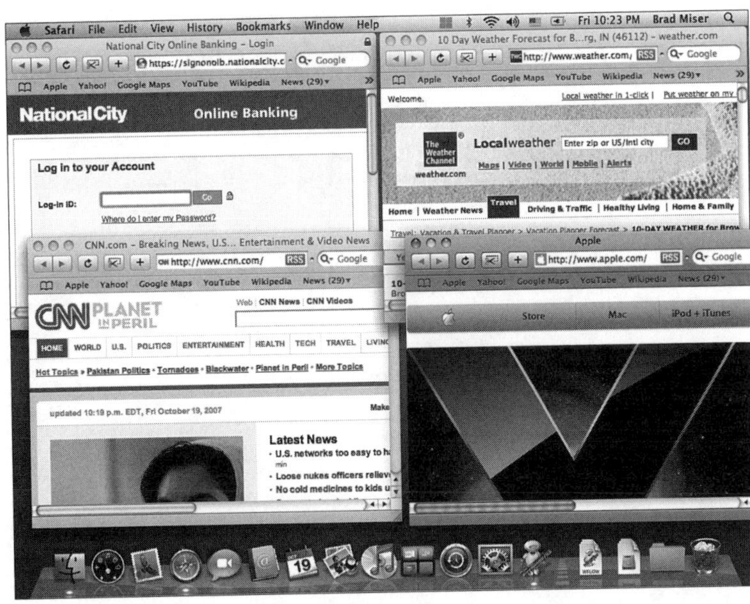

**Figure 29.7**
Here you can see that the four URLs that are part of the workflow have been opened in Safari. Because each is a separate window, the desktop can be cluttered (we'll add to the workflow to fix that).

17. While in the workflow, click the Record button. A new step called "Watch Me Do" is added to the workflow and Automator begins recording your actions. The workflow window will not be visible while you are recording; instead an Automator: Recording window is visible above all other open windows.

**NOTE**

> If you have not recorded in Automator before, you will be prompted to enable Accessibility. Click the Open Universal Access button and then click "Enable access for assistive devices" check box. After you have completed this you can quit the System Preferences application and return to Automator.

18. Switch to Safari and choose Window, Merge All Windows.
19. Click the Stop button on the Automator: Recording window. The recording process stops and you see the events that Automator recorded in the "Watch Me Do" action (see Figure 29.8).

**TIP**

> In a "Watch Me Do" action, each event is recorded separately. If you select an event, you see the application involved and the action that was recorded in the panel at the right side of the action. You can delete events you don't want to keep by selecting them and pressing the Delete key. You can configure individual events by selecting them and using the Timeout tool to add a pause before the action and the Playback Speed slider to change the speed at which it happens.

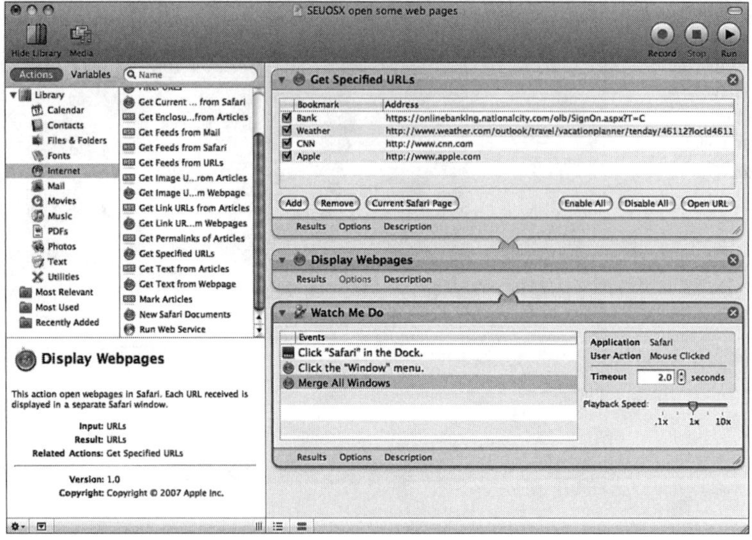


**Figure 29.8**
The "Watch Me Do" action contains the events Automator recorded.

20. Save the workflow.
21. Quit Safari.
22. Run the workflow again. This time, after the web pages have opened, you see the Window menu being opened and the Merge All Windows command selected automatically. When the workflow completes, you see a single Safari window with each page on a tab.

After you have created and tested a workflow, you can save it as an application so you can run it just like other applications. To create an application from a workflow, perform the following steps:

1. Open the workflow you want to save as an application.
2. Choose File, Save As. The Save As sheet appears.
3. Name the application (you can use the same name as the workflow if you want because they are different types of files, so you don't have to worry about replacing the workflow).
4. Choose the location in which you want to save the application you are creating. Consider creating a folder in which to store all your applications so you can locate them easily. For example, you might want to create a folder called My Applications within the Applications folder.
5. On the File Format pop-up menu, select Application.
6. Click Save. An application is created from the workflow.
7. Open the location you selected in step 4. You'll see the application you created (see Figure 29.9).

29

**Figure 29.9**
To open a number of websites at the same time, all I have to do is run the application called "webpages.app."

8. Launch the application. The application runs; as it does, you'll see the application name and progress information in the menu bar.

Just like other applications on your Mac, you can open an application you've created in many ways, such as by adding it to the Dock and clicking its icon, adding it to the Places sidebar and clicking its icon, adding it to your Login items, and so on.

## Sending Files via Email

For this example, suppose that you regularly send files to someone via email (maybe you are an author and you send your chapters to your editor). You can create a workflow that will archive files you select into a Zip file, create and address an email, and attach the Zip file to the email. Here's how to create this workflow:

1. Launch Automator or select Custom as the starting point for a new workflow.
2. In the Library pane, click the Files & Folders application and then click the Get Selected Finder Items action. You see that this action gets items you have selected in the Finder and passes them to the following action.
3. Drag the Get Selected Finder Items action onto the workflow or double-click it to add it to the workflow.
4. Select the Create Archive action (which creates a Zip archive of files or folders), drag it onto the workflow, and place it after the Get Selected Finder Items action. Notice that the output of the first action (Files/Folders) matches the input of the second one (also Files/Folders).

   Next, you configure the Create Archive action to choose a filename and save location for the archive file.
5. In the "Save as" box, enter a name for the archive file that will be created.

**TIP**

Check out the options for actions by clicking the Options button. There are a number of useful selections on the resulting menu, such as "Show this action when the workflow runs."

6. Use the Where pop-up menu to choose the location in which the archive file will be saved (see Figure 29.10).

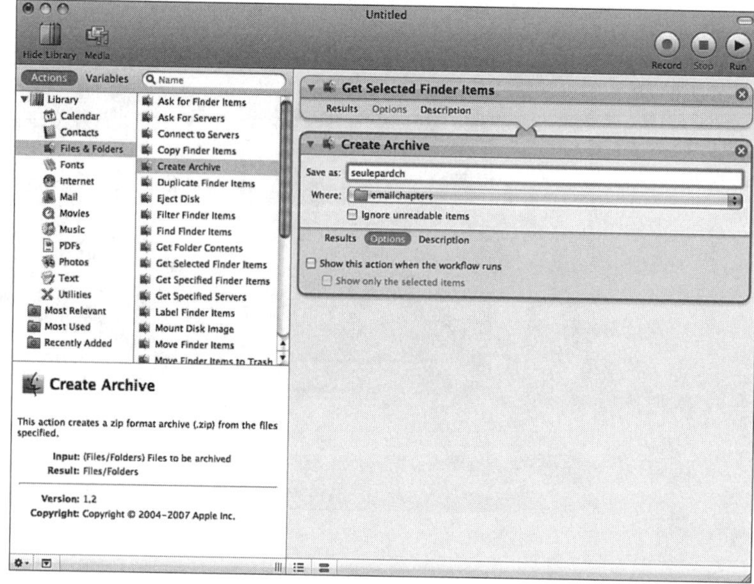

**Figure 29.10**
So far, this workflow will take selected Finder items and save them in a `.zip` file called `seuleopardch` in the folder called emailchapters.

Because you're going to using this workflow many times, you don't want each file to have the same name or they'll get replaced each time the workflow runs. So, you want to add an action to rename the files.

7. Drag the File & Folders action Rename Finder Items to the workflow and place it after the Create Archive action. A warning sheet appears explaining this action will change the name of the Finder Items and presents you with an option to add a copy action.
8. Click Don't Add to keep the rename action. The Rename Finder Items action is added to the workflow. Notice that the output of the previous action matches the input of this action.
9. Use the tools in the Rename Finder Items action to configure the name of the archive file created. For example, you can add the date or time to it, make it sequential, and so on. Choose Make Sequential on the top pop-up menu; the tools in the action change to reflect the selection you made. To have a sequential number added after the name separated by an underscore, choose "underscore" on the "separated by" pop-up menu. Enter the first sequential number you want to be used in the "Start numbers at" box.

It's a good idea to test workflows as you create them, so test what you've done so far.

29

**TIP**

> You can double-click an action's title bar to collapse or expand it.

10. Move to the Finder and select a couple of files.
11. Move back to the workflow and click the Run button. The workflow runs. If it can't complete for some reason, you see information about what happened. If it does complete, you hear the whistle tone. Look in the save location you configured. You see the file the workflow created (see Figure 29.11).

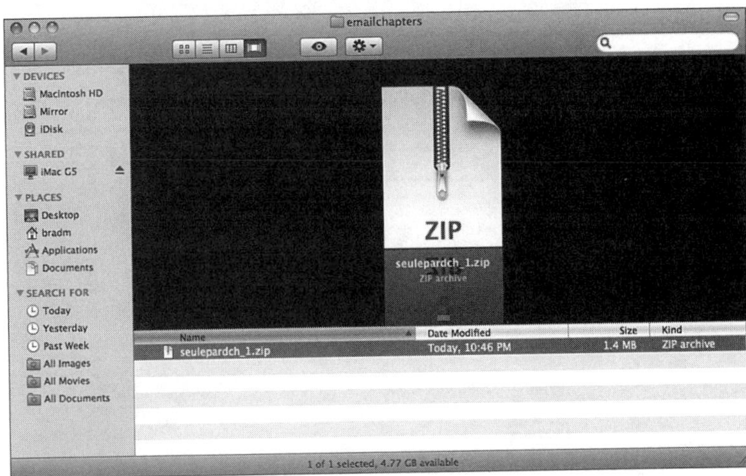


**Figure 29.11**
This file was created by an Automator workflow and saved in the designated location.

The file that was created is a `.zip` file containing the files that were selected when you ran the workflow.

Now, add the actions to send the archived file.

12. Move back to the workflow.
13. Select the Mail application and then drag the New Mail Message action into the workflow and place it below the Rename Finder Items action. Notice that the output of the Rename Finder Items action fits with the input of the New Mail Message action (see Figure 29.12).
14. Enter the email address for the person to whom you want to send the file in the To box or click the Address Book icon to select an address in your Address Book.
15. Type a subject for the message in the Subject field.
16. If you want some text to appear in the message every time, enter it in the Message box.
17. Choose the email account that should be used to send the message on the Account pop-up menu.
18. Review the workflow to see whether the actions you need it to run are available, configured, and in the correct order (see Figure 29.13).
19. Save the workflow.

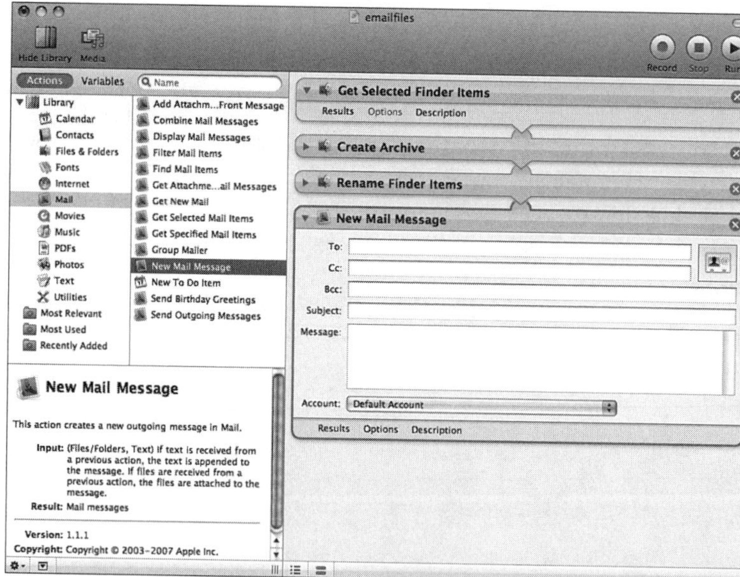


**Figure 29.12**
Now the workflow implements Mail to send the results of the previous actions.

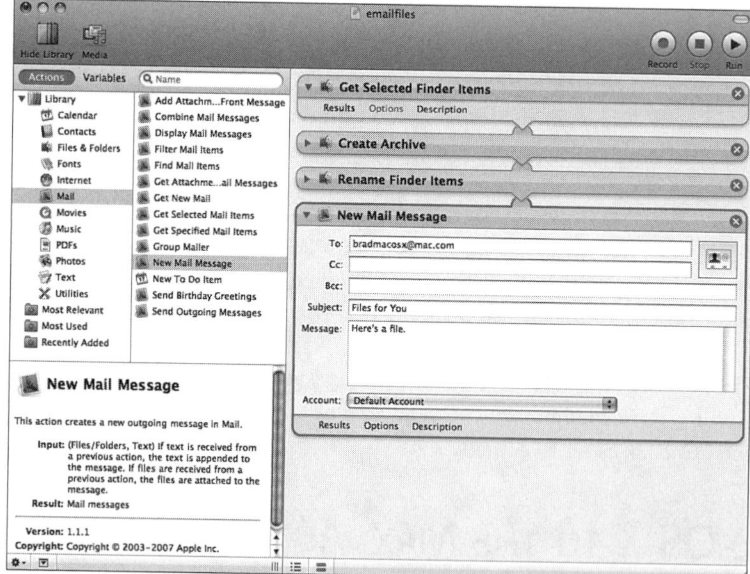


**Figure 29.13**
This workflow creates and archive of selected files and emails them to me.

**CAUTION**

> You should always save a workflow before you run it. If it doesn't work properly, Automator might quit, in which case you could lose your workflow.

29

Now that you have created the workflow, it is time to test it by performing the following steps:

1. Move to the Finder and select one or more files.
2. Move back into the Automator and click Run to run the workflow. The workflow runs; when it completes, you see a new email message with the default text entered and the archive file attached (see Figure 29.14).

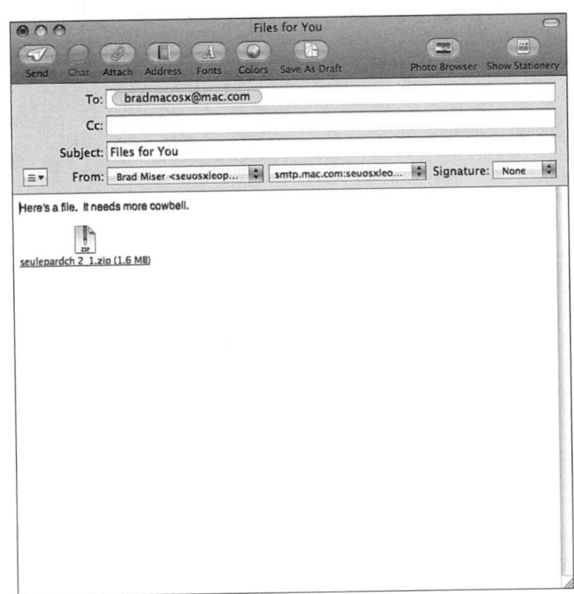


**Figure 29.14**
The workflow took selected files, created a `.zip` file containing them, and then attached that file to a new Mail message.

3. If the result is correct, you can save the workflow as an application. If not, you need to troubleshoot it until it does work as you want.

After the workflow creates the email message and attaches the file to it, you can edit the message as needed before you send it. The workflow won't actually send the message so you need to click Send to actually send it.

## MAC OS X TO THE MAX: AUTOMATOR ALTERNATIVES

Automator is a powerful, but easy-to-use, way to create custom applications to automate work you do. However, it does have its limitations. If an application you need to use to complete a task isn't supported or if you aren't able to record it, you can't use Automator to automate it. There are other options for automating your Mac; in this section, you'll learn about two other ways to automate your Mac.

## USING QUICKEYS TO AUTOMATE YOUR MAC

One of my favorite automation utilities is Startly Technology's QuicKeys. The best thing about QuicKeys is that you can record your actions to create a script. This is often much easier than programming each step manually. To automate a task, you start the QuicKeys recorder and perform the task yourself. As you do so, QuicKeys records your actions and builds a script for you. You can edit the scripts you record, allow user input, and do many other actions that Automator can't match. You can also easily assign keyboard shortcuts to all the scripts you create or add them to menus. If you need to automate your work, QuicKeys is indispensable.

**NOTE**

For more information or to download a trial version, check out the QuicKeys website at www.cesoft.com.

## USING APPLESCRIPT TO AUTOMATE YOUR MAC

AppleScript is Mac OS X's built-in scripting tool, which you can use to create AppleScript programs to perform all kinds of actions. AppleScript is much more powerful than the Automator, but it also has a higher learning curve because you use a scripting language (AppleScript) to create programs rather than the Automator's easier graphical programming. The tools you use to work with AppleScript are in the AppleScript folder located in the Applications folder.

**NOTE**

You can use AppleScript and Automator together. For example, you can create an AppleScript and then use that as a step in an Automator workflow.

**NOTE**

To learn about AppleScript in more detail, visit www.apple.com/applescript/.

PART V

# PART V EXPANDING THE SYSTEM

CHAPTER 30

# Understanding Input and Output Technology

## In this chapter

## UNDERSTANDING INTERFACE TECHNOLOGY

The processor is the heart of any computer. For the processor to be capable of doing anything, it has to have data on which to operate. There are many ways in which data is moved into, out of, and within your Mac. To use a Mac, you do not need to understand the various technologies involved in this transfer of data among the various components of the system, such as the processor. However, if you add enhancements to your machine—whether they are external peripherals or internal system upgrades—you do need to understand these interface technologies.

**NOTE**

The term *interface* refers to the location at which two devices are physically connected. The term also refers to the technology that particular interface uses. For example, when someone refers to devices that use a USB interface, this implies that a specific physical connector is used (a USB connector) over which data following the USB specification is communicated.

On your Mac, there are two general types of input and output interfaces: those with external interfaces (ports) and those whose interfaces are internal to the machine.

In the current lineup of Macintosh computers, only the Mac Pro is designed to enable you to easily interact with internal interfaces, such as to add additional hard drives or PCI-X cards. The exceptions to this generality are the RAM slots that you can use to upgrade iMac, MacBook, and MacBook Pro computers (you can also upgrade the memory in a Mac mini, but unless you are very comfortable working with hardware, I wouldn't recommend it). On all Mac models, including the Mac Pro, you are much more likely to use external interfaces to connect a variety of devices to your computer. So, that is the primary focus of this chapter.

In this chapter, you will gain a fundamental understanding of the various input and output technologies your Mac uses to move data. This understanding will help you when the time comes to add devices or make other improvements to your system. However, you won't get a detailed explanation of the technical intricacies of all of these interfaces. Unless that kind of information floats your boat, you really don't need to know the ins and outs of these technologies. Mostly, you just need to be able to match the technologies that your particular Mac supports with peripheral devices or upgrades you want to add to it. Equipping you with the information you need to be able to do this is the goal of this chapter.

**CAUTION**

Obviously, the types of interfaces available depend on the model of Mac you are using and whether you have added other components to it. This chapter focuses on modern Mac models, such as the Intel iMac, MacBook, and so on. Newer machines generally support newer and better technologies. For example, the Mac Pro offers faster interface technologies than the Power Mac G5 did. Similarly, newer models of machines of the same class also support faster technologies. For example, some models of the Intel iMac added support for FireWire 800, whereas earlier models did not support this. In this chapter, you will find information on the more common interfaces used on modern Macintosh computers, but this chapter is not intended to explain all the interfaces that can be used. To be familiar with the technologies your specific Mac supports, you should study the specifications for your Mac.



# ETHERNET

Ethernet is the interface that is used for almost all local area networks (LANs) that use wires to connect. Ethernet is designed for hub-based networks, which means information flowing across the network is controlled to some extent by a central hub of one type or another.

All Macs have built-in Ethernet ports to enable you to network with other machines; Ethernet on all modern Macs uses an RJ-45 connector, which looks like an overgrown telephone connector (see Figure 30.1).

**Figure 30.1**
All modern Macs have an Ethernet port. The only variation is in the speed the port supports.

Three different speeds of Ethernet are supported by the Mac. These are the following:

- **10 megabits per second (Mbps)**—This was the speed of the "original" Ethernet.
- **100BASE-T**—This flavor of Ethernet is 10 times as fast as the original and is also known as *Fast Ethernet*. It communicates at speeds up to 100Mbps. All modern Macs support at least 100BASE-T Ethernet.
- **Gigabit Ethernet**—The newest Ethernet standard can communicate at 1,000Mbps. All current Mac models support Gigabit Ethernet.

**NOTE**

> The Power Mac G4 was the first PC to support Gigabit Ethernet as a standard feature. It follows in the tradition of earlier Macs, which were the first to provide built-in Ethernet support as standard equipment.

Ethernet-capable devices can communicate at various levels of speed up to their maximum speeds (such as Gigabit Ethernet). Higher-speed devices can communicate at lower speeds, but lower-speed devices can't communicate at the higher speeds. Therefore, the speed at which devices communicate over Ethernet connections always defaults to the maximum speed of the lower-speed device.

**NOTE**

> All data that travels around your Mac eventually moves from one device to another. When data "crosses over," it is said to have crossed a bus. A data *bus* is simply a channel through which data flows. Many buses exist inside your Mac, and all devices have at least one bus (the point at which data enters or leaves the device).

**NOTE**

> If you want to really dive into the details of computer buses and other technology, check out www.pcguide.com/ref/. Although this site is PC-focused, it does contain lots of great general information that is equally applicable to the Mac. For example, you can learn all you need to know about the various hard drive technologies at this site in addition to finding detailed information on memory buses, monitors, and just about anything else about which you want to learn.

A *protocol* is the "language" in which data is communicated over a particular interface at a particular time. The physical interface might be capable of transmitting data in more than one protocol. For example, Ethernet can be used to transmit data in the AppleTalk protocol as well as using the Transmission Control Protocol/Internet Protocol (TCP/IP).

All Ethernet devices are designed to work with an Ethernet hub (or router) that acts as a traffic controller for the data being communicated among the attached devices.

Ethernet is used exclusively for networking computers to hubs, routers, or other computers.

⇨ To learn more about creating and using an Ethernet network, **see** Chapter 17, "Building and Using a Wired Network," **p. 359**.

---

**Direct Connect Ethernet**

Because Ethernet is designed to be used with hubs, you usually can't simply connect two Ethernet ports together to connect two machines. Instead, you have to use a special Ethernet cable, called a *crossover cable*. Using such a cable, you can connect any two Ethernet devices directly. If you use a standard Ethernet cable, the devices must be connected with an Ethernet hub.

An exception to this is the Ethernet port on some modern Mac models. It can sense whether it is connected to another device or a hub and configure itself appropriately for either situation using a standard Ethernet cable. Check the documentation for your machine to determine whether you need to use a crossover cable to connect it to another device via Ethernet.

---

# FireWire

FireWire is a very fast external interface that you can use to connect a wide variety of devices to your Mac, including hard drives, video cameras, and others that require that large amounts of data to be moved quickly.

There are two kinds of FireWire: FireWire 400 and FireWire 800. All modern Macs have FireWire 400 ports and several models also support FireWire 800. If your Mac doesn't have enough FireWire ports, you can add external hubs so that you can connect even more devices to your Mac at the same time.



## FireWire 400

FireWire 400 (more commonly referred to as just *FireWire*) is a fast technology that provides an interface for many types of peripheral devices. FireWire was designed to enable very high data rate transfers (it communicates at 400Mbps), such as those required to move digital video data. At least one FireWire 400 port is available on all modern Mac models. Some models have more than one FireWire 400 port, such as the Mac Pro, which has two FireWire 400 ports.

**NOTE**

> FireWire is Apple's brand name for an industry-standard interface definition. The actual specification for the interface is IEEE 1394. Other companies use specific names for their implementations of the interface, such as Sony's term for it: iLink.

FireWire offers several major advantages, which are the following:

- **High speed**—FireWire is capable of communicating at up to 400 Mbps, making it suitable for many high-bandwidth applications.
- **Chainable**—FireWire devices can be chained together; the interface supports up to 63 devices per port. Many FireWire devices have two ports; one is an input port that you connect to a Mac's FireWire port or another FireWire device and the other is an output port that enables you to connect another FireWire device. This enables you to add multiple devices to a single FireWire port on a Mac without requiring a hub.
- **Hot-swappable**—FireWire devices can be connected to and disconnected from your Mac while the Mac is running.
- **Powered connection**—The FireWire interface is capable of providing power to a peripheral device through the bus. Devices that use the capability don't require a separate power supply. Also, this enables some FireWire devices that have batteries, such as an iPod, to be charged by the Mac while it is connected.

FireWire connectors are an unusual shape and consist of a rectangle with a triangular top section (see Figure 30.2). FireWire ports are marked with a high-tech-looking *Y*.

**Figure 30.2**
FireWire ports can be used for various devices, the most prominent of which are digital video cameras and hard drives.

The connector shown in Figure 30.2 is that used to connect FireWire devices to your Mac. Consumer and other FireWire-equipped devices can use differently configured FireWire ports. For example, you won't find a port like that shown in Figure 30.2 on a DV camcorder. Because of size limitations, DV camcorders use a much smaller FireWire port that looks quite different from the FireWire ports on a Mac. Typically, these devices include the specialized cable you need to attach their ports to a FireWire port on your Mac.

**CAUTION**

FireWire connectors are relatively delicate. You should always exercise care when connecting a FireWire device to a FireWire port. The pins in the connector are somewhat fragile and can be bent if you attempt to insert the connector when it is not aligned properly.

Because of its capability to move large amounts of data quickly, the FireWire interface is used for many devices, including the following:

- Digital video cameras
- External hard drives
- External removable media drives, including CD-RW, DVD-R, and tape drives
- Other devices, such as early generations of iPods
- Scanners

**Competition**

Apple's implementation of FireWire has led the industry. For example, Apple is almost single-handedly responsible for the dramatic rise in the use of digital video technology. Many other computers still require that a separate card be added to be able to use devices that transfer data via the FireWire interface.

FireWire's competitor is the USB 2 interface. USB 2 is much faster than the previous USB specifications and is slightly faster than FireWire 400. Although support for FireWire is built in to Macs, it isn't built in to all Windows PCs. Most Windows PCs have USB 2 support by default, which means the market for USB 2 devices is much larger than for FireWire devices. Want some good news? All modern Macs also support USB 2 and many also support FireWire 800, which is much faster than USB 2. As usual, when it comes to innovative technologies, the Mac is leading the way.

## FireWire 800

FireWire 800, as you can probably guess from its name, is faster than FireWire 400. As you can also probably guess, FireWire 800 communicates at 800Mbps. FireWire 800 supports similar devices such as hard drives but can move data at twice the rate of FireWire 400 devices. Currently, FireWire 800 devices are mostly limited to data storage, such as hard drives, but as the technology matures, it can be expected to enable other devices as well.

Another advantage of FireWire 800 over FireWire 400 is the length over which data can be communicated. FireWire 800 works over distances up to 100 meters.

FireWire 800 uses a different port than does FireWire 400 (see Figure 30.3).



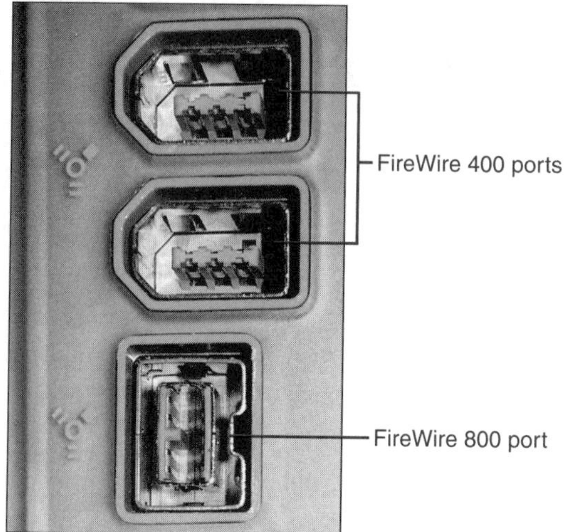


**Figure 30.3**
FireWire 800 and FireWire 400 cables are not interchangeable, as you can see in this photo.

## Using FireWire Hubs

Because many Macs include only two FireWire ports (some mobile Macs have only one), and peripheral devices such as keyboards and monitors don't include additional FireWire ports, you are somewhat limited in the number of FireWire devices you can attach to your Mac at the same time.

A FireWire hub is a device that provides additional FireWire ports to which you can connect FireWire devices (see Figure 30.4).

---

**Daisy-chaining on FireWire Hubs**

FireWire supports daisy-chaining, which means some FireWire devices, such as hard drives, have two FireWire ports. One port receives the FireWire connection coming in, whereas the other can support a connection going out. You can link FireWire devices in this way so that you can support many devices from a single FireWire port. However, this can be problematic for some devices that require large amounts of data to flow smoothly, such as a digital camcorder. Because all the data in a FireWire chain flows across each device, the data flow can be turbulent when many devices are connected on a single chain. For best performance, devices with higher data

30

speed requirements should be placed closer to the Mac, preferably actually connected to the Mac's FireWire port. A FireWire hub can help manage the data flow so you can connect more devices without the interference that can be experienced when you use a FireWire daisy-chain.

**Figure 30.4**
This Belkin FireWire hub offers six additional ports (one port is required for the upstream connection).

If you use multiple FireWire storage devices, such as an older iPod, hard drive, tape drive, or other devices that you will want to be connected at all times, you might need to add more FireWire ports to your system.

FireWire hubs are relatively simple devices, and they have a set of specifications you can choose from:

- FireWire (AKA FireWire 400) or FireWire 800
- Number of available ports (most FireWire hubs include either three or six ports)
- Self-powered, bus-powered, or both

The process of choosing, installing, and using a FireWire hub is straightforward. First, determine whether you need to support FireWire 800. FireWire 800 is a faster protocol than FireWire so you need a hub that is capable of supporting it (you can't use FireWire 400 devices with a FireWire 800 hub, and vice versa). Second, decide how many ports you need. Third, decide whether you need a more mobile hub that can take its power from the bus. Fourth, look for any special features you might need (there aren't many available, so this won't take much time).

Installing and using a FireWire hub is easy to do. Simply connect the hub to your Mac using a FireWire cable, connect its power supply (if applicable), and then connect FireWire devices to ports on the hub.

NOTE

> Remember that one port is used to connect the hub to the Mac or to another hub. Most of the time, you can connect one fewer device to a hub than the number of ports it offers. Because FireWire devices are also hot-swappable, you need only a dedicated port for those devices you want to be connected to your Mac at all times. As long as you have at least one available port for the devices you use only periodically, it isn't a big deal to connect and disconnect those devices. Even if you have more devices than ports, you still might not need a hub unless you want to have all those devices connected at the same time and can't daisy-chain them together.



The FireWire cable you use depends on the device and the type of FireWire being supported; FireWire 800 cables are different from standard FireWire cables. Many devices use a FireWire cable with a standard FireWire connector on each end, but some devices, such as digital video cameras, have a uniquely shaped FireWire port. The specialized cable you need for such devices is usually included with the device.

TIP

> You can chain both USB and FireWire hubs. So, you can connect hubs of the same type to one another to continue to add devices to your system, up to the maximum number of devices supported by that interface.

# USB

The universal serial bus (USB) is an interface that, like FireWire, also provides access to external peripheral devices for your Mac. Also like FireWire, there are two types of USB: USB 1 and USB 2. The similarities continue in that you can also add a USB hub to your system to enable you to connect more devices to your Mac at the same time.

All Macs include at least two USB 2 ports and all USB ports on a Mac itself are USB 2. Keyboards that ship with Macs have USB 1 ports to which you can attach USB 1 devices. USB ports on Macs have a thin rectangular shape (see Figure 30.5). USB 1 and USB 2 ports are identical in appearance; you can't tell which is which just be looking at them (except if the port is on an Apple keyboard, in which case you know it is a USB 1 port).

## USB 1.1

USB 1.1 is a fairly slow interface and is capable of transferring data at the rate of 12Mbps (compared to 400Mbps for FireWire 400). Although slower than many other interfaces, this speed is more than adequate for many peripheral devices.

NOTE

> Similar to FireWire, the USB ports on peripheral devices can look quite different from the USB ports on a Mac. Many USB devices have a USB port that is almost square; others have specialized shapes (such as those on digital still cameras that tend to be small).

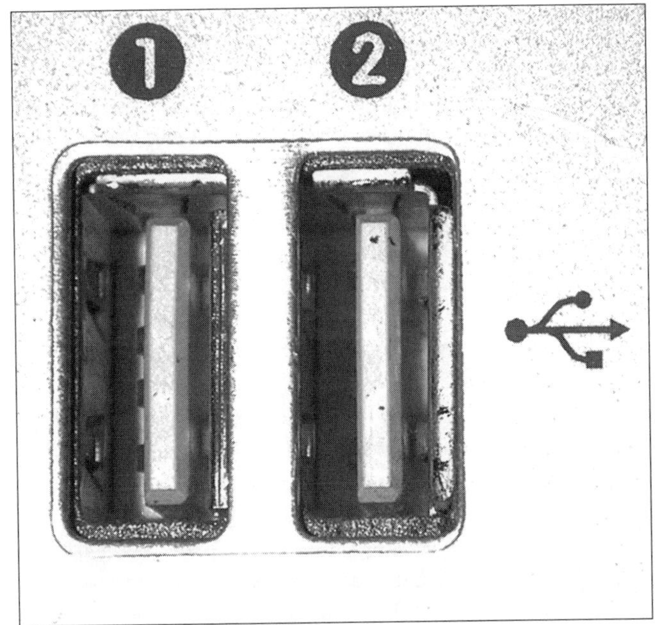


**Figure 30.5**
USB ports enable you to connect your Mac to a large variety of devices.

USB offers advantages similar to those offered by FireWire, including

- **Chainable**—As with FireWire, USB devices can be chained together. A single USB port can support up to 127 devices.
- **Hot-swappable**—USB devices can be connected to or disconnected from your Mac while it is running.
- **Self-powered**—The USB interface can also provide power to a peripheral device, so such devices do not require a separate power supply.

---

**Apple Leads Again**

Adoption of the USB interface across the entire computer industry can also be largely attributed to Apple. Although USB is an industry-standard interface, it was not widely used until Apple released the original iMac. The success of the iMac encouraged other computer manufacturers to more strongly support the adoption of USB. All PCs are now also equipped with USB ports. USB has mostly replaced several different ports on the PC (such as the parallel port) as it has on the Mac.

Because USB is an industry-standard interface, Macs can use the same USB hardware as PCs do. The manufacturer only has to provide Mac-specific software for the device to be Mac compatible.

---

Numerous devices can use the USB interface, including the following:

- Mice
- Keyboards
- Printers

- Digital cameras
- Microphones
- Speakers
- CD-RW and DVD-RW drives
- Cradles for PDAs
- Scanners



**NOTE**

Although USB supports up to 127 devices and FireWire supports up to 63, these are somewhat theoretical limits. The actual number of devices you can connect to these ports depends on the power requirements of the devices. For example, you could not connect 127 USB devices that get their power from the USB interface to a single Mac because the bus could not provide enough power for all those devices.

## USB 2

USB 2 is a much faster implementation of the USB interface. It communicates at 480Mbps, which is slightly faster than FireWire 400. In fact, USB 2 is so fast that it is suitable for hard drives and other high data rate transfer devices.

USB 2 is supported by all modern Macs, and USB 2 has become a standard on Windows PCs. USB and USB 2 share the same hardware, so USB 2 and USB 1 devices can exist on the same USB chain.

If your Mac does support USB 2 (which it likely does unless it is pretty old), many USB 2 devices are available, most of which your Mac can use even if they are not designed for the Mac. This is the benefit of supporting dominant technologies on Windows PCs—little to no development has to be done for a device to support Macs and Windows PCs. (Of course, if software is required to support the device, a Mac OS X version of the software must be available for you to use that device with a Mac.)

Most current USB devices that move data, such as hard drives, iPods, digital TV tuners, and so on, use the USB 2 specification. USB 1 is mostly used for low bandwidth devices, such as keyboards and mice.

## Using USB Hubs

Because so many peripheral devices use the USB interface, you might run out of available USB ports before you run out of devices you want to attach to your Mac. That's where a USB hub comes in.

Like a FireWire hub, a USB hub expands the number of USB ports available on your Mac; USB hubs are one of the simpler devices you will use. USB ports offer the following features:

- **Number of ports**— The number of ports a USB hub offers determines the number of devices you can attach to it. Typical USB hubs offer four ports, but some offer more than that (such as seven ports).

CAUTION

> Sometimes the number of ports offered by a hub can be a bit deceiving. Remember that you have to use one port to connect the hub to your Mac or to another USB hub. Some hubs count this "upstream" port, but others do not. For example, some four-port hubs allow you to connect only three USB devices because one port is required to connect the hub to your Mac or to another hub. Other four-port hubs provide an additional port for the upstream connection so that you can actually connect four devices to them.



- **USB 2 or USB 1 support**—The two types of USB are USB 1 and USB 2. USB 2 is faster than USB 1. If you are using USB 2 devices, you should get a hub that supports USB 2. USB 1 devices are mostly keyboards, mouse devices, and other low-bandwidth devices. USB 2 devices are typically hard drives, cameras, and other devices that require large amounts of data to be moved quickly. USB 2 hubs support USB 1, but USB 1 hubs do not support USB 2.
- **Self-powered or bus-powered**—Some hubs get the power they need from an external power supply (they provide this power to the devices that are attached to them if needed). Others take power for the hub and the USB devices from the USB bus itself.

NOTE

> Although most Macs include two or more USB ports, you can often find additional ports in the other devices attached to your Mac. For example, the Apple keyboard has two USB 1 ports built in to it. Apple monitors, such as the Apple Cinema Display, also include additional USB ports. Make sure that you account for these available ports before adding a dedicated USB hub to your system.

Choosing a USB hub is mostly a matter of deciding whether you need to be able to support USB 2 devices and the number of USB devices you want to be able to connect to your Mac at the same time (see Figure 30.6).

TIP

> Remember that USB is hot-swappable, meaning you can connect and disconnect USB devices at any time. There are many devices you will need to connect only periodically, such as a digital camera. So you don't really need a USB port dedicated to every USB device you have—just those you want to always be available. Having one or more extra ports above that number enables you to add other devices as you need them.

**Figure 30.6**
This Kensington four-port hub is an example of a simple, inexpensive USB hub you can add to your system.

Next, you should decide whether you want a self-powered or bus-powered hub. Because some devices take their power from the USB interface, you should get a USB hub that is capable of providing its own power (many hubs can operate either on their own power or on power from the USB bus). If you are going to use the hub primarily on the move, such as with your MacBook, a bus-powered hub might be a better choice (it will be smaller than a powered hub).

Some hubs offer other features that aren't required but can be useful. For example, some hubs provide status lights for each port. These lights show you when a device is actively using the port; this can be helpful when you are troubleshooting problems with a specific peripheral device.

Installing a USB hub is quite simple. You just attach its uplink port to a USB port on your Mac or on another USB hub. Then, attach each device to a port on the hub. If the hub is self-powered, you attach its power source. That's it.

**NOTE**

> USB 2 and USB 1 cables use the same connector, so you can't tell the difference just by looking at the cables. Be sure you don't try to support a USB 2 device over a hub that supports only USB 1.

There isn't anything complicated to using a USB hub, either. They just work.

# AirPort

All modern Mac models provide an AirPort card slot in which you can install an AirPort card to add wireless networking capabilities to the machine. There are two types of AirPort: AirPort and AirPort Extreme. The primary difference between these is the speed at which they communicate. All modern Macs use AirPort Extreme, which is good because it is considerably faster than AirPort. Most modern Macs include an AirPort Extreme card as standard equipment, and it is an option on all the other models. If you didn't order your Mac with an AirPort card installed in it, you can purchase a card separately and install it yourself.

⇨ To learn more about AirPort, **see** Chapter 18, "Creating and Managing AirPort Wireless Networks," **p. 393**.



## BLUETOOTH

*Bluetooth* is a wireless standard for communicating with peripheral devices, such as PDAs, cell phones, printers, mouse devices, keyboards, and so on. Bluetooth is similar in performance to USB 1 except that it is a wireless technology.

Mac OS X has built-in support for Bluetooth devices, but to use this capability, your Mac must have the hardware required to communicate via Bluetooth. This can be obtained in two ways: either as an installed feature or by a Bluetooth adapter.

Most modern Macs offer built-in Bluetooth as a standard feature along with AirPort whereas the rest of the models offer it as an option.

If your Mac doesn't have Bluetooth built-in, the good news is that you can purchase a Bluetooth adapter to install in one of your Mac's USB ports (see Figure 30.7). These adapters are inexpensive, simple to install, and easy to use.

**Figure 30.7**
A Bluetooth adapter enables any Mac OS X Mac to communicate with Bluetooth devices.

The most common uses of Bluetooth are the following:

- **Synchronize contact information with cell phones and PDAs**—Using Bluetooth, iSync, and Address Book, you can manage your contact information among several devices and synchronize them easily.

- **Print wirelessly**—You can also add Bluetooth adapters to many types of printers so you can communicate with them without using wires. Some printers include Bluetooth capabilities built-in.
- **Use wireless keyboards and mice**—There are many wireless keyboards and mice that use the Bluetooth interface.
- **Transfer photos from a digital camera to your Mac without wires**—If your camera has Bluetooth, you can transfer its photos to the Mac with no wires.



**NOTE**

Bluetooth is an electronics industry standard, so many wireless devices are Bluetooth compatible.

⇨ To learn how to connect and configure Bluetooth keyboards and mice, **see** Chapter 31, "Working with Mice, Keyboards, and Other Input Devices," **p. 763**.

⇨ To learn how to sync your Mac with a Bluetooth cell phone, **see** Chapter 36, "Synchronizing Information on Macs and Other Devices," **p. 859**.

# AUDIO INTERFACES

With the great digital media applications available for Mac OS X, sound has never been a more important part of any Mac system. All Macs have built-in speakers. On the Mac Pro and Mac mini, these consist of a single speaker that isn't really intended to be used for anything beyond audio feedback. The MacBook and MacBook Pro have built-in stereo speakers, but these don't really sound that good unless you like tinny sound with little bass or treble. The iMacs have the best built-in stereo speakers in the Mac family.

For the desktop Macs, you'll almost certainly want to connect external speakers, especially to take advantage of 5.1 sound systems for DVD movies and games. If you use a mobile Mac as part of a workstation, you'll likely want to do this as well.

Of course, getting sound out of your Mac is only half the battle, you'll want to get audio into it as well.

All Macs have audio ports to which you can connect a variety of audio devices.

## AUDIO OUTPUT

All Macs except the Mac Pro include a single audio output minijack port that supplies both an analog and digital audio signal. Which is used depends on the connector and device you attach to the port. If you attach an analog minijack connector, you can use a standard pair of headphones or analog speakers. If you use an optical minijack connector/adapter, you can connect a digital sound system to enjoy the benefits such a system provides.

The technical specification for the Mac's (except the Mac Pro) digital audio output port is called a mini-Toslink (which comes from Toshiba Link) port. This is a smaller version of the standard Toslink connector that is used on audio home receivers and other digital audio equipment.

The Mac Pro provides a full size Toslink digital audio output port so that you don't need to use any adapters to connect it directly to a digital audio device (see Figure 30.8). It also provides a separate analog audio out minijack to which you can connect analog audio devices, such as headphones or stereo speaker systems.

**Figure 30.8**
You can connect digital audio devices to a Mac Pro using the standard Toslink ports.

⇨ To learn how to get the most out of your Mac's audio capabilities, **see** Chapter 33, "Working with Your Mac's Sound," **p. 801**.

### AUDIO INPUT

Like the audio output side, all Macs except the Mac Pro have a single audio input minijack that can process analog or digital input (digital with an appropriate connector/adapter). You can connect audio input devices, such as microphones or voice recorders, to these to move the output of these devices onto your Mac.

iMacs, MacBooks, and MacBook Pros also have built-in microphones that you can use to capture sound, such as when you are using iChat for audio and video conferencing.

You might also use the audio input port on your Mac to connect it to other audio devices. For example, many musicians will connect their instruments or digital equipment to their Mac so they can import tracks into GarageBand.

Mac Pros have a Toslink digital audio input port to which you can connect digital audio devices to use their output on the Mac Pro. They also have a separate analog audio input minijack to which you can connect analog devices, such as microphones.

## VIDEO INTERFACES

In order to use a Mac Pro or Mac mini, you need to connect a video display using their video interface. All other Macs include a built-in display, but you are likely to want to maximize your desktop real estate by connecting a second display using their video interfaces.

The video interface in the Mac provides the video output of the machine to a monitor or other device. Depending on the particular Mac model you are dealing with, there are two primary types of video interfaces available as built-in ports on the machines.

## DVI

The digital video interface (DVI) is designed for flat-panel digital displays. The DVI interface is standard on all digital flat-panel displays—including Apple's. Mac Pros and Mac minis have at least one DVI port to which you an connect a digital display (see Figure 30.9).

**Figure 30.9**
This DVI port will allow you to connect an additional monitor to your Mac.



Mac Pros also feature dual-link DVI ports that you can use to connect display devices that require extreme graphic processing power, specifically Apple's 30-inch Cinema HD Display.

⇨ To learn how to get the most out of your Mac's display capabilities, **see** Chapter 32, "Working with Your Mac's Displays," **p. 785**.

## MINI-DVI

MacBooks, MacBook Pros, and iMacs have a mini-DVI port. This port provides similar functionality to a standard DVI port, but uses a different connector. You can purchase an adapter to connect a variety of displays to these ports, such as an external DVI monitor to add a second display to your system (see Figure 30.10). You can also use similar adapters to output your Mac's video to a television or to an older VGA display.

**Figure 30.10**
An adapter cable is needed to connect an external display to a mini-DVI port.

## S-VIDEO

Different Macintosh models have included S-video ports in the past. If you have a need to connect an S-video device to your Mac, there are adapters available that will enable you to accomplish this task.

### iSight

Including an iSight camera in this section isn't really correct from the technical point of view because it isn't a video interface. But from the a functional perspective, iSight is a video interface because it enables you to capture video on a Mac. Because iSight cameras are built-in on MacBooks, MacBook Pros, and iMacs, they become, in effect, a video interface for the Mac. A standalone iSight camera that connected via the FireWire interface has recently been discontinued.



## IR

Most modern Macs except the Mac Pro include a built-in infrared (IR) receiver that can be used to work with IR devices, primarily the Apple Remote that is included with these Macs. You can use this remote to control Front Row as well as many of the Mac's digital media applications, such as iTunes and DVD Player.

## ExpressCard

MacBook Pros support the ExpressCard interface. This interface provides a slot into which you can plug express cards to add additional capability to these mobile Macs.

## RAM

The internal interfaces that you are most likely to deal with are the Random Access Memory (RAM) slots. RAM is a critically important factor in your system's performance, and unless you ordered your Mac with its maximum amount of RAM, you'll probably want to upgrade your Mac's RAM at some point.

Current Macs use various flavors and types of double data rate synchronous dynamic random access memory (DDR2 SDRAM) modules.

In all cases, when you expand your Mac's RAM (which is one of the best things you can do), you need to ensure that you get memory modules that are the type and speed your Mac supports. See your Mac's documentation to determine the type of memory modules you need for it.

You also need to determine whether your Mac requires that memory be installed in pairs.

Installing additional RAM in most Macs is a relatively simple task. The easiest models are the Mac Pro followed by the iMac. Installing RAM in mobile Macs is only slightly more difficult. Installing RAM in Mac minis is not for the faint of heart.

## PCI Express

PCI Express cards provide expandability in the Mac Pro at very high data rates, up to 8Gbps. PCI Express cards are mostly used for high-end digital video and audio tasks. Note that the new PCI Express slots are not backward compatible, so you cannot install a standard PCI or PCI-X card in a PCI Express slot.

Only Mac Pros support PCI Express cards. The current Mac Pro model has three PCI Express slots

Many PCI Express cards are available for Mac Pros, including the following:

- Graphics cards
- Video digitizers
- Other interfaces (such as Fibre Channel)
- Advanced audio cards



Adding more PCI Express cards is a simple matter of opening the case and installing a new card in an available slot.

**NOTE**

A great resource on the Net from which you can learn about various interface technologies is http://webopedia.internet.com/. In addition to plenty of information about input and output technologies, you can find information on just about any computer-related terminology you encounter. When you find a term, you are also presented with links to additional sites at which you can get more detailed information.

## ATA

The AT attachment (ATA) interface is a PC standard specification for hard disk drives and has been adopted on modern Macs. The ATA interface provides high-speed communication, and because it is a PC standard, ATA hard drives are inexpensive.

As with other specifications, there are various "flavors" of the interface, with each offering a specific speed. For example, current Mac Pros use the serial ATA 3Gb/s standard, which means the throughput of devices using this standard is 3 gigabytes per second (GBps).

Current Mac Pros offer four internal hard drive bays; at least one of these will be filled by a drive. It is quite easy to expand a Mac Pro's internal disk space by adding additional drives to available bays.

All other models include only one hard drive bay, which is occupied by its hard drive. Although you can replace these drives with higher capacity versions, in most cases it is better to add an external FireWire or USB 2 hard drive to expand your system's disk capacity.

**NOTE**

When you deal with internal devices, you might also hear the term *IDE*, which stands for *integrated drive electronics*. IDE devices are those on which the controller is integrated into the device rather than provided by the computer. This term is often used as a synonym for ATA because ATA devices are also IDE devices. But IDE refers to the general technology, whereas ATA refers to a specific specification.

# CHAPTER 31

# Working with Mice, Keyboards, and Other Input Devices

## In this chapter

# CHOOSING AN INPUT DEVICE

Technically speaking, an *input device* is any device you use to move data into your Mac. Some input devices enable you to input data to create documents, images, movies, and so on. The other type of data input device enables you to control your Mac.

In the context of this chapter, the term *input device* refers to the essential devices you use to input data and to control your Mac. Other sorts of input devices used only for data input, such as cameras, scanners, and so on, are covered elsewhere in this book.

There are two types of essential input devices: keyboards and mouse devices. However, many varieties of each device exist, and in the case of mouse devices, some of the varieties are hardly recognizable as being a device of that type. There are other types of input devices you might want to use, such as a graphics tablet.

Many of the devices described in this chapter use the USB interface.



⇨ To learn more about USB, **see** "USB," **p. 751**.

**NOTE**

> Introduced in Mac OS X version 10.2 was the built-in handwriting-recognition system called Ink. Now called Inkwell, this technology allows you to use a tablet to write or draw and the Inkwell system converts your writing into text and graphics. Because of space limitations, I can't provide detail about using Inkwell in this chapter. However, if you have a graphics tablet, you can use the Ink pane of the System Preferences application to configure Inkwell. Then, you can write on your graphics tablet to input text and graphics and to control your Mac.

Since Mac OS X version 10.2, Mac OS X has supported wireless devices that use Bluetooth technology. Many of these devices are available, including keyboards, mouse devices, PDAs, cell phones, and so on. Bluetooth enables your Mac to wirelessly communicate with multiple devices at the same time.

⇨ To learn more about Bluetooth, **see** "Bluetooth," **p. 756**.

# FINDING, INSTALLING, AND CONFIGURING A KEYBOARD

The keyboard is one of the most fundamental, and at the same time, simplest devices in your system. You are likely to spend most of your "Mac" time pounding on its keys, so it pays to make sure you have a keyboard you like.

## CHOOSING AND INSTALLING A KEYBOARD

All Macs come with a keyboard of one type or another, so if you are happy with the keyboard that came with your Mac, there is no need to consider another type. The most recent Apple Keyboard combines a very nice feel with good ergonomics and features. The Apple Keyboard also provides several control keys, which are the mute, volume, and eject keys; these are located along the top of the number pad. And it looks pretty cool, too. Apple has also recently introduced the Apple Wireless Keyboard that connects to your Mac using Bluetooth wireless technology.

However, other types of keyboards are available, such as those designed for maximum ergonomics, to provide additional controls (such as an Internet button), and so on.

Many modern keyboards use the USB interface, so installing a keyboard is a trivial matter of plugging it in to an available USB port. (And remember that, as you read in Chapter 30, "Understanding Input and Output Technology," USB devices are hot-swappable so you can connect and disconnect them without turning off the power to your Mac.)

Some keyboards are wireless; two basic types of these devices are available. One type includes a transmitter you plug in to an USB port. The other type, such as the Apple Wireless Keyboard, uses Bluetooth. The advantage of Bluetooth is that you don't consume an USB port and can communicate with many Bluetooth devices at the same time. The disadvantage is that your Mac must have a Bluetooth module built in or have a Bluetooth adapter installed.



If at all possible, you should obtain a wireless keyboard; being without wires is very freeing, especially if you move your keyboard or mouse around much. And who needs all the clutter that so many wires bring? If you use a USB-based wireless keyboard, you connect its transmitter to a USB port and then use its controls to get the transmitter and keyboard communicating. If you use a Bluetooth keyboard, you use the Bluetooth configuration tools to install and configure it.

⇨ To learn more about Bluetooth devices, **see** "Finding, Installing, and Using Bluetooth Devices," **p. 775**.

If the keyboard you select includes additional features, such as additional buttons and controls, it probably also includes software you need to install. This typically adds a new pane to the System Preferences application that you use to configure the device. An example of this is provided in the next section.

## Configuring a Keyboard

With the Keyboard & Mouse pane of the System Preferences application, you can change the key repeat rate and the delay-until-repeat time. You can also configure the function keys and set the language in which your keyboard is configured. Here's how:

1. Open the System Preferences application, click the Keyboard & Mouse icon to open the Keyboard & Mouse pane, and click the Keyboard tab if it isn't selected already (see Figure 31.1).

**NOTE**

> If you use a mobile Mac (MacBook or MacBook Pro), you will see additional controls for configuring the trackpad and function keys.

⇨ To learn how to configure the keyboard and trackpad on a mobile Mac, **see** "Using and Configuring the Trackpad," **p. 327**.

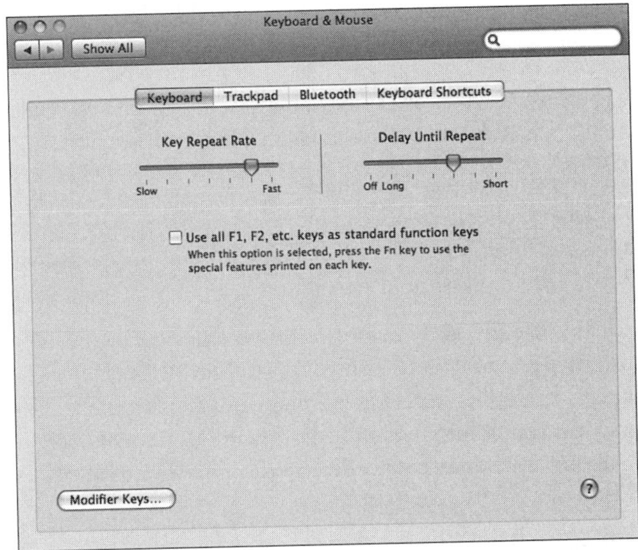


**Figure 31.1** Use the four (three if your Mac isn't Bluetooth capable) tabs of the Keyboard & Mouse preferences pane to configure your mouse and keyboard.

31

2. Use the Key Repeat Rate slider to set how fast a key repeats itself. Move the slider to the right to cause keys to repeat more quickly.
3. Use the Delay Until Repeat slider to set the amount of time it takes for a key to repeat itself. You can test your settings in the text area below the sliders.
4. Click the Modifier Keys button. The Modifier Keys sheet appears.
5. For each of the four modifier keys, select the action that you want to occur when you press that key. The options are one of the modifier keys or No Action. For example, if your keyboard preference is such that the Control key is more convenient for you, you might want to set it to be the Command key because you use that key more frequently. You can select No Action to disable a key.
6. Click OK to set your preferences and close the sheet.

**NOTE**

The greatest Mac OS X feature ever (okay, that is a bit of an exaggeration) might be the ability to disable the Caps Lock key. I have never discovered a real use for this key, but have accidentally turned it on thousands of times and found myself TYPING IN ALL CAPS, which is very annoying for readers and it seems like you are shouting. Finally, I can disable this most annoying of keys without additional software!

## Configuring Keyboard Shortcuts

One of the best things you can do to increase your personal productivity is to learn to use keyboard shortcuts. In the "Mac OS X to the Max" sections of other chapters in this book, you will find many lists of keyboard shortcuts. You should take the time to learn and practice the shortcuts for the OS, as well as shortcuts for any applications you use frequently. The Mac Help Center also lists some keyboard shortcuts if you need to look them up.

Using the Keyboard Shortcuts tab of the Keyboard & Mouse pane, you can configure many of the available keyboard shortcuts. You can enable or disable some of the standard keyboard shortcuts and add keyboard shortcuts for commands in applications you use.

Using the Full Keyboard Access feature, you can access the interface elements with the designated keys. Open the Keyboard & Mouse pane of the System Preferences application and click the Keyboard Shortcuts tab (see Figure 31.2). You will see a list of standard OS keyboard shortcuts in a number of areas, such as Screen Shots, Universal Access, Keyboard Navigation, and so on.

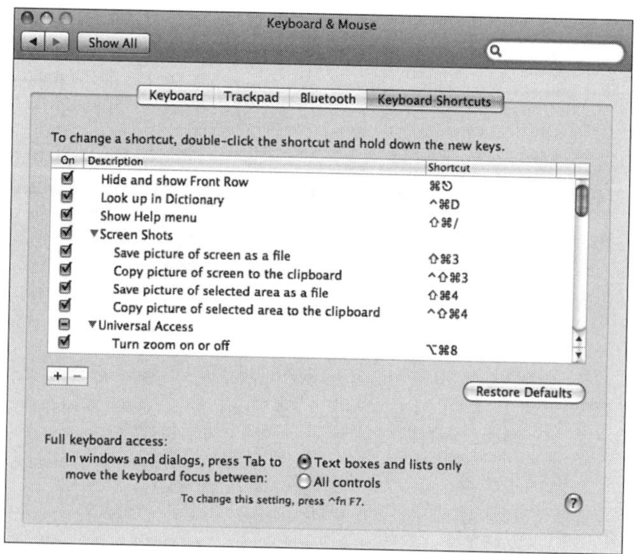


**Figure 31.2**
Use the Keyboard Shortcuts tab to configure your own keyboard shortcuts.

Disable any of the listed shortcuts by unchecking the shortcut's On button. Typically, you would do this when that shortcut conflicts with a shortcut in an application you use. For example, the default shortcut to capture the screen to an image file is Shift-⌘-3. The screenshot application I use, Snapz Pro X, also uses this shortcut by default. Because I don't use the Mac OS X's built-in shortcut, I disable the default screenshot shortcut so it won't interfere with the default Snapz Pro X shortcut.

⇨ To see an explanation of the standard keyboard shortcuts you can configure and use, **see** "Getting the Most from Keyboard Shortcuts," **p. 779**.

In the Keyboard Navigation section, many of the commands start with the phrase "Move focus to." *Moving the focus* means highlighting the item to which you want to access via the keyboard. For example, if you want to use the keyboard to access a menu command for which a keyboard shortcut isn't defined, you can press Control-F2 (the default) to highlight the first item on the active menu bar, which is always the Apple menu. Then use the right-arrow key to select the menu you want to open. Then press the down-arrow key to open the menu move to the command you want to activate. Press Return to activate the command.

## CONFIGURING YOUR KEYBOARD'S LANGUAGE SETTINGS AND THE INPUT MENU

You can configure the languages you use for the keyboard along with other input preferences by using the International pane of the System Preferences application. You can also configure the Input menu, which enables you to quickly choose among languages and select some other handy keyboard tools:

1. Open the International pane of the System Preferences application.
2. On the Language tab, move the language you want to be the default to the top of the list by dragging it there. Move the other languages on the list to set the order in which they are used.
3. Click the Input Menu tab. You use this area to show the Input menu on the Finder menu bar and to configure the items you see on it (see Figure 31.3).

31

**Figure 31.3**
You can configure the Input menu with the Input Menu tab of the International pane.

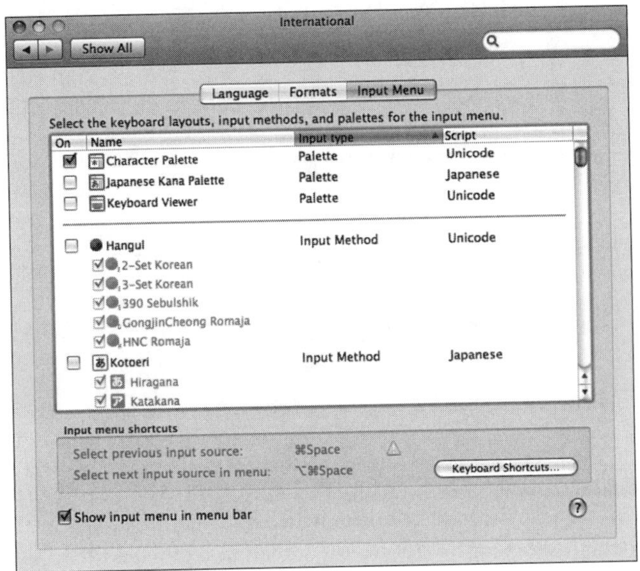


4. Check the "Show input menu in menu bar" check box.
5. Check the boxes next to the other languages you want to be available on the Input menu.
6. Check the Character Palette check box to add that to the menu. You can use this to select, configure, and use special characters such as accent marks.
7. Check the Keyboard Viewer check box to add that to the menu. This viewer shows you the keys for a selected font.
8. If you want to change the keyboard shortcuts for selecting the source on the Input menu, click Keyboard Shortcuts and use the controls you learned about in the previous section to set the appropriate keyboard shortcuts.

When you open the Input menu, which is indicated by a flag representing the language you have made the default, you will see the items you configured there (see Figure 31.4). You can change the current input source, which is indicated by the check mark, to a different one by selecting a different source on the menu. You can open the Character Palette or Keyboard Viewer by selecting the command from the Input menu for the item you want to show. If you select Show Input Source Name, the source name appears as the menu title in addition to the flag icon.

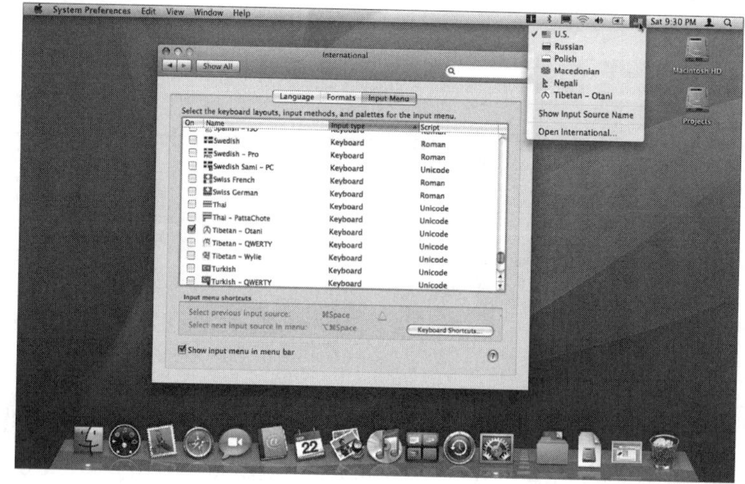


**Figure 31.4**
The Input menu enables you to select the language setting for your keyboard and open palettes and viewers related to the keyboard.



## Configuring a Third-Party Input Device

If you use a non-Apple keyboard and it includes software, you can use it to configure that keyboard.

Open the System Preferences application and then open the pane relating to the keyboard you are using (see Figure 31.5).

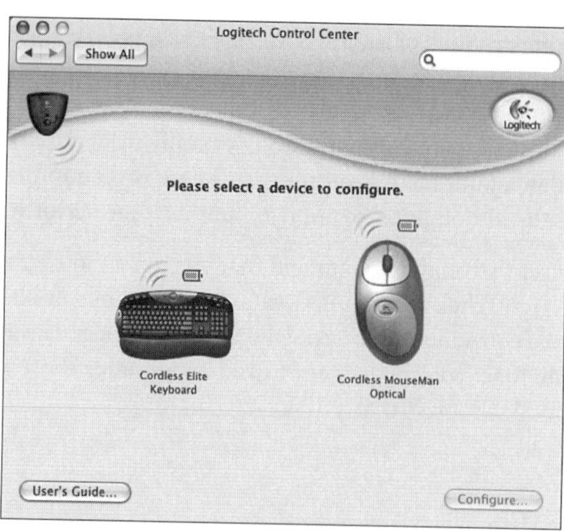


**Figure 31.5**
I use a Logitech Cordless Elite keyboard and mouse; the Logitech Control Center pane enables me to configure many aspects of these devices.

Use the controls provided by that pane to configure the device (see Figure 31.6).

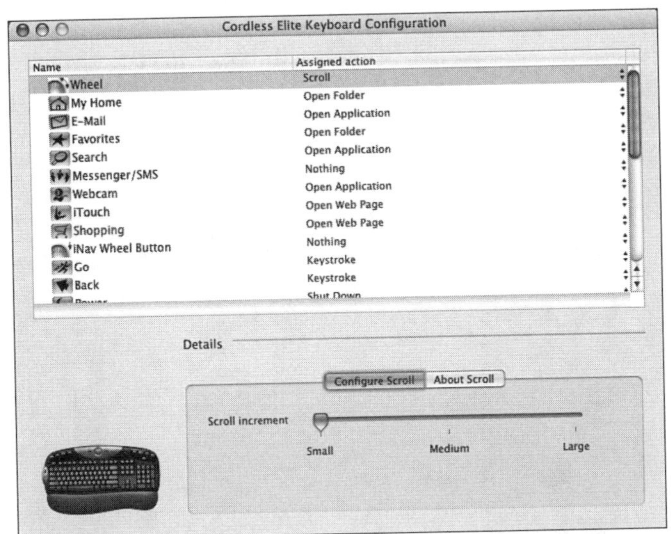


**Figure 31.6**
Here you can see some of the many additional controls provided on the Logitech Elite keyboard; you can customize the keys and other controls it provides to perform many actions.



# Finding, Installing, and Configuring a Mouse

When the Mac was first introduced, its mouse separated it from all the computers that came before it, and those that came after it, for a long time. Until Windows and other platforms adopted the mouse as one of their primary input devices, the Mac and its mouse really stood out from the crowd. Now, the default Mac Mighty Mouse mouse stands out because its design and controls are quite different from most other mice.

## Choosing and Installing a Mouse

All desktop Macs come with the Apple Mighty Mouse. This is an optical mouse, which means it uses light to translate your movements into input information (as opposed to the rolling ball in previous generations of mouse devices). The Apple Mighty Mouse uses the entire top half as its two "buttons," which makes using it even easier (if that is even possible). And it shares the same clear or white plastic look as the Apple keyboard. It also includes a tiny scroll ball that you can use to scroll vertically or horizontally and you can press the ball down for an additional button control. There is yet another button at the base of the mouse on each side (although there are two buttons, they perform the same action).

Whatever mouse you use, I strongly recommend that you get a mouse that has at least two buttons. The ability to right-click things to activate contextual menus and to perform other commands is much more convenient than using a key and clicking the single mouse button. Plus, if you use a mobile Mac, you might want to add a mouse for those times when you are using your MacBook or MacBook Pro at a desk.

There are three main considerations when choosing a mouse.

First is its comfort in your hand. Mouse devices come in various shapes and sizes. Using one that is suited to your own hand cuts down on fatigue in your hand and lower arm.

Second is the number of buttons and other features on the mouse. Apple's mouse devices all provide four mouse buttons, but other mouse devices come with even more or fewer buttons. These buttons can be programmed to accomplish specific tasks, such as opening contextual menus. Also, most mouse devices include a scroll wheel that enables you to scroll in a window, such as a web page, without moving the mouse (the Mighty Mouse's scroll ball enables you to scroll in two directions).

Because support for a two-button mouse with a scroll wheel is built in to the OS (even though you won't find this indicated on the Mouse tab of the Keyboard & Mouse pane of the System Preferences application unless you have such a device installed), you should get at least a two-button mouse. This makes opening contextual menus, which are used throughout the OS and in most applications, much easier. Even better, get a mouse that includes a scroll wheel or a scroll ball like the Mighty Mouse has. This makes scrolling much more convenient and faster at the same time.



Third, you need to decide whether you want a wireless mouse. Because of the amount of time you spend moving a mouse, you should really consider a wireless mouse. Getting rid of the wire provides much more freedom of movement for you. As with keyboards, two types of wireless mouse devices are available—those that use a USB transmitter and those that use Bluetooth (such as Apple's Wireless Mouse).

Like installing a keyboard, installing a mouse isn't hard.

If you use a wired mouse, just plug it in to an available USB port; Apple keyboards include USB ports that you can use for this. If you use a USB-based wireless mouse, plug its transmitter in to an available USB port and use its controls to get the mouse and transmitter communicating.

If you use a Bluetooth mouse, use the Bluetooth configuration controls to set it up

⇨ To learn more about Bluetooth devices, **see** "Finding, Installing, and Using Bluetooth Devices," **p. 775**.

**NOTE**

> Apple's wireless keyboard and mouse use Bluetooth to communicate with a Mac. You must purchase these devices separately. Hopefully, someday soon Apple will include Bluetooth support in all Macs and include the wireless keyboard and mouse for all desktop models.

## Configuring a Mouse

Configuring a mouse is much like configuring a keyboard; however, if you use a mouse that offers additional features, you need to install and configure the software that comes with that device first to take advantage of all its features. Without this software, the second button and scroll wheel will likely work as you expect but more advanced features might not.

To configure an Apple Mighty Mouse, do the following:

1. Open the Keyboard & Mouse pane of the System Preferences application.
2. Click the Mouse tab (see Figure 31.7).

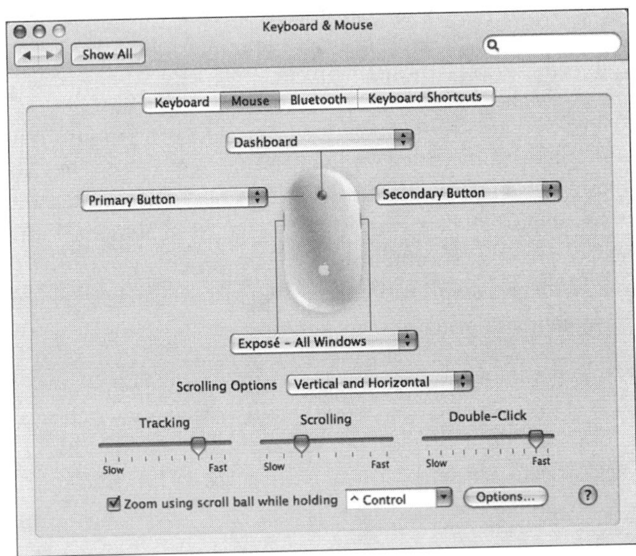


**Figure 31.7**
Configuring a Mighty Mouse isn't hard to do.

3. Use the Tracking slider to set the tracking speed of the mouse. A faster tracking speed means that the pointer moves farther (faster) with less movement of the mouse.
4. Use the Scrolling slider to set the speed at which the scroll ball scrolls. Moving the slider to the right makes the scroll action faster, meaning you move up or down or across the screen faster.
5. Use the Double-Click slider to set the rate at which you have to click the mouse buttons to register a double-click. You can use the test area to check out the click speed you have set.
6. Click the pop-up menu for the left mouse button to open its contextual menu and choose the action that you want to be performed when you click the button. For example, if you want the left button to be your primary button, choose Primary Button (which is the default). Other actions include
   - **Secondary button**—Choose this to have a button perform the secondary action, such as opening an item's contextual menu.
   - **Exposé**—Choose one of the Exposé actions to trigger Exposé. The All Windows option minimizes all windows on the desktop. The App Windows minimizes all windows open in the current application and presents them on the desktop. The Desktop option shows the desktop.

- **Dashboard**—Choosing this option causes the Dashboard to open when you press the button.
- **Application Switcher**—This option causes the Application Switcher to open so that you can quickly move among your open applications.
- **Spotlight**—This action moves you into Spotlight so you can search for information.
- **Other**—If you choose Other, you'll be prompted to select a script or other executable file to associated with the button. For example, if you've created an application with Automator, you can associate it with a mouse button so it runs when you click that button.

7. Using the same menu options, configure the action for the right button, the side button, and the scroll ball button (when you press on the scroll ball).
8. If you want to be able to zoom using the scroll ball, check the "Zoom using scroll ball while holding" check box and choose the modifier key you'll need to press to trigger zooming on the pop-up menu. Click the Options button and use the resulting sheet to control how zooming occurs. You can control how the screen image moves when zoomed (stays with pointer, moves when the pointer reaches an edge, or so the pointer is always at the center of the image). Check the "Smooth images" check box to have your Mac smooth zoomed images. Click Done to save your zoom preferences.



If you use a third-party mouse that comes with its own software, use the software that came with it to configure its additional controls. A pane should be installed in the System Preferences application that enables you to access its configuration software (see Figure 31.8).

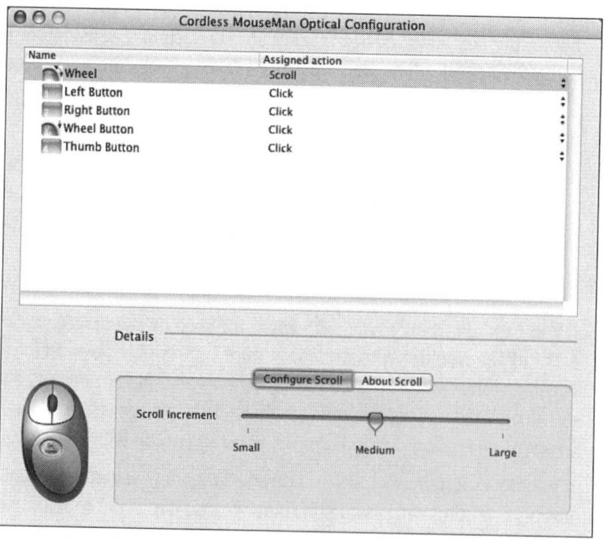


**Figure 31.8**
If you use a third-party mouse, use its software to configure it.

**NOTE**

Mobile Macs use a trackpad instead of a mouse (although you can connect a mouse to one of these machines just as you can any other Mac).

⇨ For information about working with a trackpad, **see** "Using and Configuring the Trackpad," **p. 327**.

# Finding, Installing, and Using a Trackball

Trackballs are really upside-down, roller-bearing mouse devices. Instead of the ball being inside the body (well, modern mice don't use a ball anymore, but I'm sure you get the idea), the ball is on the top of a trackball-style mouse and you move just the ball instead of the mouse body. Trackballs have several advantages over mouse devices. Because you don't actually move the trackball itself, it takes up less space than a mouse does. And you don't have to lift it up to move it when you run out of room or reach. Because your hand remains stationary, you don't rub the sensitive areas of your wrist across the edge of your desk, which can lead to damage of the tissues in your forearm. Trackballs also have more than one button, and you can program the other buttons to perform various functions. For example, you can set a button to add a modifier key when you click with the trackball. In addition, trackballs can move the cursor either more quickly to cover more screen real estate or more slowly to give you more precise control than a mouse.

Choosing a trackball is similar to choosing a keyboard or mouse (except that desktop Macs don't ship with a default trackball). Look for one that fits your hand and has the features you want—such as the number of buttons it has.

**NOTE**

Two of the best input device makers are Logitech and Kensington. You can learn more about their products at their websites: www.logitech.com and www.kensington.com.

Installing trackballs is also similar to installing keyboards and mouse devices. You attach the device through an available USB port and then install and configure its software. Some of these devices are wireless and are set up similarly to wireless keyboards and mouse devices.

**NOTE**

If you experience fatigue or pain when using any input device, make sure that you experiment to see whether you can find a more comfortable position for the device. If you can't, consider replacing the device with another type that is more suited to you. Discomfort, even of a mild nature, can indicate that some damage is being done to your body. If this happens over a long period of time, you can end up with serious health problems.

If you do experience problems, consider obtaining several different devices and set up positions among which you can rotate so you can avoid repeating exactly the same actions over an extended period of time. For example, you might want to have both a mouse and a trackball and switch between those devices every so often.

**Providing Universal Access**

You can use the Universal Access pane of the System Preferences application to configure input devices in different ways to enable those with disabilities to be better able to use a Mac. For example, you can use the Sticky Key feature to cause a series of modifier keypresses (such as ⌘ or Option) to be treated like those keys are pressed at the same time. You can also use Mouse Keys to enable the pointer to be moved with the keyboard for folks who have difficulties using a mouse.

⇨ For the details of configuring Universal Access, **see** Chapter 13, "Making Your Mac Accessible to Everyone," **p. 277**.

# FINDING, INSTALLING, AND USING BLUETOOTH DEVICES

Bluetooth is a wireless communication standard used by many devices, including computers, keyboards, mouse devices, personal digital assistants (PDAs), cell phones, printers, and so on. Mac OS X is designed to be Bluetooth capable so your Mac can communicate with Bluetooth devices, such as to synchronize your iCal calendar on your Mac with the calendar on your Palm PDA.



## PREPARING FOR BLUETOOTH

Two elements are required to be able to use Bluetooth devices.

One is the software component, which is installed as part of Mac OS X.

The other is the transmitter and receiver that sends and receives Bluetooth signals. Some Mac models have this device built in. For those models, you don't need anything else. For models without this, however, you need to obtain and install a Bluetooth USB adapter. This device connects to a USB port and enables a Mac to send and receive Bluetooth signals (see Figure 31.9).

**Figure 31.9**
For less than $40, you can add Bluetooth support to any Mac that has USB ports and is running Mac OS X.

Bluetooth communication is set up between two devices—a single device can be communicating with more than one other Bluetooth device at the same time. Each device with which your Mac communicates over Bluetooth must be configured separately so your Mac recognizes that device and that device recognizes your Mac.

Two steps are involved in setting up Bluetooth. First, you configure Bluetooth for your Mac using the Bluetooth pane of the System Preferences application. Then you configure your Mac to work with each Bluetooth device you want to use.

## Configuring Bluetooth on Your Mac

**NOTE**

> If your Mac isn't capable of using Bluetooth, the Bluetooth pane won't appear in the System Preferences application.

31

When your Mac recognizes that it has the capability to communicate via Bluetooth, the Bluetooth pane appears in the System Preferences application (see Figure 31.10). You use this to configure the general aspects of Bluetooth on your Mac and to see the list of devices your Mac recognizes.

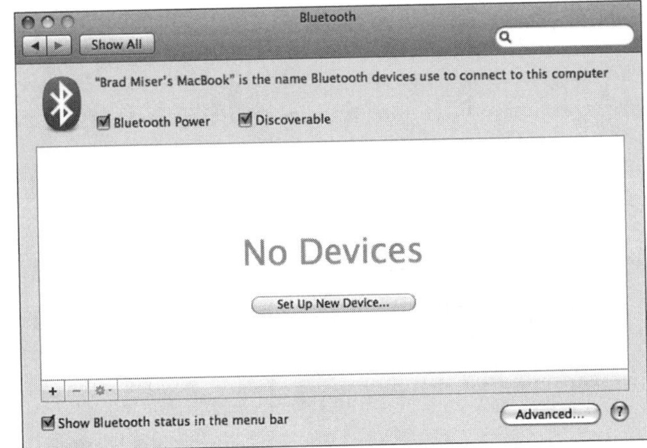


**Figure 31.10** Use the Bluetooth pane of the System Preferences application to control general aspects of Bluetooth on your Mac.

You use the the Bluetooth pane to configure your Mac's Bluetooth configuration. It includes the following controls:

**NOTE**

> In most cases, the default settings will work for you. You should try to configure a Bluetooth device before you adjust your Mac's Bluetooth settings. If it doesn't work properly, come back to these controls to make adjustments.

- **Bluetooth Power**—Use the check box at the top of the pane to turn Bluetooth services on or off. Obviously, Bluetooth has to be turned on for your Mac to be able to communicate with Bluetooth devices.
- **Discoverable**—This makes your Mac "discoverable" by other devices because your Mac transmits signals that other devices can detect. If you don't want this, you can uncheck the check box. For example, if you work in a area in which there are many Bluetooth devices, you might want to hide your Mac so other devices won't be able to detect it. You can still connect to your configured Bluetooth devices when this box is unchecked; your Mac just won't be capable of being detected by other devices automatically.
- **Device list**— If you have already configured your Bluetooth devices to communicate with your Mac, you will see them in this list (assuming that they are turned on). If you have not yet paired your device to your Mac, you can click "Set Up New Device" to open the Bluetooth Setup Assistant to guide you through this process.
- **Advanced**—Several additional configuration options are available on the Advanced sheet of the Bluetooth pane. If your primary keyboard and mouse connect to your Mac with Bluetooth, you can have the Bluetooth Setup Assistant start automatically if your Mac doesn't recognize a keyboard or mouse. You can make sure that your keyboard or mouse can wake your Mac. You can even share your Internet connection with Bluetooth devices. Explore the Advanced sheet to see what settings make the most sense for your computer.
- **Bluetooth menu**—Check the "Show Bluetooth status in the menu bar" check box to add the Bluetooth menu to the menu bar.

31

Many Bluetooth interactions allow the transfer of files between the devices. You configure this using the Sharing pane of the System Preferences application (see Figure 31.11). For example, you can use these settings to move files from your Mac to a Bluetooth cell phone or PDA.

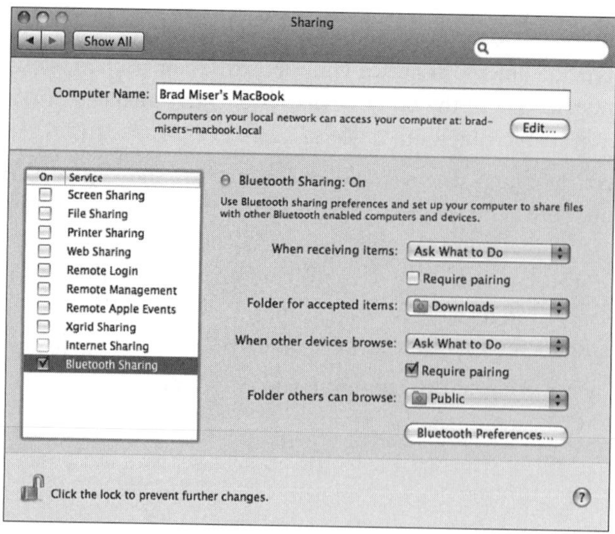


**Figure 31.11**
Use the Sharing pane of the System Preferences application to configure file transfers over Bluetooth.

## Installing a New Bluetooth Device

Before your Mac can communicate with a Bluetooth device, that device must be configured on your Mac. And because Bluetooth devices are paired, your Mac must also be configured on the Bluetooth device with which you are communicating. After you have established a pair, your Mac can communicate with its partner via Bluetooth, and vice versa.

To set up a new device, you use the Bluetooth Setup Assistant. The general steps to do this are the following:

1. Open the Bluetooth Setup Assistant by either clicking the Set Up New Device button on the Devices list of the Bluetooth pane of the System Preferences application or selecting Set up Bluetooth Device on the Bluetooth menu. The Bluetooth Setup Assistant opens (see Figure 31.12).



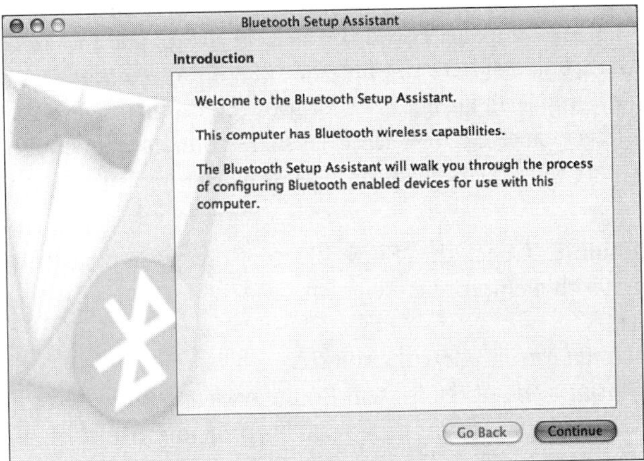


**Figure 31.12**
The Bluetooth Setup Assistant walks you through the steps required to set up a Bluetooth device.

2. Click Continue.
3. Select the type of Bluetooth device you want to set up, such as Mouse, Keyboard, Mobile phone, or one of the other devices listed, and then click Continue. Your Mac searches for available Bluetooth devices.
4. If the device is not auto-discoverable, and most mice and keyboards are not, press the communicate button on the device. This causes the device to start broadcasting a Bluetooth signal that your Mac can detect. As your Mac discovers devices, they are listed in the search results pane of the Bluetooth Setup Assistant window. The devices should be easily recognizably by their names, such as Kensington PocketMouse For Bluetooth when a mouse of that type is detected.
5. Select the device you want to configure and click Continue.

6. Follow the onscreen instructions to configure the device. When the process is complete, the devices can communicate. When Bluetooth devices are connected as a trusted pair, the same passkey is required on each device for those devices to communicate. Depending on the device, you may need to enter a passcode the Mac generates and shows in the assistant window on the device or enter a passcode the device generates on the Mac. When dealing with a mouse, keyboard, or other "dumb" device, this is done automatically and you'll seem to skip over this part of the process.

   When the process is done, you see the Conclusion screen in the assistant.

7. Click Set Up Another Device to configure another Bluetooth device or Quit to stop the assistant.

### Working with Bluetooth Devices

After you have configured a Bluetooth device to work with your Mac, you use the device's applications or controls to communicate with your Mac or use a Mac application to work with the device.



For example, one of the most useful Bluetooth devices is a Bluetooth-capable cell phone. You can use the iSync application to synchronize the phone's contact list with your Address Book so that you have the same information available on both devices. Because you can communicate wirelessly, you don't need to bother connecting any wires to synchronize. You can also transfer files between the two devices, such as to install applications on the cell phone if it supports them.

⇨ To learn how to use iSync, **see** Chapter 36, "Synchronizing Information on Macs and Other Devices," **p. 859**.

Although synchronizing a cell phone wirelessly is one of the most useful Bluetooth-enabled tasks, it isn't the only one. Consider the following examples:

- Using wireless keyboards and mouse devices
- Printing wirelessly
- Connecting to the Internet through a Bluetooth modem or cell phone
- Communicating with other Bluetooth-equipped Macs to share files
- Transferring photos wirelessly from a Bluetooth digital camera

## Mac OS X to the Max: Inputting More Better and Faster

No matter what you do, you will be inputting information continually. Use the information in this section to do that better and faster.

### Getting the Most from Keyboard Shortcuts

Using keyboard shortcuts is a great way to work both faster and smarter. Mac OS X includes support for many keyboard shortcuts by default. As you have seen throughout this book, many areas of the OS and within applications provide keyboard shortcuts you can use.

31

### Using Keyboard Navigation

One of the least used, but most useful, aspects of using keyboard shortcuts is keyboard navigation. You can use the keyboard to access almost any area on your Mac in any application, including the Finder. For example, you can open any menu item by using only keys even if that item does not have a keyboard shortcut assigned to it.

First, configure keyboard navigation:

1. Open the Keyboard Shortcuts tab of the Keyboard & Mouse pane of the System Preferences application.
2. Review the list of Keyboard Navigation and Dock, Exposé, and Dashboard shortcuts to make sure the ones you want to use are enabled (see Table 31.1 for the default shortcuts).
3. If you want to use a keyboard shortcut that is different from the default, click the default shortcut, wait for a moment for it to become editable, and change it to a new combination.

**Table 31.1 Keyboard Navigation and Dock, Exposé, and Dashboard Keyboard Shortcuts**

| Shortcut | What It Does | Default Keyboard Shortcut |
|---|---|---|
| Turn keyboard access on or off | Enables or disables the use of certain keys to navigate. | Control-F1 |
| Move focus to the menu bar | Opens the first menu on the current menu bar; use the Tab or arrow keys to move to other menu items. | Control-F2 |
| Move focus to the Dock | Makes the Dock active; use the Tab or arrow keys to move to icons on the Dock. | Control-F3 |
| Move focus to the active window or next window | Moves into the currently active window or takes you to the next window if you are already in a window. | Control-F4 |
| Move focus to the window toolbar | If you are using an application with a toolbar, such as the System Preferences application, this makes the toolbar active. Use the Tab or arrow keys to select a button on the toolbar. | Control-F5 |
| Move focus to the floating window | If you are using an application that has a floating window, this takes you into the floating window so that you can control the corresponding application. | Control-F6 |
| Move focus to next window in active application | Moves you among the open windows in any application, such as the Finder, Word, and so on. | ⌘-` |

| Shortcut | What It Does | Default Keyboard Shortcut |
|---|---|---|
| Move between controls or text boxes and lists | If "Text boxes and lists only" is active, when you are viewing windows or dialog boxes with controls, pressing the Tab key moves you among only the text boxes and lists in that open window or dialog box. If "All controls" is selected, pressing Tab moves you among all the elements of the window This command changes the mode. You can uncheck its check box to disable this action entirely. | Control-F7 |
| Move focus to window drawer | If the application you are using has a drawer, such as iDVD, this moves you into that drawer so you can use its tools. | ⌘-Option-` |
| Move focus to status menus in the menu bar | If you have enabled additional menus in the Mac OS X menu bar, such as the Displays menu, this command enables you to open them. | Control-F8 |
| Show or hide the Character Palette | Shows or hides the Character Palette that you can use to select special characters. | ⌘-Option-T |
| Automatically hide and show the Dock | Hides or shows the Dock. | ⌘-Option-D |
| All windows | Causes Exposé to present reduced versions of all open windows on the desktop. | F9 |
| Application windows | Causes Exposé to present a reduced version of all windows currently open in the active application on the desktop. | F10 |
| Desktop | Moves all open windows off the desktop. | F11 |
| Dashboard | Opens the Dashboard. | F12 |
| Spaces | Moves your Mac into Spaces mode. | F8 |
| Show Spotlight Search field | Opens the Spotlight. | ⌘-Spacebar |
| Show Spotlight window | Open the Spotlight results window. | ⌘-Option-Spacebar |

**NOTE**

> If you use a mobile Mac, some of the defaults might be different from those listed in Table 31.1. Check the Keyboard Shortcuts pane to see the current shortcuts for your specific system.

Using the shortcuts in Table 31.1, you can move to and select just about anything you can see. For example, to select a menu command, press the Focus on Menu shortcut

(Control-F2 by default) and use the right-arrow or Tab key to move to the menu on which the command is located. Use the down-arrow key to move to the command on the menu that you want to select and press Return to activate the command.

As another example, when you are working with an application that has a toolbar, press the shortcut for the "Move focus to the window toolbar" command, use the Tab key to select the tool you want to use, and press Return to use it.

**NOTE**

Some applications don't support all aspects of keyboard navigation. For example, in some versions of Microsoft Word, you can't select radio button options using the arrow keys, which is too bad.

31

### Adding Keyboard Shortcuts for Application Commands

You can add keyboard shortcuts to commands within Mac OS X applications using the following steps:

1. Open the Keyboard Shortcuts tab of the Keyboard & Mouse pane of the System Preferences application.
2. Click the Add Shortcut button (+) at the bottom of the pane. The Add Application sheet appears (see Figure 31.13).

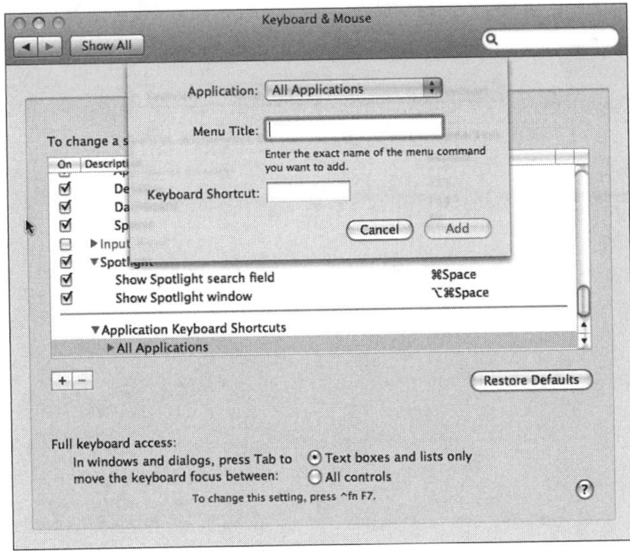


**Figure 31.13**
Using this simple sheet, you can add a keyboard shortcut for any command in any application.

3. Select the application for which you want to create a shortcut on the Application pop-up menu. If the application for which you want to create a shortcut isn't listed, select Other and use the Open Application dialog box to select the application. To create a shortcut for all applications, select All Applications.

4. In the Menu Title box, type the exact command name for which you want to create a shortcut. If the command contains an ellipsis, you need to include that as well.

**TIP**

> To type an ellipsis, use the Character palette to select it or press Option--.

5. In the Keyboard Shortcut field, press the key combination for the shortcut that you want to use to access the command. You need to be careful not to use a keyboard shortcut that is used elsewhere or you might get unexpected results.
6. Click Add. When you return to the Keyboard Shortcuts tab, the shortcut you added is listed under the related application under the Application Keyboard Shortcuts section.

**TIP**

> You can expand or collapse the applications listed in the Application Keyboard Shortcuts section to see all the keyboard shortcuts configured using this tool.

7. If the application for which you configured a shortcut is currently running, quit and restart it. If it isn't currently running, open it. The keyboard command you created will be shown next to the command on the application's menu and you can execute the command by pressing the keyboard shortcut.



---

**Get Serious**

If you want to make keyboard shortcuts work even better, consider adding a macro application to your Mac. My favorite is QuicKeys. Using this application, you can create macros to perform almost any series of steps and then activate the macro with a keyboard shortcut or by clicking a button on a toolbar.

Using QuicKeys you can easily create a keyboard shortcut for any action or series of actions you want to perform. For example, you can record a series of steps and perform those steps by pressing the keyboard shortcut you assign to the macro you create. If you want to take your personal (and your Mac's) productivity to the next level, get a copy of QuicKeys as soon as you can.

---

**NOTE**

> To learn more about QuicKeys, visit www.cesoft.com/products/quickeys.html.

# CHAPTER 32

# WORKING WITH YOUR MAC'S DISPLAYS

## In this chapter

# Getting the Most Out of Your Mac's Displays

Next to your Mac itself, your Mac's display might be the most important element of your system. Having the correct type and size of display can make working with your Mac more efficient and more enjoyable.

iMacs, MacBooks, and MacBook Pros include a built-in display of various sizes (up to the top-of-the-line 24-inch iMac display). You should understand how to configure these displays to get the most from them.

If you use a Mac mini or Mac Pro, you need to add and then configure a display for your system to be able to use it.

⇨ Choosing a first display is similar to choosing a second one; for some advice about choosing displays, **see** "Choosing a Display," **p. 789**.

There's one guiding rule about display space: More space is better. The more display space you have available to you, the more you can have on the screen at the same time, which makes working or playing more efficient and more enjoyable.

The good news is that you can easily add a second display to all Macs except the Mac mini; the Mac Pro will support up to eight displays.



In the next section, you'll learn how to configure a Mac's display. From there, you'll learn about adding and configuring a second display (or even more if you have a Mac Pro) to your system to expand your desktop real estate. And for maximum effectiveness, synchronize the color across the various devices you use with your Mac.

# Configuring a Mac's Display

Use the Displays pane of the System Preferences application to configure the displays connected to your Mac. If you use a single display, this pane has two tabs—Display and Color. If you use multiple displays, the pane also includes the Arrangement tab, which you'll learn about later in this chapter (see Figure 32.1).

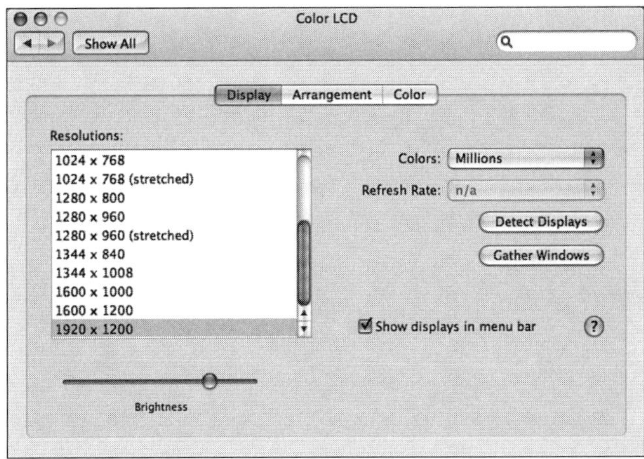


**Figure 32.1**
Here's the Display pane for a 24-inch iMac's screen (you can tell this iMac has a second display attached to it because the Arrangement tab appears).

You use the Display tab to configure the resolution, color depth, refresh rate, and, depending on the display you are using, the brightness of the display. The specific options you have depend on the graphics card and display you are using. In any case, you use the menus, sliders, pop-up menus, and other controls to configure the display. Generally, you should use the highest resolution that is comfortable for you to view. Then, choose the largest color depth and highest refresh rate that are available at that resolution. Finally, set the brightness to a comfortable level for you.

A display's resolution is the number of pixels (picture elements) shown in the horizontal direction by the number of pixels in the vertical direction. For example, a setting of 1024×768 means the display presents 1024 pixels horizontally and 768 pixels vertically.

When you increase the resolution for a display, the objects on the screen get smaller. That's because a display has a fixed physical display size, such as a 23-inch Apple Cinema HD Display. As you increase a display's resolution, the number of pixels displayed on the fixed screen area of the display increases. This means that each pixel gets smaller. Higher resolutions display more information in the same physical space, requiring that the information is smaller.

Setting the resolution of a display is a matter of personal preference, but generally you can use higher resolutions on larger displays. For example, on the 24" iMac, a resolution of 1920×1200 is comfortable for many people. On smaller displays, such as a 13-inch MacBook, 1024×768 might be appropriate. The resolution also depends on the sharpness and clarity of the display. Higher-quality displays, such as those produced by Apple, can display higher resolutions more clearly so that they are more comfortable to view.



All displays also have a maximum resolution that can be used. This maximum is determined by the Mac's video capabilities and the display's hardware. For example, a 24-inch iMac can display resolutions up to 1920×1200 while a 13-inch MacBook's maximum resolution is 1280×800.

Your Mac can resize the resolution on-the-fly (you don't have to restart for the change to be applied) by simply clicking the resolution that you want to try on the Displays pane. The display will be immediately resized according to the resolution you selected. So trying different resolutions to see which works best for you is easy. The trade-off is between more screen space at higher resolutions versus everything appearing smaller. Find the best fit for the type of data you work with and your eyesight.

Some displays support a "stretched" resolution, such as 1024×768 (stretched). This takes the standard 1024×768 resolution and "stretches" pixels in the horizontal direction so the image fills a widescreen display. (If you use a nonstretched resolution on these displays, black vertical bars appear on each side of the screen.)

**NOTE**

> The "standard" resolution for Macs has continued to increase along with the size and clarity of displays. For most of the Mac's early life, the standard display resolution was 640×480 (which also happens to be the resolution of non-HD television by the way). When Macs included larger screens and bigger displays became available, this increased to 800×600. Currently, the minimum resolution you will likely use on most displays is 1024×768. In fact, some applications, such as iMovie, won't even run at 800×600 or less.

After you have selected a resolution, select the color depth on the Colors pop-up menu. In almost all cases, you should select Millions. However, if you use an older graphics card and display, you might have to settle for Thousands.

Select the highest refresh rate available on the Refresh Rate pop-up menu. If you use a digital signal with a flat-panel display, the Refresh Rate pop-up menu is grayed out because refresh rate isn't applicable to these displays when you use a digital signal over the DVI interface.

Some displays support software brightness controls, in which case you will see a Brightness slider on the Displays pane. If you don't see this, use the physical controls located on the display itself to set its brightness (and contrast, if applicable). If you do see the Brightness slider in the Displays pane, move it to the right to increase the brightness of the display or to the left to decrease it.



**NOTE**

> Non-Apple displays provide hardware controls for lots of display settings, such as brightness and contrast, color adjustments, and so on. If you use one of these displays, check out its configuration menu to see what options you have.

Use the "Show displays in menu bar" check box to turn on the Displays menu in the menu bar. You can configure a display, such as setting its resolution, by selecting the resolution you want to use from the Displays menu (see Figure 32.2).

If you display this menu, use its Number of Recent Items menu to set the number of resolution settings to display. For example, if you select 3 on this menu, the Displays menu on the menu bar shows the three most recent settings you have selected. This makes changing among your most commonly used resolution settings even easier.

You can also select the Displays command to open the Displays pane of the System Preferences application. The rest of the commands on the menu appear and are used when you have multiple displays connected to your Mac. You'll learn about those commands later in this chapter.

After you have configured the Display tab, use the Color tab to select a ColorSync profile for your display.

⇨ To learn more about ColorSync, **see** "Synchronizing Color Among Devices," **p. 797**.

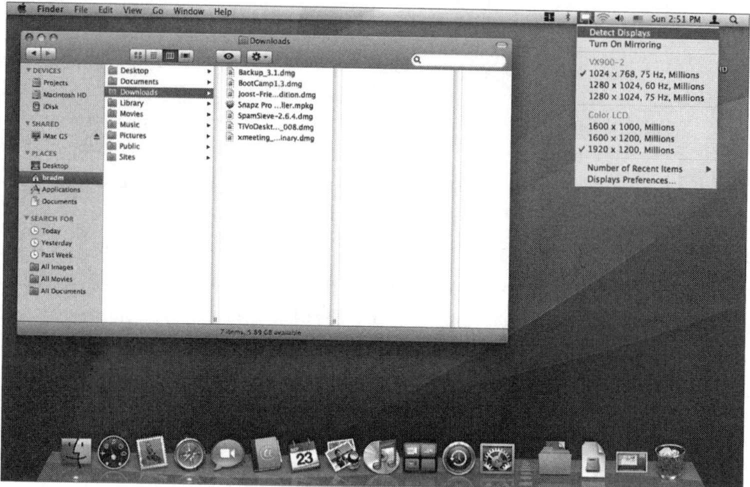


**Figure 32.2**
This system has two displays attached to it. The current main display is a ViewSonic VX900-2 while the Apple 24" iMac's display is identified as the Color LCD. The Displays menu on the menu bar makes configuring all the displays attached to a machine easy.

# Setting Up and Using Multiple Displays



To create the ultimate amount of desktop working space, consider adding multiple displays to your system. With the Mac OS, you have always had the capability to have two or more displays working at the same time, with each display displaying different portions of the desktop. For example, you can display a document on which you are working on one display and all the toolbars and palettes you are using on a second. Or you might want to have a document open on one screen and your email application open on the other.

More screen space is better and with all Macs except the Mac mini, it is easy to connect a second display to your system to give yourself even more working room. If you have a Mac Pro, you can use up to eight displays at the same time.

There are three basic steps to adding an additional display to your Mac. First, choose and obtain the second display you are going to use. Second, connect the display to your Mac. Third, configure your Mac to work with multiple displays.

## Choosing a Display

The fundamental factors you need to take into account when choosing a display are detailed in the following sections.

### Display Type

There are two options in the way a display displays information. With a *cathode-ray tube (CRT)* display, information appears on the screen as the result of an electron gun spraying electrons against the inside of the display screen, which is covered with phosphors that glow when struck by those electrons. The other choice is a *liquid crystal display (LCD)*, which uses a liquid-based display medium. This technology enables the viewing area to be very thin and light, which is why all laptops are equipped with LCDs.

**NOTE**

> Because LCD displays are so thin and their screen is completely flat, they are also called flat panel displays.

Because LCD displays offer many benefits over CRTs, CRTs have mostly gone the way of the eight-track tape player, the cassette, and other obsolete technology. One reason is their size and weight; a comparably sized LCD display is much thinner and lighter than a CRT display. And a high-quality LCD display has a sharper and more vibrant picture than its CRT cousin. Because of these reasons, LCD displays now dominate the computer landscape. All the displays Apple produces are now LCDs.

The cost of LCD displays has dropped drastically over the past few years so there's really no reason to use a CRT, even if you can find one.

### Display Size

Display size might be the single most important factor when considering a display. Various sizes of display area are available. Common LCD display sizes are 15", 17", 19", and 20" along with Apple's spectacular Cinema Displays, which come in a 20" model or the 23" and 30" high-definition models. When it comes to display size, bigger is better. You should get a quality display in the largest size you can afford because more display space yields more working area.



### Interface Type

All modern Macs support the digital video interface (DVI). Almost all flat panel displays use DVI, although you might find some cheap displays that actually use the video graphics array (VGA) interface. You should get a display that uses DVI if possible.

⇨ To learn more about video interfaces, **see** "Video Interfaces," **p. 758**.

**TIP**

> If you use an Apple display (one of its flat-panel displays), you can power up your Mac by pressing the Power button on the display and put your Mac to sleep by pressing the Power button again. Press the Power button while your Mac sleeps, and it will wake up.

### Picking a Display

Choosing a display can be difficult because of the number of choices that are available. However, you can use several factors to quickly narrow down the options to a few displays that meet your criteria. First and most importantly, decide how much you can afford to spend. You can spend as little as $150 for a 15" flat panel to around $1,799 for the top-of-the-line Apple 30" Cinema HD Display. Second, consider any other special features such as additional ports. Third, choose the largest size in a quality brand of the type you choose that fits your budget.

I hate to sound like a commercial here, but Apple's displays are the best available. If you can afford to get one, you won't be disappointed. At $599, even the "small" 20" model offers plenty of desktop space and excellent image quality. For the maximum in size and image quality, consider the 30" Cinema HD display that supports high-definition signals.

Other brands can provide excellent displays at significantly lower prices. One of my favorite brands is ViewSonic. You can get a very good ViewSonic 19" flat panel display for about $250.

Whatever brand and model you choose, I don't recommend anything less than a 19" display unless you really can't afford one that big. Having sufficient display size is important to be able to work efficiently.

**NOTE**

> Another output option is a projector. Although covering these is beyond the scope of this chapter, the cost of the devices has decreased such that obtaining a decent-quality projector is in the realm of possibility for many Mac users. Adding a projector to your Mac system has all sorts of uses, such as for a home theater.

## Installing Displays



Installing a display requires two steps. First, connect the appropriate cable to the display and the Mac. Second, install any software that was provided with the display (you won't need to do this for most displays, such as Apple displays). Some displays include a ColorSync profile; if yours does, you should install and use it. If you have to install an additional graphics card in a Mac Pro, the graphics card you install might also have software that provides its special features.

⇨ To learn more about ColorSync, **see** "Synchronizing Color Among Devices," **p. 797**.

The details of these steps depend on the kind of Mac you have. Each type is covered in the following sections.

### Installing a Second Display for iMacs, MacBooks, and MacBook Pros

In addition to their internal displays, iMacs, MacBooks, and MacBook Pros have a mini-DVI port. To attach a display to this port, you need one of Apple's adapters. There are three types, and the type you need depends on the type of display you are going to connect. If you have a DVI display, you'll need the Mini-DVI to DVI Adapter (see Figure 32.3). If you use a VGA display, you should get the Mini-DVI to VGA Adapter. If you want to connect the Mac to a television or other video device, you'll need the Mini-DVI to Video Adapter. Each of these is available for about $20 from Apple or other retailers.

Connect the mini-DVI end of the adapter to the mini-DVI port on your Mac. Connect the other end to the display. If you are using the Video Adapter, you can use its S-video connector or the composite (RCA) video connector depending on the input port available on the video device you are using.

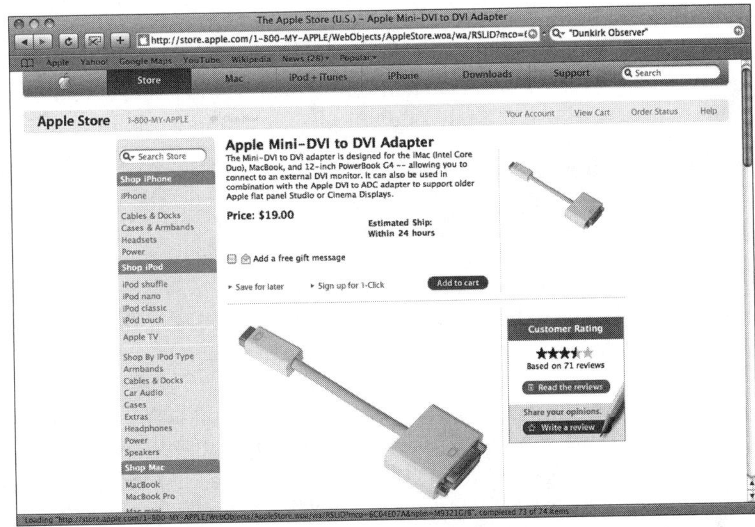


**Figure 32.3**
With a Mini-DVI to DVI Adapter, you can easily connect a second display to iMacs, MacBooks, and MacBook Pros.

Once connected, you are ready to configure the Mac to work with the second display.

⇨ To learn how to configure your Mac for multiple displays, **see** "Working with Two (or More) Displays," **p. 794**.

### Installing a Second Display for Mac Minis

The Mac mini is the most limited model with respect to displays. That's because the mini only has one DVI port, so it is the only Mac that doesn't support multiple displays "out of the box." You can use Apple's DVI to Video Adapter to connect the mini to a television or other video device. This can be useful to view the mini's output over a big screen TV, but isn't all that useful for working with your Mac because it doesn't expand your working space (although, if you connect your mini to a big screen television, it certainly appears to be larger).

> **NOTE**
>
> There are lots of splitters and other specialized devices that enable you to connect more than two displays to iMacs, MacBooks, and MacBook Pros. Some of these devices also enable you to connect two displays to a Mac mini. Providing details about these devices is beyond the scope of this chapter, but if you do a quick search of the web, you'll find lots of information about this topic.

### Installing Multiple Displays for Mac Pros

The Mac Pro is definitely the most expandable in all ways, including multiple display support. All Mac Pro models support two displays out of the box. For even more displays, you can add more graphics cards to a Pro, with each supporting up to two displays for a grand total of eight displays.

The specific number and type of display a Mac Pro supports depends on the video cards installed in it. The current "low end" (which is a relative term) graphics card includes one DVI port and one dual-link DVI port. You can connect a display to each port; you can connect one of Apple's monster 30-inch cinema displays to the dual-link port. Other cards include two dual-link ports in case you have the means to acquire two of the 30-inch displays.

**NOTE**

> Apple offers extensive "build to order" options when it comes to the video configuration of a Mac Pro. You can get a Pro with up to four video cards installed in it. Apple currently offers three different types of video cards from the capable GeForce 7300 GT to the monster Quadro FX 4500.

After you've connected displays to both ports on the Pro's first graphics card, you can add additional graphics cards to work with more than two displays.

Many graphics cards are available, each offering differing levels of performance and special features. When choosing a graphics card, consider the following factors:

- **Mac OS X compatibility**—Not all graphics cards are Mac OS X–compatible, so any that you consider should be.
- **Performance**—Graphics cards offer varying levels of performance, such as 2D and 3D acceleration and the display resolution they support. The amount of memory installed on a card is a large determinant of this performance, with more memory being better. Common memory amounts are 256MB or 512MB. Generally, you should obtain the highest performance you can afford.
- **Video interface support**—Most modern graphics cards support the DVI interface used by almost all flat-panel displays. Some offer support for multiple interfaces, such as DVI and VGA.
- **Special features**—These include video digitizers that enable you to digitize video from analog sources, TV tuners that enable you to watch TV or the output from a VCR on your display, and other features for which you might have a use.

Installing a PCI Express graphics card in a Mac Pro is a relatively easy process.

**NOTE**

> If software is provided for the card, such as drivers and applications, you should install the software before you install the card. However, check with the instructions that came with the card to see the order in which the manufacturer recommends the items be installed.

To install an additional graphics card, do the following:

1. Power down your Mac Pro.
2. Open the case.

3. Locate the PCI Express slot in which you want to install the card. You can use any open PCI Express slot; they are functionally identical.
4. Remove the blank cover from the PCI Express slot you are using.
5. Install the PCI Express card in the slot and secure it with the screw that was used to hold the blank cover in place.
6. Close the case.
7. Attach displays to the DVI ports of the graphics card.
8. Restart your Mac.

## Working with Two (or More) Displays

After your Mac is connected to multiple displays, you need to configure the displays to work together. When you have more than one display installed, one of the displays will be the primary display. This is the display on which the menu bar, Dock, mounted volumes, and other desktop items are displayed. The rest of the displays contain the windows that you place on them.

To view items on more than one display, do the following:

32

1. Open the Display pane of the System Preferences application. When you do so, you see a Displays pane on each display. On the primary display, this is included in the System Preferences application window. On the other displays, this is an independent window with the name of the display at the top of the window. The settings shown in each Displays pane are those that are currently being used for that display. On the primary display, a third tab called Arrangement appears in the Displays pane (see Figure 32.4). The Displays pane on the other displays contains the normal tabs, but it does not contain any part of the System Preferences interface (see Figure 32.5).

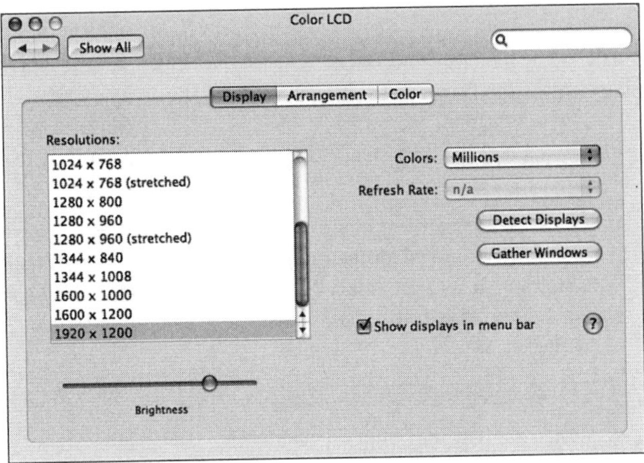


**Figure 32.4**
This Display pane contains the Arrangement tab, which means it is for the primary display.

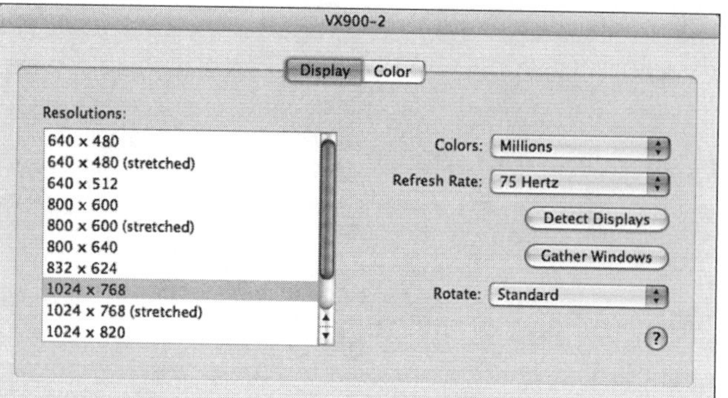


**Figure 32.5**
This Displays pane is shown on a secondary display; note that the resolution setting is different from that of the primary display shown in Figure 32.4.

**TIP**

> The Display preferences window for each display is independent. By default, each Display preference window appears on the display it controls. If you want to move all the open Display preference windows together, click the Gather Windows button. This will stack all the open Display preference windows under the current one.

If you want your Mac to detect the displays you have attached to it, click the Detect Displays button (it won't be available in all circumstances). The name shown at the top of the System Preferences application and each Display settings window (there will be one for each display) should identify the display you are using.



**TIP**

> If you connect another display to your Mac but it doesn't become active, click the Detect Displays button. Your Mac should recognize and start using the additional display.

2. Set the resolution, color depth, and refresh rates for each display using its Displays pane. You can use different settings for each display; for example, if one display is larger than the other, you might want a higher resolution on the larger display.
3. Click the Arrangement tab on the primary display's Display pane. You will see a graphical representation of the displays attached to your system (see Figure 32.6). The primary display is indicated by the menu bar across the top of the display window (on the right display in Figure 32.6.
4. Organize the displays by dragging them on the pane so they correspond to the physical arrangement of the displays. For example, drag the display you want to display "to your left" to the left side of the pane. This configures the virtual desktop so you move the mouse pointer to the left to work on the left display. The display icons should be in the same orientation as the physical displays.

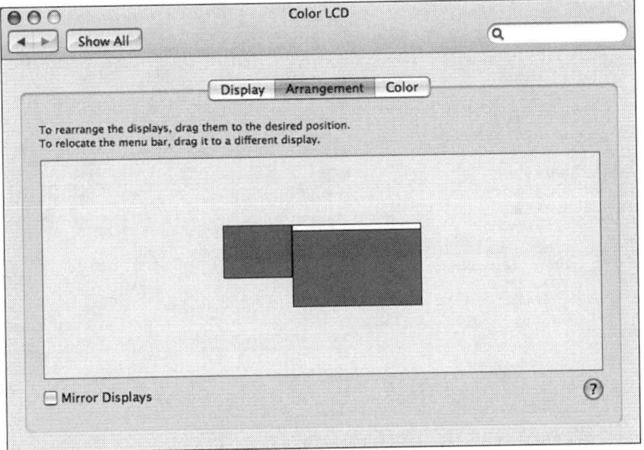


**Figure 32.6**
This system has two displays attached to it; the relative resolution settings are indicated by the size of the displays in this pane. The primary display, located on the right, is set to a higher resolution than the display on the left.

**NOTE**

If a display supports additional features, controls for those features may appear in the Displays pane. For example, in Figure 32.5 you can see that the display can be rotated and the current orientation of the display can be selected on the Rotate pop-up menu.



5. Set the primary display by dragging the menu bar onto it. The menu bar, Dock, and other elements will move onto the primary display.

*If you can't get both displays working, see "My Second Display Doesn't Work" in the "Troubleshooting" section at the end of this chapter.*

Because the desktop stretches across all the displays connected to your system, they act as one large desktop. You can drag windows, palettes, and other elements from one display to another by moving them from one side of the desktop to the other. You can move between the displays by moving the pointer "across" the divide between them. For example, you might have an image open in Photoshop on one display and all the Photoshop palettes on another. Or, you can have a Word document open on one display and a web browser on another. After you use multiple displays for even a short time, you might find that you can never get along with just one again.

**NOTE**

You can drag windows between the displays, but the menu bar and Dock always remain on the primary display.

You can have multiple displays show the same image by turning on display mirroring. When you do this, each display shows the same desktop. You are limited to the same amount of working space, but that same space is displayed on multiple displays. This is especially useful when you connect a projector to one video port and use a display on the other. You can work using the display while the audience sees what you are doing via the projected image.

Or, if you connect a mobile Mac to an external display, you can have that display face the audience while you work on the internal display.

To configure display mirroring, set the displays to the same resolution. In the Arrangement tab of the Displays pane, check the Mirror Displays check box. All displays connected to the machine then display the same image.

If you add the Displays menu to your menu bar, you can control display mirroring, the resolution, and the color depth of each display by choosing the setting you want from the menu (see Figure 32.7).

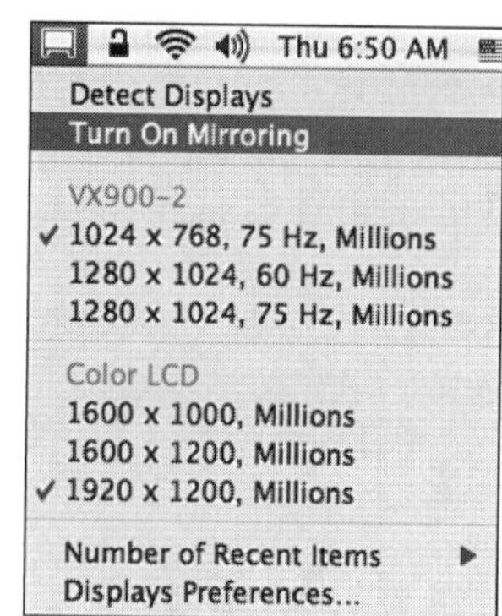


**Figure 32.7**
Control the resolution and other settings of all the displays attached to your Mac from the Displays menu in the Mac OS X menu bar.

32

## Synchronizing Color Among Devices

One of the most challenging aspects of creating color documents for output on paper or electronically is maintaining consistent color among the images and text in those documents. Each device you use, such as displays, printers, scanners, cameras, and so on, can have a slightly different interpretation of particular colors and can use a different color space. This makes creating a document that contains the exactly colors you really want difficult.

Apple's *ColorSync* technology is an attempt to solve this problem. With ColorSync, you configure a ColorSync profile for each device you work with. If all your devices use a ColorSync profile, the colors across the elements of your document should be more consistent because ColorSync translates colors across different color spaces.

The two general steps to use ColorSync are the following:

1. Use the ColorSync Utility to select and configure a ColorSync profile for each device you will use.
2. Use the color management features of the application you want to use to create a document to select the ColorSync workflow for that project.

## CONFIGURING COLORSYNC

To configure a ColorSync profile for your devices, do the following:

**NOTE**

> To use ColorSync, a device must have a ColorSync profile installed. For many devices, this profile is built in to Mac OS X. For others, the profile is installed when you install software related to that device.

1. Open the ColorSync Utility (found in Applications, Utilities). The first time you run this, you'll be prompted to run Profile First Aid, which will attempt to repair the various profiles stored on your Mac.
2. Click Verify. The Profile First Aid utility runs and finds all the profiles stored on your Mac. It will find problems and report about any that it can.
3. Click the Devices button to open the Devices pane. On this pane, you will see the list of devices with color implications connected to your Mac, such as cameras, printers, displays, and so on (see Figure 32.8).

32

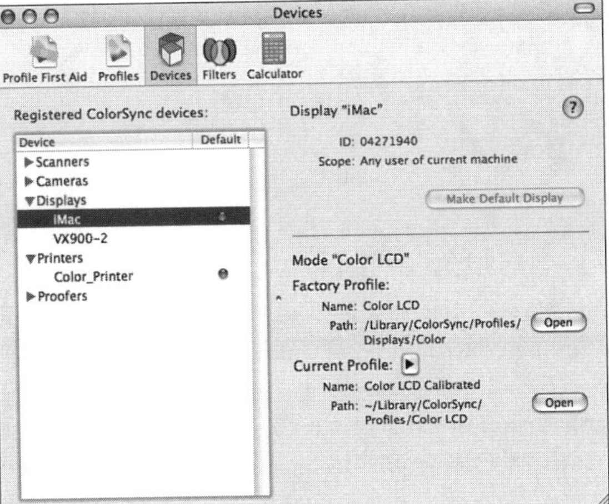


**Figure 32.8**
Expand a device type to see a list of devices of that type connected to your Mac.

4. Choose the device you want to configure. The current ColorSync profile for that device will be shown.
5. To select a different profile, click the Current Profile pop-up menu and choose the profile you want to use. If the one you want to use is not shown on the menu, choose Open and then move to and select the profile you do want to use.
6. Repeat steps 4 and 5 for each device you want to use with ColorSync.

*If you can't find profiles for the devices you want to use, see "I Don't See a ColorSync Profile for My Device" in the "Troubleshooting" section at the end of this chapter.*

NOTE

Understanding and using ColorSync effectively is a very complex topic. For detailed information, see Apple's ColorSync website located at www.apple.com/colorsync.

### USING COLORSYNC

After you have installed and configured your device profiles and workflows, the way you use ColorSync depends on the particular applications you use. For example, you can employ the ColorSync profiles when you print a document by using the ColorSync option on the Options pop-up menu in the Print dialog box. Other applications, such as Photoshop, enable you to employ more sophisticated ColorSync features.

## TROUBLESHOOTING

### MY SECOND DISPLAY DOESN'T WORK

*When I install and connect a second display, it remains dark when I restart my Mac. Why isn't the second display working?*

First, try the easiest steps. Power the Mac all the way down using the Shut Down command. Restart it. After it restarts, if the display is still dark, open the Displays pane. If there is only one pane, the Mac is not recognizing that there is a second display connected to it. Click the Detect Displays button. If the display is still not recognized, the problem lies with the display itself, the cable connecting the display to the Mac, or with the Mac's graphics hardware.

Isolate the problem to the graphics card or the display by connecting the display that is working to the port to which the display that isn't working is currently connected and the display that isn't working to the port to which the display that is working is connected.

If you are using a Mac with an internal display, you won't be able to do this because it has only one external port. You'll have to connect the display to another computer to test it. If possible, use an adapter or cable that you are sure is working.

If the second display (now connected to a working port) works but the other display does not, you know that the problem is related to the graphics card. The most likely cause is an incompatible card. Check the manufacturer's website to ensure that card is supported on Mac OS X. Download and install any updated drivers for that card. Finally, make sure that the card is properly seated in the PCI Express slot.

If the second display doesn't work when it is connected to a working port, you know the problem lies with the display itself. You'll likely have to get help from the manufacturer to repair it.

### I DON'T SEE A COLORSYNC PROFILE FOR MY DEVICE

*I don't see a profile for a specific device I want to use. How do I obtain the correct profile?*

For you to be able to choose a profile for a device, that profile has to be installed. It should have been installed when you installed that device's software. However, if it wasn't, check the website of the manufacturer of the device. Locate a ColorSync profile and download it. Install it in the `Mac OS X/Library/ColorSync/Profiles` directory where `Mac OS X` is the name of your startup volume.

If you still can't find a profile even after you have downloaded and installed it, the profile might be damaged. Run the ColorSync Utility (Applications/Utilities) to verify and repair your profiles.

CHAPTER 33

# Working with Your Mac's Sound

## In this chapter

# Understanding Mac Audio

Sound is an important part of any Mac. From alert sounds that tell you something is happening to enjoying DVD movies, it's important that you have sound capabilities that match what you want to do. Sound goes both ways; you'll probably want to connect a speaker system to get sound out of your Mac, and you might want to use input devices so that you can record various audio on a Mac.

# Understanding Audio Output Options

You're likely to use your Mac for a lot more than just work. From listening to music and watching video with iTunes to enjoying DVDs with the DVD Player to creating your own masterpieces with iLife applications, sound is a very important component of your system. Modern Macs support at least three audio output options, and the Mac Pro supports even more than that.

When it comes to Mac audio, there are two fundamental options from which you can choose. You can use analog sound or digital sound. Adding good quality analog sound to your Mac is easy and inexpensive. But, most Mac users should opt for digital sound instead. Digital sound enables your Mac to take advantage of the highest quality speakers along with benefits, such as surround sound, so that your Mac's sound quality can rival that of a home theater system. And since you are likely to enjoy so much rich audio content on your Mac, why not opt for the highest quality?

When it comes to getting sound from your Mac, your options include the following:

33

- **Built-in speakers**—iMacs, MacBooks, and MacBook Pros include built-in speakers. The speakers in some iMac models are pretty good, but they don't come anywhere close to the sound quality you can get with even a basic set of external analog speakers, and they completely pale in comparison to a set of digital surround sound speakers.

**NOTE**

> Mac Pros and Mac minis include a single built-in speaker. Unless you have absolutely no interest in sound quality, you won't want to rely on these speakers to hear what your Mac puts out.

- **Analog speakers**—Analog speakers connect to the Mac's audio mini-jack port. You can find very high-quality analog computer speakers, some of which rival their home stereo counterparts in sound quality. Analog speakers tend to be inexpensive, but they don't provide you with surround sound capabilities. Unless your budget is extremely limited, I'd recommend going digital.
- **Digital speakers**—For Mac users who are interested in high quality audio for music, video, movies, and so on, a digital sound system is the way to go. The good news is that all Mac's support digital sound output so you can connect a set of digital speakers (such as a 5.1 surround sound system) to any Mac to enjoy all the quality that digital sound offers. There are several ways to do this as you'll see later in this chapter.

# CHOOSING SPEAKERS

As with other system components, choosing speakers is primarily a task of balancing how much you want to spend versus how demanding you are in terms of quality. At the low end, you can get a basic analog set that has two speakers; however, unless you have a very small budget, you should get a set that also includes a subwoofer. From there, you can move up to more advanced digital systems, such as a 5.1 speaker set that includes six speakers, to provide full surround sound.

There are a mind-boggling variety of speaker systems available, and there's no way to provide even a reasonable overview of them in this short chapter. So, I'll stick with some general guidelines about how to choose a speaker system.

First, assess your Mac's current capabilities. If you use a Mac with built-in speakers that sound fine to you, and you don't use your Mac for movies, the built-ins might be good enough. (Ok, I don't think many people should stick with this option, but you might choose to.)

Second, determine how important sound quality is for you. If you don't really care that much, you can get a basic set of speakers, such as a 2.1 system, and you'll probably be satisfied. If you use your Mac to listen to and watch content and you care about quality, you'll want to move toward the middle and upper end of the spectrum by obtaining at least a 5.1 sound system for your Mac.

Third, set a budget. Quality speaker systems can get expensive. Decide how much you can afford to spend and let that drive your selection of speakers. (Of course, you'll want to do some shopping to make sure you get the best speakers available for your budget.) To get a good quality 5.1 system, you can expect to pay about $350 (see Figure 33.1).



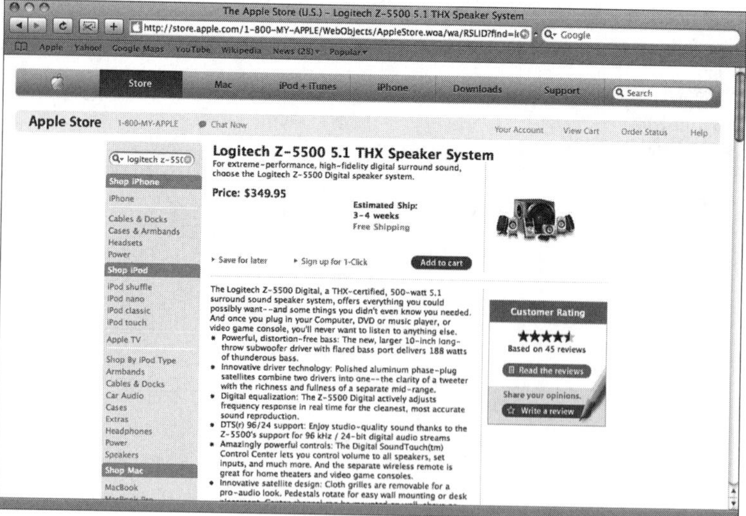


**Figure 33.1**
These Logitech Z-5500 5.1 speakers transform Mac audio into something special.

# INSTALLING SPEAKERS

Figuring out which speakers to add to your system is a lot more complicated than installing them. Although installing a speaker system with your Mac depends on the kind of system and Mac you are using, none of the options require much in the way of time or effort.

## INSTALLING ANALOG SPEAKERS

Analog speakers are the simplest to install. If you have a two-speaker set, you'll want to place one speaker on your right and one on your left, preferably at ear level. If you have a three-speaker set, you'll want to place the bass unit on the ground or on your desktop. Connect the input line for the speaker set (which will be connected to one of the satellite speakers or to the bass unit) to the audio output minijack on the Mac. Connect the speakers to the bass and power the system. That's all there is to it.

## INSTALLING DIGITAL SPEAKERS USING THE MAC'S MINI-TOSLINK DIGITAL AUDIO OUT PORT

All modern Macs include a combo analog/digital audio out mini-jack port. To connect a digital speaker system to the Mac, you need a cable that has a mini-Toslink connector on one end; typically, the cables you'll use include an adapter that connects to one end of the cable (see Figure 33.2). What's on the other end of the cable needs to be determined by the input connector on your speaker system. There are two basic options: digital coax or Toslink (which is often called optical digital). If you use a 5.1 system, it probably includes a control unit with the input jacks; which cable you need to get is determined by the jacks available on the control unit.



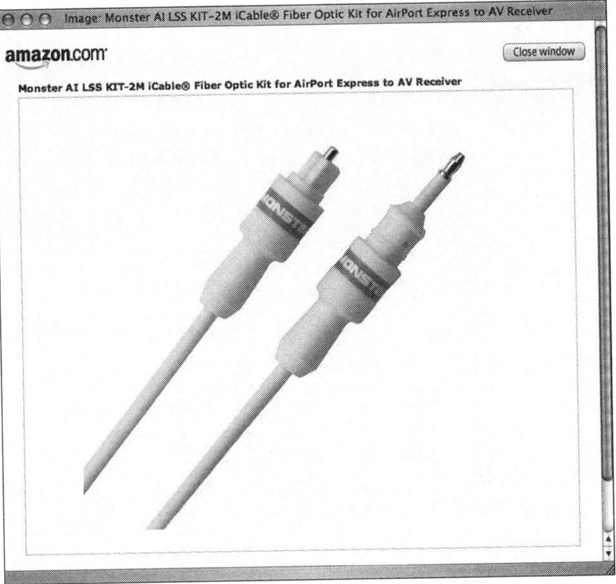


**Figure 33.2**
This Monster Fiber Optic Cable kit includes an adapter so the cable has a Toslink connector on end and a mini-Toslink connector on the other.

The most difficult part of installing a 5.1 or higher sound system is being able to place the speakers in appropriate locations, so you get the maximum benefit of surround sound. Generally, you'll want to arrange the speakers so that they are all at ear level. With a 5.1 system, you'll have three front speakers, which are arranged one on the left, one in the center, and one on the right. You'll have two or more rear speakers, which should be arranged similar to the front speakers, except behind you; these are often the tricky ones to arrange depending on how hard it is to route speaker wires to the speaker locations. You'll usually want to place the bass unit on the floor; where it is in location to you really doesn't matter as you'll hear the bass well (assuming it's at least in the same room with you).

After you've placed the speakers, you'll need to connect their wires together at a central point; typically, you connect them to the bass speaker along with the power. Then you connect the bass input wire to the control unit, and use the cable you purchased to connect the control unit's input jack to your Mac's output.

### Installing Digital Speakers with a Mac Pro

The Mac Pro includes digital output ports. One is the same mini-Toslink port included on all Macs. The other is a full-sized Toslink port. The capabilities of these ports are similar, so you can use either port to connect a set of digital speakers to a Mac Pro. Otherwise, the steps are the same as in the previous section.

### Installing Digital Speakers Using USB

Some speaker systems use USB to connect a Mac. These systems are limited to two- or three-speaker sets, but if you don't need more advanced audio capabilities, they might be a good choice for you.

A more likely option for USB sound is to connect a USB adapter to a Mac and then connect the adapter to the speaker system. You might use an adapter when the Mac's built-in audio capabilities are not sufficient for your needs, such as if you want to use specific types of microphones to input sound to your Mac.



### Installing Digital Speakers Using a PCI Express Card (Mac Pro)

If you use a Mac Pro, you can install a high-end audio PCI Express card and then connect the speaker system to that card. Mac Pros (and other Macs for that matter) have pretty good built-in audio capabilities so you'll likely only need to add such a card for specific purposes, which are beyond the scope of this chapter.

## Understanding Audio Input Options

There are many situations in which you'll want to put sound into your Mac. If you use GarageBand, you'll want to record instruments and vocals. You might want to add narration to a slideshow you create in iPhoto. Or, you might want to use iChat for audio and video conferencing.

The options for inputting sound to a Mac range from the simple to complex. On the simple side, you can use the built-in microphone on iMacs, MacBooks, and MacBook Pros to record voice narration or other sounds.

You can also attach sound input devices to USB ports or to the Mac's input sound jacks. For example, you can attach the output of another device, such as a portable cassette recorder, to a Mac's audio input jack to be able to record the device's output on the Mac. Like the audio output jack, the input jack is a combo analog and digital port. To use its digital capabilities, you'll need to obtain a cable with a mini-Toslink adapter to connect a device to that port digitally.

As with other areas, Mac Pros include the most sophisticated sound input capabilities and both the standard analog/digital input port along with a full Toslink digital input port. You can also install many kinds of audio PCI Express cards for more sophisticated capabilities.

Choosing and installing audio input devices is more complex than choosing a speaker system. There are so many more options, and the options become more complicated as there is a large variety of audio sources from which you might want to input sound.

If you want to record only voice input, the Mac's built-in microphone or a simple USB headset microphone will probably meet your needs just fine. If you want to record output from other devices, you'll probably be able to connect their output to the Mac's input mini-jack using a cable similar to one you use to connect speakers to the output mini-jack. Being able to record multiple or MIDI instruments will require either a USB adapter or a sound card (Mac Pro only).

After you've installed an input device, you'll be able to use its output in a variety of ways, such as recording narration for your projects.



## Controlling a Mac's Audio

After you've set up a Mac for sound output and input, it's time to take control of all that audio.

There are three ways you control audio on a Mac. First, you can use the Sound pane of the System Preferences application to configure general sound properties for the system. Second, all applications that have audio components provide audio controls; at the least, they enable you to configure the relative volume level of that application's output (versus the overall system volume setting), but most provide other controls as well, such as enabling you to choose an input source for applications to record sound. The third way is to use audio hardware connected to your Mac; for example if you use an external speaker system, it probably has volume controls. (Most 5.1 systems include a remote to enable you to control output volume, input source, settings, and so on.)

In the remainder of this section, you'll discover the details of using the Sound pane of the System Preferences application to control your system's audio. The other means of controlling audio depend on the specific applications or hardware with which you are working.

The Sound pane of the System Preferences application has three tabs: Sound Effects, Output, and Input (see Figure 33.3). As you've probably guessed, each tab controls a specific aspect of a Mac's audio.

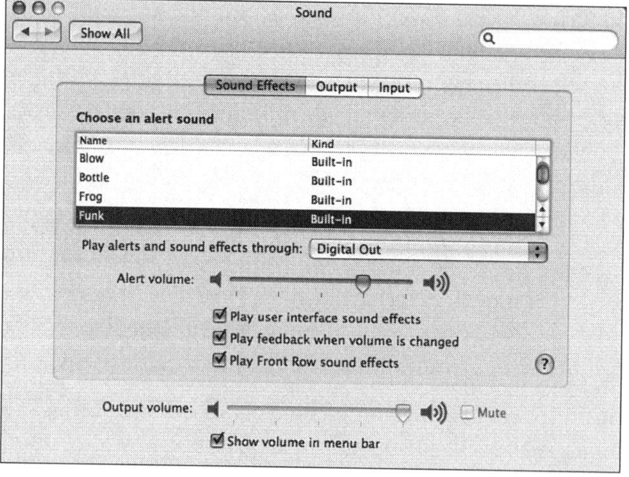


**Figure 33.3**
The Sound Effects pane of the System Preferences application provides complete control over your Mac's sound effects, such as the alert sound.

At the bottom of the Sound pane, you can use the "Output volume" slider to set the general sound level for your system, or you can mute it by checking the Mute check box. You can also choose to install the Volume menu on the Mac OS X menu bar by checking the "Show volume in menu bar" check box. If you do so, you can set the volume level by clicking the speaker icon on the menu bar and setting the volume level with the slider.

If your Mac is connected to a digital sound system, these controls are disabled because you control the system volume with the digital sound system's controls.



**NOTE**

> You can also control volume using controls within specific applications, such as iTunes or iMovie. When you do so, the volume control in the application changes the volume of that application's output relative to the system volume level.
>
> When you use the volume controls on an Apple keyboard, you change the system volume level.

## CONFIGURING SOUND EFFECTS

On the Sound Effects tab, you can configure several aspects of the sound effects your Mac uses to communicate information to you.

When a Mac needs your attention, such as when an error has occurred, it will play the alert sound. Select the alert sound you want to use by clicking it on the list shown on the Sound Effects pane (refer to Figure 33.3). You then hear a sample of the sound you select. When your Mac needs to get your attention, it will play this sound.

⇨ To learn how to add and use custom alert sounds, **see** "Mac OS X to the Max: Installing Additional Alert Sounds," **p. 810**.

On the "Play alerts and sound effects through" pop-up menu, choose the output device on which you want the alert to be played. The options on the menu are determined by the output devices connected to your Mac. If your Mac can output sound through different devices simultaneously, such as via internal speakers and a sound system connected to a USB port, you'll be able to select the system on which you want the sounds to be played. This prevents you from being jarred by an alert sound when listening to loud music or movies. If a Mac is connected to only one sound output system, such as a digital speaker system, you'll have to have alert sounds played on that device.

Set the volume level of alerts by using the "Alert volume" slider. If you do have alerts play through internal speakers while other sound plays through external speakers, you'll likely need to set the alert volume level relatively high to be able to hear it over the sound coming from the external speakers. If you play all audio through one device, you might want to test the volume level of the alert sound while listening to other content at a typical sound level.

If you check the "Play user interface sound effects" check box, you will hear sound effects for various actions, such as when you empty the Trash.

If you check the "Play feedback when volume is changed" check box, you will hear a sound when you change the system volume level using the volume keys on your keyboard. The louder the volume setting, the louder the feedback sound. You also see a visual slider appear briefly on the screen to show you the relative sound level you are setting.

If you check the "Play Front Row sound effects" check box, Front Row will use its cool sounds when you activate it, open menus, and so on.



## Controlling Sound Output

Use the Output tab to select and configure the output devices you want to use to play all sound other than system alerts (see Figure 33.4). The list of devices through which you can play audio appears at the top of the pane. Select the device you want to use to play sound, and then configure the settings for that device (if additional controls appear under the device list). The settings you have depend on the device you have installed. For example, with analog speakers, you can control the balance of the satellite speakers using the Balance slider. If you connect a digital system or other device that Mac OS X doesn't recognize, the message "The selected device has no output controls" appears to let you know that you should use the device's controls to configure it, such as selecting specific output settings.

**NOTE**

> Some hardware devices include control panels you can use to perform detailed configuration of those devices. In such cases, a pane will be added to the System Preferences application for that device. Open its pane to configure it.

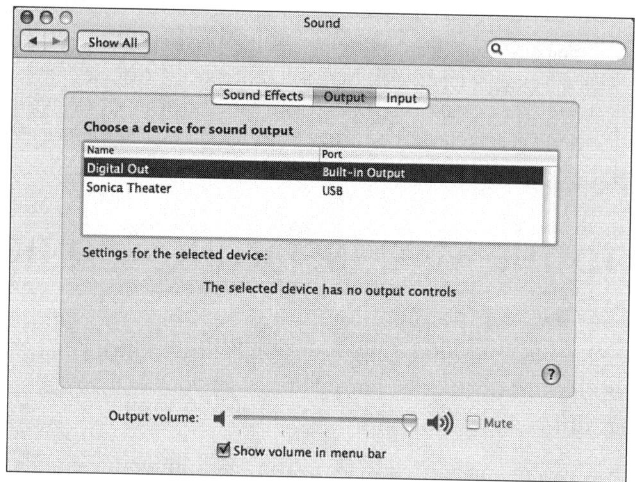


**Figure 33.4**
The Output tab of the Sound pane of the System Preferences application enables you to select and configure a Mac's sound output.

## Controlling Sound Input

Use the Input tab to configure sound input devices, such as an internal microphone, the audio in port, or a USB microphone (see Figure 33.5). A list of all sound input devices appears in the upper part of the pane. To capture input from a device, select it on the list. Then use the "Input volume" slider to set the input volume level for the selected device. Use the "Input level" display to monitor the input volume being received by the input device. The "blips" show you how "loud" the input sound is. A blip remains at the highest level of sound input to show you where the maximum is. Generally, you should set the level so that most of the sound is coming in at the middle of the slider's range.

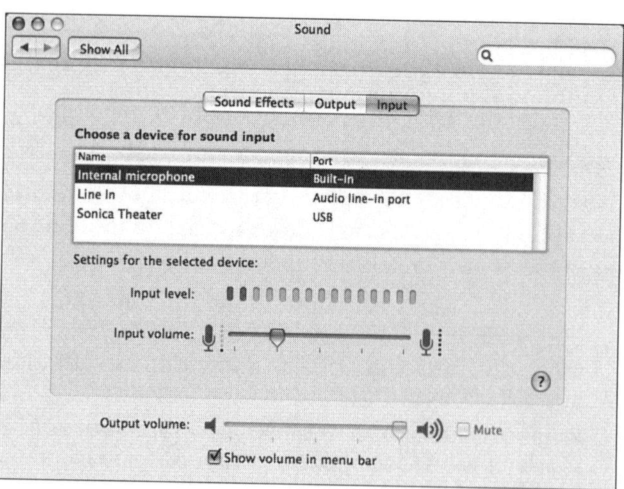


**Figure 33.5**
You can use the Input tab to set the input volume for devices you will use to record sound or for other reasons (such as speech recognition).

33

**NOTE**

Using the Sound pane only configures the general system settings. When you use sound in other applications, make sure you configure the audio settings for that specific application. For example, when you record narration in an application, use its controls to select the appropriate device and to set the input volume level and other settings.

# MAC OS X TO THE MAX: INSTALLING ADDITIONAL ALERT SOUNDS

Mac OS X includes a number of default alert sounds from which you can choose. However, you can also create your own alert sounds if you want your Mac to sport a unique way of communicating with you.

Under Mac OS X, system alert sounds are in the Audio Interchange File Format (AIFF). This is a good thing because you can use many sounds as your alert sound, and by using iTunes and other applications, you can convert or record almost any sound into the AIFF format and use that sound as a custom alert sound.

**NOTE**

Under Mac OS X, AIFF files have the `.aiff` filename extension. By default, iTunes appends the `.aif` filename extension to files when you convert them to the AIFF format. Be sure to add the second *f* to the filename extension for the sound you want to add as an alert sound. If you don't, the file will not be recognized as a valid alert sound.

33

There are two basic ways to add alert sounds. You can add them to specific user accounts or to the system so they are accessible to everyone who uses your Mac.

To add an alert sound to a specific user account, perform the following steps:

1. Create or download the AIFF files you want to add to your available alert sounds.
2. Log in to the user account under which you want to make the alert sounds available.
3. Drag the new alert sounds to the following directory: **/*shortusername*/Library/Sounds**. The new alert sound is available to that user account on the Alert Sounds list in the Sound pane of the System Preferences application.

**NOTE**

If the System Preferences application is open when you install a new alert sound, you must quit and restart it to see the new sound on the list.

When you install your own system alert sounds in the alert sound list, the type for the sounds you add is Custom instead of Built-in. Built-in sounds are stored in the Sound folder in the System Library folder instead of the user's Library folder.

You can also add alert sounds to the system so they are available to all the user accounts on your machine. However, to do this, you must log in under the root account.

**CAUTION**

> You can't modify files or directories that are within the Mac OS X system directory without authenticating as an administrator or being logged in under the root account. Be careful when you are logged in under the root account because you can change anything on your system, including changing vital system files in such a way that your Mac fails to work. You can also delete any files on the machine while you are logged in as root.

⇨ To learn how to enable and log in under the root account, **see** " Enabling the Root User Account," **p. 261**.

To add alert sounds to your system, do these steps:

1. Create or download the AIFF files you want to add to your alert sounds.
2. Drag the AIFF file into the directory `Mac OS X/System/Library/Sounds`, where `Mac OS X` is the name of your Mac OS X startup volume.
3. You will be warned that the Sounds directory cannot be modified. Click Authenticate and enter an administrator username and password to finish moving the files. The new sounds are available on the Alert Sounds list on the Sound pane of the System Preferences application.

**NOTE**

> The kind of alert sounds you add to the system when logged in under the root account are Built-in, just as the alert sounds that are installed with Mac OS X.

CHAPTER 34

# Installing, Configuring, and Using Printers

## In this chapter

# Finding, Installing, and Using Printers

If you want to get your work out on paper, you can use many types of printers to get the job done. Under Mac OS X, you install and manage printers using the Print & Fax pane of the System Preferences application, the Printer Browser, and the Printer Setup Utility application. In addition, Mac OS X includes support for a large number of printers by default.

Four basic categories of printers are available, based on the technology the printer uses to imprint the paper:

- **Inkjet**—Inkjet printers spray small dots of ink on the paper to form images and text. Inkjet printers produce excellent quality text and good-to-excellent quality graphics. For personal printers or those shared by only a few people, inkjets are hard to beat. A good quality inkjet printer costs less than $100, so they are also an excellent value. Support for many Hewlett-Packard, Lexmark, Epson, and Canon inkjet printers is built in to Mac OS X.
- **Laser**—Laser printers produce superb quality for both text and graphics. They are also very fast and are the best choice for network printing. Lower-end laser printers are affordable enough to also be a good choice for a personal printer.
- **Color laser**—Color laser printers produce excellent text and graphics and also have color capability. High-quality color laser printers are very expensive and are unlikely to be an option for you unless high-quality color printing and network support are required and you have a business that can justify their expense. But lower-end color laser printers are now priced so they are a feasible option for people who use them for a home-based business.
- **Other printers**—Beyond color laser printers are dye-sublimation and other higher-quality printers that are used in graphic design and other high-end businesses.

**NOTE**

> A factor to consider when selecting a printer is that inkjets use a lot of ink and cartridges are expensive. If you do more black-and-white printing, a laser printer can be a less expensive option in the long run when you consider the cost of the consumable supplies (ink versus toner). If you do a lot of printing, consider a laser printer for black and white printing and an inkjet for color printing.



There are two ways you can connect a printer to your Mac: directly or through a network. To connect a printer directly to your Mac, you simply attach the printer cable to the appropriate port on your Mac (USB or Ethernet). How you connect a printer to your network depends on the type of network you are using. If you are using an Ethernet network, you can attach a cable from the nearest hub or print server to your printer. You can also choose to share either type of printer over a wired or wireless network. If your network includes an Apple AirPort Base Station or an AirPort Express Base Station, you can connect a USB printer to the base station's USB port on either kind of base station or to one of the Ethernet ports on the AirPort Base Station.

Mac OS X supports several printer communication protocols, including AppleTalk, IP Printing, Open Directory, Bonjour, direct connection through USB, and Windows Printing.

Using Bonjour enables your Mac to actively seek devices in the network. In the case of Bonjour printers, your Mac can discover the printers it can access and automatically configure itself to use those printers. No configuration on your part is required. However, printers have to be Bonjour capable for this to work. Although Bonjour has been supported since Mac OS X version 10.2, few printers support this technology.

## Installing and Configuring Printers

There are many types of printers you can use with Mac OS X. In this section, you will learn how to work with the most common types of printers.

### Installing and Configuring a Local USB Printer

As long as it offers Mac OS X–compatible drivers, you can install and use just about any USB printer.

#### Installing a Local USB Printer

Using such devices is relatively straightforward:

1. Connect the printer to the power supply and to your Mac's USB port.
2. Install the printer driver software, if necessary. If the printer you are using is an inkjet from HP, Lexmark, Canon, or Epson, the drivers are probably already built in to Mac OS X.

> **TIP**
>
> To see which specific printer models are supported natively by Mac OS X, open `Mac OS X/Library/Printers`, where `Mac OS X` is the name of your Mac OS X startup volume. You will see folders for each brand of printer you elected to include when you installed Mac OS X.

3. Configure the printer via the Print & Fax pane of the System Preferences application.



#### Configuring a Local USB Printer

Support for many inkjet printers is built in to Mac OS X. For example, you can use the following steps to install, configure, and use an Epson Stylus inkjet. Other models of inkjet printers work similarly:

1. Connect power to the printer.
2. Connect the printer's USB cable to a USB port on your Mac.
3. If the printer has Mac OS X–compatible software, install it—support for many printers is built in to the operating system.

4. Open the Print & Fax pane of the System Preferences application (see Figure 34.1).

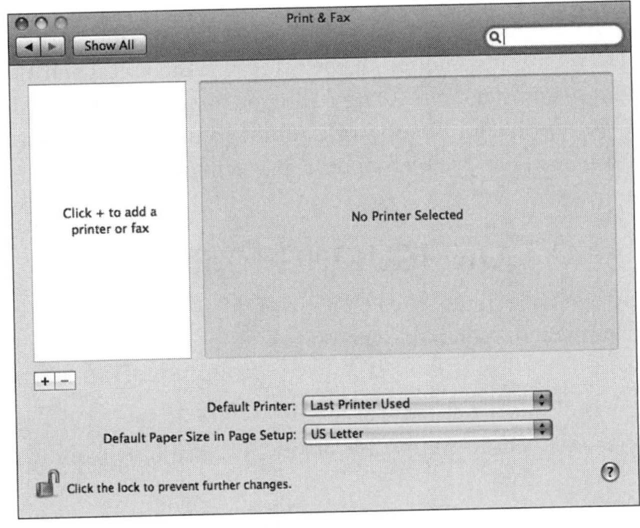


**Figure 34.1**
Use the Print & Fax pane of the System Preferences application to configure the printers your Mac uses.

5. Click the Add Printer button (the plus sign). The Printer Browser appears and immediately seeks out all the printers it can find. At the top of the browser, you'll see buttons for each type of printer that Mac OS X supports, including Default, which finds all the printers your Mac can access; IP Printers, which you use to configure printers via their IP addresses; Bluetooth, which you select to find and configure Bluetooth printers, and so on. When you select one of these types, the browser's lower pane is reconfigured for the type of printer you selected.
6. For a printer connected to your Mac's USB port, select the Default button in the toolbar. The list of printers shown in the lower pane of the browser will be refreshed (see Figure 34.2).
7. Select the printer you want to configure by clicking its name in the list. Information about that printer is gathered, and Mac OS X attempts to choose the best driver software for it, which will be shown on the Print Using pop-up menu (see Figure 34.3).
8. If you don't want to use the default printer name shown in the Name box, select it and type a new name.
9. If the default location isn't what you want, select it and change that, too.
10. If Mac OS X found a driver for your printer and selected it on the Print Using pop-up menu, leave that selection as it is; if a driver wasn't found, open the pop-up menu and choose the appropriate driver. If you can't find a driver for your printer, you need to get one from the printer's manufacturer.

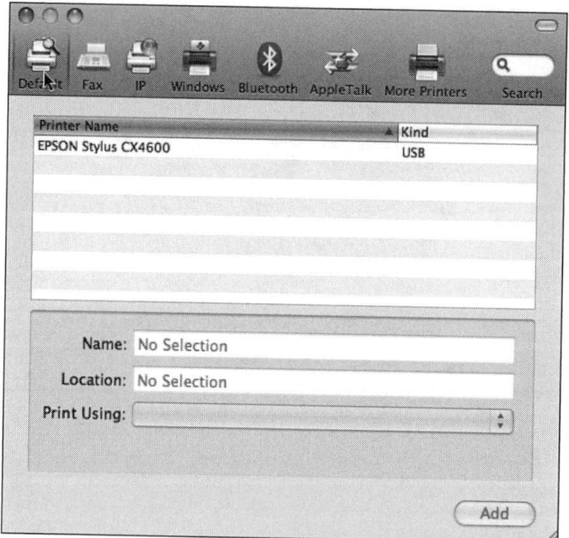


**Figure 34.2**
The Printer Browser finds printers with which your Mac can communicate.

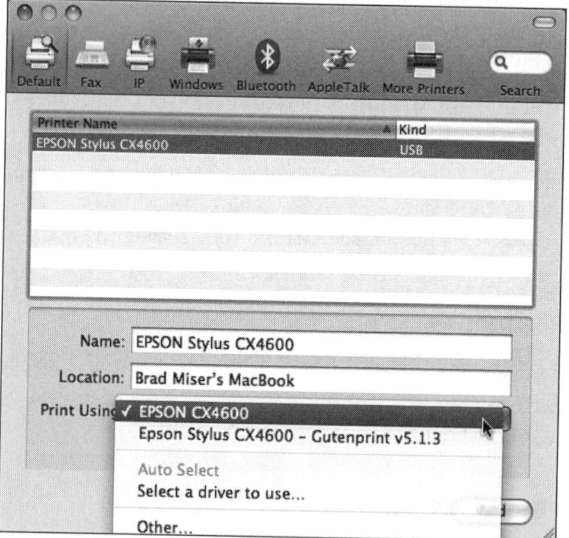


**Figure 34.3**
Mac OS X can configure most printers automatically, as it did for this one when I selected the Epson Style CX4600 on the printer list.

11. Click Add. You'll return to the Printer List on the Print & Fax pane and the printer you selected and configured appears on the list (see Figure 34.4). The printer will be ready to print your documents.

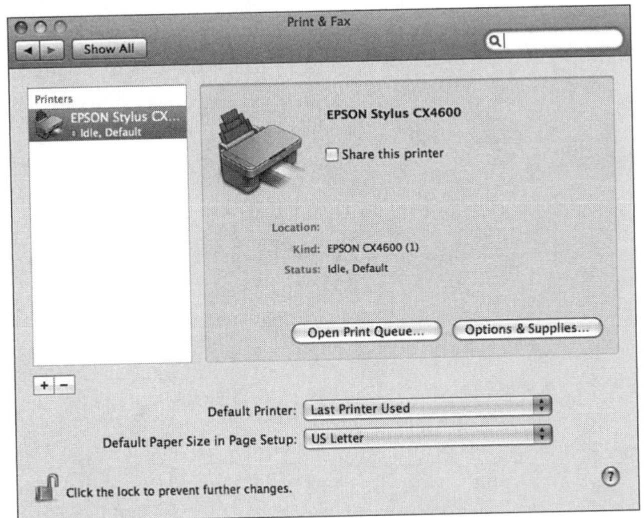


**Figure 34.4**
An Epson Stylus multi-function ink jet printer has been installed on this Mac.

## Installing and Configuring a Network Printer

Using a network printer is a good way to share a printer among multiple users; with the rise of home networks and the decrease in the cost of networkable printers, installing networked printers in a home or home office is also a practical option. Using an AirPort Base Station, any USB printer can be shared over a wireless network.

⇨ To learn how to establish a wired network, **see** Chapter 17, "Building and Using a Wired Network," **p. 359**.

⇨ To learn about sharing a printer via AirPort, **see** Chapter 18, "Creating and Managing AirPort Wireless Networks," **p. 393**.

### Installing a Network Printer

Installing a network printer is similar to installing a local printer. The specific steps you use depend on the network you are using and the particular printer model. Support for most laser printers is built in to Mac OS X.

34

### Configuring a Network Printer

In the following example, a printer is installed on a small Ethernet network. The steps to configure such a printer are:

1. Connect power to the printer.
2. Connect the printer to an Ethernet hub.
3. If the printer has Mac OS X–compatible software, install it—support for most laser printers is built in to the operating system.
4. Open the Print & Fax pane of the System Preferences application.
5. Click the Add Printer button (the plus sign). The Printer Browser appears. It will begin to search for printers with which your Mac can communicate. The printers it finds are shown on the printer list.

6. Select the printer you want to install. Mac OS X will attempt to find the driver and configure the printer. If it can do so, you will see the printer's name, its location, and the driver Mac OS X has selected.
7. If you don't want to use the default printer name shown in the Name box, select it and type a new name.
8. If the default location isn't what you want, select it and change that, too.
9. If Mac OS X found a driver for your printer and selected it on the Print Using pop-up menu, leave that selection as it is; if a driver wasn't found, open the pop-up menu and choose the appropriate driver. If you can't find a driver for your printer, you need to get one from the printer's manufacturer either on the disc that accompanied the printer or on the manufacturer's web site.
10. Click Add. You'll return to the Printer List on the Print & Fax pane and the printer you selected and configured appears on the list. The printer will be ready to print your documents (see Figure 34.5).

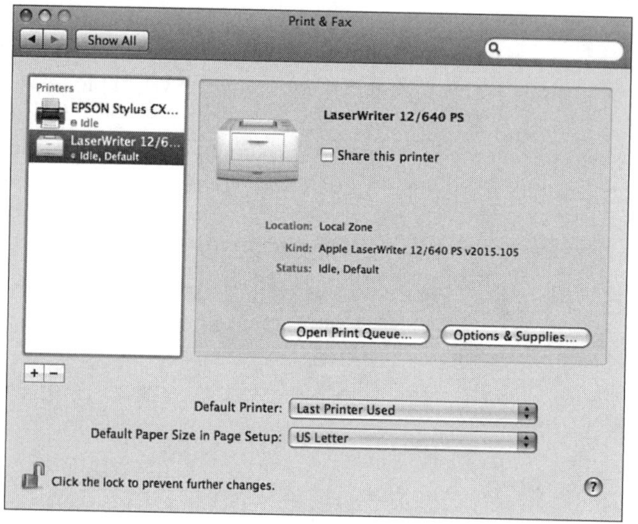


**Figure 34.5**
The LaserWriter printer is connected to a hub on a local network.

## INSTALLING AND CONFIGURING OTHER TYPES OF PRINTERS

34

Mac OS X supports many types of printers connected in a variety of ways. Although you are most likely to use a printer connected directly to your Mac or through a network—in which case the Printer Browser will likely do most of the configuration work for you—you might have a more unusual situation, such as wanting to use Bluetooth to print.

In the event that the Printer Browser doesn't automatically find and configure a printer, you can use its advanced tools to do the configuring:

1. Open the Print & Fax pane of the System Preferences application and click the Add Printer button (the plus sign). The Printer Browser appears.

2. If the printer you want to install doesn't appear in the list, click the button for the type of printer you want configure. Commonly used options are in the following list:
   - **IP Printer**—If a printer is installed on a network, but the browser doesn't find it automatically, you can use this tool to configure a printer by entering its IP address on the network. The only challenge of using this option is determining the printer's address. Most network printers have a function that will print the printer's current configuration options, including its IP address. See your printer's documentation to determine how to print this information.
   - **Windows printers**—If your Mac is connected to a Windows printer, use this tool to configure it.
   - **Bluetooth**—To use a Bluetooth printer, select the Bluetooth tool. The Browser attempts to find all the Bluetooth printers with which your Mac can communicate. You can then use the other tools on the pane to configure a printer that you select.
   - **AppleTalk**—AppleTalk is a local network protocol that can also be used by a Mac to communicate with a printer. To use AppleTalk, AppleTalk services must be enabled on your Mac. When you select the AppleTalk tool, your Mac will identify all the printers with which it can communicate via AppleTalk.

After you select a tool, the browser will be reconfigured with the controls you will use to configure printers of the type you selected (see Figure 34.6).

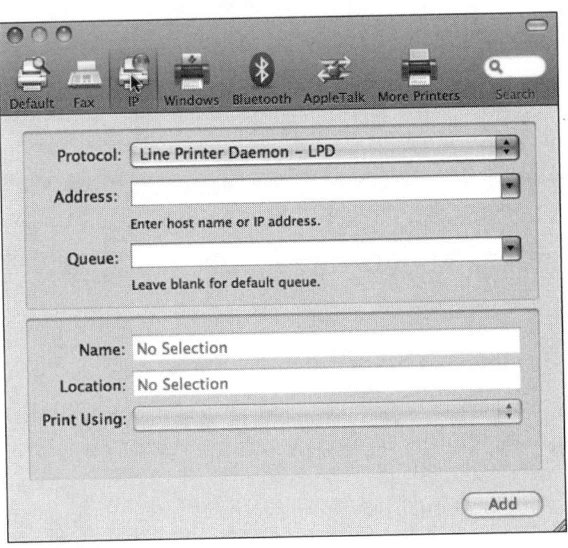


**Figure 34.6**
Use the IP Printer tool to configure a printer based on its IP address.

3. Use the tools on the browser to configure the printer. Each offers a different tool set, but the general tasks are the same. You select the printer you want to configure, choose its driver, name it, and so on. For example, to configure an IP printer, you select the

protocol on the Protocol pop-up menu, enter the IP address, and choose a queue for that printer. Then, you name it, create a location name, and choose its driver. Other tools have similar tasks.

4. Click Add. The printer is installed on your Mac and you see it on the Printer List on the Print & Fax pane of the System Preferences application.

# MANAGING PRINTERS

You manage the printers that your Mac can work with using the Print & Fax pane of the System Preferences application (see Figure 34.7). In the left part of this pane, you will see the printers installed on your Mac. For the selected printer, you'll see information in the area to the right of the Printers list pertaining to it's location and status, as well as have access to other options. At the bottom of the pane are a number of controls you can use to set your printing preferences. These include the following:

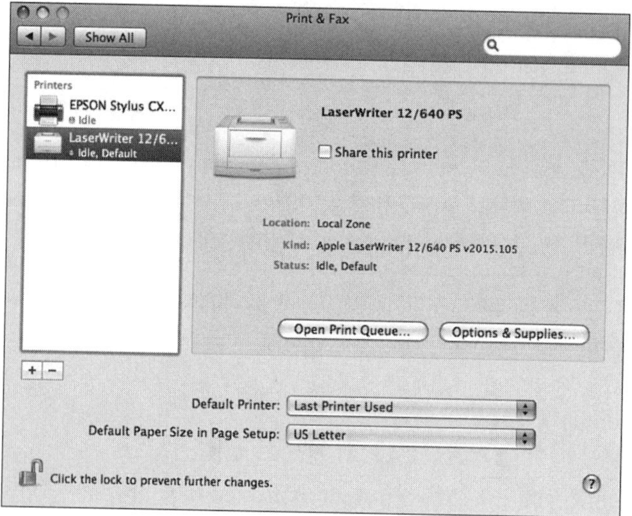


**Figure 34.7**
Use the Print & Fax pane to set printer preferences for your system.

- Click the Add button (+) to add a new printer. This will take you to the Printer Browser.
- Select a printer and click the Delete button (-) to remove the printer from the list of available printers.
- Select a printer and click Open Print Queue to open its Print Queue window (more on this later in the chapter).
- Select a printer and click Options & Supplies to open its Info sheet (see Figure 34.8). This sheet has three tabs. Use the General tab to update the printer's name and location information. You'll also see configuration information for the printer, such as the version of the driver being used, its URL, and so on. Use the Driver tab to change the

driver being used for the printer and to configure additional options it supports, such as paper trays, memory configuration, and the like. The Supply Levels tab provides you with information about the consumables for your printer (if supported). This is a handy way to find out how much ink is left in one of your printer's cartridges. When you click the Supplies button, Mac OS X opens your default web browser and attempts to locate supplies for the printer, such as ink cartridges in the Apple Store.

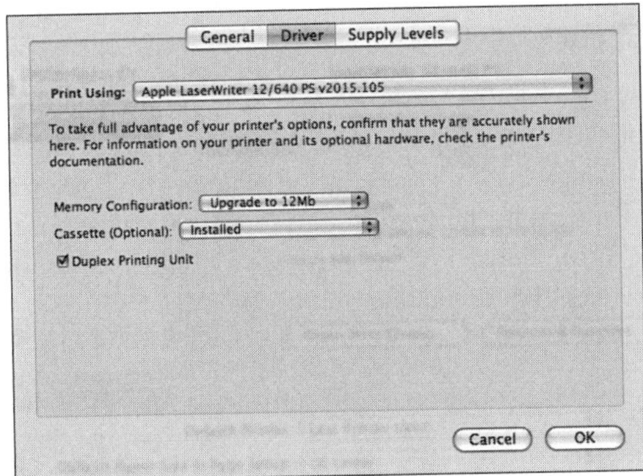


**Figure 34.8**
The Options & Supplies sheet enables you to configure additional options for a selected printer.

- Use the Default Printer pop-up menu to determine which printer is selected automatically in the Print dialog box. The Last Printer Used selection will cause the dialog box to remember the last printer you printed with. If you choose one of the installed printers, that printer is selected each time you print. (It becomes the default printer.)
- Use the Default Paper Size in Page Setup to choose the default size of paper for the selected printer when you print.

## Working with Shared Printers

34

Under Mac OS X, you can share printers connected to your Mac over wired and wireless networks, as well as those connected directly to your Mac through USB or Ethernet. If your Mac can communicate with a printer, it can also share that printer with other computers with which it can communicate. You can also access printers being shared with you.

### Sharing a Printer Connected to Your Mac

To share a printer, perform the following steps:

1. Install and configure the printer you want to share on your Mac.
2. Open the Sharing pane of the System Preferences application. On this pane, you will see the list of services you can share on your Mac.
3. Click the "Printer Sharing" check box. This activates the printer sharing function.
4. Check the check box next to each printer you want to share (see Figure 34.9). The selected printers will be accessible to other Macs on the same network.

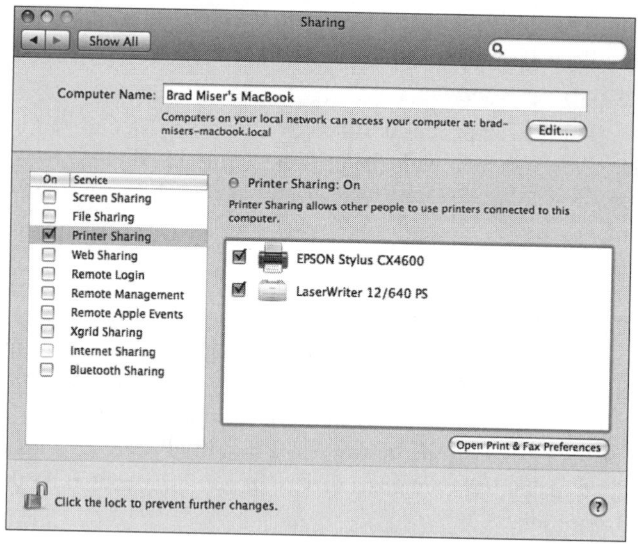


**Figure 34.9**
The LaserWriter and Epson Stylus printers connected to this Mac can be used by other Macs on the same network.

**NOTE**

> You can also share printers that are connected to your Mac through a network connection, but you don't need to do this. Instead, just install the network printer on each machine from which it should be available.

When you share a printer, the Mac from which it is being shared must be running for the printer to be available to other computers on the network. If it isn't, the printer won't be accessible to those other Macs.

**TIP**

> If your network includes an AirPort Extreme or AirPort Express Base Station, you can connect a USB printer to the Base Station to share it.

## Adding Shared Printers to Your Mac

To access printers being shared on a network, use the following steps:

1. Open the Print & Fax pane of the System Preferences application.
2. Click the Add Printer button. The Printer Browser appears and searches for printers with which your Mac can communicate. Printers that are being shared with your Mac will have "Bonjour" or "Shared Printer" displayed.
3. Select the shared printer you want to access.
4. Change the name and location if you want to; in most cases, you should leave the default selections.

5. If your Mac was able to find a driver for the printer, leave the default driver as the selection on the Print Using pop-up menu. If no driver was found, use the pop-up menu to select a driver for the printer.
6. Click Add. The shared printer is added to the printer list and you will be able to print with it just like you would with the printers connected directly to your Mac or through a network.

## Printing Under Mac OS X

When you print a document, you see the print dialog box for the current printer; the printer shown on the Printer pop-up menu is determined by the preference you set (either the last printer you used or the default). You can choose any other printers that are installed on your Mac or those being shared on the network by using the Printer pop-up menu (see Figure 34.10). The Print dialog box contains a variety of pop-up menus and other tools you can use to configure a print job.

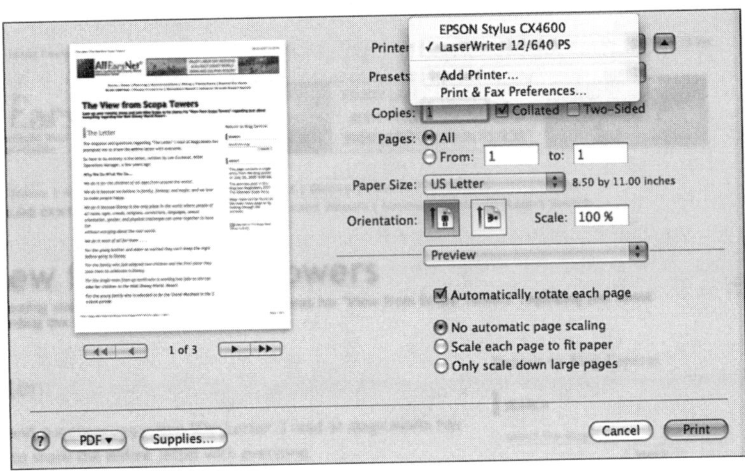


**Figure 34.10** The list of printers available to your Mac, including any that are being shared with you over a network, are shown on the Printer pop-up menu.



There are two versions of the Print dialog box. The expanded version is shown in Figure 34.10. If you click the expansion triangle next to the Printer pop-up menu, the dialog box will expand to that version or will collapse to the simple version, depending on its current state. In the simple version, you only see the Printer and Presets pop-up menus and the print controls.

In many Apple applications, the print sheet appears; this is functionally identical to the Print dialog box, but it remains attached to the top of the document that you are printing.

The specific options you see in the Print dialog box or sheet depend on the printer you are using and the application from which you are printing. You select the settings you want to configure from the third pop-up menu (counting the Printer and Preset pop-up menus as the first and second ones) and then configure those settings with the controls that appear in the lower part of the dialog box. Depending on the printer and application you are using, the options you have can include the following:

- **Printer**—You can use this pop-up menu to select a printer to use. You can also open the Printer Browser by selecting Add Printer. You can open the Print & Fax pane of the System Preferences application by choosing "Print & Fax Preferences."
- **Presets**—You can switch between the standard settings for the selected printer, or you can save a custom configuration and switch to that one.
- **Copies & Pages**—These controls enable you to set the number of pages you want to print and choose the part of a document you want to print. Several applications also show a mini-preview of a document on the left side of the Print dialog or sheet.
- **Two-Sided**—If a printer is capable of duplexing, you can select the check-box to save paper when printing.

Most applications have specific print settings that you can configure, as well. A pop-up menu with the name of the current application appears on the Print dialog box or sheet and allows you to adjust the following print options:

- **Layout**—These commands enable you to control how many pages print per sheet of paper, the direction in which your document layout prints, and whether a border is printed.
- **Scheduler**—This pane enables you to schedule a print job.
- **Paper Feed**—These controls enable you to select a paper tray for the print job, or you can choose to do a manual feed.
- **Print Settings**—Controls in this pane enable you to choose a paper type and select from the print modes offered by a printer (such as color, black and white, draft, and so on).
- **Image Quality**—These controls enable you to determine the quality with which images are printed—to save toner, for example.
- **ColorSync**—This pane enables you to choose ColorSync options for the selected printer.
- **Summary**—The Summary area displays a description of the print job you have currently configured. This can be useful if you have configured a complex print job and want to check it before you run it.

34

TIP

> In the Copies & Pages pane for most printers, you have the option to collate documents by checking the Collated check box. If you ever had to hand-collate a large document, you will really appreciate this feature.

Some applications allow you to preview a print job by clicking the Preview button. The document will open in the Preview application and appears as it will in the printed version. When you're ready to print, you can print it from that application. You can also see a preview by clicking the PDF pop-up menu and selecting Open PDF in Preview.

When you are ready to print, click Print or press Return.

After you have sent a document to a printer, the print proxy application for that printer will open. You'll know this because the Printer's icon opens on the Dock and begins to bounce; you can click this to open a printer to access its queue application (see Figure 34.11).

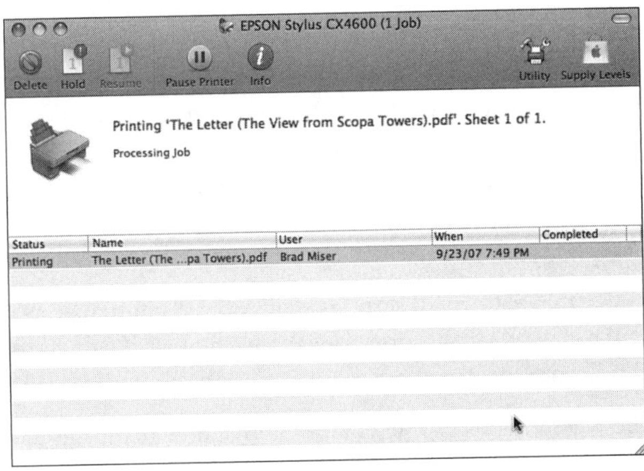


**Figure 34.11**
You can monitor the status of print jobs by double-clicking a printer in the printer list on the Print & Fax pane or by clicking the Printer's icon on the Dock to open the queue for that printer.

With this tool, you can perform the following tasks:

- Select a print job on the list and click Delete to remove the job from the queue.
- Click a print job and click Hold. The printing process will stop.
- Click Resume and the current job on hold will start printing again.
- Click Pause Printer to pause the current print job.
- Click the Info button to open the Options & Supplies information for the printer.
- Click Utility to open the printer's utility software.
- Move print jobs up or down the list to change the order in which they will print.

34

**TIP**

Some additional actions can be useful for some printers. For example, you can click the Supply Levels button to check the amount of ink left in a printer's cartridges (if that action is supported by the printer you are using).

# SENDING FAXES WITH MAC OS X

With the rise of email, faxing documents isn't something you are likely to need to do that often, but it can come in handy from time to time. Mac OS X has the capability to send and receive faxes. Of course, to use this capability, your Mac must have a modem installed and that modem must be connected to a working phone line. With the rise of broadband, this isn't always the case. Modern Macs don't include a dial-up modem by default; it is an optional device.

**NOTE**

> If you're like me and no longer have a dial-up modem, but you need to send a fax, check out the email to fax services that are available. These services allow you to send and receive faxes via an email application. A quick web search will enable you to find lots of these services to choose from.

## Receiving Faxes on Your Mac

To configure your Mac to receive faxes, do the following steps:

1. Connect your Mac's dial-up modem to a working phone line.
2. Open the Print & Fax pane of the System Preferences application.
3. Select your fax modem in the Printers list.
4. Enter the phone number to which you have connected your Mac's modem in the Fax Number field.
5. Click on Receive Option, then select "Receive faxes on this computer."
6. Use the "Answer after" field to set the number of rings before your Mac answers the phone. Make sure this number is set before any answering machine or voice mail will pick-up the call.
7. If you want the fax to be saved as a file, check the "Save to" check box and select the location in which you want fax files to be saved on the pop-up menu.
8. If you want the fax to be printed, click the "Print to" check box and select the printer to which it should be printed on the pop-up menu.
9. If you want to be able to control faxing from the desktop, check the "Show fax status in menu bar" check box. The Fax menu will be added to the Mac OS X menubar.

When the phone number to which your Mac is connected receives a call and the number of rings you set have occurred, your Mac answers the phone and attempts to receive a fax. If it receives one, it is saved or printed as indicated by your configuration choices.

**TIP**

> If you want to share your Mac's faxing capability, such as when it is the only Mac connected to a phone line, check the "Share this fax" check box on the Print & Fax pane of the System Preferences application.



## Sending Faxes from Your Mac

You can send faxes from within any application on your Mac as easily as you can receive them.

Open the Print dialog box and then click the PDF menu. Choose Fax PDF and use the resulting tools to configure and send the fax.

# Working with PDFs

Portable Document Format (PDF) files are one of the most useful ways to output documents for electronic viewing. Any PDF document can be easily read by anyone using any computer platform. PDF documents maintain their appearance because they do not rely on fonts and other aspects of the system on which they are viewed.

Under Mac OS X, PDFs are a native file format. You can create PDFs from within any Mac OS X application, and you can read PDF files with the Preview application.

**NOTE**

> The free Adobe Reader application is also available for Mac OS X. This application offers more features for viewing PDFs than does Preview, but either application will get the job done. To download a copy of Adobe Reader, visit www.adobe.com/products/acrobat/readstep2.html.

## Creating PDF Files

Creating PDF files is an extremely simple task:

1. Open the document for which you want to create a PDF.
2. Select File, Print.
3. Open the PDF pop-up menu and choose "Save as PDF" (see Figure 34.12). The "Save to File" dialog box appears (see Figure 34.13).

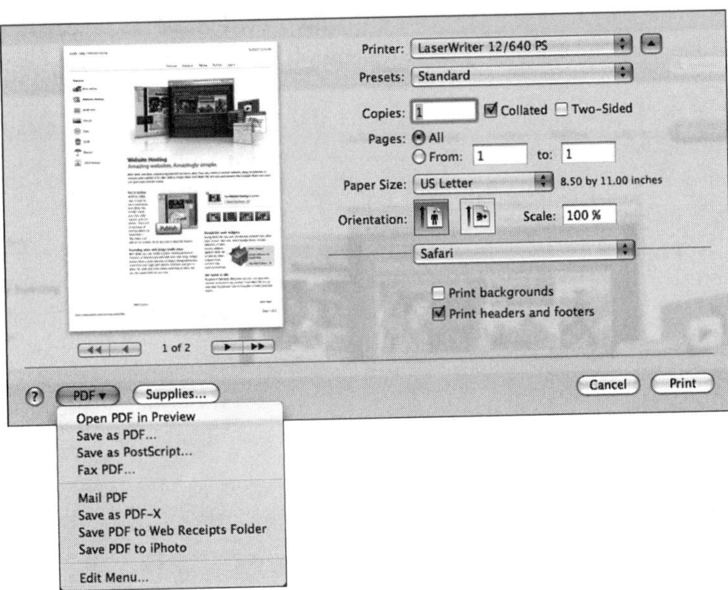


**Figure 34.12** You can quickly and easily create a PDF of any file by choosing "Save as PDF" on this menu.

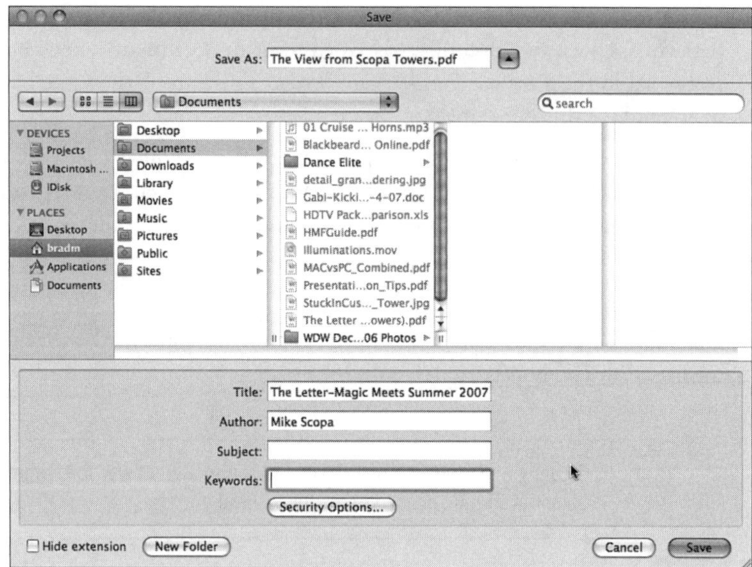


**Figure 34.13**
Use the Save dialog box to name a PDF and associate attributes, such as keywords, with it.

4. Name the document and select a location to save it. Use the filename extension `.pdf`.
5. Complete the fields that appear for the PDF, which are Title, Author, Subject, and Keywords. This information will be associated with the PDF file and will be available to anyone who accesses the PDF.
6. Click Security Options. The Security Options dialog box appears (see Figure 34.14).

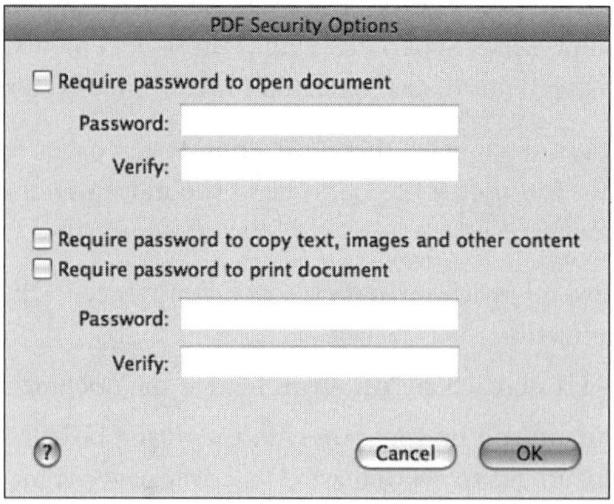

PDF Security Options

Require password to open document

Password:

Verify:

Require password to copy text, images and other content

Require password to print document

Password:

Verify:

? Cancel OK

**Figure 34.14**
You can secure a PDF you create using the Security Options dialog box.

7. To require that the viewer enter a password to be able to view the PDF, check "Require password to open document" and enter the password in the Password and Verify boxes. In order to open the document, you'll need to provide the password to the people who need to access it.

8. If you want to restrict the PDF from being printed unless the viewer has the correct password, check the "Require password to print document" check box and enter the password in the Password and Verify boxes. This can be the same as the open password or it can be a different one.
9. To protect content from being copied, check the "Require password to copy text, images and other content" check box. With this checked, viewers will not be able to select and copy the document's content and paste it into other documents.
10. Click OK. The options you selected are set and the dialog box closes. You return to the Save dialog box.
11. Click Save. The PDF is created in the location you specified with the settings and other information you configured.

**TIP**

> Creating a PDF version of a document is also a great way to capture versions of that document at specific points in time for archival purposes.

One thing to note is that creating a PDF in this way does not always create or preserve any hyperlinks in a document. For example, if you create a PDF of a web page in Safari, the links on that page will be functional. However, if you create a text document that contains a table of contents in which the entries are hyperlinked to the sections in the document, the resulting PDF may not contain active links. Being able to create a PDF from any document using the Print command is useful when you want to send your documents to other people.

To create PDFs that contain hyperlinks and other electronic document features, you may need to use a more sophisticated application. For example, Adobe applications can save documents in PDF format and preserve hyperlinks within those documents. Or, you can use the full Acrobat application to create more sophisticated PDFs from any application.

In addition to a standard PDF document, there are a number of other options on the Save As PDF pop-up menu (refer to Figure 34.13). Some of the more useful of these are the following:



- **Open PDF in Preview**—This command creates a temporary PDF of the page and opens the Preview application.
- **Save as PostScript**—This creates a PostScript file for the document.
- **Fax PDF**—This command will present you with the dialog boxes to specify the fax number to send the document to, as well as add a cover page. When you are ready, click Fax. Note that you must have a fax modem connected to your Mac for this option to work.
- **Mail PDF**—This creates a PDF of the document and attaches it to an email message in your default email application.
- **Save as PDF-X**—This commands saves the document in the PDF/X format which adds information intended to improve the reliability of printing the document. This

format is intended to be used when the desired output of the document will be a high-quality printed version. PDF/X files can be sent directly to a printer and will be rendered more reliably than standard PDF files.

- **Save PDF to Web Receipts Folder**—This create a Web Receipts folder in your Documents directory (if it does not already exist.) This is a handy place to store all of the receipts for those late-night Amazon.com buying sprees.
- **Save PDF to iPhoto**—This creates a PDF version of the document and adds it to iPhoto.
- **Edit Menu**—Use this command to edit the contents of the Save as PDF menu. You can use the Add Command button (the plus sign) to add commands to the menu or the Remove Command button (the minus sign) to remove commands from the menu. These tools enable you to configure the menu so that it contains only those commands that you use regularly.

## Viewing PDFs with Preview

To view PDF documents you create, open them. Unless you have configured PDFs to open in a different application, Preview launches and you can view the PDF.

⇨ To learn how to use Preview, **see** "Working with Preview," **p. 699**.

**TIP**

> Because Adobe Reader enables you to take advantage of all the features PDF documents offer, you might want to designate it as the default application for all PDF documents so it opens automatically when you view PDFs.

⇨ To learn how to associate file types with applications, **see** "Determining the Application That Opens When You Open a Document," **p. 156**.

# CHAPTER 35

# Understanding and Using Data Storage Devices

## In this chapter

## Understanding Data Storage Options

A general law of Mac use—especially when you start working with digital video, music, and images—is that you can never have too much room to store your data. As you work with a Mac, you're likely to work with a number of types of data storage devices, including the following:

- Hard drives
- DVD/CD writers, such as Apple's SuperDrive
- Flash drives
- Tape drives

All Mac users have at least one hard drive, and most have a disc drive capable of reading and writing CDs and DVDs. Flash drives are also relatively common. Tape drives are used for backing up large amounts of data. In this chapter, you'll learn about hard drives and CD/DVD writers.

**NOTE**

> One data storage device that you might not think of is an iPod. iPods and iPod nanos can be used as hard drives. iPod shuffles can be used as flash drives.

## Using Disks and Discs

Working with hard drives, CDs, DVDs, and other similar types of storage devices is an important part of using Mac OS X. The following bullets provide information about some useful disk- and disc-related tasks:

- You can control whether mounted disk, disc, and volume icons are automatically shown on the desktop using the Finder Preferences window (select Finder, Preferences and click the General tab). Check the "Show these items on the Desktop" check boxes to show icons on the desktop, or uncheck them to keep those icons from appearing on the desktop. (If you choose not to have disk icons mounted on the desktop, you can access the mounted disks and volumes using the Computer folder and the Sidebar.)
- You can eject removable disks by dragging them to the Trash; selecting them and selecting File, Eject; pressing ⌘-E or your Apple keyboard's eject button; using the contextual menu's Eject command; or using the Eject icon that you can place on the Finder toolbar. You can also eject any ejectable item by clicking the Eject button that appears next to that item in the Sidebar. You should always eject any kind of disk before you disconnect it from your Mac; if you don't, some or all of the data it contains might be damaged.

**TIP**

> When you select a mounted volume (such as a CD), the Trash icon on the Dock becomes an eject symbol to indicate you are unmounting a volume rather than deleting it.

- To erase a disk under Mac OS X, you use the Disk Utility application (Applications/Utilities). Open the application; select the disk you want to erase; click the Erase tab; select the format on the Volume Format pop-up menu; enter the volume name; and click Erase.
- Disk Image is a file type that mimics the behavior of a disk. When you open a disk image, it acts just as if it were a real disk. Disk images are most commonly used to distribute applications. When a disk image is mounted, you can open it as you would a physical disk, eject it, and so on.

⇨ To learn more about disk images, **see** "Installing Mac OS X Applications," **p. 141**.

⇨ To learn how to configure the action when you insert blank media, **see** "Configuring Disc Actions," **p. 845**.

# Choosing, Installing, and Using a Hard Drive

Your Mac's hard drive is one of its most important devices, and its performance and operation have a major impact on the performance and operation of your system. At some point, you will probably want to increase the amount of hard disk space available to you. Adding more hard drive space is relatively simple in most cases and offers many benefits to you.

## Choosing a Hard Drive

When it comes to choosing a hard drive to add to your system, you should consider the following factors:

- **Will your Mac support additional internal hard drives?**—If you use a Mac Pro, the answer to this question is yes. If you have one of the other current Mac models, the answer is no.
- **Should you add an external drive?**—If your Mac won't support the addition of another internal hard drive, you will likely want to add more hard drive space by using an external hard drive. Even if your Mac can handle an additional internal hard drive, you might choose to get an external drive instead because external drives are simpler to install and easier to use with different machines. For example, you can share the same external hard drive among several Macs. Because FireWire and USB 2 offer good enough performance for all but the most demanding tasks, you won't face much of a performance penalty if you choose to use an external hard drive.
- **Which drive interface does your Mac use?**—For internal drives, you'll use SATA. For external drives, the choices are FireWire, FireWire 800, or USB 2.

**NOTE**

> Many external hard drives use the USB 2 interface, which is a dominant interface on Windows computers and is supported on all modern Mac models. However, in most cases, FireWire external drives should be your first choice. FireWire (both varieties, but especially FireWire 800) offers excellent performance and you won't have to use a USB port on your Mac (which is good because you tend to need more USB ports than FireWire ports). Many external drives offer multiple kinds of interfaces, such as both FireWire 800 and USB 2.

- **What size drive do you need?**—Drives come in various sizes; generally, you should get the largest drive you can afford in the format you select.
- **Does your Mac need to meet specific performance requirements?**—If you intend to use the drive for high data rate work, such as for digital video, typically, you need to get a drive that spins at least 7,200rpm. Some drives spin even faster, which means they can transfer data at a greater rate. (Some drives that spin at slower rates are also acceptable; check with the drive's manufacturer to see what data rate the drive can sustain.)

**NOTE**

> If you have a Mac with room for only one internal hard drive, you can replace that drive with one of a higher capacity. For MacBooks and MacBook Pros, this is a relatively simple operation. For iMacs and Mac minis, this is a more complex task and is not recommended unless you are very comfortable working with hardware.

⇨ To learn about the various interfaces related to hard drives, **see** Chapter 30, "Understanding Input and Output Technology," **p. 743**.

After you have answered these questions, you should have a good idea about the type of drive you need, such as an external FireWire hard drive that offers performance suitable for the kind of tasks you do and has as much space as you can afford to purchase.

Head to your favorite retail site to research or purchase hard drives (see Figure 35.1).

**CAUTION**

> Before you purchase a drive, check the owner's manual for your Mac to ensure that the specifications for the drive are compatible with your Mac.

To begin using a drive, you must install the drive, and then initialize and partition it.



## Installing an External Hard Drive

Installing an external hard drive is about as simple as things get. You connect the power supply to the drive and to an electrical outlet, if needed (some drives take their power from the interface). Then, you connect a FireWire, USB 2, or FireWire 800 cable to the drive and your Mac.

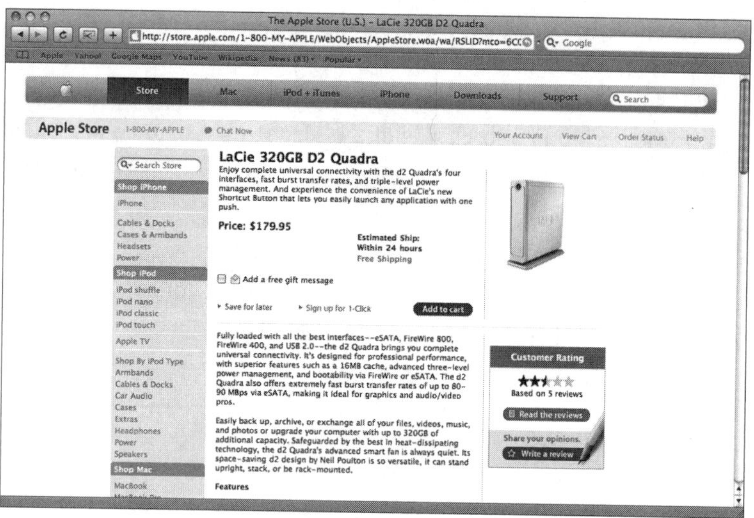


**Figure 35.1**
Check out this LaCie 320GB drive that supports both flavors of FireWire and USB 2, which means it is compatible with all modern Macs.

After you have connected the drive and powered it up, the installation part is complete (easy installation is a good reason to use an external drive). Because FireWire and USB are hot swappable, you don't even need to shut your Mac down to connect it to an external hard drive. The disk will probably mount on your desktop, and you could start using it if it does. However, you should immediately initialize and partition the disk before you place any data on it.

## INSTALLING AN INTERNAL HARD DRIVE

Installing an internal hard drive is a bit more complicated than installing an external drive, but it is still relatively easy to do.

**NOTE**

> Because I don't recommend that most users replace a hard drive in most Macs, this section provides information only on adding additional hard drives to a Mac Pro. If you are comfortable enough working inside a Mac to be able to replace a hard drive, you probably don't need any help doing so.

Before you get started, read through the instructions contained in your Mac's user manual. Then do the following:

1. Get the drive ready to install by configuring it as a slave drive (if necessary); see the instructions that came with the drive for help with this. Typically, this involves configuring jumper clips on specific pins at the back of the drive. Most of the time, these pins are already set in the appropriate configuration.
2. Back up the data on your Mac (just in case).
3. Power down your Mac.
4. Open the case.

5. Locate the bay in which you are going to install the drive; Mac Pros have a total of four drive bays, at least one of these will be occupied, but you can install a new drive in any of the open bays.
6. Lift the latch on the back side of the Mac Pro's case to unlock the hard drive carriers.
7. Pull the carrier in which you are going to install the drive out.
8. Install the new drive in the upper part of the drive carrier using the four screws.
9. Install the drive carrier back in the Mac by lifting the latch and pushing the carrier in place until it snaps into the connectors mounted in the Mac.
10. Replace the side panel and push the latch down.
11. Power the Mac up.

The Mac should restart normally. When it boots up, you might not notice any difference because you can't use the drive until you initialize it.

## INITIALIZING AND PARTITIONING A HARD DRIVE

Before you use a hard drive, whether it is internal or external, you should initialize it. (You have to initialize most internal drives before you can use them, but most external drives can be used out of the box.) You can also partition a hard drive to create multiple volumes on a single drive. (For example, you might want to be able to install more than one instance of Mac OS X on a single disk.)

When you partition a hard drive, logical volumes are created for each partition on the disk. For most practical purposes, a logical volume looks and acts just like a separate hard drive. There can be some small performance advantages to partitioning a disk, or you might choose to partition it to help you keep your system organized. The most likely reason to partition a drive is to be able to run more than one version of the Mac OS on your computer—each version needs to be installed on a separate volume. For example, you should create at least one partition to install an alternate startup version of Mac OS X in case your primary stops working correctly.

One of the results of partitioning a drive is that all the volumes outside of the startup volume are not a part of the default Mac OS X organization scheme. This can be a benefit or a problem depending on what you are doing. For example, documents you store on a separate volume aren't secured using Mac OS X's default permissions, like documents you store within your Home folder are. If you want to provide broader access to files, this is a good thing. If you don't want people to access these documents outside the control of Mac OS X's security, it isn't.



Be aware though that when you partition a drive, the size of each partition becomes a size limitation, just as if the volume was a separate disk. If your partition sizes are too small, you might run out of free space in a specific volume even though the disk on which that volume is stored still has plenty of space. Generally, you should keep your partitions pretty large. If you run out of space on a partition, you have to delete files from it or re-partition the disk, which means that you must start over and reformat the disk (resulting in all files being erased). Unless you have a very specific reason to do so, you typically shouldn't partition a drive into more than two volumes. If you aren't going to have multiple versions of the Mac OS installed, you might not want to use multiple partitions at all.

**NOTE**

> Mac OS X 10.5 introduces the ability resize a live partition. Specifically, if you have your hard drive partitioned into two volumes and the first volume is running out of room you can use Disk Utility to delete the second volume and allow the first volume to use all of the drive space available. Of course, anything on that second volume will be deleted, so make sure you move it to another drive or a network volume before you remove that volume.

**How Many Partitions?**

Because the size of a partition can't be changed without erasing the disk on which it is stored, you should avoid creating partitions unless you have a specific reason to do so. The size of a partition limits space just as if it were a separate disk. Because erasing and recovering all the data on a drive isn't a lot of fun, don't set yourself up to do it by creating small partitions.

I recommend that you have at least two volumes available to you, and it is even better if you have these on more than one drive. Then, install a version of Mac OS X on each volume. One should be your primary startup volume on the internal disk in your Mac. Create a relatively small (20GB or so) partition on a different disk (or the same one if you have only one drive available to you), and install Mac OS X on it. Keep this as an alternative startup volume in case your main startup volume has problems.

An ideal configuration is to have at least one external drive along with your Mac's internal drive. Have only one partition on the internal drive and make that your startup volume. This ensures you have as much storage space on that volume as possible. Partition the external drive into two volumes, one relatively small (20GB) and the other with the remainder of the drive's space. Install your alternative OS installation on the smaller volume. Use the large partition for data storage, such as for projects or backups. Ideally, you should have one volume that can be a mirror of your startup volume for back-up purposes, in which case the size of that volume needs to be equal to or greater than the size of the startup volume.

**NOTE**

> Most external hard drives come initialized, in which case you can use them without doing the following steps. However, even in those cases, you might want to partition the drive, especially if it is a large one.

To initialize and partition a disk, perform the following steps:

1. Launch Disk Utility (Applications/Utilities). In the Disk Utility window, you see two panes. In the left pane, you see the drives installed in your system (the drives are labeled by their capacities and types). Under each disk, you'll see the volumes into which that disk has been partitioned.
2. Select the drive with which you want to work. At the top of the right pane are five tabs; each tab enables you to view data about a drive or to perform a specific action. At the bottom of the window, you see detailed information about the drive that you are working with, such as its connection bus, type, capacity, and so on (see Figure 35.2).

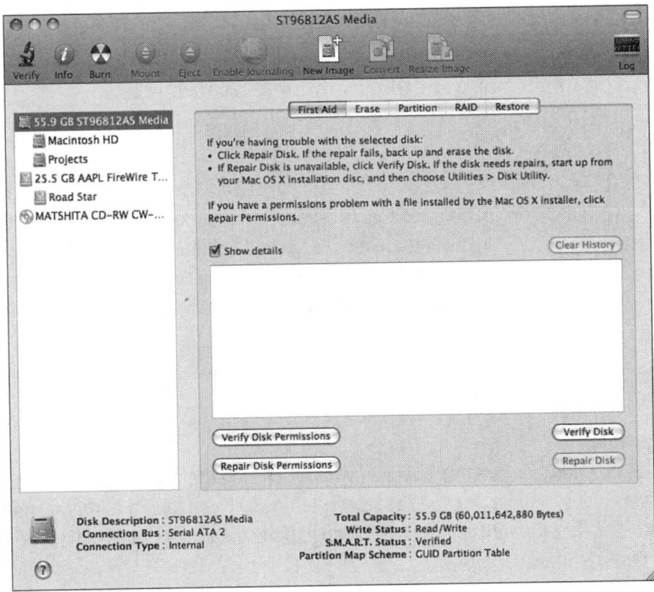


**Figure 35.2**
The Source pane of the Disk Utility application shows one internal hard drive, and one external FireWire drive. Information about the selected drive appears at the bottom of the window.

3. Click the Partition tab. In the left part of this pane, you see a graphical representation of the partitions on the disk. If the disk is currently partitioned, you see its current partitions. If you are working with a new disk or one with a single partition, you see one partition called "Untitled" (if you've not named it before). In the right part of the pane, you see information about the selected volume, such as its name, current format, and size.

**NOTE**

> Another reason you might want to partition a hard drive is to more easily share files with other users of your Mac. Because volumes outside the startup volume don't use Mac OS X's default security settings, it can be easier to provide access to a volume that all users share. For example, you might want to store files related to an iMovie project that other people are helping you with. They can then access these files without needing access to your Home folder.

4. Select the number of partitions you want to have on the drive by using the Volume Scheme pop-up menu. You can choose Current, which leaves the partitions as they are, or the number of partitions you want from 1 to 16. After you choose the number of partitions, each partition is represented by a box in the disk graphic shown under the Volume Scheme pop-up menu. The partitions are called `Untitled 1`, `Untitled 2`, and so on.
5. Select a volume by clicking its box. The volume's partition is highlighted and information for that volume is shown in the Volume Information area.

**TIP**

> You can divide a volume into two partitions of the same size by selecting the partition and clicking the Split button. This does the same thing as choosing 2 Partitions on the Volume Scheme pop-up menu.

6. Name the selected volume by typing a name in the Name box. As you type the name, it will be shown in the partitions box.
7. Select the format type from the Format pop-up menu. You should almost always select Mac OS Extended (Journaled) or Mac OS Extended. The journaling option is the best choice if it is available because it improves Mac OS X's capability to recover from unexpected power losses and other such circumstances. For each of these options, you can choose Case-sensitive. If you select a Case-sensitive format, file names are case sensitive meaning that a file called `filename.file` is not the same as a file called `FileName.file`. In most cases, you should choose Mac OS Extended (Case-sensitive, Journaled) to take advantage of the most sophisticated format option.

**NOTE**

> The other format options include MS-DOS, Unix File System, and Free Space. These are useful in some special circumstances. For example, if you are going to run a Unix OS system (apart from Mac OS X) on your machine, you might want to use the Unix File System for one partition.

8. Enter the size of the partition in the Size box. You can also set the size of a partition by dragging its Resize handle in the Volumes pane.

   If you check the "Locked for editing" check box, the information is reset and locked (you won't be able to change it). This is useful when you are creating multiple partitions and want to make sure that changes you make to other partitions won't impact the one you have configured.
9. Select the next partition.
10. Repeat steps 6–8 for each of the volumes (see Figure 35.3).

**CAUTION**

> Partitioning a drive erases all the data on it. If the drive has data on it, make sure you back it up before your partition the drive.

13. Click Options. The Options sheet appears (see Figure 35.4). If you want to use the disk as a startup disk for a PowerPC Mac or with any other kind of Mac, click Apple Partition Map. If you want to use the disk for a Windows startup disk, click Master Boot Record. If you are using an Intel Mac, leave the default GUID Partition Table option selected. Click OK.
12. Click Partition.

35

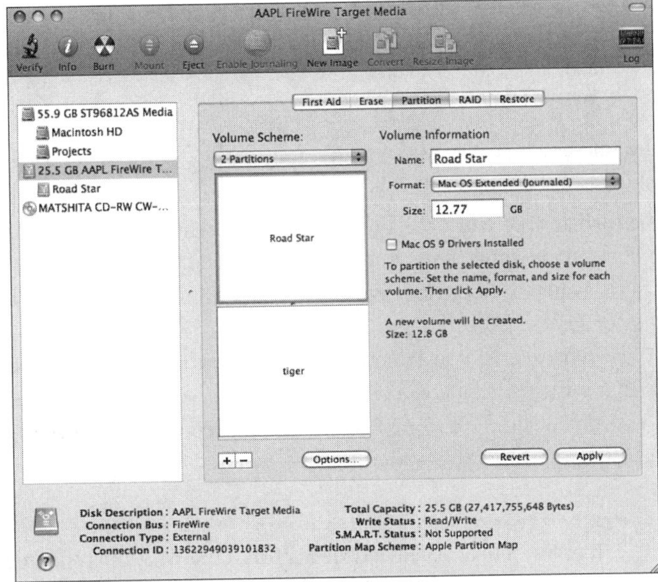


**Figure 35.3**
This drive will contain two volumes after it has been partitioned; one will be called `Road Star` and the other will be called `tiger`.

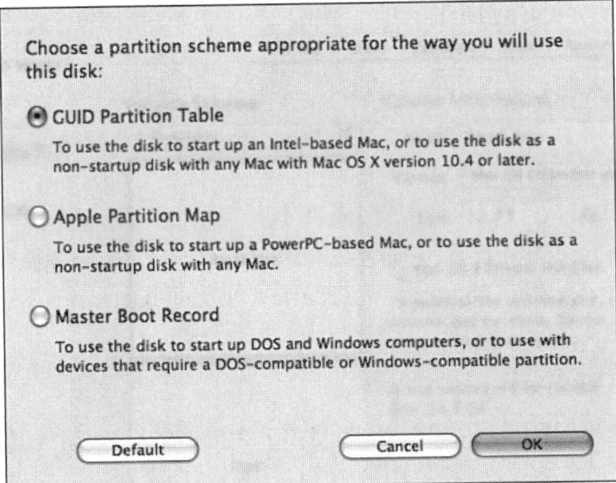


**Figure 35.4**
If you use an Intel Mac, you won't need to choose one of the other options when you partition a drive.

13. If you are sure that you want to initialize and partition the drive, click Partition in the Warning sheet. You return to the Disk Utility window and a progress bar appears in the lower right corner of the window. You can use this to monitor the process.
14. When the process is complete, select the drive you partitioned. Confirm that the drive has been partitioned properly.
15. Under the hard drive icon, select one of the partitions you just created. The Information pane at the bottom of the window will reveal details about that partition, such as the format, capacity, available space (which will be about the same as capacity immediately after you partition a drive), and so on (see Figure 35.5).
16. Explore each partition to ensure that they are configured properly.
17. Quit Disk Utility.

When you return to your desktop, you see the new volumes that are ready for your data (see Figure 35.6).

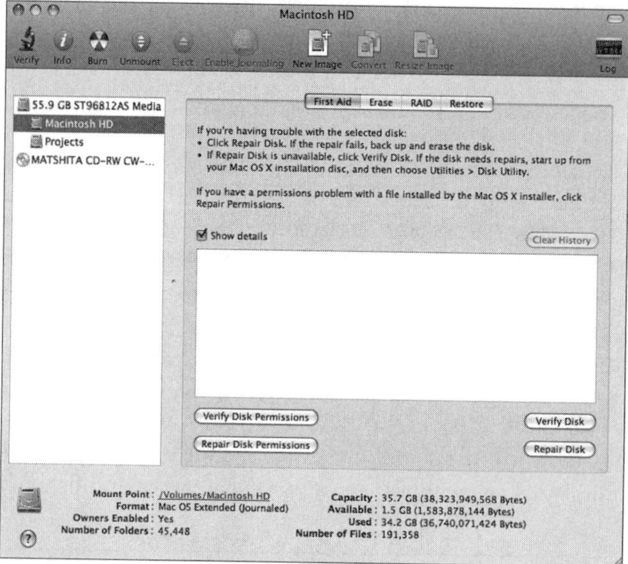


**Figure 35.5**
At the bottom of the Disk Utility pane, you see information about the selected partition.

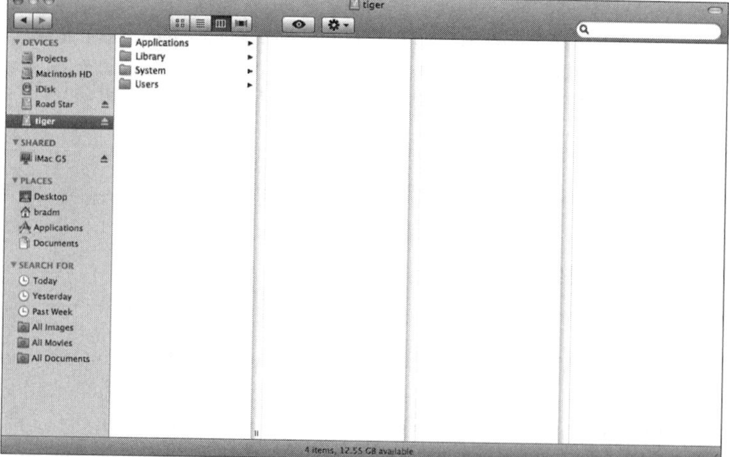


**Figure 35.6**
The `Road Star` and `tiger` volumes are ready to use.

*Disk Utility can't see your new drive? See "Disk Utility Can't See My Drive" in the "Troubleshooting" section at the end of this chapter.*

35

You can also use Disk Utility for various other tasks, such as erasing a disk or a volume, managing disk images, disk maintenance, and creating a RAID disk.

⇨ To learn how to use Disk Utility for disk maintenance tasks, **see** "Maintaining Your Disk Drives," **p. 800**.

# Working with Optical Discs

CDs and DVDs are the dominant removable media storage devices for Macs. They offer many benefits including large capacity per disc, inexpensive media, and ease of use. All modern Macs include an optical disc drive that reads CDs and DVDs and at least writes to CD too. Most Macs include an Apple SuperDrive that also writes to DVD in a variety of formats.

**NOTE**

Just as with hard drives, third-party DVD-R/DVD-RW drives are available. However, because Apple's optical disc technology works so well and is included with Mac hardware and as part of Mac OS X, Apple's technology is the focus of this section.

Before you burn your own discs, you should understand the type of drive your Mac has because that determines what kind of media you can use. CDs can hold about 700MB of data. Single layer DVDs can hold up to 4.7GB of data while dual layer discs can hold more than twice as much data. The other significant variable is the speed of your drive, but that doesn't really come into play as you will just use the drive you have regardless of how fast it is.

**CAUTION**

Depending on the specific model of Mac you use and the application you use to create DVDs, you might be able to use third-party DVD-R or DVD-RW discs, which are less expensive than Apple's media, to create DVDs. It isn't possible to list all situations in which you can use third-party discs. If you want to try to save some money, purchase a single disc from various manufacturers rated for your drive's speed and try to burn them with the application you intend to use. If that works, you can save some money by using the third-party media. If not, you'll have to keep trying other brands or just use Apple's media.

## Assessing Your Mac's Disc Drive

There are a number of ways to determine which type of optical drive your Mac has.

Currently, only the lowest end MacBook, iMac and Mac mini models have a combo drive, which reads CDs and DVDs, but can only write to CD. All other models have some version of the SuperDrive that can also write to DVD, including dual layer DVDs; there are some speed differences among the drives in some models, with the higher end Macs having faster drives.



You can check the documentation that came with your Mac to determine which formats it supports. For example, if your Mac includes an 8x SuperDrive with 2.4x Dual Layer burn, you can use single layer DVDs, dual layer DVDs, and writable CDs. (You can also use erasable versions of these formats.)

You can also assess your Mac's drive using the System Profiler.

1. Choose Apple, About This Mac.
2. Click More Info. The System Profiler launches.
3. Click the Disc Burning category in the left pane. In the right pane, you see the formats your Mac's drive supports (see Figure 35.7).

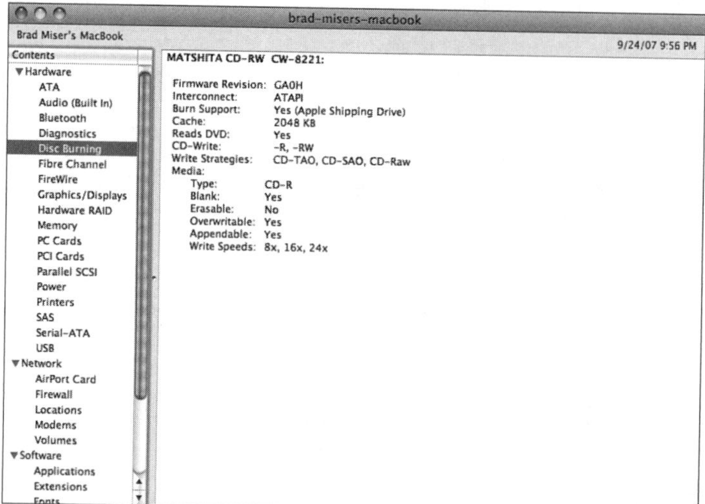


**Figure 35.7**
This entry level MacBook can read CDs and DVDs, as well as burn CDs.

4. To see information about the performance you'll achieve with specific media, insert a disc into the drive and choose View, Refresh. Under the Media section, you see the type of media along with whether it is erasable and the write speeds it supports. (In Figure 35.7, you can see that a CD-R disc is in the iMac's drive.)

> **TIP**
>
> Any media you purchase should match one of the supported formats shown for your drive. For example, to burn to a dual layer DVD, the +R DL format should be listed in the DVD-Write section.

## Configuring Disc Actions

You should configure Mac OS X to work with the disc drive you have installed. You do this through the CDs & DVDs pane of the System Preferences application.

Open the System Preferences application and click the CDs & DVDs icon to open that pane (see Figure 35.8).

**Figure 35.8**
You use the CDs & DVDs pane of the System Preferences application to configure the actions your Mac takes when you insert CDs and DVDs of various types.

Use the "When you insert a blank CD" and the "When you insert a blank DVD" pop-up menus to select the action you want your Mac to take when you put a blank CD or DVD into your machine. (If your Mac's drive doesn't support DVD burning, you see only the CD menu.) You have the following options:

- **Ask what to do**—When you insert a blank disc, your Mac prompts you and provides an Action pop-up menu containing a list of possible actions from which you can choose (see Figure 35.9).

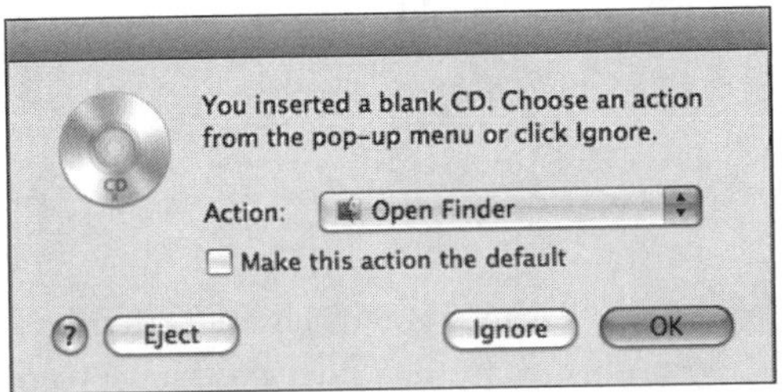


**Figure 35.9**
Use the Action dialog box to choose what you want your Mac to do when you insert a blank disc.

The Action pop-up menu contains a set of choices similar to those on the "When you insert a blank disc" pop-up menus on the CDs & DVDs pane, such as Open Finder or Open iDVD (when you insert a blank DVD and iDVD is installed on your Mac). You can make the action you select on the Action pop-up menu be the default (checking the "Make this action the default" check box in the prompt window does the same thing as selecting that option in the CDs & DVDs pane). The Eject, Ignore, and OK buttons in the dialog box do what you expect (eject the disc, ignore it, or implement the changes you make, respectively).

Because the "Ask what to do" options provides the most flexibility, I recommend that you choose this option. However, for specific situations, the other choices might be more appropriate for you.

- **Open Finder**—When this option is the default or if you select it in the Action dialog box, the blank disc is mounted and a burnable folder will be created. You can then use the Finder to name the folder, add content to it, and burn the disc. If you usually burn discs from the Finder and don't like to be interrupted by the Action dialog box, this option is probably for you.

- **Open iDVD**—When a DVD is mounted, iDVD becomes the active application. If you mostly burn DVDs using iDVD, this setting can make the process more convenient. (iDVD must be installed on your Mac for this to appear.)
- **Open iTunes**—When a DVD or CD is mounted, iTunes becomes the active application. If you regularly burn discs for your iTunes content, this might be your best choice.
- **Open Disk Utility**—You can also burn discs using the Disk Utility application. If that is your preference, you can choose this option to have Disk Utility launch when you insert a recordable disc into your Mac's drive.
- **Open other application**—You can use this option to select a different application to open when a disc is inserted.
- **Run script**—With this option, an AppleScript you select is launched when you insert a blank disc. After you select the script you want to launch, it appears on the "When you insert a blank disc" pop-up menus. If you have a custom burn process implemented through an AppleScript, this is the option you should choose.
- **Ignore**—When you insert a blank disc, your Mac takes no action. In fact, this disc is not even mounted in the Finder. You have to manually take some action later, such as opening an application that can burn DVDs, to do something with the disc. If you prefer to keep blank discs in your Mac and don't want to be interrupted when you insert them, this might be the option you want to choose.

**TIP**

Use the other pop-up menus on the CDs & DVDs pane to set default actions for specific kinds of discs. For example, if you want iTunes to launch when you insert a music CD, choose Open iTunes on the "When you insert a music CD" pop-up menu.

# Burning Discs from the Finder

After you have configured your Mac, burning discs from the Finder is very straightforward, as the following steps demonstrate. (These steps assume that you have selected the "Ask me what to do" option; however, using the Open Finder option works similarly.) Do the following:

**CAUTION**

Because burning CDs or DVDs from the Finder is a single session, you can burn to a disc only once. After it has been burned, you won't be able to add files to it (unless it is a rewritable disc, in which case you can erase it and burn a new set of files to it). Make sure you have all the files on the disc that you want before you burn it. If you want to burn to a disc in more than one session, use Disk Utility instead.

⇨ To learn how use Disk Utility to burn discs, **see** "Burning CDs/DVDs with Disk Utility," **p. 850**.



1. Insert a blank disc into the drive. You are prompted to select an action (refer to Figure 35.9).

2. Select Open Finder on the Action pop-up menu. The blank disc is mounted on your desktop and you see a burnable folder icon on the Sidebar.
3. Select "Untitled CD" or "Untitled DVD" on the Sidebar or double-click the disc's icon on the Desktop to open it in a Finder window (see Figure 35.10).

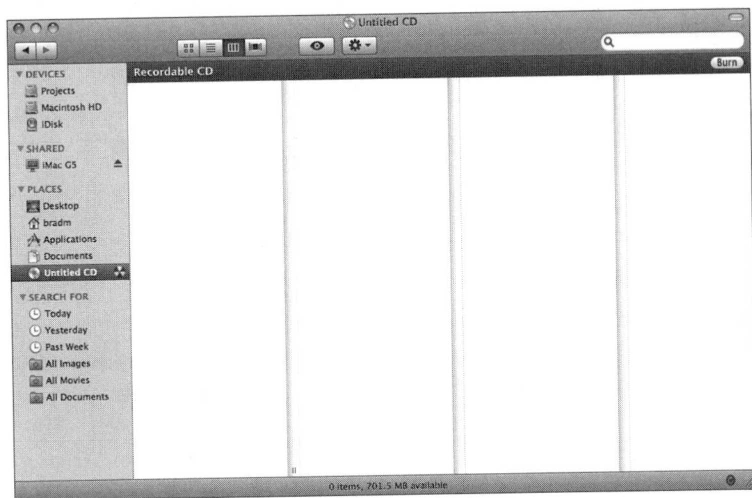


**Figure 35.10**
The selected burnable folder called `Untitled CD` is a blank CD.

4. Select the burnable folder on the Sidebar, open its contextual menu, and choose the Rename command. The disc's name becomes editable.
5. Type the name of the disc and press Return to save the new name.
6. Drag the folders and files you want on the disc to the mounted disc, just like any other volume to which you can copy or move files. Aliases to those files and folders are created in on the disc.
7. Arrange and organize the files as you want them to be on the disc (see Figure 35.11). At the bottom of the Finder window, you see the amount of space still available for more files.
8. When you are ready to record the files on to the disc, click the Burn button in the disc's window; select the disc and choose File, Burn Disc; click the Burn button next to the disc in the Sidebar; or choose Burn Disc on the Action pop-up menu. The Burn Disc dialog box appears (see Figure 35.12).
9. If you want to change the name of the disc, type a new name for the disc in the Disc Name field. You can choose any name you'd like. If you will be sharing the disc with people who use other kinds of computers, keep the name relatively short, such as less than eight characters.
10. Select the speed at which you want to burn the disc on the Burn Speed pop-up menu. In most cases, choose the fastest speed available. However, if you are having problems burning discs at your drive's maximum speed, you can try to burn at a lower speed, which might solve the problems.

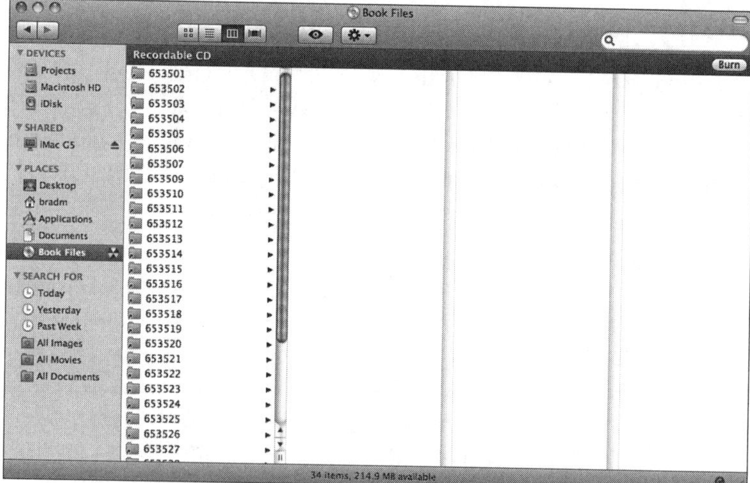


**Figure 35.11**
Here, I have moved files from some book projects onto the CD (note the CD icon in the Finder window's title bar).

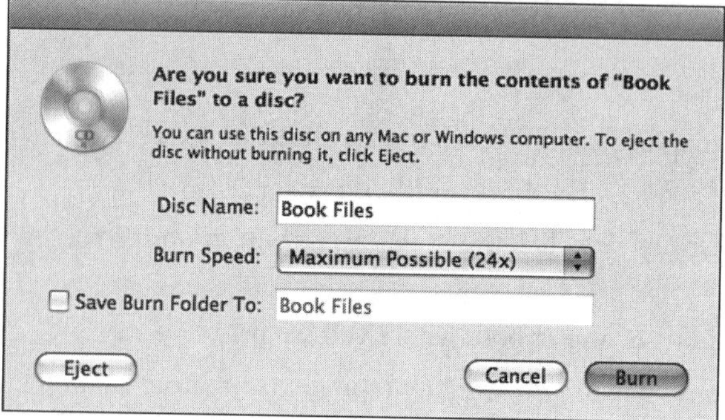


**Figure 35.12**
The CD called `"Book Files"` is ready to burn.

11. If you want the data saved to a Burn folder, so you can make multiple copies of the disc, check the "Save Burn Folder To" check box and name the Burn folder. (The default name will be the name of the current disc, but you can rename it if you want to.)
12. Click Burn. If the files fit onto the disc, the burn process starts. If not, you see a prompt explaining that the selected files are too large for the disc; you need to remove some of the files until they fit on the disc and then start the burn again. As it proceeds, you see a progress window as the data is prepared and the disc is recorded and verified. When the process is complete, the disc is mounted on your Mac and is ready to use. The time it takes to burn a disc depends on the amount of data, type of disc, and the speed of your system. Fortunately, you can work on other tasks during the burn process.

**TIP**

> In the CD Burn progress window, click the Stop button (the *x*) to abort the burn process. This might destroy the disc if the burn process is underway, so most of the time it's better to just let the process complete unless you are using erasable media.

# Burning CDs/DVDs with Disk Utility

In addition to helping you maintain your disks, Disk Utility can also burn CDs and DVDs. It is especially useful when you want to burn a CD or DVD from a disk image file. Another great use of this is to back up image files for the applications you download from the Internet; rather than keeping a folder of these items on your hard drive, you can use Disk Utility to burn a folder of images onto a CD or DVD.

The benefit to burning a disk image onto a CD or DVD using Disk Utility rather than just using the Finder is that, when you use Disk Utility, the image is mounted when you insert the CD—you don't have to first open the disk image file to mount it.

**TIP**

> One of the best reasons to use Disk Utility to burn CDs or DVDs is that you can leave a disc open so you can burn to it multiple times. When you use the Finder, you have only one recording session for a disc. When you use Disk Utility, you can choose to make a disc *appendable*, meaning you can burn to it more than one time.

## Creating a Disk Image to Burn

Before you can burn a disc using Disk Utility, you create a disk image containing the folders and files you want to place on the disc using the following steps:

1. Launch Disk Utility and click the New Image button on the toolbar. The New Image sheet appears.
2. Name the disk image and choose where you want to save it.
3. Name the volume you are creating by typing a name in the Volume Name field. The name of the volume becomes the name of the disc you burn it onto.
4. Use the Volume Size pop-up menu to choose the size of the disk image. Since you are going to burn the image to disc, you want to choose one of the disc options, such as "660MB (CD-ROM 80 min)" if you're putting the image on CD or "4.7GB (DVD-R/DVD-RAM)" if your putting the image on a single layer DVD.
5. Choose the format on the Volume Format pop-up menu. You have the same options as when you format a hard disk. In most cases, you want to use one of the Mac OS Extended formats.
6. If you want to protect the contents of the image with encryption, choose the level of encryption you want to use on the Encryption pop-up menu.
7. Leave CD/DVD selected on the Partitions pop-up menu.
8. Leave "read/write disk image" selected on the Image Format pop-up menu.
9. Click Create. The disk image is created and mounted on your Mac; you can access the disk image just like other volumes such as hard disks (see Figure 35.13).

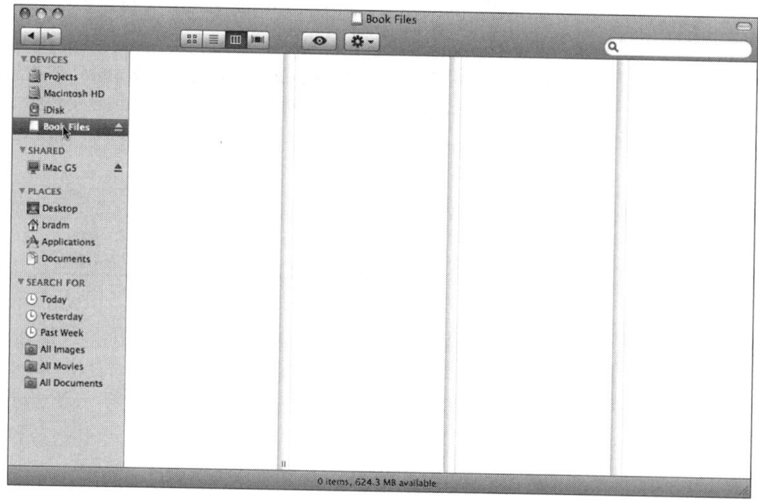


**Figure 35.13**
The disk image called `"Book Files"` is mounted and can be used just like other volumes available to this Mac.

10. Open the disk image by selecting it on the Sidebar, and drag folders or files onto it to add them to the image. Do this until all the files and folders you want to put on the disc are part of the disk image. You are limited to the size of the image you selected using the Volume Size pop-up menu; for example, if you selected the 660MB option, the files can't consume more than 660MB if you want them to fit on a single disc. If you try to place more files on the disk image than will fit, you'll be prevented from moving the files onto the image and a warning prompt appears.

**TIP**

> To see how large a disk image currently is, select it in the Sidebar and use its contextual menu to choose Get Info. In the resulting Info window, expand the General section. In the middle of this section, you'll see the size of the image listed next to the text "Capacity."

## BURNING A SINGLE DISK IMAGE ON CD OR DVD

To put a disc image on CD or DVD using Disk Utility, do the following:

1. Launch Disk Utility. If you have worked with the disk image recently, it will be listed in the lower part of the left pane of the Disk Utility window (which Disk Utility calls being *attached*); you can skip to step 4. If it isn't listed, you will need to locate it using Disk Utility.
2. Locate the disk image by choosing File, Open Disk Image. The "Select Image to Attach" dialog box appears.
3. Move to and select the disk image you want to place on disc; then click Open. The image you selected is attached to Disk Utility, and you will see it in the left pane of the window.

**TIP**

> Disk images are separated from physical disks by the dividing line that appears in the left pane of the Disk Utility window when at least one disk image is attached. Anything above the line is a physical disk of volume; anything below the line is a disk image.

4. Select the disk image you want to burn to disc.

**NOTE**

> If the disk image is currently mounted, you will see its mounted icon below the disk image file itself. You need to select the image file, not the mounted icon.

5. Choose Images, Burn, press ⌘-B, or click the Burn button. The Burn sheet appears.

**TIP**

> If you have more than one drive that can burn discs available to you, choose the drive you want to use on the “Burn Disc In” pop-up menu.

6. Insert the disc on which you want to burn the image. The drive is prepared, and the Burn button becomes active if the disc has enough space to hold the image. If not, you see a message saying so; click Cancel and use a smaller disk image or use a larger capacity disc. Then start the burn process again.

**TIP**

> If you move files from the disk image into the Trash, empty the trash to see the image’s current size.

7. Click the downward facing triangle next to the Burn Disc In text to see additional options (see Figure 35.14).
8. Set the burn speed by using the Speed pop-up menu. In most cases, Maximum Possible is the best choice. However, if you have problems burning discs, a slower speed might help.
9. If you want to test the burn process without actually burning the disc, check the Test Only check box. If the test is successful, you can come back and burn the disc; if not, you’ll need to fix any issues you encounter. This can be a good way to prevent the creation of coasters during the burn process.
10. If you are burning to an erasable disc, check the “Erase disc before burning” check box to erase the disc before you burn to it.
11. If you want to be able to add more data to the disc at a later time, check the “Leave disc appendable” check box. This is one of the best reasons to use Disk Utility to burn discs; you can add data to discs during multiple burn sessions.

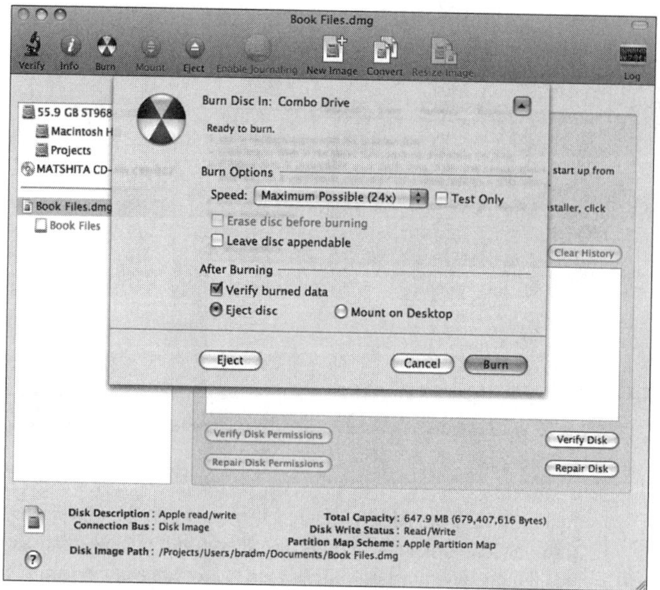


**Figure 35.14**
Use the options on this sheet to configure a burn session.

12. Make sure the "Verify burned data" check box is checked to have your Mac verify the disc after the burn is complete; if you are confident and want to save some time, you can uncheck this box.
13. Click the "Eject disc" radio button if you want the disc ejected when it has been burned, or click the "Mount on Desktop" radio button if you want the disc to be mounted instead.
14. Review the options you have selected and either click Burn or press Return when you ready to burn the disc. You will see the Progress window that displays the progress of the burn.
15. When the process is complete, you'll hear the "burn complete" tone and the finished prompt will appear; click OK and the disc is ejected or mounted on the desktop, depending on the option you selected in step 13 (see Figure 35.15).

**TIP**

> To unattach disk images from Disk Utility, select the disk image file and press Delete or drag its icon out of the window. This does not delete the image file itself–it just removes it from the Disk Utility window.

If you leave a disc appendable, you can repeat these steps to add disk images to it. When you append files to a disc, the Burn button becomes the Append button to indicate that you are adding files to the disc rather than burning it for the first time.

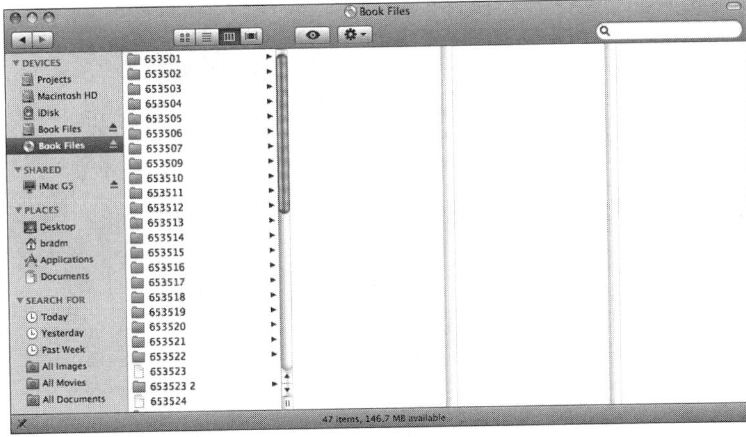


**Figure 35.15**
Here, I have placed a disk image (called `book_files`) containing book files on a CD; above the CD of the same name, you can also see the disk image which is still mounted.

**CAUTION**

> If you want a disk image to mount when you insert the CD on which you want it burned, burn only one disk image on the disc. If you add multiple disk images to the same disc, only the one you most recently burned is accessible in the Finder. You should use the multiple session option only when you are burning other types of files onto a disc or when you are adding files to the same disk image.

**TIP**

> You can use Disk Utility to erase CD-RW or DVD-RW discs. To do so, launch the application; insert the CD-RW or DVD-RW you want to erase; select the icon for the disc drive; and use the tab's tools to erase the disc. You can also erase such discs by using the "erase" check box in the Burn sheet.

## Burning a Folder on CD or DVD

Using the following steps, you can create a disk image from a folder and then burn that image onto a disc:

1. Gather all the files you want to put onto a disc in a single folder.
2. Open Disk Utility.
3. Select File, New, Disk Image from Folder.
4. Move to and select the folder from which you want to create an image.
5. Click Image. You will see the New Image from Folder dialog box (see Figure 35.16). Use this dialog box to name the disk image and choose the options for the image.
6. Name the disk image file and select the location in which you want to store it.
7. On the Image Format pop-up menu, select a format for the image you are creating. The read/write option creates an image you can add more files to later. The read-only

option creates a "closed" image to which files can't be added later. The compressed option creates a compressed version of the folder, so you can get more files in a smaller space. The DVD/CD master creates a disk image ready to be put on disc, so choose that one if you want to put the folder on a disc.

8. Use the Encryption pop-up menu to choose an encryption scheme for the image file if you want to protect the data it contains. If you select none, the image is not encrypted.
9. Click Save. You will see a Progress window as the image file is created. When the process is complete, the disk image you created is shown in the Source pane.
10. Select the disk image you just created and follow the steps in the previous section to put that image on disc.

**Figure 35.16**
The New Image From Folder dialog box enables you to configure a disk image you are creating.

### Burning a Volume on CD or DVD

You can also create a disk image from an entire volume. Then you can place that image on a disc for backup or other purposes. The steps you follow are very similar to those in the previous section. The only difference is that you select the volume from which you want to create a disk image and then select File, New, Image from (*volume* where *volume* is the name of the volume you selected). That volume is then selected and you move to the Convert Image dialog box.

## Burning Discs with Applications

The Finder and Disk Utility work great for burning data discs that you can mount on your Mac. However, many different applications also support disc burning. For example, you can use iTunes to burn a number of kinds of discs including backups of your iTunes content, audio CDs, and data discs. Using iDVD, you can create DVDs with video content. Likewise, you can use iPhoto to put slideshows and photos on disc. If you need to create professional DVDs, you can use DVD Studio Pro application, part of Apple's Final Cut Studio suite.

# Troubleshooting

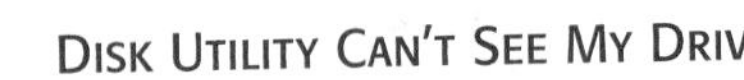

## Disk Utility Can't See My Drive

*When I launch Disk Utility, it does not recognize the drive I installed.*

The fundamental problem is that the drive is not registering with your Mac. There can be many causes for this problem, but the most likely are the following:

- **The drive is incompatible with your Mac.**—Double-check the drive's specifications against those in your Mac's owner's manual.
- **The drive is improperly installed.**—Repeat the installation steps to ensure that the drive is installed and connected properly.
- **An internal drive is not set to be the slave.**—You must set any additional drive to be the slave; your Mac's "first" preinstalled drive must be the primary drive. See the instructions that came with your drive to see how to set it as the slave.

**NOTE**

> Different Mac configurations might require slightly different configurations of drives. Check the user's manual for your Mac before installing an internal drive.

If the drive is external, try disconnecting its FireWire or USB cable and then reconnecting it. Sometimes this will cause the Mac to recognize the drive. If this fails, restart the Mac. If this fails, try using a different type of connection (such as switching from FireWire to USB) or a different port.

Hard drives do wear out over time. If a drive becomes noisy, you should be prepared for it to fail, such as by making sure you have all its data backed up.

## I Can't Burn a Disc

*When I try to burn a disc, the drive can't be found or the process is never completed.*

Burning discs can be a finicky process.

One complexity associated with using disc-burning software is that these applications support only specific drives. If a particular drive isn't supported by the application you want to use, it won't work. Your only option is to find a version that will support your drive or find another application that will.

Burning applications can also interfere with one another. If you have more than one burning application installed on your Mac and have trouble creating discs, remove all the applications but one.

You can also have data transfer speed problems. Most drives include a buffer to which data is written before it is placed on the disc. This buffer ensures that a steady stream of data is written to the disc. If this stream is interrupted and the buffer becomes empty, the process will fail or it will appear to finish, but the disc will be unusable. If this happens, make sure no other applications are running before you attempt to create discs. You can also try to burn at slower speeds.

You can also have trouble with specific kinds of media. For example, if you try to burn onto media that doesn't support your drive's speed, the process can fail. Or, if you try to use media that has a format that isn't supported by your drive, you'll be unable to burn discs. If you use non-Apple media, it's a good idea to buy a small amount of specific media to make sure it works with your system so that you don't waste money.

# CHAPTER 36

# Synchronizing Information on Macs and Other Devices

## In this chapter

# Synchronizing Information

The odds are that you use more than one "information device." Since you're reading this book, you must use at least one Mac to manage information, and most people who use one Mac have more than one to work with. You might have more than one computer at home or have one Mac at work and another at home. Or, you might have one desktop and one mobile Mac. You might also have other devices you use to manage information such as cell phones, iPods, and so on.

It's great having all these devices at your disposal, but this does present a challenge; the odds are that you want to use the same information on each of these devices. Obvious examples are your contact information and calendars. You probably also want to access your Safari bookmarks and even files on which you're working from multiple devices. It's not a lot of fun entering this kind of information more than once (assuming you have a better memory than I do and can remember to add it in each place). Plus, it's easy to forget which device has the information you need when you need it.

It's better to learn how to synchronize information among the devices you use as much as possible; enter information once, access it anywhere. When you change information on one device, you want it to be changed on other devices automatically.

In this chapter, synchronization is covered in two primary situations. The first is synchronizing information between Macs. The second is synchronizing information between Macs and other devices, namely cell phones and iPods.

**NOTE**

> If you have an iPhone and want information on how to sync it with your Mac as well as how to use all the various features, check out *My iPhone* by Brad Miser (Que Publishing, October 2007).

# Synchronizing Information Between Macs

If you use more than one Mac, you'll probably want some of the same data available to you on each of those Macs. There are many examples of this type of information including your contact information, calendars, Safari bookmarks, keychains, and so on. Likewise, you'll probably work on the same files on more than one of your Macs, so you'll need to be able to synchronize the files you use on each machine.

## Synchronizing Information with .Mac

Using .Mac to keep Macs in sync is one of the best ways to work with the same information from multiple Macs, even if all the Macs you use are on the same local network. Plus, you get other benefits, such as email, websites, and so on. Using Apple's .Mac service makes synchronizing information between many Macs easy and automatic. Using Mac OS X's built-in .Mac sync tool, you can synchronize any or all of the following information on as many Macs as you want:

- Bookmarks
- Calendars
- Contacts
- Dashboard widgets
- Dock items
- Keychains
- Mail accounts
- Mail Rules, Signatures, and Smart Mailboxes
- Notes
- Preferences

When you have synchronized with this information, each Mac you use will reflect the same information in the areas you choose to synchronize. For example, if you synchronize your Safari bookmarks, you'll have the same bookmarks available on each machine.

You can configure synchronization in a number of ways too. For example, you can use one Mac as a master so that you use it to enter or change information, and then set up the other Macs as subscribers so that they always contain the same information as the master. Or, you can set up the synchronization so that changes you make on any of the synchronized Macs are made on all of them.

Using an iDisk, you can easily keep files you need to access on more than one Mac synchronized as well. Store the files you need to access from each machine on the iDisk, and you'll be able to use those same files from any Mac that can access your iDisk.

⇨ To learn about .Mac, **see** Chapter 20, "Using .Mac to Integrate a Mac onto the Internet," **p. 435**.

⇨ To learn how to use .Mac to keep information in sync, **see** "Using .Mac to Synchronize Important Information on Multiple Macs," **p. 454**.

⇨ To learn how to use an iDisk, **see** "Using Your iDisk," **p. 441**.

## Synchronizing Information on a Local Network without .Mac

If you don't use .Mac, but do have more than one Mac on a local network, keeping the Macs in sync is a bit more difficult, but still worthwhile.

**NOTE**

> Remember that some applications you use to manage information you'll want to share, such as iTunes music or iPhoto photos. These can be shared using those applications' sharing tools so that you can access that information from any Mac on the network. Often you will configure the application's sharing tools from the Preferences of that application.

Unfortunately, Mac OS X doesn't include any built-in tools to help you with this kind of synchronization. The good news is that there are third-party applications that can help you move specific files among machines automatically, in different ways, such as master/subscribers or keeping the same files on all machines.

⇨ To learn how to automate synchronization on a local network, **see** "Mac OS X to the Max: Automatic File Syncing," **p. 870**.

If you don't use one of these synching applications, you can still share information among the machines you use.

First, you need to configure file sharing on each machine that will be sharing information so that those machines can "see" each other on the network.

⇨ To learn how to share files, **see** "Configuring the Services on a Network," **p. 369**.

Synchronizing information on these machines will be easier to manage if you designate one machine as the master and the others as subscribers. You'll need to make changes to data only on the master machine and then move the information you've changed onto the subscriber machines.

**TIP**

> Of course, you can make exceptions to this if you work on a specific file on one of the subscribers and then move the changed file back to the master Mac. For example, if you sync your contacts between your desktop and laptop, but make a change to a friend's address information while using the laptop, you will need to sync from the laptop back to the desktop.

While moving the files among the Macs on the network isn't difficult, determining which files you need to move can be. Obvious files you'll want to move are documents that you've changed on one machine that you want to be available on another.

Less obvious are things like contact information, bookmarks, and so on. The good news is that most of this information is stored in the same folder, which is the Library folder in your Home folder. For example, Safari settings, including bookmarks are stored in the Safari folder within your Library folder. To make the same set of bookmarks available on each Mac, copy the Safari folder from your Library folder to the same location under your user account on each Mac. Likewise, if you want to have the same keychains available, you can copy the Keychains folder from the master to each of the subscribers. (Hey, I did say this wouldn't be as easy as using .Mac.)

**TIP**

> One idea to consider is to use your Home folder on the master machine as your master folder. Copy that folder to each of the subscriber machines and replace the current Home folder. When you use one of the subscriber machines, you'll have access to the same data you have in the Home folder on your master machine. Of course, this can consume lots of disk space so you'll only be able to do this if you can afford to have a copy of your Home folder on each machine. And, you need to make sure nothing in the Home folder on a subscriber machine can't be replaced when you copy the master Home folder onto that machine.

You can also use Mac OS X's search tools and smart folders to identify files that have changed recently so you know which files you need to move from the master to subscribers. For example, you can create a smart folder to automatically locate any documents or files that have been changed "today" so you know which files you need to synchronize.

⇨ To how to find information and create smart folders, **see** Chapter 4, "Finding Things on Your Mac," **p. 101**.

**NOTE**

Another way to share information on a local network is by publishing that information on a website.

⇨ To learn how to publish a website on a local network, **see** "Mac OS X to the Max: Using Mac OS X to Serve Web Pages," **p. 458**.

# Synchronizing Information on Macs to Other Devices

If you use a cell phone or PDA, you'll probably want to keep the information on those devices in sync with your Mac. Mac OS X's iSync application enables you to synchronize calendar and contact information among multiple devices, such as Macs, cell phones, or PDAs.

**NOTE**

You can use iTunes to move your Mac's calendar and contact information onto an iPod, just like you move audio and video content onto it. While you can't change information on the iPod, you can view it, such as looking up contact information or viewing your calendar.

## Determining If You Can Sync a Device with iSync

You need to determine if the device with which you want to sync information is compatible with iSync. The good news is that many devices are; however, even if a device is compatible, it might not be able to synchronize all information (such as associating photos included in your Address Book with contact information on the cell phone).

To determine if the device you want to sync is compatible, visit www.apple.com/macosx/features/isync/devices.html (see Figure 36.1).

**Figure 36.1**
Mac OS X's iSync is compatible with many PDAs and cell phones.

If your device is on the list, you can be sure that you'll be able to synchronize it; and you'll even see which information can be synchronized. If your device isn't on the list, you can always try to synchronize it anyway, but don't be too surprised if it doesn't work.

## Configuring iSync Preferences

To get started, launch iSync and configure the relevant iSync preferences with the following steps:

1. Launch iSync (Applications folder) and open the iSync Preferences dialog box by selecting iSync, Preferences (⌘-,).
2. Enable iSync by checking the "Enable syncing on this computer" check box (see Figure 36.2).

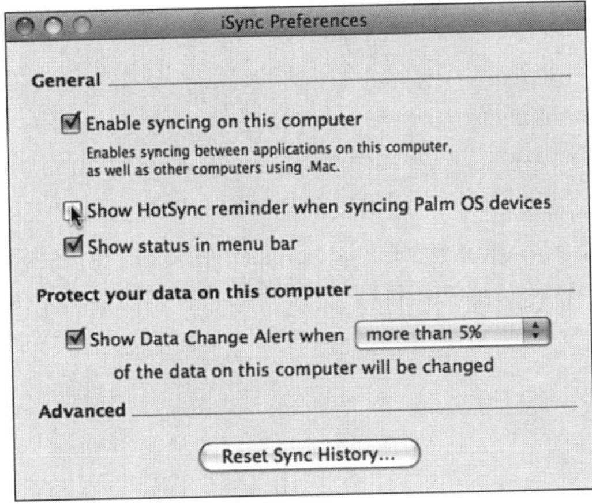


**Figure 36.2**
Setting iSync preferences isn't a challenge.

3. If you want iSync to warn you when you attempt to sync a Palm device, check the "Show HotSync reminder when syncing Palm OS devices" check box. When you attempt to synchronize a Palm device, you are instructed to use the HotSync software instead. iSync doesn't actually perform the synchronization between Macs and Palm OS devices, and this setting will make the process more smooth. If you don't use a Palm OS device, you can uncheck this box.
4. To show the iSync menu in the menu bar, check the "Show status in menu bar" check box.
5. If you want to be alerted when data on your Mac will be changed, check the "Show Data Change Alert when" pop-up menu, and select the amount of data that must be changed before you see a warning. Your options are "any," "more than 5%," "more than 25%," or "more than 50%." It's a good idea to use this to make sure you are aware of the change to prevent significant changes to your Mac's data unless you're very sure you want those changes made.
6. Close the Preferences dialog box.

**TIP**

To clear iSync's memory, click the Reset Sync History button.

**TIP**

To sync with a Palm device, launch iSync and choose Devices, Enable Palm OS Syncing. Follow the onscreen instructions to set up syncing between your Mac and a Palm OS device, such as a PDA.

## SYNCHRONIZING A MAC WITH A CELL PHONE

One of the most common devices with which you'll sync your Mac's information is a cell phone. You can create one set of contact and calendar information and use the same information on your Mac and cell phone. Changes you make on the Mac can be moved to the cell phone and vice versa.

To synchronize a cell phone with a Mac, the two devices must be able to communicate. This can be done wirelessly with Bluetooth or using a USB connection. The first time you synchronize, you need to configure the synchronization between the devices. After that, syncing them is a snap.

### CONFIGURING SYNCHRONIZATION BETWEEN A MAC AND CELL PHONE

The general steps to configure syncing between a Mac and a cell phone are the following:

**NOTE**

These steps describe syncing a Bluetooth cell phone. Syncing a phone using USB is similar; obviously, you won't use the Bluetooth Assistant. After choosing the Add Devices command, follow the onscreen instructions to configure the sync.

1. Enable Bluetooth services on your Mac and on the phone.

⇨ To learn how to configure Bluetooth on a Mac, **see** "Finding, Installing, and Using Bluetooth Devices," **p. 775**.

2. Launch iSync and Choose Devices, Add Device. The Bluetooth Assistant will open.
3. Click Continue.
4. Click Mobile phone. iSync will locate phones with which your Mac can communicate (see Figure 36.3).

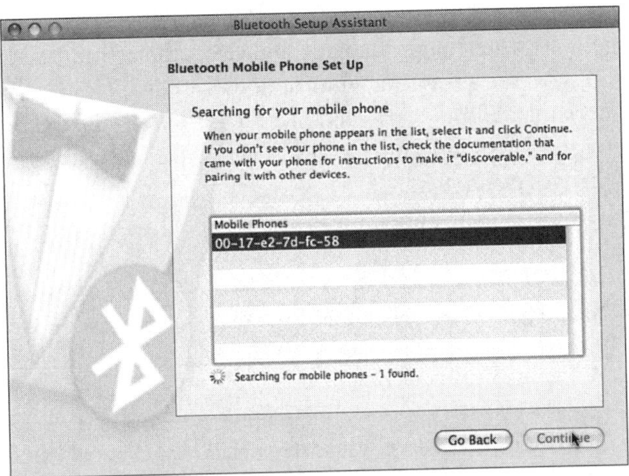


**Figure 36.3**
A phone has been found.

If the Assistant can't find the phone, make sure that it is set to be discoverable and that its Bluetooth services are turned on. Check the documentation that came with your phone to learn how to do this.

5. Select the device you want to sync with and click Continue.
6. Click Continue to allow your Mac to gather information about the device. When this process is underway, you'll be shown a passkey in the Assistant window.
7. Using the cell phone's controls, allow the connection to be made and enter the passkey shown in the Assistant. When this is done correctly, the two devices will be paired and will be able to communicate and you see the Bluetooth Mobile Phone Set Up screen (see Figure 36.4). The options you see on this screen will depend upon the specific phone you are using.
8. To enable iSync to transfer contacts and calendar information, check the "Set up iSync to transfer contacts and events" check box.
9. If you want to be able to use the phone as a modem to access the Internet, check the "Access the Internet with your phone's data connection" and then choose the appropriate radio button. This can be useful if you use a mobile Mac and want to be able to connect to the Internet via your phone.
10. Click Continue.

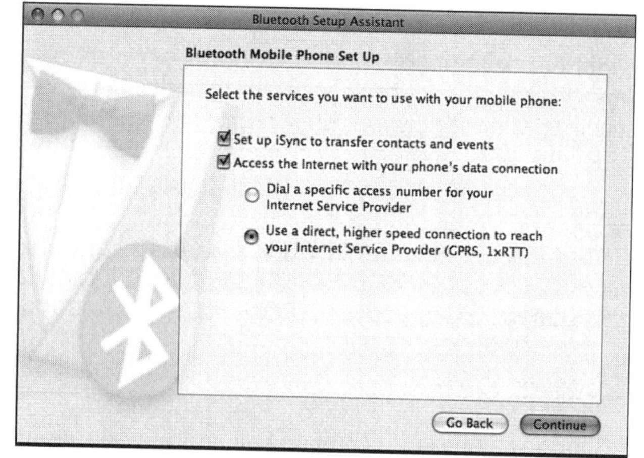


**Figure 36.4**
Use this window to choose the information that you want to exchange between the Mac and the mobile phone.

11. If you choose to use the phone for an Internet connection, you'll see a configuration screen; on that screen complete the information for the type of Internet connection your phone has and click Continue. If you don't use the phone for an Internet connection, you'll skip this step.
12. Click Quit when you see the Conclusion screen. The phone is now ready to be synced and you'll see the phone's configuration screen in iSync (see Figure 36.5). At the top of the iSync window, you'll see an icon for the device you've configured while in the lower part of the window, you see the options for that device.

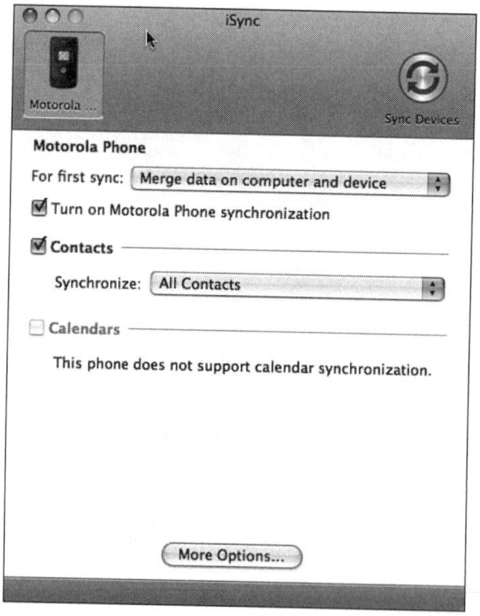

**Figure 36.5**
Back in iSync, you'll see the configuration screen for the device you are configuring, such as this Motorola Razor cell phone.

13. Use the "For first sync" pop-up menu to determine how you want iSync to handle the data on both devices. Choose "Merge data on computer and device" if you want the unique information on each device to be moved onto the other device so that they both have the same data. Choose "Erase data on device then sync" if you want all the data on the cell phone to be replaced with data on the Mac.

**NOTE** The specific options you see in the iSync device configuration window depend on the specific device with which you're working. For example, if you use a Motorola cell phone, you can enable its synchronization by checking the "Turn on Motorola Phone synchronization" check box.

14. Use the configuration options to configure how and when the device will be synchronized. For example, if the device can store contact information, check the Contacts check box and use the pop-up menu to choose which contacts will be synchronized. If the device can store calendar information, check the Calendars check box and choose the calendars with information that you want to sync.
15. Click More Options. The More Options sheet appears (see Figure 36.6).

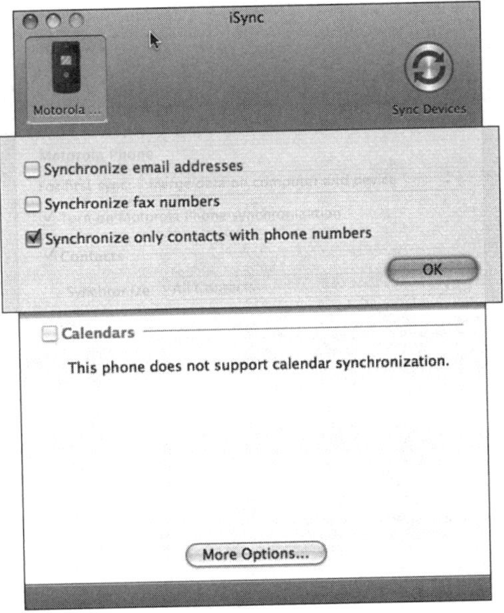


**Figure 36.6**
Use the More Options sheet to configure specific kinds of data that will be moved from the Mac to the cell phone.

16. Set the additional synchronization options, such as "Synchronize only contacts with phone numbers" if you don't want to sync contacts who don't have phone numbers on your cell phone. Click OK.
17. Click the Sync Devices button on the iSync toolbar to synchronize the device. You see a progress window that shows you how the sync is going (see Figure 36.7).

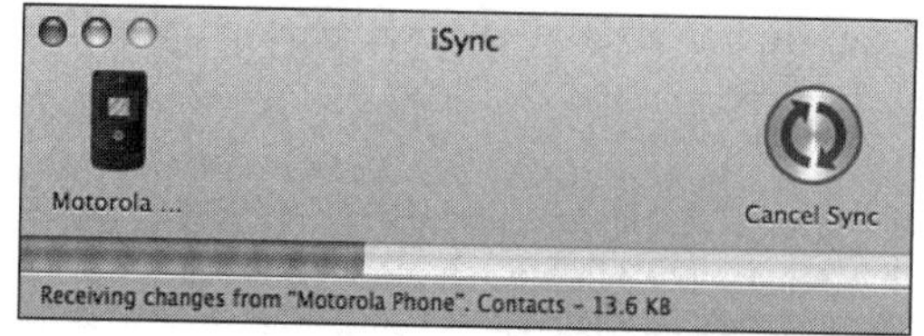


**Figure 36.7**
A sync is underway.

18. If you enabled the data change warning and the threshold you set is reached, you see the Sync Alert window. At the top, you see a summary of the type (such as contacts) and amount of data (number added, modified, or deleted) that will be changed if you allow the sync to complete. To get more details, click the More Info expansion triangle and details about the data changes appear at the bottom of the window (see Figure 36.7). You can use the left and right scroll buttons to see each change in detail.

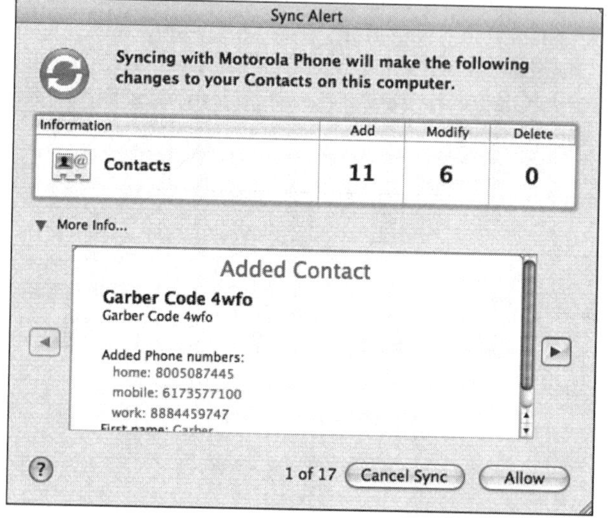


**Figure 36.8**
iSync warns you when your Mac's data will be changed more than the threshold warning level you set.

Click Allow to allow the sync to continue or Cancel Sync to stop it.

When the process is complete, the progress bar will go away and you see the Synchronization complete message.

**TIP**

> iSync can synchronize multiple devices at the same time. Configure each device separately; you see the icon for each configured device at the top of the iSync window.

## Synchronizing Information on a Mac and on a Cell Phone

After you have configured a device for synchronization, you can sync it manually either by opening iSync and clicking the Sync Devices button or by choosing Sync Now on the iSync menu if you added it to the Finder menu bar. The device's data is synced with your Mac's information. If the change threshold warning is set and reached, you'll need to allow changes to be made during the sync process.

**TIP**

> When you have configured a device in iSync, it appears in the iSync toolbar. Click the device to reconfigure its sync options.

You can view the synchronization history for your Mac by choosing Window, iSync Log. The resulting window shows the synchronization activity by date. You can expand a date to view details for each synchronization that occurred on that date.

## MAC OS X TO THE MAX: AUTOMATIC FILE SYNCING

Manually managing files between Macs isn't a lot of fun, and it consumes time and effort that could be better spent doing something else. Fortunately, there are applications that enable you to automatically synchronize data between hard drives, computers, and even across a local network. One of the best of these applications is Econ Technologies' ChronoSync (see Figure 36.9).

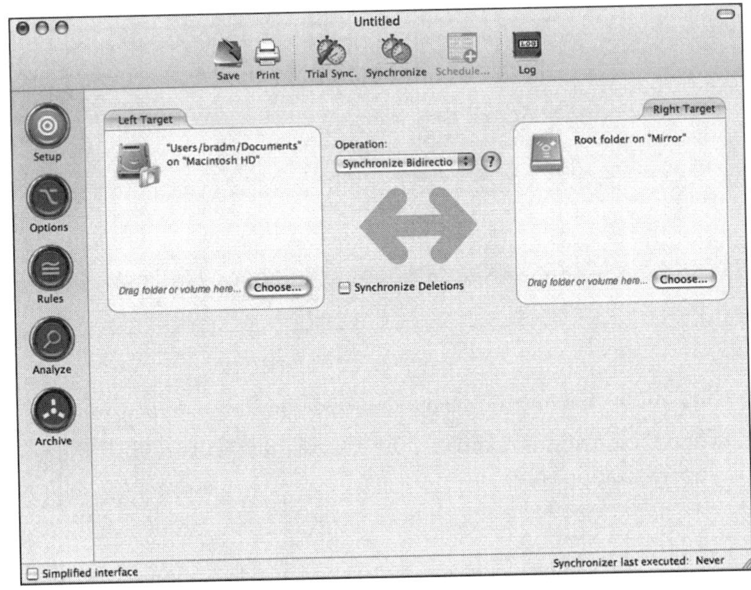


**Figure 36.9**
ChronoSync is a great way to keep files on multiple Macs or multiple hard drives in sync.

Using ChronoSync, you can set up two targets for synchronization. For either target, you can select a folder, set of folders, or even an entire hard disk for synchronization. Then, you can choose the operation you want to perform, such as Synchronize Bidirectional to keep the data on the drives the same. Another really useful option is to make one target a mirror of the other for back-up purposes.

ChronoSync allows you to synchronize Macs across a local network just as easily as you can synchronize folders among the hard drives connected to a Mac. And, you can set up schedules so the synchronization happens automatically at the times you determine.

If you need to keep Macs on a local network synchronized or need a more capable back-up application than Mac OS X's Time Machine, ChronoSync is a great tool. You can learn more about it and download a free trial version from www.econtechnologies.com/site/Pages/ChronoSync/chrono_overview.html.

PART VI

# Protecting, Maintaining, and Repairing Your Mac

# CHAPTER 37

# Maintaining a Mac

## In this chapter

# MAINTAINING YOUR MAC

Time and effort you have to spend troubleshooting problems is time and effort you don't have available to accomplish what you want to accomplish. To minimize the time you have to spend solving problems, you should take specific steps to maintain your Mac. In this chapter, the following preventive activities are described:

- Maintaining your system software
- Maintaining your hard disks
- Maintaining alternative startup volumes and discs
- Building and maintaining a Mac toolkit
- Maintaining your applications

Maintaining your Mac in good condition with these tasks isn't terribly difficult, and the effort you do put in will pay off in having to spend less time and effort solving problems.

The previous list will certainly get your started with good Mac maintenance practices. There are a couple of other areas that are equally or more important to keeping your Mac working and in good condition. These topics are so important that the next two chapters are dedicated to them.

⇨ To learn about the most important Mac maintenance task you can and should do, **see** Chapter 38, "Backing Up a Mac," **p. 895**.

⇨ To learn how to prevent problems using Mac OS X's security features, **see** Chapter 39, "Securing a Mac," **p. 921**.

# USING SOFTWARE UPDATE TO MAINTAIN YOUR SYSTEM SOFTWARE

Apple regularly updates Mac OS X (and other applications, such as the iLife applications) to solve problems, enhance performance, and introduce new features. Keeping track of the updates manually would be time-consuming. Fortunately, you don't have to. You can use the Software Update tool (which consists of a pane in the System Preferences application and the Software Update application) to check, download, and install updates to Mac OS X and related software (including firmware updates, updates to Apple applications you use, and so on).

## CONFIGURING SOFTWARE UPDATE

To configure Software Update, follow these steps:

1. Open the System Preferences application, and then open the Software Update pane (see Figure 37.1).
2. Use the check boxes, pop-up menu, and other buttons to configure the Software Update schedule (the options are described in the following bulleted list).

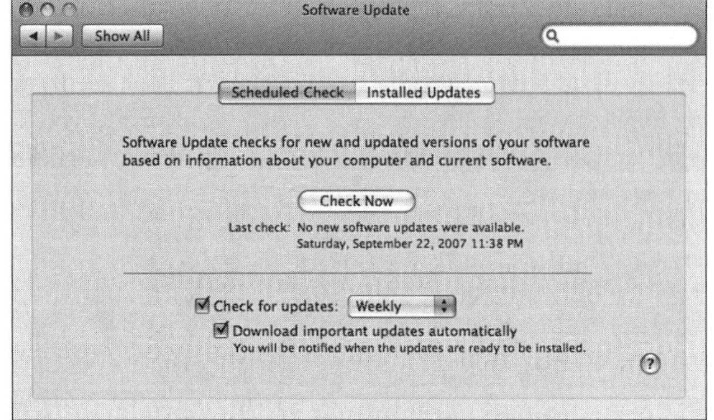


**Figure 37.1**
The frequency with which you check for updates depends on your connection to the Internet; for most people, weekly updates are sufficient.



When configuring Software Update, you have the following options:

- **Manual or Automatic Updates**—Use the "Check for updates" check box to determine whether your system will automatically check for updates when you have a network connection. If you check this box, use the pop-up menu to set the frequency of checking for updates. Your choices are Daily, Weekly, or Monthly. I recommend you use the Weekly or Daily options.
- **Download Updates in Background**—If you check the "Download important updates in the background" check box, Software Update automatically (you have to select the automatic option for this option to be available) downloads important updates (such as updates to the OS) without bothering you first. When the update has been downloaded and is ready to be installed, you are prompted to allow the operating system to start the installation process.
- **Check Now**—You can click the Check Now button to manually check for updates. You see a progress bar at the bottom of the pane to indicate how the process is proceeding. If no updates are available, you'll see a message saying so along with the date and time you last checked for updates. If updates are available, the Software Update application opens.
- **Installed Updates tab**—Here you can see the history of all the updates Software Update has installed for you. Click the tab to see the list of files that were changed and when the changes were made. If you click the "Open as Log File" button, you will see a Console window that provides the same list, but in a different format and in a bit more detail.

## Working with Software Update

When you have configured your system to check for updates automatically and an update is available (and you haven't selected the "download in background" option), or when you use the Software Update command on the Apple menu to check for updates manually, the

Software Update application opens (see Figure 37.2). It will check for updates for Mac OS X along with any Apple applications installed on your Mac, firmware updates, and so on. If it doesn't find any, it will quit automatically if the check was done according to a schedule. If it doesn't find any updates when you performed the check manually, you'll see a message stating that there isn't any new software for your computer; when you click OK, the Software Update application will close.

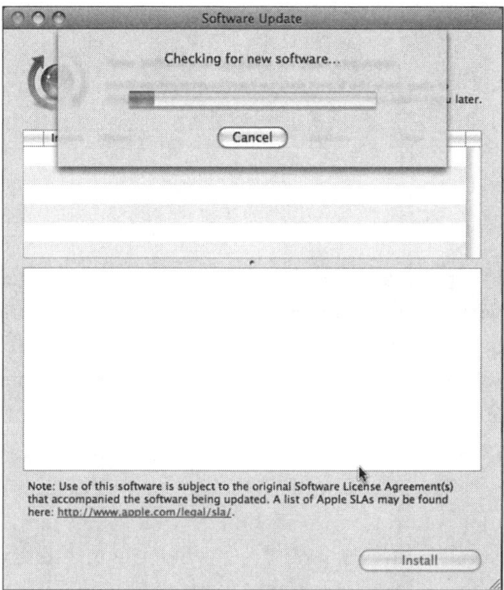


**Figure 37.2**
The Software Update application manages the download and installation of available updates for you.

If updates are available, in the top pane of the application's window you'll see a list of all available updates. If you select an update, information about that update appears in the lower pane of the window. You can download and install one or more updates by checking the check box next to the updates you want to install and clicking the Install button or choosing a specific option from the Update menu.

**TIP**

You can jump into the Software Update application (without opening the Software Update pane first) by selecting Apple menu, Software Update. The application will launch and immediately check for updates.

**NOTE**

As with other application installs, you have to authenticate yourself as an administrator to be able to install updates via Software Update. Depending on the type of update you install, you might have to agree to a license before the update can be installed on your computer (such as a new version of an iLife application).

When the Software Update application is open, you can select one of the following download options from the Update menu:

- **Download only**—This option causes the update to be downloaded to your Mac. You have to run the installer manually to install it. Updates are provided as packages you can run just like other application installers. These packages are stored in the `Mac OS X/Library/Packages` folder, where `Mac OS X` is the name of your Mac OS X startup volume. When you want to install the update, open this folder and run the update's installer. After the file has been downloaded, a Finder window showing the installer is opened so you can run it easily.
- **Install**—This one downloads and installs the update and then removes the package from your Mac.
- **Install and Keep Package**—This option downloads and installs the update, but it also keeps the package so you can install the update again later if you need to. The update's installer is located in the `Mac OS X/Library/Packages` folder, where `Mac OS X` is the name of your Mac OS X startup volume. You can run the installer again from this location.



TIP

> If you have more than one Mac and a slow Internet connection, the first or third option can be a good choice because you can put the updater on a CD and install it from there on each machine rather than downloading it to each machine one at a time.

NOTE

> When you click the Install button in the Software Update application, the Install option on the Update menu is selected. To select one of the other options, you must use the Update menu.

If you selected the "download in background" option, you won't see the Software Update application until the updates have been downloaded to your Mac.

Occasionally, updates are released that are of no value to you, such as updates for languages you don't use, devices you don't have, and so on. Software Update regularly reminds you of these updates until you download them. However, if you see an update that you are sure you won't want to download and install, you can have Software Update ignore that specific update. To do so, use the following steps:

TIP

> Ignoring an update removes it from the list of available updates. If you don't want to install a specific download, just uncheck its check box. To install that update, check its box before you click the Install button.

1. In the Software Update application, select the update you want to ignore.
2. Select Update, Ignore Update or press the Delete key.
3. Click OK in the resulting warning sheet. The update is removed and you will no longer be prompted to download the current or future versions of the update you ignored.

37

You can see ignored updates again by selecting Software Update, Reset Ignored Updates. All the updates you have ignored are added back to the Software Update application, and you are prompted to download and install them again. You can't choose to restore a single update; you have to restore them all. Of course, you can choose to ignore specific updates again to remove them from the list.

**NOTE**

> Whether the "download in background" option is good for you or not mostly depends on the type of Internet connection you have. If you have a broadband connection, this option doesn't hurt because you aren't tying up a phone line while updates are downloading. You can just choose not to install any updates you don't want. If you use a dial-up connection, it is better not to download updates in the background because some of the updates are quite large, and you might tie up a phone line for a long time downloading an update you aren't going to install anyway.

After you have downloaded and installed an update, use the Installed Updates tab of the Software Update pane of the System Preferences application to verify that the updates were installed.

---

**Seeing Installed Files**

To view all installs that have been done on your Mac, including but not limited to software updates, open the folder `Mac OS X/Library/Receipts`, where `Mac OS X` is the name of your Mac OS X startup volume.

In this folder, you will see all the installs that have been performed on your Mac. Most are in `.pkg` files, but you can't open these to reinstall the software. Because they are receipts, they are for information purposes only.

---

**NOTE**

> If you want to manually check for Apple software updates, go to www.apple.com/support. Use the tools on the Apple Support pages to locate and download updates. For example, in the Downloads section, you will see a list of the current updates that are available.

# MAINTAINING YOUR DISK DRIVES

Maintaining your disk drives will go a long way toward maximizing performance and preventing problems. You can use the Mac OS X Disk Utility application to do basic disk maintenance and repair. For maximum performance, you can also consider defragmenting and optimizing your disks.

## Checking and Repairing Disks with Disk Utility

Among other things, the Disk Utility application (located in the Applications/Utilities folder) enables you to check for problems with your disks and then repair problems that are found.

**NOTE**

> A volume is a disk that has been partitioned into two or more partitions. Each partition behaves as if it were on a separate hard disk. There are several reasons you might want to partition a disk into multiple volumes, such as for organization purposes or to create multiple startup volumes.



To check and repair a volume, perform the following steps:

1. Launch Disk Utility. In the left pane of the window are all the disks mounted on your Mac, including drives installed in your computer and those that are connected via FireWire or USB (see Figure 37.3). Each volume on each disk is listed under that disk's icon. You will also see any disk images that have been mounted on the machine.

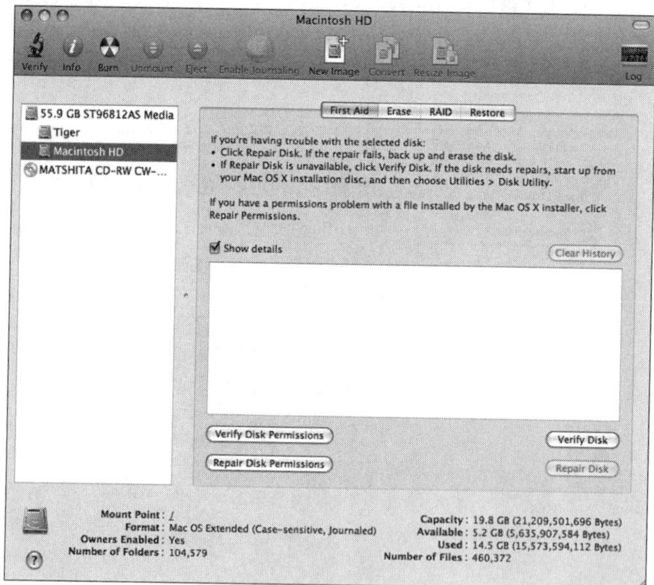


**Figure 37.3**
Use Disk Utility to check the condition of your hard disks.

**NOTE**

> Even if a disk has only one volume on it, you will see that disk's volume listed under the disk's icon.

2. Highlight a disk, a volume on a disk, or a disk image you want to check. When you select a disk or volume, a number of tabs appear in the right pane of the window. How many tabs appear depends on what you select.

**NOTE**

> In this context, *volume* and *partition* are the same thing. When you partition a disk, each partition becomes a mounted volume on that disk.



If you select a hard disk, the following tabs appear: First Aid, Erase, Partition, RAID, and Restore.

If you select a mounted volume, CD, or DVD, you will see the following tabs: First Aid, Erase, and Restore.

If you select a disk image, the First Aid, Erase, and Restore tabs appear.

3. Check the bottom of the Disk Utility window for information about the disk, volume, disc, or image you selected. Again, what you see here depends on what you have selected.

If you select a hard drive, you see the disk type, connection bus (such ATA for internal drives or FireWire for an external drive), connection type (internal or external), capacity, write status, S.M.A.R.T. status, and partition map scheme (see Figure 37.4).

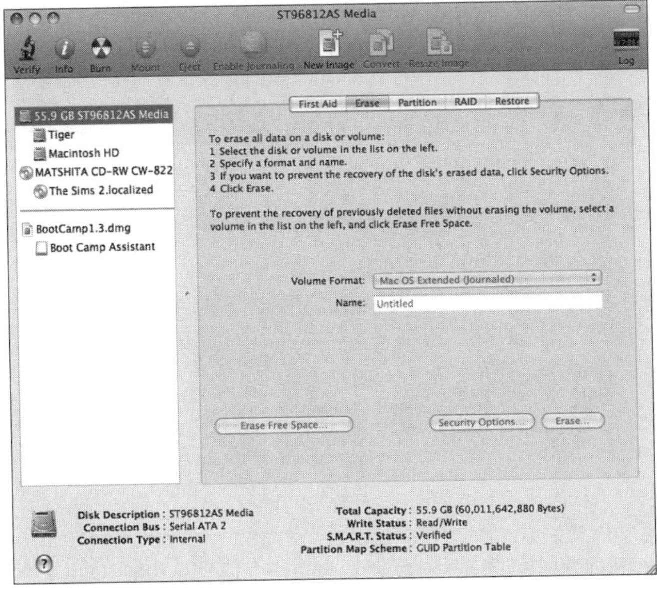


**Figure 37.4**
At the bottom of the Disk Utility window, you see information about the selected hard disk; the name of the window is the name of the selected disk or volume.

For most disks, the S.M.A.R.T. status provides an indication of the disk's health: This is Verified if the disk is in good working condition or About to Fail if the disk has problems. If a disk doesn't support S.M.A.R.T., the status will be Not Supported.

If you select a volume on a disk, you will see various data about the volume, such as its mount point (the path to it), format, whether owners are enabled, the number of folders it contains, its capacity, the amount of space available, the amount of space used, and the number of files it contains (see Figure 37.5).

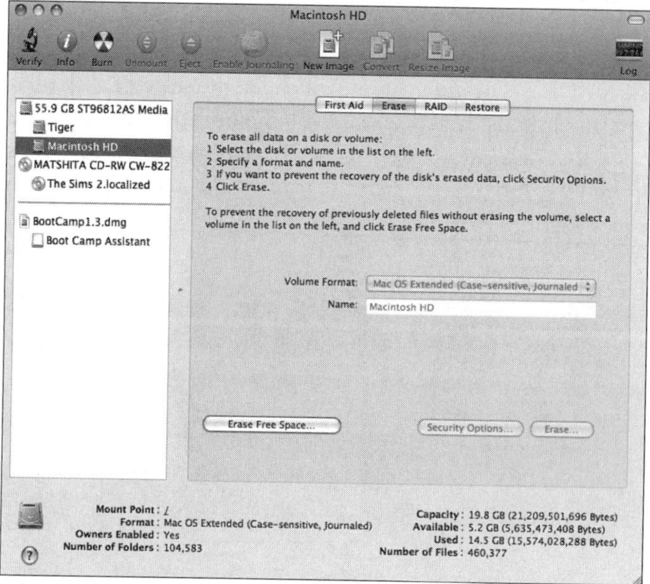


**Figure 37.5**
A partition on a disk has been selected, and information relevant to a volume is now shown at the bottom of the Disk Utility window.



**NOTE**

> S.M.A.R.T. stands for self-monitoring analysis and reporting technology. Most modern disk drives support this technology, which means potential problems with a disk are identified and reported before the problem occurs. The goal of this technology is for you to be able to repair a disk before you lose any data or to at least transfer the data on that disk to another disk.

If you select a CD or DVD disc drive, you see the drive's specifications and the types of discs with which the drive can work.

If you select a mounted CD or DVD, you see where the disc is mounted and its name, its format, its write status, the number of folders it contains, the disc's capacity, the available space, the used space, and the number of files stored on it.

If you select a disk image, you see its description, size of the image file, write status (mounted or not), connection bus, and where it is located (the path to it).

4. Click the First Aid tab to see some information explaining how Disk Utility works.

**NOTE**

> You can't repair a disk with open files, which means you can't do these tasks with your Mac OS X startup volume. You can verify your startup volume to learn about any issues on that disk. To repair that volume, restart your Mac from the Mac OS X installation CD and select Disk Utility from the Installer menu. Or start up your Mac from an alternate startup volume, which should be part of every Mac user's toolkit.



5. Click Repair Disk. The application will check the selected disk or volume for problems and repair any it finds. If you select a volume on a disk, the application will check all the volumes on that disk automatically. As Disk Utility works, you will see progress messages in the First Aid pane. When the process is complete, a report of the results appears (see Figure 37.6).

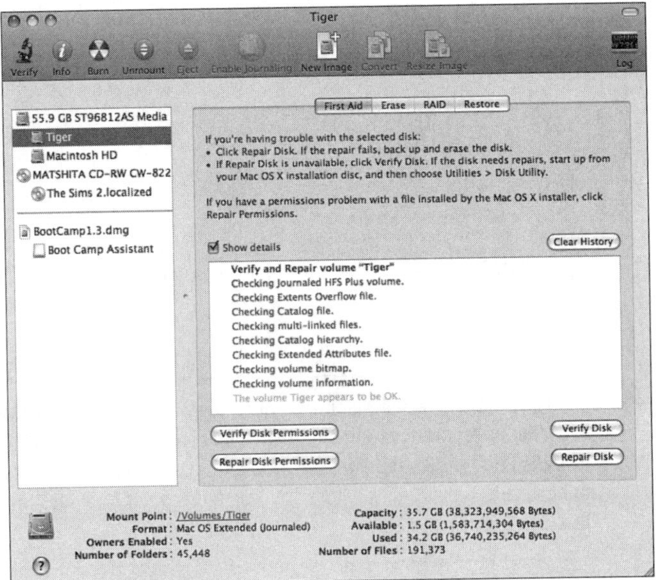


**Figure 37.6**
The selected disk appears to be okay.

**NOTE**

> For the Mac OS X startup volume, you never really need to run Disk First Aid. That is because the disk is checked and repaired during startup. You can also run a Unix disk repair utility during startup.

⇨ To learn how to run a Unix disk repair utility during startup, **see** "Starting Up in Single-User Mode," **p. 210**.

You can choose to verify a volume rather than to repair it. When you do so, the application finds problems with the disk and reports back to you. You then have to tell the application to repair those problems. Generally, you should use the Repair button to save the extra step because you will always choose to repair problems Disk Utility finds.

⇨ To learn how to use the Disk Utility to initialize and partition hard disks, **see** "Initializing and Partitioning a Hard Drive," **p. 838**.

You can also use Disk Utility to check or repair the permissions on the startup volume you are using. This can solve access problems with specific files on the machine when you don't have the required permissions. Even if you aren't currently having permissions related problems, it's a good idea to use the following steps periodically as part of your disk maintenance tasks:

1. Select your current startup volume (if your startup disk has more than one volume, you have to select the startup volume, not the disk on which the volume is stored).
2. Click Repair Disk Permissions. The application will start searching for permission problems and repairing those it finds. As it works, you can view the status of the process in the window. When the process is complete, you see the results in the information window on the First Aid tab.

You can use the Verify Disk Permissions button to find permission problems. Then you have to tell the application to repair them. Like disk problems, you will almost always repair any problems the application finds, so you can save yourself a step by using the Repair button instead.

**TIP**

Disk Utility has a toolbar, which you can configure by Control-clicking it and using the resulting pop-up menu to configure the toolbar.



## Erasing Disks with Disk Utility

You can also use Disk Utility to quickly erase and reformat volumes or erasable disks (such as CD-RW discs):

1. Select the disk, disc, or volume you want to erase.
2. Click the Erase tab.
3. Choose the format you want to use for the volume on the Volume Format pop-up menu. The format options are Mac OS Extended (Journaled), Mac OS Extended, Mac OS Extended (Case-sensitive, Journaled), or Mac OS Extended (Case-sensitive). If you select a disk, you will also see the MS-DOS File System format.
4. Name the volume in the Name field.

**TIP**

If you select a volume, you can use the Erase Free Space button to remove files that you have deleted from the volume to make it harder or impossible to recover using data recovery tools. When you click the Erase Free Space button, you can use the resulting sheet to choose how you want to overwrite the free space. There are three options, with each providing a different level of security.

5. Click the Security Options button. The Secure Erase Options sheet appears (see Figure 37.7).

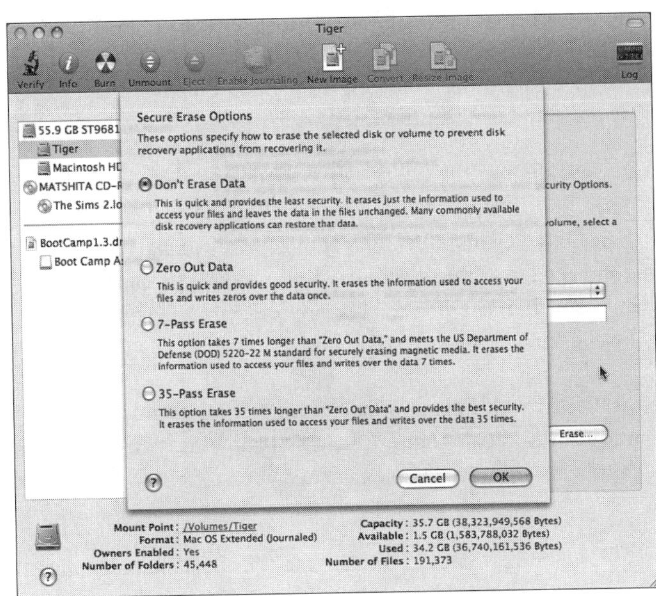


**Figure 37.7**
When you erase a volume or disk, you can choose the security with which you erase that volume's data.

There are four options you can choose to determine how your Mac handles data it is erasing.

**Don't Erase Data**—This option makes the data unviewable from the Finder but leaves the data physically on the disk. As your Mac needs to write more files to the disk, it will overwrite the erased space. Until the data is overwritten, that data can be recovered (unerased) using an application designed to recover data.

**Zero Out Data**—This option writes zeros in all sectors on the disk.

**7-Pass Erase**—This writes random data over the entire disk 7 times.

**35-Pass Erase**—This overwrites the disk 35 times.

The purpose of the last three options is to prevent data on the disk from being restored after you erase it. For example, if you were transferring a disk to someone else, you would want to select one of these options so that the data you had on the disk could not be recovered. The more overwrites you choose, the more secure the erase will be and the longer the process will take. If you are maintaining control of the disk, you probably don't need to choose one of the secure erase options, but using the Zero Out Data option doesn't add a lot of time to the process, so it isn't a bad choice.

If you want to use one of these options, click its radio button and then click OK.

6. Click Erase. The confirmation sheet appears; if you are sure you want to erase the disk, click Erase again. The drive's or volume's data is erased and is formatted with the options you selected.

**TIP**

> You can get detailed information about a device or volume by selecting it and clicking the Info button on the toolbar.

## ENABLING JOURNALING WITH DISK UTILITY



Under Mac OS X, disks can use the Mac OS (Journaled) file format. This format provides a journal function that tracks activity that has taken place in the main areas of the disk. This log helps re-create the data on the disk and makes repair operations more successful. In most cases, you should use this option because it gives you a better chance of recovering data and disks if you have problems. As you saw in the previous section, you can select the Journaled format when you erase a disk or volume. You can also enable journaling on an existing volume without erasing or reformatting it. To do the latter, use the following steps:

1. Select the volume on which you want to enable journaling.
2. Click the Enable Journaling button on the toolbar; select File, Enable Journaling; or press ⌘-J. The journaling information is tracked for the selected disk or volume. (If this option is inactive, it means that journaling is already enabled or it can't be activated on the current disk, in which case, you will have to erase the disk to activate journaling.)

**TIP**

> You can disable journaling again by selecting File, Disable Journaling.

## DEFRAGMENTING AND OPTIMIZING YOUR HARD DISKS

As you save files to a disk (again, this means any kind of disk you have mounted on your Mac, except for CD-ROMs, DVD-ROMs, and other locked disks from which you can only read data), data is written to the disk. The Mac is also frequently writing other sorts of data (such as preference changes and other system-level data) to the startup disk. As data is written to a disk, it is written in the next available space (called a *block*). After the data is laid down, the Mac returns to what it was doing. When it is time to save more data, the next batch is written in the next open space, and so on. Think of this as the Mac putting all the data down in a straight line (yes, the disk is round, but it is easier to think of it this way), one chunk after another.

As files are opened and closed, data from different files is laid down in the next available space so that, instead of all the data from one file being in a continuous block, it can be stored in blocks located in various spots around the disk. In this state, the data is *fragmented*. Although fragmentation is a normal part of the way disk drives function, excessive fragmentation can slow down the disk. Things slow down because the drive head must read data from all the blocks that make up a particular file. As those blocks become more numerous and are spread out around the disk, it takes longer and longer to read all the data for that file.

You use a process called *defragmentation* to correct this condition. You need a disk maintenance program to do this, such as Tech Tool Pro. The defragmentation process picks up all the data blocks for each particular file and writes them in a continuous block. It does this for every file on the disk. After the data is laid out nice and neat, the drive performs faster because it doesn't have to move as far to read and write the data for a particular file.

**NOTE**

To learn more about Tech Tool Pro, visit www.micromat.com.

37

Because a hard drive is made up of a round disk that spins at a constant speed, it takes longer to read and write data to various parts of the disk. Data near the center is read more quickly than data out near the rim. Data can be written to the disk in such a way that the access speed of the drive is *optimized*.

To do this, the data that is used constantly but not changed much—such as the system software and applications—are stored near the center of the disk. The documents and other data that are infrequently used are stored out toward the edge of the disk. This arrangement speeds up the disk because access to the most frequently used data is faster, and keeping the static data together means it will not become fragmented. Thus, the data is read and written in an optimized (for speed) fashion. You also need a disk maintenance tool to optimize a disk.

Usually, defragmentation and optimization are done at the same time using the same tool. The steps to perform these tasks depend on the particular software you use. Generally, this is not complicated and is a matter of choosing the drives you want to defragment and optimize and clicking Start.

Defragmentation and optimization are somewhat controversial topics. Many experts believe they do little to no good, while others believe you can gain some performance and reliability improvements by performing these tasks on your disks regularly. Personally, I think you can better spend your time by keeping your disks well-organized and using Disk Utility to check them every so often than worrying about squeezing a few microseconds of performance out of them. But you might want to obtain and use a disk maintenance application, such as TechTool Pro, if getting the best possible performance from your disks is important to you. These applications also provide additional troubleshooting tools that can be useful.

## Cleaning Up Your Drives

You can do a lot for the performance of your disks by simply keeping them cleaned up. The more data on your drive, the less room you have to store new files. If your disks get too full, their performance slows down significantly. More data means there is more information for your Mac to manage, and thus it has to work harder and use more resources. You can also run into all kinds of problems if you try to save files to disks that are full to the brim; how full this is depends on the size of the files with which you are working.

Learn and practice good work habits, such as deleting files you don't need, uninstalling software you don't use, and archiving files you are done with (such as on a DVD). Regularly removing files that you no longer need from your hard drives will go a long way toward keeping them performing well for you, not to mention maximizing the room you have to store files you do need.

**NOTE**

Many disk maintenance applications enable you to retrieve files you have deleted (an "undelete" or recover function). This is possible because during normal deletes (when you empty the Trash) the file is removed from the active system but might still exist on the disk in some form. The only way to permanently rid of a file so it can't be recovered is to write over the area in which that file was stored with other data. To do this, you need an application that writes zeros or other bogus data over the location where the file you are deleting is stored. Typically, disk maintenance and other tools enable you to "really" delete files that you don't want to be recovered. In Mac OS X , you can also do this by using the Finder's Secure Empty Trash command or by erasing a disk with Disk Utility.



# Maintaining Alternative Startup Volumes

One of the most important tasks you need to do reliably and quickly is to start up from an alternative startup volume. There are several situations in which you might need to do this. For example, if you find problems on your current startup volume, you will need to start up from another volume to repair the startup volume. If something happens to your startup volume so that your Mac can no longer use it, you need to use an alternative startup volume to keep your Mac running. An alternate startup volume can also be very helpful when you are troubleshooting problems.

Several possibilities exist for alternative startup volumes; you should maintain at least one, or preferably two, of the following options:

- **Your Mac OS X installation disc**—You can always use the disc that contains the Mac OS X installer as a startup volume. It contains the basic software you need to start up your Mac and accomplish a limited number of activities, such as re-installing the operating system. The downside to this is that any updates you have applied to your active system are not included in the version on the installation disc. If the version of Disk Utility on the installation disc is too far removed from the version of the OS installed on your Mac, it is possible (but not likely unless you are using a very old installation disc) that Disk Utility on the disc will be incompatible with the OS version installed on your startup disc. The biggest drawback to this option is that you can't really use your Mac while it is starts up with the Mac OS X installation disc. You can only install system software or use Disk Utility and the other tools that are available on the Installer's menu.
- **An alternative Mac OS X installation on a different volume**—You should install a backup installation of Mac OS X on a different volume from the one that you use for your primary system—if you can spare the disk space required to do so. Ideally, this alternative volume will also be located on a separate disk (not just a separate volume)

from your primary installation. For example, if you have an external FireWire hard drive, you can install Mac OS X on it so you can also use it as a startup volume.

> **TIP** If you choose to install a backup version of Mac OS X on an alternative startup volume, you should delete any applications in that Mac OS X installation that you won't need when you are starting up from that volume. This will reduce the storage space it consumes. You also should start up from that volume and run Software Update periodically to keep the alternative startup volume's OS software current. Plus, this will ensure that you can actually startup from that volume before you need to actually do so, such as when there is a problem with your primary startup volumes.

- **Third-party application discs**—Many third-party applications, such as disk maintenance, antivirus, and backup software, include discs that contain system software you can use to start up your Mac. These discs also enable you to run the application software with the idea that you will be able to correct a problem that has prevented you from starting up your system from the primary startup volume.

To start up your Mac from an alternative volume, restart the machine and hold down the Option key. After a few moments, each valid startup volume appears. Select the volume from which you want to start up and click the arrow pointing to that volume. The volume you selected will be used to start up your Mac. Depending on the type, such as a full installation of Mac OS X on a volume or the Mac OS X installation disc, you will be able to access various functionality from full Mac OS X capabilities (a full install on an alternative volume) or at least attempt to repair the startup volume itself (using the installation disc).

If your Mac is hung, meaning it won't respond to any commands, such as the Restart command, press and hold its Power button down until the machine shuts down. Press the Power button again to restart it and hold the Option key down so that you can select an alternate startup volume.

> **TIP** If you use a wireless keyboard and mouse, which I recommend that you do, keep wired versions handy. In some cases, you might not be able to use a wireless device to control system startup by pressing the Option key. In which case, you'll need to attach a wired keyboard and mouse to startup your machine from an alternate volume.

You can start up your Mac from a disc installed in it, such as the Mac OS X Installation disc, by holding down the C key while the machine is starting up.

A third approach is to use the Startup Disk pane of the System Preferences application to choose the volume you want to use to startup your Mac. Of course, your Mac has to be running to be able to do this.

## MAINTAINING YOUR APPLICATIONS

Along with the system software, you should also maintain the applications you use. It is good practice to regularly check for updates for the applications on which you rely. There are several ways to do this, including the following:

- **Software Update**—Mac OS X's Software Update function will also update any Apple software installed on your computer, such as the iLife applications.
- **Automatic update features**—Most modern applications include the capability to go online to check for updates, automatically or manually. For example, most Adobe applications can check for updates to keep you informed when new versions or patches are available. You should configure your applications to check for updates periodically, just as the Software Update application checks for updates to Mac OS X.
- **Company mailing lists**—Some publishers maintain a mailing list for each application. Updates are announced in the mailing list, and the link to get to the update is provided.
- **Company websites**—Software publishers announce updates to their applications on their websites. Typically, you can check for and download updates from the Support area of a publisher's website.
- **Mac news**—Many Mac news sites and mailing lists include information about updates to popular applications.
- **Version Tracker**—Most Mac applications are listed on www.versiontracker.com. You can regularly check this site to look for application updates and patches.

**NOTE**

As with the system software, it is sometimes wise to let a few days or a week pass after an update to an application is released before you download and install it in case problems are introduced by the update.

You should also organize your applications and ensure that you have all the registration and serial number information you need for each application. It is amazing how easy it is to lose this information; getting it from the publisher can be a time-consuming task (and if you have to relicense the software, it can be expensive). Consider making a list of each application along with its serial number or registration number and keeping that list with the original installation discs or the discs containing the installers and updaters you make for your applications. When you need to reinstall an application, this list will be a great timesaver.

**Downloading Applications**

If you obtain an application by downloading it rather than getting it on a disc, you should save the application installer so that you can reinstall it even if the publisher withdraws the installer for some reason (for example, sometimes the installer for one version is removed if a newer version is released). You can save hard drive space by burning these installers on a DVD or CD disc and storing that disc with your other application discs.

You should also maintain the installer for any updates or patches you download and install so you can return the application to its current condition if anything happens to the version you have installed on your hard drive.

## BUILDING AND MAINTAINING A MAC TOOLKIT

One of the best maintenance-related tasks you can do is to assemble and maintain a Mac toolkit. In times of trouble, this toolkit can enable you to get back to work quickly. Not having to find your tools in times of trouble also reduces the stress you experience. Following are some fundamental items you should keep in your toolkit:

- **Your system configuration**—When you need help or are considering adding something to your system, having a detailed understanding of your system is very important. Use the System Profiler application (in the Applications/Utilities folder) to generate a report on your system. Print that report and keep it handy (in case you can't generate it when you need it).

⇨ For more information about Apple System Profiler, **see** "Using System Profiler to Create a System Profile," **p. 954**.

- **Up-to-date backups**—Your toolkit should include everything you need to restore as much of your system as possible. This includes all your data, applications, and so on.
- **A disk maintenance application**—You need one of these applications to solve disk problems you might encounter. Examples are Disk Utility (included with Mac OS X) or Tech Tool Pro.

**CAUTION**

When selecting a disk maintenance application, make sure you get one that is written for the specific version of Mac OS X that you are using. Using one designed for an older version of the OS can be harmful to your Mac and its data.

- **An antivirus application**—You'll need this to protect your machine from infection and in the event that your system becomes infected.
- **Your Mac OS X installation disc**—Sometimes, this is the only thing that will get your Mac started again.
- **Your original application installers on CD or DVD (even if you downloaded the installer originally), serial or registration numbers, and updates**—You should maintain the current versions of all your applications by maintaining the discs on which they came. You should also create CDs or DVDs containing updates to those applications along with any applications you download from the Internet. Finally, be sure you have a list of the serial or registration numbers for your applications so you can restore them if needed.

**TIP**

Consider devising some secure way to record passwords, usernames, serial numbers, and other critical data so you don't have to rely on memory to retrieve such information when you need it. Although keeping such information in hard copy is usually not advised, some people find it safer to develop and use some sort of code for this information and then have a hard copy of the encoded information handy.

# Mac OS X to the Max: Going Further with Disk Utility

Disk Utility is a very powerful and useful application. Covering all its functionality is beyond the scope of this chapter, but you will find it covered again in several other chapters for a variety of purposes. Following are some hints about other tasks for which you can use it:

- **Create disk images**—You can create disk images from files, folders, or even drives and volumes. Just like other disk images you work with, you can easily put your disk images on CD, use them to quickly re-create a set of data in multiple locations, and so on. The commands you use to create and work with disk images are on the File and Images menus.
- **Burn CDs and DVDs**—Disk Utility enables you to burn CDs or DVDs from disk images. You can also use it to create multisession discs so that you can burn to a disc more than once. First, create a disk image for the files you want to put on disc. Then use the Burn button or the Burn command on the Images menu to access the application's burn functionality.
- **Work with disk images**—As you mount disk images in Disk Utility, it tracks those images in the lower part of the left pane so you can work with them again by selecting them. This makes accessing these images simple.

**TIP**

> To remove a disk image from Disk Utility, drag its icon out of the application window or select it and press Delete.

- **Mount, unmount, or eject volumes**—You can use the mount, unmount, and eject buttons and commands to perform those actions for disks, discs, volumes, and disk images.
- **Restore any folder, volume, or disk**—You can create a disk image from any source (such as a folder or volume) and use the application's command to restore that information on a disk. For example, if you want to replicate a set of software on multiple machines, you can create a disk image and use the Restore function on each machine to re-create that data. After you have created the disk image, use the Restore tab to restore it.
- **Access a log file**—As you perform actions with it, Disk Utility maintains a complete log of the actions it performs (see Figure 37.8). To access this log, select Window, Show Log press ⌘-L, or click the Log button in the toolbar. The Log opens and you can view its contents. This provides a complete history of your disk maintenance tasks.

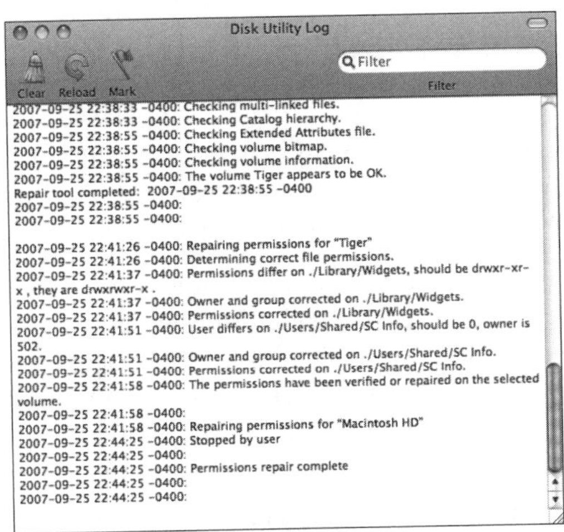


**Figure 37.8**
Disk Utility's log shows you all the actions it has performed along with the results of those actions.

- **Configure RAID disks**—Redundant array of independent disks (RAID) is a scheme whereby multiple disks can be linked to work together for performance and reliability reasons (for example, disks can be mirrored so the same information is always stored on more than one disk in case of disk failure). You can use the RAID tab in Disk Utility to configure RAID services on a machine.

CHAPTER 38

# Backing Up a Mac

## In this chapter

# BACKING UP YOUR SYSTEM

If you use a computer, at some point, your system will crash, a disk will fail, you'll delete files that you really didn't intend to, or some other problem will occur and you will lose data you would rather not lose—maybe not today or tomorrow, but it *is* the inevitable nightmare. Think of the information you have on your Mac at this very moment that would be difficult—if not impossible—to reconstruct if your computer bombed and destroyed it. This data might be a report for work, a school project, your tax information, a complex spreadsheet, or even the great American novel on which you have been working. To be more specific, think about all the content you've purchased from the iTunes Store. If you lose that content and don't have it backed up, you'll need to pay for the content again. Even worse, imagine that you have 5,000 photos in your iPhoto Library covering the last 5 years. Now imagine that the disk on which these images are stored dies. Losing all those pictures forever is not a pretty picture, is it? Without a backup, there's simply no way to recover that kind of data, and your photos are gone forever.

Whatever the information, rest assured that some day, somewhere, somehow you will suddenly lose it. When that happens, you will want to be able to restore all the information on your Mac so you can quickly re-create your data. Backing up is the means by which you ensure that you can always preserve most of your work, no matter what happens to your Mac.

---

**Backups: Insurance for Your Data**

You need a good backup for more than just catastrophic failures of your hardware. I'll bet that you have accidentally deleted a file right before you needed it again. If you have a backup, you can quickly recover a document you accidentally delete. Or perhaps you edited a document and discovered that all your changes were actually worse than the original. You can use your backup to bring the file back to the way it was. And if your Mac is ever stolen or destroyed, your backup will enable you to recover from potential disaster.

---

Although backing up your data is strongly recommended by computer authors, experts, and support personnel, it is a task that many Mac users never do for a variety of reasons. Some people don't back up data because they think their systems are infallible and won't crash. Still others are confused about how to make a backup of their system, or they lack the hardware and software necessary to maintain good backups. And then there are always those who simply don't believe that protecting their data is enough of a priority to waste their time on it. Trust me, the first time you lose something you can't re-create, such as important photos, you'll wish you'd backed up your Mac. Why wait for the inevitable? Better to get backed up now so you don't have to face losing your data.

There are four steps to creating and implementing a solid backup system. These steps are the following:

- **Define a strategy**—You need to define your own backup strategy; your strategy should define the types of data you will back up and how often you will back up your data. These choices will guide you as you decide on the type of hardware and software you use.

- **Obtain and learn to use backup hardware**—You need some kind of hardware on which to store the backed-up data. Many types of hardware can be used, including hard drives, tape drives, DVD-R drives, and CD-RW drives.
- **Obtain and learn to use backup software**—Ideally, you should use some sort of software to automate the backup process. The easier you make it on yourself, the more likely it is that your backup system will work reliably.
- **Maintain your backup system**—Like all other systems, you need to maintain your backup system and ensure that your data is safe.

## Defining a Backup Strategy

One of the first things you need to decide is what data on your machine will be backed up.

The three general categories of data you should consider backing up are



- **Documents, photos, movies, music, and other important data you create or purchase**—These items are, after all, the reason you use a Mac in the first place. You will want to back up all your own data because it doesn't exist anywhere other than on your computer. If you lose important data, it might be impossible to re-create. Even if you are able to re-create it, you will be wasting a lot of valuable time redoing what you have already done. Other data, such as your photos, simply can never be re-created. Still other data, such as music you have purchased from the iTunes Store, will cost money to replace.
- **System files**—You should have installation discs that contain your Mac OS software, so you usually don't risk losing the Mac OS software itself. What you do risk losing is any customization you have done, updates you have installed, and so on. If you have adjusted any settings or added any third-party software, all the settings you have changed will be lost in the event of a major failure.

  Additionally, don't forget about all the configuration information you have on your machine. For example, if you lose your system for some reason, you might lose all the configuration you have done to make your Mac connect to the Internet. You might also lose all the serial numbers of your software, which you will have to re-enter if you need to reinstall it.
- **Applications and other third-party software**—As with the OS software, you probably have discs containing much of your third-party software. What you lose if you have a failure without a backup is the customization of those applications. Plus, you will have to reinstall that software—not an easy task if you have a lot of applications installed on your Mac. In any case, it can be very time-consuming to reinstall your applications. Don't forget about all the updates you have applied to these applications. If you lose your system, you'll have to do that all again, too.

**NOTE**

> These days, you probably obtain a lot of your software by downloading it from the Web. If you lose the installers or patches you download without having a backup, you will have to download them again–assuming they are still available, of course. Sometimes, the version you want to use has been replaced by a newer version you don't want to use or pay for. (In my opinion, software companies should make older versions of applications available to download to handle cases where you need to reinstall it, but not all of them do.) And, occasionally, software moves from shareware to commercial, in which case it becomes unavailable to download again without paying for it. You should keep backup copies of any software installers or updates you download so you can reinstall that software if you need to–whether it is still available from the original source or not.



In conjunction with the kind of files you will back up, several types of backups you can make include

- **Full backup**—In a full backup, you back up every file on your system. The advantage of doing full backups is that restoring your entire system, as well as just particular parts of it, is possible.
- **Selected files only**—Using this scheme, you select particular files to back up; usually these are your important data (documents, photos, music, and so on) and some of your customization files (for example, preferences files). The advantage of this scheme is that you can make a backup quickly while protecting the most important files on your computer.
- **Incremental backup**—This scheme combines the first two techniques in that all files are backed up the first time, but after that, only files that have changed are backed up until the next full backup. This scheme protects all your files but avoids the time and space requirements of doing a full backup each time.

What you decide about the type of data you will back up and how you will back it up should determine the type of backup system you develop and use. For example, if you decide that you don't mind having to reinstall applications and reconfigure settings or you mainly use small document files, you might be able to simply copy your document files onto a DVD or other removable media drive. If you have a great deal of data to protect, you will need to implement a more sophisticated system.

If you can assemble the hardware and software required to do incremental backups, you should use this approach. It is the only one that is practical for frequent backups and also protects all your data.

Ideally, you want your backup system to work without any supervision or intervention by you. This is called an *unattended* backup because you don't even need to be there for the system to work. You can set the system to automatically back up during times when you are not working on your Mac. This is not only convenient, but it also means that because you don't have to *do* anything, you can't forget or be too lazy to keep your backups up-to-date.

Lastly, you'll need two basic types of backups. One is "short term," meaning that you back up daily (or more frequently) to protect your data over the short term, which can mean from a few days to a month; you keep these backups easily accessible from your Mac so that you can quickly restore files. The other is "long term," meaning that you capture snapshots of your data at specific points in time and store those in safe locations, preferably away from your Mac in case something really bad happens to it. You're likely to use different hardware and software for each of these types.

# Choosing Backup Hardware

The hardware you use for your backup system is important because having hardware that doesn't match the types of backups you want to make will doom your backup plan to failure. For example, if you go with a dedicated backup hard drive or tape drive, you will be able to do frequent, incremental backups. The easier and better you make your backup system, the less work you have to do with it, and the more likely it is that you will *do* the backups. Table 38.1 lists the major types of backup hardware and summarizes their advantages and disadvantages.



**Table 38.1 Backup Hardware**

| Drive Type | Backup Capability | Advantages | Disadvantages |
|---|---|---|---|
| Writable CD | Can handle large amounts of data for full and incremental backups. | Drive has multiple uses (mastering CDs for distribution, creating audio CDs, and so on). | Capacity of individual discs is limited so unattended backups are not always possible. |
| | | Data is easy to share and recover because all computers have CD-ROM drives. | Relatively slow. |
| | | Provides nearly permanent storage; this is a good choice for archival purposes. | |
| | | Backups can be stored away from your Mac. | |
| | | CD-RW drives are standard on all modern Macs. | |
| | | Media is very inexpensive. | |

*continues*

**TABLE 38.1 CONTINUED**

| Drive Type | Backup Capability | Advantages | Disadvantages |
|---|---|---|---|
| Writable DVD | Can store large amounts of data on each disc. | Even though this format stores more data than a writable CD, you can't store enough to make full, unattended backups in most cases. Media can be mounted in most Macs.<br>Data is easy to share because most computers can read DVD discs.<br>Provides nearly permanent storage; this is a good choice for archival purposes.<br>Backups can be stored away from your Mac.<br>Apple's SuperDrive is standard on most Mac models.<br>DVD-R and DVD-RW drives can be used for many purposes (burning DVD movie discs, restoring disks, and so on). | DVD-R media is not reusable.<br>Media is relatively expensive for backup use.<br>Relatively slow. |
| Hard drive | Depending on size, can handle large amounts of data for unattended full and incremental backups. | Very fast.<br>Data is easily accessible.<br>Drive can be mounted and used for other tasks.<br>Backup drive is likely to be used for other purposes and thus might not be available for backing up.<br>More difficult to store backups away from your Mac. | Relatively high cost per MB of data storage.<br>Data is harder to share.<br>Unlikely to have sufficient storage space to make full backups unless you purchase a dedicated backup drive. |

| Drive Type | Backup Capability | Advantages | Disadvantages |
|---|---|---|---|
| | | Backup is subject to power surges and other outside causes of failure.<br>Capacity can't be expanded. | |
| Tape | Can handle large amounts of data for full and incremental backups. | Large storage capability is perfect for unattended backups.<br>Media is inexpensive (for example, a Travan 20GB tape costs as little as $34).<br>Backups can be stored away from your Mac. Difficult to share with others because a tape drive of the same format must be available. | Tape can't be mounted; a tape drive is a single-purpose device.<br>Tapes can be affected by magnetic forces and degrade over time.<br>Relatively slow.<br>Drives can be expensive. |

Table 38.1 lists many options, but for most Mac users, I recommend that you use two primary backup devices: an external hard drive and a writable DVD or CD drive (use CDs only if your Mac doesn't have a DVD-RW drive). Although tape drives are very useful for large backups, you aren't like to use one unless you are responsible for backing up a network and you can afford to purchase and maintain a good quality drive. You'll also need specific software to support a tape drive; not all backup software supports them (notably Apple's Backup application and Mac OS X's Time Machine).

The following sections provides an overview of these hardware options.

## Using External Hard Drives for Backups

Using a hard drive for backup provides the fastest performance, and you can usually get a drive large enough to store all the files needed to back up your primary drives (see Figure 38.1). Using Mac OS X's Time Machine, you can easily configure automated backups so your data is constantly protected with no intervention on your part. And installing and using an external hard drive is literally a matter of connecting power to the drive, connecting the cable, and turning on the drive. That is all there is to it. Using an external USB or FireWire hard drive is just that simple. For performance and ease of use, a hard drive can't be beat.

And, if you're going to use Mac OS X's Time Machine, which you should, you'll need to have a hard drive that is dedicated to this purpose. That's because Time Machine can't back up to other kinds of media, such as a tape or disc.

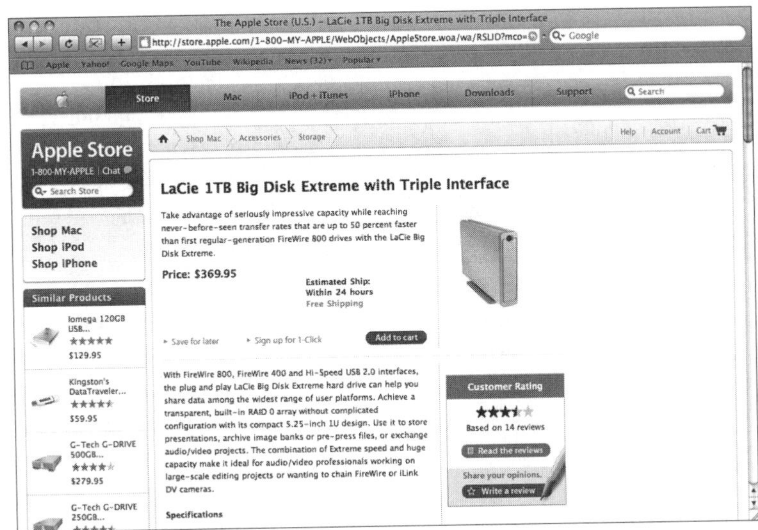


**Figure 38.1**
This LaCie 1TB hard drive provides excellent performance and lots of room.



There are several significant disadvantages to using a hard drive to back up data. One is that you can't archive data on a hard drive; a hard drive can be used only for your current backups. Another is that you can't store the backup in an alternative location, nor can you create multiple backups unless you want to invest in multiple drives and rotate among them, which you probably aren't likely to do. Still another disadvantage is that the capacity of the drive is fixed; the only way to expand the capacity of your system is to add more drives. And, hard drives can fail due to the same reasons that a drive in your Mac can fail, in which case your backup becomes worthless.

Another downside is that you will be tempted to use the backup drive for additional purposes when your other drives get full. You might delete the backup "temporarily" while you work on another project. Guess when something will go wrong and you will need your backup?

Still, even with these drawbacks you should obtain and use an external hard drive for your short term backups.

When buying an external hard drive for backup purposes, there are two primary considerations.

The first is size; you need to buy the largest drive that you can afford. At the least, you need a drive that is large enough to hold *all* the data you're going to back up. If you do full system backups, you need a drive at least as large as the amount of space you're using on your startup drive. If you're going to back up only your data, such as your Home folder, you might get by with a smaller drive. Even so, over time, your backups get larger and larger so you really can't have a backup drive that is too big.

**TIP**

> To see how large a folder that you need to back up is, select it and choose File, Get Info. In the general section, you see the size of the folder next to the text "Size." Doubling or tripling this number will give you a good idea of how large a hard drive you need to back up that folder.

The second consideration is the kind of interface the drive uses. All modern Macs support USB 2 and FireWire, which are both plenty fast for backing up data. However, if your Mac supports FireWire 800, consider a drive that supports that as well because FireWire 800 is faster than the other two options.

When purchasing a drive for backing up, size is always more important than performance so if you have to choose between a larger drive that supports FireWire or a smaller one that supports FireWire 800, go with the larger drive.

⇨ To learn how to choose, install, and use external hard drives, **see** "Choosing, Installing, and Using a Hard Drive," **p. 835**.



## Using Tape Drives for Backups

When it comes to the sole function of backing up, a tape drive is hard to beat. Because the capacity of each tape is so large, a single tape drive can handle unattended backups for all but medium or large networks (in which a more sophisticated system is required). And the media for a tape drive is relatively cheap, can be reused, and is portable (so it's easy to store the tapes away from your Mac).

One downside of a tape drive is that it serves a sole purpose, which is backing up (of course, this is also a positive because you won't ever be tempted to use it for something else). But the largest downside of a tape drive for most Mac users is that they are more difficult to use than a hard drive or writable disc; you'll need to obtain specific backup software for the kind of tape drive you use. For example, you can't use a tape drive with Mac OS X's Time Machine.

Tape drives are available in a number format and interface options (see Figure 38.2). And each is supported by specific software so you need to make sure there is software you want to use that is compatible with a tape drive. Many drives come with backup software.

Because of the complexity and expense involved with tape drives, most Mac users aren't likely to have one as part of their system so additional detail about them is beyond the scope of this book.

## Using Writable DVD Drives for Backups

Writable DVD discs provide a large amount of storage space on each disc. A single layer disc can store up to 4.7GB per disc whereas a dual layer disc can store 8.5GB per disc (your drive must be capable of burning to dual layer discs to be able to use these). And you can use as many discs as you need for a specific backup so there is no size limit for backing up to DVD. Another plus is that many Macs include a SuperDrive so you don't need to spend money on additional hardware to back up your data. Because you back up to removable media, you can store your backups at alternative locations to protect them from situations such as theft or fire. Further, DVD is an excellent option for archiving data and should provide good long-term storage for the data you don't need to work on any longer.

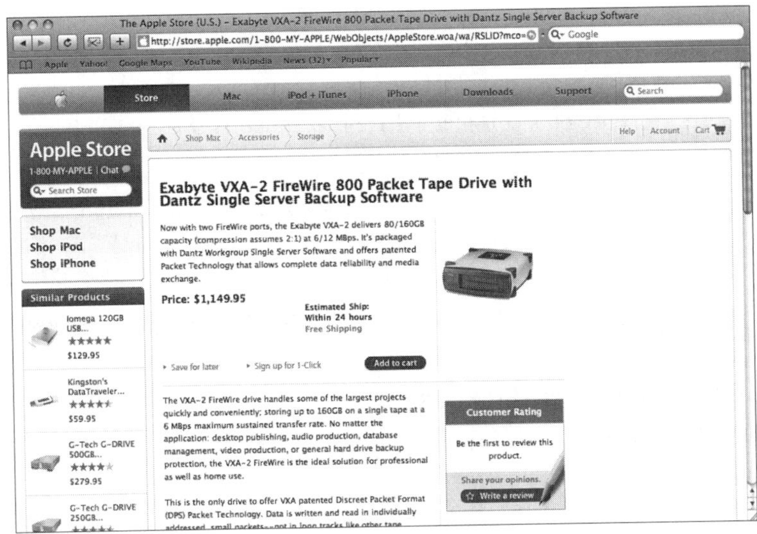


**Figure 38.2**
Tape drives are excellent for backing up, but they are also relatively expensive compared to other options.



Of course, a writable DVD drive is also very useful for other purposes, such as for creating DVDs with iDVD.

Although DVDs can store lots of data per disc, you probably won't have the patience or want to go to the expense of doing your short term backups on DVD, except for very specific purposes, such as doing incremental backups of iTunes content you purchase. For example, if you have 100GB of data in your Home folder and use single layer discs for backing up, you'll need to burn about 22 discs to back up all of it. Subsequent, incremental backups will require a few discs at a time, but backing up large amounts of data on a regular basis quickly becomes impractical.

However, you should back up your critical data, such as photos, documents, iTunes content, and so on, to DVD periodically and store the discs in a safe location as a long term backup.

There are a number of ways to back up to DVD, including backup software such as Apple's Backup or directly from the Finder. However, DVD is not supported by Mac OS X's Time Machine feature.

## Using Writable CD Drives for Backups

This option takes a back seat to the other options, in my opinion. The upsides to using writable CDs for backing up are that all modern Macs have a writable CD drive and the discs are very inexpensive. And you can store the discs away from your Mac for sakekeeping.

However, even with these benefits, writable CD drives are not an optimal choice f
up. This is primarily because a CD holds only about 700MB of data. Although th
nificant amount for everyday documents, it is inadequate for many types of data.
ple, when you consider iMovie projects, a single disc usually can't hold even one project.

You should use a writable CD as a backup only if you don't have a writable DVD or hard drive available to you or when you are backing up small amounts of data, such as individual purchases from the iTunes Store.

## Choosing Backup Software

You should use software to automate the backup process. Although you can simply drag files you want to back up from the Finder onto a hard drive, DVD, or CD, you aren't very likely to do this consistently enough to have reliable backups and it is likely that you will miss files (which of course, will be the ones you need to recover later). Plus, you'd have to spend a lot of time to do this, and who has time for that kind of stuff?



Good backup software enables you to define which files will be backed up and how often the backups will be updated. It also enables you to restore your data when the time comes. The software should enable you to automate the process as well.

The software you choose needs to be compatible with the backup hardware you use. For example, if you use a tape drive, the software you choose needs to be compatible with the specific model of drive you have. If you have a hard drive available for backing up, you can use Mac OS X's Time Machine.

Ideally, you'll want to be able to back up to more than one kind of media, such as a hard drive for your short term backups and DVD for long term backups. Most backup applications support this, with the notable exception of Time Machine that can only back up to a hard drive.

### Using Time Machine

Mac OS X includes its own backup software called Time Machine. Using Time Machine, you can automate the backup process and easily restore any data included in your backups. Time Machine is designed to work with Apple's iLife and other Mac OS X applications so it's ideal to back up your iTunes and iPhoto content along with your documents. It's also smart enough to not waste backup space on files such as temporary Internet files. You can also determine how frequently backups are made and how long they are kept. The primary limitation of Time Machine is that you can only use it to back up to a hard drive so you must have a dedicated hard drive to be able to use it. If you do use Time Machine, you really shouldn't rely on it as your only backup solution. You should back up so that you can store long term backups away from your Mac, but for everyday, short term backups, it's ideal.

⇨ To learn how to use Time Machine, **see** "Backing Up Your Mac with Time Machine," **p. 907**.

## USING APPLE'S BACKUP

Apple's Backup application is capable backup software that enables you to back up to various kinds of media, including hard drives, DVD, and CD. You can also automate backups and you can even configure different backups, such as a long term backup and a short term backup, and Backup will manage each of them for you so you can rely on it as your primary backup solution. The good news is that if you are a .Mac member, you get Backup at no cost. If you aren't, you'll need to get a different application because Backup is not available to nonmembers.

⇨ To learn how to use Backup, **see** "Backing Up Your Mac with Apple's Backup," **p. 914**.

**TIP**

> A very good backup system is to use Time Machine for your short term backups because it is so easy to configure and restore files when you need them, and Backup for long term backups because you can back up to DVD.

38

## USING CHRONOSYNC

Econ Technologies ChronoSync is complete backup software. It's named as it is because it designed to enable you to synchronize a source with a target, which is exactly what you want to do to back up your system (see Figure 38.3). ChronoSync has just about any feature you want in a backup application including the ability to specify any set of files to be included in a backup, automate the backup process, and save different sets of backup configurations so you can use them all at the same time, such as one short term backup to hard drive and one longer term backup to DVD. If you don't have access to Apple's Backup application, I recommend that you check out ChronoSync.

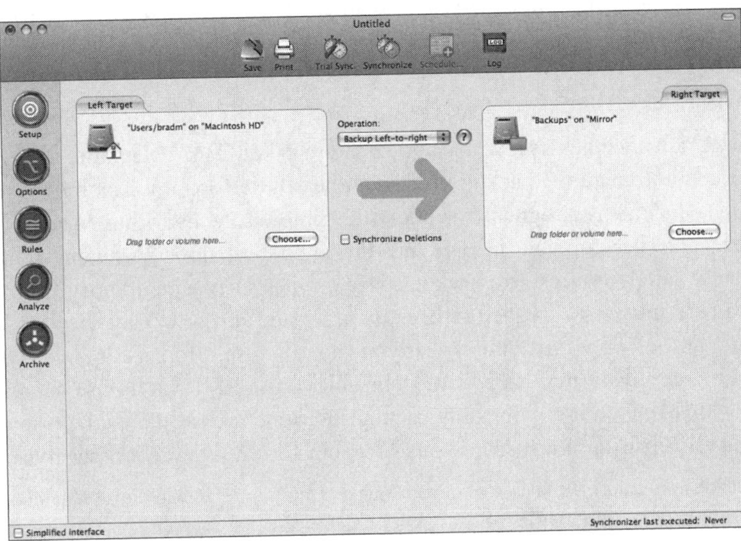


**Figure 38.3**
If you want to have the maximum amount of control over your backup system, ChronoSync might the software for you.

**NOTE**

You can learn more about ChronoSync and download a trial version from www.econtechnologies.com.

**TIP**

You can use ChronoSync across a network also to back up multiple Macs.

### Using Retrospect

Another option for Mac backup software is EMC Retrospect for Macintosh. Retrospect for Macintosh Desktop is targeted to individual users with relatively simple backup needs, whereas Retrospect for Macintosh can back up a networked workgroup, such as are in most home or small businesses.

Like ChronoSync, you can define multiple backups with different files collections that you are backed up to various kinds of media. You can also fully automate the backup process and handle just about any backup-related task. If you want to back up to a tape drive, Retrospect is likely to be your best choice.



**NOTE**

To learn about EMC Retrospect, check out www.emcinsignia.com. You can learn more about Retrospect and download a trial version.

### Using Non-backup Applications to Back Up Data

If you don't use backup software, shame on you, but you still want to protect critical data, many applications feature backup functionality. For example, you can back up your iTunes content from within iTunes by choosing File, Back Up to Disc. As you can probably guess, you back up to DVD or CD. This function enables you to back up your entire library or just the content you've purchased from the iTunes Store. You can also choose to perform incremental backups so that you copy the entire Library once and from then on you only back up new or changed files.

Other applications, such as iPhoto, also enable you to "back up" to disc by burning DVDs or CDs of their data. Although I don't recommend that you rely on this kind of functionality for your backups, it can be handy for long term backup of critical data. For example, you might use Time Machine for everyday backups, and use application backup functions to create long term backups on disc.

## Backing Up Your Mac with Time Machine

Time Machine is somewhat limited as backup software because you can only have one backup active at a time and you can back up only to a hard drive. However, it is very easy to use, which is important for backup software, and you can automate the backup process.

Time Machine also makes restoring files very easy. For some applications, such as Address Book, you can even restore individual data records.

To use Time Machine, you'll need to dedicate a hard drive for your backups. Once you're drive is configured and available on your Mac, you can configure Time Machine to back up your important data. If you need to restore files, you use the Time Machine application.

## Configuring Time Machine

To configure Time Machine, perform the following steps:

1. Open the System Preferences application and click Time Machine. The Time Machine pane opens (see Figure 38.4).



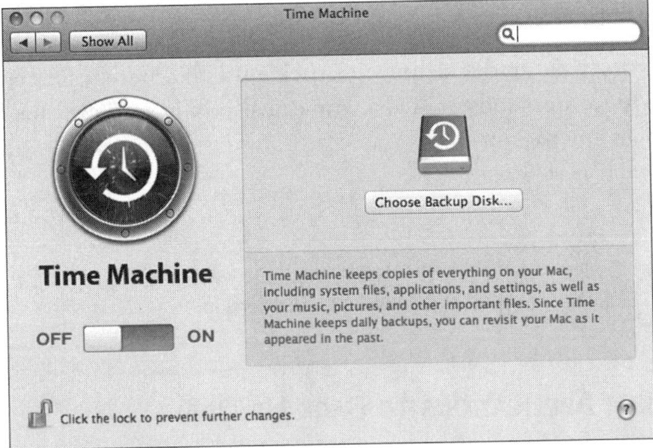


**Figure 38.4**
With Time Machine, backing up isn't hard to do.

2. You can either slide the switch to turn Time Machine on, or click the Choose Backup Disk button.
3. In the resulting sheet, select the drive where your backup files will be stored.
4. Click Use for Backup. You will return to the Time Machine pane where the top portion allows you to modify your settings. The bottom portion of the pane notes the frequency of the backups. Time Machine will create an hourly backup for the past 24 hours, daily backups for a month, and weekly backups, assuming your backup drive has enough storage space.
5. Click the Options button. Use the exclusion list to exclude files from the backup process. By default, the drive you are using to back up is excluded because it would make no sense to back up a drive onto itself.

   In an ideal world, you'd have such a large backup disk that you could back up all of your files indefinitely, but for most Mac users, that won't be the case. If it isn't true for you, you'll need to exclude files that don't really need to be in your short term backups. One candidate is your Applications folder, which tends to be pretty large.

Make sure any files you exclude from your short term backup are backed up in some way, such as on DVD or with the original installation discs.

To exclude files from the backup, click the Add button (+) and use the resulting sheet to move to and select the files you want to exclude. You can exclude entire volumes or choose specific folders to exclude the contents of those folders from the backup.

To include files in a backup again, select the folder on the exclusion list and click the Remove button (-). The folder you selected is removed from the exclusion list, which means it's included in the backup.

You can see how large the files that will be excluded from the backup are by looking just above the exclusion list toward the right side of the pane. The amount shown next to "Total Included" tells you how much room your backup is going to require.

You can decide if you would like to be warned when old backups are deleted by Time Machine. It is a good idea to have your longterm backup completed before Time Machine deletes any older backup files.

6. When you've excluded all the files you want to, click Done. The backup process will run at the next scheduled time (see Figure 38.5). The first time you run a backup, it will take a longer time because every file in the backup has to be copied to the backup drive. Subsequent runs will be faster because only changed files are copied.



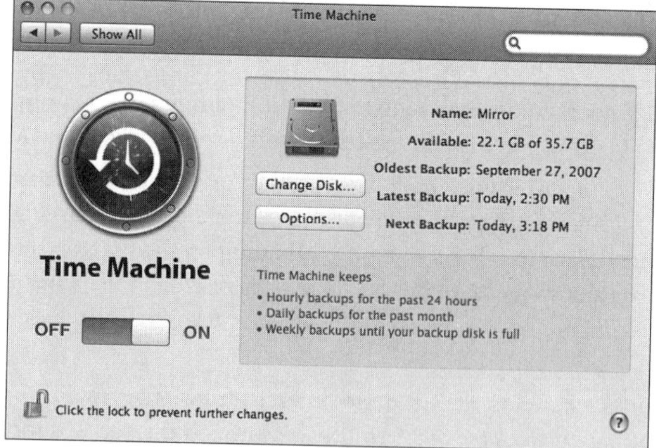


**Figure 38.5**
The Time Machine pane provides status information and the option to change the hard drive used for backup files.

**NOTE**

> If the data you selected to back up doesn't fit on the backup disk, Time Machine will abort the backup process and warn you about the situation. You'll need to exclude more data from the backup until it does fit. If the data you want to back up consumes a large part of the space available on the backup disk, you won't be able to maintain backups for very long so you should consider using a larger backup disk.

When the backup process is complete, the time and date when it was completed is shown in the status area at the top of the pane.

After you've configured Time Machine, it handles the backup process for you and keeps your backup fresh according to the parameters you set.

> **TIP**
>
> If you make significant changes to your data, such as downloading photos from a camera or making purchases from the iTunes Store, and the next backup time doesn't occur for a while, open the Time Machine pane and click the Back Up Now button to immediately add the new data to your backups. If you use the Automatically back up option, you can probably skip this because your data will be backed up relatively quickly.

## RESTORING FILES WITH TIME MACHINE



A backup system, like car insurance, is something you need to have in place but hope you never have to use. But, because losing data is inevitable (as I suppose car crashes are at some point), you're going to have to use your backup system to recover the data you've lost. Time Machine makes restoring files relatively easy, at least once you understand its "unique" interface (which you'll probably either find intuitive and amazing or odd and confusing).

There are two basic sources of data you can recover with Time Machine: files in the Finder or data within applications. Time Machine works very similarly for both kinds.

### RESTORING FILES FROM THE FINDER WITH TIME MACHINE

To restore files from your backup, perform the following steps:

1. Open the Finder window showing the location of the files you want to recover (this step is optional because you can navigate the Finder from within Time Machine).
2. Launch the Time Machine application (in the Applications folder or click its icon on the Dock). Time Machine fills the entire desktop on the primary monitor and makes all other displays dark (see Figure 38.6). Depending on the desktop resolution and window size of the folder in focus, that folder might be resized in the Time Machine window, but it will remain in focus. Along the bottom of the window, you see the Time Machine menu bar.

   The Time Machine interface is quite different from other applications. The general concept of how it works is that you browse through the backups for the item in focus until you get to the files you want to restore. Once you see the files or folder you want to restore, you select the version you want and click the Restore button located at the right end of the menu bar (this button becomes active only when you've selected something that can be restored).

   The first task is to locate the specific version of the files that you want to recover. You can do this by browsing with the browse arrows or using the backup bars along the right side of the screen to choose a specific backup (by date and time) from which you want to restore a file.

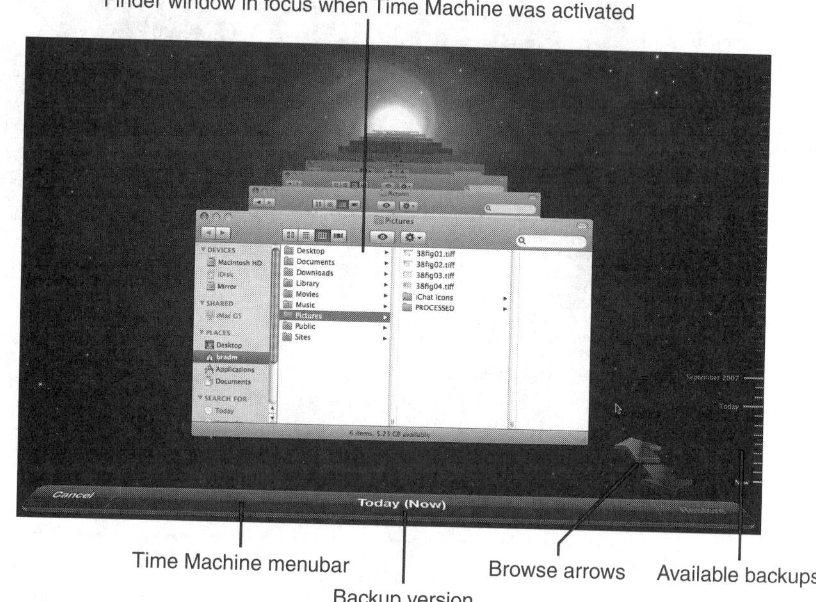


**Figure 38.6**
Time Machine takes a bit of getting used to, but once you do, you'll be able to quickly recover files and data.



3. Browse through the backups by clicking the backward-facing arrow to move to older versions of the backup or the forward-facing arrow to move to newer versions of the backup. Or, point to the Available backups bar along the right side of the screen and click a date and time to jump to that version of the backup. As you point to versions, the magnifying effect is applied to make it easier to see the specific version you are working with.

   The version of the backup that is currently in focus is shown in the center of the menu bar. When you are looking at the current files, this says "Today (Now)." When you are looking at a version of the backup, you see the date and time of the version in focus.
4. When you've reached the version of the backup from which you want to restore the file, move to the file's or folder's location in the Finder window (see Figure 38.7).

**TIP**

> To quit Time Machine without performing a restore, click the Cancel command.

5. Select the file or folder you want to restore and click the Restore command. The file or folder is restored to your desktop in the state it was in for the backup version you selected. Time Machine quits and you return to the Finder with the recovered files and folders available for your use.

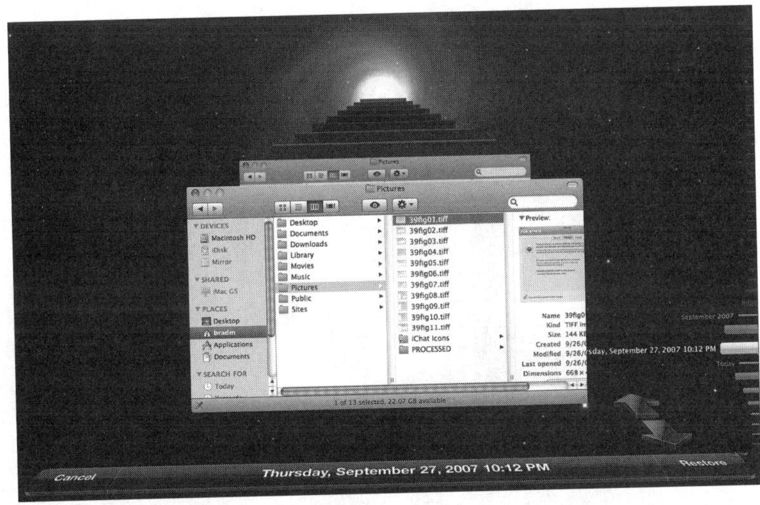


**Figure 38.7**
Time Machine enables you to move back in time to recover files and folders that have been lost.

**TIP**

> If you restore a file to a location that already has a file with that name, you will be prompted to select whether you want the restored file, the existing file, or both. Selecting both keep the existing file and save the restored file with "(original)" added to the name.

**TIP**

> Time Machine can recognize backups that were performed by another Mac using Time Machine. For instance, if an external hard drive was used to backup a Mac and you need to retrieve files from that backup, connect the hard drive to your Mac and Time Machine will automatically recognize that volume. You can then browse through the backup to restore files to your Mac.

### RESTORING DATA FROM WITHIN APPLICATIONS WITH TIME MACHINE

With certain applications, mostly Apple applications that manage data such as iPhoto, Address Book, and so on, you can also use Time Machine to restore data. For example, if you accidentally delete photos from iPhoto, you can use Time Machine to retrieve them from one of your backups.

To restore data from within an application, perform the following steps:

1. Make the application containing the data you want to restore active.
2. Launch Time Machine. The application appears and you see the application's window in the Time Machine space (see Figure 38.8).
3. Move back through the available backups until you see the data that you want to restore.
4. Select the data you want to restore and click Restore. The selected data will be added to the application. For example, if you select an address card, it is added to Address Book. If you select photos in iPhoto, they are added to your iPhoto Library.

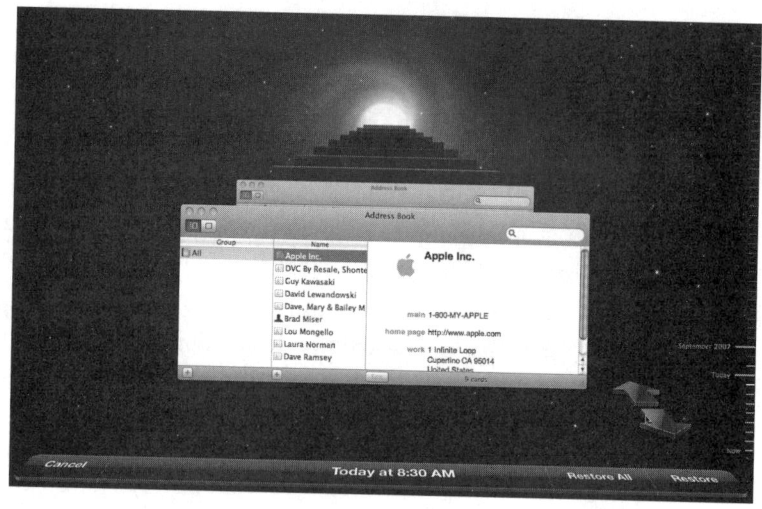


**Figure 38.8**
Time Machine allows you to recover data that you may have deleted within Apple's applications.



## Managing Your Time Machine Backups

Time Machine stores each backup on the selected backup disk. The backups are stored in a folder called "Backups.backupb". If you open that folder, you see a folder for the disk you are backing up. Open that folder and you see folders for each version of the backup that Time Machine is managing (see Figure 38.9). You can open these folders to access files that are stored within them; this means that you can try to manually recover files from these folders if Time Machine loses track of them for some reason.

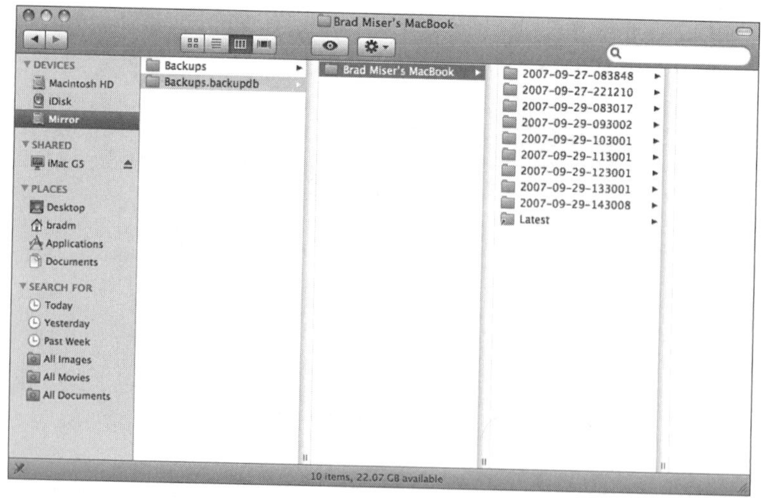


**Figure 38.9**
The various versions of your backups are stored in folders on your backup drive.

As time passes and the number of backups increases, the backup drive will become full. When that happens, Time Machine will start dropping versions of the backups, starting with the oldest first. It attempts to keep all backups for as long as indicated on the Time Machine pane, but if your drive doesn't have enough room, you'll be prompted to let Time Machine delete versions that it doesn't have room to store. If this happens frequently, you need to get a larger backup drive or reduce the size of the files included in the backups.

## Backing Up Your Mac with Apple's Backup

Time Machine is great for short term backups that you want to keep active. However, you should also create backups that are more permanently stored and that you can keep in a location away from your Mac. To do that, you need a different application.

If you have a .Mac account, you can download and use Apple's Backup application. This application provides good backup capabilities. In addition to being able to back up to CD or DVD, you can back up your files to your iDisk (which takes the idea of remote storage of your data to a new level). You can also automate your backups. The application is simple to use and is free to anyone who has a .Mac account.

38

### Obtaining and Installing Backup

To get a copy of Backup, move to the .Mac website and log in to your account. Move to the Member Central page and download the Backup application. Launch the installer and work through its steps to install Backup on your Mac.

### Configuring Backups with Backup

To configure a backup, perform the following steps:

1. Launch Backup, found in the Applications folder.
2. The first time you launch Backup you will be presented with the welcome sheet, which includes four different backup plans with descriptions of the plans to help you select the best fit for your needs (see Figure 38.10).

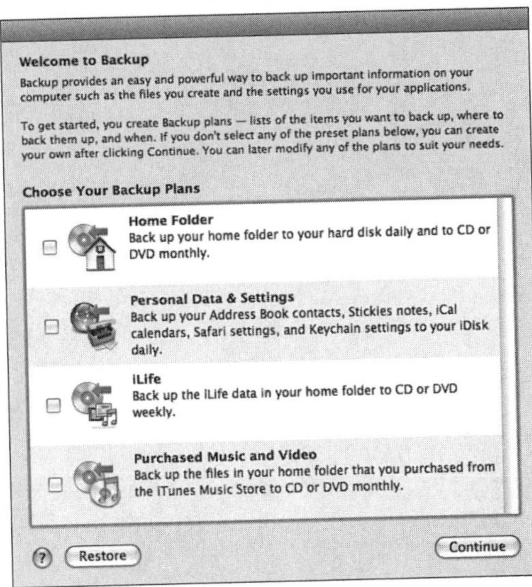


**Figure 38.10**
Backup provides a number of templates you can use to quickly create a backup configuration.

3. Select the plan you want to use and click Continue. The plan is created and the options that came from the template or that you selected are shown when you double-click the plan (see Figure 38.11). At the top of the plan window, you see three tabs. The Back Up tab enables you to configure the backup. The History tab shows you when the backup has run. You use the Restore tab to restore files from previous backups.

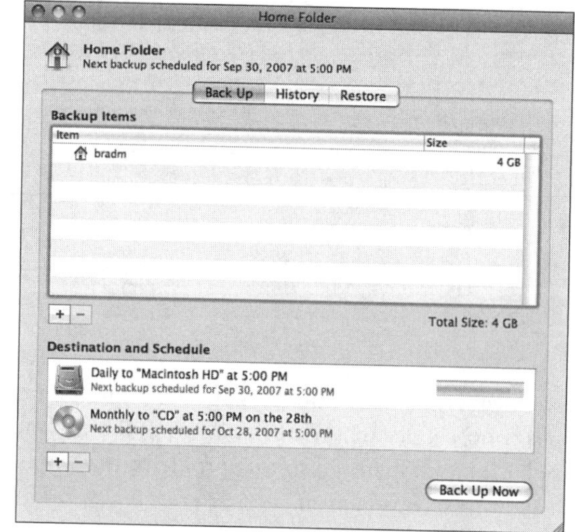


**Figure 38.11**
The plan window enables you to configure and use a backup plan.

The Back Up tab has two panes. The Backup Items pane shows the items that are included in the backup. The Destination and Schedule pane shows where the backups are stored and how often the plan backs up to each location.

4. To add folders or files to the backup, click the Add button (+) at the bottom of the Backup Items pane. Use the resulting sheet to move to and select folders or files you want to include. Anything marked with a green circle and check mark is included in the backup; if a folder is included, all its contents are included too. When you've selected all the content you want to add to the backup, click Done.
5. To remove items from the backup, select the items you want to remove and click the Remove button (-) at the bottom of the Backup Items pane.

> **TIP**
> You can also remove folders and files from the backup in the Add Item sheet by selecting them and checking the "Do not include this folder" or the "Do not include this file" radio buttons.

6. To change the location or schedule for the backup, double-click the location and schedule you want to change or to add a new location and schedule to the backup, click the Add button (+) at the bottom of the Destination and Schedule pane. The Choose a Destination and Schedule sheet appears (see Figure 38.12).

38

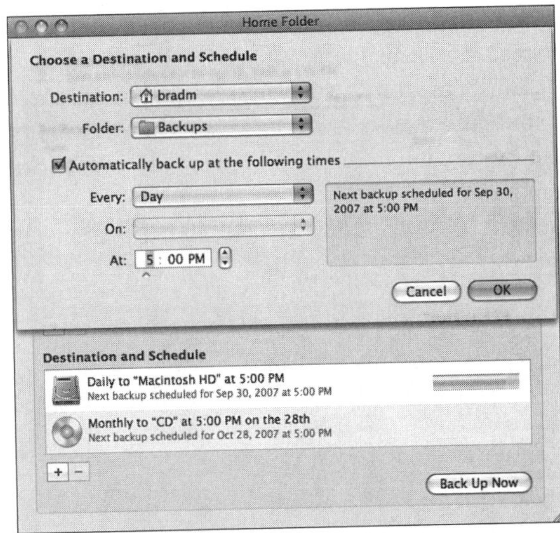


**Figure 38.12**
Use this sheet to choose a location and schedule for your backups.



7. Choose the volume on which you want the backup to be stored on the Destination pop-up menu. You should choose a destination different from the volume on which the information you are backing up is stored so that problems that wipe out what you are backing up don't also destroy your backup.
8. Choose the folder in which you want the backups stored on the Folder pop-up menu. Choose "Choose Location" and then move to and select the folder you want to store the backup in or use the New Folder button to create a new folder.
9. To enable automatic backups, check the "Automatically back up at the following times" check box, choose the frequency on the Every pop-up menu, choose the day the backup will be done (all options except Daily on the Every pop-up menu), and time for the backup. Click OK to save the changes.
10. Repeat step 9 to create as many locations and schedules for the backup that you need. For example, you might want a daily backup to hard drive and a monthly one to DVD.
11. If you want to run a backup immediately, select the location to which you want to backup and click Back Up Now. The configuration you selected runs and the backup is created.
12. Close the plan. You move to the Backup window in which you see all the backup plans you've created (see Figure 38.13).

**TIP**

> You can create as many backup plans as you need to protect your data. For example, you might want to have a backup that runs frequently (unfortunately, daily is as frequent as you can run backups in Backup) and stores important files on a hard drive while another stores all your files on disc and runs monthly.

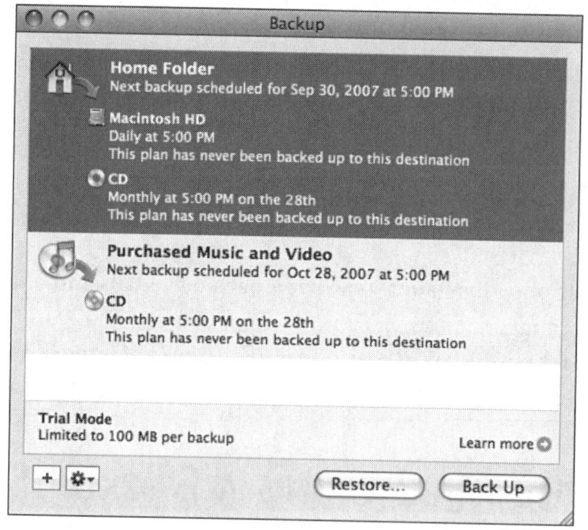


**Figure 38.13**
The Backup window shows all the backup plans you've configured.



## Backing Up with Backup

After you've configured backups, they run according to the schedules you've set. If a backup is stored on a CD or DVD, when it runs, you're prompted to insert the appropriate kind of disc.

You can manually run a backup by launching the Backup application, selecting the backup plan you want to run, and clicking Back Up. If the backup has more than one location, choose the location you want to run on the location sheet.

After the backup runs, the time and date of its last operation are shown under the plan in the Backup window. You can also open a plan and click the History tab to see when it has been run.

If a backup fails, it's marked with an exclamation point icon in the Backup window. Click it and you move to the plan's History tab where you see the backup that failed. Select it and click View Details to open a log file. Sometimes the information you see is useful, sometimes it isn't. The most common cause of a failure is not having enough room on the selected destination.

**TIP**

To remove a backup plan, select it in the Backup window, open the Action pop-up menu and choose Remove. The backup is removed from the Backup application and is no longer used. If the backup is stored on a hard drive, look in the location in which it was stored and delete any files associated with the backup if you no longer need them.

## Restoring Files with Backup

To restore files from a Backup backup, do the following:

1. Launch Backup.
2. Select the plan from which you want to restore files and click Restore. The Restore tab for the selected backup appears.

3. Select what you want to restore on the Previous Backups list.
4. If you want to restore the files to a location other than the one from which they were copied, check the "Restore to an alternate location" check box and choose the location to which you want the files restored.
5. Click Restore Selection. The selected files are restored from the backup to their previous location or to the location you selected.

If your Backup installation is lost (such as when a hard drive fails and you have to use a new one) such that you no longer see the plans in Backup, you can still restore files. Re-install Backup and launch it. Choose Plan, Restore from Backup. Then move to and select the backup from which you want to restore files.



## Mac OS X to the Max: Using a Backup System

I can't emphasize enough how important it is to maintain good backups for your data. Here are a few tips to keep in mind:

- **Develop your own strategy based on the hardware and software you have or can afford to purchase**—At the least, make sure your critical files, such as photos, iTunes content, and financial data, are protected with good backups.
- **Make sure that backing up is easy**—If you have to do a lot of work to back up or if it takes a lot of your time, you won't keep up-to-date backups. Ideally, you want to be able to do unattended backups; Time Machine and an external hard drive make it so.
- **Be consistent**—Whatever strategy you decide on, keep up with it. Old, out-of-date backups are not much better than no backups.
- **Always refresh your backups before you install any new software or make major changes to your system**—This will enable you to recover data if the changes you make to your system cause problems.
- **Be sure to test your backups regularly**—Pretend that you've lost some very important files and try to restore them to ensure that everything is working properly. If you don't, you might get a nasty surprise when you need to restore some data "for real." You need to know your backup system has a problem before you need to use it. If you don't regularly test your backups, you are asking for trouble.
- **Maintain your equipment**—Almost all equipment needs some kind of maintenance now and again, so follow the manufacturer's guidelines to keep your system in top condition. Hard drives can fail, so check the ones you use for backing up periodically to make sure they are still working (see previous bullet!).
- **Maintain more than one set of backups**—Create multiple copies of your backups in case something happens to one set.

- **Keep a set of backups offsite**—Keep a copy of your backups in a different location than your Mac is in. This will save you in the event of a catastrophic event such as fire or theft. This is especially important for data you can't replace, such as photos and financial data.

NOTE

> Archiving is slightly different from backing up. Backing up is done mostly for the "active" data on your Mac, whereas archiving is done with data you don't really need to work with anymore. Fortunately, you can use your backup system to archive data as well. For archiving smaller documents, a CD drive is a good choice because the media is very cheap and relatively permanent. For larger amounts of data, a DVD is a good way to archive. When you archive, you should use a solution that won't degrade over time, which is why optical media such as CD and DVD are good choices. After you've archived data and checked to make sure that you can recover that data from the archive, you can delete the files from your working drive to free up some space.

38

**Restoring a Disk or Files**

Using Disk Utility, you can create and save a disk image of a folder, volume, or disk. (A disk image is a file type that can be mounted and used just like a physical volume, such as a hard drive.) You can then use Disk Utility's Restore feature to restore the entire volume or specific files that are part of that disk image. This is, in effect, backing up specific parts of your system. You can choose folders, volumes, or an entire disk. To do this, you first use Disk Utility to create a disk image of the volume or folder you want to back up.

When you need to restore a file, you select the disk image you created and use the Restore tab to restore it or specific files it contains.

Although this approach has the benefit of using tools always available under Mac OS X, it does have several major drawbacks. This first is that you have to manually update the disk images you save. The second is that you still have to have the space to store those images (of course, you don't want to store them on the same volume as the files they include). However, you can use this technique to back up files if you don't have a better solution or to archive them.

# CHAPTER 39

# Securing a Mac

## In this chapter

# Securing Your Mac

An important part of maintaining your Mac in good condition is protecting it from various kinds of attacks that will be attempted assuming that you connect your Mac to the Internet. It is very likely that your Mac contains sensitive data that you don't want other people to be able to access, such as financial records. Last, but not least, if you share your Mac with other people, you might want to protect them by limiting how the Mac can be used. Learning to secure your Mac to an appropriate level is where this chapter comes in.

# Securing Your Mac with User Accounts

You should create user accounts for everyone who uses your Mac. In addition to the features user accounts provide, such as a website and well-organized file storage, user accounts prevent unauthorized users from changing the system configuration of your machine. And you can use parental controls to define how users are able to use your Mac.

⇨ To learn how to create and configure user accounts, **see** Chapter 11, "Configuring and Working with User Accounts," **p. 231**.

⇨ To learn how to limit how your Mac is used by others, **see** "Using Parental Controls to Safeguard a Mac," **p. 941**.



# Securing Your Mac with Privileges

For those who access your Mac over a network and for those who share your machine, you can control the access to specific items by setting privileges for those items. You can control access in several levels of privilege from not being able to even see the item to being able to read and write to it.

⇨ To learn how to configure privileges, **see** "Understanding and Setting Permissions," **p. 385**.

# Securing Your Mac with the Security Pane

The Security pane of the System Preferences application enables you to protect your Mac in three ways. One is by using the FileVault feature that encrypts all the files in your Home folder; these files can't be used unless you input your login password or the master password for your Mac. The second way is through the configuration and use of Mac OS X's firewall. The third way is by configuring various security settings for your Mac.

## Securing Your Mac with FileVault

Mac OS X's FileVault feature encrypts all the files in your Home folder with 128-bit encryption. Such files can't be opened unless one of two passwords is entered. One password is the one you use to log in to your account. The other is a master password you set for your Mac; with this password, you can decrypt any encrypted files on your Mac, regardless of the user account with which those files are associated.

Once configured, FileVault works in the background and you won't notice it doing its job unless you try to open encrypted files without knowing one of the two passwords. In that case, you'll definitely notice it working.

**CAUTION**

According to Apple, FileVault can interfere with backups because it makes your Home folder appear as a single file to the backup system. This can make the individual files impossible to restore. When using FileVault, be sure you test your backup system to ensure that you can still recover files if you need to.

The following steps demonstrate how to configure FileVault:

1. Open the System Preferences application, click the Security icon, and then click the FileVault tab (see Figure 39.1).

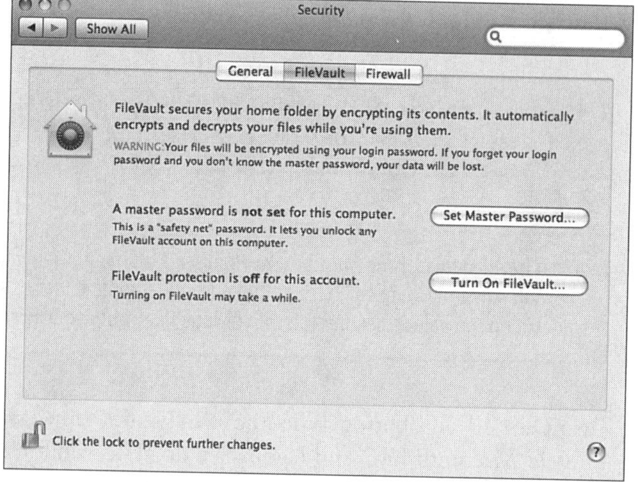


**Figure 39.1**
Use the FileVault feature if you want to encrypt the files in your Home folder so they can't be used without a valid password.

2. Click the Set Master Password button. The master password sheet opens. Generally, you should use this feature if there is some chance that any user of your Mac will forget his password; the master password enables you to decrypt encrypted files for all users. You don't really have a choice because you must create a master password before you can activate FileVault.
3. Enter the master password in the Master Password field and enter it again in the Verify field.

**TIP**

Click the key button next to the Master Password box to open the Password Assistant. You can use this tool to generate passwords based on specific criteria, such as type and length. When you have configured a password, it is placed in the box for you. You then have to type it in the Verify box.

39

4. Enter a hint for the master password in the Hint field.
5. Click OK to set the master password.

**NOTE**

> To use FileVault, a user account must have a password. If you didn't configure a password for your user account, or for any other user account, you need to do so before you can activate FileVault.

6. Click the Turn On FileVault button. If there currently isn't a password for the user account, the warning sheet appears and you can use the Password sheet to create one. If the user account already has a password, the service starts up and you are prompted to enter your password.
7. Enter your user account's login password and click OK. You see a warning sheet that explains what you are doing and that activating this service can take a while (you can't log out of your account until the service has been turned on).

**TIP**

> If you also want Secure Erase (which overwrites deleted data so that it can't be recovered as easily), check the "Use secure erase" check box.

**NOTE**

> If you have enabled Time Machine, you will see a warning when you go to turn on FileVault. Time Machine will back up the encrypted home folder as a single file, meaning you will not be able to see or restore individual files from your Home folder.

8. Click the Turn On FileVault button. The FileVault window appears; you can't do anything else on your Mac until FileVault has started up. This window shows you the progress of the encryption process. If you have a lot of data in your Home folder, this process can take quite some time. When the process is complete, you see the Login window.

**NOTE**

> If you want this feature to be active for multiple user accounts, you must log in under each account and turn on FileVault.

9. Log back in to your account. You shouldn't notice any difference, but all your Home folder files are encrypted and won't be accessible unless a valid encryption password has been entered.

**CAUTION**

> FileVault applies only to each user account in which it is activated, and it works only on the files in each user's Home folder. Files stored outside the Home folders for which it is activated are not protected.

When you log in to your account (or any other user whose account is protected by FileVault), the files in your Home folder are decrypted automatically so you won't need to do anything else to access them. The value of FileVault is for those times when you aren't logged in to your account and someone else has access to your machine. For example, suppose someone steals your MacBook. Although she can't access your user account without your login password, she could connect the machine to a FireWire drive with Mac OS X installed and start up from that volume. Because the files on your MacBook startup volume are not protected anymore (the OS on the computer to which the MacBook is connected is running the show), they are accessible. If FileVault is not on, these files are not encrypted and can be used, but if FileVault is on, these files are encrypted and are useless.

You can turn off FileVault again by clicking the Turn Off FileVault button and entering your login password.

If another user on your Mac turns on FileVault and subsequently forgets her password, you can use your Mac's master password to decrypt the files in that user's Home folder. You can provide the master password to the other user so he can decrypt his files. Then, change the master password to make sure only the "right" people have it.



**NOTE**

> When a user account is protected by FileVault, its Home folder icon looks like a cross between the normal Home folder icon and a safe.

## SECURING YOUR MAC WITH MAC OS X'S FIREWALL

If your Mac is connected to the Internet, it's critical that it be protected from Internet attacks. There are number of ways to accomplish this. Ideally, you'll connect your Mac to the Internet via a network hub that protects it from attack. However, if you connect your Mac directly to the Internet or just want a double layer of protection, you can configure Mac OS X's built-in software firewall to guard your Mac from attack.

⇨ To learn more about protecting your Mac from Internet attacks, **see** "Defending Your Mac Against Internet Hackers," **p. 940**.

You can enable your Mac's firewall by doing the following:

1. Open the System Preferences application.
2. Click the Security icon to open the Security pane.
3. Click the Firewall tab (see Figure 39.2).

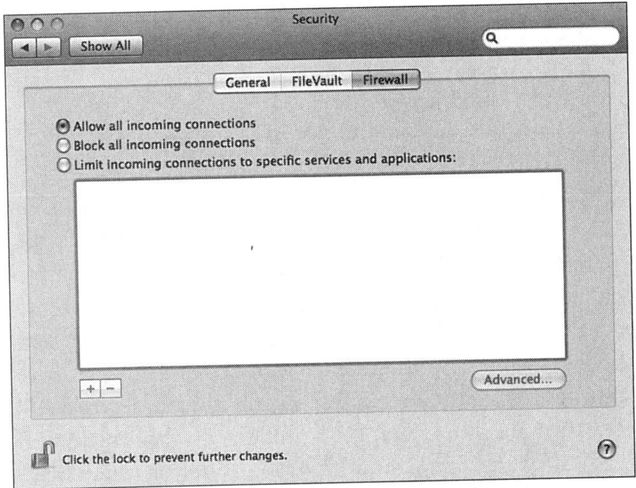


**Figure 39.2**
Use the Firewall tab to enable your Mac's built-in firewall.

39

4. To turn the firewall off so that it doesn't block any connections to your Mac, click the "Allow all incoming connections" radio button. You should use this setting only if your Mac is not connected to the Internet in any way or it is protected by a network hub or router. If you leave this radio button selected, skip the rest of these steps.
5. To prevent all connections to your Mac, click the "Block all incoming connections" radio button. With this active, you won't be able to accept any connections between your Mac and network services so you should use this only when you have a Mac that you want to completely isolate. If you block all connections, skip the rest of these steps.
6. To block some connections, click the "Limit incoming connections to specific services and applications" radio button.
7. If you have services that you have turned on in the Sharing pane of the System Preferences application, those services will appear in the list (see Figure 39.3).

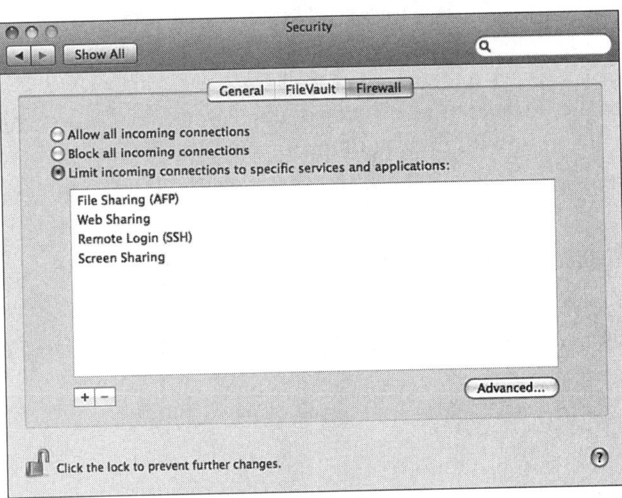


**Figure 39.3**
When you activate the Mac's firewall, you limit incoming traffic to specific services you are sharing or applications you are running.

8. Click the Advanced button to configure two other important settings. You can turn on firewall logging if you need to see what traffic is being blocked and allowed. This can be very helpful in troubleshooting connection issues that you think might be related to the firewall. Most importantly, you can turn on stealth mode for the firewall. If someone was trying to attack your computer, they would not get a response from your Mac.
9. After you configure the settings for all the services you are sharing, you can also add Applications.
10. Click the Add button (+).
11. Move to and select applications for which you want to configure the firewall and then click Add. The applications you add appear on the list; a pop-up menu appears for each application. You only need to do this for applications that communicate across the network or the Internet.
12. Use each application's pop-up menu to determine the connections that are allowed. You can choose "Block all connections" to prevent an application from any communication across the network. Select "Allow incoming connections" so that your application can communicate with other network resources.

Only the connections for the services and applications you allow are permitted to access your Mac. All others will be denied. This prevents most of the kinds of attacks you are likely to experience.



**NOTE**

> If you have trouble with some network or Internet services, make sure you check the firewall configuration to ensure it isn't configured to prevent the kind of service you are trying to use.

## Securing Your Mac with Security Settings

Several other security settings are available on the General tab of the Security pane (see Figure 39.4).

These features are described in the following list:

- **Require password to wake this computer from sleep or screen saver**—If you enable this feature, a user account's login password is required to stop the screen saver or wake up the Mac from sleep. This setting affects only the account currently active; if you want this to be required for each user account, you need to log in to each one and set it for that account.
- **Disable automatic login**—Check this box and the automatic login feature is turned off. This means that someone will have to log in into your Mac manually to be able to use it.
- **Require password to unlock each System Preference pane**—When you check this box, a login password must be entered to make any changes using the System Preferences application.

**Figure 39.4**
Check out these general security settings to protect your Mac.

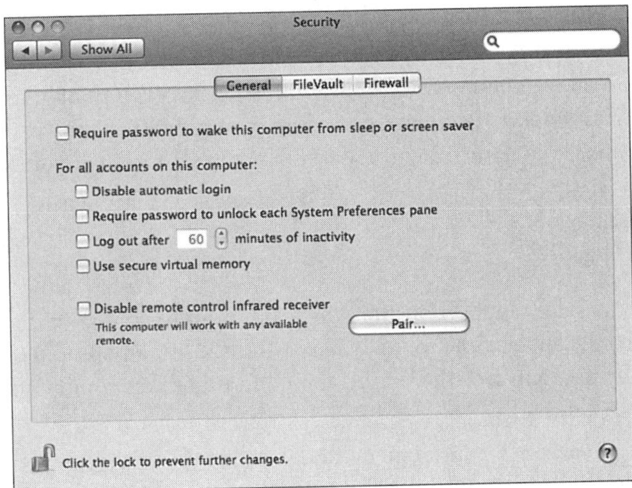


- **Log out after _ minutes of activity**—This feature logs out the current user account after the specified amount of inactivity has occurred. To use it, check the box and set the amount of time using the box. When the amount of inactive time passes, the current user is logged out automatically.
- **Use secure virtual memory**—When this feature is active, data written to disk when virtual memory is required is stored securely.
- **Disable remote control infrared receiver**—If you check this box, your Mac's infrared receiver is disabled so that it can't be accessed via infrared (such as through its remote control). You can also use the Pair button to associate a specific remote control with your Mac.

39

## Securing Your Mac by Removing Trash Securely

Normally, when you delete files, they are deleted from the system but the data for those files might or might not be overwritten by other data. If not, files you've deleted can sometimes be recovered by software restoration tools. If you want the files you delete to be overwritten with random, system-generated data so they can't be recovered, use the Secure Empty Trash command on the Finder's File menu instead of the normal Empty Trash command. This causes the files you delete to be overwritten so they can't be recovered. It takes a bit longer to empty the trash because your Mac has to overwrite the space on which the files you deleted are stored.

## Securing Your Mac with Keychains

For security and other reasons (such as making online shopping more convenient), you need usernames and passwords to access network resources, whether those resources are on a local network or the Internet. After using even a few of these, you will have a large collection of usernames and passwords. Remembering these can be a challenge. Fortunately, your Mac lets you store all your usernames and passwords along with other information you might want to secure in a keychain. You can then apply your keychain to whatever resource you want to use and the appropriate information is provided so you can access what you need. All you need to remember is the password that unlocks your keychain. By default, this is the same as your login password so that your keychain is used automatically. After you have added a password to your keychain, you can access the related resources without entering your keychain's password (because it is entered when you log in).

**NOTE**

> Safari can also remember usernames and passwords for sites you visit so you don't have to enter this information each time you log in. This saves a lot of time and keystrokes (assuming that you can even remember all your usernames and passwords, of course). What actually happens is that Safari creates an item within the Passwords category in your keychain in which all your web usernames and passwords are stored. When you return to a page for which you have had Safari remember your login information, it uses the data stored in the keychain to input the appropriate data for you.

⇨ For more information about Safari and keychains, **see** Chapter 22, "Surfing the Web with Safari," **p. 511**.



You can configure other keychains so that you can gain automatic access to secured resources during each working session. To secure those resources again, you can lock your keychain, which means the password must be entered for that keychain to use it again.

Before you can use a keychain, one has to be created. A keychain is created automatically for each user account you create. However, you can create additional keychains for specific purposes if you need to.

To use a keychain, it must be unlocked. To unlock a keychain, you enter its password when you are prompted to do so. When you log in to your user account, the default keychain for that account is unlocked automatically.

**NOTE**

> You can store information that you want to secure using notes. For example, if you want to store your credit card information so it can't be accessed unless you are logged in to your user account, you can add it to your keychain. When you need that information, you can open the secured note containing your credit card information in your keychain.

Many types of resources can be added to your keychain to enable you to access them, including the following:

- **AirPort network password**—When you add an AirPort network password to your keychain, you can join the network by selecting it via the AirPort controls. The network's password are added to your keychain automatically.

- **Application password**—Some applications require passwords to perform specific tasks. One notable example is the iTunes Store function. When you have your iTunes Store password added to your keychain, you can purchase songs with a single click of the mouse button (which can be a dangerous thing!).
- **AppleShare password**—Any passwords you use to access network volumes can also be added to your keychain.
- **Internet password**—When you need to enter passwords for Internet services, such as email accounts, adding them to your keychain makes accessing those services much more convenient because you never have to enter the passwords manually.
- **.Mac password**—When you enter your .Mac password in the .Mac pane of the System Preferences application, it is added to your keychain so you can work with your iDisk from the desktop without having to log in to your .Mac account each time.
- **Secure note**—These enable you to store information securely.
- **Internet and web form password**—When you access your account on secure websites, you can add your usernames and passwords to your keychain. When you visit those sites again (via Safari), you can log in just by clicking the Login button because your username and password are entered automatically.



## Viewing and Configuring Your Keychains and Keychain Items

You access your keychains through the Keychain Access application by doing the following:

1. Open the Keychain Access application (Applications/Utilities folder). When the application opens, two panes appear (see Figure 39.5). In the left pane is a list of categories for all the keychains that are installed under your user account. These categories include All Items, which contains all keychain items you can access; Passwords, which contains passwords for network, application, and Internet resources; and so on. Select a category and the keychain items it contains appear in the right pane of the window. You see information related to each keychain item, such as its name, its kind, the date it was last modified, when it expires, and the keychain in which it is stored.

**TIP**

> The Passwords category contains several subcategories. To view them, expand that category by clicking its expansion triangle.

2. To view all the keychains your user account can access, click the Show Keychains button at the bottom of the Keychain Access window (see Figure 39.6). The Keychains pane appears at the top of the left side of the window.
3. To get summary information about a keychain item, select it. A summary of the item appears at the top of the window, including the kind of item it is, the user account with which it is associated, where the location to which it relates is, and the modification date.

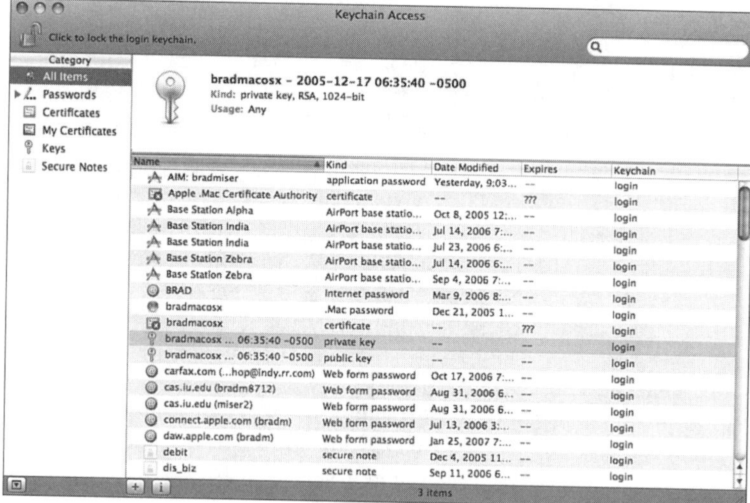


**Figure 39.5**
Over time, your keychain will start to have quite a few keys installed on it.

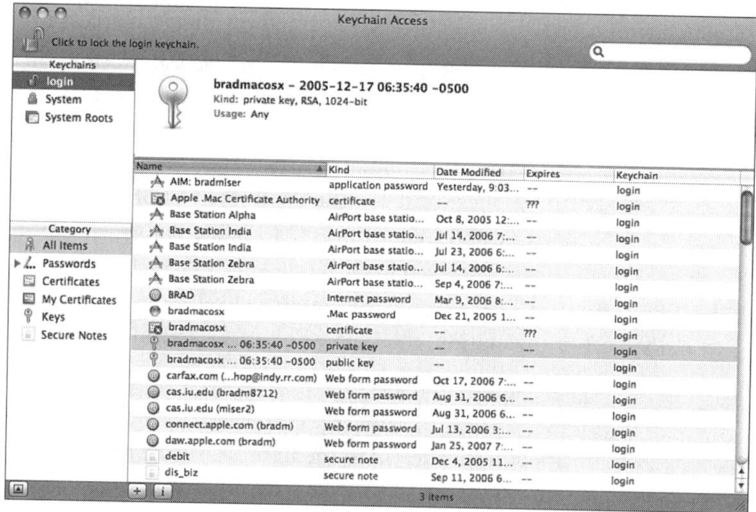


**Figure 39.6**
Here, you can see that this user has several keychains available; only the Login keychain is currently unlocked.

4. With the item still selected, click the Information button (the *i* located at the bottom of the Keychain Access window). The Information window appears. This window has two tabs: Attributes and Access Control (see Figure 39.7). The Attributes tab presents various information about the item, such as its name, its kind, the account, the location of the resource with which it is associated, comments you have entered, and the password (which is hidden when you first view an item). The Access Control tab enables you to configure how the item is used.

5. To see the item's password, check the "Show password" check box. You are then prompted to confirm the keychain's password (you'll learn more about this in the next section).

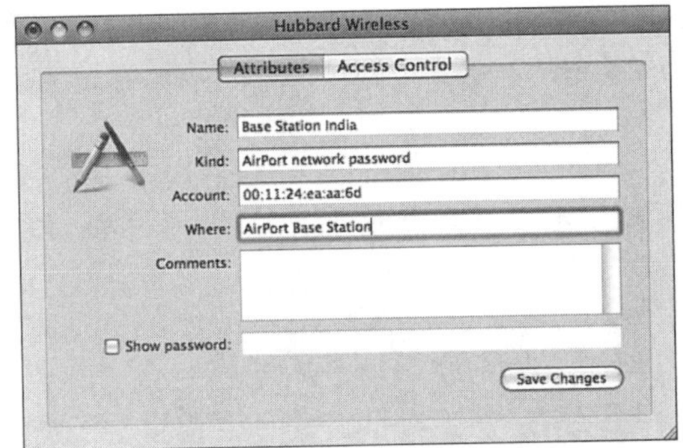


**Figure 39.7**
The Information window provides detailed information about a keychain item.

39

6. Confirm the password by entering it at the prompt and choosing to allow access to the item (the options you see are explained in the next section). When you return to the Attributes tab, you will see the item's password.
7. Click the Access Control tab. At the bottom of the tab, you see a list of the applications that have access to the keychain item. Use the access controls in the pane to control which applications can access this item and how they can access it.
8. To allow access to the item by all applications, check the "Allow all applications to access this item" radio button. You see a warning that access to the item is not restricted. This means that all applications are able to use the item. With this option, you can't configure the other options because they don't apply. If you want to configure access for specific applications, continue with the rest of these steps.
9. To allow access by specific applications but require confirmation, click the "Confirm before allowing access" radio button, and check the "Ask for Keychain password" check box if you want to be prompted for your keychain's password before access is allowed (if you don't select this option, the item will be accessed automatically).
10. To enable an application not currently on the list to access the keychain item, click the Add button (+) and select the application to which you want to provide access.
11. To remove an application's access to the item, select the application and click Remove (-).
12. Click Save Changes to save the changes to the keychain item.

## Adding Items to a Keychain

You can add items to a keychain in several ways, including the following:

- When you access a resource that can provide access to a keychain, such as a file server, look for the "Add to Keychain" check box. When you check this, an item for that resource is added to your keychain. This is the most common and easiest way to add items to a keychain.

**NOTE**

> Sometimes you have to click the Options button to be able to add an item to your keychain. For example, when you mount a network volume, click Options to reveal the "Add Password to Keychain" check box.

- Drag a network server onto the Keychain Access window.
- Drag the Internet Resource Locator file for a web page onto the Keychain Access window.
- Manually create a keychain item.

**CAUTION**

> Not all applications support keychain access. If a particular application or resource doesn't support keychains, you won't be able to access that resource automatically. However, you can still use Keychain Access to store such an item's username and password for you, thus enabling you to recall that information easily. This also stores it more securely than writing it down on a piece of paper.

To manually add a password item to your keychain, perform the following steps:

1. Open Keychain Access (Applications/Utilities).
2. View the keychains installed for your user account and select the keychain to which you want to add the item (your default keychain, which is the login keychain unless you have changed it, is selected automatically).
3. Select File, New Password Item or press ⌘-N to see the New Password Item sheet.
4. Enter the name of the item in the Keychain Item Name box. If you are adding an Internet resource, such as a web page, enter its URL.
5. Enter the account name or username for the item in the Account Name box. This is the name of the user account with which the keychain item is associated.
6. Enter the password for the item in the Password box. If you want to see the password as you type it, check the Show Typing check box. This helps you confirm you are entering the correct password. Otherwise, you see only bullets as you type. You see an indication of the strength of the password you create in the lower part of the sheet.

**TIP**

> Click the Key button to open the Password Assistant to help you configure a password for the item.

7. Click Add to return to the keychain's window and see the new item you added. You will be able to access that item using your keychain. You can view and configure the new item using the steps in the previous section.

**TIP**

> You can set the default keychain for your user account by selecting the keychain you want to make the default one and choosing File, Make Keychain *keychainname* Default, where *keychainname* is the name of the keychain you have selected.

To add a secure note to a keychain, use the following steps:

1. Open Keychain Access.
2. Select the keychain to which you want to add the note (your default keychain is selected automatically).

**NOTE**

> If you select a keychain that is currently locked, you will have to unlock it before you can add items to it.

3. Select File, New Secure Note Item or press Shift-⌘-N. The New Secured Note sheet appears.
4. Enter the name of the note in the Keychain Item Name box.
5. Enter the information you want to store in the Note box. This a freeform text field so you can enter anything you want.
7. Click Add to return to the Keychain Access window where you see the new note you added.



To view a secure note, double-click it and click the "Show note" check box. You see the note in the window.

## Adding a Keychain

You might want to add keychains to your current account, which you can do using the following steps:

**NOTE**

> You might want to move a keychain between user accounts so you don't have to re-create the items it contains.

1. Open Keychain Access (Applications/Utilities).
2. To add a keychain, select File, New Keychain or press Option-⌘-N. You see the New Keychain dialog box.
3. Move to the location in which you want to save the keychain, name it, and click Create. (By default, keychains are stored in the Keychains folder in the Library folder in your Home folder. In most cases, you should store new keychains in this folder.) You are prompted to create the password for the keychain.

**TIP**

> An exception to where you keep your keychains might be when you want to enable others to import your new keychain into their accounts, in which case you should store it in a location accessible to others, such as your Public folder. For example, you might want to create a keychain with website items on it. You could provide this to other users who would then be able to access the items contained in the keychains you install.

4. Enter the password for the keychain in the Password and Verify fields; then click OK. The new keychain is added to the list of available keychains, and you can work with it just like those already on the list.

**TIP**

> Click the Key button to open the Password Assistant to use it to create a password for the keychain you are creating.

## USING KEYCHAINS

When you have a keychain configured for an account and it is unlocked, you can access the items it contains without entering your username or password. For example, when you open a server, it opens for you immediately.



**NOTE**

> By the way, this is how Mac OS X can access your .Mac account without you having to log in each time. When you create a .Mac account, it is added to the keychain for the Mac OS X user account related to it. Mac OS X can use this keychain to access the .Mac account without requiring that you log in manually.

To prevent a keychain from being accessed, lock it. Do so by opening the Keychain Access application, selecting the keychain, and selecting File, Lock Keychain *keychainname*, where *keychainname* is the name of the keychain. You can also do so by pressing ⌘-L or clicking the Lock button (the padlock) on the toolbar.

To unlock a keychain again, select it, click the Unlock button or press ⌘-L, enter the password for that keychain, and click OK.

When an application needs to access a keychain item and it is not configured to always allow access, you see the Confirm Access to Keychain dialog box that prompts you to enter a keychain's password and choose an access option. When prompted, you have the following three options:

- **Deny**—If you click this, access to the item is prevented.
- **Allow Once**—A single access to the item is allowed. The next time you attempt to access it, you see the prompt again.
- **Always Allow**—Access to the item is always allowed.

**NOTE**

> The first time you access keychain items after the OS has been updated, such as through the Software Update application, you see the Confirm Access to Keychain prompt, even for those items for which you have selected the "always allow access" option (such as the first time you check your email after upgrading the OS). This is normal behavior. Just select the Always Allow option to re-enable that behavior.

## GOING FURTHER WITH KEYCHAINS

Keychain Access is actually a fairly complex application that can do more than just what I have room to show you in this section. Following are some pointers in case you are interested in exploring on your own:

- Your keychains are stored in the Library/Keychains folder in your Home directory. You can add a keychain from one account to another account by exporting the keychain file (use the File, Export command) to a location that can be accessed by the second account. (For example, you can copy your keychain into the Public folder of your Home directory to enable other users to add that keychain to their own accounts.) To add a keychain to a user account, open Keychain Access under that account and use the File, Import command. This is useful if you want to use the same keychain from several accounts. You can't export all keychains, so you have to try one to see whether you can export it.
- Delete a keychain by selecting it and selecting File, Delete Keychain *keychainname*, where *keychainname* is the name of the keychain.
- If you select Edit, Change Settings for Keychain *keychainname*, where *keychainname* is the name of the keychain, you can set a keychain to lock after a specified period of time or lock when the Mac is asleep.
- You can synchronize keychains on different computers by using .Mac.
- If you select Edit, Change Password for Keychain *keychainname*, where *keychainname* is the name of the keychain, you can change a keychain's password.
- Choose Keychain Access, Preferences. On the General tab, check "Show Status in Menu Bar." This adds the Keychain Access menu to the Mac's menu bar. From this menu, you can lock or unlock keychains and access security preferences and the Keychain Access application.
- If you select Edit, Keychain List or press Option-⌘-L, you see the Configure Keychain sheet. You can use this to configure keychains for a user account or the system. For example, you can check the Shared check box to share a keychain between user accounts.
- If you select Keychain Access, Keychain First Aid or press Option-⌘-A, you see the Keychain First Aid dialog box. You can use this to verify keychains or repair a damaged keychain.
- In the keychain access prompt, you can click the Show Details button to expose the details of the keychain access being requested.

# Defending Your Mac from Internet Attacks

The Internet is a major source of threat to the health and well-being of your Macs and the network to which they are connected. You face two fundamental types of threats: viruses and hackers. Although viruses receive more media attention, defending against viruses is easier than defending against attacks from hackers. However, with some relatively simple activity, you can protect yourself from both threats.

# Defending Your Mac from Virus Attacks

No matter what level of computer user you are, because of the extensive media hype about viruses, you are likely to be keenly aware of them. Although many viruses are relatively harmless, some viruses can do damage to your machine. Part of practicing smart computing is understanding viruses and taking appropriate steps to protect your machine from them.

**CAUTION**

Under previous versions of the Mac OS, there were many fewer viruses on the Mac platform than for Windows or other operating systems. And, as of the release of Mac OS X, version 10.5, this is still the case. However, because Mac OS X is based on Unix, Unix viruses can be a threat to machines running Mac OS X. Until this threat is more fully understood, Mac OS X users would do well to pay additional attention to virus threats.



## Understanding the Types of Viruses

Although there are many types of individual viruses, there are two major groups of viruses of which you need to be aware:

- **Application viruses**—These viruses are applications that do *something* to your computer. What they do might be as harmless as displaying a silly message or as harmful as corrupting particular files on your hard drive.
- **Macro viruses**—A macro virus can be created in and launched by any application that supports macros (such as the Microsoft Office applications). When you open a file that has been infected by a macro virus, that virus (the macro) runs and performs its dirty deed.

Covering the multitude of viruses that are out there is beyond the scope of this book and, besides, there is no real need to become an expert on the viruses that exist. It is more important to understand how to protect yourself from these viruses and be able to recover from an infection should one occur.

## Preventing Virus Infection

I hate to use this cliché, but when it comes to viruses, an ounce of prevention is indeed worth a pound of cure. The main way to avoid viruses is to avoid files that are likely to have viruses in them. Following are some practices to help you "stay clean":

- Find and use a good antivirus software program; keep the virus definitions for that application up-to-date.
- Be wary when you download files from any source, particularly email. Even if an email is apparently from someone you know, that doesn't mean the attachments it contains are safe. Some users will unknowingly transmit infected files to you (especially beginning users). Some viruses can use an email application to replicate themselves. Before you open any attachment, be sure it makes sense given who the sender appears to be.
- When you do download files, download them from reputable sites, such as magazine sites or directly from a software publisher's site. These sites scan files for viruses before making them available so your chances of getting an infected file are lower. Remember the expression, "Consider the source."
- After you download a file, run your antivirus software on it to ensure that it isn't infected. Most programs let you designate the folder into which you download files and automatically check files in this folder.

## IDENTIFYING VIRUS INFECTION



Even with good preventive measures, your Mac might occasionally become infected. Hopefully, you will find out you have been infected by being notified by your antivirus software—that means it is doing its job. But if you suddenly notice that your computer is acting peculiarly, you might have become infected. What does *acting peculiarly* mean? Viruses can have many different effects on your computer; some of the more common effects are the following:

- **Weird messages, dialog boxes, or other unexpected interface elements**—Sometimes viruses make themselves known by presenting something odd onscreen. So, if you suddenly see a strange dialog box, you might have stumbled across a virus (for example, one of the Word macro viruses causes a happy face to appear in Word's menu bar). They can also cause menu items to disappear or be changed in some way.
- **Loss in speed**—Viruses often make your computer work more slowly.
- **Disappearing files**—Some viruses cause files to be deleted or hidden.
- **Errors**—Many viruses cause various errors on your computer and prevent applications from working properly. If you haven't changed anything on your machine for a while and you suddenly start experiencing errors, you should check your computer for a possible infection.

**NOTE**

> The first time an application opens, Mac OS X presents a dialog box to you informing you about this. If you recognize the application because you are trying to open it, allow it to open and move along. If you don't recognize the application, it could be a virus. Deny it permission to open until you check it out to make sure it's something you want to use. It's easy to get in the habit of allowing applications by default, but you should pay attention to these warnings because they could save you a lot of trouble.

## Using Antivirus Software

Although the best defense against viruses is being very careful about the files you transfer onto your machine, you should also obtain and use a good antivirus application. Good antivirus applications generally perform the following functions:

- Monitor activity on your computer to identify potential infection
- Periodically scan your drives to look for infections
- Notify you if an infection is discovered
- Repair the infected files and eliminate the virus
- Delete infected files if repairing them is impossible
- Enable you to identify particular folders that should be scanned automatically, such as the folder into which you download files
- Update themselves automatically

**NOTE**

> Most viruses are identified by their code. The antivirus software knows about the virus's code through its virus definition file. As new viruses appear, this virus definition file needs to be updated so that the new viruses will be recognized as being viruses. You can usually obtain an updated virus definition file from the website of the manufacturer of your antivirus software. Most programs automate this process and can update the virus definition at intervals you set.

**NOTE**

> One of the important things to look for in an antivirus program is that it can detect and repair macro viruses. Macro viruses are easy to create and spread, and some of them are quite nasty.

As with previous versions of the Mac OS, there are several major antivirus applications, including Norton AntiVirus for Mac and Virex.

These applications provide most of the features in the previous list, and they work well. You should obtain and use one of these applications to protect your Mac against viruses and to repair your Mac should it become infected.

---

**Viruses and You**

Frankly, viruses are less of a problem than they appear to be from the tremendous amount of media hype they receive, especially for Mac users. Most of the time, you can protect yourself from viruses by being very careful about the files you receive in email or download from the Web. Because the only way for a virus to get onto your machine is for you to accept a file in which it is contained, you can protect yourself from most viruses by using common sense. For example, if you receive an email containing an oddly titled attachment (such as the famous I Love You file), you should either request more information from the sender before you open the file or simply delete the message.

This is one case is which being in the minority as a Mac user is beneficial. The vast majority of viruses are designed for Windows machines and have no effect on a Mac.

Adding and using an antivirus application makes your machine even safer, but if you are very careful about downloading files, you might find that you can get by just fine without one.

# DEFENDING YOUR MAC AGAINST INTERNET HACKERS

If you have a broadband connection to the Internet, such as a cable or DSL modem, being attacked by hackers is a much more real threat than are viruses. And with a broadband connection, you *will* be attacked, daily if not hourly or even more frequently. Hackers are continuously looking for machines they can exploit, either to do damage to you or to use your machine to do damage to others (such as using your machine to launch a spam attack). Most of these attacks are carried out by applications, so they can be both automatic and continuous.

**CAUTION**

> Never expose a machine containing sensitive or production data to a broadband connection without protecting that machine from network attack. Doing so makes everything on such a machine vulnerable to exposure to a hacker, and the machine itself can be used to carry out attacks on other networks and machines.



There are two fundamental ways you can prevent your Mac from being hacked through your broadband Internet connection: Use a server/hub to isolate the machines on your network from the outside world or use a software firewall to protect each machine on the network from attack.

## USING A SERVER AND FIREWALL TO PROTECT YOUR NETWORK

You can isolate the machines on your network from attack by placing a physical barrier between them and the public Internet. You can then use a Dynamic Host Configuration Protocol (DHCP) server that provides network address translation (NAT) protection for your network, or you can add or use a hub that contains a more sophisticated firewall to ensure that your network can't be violated. A benefit to these devices is that you can also use them to share a single Internet connection.

⇨ To learn how to install and use a DHCP server or firewall, **see** Chapter 19, "Sharing an Internet Connection," **p. 421**.

**NOTE**

> One of the easiest and best ways to protect machines on a local network from attack and to share an Internet connection is to install an AirPort base station. This device provides NAT protection for any computers that obtain Internet service through it, and for most users, this is an adequate level of protection from hacking.

### Using a Software Firewall to Protect Your Network

You can also install and use a software firewall; a software firewall prevents unexpected access to your Mac from the Internet. Software firewalls can be quite effective and might be the best solution if you have only a single Mac connected to the Internet.

**CAUTION**

> Unlike a hardware firewall or NAT hub, a software firewall must be installed on each computer attached to your network.

A software firewall works by blocking access to specific ports on your Mac; these ports are linked to specific services. If hackers can access these ports on your machine, they can use them to attack your machine directly to launch attacks on other computers, servers, and networks (such as denial-of-service attacks, in which a system is overloaded by repeated requests from many machines).

⇨ To learn how to configure and use Mac OS X's built-in firewall, **see** "Securing Your Mac with Mac OS X's Firewall," **p. 925**.

## Using Parental Controls to Safeguard a Mac



In addition to protecting your Mac itself from attack, you can also protect individual users from various kinds of danger by blocking specific types of access for individual accounts. For example, you might want to control the kind of email a child who uses your Mac receives. You control various types of access to your Mac and to the Internet via the Parental Controls pane of the System Preferences application.

### Using Parental Controls to Limit a User's Access to the Mac

You can limit a user's access to your Mac's resources using the tabs on the Parental Controls pane of the System Preferences application.

Use the System tab to control how users can interact with the system by doing the following:

1. Open the Parental Controls pane of the System Preferences application, select the user whose access you want to limit in the user list in the left pane of the window, and click the System tab (see Figure 39.8).

**NOTE**

> The first time you select a user, you have to click the Enable Parent Controls button before you are shown the detail page with the tabs.

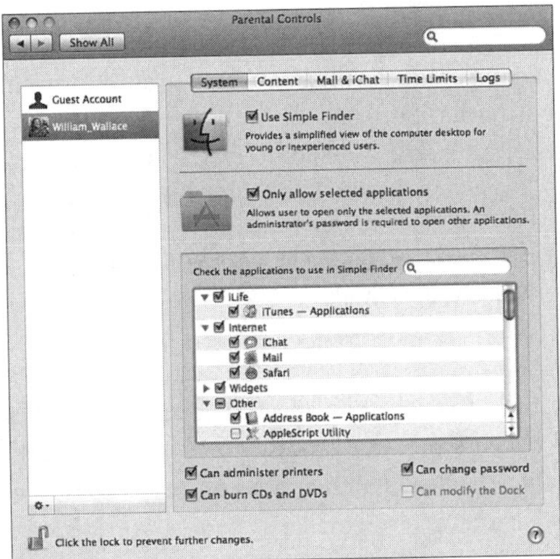


**Figure 39.8**
Use the System tab to determine what kind of system resources a user can access.



2. Use the upper check boxes to determine whether the user has access only to the Simple Finder or to limit access to specific applications.

   The Simple Finder provides the most basic level of access. As you might expect from its name, the Simple Finder provides a less complex interface for a user and greatly restricts what that user can do. When a user is logged in with the Simple Finder, the Dock contains only five icons: Finder, My Applications, Documents, Shared, and Trash. These are the only areas the user can access. For example, under the Simple Finder, a user can store documents only in his Documents folder and can't open other folders. The only Finder commands the user can access are Sleep, Log Out, About Finder, the Hide/Show Finder commands, and Close Window. The Simple Finder makes your machine more secure because it limits the actions of a user so severely. Using the Simple Finder can be a good choice if the user for whom you are creating an account has minimal computer skills, such as for very young children or someone who is totally new to the Mac.

3. To limit the user to the Simple Finder, check the Use Simple Finder check box.

4. To limit the user to specific applications, check the "Only allow selected applications" check box. Then check the check box next to each application on the application list to enable the user to use it or uncheck a box to prevent a user from using that application.

   On the list, applications are grouped; expand a group to see the applications it contains. You can enable or disable all the applications in the group by using its check box or expand a group and check or uncheck individual applications.

**NOTE**

> Apple applications are grouped pretty well, such as the iLife applications. Most other applications appear in the all-inclusive Other category.

You search for applications using the Search box at the top of the application list.

5. Check the following check boxes to determine whether the user can perform the related actions:
   - **Can administer printers**—This control allows or prevents a user from being able to configure printers.
   - **Can burn CDs and DVDs**—This one is easy to figure out; if enabled, the user can burn discs. If not, the user won't be able to write to CD or DVD.
   - **Can change password**—If enabled, the user can change her password.
   - **Can modify the Dock**—If this is enabled, the user can configure his Dock.

To limit when a user can use a Mac, do the following:

1. Open the Parental Controls pane of the System Preferences application, select the user whose access you want to limit in the user list in the left pane of the window, and click the Time Limits tab (see Figure 39.9).

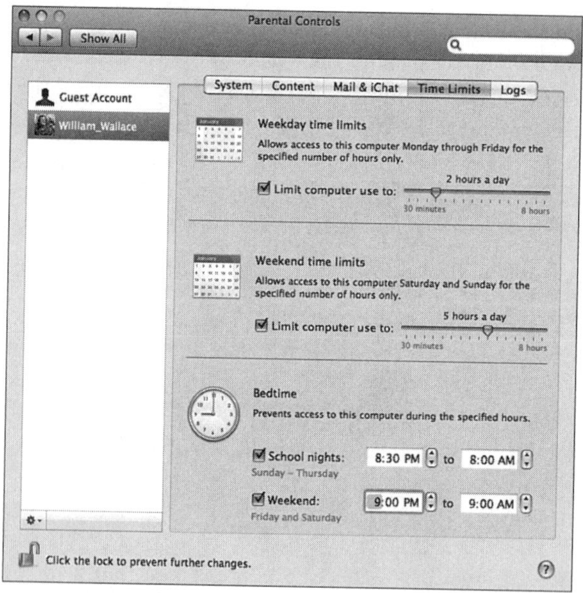


**Figure 39.9**
Use the Time Limits tab to determine when a user can use a Mac.

2. To limit the time the user can access the Mac on weekdays, check the "Limit computer use to" check box in the Weekday time limits section of the pane and set the amount of time on the slider.

3. To limit the time the user can access the Mac on weekends, check the "Limit computer use to" check box in the Weekend time limits section of the pane and set the amount of time on the slider.

4. To set an off-limits period for weekdays or weekends, use the controls in the Bedtime section. Check the "School nights" check box and enter times during which the computer can't be used by the user. Check the Weekend check box and set times to limit its use on Friday and Saturday nights.

After you set time limits, the user will be unable to use his user account outside of the limits you set. If you have your Mac configured to show the list of users on the login window, a note next to the username will indicate when that user can login again. If a user is logged in and has a Bedtime setup, they will be warned a few minutes before that time that their computer time is almost up. An option is displayed to add more time, which requires an administrative password to confirm. After the Bedtime limit is reached, the user is locked out of his account. When he can log in again, he will be able to pick up where he left off.

## Limiting the Web and Dictionary Content Your Mac's Users Can Access

The Web is often a great place to be, but it can also be a dangerous or disgusting place to be as well. You can protect users by limiting the websites they can visit by doing the following steps:

1. Open the Parental Controls pane of the System Preferences application, select the user whose access you want to limit in the user list in the left pane of the window, and click the Content tab (see Figure 39.10).

39

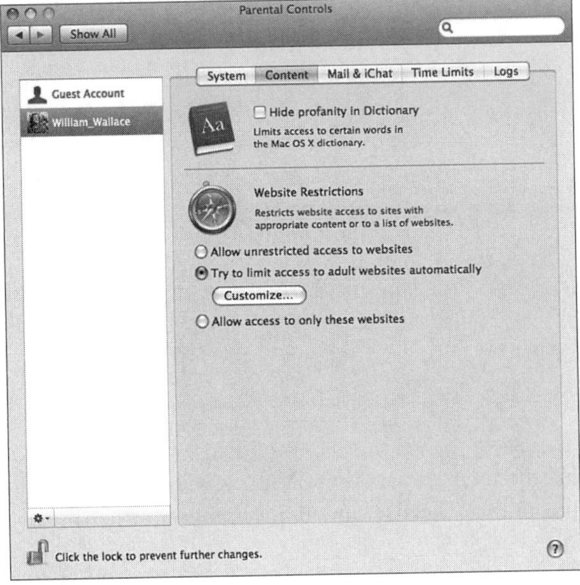


**Figure 39.10**
Use the Content tab to limit access to Dictionary and website content.

2. To hide profanity in the Dictionary, check the "Hide profanity in Dictionary" check box.

3. To determine web content the user can access, choose one of the following options:
    - **Allow unrestricted access to websites**—This option doesn't prevent access to any websites.
    - **Try to limit access of adult websites automatically**—Mac OS X will try to prevent the user from accessing websites that have adult content, such as porn sites.
    - **Allow access to the following websites only**—If this is enabled, you can configure a specific list of URLs that the user can access by doing the rest of these steps.
4. Click Customize. A list of kids-focused sites appears below the radio button. These are the sites that the user is allowed to access.

**TIP**

> To organize the bookmarks, click the Add button and choose Add folder. Name the new folder. You can use these folders to organize the bookmarks you create. Unfortunately, you can't drag bookmarks around the list to place them in folders. You must create the folder first and then create the bookmark in it.

5. Click the Add button (+) and choose Add bookmark. The bookmark sheet appears.
6. Enter the site title and URL and then click OK. The website is added to the list of approved sites.

**TIP**

> You add websites to the approved list by dragging the URLs from the Safari Address bar or from the Bookmarks page in Safari and dropping them onto the Content pane (drag them onto a folder to place them there).

7. Repeat steps 5 and 6 until you've added all the websites that you want the user to be able to access.
8. To remove a site from the list, select it and click the Remove button (-).

The user is only able to access web pages for which you have configured bookmarks. If the user attempts to access any other pages, such as by entering a URL, that access will be blocked.

**NOTE**

> The Parental Controls tools are designed to work with Apple applications, such as Safari and iChat. If you allow the user to access other applications, such as Instant Messenger, the Parental Controls tools will not prevent access to whatever resources the user wants. For maximum protection, you need to limit the user to Safari, Mail, and iChat.

## Limiting Email and Chat Access of Others to Your Mac's Users

You can determine from which email addresses a user can receive email to shield that user for unwanted emails. You can also allow a user to chat only with specific people. Set this up with the following steps:

1. Open the Parental Controls pane of the System Preferences application, select the user whose access you want to limit in the user list in the left pane of the window, and click the Mail & iChat tab (see Figure 39.11).

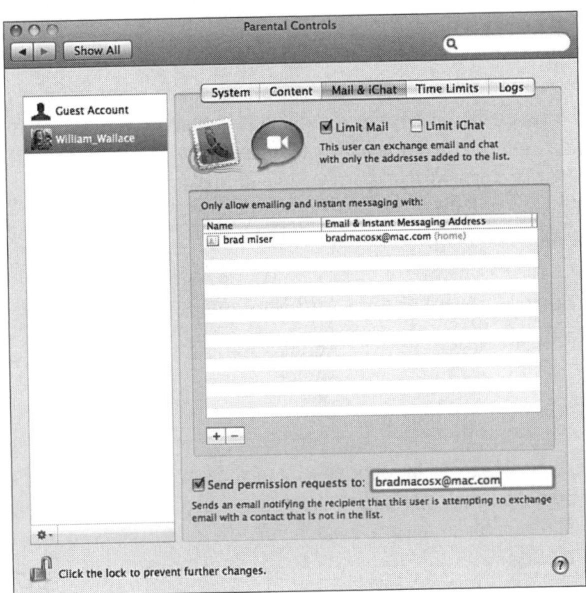


**Figure 39.11**
Use the Email & iChat tab to prevent users from communicating with anyone except those people on the approved list.

2. Check one or both of the check boxes for Limit Mail or Limit iChat.
3. Click the Add Email address button (+) located at the bottom of the allowed email list. The Add sheet appears. There are two ways to add people to the approved list. One is to create the person's information in the sheet (step 5), and the other is to select a person from your Address Book (step 6).
4. Enter the first and last names of the person with whom you are going to allow email or chat and then enter the email address in the box below the name fields. Use the pop-up menu to choose email, AIM, or Jabber. You need to enter an email address or username for each of the options you want to allow. Check "Add person to my address book" to add the person whose information you are entering to your Address Book. Click Add to add the person to the approved list.
5. Click the expansion triangle next to the Last Name field. Use the resulting Address Book browser to select the person you want to add to the approved list and click Add (see Figure 39.12). The person and all their email addresses are added to the approved list.

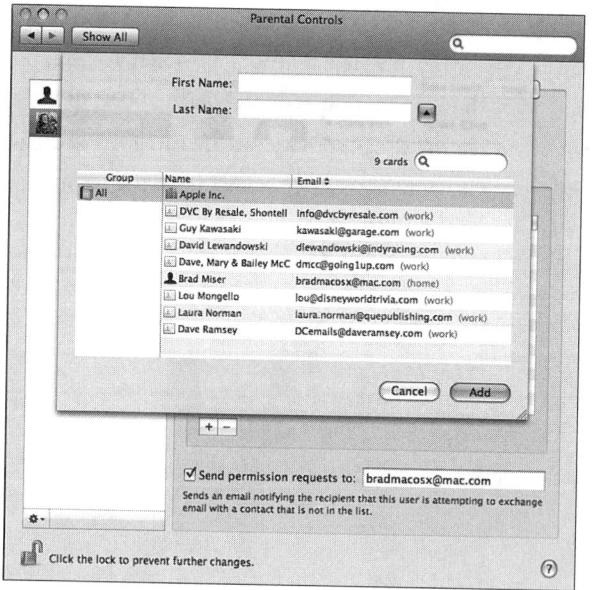


**Figure 39.12**
You can add people to the approved list by selecting them in your Address Book.

6. To remove someone from the list, select the name and click Remove (-).
7. If you want to receive a permission email each time an email from an address not on the list is received, check the "Send permission emails to" check box and enter the email address where you want the permission emails to be sent in the box. If you approve the contact, the email address is added to the approved list.



Any email or chat requests addressed to the user from addresses not on the approved list you configured are rejected. If you enabled the permission email option, a permission email is sent to the address you configured. If permission is granted via that email by clicking the Always Allow button, the email or chat request from the unlisted address is allowed, as will future emails or chat requests from the same address (it is added to the list of allowed email addresses).

**TIP**

> You can prevent additional emails from the same address by clicking the No Longer Allow button in the permission email.

## Viewing Logs of User Activity

If you want to view the activity of a user account, perform the following steps:

1. Open the Parental Controls pane of the System Preferences application, select the user whose access you want to limit in the user list in the left pane of the window, and click the Logs tab. In the Log Collections pane, you see the categories of logs you can view: Websites Visited, Websites Blocked, Applications, and iChat.

2. Select the category in which you are interested, such as Websites Visited.
3. Select the timeframe you want to view on the "Show activity for" pop-up menu.
4. Choose how you want the information grouped on the "Group by" pop-up menu.
5. In the Logs pane, you see the user's activity for the category you selected.
6. To prevent further activity with a resource, select it on the list and click Restrict. The user can no longer access the resource.
7. To view a resource, select it and click Open. You move to the resource, such as website, you selected.

CHAPTER 40

# Solving Mac Problems

## In this chapter

## HANDLING MAC PROBLEMS

Even though Mac OS X is a very stable and reliable operating system, you will inevitably experience problems. You might experience application crashes or hangs, or an application just might not work the way it is supposed to. You might even experience minor annoyances, such as having to do something in several steps that should require only one. In any case, one of these days, you will run into a situation that requires you to troubleshoot and solve a problem.

Dealing with a problem, especially related to Mac OS X, can be intimidating even if you are a power user because there is so much going on that you might not understand. Although the top-level Mac interface is relatively intuitive, the Unix underpinnings of the OS have a tremendous amount of complexity. Nowhere is this more apparent than when you are trying to solve a problem. As you use the various tools that are part of Mac OS X to diagnose and solve a problem, you are likely to run into information that doesn't make much sense to you—unless you have lived in the Unix world for a long time, in which case you'll feel right at home.

Fortunately, you don't need to be a Unix expert to be able to troubleshoot and solve Mac OS X problems. Mostly, what is required is the ability to carefully observe what is happening and to follow logical trails. Being able to communicate clearly with other people is also very important when you need to get help.

**NOTE**

If there is one troubleshooting trick or technique that I would classify as critical, it is the ability to accurately and completely (and calmly) describe a problem you are experiencing, whether you are telling someone about it or writing to them. Not only will this help your own troubleshooting work, but it also is vital when you need help from someone else. Unfortunately, many requests for help provide only partial or incomplete information that makes it almost impossible to provide the correct help.



From the title of this chapter, you might be under the impression that you will be seeing many solutions to specific Mac problems you might encounter. If that is your expectation, I must be up front with you here. There simply isn't room in this book to provide lists of problems and solutions that would be detailed enough to help you with the specific problems you will face.

Instead, the purpose of this chapter is to help you learn *how* to troubleshoot Mac OS X problems in general. You can then apply the techniques and tools you will learn about in this chapter to any problems you face; these techniques will help you solve problems on your own. In the long run, the strategies you need to know to solve problems will be much more useful to you than lists of problems that might or might not include those you actually experience.

**NOTE**

> The goal of this chapter is to help you learn general problem-solving techniques, but solutions to some specific problems you might encounter are explained in the "Troubleshooting" sections in many chapters of this book.

# UNDERSTANDING THE CAUSES OF PROBLEMS

The causes of the problems you experience will be one—or a combination—of five general types of problems:

- User error
- Bugs
- Conflicting software
- Attacks on your system
- Hardware failures

Each of these problems is detailed in the sections that follow.

## USER ERROR

The results of many investigations into aviation accidents can often be summed up with the phrase "pilot error." Similarly, this is often the case with an "accident" in the Mac world. Many problems are the direct result of a user (this means you) doing something improperly—or not doing something properly. Some of the things you might do to cause problems for yourself are the following:

- **Not following instructions**—This is the big one. At times, you will cause your own problems simply because you fail to follow instructions provided with software or hardware. You should become a believer in the old adage "if all else fails, follow the instructions."
- **Operating a machine past its limits**—If you know that a particular application requires a computer with an Intel processor, but you try to run it on a G3-equipped Mac, you are bound to have troubles. If you live on the edge of your machine's capabilities, you will have more problems than you might with a more capable machine. This is especially important related to a computer's RAM. Most minimum RAM requirements are understated; add as much RAM to your Mac as it can handle and you can afford.
- **Not doing proper maintenance on your system**—If you don't keep an eye out for patches and updates to Mac OS X as well as the applications you use, you might experience more problems than you have to. Take advantage of the many ways in which you can keep your system up-to-date. For example, Mac OS X's Software Update feature can help you keep your operating system and all your Apple applications current automatically.
- **Not keeping enough free space on a drive**—This is a fairly common cause of problems. All drives need to have free space to be capable of storing files, sometimes

temporarily. If a drive is full, or very close to being full, you will have problems as you try to store more data on it. This can be a problem under Mac OS X because virtual memory is always on—low disk space can cause problems related to insufficient RAM as well.

**NOTE**

Proper maintenance includes maintaining good backups of your data, applications, or (even better) your entire system. Using a Mac without a backup system is like playing Russian roulette. Much of the time, you'll be fine. But sometimes you lose, and when you get caught without a backup, you lose big.

## BUGS

Sometimes the cause of a problem is a bug inherent in the design of the products involved. The bug can be a design flaw, a manufacturing problem, or a conflict with some other part of your system. Although companies often do the best they can to prevent bugs, there is usually no way to prevent all the possible bugs in a product. Many bugs aren't revealed until a piece of software or hardware is combined with some other pieces of hardware or software.

## CONFLICTING SOFTWARE

One of the most common causes of problems is conflicting software. Some programs just don't play well with others. Conflicts are often associated with system-level applications and resources because they modify the low-level operations of the system. However, applications can also conflict with one another and cause you headaches.



Because Mac OS X features protected memory, these types of conflicts are much less common under Mac OS X than they were under previous versions of the Mac OS. Because of protected memory, you aren't likely to experience many conflicts between applications. However, there is still the potential for conflict between software that modifies the system and the core OS or software that uses hardware components of your system, such as heavy use of disks.

## ATTACKS ON YOUR SYSTEM

The two primary sources of attacks on your system come from the outside: viruses and hackers. Viruses can cause all sorts of problems from simple and silly messages appearing to strange dialog boxes to major system crashes and even data deletions or hard disk failures. Viruses that do serious damage have traditionally been fairly rare on the Mac, but because Mac OS X is based on Unix, it remains to be seen whether viruses will be a more significant source of concern than they have been for Mac users traditionally. Fortunately, viruses are among the easier problems to avoid. On the other hand, if you use a broadband connection to the Internet, your Mac will be subjected to all sorts of hackers who want to do damage to you or others. This is definitely the more serious of the two possible sources of attacks.

**NOTE**

Although attacks are normally associated with someone from outside your local network, this is not always the case. Sometimes, even unknowingly (such as in an email-based virus attack), users on your local network can wreak havoc on your system. The proper use of user accounts and permissions and a bit of paying attention will go a long way toward preventing incursions on your Mac from a local user.

⇨ To learn how to defend yourself against these attacks, **see** "Defending Your Mac from Internet Attacks," **p. 937**.

### Hardware Failures

The most unlikely cause of problems is a hardware failure. Although hardware does fail now and again, it doesn't happen very often. Hardware failures are most likely to occur immediately after you start using a new piece of hardware or close to the end of its useful life. Sometimes, you can induce a hardware failure when you upgrade a machine or perform some other type of maintenance on it—for example, if you install new RAM in a machine but fail to seat a RAM chip properly.

The most common problems associated with hardware devices are actually related to the device drivers that enable the OS to communicate with the device.

## Preventing Problems

It is better to prevent problems than to try to solve them. Following are three techniques you can employ to minimize the problems you experience:

- **Maintain your Mac properly and protect it**— This will go a long way toward minimizing your problems.

⇨ For information about protecting and maintaining your Mac, **see** Chapter 37, "Maintaining a Mac," **p. 875**.

- **Be cautious about upgrades, updaters, and other changes to the system software or applications**—Generally, you should wait a period of time after an upgrade is released before putting it on your system. You should always carefully evaluate the benefits of a new version of an application versus the potential for problems it might introduce. This holds true for updaters and patches as well. If you are not experiencing the problems that are solved by an updater or a patch, you might be better off without it.

  You should try to keep a log that records the date and time when you make significant changes to your system, such as adding new software, changing network settings, and so on. Such a log can help you identify possible causes of problems when a time lag exists between when you make a change and when problems occur. Mac OS X's Software Update feature maintains such a log for you automatically. But when you make changes outside of that tool, you will have to record the relevant information manually.

**TIP**

If you support more than one computer, you should have a test system on which you can install new software to test for a while before exposing other systems to it.

- **Make as few changes as possible at one time**—There are at least two reasons you should make changes to your system (such as installing software, making major configuration changes, and so on) incrementally. The first and most important is that making multiple changes at one time can obscure the cause of problems. For example, if you install three or four applications at once and then experience problems, determining which of the applications you installed is causing the problem will be difficult. The second reason is that sometimes making multiple changes at once can cause problems for you. When you change something significant, go slowly and take one step at a time. Introduce additional changes only after you are fairly sure that the changes you previously introduced are working properly.

## ASSESSING YOUR MAC

Key to troubleshooting and solving problems that you can't prevent is being able to accurately and precisely assess how your Mac is performing and knowing the specific configuration of your system. Mac OS X offers many diagnostic tools that can help you; however, several of these tools are quite complicated. Still, even if you are not able to interpret all their output, people who are trying to help might be able to, so even in this case it is useful for you to know how to use them. And, you should understand how to use these tools before you need them.



**NOTE**

If you choose Apple menu, About This Mac, you will see a window displaying the version of the Mac OS X you are running, the amount of RAM installed in your machine, the specific processors it contains, and the current startup disk. You can also click the Software Update button to move to that pane in the System Preferences application or click More Info to move into the System Profiler.

**TIP**

If you click the Mac OS X version number shown in the About This Mac window, you will see the specific build number of the version you are using. Click this information and you will see your Mac's serial number. Click it again and you will return to the Mac OS X version information.

### USING SYSTEM PROFILER TO CREATE A SYSTEM PROFILE

Mac OS X includes the System Profiler application. This application enables you to get a detailed view into your system at any particular point in time.

To create a profile of your system, launch System Profiler (Applications/Utilities directory). System Profiler provides a window with two panes (see Figure 40.1). In the left pane is a list of areas about which you can get information, including Hardware, Network, and Software. Each of these sections is broken down into component areas. For example, the Hardware section is further organized into various aspects of your system, such as ATA, Audio, Bluetooth, Diagnostics, and so on. The Software area is organized into Applications, Extensions, Fonts, and so on. When you select an item in the left pane, detailed information about that item appears in the right pane. For example, in Figure 40.1, the Hardware item is selected, which provides an overview of a machine's hardware configuration.

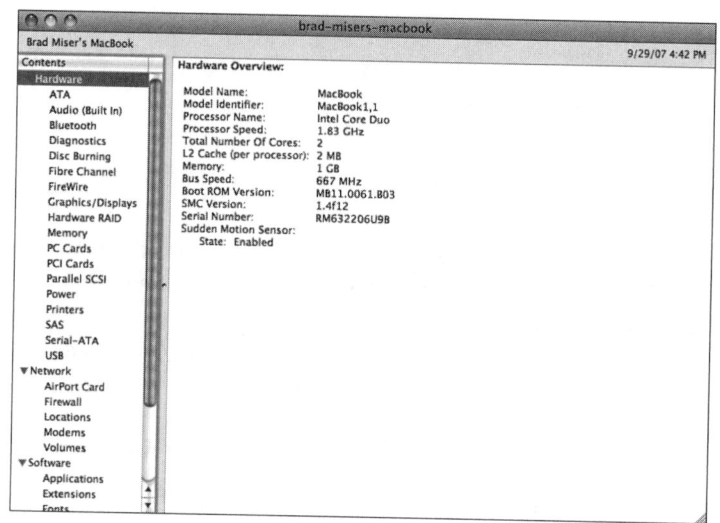


**Figure 40.1**
System Profiler provides detailed information about the hardware and software that make up your system.

**TIP**

You can also open System Profiler by clicking the More Info button that appears in the About This Mac widow.

Click the category for the part of the system about which you want information. For example, to see the memory configuration of your machine, click the Memory category. In the right pane is each memory slot the machine contains. When a chip is installed in a slot, you can select the chip and see detailed information about it in the lower part of the pane (see Figure 40.2).

**TIP**

Click the expansion triangle next to a category to expand or collapse its detail.

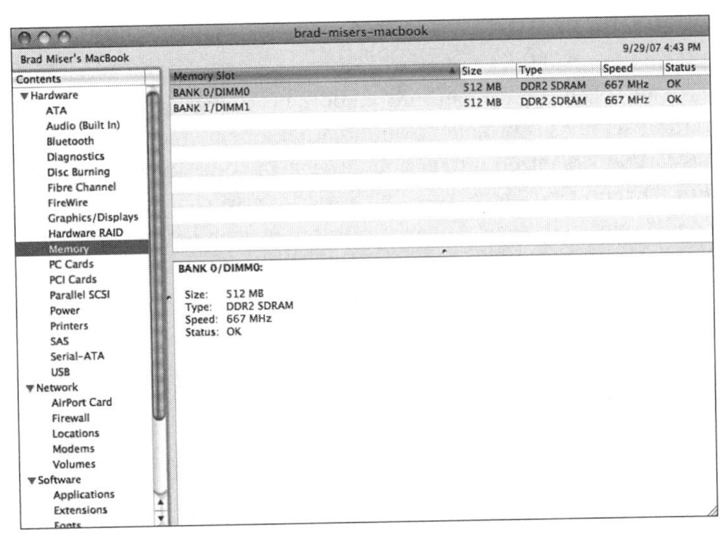


**Figure 40.2**
The Memory category enables you to get information about the memory configuration of your Mac.

Three views are available in System Profiler; you can select the view on the View menu. The Full Profile (press ⌘-3) is the default view and provides the most information. The Mini Profile (press ⌘-1) hides details under the Software and Network categories; you can expand these sections to view the detail. The Basic Profile (press ⌘-2) includes more detail in the Hardware and Network sections but no additional detail in the Software section. Frankly, there's really no reason to use any view other than the Full Profile. After all, you use System Profiler to get information, so why not get as much as is available?

The categories available in System Profiler in the Full Profile view can include those shown in Table 40.1.



**TABLE 40.1 SYSTEM PROFILER IN THE FULL PROFILE VIEW**

| Category | Subcategory | Summary |
|---|---|---|
| Hardware | None | This area provides an overview of the hardware that is part of your machine. You will see the type of Mac, the CPU(s) it includes, cache information, memory details, and other hardware information. |
| Hardware | ATA | Use this category to view detailed information about the ATA disk or disc drives in your Mac. |
| Hardware | Audio (Built In) | Use this section to view information about the audio capabilities of your Mac. For example, you see the type of Line In port your Mac has; Combo means that it's both an analog and digital port. |
| Hardware | Bluetooth | If your Mac supports Bluetooth, this tool provides a lot of information about it, such as the Mac's current settings, the services that are enabled, and the devices with which the Mac is paired. |

| Category | Subcategory | Summary |
|---|---|---|
| Hardware | Diagnostics | This section provides information about diagnostics that your Mac will sometimes run, such as those that occur during the self-test when you power up your Mac. |
| Hardware | Disc Burning | Use this to view information about CD or DVD burners in your system or that are connected via FireWire or USB. |
| Hardware | Fibre Channel | This section applies if you use fibre channel to link machines together. |
| Hardware | FireWire | This provides information about your Mac's FireWire ports, including the devices that are currently connected. If a FireWire device is connected to your Mac, but is not listed in this section, you know there is a problem with the device or the cable connecting it to your Mac. |
| Hardware | Graphics/Displays | This section provides details about the graphics cards installed in your Mac and the displays connected to those cards. |
| Hardware | Hardware RAID | If you have a Mac with a hardware RAID, you will be able to gather information about it in this category. |
| Hardware | Memory | Use this category to view detailed information about the composition of your machine's RAM memory. |
| Hardware | PC Cards | If you use a mobile Mac and PC cards, you can view information about them here. |
| Hardware | PCI | This area provides information about PCI cards you have installed in your Mac. If you have physically installed a card, but it is not listed here, the card is not working. The most likely cause is that the correct driver isn't installed. |
| Hardware | Parallel SCSI | Here you see information about any SCSI devices included in your system. |
| Hardware | Power | This area displays the current power settings for your Mac, such as sleep time. |
| Hardware | Printers | This provides information about any printers with which your Mac can communicate. |
| Hardware | SAS | Serial Attached SCSI devices are listed on in this part of the report. |
| Hardware | Serial-ATA | In this area, you'll see information about serial ATA drives connected to your Mac or installed in it. |
| Hardware | USB | This particularly useful section shows all the USB devices attached to your system. If you are having trouble with a specific device, use this information to see whether your Mac recognizes a device properly. You can also see the speed at which USB devices are communicating with your Mac. |

*continues*

TABLE 40.1 CONTINUED

| Category | Subcategory | Summary |
|---|---|---|
| Network | None | This category provides an overview of your Mac's current network connections. |
| Network | AirPort Card | View this to see the type of AirPort card installed in your Mac and the current AirPort network you are using, along with other AirPort information. |
| Network | Firewall | This area provides information about the firewall configured for your Mac. |
| Network | Locations | This section provides a list of all the locations configured on your Mac. If you select a location in the upper pane, details about it will be shown in the lower pane. |
| Network | Modems | This provides information about modems installed in or connected to your Mac, such as an internal dial-up modem, or an external modem, such as a cable modem to which your Mac is directly connected. |
| Network | Volumes | This section provides information about network volumes that are currently mounted on your Mac, such as your iDisk. |
| Software | None | This provides an overview of your system software, including version and build, kernel version, boot volume (startup volume), computer name, and current user. |
| Software | Applications | This category displays information about the applications installed on your startup volume. The upper part of the pane shows the application name, version number, and modification date. If you select an application, in the lower part of the pane you will see its version, modification date, location, info string (which is usually a copyright statement from the manufacturer), the location in which it is stored, and the kind of application it is. |
| Software | Extensions | Here you will see the Mac OS X extensions installed on your startup volume. This information can sometimes be useful when troubleshooting. For example, you can determine if an extension associated with a piece of hardware is currently recognized by your system. |
| Software | Fonts | This provides the details about all the fonts on your Mac. Select a font listed in the upper pane to see more details about it in the lower pane. |

| Category | Subcategory | Summary |
|---|---|---|
| Software | Frameworks | This category lists the Mac OS X frameworks installed on your startup volume. In the upper pane, you see the name of the framework, its version, and when it was last modified. If you select a framework, in the lower part of the pane you will see its version, modification date, location, info string (which can sometimes tell you more about the framework), and whether it is private. |
| Software | Logs | This section provides access to various logs the system and some applications keep to record significant events, such as crashes. Each log can be selected to reveal its details. In the upper pane are all the logs available to you. For each log, you'll see its name, a description, its size, and when it was last modified. If you click a log, its information will be displayed in the lower pane. The specific information you see will depend on the log you select.<br>Some of the information in these logs is quite technical. However, you can often review the logs for a specific point in time during which you were having trouble, to assess what was happening with your system. For example, you can see significant events that occurred or didn't occur successfully. This can often reveal the source of a problem. Also, if you need to ask for help, accessing these logs can enable you to provide more specific information to the person trying to help you and might result in a problem being solved more quickly. Other logs, such as those for applications, are quite easy to understand and will often reveal information about problems you have experienced. |
| Software | Managed Client | This portion of the report details the preferences that your Mac receives when it is connected to the Workgroup Manager functions of a Mac OS X server. |
| Software | Preference Panes | This list shows you all the preference panes currently installed in the System Preferences application. Select a preference pane in the upper pane of the window to see details about it in the lower pane. |
| Software | Startup Items | This list shows all processes that start up when your Mac does. As with other panes, select the item in which you are interested in the upper pane and view the details in the lower pane. |
| Software | Universal Access | This list displays the current settings for the Mac's Universal Access features, such as cursor magnification. |

You should periodically save a Profiler report, called a *profile*, to disk and print it. Then, if you need to get help with a problem but can't open System Profiler at the time, you can use the saved version or the hard copy of the profile to help troubleshoot the issue. You can also email the profile file to people trying to help you solve a problem. To save a profile for your system, do the following steps:

1. Launch System Profiler.
2. Select File, Save As.
3. In the resulting Save sheet, name the file, choose a location in which to save it, and select the file format in which you want to save the profile. The options are System Profiler 4.0 (XML), Rich Text Format (RTF), and Plain Text. The format you choose depends on how you are going to use the profile. In most cases, you should choose System Profiler or Rich Text because the resulting profile will retain some formatting.
4. Click Save. The profile is saved in the format you selected.
5. Open the profile to view it (see Figure 40.3).

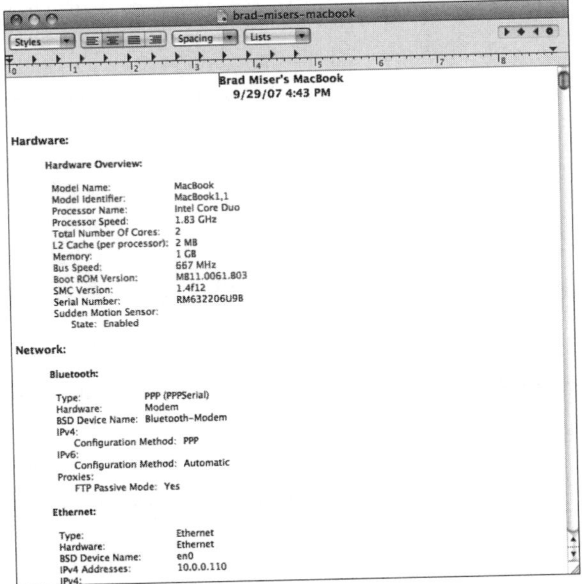


**Figure 40.3**
Here is a profile saved in the RTF format.

**TIP**

> When you need help from Apple, you can send a profile to it by choosing File, Send to Apple. Click the Send to Apple button in the resulting sheet and your profile will be transmitted to Apple. An Apple representative will be able to access the profile to help you solve a problem. Apple can also use the profile to help identify bugs and other issues with its software, including Mac OS X.

The System Profiler menus contain some additional commands that might be useful. For example, View, Refresh causes System Profiler to refresh all its information.

## Using Activity Monitor to Understand and Manage Processes

To provide services, your Mac runs a lot of processes. These processes fall into many categories. User processes are those that are related to specific user accounts, such as running an application. Administrator (also called root) processes are those that are fundamental to the OS and are controlled by it, such as the Desktop database.

The Activity Monitor application enables you to get detailed information about any process running on your Mac at any point in time. This information can be useful when it comes time to troubleshoot your system. You can also use Activity Monitor to kill any running process; this is useful when a process is hung and needs to be stopped.

The following steps walk you through using Activity Monitor:

1. Open Activity Monitor (Applications/Utilities directory). You will see a window providing a listing of all the processes on the machine (see Figure 40.4).

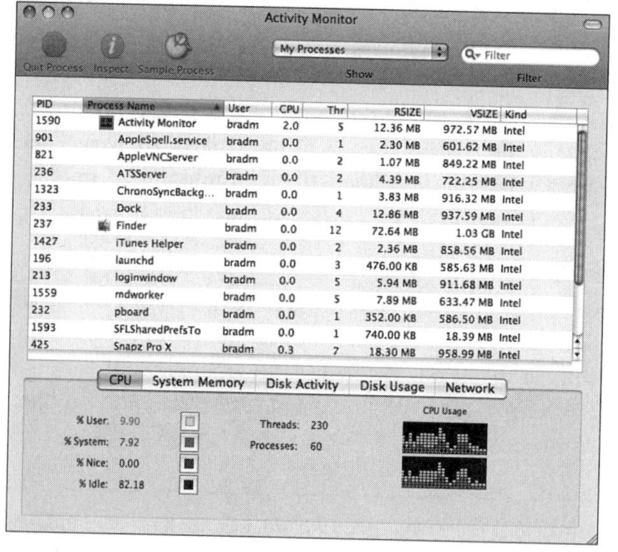


**Figure 40.4**
Activity Monitor enables you to get detailed information about any process on your Mac.

2. Select the category of process you want to view from the pop-up menu at the top of the window. There are many options from which to choose, and the option you choose will depend on the types of processes in which you are interested. For example, select My Processes to see the processes that are related to your user account. The processes shown in the window are refreshed according to the category you select.

**TIP**

> One of the more useful process categories to view is the Active Processes option. This shows only processes that are currently doing something. When you are troubleshooting, these are typically the processes in which you are interested.

For each process shown in the Activity Viewer window, you can see the following information (you may need to expand the column to see the full name):

- **Process ID**—Each process running on your Mac is assigned a unique ID number. This number can change each time the process is started.
- **Process Name**—Unlike a process ID number, a process's name is constant.
- **User**—This identifies the specific user running the process. In addition to the user accounts on your machine, you will see processes with root as the user. These are processes that are part of the OS and are started and managed by your Mac when it starts up.
- **CPU**—This percentage indicates the amount of CPU processing that a process is consuming. This is one of the more useful pieces of data. Any process should be consuming a small percentage of the available CPU processing power. If a process is consuming a large amount, such as something more than 90%, over a long period of time that usually indicates the process is having trouble and should be stopped.
- **# Threads**—Processes can run in different threads within the processor. This column indicates how many threads a process is using. Unless you have a detailed understanding of how processors work, this isn't likely to be meaningful.
- **Real Memory**—This indicates how much physical RAM is being used by the process.
- **Virtual Memory**—This indicates how much virtual RAM is being used by the process.
- **Kind**—This indicates whether the process is designed for Intel processors or PowerPCs. If you have an Intel Mac, you want more processes to be of the kind Intel because you will get the best performance. Older applications are likely to have the type PowerPC. They'll probably work fine on an Intel Mac, but won't perform as well as Intel processes do.



**NOTE**

> Virtual RAM is your Mac using its hard drive like it uses real RAM—that being to temporarily store data with which it is working. Virtual memory is much slower than real RAM, but you usually have a lot more available to you. Fortunately, Mac OS X takes care of managing both kinds of memory for you.

The following list outlines some additional process tasks you can perform in Activity Monitor:

- **Open a sheet that enables you to quit a process normally or to force it to quit**—Select a running process and either click Quit Process or press Option-⌘-Q to open this sheet. You can use this to stop a process that is hung. For hung processes, use Force Quit; for processes that are running normally, use Quit.

- **Sort the processes shown in the window**—You do this by clicking the column by which you want them sorted. The current sort criterion is shown by the highlighted column name. You can reverse the direction of the sort with the sort order button that is located next to the column heading.

**TIP**

Sorting the window by the Real Memory or CPU column is useful because you can see which processes are consuming the most system memory or processing power. If a process is consuming a large amount of memory (such as 80%), that can indicate something is wrong with the application that is generating the process.

- **Find specific processes**—You do this by typing in the Filter box. The list is reduced to only those processes that contain the text you type.
- **Open the Inspector window**—When you double-click or select a process and then either click Inspect or press ⌘-I, the Inspector window opens and you see additional information about the process, including the parent process and recent hangs (see Figure 40.5). You can click the Memory tab to see detailed memory usage information for the process. Click the Statistics tab to get information about the threads, CPU time, and other technical specifications. Click Open Files and Ports to see the open files and network ports related to the process. Click the Quit button to open the Quit/Force Quit sheet.

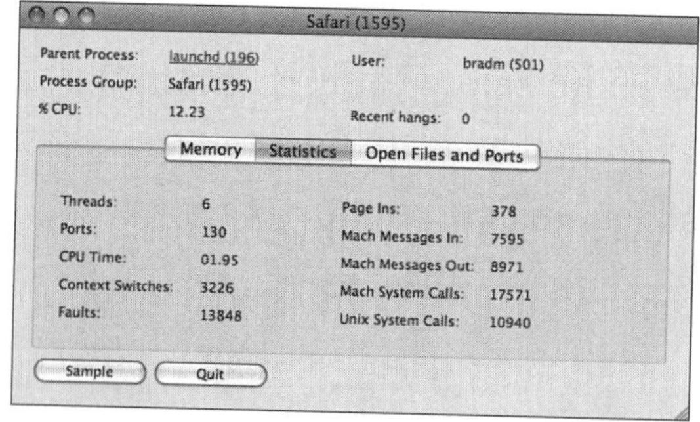


**Figure 40.5**
With the Process Inspector, no process can hide.

**TIP**

If you click the Sample button, you will see yet another window that provides even more technical information about a process.

- **Change the rate at which process information is updated**—You do this by selecting View, Update Frequency; then you select the frequency you want to use, such as every .5 seconds. Increasing the sample rate provides data closer to real time.

40

## USING THE ACTIVITY MONITOR TO MONITOR SYSTEM ACTIVITY

Using the tabs along the bottom of the Activity Monitor application enables you to gain insight into the following system activities:

- **CPU Usage**—You can monitor the CPU activity of the processors in your Mac. This gives you a good idea of the resources being used at any moment in time. When CPU usage becomes close to the upper limit, this usually indicates a problem.
- **System Memory**—Using this tool, you can view the usage of various types of system memory, such as physical RAM and virtual memory. You can also view the free memory of your system, which can be useful to determine whether you need to add more memory resources to your Mac.
- **Disk Activity**—This tool enables you to view the performance of your machine when reading and writing data to disk.
- **Disk Usage**—This area enables you to see the space breakdown of a selected disk (see Figure 40.6). This is particularly useful to make sure your disks aren't running close to their maximum capacity.

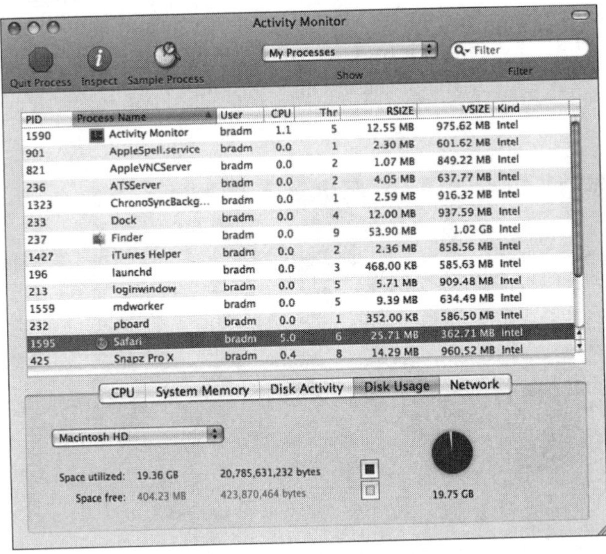


**Figure 40.6**
The Disk Usage information shows that the disk called Macintosh HD currently has about 404MB of free space: time for a little housekeeping.



- **Network**—This tool provides information about the communication across your network interface, such as via Ethernet.

Using Activity Monitor, you can display system activity monitoring information on your desktop in a number of ways. For example, you can display CPU usage information on the desktop and display an icon showing other information on the Dock (see Figure 40.7). The monitoring options you have are listed in Table 40.2.

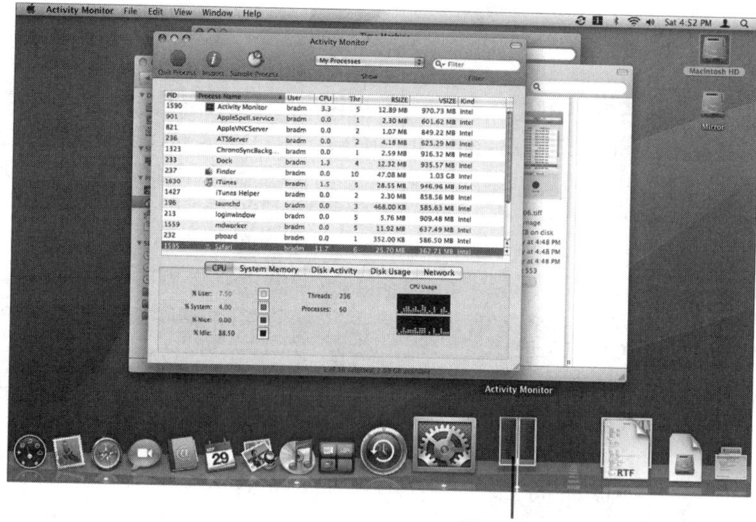


**Figure 40.7**
Several options are available for real-time performance monitoring from the desktop, such as viewing CPU usage on the Dock.

## Table 40.2 Monitoring Options in Activity Monitor

| Menu | Command | Keyboard Shortcut | What It Does |
|---|---|---|---|
| Window | Activity Monitor | ⌘-1 | Opens the Activity Monitor window. |
| Window | CPU Usage | ⌘-2 | Opens a window on the desktop containing a bar for each processor that graphically displays its activity level. This is disabled if the Dock icon is showing CPU usage. |
| Window | CPU History | ⌘-3 | Opens a window that tracks processor activity over time. |
| Window | Floating CPU Window, Show Horizontally | ⌘-4 | Opens a bar showing activity for each processor. The bar appears in the lower-left corner of the desktop and is oriented horizontally. |
| Window | Floating CPU Window, Show Vertically | ⌘-5 | Opens a bar showing activity for each processor. The bar appears in the lower-left corner of the desktop and is oriented vertically. |
| Window | Floating CPU Window, Do Not Show | | Closes the Floating CPU window. |
| View | Clear CPU History | ⌘-k | Starts the CPU history over again. |
| View | Columns, *Column* (where *Column* is the name of an Activity Monitor column) | | Enables you to show or hide all the columns Activity Monitor can display. |

*continues*

TABLE 40.2 CONTINUED

| Menu | Command | Keyboard Shortcut | What It Does |
|---|---|---|---|
| View | Show CPU monitors on top of other windows | | When this option is selected, all CPU monitor windows always appear on top of other windows. When not selected, the CPU monitoring windows can be hidden by other windows. |
| View | Dock Icon, Show CPU Usage | | Shows a CPU Usage window on the Dock. |
| View | Dock Icon, Show CPU History | | Shows a CPU History window on the Dock. |
| View | Dock Icon, Show Network Usage | | Shows a Network Usage window on the Dock. |
| View | Dock Icon, Show Disk Activity | | Shows a Disk Activity window on the Dock. |
| View | Dock Icon, Show Memory Usage | | Shows a Memory Usage window on the Dock. |
| View | Dock Icon, Show Application Icon | | Shows the Activity Monitor icon on the Dock instead of a monitoring window. |
| View | Update Frequency, *Frequency* (where *Frequency* is the frequency you choose) | | Changes the frequency at which the Activity Monitor monitors processors. The frequency can be .5 second, 1 second, 2 seconds, or 5 seconds. |

40

**TIP**

When you choose a frequency, it affects only the monitoring of processes. The monitors always display information in real-time.

Monitoring is available only while Activity Monitor is running. When you quit the application, all monitoring disappears. If you want to display the monitoring tools but hide the Activity Monitor window itself, you can minimize or close the Activity Monitor window.

## VIEWING SYSTEM ACTIVITY WITH TOP

The Top window is a Unix window that provides detailed information about the current operation of your Mac. To access it, open a command-line application such as Terminal, type **top**, and press Return.

The Top window provides detailed information about your system, although not in the most easily understood format (see Figure 40.8). At the top of the Top window, you see a summary of the activity on your machine; the lower part of the window lists all the running processes and detailed information about each.

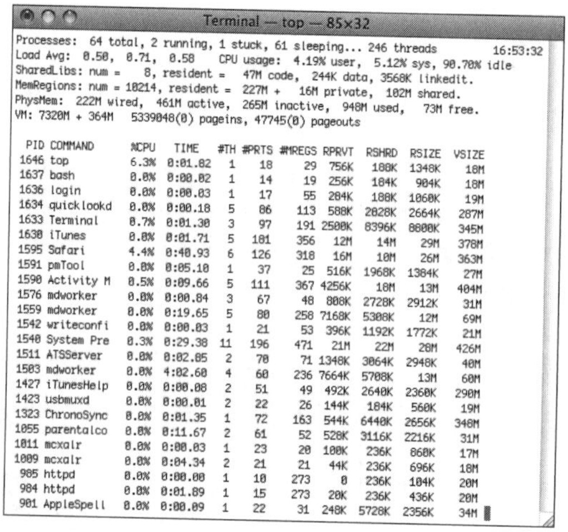

```
Terminal — top — 85×32
Processes:  64 total, 2 running, 1 stuck, 61 sleeping... 246 threads          16:53:32
Load Avg:  0.50, 0.71, 0.58    CPU usage:  4.19% user,  5.12% sys, 90.70% idle
SharedLibs: num =    8, resident =  47M code,  244K data, 3568K linkedit.
MemRegions: num = 10214, resident =  227M +  16M private,  102M shared.
PhysMem:  222M wired,  461M active,  265M inactive,  948M used,   73M free.
VM: 7320M + 364M   5339048(0) pageins, 47745(0) pageouts

  PID COMMAND      %CPU   TIME    #TH #PRTS #MREGS RPRVT  RSHRD  RSIZE  VSIZE
 1646 top          6.3%  0:01.82   1   18     29   756K   108K  1348K    18M
 1637 bash         0.0%  0:00.02   1   14     19   256K   184K   904K    18M
 1636 login        0.0%  0:00.03   1   17     55   204K   188K  1060K    19M
 1634 quicklookd   0.0%  0:00.18   5   86    113   588K  2028K  2664K   287M
 1633 Terminal     0.7%  0:01.30   3   97    191  2500K  8396K  8800K   345M
 1630 iTunes       0.0%  0:01.71   5  101    356    12M    14M    29M   378M
 1595 Safari       4.4%  0:40.93   6  126    318    16M    10M    26M   363M
 1591 pmTool       0.0%  0:05.10   1   37     25   516K  1968K  1384K    27M
 1590 Activity M   0.5%  0:09.66   5  111    367  4256K    18M    13M   404M
 1576 mdworker     0.0%  0:00.84   3   67     48   808K  2728K  2912K    31M
 1559 mdworker     0.0%  0:19.65   5   80    258  7168K  5308K    12M    69M
 1542 writeconfi   0.0%  0:00.03   1   21     53   396K  1192K  1772K    21M
 1540 System Pre   0.3%  0:29.38  11  196    471    21M    22M    28M   426M
 1511 ATSServer    0.0%  0:02.85   2   70     71  1348K  3064K  2948K    40M
 1503 mdworker     0.0%  4:02.60   4   60    236  7664K  5708K    13M    60M
 1427 iTunesHelp   0.0%  0:00.08   2   51     49   492K  2640K  2360K   290M
 1423 usbmuxd      0.0%  0:00.01   2   22     26   144K   184K   560K    19M
 1323 ChronoSync   0.0%  0:01.35   1   72    163   544K  6440K  2656K   348M
 1055 parentalco   0.0%  0:11.67   2   61     52   528K  3116K  2216K    31M
 1011 mcxalr       0.0%  0:00.03   1   23     20   100K   236K   860K    17M
 1009 mcxalr       0.0%  0:04.34   2   21     21    44K   236K   696K    18M
  985 httpd        0.0%  0:00.00   1   10    273      0   236K   104K    20M
  984 httpd        0.0%  0:01.89   1   15    273    20K   236K   436K    20M
  901 AppleSpell   0.0%  0:00.09   1   22     31   248K  5728K  2356K    34M
```

**Figure 40.8**
Using Top can be a bit intimidating, but the information it provides is worth getting to know.

In the summary area of the window, you can see how many processes are running versus the number sleeping, how many threads are running, the average loads, and the percentage of CPU usage of user processes versus system usage. The PhysMem information contains data about your RAM. For example, the amount shown as active is the RAM currently being used by running processes. The VM information provides data about the virtual memory being used.

40

**NOTE**

> You can get similar information in an easier-to-use format by using Activity Monitor.

In the lower part of the window, you see a table that provides data on each process that is similar to the information in Activity Monitor. For example, you see the PID, which is the same process ID as is displayed for a process in Activity Monitor. You can also see the percentage of CPU use, the processor time, and other more technical information. Much of this information will probably not be useful to you unless you are quite technically oriented; however, it can be useful to others when you are trying to get help.

You can save the information seen in the Top window by selecting the information in the window and selecting File, Save Selected Text As. This text file can be useful or can be provided to someone else when you are getting help with a problem.

> **TIP**
>
> To stop the Top process, press Ctrl-C.

## USING THE CONSOLE TO VIEW LOGS

The Console application (Applications/Utilities) provides a window to which Mac OS X writes system messages you can view, most notably various logs your Mac creates as it works (or doesn't work as in the case of crash logs). These messages are mostly error messages; some of these can be useful when you are troubleshooting problems (see Figure 40.9). The messages you see are quite technical; unless you are a programmer or are extremely technically knowledgeable, you might not be able to understand all their detail. However, Console messages can be helpful to understand what was happening when something went wrong and when you are communicating a problem to someone else.

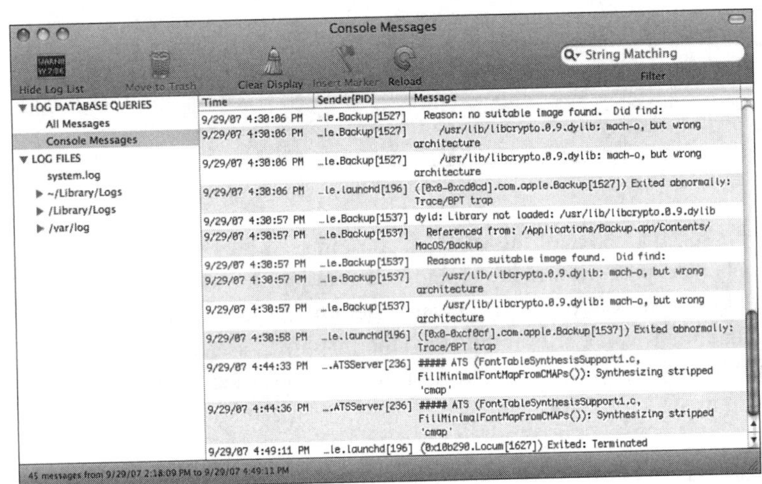


**Figure 40.9**
The Console enables you to view the contents of a log in detail.

You can choose the log that is displayed in the Console window in a number of ways:

- **Click the Show Log List button in the toolbar**—You will see a list of all available logs organized into categories. You can expand a category to show the logs contained in that category. When you select a log, it appears in the Console window.
- **Select File, Open Console Log (or press Shift-⌘-O)**—This opens that log. Or, you can select Open System Log (or press Option-⌘-O) to open the System log.
- **Select File, Open Quickly**—Then choose the log you want to see on the hierarchical menu that appears.

A number of logs are available through the Console, and each provides a specific type of information, as you can see in Table 40.3.

**Table 40.3 Logs Available in the Console**

| Log Name | Information It Provides |
|---|---|
| Console Messages | This log lists events related to the core operation of your Mac, such as when specific events occurred. Reviewing this log can sometimes give you insight into failed processes that might be causing problems for you, but that you might not be aware of because an application didn't crash. |
| All Messages | Whereas `console.log` displays mostly errors, `system.log` shows all events that have occurred for the system, such as when specific processes start up. You see the date and time for each event. |
| ~/Library/Logs | This category of logs provides information related to your user account (indicated by the ~). The specific logs you see in this category depend on what you are running at any point in time. You will always see the CrashReporter log for each application that has crashed. You might also see logs for various processes, such as the `MirrorAgent.log` when you are using an iDisk that is synchronized on your Mac. |
| /Library/Logs | This category presents a set of logs related to the system. These include various error logs along with logs for various system services. |
| /var/log | This category contains many logs related to various processes. For example, you can choose `install.log` to see a list of all installations you have done on your Mac or `ftp.log` to see information related to FTP access of your machine. |

**NOTE**

You must be logged in under an account to see its logs. Even if another user is currently logged in while you are using your user account, you will still see only your logs.

40

You are most likely to use the Console to troubleshoot problems. To do so, use the following steps:

1. Open the Console and choose the log you want to view. For example, if an application has crashed, find that application's crash log, which will be located in the CrashReporter category within the ~/Library/Logs set of logs.
2. View the information you see. At the top of the log window, you will see summary information. Moving down the screen shows you the very technical log detail (see Figure 40.10).
3. Save a copy of the log by selecting File, Save a Copy As.
4. Name the log, select a save location, and press Return.
5. In the Console, click the Clear Display button on the toolbar. The log's information is erased.
6. Repeat the steps that lead to the crash if you can. If not, just keeping doing what you were trying to do.

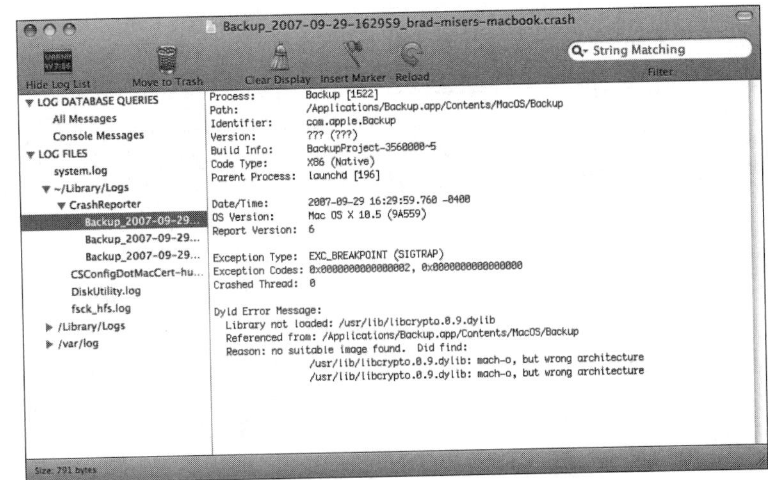


**Figure 40.10**
This CrashReporter log shows information about a crash of the Backup application.

7. If the crash occurs again, repeat steps 1–4 to view the crash log. Compare the log to what you viewed in step 2. This might tell you whether it is the same problem.
8. If you can't solve the problem on your own, save the new log information so you can provide both logs to whomever you contact for help.

If you aren't very technically inclined, the information you see in the logs won't be understandable. However, you can still glean useful information such as the general cause of a problem and specific information about when it occurred. That information will often help you pinpoint exactly what was happening when a problem occurred, which is often critical to being able to solve it.



Here are a few other Console tips:

- You can open multiple Console windows at the same time by selecting File, New Log Window or pressing ⌘-N. This is useful when comparing different logs.
- You can reload the information in a log by viewing it and clicking the Reload button; by selecting File, Reload; or by pressing shift-⌘-R.
- You can get rid of old logs by selecting them and clicking the Move to Trash button.
- You can use the Filter tool to search for specific log items.

# SOLVING PROBLEMS

If you understand the general techniques you should use when troubleshooting, you will be able to handle most of the problems you are likely to encounter. Having a good understanding of what you need to do will also make you more confident, which in turn will help you be more effective.

The general process of solving problems can be broken down into four phases, which are the following:

1. Implementing a workaround.
2. Understanding and describing your problem.
3. Fixing problems yourself.
4. Getting help.

You should work through these phases in the order in which they are listed. Doing so will help you solve your problem as efficiently as possible.

## IMPLEMENTING A WORKAROUND

One of the tough things about troubleshooting is that you usually have to do it at an inconvenient time—for example, in the middle of a big project. At times like these, you are likely to feel stress, which can lead to frustration, which in turn often leads to hasty actions. Haste will often drive you down the wrong path.

Effective troubleshooting requires a cool head. The best approach when you are working under a deadline is to find a quick workaround for the problem that will enable you to complete the job you need to get done immediately. Then you can come back and really fix the problem later when you are more in a "troubleshooting" frame of mind.

There are many types of workarounds you might be able to implement to get you working well enough to meet your immediate needs. Some examples are the following:

- **Use a different application to complete the project**—If your trouble is with a specific application, use an alternative one to get the project done.
- **Log in from a troubleshooting user account**—Some problems are related to corrupted preferences and other files that are part of your user account. If you followed my recommendation to create an alternative user account, log in under that account and try to complete your work.
- **Restart from an alternative startup volume**—If the problem is related to the system itself, use one of your alternative startup volumes until you have time to fix your current one.
- **Use a different Mac**—If you use your Mac for important work, you should consider having a backup machine so you can switch to it in times of trouble.

## UNDERSTANDING AND DESCRIBING YOUR PROBLEM

When you start to troubleshoot, the most important thing you can do is to understand your problem in as much detail as possible. This understanding will enable you to know what you need to do to correct the problem. As you gain insight into your problem, you should be able to describe it in detail; this will help you get help from others if you are not able to solve the problem yourself.

Use the assessment tools, such as System Profiler and Activity Monitor, that you learned about earlier in this chapter to help you understand what is happening.

### PUTTING THE PROBLEM IN CONTEXT

Many problems are triggered by something you do (this doesn't mean you cause the problem, but that some action you take initiates the problem). When a problem happens, think about what you were doing immediately before the problem occurred. Following are some questions you need to answer:

- Which applications and processes were running (not only the particular one with which you were working)?
- What, specifically, were you trying to do (print, save, format, and so on)?
- Have you made any changes to the computer recently (installed software, changed settings, and so on)?

> **NOTE** If you create a system change log as was suggested earlier, answering the last question in the previous list will be much easier. Remember to use the Software Update logs to track changes to your Apple software, including those made to the OS itself. You can also view the install log as explained in the previous section to see which installers have been run recently.

The answers to these questions provide significant clues to help you figure out what is triggering the problem. Identifying the trigger goes a long way toward identifying the cause.



### USING YOUR TROUBLESHOOTING ACCOUNT

Some problems you encounter might be related to files that are associated only with a user account. Examples of these include preference files for applications, other application support files, and so on. One of the best troubleshooting steps—which can also be a workaround—is to create a troubleshooting user account. Keep this account as basic as you can, meaning don't install applications that modify the system (such as applications associated with specific hardware) while logged in under this account. Leave all its settings in their default configurations, such as login items, preferences, and so on.

When you encounter a problem, log in under your troubleshooting account. If the problem goes away, you know that it is related to the user account under which you were logged in when the problem occurred. This can give you a good idea of where to start solving the problem. If the problem doesn't go away, you know that it is a more general issue.

> **TIP** Your troubleshooting account should have administrator privileges.

⇨ To learn how to create and configure user accounts, **see** Chapter 11, "Configuring and Working with User Accounts," **p. 231**.

### TRYING TO REPEAT THE PROBLEM

When a problem occurs, you should recover the best you can and then try to make the problem happen again. Try to re-create everything that was happening when the problem first appeared.

**CAUTION**

> Obviously, you shouldn't intentionally re-create a problem in such a way that you will lose data. Make sure that your data is safe by having a good backup before you do much troubleshooting.

If you can replicate the problem, figuring out what is happening will be much easier. The hardest problems to fix are those that occur only occasionally or intermittently.

### DESCRIBING THE PROBLEM IN DETAIL

After you have developed an understanding of how and when the problem is happening, write down a description of the problem. Be as detailed as you can. This description will help you decide on the best course of action, and if you are unable to solve the problem yourself, you will be in an excellent position to ask for help.

Use the Console to save logs related to the problem and System Profiler to create a report about your system's configuration. This will create much of the detail that will enable you or someone else to solve the problem.

## FIXING PROBLEMS YOURSELF



After you have described your problem, you should have some idea of where it lies. The four general areas in which you will experience problems are applications, system, hardware, and during startup.

### CORRECTING APPLICATION ERRORS

Application errors usually fall into one of the following categories:

- **Hangs**—Sometimes application errors cause your application to hang. Fortunately, because Mac OS X has protected memory, a hung application usually affects only the application itself and your other applications continue to work normally. You are likely to lose unsaved data in the hung application, but at least your losses are limited to a single application.
- **Quits**—Sometimes, the application you are using suddenly quits. You might or might not get an error message saying something like, `The application has unexpectedly quit because of an error`. When this happens, you lose all the changes you made to the open document since the last time you saved it.
- **Won't do what it is supposed to do**—Many times, errors occur that prevent you from doing what you want to do—whether using a particular function of the software, printing, saving files, and so on.

**NOTE**

> When you see an error alert that provides an error ID number, you should make a note of it. Although the number is not likely to be meaningful to you unless you have seen it before, it might be very meaningful to someone else when you ask for help.

Obviously, application problems are usually unpredictable. And when they happen, there isn't much you can do to recover your unsaved data (if you are saving frequently, you will limit your losses when the inevitable does happen). With an application problem, your real task is to figure out how to *prevent* future occurrences of the problem.

**TIP**

> Some applications, such as Microsoft Office, have a recover feature that attempts to recover documents on which you were working when the application crashed or hung. This sometimes works and sometimes doesn't. However, you should take a look at recovered documents when you restart the application to see how much of your work you can restore.

Mac OS X includes a crash reporter feature. When an application crashes, the crash reporter appears. At the top of this window, you can enter information about what you were doing at the time of the crash. When you have described this in as much detail as possible, you can send the information to Apple. Apple collects this information and uses it to identify problems that need to be fixed.

Typically, there are many things you can try to correct an application error. Following are the general tasks you should attempt to get the application working properly again.



**HUNG APPLICATION** When an application is hung, your only option is to force it to quit. You can do this by bringing up the Force Quit Applications window by pressing Option-⌘-Esc or by choosing Apple, Force Quit. Select the application you want to force quit and click Force Quit. After you confirm that you really do want to force the application to quit, it will be shut down. You can also use Activity Monitor to force an application to quit—the benefit of Activity Monitor is that you can see all the processes that are running along with their statuses. If other processes are also hung, you will be able to see them by looking at the Activity Monitor window. This can provide important clues as to the source of the problem (where two or three hung processes are gathered, there is likely a problem in their midst).

After you unhang the application, try to replicate the conditions under which it hung. If the problem is repeatable, it is either a bug in the application or a conflict with another part of the system.

Try running the application by itself while re-creating the situation in which the problem occurred (use your problem description to do this). If the hang doesn't occur again, you know that the problem is some type of conflict with another part of your system—be aware that this is much less likely to occur under Mac OS X than with previous versions of the OS.

If the hang is repeatable, the most likely solution is to install an update to the application. Visit the support area of the manufacturer's web page to see whether the problem you have is a known one. If so, an update is probably available to correct it. If not, report the problem to tech support to see what the application's manufacturer recommends.

**TIP**

> When an error dialog box appears or an application hangs, it can be useful to capture a screenshot so you can reproduce it later when you are writing down the description of your problem. In the case of a hung application, capturing a screenshot can help you re-create at least a screen's worth of data if you lose it all. Sometimes this can be helpful (such as for a table of data). To capture a screenshot, use the Grab application or download and use the much more capable Snapz Pro X.

⇨ To learn how to capture screenshots, **see** "Capturing Screen Images," **p. 717**.

**Quits** When an application unexpectedly quits, you should do the same tasks as when it hangs—except that you don't need to force it to quit because it already has. When an application quits, you will see a dialog box that enables you to reopen the application. If it reopens, continue working—while saving frequently, of course.

**NOTE**

> Although Mac OS X's protected memory guards applications, unexpected quits and other issues can affect the application's memory space. Because of this, you should save all work in open applications and restart your Mac when you experience an application quitting or hanging.

If the application quits again, restart your Mac and try again using a different file (if the application involves working with a file). If you are able to work with a different file, you know the issue is specific to the file you were using when it quit. If it continues to quit, the most likely solution will be to get an updated version of the application from the manufacturer.

**TIP**

> Applications under Mac OS X are like applications under other versions–they don't always work as they should and will sometimes crash or hang, in which case you lose any changes you have made since you last saved your document. Make it a practice to save your documents frequently; make sure you take advantage of auto-save features to automate this task, such as in Microsoft Office applications. You can also use automation tools, such as QuicKeys, to save any documents at regular intervals. Of course, you should always back up your data at regular intervals.

**Unexpected Behavior** If the application isn't working as you expect it to, the most likely causes are that the application has a bug or you aren't using it in the way it was intended.

Eliminate the second possibility first. Check the application's documentation, help, or readme files to ensure that you are doing the task in the way the manufacturer intends. If you ask for help for something that is covered in the application's documentation, the responses you get might be embarrassing or unpleasant.

If you seem to be using the application properly, a likely cause is a bug and the solution is to get an update from the manufacturer.

**TIP**

> Occasionally, an application's preferences can become corrupted, and cause problems for you. One way to eliminate this as a cause of a problem is to log on under your troubleshooting user account. If the problem doesn't occur under that user account, the cause might be corrupted preference files. Log back in to the previous user account and delete preferences related to the application that are stored in that user account's Library folder. Preference files have the extension `.plist` so look for the name of the application and that extension to find its preference files.

### CORRECTING SYSTEM ERRORS

System errors can be tougher to solve because they are usually harder to isolate. Even so, your goal should be to isolate the problem as much as you can. If you have carefully investigated and described your problem, you should have some idea where it originates.

Your first step should be to ensure that your system software is current—use the Software Update tool to check this.

The following list provides some general things to try for various sorts of system errors:

- If the problem seems to be related to a disk, run Disk Utility or other disk maintenance application to correct it. The problem might be related to the disk being too full, so check that as well.

⇨ To learn how to use Disk Utility for disk repair, **see** "Checking and Repairing Disks with Disk Utility," **p. 881**.

  Many Unix commands can be helpful when you are trying to solve system problems, such as getting rid of files you can't delete in the normal way and working with directories.

⇨ To learn how to use some basic Unix commands, **see** Chapter 14, "Unix: Working with the Command Line," **p. 297**.

- If the problem seems to be related to a specific user account, try repeating the same action under a different account. If the problem goes away, you know that something is wrong in the user account configuration.

  The best option for this is to use your troubleshooting user account to assess this. Because this account should have little or no third-party software installed, it often helps you determine whether a problem is part of the system or is related to something happening under a specific user account.

Some troubleshooting tasks are possible only when you are logged in to your Mac as root. Logging in as root can be dangerous, so you should know what you are doing before you try any action under the root account.

⇨ To learn about logging in as root, **see** "Enabling the Root User Account," **p. 261**.

- If the problem is more general, you might have to reinstall the system or specific components of it.

### CORRECTING HARDWARE ERRORS

Hardware problems are almost always caused by one of the following two conditions: improperly installed hardware or problematic drivers.

Eliminate the first cause by reviewing the steps you took to install the hardware. Check out the instructions that came with the device to make sure you are following the manufacturer's recommendations.

If the hardware is an external device, check the cable you used to connect it; if you have another cable, try that. If the device is connected to a hub, reconnect it to a port on the Mac itself.

**NOTE**

> A good way to check whether a device is successfully communicating with your Mac is to use System Profiler. Use the bus type information (such as FireWire) for that device to see whether the device with which you are having trouble is listed.

If the hardware is internal, repeat the installation process to ensure that it is correct.

The most likely cause of hardware problems is a faulty or buggy driver. Your only solution to this problem is to get an updated driver from the manufacturer. Visit the manufacturer's website for help or use the related application's check for updates command.

The hardware might simply be defective. Although this doesn't happen very often, it can occur. If none of the other solutions works, you might be left with this possibility, in which case all you can do is exchange the unit for a different one or repair it. Hardware failures are most likely to occur immediately after installing and starting to use a device or at the end of its useful life.

### SOLVING THE STARTUP PROBLEM

One of the worst problems you can have is when your Mac won't start. This can be caused by many things, including software conflicts, buggy software, disk problems, failed hardware, or a combination of all of these. Instead of loading the system, the machine just sits there and flashes a broken folder icon, meaning your Mac can't find a suitable System folder to use to start up the machine. (If the system doesn't try to start up at all, but you just hear the chimes of death, that means you definitely have a hardware problem.)

If the startup problem is because of failed hardware, you will have to correct the issue before you can get going again.

If the startup problem is related to your system software, the best solution is to start up from an alternative startup volume. Just like the troubleshooting user account, maintaining an alternative startup volume, with as little modification as possible, will enable you to get back to work as quickly as possible and fix the problems with your regular startup volume when you have time to do so.

If you have an alternative startup volume available, use it to start up your Mac. Run Disk Utility on your normal startup volume to see whether it can find and correct issues.

**NOTE**

> Make sure you start up under your alternative startup volume every so often and update its software so its system stays current. This will ensure it is ready to use when you need it.

If you do not have an alternative startup volume, you can start up from the Mac OS X installation DVD. When the Installer opens, you can use the Utility menu to run Disk Utility on your normal startup volume. Be aware that the version of Mac OS X on your installation DVD will likely be older than the version you are currently using. This can sometimes cause problems, but you might not have a choice if you don't have an alternative startup volume to use.

If you can't repair the disk on which Mac OS X is installed, you might have to reinstall the system. Try using the Archive option so that you maintain your user accounts; this might not work if the version of Mac OS X you are currently using is much newer than the one on the DVD, but it is worth a shot.



**NOTE**

> If you have a backup of your entire system when it was working properly, you can restore that version instead of reinstalling a new one. The advantage of this is that you won't have to reinstall your third-party software.

## MAC OS X TO THE MAX: GETTING HELP FOR YOUR PROBLEM

Unless you can instantly see how to solve your problem or one of your tools takes care of it, you will probably need to get help. There are plenty of sources for troubleshooting help, including the following:

- Manuals and online help
- Technical support from the manufacturer

- Websites, many of which include forums that can be used to look for help
- Magazines
- Troubleshooting software
- Mailing lists
- Co-workers and other people you know personally

When asking for help from people—regardless of the means you use, such as the telephone or email—be sure that you keep the following in mind:

- **Use basic manners**—You have no call to be rude to people who are trying to help you, even if they happen to work for the manufacturer of the software or hardware that is giving you trouble. Besides being the right thing to do, using good manners will probably get you better help. Manners are equally important when making requests via email or other online sources. "Please" and "thank you" go a long way toward encouraging people to help you. Sometimes this basic rule can be hard to remember when you are stressed out about a problem.
- **Give accurate, specific, and complete information**—Use the work you did earlier to provide a complete description of your problem. For example, provide information from logs you captured and be prepared to provide System Profiler information. Unless you give the person who is trying to help you a good idea of what is really going on, that person is unlikely to be able to help.
- **Don't wear out your welcome with someone who is only trying to help**—You need to be careful not to impose on people who are trying to help you only out of the goodness of their hearts. If you are asking a friend, co-worker, or even a complete stranger to help you with a problem, use her time efficiently. Be prepared to describe your situation. Be specific. And if the person can't help you after a reasonable amount of time, go to someone else. It is not fair to ask a volunteer to spend large amounts of her time trying to solve your problems. You can usually tell if someone is willing and able to help you quite quickly. If you sense that you are butting up against a dead-end, bow out gracefully and try another path.



**Getting Help More Effectively**

An ineffective request for help goes something like this, "I was printing and Word quit. Help!" This kind of question–which happens more than you might imagine–is just about impossible to answer.

A more effective question might be something like this: "I am using a 500MHz Power Mac G4 running Mac OS X version 10.4.1 that is connected to an Epson 740i. While I was trying to print from Microsoft Word for Mac OS X version 1.1, Word unexpectedly quit. I didn't get any sort of error message. I am able to print from other Mac OS X applications, and I have installed the latest printer drivers. Do you have any suggestions that might help?"

Table 40.4 lists some specific sources of online help with Mac OS X issues.

**TABLE 40.4 SOURCES OF GENERAL HELP FOR PROBLEMS**

| Source | Contact Information | Comments |
|---|---|---|
| Apple | www.apple.com/support | Apple's support pages are a great source of information about problems, and you can download updates to system and other software. You can search for specific problems. You can also read manuals and have discussions about problems in the forums available here. If the problem you are having seems to be related to the OS, Apple hardware, or an Apple application, this should be your first stop. |
| MacFixIt | www.macfixit.com | This is a good source of information related to solving Mac problems. Access to much of the information is not free, but you can get help on literally every aspect of using a Mac. Most of the information comes from Mac users, and you can ask specific questions—although the answer to your question is probably already available. You can get access to some current information free; however, you must pay to access older information maintained in an exhaustive set of archives. The fee is quite reasonable for the quality of the information to which you have access. |
| MacInTouch | www.macintouch.com | This site offers a lot of Mac news that can help you solve problems, especially if those problems are solved by a software update of which you are unaware. |
| MacWorld | www.macworld.com/news | Another source of Mac news. Be aware that some of this "news" is press releases from various companies. However, you sometimes learn useful information from press or marketing information. |
| Version Tracker | www.versiontracker.com | You can quickly find find out whether updates have been released for applications with which you are having trouble. |
| Me | bradmacosx@mac.com | You can email me to ask for help, and I will do my best to provide a solution for you or at least point you to a more helpful source if I can't help you directly. |

# INDEX

## Symbols



## A

## D

## F

## G



## H



## I

## J



## K

## L

## M

## N

## O

## S

*How can we make this index more useful? Email us at indexes@quepublishing.com*

## T

## U

## V

## W

## X-Z

# THIS BOOK IS SAFARI ENABLED

## INCLUDES FREE 45-DAY ACCESS TO THE ONLINE EDITION

The Safari® Enabled icon on the cover of your favorite technology book means the book is available through Safari Bookshelf. When you buy this book, you get free access to the online edition for 45 days.

Safari Bookshelf is an electronic reference library that lets you easily search thousands of technical books, find code samples, download chapters, and access technical information whenever and wherever you need it.

### TO GAIN 45-DAY SAFARI ENABLED ACCESS TO THIS BOOK:

- Go to **http://www.quepublishing.com/safarienabled**
- Complete the brief registration form
- Enter the coupon code found in the front of this book on the "Copyright" page

If you have difficulty registering on Safari Bookshelf or accessing the online edition, please e-mail customer-service@safaribooksonline.com.